Marianne Koster

Application Software

Version A

- ➢ WordPerfect® 5.1
- ➢ DOS Versions 2.x-5.x
- ➢ Lotus® 1-2-3® Releases 1A-2.4
- ➢ dBASE III Plus®

Third Edition

Dennis P. Curtin

REGENTS/PRENTICE HALL
Englewood Cliffs, New Jersey 07632

Library of Congress Cataloging-in-Publication Data
Curtin, Dennis P.
Application software: version A / Dennis P. Curtin — 3rd ed.
p. cm. — (Computer application software series)
Includes indexes.
ISBN 0-13-041971-0
1. Business—Computer programs. 2. WordPerfect—(Computer program)
3. Lotus 1-2-3 (Computer program) 4. MS-DOS (Computer file)
5. dBASE III plus (Computer program) I. Title. II. Series.
HF5548.2.C877 1993
005.365—dc20 92-14812
CIP

Acquisitions editor: Liz Kendall
Editorial/production supervision: Cecil Yarbrough
Copy editor: Robert Fiske
Designer and half-title illustrator: Janis Owens
Cover designer: Marianne Frasco
Interior art production: Dennis P. Curtin
Desktop publishing: Cathleen Morin
Prepress buyer: Ilene Sanford
Manufacturing buyer: Ed O'Dougherty
Supplements editor: Cindy Harford
Editorial assistant: Jane Avery

Cover art: Compass dial printed from a copper plate
made by Samuel Emery of Salem, Massachusetts (1809-1882),
by permission of the Peabody Museum of Salem

Printed in the United States of America
10 9 8 7 6 5 4 3 2 1

ISBN 0-13-041971-0

Prentice-Hall International (UK) Limited, *London*
Prentice-Hall of Australia Pty. Limited, *Sydney*
Prentice-Hall of Canada Inc., *Toronto*
Prentice-Hall Hispanoamericana, S.A., *Mexico*
Prentice-Hall of India Private Limited, *New Delhi*
Prentice-Hall of Japan, Inc., *Tokyo*
Simon & Schuster Asia Ptd. Ltd., *Singapore*
Editora Prentice-Hall do Brasil, Ltda., *Rio de Janeiro*

CONTENTS

CONTENTS

WordPerfect 5.1

CHAPTER 1

Getting Started WP51-2

CHAPTER 2

Basic Entering, Editing, & Printing WP51-47

CHAPTER 3

Basic Formatting WP51-75

CONTENTS

Lotus 1-2-3

PREFACE

Do you need Incentive?
Workers who use computers, but who are similar in every other respect to workers who do not use them, earn a fat bonus of 10 to 15 percent for their knack with these machines.
The New York Times, *February 14, 1992, page D2, referring to a study by Alan B. Krueger of Princeton University.*

Whether you take college courses, go to graduate school, enter business or the professions, or join the military, you are often expected to understand how to use a microcomputer—the type of computer that fits on your desktop. The microcomputer, also called the *personal* or *desktop computer,* has become the standard tool for information processing. It has achieved this status partly because of its low cost but mainly because of its flexibility. The same machine can process numbers, text, and graphics. For example, you can use a microcomputer to prepare a financial analysis; then to write, edit, and illustrate a report on the results of that analysis; and then to send the final document over the telephone lines to an office halfway around the world.

A computer is a very sophisticated piece of hardware, but it is software that makes it useful. Software programs enable the computer to do word processing, spreadsheet analysis, and database management, among other things. The software used in each of these areas allows you to apply the computer to specific tasks—therefore it is called *application software.* This text is designed to be used in a lab-oriented course that introduces you to the most widely used application software packages, including:

- DOS versions 2 through 5
- WordPerfect® 5.1
- Lotus® 1-2-3® Releases 1A through 2.4
- dBASE III Plus®

ASK THE AUTHOR

Dennis Curtin welcomes your questions about his textbooks and hardware and software issues. Please feel free to call him at 1-800-926-7074. For examination copies or ordering issues, call your Regents/ Prentice Hall representative.

Topics: The Basic Unit

The basic unit of this text is the topic, a short section that is narrowly focused on a specific procedure. This narrow focus, and the precise beginning and end of a topic, make it easier for you to study procedures than does a traditional chapter organization. Short topics are less intimidating than long chapters, and they make it easier for your instructor to assign specific sections.

Each topic contains the following elements.

- *Objectives* tell you what you should be able to accomplish when you have finished the topic.
- *Introductory concepts* introduce the basic principles discussed in the topic. These principles all apply to the programs discussed in this text, but many also apply to other programs you will eventually use on a microcomputer. When you understand concepts, procedures are easier to learn because they fit into a framework. Understanding concepts also makes it much easier to transfer your understanding to other programs and other computers.
- *Tutorials* demonstrate step by step how to use the procedures discussed in the topic. If you follow the instructions, you quickly see how each procedure is performed and the results it has. This establishes a framework on which you can build a better under-

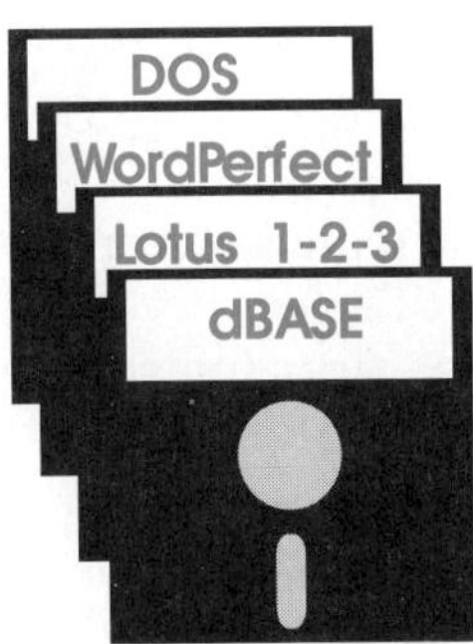

Application Software Packages
Application software such as WordPerfect, 1-2-3, and dBASE makes the microcomputer a useful tool.

PROBLEM SOLVING

It would be wonderful if the real world were neatly structured like a textbook—with all of the necessary information neatly provided. Unfortunately, a boss rarely tells us to "use a spreadsheet to analyze breakeven and enter the formulas shown in Figure 1 to do so." More often we are just told to analyze a product's profit potential and risk. It's up to us to choose the tools and approach. This is problem solving, and it takes practice.

standing of the procedures that are discussed in detail in the section that follows.

- *The Quick Reference Section* describes step by step how you execute commands. This section serves a dual function: You can refer to it when working on the activities in this text or when working on your own projects. Many of the procedures are presented step by step in easy-to-find highlighted KEY/Strokes boxes.
- *Exercises* provide you with additional opportunities to practice and gain experience with the concepts and procedures discussed in the topic. Unlike tutorials, the exercises do not guide you step by step. You have to refer to the Quick Reference section if you cannot recall the procedures to follow.
- *Tips* in many topics suggest shortcuts or discuss advanced procedures.

Chapters: A Pause for Reinforcement

Related topics are grouped into chapters so you can pause to review and test yourself. At the end of each chapter are the following sections you should complete:

- A review of the key concepts and procedures that were discussed in the chapter.
- A series of questions that test your understanding of the concepts and procedures discussed in the chapter. There are three types of questions: fill in the blank, match the columns, and write out the answer.
- Projects that build skills and introduce problem solving. Background material is provided for each project, but no specific procedures are given. To complete the projects, you must already have mastered the topics in the chapter or go back and look up the information that you need.

Parts: Software Applications

This text is organized into five parts (the first four of which are available as separate stand-alone "Short Course" volumes).

- Part One, *Microcomputers and DOS*, introduces you to microcomputer systems and to PC-DOS and MS-DOS operating system commands that you use to manage your files and application programs on a floppy or hard disk system. Because all commands are discussed from a command prompt perspective (except the final topics on DOS 5 special features), the tutorials can be used with DOS versions 2 through 5.
- Part Two, *WordPerfect 5.1*, introduces you to the principles of word processing and the procedures you use with WordPerfect 5.1.
- Part Three, *Lotus 1-2-3*, introduces you to the principles of spreadsheets and the procedures you use with Lotus 1-2-3 Releases 1A through 2.4.
- Part Four, *dBASE III Plus*, introduces you to the principles of database management programs and the procedures you use with dBASE III Plus.
- Part Five, *Exchanging Files Among Programs*, discusses moving data among the programs covered in this text. For example, you'll

see how to move 1-2-3 graphs or models into WordPerfect documents and move dBASE files into 1-2-3.

JUMP-START TUTORIAL

As the author of many books on computer applications, I teach teachers in seminars and workshops all over the country. If the room has computers, teachers are already punching keys while I'm still giving the introduction. Just like students, they can't wait to do something. The computer is an enticing, interactive tool, not a passive device you just read about. To encourage this hands-on flavor, each part of this text begins with a Jump-Start tutorial that lets you work with the computer and application programs immediately. The tutorials not only let you begin sooner but also show you what the programs can do.

Hands-On Lab Activities

In a lab-oriented course, your progress and enjoyment are highly dependent on the quality of the hands-on activities used as vehicles to teach you concepts and procedures. Ideally, these hands-on activities perform a number of useful functions.

- They build skills in the specific procedures you need to know.
- They provide motivation.
- They demonstrate a variety of situations in which specific procedures are useful.
- They introduce important business and other principles that have been or will be introduced in other courses in the curriculum.
- They develop problem-solving skills.

This text includes hundreds of such activities and presents them on four levels: tutorials, exercises, projects, and real-world applications. Each level requires an increasingly better understanding of the application programs to complete it successfully.

- Tutorials introduce a specific procedure or a group of closely related procedures. Their purpose is to demonstrate how the procedures work and show the effects they have.
- Exercises at the end of each topic reinforce the concepts and procedures discussed in the topic. They focus on the topic of which they are a part. You will have to rely on your experience with the tutorial and refer to the Quick Reference section to find the information you need to complete exercises. This refines your ability to look up information you need to complete tasks—something you will have to do on your own when the class is over.
- Projects at the end of each chapter are like exercises, but require an understanding of more than one topic to complete them.
- Real-world applications are threaded through the final chapters in the WordPerfect, 1-2-3, and dBASE parts. These applications develop your skills by having you use a word processing, spreadsheet, and database program to attack integrated problems that cannot be solved with a single program. These real-world applications are organized into three separate tracks: a job-search kit, a research paper, and a business plan. Different applications may be assigned to different classes or to different groups within the same class. Moving through this sequence of activities challenges you to think about what you should do and why you need to do it.

Key Features

This text has a number of features that distinguish it from other texts in this area.

- *Jump Start tutorials* open each part of the text so you can begin working from the very first day. These tutorials are designed to give you an overview of how the programs work and demonstrate some of the things they can do.
- The documents, spreadsheet models, or databases used in all lab activities are designed to be *real-world* in nature and representa-

tive of the kinds of activities that you will encounter in other courses in the curriculum and in business.

- This text goes beyond procedures. Its activities are not boring "make-work" activities. In many cases they introduce you to other subject areas and require you to think about *problem solving* and not just button pushing.
- To reduce the amount of typing or data entry time, many exercises are based on files that are provided on the *Application Software Student Resource Disk*. This disk is available from your instructor in either the 3 ½" or 5 ¼" format.
- You will find that you first use this text to structure your learning and then later as a reference. By referring to the list of topics on the back cover, you can immediately locate a topic of interest and then skim the Quick Reference section in that topic for the information that you need.
- At the back of the text are cardboard punch-out *keyboard templates* and *pocket guides* for DOS, WordPerfect, 1-2-3, and dBASE.

REAL-WORLD APPLICATIONS

Real-world applications are threaded through the last chapters in the WordPerfect, 1-2-3, and dBASE parts of this text.

Application 1: A Job-Search Kit
As you progress through the text you create a cover letter and résumé with WordPerfect, track travel expenses with 1-2-3, and organize your company contacts with dBASE.

Application 2: A Research Paper
As you progess through the text you edit and revise the body of the paper with WordPerfect, analyze the cost of a microcomputer system for your own use with 1-2-3, and track references with dBASE.

Application 3: A Business Plan
As you progress through the text you format the written portion of the plan with WordPerfect, calculate the cost of the computer system and prepare financial statements with 1-2-3, and track inventory with dBASE.

Supplements

The publisher has developed many supplements for this text that are free to instructors on adoption. These supplements include:

- *Instructor's Manual with Tests and Resource Disks* by Linda Dowell and Donna M. Matherly contains suggested course outlines for a variety of course lengths and formats, chapter summaries, teaching tips for each topic, competencies to be attained, solutions and answers to in-text activities, competency production tests, a test bank of objective questions, and a number of supplementary problems.

  Two types of disks are included with this supplement, and both are available as either 3 ½" or 5 ¼" disks.
  - *Student Resource Disk* contains the unformatted files to be used to complete the hands-on activities in this text. This master disk can be duplicated for students. Arrangements can be made to have the *Student Resource Disk* bound to copies of this text for an additional fee — contact your Regents/Prentice Hall representative to make arrangements.
  - *Instructor's Resource Disk* contains files for chapter summaries, competencies, topic goals and tips, solutions for hands-on activities, competency tests, and supplementary problems.
- *Course Outlines on Disk* contains files and other information from the Instructor's Manual which allow the professor to customize lecture outlines and course syllabi with ease.
- Transparencies illustrate essential screen displays for the application software programs.
- *Test Manager* (3 ½" and 5 ¼" disks) is a test generating package that allows professors to customize the test questions contained in the Instructor's Manual. Users can edit, add to, and scramble test questions.
- Videos covering DOS, WordPerfect, Lotus 1-2-3, and dBASE (by Video Professor) are available to qualified adopters.

Activities Build on Previous Work
Exercises, projects, and applications build on previous work as you progress through the text. Exercises build on exercises completed at the end of previous topics, projects build on projects completed at the end of previous chapters, and real-world applications build on applications completed in previous parts. This sequential approach to developing files allows you to see how documents, models, or databases can evolve and become increasingly more refined, powerful, and useful.

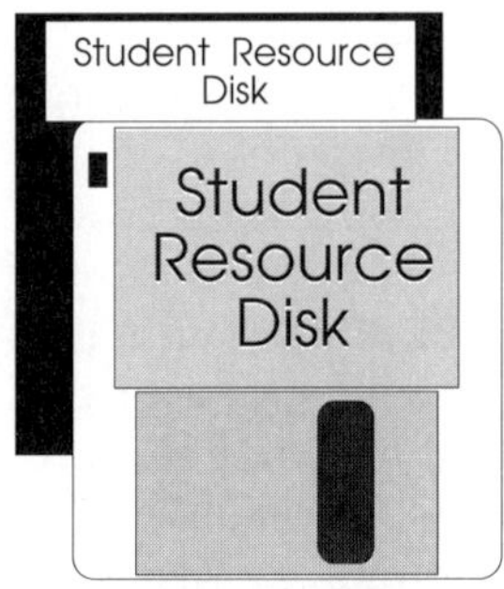

Student Resource Disks
Many of the files on which you work are on the *Student Resource Disk* available from your instructor.

The COMPASS Series

This text is part of the COMPASS (**COMP**uter **A**pplication **S**oftware **S**eries) series. The DOS, WordPerfect, Lotus 1-2-3, and dBASE III Plus parts of this text are also available as separate "Short Course" volumes. If you cover only some of these programs in your course, you can use these separate stand-alone texts instead of this combined volume. Also, as programs are updated or new programs become accepted in the academic community, new short-course texts are developed. Contact your local Regents/Prentice Hall representative for a current list of the titles available in this series.

Acknowledgments

No book is the result of the efforts of a single person, and that is especially true of this text, where many people went the extra mile to create the best possible text. Although I accept full responsibility for any of the text's shortcomings, full credit for the things that were done correctly belongs to others.

The following teachers took time out of their busy schedules and traveled to another state to sit down with me in an all-day session. At that meeting they laid out a plan for me to follow to create the best possible revision of this text:

- Richard Bernardin, Cape Cod Community College
- Catherine Brotherton, Riverside Community College
- Linda Dowell, St. Johns River Community College
- Nancy P. Houston, Grove City College
- Toni M. Hutto, Wake Technical Community College
- Sarah J. MacArthur
- James A. Pope, Old Dominion University
- Howard Pullman, Youngstown State University
- Frederick L. Wells, DeKalb College at Gwinnett Center
- Myrna Wulfson, Rockland Community College

A number of people reviewed the outline and/or the final manuscript with care and attention that the author had not previously seen. Many of these instructors spent days reading the manuscript and sharing

Procedures vs Applications

Survey after survey shows that the massive introduction of microcomputers in business has not improved productivity. Part of the problem is that users are not skilled in procedures. However, the much greater problem is that users do not know how to use computers productively. The computer is a wonderful problem-solving tool, but users need more training and experience in using it as such. In computer courses, problem-solving must be introduced at the earliest possible time.

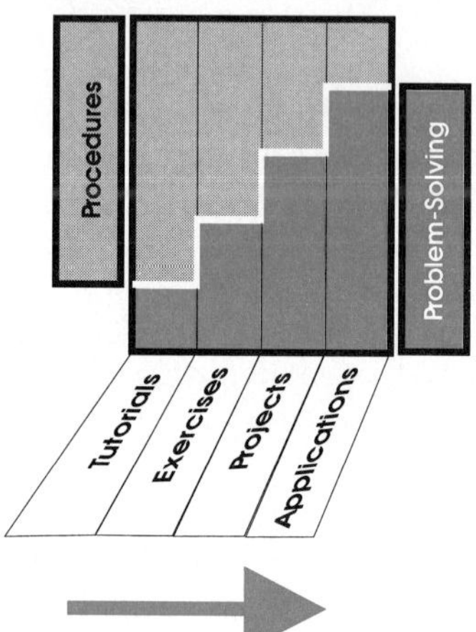

As you progress from tutorials through exercises, projects, and real-world applications, the focus of the activities gradually shifts from an emphasis on procedures (keystrokes) to an emphasis on applications (problem solving).

their insights with the author. Their efforts often required that I reorganize and rewrite major sections of the text; and the final text has been greatly improved as a result.

- Nancy M. Acree, University of Puget Sound
- Nicki Baxter, Waukesha County Technical College
- Richard Bernardin, Cape Cod Community College
- Catherine Brotherton, Riverside Community College
- Bruce Case, Thomas Jefferson High School
- Lee D. Cornell, Mankato State University
- Diane C. Davis, Southern Illinois University
- Linda Dowell, St. Johns River Community College
- Lois T. Elliot, Prince George's Community College
- William J. Ferns, Jr., Baruch College
- Debbie Fields, Las Positas College
- Deborah Haseltine, State Technical Institute at Memphis
- Dennis R. Heckman, Portland Community College
- Vicki Hightower, Elon College
- Toni M. Hutto, Wake Technical Community College
- Donal Janes, Los Medanos College
- M. Kathleen Malenky, Cape Cod Community College
- Donna M. Matherly, Tallahassee Community College
- Mike Michaelson, Palomar College
- Elise S. Patterson-Crate, Florida Community College
- James A. Pope, Old Dominion University
- Jane Rada, Western Wisconsin Technical College
- Bonnie M. Skelton, Radford University
- Eugene F. Stafford, Iona College
- Frederick L. Wells, DeKalb College at Gwinnett Center
- Donna Yoder, Pima Community College

I would also like to express my appreciation to many others who helped me implement the plan for this text. The supplements that accompany this text were prepared by Linda Dowell and Donna Matherly. Their work expands on, and improves upon, the content of this text, and both are a joy to work with. Donna Matherly, Meredith Flynn, and Robert Fiske tested tutorials, exercises, projects, and applications for various parts of the book. They tried to chase down every error in concept or keystroke, and any that remain are not a result of their efforts.

Thanks also to all of those at Regents/Prentice Hall who brought the final result into print. Cecil Yarbrough coordinated all aspects of the book's production and worked as hard as anyone has ever worked to make it the best possible text. His efforts are greatly appreciated and are vividly illustrated in all aspects of this text. Liz Kendall helped plan the revision, coordinated all aspects of the project's development, and encouraged me over long months of writing and rewriting. Liz's assistant, Jane Avery, successfully juggled all of the reviewing and author contacts to keep information flowing at all times. Cathy Morin electronically published the manuscript and worked side by side with me, laying out the pages and suggesting many improvements along the way.

Dennis P. Curtin
Marblehead, Massachusetts

CONVENTIONS

NOTATION USED IN QUICK REFERENCE COMMANDS

In this text, you will occasionally find notations such as **COPY A:**<*filename.ext*> **B:** or **REN** <*oldname.ext*> <*newname.ext*>. The names in brackets indicate the data that you should enter in your own commands. Substitute your own filenames for the brackets and the text within them. Thus, to copy a file named MYFILE.WP5 from drive A to drive B, you would type **COPY A:MYFILE.WP5 B:**. To rename a file named JUMPSTRT.WP5 as MYFILE.WP5, you would type **REN JUMPSTRT.WP5 MYFILE.WP5**.

This text uses the following conventions for commands and prompts.

Commands

All keys you press (except those in boxes such as [Enter←]) and all characters you type are shown in the typeface used here for **FILENAME**.

- Keys you press in sequence are separated by commas. For example, if you are to press [Y], release it, and then press [Enter←], the instructions read [Y], [Enter←].
- Keys you press simultaneously are separated by dashes. For example, if you are to hold down [Ctrl] while you press [PrtScr], the instructions read [Ctrl]-[PrtScr].

Prompts

All prompts, messages, and menu choices are shown *in this typeface*. When a prompt appears, read it carefully and do as it says.

Summary

Now that you have read about how keys and commands are presented, see if you can understand the following instructions.

 KEY/Strokes

To List the Files on a Disk

1. Insert the disk with the files to be listed into the drive.
2. Type **DIR** <*drive:*> and press [Enter←].

To follow these instructions, you begin by inserting the disk with the files to be listed into one of the disk drives. If you insert the disk into drive A, you then type the command **DIR A:** and press [Enter←]. If you insert the disk into drive B, you would type **DIR B:** and press [Enter←].

Microcomputers and DOS

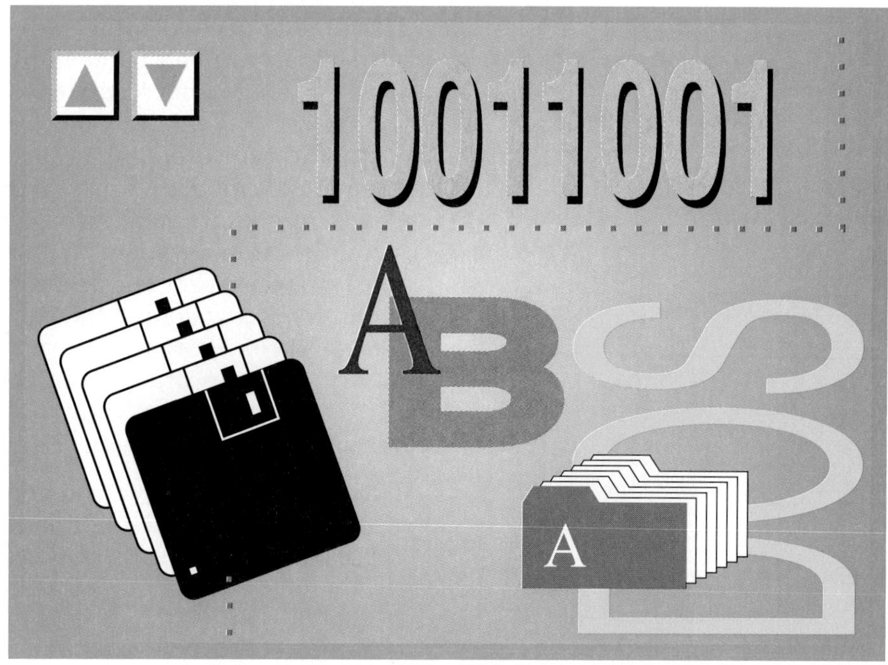

CHAPTER 1

The Computer System

TOPIC 1

The Digital Revolution

After completing this topic, you will be able to:

- Explain the concepts behind the term *digital*
- Describe how information is stored, processed, and communicated in a computer
- Explain the difference between a bit and a byte

A single concept, called *digital processing*, makes possible the computer and many other modern electronic devices such as compact disc players. Digital processing simply refers to a way information—be it music, numbers, words, or images—is stored, processed, and used.

The term *digital* comes from the word *digit*, which means a single number. When you write a check or count your change, you use the digits 0 through 9. For example, the digits 1 and 9 can convey $1 or $9, or they can be combined to convey $19, $91, $19.19, and so on. This numbering system is called the decimal system. You use this system when you dial the phone, look up pages in the index of a book, or address a letter to a specific street address.

The familiar decimal system is complicated. To master the system in grade school, you had to memorize numerous tables. For example, to add 2 + 2, you do not calculate, you recall the answer 4 from memory. To multiply 3 × 2, you recall the answer 6 from memory. If you never learned the tables or forgot them, you would find it hard or even impossible to calculate with the decimal system.

Computers and other digital equipment use a simpler numbering system, the binary system. The binary system uses only two numbers, 0 and 1, to store, process, and display all digits. As the table "Decimal and Binary Equivalents" shows, any number can be conveyed with these two digits.

Binary numbers are used in computers because their two components, the 0 and 1, can be stored, processed, and communicated by devices that have two states. For example:

- If a device can be turned on and off, on can represent 1 and off 0.
- If a device can emit high or low voltage, the high voltage can represent 1 and the low voltage 0.

DECIMAL AND BINARY EQUIVALENTS

Decimal Number	Binary Equivalent
0	0
1	1
2	10
3	11
4	100
5	101
6	110
7	111
8	1000
9	1001
10	1010
11	1011

- If magnetic particles can be aligned on a surface so that they point in opposite directions, one direction can represent 1 and the other 0.
- If dots on a display screen can be either illuminated or dark, 1 can tell the screen to illuminate a dot and 0 to leave it dark.
- If a printer can print black spots onto a white sheet of paper, 1 can tell the printer to print a black dot and 0 to leave it white.

All these techniques are used in microcomputer systems to store, process, and communicate data. To take it one step further, you can convey information with these two digits if you have an agreed-on code. Let's now see how various devices and codes can be used to convey information.

The Lanterns in the Belfry

Two lanterns were used to signal Paul Revere which way the British were heading.

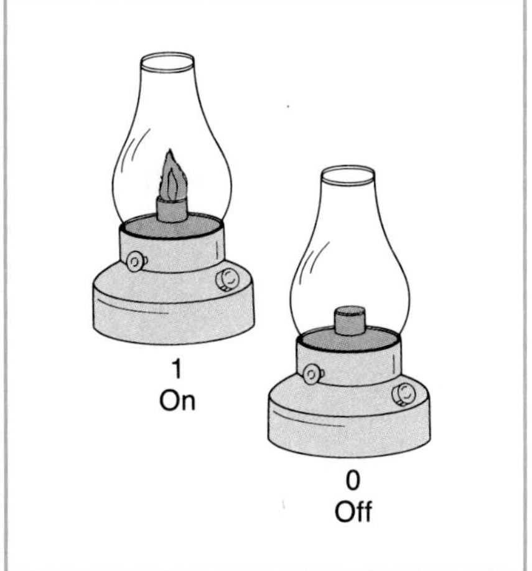

When one lamp was on (1) and the other was off (0), it meant the British were moving by land.

When both lamps were on (1), it meant the British were moving by sea.

Paul Revere's Ride—The First Digital Revolution?

You may have heard or read Longfellow's poem *Paul Revere's Ride*. Here are a few stanzas of the poem.

Listen, my children, and you shall hear
Of the midnight ride of Paul Revere,
On the eighteenth of April, in Seventy-five;
Hardly a man is now alive
Who remembers that famous day and year.

He said to his friend, "If the British march
By land or sea from the town tonight,
Hang a lantern aloft in the belfry arch
Of the North Church as a signal light,—
One, if by land, and two, if by sea;
And I on the opposite shore will be,
Ready to ride and spread the alarm
Through every Middlesex village and farm,
For the country folk to be up and to arm."

"One, if by land, and two, if by sea" is a digital message. When America was a colony of England, Paul Revere was assigned the responsibility of notifying the Minutemen who lived in the countryside if the British left Boston to attack them. He and his friend Robert Newman, the sexton of Old North Church, decided that Revere would wait on the other side of the harbor so that he had a head start should the British troops begin to move. Newman would remain in Boston to watch for any troop movements. Newman would light one lantern in the belfry of Old North Church if the British were leaving Boston by land and two lanterns if they were going by sea. This simple digital signal sent Paul Revere on his famous ride that resulted in "the shot heard round the world" at the bridge in Concord.

The Telegraph—The First Digital Code

Lanterns have their limits when it comes to sending information. It is hard to spell out messages. For example, if the British had been able to take an unexpected route, Paul Revere's prearranged code would not have been able to convey the message. This problem was solved by Samuel Morse's invention of the telegraph in the late 1830s.

The First Digital Code
The telegraph was used to send dots and dashes down a wire to a recipient at the other end of the line.
Bettmann Archive, Inc.

To send a telegraph message, you tap on a key to transmit pulses of electricity down a wire to a distant listener. At the listener's end, a device called a sounder clicks when each pulse arrives. Like the lanterns in the belfry, this is a digital process. However, random clicks do not convey information, so Morse developed a code based on the pauses between the clicks, using a short pause and a long pause. When printed, these were represented as dots and dashes. An experimental telegraph line was constructed between Baltimore and Washington, and on May 24, 1844, a series of long and short pauses between clicks sent the historic message "What hath God wrought" down this first telegraph line.

A Silicon Chip
In computers, hundreds of "chips" are etched together onto a large silicon wafer (top). Each chip contains millions of transistors and is cut from the wafer and mounted on a larger board to which wires can be connected (bottom). These chips are the reason modern computers are so small.
Courtesy Hewlett Packard

The Digital Computer

Like these early message systems, computers need a device that can send, process, or store information and a code to give the information meaning. Instead of lanterns or a key to send electrical pulses down a wire, a computer uses transistors. Like lanterns, transistors have only two possible states: on and off. When thousands of transistors are packed together, it is called an integrated circuit, or silicon chip. These chips store and process large amounts of information. Instead of using a code of long and short pauses, as Morse did, a microcomputer uses the transistor's on and off states. The code is based on *bits* and groups of bits called *bytes*.

Bits

The smallest unit stored or processed in a computer is the *bit*, a contraction of the more descriptive phrase **bi**nary digi**t**. In the computer, on (or 1) is represented by a high voltage, and off (or 0) is represented by a low voltage. On a magnetic disk, the same information is stored by changing the direction in which magnetized particles on the disk's surface are aligned.

To visualize a bit, imagine a light bulb. When the light bulb is on, it represents the number 1. When it is off, it represents the number 0. You could send a message to a nearby recipient by turning the bulb on and off, but to send even a short message would take a long time.

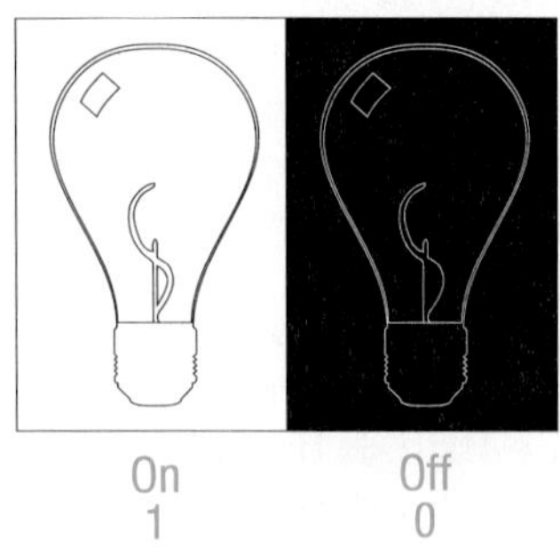

A Bit
A bit is like a light bulb–it is either on to indicate 1 or off to indicate 0.

Bytes

Since bits are small units and can convey only two possible states, they are organized into larger units to convey more information. This larger unit is a *byte*, and it contains 8 bits. Since each bit has two states and there are 8 bits in a byte, the total amount of information that can be conveyed is 2^8 (2 raised to the 8th power), or 256 possible combinations.

A Byte
To understand a byte, imagine using eight light bulbs instead of one. Each letter in the alphabet could be assigned a pattern of lights. For example, this pattern could represent the letter A.

CHARACTERS AND THEIR ASCII CODES

Character	ASCII Code
A	0100 0001
a	0110 0001
B	0100 0010
b	0110 0010

To give meaning to each of these combinations, they must be assigned a code. The code can specify that each of them represents a letter, number, symbol, or command to the computer. For example, the number 0100 0001 can stand for the letter A.

Usually, you see these numbers converted to characters such as letters, numbers, and symbols displayed on the screen. To standardize the meaning of these number combinations, the computer industry uses several codes, including the **A**merican **S**tandard **C**ode for **I**nformation **I**nterchange, or ASCII (pronounced "as-key"), the code frequently used on microcomputers. The table "Characters and Their ASCII Codes" lists some typical characters and their ASCII codes.

FROM BYTES TO GIGABYTES

Power	Actual Bytes	Shorthand
2^0	1	1 byte
2^1	2	2 bytes
.	.	.
2^{10}	1,024	1KB (kilobyte)
2^{11}	2,048	2KB
2^{12}	4,096	4KB
.	.	.
2^{18}	262,144	256KB
2^{19}	524,288	512KB
2^{20}	1,048,576	1MB (megabyte)
2^{21}	2,097,152	2MB
2^{22}	4,194,304	4MB
.	.	.
2^{30}	1,073,741,824	1GB (gigabyte)

Shorthand
Most references to a computer's storage and processing capacity use the byte as the basic unit of measurement. The number of bytes is usually given in shorthand. For example, you'll see advertisements that say a computer's memory is 640,000 bytes, or 640KB. The KB (for kilobyte) indicates a magnitude of 1,000. As memory increases, the KB is replaced by an MB (for megabyte), which indicates a magnitude of 1,000,000. For example, you can say the computer's memory is 1,000,000 bytes, 1,000KB, or 1MB. As computer capacity expands, you'll begin to encounter the next levels of magnitude: the gigabyte (1 billion bytes) and the terabyte (1 trillion bytes).

When we refer to bytes in this way, we round the numbers to make them easier to remember. Bytes are calculated by raising the number 2 to various powers. The number 2 is used because digital devices have two states—on and off. The number 2 raised to the 10th power is 1,024. This is usually rounded off to 1,000 (or 1KB). The table "From Bytes to Gigabytes" shows the number 2 raised to some of the powers between 0 and 30, the actual bytes that result, and how these bytes are expressed in shorthand as kilobytes, megabytes, or gigabytes.

EXERCISE

BYTES, KILOBYTES, AND MEGABYTES

Bytes	Kilobytes	Megabytes
1,024	________	______
524,288	________	______
1,048,576	________	______
2,097,152	________	______
16,777,216	________	______

EXERCISE 1

CONVERTING BYTES, KILOBYTES, AND MEGABYTES

Memory and other devices are frequently described in terms of bytes, kilobytes, and megabytes. In the table "Bytes, Kilobytes, and Megabytes," bytes are listed in the first column. In the next two columns, indicate the number of bytes in kilobytes and then in megabytes. Round off where necessary.

TOPIC 2

The Anatomy of a Microcomputer

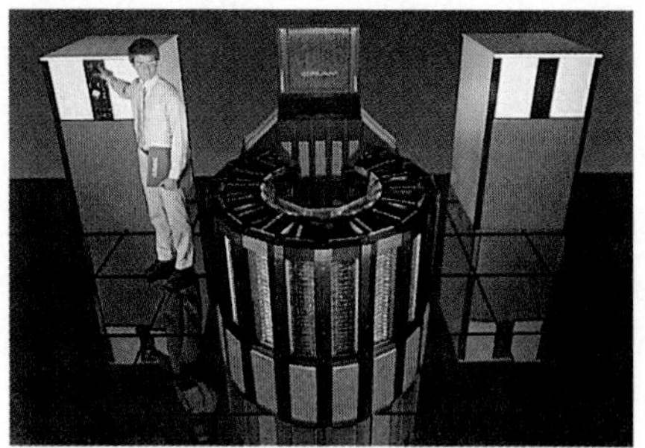

Supercomputers
Supercomputers are powerful computers used to solve scientific problems and manipulate large graphic files.
Courtesy of Cray Research Inc.

After completing this topic, you will be able to:

- Describe the function of the central processing unit (CPU)
- Explain how peripheral equipment such as a printer is attached to the computer
- Describe how "boards" can be plugged into expansion slots in the computer to expand its capabilities and improve its performance
- List things to do and to avoid doing with your computer

Computers come in many designs, but one way to classify them is according to their size, power, and portability.

- Supercomputers are the most powerful computers available. They are used for many scientific and technical applications, including weather forecasting and automotive design. They are also used to generate the extremely realistic graphics seen in many movie special effects.
- Mainframe computers are room-sized computers operated by a special staff. They are normally used for centralized business functions such as accounting and inventory control.
- Minicomputers are less powerful than mainframe computers and are anywhere from refrigerator size to desktop size. They are frequently used by small companies or by departments within large corporations.

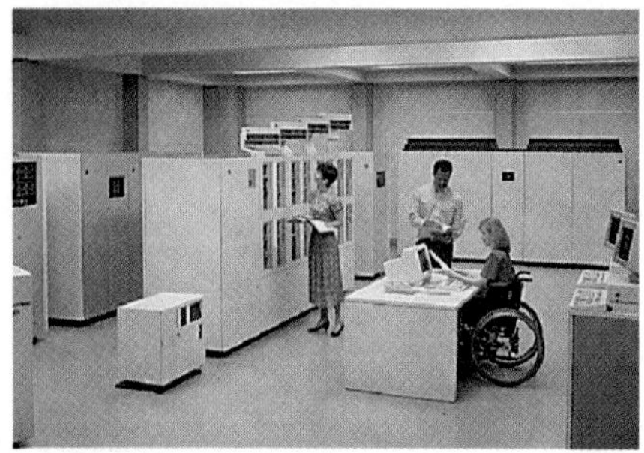

Mainframe Computers
The mainframe computer is often the corporate workhorse, occupying an entire room all by itself and maintained and operated by a highly trained staff of specialists.
Courtesy of IBM Corporation

More recently, advances in technology allowed for the development of smaller, more personal computers.

- Desktop computers, those used by individuals, are designed to be permanently positioned on a desk. Portable computers (also called *transportables*) are smaller than desktop computers so that they can be carried, but you wouldn't want to carry one with you on a subway or a long walk through an airport terminal.
- Laptop computers can be carried like a small attaché case or packed in a suitcase. They are designed so that they can run on rechargeable battery packs. Notebook computers are like laptops but even smaller, so they can be easily carried in a briefcase. In that sense, they are almost as convenient as a pocket calculator. However, they are working computers that can run programs and exchange information with other, larger computers.
- Handheld, or palm-top, computers have very small keyboards, so they cannot be easily used for word processing or other applications that require you to enter a lot of data. However, their small size makes them useful in many special applications. For example, salespeople use them to record customers' inventories,

Minicomputers
Minicomputers are smaller than mainframes and are normally used for departmental computing.
Courtesy of IBM Corporation

and others use them to make calculations and maintain appointment schedules and phone numbers and addresses.

Desktop Computers
Desktop computers are currently the fastest selling microcomputers.
Courtesy of IBM Corporation

Laptop and Notebook Computers
Laptop, and the slightly smaller, notebook computers are designed so that you can take them with you on trips or between the office and home.
Courtesy of IBM Corporation

Handheld or Palm-Top Computers
Handheld, or palm-top, computers are the smallest of all computers. Their functions are still somewhat limited, but their portability makes them very popular for many applications.
Courtesy of Hewlett-Packard

The Central Processing Unit

The heart of a computer is the central processing unit (CPU). In microcomputers, the CPU is a microprocessor—the device that made microcomputers possible in the first place. Though small, a microprocessor is extremely powerful; it (along with its operating system software) performs three key functions:

- It coordinates all the computer's activities. For example, it retrieves files from the disk, interprets data and commands entered from the keyboard, and sends data to a printer.
- It performs arithmetic calculations like addition and subtraction. For example, if you enter a list of numbers in a spreadsheet and ask for the total, the microprocessor performs the addition.
- It performs logical operations using equal to, greater than, and less than comparisons. For example, it can determine if your grades are higher or lower than those of other students in the same course, and it can print a list ranking everyone in descending order of the grades they received.

The speed and power of a computer are largely determined by the microprocessor that is used for its CPU. New microprocessors are periodically introduced as advances in technology allow them to be improved, and quite a number of versions are in widespread use. For example, the earliest IBM PCs used the Intel 8088 or 8086 chip. The IBM AT computers introduced next used the Intel 80286 (called the 286). Today, the most widely used chip in IBM and compatible computers is the Intel 80386 (called the 386), but it is being replaced on newer computer models by the Intel i486 (called the 486), and widespread use of the i586 is in the near future.

The most recent microprocessors are available in at least two versions and sometimes three. The full-featured versions are referred to by their numbers alone, for example, 386 and 486, or with the suffix *dx*, for example, 386dx and 486dx. Slightly less powerful but also less expensive versions use the suffix *sx*, for example, 386sx and 486sx. Finally, there is a version called the 486dx2 that is faster than a 486sx but slightly slower than a 486dx. The 2 following the dx indicates that the chip runs twice as fast internally as it does when it communicates with other parts of the computer.

The Microprocessor
The microprocessor is an extremely small but powerful device that is used as the central processing unit (CPU) in the microcomputer.
Courtesy of IBM Corporation

Clock Rates
The clock rate of a computer determines how fast it runs and affects how powerful it is.

IBM MICROPROCESSOR CHIPS

Microprocessor	Speed (MHz)	Date
8086 or 8088	4.7	1981
80286	8-12	1982
80386dx	25	1988
80386sx	16	1988
80386dx	33	1989
i486dx	25	1989
80386sx	20	1989
i486dx	33	1990
i486sx	20	1991
i486dx	50	1991
i486dx2	50	1992
i486dx2	66	1992

The version of the microprocessor is not the only consideration when you are choosing a computer. Another important variable is the *clock rate*, which is specified in megahertz (millions of cycles per second, or MHz). The clock rate indicates the speed at which the chip processes data. Like a caller at a square dance, it sets the pace for all activity. The higher the clock rate, the faster the computer. For example, a 33 megahertz 386 is faster than a 20 megahertz 386.

For most applications in a work environment where speed is essential, computers with 386sx chips are now becoming the minimum requirement.

The table "IBM Microprocessor Chips" lists the Intel microprocessor chips used in various IBM and compatible computers and the date they were first shipped to manufacturers.

Memory

For the computer's CPU to process data, it must have access to the data and instructions, called programs. The data and programs are normally stored in the computer's internal memory when they are being used. There are two types of internal memory—read-only memory (ROM) and random-access memory (RAM).

Read-Only Memory (ROM)

Read-only memory (ROM) is static, unchanging memory. Your computer can read data stored in ROM, but you cannot enter data into ROM or change the data already there. The data in ROM are permanently recorded on memory chips by the computer's manufacturer. Neither turning the computer off nor electrical failure affects it; the data will still be there when you resume. ROM is generally used to store programs and instructions that the computer frequently needs. For example, it contains the instructions your computer follows to start up when you first turn it on.

Random-Access Memory (RAM)

Random-access memory (RAM) is also called main, primary, or user memory. When you load a program into the computer or create a document with an application program, the program you load and the data you enter from the keyboard are temporarily stored in RAM. Usually, if you turn off the computer, any programs or data stored in this memory are lost; thus RAM is said to be volatile memory.

The term *random* comes from the way the data in memory can be located, or accessed, by the computer. One way to understand random access is to think of the differences between a tape player and a compact disc player. If you want to play the third song on a tape, you must advance the tape past the first two songs. This is called sequential access because you must access each song in sequence. On a compact disc player, you can advance directly to the track where the third song begins without having to play the first two songs. This is called random access because you can access songs in any order.

Ports

A computer system's external components, or peripherals, may include a printer, display screen, modem, keyboard, and mouse. You connect these peripherals to the computer with cables that plug into sockets mounted on the computer's cabinet. These sockets are called ports because, like seaports where ships enter and leave a country and airports where airplanes enter and leave a city, they are where signals carrying information enter and leave the computer. Some ports are dedicated to specific devices such as the keyboard, but there are two versatile ports—serial ports and parallel ports.

Memory
The Scrabble brand crossword game is like a computer's memory. The instruction book is like ROM—you can read it, but you cannot change it. The game board is like RAM—you can add, delete, or move data around on it.

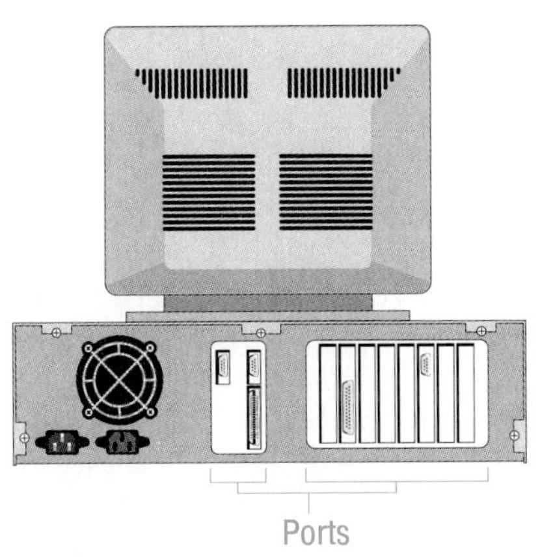

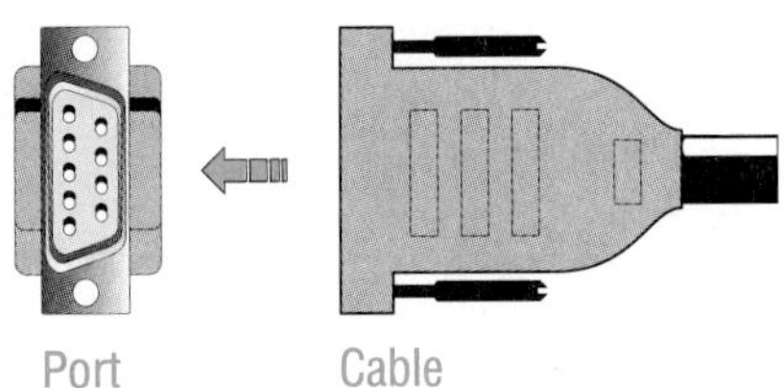

Ports
Ports are where data enter and leave the computer. Ports are mounted on the back of the computer. You plug cables into ports to connect peripherals such as printers and mice.

Serial Ports
Serial ports (sometimes called RS-232-C ports) are where you attach mice, modems (devices used to communicate with other computers), and some types of printers. When data are sent out of a serial port, they are sent 1 bit at a time. Since the data are processed inside the computer 8, 16, or even 32 bits at a time, a serial port is like a narrowing on a highway where it enters a narrow tunnel. Data slows down, just as the highway traffic does, so that they can funnel out of the computer in single file.

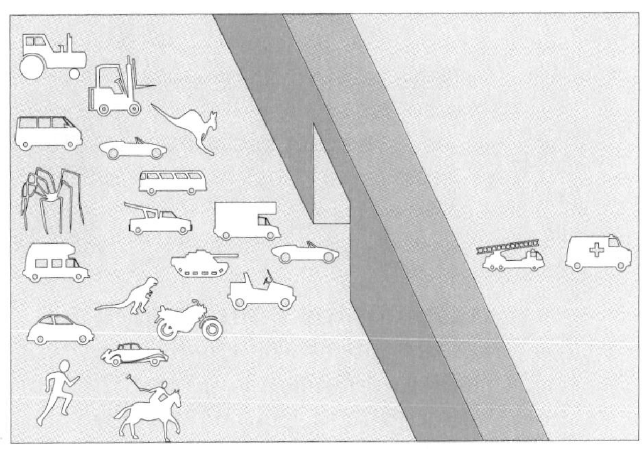

Serial Ports
A serial port is like a single-lane tunnel. Information fed to it has to squeeze through the port a single bit at a time.

Parallel Ports

Parallel ports (sometimes called Centronics interfaces) carry data 8 bits at a time on parallel paths. Because they can transmit data 8 bits, or 1 byte, at a time, they are a faster way for the computer to communicate with input and output devices. There is less narrowing than on a serial port, so traffic moves faster. Parallel ports are usually used to plug in certain types of printers.

Parallel Ports
A parallel port is like a tunnel with almost the same number of lanes as the highway that feeds it. Information flows through faster since there is little or no constriction.

Expansion Slots and Boards

Many users like to customize or update their computers to better serve their needs. To make this possible, most computers have expansion slots inside the cabinet into which you can plug boards (also called *cards* and *adapters* and sometimes prefaced with *add-on*, *add-in*, or *expansion*). Boards plugged into these slots perform just as if they were built into the computer. Boards can serve any one of many functions. For example, boards can be added to expand the computer's memory, allow the computer to display colors or graphics, send and receive FAXes, or call up other computers. Still others connect peripherals or are the peripherals themselves. For example, you can plug in a board that controls a hard disk drive located elsewhere in the system, or you can plug in a board that contains the hard disk drive itself.

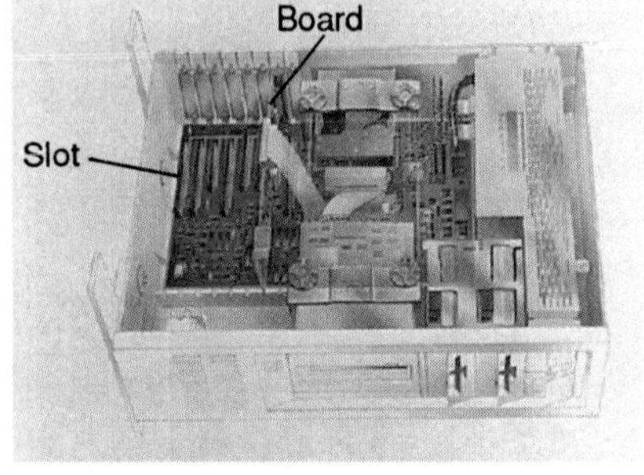

Expansion Slots and Boards
Expansion slots inside the computer allow you to plug in boards that expand the computer's capabilities.
Courtesy of IBM Corporation

Inside a Computer
If you were to remove the cover from a microcomputer, you would see a green circuit board (called the motherboard). All other elements are either mounted onto this board or connected to it. In this photograph, you can see the power supply (upper right) and a silver-colored floppy and black hard disk (bottom).
Courtesy of IBM Corporation

Caring for Your Computer

Computers are rugged and will provide good service with minimal maintenance if you treat them properly. Here are a few important dos and don'ts that will ensure you get the maximum life out of your equipment.

- **DO** turn down the screen intensity or use a screen-saving program if you will not be working on the computer for a while so that an image is not burned into the display screen's phosphor surface.
- **DO** use a surge protector between the computer and the wall outlet to protect the computer from any surges of electricity that might come down the power line. Surges occur when the power company restores service after it has been lost or when a nearby line is struck by lightning. A surge temporarily increases the current in the line, much as a wave of water is created when you suddenly remove a dam from a river. This surge of current can damage a computer.
- **DON'T** use it during lightning storms. If fact, to be completely safe, unplug it when there is lightning.
- **DON'T** get it wet.
- **DON'T** drop it.
- **DON'T** smoke around it.
- **DON'T** leave it where it is exposed to direct sunlight.
- **DON'T** turn it off more often than necessary. Computers, like other electronic equipment, are harmed more by the surge of power that runs through them when you first turn them on than they are by being left on all the time. Some users never turn their computers off; others turn them off only at the end of the day or on weekends.
- **DON'T** use an ultrasonic humidifier without a mineral filter near the computer. These units break the water and minerals into particles that are then distributed throughout the room. When the particles land on a computer, the water evaporates, leaving behind a powder that can damage sensitive equipment.

MAINFRAMES AND MICROS

As late as 1977, nearly 100% of the world's computer power was commanded by mainframe and other large computers with dumb terminals attached. (A dumb terminal is a screen and keyboard that can send and receive data to and from a computer, but which isn't a computer itself.) By 1987, less than 1% of the world's computer power was commanded by large computers. U.S. companies controlled some two-thirds of a global computer market of 90 million personal computers, more than half of them in the U.S.*

*From "The Drexel Era," *The Wall Street Journal*, February 16, 1990, p. A12.

THE DEVELOPMENT OF THE COMPUTER

The first electronic digital computer built in the United States, ENIAC, was unveiled at the University of Pennsylvania in 1946. It weighed 30 tons, filled the space of a two-car garage, and contained 18,000 vacuum tubes, which failed on average at the rate of one every seven minutes. It cost half a million dollars at 1946 prices.

Today, the same amount of computing power is contained in a pea-sized silicon chip. Almost any home computer costing as little as $100 can outperform ENIAC. Put another way, if the automobile and airplane businesses had developed like the computer business, a Rolls Royce would cost $2.75 and run for 3 million miles on one gallon of gas. And a Boeing 767 would cost just $500 and circle the globe in twenty minutes on five gallons of gas.*

*Tom Forester, ed., *The Information Technology Revolution* (Cambridge, Mass.: MIT Press, 1985).

EXERCISES

EXERCISE 1

DESCRIBING COMPUTERS IN THE LAB

List and describe in the table "Computers in the Lab" one or more of the computers in your lab. Because some of the information is not noted on the computer, you may have to ask your instructor or refer to the computer's manual.

A. Who is the manufacturer of each computer? Typical manufacturers are IBM and Compaq. If the computer is not one of these brands, does it act as if it were; for example, is it compatible with IBM's products?
B. What models are the computers? For example, they might be IBM PCs, XTs, ATs, or PS/2s.
C. How much random-access memory (RAM) does each computer have?
D. What kind of microprocessor (chip) does each use?
E. How many expansion slots does each have?

COMPUTERS IN THE LAB

Manufacturer/ID	Model	RAM	Chip	Number of Slots

EXERCISE 2

IDENTIFYING YOUR COMPUTER'S PORTS

Sketch the back of one of the computers in the lab, and then label the ports to which the peripherals are attached. They are probably not labeled on the computer, so you may have to ask your instructor or lab assistant. Try to identify the following ports, and then list what is attached to them:

A. Parallel port
B. Serial port
C. Keyboard port
D. Mouse port

TOPIC 3

Input and Output Devices

After completing this topic, you will be able to:

- Describe the keys on the computer's keyboard
- Describe how a mouse works
- Explain how scanners can input text and graphics
- Explain the differences between character and graphics display modes
- Explain how different types of printers form images on paper
- List and describe common printer features and controls

For a computer to be useful, you must be able to get information into or out of it. It is the input and output devices that perform this crucial role. The most common input device is the keyboard. The most common output devices are the display screen and printer.

The Keyboard

Keyboards vary in design and layout from computer to computer, but all have essentially the same types of keys. For example, two types of keyboards are used with most IBM or compatible computers—the original IBM PC keyboard and the enhanced keyboard introduced with the IBM AT. The main differences between the older and newer keyboards are the locations of the function keys and the directional arrow keys.

When you press keys on a keyboard, you should do so smoothly and quickly, just as if you were typing on a typewriter. Many keys have an autorepeat feature. If you hold one of these keys down, it will continue entering the key's character or repeating its function until you release it. Although this feature is occasionally useful, it can cause problems when you are first learning because strange things may happen when you hold a key down too long.

The Cursor
The cursor is a one-character-wide highlight that you move about the screen to enter, edit, and format text. Its shape can vary, but it is usually an underline or rectangle that highlights a single character.

Keyboard Lights

Many keyboards have lights that indicate the status of the CapsLock, NumLock, and ScrlLock keys. Each of these keys toggles like a wall switch. If it is not engaged when you press it, it becomes engaged. If it is engaged when you press it, it becomes disengaged. When any of these keys are engaged, the corresponding keyboard indicator light will be lit.

Cursor Movement Keys

Cursor movement keys move the cursor around the screen. You use the cursor to point to where you want to enter or edit data on the screen. Because program designers can change their functions, the keys used to move the cursor vary from program to program. However, the directional arrow keys move the cursor one line or character at a time in the direction of the arrow. On most programs, the PgUp and PgDn keys move the cursor a screen or page at a time.

Keyboards
These figures show the regular and enhanced keyboards. They are similar except for the location of the function keys and an extra set of cursor movemenet keys on the enhanced keyboard.

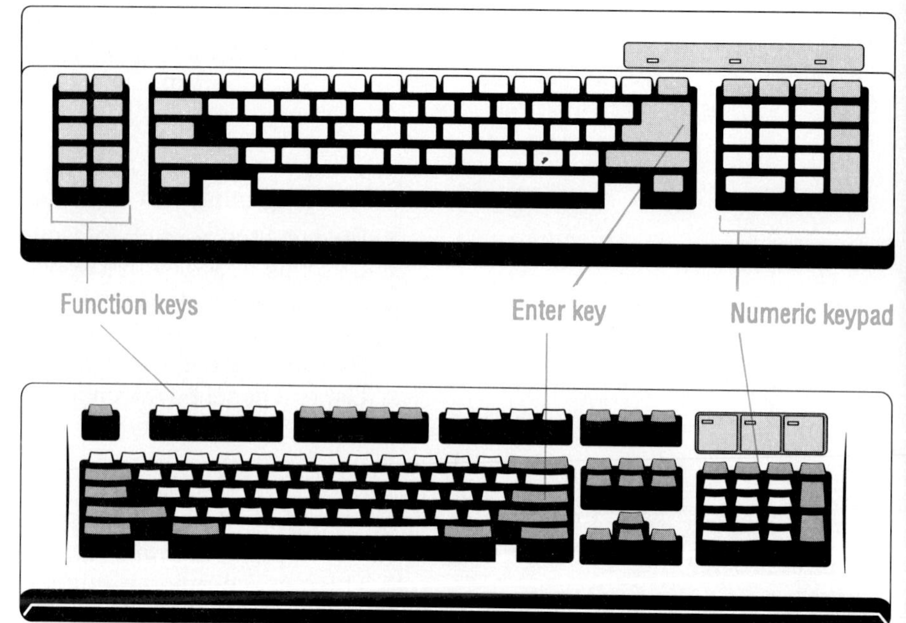

The Regular Keyboard

The Enhanced Keyboard

Entering and Editing Keys
Most of the keys on a keyboard are used to enter or edit data. The alphabetic keys are arranged just as they are on a typewriter. When you press these keys, you enter lowercase letters. If you hold down the Shift key when you press them, or if you engage the CapsLock key, you enter uppercase (capital) letters. If you engage CapsLock and then hold down Shift while typing, you enter lowercase letters.

If you are an experienced typist and are used to typing a lowercase L for 1 or an uppercase O for 0 (zero), do not do this on your computer. The computer treats numbers and letters differently, and you will run into difficulties by disregarding this distinction.

Numeric keys are located above the alphabetic keys and are labeled with both numbers and symbols. When you press these keys, you enter either the indicated numbers or, if you hold down Shift, the indicated symbols. On many computers, you can also enter numbers using the numeric keypad at the right end of the keyboard. Since some of the keys on the numeric keypad also move the cursor, you must press NumLock to switch back and forth between entering numbers and moving the cursor. When NumLock is engaged, the keys enter numbers. When it is not engaged, they move the cursor.

The Spacebar moves the cursor one character to the right and enters a space. If there is a character to the right of the cursor, it may be pushed to the right or replaced by a blank space depending on how the program is set up.

The ←Bksp key backs the cursor up and usually deletes characters as it does so. This lets you quickly back over and delete characters when you discover a mistake while entering text.

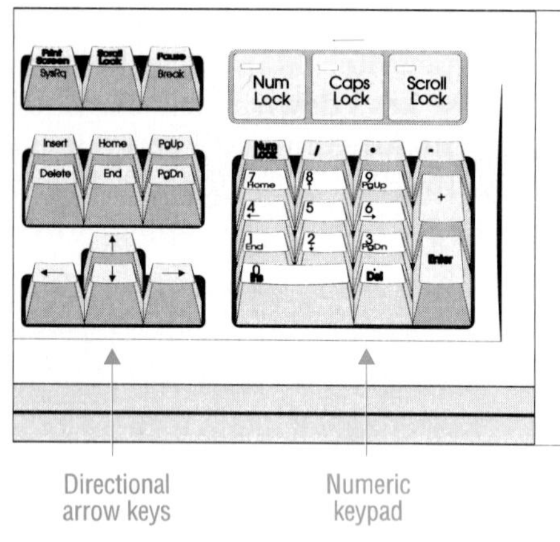

Directional Arrow Keys
All computers have directional arrow keys on the numeric keypad that work only when NumLock is not engaged. Enhanced keyboards have a separate set of directional arrow keys that work whether NumLock is engaged or not.

Tab and Backtab
The tab and backtab functions are both on the same key. It acts as backtab when you hold down [Shift].

The [Tab] key moves the cursor to the next tab stop, and the [Shift]-[Tab] key moves it back to the previous tab stop.

Command Keys
Many keys on the keyboard are used to execute commands rather than to enter or edit data. Although the function of many keys varies from program to program, the following functions usually apply:

The [Enter] key (also called the **Return** key) is often pressed as the final keystroke of an operation. For example, when you type a command or highlight one on a menu, you have to press [Enter] to send the command to the CPU.

The [Esc] (Escape) key is often (but by no means always) used to cancel a command in progress.

Function keys (designated [F1], [F2], [F3], and so on) perform functions assigned to them by the programmer. For example, on a word processing program, function keys are often assigned to select, copy, move, or delete text. On some keyboards, the function keys are grouped at the left side of the keyboard. On other computers, they are the top row of keys.

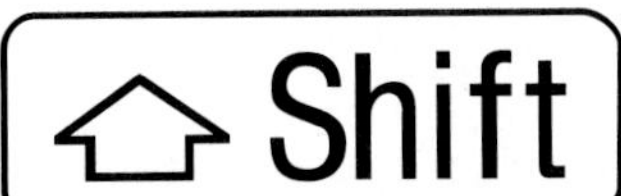

The Shift Key
The [Shift] key has an up arrow on it to indicate that it shifts to uppercase letters when held down.

Many keys are assigned more than one function. For instance, pressing the right directional arrow key may move the cursor one column or character at a time, but pressing the same key while holding down the [Ctrl] (Control) key may move the cursor several columns or characters at a time. Pressing the letter [B] enters the letter alone, but pressing [B] while holding down the [Alt] (Alternate) key might enter a code that tells the printer to begin boldfacing text. [Ctrl] and [Alt] do not send characters to the computer; they change what is sent when you press other keys. Using combinations of keys in this way lets software designers assign many more functions to the keyboard than there are keys. This is much like the standard typewriter, which uses **Shift** to enter fifty-two characters (twenty-six uppercase and twenty-six lowercase letters) with only twenty-six keys.

When you use these modifier keys, you hold them down first and then press the other key. The sequence in which you press the keys is important, so follow these procedures:

1. Hold down the [Alt], [Shift], or [Ctrl] key. These keys do not repeat or send commands to the computer, so you can hold them down as long as you want.
2. Press the function key just as if you were typing a character, then release both keys. If you hold the second key down, the command may repeat over and over until you release it, and this can create problems.

Mice

Many programs have added support for a mouse. As you move the mouse around on a flat, smooth surface, it moves a mouse pointer on the screen so that you can point to items. You can use a mouse for several procedures, including the following:

- Making menu choices from pull-down menus
- Moving the cursor through a document or other file
- Selecting (blocking) data so that they can be copied, moved, deleted, or formatted

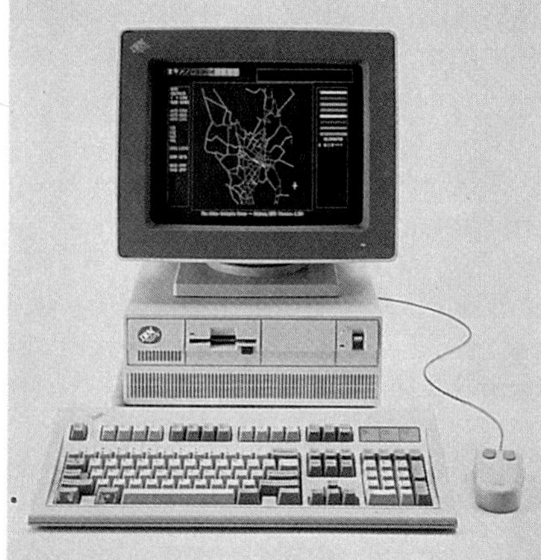

A Mouse
Mice are used to point to and then click on commands to execute them or to drag items about on the screen.
Courtesy of IBM Corporation

When you use a mouse for the first time, you will experience some frustration. It seems hard to point to just the right place and to click or hold the button at the right time. Don't let these frustrations get you down; everyone experiences them. In a few days, you'll wonder how you ever got along without a mouse. However, once you have mastered it, you have to decide when to put it down. Many operations can be performed faster from the keyboard. Users who continually switch back and forth between the keyboard and a mouse actually work slower than those who think through the fastest approach to a task.

When you use a mouse, you roll it across the surface of the desk. This motion tells the mouse which way to move the mouse pointer on the screen. To make the mouse pointer move in a predictable direction, it is important that you hold the mouse so that it is oriented parallel to the center line of the screen. This way, when you move the mouse up, down, or sideways, the mouse pointer moves in the expected direction. If you hold the mouse at an angle, your hand motion and the motion of the mouse pointer will not be coordinated.

When you use a mouse, here are some basic terms to remember:

- The *mouse pointer* refers to the arrow or other symbol on the screen that moves when you move the mouse.
- *Point* means to position the mouse pointer over or on some items on the screen.
- *Clicking* refers to pressing one of the buttons on the mouse.
- *Double clicking* refers to pressing one of the buttons on the mouse twice in rapid succession.
- *Drag* means to hold down one of the mouse buttons while you move the mouse. You do this frequently when you want to highlight a block of text so that you can format it. In other situations, this action drags the highlighted item to a new position on the screen.

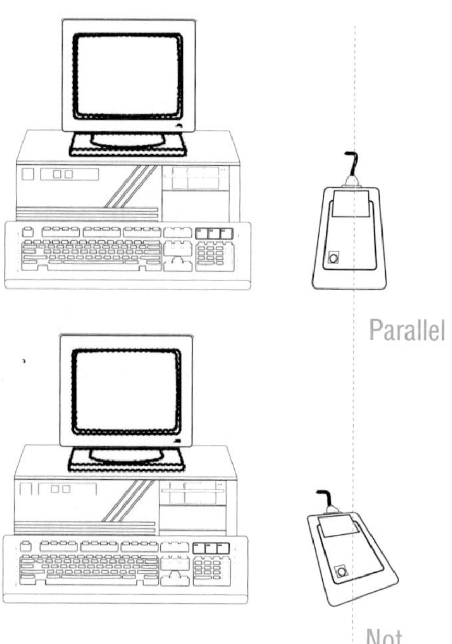

Holding and Dragging a Mouse
Hold the mouse parallel to the center line of the screen and when you move it, the mouse pointer on the screen will move in a predictable direction.

Scanners

You do not have to type everything into a computer. Scanners allow you to enter text and graphics from hardcopy such as printed or typed documents, photographs, or line drawings. You have seen scanners at work whenever you visit the supermarket. At the checkout counter, a clerk runs a handheld wand over a product or passes the product over a slot in the counter. These devices read the bar code on the product and display its price on the register. They also record the sale and make adjustments in inventory so that the store knows when to reorder. In most situations, however, scanners are used to scan text and graphics into the computer.

Text Scanners

When you type text into a computer and then print it out on a printer, you are actually converting the text from a digital form (the form used by the computer) to a printed form. Until recently, it was not easy to go the other way—to convert printed copy into an electronic form that could be processed by a computer. To make this conversion more efficient, scanners and optical character recognition (OCR) software have been developed to automate the process.

The scanner reads the pattern of dark characters against a light background, and the software converts each character to its digital ASCII number. This ASCII number is then stored in the computer's

CRT Displays
CRT displays create a sharp and readable image with a TV-like tube.
Courtesy of IBM Corporation

Flat Panel Displays
Flat panel displays are very thin, so they are used mostly in laptop and notebook computers.
Courtesy of IBM Corporation

memory or on a disk. Because the text is converted into its ASCII numbers, it can be stored, displayed, printed, and otherwise manipulated just as if it had been entered into the computer with the keyboard.

Graphics Scanners
To scan graphic images such as photographs, line drawings, charts, and maps into the computer, you use a scanner and graphics scanning software. The scanner works by breaking the image up into small spots, called pixels (for picture elements). It then assigns a numeric value to each pixel and stores it in memory or on the disk. The image can then be incorporated into a word-processed or desktop published document or manipulated with a program designed to work with images of this kind.

Display Screens

Many microcomputer display screens (also called monitors) are based on a cathode ray tube (CRT) like the one used in television sets. Others, such as those used in laptop and notebook computers, use light-emitting diodes (LEDs) or liquid crystal displays (LCDs), among other technologies, to create the image.

When you load a program, the display that you see on the screen is either a character display or a graphics display. These two types of screen displays are referred to as character mode and graphics mode. Which mode you see depends both on the system you are using and the program you are running. Most computer systems today are capable of displaying graphics, but many programs do not yet take advantage of this feature; they run in character mode.

Character Mode
When microcomputers were first developed, most systems displayed just letters, numbers, and a very limited set of other special characters (such as ▪). Altogether, 256 characters, called the character set, could be displayed and nothing else. Because of this limitation to a fixed set of characters, this is called character mode.

Character mode has the advantage of requiring little memory and operating very fast. Unfortunately, it also has several disadvantages. Since it can display only the characters in the computer's character set, it can display only simple graphics such as lines and boxes. Moreover, characters must occupy a fixed position on the screen and are all the same size. This prevents you from seeing different typefaces and type sizes until you make a printout. Finally, character mode cannot display photographs or line drawings.

Character Mode
Character mode displays only a limited number of characters and simple graphics. Here, a typical character mode program is shown.

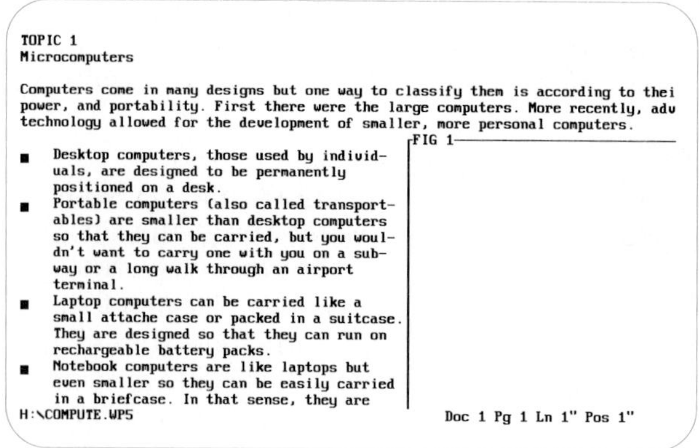

Graphics Mode
In graphics mode, the screen is divided into a grid of picture elements, or pixels. When an image is displayed on the screen, some of the pixels are illuminated, and some are left dark. On a color monitor, the colors of each pixel can also be set. The patterns of illuminated or colored pixels form characters and other images on the screen. This flexibility allows text and illustrations to be displayed on the screen.

Graphics Mode
Graphics mode can display any character and any graphic because each is created from a pattern of small dots, called pixels. Since these dots can be arranged in any pattern, any image can be displayed. Here, the same document as shown in the figure "Character Mode" is displayed in graphics mode.

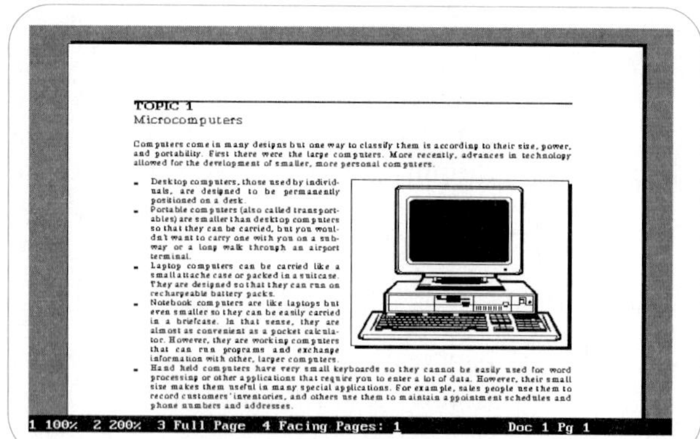

The resolution (sharpness) of a graphics display is determined by the number of pixels the screen is divided into. The resolution is indicated by the number of pixels displayed horizontally on the screen by the number displayed vertically. For example, a resolution of 320 by 200 pixels indicates the screen has 320 pixels horizontally and 200 vertically.

The resolution of a system is determined by which of the four most widely used standards, called display modes, it is using. In ascending order of sharpness, these modes are as follows:

- Color graphics adapters (CGA) display 320-by-200 resolution.
- Enhanced color graphics adapters (EGA) display 640-by-350 resolution.
- Video graphics arrays (VGA) display 640-by-480 resolution.
- Extended graphics arrays (XGA) display 1024-by-768 resolution. Many systems achieve this high resolution using a mode called Super VGA.

Screen Resolution

A high-resolution display screen is divided into more pixels than a low-resolution display is. The result is a sharper image because each character is formed from more dots.

High Resolution

Low Resolution

The graphics standard that your system uses is determined by the video display that is built into your computer or that was added by inserting a board into an expansion slot inside the computer. The monitor must exactly match the mode of the board, or it must be a multisync monitor that can display any of the popular modes. Multisync monitors are initially more expensive, but they allow you to upgrade to a higher resolution without buying a new monitor.

Although all the display modes can display colors, it is not essential that the monitor also do so. Since most printers cannot print colors, formatting a document for color is not usually important. There are several gray-scale monitors that are inexpensive (about one-third the cost of a color monitor of comparable quality) and give display quality similar to that of more expensive color monitors.

Graphics displays have several advantages. They can display different fonts, type sizes, and enhancements such as italics and proportional spacing. Also, both text and graphics can be displayed on the screen at the same time, which is especially important in desktop publishing applications. But there are also disadvantages; graphics displays require a lot of memory, and they operate more slowly than character displays.

WYSIWYG

The latest programs allow you to see on a graphics screen exactly what your document will look like before it is printed out. This is called WYSIWYG (pronounced "wizzy-wig"), or "What You See Is What You Get." WYSIWYG is now incorporated into high-end word processing and spreadsheet programs that have desktop publishing features. On programs that do not yet display a document for editing in WYSIWYG, this feature is offered as a document preview command that lets you see how the document will look when it is printed. Although you cannot edit a document in this preview mode, you can see where improvements might be made before you print it out. A true WYSIWYG display has the following features:

- Characters are displayed in the actual typeface, typestyle, and type size in which they will be printed.
- Paragraphs are displayed with the same line endings and line spacings with which they will be printed.
- Line drawings or photographs that are inserted into the document are displayed on the screen.
- Pages are displayed as they will print, including headers and footers, margins, and page numbers.
- Many programs have pull-down menus, icons, and scroll bars that make the programs easy to operate. These items make up what is known as a graphical user interface (GUI—pronounced "goo-ey").

Unfortunately, WYSIWYG displays are slow, even on the fastest computers. This is because much of the computer's processing power must be devoted to updating the screen display. For this reason, some programs allow you to switch back and forth between a WYSIWYG mode and a draft mode. In draft mode, graphics are not displayed, and some fonts are not displayed as they will appear when printed. This reduced display allows you to scroll through the document and make corrections much faster than when in WYSIWYG mode.

WYSIWYG
The latest programs designed for graphic displays feature WYSIWYG (What You See Is What You Get). This means the document on the screen looks almost exactly as it will look when printed. You might compare this figure with the "Character Mode" and "Graphics Mode" figures since all three show the same document.

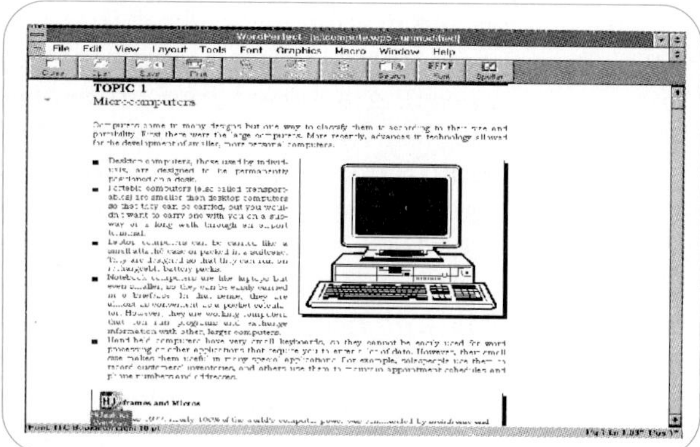

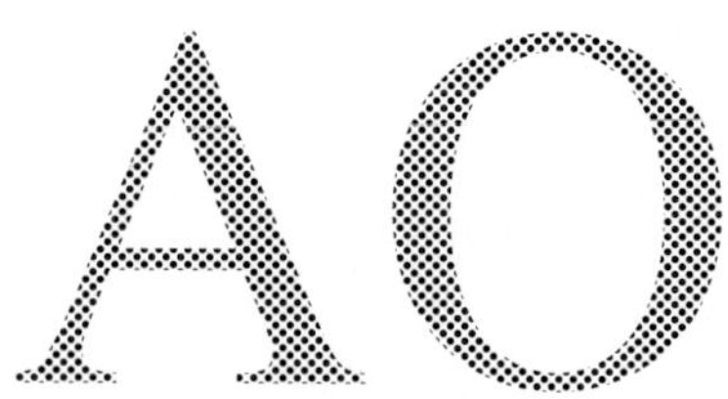

Printer Resolution
The quality of a printed character is determined by the spacing of the dots. This enlargement shows that the closer the dots are, the better the quality of the character.

Printed Graphics
Graphic images such as photographs are printed with dots. Here a partial enlargement shows how the image is formed from dots.

Printers

Most modern printers form characters using an array of dots. These printers are called raster printers, and there are several different types. The spacing of the dots affects the resolution, or quality, of the characters. For comparison, display monitors use about 50 to 100 dots per inch (dpi) to display text and images, dot-matrix printers 100 to 200, laser printers 300 to 600, and commercial typesetting machines 1,000 to 2,400.

Printers that print using an array of dots can also print graphics. By controlling the position dots are printed in, an illusion of brightness can be conveyed. The ability to convey brightness allows dot-matrix printers to print detailed line art and photographs.

Dot-Matrix Printers

One of the most common printers is called a dot-matrix printer. This printer uses a printhead containing pins, or wires, arranged in a column to print characters. As the printhead passes across the paper, the computer tells it which pins are to be fired to form a particular character. As the pins are fired, they strike an inked ribbon against the paper. The number of pins and dots determines the character's resolution. Less-expensive printers usually use 9 pins to create characters. More-expensive printers have 24 pins in their printheads.

Laser Printers

Laser printers, the most desirable type of printer, are very fast, usually printing eight or more pages per minute.

The resolution of laser printers is greater than that of dot-matrix printers because of the higher number of dots and their greater density. Most laser printers can print 300 dpi, and printers with 400 and more dpi are available. Despite the great number of dots, laser printers are fast and quiet because the dots are not transferred to the paper by mechanical devices that strike a ribbon.

Printer Features

Even with the best printers, there are differences that affect their use. Two of the more significant are memory and fonts.

Memory

Unlike dot-matrix printers, where data are taken from the computer and then printed a line at a time, laser printers make up an entire page before printing it. The page is temporarily stored in the printer's

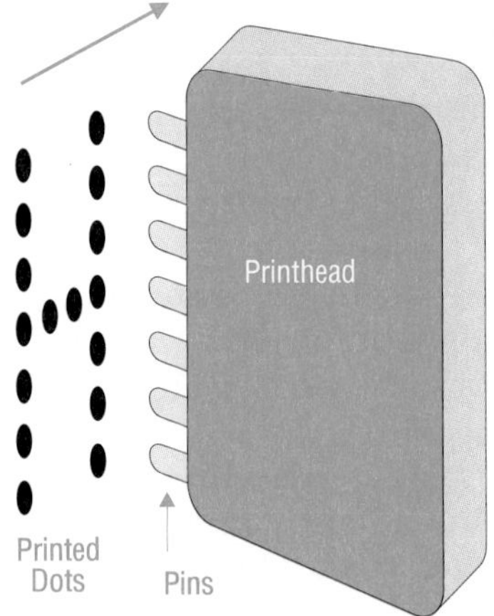

Dot-Matrix Printhead
Dot-matrix printers have a printhead that contains pins. These pins are "fired" against the inked ribbon to print characters on the page.

Laser Printers
Laser printers are now the printer of choice. They give superb results at a reasonable cost.
Courtesy of Hewlett Packard

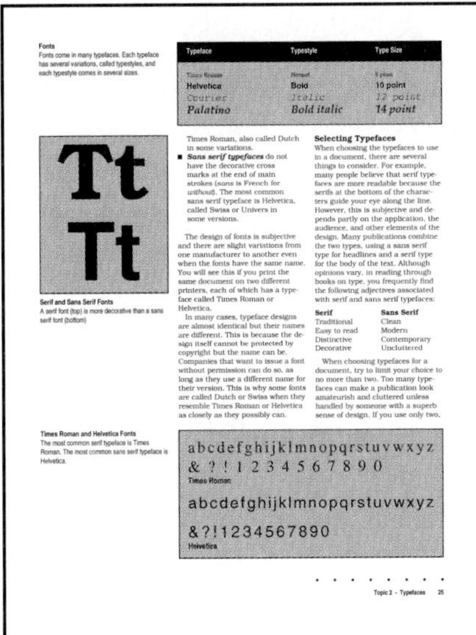

Fonts
Fonts come in many typefaces. Each typeface has several variations, called typestyles, and each typestyle comes in several sizes.

Typeface	Typestyle	Type Size
Times Roman	Normal	8 point
Helvetica	Bold	10 point
Courier	Italic	12 point
Palatino	Bold italic	14 point

Tt
Tt

Serif and Sans Serif Fonts
A serif font (top) is more decorative than a sans serif font (bottom)

Times Roman, also called Dutch in some variations.

- ***Sans serif typefaces*** do not have the decorative cross marks at the end of main strokes (*sans* is French for *without*). The most common sans serif typeface is Helvetica, called Swiss or Univers in some versions.

The design of fonts is subjective and there are slight variations from one manufacturer to another even when the fonts have the same name. You will see this if you print the same document on two different printers, each of which has a typeface called Times Roman or Helvetica.

In many cases, typeface designs are almost identical but their names are different. This is because the design itself cannot be protected by copyright but the name can be. Companies that want to issue a font without permission can do so, as long as they use a different name for their version. This is why some fonts are called Dutch or Swiss when they resemble Times Roman or Helvetica as closely as they possibly can.

Selecting Typefaces
When choosing the typefaces to use in a document, there are several things to consider. For example, many people believe that serif typefaces are more readable because the serifs at the bottom of the characters guide your eye along the line. However, this is subjective and depends partly on the application, the audience, and other elements of the design. Many publications combine the two types, using a sans serif type for headlines and a serif type for the body of the text. Although opinions vary, in reading through books on type, you frequently find the following adjectives associated with serif and sans serif typefaces:

Serif	Sans Serif
Traditional	Clean
Easy to read	Modern
Distinctive	Contemporary
Decorative	Uncluttered

When choosing typefaces for a document, try to limit your choice to no more than two. Too many typefaces can make a publication look amateurish and cluttered unless handled by someone with a superb sense of design. If you use only two,

Times Roman and Helvetica Fonts
The most common serif typeface is Times Roman. The most common sans serif typeface is Helvetica.

abcdefghijklmnopqrstuvwxyz
& ? ! 1 2 3 4 5 6 7 8 9 0
Times Roman

abcdefghijklmnopqrstuvwxyz
&?!1234567890
Helvetica

Topic 2 · Typefaces 25

Laser-Printer Quality
Laser printers can print both text and graphics. The dots making up the image are so closely spaced that they look as if they were professionally printed.

memory while it is being processed and printed. If a page contains a graphics image, the memory required for it can be substantial. For example, it takes 1 megabyte to store a full-page black-and-white graphics image that is to be printed with a 300-dpi resolution. To fill the page, the printer has to address over 8 million dots (1 megabyte × 8 bits = 8 million bits). This is obviously a big chore.

If there isn't enough memory in the printer, only part of a page or image may be printed. As a rule of thumb, a laser printer should have at least 1 megabyte of memory, but if you are planning on printing large graphics or downloading fonts to the printer, you may need more.

Fonts

When you print a document, the way the characters look depends on the font used to print them. There are thousands of designs for type, each one different from the next. These different designs are referred to as fonts. All printers can print using fonts that are permanently stored in the printer's ROM (read-only memory). For some printers, other fonts are available in cartridges that are plugged into the printer. You can quickly access fonts stored in ROM and cartridge fonts, and they do not take up room on your computer's hard disk. Some printers, however, will accept downloadable fonts stored on the computer's hard disk. You can choose from the fonts on the disk and load them into the printer when you need them. This way, the printer has access to any fonts you want to use. Two types of fonts are available—bit-mapped and scalable.

- Bit-mapped fonts are made up of a series of dots and can be printed in only one size, the size they come in. If you need 8-, 10-, 12-, and 14-point versions, you must have a complete font in each size. Storage can be a problem as a result.
- Scalable fonts (also called *outline fonts*) are created on the fly while text is being printed by formulas stored in the computer or printer. These fonts allow a wide range of sizes while requiring very little space on the disk or in a printer's memory.

Using Printers

When you want to send a document to the printer, you first load the printer with paper and turn the printer on. The way you load paper depends on the type of printer and paper you are using. If you are using single sheets, you usually stack them in a paper tray or bin. If you are using fan-fold paper (also called continuous form paper), you feed it into the printer.

The settings you can make on the printer vary. However, many have some or all of the following switches:

- *On/Off* turns the power to the printer on and off. Knowing when to use this switch is important.
  - If you turn the printer off while it is operating, all data in its memory will be lost.
  - If you have canceled a print job and want to start over, turning the computer off and back on is a good way to ensure that text from the previous job does not remain in the printer's memory.
  - When you turn a dot-matrix printer on, it uses the line that the print element is resting on as the starting point when calculating top margins and page length. This is useful since you can

Courier
Times Roman (or Dutch)
Helvetica (or Swiss)

Printer Fonts
All printers have at least one built-in font. These are simply sets of characters that have different appearances. Here, the most common built-in fonts are shown.

turn off the printer, adjust your paper, and then turn it back on to set the top of the form.

- *Off-Line/On-Line* connects the printer to and disconnects it from the computer. The printer must be on line to print documents, but it must be off line to use some of the other switches on the printer, such as Form Feed and Line Feed.
- *Form Feed* (sometimes labeled FF) advances a sheet of paper out of the printer. If the printer has an automatic sheet feeder, it inserts a new sheet. For this switch to work, the printer must be off line.
- *Line Feed* (sometimes labeled LF) advances paper in the printer by one line. This is useful when making fine adjustments to the paper's position in the printer. For this switch to work, the printer must be off line.
- *Letter Quality/Draft Quality* switches a dot-matrix printer between its letter-quality mode (which is high quality but slower) and its draft-quality mode (which is lower quality but faster).
- *Font* changes the default font so that the entire document is printed in that font unless you specified otherwise within the document being printed.

EJECTING PAPER

Many printers do not eject a printed sheet automatically. To manually advance a printed page out of your printer:

1. Press the printer's on-line switch to take it off line.
2. Press the printer's form-feed switch to advance or eject the page.
3. Press the printer's on-line switch to put it back on line.

EXERCISES

EXERCISE 1

IDENTIFYING KEYS ON THE KEYBOARD

Match the keyboard on your computer with one of those shown in the figures "Regular Keyboard" or "Enhanced Keyboard." Then identify the location of the following keys on the figure:

A. Alphabetic keys
B. Numeric keys
C. Numeric keypad
D. Enter↵ **(Return)**
E. Arrow keys
F. Spacebar
G. ←Bksp key
H. Esc key
I. ⇧Shift keys
J. Ctrl key
K. Function keys
L. NumLock key
M. CapsLock key

Regular Keyboard

Enhanced Keyboard

EXERCISE 2

IDENTIFYING KEYBOARD INDICATORS

If one of the keyboards in the lab has indicator lights built into it, sketch the lights, and then label each of them as follows:

A. On/off indicator
B. NumLock indicator
C. CapsLock indicator
D. ScrlLock indicator

EXERCISE 3

IDENTIFYING THE PRINTER'S CONTROLS

Sketch and label the controls on one of the printers in the lab. Briefly describe the purpose of each control listed in the table "The Printer's Controls," and indicate the procedures you follow to use the control. For some of this information, you may have to ask your instructor or refer to the printer's manual.

THE PRINTER'S CONTROLS

Control	Description
On/off switch	______________
On line	______________
Form feed	______________
Line feed	______________
Fonts	______________
Other	______________

TOPIC 4

External Storage Devices

After completing this topic, you will be able to:

- List and describe the main features of floppy disks
- Explain how floppy and hard disk drives work
- Describe how data are stored on magnetic media
- Describe CD-ROM players and CD-ROM discs
- List and describe ways to protect and secure your data

When you work on a computer, the programs and files on which you work are stored internally in the computer's random-access memory (RAM). This memory is a limited resource, yet it must serve many uses. Not only do you load different application programs, you also create numerous files of your own work. The computer's memory is not large enough to store all the programs, documents, and other computer-generated files you work on. Moreover, most internal memory will lose its data when you turn the computer off.

External Storage
External storage is used to permanently store data and programs. Any data stored on an external storage device can be quickly moved into the computer's memory when needed.

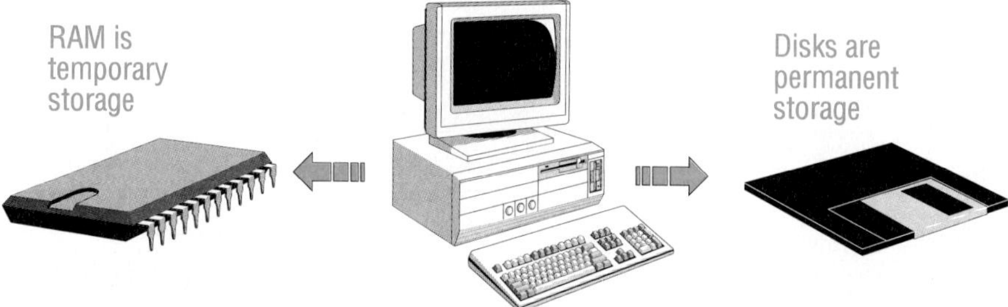

For these reasons, external storage (also called auxiliary or secondary storage) is provided to store program files and data files that you are not using at the moment. Once data files are stored externally, you can reload them into the computer's internal memory without having to rekeyboard the data.

Computers usually use magnetic disks to store programs and files externally. Magnetic disks, and the devices used to store and retrieve data on them, fall into two major classes—floppy and hard disks and drives.

Floppy Disks

Floppy disks for microcomputers come in two sizes: 5¼ and 3½ inches. Each size works only with drives specifically designed to accept it. Though they vary in size, they have certain features in common:

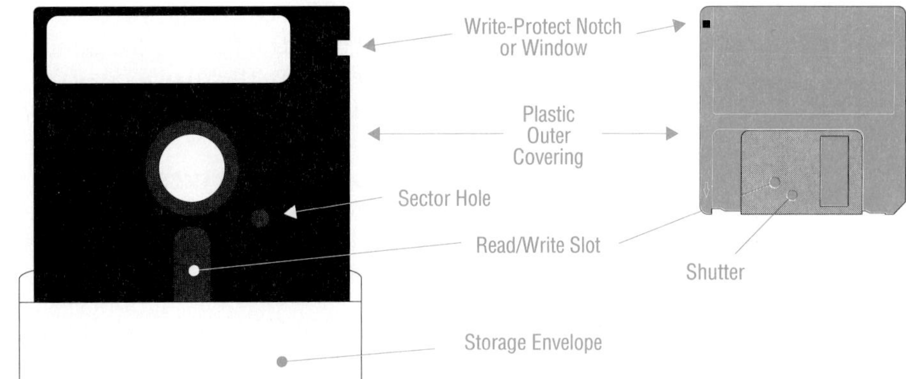

Floppy Disk Characteristics
5¼-inch and 3½-inch disks have many features in common.

1. A plastic outer covering protects the disk itself while allowing it to spin smoothly. A 5 -inch disk is protected by a flexible plastic jacket, whereas a 3 -inch disk is mounted in a rigid plastic housing. The jacket or housing is permanently sealed and contains lubricants and cleaning agents that prolong the life of the disk. A storage envelope protects 5 -inch disks from scratches, dust, and fingerprints. These envelopes are not used on the better-protected 3 -inch disks.
2. The read/write slot in the jacket is where the disk drive's read/write head contacts the surface of the disk. This read/write head stores data on (writes) and retrieves data from (reads) the surface of the disk as the disk spins inside the drive. On 3 -inch disks, the read/write slot is protected by a sliding metal cover called the shutter. When you insert the disk into the drive, this shutter is automatically pushed aside so that the read/write slot is exposed, and the drive can come in contact with the floppy disk within.
3. The write-protect notch or window allows you to write data to a disk when it is not write-protected and prevents you from writing to the disk when it is. (See the section "Write-Protecting Your Disks" on page 28.) A switch, or photoelectric circuit, inside the disk drive determines if the disk is write-protected. When it is, the switch disables the drive's ability to write data onto the disk.

If you were to remove the plastic jacket or housing of a floppy disk, you would find a round piece of plastic covered with a metallic oxide similar to the magnetic recording material used on audiotapes and videotapes. The round disk is sandwiched between two sheets of a soft, feltlike material, which is impregnated with a lubricant that protects the disk when it is spinning in the drive. The blank disk has three key features:

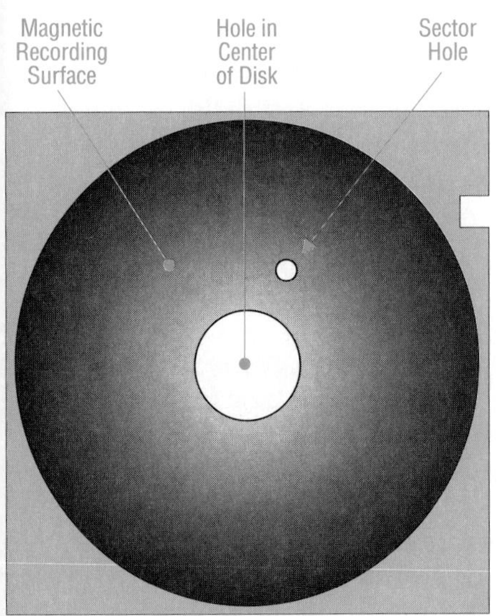

Inside a Floppy Disk
Inside a floppy disk there is a plastic disk, that has three key features.

1. The magnetic recording surface on which the data are stored occupies the outer portion of the disk. The density used to store data on this surface varies depending on your system. (For a detailed discussion of disk densities, see Topic 9.)
2. The large hole in the center of the disk is used by the drive to align and spin the disk. This hole is sometimes reinforced with a plastic hub and, on 3 -inch disks, is covered by a metal hub.
3. The sector hole, which is punched through the disk, is used by the computer to know where to store data to and retrieve data from the disk. A light is positioned in the drive so that it shines through the

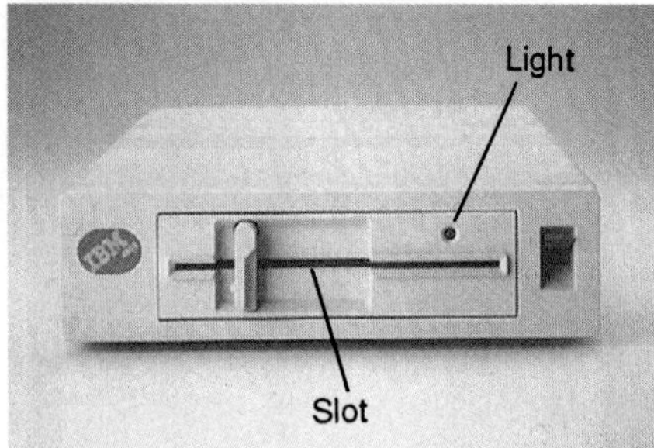

A Floppy Disk Drive
The floppy disk drive has two parts that you should be familiar with: the slot and the light. Here, they are shown on a standalone drive, but most disk drives are built into the computer.
Courtesy of IBM Corporation

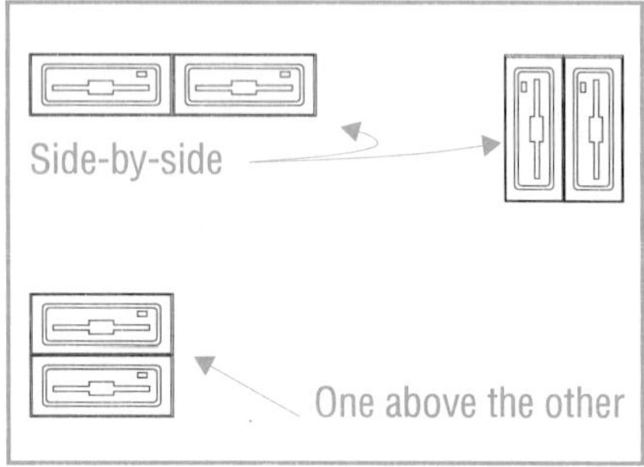

Inserting a Floppy Disk
The arrangement of floppy disk drives varies from computer to computer. If your floppy disk drives are side by side, drive A is usually the one on the left. If one drive is above the other, drive A is usually the one on the top.

Hard Disks
A hard disk uses rigid metal platters instead of a floppy disk to store data. These disks spin at over 3,000 revolutions per minute as data are written to the disk and read from it by a movable read/write head.
Courtesy of Seagate

sector hole on each revolution. When this happens, a photoelectric cell sees the light and signals the computer so that it can keep itself oriented to the disk's position, much as a ship can orient itself from a lighthouse beacon.

Floppy Disk Drives

The floppy disk drive is the device that the floppy disk is inserted into so that you can store data to and retrieve data from it. The floppy disk drive has two parts you should be familiar with: the slot and the light.

1. The slot is where you insert a floppy disk into the drive. The way you insert floppy disks depends on the type of system you are using.
   - To insert a 5¼-inch disk, open the door to the disk drive. Hold the disk with the label facing up to insert it into a horizontal drive or with the label facing to the left to insert it into a vertical drive. Point the oblong read/write slot toward the slot in the drive, and insert the disk into the slot. (On some systems, it clicks into place.) Never push hard because a 5¼-inch disk will buckle if it gets caught on an obstruction. Carefully jiggle the disk to make sure it is inserted all the way into the disk drive. Gently close the disk drive's door, or press the button that locks the disk into the drive. If you encounter any resistance, jiggle the disk, and then close the door or press the button again. To remove the disk, open the door and pull the disk out. On some drives, gently pushing it in and quickly releasing the pressure pops it out of the drive; on others, you have to press a button.
   - To insert a 3½-inch disk, hold it so that the arrow embossed on the case is facing up or to the left and pointing toward the drive's slot. Insert the disk gently into the drive, and then press until it clicks into place. To remove the disk, press the disk-eject button located near the drive's slot.
2. The light on the front of the drive goes on when the drive is operating. When the light is on, you should not open or close the door or eject a disk. Doing so can damage the disk or cause you to lose data. If you make a mistake and the drive spins when the door is open or without a disk inserted, do not close the door or insert a disk. In a few moments, a message will usually appear on the screen telling you the drive's door is open or no disk is in the drive. When the light goes out, close the door or insert a disk, and then follow the instructions displayed on the screen.

Hard Disk Drives

Hard disk drives (also called fixed disks) are now a necessity for serious computer users. Newer programs frequently require 2 or more megabytes of disk storage space. (One new word processing program requires 16 megabytes.) These programs cannot be run without a high-capacity hard disk drive.

Instead of a floppy disk, hard disk drives use rigid metal platters to store data. On such a platter, data can be stored more densely than on a floppy disk, and a drive can use more than one platter. As a result, hard disks with over 100 megabytes of storage capacity are now common. In addition, a hard disk drive spins at 3,600 rpm, about ten times faster than a floppy disk drive, allowing data to be stored and retrieved faster.

In a floppy disk drive, the read/write heads are in contact with the disk. In a hard disk drive, they fly over its surface on a cushion of air with a space smaller than a piece of dust separating the head from the rapidly spinning disk. To imagine the very small tolerances involved, picture an airplane flying at high speed ½ inch above the ground without making contact. With the high speeds and small spaces involved, even a dust particle can cause the read/write head to come in contact with the disk's surface, creating what is called a head crash. With the disk spinning at almost 60 mph, this can cause a lot of damage to the disk and the data stored on it.

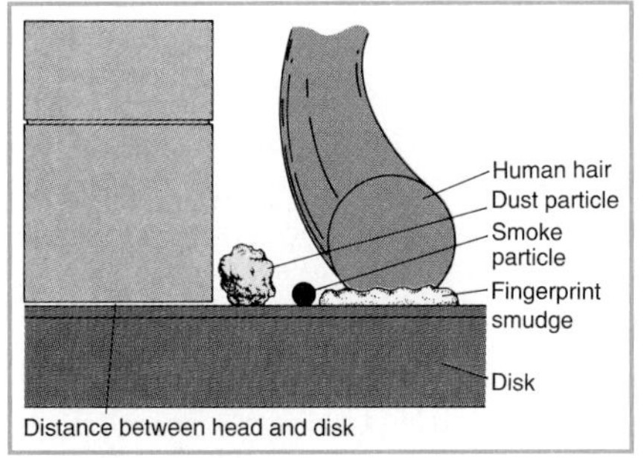

Hard Disk Tolerances
Hard disks have very small tolerances. When the read/write head is flying over the surface of the disk, the two are so close that smoke, a dust particle, a strand of hair, or even a fingerprint could cause the head to crash into the disk, causing damage to data.

To prevent small objects from damaging the drive or affecting its performance, hard disks are hermetically sealed in a case. When you use a hard disk drive, the read/write head is positioned on the disk where data are stored. Even slightly jarring your computer may damage your files. If you are going to move your computer, use the park program (usually found on a disk that comes with your computer) to park the read/write head. This program moves the read/write head to a section of the disk that has no data, thus preventing the head from damaging data on the disk should it move. You needn't do this on all systems because some have an autopark feature that parks the disk whenever you turn off the computer.

How Data Are Stored to and Retrieved from a Disk

Data are stored on a disk magnetically. If you have ever played with two magnets, you know that when held end to end, they attract each other. When one of them is then reversed, they repel each other. This is caused by a difference in polarity. Opposite polarities attract, and identical polarities repel. These two magnetic states are used to record data on a disk. As the disk spins, electrical signals in the read/write head change the polarity of magnetic particles on the disk's surface to record 0s and 1s. When you retrieve a file from the disk, the effect is reversed. The polarity of the disk immediately under the read/write head induces an electrical current in the read/write head that is transmitted to the computer as 0s and 1s.

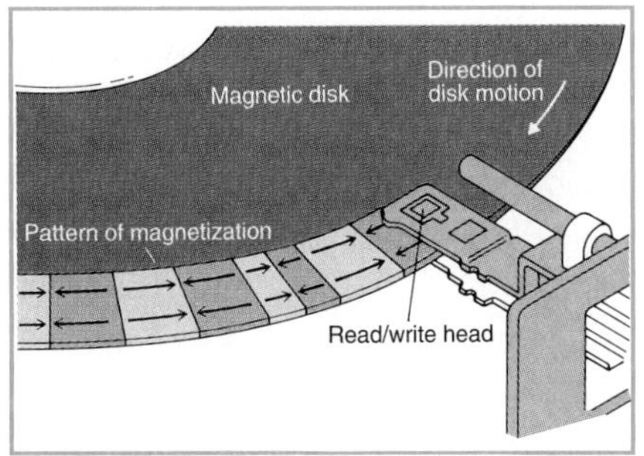

How Data Are Stored
Data are stored magnetically as the drive's read/write head moves over the disk. If the polarity of the magnetized area points in one direction, it is a 1; in the other, it is a 0.

CD-ROM

One of the most recent and far-reaching developments in the microcomputer field is the new technology of optical disks. Data are stored on and retrieved from these disks with a laser. One of the most popular kinds of optical disks is called a CD-ROM disc. These discs are similar in concept to the compact discs (CDs) now popular in the music industry. A small 4 3/4-inch CD-ROM disc can store up to 600MB of data. This is equivalent to about 250,000 pages of text or 40,000 images.

These discs are changing the way information is stored, distributed, and accessed. One of the first to be published was *Microsoft's Bookshelf CD-ROM Reference Library*. This CD-ROM disc contains ten of the most widely used reference works, including *The World Almanac and Book of Facts*, *Bartlett's Familiar Quotations*, *The Chicago Manual of Style*, and the *U.S. ZIP Code Directory*. It also includes search and retrieve software, which makes it possible to look for information while working on another program. With just a few keystrokes, you can find informa-

CD-ROM
CD-ROM discs look like compact discs for music. These discs can store an enormous amount of information.
Courtesy of IBM

tion in any of these references and insert it into a document on the screen.

Protecting and Caring for Your Files and Disks

When you enter information into the computer, it is not stored permanently until you save it onto disks. But even then the data are not protected from loss or damage. No one ever heeds advice on this matter until she or he loses important information and has to spend hours or days recreating it. Don't be like everyone else; follow these recommendations before you lose data.

CLASS FILES--ORIGINAL
Your Name / The Date
Formatted with DOS 5

Disk Labels
Disks labels should indicate the type of disk, whether it is an original or backup copy, your name, the date the disk was formatted, and the format used.

Labeling Your Disks

An unwritten rule among computer users is that an unlabeled disk contains no valuable files. People often do not take the time to check what files, if any, an unlabeled disk contains. Thus the first step when you use a disk is to label it. Always write the disk title, your name, the date, and the operating system version that you are using on the labels.

If you are using 5¼-inch floppy disks, be sure also to fill out labels before you affix them to the disks. If you write on a label that is already on a disk, you can damage the disk if you press down too hard. If you must write on a label that is already on a disk, use a felt-tip pen, and write very gently. Do not apply pressure.

Write-Protecting Floppy Disks
You write-protect your disks by taping over the write-protect notch on a 5¼-inch disk or opening the write-protect window on a 3½-inch disk.

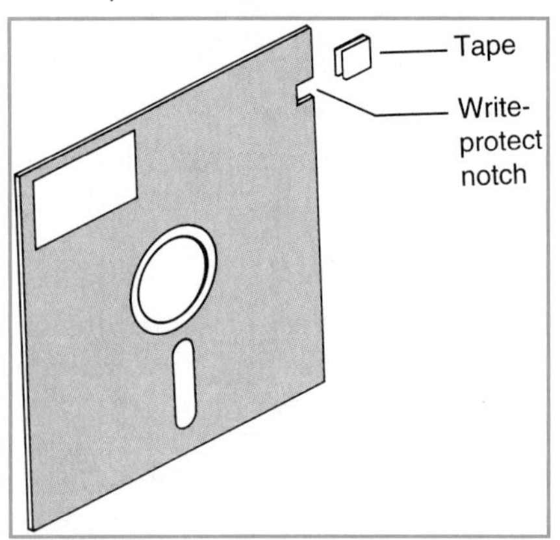

Write-protecting a 5¼-inch disk

Write-protecting a 3½-inch disk

Write-Protecting Your Disks

When you work with files and disks, you can lose work if you make a mistake. To protect important files, write-protect the disk. If a disk is write-protected, you can read files on the disk, but you cannot save files on it, format it, or erase files from it.

- To write-protect a 5¼-inch floppy disk, cover the write-protect notch with a piece of tape. You must use a write-protect tape that light cannot shine through since some drives use a light to determine whether the notch is covered. If you use a transparent tape, the light will shine through the notch just as if it were not covered, and the drive will assume it is not write-protected.
- To write-protect a 3½-inch floppy disk, open the sliding tab in the write-protect window.

Making Backup Copies

Always make backup copies of your important files and disks, and save them a safe distance from your working area. Make sure the same accident cannot happen to both the original disk and its backup copy. The information on the disk is usually worth much more than the disk itself, so don't take chances. You can back up floppy disks using the COPY or XCOPY commands described in this text. Backing up hard disks using the BACKUP command is described in the DOS manual.

Caring for Your Disks

Disks, both hard and floppy, are very reliable storage media. However, the data they contain can be lost or damaged if you do not take a few precautions. Floppy disks are relatively durable under ordinary conditions and have a useful life of about 40 hours' spinning time. But that life can be shortened or abruptly ended by improper handling. Proper

A CONSPIRACY OF DIFFICULTY?

You may have noticed that you write-protect one type of disk by *covering* the notch and the other by *uncovering* the window. If you are paranoid and believe in conspiracies, this may be evidence that there is a plot to make computers as difficult as possible.

care ensures that disks will accurately store and play back the data you need.

Care of Hard Disk Drives

- *DON'T* drop or jar them. They are very sensitive.
- *DO* use the park program, if necessary, to move the drive's read/write head to a safe place on the disk before moving the computer.

Care of Floppy Disk Drives

- *DON'T* use commercial cleaning kits too often. Overuse can cause problems with the drive.
- *DO* insert the cardboard protectors that came with 5¼-inch disk drives and close the doors when moving the computer.

Care of Floppy Disks

- *DO* keep disks in their protective storage envelopes. These envelopes reduce static buildup, which can attract dust that might scratch the disks.
- *DO* keep disks dry, away from sneezes, coffee, or anything else wet. A wet disk is a ruined disk.
- *DO* prevent disks from getting too hot or too cold. They should be stored at temperatures of 50°-150°F (10°-52°C). Extremes of temperature can destroy a disk's sensitivity, so treat them the same way you treat photographic film; that is, keep them out of direct sunlight, do not leave them in a car exposed to temperature extremes, and so forth.
- *DO* keep disks at least 2 feet away from magnets. The magnets found in copy stands, telephones, radio or stereo speakers, vacuum cleaners, televisions, air conditioners, novelty items, electric motors, or even some cabinet latches can ruin a disk's data.
- *DON'T* touch a disk's recording surface. Handle disks only by their protective covers.
- *DON'T* use a hard-tipped pen to write on a 5¼-inch disk's label that is affixed to the disk. This can crease the disk inside the protective cover and cause you to lose data. Write on the label before affixing it to the disk, or use a felt-tip pen with very light pressure.
- *DON'T* leave a disk in a nonoperating disk drive with the door closed for long periods. Open the drive door to lift the read/write head from the surface of the disk.
- *DON'T* insert or remove a disk from the drive when the disk drive is running (that is, when the drive's light is on).
- *DON'T* bend, fold, or crimp disks.
- *DON'T* use paper clips to attach a floppy disk to a file folder or copy of a printout. Special folders are available that let you keep disks and printed documents together.
- *DON'T* expose disks to static electricity. In dry climates or in heated buildings, static builds up when you walk on carpeted and some other kinds of floors. If you experience shocks when you touch metal objects, you are discharging the static that has built up. If you touch a disk when still charged with this static, you can

damage the data. To prevent this, increase the humidity in the air, use static-proof carpets, or touch something like a lamp to discharge the static before you pick up a disk.

Even with the best of care, floppy disks can last only so long. Close to the end of their useful life, they show their own form of senility by losing information or giving invalid commands. These are signs that it is time to replace them.

EXERCISES

EXERCISE 1

IDENTIFYING PARTS OF A FLOPPY DISK

Sketch a floppy disk used on your system, and then label each of its parts.

EXERCISE 2

PRACTICING INSERTING AND REMOVING FLOPPY DISKS

Practice inserting and removing floppy disks from your system's floppy disk drive. When you have it mastered, summarize the steps for inserting and removing them.

___

___

___

___

___

TOPIC 5

Application Software & the Operating System

After completing this topic, you will be able to:

- Briefly list and describe the main types of application software programs that you run on a computer
- Describe the functions of an operating system and graphical user interfaces such as Windows
- Explain program updates
- Describe installing programs, and explain why it is necessary

Microcomputers are general-purpose machines with many abilities. You determine their specific applications by the software you use. The computer is like an actor, and the software is like a script. When the actor changes scripts, he or she can perform a different role. By changing software, you can make your computer perform different applications. For example, to use your computer for word processing, you load a word processing program like WordPerfect® into your computer's memory from the disks it is stored on. To use your computer for financial analysis, you load a spreadsheet program like Lotus® 1-2-3®. You do not have to learn programming to make the computer a valuable tool. Instead, you learn how to effectively use these application software programs. Let's look briefly at some of the most popular types of application software and the operating system software that makes them possible.

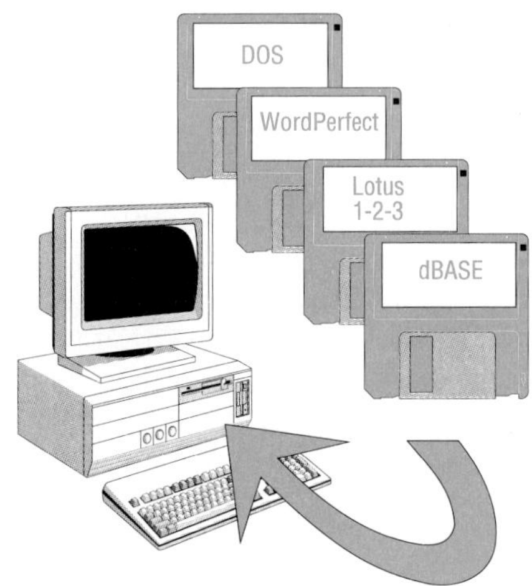

The Computer System's Software
Microcomputers allow you to load a variety of application software into memory so that you can use the same piece of equipment to process words, numbers, data, and graphics.

Word Processing and Desktop Publishing Programs

Word processing programs are used to enter and edit text. They are typically used to prepare memos, letters, reports, manuscripts, contracts, and other types of documents. In addition to entering and editing, these programs allow you to format documents so as to control how they look when printed. For example, you can set margins and tab stops, boldface headings, and automatically print personalized copies of form letters.

Since the introduction of the laser printer, new formatting procedures have become available. For example, you can print in different typestyles and type sizes, and you can combine graphics with text. To take advantage of these new possibilities, a new class of desktop publishing programs was introduced. These programs offer a wide selection of typestyles and make it easy to organize type into columns, add ruled lines, and combine text with graphics on the same page. To use one of these programs, you first enter and edit a document on a word processing program, and then you transfer it to a desktop publishing program where you lay out and design the final document. Increasingly, however, the features offered by desktop publishing programs are being incorporated into word processing programs, so you can now desktop publish documents without learning a second program.

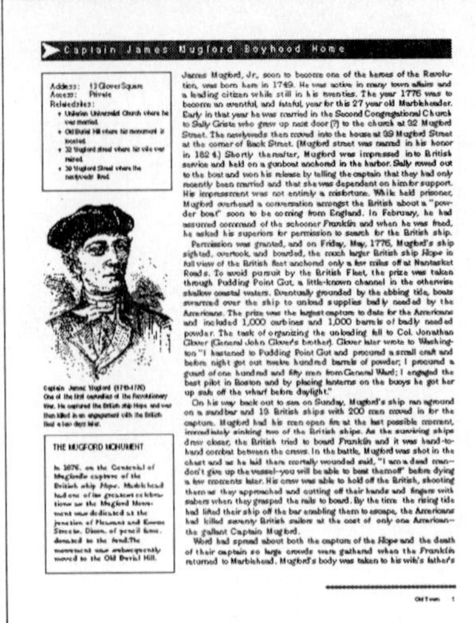
Captain James Mugford Boyhood Home

Word Processing and Desktop Publishing Programs
Word processing and desktop publishing programs allow you to create formatted documents that include both text and graphics.

Spreadsheet Programs

Spreadsheet programs have taken the drudgery out of working with numbers. On a spreadsheet, you quickly create a model of a numeric situation by entering labels, numbers, and formulas. You use the program's built-in features, called functions, to perform complicated calculations, such as the monthly payments due on a loan. You then use the completed model to explore what-if questions. For example, when you change the interest rate for the loan, the spreadsheet instantly recalculates your new monthly payment.

All modern spreadsheet programs include built-in graphics capabilities that allow you to quickly create graphs of any data that you enter into the spreadsheet. If you change the data in the spreadsheet, the graphs based on it change automatically. This makes graphs a usable tool for analysis.

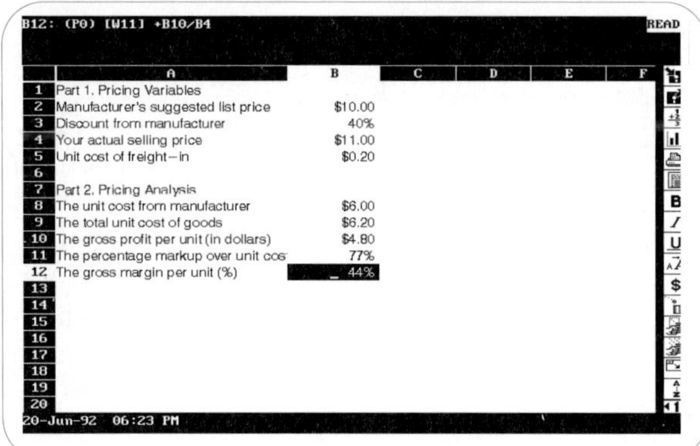

Spreadsheet Programs
A spreadsheet program has a screen divided into rows and columns. Where a row intersects a column, there are rectangular cells, which are used to enter labels, numbers, or formulas that make calculations.

Database Programs

You use database management programs (sometimes called record or file management programs) for tasks as simple as keeping a phone list or as complicated as controlling inventory. These programs allow you to store information in an organized way so that you can retrieve, update, or analyze it when you need to.

These programs do the same things you can do with a set of index cards, but they let you do it faster and more easily. You can store large amounts of information, such as mailing lists, inventory records, or billing and collection information, in tables. You can then sort, edit, add to, or delete from the information in these tables. Database management programs are often used to maintain mailing lists, which are then used automatically to print names and addresses on letters, envelopes, and mailing labels. They are also frequently integrated into other application software, such as word processing and spreadsheet programs.

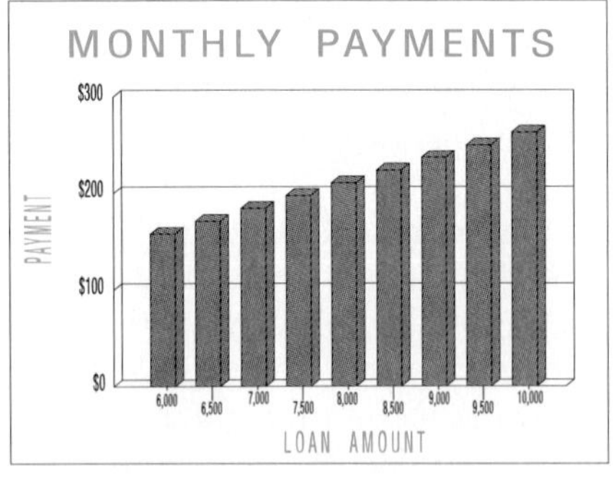

Business Graphs
Business graphs are used to convey a great deal of information in a single picture.

The Operating System

Although you do your computer work with application programs like word processors and spreadsheets, the heart of the computer's software is another type of software called the operating system. The operating system coordinates activity between you and the computer and between parts of the computer like the keyboard and display screen.

When IBM developed the original IBM PC, it contracted the development of its operating system to Microsoft, which developed an operating system called MS-DOS (Microsoft Disk Operating System). The IBM PC version of this program was named PC-DOS. The PC-DOS version usually runs on IBM PC computers, and the MS-DOS version usually runs on compatibles made by manufacturers other than IBM. These two versions of the operating system are essentially identical in the way they work and the commands you use to operate them; usually they are interchangeable.

Because the operating system coordinates activity between any application program you run and the computer hardware, you must load the operating system into the computer's memory before you load an application program. The primary functions of the operating system are to coordinate, or supervise, the activities of the computer and help you manage your files. When the operating system controls your computer, it performs two main functions: controlling input and output and processing commands.

Controlling Input and Output

The operating system decides where programs and data are stored in the computer's memory and handles communication among the computer's components such as the printer and display screen, the application programs, and you—the user. The operating system controls your computer without your involvement or awareness. In this respect, it is like your body's respiratory system, which keeps you breathing even though you are hardly aware of it.

The Operating System Coordinates Traffic
Intersections without traffic control are confusing. Those with traffic control are more efficient; everyone knows when to stop and when to go. The operating system performs traffic control functions within the computer.

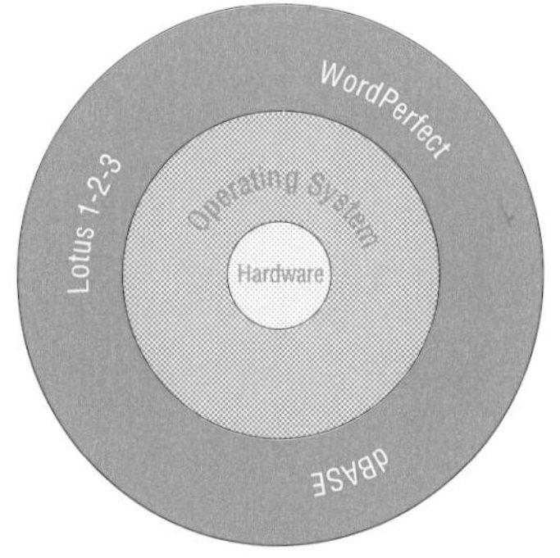

The Operating System and Application Software
The operating system communicates between application software and the hardware. The operating system must always be loaded into the computer's memory before application software such as WordPerfect or 1-2-3 is loaded.

Processing Commands

The command processor portion of the operating system interprets what you enter from the keyboard. In this respect, it is rather like an interpreter. If you spoke only English and tried to carry on a discussion with someone who spoke only French, you both would need an interpreter to translate what was being said so that you could understand each other. The same is true of a computer. When you use an application program, the program's commands are interpreted by the operating system for the hardware. For example, on one program, you might save a file you are working on by pressing F10 and then pressing Enter ←. On another, you might press / F S and then press Enter ←. The operating system interprets these commands and instructs the disk drive to spin while it copies the file to the disk from the computer's internal memory.

The Operating System Interprets
Command processing is a form of interpreting. The commands you enter on the keyboard are interpreted by the operating system and sent to the computer's central processing unit.

File and Disk Management Functions
In addition to the things the operating system does automatically, it contains commands that you use to manage your files and disks. These commands perform tasks such as copying or deleting files and preparing disks for use on your computer. Many of these commands are described in this text.

Graphical User Interfaces

Graphical user interfaces (also called GUIs—pronounced "goo-ees") like Microsoft's Windows make using the computer easier and more efficient. Windows incorporates a graphic display that allows you to choose commands from pull-down menus and to divide the screen into windows in which multiple application programs can be displayed and run at the same time. You can run your favorite spreadsheet in one window and your favorite word processor in another. The program you are currently working on is in the foreground. The other programs, which you are not currently working on, are in the background.

Icons
Icons are graphic symbols on the screen that you click on with a mouse to run the associated program. For example, if you clicked on the icon shown here, you would load WordPerfect for Windows.

Microsoft Windows
Microsoft Windows, a typical operating system environment, allows you to load more than one program into memory so that you can quickly switch between them. It also allows you to perform many operating system functions, such as copying files, without having to learn the commands usually required.

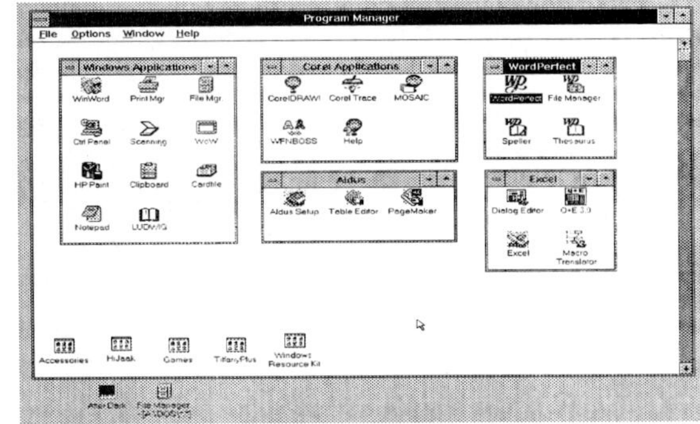

The Windows Program Manager screen (top) displays icons, graphic symbols that represent programs. To run a program, you just point to it and double click one of the buttons on a mouse.

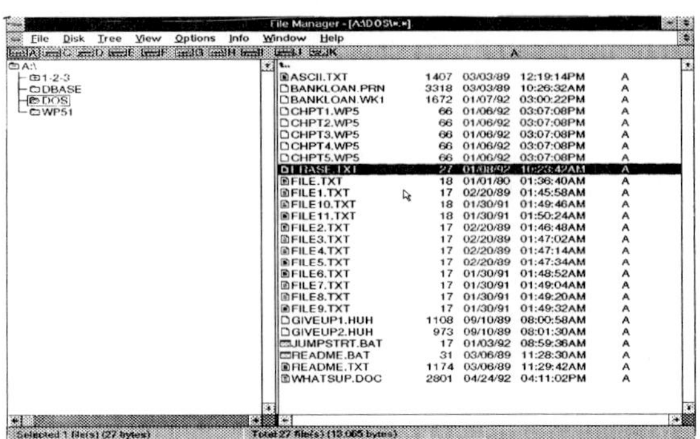

One of the Windows programs is the File Manager (bottom) that displays a graphic tree of the directories on the disk (subdivisions of the disk in which related files are stored) and any files they contain.

Windows also gives a common look to most programs that are developed to take advantage of its features. For example, it allows you to operate the computer using standardized commands to load programs, call up help, cancel commands, and quit to return to the operating system. This makes it easier to learn new programs because your existing skills are transferable.

Program and Operating System Updates

Companies that publish programs and operating systems generally update them every year or so. Updates (also called upgrades) generally include corrected old features as well as new features that improve the program. To identify new versions, version or release numbers are changed. For example, DOS has been revised several times, so there are versions 3, 3.1, 4, 4.01, and 5 in widespread use. Changes in the decimal number usually indicate relatively minor changes. Changes in the whole number indicate major revisions. For example, version 3.1 is only slightly different from 3.0, but version 5.0 was a big change from version 4.01.

New versions usually add new features. If these just build on the previous version, you need learn only the new features. When faced with a new version, you should be an informed consumer. Find out what features the new program has. If it does not have any that you need, you probably should not buy the new version.

Installing Programs and Operating Systems

Drivers
Reprinted from INFOSYSTEMS, May 1985, © Hitchcock Publishing Company.

Before you actually use a new application program or operating system, you must install it by running an installation program (also called a setup program). The installation process copies the program's or operating system's files to your working disk or disks and customizes it for your system's hardware based on your responses to questions. Installing a program is generally a one-time task unless you change equipment. When you add a new printer or other device, you may have to reinstall the program so that it is aware of the change.

Based on the information you supply about your screen and printer when you install a program, the program then knows what device drivers to use. Drivers are small programs that translate the programmer's generic instructions into instructions for a specific piece of hardware. When a new piece of hardware comes on the market, the programmers of the application software just write a driver for it; they don't have to revise the program itself.

Application software programs generally have a library of device drivers, one for each specific hardware item. If you have a piece of hardware that the program does not include a driver for, you may be unable to use it with the program. Using a printer or display screen without the correct driver can give totally unexpected results. When buying an application software program, always be sure it contains the drivers needed to work with your equipment.

There is often a way around this problem, however. Many pieces of computer hardware are designed to emulate (act like) other brands of the same equipment. Thus, many printers will emulate the Hewlett-Packard LaserJet, and many display screens can emulate IBM's video graphics adapter (VGA). If your program doesn't list the drivers for your printer or screen, but your printer or screen can emulate another, you may be able to install that driver, and the program will run correctly.

Theft of Software

When you walk into a computer store and pay $100 or more for a program, you may think you have bought the program, but usually you would be wrong. You have actually bought the *license*, or right, to use the program and its documentation. The physical materials still belong to the publisher. Read these licenses carefully; they spell out your rights in detail. Most specify that you can use the program only on one computer and cannot make copies for distribution to others. You can, however, make copies for your own use because you should never run the program from the original disk.

Users do not have the right to make copies of software for distribution to others. Doing so infringes on the publisher's copyright and is a federal offense. Called software piracy, this practice costs software companies lost revenues, and they are increasingly taking legal action to prevent the distribution, sale, and use of these disks, especially in colleges and large corporations. Colleges and corporations are even being held accountable for the actions of students and employees who illegally copy programs.

A site license allows a school or company either to run programs on networks without having a copy for each computer or to make a limited number of copies for use within a single department or location. Site licenses reduce the company's total software costs, lessen the likelihood of violating the publisher's legal rights, and make it easier on all network users because they do not need individual copies of the program.

THE VIRUSES ARE COMING

- A virus introduced into the computers at several universities counted the number of times it copied itself to other disks. When it had reproduced itself four times, it erased all files on the current disks in the computer.
- ARC, a major shareware program used to compress files so that they take up less space on the disk and can be telecommunicated faster, was altered and then uploaded to bulletin board systems. When it was then downloaded to a user's computer and run, it erased the part of the hard disk that is needed to boot the computer.
- A Christmas message sent over IBM's worldwide network looked up the mailing list of each person it was sent to and then sent itself to all those people. The avalanche of messages that were sent to more and more people slowed down the system and eventually brought it to a halt.
- A virus attached to Aldus's Freehand program displayed a peace message on users' screens on March 2, 1988, the anniversary of Apple's introduction of the Macintosh II. This was the first virus to be distributed in a commercial software program.

Viruses

One of the fastest growing problems in the microcomputer field is the introduction of viruses by antisocial users. A virus is a small program, either stored on a disk by itself or appended to an existing file called a Trojan horse. When the file is loaded or the Trojan horse program is run, the virus loads itself into the computer's memory. Once there, it can secretly attach itself to other files or programs or store itself on any other disks run on the computer, including the hard disk. What happens next depends on the intent of the vandal who created the virus:

- The virus may cause problems immediately.
- It may count specific occurrences, for example, how many times it is copied, and then cause damage.
- It may look at the computer's clock and cause damage on a specific date.
- It may reproduce itself and then cause damage. Like a biological virus, a computer virus can infect other files and then spread from them.

The number of instances in which viruses cause damage is increasing. Once introduced, viruses are hard to detect and remove. For individual users, the best defense is to use only commercial programs and not to exchange files with other users. Using a virus scan program will help you detect the presence of viruses on your system.

EXERCISE 1

ATTENDING A DEMONSTRATION

Application software is demonstrated in college labs, in computer stores, and in computer groups. Try to attend a demonstration of any program to see how it operates, and then summarize your observations.

EXERCISE 2

READING A REVIEW

Obtain a copy of a recent computer magazine and read a review of any new program. List its main applications, and briefly describe some of the features that the reviewer thought important.

EXERCISE 3

READING A LICENSE AGREEMENT

Ask the person in charge of your computer lab to show you a license agreement covering a software program that you will be using. Read the agreement, list the rights it gives you, and list the things it prohibits.

CHAPTER 1 REVIEW

- Bytes can be indicated using the shorthand terms kilobyte (KB) for thousands, megabyte (MB) for millions, gigabyte for billions, or terabyte for trillions. They are calculated by raising the number 2 (for the two possible states of the transistor) to a power. For example, 2^{18} is 262,144 bytes or 262 kilobytes (rounded off to 256 for most purposes).
- The central processing unit (CPU) coordinates the computer's activities and performs arithmetic and logical calculations. The microcomputer's CPU is a microprocessor.
- Microprocessors come in full featured versions (dx) and more limited but less expensive versions (sx).
- There are two basic types of internal memory: read-only memory (ROM) and random-access memory (RAM). ROM is unchangeable, but your programs and data are stored in RAM. Because you can change the data in RAM, it is called volatile memory.
- Data can enter and leave the computer through ports. Serial ports send data a bit at a time, and parallel ports send data a byte at a time.
- Many computers have expansion slots into which you can plug boards to improve the performance of your system.
- WYSIWYG displays show a document on the screen almost exactly as it will appear when printed.
- Off-Line/On-Line connects and disconnects the printer from the computer, and Form Feed advances the paper out of the printer.
- The most common external storage devices are floppy and hard disks. Hard disks not only store more data but also allow you to store and retrieve it faster than floppy disks do.
- To protect your files, you should label your disks, make backup copies, and write-protect the disks when executing commands that could damage the files.
- The operating system controls the computer's operations and must always be loaded before you load an application program.
- When new features are added to an existing program, it is released by the publisher as an update.

CHAPTER 1 QUESTIONS

FILL IN THE BLANK

1. The smallest unit of information in a computer is the ___________.
2. Bytes contain ___________ bits.
3. The abbreviation for a kilobyte is ___________ and for a megabyte it is ___________.

4. The abbreviation CPU stands for ___________ ___________ ___________.
5. Memory in the computer where you store your files and programs when you are using them is called ___________.
6. The port where data are sent through a bit at a time is called a ___________ port.
7. The port where data are sent through a byte at a time is called a ___________ port.
8. When a display screen can display only a fixed set of characters, it is called a ___________ display.
9. When a display screen can show a photograph, it is called a ___________ display.
10. If the screen shows a document almost exactly as it will be when printed, it is called a ___________ display.
11. To change the style of type in a printed document, your printer must have more than one ___________.
12. Installing a program tells it which ___________ to use to communicate with devices such as printers and display screens.

MATCH THE COLUMNS

1. DOS
2. The smallest unit of computer information
3. Contains 8 bits
4. CPU
5. Storage for documents
6. Memory you cannot change
7. Attach peripherals
8. Expand the computer's capabilities
9. Enters uppercase letters
10. Cancels commands
11. Enters commands
12. Deletes characters
13. Fonts

__ Esc
__ CapsLock
__ Byte
__ An operating system
__ Read-only memory
__ Ports
__ Expansion slots and boards
__ Central processing unit
__ Enter ←┘
__ Determine the style of type you can print with
__ Bit
__ ← Bksp
__ Random-access memory

WRITE OUT THE ANSWERS

1. What is the difference between a bit and a byte?
2. Describe the differences between RAM and ROM.
3. What is the function of a port? List the two kinds of ports on a computer, and describe the basic difference between them.
4. What is the purpose of the expansion slots inside a computer? What can they be used for?
5. What does it mean when you say a key toggles?
6. What is the difference between a graphics display and a character display?
7. What is the primary difference among CGA, EGA, VGA, and XGA?
8. What are fonts?
9. What does it mean to say a printer is on line or off line? What switch on the printer do you use to take the printer off line and then put it back on line?
10. What switch on the printer do you press to advance the paper to the top of the next sheet?
11. List and briefly describe the two main types of external storage media and devices.
12. When you are going to move a microcomputer, what step should you take to protect the hard disk drive?
13. What is the purpose of the write-protect notch or window on a floppy disk? What can you do when the disk is write-protected, and what can you not do? What can you do when it is not write-protected?
14. Why does a computer need an operating system?
15. What are the operating system's utility programs used for?
16. Do you think it is legal or ethical to copy disks when a publisher has asked you not to? Why or why not?
17. When you buy a program, do you usually buy all rights to it?

CHAPTER 1

PROJECTS

PROJECT 1

LOCATING LIBRARY RESOURCES

When learning about computers, you can find much useful and interesting information in magazines and newspapers devoted to the field. Most libraries subscribe to at least some of the major computer magazines. Visit the library, and list the computer magazines or other periodicals to which your library subscribes. Read some of the articles and ads in these magazines to become familiar with computer terms and applications.

- ❑ *PC World*
- ❑ *MacWorld*
- ❑ *PC Week*
- ❑ ___________
- ❑ ___________
- ❑ *PC Magazine*
- ❑ *BYTE*
- ❑ *InfoWorld*
- ❑ ___________
- ❑ ___________

Read a review in one of the computer magazines on a desktop or laptop computer, and fill in the information below.

Manufacturer: ______________________________
Model: ______________________________
Size of internal memory (RAM): ______________________________
Type of microprocessor: ______________________________
Type of display (CRT or flat panel): ______________________________

PROJECT 2

VIEWING A VIDEO

Many videocassettes have been developed to introduce users to specific computers. Visit your library, learning center, or computer lab to see if any are available for you to view. You might also find one in a local video store. If you do, you can share the rental cost with other students and view the video together.

PROJECT 3

ATTENDING A USER GROUP MEETING

Many towns have computer groups that hold periodic meetings. Frequently, these groups are divided into smaller groups called Special Interest Groups, or SIGs, where particular computer systems or programs are discussed. Ask around to see if there is a computer group in your area, and if so, attend one of its meetings.

CHAPTER 2

Getting Started with DOS

TOPIC 6

DOS—An Overview

After completing this topic, you will be able to:

- Load DOS on a floppy or hard disk system
- Determine the version number of DOS that your system is running
- Quit DOS and turn off your equipment

To use a computer, you must first load the operating system. This is called booting the system. The term *booting* comes from the expression "pulling oneself up by one's bootstraps." Once the operating system is loaded, you can load your application programs or use the operating system's commands to manage your files and disks.

If your computer is off, you load the operating system by turning it on. When you do so, the computer automatically looks to the startup drive for the operating system files that it needs to start up.

- On a floppy disk system, the startup drive is drive A, so you have to insert a disk that contains the operating system files into that drive.
- On a hard disk system, the startup drive is drive C, but the computer still looks to drive A first. Therefore, before you turn on a hard disk system, be sure to open the door to drive A or eject the disk so that the program does not try to load the operating system from that drive (see the section "Things That Can Go Wrong").

If the files it needs to start are on the disk in the startup drive, that disk is called a *system disk*. If the files are not on the disk in the startup drive, an error message is displayed, and the system will not boot.

Turning a computer on to boot it is called a cold boot. However, you can also reboot a computer if it is already on—called warm booting. To warm-boot the system, you hold down Ctrl and Alt and then press Del. (This command is usually written out as **Ctrl**-**Alt**-**Del**.). Warm booting clears all data from the computer's memory and has almost the same effect as turning the computer off and then back on again. You normally use this procedure only when you encounter a problem with your system. Whenever possible, you should exit any application program you are using before warm booting your system, or you may lose data.

In this tutorial, you take a quick guided tour of some of the most commonly used DOS procedures. You load DOS, check which version you are using, format a disk so that you can store your own work on it, explore directories, and copy files. Everything you do here will be explained in much greater detail later in this text, so relax. The purpose of this Jump-Start Tutorial is to get you over the initial hurdle of using DOS and to make it possible for you to perform basic procedures should the need arise at home, at work, or in other courses.

To load DOS on some systems, such as those connected to networks or with special startup menus, you follow procedures specific to your system. In these cases, ask your instructor how to display the DOS command prompt, and then start this tutorial at the section headed "Changing the Command Prompt."

GETTING STARTED

1. If your computer is on, turn it off. The location of the On/Off switch varies, but it may be located on the right side of the computer toward the rear.
2. Before proceeding:
   - If you are working on a hard disk system, open the door to drive A or eject the disk in that drive. Drive A is the name of the floppy drive if there is only one. If there are two (or more) drives, drive A is usually the one on the top or on the left.
   - If you are working on a floppy disk system, insert the DOS disk into drive A. If there are two (or more) drives, drive A is usually the one on the top or on the left. (On some systems, there may be more than one DOS disk. If you are working on such a system, the disk you use to boot the computer might be named the DOS startup, boot, or system disk. If you are unsure of which disk to use, ask.)

LOADING THE OPERATING SYSTEM

3. Turn on the computer. In a few moments, the computer may beep, and then drive A spins, and its light comes on while the operating system is loaded. If there is no disk in drive A, the computer looks to drive C for the program if the system contains a hard disk drive.
   - If a list of files is displayed, and the screen has the title *MS-DOS Shell*, *IBM DOS Shell*, or *Start Programs*, press F3 to display the command prompt.
   - If nothing appears on your screen, your display screen may not be on. On some systems, the display screen has a separate On/Off switch.
   - If your computer does not have a clock that is set automatically, in a moment the prompt reads *Enter new date:*. If this prompt appears, refer to the section "Entering or Changing the Date and Time" in the Quick Reference section of this topic.

   The command prompt appears and should read *C:\>*, *C>*, *C:\DOS>*, *A:\>*, *A>*, or something similar. This prompt indicates that DOS has been loaded.

LOOKING AHEAD: ENTERING COMMANDS

- In all the instructions in this text, the characters you type are shown in uppercase letters, but whether you use uppercase or lowercase letters usually does not matter. For example, you can type **PROMPT PG** or **prompt pg**.
- If you make a typo when entering any commands, press ←Bksp to delete the incorrect characters, and then type them in correctly before pressing Enter←.

LOOKING AHEAD: DEFAULT DRIVES

Most computers have more than one disk drive. For this reason, disks are assigned names: A, B, C, and so on. Just as you can be in only one place at a time, so it is for your computer. It is always on one and only one of the drives. The drive it is on is called the *default drive*. To have a command affect a disk in any other drive, you must indicate the letter of that drive in the command. This is called *addressing* the drive.

CHANGING THE COMMAND PROMPT

4. If your command prompt does not read *C:\>*, *C:\DOS>*, or *A:\>*, type **PROMPT PG** and press Enter← so that it does (although the *DOS* part may be different).

CHECKING THE VERSION NUMBER

5. Type **VER** and press Enter← to display the version number of the operating system you are using. Write it down so that you don't forget it. The commands you use vary somewhat depending on which version of DOS your system is running.

FORMATTING A DATA DISK

6. Locate a blank disk that **DOES NOT** contain any valuable files. The command you are about to use effectively erases all data from the disk.
7. Insert your disks as follows:
   - On a hard disk system, insert the blank disk into drive A.
   - On a floppy disk system with two disk drives, insert the DOS disk into drive A and the blank disk into drive B.
8. Set your drives as follows:
   - On a hard disk system, type **C:** and press Enter← to change the default drive to drive C. The command prompt should read *C:\>* or *C:\DOS>*.
   - On a floppy disk system, type **A:** and press Enter← to change the default drive to drive A. The command prompt should read *A:\>*.
9. Enter the FORMAT command as follows:
   - On a hard disk system, type **FORMAT A:** and press Enter←.
   - On a floppy disk system, type **FORMAT B:** and press Enter←.

   In a moment, a prompt asks you to insert a disk into the drive you entered in the FORMAT command and press or strike Enter← when ready. You already inserted the disks in a previous step. (If you get the message *Bad command or filename*, or something similar, ask your instructor on what disk or in which directory the FORMAT.COM file can be found, and insert that disk or ask how you change to that directory.)
10. Press Enter←, and the drive spins as it formats the disk. (On DOS 4 and later versions, a message on the screen keeps you posted on the progress.) When the message reads *Format complete*, the drive stops.
11. If you are using DOS 4 or a later version, you are prompted to enter a volume label. Type your last name (abbreviate to 11 characters if necessary), and press Enter← to continue.)
12. When the prompt reads *Format another (Y/N)?*, press N and then press Enter←.

EXPLORING YOUR STUDENT RESOURCE DISK

13. Insert the *Student Resource Disk* into drive A. (The *Student Resource Disk* is a special disk that contains all the files you need to complete the tutorials and exercises in this text.)

> **LOOKING AHEAD: DIRECTORIES**
>
> Disks can store a lot of files. To keep them organized, experienced users divide the disk into directories that are like file folders in which related files can be stored. Knowing which directory a file is in is important since you may not be able to run a program or copy a file unless you do. Directories are discussed in detail in Topic 14. For now, think of them as an address. Just as you may live in San Francisco in the state of California, a file may be stored in a directory named DOS on a drive named C.

14. Type **A:** and press Enter↵ to change the default drive to A, and the command prompt reads *A:\>*.
15. Type **DIR** and press Enter↵ to list the directories on the disk. Directories are like file folders in which you can store related files. They are used to organize your work and programs on the disk. You can tell 1-2-3, DBASE, DOS, EXCHANGE, and WP51 are directories because they are followed by the notation *<DIR>*.
16. Type **CD \DOS** and press Enter↵ The prompt changes to *A:\DOS>* to indicate that DOS on drive A is the current directory.
17. Type **DIR** and press Enter↵ to display a list of the files in the DOS directory along with information about each file. The list is too long to be displayed on the screen, so the topmost files scroll off the top. However, notice how each file has a name such as WHATSUP, an extension such as DOC, a size (in bytes), a date, and a time.
18. Type **DIR/W** and press Enter↵ to display the filenames in five columns without additional information so that more names can be displayed at one time.
19. Type **CD \DBASE** and press Enter↵ to move to the DBASE directory.
20. Type **DIR** and press Enter↵ to display a list of the files in that directory.
21. Type **CD \DOS** and press Enter↵ to return to the DOS directory.
22. Type **DIR *.DOC** and press Enter↵. The command told DOS to list any file with a period followed by the three letters DOC.

> **LOOKING BACK: WRITE-PROTECTION**
>
> As you saw in Topic 4, a disk must not be write-protected when you copy files to it.
>
> - To remove write-protection from a 5¼-inch floppy disk, remove the tape covering the write-protect notch.
> - To remove write-protection from a 3½-inch floppy disk, close the sliding tab in the write-protect window.

COPYING FILES

23. Type **COPY *.* A:** and press Enter↵ to copy all the files from the DOS directory to A:\, the topmost directory on the disk—called the *root directory*. Files are listed on the screen as they are copied, and when all have been copied, the command prompt reappears. The *.* (called star-dot-star) part of the command uses wildcards to tell DOS "all files."
24. Type **DIR** and press Enter↵ to see that all the files are still in the DOS directory.
25. Type **CD ** and press Enter↵ to move back up to the root directory. The command prompt should change to A:\> to indicate that you are there.
26. Type **DIR** and press Enter↵ to see that copies of all the files that were in the DOS directory are now in the root directory.

FINISHING UP

27. Either continue to the next activity or quit for the day. To quit, remove your disks from the drives and turn off the computer.

QUICK REFERENCE

You have to load the operating system only once during a session. If you are already running an application program, you use the application program's Quit or Exit command to return to the operating system or the menu from which you loaded the program.

KEY/Strokes

Loading DOS

1. Set your disk drives as follows:
   - To boot from a hard disk, open the door to drive A or eject any disk from the drive.
   - To boot from a floppy disk, insert a system disk (a disk with the DOS files needed to start up the computer) into drive A.
2. Turn on the computer. What happens next depends on how your system has been set up. Any of the following events may happen:
   - If your system's clock is not set automatically, you are prompted to enter the date and time each time you turn it on. If you are prompted to do so, see the section "Entering or Changing the Date and Time."
   - If your system is connected to a network, or has been customized, a menu may appear on the screen listing actions you can take.
   - The command prompt may appear and will normally be *A>* or *A:\>* if you booted from a floppy disk or *C:\>* if you booted from a hard disk drive. However, the command prompt can be customized, so it may be different on your system. The command prompt tells you that DOS has been loaded, that the default, or active, disk drive is drive A or C; and that the drive is ready to receive commands. From this command prompt, you can execute all DOS commands or start application programs such as WordPerfect, Lotus 1-2-3, or dBASE.
   - The DOS Shell, a menu-operated screen, may appear on systems using DOS 4 or later versions. To display the command prompt from this Shell, press F3.

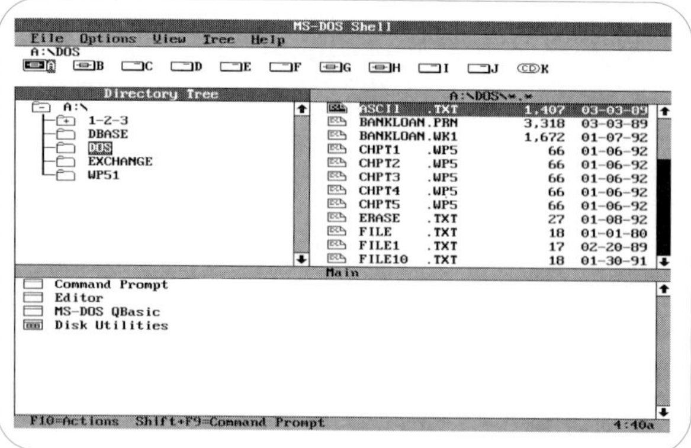

The DOS 5 Shell
DOS 4 and later versions contain a Shell with pull-down menus you can use to execute commands. This illustration shows the screen that appears when the DOS 5 Shell is loaded.

MAIN MENU

1. WordPerfect
2. Lotus 1-2-3
3. dBASE III Plus
4. DOS Command Prompt
5. E-Mail

Enter Choice: __

Network Menus
Many computers are connected to networks so that they can communicate with one another. On these systems, special screens may appear that list programs you can run or commands you can execute.

Entering or Changing the Date and Time

When you first turn on some computers, you are prompted to enter the date and time. Entering the correct date and time is important because the computer's clock date-and-time-marks files that you save. The clock is also used by some programs to enter dates and times into files and to display them on the screen.

If you are prompted to enter the date, type it in the format MM-DD-YY, where MM (month) is a number from 1 to 12, DD (day) is a number from 1 to 31, and YY (year) is a number from 80 to 99 or from 1980 to 1999. For example, to enter the date January 10, 1993, type 1-10-93 and press Enter←.

To enter the time when prompted to do so, use the format HH:MM, where HH (hours) is a number between 0 and 23, and MM (minutes) is a number between 0 and 59. For example, to set the clock to 1:30 p.m., type **13:30** (for military time—see box) and press Enter←. If you are using DOS 4 or later, you could also enter the time as 1:30p (for p.m.).

MILITARY TIME

Versions of DOS prior to 4.0 do not recognize **a** and **p** after the time to indicate a.m. or p.m. With those versions, to set the computer's clock accurately in the afternoon or evening, so that its date will change at midnight, you must use military time. Military time is based on the 24-hour clock. In military time, the hours from 1 a.m. until noon have the same names as they do with the 12-hour clock. But at 1 p.m., the hour is 13:00 (called "thirteen hundred hours"); 2 p.m. is fourteen hundred hours; and so on until midnight, which is zero hours, when the sequence begins again.

Things That Can Go Wrong

It is not at all likely that anything you type on a computer will really harm the system, but it is easy to make mistakes that affect your own work. That's why you should always keep backup copies of important files and take care to follow the directions in this text as you enter commands that are new to you. Here are some problems to look out for when working with DOS:

- When you boot an IBM computer system, you may see the error message *Non-System disk or disk error* (or a similar message on compatible computers). This appears when you turn on the computer with a disk in drive A that does not contain the operating system files that the computer needs. If you get this message, insert the DOS disk into drive A or open the drive's door if it is a hard disk system, and press Enter←.
- The message *Bad command or filename* appears when you type a command incorrectly or when DOS cannot find the file you have tried to run. If you get this prompt, retype the command, or find a disk with the DOS utility program that you want to use.
- If you make a typo and notice it before you press Enter←, press ←Bksp to delete it, and then retype it.
- If you or the computer addresses a drive (for example, type **A:** and press Enter←) and the drive doesn't contain a disk, a message tells you the computer is not ready reading the drive and then offers you options to *abort*, *retry*, *fail*, or *ignore* (although the choices vary depending on the version of DOS you are using).
    - *Abort* cancels the command and returns you to the command prompt (or Shell).
    - *Retry* retries the command, perhaps after you have closed a drive door or inserted a disk.
    - *Fail* cancels the current portion of the command and then continues.
    - *Ignore* ignores the problem and continues processing the command.
- To cancel a command in progress, press Ctrl-C or Ctrl-Break.

Quitting DOS

When you are done for the day, you should always exit the program you are using to return to the operating system, and then:

- Open the floppy disk drive doors or eject the disks in the drives so that the disk drives' read/write heads don't leave indentations in the disks' surfaces.
- Remove your disks from the disk drives to prevent their loss, increase security, and ensure that no one mistakenly erases them.
- Turn off the computer or use the display monitor's controls to dim the screen so that an image will not be "burned" into its phosphor surface.

On some systems, after turning your computer off, you should wait 20 to 30 seconds before turning it back on. Some systems will not reboot without this pause. If you turn one of these systems back on too quickly, nothing happens.

EXERCISES

EXERCISE 1

LOADING DOS ON YOUR OWN SYSTEM

Many computers are now networked or have other special startup procedures. If your system is one of these, list the steps here that you use to access the DOS command prompt so that you have it for future reference.

1. ______________________________

2. ______________________________

3. ______________________________

4. ______________________________

5. ______________________________

EXERCISE 2

IDENTIFYING YOUR SYSTEM'S FLOPPY DISK DRIVES

If your system has more than one floppy disk drive, make a sketch of them and label them A, B, and so on. Use this sketch for later reference when you are asked to insert a disk into a specific floppy disk drive.

TOPIC 7

Executing Commands

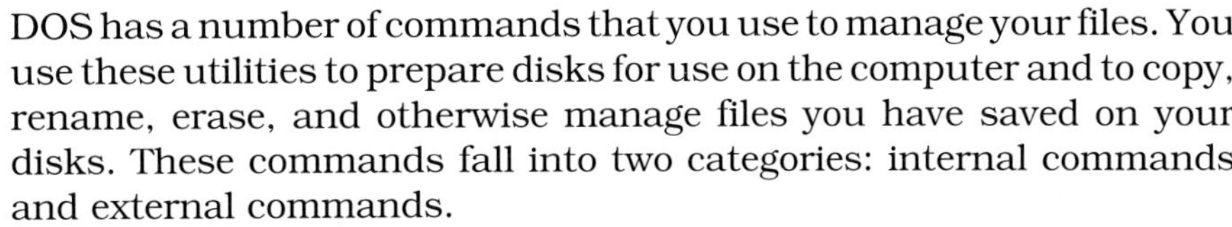

After completing this topic, you will be able to:

- Describe the difference between internal and external commands
- Execute commands from the command prompt
- Print the screen display

DOS has a number of commands that you use to manage your files. You use these utilities to prepare disks for use on the computer and to copy, rename, erase, and otherwise manage files you have saved on your disks. These commands fall into two categories: internal commands and external commands.

Internal commands are available whenever the command prompt is displayed. Internal commands are automatically loaded into the computer's memory whenever you load DOS because they are included in the COMMAND.COM file that is loaded automatically whenever you boot the system.

External commands are stored on the DOS disk or hard disk until you need them. These commands are used less often than internal commands. Not loading them into memory until they are needed leaves room for other programs and data.

External commands are little more than small programs that are loaded into the computer's memory and then executed when you type their name and press Enter←. If you enter an external command and its program is not on the disk in the drive, the computer displays an error message indicating you have used a bad command. When this occurs, you first make sure you entered the correct command. If you did, you then use the DIR command (which you'll learn more about later) to check if the command's file is on the disk and, if not, locate the disk it is on. If you use an external command frequently, copying the appropriate program file from the DOS disk onto an application program disk may be helpful.

Relax!
There is almost nothing that you can do from the keyboard that will damage the system or cause serious problems. If there were, it would be the system designer's fault and not yours.

EXTERNAL COMMANDS ON HARD DISK SYSTEMS

This tutorial and all other DOS activities in this text assume that your hard disk system's AUTOEXEC.BAT file contains a PATH command listing the directory in which the DOS program files are stored. All hard disk external commands are given in this text without specifying the location of the DOS files needed to execute them.

Usually DOS files are stored in a directory of their own on the hard disk. As you may recall, directories are like file folders in which you can store related files. If you are working on a hard disk system, ask your instructor where the DOS files are stored and write down the name of the directory because you may need to know it to complete the activities in this text. Now, let's look at two ways you can execute DOS's external commands.

1. The best way to execute commands is to have the DOS directory listed in the PATH command in the AUTOEXEC.BAT file that the system reads when you boot it. Type **C:** and press Enter↵ to make drive C the default drive. Then, type **C:** and press Enter↵ to be sure you are in the topmost directory of drive C. Finally, type **TYPE AUTOEXEC.BAT** and press Enter↵. If you get the message *File not found*, or if no line in the file begins with the word *PATH*, your system does not have a PATH command, so proceed to Step 2. If a line in the file does begin with *PATH*, look to see if the name of your DOS directory is listed on the line. For example, if your DOS files are in a directory named DOS, one part of the line should read *C:\DOS*. If your directory is listed, you can execute DOS external commands without any concern for the directory they are stored in. The PATH command tells DOS to look for them in the listed directory.
2. If your system does not have a PATH command, you have to either be in the DOS directory to execute an external command or refer to the directory in the command. For example, to move into the DOS directory, assuming it is named DOS, type **CD \DOS** and press Enter↵.

LOOKING AHEAD: THE AUTOEXEC.BAT FILE

When you boot your system, one of the first things it does is look for a file on the startup drive named AUTOEXEC.BAT. This file contains commands that are then executed before the command prompt is displayed.

TUTORIAL

In this tutorial, you experiment with some basic commands. (To execute the CHKDSK command described in this tutorial, you will need a copy of the DOS utility file CHKDSK.COM or CHKDSK.EXE.) If your system uses more than one DOS disk, ask which disk it is on.

GETTING STARTED

1. Load DOS so that the command prompt is displayed.
2. Insert the original write-protected copy of the *Student Resource Disk* into drive A.
3. Type **A:** and press Enter↵, and the command prompt indicates that drive A is the default drive.
4. Check that the printer is on and has paper in it.

EXECUTING SOME INTERNAL COMMANDS

5. Type **DATE** and press Enter↵ to display the current date and a prompt asking you to enter a new date.
6. Press Enter↵, and the date is left unchanged. The command prompt reappears.
7. Type **TIME** and press Enter↵ to display the current time and a prompt asking you to enter a new time.
8. Press Enter↵, and the time is left unchanged. The command prompt reappears.
9. Type **CLS** and press Enter↵ to clear the screen and move the command prompt to the upper left corner of the screen.

LOOKING AHEAD: THE CHKDSK COMMAND

You use the CHKDSK command to find out how much space is still available on a disk and in the computer's memory. This command also tells you if all the files on your disk are stored correctly. If it finds that they are scattered, you will see a message that files are in noncontiguous blocks. This is discussed in Topic 19.

10. Type **DIR** and press Enter↵ to list the names of the files on the disk.

EXECUTING SOME EXTERNAL COMMANDS

11. If you are working on a floppy disk system (leave things as is on a hard disk system):
    - Move the *Student Resource Disk* to drive B.
    - Type **B:** and press Enter↵ to change the default drive to B.
    - Insert the DOS disk containing the DOS utility file CHKDSK.COM or CHKDSK.EXE into drive A. (Ask your instructor if you are not sure of which disk to use.)
12. Enter a command as follows:
    - On a hard disk system, type **CHKDSK** and press Enter↵.
    - On a floppy disk system, type **A:CHKDSK** and press Enter↵.

    The screen indicates how much room is on your disk and in your internal memory and how much of it has been used. If you get a message that tells you it is a bad command or filename, see the box "External Commands on Hard Disk Systems" in the introduction to this topic
13. Type **TYPE WHATSUP.DOC** and press Enter↵. The contents of the file are scrolled up the screen too fast to read them.
14. If you are working on a floppy disk system, insert the DOS disk containing the DOS utility file MORE.COM into drive A. (It's probably on the same disk you inserted into drive A earlier.)
15. Enter a command as follows: (The | character is the split vertical bar(¦) on the backslash (\) key. You must press ⇧Shift to enter it.)
    - On a hard disk system, type **TYPE WHATSUP.DOC |MORE** and press Enter↵.
    - On a floppy disk system, type **TYPE WHATSUP.DOC |A:MORE** and press Enter↵.

    The list of Bugs Bunny films directed by Chuck Jones scrolls onto the screen until the screen is full. Then, the screen pauses, and the prompt -- *More* -- is displayed at the bottom of the screen.
16. Press any key to scroll through the document a screenful at a time until the command prompt reappears.

LOOKING AHEAD: SPECIFYING PATHS TO A PROGRAM

The CHKDSK command is an external command, so DOS needs to know where this file is located when you execute the command. If it is not on the default drive, you have to specify which drive it is on. If the file is on drive A, you indicate its location by specifying A:CHKDSK. The A: part of the command is called a path since it tells DOS what path to follow to find the file.

LOOKING AHEAD: THE MORE COMMAND

When you display directories or files from DOS, they may scroll off the top of the screen too fast to be read. In these cases, you can use the |MORE command to pause the screen whenever the screen is full. The command then displays a message -- *More* -- and you press any key to scroll to the next screenful of data.

FINISHING UP

17. Either continue to the next activity or quit for the day. To quit, remove your disks from the drive and turn off the computer.

QUICK REFERENCE

To execute commands, you type them in and press Enter↵. However, you can also save time by executing a command you have used previously without having to retype it or by editing it into a new form.

Executing Commands

To execute commands from the command prompt, you type the name of the command and press Enter↵ When the command is finished executing, the command prompt reappears.

When you type commands, there are certain conventions that you must follow. Getting used to these conventions takes practice. If you do not follow them exactly, an error message is displayed, but no harm is done. When entering commands, keep the following conventions in mind:

- You can use uppercase, lowercase, or any combination of case. For example, when checking a disk, you can type **CHKDSK**, **chkdsk**, or **Chkdsk**, and the computer accepts them all.
- Parts of many commands must be separated from each other by *delimiters*. Delimiters, which are like punctuation marks in English, indicate where parts of a command begin or end. DOS delimiters include spaces, colons, and slashes.
  - Spaces should not be used at times. For example, you do not enter spaces between the drive, path, and filename. You type **B:**<*filename*> not **B: **<*filename*>. The colon and backslash act as the delimiters.
  - Spaces should be used at other times. For example, when displaying a directory of a disk other than the default, you type **DIR B:** not **DIRB:**.
- Many commands can include optional *switches* that modify them. These switches must be separated from the command by a delimiter. For example, to display the directory of a disk in drive B across the screen, you type **DIR B:/W**.

GETTING HELP

On-line help was added to DOS beginning with DOS 4, but in that version it is available only from the Shell. Beginning with DOS 5, you can obtain help when working from the command prompt. Microsoft customizes DOS 5 for its customers so versions from Microsoft, IBM, Compaq, and others may vary slightly from one another. On the original Microsoft version, the following commands work as described. On other versions, you may find slight differences but the following commands should get you pointed in the right direction.

- For brief help, type **HELP** and press Enter↵ to display a list of commands with a brief description of each. Since all the commands cannot be listed at once, the screen periodically pauses. To see the next screen, press any key. To return directly to the command prompt at any point, press Ctrl-C.
- For detailed help on a specific command, type **HELP** <*command*> and press Enter↵. For example, for help on the DIR command, type **HELP DIR** and press Enter↵.

Responding to Prompts

When working with DOS and application programs, you often encounter prompts, which are simply requests for you to supply the computer with information it needs. Some prompts, like the command prompt, are cryptic. Others are more helpful; for example, a prompt may ask *Insert new diskette for drive A Press Enter to continue.* To enter responses to these prompts, you take the requested actions. Some commands then continue automatically. With others, you have to enter a response like **Y** or **N** (for Yes or No), and then you sometimes have to confirm that response by pressing Enter↵ to continue.

Editing Commands

When you type commands, you might make a mistake, or you might want to repeat the same command, perhaps with a few changes. DOS has editing keys and commands that allow you to do each of these things.

To cancel a command that you have not yet executed by pressing Enter↵, press Ctrl-Break or Ctrl-C (hold down Ctrl while you press the second key) to return to the command prompt.

When entering a command, you can press ←Bksp to delete typos. To cancel a partially entered command, press Esc. This places a backslash (\) character at the end of the current line and moves the cursor down one line ready for a new command. At this point, you can either press Enter↵ to return to the command prompt, or enter a new command and press Enter↵.

The last command you typed is stored in a buffer, a small area of memory used to store keystrokes. You can recall the command from that buffer to edit it. There are many commands you can use to do so, but the two most popular are F1, which displays the previous command one character at a time, and F3, which displays the complete command. Once the command is displayed on the command line, you can press Enter↵ to execute it or press ←Bksp to delete characters and type new ones at the end of the line.

DOS 5 added a new feature called DOSKEY that makes it easy to repeat or edit previous commands. To use this feature, type **DOSKEY** and press Enter↵ to load this external command. Once it has been loaded, it stores each command you use so that you can redisplay any of them on the command line. To display a list of all commands that have been saved, type **DOSKEY /HISTORY** and press Enter↵ or press F7.

To display a specific command so that you can repeat it or edit it, press ↑ or PgDn to display the command you used most recently, or press PgUp to display the oldest command you used. Once you have displayed a command, you can use ↑ and ↓ to scroll back and forward through them.

Once the command you want is displayed on the command line, you can press Enter↵ to execute it, or you can edit it by moving the cursor through the command and inserting or deleting characters. To delete a character, you move the cursor under it, and type a new character or press Del. You can also move the cursor to the right of a character, and press ←Bksp to delete it. To insert characters, press Ins to turn on insert mode, and the cursor should change shape to indicate that you are in insert mode. Move the cursor to where you want to insert one or more characters, and type them in. The characters above the cursor and those to its right move aside to make room for the new characters. The commands used most frequently with DOSKEY are described in the table "DOSKEY Edit Commands."

TIP

If numbers appear when you press the arrow keys on the numeric keypad, the NumLock key is engaged. To disengage it, press it once.

DOSKEY EDIT COMMANDS

Key	Description
↑ or PgDn	Displays the command you used most recently.
PgUp	Displays the oldest command you used.
↑ and ↓	Scrolls back and forward through the displayed commands.
← or →	Moves the cursor left or right one character.
Ctrl-← or Ctrl-→	Moves the cursor left or right one word.
Home or End	Moves the cursor to the beginning or end of line.
Esc	Removes the command from the display.
F7	Displays all stored commands as a numbered list.
Alt-F7	Erases all stored commands.
F8	Searches for the stored command you want. Type the first few characters in the command, and press F8 to display the most recent version you used. Press F8 to cycle through any other versions being stored.
F9	Prompts you to type the number of a command you want to repeat. (Use F7 to find numbers.)

EXERCISES

EXERCISE 1

PRINTING THE SCREEN

In some cases, your instructor may want a printed record of the commands you execute in the activities in this text. If you are requested to submit printed results, there are two ways to do so. You can print the current screen, or you can turn on printing so that everything that appears on your screen is printed. Complete this exercise only if your instructor approves since the commands discussed here can cause problems on some systems.

1. Be sure your printer is on. If you use one of the commands in this exercise when your printer isn't on, your system may "hang" and not accept keyboard input until you turn the printer on.
2. Type **DIR/W** and press Enter↵ to display a list of the files on the disk.
3. Press ⇧Shift-PrtScr (or just PrtScr on an enhanced keyboard) to print what is currently displayed on the screen. (To see the printout on some printers, you may have to press On Line to take the printer off line, FF for Form Feed, and then On Line again to put the printer back on line.)
4. Press Ctrl-PrtScr to turn on screen printing so that you will have a running, printed record of what you do while working from the command prompt.
5. Repeat the tutorial at the beginning of this topic. When finished, press Ctrl-PrtScr again to turn printing off.

EXERCISE 2

EXECUTING INTERNAL AND EXTERNAL COMMANDS

In this exercise, you practice executing internal and external commands. All the commands that you enter here are similar to those you entered in this topic's tutorial. If you need help on a command, refer to the tutorial to see how you executed it there.

1. Insert your disks as follows:
   - On a hard disk system, insert the *Student Resource Disk* into drive A.
   - On a floppy disk system, insert the DOS startup disk into drive A and the *Student Resource Disk* into drive B.
2. If your instructor approves, press Ctrl-PrtScr to turn on printing.
3. Change the date to January 2, 1993.
4. Change the time to 10:30 a.m.
5. Display the path if your system has one.
6. Clear the screen.
7. Use the CHKDSK command to check the disk in drive A.

8. Display a directory of the disk in drive A in five columns.

EXERCISE 3

EXPLORING DOS 5'S DOSKEY FEATURE

In this exercise, you explore DOS 5's DOSKEY feature that allows you to repeat or edit previous commands. For this feature to work, the DOSKEY program must be loaded into memory.

1. Insert your disks as follows:
   - On a hard disk system, insert the *Student Resource Disk* into drive A.
   - On a floppy disk system, insert the DOS startup disk into drive A and the *Student Resource Disk* into drive B.
2. Enter the following command:
   - On a hard disk system, type **DIR A:** and press Enter↵.
   - On a floppy disk system, type **DIR B:** and press Enter↵.
3. Press ↑ to see if it displays the previous command on the command line. If so, your DOSKEY program has been loaded. If the previous command does not appear on the command line, DOSKEY has not been loaded. To load it, type **DOSKEY** and press Enter↵. (Immediately after it loads, a message reads *DOSKey installed.* If this message doesn't appear, ask your instructor for help.)
4. If DOSKEY is operating correctly on your system, repeat Exercise 1. Then repeat it again, but this time press ↑ until any command you want is displayed on the command line (once you have scrolled up, you can also press ↓ to back down through commands), and press Enter↵ to execute it.
5. You can edit previous commands. To see how this works, display a previous command, and press ← and → to move the cursor through it. Type new characters, and then press Ins and type some more. Before you press Ins, characters you type replace any character in the cursor's position. After pressing it, new characters are inserted and text to the right is pushed aside. Use Del and ←Bksp to delete characters. To cancel the command without executing it, press Ctrl-C.

DOS EXTERNAL COMMAND FILES

File	Disk
CHKDSK	
COMP	
DOSKEY	
FORMAT	
LABEL	
MORE	
PRINT	
SORT	
SYS	
TREE	
TYPE	
XCOPY	

EXERCISE 4

LOCATING DOS FILES NEEDED FOR EXTERNAL COMMANDS

When you execute an external command, the DOS file for that command must be on a disk in one of the disk drives. If you are working on a floppy disk system that has more than one DOS disk, locate the disks that contain the files listed in the table "DOS External Command Files." The files will have the name shown in the table, but their extensions may be either .EXE or .COM. To locate the files, put each DOS disk into drive A one at a time, type **DIR A:** and press Enter↵ to list the files on the disk. If the filenames scroll by too fast to read, type **DIR A:/W** and press Enter↵.

TOPIC 8

Changing the Default Drive

After completing this topic, you will be able to:

- Describe the difference between the default drive and other drives
- Change default drives
- Customize the command prompt

When you first turn on your computer to boot the system, drive A spins. If a disk in that drive contains the necessary operating system files, the operating system is loaded. Drive A operates because the computer's designers have placed a program in the computer's ROM telling it that it should address this drive when first turned on. Since it addresses drive A automatically, drive A is the default startup drive. (On a hard disk system, it then looks to drive C if no disk is in drive A.)

Although you cannot change the default drive that the computer addresses when you first turn it on, you can, and often do, copy, rename, delete, and save files on a drive other than the default drive. To do so, you can change the default drive.

The Default Drive
The default drive is the drive your computer automatically addresses when you execute commands. It's like a model railroad where you can set a switch to send a train down one track or another.

Changing the Default Drive
You can change the default drive so that the program automatically addresses another drive. It's like changing the position of the switch on a model railroad to send the train down another track.

TUTORIAL

In this tutorial, you change the default drive.

GETTING STARTED

1. Load DOS so that the command prompt is displayed.
2. Insert your disks as follows:
   - On a hard disk system, insert the *Student Resource Disk* into drive A.
   - On a floppy disk system, insert the DOS disk into drive A and the *Student Resource Disk* into drive B.

CHANGING THE COMMAND PROMPT

3. Type **PROMPT What can I do for you?** and press Enter← to change the prompt. Changes in the prompt stay in effect until you turn off the computer unless you use the PROMPT command again to change it.
4. Type **PROMPT PG** and press Enter←. The PG at the end of the text is a DOS command that tells the computer to display the current default drive, in this case, *C:*\> or *A:*\>.
5. Type **PROMPT The default drive is now PG** and press Enter← to have the prompt indicate the current default drive as you complete the steps that follow.

CHANGING THE DEFAULT DRIVE

6. Enter the command as follows:
   - On a hard disk system, type **C:** and press Enter←.
   - On a floppy disk system, type **B:** and press Enter←.

   When you enter this command, the command prompt changes to indicate the current default drive.
7. Type **DIR** and press Enter← to display a list of files on the current default drive.
8. Type **A:** and press Enter← to change the default drive to A.
9. Type **DIR** and press Enter← to display a list of files on the new default drive.
10. Enter the command as follows:
    - On a hard disk system, type **C:** and press Enter←.
    - On a floppy disk system, type **B:** and press Enter←.
11. Type **A:** and press Enter←.

FINISHING UP

12. Type **PROMPT PG** and press Enter← to have the prompt indicate the default drive without the preceding text.
13. Either continue to the next activity or quit for the day. To quit, remove your disks from the drives and turn off the computer.

QUICK REFERENCE

When working with DOS and application programs, you need to change the default drive. At times, it is helpful to customize the command prompt so that it provides you with information that you need.

Changing the Default Drive

To change the default drive from the command prompt, type the letter of the drive and a colon and press Enter←. For example, if the default drive is set to A and you want to change it to B, type **B:** and press Enter←. The command prompt is usually set to indicate the current default drive. For example, *B>* or *B:\>* indicates that drive B is the default drive.

In a system with a single floppy disk drive, the drive functions as both drive A and drive B. If the command prompt reads *A>* and you type **B:** and press Enter←, the command prompt changes to *B>*. On such systems, when you execute DOS commands such as copying files from one disk to another, you are frequently asked to swap disks in the drive.

Changing the Command Prompt

The default command prompt (which you get if you type **PROMPT** and press Enter←) is the letter of the current default drive followed by a greater-than sign, but you can customize the prompt to display other useful information. To change the command prompt, you can use any of the commands, either alone or in combination, described in the table "Prompt Commands." Note that each of these commands is preceded by a dollar sign so that it will not be treated as text and appear just as typed. The prompt command **PROMPT PG** is probably the most frequently used version. It displays the current drive (and directory, as you will see later).

PROMPT COMMANDS

Character	Description
$_	Inserts a carriage return and line feed when you want to create two or more lines on the prompt; for example, **PROMPT TIME = T_DATE = D_PG** displays the time on one line, the date on the next, and the current drive and directory on the third.
$B	Displays a ¦ (split vertical bar).
$D	Displays the current date.
$E	Displays an ← (Esc) character.
$G	Displays a > (greater-than) character.
$H	Backspace that deletes the previous character in the prompt.
$L	Displays a < (less-than) character.
$N	Displays the default drive.
$P	Displays the current directory of the default drive. (If you use this character on a floppy disk system, the disk drive must always have a disk in it when you make it the default drive; otherwise, you get the error message *Not ready reading drive x.* (The *x* is the specified drive and varies depending on the system you are using.) If this prompt appears, press F (for *Fail*) to continue.
$Q	Displays an equal sign (=).

PROMPT COMMANDS (CONTINUED)

Character	Description
$T	Displays the current time.
$V	Displays the DOS version number.
$<*spaces*>	Type **$** and then press Spacebar to insert spaces. If you insert a space after the last character in the PROMPT command, the cursor will be spaced one character to the right of the prompt.

EXERCISE

EXERCISE 1

CHANGING BETWEEN DRIVES A AND B ON A SYSTEM WITH A SINGLE FLOPPY DISK DRIVE

If your system has only a single floppy disk drive, you can explore how it acts as both drive A and drive B. You will find this feature very useful when you want to copy files between disks in later tutorials and in your own work. As you complete the following steps, watch the prompts that appear on the screen; then press Enter← to remove them before proceeding to the next step. Whenever you see the prompt asking you to insert a disk, you can remove one disk and then insert another before continuing. This way you can use the single drive in your system as though it were two separate drives.

1. Load DOS.
2. Insert your *Student Resource Disk* into drive A.
3. Type **A:** and press Enter← so that the command prompt *A>* or *A:\>* is displayed.
4. Type **B:** and press Enter←.
5. Type **A:** and press Enter←.
6. Type **DIR B:** and press Enter←.
7. Type **DIR A:** and press Enter←.

CHAPTER 2 REVIEW

- Loading the operating system is called booting the system. If the computer is off, it is called a cold boot. If the system is already on, it is called a warm boot.
- When you load DOS, either the command prompt or the DOS Shell is displayed, depending on which version of DOS you're using and how your system has been set up.
- DOS has internal and external commands. The internal commands are part of the COMMAND.COM file and are always available whenever the command prompt is displayed on the screen. External commands are stored in their own files. To use one of them, the file must be on a disk in one of the drives.
- The default drive is the drive that the computer addresses unless you specify another drive. To change the default drive, you type its letter and a colon and press Enter↵.

CHAPTER 2 QUESTIONS

FILL IN THE BLANK

1. If you make a typo when typing a command, you can press ___________ to delete it.
2. After typing a command, you press ___________ to send it to the CPU.
3. The *A>*, *A:\>*, *C>*, *C:\>* or something similar that appears on the screen when you boot your system is called the ___________ ___________.
4. To enter the date January 10, 1994, into a computer, you would type ___________.
5. To enter the time ten-thirty a.m. into a computer, you would type ___________.
6. To warm-boot many computers, you hold down ___________ and ___________ and then press ___________.
7. To find out what version of DOS is in your computer's memory, you use the ___________ command.
8. Commands that are always available when the command prompt is on the screen are called ___________ commands.
9. Commands that are available only when the file that contains them is on a disk in one of the disk drives are called ___________ commands.
10. To repeat the previous command, you press ___________ and then press ___________.
11. To print the text currently on the screen, you would press ___________.

12. To print all text that will appear on the screen with subsequent commands, you would press __________.
13. To change the way the command prompt looks, you use the __________ command.
14. To change the default drive from drive A to drive B, you type __________ and press __________.
15. To change the default drive from drive B to drive A, you type __________ and press __________.

MATCH THE COLUMNS

1. VER	__ Repeats the previous command
2. F3	__ Command prompt
3. Ctrl-Alt-Del	__ Command that customizes the command prompt
4. ← Bksp	__ Changes the default drive to drive A
5. Prompts	__ Computer's request for you to type something
6. ⇧ Shift-PrtScr or PrtScr	__ Prints all screen text until you turn it off
7. Ctrl-PrtScr	__ Prints text currently on the screen
8. PROMPT	__ Deletes typos when entering commands
9. *A>* or *A:\>*	__ Keys you press to warm-boot many computers
10. **A:** and then Enter ↵	__ Changes the default drive to drive B
11. **B:** and then Enter ↵	__ The command that tells you what version of DOS is in memory

WRITE OUT THE ANSWER

1. What does booting a computer mean?
2. What is the startup drive? Which drive is it on a floppy disk system? On a hard disk system?
3. What is the difference between a warm boot and a cold boot? How do you do each?
4. What is the basic difference between an internal and an external DOS command?
5. Name and describe the use of three function keys that can be used with DOS.
6. What is the default drive? Describe how you change it.
7. What does the *A>* prompt mean? The *B>* prompt?

CHAPTER 2

PROJECTS

PROJECT 1

VIEWING A VIDEO

Many videocassettes have been developed to introduce users to specific operating systems. Visit your library, learning center, and computer lab to see if any are available for you to view. If there are, view one, and then summarize its key points.

PROJECT 2

CREATING A DOS REFERENCE CARD

The table "Summary of DOS Commands" lists some of the most frequently used DOS command procedures. Complete the table by entering in the Command column the command you would use to perform each of the tasks. In the Type column, indicate if the command is an internal or external command.

SUMMARY OF DOS COMMANDS

Description	Command	Type
Basic Commands		
Displays DOS version number	__________	____
Displays system date	__________	____
Displays system time	__________	____
Changes the command prompt	__________	____
Clears the screen	__________	____
Changing Default Drives		
Makes drive A the default drive	__________	____
Makes drive B the default drive	__________	____
Makes drive C the default drive	__________	____

CHAPTER 3

Basic DOS Utilities

TOPIC 9

Formatting Disks

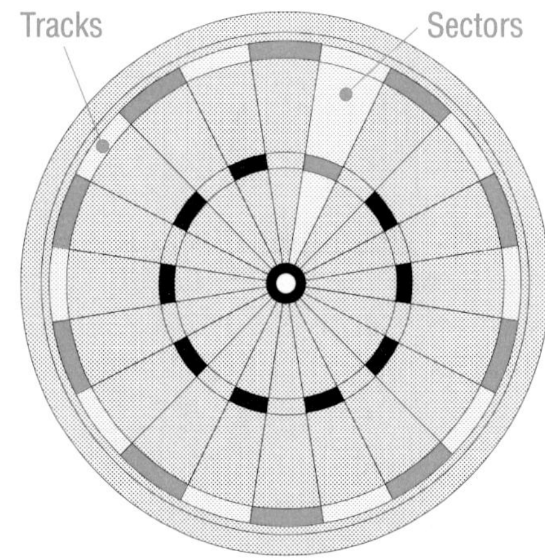

A Formatted Disk

One way to visualize a formatted disk is as a dart board. Tracks run in circles around the disk. The number of tracks per inch determines the density of the disk. A high-density disk has more tracks per inch than a low-density disk and can therefore store more data. Since the tracks can store a great deal of data, the computer divides them into sectors, which makes it easier to find a location on the disk. These sectors are like pie-shaped wedges that radiate from the center of the disk.

After completing this topic, you will be able to:

- Describe why you format a disk and what happens when you do
- Format your own data disks
- Explain the difference between a data disk and a system disk
- Format a disk as a system disk
- Transfer the operating system files to a disk that has already been formatted

When you open a box of new floppy disks, they will usually not work properly on your computer because they have been designed to work with a variety of computer systems. To customize them so that they will work with the equipment you are using, you format the disks. Formatting checks the disk surface for unusable spots, divides the disk into tracks and sectors, and creates a directory.

Formatting a disk effectively erases any data that may already have been saved on it. You therefore have to be careful with this command. You should never format a previously used disk unless you are sure you will not need any of the files on it. Moreover, you should never format a hard disk drive unless you are willing to lose every file on the disk. However, since no one is perfect and mistakes do happen, DOS 5 added an unformat command that helps you recover files should you format a disk by mistake.

TUTORIALS

(your name)
Resource Disk—Backup
Formatted with DOS (version number)

The Resource Disk—Backup Label

In this tutorial, you format a blank data disk for use in the tutorials and exercises in this text.

GETTING STARTED

1. Load DOS so that the command prompt is displayed.
2. Label a blank disk, using as a guide the information shown in the figure "The Resource Disk—Backup Label."
3. Insert your disks as follows:
   - On a hard disk system, insert the disk labeled *Resource Disk—*

Backup into drive A.
- On a floppy disk system, insert the DOS disk that contains the file FORMAT.COM into drive A and the disk labeled *Resource Disk—Backup* into drive B.

4. Set your drives as follows:
   - On a hard disk system, change the default drive to drive C.
   - On a floppy disk system, change the default drive to drive A.

FORMATTING A DATA DISK

5. Enter the command as follows:
   - On a hard disk system, type **FORMAT A:** and press Enter←.
   - On a floppy disk system, type **FORMAT B:** and press Enter←.

   In a moment, a prompt asks you to insert a disk into the drive you entered in the FORMAT command and press or strike Enter← when ready. You already inserted the disks in Step 3.
6. Press Enter← and the drive spins as it formats the disk.
   - On DOS 4 and later versions, a message is displayed on the screen to keep you posted on the progress. When the message reads *Format complete*, the drive stops.
   - If you are using DOS 4 or later, you are prompted to enter a volume label. Type your last name (abbreviate to 11 characters if necessary), and press Enter← to continue.
7. When the prompt reads *Format another (Y/N)?*, press N and then Enter←.

   Information is displayed on the screen about the disk's status. The information varies slightly between DOS 3 and later versions but includes the following:
   - The number of bytes of total disk space and how many bytes are currently available. Usually the two numbers are the same; if they are different, DOS may have found bad sectors on the disk. If it did, it marked them so that no data can be stored on them.
   - The number of bytes in each allocation unit and the number of allocation units are displayed on DOS 4 and later versions.
   - The volume's serial number is displayed on DOS 4 and later versions.

FINISHING UP

8. You have now completed this tutorial. Either continue to the next activity or quit for the day.

QUICK REFERENCE

To format a data disk, you use the FORMAT command. The FORMAT.COM file must be on one of the drives since this is an external command.

DOS always formats a disk to match the drive it is being formatted in unless you specify otherwise. To change the way a disk is formatted, you add switches to the FORMAT command to control the formatting process. For example, you may want to format a 360KB disk in a 1.2MB drive or a 720KB 3½-inch disk in a 1.44MB drive. To format a 360KB disk in a 1.2MB 5¼-inch drive, use the command FORMAT <*drive:*> /4. To format a 720KB disk in a 1.44MB 3½-inch drive, use the command FORMAT <*drive:*> /T:80 /N:9 (or FORMAT <*drive:*> /F:720 on versions 4.0 and later).

> **LOOKING AHEAD: SWITCHES**
>
> Many DOS commands have options you can specify to control or vary the results of the command. To tell DOS to use these options, you add switches to the command. Most switches are specified by typing a slash followed by a letter or number. For example, to format a disk you might use command FORMAT /4 instead of simply FORMAT.

 KEY/Strokes

Formatting Floppy Disks

1. Insert your disks as follows:
   - On a hard disk system, insert the disk to be formatted into drive A.
   - On a floppy disk system, insert the disk with the file FORMAT.COM into drive A and the disk to be formatted into drive B.
2. Set your drives as follows:
   - On a hard disk system, make drive C the default drive.
   - On a floppy disk system, make drive A the default drive.
3. Enter the command as follows:
   - On a hard disk system, type **FORMAT A:** and press [Enter←].
   - On a floppy disk system, type **FORMAT B:** and press [Enter←].

   In a moment, a prompt asks you to insert a disk into the drive you entered in the FORMAT command and press or strike [Enter←] when ready. You inserted the disks in Step 1.
4. Press [Enter←] to continue and the drive spins as it formats the disk. On DOS 4 and later versions, a message is displayed on the screen to keep you posted on the progress. (DOS 5 also saves UNFORMAT information.) When the message reads *Format complete*, the drive stops.

   If you are using DOS 4 or later, a prompt reads *Volume label (11 characters, ENTER for none)?*. Either type a volume name to identify the disk and press [Enter←] or press [Enter←] without entering a volume name.

   The prompt reads *Format another (Y/N)?*.
5. Either: Press [N] and then [Enter←] to quit formatting and return to the command prompt.

   Or: Insert a new disk into the same drive as you did in Step 1, press [Y] and then [Enter←] to display the prompt asking you to insert a new disk. Press the designated key to continue.

Creating System Disks

When you boot the computer, it looks in the startup drive for the file COMMAND.COM and two hidden system files named IBMBIO.COM and IBMDOS.COM (or something similar on some versions of DOS). The DOS startup disk contains these files, but you can also put them onto your own floppy disks, which are then called system disks because they can be used to boot the system.

There are two ways to transfer these files to your own floppy disk: either during or after formatting.

- To transfer the files during formatting, add the /S switch to the FORMAT command. For example, to format a disk on drive A as a system disk, type **FORMAT A: /S** and press Enter←. On most systems this switch copies the two hidden system system files and the file COMMAND.COM to the floppy disk. On some systems, however, it does not copy COMMAND.COM and you must copy it separately with the COPY command. (See the box "Copying COMMAND.COM.")
- If there is room for them on an already formatted floppy disk, you can transfer the two hidden system files to it with the external command SYS. For example, to transfer the system files to an already formatted disk in drive A, type **SYS A:** and press Enter←. The SYS command does not copy the file COMMAND.COM. You have to copy it separately with the COPY command. (See the box "Copying COMMAND.COM.")

LOOKING AHEAD: COPYING COMMAND.COM

You will learn about copying files in Topic 11. For now, just follow these directions to copy COMMAND.COM to a floppy disk.

1. Insert the DOS startup disk into drive A.
2. Insert the formatted system disk into drive B.
3. Make drive A the default drive by typing **A:** and pressing Enter←.
4. Type **COPY COMMAND.COM B:** and press Enter←.

Unformatting a Disk

If you format a disk by mistake, you can lose valuable files because the FORMAT command erases them. For this reason, many companies have published special programs you can use to restore deleted files. With the introduction of DOS 5, an UNFORMAT external command was added so that you can use DOS to unformat a disk and restore the lost files. To unformat a disk, type **UNFORMAT** <*drive*> and press Enter←. For example, to unformat a disk in drive A, type **UNFORMAT A:** and press Enter←.

To ensure that this command works, you should load DOS 5's Mirror program before formatting a disk. This program saves data that can be used to unformat the disk (specifically the file allocation table and the root directory) in a file named MIRROR.FIL. To load the Mirror program, type **MIRROR** <*drive*> and press Enter←. To mirror more than one drive, list each drive after the command. For example, to mirror drives A and C, type **MIRROR A: C:** and press Enter←. The UNFORMAT command may work on a disk that was formatted without MIRROR loaded, but your risks of not being successful increase, and the process takes longer. Moreover, for the most likelihood of success, unformat the disk immediately. If you save any files on it, they may overwrite files from the previous format, and the overwritten files will not be recoverable.

Selecting Floppy Disks for Your System

When you format a disk, the operating system divides it into tracks and sectors, an invisible magnetic pattern something like a dart board. On a formatted disk, tracks run in circles around the disk. Because tracks can store a great deal of data, the computer needs to divide them into sectors, which makes it easier to find a location on the disk. These sectors are like pie-shaped wedges that divide each track into the same number of sectors.

On early computers, disks were single-sided. All disks used now are double-sided. To store more data, the tracks on the disk are placed closer together. The spacing of these tracks is measured as tracks per inch (TPI). The number of TPI determines the density of the disk and the amount of data that can be stored on it. A high-density disk has more tracks per inch than a low-density disk and can therefore store more data. The maximum density that can be used to store data on a disk is indicated on the disk label and box. For example, on 5¼-inch disks:

- Double-density disks can store data on 48 TPI or up to 360KB.
- High-density disks (also called high-capacity or quad-density disks) can store data on 96 TPI or up to 1.2MB.

The smaller 3½-inch floppy disks can store 720KB or 1.44MB. These disks can store more data than the larger 5¼-inch disks because they can store data on 135 TPI. You can tell the two types of disks apart as follows:

- A 720KB disk is labeled 1.0MB or 2HC and has a single square cutout.
- A 1.44MB disk is labeled 2.0MB or HD and has two square cutouts.

Because of these variations in the way computers assign tracks and sectors, the disks you use must be appropriate for your system. Some of the possible combinations are shown in the tables "Formatting and Reading 5¼-Inch Disks" and "Formatting and Reading 3½-Inch Disks."

FORMATTING AND READING 5¼-INCH DISKS

Procedure	360KB Drive	1.2MB Drive
Format a 360KB disk	Yes	Yes*
Format a 1.2MB disk	No	Yes
Read a 360KB disk	Yes	Yes
Read a 1.2MB disk	No	Yes

** With switches*

FORMATTING AND READING 3½-INCH DISKS

Procedure	720KB Drive	1.44MB Drive
Format a 720KB disk	Yes	Yes*
Format a 1.44MB disk	No	Yes
Read a 720KB disk	Yes	Yes
Read a 1.44MB disk	No	Yes

** With switches*

Volume Labels

It can be useful to give your disks a label (name) that will appear on the screen whenever you look at their directory or use the VOL command. When you format a disk, DOS 4 and later versions automatically prompt you to enter a volume label. On earlier versions, you can add a label by using the command **FORMAT B: /V**. You can also add or change a label after a disk has been formatted with the LABEL command (an external command).

→ KEY/Strokes

Labeling a Formatted Disk

1. Insert your disks as follows:
   - On a hard disk system, make drive C the default drive.
   - On a floppy disk system, insert the disk with the LABEL.COM or LABEL.EXE file into drive A and the disk to be labeled into drive B. Make drive A the default drive.
2. Enter a command as follows:
   - On a hard disk system, type **LABEL A:** and press Enter↵.
   - On a floppy disk system, type **LABEL B:** and press Enter↵.

   A prompt reads *Volume label (11 characters, ENTER for none)?*.
3. Type a new label, and press Enter↵.

EXERCISES

EXERCISE 1

FORMATTING ADDITIONAL DATA DISKS

Format any additional data disks that you might need for your own work.

EXERCISE 2

ADDING A VOLUME NAME

If you are using a version of DOS earlier than DOS 4, you were not prompted to enter a volume label when you formatted the *Resource Disk—Backup* in the tutorial. Use the LABEL command to label this disk with your last name (if necessary, abbreviate to 11 characters).

EXERCISE 3

CHECKING VOLUME NAMES

Use the VOL command to display the volume names for each of your floppy disks. If you find any disk with a name, write it down.

EXERCISE 4

SPECIFYING YOUR SYSTEM'S DISKS

List the specifications for the disks your system requires in the table "Disk Specifications." You will find this information in the manual that accompanies the computer. Look up "disks" or "disk drives" in the index, and refer to the listed sections. If you cannot find the information in the manual, refer to the specifications printed on the box that your disks came in.

DISK SPECIFICATIONS

Specification	Your System's Disks
Size	__________
Sides	__________
Density	__________
TPI	__________

TOPIC 10

Assigning and Listing Filenames

The file's name can have up to eight characters

The file's extension must begin with a period and can have up to three characters

Filenames
Filenames have two parts: the file's name and an optional three-character extension separated from the file's name with a period.

After completing this topic, you will be able to:

- Describe the number and types of the characters that you can use when naming files
- List the names of files on a disk
- Use switches to modify a basic command
- Describe the function of the question mark and asterisk wildcards
- Use wildcards to specify files in commands

The files for the application programs you use have already been assigned names. When you use these programs to create and save your own work, you must assign names to your files. With DOS, you can assign names to files that have up to eight characters and an optional extension of up to three characters separated from the name by a period.

Character	Example
Letters	A - Z
Letters	a - z
Numbers	0 - 9
Underscore	_
Caret	^
Dollar sign	$
Tilde	~
Exclamation point	!
Number sign	#
Percent sign	%
Ampersand	&
Hyphen	-
Braces	{ }
Parentheses	( )
At sign	@
Grave accent	`
Apostrophe	'

Legal Filename Characters
You can use any of the characters shown here in your files' names and extensions. You can type filenames in uppercase letters, lowercase letters, or a combination of uppercase and lowercase. If you enter lowercase letters, the computer automatically converts them to uppercase.

File Names

The characters that you can use in a filename are called *legal characters* and are shown in the figure "Legal Filename Characters." Using any other character results in a name the computer will not accept.

Each filename you use must be unique. If you assign a file the same name and extension as a file that is already on the disk, the new file will overwrite the previous file and erase it. However, you can use the same name with different extensions—for example, LETTER.DOC and LETTER.BAK. You can also use the same extension with different names.

Filename Extensions

Many application programs automatically enter extensions that identify files that they create. For example, Lotus 1-2-3 adds extensions such as .WK1 or .PIC to files it creates. dBASE adds extensions such as .DBF and .NDX. Conventions also dictate that some extensions are to be used only in specific situations. For instance, .EXE and .COM are normally used for program files, and .BAT is used for batch files. The extension .SYS is used for files containing information about your system's hardware. In many cases, if you don't use the extension the program automatically adds, the program will not be able to identify the file as its own. This can cause problems when you want to retrieve a file later.

Listing Files

Since a disk can hold many files, it is often necessary to find out what files are on a particular disk. The names of the files on a disk are held in a directory, which you display with the DIR command. When you use this command, you control which files are listed and how they are listed using wildcards and switches. A wildcard is simply a character that stands for one or more other characters, much like a wildcard in a card game. DOS wildcards are the question mark (?) and the asterisk (*). A switch is an add-on to a command that modifies the command's performance. For example, you can use a switch to list filenames across the screen instead of down it, or to sort the listing by name, extension, date, or size.

TUTORIAL

In this tutorial, you list filenames with the DIR command and explore both wildcards and switches. Study carefully how wildcards are used. Although you are introduced to wildcards in this tutorial on the DIR command, keep in mind that they can be used with many DOS commands and with many application programs.

GETTING STARTED

1. Load DOS so that the command prompt is displayed.
2. Insert your disks as follows:
   - On a hard disk system, insert the *Student Resource Disk* into drive A.
   - On a floppy disk system, insert the DOS disk into drive A and the *Student Resource Disk* into drive B.
3. Set your drives as follows:
   - On a hard disk system, make drive A the default drive.
   - On a floppy disk system, make drive B the default drive.
4. Type **CD\DOS** and press Enter↵ to move to the DOS directory.

DISPLAYING A LIST OF FILENAMES

5. Type **DIR** and press Enter↵ to list all the files in the DOS directory on the *Student Resource Disk*.
6. List the files on the disk in another drive as follows:
   - On a hard disk system, type **DIR C:** and press Enter↵.
   - On a floppy disk system, type **DIR A:** and press Enter↵.

   Note how the periods between the files' names and extensions have been replaced with spaces.

```
 Volume in drive A has no label
 Directory of A:\DOS

.            <DIR>        05-27-92   7:39p
..           <DIR>        05-27-92   7:39p
ERASE    TXT           27 01-08-92  10:23a
ASCII    TXT         1407 03-03-89  12:19p
BANKLOAN PRN         3318 03-03-89  10:26a
BANKLOAN WK1         1672 01-07-92   3:00p
CHPT1    WP5           66 01-06-92   3:07p
CHPT2    WP5           66 01-06-92   3:07p
CHPT3    WP5           66 01-06-92   3:07p
CHPT4    WP5           66 01-06-92   3:07p
CHPT5    WP5           66 01-06-92   3:07p
FILE     TXT           18 01-01-80   1:36a
FILE1    TXT           17 02-20-89   1:45a
FILE10   TXT           18 01-30-91   1:49a
FILE11   TXT           18 01-30-91   1:50a
FILE2    TXT           17 02-20-89   1:46a
FILE3    TXT           17 02-20-89   1:47a
FILE4    TXT           17 02-20-89   1:47a
FILE5    TXT           17 02-20-89   1:47a
FILE6    TXT           17 01-30-91   1:48a
FILE7    TXT           17 01-30-91   1:49a
FILE8    TXT           17 01-30-91   1:49a
FILE9    TXT           17 01-30-91   1:49a
GIVEUP1  HUH         1108 09-10-89   8:00a
GIVEUP2  HUH          973 09-10-89   8:01a
README   BAT           31 03-06-89  11:28a
README   TXT         1174 03-06-89  11:29a
JUMPSTRT BAT           17 01-03-92   8:59a
WHATSUP  DOC         2801 04-24-92   4:11p
       29 file(s)       13065 bytes
                      1229824 bytes free
```

A Directory Displayed from the Command Prompt
Besides listing a file's name and extension, the DIR command displays the volume name, the size of each file in bytes, the date and time the file was last saved, the number of files on the disk, and how much free space is left on the disk. (Your list will be slightly different than the one shown here).

USING THE /W SWITCH TO DISPLAY THE FILENAMES HORIZONTALLY

7. Type **DIR/W** and press Enter↵ to list the files on the default drive in five columns. The /W switch lists the files on the *Student Resource Disk* in five columns. To make room for the new columns of filenames, the size, date, and time have been dropped.
8. Display the files on the other drive in the same way:
   - On a hard disk system, type **DIR C:/W** and press Enter↵.
   - On a floppy disk system, type **DIR A:/W** and press Enter↵.

USING THE /P SWITCH TO PAUSE THE DISPLAY OF FILENAMES

9. Enter a command as follows:
   - On a hard disk system, type **DIR /P** and press Enter←.
   - On a floppy disk system, type **DIR /P** and press Enter←.

   The /P switch displays the filenames in the DOS directory on the *Student Resource Disk* until the screen is full and then pauses and displays a prompt asking you to press or strike a key to continue. Do so, and the list continues to scroll.

USING THE * WILDCARD

10. Type **DIR** and press Enter← to list all the files on the default drive. (The filenames followed by <*DIR*> are subdirectories, which you will learn about later in this text.)
11. Type **DIR *.*** and press Enter← to list all the files on the default drive again.
12. Type **DIR F*.*** and press Enter← to list all files that begin with the letter F.
13. Type **DIR C*.*** and press Enter← to list all files that begin with the letter C.
14. Type **DIR *.TXT** and press Enter← to list all files with the extension *.TXT*.
15. Type **DIR *.BAK** and press Enter← to list all files with the extension *.BAK*.
16. Type **DIR *.DOC** and press Enter← to list all files with the extension *.DOC*.

USING THE ? WILDCARD

17. Type **DIR** and press Enter← to list all the files on the default drive again.
18. Type **DIR FILE?.TXT** and press Enter← to list all files that begin with *FILE*, have up to one additional character, and have the extension *.TXT*. The files with the names FILE10.TXT and FILE11.TXT are not listed.
19. Type **DIR FILE??.TXT** and press Enter← to list all files that begin with *FILE*, have up to two additional characters, and have the extension *.TXT*. Now the files with the names FILE10.TXT and FILE11.TXT are listed.
20. Type **DIR CHPT?.???** and press Enter← to list all files that begin with *CHPT*, have up to one additional character, and have any extension.
21. Type **DIR C*.???** and press Enter← to list all files beginning with *C* and with any extension of three or fewer characters.
22. Type **DIR ?????.*** and press Enter← to list all filenames with five or fewer characters and any extension.
23. Type **DIR F??E?.*** and press Enter← to list all filenames with four or five characters that begin with F and have E as its fourth character and any extension.
24. Press F3 and then Enter← to repeat the previous command.

SORTING THE DIR LISTING

25. To list files in alphabetical order by name, enter a command as follows:
    - If you are using DOS 4 or earlier, type **DIR | SORT** and press Enter.
    - If you are using DOS 5 or later, type **DIR /ON** and press Enter.

    SORT is an external command, so if you use that command and a message tells you that it is a bad command or filename, the SORT.EXE file is not on the disk you are using. Ask your instructor which disk contains the file.
26. To list files in alphabetical order by extension, enter a command as follows:
    - If you are using DOS 4 or earlier, type **DIR SORT /+10** and press Enter.
    - If you are using DOS 5 or later, type **DIR /OE** and press Enter.
27. To list files in order by size, enter a command as follows:
    - If you are using DOS 4 or earlier, type **DIR SORT /+14** and press Enter.
    - If you are using DOS 5 or later, type **DIR /OS** and press Enter.
28. To list files in order by date, enter a command as follows:
    - If you are using DOS 4 or earlier, type **DIR SORT /+24** and press Enter, to sort by the month but not the year.
    - If you are using DOS 5 or later, type **DIR /OD** and press Enter, to sort by the month and the year.

FINISHING UP

29. You have now completed this tutorial. Either continue to the next activity or quit for the day.

QUICK REFERENCE

The names of files on a disk are stored in a directory that you can display with the DIR command. You can control which files are listed, and how they are listed, by adding wildcards and switches to the command.

The DIR Command

In its simplest form, the DIR command displays a listing of the directory of the disk in the default drive. For example, with the *A>* command prompt on the screen:

- To list the files in drive A, type **DIR** or **DIR A:** and press Enter.
- To see the files in drive B, type **DIR B**: and press Enter.

Besides listing filenames, the DIR command also displays the size of each file in bytes, the date and time the file was last saved, and the number of files in the current directory and the amount of free space left on the disk. DOS 5 and later versions also indicate the number of bytes occupied by the files in the current directory.

Using Switches with the DIR Command

If a list of files is too long to be displayed on the screen, some of the filenames will quickly scroll up and off the top of the screen. Two commands prevent this: DIR <*drive*> /W and DIR <*drive*> /P. The /W and /P following the commands are called switches and they modify the basic command.

With DOS 5, other switches can be used to arrange ("or sort") the list by name, extension, date, or size in ascending or descending order. All switches that can be used with the DIR command are listed and described in the table "DIR Command Switches."

DIR COMMAND SWITCHES

DOS 5 Switch	DOS 4 Switch	Description
/W	/W	The /W (for Wide) switch displays five columns of filenames instead of a single vertical list. This command drops the file size, date, and time information to make room for the additional columns of filenames. Because only the filenames are displayed and they are arranged horizontally on the screen, many filenames can be displayed on the screen at one time.
/P	/P	The /P (for Pause) switch displays filenames until the screen is full. The list then pauses, and a prompt reads *Press any key to continue.* To display more filenames, simply press any key.
/ON	ISORT	Lists file names in ascending alphabetical order.
/O-N	ISORT /R	Lists file names in descending alphabetical order.
/OE	ISORT /+10	Lists file extensions in ascending alphabetical order.
/O-E	ISORT /+10 /R	Lists file extensions in descending alphabetical order.
/OS	ISORT /+14	Lists files by size from smallest to largest.
/O-S	ISORT /+14 /R	Lists files by size from largest to smallest.
/OD	ISORT /+24	Lists files by dates from newest to oldest (DOS 4 and earlier versions sort only by month, not year.)
/O-D	ISORT /+24 /R	Lists files by dates from oldest to newest (DOS 4 and earlier versions sort only by month, not year.)

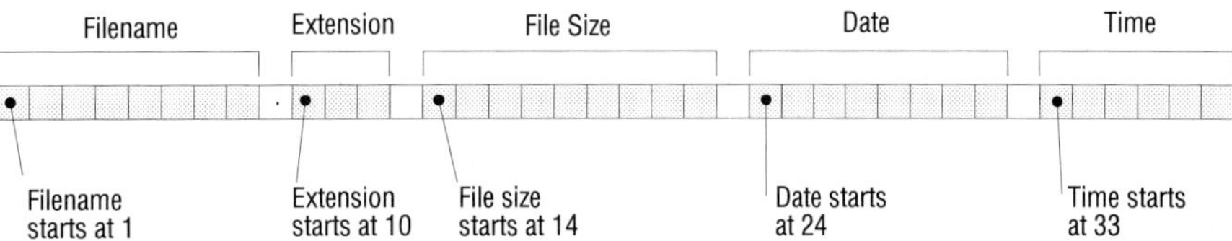

The Directory Arrangement
A directory is actually arranged into 38 columns. Each section begins in its own column, which you can specify to sort the directory by that section. For example, to sort on the extension, you specify /+10. To sort on the file's size, you specify /+14.

On DOS 4 and earlier versions, sorting directories is more complicated. First of all, you cannot use a sort switch with the DIR command directly. Instead, you have to use the pipe character [¦] (the split vertical bar above the [\]) with the SORT command and add a switch to that command as shown in the table. You then have to use a second switch to sort directories in reverse order. If you look at a directory listing carefully (see the figure "The Directory Arrangement"), you will see that each element, be it name, extension, size, or date, begins in a specific column. The numbers in the switches are the columns in which the first character of the element appears in the directory. For example, the file

Wildcards

The term *wildcard* comes from card games where a designated card, say a jack, can substitute for any other card in the deck. For example, in the card sequence 4-5-J-7-8, the jack stands for the 6 card.

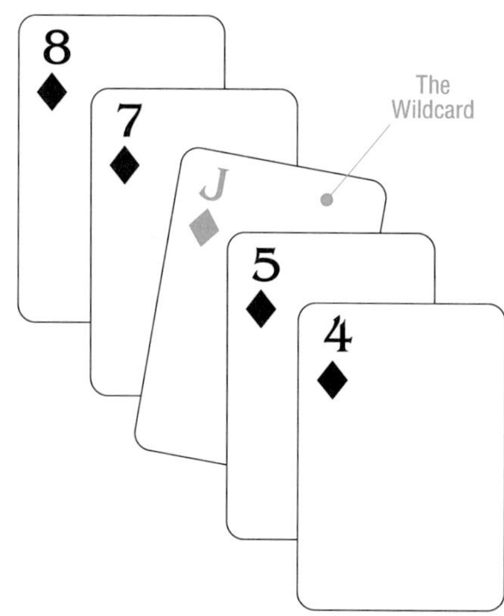

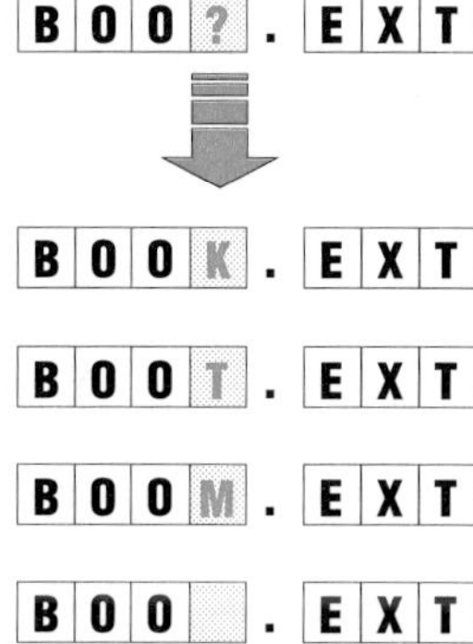

The Question Mark Wildcard

In this figure, the question mark will substitute for any character in the fourth and last position in the file's name. All other characters in filenames must be exactly as shown for a match to occur. This filename specification will therefore match files with names such as BOOK.EXT, BOOT.EXT, BOOM.EXT, and BOO.EXT.

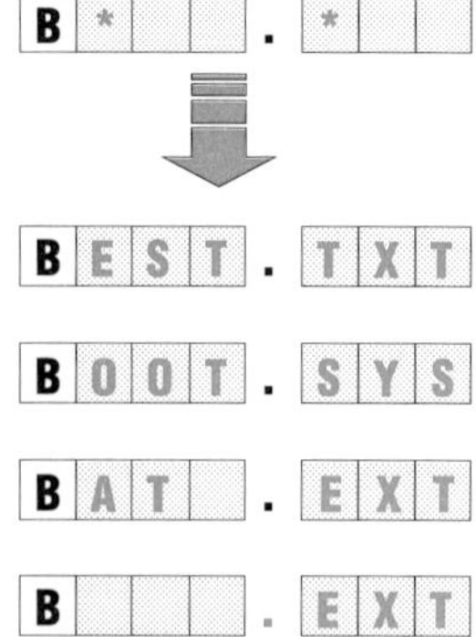

The Asterisk Wildcard

In this figure, the asterisk will substitute for all characters following the first character in the file's name and all characters in the extension. This filename specification will therefore match files beginning with the letter B that have up to eight characters in their name and any extension.

extensions are listed in the directory beginning in column 10, sizes in column 14, and dates in column 24.

Using Wildcards with the DIR Command

You use the ? and * wildcards to specify groups of files.

Using the ? Wildcard

The question mark substitutes for any single character. If you think of all filenames fitting into a grid with eight columns for the name and three columns for the extension, you can see how the question mark wildcard works.

- **????????.???** stands for the names of all files on the disk.
- **BOO?.EXT** stands for any name that has three or four characters and that begins with BOO followed by the extension .EXT.
- **BO??.EXT** stands for any name that has two to four characters and that begins with BO followed by the extension .EXT.
- **B???.???** stands for any name that has one to four characters and that begins with B followed by any extension of three or fewer characters.
- **????.E??** stands for any name that has four or fewer characters followed by any extension that begins with E.

Using the * Wildcard

The asterisk represents any character in a given position and all following characters in the part of the filename (either the name or extension) where it is used. For example, to display all filenames with the extension .DOC, type **DIR *.DOC**. Again, if you think of all filenames fitting into a grid with eight columns for the name and three columns for the extension, you can see how the asterisk wildcard works.

- ***.*** stands for any name and any extension.
- **B*.*** stands for any name that begins with B and has any extension.
- **B*.EXE** stands for any name that begins with B and has an .EXE extension.
- ***.E*** stands for any name that has an extension that begins with E.

EXERCISES

EXERCISE 1

PRINTING DIRECTORIES

1. Turn on your printer.
2. If your instructor approves, press Ctrl-PrtScr to turn on printing.
3. Insert the *Student Resource Disk* into a floppy drive and make that drive the default drive.
4. Type **CD\DOS** and press Enter↵ to change to the DOS directory.
5. Display filenames on your original *Student Resource Disk* so that names, extensions, sizes and dates are listed.
6. Display filenames on your original *Student Resource Disk* so that just the filenames are listed in five columns.
7. Turn off printing if you turned it on.

EXERCISE 2

USING WILDCARDS

1. Insert the *Student Resource Disk* into drive A and make that the default drive. Then type **CD\DOS** and press Enter↵ to change to the DOS directory.
2. Using the *.<*ext*> filename specifications, list in the table "Student Resource Disk Filename Extensions" the number of files there are with each extension. For example, to complete the first entry, type **DIR *.BAK** and press Enter↵. Then list in the table the number of filenames displayed.

STUDENT RESOURCE DISK FILENAME EXTENSIONS

Extension	Number
BAK	________
BAT	________
DOC	________
HUH	________
PRN	________
TXT	________
WK1	________
WP5	________

TOPIC 11

Copying Files

After completing this topic, you will be able to:

- Describe the difference between the source and target drives
- Copy files from one disk to another

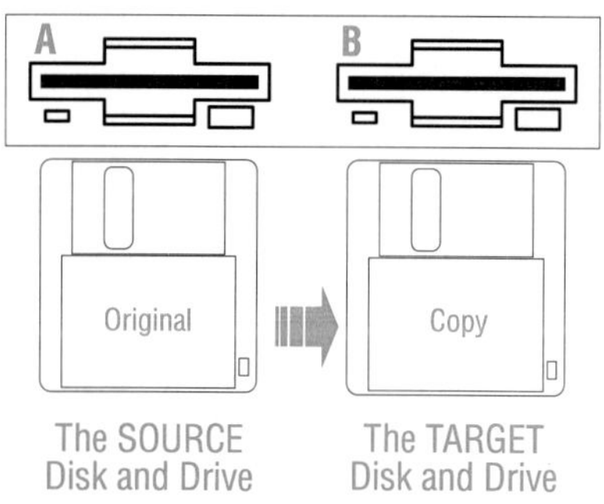

Source and Target Drives
The source drive is the one containing the files you want to copy. The target drive is the one you want them copied to.

To copy files from one disk to another, you use the COPY command. This command is often used to make backup copies of important files. When you use this command, you usually must specify three things:

1. The drive containing the disk the files are to be copied from—the source drive unless it is the default drive.
2. The name of the files to be copied.
3. The drive containing the disk the files are to be copied to—the target drive unless it is the default drive.

Keep in mind that the source is the drive containing the disk that you want the action performed on. The target is the drive containing the disk that you want to be affected by the source. For example, to copy a file from drive A to drive B, you use the command COPY A:FILENAME.EXT B:. The A: specifies the source drive that contains the file to be copied, and the B: specifies the target drive that you want the file copied to.

If your system has only one floppy disk drive, specify the source drive as drive A and the target drive as drive B. The operating system will then prompt you to swap disks whenever it needs access to the source or target disk and it is not in the drive.

TUTORIAL

In this tutorial, you copy the files from your original *Student Resource Disk* to the disk labeled *Resource Disk—Backup* that you formatted in Topic 9.

GETTING STARTED

1. Load DOS so that the command prompt is displayed.
2. Insert your disks as follows:
   - On a hard disk system, insert the *Student Resource Disk* into drive A.
   - On a floppy disk system, insert the *Student Resource Disk* into drive A and the disk you labeled *Resource Disk—Backup* into drive B.
3. Make drive A the default drive.

> **NOTE ABOUT SINGLE FLOPPY DISK SYSTEMS**
>
> If your system has a single floppy disk drive, it will act as both drive A and drive B during this tutorial. You will be periodically prompted to swap disks during the procedure.
>
> - When the prompt asks you to insert a disk into drive A, insert the original *Student Resource Disk*.
> - When the prompt asks you to insert a disk into drive B, insert the *Resource Disk—Backup*.
>
> After swapping disks, press any key to continue.

> **LOOKING AHEAD: XCOPY COMMAND**
>
> When you use the COPY A:*.* B: command on a single disk drive system, you have to swap disks for each and every file. To avoid this problem, use the command XCOPY A:*.* B: instead. This command is discussed in detail in Topic 16.

COPYING A SINGLE FILE

4. Type **COPY WHATSUP.DOC B:** and press [Enter↵]. A message reads *1 file(s) copied*, and the command prompt reappears.
5. Type **DIR B:** and press [Enter↵] to see that the file was copied.

COPYING FILES USING A WILDCARD

6. Type **COPY C*.WP5 B:** and press [Enter↵] to copy all files beginning with the letter *C* and ending with the extension .WP5. As each file is copied, its name is listed on the screen.
7. Type **DIR B:** and press [Enter↵] to see that only those files beginning with the letter *C* and ending with the extension .WP5 were copied to drive B.

COPYING A FILE WITH THE TARGET DIRECTORY AS THE DEFAULT

8. Make drive B the default drive.
9. Type **COPY A:FILE1.TXT** and press [Enter↵] to copy the file FILE1.TXT from drive A to drive B.
10. Type **DIR** and press [Enter↵] to see that the file was copied to the disk in drive B even though that drive wasn't specified in the command.

COPYING ALL FILES

11. On a hard disk system, be sure the original *Student Resource Disk* is in drive A. (If your system has one floppy drive, see the box "Looking Ahead: XCOPY Command.")
12. Type **COPY A:*.* B:** and press [Enter↵] to copy all the files on drive A to the disk in drive B. As each file is copied, its name is listed on the screen.
13. Type **DIR B:** and press [Enter↵] to see that all files were copied. You have a duplicate of the *Student Resource Disk* (except for the subdirectories you will learn about later).

FINISHING UP

14. Either continue to the next activity or quit for the day.

QUICK REFERENCE

The COPY command is an internal command that you can use to copy single files or groups of files. When using it, you must specify the source and target drives only if they are not the default drives. For example:

- If the default drive is set to A, and you want to copy a file named LETTER on drive A to drive B, you would type **COPY LETTER B:**. This command reads "copy the file named LETTER in the default drive to drive B." You do not need to specify drive A because that is the default drive.
- If the default drive is set to B, and you want to copy a file named LETTER on drive A to drive B, you would type **COPY A:LETTER**. The command reads "copy the file named LETTER in drive A to the

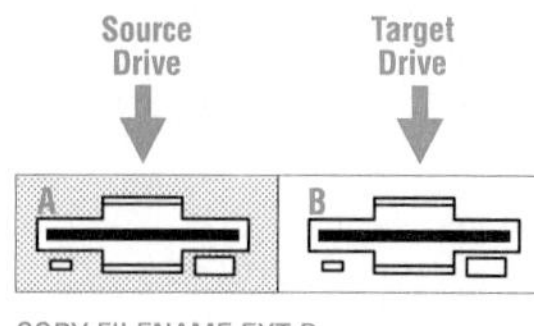

COPY FILENAME.EXT B:

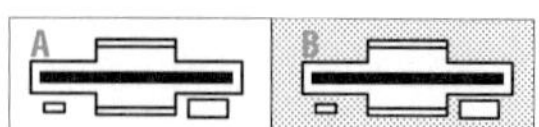

COPY A:FILENAME.EXT

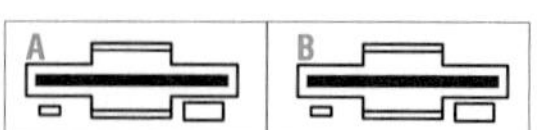

COPY A:FILENAME.EXT B:

Specifying Drives in Commands
Three possible copying situations are illustrated here. In the first, the source drive is the default (shown tinted), so you need to specify only the target drive in a command. In the second, the target drive is the default, so you need to specify only the source drive in a command. In the third, neither drive is the default, so you must specify both the source and target drives in a command.

default drive." You do not need to specify drive B because that is the default drive.

- Regardless of which drive is the default, you can specify both the source and target drives as a precaution. For example, to copy the file named LETTER from drive A to drive B regardless of which drive is the default drive, type **COPY A:LETTER B:**. This command reads "copy the file named LETTER in drive A to drive B."

If you copy a file to a disk or directory that already has a file by the same name, the copied file overwrites and replaces the original file.

KEY/Strokes

Copying Files

1. Insert your disks as follows:
   - On a hard disk system, insert the source disk into drive A. You will be prompted to swap disks periodically.
   - On a floppy disk system, insert the source disk into drive A and the target disk into drive B.
2. Either: Type **COPY A:*.* B:** and press Enter↵ to copy all files.
   Or: Type **COPY A:**<*filename.ext*> **B:** and press Enter↵ to copy a single file.

EXERCISE

EXERCISE 1

COPYING FILES

1. To copy all files with the extension .DOC from drive A to drive B, you would type ____________________.
2. To copy all files with the extension .TXT from drive B to drive A, you would type ____________________.
3. To copy all files beginning with the letter A and with the extension .DOC from drive A to drive B, you would type ____________________.
4. To copy all files beginning with the letters CHPT followed by any single digit number (for example, CHPT1, CHPT 2, and so on) from drive A to drive B, you would type ____________________.

TOPIC 12

Renaming Files

After completing this topic, you will be able to:

- Rename files one at a time
- Rename groups of files using wildcards

There are times when you want to change the name of a file on a disk. For example, you may rename them to make your filenames consistent or to free up a name so you can use it for another file.

TUTORIALS

In this tutorial, you rename some of the files on the disk labeled *Resource Disk—Backup*. To do so, you use both the RENAME command and the shorthand version REN, which has the same effect.

Renaming Files
When you rename a file, you don't affect its contents, just the name it goes by.

GETTING STARTED

1. Load DOS so that the command prompt is displayed.
2. Insert the disk labeled *Resource Disk—Backup* into drive A, and make that the default drive.

SELECTING FILES TO BE RENAMED

3. Type **DIR CHPT** *.* and press Enter↵ to display all files beginning with the letters CHPT.

RENAMING SINGLE FILES

4. Type **RENAME CHPT1.DOC CHPT6.WP5** and press Enter↵ to rename the file.
5. Type **DIR** *.**WP5** and press Enter↵ to see that the file is now listed under its new name, CHPT6.WP5, instead of its old name, CHPT1.DOC.

RENAMING GROUPS OF FILES USING WILDCARDS

6. Type **REN CHPT?.WP5 CHPT?.NEW** and press Enter↵ to rename all files that begin with CHPT, have one or fewer additional letters, and end with the extension .WP5.
7. Type **DIR CHPT?.*** and press Enter↵ to see that the files are listed under their original filenames but end with the extension .NEW instead of .WP5.

8. Type **REN CHPT?.NEW CHPT?.WP5** and press Enter↵ to change the names back to the way they were.
9. Type **DIR CHPT?.*** and press Enter↵ to see that the files are now listed under their original filenames.

FINISHING UP

10. Either continue to the next activity or quit for the day.

QUICK REFERENCE

To rename files, you use the RENAME or REN command and specify both the old name and the new name for the file. You can also specify a path for the original file if it is not on the default drive. For example, to rename a file on drive A named OLDNAME.EXT to NEWNAME.EXT, you would use the command RENAME A:OLDNAME.EXT NEWNAME.EXT.

You can also use wildcards to rename groups of files. For example, to rename all files named CHPT1.WP5 through CHPT9.WP5 so that their extension becomes .DOC, you use the command REN CPTH?.WP5 CHPT?.DOC.

→ KEY/Strokes

Renaming Files

1. Select the file that you want to rename, and make the drive that it's on the default drive.
2. Type **REN** *<oldname.ext>* *<newname.ext>* and press Enter↵.

You can also change the name of a file while copying it. For example, to copy and change the name of a file named OLDNAME.EXT, you type **COPY OLDNAME.EXT NEWNAME.EXT** and press Enter↵.

EXERCISES

EXERCISE 1

RENAMING A FILE

1. Insert the disk labeled *Resource Disk—Backup* into one of the disk drives, and make that drive the default drive.
2. Use the command **REN FILE?.TXT PART?.TXT** to rename all the files that begin with FILE, have four or five characters, and end with the extension .TXT.
3. Use the DIR *.TXT command to see the results. Why were the files named FILE10.TXT and FILE11.TXT not renamed? What command would you use to change the FILE part of their name to PART?

EXERCISE 2

COPYING AND RENAMING FILES

1. Copy the file WHATSUP.DOC from the original *Student Resource Disk* to the *Resource Disk—Backup*, and change its name to MYFILE.DOC.
2. Copy the CHPT files with the extension .WP5 from and to the *Resource Disk-Backup* disk, changing their extensions to TXT as you do so. (*Hint*: You can specify the source files as CHPT?.WP5 and the target files as CHPT?.TXT to copy them in one step since they all contain five characters and only the last one varies.)

TOPIC 13

Deleting Files

After completing this topic, you will be able to:

- Preview files that will be deleted
- Delete files from a disk
- Undelete files with DOS 5 and later versions

Monitoring the amount of free space on a disk is important because many application programs misbehave when you ask them to save files on a full disk. Some programs, for example, create temporary files on your disks, and they cannot do so if the disk is too full. Most people tend to keep files long after they are useful. It is good practice to occasionally use the DIR command to list the files on a disk and then delete any of them that you no longer need.

TUTORIAL

In this tutorial, you delete files from the disk labeled *Resource Disk—Backup* using the ERASE and DEL commands.

Deleting Files
When you delete a file, you permanently remove it from the disk and can no longer use it (although you can recover it in some situations).

GETTING STARTED

1. Load DOS so that the command prompt is displayed.
2. Insert the disk labeled *Resource Disk—Backup* into drive A, and make that the default drive.

PREVIEWING THE FILES TO BE DELETED

3. Type **DIR *.BAK** and press Enter↵ to display a list of files with the extension .BAK.

DELETING A SINGLE FILE

4. Type **ERASE CHPT1.BAK** and press Enter↵ to delete the file.
5. Type **DIR *.BAK** and press Enter↵ to see that the file CHPT1.BAK is no longer listed in the directory.

DELETING ALL FILES WITH THE SAME EXTENSION

6. Type **DIR *.BAK** and press Enter↵ to preview which files would be deleted using the *.BAK filename specification.
7. Type **DEL *.BAK** and press Enter↵ to delete all files with the .BAK extension.

8. Type **DIR *.BAK** and press Enter← to see that a message reads *File not found* since all files with the extension .BAK have been deleted.

FINISHING UP

9. Either continue to the next activity or quit for the day.

QUICK REFERENCE

To manage your files you have to use the ERASE or DEL command to delete unneeded files. If you are using DOS 5 or later versions, you can also often recover or undelete files should you delete them by mistake.

Deleting Files

To delete one or more files, you use the ERASE or DEL command. These two internal commands are interchangeable—they work exactly alike. For example, to delete a file on drive B named FILENAME.EXT, you type either **ERASE B:FILENAME.EXT** or **DEL B:FILENAME.EXT** and press Enter←.

You can use wildcards with the ERASE and DEL commands, but it is dangerous to do so. Even a slight miscalculation can cause the wrong files to be deleted. However, there are precautions you can take:

- One way to use wildcards safely is to preview what files will be affected by specifying the planned wildcards in the DIR command. If only the files you want to delete are listed, the same wildcards are safe to use with the ERASE or DEL command. For example, if you want to delete all files with the extension .BAK, type **DIR *.BAK**. If the displayed list of files can all be deleted, type **DEL *.BAK** (or type **DEL** and press F3).
- To be prompted for each file when using DOS 4 or later, use the /P switch. For example, to delete all files with the extension .BAK, type **DEL *.BAK/P**. Before each file is deleted, a prompt reads *Delete (Y/N)?*. Press Y to delete the file, or press N to leave the file on the disk.
- If you use the *.* wildcards, a prompt reads *Are you sure (Y/N)?*. Press Y to continue and delete all the files, or press N to cancel the command.

→ KEY/Strokes

Deleting Files from the Disk

1. Select the name of the file you want to delete, and make the drive that it's on the default drive.
2. Type **ERASE** <*filename*> or **DEL** <*filename*> and press Enter←.

Undeleting Files with DOS 5

The ERASE and DEL commands do not actually delete a file from the disk. They merely change the first letter of its name so that the name no longer appears when you display the disk's directory. This also makes the space the file occupies on the disk available for overwriting by another file. If you delete a file by mistake, do not save any files on the disk because utility programs are available that you can use to restore deleted files by putting the first letter back into their filename. One such utility program, the UNDELETE command, has been included with DOS 5 and later versions.

To undelete a file, type **UNDELETE** <*filename*> and press Enter ↵. For example, to undelete a file named LETTER91.WP5 on a disk in drive A, type **UNDELETE A:/LETTER91.WP5** and press Enter ↵. You can also use wildcards to undelete groups of files. For example, to undelete all files with the extension .WK1 of drive B, type **UNDELETE A:/*.WK1** and press Enter ↵. If you are not using the Mirror program to track deletions (see below), you are prompted to enter the first character in the file's name. You can also use the /ALL switch to undelete all files. If you use this switch and are not using the Mirror program to track deletions, the number sign (#) is used as the first character in each file's name. You can then use the REN command to rename the files.

To ensure that the UNDELETE command works, you should use the command MIRROR /T<*drive*> to store data about files that have been deleted. For example, to store data that can be used to undelete files on drive A, type **MIRROR /TA** and press Enter ↵. To mirror more than one drive, list each drive after the command. For example, to mirror drives A and C, type **MIRROR /TA /TC** and press Enter ↵. The first time you delete a file after loading this program, a file named PCTRACKR.DEL is created in the root directory of the drive. This file contains data that can be used to undelete files. As you delete additional files, information about them is added to the PCTRACKR.DEL file. With deletion tracking on, you can display a list of deleted files with the /LIST switch. For example, to list all deleted files on drive A, type **UNDELETE A: /LIST** and press Enter ↵.

The UNDELETE command may work without the Mirror program tracking deletions, but your risks of not being successful increase and you have to enter the first letter of each filename when prompted to do so. Moreover, for the highest degree of success, undelete the files immediately.

EXERCISES

EXERCISE 1

COPYING AND THEN DELETING FILES

1. Insert the disk labeled *Resource Disk—Backup* into one of the disk drives.
2. Copy and rename all CHPT?.WP5 files to CHPT?.BAK files.
3. Delete the CHPT?.BAK files.

EXERCISE 2

DELETING A FILE

1. Insert the disk labeled *Resource Disk—Backup* into one of the disk drives.
2. Delete the ERASE.TXT file if it is on the disk.

EXERCISE 3

UNDELETING FILES WITH DOS 5

1. Insert the disk labeled *Resource Disk—Backup* into one of the disk drives.
2. Use the /LIST switch to list all deleted files.
3. Undelete one of the files.

CHAPTER 3 REVIEW

- To use a new disk on your computer, you must first format it with the FORMAT command. This is an external command.
- To specify a drive other than the default, you must enter its address in the command. To display a directory of the files on the default drive, you type **DIR** and press Enter. To display them on drive B when that is not the default drive, you type **DIR B:** and press Enter.
- Filenames on DOS computers can have eight characters followed by an extension of up to three characters (separated from the filename by a period).
- To specify more than one filename in a command on DOS computers, you use wildcards. The question mark wildcard stands for any character in the position you enter it. The asterisk wildcard stands for any character in the position you enter it and all the characters that follow up to the end of either the filename or the extension.
- The command you use to list the files on a disk is DIR, which is an internal command. You can add switches to the DIR command. DIR/W displays filenames across the screen, and DIR/P displays a screenful of names and then stops.
- The command you use to copy files is COPY, an internal command. You can use wildcards to copy groups of files. For example, COPY A:*.* B: copies all files on the disk in drive A to the disk in drive B.
- The command you use to erase files is ERASE or DEL, both of which are internal commands.
- The command you use to rename a file is RENAME (or REN), which is an internal command.

CHAPTER 3 QUESTIONS

FILL IN THE BLANK

1. To prepare a disk for use on your system the first time, you usually must ____________ it.
2. The command you would use to format a disk on drive B is ____________.
3. DOS filenames can have up to ____________ characters and an optional ____________-character-long extension.
4. To list the files on a disk in drive B, you would use the command ____________.
5. To list the files on a disk in drive B so that the screen display pauses when it is full, you would use the command ____________.
6. To list the files on a disk in drive B in five columns, you would use the command ____________.

7. To list all files with the extension .DOC on a disk in drive A, you would use the command __________.
8. To list all files with the filename LETTER and any extension on a disk in drive A, you would use the command __________.
9. To sort a directory listing of drive B by filename extension, you would enter the command __________.
10. To copy a file named REPORT.WK1 from a disk in drive A to a disk in drive B when neither drive is the default, you would use the command __________.
11. To copy a file named REPORT.WK1 from a disk in drive A to a disk in drive B when drive A is the default, you would use the command __________.
12. To copy all files from a disk in drive B to a disk in drive A, you would use the command __________.
13. To change the name of a file on drive A from OLDFILE.TXT to NEWFILE.DOC, you would use the command __________.
14. To delete a file named OLD.TXT from a disk in drive A, you would use the command __________.

MATCH THE COLUMNS

1. FORMAT	__ A switch added to the DIR command to pause the screen when it is full
2. FORMAT/S	__ A wildcard that stands for a single character
3. DIR	__ Changes the name of a file
4. /P	__ Command used to copy files
5. /W	__ Displays a list of files on the disk
6. *	__ Formats a disk as a system disk
7. ?	__ Erases specified files
8. COPY	__ A switch added to the DIR command to display filenames in five columns
9. COPY *.*	__ A wildcard that stands for more than one character
10. RENAME	__ Command that copies all files
11. ERASE	__ Prepares a disk so that you can store data on it

WRITE OUT THE ANSWERS

1. What is the difference between a system disk and a data disk?
2. What are the two parts of a filename called? How many characters are allowed for each part? What are the parts separated with?
3. What switch do you use to display filenames horizontally across the screen? What switch do you use to display filenames one page at a time?
4. What are wildcards used for? What two wildcards are used with DOS? Describe what each does.

5. If you are using commands that erase or copy files, how can you preview the results the commands will have?
6. When the default drive is set to A, what command do you enter to copy a file named FILENAME.EXT from drive A to drive B?
7. When the default drive is set to A, what command do you enter to copy a file named FILENAME.EXT from drive B to drive A?
8. What command do you use to rename a file? Is this command internal or external?
9. Can you rename a file while copying it? If so, how?
10. What command do you use to delete files?
11. Why must you be careful when using wildcards to delete files?
12. When using wildcards to delete groups of files, how can you preview the names of the files to be deleted?
13. Can you retrieve a file that you inadvertently deleted? What should you do to salvage it?

CHAPTER 3

PROJECTS

PROJECT 1

SPECIFYING COMMANDS

Assume that drive C is the default drive and your system has two floppy disk drives, A and B. Write out the commands you would use to accomplish the following procedures:

1. Format a disk in drive A.
2. List the files on a disk in drive B so that the screen pauses when full.
3. Copy a file named LETTER.91 from drive A to B.
4. Erase all files on drive A that have the extension .BAK.

PROJECT 2

CREATING A DOS REFERENCE CARD

Complete the table "Summary of DOS Commands" by entering in the Command column the command you would use to perform each of the tasks. In the Type column, indicate if the command is an internal or external command.

SUMMARY OF DOS COMMANDS

Description	Command	Type
Formatting Disks		
Formats a data disk in drive A	________	____
Formats a data disk and adds a volume label	________	____
Adds a volume label to any disk	________	____
Formats a system disk in drive A	________	____
Displaying Lists of Files		
Lists the files on drive A	________	____
Lists all files on drive B with a .DOC extension	________	____
Wildcards		
Stands for any single character	________	____
Stands for any group of characters	________	____
Copying Files		
Copies individual files	________	____
Copies all files from drive A to B	________	____
Renaming and Erasing Files		
Renames files	________	____
Deletes files	________	____

CHAPTER 4

Directories & Paths

TOPIC 14

Using Directories

File Drawers
Directories are a way to organize electronic files on a disk, just as paper files are easier to work with when organized in filing cabinets.

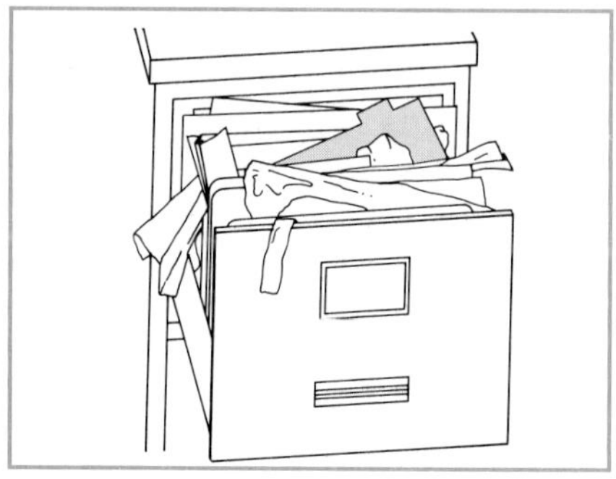

Unorganized file drawers make it difficult to find files when you need them.

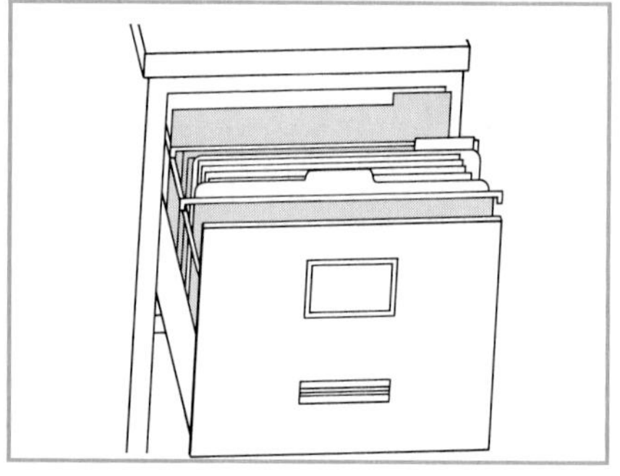

Organized file drawers make it easy to find the files you want.

After completing this topic, you will be able to:

- Explain how disks can be organized into directories and subdirectories
- Change directories
- Display lists of directories and files

Dividing a disk into directories helps you organize your files better. Imagine using a file drawer to store all of your memos, letters, and reports. Before long, the drawer would become so crowded and disorganized that you could not find anything. But with a little organization and planning, the documents could be organized into folders, making it easier to locate the one you needed.

A hard disk is like an empty drawer in a new filing cabinet: It provides a lot of storage space but no organization. To make it easier to find items in the drawer, you can divide it into categories with hanging folders. You can file documents directly into the hanging folders, or you can divide them into finer categories with manila folders. A directory is like a hanging folder, and a subdirectory is like a manila folder within a hanging folder. A file in a directory or subdirectory is like a letter, report, or other document within either a hanging folder or a manila folder.

Directories on a hard disk drive are organized in a hierarchy. The main directory, the one not below any other directory, is the root directory. Below it, directories can be created on one or more levels. These directories can hold files or subdirectories. The terms *directory* and *subdirectory* are used somewhat loosely. Strictly speaking, there is only one directory—the root directory—and all others are subdirectories. In most discussions, however, any directory above another is called a directory, and those below it are called its subdirectories.

TUTORIAL

In this tutorial, you explore changing directories on the original *Student Resource Disk*.

GETTING STARTED

1. Load DOS so that the command prompt is displayed.

2. Insert your disks as follows:
   - On a hard disk system, insert the *Student Resource Disk* into drive A.
   - On a floppy disk system, insert the disk with the DOS file TREE.COM into drive A and the *Student Resource Disk* into drive B.
3. Set your drives as follows:
   - On a hard disk system, make drive A the default drive.
   - On a floppy disk system, make drive B the default drive.
4. Type **PROMPT PG** and press Enter ← so that the prompt indicates the current drive and directory.

CHANGING THE CURRENT DIRECTORY

5. Type **DIR** and press Enter ← to list all the files on the disk.
6. Type **DIR *.** and press Enter ← to display just directories off the current directory. On this disk, there are four directories, each followed by *<DIR>*.
7. Type **CD\1-2-3** and press Enter ← to make the 1-2-3 directory the current directory, and the command prompt reads *A:\1-2-3* or *B:\1-2-3*.
8. Type **DIR** and press Enter ← to see that the 1-2-3 directory contains a subdirectory named *OLD <DIR>*. The two *<DIR>*s listed next to the periods indicate hidden files and can be ignored.

MOVING BETWEEN DIRECTORIES

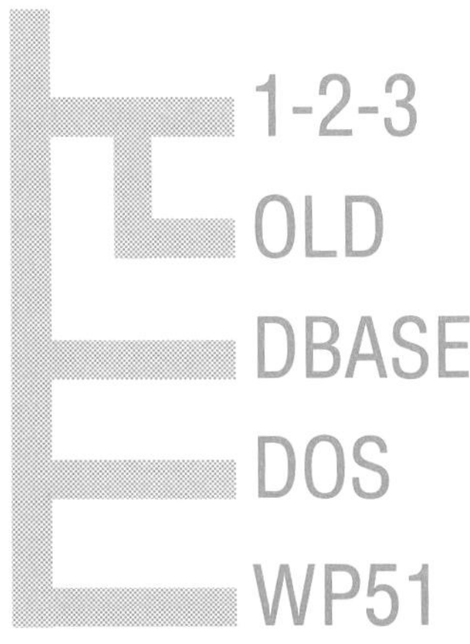

The Student Resource Disk Directories
The *Student Resource Disk* directories are organized as shown here.

9. Type **CD OLD** and press Enter ← to move down one level, and the prompt now reads *A:\1-2-3\OLD>* or *B:\1-2-3\OLD>*. This indicates that you are in a subdirectory named OLD below the directory named 1-2-3, which is below the root directory A:\ or B:\.
10. Type **CD..** and press Enter ← to move up one level, and the prompt now reads *A:\1-2-3>* or *B:\1-2-3>*.
11. Type **CD** and press Enter ← to return to the root directory, and the prompt now reads *A:\>* or *B:\>*.

DISPLAYING A LIST OF DIRECTORIES AND FILES

12. Enter a command as follows:
    - On a hard disk system, type **TREE A:** and press Enter ←.
    - On a floppy disk system, type **A:TREE B:** and press Enter ←.

    A list of the directories is displayed. DOS 4 and later versions show them graphically whereas DOS 3 and earlier versions just list them.
13. Enter a command as follows:
    - On a hard disk system, type **TREE A:/F** and press Enter ←.
    - On a floppy disk system, type **A:TREE B:/F** and press Enter ←.

    Both the directories and the files on the disk are displayed. Notice how when you execute this command, the files cannot all be displayed on the screen at the same time.
14. Press F3 and then Enter ← to repeat the command. Press Ctrl-S or Pause to pause the screen display at any point. Press any key to

resume scrolling. Practice these commands until you can pause the screen before all the files scroll past.

FINISHING UP

15. Either continue to the next activity or quit for the day.

QUICK REFERENCE

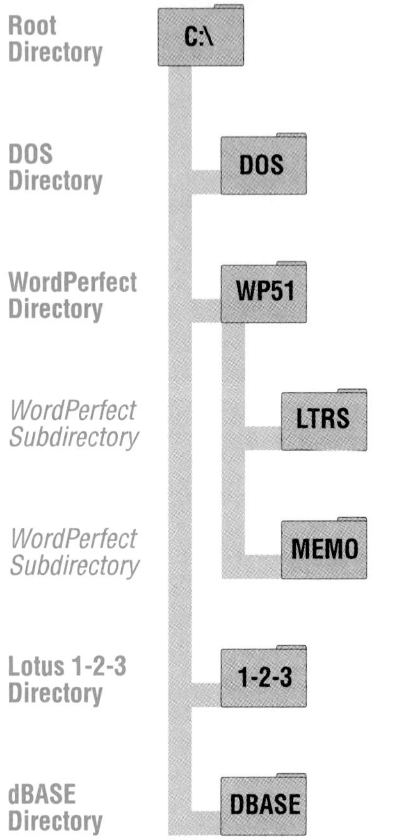

Root Directory — C:\

DOS Directory — DOS

WordPerfect Directory — WP51

WordPerfect Subdirectory — LTRS

WordPerfect Subdirectory — MEMO

Lotus 1-2-3 Directory — 1-2-3

dBASE Directory — DBASE

Directory Trees
Directories and subdirectories are organized into a treelike hierarchy. The topmost directory is called the root directory. Directories below the root directory are called directories. When directories are subdivided into additional directories, they are called subdirectories.

Any disk may be divided into directories and subdirectories. You will often find floppy disks with directories, and almost every hard disk has them. To work with these disks, you have to know how to move between directories and see how they are organized.

Changing Directories
To change directories on the current drive, you use the CHDIR or CD command. To change the default directory, type **CD**<*drive:\directory*> and press Enter←. If you are changing more than one level, list the directories in order, separated by a backslash. There are several versions of these commands. For example, in the figure "Moving Through Directories," the following commands would work:

- To make the subdirectory OLD the default directory, you would type **CD\LETTERS\OLD** and press Enter←.
- To move up one directory, for example, from OLD to LETTERS, you would type **CD..** and press Enter←.
- To move down to a subdirectory within the current directory, for example, from LETTERS to NEW, you would type **CD NEW**.
- To return to the root directory from any other directory, you would type **CD** and press Enter←.

To display the default directory on the current drive, type **CD** and press Enter←. To display the current default directory on another drive, type **CD** followed by the drive identifier, and press Enter←. For example, to display the current directory on drive C, type **CD C:** and press Enter←.

KEY/Strokes

Changing Directories

- To move to a directory, type **CD**<*directory*> and press Enter←.
- To return to the root directory, type **CD** and press Enter←.
- To move up one level, type **CD..** and press Enter←.
- To move down one level, type **CD** <*directory*> and press Enter←.
- To display the current directory, type **CD** and press Enter←.
- To display the default directory on drive C, type **CD C:** and press Enter←.

Displaying Files
To list your hard disk's organization, you use the TREE command (an external command). For a list of the directories and the files they

contain, you use the /F switch: TREE/F. This command, unlike the DIR command, lists files in all directories.

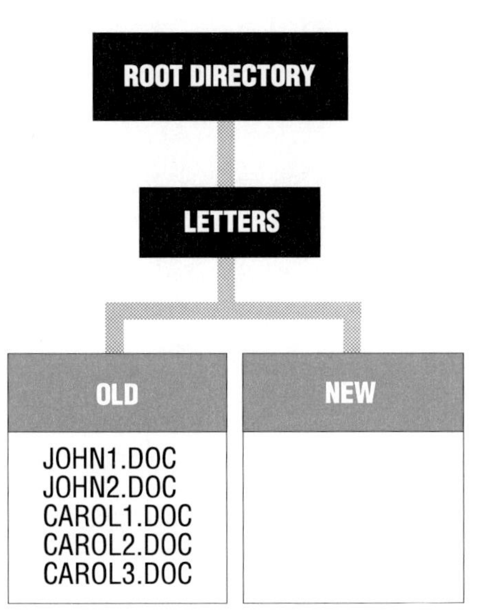

Moving Through Directories
This figure shows the root directory, a LETTERS directory, and two subdirectories, OLD and NEW.

KEY/Strokes

Listing Directories and Files

- To display a list of directories, type **TREE** and press Enter↵.
- To display a list of directories and the files they contain, type **TREE/F** and press Enter↵.

TIPS

- When you change the default directory on one drive, and then change default drives, the directory on the previous drive remains set as the default for that drive. When you switch back to that drive, you return to that directory. If you copy files to that drive without specifying otherwise, they are copied to the current default directory.
- Most directory and file management commands work only within the current directory. For example, if you used the ERASE *.* command in a subdirectory, it would erase files only in that subdirectory, not on the entire disk.

EXERCISE

EXERCISE 1

PRINTING A DIRECTORY TREE

1. Use the TREE command to display the tree for the original *Student Resource Disk.*
2. Use the TREE/F command to display the directories and files on the same disk.
3. Describe how the two commands differ.

TOPIC 15

Making and Removing Directories

After completing this topic, you will be able to:

- Make directories on your own disks
- Remove directories on your own disks

To organize your work on a hard disk drive, you create directories. When the directories are no longer needed, you remove them (after deleting all the files they contain). When creating directories, you should have a plan.

- Keep only essential files in the root directory.
- Store all program files related to a program in their own directory. For example, you might want a directory for DOS, 1-2-3, WordPerfect, and dBASE.
- Do not store the data files that you create in the same directory as the program files. Keep all related data files in their own directories. For example, you might have separate directories for letters, reports, financial documents, and name and address lists. You might also create separate directories for the files you create with different programs. For example, you might have separate directories for WordPerfect documents, 1-2-3 worksheets, or dBASE database files.
- Do not create too many levels since it takes time to move around them. Most disks can be well organized with no more than three levels, including the root directory.

TUTORIAL

In this tutorial, you create and remove subdirectories on the disk labeled *Resource Disk—Backup.*

GETTING STARTED

1. Load DOS so the command prompt is displayed.
2. Insert the disk labeled *Resource Disk—Backup* into drive A, and make that the default drive.
3. Type **PROMPT PG** and press Enter ↵ so that the prompt will indicate the drive and directory that you are in.

The Student Resource Disk—Backup Directories
This figure shows the organization of the directories and subdirectories that you create and remove in this tutorial.

CREATING DIRECTORIES

4. Type **MD\LETTERS** and press Enter← to create a directory named LETTERS.
5. Type **MD\MEMOS** and press Enter← to create a directory named MEMOS.
6. Type **MD\REPORTS** and press Enter← to create a directory named REPORTS.
7. Type **DIR *.** and press Enter← to see that the three new directories are listed.

CREATING SUBDIRECTORIES

8. Type **MD\LETTERS\NEW** and press Enter← to create a subdirectory named NEW below the directory named LETTERS.
9. Type **MD\LETTERS\OLD** and press Enter← to create a subdirectory named OLD below the directory named LETTERS.

MOVING DOWN THROUGH DIRECTORIES

10. Type **CD\LETTERS** and press Enter← to move down to the LETTERS directory, and the prompt reads *A:\LETTERS>*.
11. Type **DIR** and press Enter← to see that the directory contains the two new subdirectories, NEW and OLD.
12. Type **CD NEW** and press Enter← to move down to the NEW subdirectory, and the prompt reads *A:\LETTERS\NEW>*.

MOVING UP THROUGH DIRECTORIES

13. Type **CD..** and press Enter← to move up one level, and the prompt reads *A:\LETTERS>* to indicate that you have moved up to the LETTERS directory.
14. Type **CD** and press Enter← to return to the root directory, and the prompt now reads *A:\>*.

JUMPING BETWEEN DIRECTORIES

15. Type **CD\LETTERS\NEW** and press Enter← to move down to the NEW subdirectory in one step.
16. Type **CD\LETTERS\OLD** and press Enter← to move directly to the OLD subdirectory.
17. Type **CD..** and press Enter← to move up one level to the LETTERS directory.
18. Type **CD NEW** and press Enter← to move back down to the NEW subdirectory.

REMOVING DIRECTORIES

19. Type **CD** and press Enter← to move back up to the root directory in one step.
20. Type **RD\LETTERS** and press Enter← to remove the LETTERS directory, and a message indicates that you cannot do so because the current directory is not empty. (It still contains subdirectories.)
21. Type **RD\LETTERS\NEW** and press Enter← to remove the NEW subdirectory.

22. Type **RD\LETTERS\OLD** and press Enter ↵ to remove the OLD subdirectory.
23. Type **RD\LETTERS** and press Enter ↵ to remove the LETTERS directory.
24. Type **RD\MEMOS** and press Enter ↵ to remove the MEMOS directory.
25. Type **RD\REPORTS** and press Enter ↵ to remove the REPORTS directory.
26. Type **DIR *.** and press Enter ↵. The message reads *File not found* because there are no directories.

FINISHING UP

27. Either continue to the next activity or quit for the day.

QUICK REFERENCE

To organize your disk, you need to make and remove directories.

Making Directories

To make a directory, you use the internal command MKDIR <*directory name*> (or MD <*directory name*>). Directory names follow the same conventions that you use for filenames. However, you should not use a period and extension, or you might confuse directories with filenames at some later date. Files and subdirectories in one directory can have the same names as files and subdirectories in other directories.

The form of the command depends on whether you are working in the directory below which you want to make a directory or subdirectory. For example, if you wanted to create the directories shown in the figure "Making Directories," you would type:

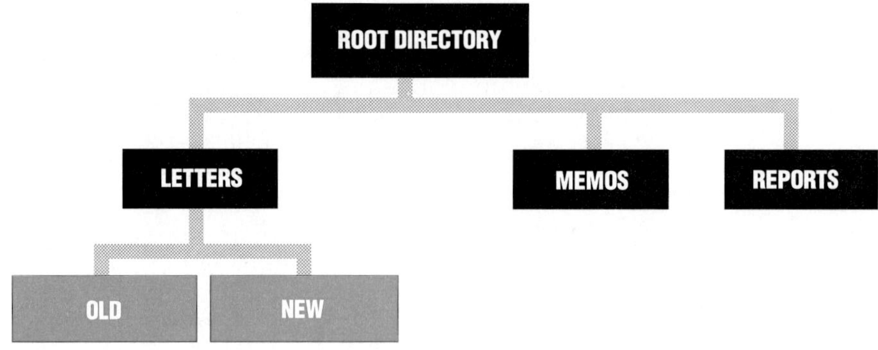

Making Directories
This tree shows the root directory, a LETTERS, MEMOS, and REPORTS directory, and two subdirectories of the LETTERS directory, NEW and OLD.

- **MD\LETTERS** and press Enter ↵
- **MD\MEMOS** and press Enter ↵
- **MD\REPORTS** and press Enter ↵

To make the two subdirectories off the LETTERS directory, you would type:

- **MD\LETTERS\NEW** and press Enter ↵
- **MD\LETTERS\OLD** and press Enter ↵

If you had first changed directories so that LETTERS was the default directory, you could make the two subdirectories by typing:

- **MD NEW** and pressing [Enter ←]
- **MD OLD** and pressing [Enter ←]

→ KEY/Strokes

Making Directories

- To create a directory below the root directory regardless of the directory you are in, type **MD** *<directory name>*.
- To create a directory below the root directory of another drive, type **MD** *<drive:\directory name>*. For example, to create a directory named 1-2-3 on drive C when drive B is the default drive, type **MD C:\1-2-3** and press [Enter ←].
- To create a subdirectory in the current directory, type **MD** *<directory name>*. For example, to create a subdirectory named BUDGETS below the 1-2-3 directory when 1-2-3 is the current default directory, type **MD BUDGETS** and press [Enter ←].

Removing Directories

To remove a directory, you use the internal command RMDIR *<directory name>* (or RD *<directory name>*). For example, to delete a directory named LETTERS, you would type **RD LETTERS** and press [Enter ←]. To delete a subdirectory named NEW below a directory named LETTERS, you would type **RD LETTERS\NEW** and press [Enter ←]. The directory you want to remove must not contain any files or subdirectories, and it cannot be the current default directory.

EXERCISE 1

CREATING AND DELETING DIRECTORIES

1. Insert the disk labeled *Resource Disk—Backup* into one of the disk drives, and make it the default drive.
2. Create a directory named 1992.
3. Create two subdirectories in the 1992 directory named SALES and BUDGETS.
4. Display a tree of the directories.
5. Delete all the new directories and subdirectories from the disk.
6. Display another tree of the directories.

TOPIC 16

Specifying Paths

After completing this topic, you will be able to:

- Explain what a path is
- Specify paths in your own commands
- Use the XCOPY command with paths to copy files in subdirectories

In previous topics, you frequently specified source and target drives when executing commands that copied, moved, or deleted files. When a disk is divided into directories, you not only must specify a drive, you also must specify a directory or directories in many commands. Specifying the drive and directories is called specifying a path.

Paths are simply a listing of the directories and subdirectories that specify exactly where a file can be found or where it is to be copied to. It is like telling someone that "the letter to ACME Hardware is in the manila folder labeled ACME in the hanging folder labeled Hardware in the third file cabinet from the right." These precise instructions make it easy to locate the file.

TUTORIAL

In this tutorial, you use paths to copy files on the *Resource Disk—Backup.*

GETTING STARTED

1. Load DOS so that the command prompt is displayed.
2. Insert the disk labeled *Resource Disk—Backup* into drive A, and make that the default drive.

CREATING DIRECTORIES

3. Type **MD\WP51** and press Enter↵.
4. Type **MD\TEXT** and press Enter↵.
5. Type **MD\TEXT\BATCH** and press Enter↵.
6. Type **DIR *.** and press Enter↵ to display the new directories but not the BATCH subdirectory.

COPYING FILES

7. Type **COPY A:CHPT?.WP5 A:\WP51** and press Enter↵ to copy the files into the WP51 directory.

8. Type **DIR A:\WP51** and press [Enter←] to see that the files were copied into the WP51 directory.
9. Type **COPY A:*.TXT A:\TEXT** and press [Enter←] to copy the files into the TEXT directory.
10. Type **DIR A:\TEXT** and press [Enter←] to see that the files were copied into the TEXT directory.
11. Type **COPY A:*.BAT A:\TEXT\BATCH** and press [Enter←] to copy the files into the BATCH subdirectory below the TEXT directory.
12. Type **DIR A:\TEXT\BATCH** and press [Enter←] to see that the files were copied into the BATCH subdirectory.

ERASING FILES IN THE WP51 DIRECTORY

13. Type **DIR A:\WP51*.*** and press [Enter←] to preview which files would be deleted with the path and filename specification.
14. Type **ERASE A:\WP51*.*** and press [Enter←]. In a few moments, the prompt reads *Are you sure (Y/N)?*.
15. Press [Y] and then [Enter←] to delete the files.
16. Type **DIR A:\WP51** and press [Enter←] to see that the directory is now empty. The two listings, *. <DIR>* and *.. <DIR>*, indicate hidden files.

ERASING FILES IN THE TEXT DIRECTORY

17. Type **DIR A:\TEXT*.*** and press [Enter←] to preview which files would be deleted with the path and filename specification.
18. Type **ERASE A:\TEXT*.*** and press [Enter←]. In a few moments, the prompt reads *Are you sure (Y/N)?*.
19. Press [Y] and then [Enter←] to delete the files.
20. Type **DIR A:\TEXT** and press [Enter←] to see that the directory is now empty except for the BATCH subdirectory.

ERASING FILES IN THE BATCH SUBDIRECTORY

21. Type **DIR A:\TEXT\BATCH*.*** and press [Enter←] to preview which files would be deleted with the path and filename specification.
22. Type **ERASE A:\TEXT\BATCH*.*** and press [Enter←]. In a few moments, the prompt reads *Are you sure (Y/N)?*.
23. Press [Y] and then [Enter←] to delete the files.
24. Type **DIR A:\TEXT\BATCH** and press [Enter←] to see that the directory is now empty. The two listings, *. <DIR>* and *.. <DIR>*, indicate hidden files.

FINISHING UP

25. Either continue to the next activity or quit for the day.

QUICK REFERENCE

To specify a path, you must indicate the drive, then the name of all subdirectories leading to the file, and then the filename. All elements

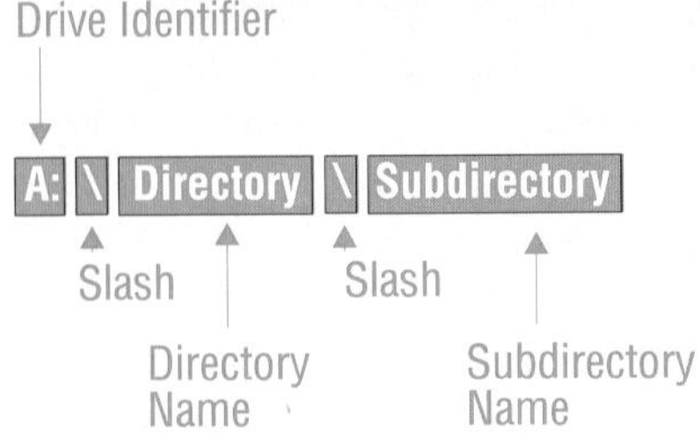

Specifying Paths
When specifying a path, you use a drive identifier and then list a directory and any subdirectories. Each item is separated from the next by a backslash.

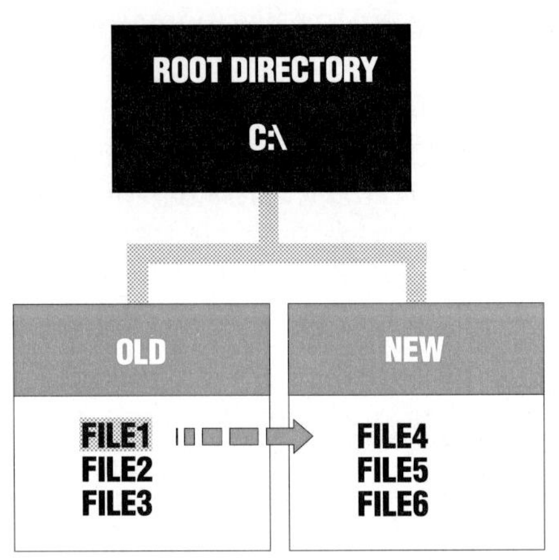

COPY C:\OLD\FILE1 C:\NEW

Paths
When copying files, displaying directories, or deleting files from the command prompt, you have to specify a path when the source or target directory is not the default.

must be separated from one another by backslashes (\), for example, C:\LETTER\NEW\FILE1.DOC.

When specifying paths, you have to consider both the source and target directories:

- If the source directory is the default, you have to specify only the source filename and the path to the target.
- If the target directory is the default, you have to specify only the path to the source and the source filename.
- If neither the target nor the source directory is the default, you have to specify the path for both.

For example, let's assume your disk has the directories and files shown in the figure "Paths."

- To copy files, you have to specify a path only when the source or target directory is not the default.
  - When OLD is the default, the path you specify to copy FILE1 to the NEW directory is only for the target. For example, type **COPY FILE1 C:\NEW**.
  - When NEW is the default, the path you specify to copy FILE1 to the NEW directory is only for the source. For example, type **COPY C:\OLD\FILE1**.
  - When the root directory is the default, the paths you specify to copy FILE1 to the NEW directory are for both the source and the target. For example, type **COPY C:\OLD\FILE1 C:\NEW**.
- To display a list of the filenames in a directory, the same principles work.
  - When the root directory is the default, you can display its directory by just typing **DIR** and pressing Enter←.
  - To display the files in the OLD directory, you type **DIR C:\OLD** and press Enter←.
  - To display the files in the NEW directory, you type **DIR C:\NEW** and press Enter←.
- To delete a file, the same principles also work. For example, when OLD is the default directory:
  - To delete FILE1, you type **DEL FILE1** and press Enter←.
  - To delete FILE4 in the NEW subdirectory, you type **DEL C:\NEW\FILE4** and press Enter←.

The XCOPY Command

Your can use the XCOPY command to copy files in subdirectories, files created after a certain date, or only files that weren't copied previously using the switches described in the table "XCOPY Switches." For example:

- To copy all files on a disk in drive C to a disk in drive A, type **XCOPY C:\ A:\/S**.
- To copy all files in the 1-2-3 directory on drive C, and all its subdirectories, to a disk in drive A, type **XCOPY C:\1-2-3 A:/S**.
- To copy just the files in the root directory on the disk in drive C to a disk in drive A, type **XCOPY C:\ A:**.
- To copy just the files in the 1-2-3 directory on drive C, without copying files in any of its subdirectories, type **XCOPY C:\1-2-3 A:**.

ARCHIVE BITS

When you create a file, DOS sets one of its bits—the archive bit—to 1 to indicate that it is a new file. If you then copy the file with the XCOPY command using the /M switch, DOS changes the archive bit to 0, to indicate that the file has been copied. If you later revise the file and save it again, DOS changes the archive bit back to 1, to show that it is a new file. This property of the /M switch means that you can use it repeatedly and have DOS XCOPY only those files that have not been changed since the last time you used it, ignoring all files that it has previously copied.

If you want to change the archive bit back from 0 to 1 manually, you can do it with the ATTRIB <*filename or wildcard*> +A command. For example, to reset the archive bit to 1 for every file in the current directory with the extension .DOC, type **ATTRIB *.DOC +A** and press Enter ↵.

- To copy all files on a disk in drive C, with a date later than December 31, 1992, to a disk in drive A, type **XCOPY C:\ A:\/S/ D:12-31-92**.
- To copy all files on a disk in drive C that have been changed since you last used the XCOPY command to a disk in drive A, type **XCOPY C:\ A:\/S/M**.

XCOPY SWITCHES

Switch	Description
/P	Prompts you before copying each file.
/D:mm-dd-yy	Copies only files created on or after the specified date.
/W	Waits for you to insert a disk and press any key before copying.
/S	Copies all files in the source directory and its subdirectories.
/E	Creates subdirectories on the target to match those on the source.
/V	Verifies that files are copied correctly.
/M	Copies only those files whose archive bit is 1; after the file has been copied, the archive bit for the source file is set to 0. (The archive bit is a marker that indicates if a file has been backed up or not.) When using this switch, the source disk cannot be write-protected.
/A	Same as /M but does not change the archive bit for the source file.

XCOPY with the /M switch is very useful for copying files when the target disk does not have enough room for all the files on the source. Say you want to copy all the files in the 123 directory of drive C to a disk in drive A but a disk in that drive won't hold all of them. Type **XCOPY C: \123 A: /M**. When the first disk is full, the message *Insufficient disk space* is displayed and the command prompt reappears. Put a new floppy into the drive and repeat the XCOPY command (press F3). XCOPY will copy another diskful of files, but it will not copy any files it has already copied, because the /M switch changed their archive bit to 0 after copying them. Continue to do this until all the files have been copied and the command prompt reappears without the *Insufficient disk space* message. If you want XCOPY to copy the files in subdirectories of the source directory too with this procedure, remember to use the /S switch along with the /M one. If you want it to create subdirectories to match those of the source disk even if those subdirectories are empty, use the /E switch too.

EXERCISE

EXERCISE 1

PRINTING DIRECTORIES

1. Insert the *Student Resource Disk* into drive A.
2. Change the default drive to A.
3. Without changing the default directory, use the DIR command to display a directory of all the files in the root directory and the subdirectories on the disk.

CHAPTER 4 REVIEW

- A disk can be divided into directories and subdirectories. The highest-level directory is called the root directory.
- To change directories, you use the CD or CHDIR command. For example, to change to a directory named LETTERS, you type **CD\LETTERS** and press Enter↵.
- To display a list of directories on a hard disk drive, you use the TREE command. To display a list of directories and the files they contain, you use the TREE/F command.
- The command you use to make new directories on a disk is MKDIR (or MD), which is an internal command.
- The command you use to remove a directory is RD or RMDIR, which is an internal command. You can remove a directory only if it is empty—that is, it can't contain files or subdirectories.
- To specify a path, you specify the drive and any directories between the root directory and the file. For example, to copy a file named FILENAME on drive C from the directory LETTERS to the directory MEMOS, type **COPY C:\LETTERS\FILENAME C:\MEMOS**.

CHAPTER 4 QUESTIONS

FILL IN THE BLANK

1. To move to a directory named LETTERS on drive C, you would enter the command ___________.
2. To move to a directory named OLD below a directory named LETTERS on drive C, you would enter the command ___________.
3. To move back to the root directory from any subdirectory, you would enter the command ___________.
4. To move up one level in the directory tree, you would enter the command ___________.
5. To create a directory named LETTERS on drive C, you would enter the command ___________.
6. To create a directory named OLD below a directory named LETTERS on drive C, you would enter the command ___________.
7. To remove a directory named LETTERS on drive C, you would enter the command ___________.
8. To remove a directory named OLD below a directory named LETTERS on drive C, you would enter the command ___________.
9. To copy a file named JOHN.DOC to a directory named LETTERS on drive C, you would enter the command ___________.

10. To copy a file named JOHN.DOC to a directory named OLD below a directory named LETTERS on drive C, you would enter the command ____________.

MATCH THE COLUMNS

1. CD\	__ Indicates a directory when you use the DIR/W command
2. CD ..	__ Displays a list of directories, subdirectories, and files
3. <DIR>	__ Returns you to the root directory
4. [1-2-3]	__ A path to a subdirectory on drive C
5. TREE	__ Makes a directory
6. TREE/F	__ Indicates a directory when you use the DIR command
7. MD	__ Moves you up one level in the directories
8. RD	__ Displays a list of directories and subdirectories
9. C:\TEXT\BATCH	__ Removes a directory

WRITE OUT THE ANSWERS

1. What is the topmost directory on a disk called?
2. What command do you use to change directories? What command do you use to move up one level? Are these internal or external commands?
3. What must you do before you can remove a directory from a hard disk?
4. What command do you use when you want to display the directories on a hard disk? When you want to display both the directories and the files?
5. What command do you use to make directories?
6. What command do you use to remove directories?
7. If you wanted to create a directory named FIRST below the root directory, what command would you use?
8. If you wanted to create a subdirectory named SECOND below the directory named FIRST, what command would you use?
9. If the SECOND directory was the current default directory, what two commands could you use to create a new subdirectory below it named THIRD?
10. To copy a file named JONES from the root directory of drive A to a directory named LETTERS on drive C, what command would you use?
11. To display a listing of the files in a subdirectory named SECOND below a directory named FIRST, what command would you use from the root directory?

CHAPTER 4 PROJECTS

PROJECT 1

PLANNING AND DRAWING A DIRECTORY TREE

Sketch out a directory tree for the following directories and subdirectories. Name each of the directories and subdirectories as you see fit.

1. The root directory is drive C.
2. Below the root directory are directories for DOS, Lotus 1-2-3, WordPerfect 5.1, dBASE III Plus, budgets, reports, memos, and letters.
3. Below the budgets, reports, memos, and letters directories are subdirectories for 1993, 1994, and 1995.

PROJECT 2

CREATING A DOS REFERENCE CARD

The table "Summary of DOS Commands" lists some of the most frequently used DOS command procedures. Complete the table by entering in the Command column the command you would use to perform each of the tasks. In the Type column, indicate if the command is an internal or external command.

SUMMARY OF DOS COMMANDS

Description	Command	Type
Making and Changing Directories		
Creates a new directory	____________	______
Changes the default directory	____________	______
Removes a directory	____________	______
Returns to the root directory	____________	______
Returns to one level up	____________	______
Displays a list of directories	____________	______
Displays a list of directories and files	____________	______

CHAPTER 5

Advanced DOS Procedures

TOPIC 17

Checking Disks and Files

After completing this topic, you will be able to:

- Explain why disks should be checked periodically
- Check disks and files on your own system

When you save a file on a new disk, it is stored neatly on adjacent sectors around adjacent tracks on the disk. But after the disk begins to fill up and you delete some files and add others, the disk drive has to work harder to store a file. It tends to store different parts of the file wherever it can find free sectors. After a while, a file may end up scattered all over the disk on noncontiguous blocks (parts of the file that do not adjoin each other on the disk). Files stored this way are called fragmented files.

When files are stored in widely separated sectors, some blocks may get lost and not be retrievable. Moreover, the drive's read/write head will have to move back and forth more frequently. This puts increased wear and tear on the drive because the drive's read/write head must keep moving over the disk's surface to reach parts of the files. It also slows down any save and retrieve operations.

To determine if files are fragmented, use the CHKDSK command. To correct the disk, copy all files onto another disk using the COPY *.* command. If the disk contains subdirectories, use the XCOPY command with the /S switch.

```
B:\PART1.DOC
Contains 3 non-contiguous blocks
B:\PART2.DOC
Contains 2 non-contiguous blocks
```

The CHKDSK Command

If you use the CHKDSK *.* command and get a message that your disk contains noncontiguous blocks, you need to unfragment your disk.

TUTORIAL

In this tutorial, you check the disk labeled *Resource Disk—Backup*.

GETTING STARTED

1. Load DOS so that the command prompt is displayed.
2. Insert your disks as follows:
   - On a hard disk system, insert the disk labeled *Resource Disk—Backup* into drive A.
   - On a floppy disk system, insert the disk that contains the CHKDSK.COM or CHKDSK.EXE file into drive A and the disk labeled *Resource Disk—Backup* into drive B.

3. Set your drives as follows:
   - On a hard disk system, make drive C the default drive.
   - On a floppy disk system, make drive A the default drive.

CHECKING A DISK

4. Enter a command as follows:
   - On a hard disk system, type **CHKDSK A:** and press Enter↵.
   - On a floppy disk system, type **CHKDSK B:** and press Enter↵.

   When you use this command, the screen indicates the following information about your system:
   - The total disk space, the space allocated to data files, and the remaining space available on the disk
   - The size and number of hidden files (if any)
   - The size and number of directories
   - The size and number of user files
   - If you are using DOS 4 or 5, the number of bytes in each allocation unit, the total number of allocation units, and the remaining allocation units available for new files
   - The total memory in the computer and the amount that is currently free (not occupied by programs or data)

CHECKING THE FILES ON A DISK

5. Enter a command as follows:
   - On a hard disk system, type **CHKDSK A:*.*** and press Enter↵.
   - On a floppy disk system, type **CHKDSK B:*.*** and press Enter↵.

   If all the files on the disk are contiguous, a message reads *All specified file(s) are contiguous*. If some are not, a series of messages tells you which files contain noncontiguous blocks.

FINISHING UP

6. Either continue to the next activity or quit for the day.

QUICK REFERENCE

To check a disk, you use the CHKDSK command (an external command). You can also use variations of the CHKDSK command to check individual files. For example:

- To check a single file, type **CHKDSK B:**<*filename*> (where <*filename*>is the name of the file).
- To list the names of files as they are being checked, use the /V switch. For example, to list the names of all files on drive B as they are being checked, type **CHKDSK B:/V**.
- To check the status of all files on a disk, type **CHKDSK B:*.*** and press Enter↵. This command gives you the same information as the other CHKDSK commands but also tells you if all files occupy contiguous, or adjacent, blocks (as they should) or lists the files

Contiguous and Noncontiguous Sectors
Disks with files located in contiguous sectors put less wear and tear on the drive and allow faster file saving and retrieving.

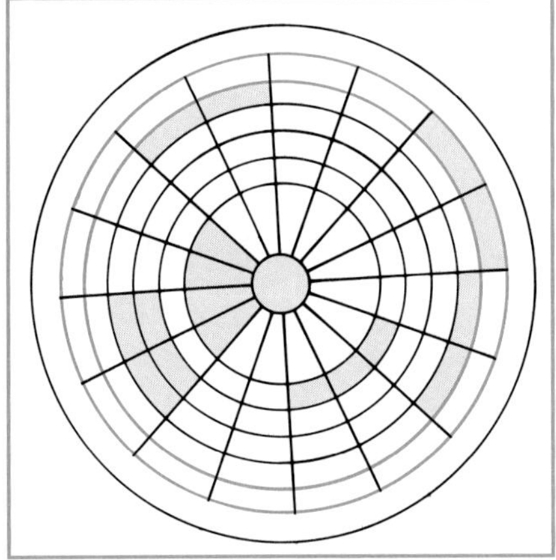

When a file is stored in noncontiguous sectors, parts of it are scattered about the disk. For the disk drive to retrieve such a file, it must move back and forth all over the disk.

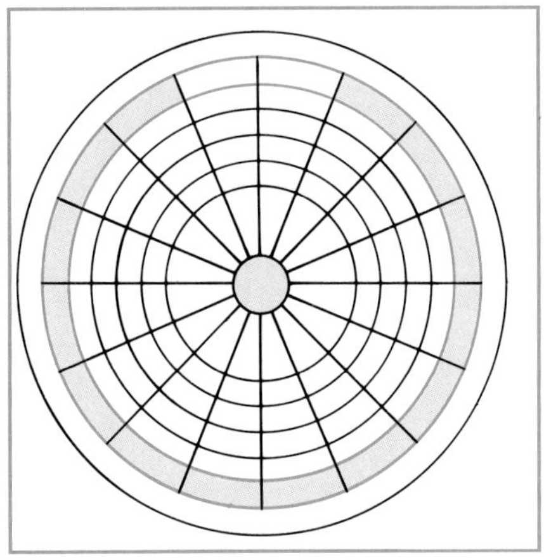

When a file is stored in contiguous sectors, it is stored on the disk in adjacent sectors. The disk drive can retrieve such a file in one smooth, continuous operation.

that contain noncontiguous, or scattered, blocks as shown in the figure "The CHKDSK Command."

If your disk contains noncontiguous blocks, you should copy the files to a new disk so that they are contiguous. To do so, copy all the files to a new formatted disk with the COPY *.* or XCOPY /S command. You can also use utility programs such as Norton Ulitities to move files together into contiguous sectors. This is the only practical way to do it on hard disks.

→ KEY/Strokes

Checking the Files on a Disk

1. On a floppy disk system, insert the DOS disk that contains the CHKDSK.COM or CHKDSK.EXE file into drive A, and make that the default drive.
2. Insert your disks as follows:
   - On a hard disk system, insert the disk you want to check into drive A.
   - On a floppy disk system, insert the disk you want to check into drive B.
3. Enter one of the following commands:
   - On a hard disk system, type:
     - **CHKDSK A:** and press Enter↵ to check the disk
     - **CHKDSK A*.*** and press Enter↵ to check files on the disk
     - **CHKDSK A:/V** and press Enter↵ to list files as they are checked
   - On a floppy disk system, type:
     - **CHKDSK B:** and press Enter↵ to check the disk
     - **CHKDSK B*.*** and press Enter↵ to check files on the disk
     - **CHKDSK B:/V** and press Enter↵ to list files as they are checked

TIPS

- If sectors of a file become scattered, the operating system may not be able to find sections called allocation units, or blocks. The CHKDSK command occasionally displays the following message:

```
Errors found, F parameter not specified
Corrections will not be written to disk

Convert lost chains to files (Y/N)?
 4096 bytes disk space would be freed
```

- If you see this message, press N and then Enter↵ to return to the command prompt. Type **CHKDSK /F** and press Enter↵. When the message reappears, press Y and then Enter↵ to store the lost allocation units in one or more files named

FILEnnnn.CHK (where nnnn is a sequential number) in the root directory. You can then retrieve these files to see if any contain useful data that you want to recover. You can retrieve these files with any application program that reads ASCII text files, or you can see their contents with the command TYPE FILE<*nnnn*>.CHK or TYPE FILE<*nnnn*>.CHK |MORE.

EXERCISE

EXERCISE 1

CHECKING DISKS

Check any of your disks with the CHKDSK, CHKDSK *.*, and CHKDSK/V commands.

TOPIC 18

Displaying and Printing ASCII Text Files

After completing this topic, you will be able to:

- Describe the different types of files that your system creates
- Display and print ASCII text files from DOS
- Stop a print job or remove files from the print queue

Files on the disk that are in ASCII text format can be displayed on the screen or printed from DOS. To understand ASCII text files, you have to understand something about the other files that you create with your application programs.

Binary files contain formatting codes specific to the application program that created them. For example, when you underline words, add page numbers, change margins or line spacing, or add headers and footers, you are actually entering codes into the document. These format codes are specific to the program you are using; there is no established standard. Thus these codes cannot be interpreted by other programs, which have their own codes. To use binary files with another program, the program-specific codes must be either removed or converted into codes the other program will understand. This is generally done by saving them with a command designed for this purpose or by using a separate program to convert them.

ASCII files are saved in a standard format understood by almost all programs. They can thus be used by other programs or easily transmitted by a modem over telephone lines. Since binary files can rarely be interpreted by other programs or telecommunicated by modem without first making special provisions, many programs let you save files for these purposes as ASCII text files. When files are saved in this way, all format codes specific to the program are removed. These files are identified with a variety of extensions, the most common being .TXT (for text).

Print files are like ASCII files, but all format codes are interpreted rather than removed. A print file is created just like a printout on the printer. The only difference is that the output is sent to a file on a disk instead of to the printer. For example, headers, footers, page numbers, top and bottom margins, and other formats that would appear on a printout also appear in the print file on the disk. Print files can also be printed directly from the operating system and, in some cases, can be used by other programs. For example, you can print a Lotus 1-2-3 file to the disk and then retrieve it into a WordPerfect document. Print files are usually identified with an extension such as .PRT or .PRN.

TUTORIAL

In this tutorial, you display ASCII text files on the *Student Resource Disk* and create an ASCII text file using the COPY CON command. You also print an ASCII text file named README.TXT from the command prompt. README files are frequently put on program disks to inform users of changes that have been made since the program's user manual was printed. Before you can use the PRINT command to send output to your printer, you need to know what port it is connected to. Typical ports are LPT1, LPT2, COM1, or COM2. Ask which yours is connected to and write it down so that you won't forget it. If it is not LPT1, substitute its name for PRN in the steps that follow.

GETTING STARTED

1. Load DOS so that the command prompt is displayed.
2. Insert the original *Student Resource Disk* into drive A.
3. Make drive A the default drive.

DISPLAYING ASCII TEXT FILES

4. Type **TYPE WHATSUP.DOC** and press [Enter←] to display the file on the screen.
5. Now repeat the same command. (You can press [F3] and then [Enter←] to do so.) Practice pressing [Ctrl]-[S] or [Pause] to pause the display. After pausing, press any key to continue. Repeat the procedure a few times until you are comfortable with it.
6. Type **TYPE ASCII.TXT** and press [Enter←] to scroll an illustration of the characters in the IBM PC character onto the screen.

PRINTING THE README.TXT FILE

7. On a floppy disk system, insert the DOS disk with the PRINT.COM or PRINT.EXE file into drive A. Insert the *Student Resource Disk* into drive B.
8. Enter a command as follows:
   - On a hard disk system, type **PRINT A:README.TXT** and press [Enter←].
   - On a floppy disk system, type **PRINT B:README.TXT** and press [Enter←].

   The first time you use the PRINT command in a session, the prompt may read *Name of list device [PRN]:*. If this happens, press [Enter←] to answer the prompt for the name of the list device or type the name of the port your printer is connected to, and then press [Enter←]. The message then reads *Resident part of PRINT installed. x:\README.TXT is currently being printed.* In a moment, the text file is printed on your printer, and then the command prompt reappears.

CREATING AN ASCII TEXT FILE

9. Type **COPY CON MYFILE.TXT** and press [Enter←].
10. Type **This is my first text file created from DOS** and press [Enter←].

11. Type **I press Enter to end lines of text** and press [Enter ↵].
12. Type **and press F6 when finished**.
13. Press [F6] to end the batch file, and a ^Z is displayed.
14. Press [Enter ↵] to save the file, and the message *1 File(s) copied* is displayed.
15. Type **TYPE MYFILE.TXT** and press [Enter ↵] to display the ASCII text file that you created.

FINISHING UP

16. Either continue to the next activity or quit for the day.

QUICK REFERENCE

To display and print ASCII files, you use the TYPE and PRINT commands.

Displaying ASCII Text Files

To display an ASCII text file from the command prompt, you use the internal TYPE command. To do so, type **TYPE** *<filename>* and press [Enter ↵]. Sometimes long files scroll by too fast to read. You can pause the screen while it is scrolling by pressing [Ctrl]-[S] or [Pause]. To resume scrolling, press any key.

Printing ASCII Text Files

To print an ASCII text file from the command prompt, you use the external PRINT command. To do so, type **PRINT** *<filename>* and press [Enter ↵]. The first time you use this command in a session, a prompt asks you for the name of the print device and suggests PRN. If your printer is attached to the LPT1 port, you just press [Enter ↵] to print the file. If your printer is attached to a different port, for example, LPT2, COM1, or COM2, you type the name of the port, and press [Enter ↵].

This command allows you to send one job after another to the printer. If one isn't finished printing before the next arrives, the new file is added to a print queue, which is just a list of jobs waiting to be processed. PRINT is also a background program. When you use this command to print files, you can continue working on other tasks while your files are being printed.

When printing files from the command prompt, you can use additional commands:

- To display a list of files in the print queue if there is more than one, type **PRINT** and press [Enter ↵].
- To stop printing a file, type **PRINT/T** (for "terminate") and press [Enter ↵]. This command removes all jobs from the print queue.
- To remove a single file from the print queue, type **PRINT** *<filename>* **/C** (for "cancel") (where *<filename>* is the name of the file to be removed from the queue). For example, to cancel a job named FILENAME.EXT, type **PRINT FILENAME.EXT/C**.

KEY/Strokes

Printing ASCII Text Files

1. Insert your disks as follows:
   - On a hard disk system, insert the disk with the ASCII text file into drive A.
   - On a floppy disk system, insert the DOS disk with the PRINT.COM or PRINT.EXE file into drive A and the disk with the ASCII text file into drive B.
2. Set your drives as follows:
   - On a hard disk system, make drive C the default drive.
   - On a floppy disk system, make drive A the default drive.
3. Enter the command as follows:
   - On a hard disk system, type **PRINT A:**<*filename.ext*> and press Enter.
   - On a floppy disk system, type **PRINT B:**<*filename.ext*> and press Enter.

   The prompt may read *Name of list device [PRN]:*. If this happens, press Enter to answer the prompt for the name of the list device or type the name of the port your printer is connected to, and then press Enter. The message then reads *Resident part of PRINT installed, B:filename.ext is currently being printed.*

EXERCISES

EXERCISE 1

DISPLAYING TEXT FILES

Use the TYPE command to display the following ASCII text files: ASCII.TXT, WHATSUP.DOC, and JUMPSTRT.BAT.

EXERCISE 2

DISPLAYING BINARY FILES

The file BANKLOAN.WK1 is a binary file saved with the Lotus 1-2-3 program. Use the TYPE command to display it from the command prompt. Describe what happens.

EXERCISE 3

PRINTING A 1-2-3 PRINT FILE

The BANKLOAN.PRN file on the original *Student Resource Disk* is a Lotus 1-2-3 print file. Use the PRINT command to make a printout of this file from the command prompt.

EXERCISE 4

PRINTING THE WHATSUP.DOC FILE

Use the PRINT command to make a printout of the WHATSUP.DOC file from the command prompt.

TOPIC 19

Using Redirection and Filters

After completing this topic, you will be able to:

- Send lists of files displayed with the DIR command to the printer and to a file on the disk
- Sort filenames on the disk
- Pause lists so that they don't scroll off the screen

DOS has several commands that allow you to manage your files better. The basic procedures involve using filters, pipes, and redirection commands. Filters sort files or directory listings or pause text that scrolls across the screen too quickly for you to read. Pipes send the output of one command to another command where it is used as input. Redirection commands redirect output from its normal device to another devicc. For example, you can send a directory listing to the printer or to a disk file, or you can copy a file to the printer instead of to another file on the disk.

TUTORIAL

In this tutorial, you send a directory of the filenames on a disk to the printer and then to a file on the disk. (If necessary substitute the name of your output device or port for PRN in the steps that follow.)

GETTING STARTED

1. Load DOS so that the command prompt is displayed.
2. Insert your disks as follows:
   - On a hard disk system, insert the *Resource Disk—Backup* into drive A.
   - On a floppy disk system, insert the *Resource Disk—Backup* into drive B.
3. Set your drives as follows:
   - On a hard disk system, make drive A the default drive.
   - On a floppy disk system, make drive B the default drive.
4. Be sure that the printer is on and has paper in it and that the paper is aligned.

PRINTING DIRECTORIES

5. Type **DIR >PRN** and press Enter← to send a directory listing to the printer. (You may have to press On Line, Form Feed (FF), and then On Line again to eject the paper from the printer.)
6. Type **DIR *.DOC>PRN** and press Enter← to send a listing of files with the extension .DOC to the printer.

STORING DIRECTORY LISTINGS IN A DISK FILE

7. Type **DIR *.TXT >FILELIST.TXT** and press Enter← to send a listing of files with the extension .TXT to a file named FILELIST.TXT on the disk.
8. Type **TYPE FILELIST.TXT** and press Enter← to display the contents of the FILELIST.TXT file.
9. Type **DIR *.DOC >>FILELIST.TXT** and press Enter← to append a list of additional files with the .DOC extension to the FILELIST.TXT file.
10. Type **TYPE FILELIST.TXT** and press Enter← to see that the new files have been appended to the end of the file.

REDIRECTING AN ASCII TEXT FILE TO THE PRINTER

11. Type **TYPE FILELIST.TXT >PRN** and press Enter← to print the file.

USING THE MORE FILTER

12. On a floppy disk system, insert the disk with the MORE.COM file into drive A and the *Resource Disk—Backup* into drive B.
13. Reset your drives as follows:
    - On a hard disk system, make drive C the default drive.
    - On a floppy disk system, make drive B the default drive
14. Enter a command as follows: (The | character is the split vertical bar (¦) on the backslash (\) key. You must press ⇧Shift to enter it.)
    - On a hard disk system, type **DIR A: | MORE** and press Enter←.
    - On a floppy disk system, type **DIR | A:MORE** and press Enter←.

    The directory is listed on the screen until the screen is full. The screen stops scrolling at that point, and the message -- *More* -- is displayed on the last line.
15. Press any key to continue scrolling the list.
16. Enter a command as follows:
    - On a hard disk system, type **MORE <A:WHATSUP.DOC** and press Enter←.
    - On a floppy disk system, type **A:MORE <WHATSUP.DOC** and press Enter←.

    The file is displayed on the screen until the screen is full. The screen stops scrolling at that point, and the message -- *More* -- is displayed on the last line.
17. Press any key to display another screenful of the file. When the command prompt reappears, the file has been displayed in its entirety.

SORTING AND PAUSING

18. Enter a command as follows to sort the directory of drive A in alphabetical order by filename and list the names so that they do not scroll off the screen:
    - On a hard disk system, type **DIR A: |SORT |MORE** and press Enter.
    - On a floppy disk system, type **DIR |A:SORT |A:MORE** and press Enter.
19. Press any key to see the rest of the filenames.
20. Enter a command as follows to sort the list of files by month but not by year:
    - On a hard disk system, type **DIR A: |SORT/+24 |MORE** and press Enter.
    - On a floppy disk system, type **DIR |A:SORT/+24 |A:MORE** and press Enter.
21. Press any key to see the rest of the filenames.

SORTING AND PRINTING A DIRECTORY

22. Enter a command as follows to print a directory sorted by file size:
    - On a hard disk system, type **DIR A: |SORT/+14 >PRN** and press Enter.
    - On a floppy disk system, type **DIR |A:SORT/+14 >PRN** and press Enter.

FINISHING UP

23. Either continue to the next activity or quit for the day.

QUICK REFERENCE

When working with ASCII text files, it is helpful to use commands that direct output of a command to the printer or a disk file, sort lists, and pause long file listings on the screen.

Redirecting Data

DOS commands accept input from devices like the keyboard, disks, programs, and mice. They then process the input and send it to output devices like the display or printer. The input devices and output devices that the commands use by default are called the standard devices. You can, however, specify other input and output devices. Doing so is called redirection since you direct the input or output from or to another device. For example, you can send text that is normally displayed on the screen to a printer or to a file on the disk. To redirect input and output, you use two characters, < and >.

- The > character redirects the output from a command. For example, DIR >FILELIST.TXT redirects the directory of a disk to a disk file named FILELIST.TXT and replaces that file's previous contents, if any. A special version of this command, >>, appends the output to the end of an existing file. For example, DIR >>FILELIST.TXT appends a directory of a disk to an existing file named FILELIST.TXT. If the file does not already exist, it is created. You can also use the > character with the COPY and TYPE commands to send ASCII text files to the printer. For example, to print a file named FILELIST.TXT, you could use either COPY FILELIST.TXT >PRN or TYPE FILELIST.TXT >PRN.

- The < character directs the input to a command. For example, MORE <DIR B: redirects the output from the DIR command to the MORE filter before it is sent to the screen.

One of the most frequent uses of redirection is to send directories of the files on your disk to a printer or disk file for future reference. Here are some typical examples:

- DIR >LPT1 or >PRN sends the directory to the printer attached to LPT1 (a port on the computer).
- DIR >FILELIST.TXT redirects the directory of a disk to a disk file named FILELIST.TXT.
- DIR >>FILELIST.TXT appends a directory of a disk to an existing file named FILELIST.TXT. If the file does not already exist, it is created.
- DIR B:*.DOC >>B:FILELIST appends a directory of all files with the extension .DOC on a disk in drive B to an existing file named FILELIST.TXT on drive B. If the file does not already exist, it is created.
- TREE >PRN sends the tree listing directories to the printer.
- TREE/F >PRN sends the tree listing directories and files to the printer.

Filters and Pipes

Filters are programs that take the output from one command, process it in some way, and then send it to the standard output device. DOS filters include the utility programs MORE and SORT, which respectively, pause output on the screen and sort files and directories. You can use redirection along with these filters.

When you use a filter, you have to send the output from one command as input to another command. To do so, you can use redirection, but using a pipe is easier. A pipe connects two programs so that the output from the first is sent to a temporary file on the disk. The information stored in this file is then used as input for the second program. To connect the two programs, you use a pipe character (¦). (This character is the split vertical bar found on the \ key. To enter it, you hold down Shift and press that key.) For example, to sort a directory listing, you use the command **DIR | SORT** or **DIR|SORT**. (Spaces are optional.) The DIR command sends the directory listing to a temporary file on the disk, which the SORT program then sorts. The sorted directory is then sent to the standard output device, in this case, the screen. You can also redirect the output from the SORT program to the printer with the command DIR | SORT >PRN.

Pausing a Scrolling Screen Display

When you are displaying information on the screen, it frequently scrolls by so quickly that you cannot read it. When this happens, you can use the MORE command (an external command). This command specifies that output from a command be displayed a screenful at a time. When the screen is full, the message *-- More --* is displayed. You then press any key to continue. You can also press Ctrl-Break to cancel the command. Here are some typical examples of how you use the MORE command:

- DIR | MORE displays the directory of the disk until the screen is full and then displays the message -- *More* --. You press any key to continue.
- MORE < FILENAME.EXT or TYPE FILENAME.EXT | MORE displays the specified file a screen at a time.
- TREE | MORE or TREE/F | MORE displays a directory tree a screen at a time.

The MORE command writes a temporary file on the default drive, so the disk in that drive cannot be write-protected or you will get an error message.

Sorting Files

SORT (an external command) can be used to sort the contents of a file into alphabetical or numerical order. You can sort by complete lines or specify a column that should be used to determine the order of the sort. Here are some typical examples:

- SORT <FILENAME.TXT sends the output of the file named FILENAME.TXT to the SORT command where it is processed and then displayed on your screen in sorted order.
- SORT <FILENAME.TXT>PRN sends the output of the file named FILENAME.TXT to the SORT command and then sends the results to the printer.
- SORT <FILE1.TXT>FILE2.TXT sorts the file named FILE1.TXT and then sends the output to a file named FILE2.TXT.
- SORT/R <FILE1.TXT>FILE2.TXT sorts a file named FILE1.TXT in reverse order and then sends the output to a file named FILE2.TXT.
- SORT/+10 <FILENAME.TXT sorts the specified file based on the contents of the line beginning with the tenth column, which is the extension.

EXERCISE

EXERCISE 1

USING THE MORE FILTER AND REDIRECTING OUTPUT

1. Use the MORE filter to pause a TREE/F display of the files and directories on the original *Student Resource Disk*.
2. Use the >PRN redirection command to send the output from the TREE/F command to the printer.

TOPIC 20

Creating Batch Files

After completing this topic, you will be able to:

- Explain the purpose of batch files
- Create and execute batch files
- Display the contents of a batch file

With batch files, you can tell the computer to do a series of tasks by entering a single command. Suppose you want to send the directories for a series of floppy disks to a disk file so that you can print it out as a permanent record. To do so, you would insert disks into drive A one at a time and then type **DIR A: >>A:DIRLIST.TXT**. You can store these keystrokes in a batch file, along with prompts to insert the disks. You can then execute the command by just typing the name of the batch file. If the name of the batch file is DIRLIST, you save at least ten keystrokes each time you use the command. Batch files can be very simple and great time savers. They can also be very complex, powerful programs.

TUTORIAL

In this tutorial, you first execute a batch file on the *Student Resource Disk* and then use the COPY CON command to create your own. The batch file that you create stores the directory of a disk in drive A into a disk file and then copies that file to the printer.

GETTING STARTED

1. Load DOS so that the command prompt is displayed.
2. Insert the disk labeled *Resource Disk—Backup* into drive A and make that the default drive.

EXECUTING A BATCH FILE

3. Type **README** and press Enter↵ to execute the batch file named README.BAT, which displays a box on the screen.

DISPLAYING THE CONTENTS OF A BATCH FILE

4. Type **TYPE README.BAT** and press Enter↵ to display the contents of the README.BAT file—the commands that are executed whenever you type the name of the batch file.
   - ECHO OFF prevents commands from being displayed on the screen as they are executed.

- CLS clears the screen.
- TYPE README.TXT displays the contents of the file named README.TXT.

CREATING A BATCH FILE

5. Type **COPY CON DIRLIST.BAT** and press Enter.
6. Enter the text and commands shown in the figure "The DIRLIST.BAT Batch File." Two versions are shown, a long and a short. Since each line of the file must be perfect before you press F6 to end it, you have to start over if you make a mistake. If you are having problems entering the long version, enter the shorter version. When entering either version:

The DIRLIST.BAT Batch File
You use the COPY CON command to enter the long or short version of this batch file in this tutorial. Both versions accomplish the same task, but the longer version displays more prompts.

```
CLS
ECHO Check that the printer is on!!
ECHO And that the disk in drive A is not write-protected!
PAUSE
CLS
ECHO These files are now being added to the DIRLIST.TXT file:
A:
DIR A:/W
DIR A: >A:\DIRLIST.TXT
COPY A:DIRLIST.TXT PRN
ERASE A:DIRLIST.TXT
ECHO All done!
ECHO You may have to advance the paper out of the printer.
```

Long Version

```
A:
DIR A:/W
DIR A: >A:\DIRLIST.TXT
COPY A:DIRLIST.TXT PRN
ERASE A:DIRLIST.TXT
```

Short Version

- Proofread each line carefully when you have finished typing it; once you have gone to the next line, you can't go back.
- Press Enter after entering each line but the last.
- After typing the last line, do not press Enter. Instead, press F6 or Ctrl-Z to end the batch file, and a ^Z then appears on the screen. Press Enter to save the file. The drive spins as the file is saved onto the disk, and then the command prompt reappears.

7. Type **TYPE DIRLIST.BAT** and press Enter to display the contents of the batch file.

EXECUTING A BATCH FILE

8. Type **DIRLIST** and press Enter to execute the batch file.
   - If you entered the short version, your directory listing will immediately print out.
   - If you entered the long version, the messages that you entered following the ECHO commands are displayed, and the prompt reads *Press any key to continue.* Follow the instructions displayed on the screen, and then press any key.

FINISHING UP

9. Either continue to the next activity or quit for the day.

QUICK REFERENCE

To create a batch file, you can use a word processing program that allows you to save files in ASCII text format, or you can use the DOS COPY CON command or DOS 5's EDIT command.

1. Load the operating system so that the command prompt is displayed on the screen. (If you are creating the batch file on a floppy disk, insert the program disk on which you want to create a batch file into drive A.) Make the drive on which you are creating the file the default drive.
2. Type **COPY CON** then the drive, then the name of the batch file (it must always have the extension .BAT), and then press Enter↵. The COPY CON command tells the computer to copy anything you type on the keyboard (console) to the specified file. The filename specification, for example, A:WP51.BAT, indicates the drive and file that the commands you type are copied to.
3. Type in the commands you want executed, just as you would normally enter them from the keyboard. End each command but the last by pressing Enter↵.
4. When you have finished entering commands, press F6 (or Ctrl-Z). This displays a ^Z on the screen.
5. Press Enter↵ to save the file, and the drive spins. In a moment, the command prompt reappears. You can now execute the batch file by typing its name (without the extension) and pressing Enter↵.

TIPS

- You cannot use a DOS program's name for a batch file because the operating system executes programs before it executes batch files with the same name. You can use the name of a program only if you put the batch file and program in separate directories or on separate disks. Even if you put them in separate directories, however, you may have problems depending on your system's PATH command.
- To display or print the contents of a batch file, use the TYPE or PRINT command.

Batch files can contain text or commands. In the simplest form, the commands are just a list of program names or DOS commands. For example, you can create a batch file named WP51.BAT that automatically changes to the directory that contains WordPerfect and then executes the program. However, you can also use special commands to make your batch files more powerful. The table "Basic Batch File Commands" describes some typical commands.

BASIC BATCH FILE COMMANDS

Command	Description
ECHO ON	Allows commands being executed to be displayed on the screen.
ECHO OFF	Prevents commands being executed from being displayed on the screen.
ECHO <*message*>	Displays a message on the screen.
PAUSE	Pauses a batch file and displays the prompt *Strike a key when ready.* (When you press any key, the batch file continues.)
REM <*text*>	(For "remark") Typed at the beginning of a line that is not to be executed—used, for example, to remind yourself what the file does.

EXERCISE

EXERCISE 1

CREATING A BATCH FILE

```
DIR *.* >LIST.TXT
TYPE LIST.TXT
```

The LIST.BAT Batch File
You enter the batch file shown in this figure in this exercise.

1. Create on the *Resource Disk—Backup* the file shown in the figure "The LIST.BAT Batch File." Name it LIST.BAT.
2. Execute the batch file, and describe what each command does.

TOPIC 21

Special DOS Files

After completing this topic, you will be able to:

- Describe the functions of the CONFIG.SYS file
- Describe the functions of the AUTOEXEC.BAT file

When you boot the computer, it always takes a few moments for the command prompt, Shell, or a custom menu to appear on the screen. During this pause, the computer is very busy.

1. The computer first executes a small diagnostic program that is permanently stored in its read-only memory (ROM). This program checks the computer's memory to make certain it is operating correctly. If the computer finds a problem, it displays a message on the screen indicating where the problem is located and then stops.
2. If the diagnostic program finds no problems, the program in ROM executes two hidden operating system programs on the disk in the startup drive (named IBMBIO.COM and IBMDOS.COM on IBM versions of DOS). If the disk does not have the two system files (which are put on the disk when it is formatted), the computer displays an error message and stops.
3. Once the two operating system programs are executed, the computer looks for a program called COMMAND.COM, which contains the most frequently used internal operating system commands. Executing this program loads a copy of it into RAM, where it remains as long as the computer has power.
4. The computer then looks for a configuration file named CONFIG.SYS. This file contains commands that customize the system.
5. The computer next looks on the disk for a batch file named AUTOEXEC.BAT. If this file is present, the computer executes whatever commands are listed there. (On some older systems, you are then asked to enter the date and time.) The process is now complete. The screen display depends on the operating system you are using and the contents of the AUTOEXEC.BAT file.

TUTORIAL

In this tutorial, you display and print your system's CONFIG.SYS and AUTOEXEC.BAT files if it has them.

GETTING STARTED

1. Load DOS so that the command prompt is displayed.
2. On a floppy disk system, insert your startup disk into drive A.
3. Set your drives as follows:
   - On a hard disk system, make drive C the default drive.
   - On a floppy disk system, make drive A the default drive.
4. Be sure that your printer is on.

DISPLAYING AND PRINTING YOUR SYSTEM'S CONFIG.SYS FILE

5. Type **TYPE CONFIG.SYS** and press Enter↵.
   - If your startup disk contains a CONFIG.SYS file, it is displayed on the screen.
   - If the message reads *File not found*, your system doesn't have the file. Proceed to Step 7.
6. If your system has a CONFIG.SYS file, type **COPY CONFIG.SYS PRN** and press Enter↵ to print it out.

DISPLAYING AND PRINTING YOUR SYSTEM'S AUTOEXEC.BAT FILE

7. Type **TYPE AUTOEXEC.BAT** and press Enter↵.
   - If your startup disk contains an AUTOEXEC.BAT file, it is displayed on the screen.
   - If the mcssage reads *File not found*, your system doesn't have the file. Proceed to Step 9.
8. If your system has an AUTOEXEC.BAT file, type **COPY AUTOEXEC.BAT PRN** and press Enter↵ to print it out.

FINISHING UP

9. Either continue to the next activity or quit for the day.

QUICK REFERENCE

When you first turn on your computer, it looks on the system disk in the startup drive for files named CONFIG.SYS and AUTOEXEC.BAT and executes the commands that are contained in those files.

CONFIG.SYS Files

CONFIG.SYS is called a configuration file because it stores commands that "configure" or set up your system. By changing the commands stored in this file, you can change the way your system operates. For example, many application programs work better and faster when there are BUFFERS and FILES statements in the CONFIG.SYS file. The table "Typical CONFIG.SYS Commands" describes these and other commands frequently used in CONFIG.SYS files.

A Typical CONFIG.SYS File
A typical CONFIG.SYS file might contain some or all of commands shown here.

```
DEVICE=C:\DOS\EGA.SYS
DEVICE=C:\QEMM\QEMM386.SYS RAM
DEVICE=C:\QEMM\LOADHI.SYS /R:2 /RES=13776 /SQF RCD.SYS /F /P
DOS=HIGH
DEVICEHIGH=DASDDRVR.SYS
BREAK=ON
BUFFERS=20
SHELL=C:\DOS\COMMAND.COM C:\DOS\ /E:256 /p
DEVICE=C:\WINDOWS\MOUSE.SYS /Y
DEVICE=C:\WINDOWS\SMARTDRV.EXE /DOUBLE_BUFFER
LASTDRIVE=Z
```

TYPICAL CONFIG.SYS COMMANDS

Command	Description
BUFFERS=<#>	Sets the number of disk buffers used by the system.
FILES=<#>	Sets the number of files that can be opened at one time.
LASTDRIVE=<*drive*>	Sets the maximum number of drives that can be addressed; for example, LASTDRIVE=B means you can address only drives A and B.
COUNTRY=<*country*>	Sets the country for keyboards and other country-dependent information, such as date formats.
DEVICE=<*name*>	Loads the specified device driver so that the device works with your system. For example, if you are using a mouse, your file may have a line such as *DEVICE=MOUSE.SYS /Y.*

AUTOEXEC Files

You use the AUTOEXEC.BAT file to store all commands that you want executed every time you turn on the computer. A typical AUTOEXEC.BAT file on a hard disk system might contain some or all of the commands shown in the figure "A Typical AUTOEXEC.BAT File." You could enter these commands from the keyboard each time you turn on the computer, but that would require 75 keystrokes. You can replace these keystrokes with a single AUTOEXEC file that automatically executes these commands when you turn on the computer. The AUTOEXEC.BAT file shown in the figure contains these commands:

A Typical AUTOEXEC.BAT File
A typical AUTOEXEC.BAT file might contain some or all of the commands shown here.

```
ECHO OFF
PATH C:\;C:\DOS;C:\123;C:\WP51;C:\DBASE
PROMPT $P$G
CLS
DIR *.BAT
```

- The *ECHO OFF* command prevents commands being executed from being displayed on the screen.
- The *PATH* command tells the computer which directories and subdirectories to look into (and in what order to do the looking) to find a command you execute that is not in the current default directory. It lays out a list of directories for the computer to search for a program, and the order in which to search them, so you don't have to change to the directory that contains a program to run it. Note how the specified directories are separated from one another by semicolons. (You can enter a PATH command from the command prompt by typing **PATH** followed by the directories you want searched. For example, to list directories named DOS, WP51, 123, and dBASE, you would type **PATH C:\;C:\DOS;C:\WP51;C:\123;C:\DBASE** and press Enter←.
- The *PROMPT PG* command sets the prompt so that it displays the current directory followed by a greater-than sign.
- The *CLS* command clears the screen.
- The *DIR *.BAT* command displays a list of all batch files in the root directory. This is useful if you have a number of batch files that automatically load your programs and you would like to be reminded of their names.

Creating or Editing AUTOEXEC.BAT and CONFIG.SYS Files

If your system does not have an AUTOEXEC.BAT or CONFIG.SYS file, you can easily create them with the EDLIN program or DOS 5's EDIT program (see your DOS manual) or with any word processing program that allows you to save and retrieve ASCII text files. You can also create them from the command prompt using the COPY CON command. This command has very limited editing procedures, so you can correct errors only on the current line. If you notice a mistake on a previous line, you have to press F6 and then Enter← to close the file. Then, you can reenter the file correctly.

Since these two files are important, you should not edit them unless you are sure of what you are doing. Before editing or revising either, you should make a backup copy of the original version so that you can recover it if something goes wrong. A good way to back it up is to copy it and change its name to AUTOEXEC.OLD or CONFIG.OLD. Before doing so, use the command DIR AUTOEXEC.* or CONFIG.* to see what versions already exist. When you install many application programs, they revise these files and rename the old file with a new extension. If anything goes wrong with the new version, you can just rename the backup file so that it has its original name.

KEY/Strokes

Creating an AUTOEXEC.BAT or CONFIG.SYS File

1. Load the operating system so that the command prompt is displayed on the screen.
2. If you are creating the batch file on a floppy disk, insert the application program disk you want to create a batch file on into drive A.
3. Make the drive on which you are creating the file the default drive.
4. Type **COPY CON AUTOEXEC.BAT** or **COPY CON CONFIG.SYS** and press Enter←.
5. Type in the commands you want executed just as you would normally enter them from the keyboard. Press Enter← after entering each command except the last.
6. When you are finished entering commands, press F6 and a ^Z is displayed.
7. Press Enter← to save the file and return to the command prompt.
8. You can now execute the batch file by typing its name and pressing Enter← or by booting the computer with the disk containing the AUTOEXEC.BAT or CONFIG.SYS file in the startup drive. On the IBM PC and compatible computers, you can press Ctrl-Alt-Del to warm-boot the system if it is already running.

EXERCISE 1

CREATING AN AUTOEXEC.BAT FILE

1. Insert your *Resource Disk—Backup* into drive A and make that the default drive. (Be sure drive C isn't the default drive on a hard disk system or you'll overwrite the existing AUTOEXEC.BAT file.
2. Create the following AUTOEXEC.BAT file:

```
PROMPT $P$G
DIR
```

3. Make a printout of the file.

TOPIC 22

Using the DOS 5 Shell

After completing this topic, you will be able to:

- Describe the parts of the DOS Shell
- Use DOS Shell menus to execute commands

DOS 5 contains a built-in Shell that gives you a visual representation of the drives, directories, and files on your system as shown in the figure "The DOS 5 Shell." You can select any of these items and then execute the most frequently used DOS commands on them by making choices from menus like the one shown in the figure "The Shell's Pull-Down Menus." You can also list your own application programs on the Shell's program list so that you can run them directly from the Shell.

The DOS 5 Shell
The DOS 5 Shell contains all the elements shown in this figure. However, your screen display may differ from the MS-DOS 5 shell shown here. The Shell can be displayed in character or graphics mode, and the areas shown and the programs listed can be modified. There are also differences between the MS-DOS and IBM-DOS versions of the Shell.

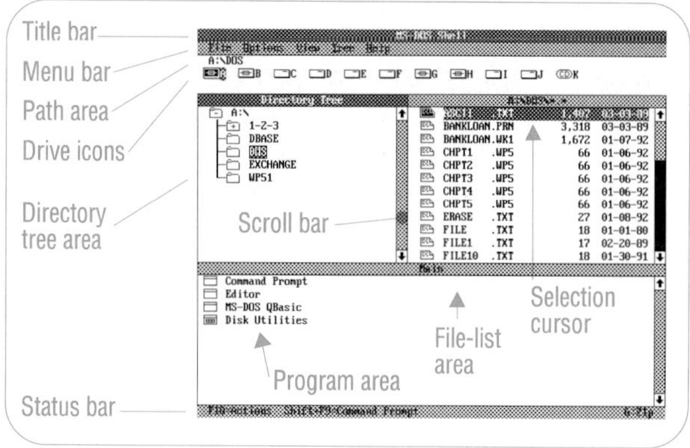

The Shell's screen display is divided into a number of areas, each of which displays a different type of information.

- The *path area* lists the current default path. For example, when it reads *C:*, the current directory is the root directory on drive C. If it reads *C:\DOS*, then DOS is the current directory.
- The *drive icon area* indicates the drives on your system with graphic symbols, called icons. The icon for the current default drive is always highlighted.
- The *directory-tree area* lists directories and subdirectories on the disk in the default drive. The current directory is always highlighted.
- The *file-list area* lists the files in the current directory. When you change the current directory on the directory tree, or select another drive in the drive-icon area, the list of files automatically changes.
- The *program-list area* lists programs that you can run without leaving the Shell.

In addition to these areas, the Shell displays the following items:

- The *menu bar* lists the names of menus that you can pull down to display commands.
- The *selection cursor* is a reverse-video or colored highlight that you move among areas of the screen to select drives, directories, files, or program names.
- A *mouse pointer* is displayed if your system has a mouse and DOS has been set up for it.
- The *status bar* lists messages and keys you can press to execute commands.

The Shell's Pull-Down Menus
When you press Alt or click on the menu bar with the mouse pointer, you can pull down menus listing many DOS commands.

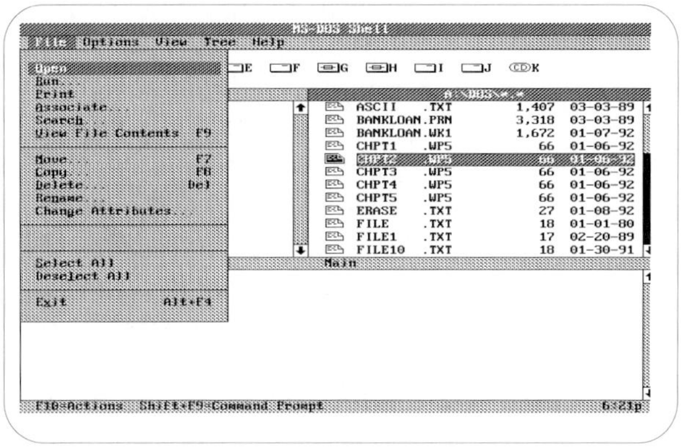

TUTORIAL

In this tutorial, you use the Shell that is built into DOS 5. As you do so, you select commands from the keyboard, not with a mouse. If your system has a mouse, you can repeat the tutorial using the mouse instead of the keyboard to execute commands.

GETTING STARTED

1. Load DOS so that the Shell is displayed. If the Shell is not displayed automatically:
   - On a hard disk system, type **DOSSHELL** and press Enter↵.
   - On a floppy disk system, insert the disk that contains the Shell program into drive A, type **DOSSHELL** and press Enter↵.
2. Insert your disks as follows:
   - On a hard disk system, insert the disk labeled *Resource Disk—Backup* into drive A.
   - On a floppy disk system, insert the disk labeled *Resource Disk—Backup* into drive B.

CHANGING DEFAULT DRIVES

3. Press → to move the selection cursor from drive icon to drive icon. (If the selection cursor is not in the drive-icon area of the screen, press Tab one or more times to move it there.)
4. Select one of the drive icons as follows:

- On a hard disk system, highlight the icon for drive A and press [Enter ←].
- On a floppy disk system, highlight the icon for drive B and press [Enter ←].

EXPLORING HELP

5. Press [Alt] to select the menu bar, and the first letter in each menu name is highlighted.
6. Press [H] (for ***H**elp*), and the Help menu descends from the menu bar.
7. Press [S] (for ***S**hell Basics*), and a help panel appears that describes Shell basics.
8. Press [↓] or [PgDn] to scroll down through the help text, and press [↑] or [PgUp] to scroll back up. Additional topics on which you can display help are highlighted in color or reverse video.
9. Press [↓] or [↑] to display the list of related help topics. The first topic listed is *Welcome to MS-DOS Shell* (or *Welcome to IBM DOS Shell* on the IBM version of DOS).
10. Press [Tab ⇆] repeatedly to move the selection cursor to the *Index* command button at the bottom of the help window, and press [Enter ←] to display an index of help topics.
11. Scroll through the list, highlight any topic of interest, and press [Enter ←] to display help on it.
12. Continue exploring help until you are comfortable with how it works.
13. When you have finished exploring help, press [Esc] to remove the help panel and return to the Shell.

EXPLORING MENUS WITH ARROW KEYS

14. Press [Alt] to activate the menu bar, and the File menu's name is highlighted.
15. Press [↓] to pull down the File menu, and all available commands are listed.
16. Press [→] to pull down the Options menu.
17. Press [→] to pull down the View menu.
18. Press [→] to pull down the Tree menu.
19. Press [→] to pull down the Help menu.
20. Press [→] to pull down the File menu again.
21. Press [↓] to highlight *Create directory*, and press [Enter ←] to display a dialog box with a space into which you type the name of the new directory.
22. Type **MYDIR** and press [Enter ←] to add a new directory named MYDIR to the menu tree.

EXPLORING MENUS WITH MNEMONIC KEYS

23. Press [Tab ⇆] to move the selection cursor to the Directory Tree and highlight *MYDIR* directory.
24. Press [Alt] and then [F] (for ***F**ile*) to pull down the File menu.

25. Press [D] (for ***D**elete*) to remove the highlighted directory from the disk and the directory tree. If the confirmation on delete option is on, a prompt reads *Delete A:\MYDIR?* or *Delete B:\MYDIR?*. If this prompt appears, highlight *Yes* and press [Enter←].

RENAMING A FILE

26. Press [Tab] to move the section cursor to the File list.
27. Highlight the file named *WHATSUP.DOC*.
28. Press [Alt] to select the menu bar.
29. Press [F] (for ***F**ile*) to pull down the File menu.
30. Press [N] (for *Re**n**ame*) to display a dialog box.
31. Type **NEWFILE.DOC** and press [Enter←] to change the file's name on the File list to NEWFILE.DOC.

COPYING A FILE

32. Highlight the file named NEWFILE.DOC, and press [Alt] to select the menu bar.
33. Press [F] (for ***F**ile*) to pull down the File menu.
34. Press [C] (for ***C**opy*) to display a dialog box.
35. Type **WHATSUP.DOC** and press [Enter←] to add the filename WHATSUP.DOC to the File list.

ERASING A FILE

36. Highlight the file named *NEWFILE.DOC*.
37. Press [Alt] to select the menu bar.
38. Press [F] (for ***F**ile*) to pull down the File menu.
39. Press [D] (for ***D**elete*) to delete the highlighted file from the disk and remove it from the file list. If the confirmation on delete option is on, a prompt reads *Delete A:\NEWFILE.DOC?* or *Delete B:\NEWFILE.DOC?*. If this prompt appears, highlight *Yes* and press [Enter←].

FINISHING UP

40. Either continue to the next activity or quit for the day.

QUICK REFERENCE

You can execute the Shell's commands with the keyboard or with a mouse. When doing so, you can display help at any time.

Getting Help

Whenever the Shell is displayed, you can display help by pressing [F1] or by pulling down the Help menu and selecting a topic. Help is context sensitive, which means the help text displayed (called a help panel) depends on the cursor's position. Many help panels have lists of related commands displayed in color or reverse video. You press [Tab] to move a highlight or a small arrow from one of these topics to another. With the topic highlighted or with the small arrow pointing to it, press [Enter←]

to display help on it. To remove the help panel, press Esc. At the bottom of each help panel are command buttons that close the help window, move you back, display help on keys, show an index, or display help on help. To choose one of these, press Tab to move the selection cursor to the desired button, and press Enter. If you are using a mouse, you can click on topics or command buttons to choose them. To do so, you use the mouse to move the mouse pointer on the screen. When the mouse pointer is pointing to the desired topic or button, you click the left button.

The Help System
You can press F1 at any point, and help is displayed on the screen. You can use the arrow keys to scroll through the text or select other related help topics that are highlighted.

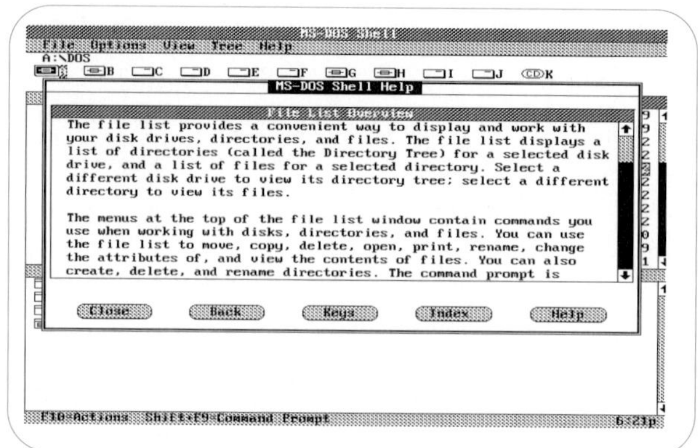

Moving Between Areas of the Shell

When the Shell is loaded, the screen displays the DOS Shell window. This window is divided into a number of areas, each of which displays a different type of information. The areas include those that display drive icons, a directory tree, a file list, and a program list. Commands listed on the View menu govern which of these areas is displayed on your system.

- You move the selection cursor between areas by pressing Tab or **Backtab**. (Hold down Shift and press Tab.)
- You move within areas by pressing the arrow keys.

Using the Shell's Pull-Down Menus

The menu bar contains pull-down menus with the choices listed in the table "The DOS Shell Menu Choices." (The choices on the File menu are different when the selection cursor is in the Program list.)

- To activate and deactivate the menu bar, you press Alt or F10. Once the menu is activated, press → or ← to move between menu choices and then press ↓ to pull down the highlighted menu. You can then press → or ← to pull down other menus.
- If using a mouse, you point to the menu name, and then click to pull it down. The mouse pointer is displayed as a highlighted box (in text mode) or as an arrow (in graphics mode). If you pull down a menu and decide not to make a choice, point to any area outside the menu, and then click the mouse button. The table "Executing Commands with a Mouse" describes the procedures you follow to execute commands with a mouse.

EXECUTING COMMANDS WITH A MOUSE

To	Point To	Click
Pull down a menu	Menu's name	Left button
Start a program	Program's name	Left button twice
Exit a pull-down menu without making a choice	Outside menu	Left button

When the menu bar is activated, you can pull down the menus in three ways:

- By pressing the letter that is underlined or highlighted (called a mnemonic) in the choice's name. For example, you can press F to pull down the File menu or H to pull down the Help menu.
- By using the arrow keys to highlight the name with the selection cursor and pressing Enter ↵ or ↓ to pull down the menu.
- By clicking on the desired menu name with a mouse.

If you do not want to make a selection, press Esc or point with the mouse to another area of the screen and click.

The table "Executing Commands from the Keyboard" summarizes the keys you use to execute menu commands.

EXECUTING COMMANDS FROM THE KEYBOARD

To	Press
Activate or deactivate the menu bar	Alt or F10
Pull down a menu from the activated menu bar	
with arrow keys	← or → and then ↓
with mnemonic keys	Mnemonic letter
Select a choice from a pull-down menu	
with arrow keys	↓ or ↑ and then Enter ↵
with mnemonic keys	Mnemonic letter
Exit a pull-down menu without making a choice but leave the menu bar activated	Alt or F10
Exit a pull-down menu without making a choice and deactivate the menu bar	Esc
Move the selection cursor between areas of the Shell	Tab ⇆

The choices on the menu bar provide additional information other than the command they execute.

- Choices on pull-down menus followed by an ellipsis (...) display dialog boxes when selected. Dialog boxes are like on-screen forms that you fill out with information the computer needs.
- Choices on pull-down menus that are dimmed or not listed are not selectable from where you are in the procedure.

THE DOS SHELL MENU CHOICES

Menu	Description
File	
***O**pen*	Runs the selected executable program file that ends with the extension .COM, .EXE, or .BAT and opens an associated file if you selected one (see ***A**ssociate*).
***R**un...*	Displays a dialog box in which you enter the name of a program you want to run.
***P**rint*	Prints up to ten selected ASCII text files.
***A**ssociate...*	Links filename extension to programs so that if you select a data file with the specified extension, the associated program is automatically run.
*Searc**h**...*	Searches for files that you specify in a dialog box that appears when you select this choice. If you check the *Search entire disk* option, DOS searches the disk in the default drive. If you leave this unchecked, DOS just searches the current directory.
***V**iew File Contents*	Displays the contents of the selected file.
***M**ove...*	Moves selected files to another drive or directory and deletes the original file.
***C**opy...*	Copies selected files to another drive or directory or to the current one if you specify a new name in the dialog box.
***D**elete...*	Deletes selected files.
*Re**n**ame...*	Renames selected files.
*Chan**g**e Attributes*	Changes a selected file's attributes to Hidden, Read-Only, or Archive. (See your DOS manual.)
*Cr**e**ate Directory...*	Creates a new directory.
***S**elect All*	Selects all files in the File List.
*Dese**l**ect All*	Deselects any previously selected files in the File List.
*E**x**it*	Closes the Shell and displays the command prompt.
Options	
***C**onfirmation...*	Turns confirmation prompts on and off for ***D**elete*, ***C**opy*, and ***M**ove* commands; also specifies if files are to be selected in more than one directory or not.
***F**ile Display Options...*	Displays selected files and sorts files in the File List.
*Select **A**cross Directories...*	Allows you to select files in more than one directory at the same time so that you can copy, move, or delete them.
***S**how Information...*	Displays information on the highlighted file.
***E**nable Task Swapper*	When enabled, you can run more than one program at the same time and switch back and forth between them.
***D**isplay...*	Changes the way the Shell is displayed.
*C**o**lors...*	Changes the colors used in the Shell display.
View	
***S**ingle File List*	Displays Directory Tree and File List for current drive.
***D**ual File Lists*	Displays Directory Tree and File List for two drives or directories.
***A**ll Files*	Displays a list of all files on a disk regardless of the directories they are stored in.
*Program/**F**ile Lists*	Displays Directory Tree and File List for current drive and a list of DOS programs.
***P**rogram List*	Displays just a list of DOS programs.

THE DOS SHELL MENU CHOICES (CONTINUED)

Menu	Description
Repaint Screen	Updates the screen display.
Refresh	Updates the list of files after you delete or restore any.
Tree	
Expand One Level	Shows one more level of subdirectories for the selected directory.
Expand Branch	Shows all levels of subdirectories for the selected directory.
Expand All	Shows all levels of subdirectories for all directories.
Collapse Branch	Hides all subdirectories below the selected directory.
Help	
Index	Displays a list of topics on which help is available.
Keyboard	Displays a list of topics on keys you use to execute commands.
Shell Basics	Displays basic help on using the Shell.
Commands	Displays all menu commands so that you can get help on them.
Procedures	Displays a list of procedures you may need help with.
Using Help	Displays help on using help.
About Shell	Displays the version number and copyright information on the Shell.

Responding to Dialog Boxes

All menu choices followed by an ellipsis (...) display dialog boxes when you select them. Dialog boxes are requests for additional information, which you enter into the dialog boxes' text boxes or select from lists. When the text that you type into a text box reaches the right end of the box, the entry scrolls off the screen to the left. If your entry is too long, eventually the computer beeps, and you have to stop typing.

When entering text into text boxes, you can use the following editing commands:

- You can press ← and → to move the cursor through the text. You can also press End to move the cursor to the end of the entry or Home to move it to the beginning.
- If the text box already contains an entry, the first character you type will delete it. If you want to just edit the existing entry, press ← or → before typing any other character, and you will enter edit mode. In this mode, you can then move the cursor through the entry to insert characters or use Del or ←Bksp to delete them.

Changing Default Drives

The drive-icon area lists the drives on your system. The current default drive is highlighted. To change the default drive:

- Press Tab to move the selection cursor to this area, press ← or → to highlight the drive you want to make the default, and press Enter. You can also hold down Ctrl and press the letter of the drive when the selection cursor is in the drive-icon area.
- If using a mouse, point to the drive and then click.

As you change the default drive, the path area, the directory tree, and the file list reflect the change.

Changing Default Directories

The directory-tree area lists all directories and subdirectories, if any, on the disk. To change the default directory:

- Press Tab to move the selection cursor to this area, press ↓ or ↑ to highlight the directory you want to make the default, and press Enter.
- If using a mouse, point to the directory, and then click.

As you change the default directory, the path area and file list reflect the change.

Selecting Files

The file-list area normally lists the files on the default drive and directory. At the top of this area the current file specification is listed. You can change this specification with the ***F**ile Display Options* command listed on the Options menu. The default file specification is *.* which displays all the files on the disk.

- If there are too many filenames to be displayed at one time, the list extends off the bottom of the area. To scroll through the list of files, press Tab to move the selection cursor to this area. You then press ↑, ↓, PgUp, and PgDn to scroll the list. You can also press Ctrl-Home to move to the top of the list or Ctrl-End to move to the bottom.
- To select a single file, press Shift-F8, and *ADD* is displayed on the status bar and the file's icon remains highlighted when you move the selection cursor off it. To unselect a selected file, highlight the file, and press Spacebar.
- To select files that are adjacent to one another on the list, you select the first filename, and then extend the selection. To do so, highlight the first file you want to select, and then hold down Shift while you press ↑ or ↓ to extend the selection to the other files.
- To select or deselect files that are not adjacent to one another, highlight the first file, and press Shift-F8. When you do so, *ADD* is displayed on the status bar, and the file's icon remains highlighted when you move the selection cursor off it. To select additional files, highlight them and press Spacebar. After selecting all the files you want, press Shift-F8 again, and *ADD* disappears from the status bar.
- To select or deselect all files, press Tab to move the selection cursor to the file-list area, pull down the File menu, and then choose ***S**elect all* or *Dese**l**ect all.*

If your Shell has been installed for a mouse, the arrows or scroll bar can be used instead of PgUp and PgDn to scroll the file list or directory tree. The scroll bar contains both up and down arrows and a slider box. The slider box indicates which part of the list is currently displayed. To scroll any list:

- Point to the arrows at the top or bottom of the scroll bar, and then click. Hold the mouse button down to scroll continuously.

- Point to the slider box within the scroll bar, hold down the mouse button, and drag the slider box up or down. Release the button to scroll the list to that point.
- To select files that are adjacent to one another on the list, click the first name, and then hold down [⇧Shift] and click the last name.
- To select or deselect files that are not adjacent to one another, hold down [Ctrl] while you click each filename.

Running Programs

A program list is displayed when you select *Program/File Lists* from the View menu. This area lists programs that you can execute. Some programs are directly listed in this area, but others have been grouped together under a single heading. For example, if you select *Command Prompt* or *Editor* (called *IBM DOS Editor* on IBM's version of DOS 5), the command is immediately executed. However, if you select *Disk Utilities*, another list is displayed. It is from this second list that you actually execute the commands.

The default program list (yours may have been modified) is named Main, and it contains those programs shown in the table "The Program-List Area Commands." To select one of the listed commands, highlight it and press [Enter↵] or double-click it with a mouse. (Click on it twice in rapid succession.)

THE PROGRAM-LIST AREA COMMANDS FOR MS-DOS (DIFFERENT ON IBM VERSION)

Choice	Description
Command Prompt	Displays the command prompt. Type **EXIT** and press [Enter↵] to return to the Shell.
Editor	Displays a dialog box asking you the name of the file that you want to edit.
MS-DOS QBasic	Displays a dialog box asking you the name of the file that you want to run.
Disk Utilities	Displays a list of utility programs you can run. • *Main* returns you to the main program list. • *Disk Copy* makes duplicate disks. • *Backup Fixed Disk* backs up a hard disk onto floppy disks. • *Restore Fixed Disk* restores a hard disk's files from backups on floppy disks. • *Quick Format* formats a disk more quickly if it has already been formatted once. • *Format* formats data and system disks. • *Undelete* recovers deleted files.

When the selection cursor is in the program-list area, the commands listed on the File menu change from those that are normally displayed. These commands are described in the table "File Menu Choices with the Selection Cursor in the Program List."

FILE MENU CHOICES WITH THE SELECTION CURSOR IN THE PROGRAM LIST

Choice	Description
New...	Adds a program or group of programs to the currently selected group
Open	Runs a program or displays the contents of a group
Copy	Copies a program or group of programs to another group
Delete...	Deletes the selected group or selected item within a group
Properties...	Describes the program to be run
Reorder	Rearranges programs and groups to a different position in the list
Run...	Displays a dialog box in which you enter the name of a program to run
Exit	Closes the Shell and displays the command prompt

EXERCISE

EXERCISE 1

USING THE SHELL'S MENUS

1. Insert your *Resource Disk—Backup* into drive A on a hard disk system or drive B on a floppy disk system.
2. Change the default drive, if necessary, to the drive into which you inserted the disk.
3. Use the Shell's menus to create three directories, SHELL1, SHELL2, and SHELL3.
4. Use the Shell's menus to copy all the files that begin with CHPT to the SHELL1 directory.
5. Use the Shell's menus to copy all the files that begin with FILE to the SHELL2 directory.
6. Use the Shell's menus to copy the WHATSUP.DOC file to the SHELL3 directory.
7. Use the Shell's menus to erase all the files in each directory, and then delete the directories.

CHAPTER 5 REVIEW

- The command you use to check your disks is CHKDSK, an external command. When files are deleted and then new files are saved onto a disk, files that you copy to the disk or save onto it with an application program may be stored in noncontiguous sectors. To find files like this, use the CHKDSK *.* command.
- The command you use to display an ASCII text file on the screen is TYPE. To freeze a file scrolling on the screen, press Ctrl-S. To resume scrolling, press any other key.
- The command you use to print an ASCII text file is PRINT, an external command. To stop a file being printed with this command, use the PRINT/T command.
- The > character is used to redirect a file to a disk file or the printer. The >> characters append a file to an existing disk file.
- The MORE command pauses data on the screen if the screen becomes full. You then have to press any key to continue.
- The SORT command sorts files and their contents.
- To create a batch file from the command prompt, you use the COPY CON command, an internal command. To end it, you press Ctrl-Z, and then press Enter↵.
- When you first boot your system, the computer looks for two files, CONFIG.SYS and AUTOEXEC.BAT. It automatically executes the commands that it finds in these files.
- Because DOS commands can be hard to remember, Shells have been developed that allow you to execute DOS commands by making menu selections. You can display DOS 4 and later Shells by typing **DOSSHELL** at the command prompt.

CHAPTER 5 QUESTIONS

FILL IN THE BLANK

1. To check the disk in drive A, you would enter the command ___________.
2. To display an ASCII text file named README.TXT, you would enter the command ___________.
3. To print an ASCII text file named README.TXT, you would enter the command ___________.
4. To stop printing an ASCII text file that is being printed with the PRINT command, you would enter the command ___________.
5. To pause a directory listing for drive C that is listed with the DIR command, you would enter the command ___________.
6. To send a directory listing of drive B to the printer, you would enter the command ___________.

7. To send a directory listing of drive B to a disk file on drive A named LIST.TXT, you would enter the command ___________.
8. To create a batch file named BATCH.BAT, you would enter the command ___________.
9. The file your system reads first when you boot it up is named ___________.
10. The file your system reads next when you boot it up is named ___________.
11. To load the DOS Shell from the command prompt, you would type ___________.

MATCH THE COLUMNS

1. CHKDSK
2. CHKDSK *.*
3. CHKDSK /V
4. CHKDSK /F
5. TYPE
6. PRINT
7. >
8. >>
9. | MORE
10. | SORT
11. COPY CON
12. F6
13. CONFIG.SYS
14. AUTOEXEC.BAT
15. DOSSHELL
16. Alt

- __ Sorts files or their contents
- __ Pauses the screen when it is full
- __ Fixes a disk that has lost chains
- __ Creates an ASCII text file
- __ Prints ASCII text files
- __ Gives you the status of a disk
- __ Redirects data to a disk file or the printer
- __ Activates the DOS Shell's menu bar
- __ Gives you the status of a disk and the files on it
- __ Displays the Shell built into DOS 4 and later versions
- __ A file that contains information about your system's setup
- __ Appends data to an existing disk file
- __ A file that contains commands to be executed when you boot the computer
- __ Lists files as it checks a disk's status
- __ Displays ASCII text files on the screen
- __ Ends an ASCII text file you are creating with COPY CON

WRITE OUT THE ANSWERS

1. What command do you use to check disks? Is the command an internal or external command?
2. What happens to files, when the disk begins to get full, that makes the drive work harder and take longer to retrieve and save the files?
3. If you get a message telling you your files have noncontiguous sectors, what does it mean?
4. If a disk has noncontiguous sectors, how can you fix the files so that they are all in adjacent sectors on the disk?
5. What is the difference between the CHKDSK and CHKDSK *.* commands?

6. What command do you use to display ASCII files on the screen? Is this an internal or external command?
7. What two commands can you use to stop text from scrolling off the screen?
8. To redirect the output from the standard output device, what redirection character do you use?
9. What is the function of a filter?
10. If you want to sort a file, what filter do you use?
11. What is the function of a pipe?
12. What character do you use to direct the list of files to the printer or a file?
13. What command would you use to redirect the output from the DIR command to the printer? To a file named FILELIST on a disk in drive B?
14. Why can't the disk in the default drive be write-protected when you use the MORE filter?
15. What are batch files, and what are they used for?
16. What is the command you type to begin creating a batch file from the command prompt?
17. What key(s) do you press to end a batch file and save it to the disk?
18. What command do you type to display the DOS Shell from the command prompt?
19. When the DOS Shell is displayed, what key do you press to activate the menu bar?

CHAPTER 5

PROJECT

PROJECT 1

CREATING A DOS REFERENCE CARD

The table "Summary of DOS Commands" lists some of the most frequently used DOS command procedures. Complete the table by entering in the Command column the command you would use to perform each of the tasks. In the Type column, indicate if the command is an internal or external command.

SUMMARY OF DOS COMMANDS

Description	Command	Type
Checking Disks		
Gives status of memory, disk space, and any noncontiguous blocks	____________	______
Displays each filename as it is checked	____________	______
Displays a prompt that asks you if you want to correct errors	____________	______
Displaying and Printing ASCII File Commands		
Displays ASCII text file on screen	____________	______
Freezes scrolling screen display	____________	______
Prints ASCII text file	____________	______
Stops a printing ASCII text file	____________	______
Batch File Commands		
Copies from console (keyboard) to disk file	____________	______
Ends a COPY CON command	____________	______

INDEX

Note: DOS commands are in **boldface**.

WordPerfect® 5.1

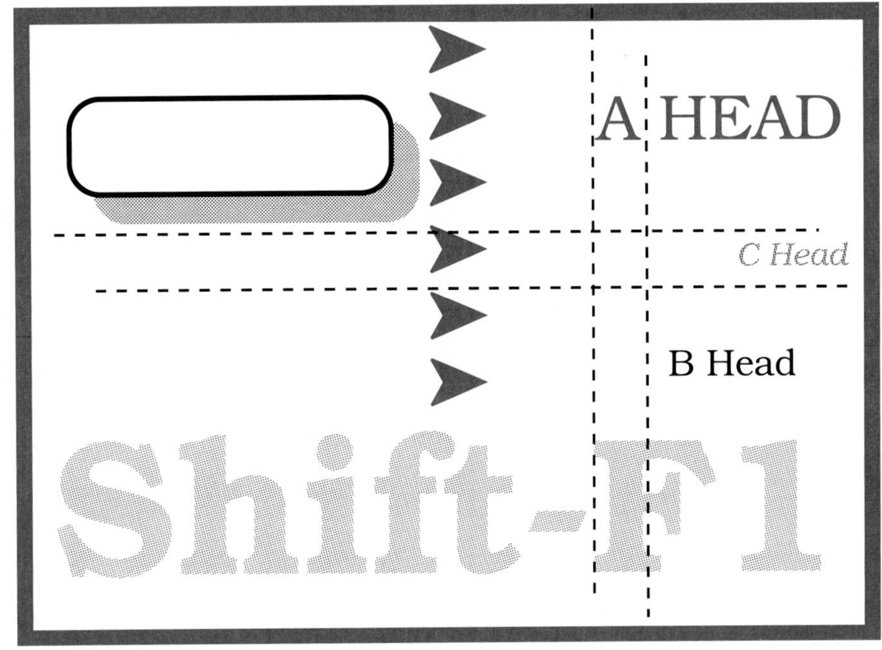

CHAPTER 1

Getting Started

TOPIC 1

WordPerfect 5.1—An Overview

After completing this topic, you will be able to:

- Explain some of the applications of word processing
- Load WordPerfect from a floppy disk drive or a hard disk drive
- Describe the elements that make up the Edit screen
- Exit the WordPerfect program

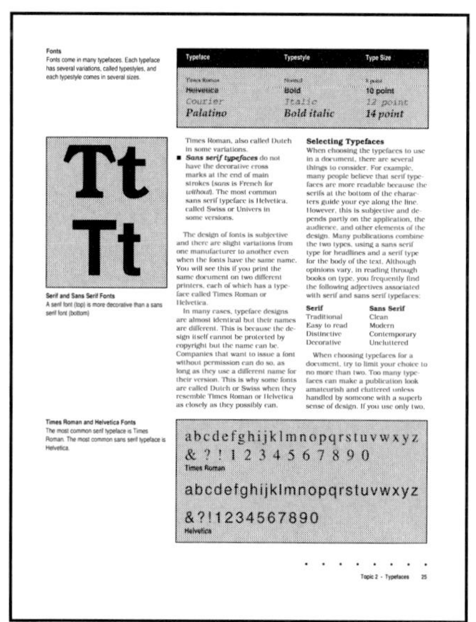

Fonts
Fonts come in many typefaces. Each typeface has several variations, called typestyles, and each typestyle comes in several sizes.

Typeface	Typestyle	Type Size
Times Roman	Normal	8 point
Helvetica	Bold	10 point
Courier	Italic	12 point
Palatino	Bold italic	14 point

Serif and Sans Serif Fonts
A serif font (top) is more decorative than a sans serif font (bottom)

Times Roman, also called Dutch in some variations.

- ***Sans serif typefaces*** do not have the decorative cross marks at the end of main strokes (*sans* is French for *without*). The most common sans serif typeface is Helvetica, called Swiss or Univers in some versions.

The design of fonts is subjective and there are slight variations from one manufacturer to another even when the fonts have the same name. You will see this if you print the same document on two different printers, each of which has a typeface called Times Roman or Helvetica.

In many cases, typeface designs are almost identical but their names are different. This is because the design itself cannot be protected by copyright but the name can be. Companies that want to issue a font without permission can do so, as long as they use a different name for their version. This is why some fonts are called Dutch or Swiss when they resemble Times Roman or Helvetica as closely as they possibly can.

Selecting Typefaces
When choosing the typefaces to use in a document, there are several things to consider. For example, many people believe that serif typefaces are more readable because the serifs at the bottom of the characters guide your eye along the line. However, this is subjective and depends partly on the application, the audience, and other elements of the design. Many publications combine the two types, using a sans serif type for headlines and a serif type for the body of the text. Although opinions vary, in reading through books on type, you frequently find the following adjectives associated with serif and sans serif typefaces:

Serif	Sans Serif
Traditional	Clean
Easy to read	Modern
Distinctive	Contemporary
Decorative	Uncluttered

When choosing typefaces for a document, try to limit your choice to no more than two. Too many typefaces can make a publication look amateurish and cluttered unless handled by someone with a superb sense of design. If you use only two,

Times Roman and Helvetica Fonts
The most common serif typeface is Times Roman. The most common sans serif typeface is Helvetica.

abcdefghijklmnopqrstuvwxyz
& ? ! 1 2 3 4 5 6 7 8 9 0
Times Roman

abcdefghijklmnopqrstuvwxyz
&?!1234567890
Helvetica

Topic 2 · Typefaces 25

Desktop Publishing
WordPerfect has become so powerful that it can be used to desktop-publish documents such as newsletters with graphics, multiple columns, and shaded headings.

Word processing is probably the most common application of computers. The ease with which you can draft and revise memos, letters, reports, and other documents with a word processing program increases both the speed and the quality of your writing. You can enter, edit, change, reorganize, format, and print text without having to retype all of it each time you make a change. This ease of use encourages you to revise and reorganize your material more frequently so that you can express your ideas more clearly and prepare more professional-looking documents.

The applications of word processing software are almost endless, ranging from the same tasks that can be done on a typewriter, such as writing memos, letters, and reports, to entirely new kinds of tasks that aren't possible without the power of the computer. For example, you can prepare a form letter that you can then use over and over again, with just a name or phrase changed here and there. Contracts, sales letters, and collection notices are typical form documents. You can also prepare electronic mail documents for telecommunication over a network, or over the telephone lines with a modem. Finally, you can desktop-publish documents. WordPerfect can change fonts, print in columns, and print graphics along with text. These features open up a new world of opportunities since you can now inexpensively desktop-publish catalogs, advertising circulars, reports, articles, and even books.

➤ JUMP-START TUTORIAL

In this tutorial, you get a jump start on WordPerfect by following steps that introduce you to the program using an existing document file. Some of the procedures you will be using may seem confusing at first, but keep in mind that this is an overview and you are not expected to retain any of the procedures except those you use to load the program and open your files. All the other procedures will be covered in more depth and at a much slower pace as you proceed through this text. *Relax* and see what WordPerfect can do for you!

GETTING STARTED

1. Load WordPerfect into your computer's memory.
   - If you load the program from the operating system command prompt (for example, *A:* or *C:*), load the operating system and then refer to one of the KEY/Strokes boxes "Loading WordPerfect from a Hard Disk" or "Loading WordPerfect from a Floppy Disk" in the Quick Reference section on page 8.
   - If you use other procedures to load the program, such as selecting it from a menu, load it, and then start this tutorial at the section "Retrieving a File Using List Files." Write down the steps that you follow to load the program in Exercise 1 at the end of this topic so that you have them to refer to later.

THE WORDPERFECT EDIT SCREEN

When you load WordPerfect, the Edit screen appears automatically. Except for the bottom line, this screen is devoted entirely to the document you create.

Doc 1 Pg 1 Ln 1" Pos 1"

- The edit area is initially empty except for a blinking cursor in the upper-left corner that indicates where the next character you type will appear. If you are using a mouse, a rectangular mouse pointer (▮) is displayed on the screen when you move the mouse and disappears when you press a key.
- The status line at the bottom of the screen displays information about the file you are working on.
  - The name of the file currently on the screen, if any, is displayed at the left end of this line.
  - *Doc* indicates the document. (You can have two documents in memory at the same time.)
  - *Pg* indicates the page the cursor is on.
  - *Ln* shows the distance of the cursor from the top of the page.
  - *Pos* serves a dual function: It indicates both the distance of the cursor from the left edge of the page and the status of the CapsLock and NumLock keys. (See the table "Key Lock Indicators.")

RETRIEVING A FILE USING LIST FILES

2. Insert the original *Student Resource Disk* accompanying this text as follows:
   - On a hard disk system, insert the disk into drive A.
   - On a floppy disk system, insert the disk into drive B.
3. Press F5, and a message on the status line reads *Dir* followed by the current default drive. At the right end of the status line, a prompt reads *(Type = to change default Dir)*.
4. Press = (the equal sign), and the prompt reads *New directory =* followed by the current default directory.
5. Set the default drive as follows:
   - On a hard disk system, type **A:\WP51** and press Enter↵.
   - On a floppy disk system, type **B:\WP51** and press Enter↵.

   The prompt reads *Dir x:\WP51*.** (where *x* stands for the drive you specified in the command).
6. Press Enter↵ to display a list of the files.

KEY LOCK INDICATORS

KEY	When Engaged	When Not Engaged
CapsLock	*POS* in uppercase	*Pos* in lowercase
NumLock	*Pos* flashes	*Pos* doesn't flash

The List Files Screen
The List Files screen displays all the files on the current drive.

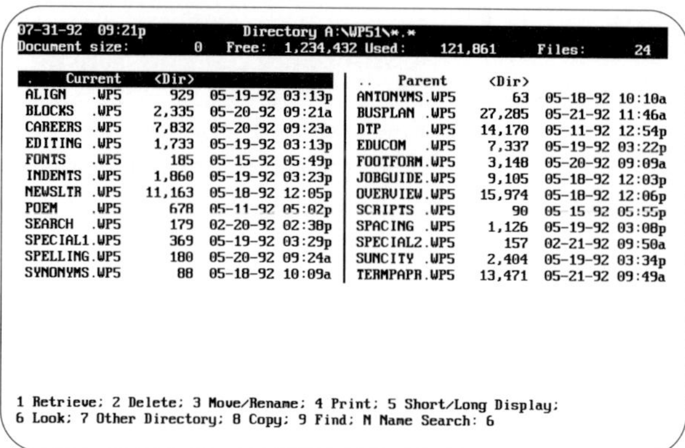

```
07-31-92  09:21p              Directory A:\WP51\*.*
Document size:       0   Free:  1,234,432 Used:     121,861      Files:      24

 .    Current     <Dir>                      |  ..   Parent      <Dir>
 ALIGN    .WP5       929  05-19-92 03:13p    |  ANTONYMS.WP5        63  05-18-92 10:10a
 BLOCKS   .WP5     2,335  05-20-92 09:21a    |  BUSPLAN .WP5    27,285  05-21-92 11:46a
 CAREERS  .WP5     7,832  05-20-92 09:23a    |  DTP     .WP5    14,170  05-11-92 12:54p
 EDITING  .WP5     1,733  05-19-92 03:13p    |  EDUCOM  .WP5     7,337  05-19-92 03:22p
 FONTS    .WP5       185  05-15-92 05:49p    |  FOOTFORM.WP5     3,148  05-20-92 09:09a
 INDENTS  .WP5     1,860  05-19-92 03:23p    |  JOBGUIDE.WP5     9,105  05-18-92 12:03p
 NEWSLTR  .WP5    11,163  05-18-92 12:05p    |  OVERVIEW.WP5    15,974  05-18-92 12:06p
 POEM     .WP5       678  05-11-92 05:02p    |  SCRIPTS .WP5        90  05-15-92 05:55p
 SEARCH   .WP5       179  02-20-92 02:38p    |  SPACING .WP5     1,126  05-19-92 03:08p
 SPECIAL1.WP5        369  05-19-92 03:29p    |  SPECIAL2.WP5       157  02-21-92 09:50a
 SPELLING.WP5        180  05-20-92 09:24a    |  SUNCITY .WP5     2,404  05-19-92 03:34p
 SYNONYMS.WP5         88  05-18-92 10:09a    |  TERMPAPR.WP5    13,471  05-21-92 09:49a

1 Retrieve; 2 Delete; 3 Move/Rename; 4 Print; 5 Short/Long Display;
6 Look; 7 Other Directory; 8 Copy; 9 Find; N Name Search: 6
```

7. Use the arrow keys to move the highlight over the file named *OVERVIEW.WP5*. (Press NumLock first if the POS indicator is flashing.)
8. Press R (for ***R**etrieve*), and the document appears on the screen.

The OVERVIEW File
When you retrieve the OVERVIEW.WP5 file, it will look something like this although the line endings on your screen may be different.

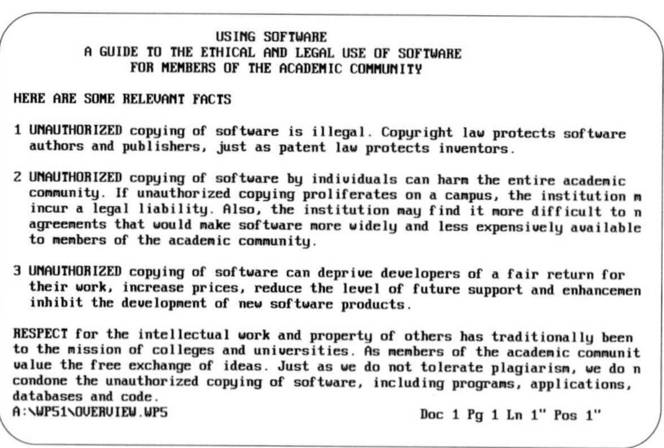

```
                              USING SOFTWARE
            A GUIDE TO THE ETHICAL AND LEGAL USE OF SOFTWARE
                  FOR MEMBERS OF THE ACADEMIC COMMUNITY

HERE ARE SOME RELEVANT FACTS

1 UNAUTHORIZED copying of software is illegal. Copyright law protects software
  authors and publishers, just as patent law protects inventors.

2 UNAUTHORIZED copying of software by individuals can harm the entire academic
  community. If unauthorized copying proliferates on a campus, the institution m
  incur a legal liability. Also, the institution may find it more difficult to n
  agreements that would make software more widely and less expensively available
  to members of the academic community.

3 UNAUTHORIZED copying of software can deprive developers of a fair return for
  their work, increase prices, reduce the level of future support and enhancemen
  inhibit the development of new software products.

RESPECT for the intellectual work and property of others has traditionally been
to the mission of colleges and universities. As members of the academic communit
value the free exchange of ideas. Just as we do not tolerate plagiarism, we do n
condone the unauthorized copying of software, including programs, applications,
databases and code.
A:\WP51\OVERVIEW.WP5                                  Doc 1 Pg 1 Ln 1" Pos 1"
```

EXPLORING KEY LOCK AND CURSOR POSITION INDICATORS

9. Press CapsLock a few times, and watch the *POS* indicator on the status line toggle between *POS* and *Pos* to indicate whether CapsLock is on. (A light on your keyboard may also toggle on and off.) When CapsLock

is on, any characters that you type will be in uppercase. When you have finished, leave the indicator set to *Pos*.

10. Press [NumLock] a few times, and watch the *Pos* indicator toggle between flashing and not flashing to indicate whether [NumLock] is on. (A light on your keyboard may also toggle on and off.) The keys on the numeric keypad can produce two different results, indicated by the numbers, arrows, or words printed on them. When [NumLock] is on, they enter numbers. When [NumLock] is off, they move the cursor. When you have finished, leave the indicator set so that it isn't flashing.

GETTING AROUND A DOCUMENT

11. Press the arrow keys to move the cursor through the text while watching the *Ln* and *Pos* indicators on the status line.
12. Practice moving the cursor with the commands described in the table "Cursor Movement Keys," and notice how the cursor moves through the text. Keys whose names are connected with hyphens in the table (for example, [Ctrl]-[←]) are pressed simultaneously, whereas those separated by commas (for example, [Home], [↑]) are pressed one after the other. Hold down some of the keys to see how they repeat until you release them. If you get lost, just press [Home] twice and then [↑] to move the cursor to the top of the document. Any dashed lines across the screen are called page breaks; they indicate where one page ends and another begins when you print the document.

CURSOR MOVEMENT KEYS

To Move the Cursor	Press
Horizontally	
One character left or right	[←] or [→]
One word left or right	[Ctrl]-[←] or [Ctrl]-[→]
To left or right edge of text on screen	[Home], [←] or [Home], [→]
To end of line	[End]
Vertically	
One line up or down	[↑] or [↓]
To top or bottom line on screen	[Home], [↑] or [Home], [↓]
To top line of document	[Home] (twice), [↑]
To end of document's last line	[Home] (twice), [↓]
To top of screen and then to top of previous screen*	[-]
To bottom of screen and then to bottom of next screen*	[+]
To top of next page	[PgDn]
To top of previous page	[PgUp]

*The [+] and [-] keys that scroll the screen are at the far right of the keyboard on the numeric keypad. To use them, [NumLock] must not be engaged.

ENTERING NEW TEXT

13. Press [Home] twice, and then press [↓] to move the cursor to the bottom of the document.

14. Press Enter↵ to move the cursor down one line.
15. Type **I have read and understand this statement:** Press Spacebar, and then type your name. As you do so:
    - Notice how the cursor moves as you type. It indicates where the next character you type will appear.
    - If you make any typos, press ←Bksp to back up the cursor to erase them, and then enter the correct letters.
16. Press Enter↵ to move the cursor down one line.
17. Type today's date, for example, January 10, 1993, and press Enter↵. (On some systems, a dashed line appears across the screen when you press Enter↵. This indicates a page break where the paper will advance in the printer to the top of a new page.)

Entering Text
After you enter your name and date at the bottom of the document, your screen should look similar to this.

```
2. make unauthorized copies of software for others.

If you have questions not answered by this brochure about the proper use and dis
software product, seek help from your computing office, from the software develo
publisher.

This brochure has been produced as a service to the academic community by EDUCOM
profit consortium of over 450 colleges and universities committed to the use and
of information technology in higher education, and ADAPSO [now called the Inform
Technology Association of America], the computer software and services industry
Although this brochure is copyrighted, you are authorized to make and distribute
whole or in part, providing the source is acknowledged.  For additional  copies
contact:

EDUCOM            Information Technology Association of America
Software Initiative 1300 North 17th Street
P.O. Box 364        Suite 300
Princeton, NJ 08540 Arlington, VA 22209

■ 1987 EDUCOM and ADAPSO

I have read and understand this statement:
January 10, 1993

A:\WP51\OVERVIEW.WP5                              Doc 1 Pg 3 Ln 8.57i Pos 1i
```

SAVING A DOCUMENT

18. Press F10, and the prompt reads *Document to be saved: x:\WP51\OVERVIEW.WP5* (where *x* stands for the drive you specified when retrieving the file).
19. Press Enter↵, and the prompt reads *Replace x:\WP51\OVERVIEW.WP5? **No** (**Y**es).*
20. Press Y (for ***Y**es*), and the drive spins as the document is saved onto the disk.

REVEALING CODES

21. Press Home twice, and then press ↑ to move the cursor to the top of the document.
22. Press Alt-F3 or F11 to reveal codes, and the screen divides into two parts. In the lower half, you can see a number of codes that do not appear in the upper half. These codes, enclosed in square brackets, are entered as you create and format documents. You will learn about these codes as you complete the topics in this text.

Revealing Codes
Revealing codes allows you to see how elements are formatted.

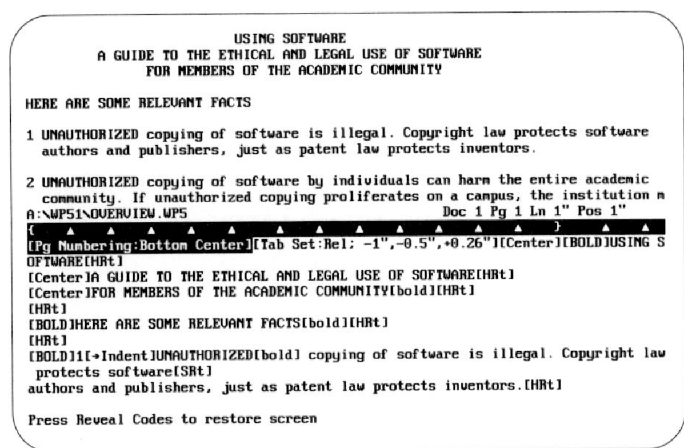

23. Press [Alt]-[F3] or [F11] to hide codes, and the lower half of the screen disappears and codes can no longer be seen.

PREVIEWING AND PRINTING A DOCUMENT

24. Be sure the printer is on and has paper in it, then press [⇧Shift]-[F7] to display the Print menu.
25. Press [V] (for ***View** Document*), and in a moment the document is displayed on your screen just as it will appear when you print it. (If it does not appear, your system may not be designed to accommodate this feature.) You can press [PgDn] and [PgUp] to scroll through the document page by page. You can use this mode to preview your documents before sending them to the printer and wasting paper if they should not look the way you intended.
26. Press [1], [2], [3], and then [4] in turn to see how the document can be displayed at various sizes.

Previewing the Document
The View Document command allows you to see what your document will look like when you print it.

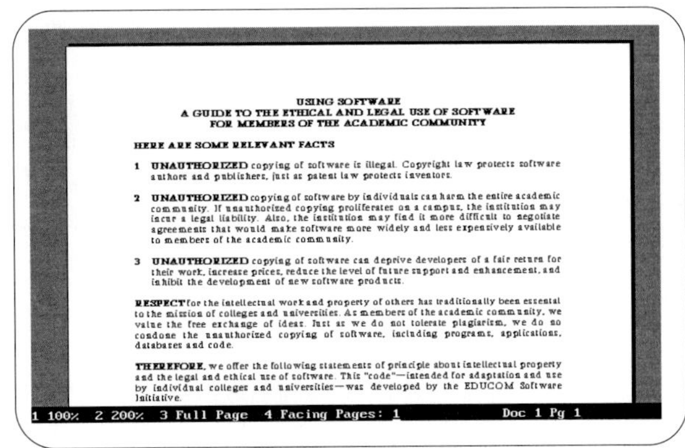

27. Press [F1] to return to the Print menu.
28. Press [F] (for ***Full** Document*) to print the entire document. It is a three-page document prepared by EDUCOM and ADAPSO on software rights and responsibilities. On your printout, headings should be boldfaced and some paragraphs printed in italic type. Page numbers should be printed at the bottom of each page.

FINISHING UP

29. Press [F7], and the prompt reads *Save document? **Yes** (**N**o).*
30. Press [Y], and the prompt reads *Document to be saved: x:\WP51\OVERVIEW.WP5.*

31. Press [Enter↵], and the prompt reads *Replace x:\WP51\OVERVIEW.WP5? **No** (**Yes**).*
32. Press [Y], and the file is saved. The prompt then reads *Exit WP? **No** (**Yes**).*
33. Press [Y] to exit the program. Remove your program and data disks, and then turn off the computer or load another program.
34. Read the printout that you made, and then sign your name following the line that you entered at the bottom of the document.

QUICK REFERENCE

To use WordPerfect, you must first understand the basic procedures that you follow to load and exit the program.

Loading WordPerfect

Once the operating system is loaded, the way you load WordPerfect depends on the type of computer you are using. You have to follow only one of the two procedures described. If your system is on a network, or you use a customized menu to load programs, refer to Exercise 1 at the end of this topic.

Hard Disk System

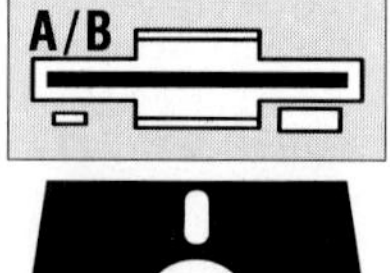

Loading WordPerfect on a Hard Disk System
To save your work on a floppy disk, you insert a formatted data disk into drive A.

KEY/Strokes

Loading WordPerfect from a Hard Disk

1. Load the operating system (DOS).
2. If the command prompt is not *C>* or *C:\>* type **C:** and press [Enter↵] to change the drive.
3. Change the default directory to the one containing the WP.EXE file. To do so, type **CD** then type the name of the directory and press [Enter↵]. For example, if the program files are in a directory named WP51, type **CD\WP51** and press [Enter↵].
4. Type **WP** and press [Enter↵]. In a moment, a copyright notice appears, and a message reads ** Please wait **. In a moment, the Edit screen appears.

Floppy Disk System

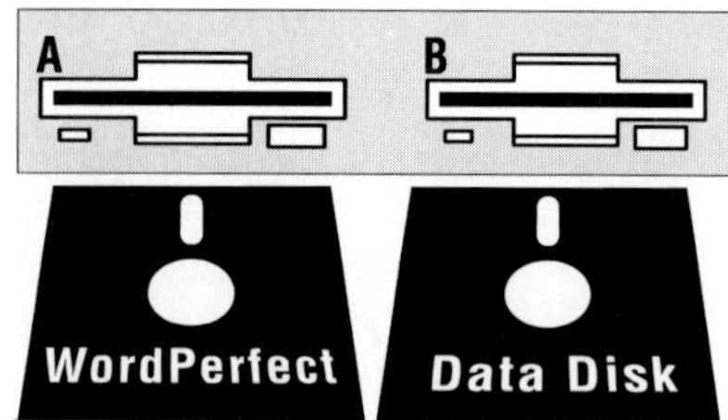

Loading WordPerfect on a Floppy Disk System
To load WordPerfect from a floppy disk, you insert the *WordPerfect 1* disk into drive A and type **WP**. To save your work, you insert a formatted data disk into drive B.

KEY/Strokes

Loading WordPerfect from a Floppy Disk

1. Load the operating system (DOS).
2. Insert the disk labeled *WordPerfect 1* or *WordPerfect 1/ WordPerfect 2* into drive A.
3. If the command prompt is not *A>*, type **A:** and press [Enter↵].
4. Type **WP** and press [Enter↵] to load the program.

   On some systems, a copyright notice appears, and then a prompt reads *Insert diskette labeled "WordPerfect 2" and press any key.* If this prompt appears, insert the requested disk, and press any key to continue. The message reads ** Please wait ** and in a moment, the Edit screen appears.

ARE OTHER COPIES OF WORDPERFECT CURRENTLY RUNNING? (Y/N)

If you did not quit the program correctly the last time you used it, the prompt reads *Are other copies of WordPerfect currently running? (Y/N)* when you load the program. If you are not running the program on a network, press N. If you are running on a network and this prompt appears, ask your instructor what action you should take.

Loading WordPerfect and Setting the Default Drive

When you load WordPerfect, the default drive for saving files is whatever drive (and directory) you have previously set as the default on your system. This means that files you save are automatically saved on that drive (and directory). You can load WordPerfect so that it will automatically save files to the drive in which you have your data disk. This saves you a step whenever you want to save a file. You do this by making the drive that holds your data disk the default drive and then loading WordPerfect from it. Follow the instructions in the KEY/Strokes box "Loading WordPerfect and Setting the Default Drive."

➜ KEY/Strokes

Loading WordPerfect and Setting the Default Drive

1. Insert your disks as follows:
   - On a hard disk system, insert a data disk on which to save your files into drive A.
   - On a floppy disk system, insert the *WordPerfect 1* disk into drive A and a data disk on which to save your files into drive B.
2. Set your drives as follows:
   - On a hard disk system, make drive A the default drive.
   - On a floppy disk system, make drive B the default drive.
3. Enter a command as follows:
   - On a hard disk system, type **C:**<*WordPerfect directory*>**\\WP** and press Enter←. (<*WordPerfect directory*> indicates where you should substitute the name of the directory in which your WordPerfect program files are stored. For example, if they are in a directory named WP51, enter the command as C:\WP51\WP.)
   - On a floppy disk system, type **A:WP** and press Enter←.

   The program is loaded with the default drive set to the one in which you placed the data disk.

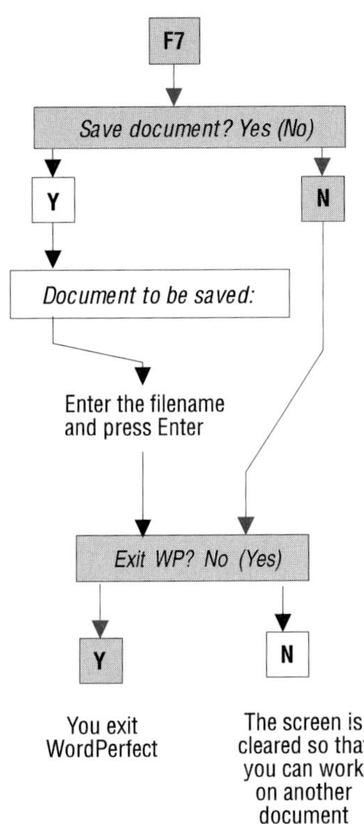

Exiting Options
When you press F7 to exit WordPerfect, you are presented with a number of options, as shown in this flow chart. The path you would take to exit the program without saving a file is shaded.

Exiting WordPerfect

It is important to exit WordPerfect using the commands designed for this purpose. Although you can exit the program by simply turning off the computer, this is a bad habit to get into because WordPerfect creates temporary files on the disk while you are working and these are deleted only if you exit correctly.

To exit WordPerfect when you want to load another program or turn the computer off, you press F7 and then answer a series of yes/no questions. One of the questions asks if you want to save the document on the screen. (Saving documents is discussed in a later topic.) The KEY/Strokes box "Exiting WordPerfect" describes how to exit the program without saving the document. You may want to exit without saving a document if you have no further use for it or because you saved it earlier and have not made any changes that you want to save. If you have not made any changes since you retrieved the document or last saved it, when you press F7 to exit, a message on the right end of the status line reads *(Text was not modified)*. If this message appears, there is no need to save the file.

After pressing F7 to begin the exit sequence, you can always press F1 at any point to cancel the command and leave the current document on the screen.

→ KEY/Strokes

Exiting WordPerfect

1. Either: Press F7.

   Or: Press Alt-= to display the menu at the top of the screen, Press F to pull down the ***File*** menu and select ***Exit***.

   The prompt reads *Save document?* ***Yes*** *(**No**)*. (If a screen with the heading *Document Summary* is displayed, it means that a previous user has changed a default setting. Just press Enter← to display the prompt.)
2. Press N to abandon the file, and the prompt reads *Exit WP?* ***No*** *(**Yes**)*.
3. Press Y to exit.

EXERCISES

EXERCISE 1

LOADING WORDPERFECT ON YOUR OWN SYSTEM

If your WordPerfect program is on a network, or if your system has been customized, your loading procedures may differ from those discussed in this topic. If they do, list the steps that you follow so that you have them for future reference.

1. ______________________________

2. ______________________________

3. ______________________________

4. ______________________________

5. ______________________________

Floppy Disk System

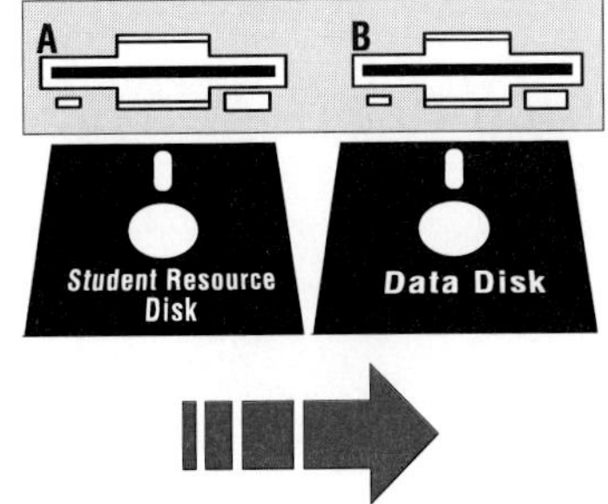

Copying Files
To work with the data files that accompany this text, you copy them from the WP51 directory on the *Student Resource Disk* to your own data disk.

EXERCISE 2

COPYING STUDENT RESOURCE DISK FILES

In this exercise, you copy files from the original *Student Resource Disk* to a formatted data disk. The instructions in this exercise assume that you are working on a system where you can display the DOS command prompt. If you are working on a system connected to a network or with a customized menu, you may have to follow different procedures. If this is the case, ask your instructor for help.

1. Load DOS so that the command prompt is displayed.
2. Insert your disks as follows:
   - On a system with only one floppy disk drive, insert the original *Student Resource Disk* into drive A.
   - On a system with two floppy disk drives, insert the original *Student Resource Disk* into drive A and the disk you want to copy the files to into drive B.
3. Type **A:** and press Enter← to make drive A the default drive.
4. Type **CD\WP51** and press Enter← to make the directory named WP51 the default directory.
5. Type **COPY *.* B:** and press Enter←. (If you are working on a system with a single floppy disk, ask your instructor if the DOS XCOPY command is available. If it is, type XCOPY *.* B: instead of COPY *.* B and you won't have to swap disks as often.)
   - On a system with only one floppy disk drive, you will be periodically prompted to swap disks.
   - On a system with two floppy disk drives, the files are listed as they are copied from one drive to the other.
6. When the command prompt reappears, remove the disks and continue with your work.

EXERCISE 3

SETTING THE DEFAULT DRIVE WHEN LOADING WORDPERFECT

Follow the instructions in the KEY/Stroke box "Loading WordPerfect and Setting the Default Drive" to load the program. After loading the program, press F5, and the current default drive will be listed at the left end of the status line. Press F1 to return to the Edit screen.

TOPIC 2A

Executing Commands—Using Function Keys

After completing this topic, you will be able to:
- Execute commands with function keys
- Use on-line help
- Make choices from menus
- Respond to prompts
- Cancel a command in progress

WORDPERFECT COLOR CODES

Color	Meaning
Black	Press the indicated function key by itself or in sequence.
Blue	Hold down [Alt] while you press the indicated function key.
Green	Hold down [⇧Shift] while you press the indicated function key.
Red	Hold down [Ctrl] while you press the indicated function key.

In its early versions, WordPerfect provided only one way to execute commands—by using the function keys. Many users still prefer its traditional function key approach. Since WordPerfect has so many function key commands, it's helpful to use a keyboard template as a memory aid or quick reference tool. Keyboard templates fit over the function keys on the left side of a standard keyboard or above the row of function keys at the top of an enhanced keyboard. Enhanced keyboards have twelve function keys, while standard keyboards have ten. WordPerfect templates use the colors described in the table "WordPerfect Color Codes" to indicate various key combinations.

TUTORIAL

THE DISK TO USE

Beginning with this tutorial, you use the data disk to which you copied files from the original *Student Resource Disk* in Exercise 2 of Topic 1. If you have not completed that exercise, you must do so before you continue.

In this tutorial, you explore WordPerfect's function key commands and on-line help.

GETTING STARTED

1. Load WordPerfect so that the Edit screen is displayed.
2. Insert the disk with your WordPerfect data files on it as follows:
   - On a hard disk system, insert the disk into drive A.
   - On a floppy disk system, insert the disk into drive B.

RETRIEVING A FILE

3. Press [⇧Shift]-[F10], and the prompt reads *Document to be retrieved:*.
4. Enter a command as follows:
   - On a hard disk system, type **A:OVERVIEW.WP5** and press [Enter ↵].
   - On a floppy disk system, type **B:OVERVIEW.WP5** and press [Enter ↵].

   The drive spins, and the document appears on the screen.

The OVERVIEW File
When you retrieve the OVERVIEW.WP5 file, it looks like this, although line endings may vary slightly on your screen.

```
                    USING SOFTWARE
       A GUIDE TO THE ETHICAL AND LEGAL USE OF SOFTWARE
            FOR MEMBERS OF THE ACADEMIC COMMUNITY

HERE ARE SOME RELEVANT FACTS

1 UNAUTHORIZED copying of software is illegal. Copyright law protects software
  authors and publishers, just as patent law protects inventors.

2 UNAUTHORIZED copying of software by individuals can harm the entire academic
  community. If unauthorized copying proliferates on a campus, the institution m
  incur a legal liability. Also, the institution may find it more difficult to n
  agreements that would make software more widely and less expensively available
  to members of the academic community.

3 UNAUTHORIZED copying of software can deprive developers of a fair return for
  their work, increase prices, reduce the level of future support and enhancemen
  inhibit the development of new software products.

RESPECT for the intellectual work and property of others has traditionally been
to the mission of colleges and universities. As members of the academic communit
value the free exchange of ideas. Just as we do not tolerate plagiarism, we do n
condone the unauthorized copying of software, including programs, applications,
databases and code.
A:\WP51\OVERVIEW.WP5                              Doc 1 Pg 1 Ln 1" Pos 1"
```

EXPLORING HELP

5. Press [F3], and a screen that introduces you to help is displayed. (On some floppy disk systems, the prompt on the status line reads *WPHELP.FIL not found. Insert the diskette and press drive letter:*. If this prompt appears, insert the disk labeled *WordPerfect 1* into drive A or B, and press [A] or [B].)

Help
When you press [F3], help is displayed.

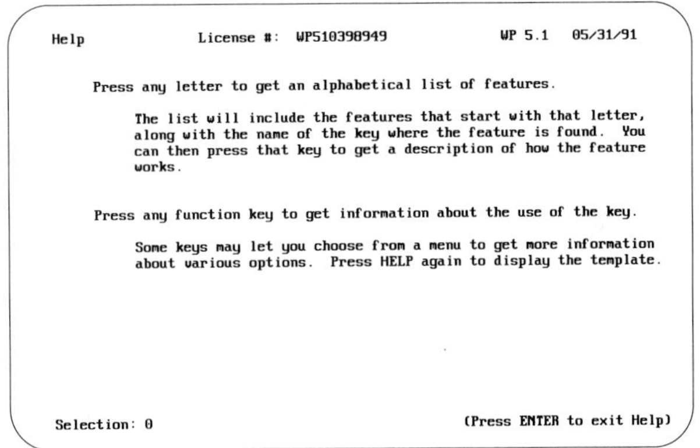

```
Help            License #:  WP510398949            WP 5.1   05/31/91

     Press any letter to get an alphabetical list of features.

          The list will include the features that start with that letter,
          along with the name of the key where the feature is found.  You
          can then press that key to get a description of how the feature
          works.

     Press any function key to get information about the use of the key.

          Some keys may let you choose from a menu to get more information
          about various options.  Press HELP again to display the template.

Selection: 0                                      (Press ENTER to exit Help)
```

6. Press [F3] again to display an illustration of the keyboard template. (If you are using a keyboard with the function keys on the left, press [1] to display a template for those function keys.)

Keyboard Template
When you press [F3] twice, a copy of the keyboard template for enhanced keyboards is displayed. If you then press [1], the keyboard template for regular keyboards is displayed.

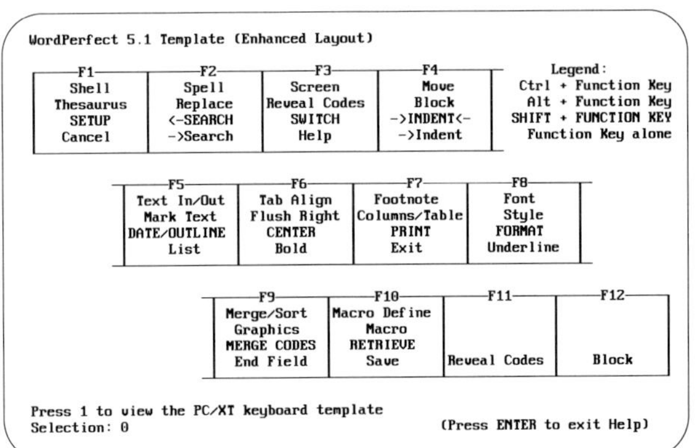

WordPerfect 5.1 Template (Enhanced Layout)

F1	F2	F3	F4
Shell	Spell	Screen	Move
Thesaurus	Replace	Reveal Codes	Block
SETUP	<-SEARCH	SWITCH	->INDENT<-
Cancel	->Search	Help	->Indent

Legend:
Ctrl + Function Key
Alt + Function Key
SHIFT + FUNCTION KEY
Function Key alone

F5	F6	F7	F8
Text In/Out	Tab Align	Footnote	Font
Mark Text	Flush Right	Columns/Table	Style
DATE/OUTLINE	CENTER	PRINT	FORMAT
List	Bold	Exit	Underline

F9	F10	F11	F12
Merge/Sort	Macro Define		
Graphics	Macro		
MERGE CODES	RETRIEVE		
End Field	Save	Reveal Codes	Block

Press 1 to view the PC/XT keyboard template
Selection: 0 (Press ENTER to exit Help)

7. Press each of the other function keys labeled [F1] through [F10] (or [F1] through [F12] on enhanced keyboards) to display a brief description of their function.

HELP SCREENS

Note that when help screens are displayed, many of them are identical to the screens that appear during the execution of commands. To let you know when you are in the help system, help screens always display the message (*Press ENTER to exit help*) in the lower right corner of the screen.

8. Hold down Alt, Shift, or Ctrl when you press each of the function keys F1 through F10 to display help on the commands these key combinations execute.
9. Press any letter key (A through Z) to display an alphabetized list of features. Each key displays a list of topics that begins with the letter you press. To get help on a topic of interest, press the appropriate key. For example, for help on deleting text, press D, and for help on the Go To command, press G.
10. Press Spacebar, and the Edit screen reappears.
11. Continue experimenting with help commands until you feel comfortable using the system. (When you have finished, if you swapped disks, remove the *WordPerfect 1* disk from the drive and insert the *WordPerfect 2* disk.)

EXPLORING MENUS

12. Press Shift-F8 to display the Format menu, which occupies the entire screen. Notice how each command on the menu has a number in front of it and how one letter in each command is highlighted. To execute commands, you can press either the number or the highlighted character. Notice that the first choice is for ***Line***, and below it are listed the settings that it controls.

The Format Menu
When you press Shift-F8, the Format menu is displayed. This full-screen menu displays commands you use to format lines, pages, and documents.

```
Format

     1 - Line
              Hyphenation                         Line Spacing
              Justification                       Margins Left/Right
              Line Height                         Tab Set
              Line Numbering                      Widow/Orphan Protection

     2 - Page
              Center Page (top to bottom)         Page Numbering
              Force Odd/Even Page                 Paper Size/Type/Labels
              Headers and Footers                 Suppress
              Margins Top/Bottom

     3 - Document
              Display Pitch                       Redline Method
              Initial Codes/Font                  Summary

     4 - Other
              Advance                             Printer Functions
              Conditional End of Page             Underline Spaces/Tabs
              Decimal Characters                  Border Options
              Language                            End Centering/Alignment
              Overstrike
Selection: 0
```

13. Press L (for ***Line***) to display the Line Format menu, which lists commands you use to format lines of text in a document. Notice that the third item is for ***Justification*** and that it is set to Full, the program's default setting.

The Line Format Menu
When the Format menu is displayed, pressing L (for ***Line***) displays the Line Format menu. This menu lists commands you use to format lines of text in a document.

```
Format: Line

     1 - Hyphenation                     No

     2 - Hyphenation Zone - Left         10%
                            Right        4%

     3 - Justification                   Full

     4 - Line Height                     Auto

     5 - Line Numbering                  No

     6 - Line Spacing                    1

     7 - Margins - Left                  1i
                   Right                 1i

     8 - Tab Set                         Rel: -1i, every 0.5i

     9 - Widow/Orphan Protection         No


Selection: 0
```

14. Press [J] (for ***Justification***) to display the Justification menu that occupies the status line.
15. Press [L] (for ***Left***) to left-align text in the document and return to the Line Format menu.
16. Press [0] (the number) to back up to the Format menu.
17. Press [0] (the number) again to back completely out of the menus.
18. Repeat Steps 12 through 14 to display the Justification menu.
19. Press [F7] to exit the menu and return directly to the Edit screen without backing up though the menus.

DISPLAYING PROMPTS

20. Press [F10] to save the document, and the prompt reads *Document to be saved: x:\OVERVIEW.WP5.* (If a screen with the heading *Document Summary* is displayed, it means that a previous user has changed a default setting. Just press [Enter←] to display the prompt.)
21. Press [F1] to cancel the command and remove the prompt.
22. The table "Help Screens" in Exercise 1 at the end of this topic lists the keys you press to start many WordPerfect commands. Use this guide to experiment with commands that display menus and prompts. Continue experimenting until you feel comfortable with the procedures. Don't worry while experimenting. The worst thing that can happen is that you inadvertently exit the program. If this happens, just reload the program and continue. Remember:
    - You cancel commands and return to the Edit screen by pressing [F1] or [F7].
    - You can back up through menus by pressing [0] (the number zero).

PRINTING A PAGE

23. Press [Home] twice, and then press [↑] to move the cursor to the top of the document.
24. Press [⇧Shift]-[F7] to display the Print menu.

The Print Menu
When you press [⇧Shift]-[F7] the Print menu is displayed. You can then press [F] or [1] to print the full document or press [P] or [2] to print the page on which the cursor is positioned.

```
Print

     1 - Full Document
     2 - Page
     3 - Document on Disk
     4 - Control Printer
     5 - Multiple Pages
     6 - View Document
     7 - Initialize Printer

Options

     S - Select Printer                    HP LaserJet III PostScript
     B - Binding Offset                    0i
     N - Number of Copies                  1
     U - Multiple Copies Generated by      WordPerfect
     G - Graphics Quality                  Medium
     T - Text Quality                      High



Selection: 0
```

25. Press [P] (for ***Page***) to print the page containing the cursor. Compare this printout with the first one you made. Notice how this printout's right margin is not even, whereas the first printout's right margin is. The first document is full justified, and this new one is left-aligned.

CLEARING THE SCREEN WITHOUT SAVING THE FILE

26. Press [F7], and the prompt reads *Save document?* ***Yes (No).***
27. Press [N], and the prompt reads *Exit WP?* ***No (Yes).***
28. Press [N], and the Edit screen is now blank.

FINISHING UP

29. You have now completed this tutorial. Either continue with the next activity or exit WordPerfect, turn off the computer, and remove your disk(s).

QUICK REFERENCE

You can execute most WordPerfect commands using function keys. As you do so, you can display help at any point.

Getting Help

WordPerfect contains extensive on-line help that you can display at any time by pressing [F3]. If you press [F3] before you begin an operation, a screen describing the help system is displayed. This screen also lists your program's registration number. You may need to know this number if you call WordPerfect's customer service for assistance.

WordPerfect's on-line help is context sensitive, so the help displayed may be directly related to what you are trying to do at the moment. For example, if you press [F10] to begin to save a file and cannot remember how to complete the sequence, pressing [F3] displays help on saving files.

Sometimes you don't even know how to start a command. In these cases, you can use the index to speed up your search. For example, let's say you want to know how to save a file. After pressing [F3], press [S] since that is the most likely index listing for the Save command. This displays a screen listing various save keystrokes. For example, it shows that to display help on saving text, you press [F10]. If you want additional help, press another letter to return to the index.

When you have finished with help, press [Spacebar], [Enter ←], or [0] to return to where you were in your procedure before you asked for help. If you are using a mouse, click the right button.

KEY/Strokes

Using On-Line Help

1. Press [F3] at any point in the program to display a help screen.
2. To display other help screens:
   - Press any letter key ([A] through [Z]) to see an alphabetized list of commands. Each key displays a list of topics that begins with the letter you press. For example, for help on deleting text, press [D]; for help on the Go To command, press [G].
   - Press any function key labeled [F1] through [F10] (or [F1] through [F12] on enhanced keyboards) for information on the command the key is used for.

- Hold down [Alt], [⇧Shift], or [Ctrl] while you press any of the function keys [F1] through [F10] for information on the commands that these key combinations execute.
- If any of the menu choices on the screen has a highlighted number or letter, you can press the number or letter to display help on that option.

Some help screens also display lists of features you can display help on by pressing the number or highlighted character in the feature's name.

3. When finished viewing help, press [Spacebar], [Enter←], or [0] to return to the Edit screen, or click the right mouse button.

SWAPPING DISKS ON A FLOPPY DISK SYSTEM

On a floppy disk system, the WordPerfect program is too large to be on one disk, so various parts of the program are located on different disks. Therefore, when you execute some commands, you are prompted to insert one of the other disks. For example, when you press [F3] for help, the program looks for the help file. If the program cannot find it, a prompt reads *WPHELP.FIL not found. Insert the diskette and press drive letter:*. If this prompt appears, insert the disk labeled *WordPerfect 1* into one of the drives (usually A or B), and press the letter of the drive. When you have finished with help, remove the disk, and replace it with the disk that was originally in the drive. Similar prompts appear at other points in the program—for example, when you execute the Speller and Thesaurus. Read the prompts that appear on the status line, and insert the requested disk.

Using Function Keys

You execute most WordPerfect commands from the keyboard by pressing one of the ten function keys, [F1] through [F10], on the keyboard. (Some newer computers and enhanced keyboards have 12 or more function keys.) The function keys are assigned more than one task; for example, the [F2] key can perform four tasks. To change its function, you hold down another key while you press it. Using combinations of keys in this way makes it possible to assign many more tasks to the keyboard than there are keys. The other keys that you hold down are called control or modifier keys: [Ctrl], [Alt], and [⇧Shift]. These keys do not send characters or commands to the computer; rather, they change what is sent when you press other keys. For example, when using [F2]:

- Press [F2] by itself to search down through a document.
- Hold down [⇧Shift] and press [F2] to search toward the top of the document.
- Hold down [Ctrl] and press [F2] to spell-check the document.
- Hold down [Alt] and press [F2] to search and replace in the document.

When you use these modifier keys, you hold them down first and press the other key. The sequence in which you press the keys is important—so follow these procedures:

1. Hold down the [Alt], [⇧Shift], or [Ctrl] key. These keys do not repeat or send commands to the computer, so you can hold them down as long as you want.
2. Press the function key just as if you were typing a character. If you hold it down, the command may repeat until you release it, and you will soon find the computer beeping. This can create problems.

Selecting Menu Options

When you execute a command with one of the function keys, any one of several things might happen:

- An action is immediately performed; for example, a line is centered.
- An action is begun that must then be stopped. You end the action either by repeating the same command (for example, boldfacing text) or by pressing [Enter←] (for example, centering a line of text).

- A prompt is displayed; for example, when you press F10 to save a file, the prompt reads *Document to be saved:*.
- A menu is displayed.

Menus are like those you get in a restaurant—they list available choices. Some menus are displayed on the status line at the bottom of the screen; others are displayed on the full screen. There are two ways to select the choices listed on these menus:

- Press the highlighted letter in the command's name. For example, if you press Shift-F8 to display the Format menu, you can then press L (for ***L**ine*), P (for ***P**age*), D (for ***D**ocument*), or O (for ***O**ther*). This is the approach used in this text—the letters for commands are given in all hands-on activities. (The way the letters are highlighted in menu commands can be changed or even turned off by pressing Shift-F1 to display the Setup menu and then selecting ***D**isplay* and ***M**enu Options*.)
- Press the number or letter that precedes your choice. When you do so, use the number keys at the top of the keyboard, or be sure NumLock is engaged before using the numeric keypad at the right of the keyboard. For example, if you press Shift-F8 to display the Format menu, you can then press 1 (for ***L**ine*), 2 (for ***P**age*), 3 (for ***D**ocument*), or 4 (for ***O**ther*).

Many menus have more than one level, so choosing a command listed on a menu may display another menu, called a submenu. Getting to the actual command you want to execute occasionally means that you must select a series of commands from the displayed submenus. When you reach the menu you want and make your choice, any one of several things might happen:

- The Edit screen may automatically reappear.
- You may have to press Enter and make another selection from the same menu.
- The cursor may automatically move to another part of the same menu choice if it has more than one part.
- A prompt may be displayed; for example, when printing a file from the disk, the prompt *Document name:* asks you to enter the name of the document.

If the menu does not automatically disappear after you finish making choices, or if you want to cancel a command in progress, you use one of the following keys:

- Press F7 to have the computer accept any changes you have made in menu choices and return directly to the Edit screen. Sometimes you may have to press it more than once to return to the Edit screen.
- Press 0 or Spacebar to have the computer accept any changes you have made in menu choices and back up through any submenus. Each time you press one of these keys, you retrace your steps one menu until you return to the Edit screen. This is helpful when you want to back up a menu or two so that you can take a new branch.
- Press F1 to cancel a command that displays a menu or a message on the status line. This command cancels any changes you have already made in the menus. You may have to press it more than once to back entirely out of the command.

If a prompt or menu is not displayed, pressing F1 executes the Undelete command, and previously deleted text may be inserted into your document. If this happens to you by mistake, press F1 again to remove the Undelete menu and any highlighted text inserted into your document.

Prompts

When you press a function key or make a choice from a menu, a prompt may appear. Prompts are questions that WordPerfect wants you to answer. For example, you may be asked to enter a page number to print, the name of a file to save or retrieve, or a word you want to find.

- To answer prompts, you type a response. For example, when you are saving a file, the prompt reads *Document to be saved:*. To save a file named LETTER, you would type **LETTER**. You can type responses to prompts in any combination of uppercase or lowercase letters—for example, **LETTER**, **letter**, or **Letter**. If you make any typos while typing an answer, press ←Bksp to delete them, and then type the answer correctly. When the response is complete and correct, press Enter↵ to enter it.
- Some prompts, when they appear a second time in the same session, display the last response you made to them. You can accept the suggested response by pressing Enter↵ or you can type a new response (The first character you type automatically deletes the previous response.) Or you can edit the previous response. To do so, press Ins or → to enter edit mode. Then:
  - Use the arrow keys to move the cursor through the text to edit it.
  - Press ←Bksp to delete the character to the cursor's left or Del to delete the character the cursor is under. You can also press Ctrl-End to delete all characters from the cursor to the end of the response.
  - Press Ins to switch between insert and typeover modes. In insert mode, new characters are inserted, and existing ones move over to make room for them. In typeover mode, new characters type over existing characters.
  - When you have finished editing the response, press Enter↵.
- Some prompts have a suggested answer, for example, *Replace B:\FILENAME.EXT? **No** (**Y**es)*. The answer *not* in parentheses is the suggested response. To accept the suggested response (in this example, ***N**o*), press N or just press Enter↵. To reject the suggested response, press Y or any key other than N.

EXERCISES

EXERCISE 1

EXPLORING WORDPERFECT'S HELP

Load WordPerfect, then press the key you use to display help. With the help screen displayed, press the keys listed in the first column of the table "Help Screens." In the second column, list the title of the help screen that is displayed in the upper-left corner of the screen. When you have finished, press one of the keys you use to exit help and return to the Edit screen.

HELP SCREENS

Key(s)	Description	Key(s)	Description
F1	______	Shift-F10	______
F2	______	Ctrl-F1	______
F3	______	Ctrl-F2	______
F4	______	Ctrl-F3	______
F5	______	Ctrl-F4	______
F6	______	Ctrl-F5	______
F7	______	Ctrl-F6	______
F8	______	Ctrl-F7	______
F9	______	Ctrl-F8	______
F10	______	Ctrl-F9	______
F11	______	Ctrl-F10	______
F12	______	Alt-F1	______
Shift-F1	______	Alt-F2	______
Shift-F2	______	Alt-F3	______
Shift-F3	______	Alt-F4	______
Shift-F4	______	Alt-F5	______
Shift-F5	______	Alt-F6	______
Shift-F6	______	Alt-F7	______
Shift-F7	______	Alt-F8	______
Shift-F8	______	Alt-F9	______
Shift-F9	______	Alt-F10	______

EXERCISE 2

PRINTING A COPY OF THE KEYBOARD TEMPLATE

If you do not have a keyboard template, you can print one from the help screen if your instructor approves. (This procedure causes problems on some systems.) Be sure the printer is on and has paper in it. Then:

1. Display help, and press the help key again to display the template for an enhanced keyboard. (If you are using a keyboard with the function keys on the left, press 1 to display a template for those function keys.)
2. Print the screen display as follows:
   - On standard keyboards, hold down Shift and press the key labeled PrtScr.
   - On enhanced keyboards, press PrtScr without holding down Shift.
3. Advance the paper out of the printer. Note that graphics characters may not print or may print as other characters.
4. Exit help and return to the Edit screen.

TOPIC 2B

Executing Commands—Using Pull-Down Menus

After completing this topic, you will be able to:

- Display the menu bar
- Make choices from pull-down menus

WordPerfect 5.1 was the first version of the program to add pull-down menus. These menus make it easier to execute many commands since you choose them from a list.

TUTORIAL

In this tutorial, you explore executing commands with WordPerfect's pull-down menus.

GETTING STARTED

1. Load WordPerfect so that the Edit screen is displayed.
2. Insert the disk with your WordPerfect data files on it as follows:
   - On a hard disk system, insert the disk into drive A.
   - On a floppy disk system, insert the disk into drive B.

RETRIEVING A FILE

3. Press Alt-= to display the menu bar at the top of the screen. The menu name ***File*** is highlighted in reverse video or color.

The Menu Bar
When you press Alt-=, the menu bar is displayed at the top of the screen. It allows you to choose commands from menus, making WordPerfect easier to learn and use.

```
File Edit Search Layout Mark Tools Font Graphics Help        (Press F3 for Help)




                                                   Doc 1 Pg 1 Ln 1i Pos 1i
```

4. Press ↓ to pull down the File menu, and the ***R**etrieve* command is highlighted.

Pull-Down Menus

A menu is pulled down from the menu bar when you press the letter that is highlighted in a menu choice's name or highlight the name and press Enter↵.

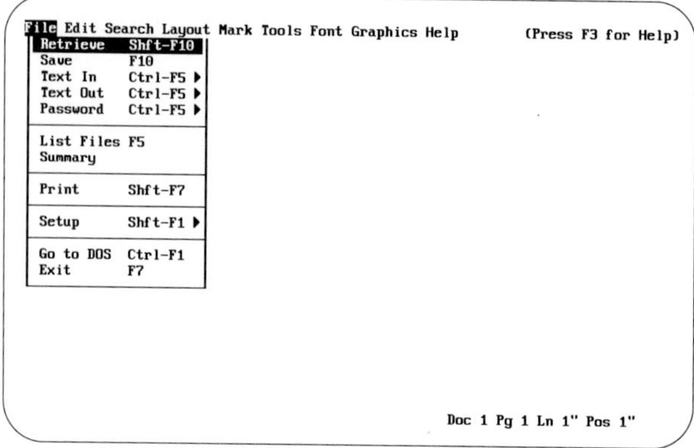

5. Press Enter↵ to select the highlighted command, and the prompt reads *Document to be retrieved:*.
6. Enter a command as follows:
   - On a hard disk system, type **A:OVERVIEW.WP5** and press Enter↵.
   - On a floppy disk system, type **B:OVERVIEW.WP5** and press Enter↵.

   The drive spins, and the document appears on the screen.

EXPLORING MENUS

7. Press Home twice, and then press ↑ to move the cursor to the top of the document.
8. Press Alt-= to display the menu bar.
9. Press ↓ to pull down the highlighted File menu.
10. Press → repeatedly to move the highlight along the menu bar and pull each menu down. When you reach the Help menu and press → again, the first menu, File, is pulled down.
11. Pull down the Layout menu.
12. Press L (for ***L**ine*) to display the Line Format menu.
13. Press S (for *Line **S**pacing*), and the cursor jumps to the number *1* on the same line as the command.
14. Type 2 and press Enter↵. The cursor returns to the number *0* following the *Selection:* prompt.
15. Press 0 (the number), and you back up to the Format menu.
16. Press 0 again, and you back out of the menus completely. The document is now double spaced on the screen.

PRINTING A PAGE

17. Press Alt-= to display the menu bar.
18. Press F to pull down the File menu.
19. Press ↓ to highlight ***P**rint*, and press Enter↵ to display the Print menu.
20. Press P (for ***P**age*) to print the page the cursor is on, and it is printed double spaced.

CLEARING THE SCREEN WITHOUT SAVING THE FILE

21. Press Alt-= to display the menu bar.
22. Press F to pull down the File menu
23. Press End to move the highlight to ***Exit***, the last choice.
24. Press Enter↵ to select the highlighted choice, and the prompt reads *Save document? **Yes** (**N**o).*
25. Press N, and the prompt reads *Exit WP? **No** (**Y**es).*
26. Press N, and the Edit screen is now blank.

FINISHING UP

27. You have now completed this tutorial. Either continue with the next activity or exit WordPerfect, turn off the computer, and remove your disk(s).

QUICK REFERENCE

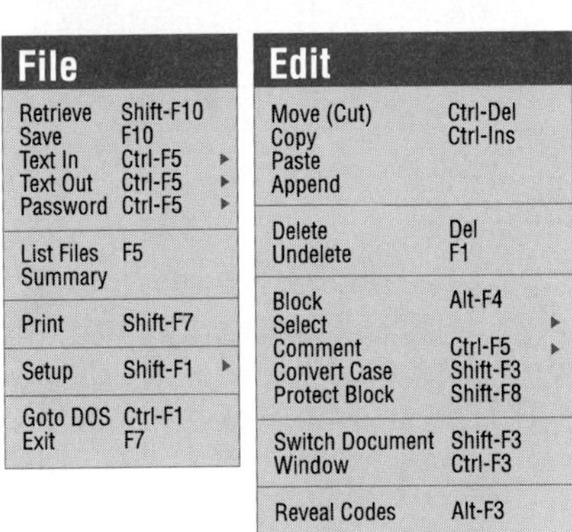

Search

Forward F2
Backward Shift-F2
Next
Previous
Replace Alt-F2
Extended
Go to Ctrl-Home

Layout

Line Shift-F8
Page Shift-F8
Document Shift-F8
Other Shift-F8
Columns Alt-F7
Tables Alt-F7
Math Alt-F7
Footnote Ctrl-F7
Endnote Ctrl-F7
Justify
Align
Styles Alt-F8

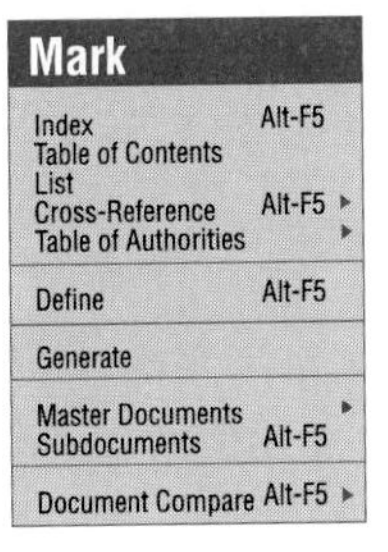

Tools

Spell Ctrl-F2
Thesaurus Alt-F1
Macro
Date Text Shift-F5
Date Code Shift-F5
Date Format Shift-F5
Outline Shift-F5
Paragraph Number Shift-F5
Define Shift-F5
Merge Codes Shift-F9
Merge Ctrl-F9
Sort Ctrl-F9
Line Draw Ctrl-F9

To display the menu bar at the top of the screen, press Alt-=. The figures to the left and on the following page show all the commands listed on the first level of pull-down menus. To operate the menus, you use the following procedures, which are also summarized in the table "Menu Bar Commands."

- To move the highlight between menu names on the menu bar:
  - Press ← or →.
  - Press Home, ← or Home, → to move the highlight to the first or last choice on the menu bar. You can also press End to move the highlight to the last choice.
- To pull down a menu:
  - Highlight its name, and press ↓ or Enter↵.
  - Press the highlighted letter in the command. The highlighted letter is called a mnemonic because it is easy to remember: ***F*** for ***F**ile*, ***E*** for ***E**dit*, and so on.
- To move the highlight between choices listed on a pulled-down menu:
  - Press ↑ or ↓ to move from one choice to the next.
  - Press Home, ↑ or Home, ↓ to move the highlight to the first or last choice on the menu. You can also press End to move the highlight to the last choice.
- To select a command from a pulled-down menu:
  - Highlight one of the command names on the menu, and press Enter↵.
  - Press the highlighted letter in the command.
- To exit the menus without making a choice, press F1 or Esc.

When choosing commands from menus, keep the following points in mind:

- Choices in brackets, like *[Copy]*, cannot be selected at the point where you are in the operation. You cannot even move the highlight over a bracketed command.

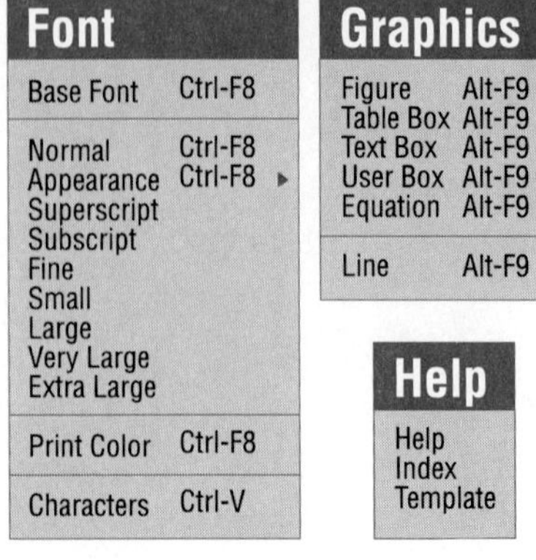

- Choices followed by an arrow head (➤), like *Appearance*, have submenus when you select them.

MENU BAR COMMANDS

To	Press
Display the menu bar	Alt-=
Remove the menu bar	F1
Pull down a highlighted menu	Enter← or ↓
Pull down a menu without highlighting it	Highlighted letter in its name
Choose highlighted command on a pulled-down menu	Enter←
Choose command on a pulled-down menu without highlighting it	Highlighted letter in its name
Exit menu without making a choice	Esc or F1

➤ EXERCISE

EXERCISE 1

LOCATING COMMANDS ON PULL-DOWN MENUS

Pull down menus and locate the commands listed in the Command column of the table "Menu Choices." In the Menu column, write down the menu on which the command is listed. In the Function Keys column, write down any function keys that are listed on the menu as an alternative way to execute the command.

MENU CHOICES

Command	Menu	Function Keys
Appearance	______	______
Base Font	______	______
Block	______	______
Copy	______	______
Delete	______	______
Exit	______	______
Go to	______	______
Line	______	______
List Files	______	______
Move	______	______
Page	______	______
Print	______	______
Replace	______	______
Retrieve	______	______
Save	______	______
Sort	______	______
Spell	______	______
Thesaurus	______	______

TOPIC 2C

Executing Commands—Using a Mouse

After completing this topic, you will be able to:

- Move the mouse pointer on the screen by moving the mouse
- Execute menu commands by clicking with the mouse

A Mouse
A mouse can have either two or three buttons.

WordPerfect supports a mouse that you can use for several procedures, including the following:

- Making menu choices from pull-down menus
- Moving the cursor through the document
- Selecting (blocking) text so that it can be copied, moved, deleted, or formatted

As you move the mouse around on a flat, smooth surface, it feeds electrical signals to the computer that move a mouse pointer on the screen so that you can point to items. When you use a mouse for the first time, you will experience some frustration. It seems hard to point to just the right place and to click or hold the button at the right time. Don't let these frustrations get you down; everyone experiences them. In a few days, you'll wonder how you ever got along without a mouse. However, once you have mastered it, you have to decide when to put it down. Many operations can be performed faster from the keyboard. Users who continually switch back and forth between the keyboard and the mouse actually work more slowly than those who think through the fastest approach to a task.

When you use a mouse, you roll it across the surface of the desk. This motion tells the mouse which way to move the mouse pointer on the screen. To make the mouse pointer move in a predictable direction, it is important that you hold the mouse so that it is oriented parallel to the middle line of the screen. This way, when you move the mouse up, down, or sideways, the mouse pointer moves in the expected direction. If you hold the mouse at an angle, your hand motion and the motion of the mouse pointer will not be coordinated.

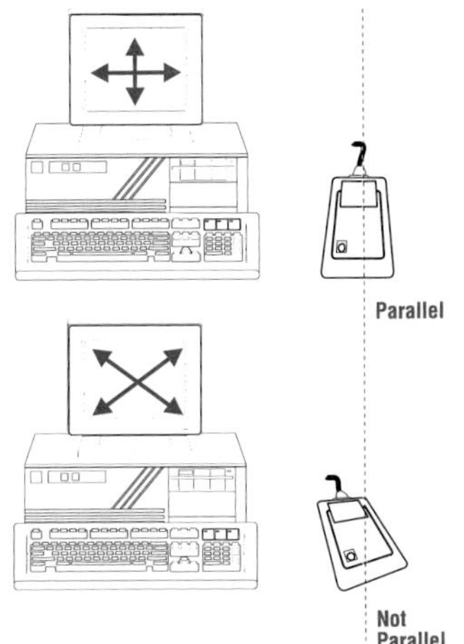

Holding and Dragging a Mouse
Hold the mouse parallel to the center line of the screen when rolling it about, and the movement of the mouse pointer will be more predictable.

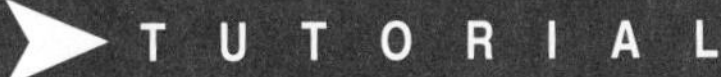

TUTORIAL

In this tutorial, you explore executing commands with a mouse.

GETTING STARTED

1. Load WordPerfect so that the Edit screen is displayed.
2. Insert the disk with your WordPerfect data files on it as follows:

BASIC MOUSE COMMANDS

When you use a mouse, here are some of the basic mouse terms to remember.

- The *mouse pointer* appears when you move the mouse and disappears when you press a key on the keyboard. The mouse pointer is not the same as the cursor. In fact, to move the cursor to where the mouse pointer is pointing, you have to click the mouse's left mouse button.
- *Point* means to position the mouse pointer over or on some item on the screen.
- *Clicking* refers to pressing one of the buttons on the mouse.
- *Drag* means to hold down one of the mouse buttons while you move the mouse. You do this frequently when you want to highlight a block of text so that you can format it. In other situations, this action drags the highlighted item to a new position on the screen.
- *Double clicking* refers to pressing one of the buttons on the mouse twice in rapid succession.

- On a hard disk system, insert the disk into drive A.
- On a floppy disk system, insert the disk into drive B.

PRACTICING WITH THE MOUSE

3. Roll the mouse around on the surface of your desk, and watch the mouse pointer appear and then move as you do so.
4. Make the pointer move vertically and horizontally.
5. Press one of the arrow keys to make the mouse pointer disappear.

RETRIEVING A FILE

6. Click the right mouse button to display the menu bar at the top of the screen.
7. Point to ***File*** on the menu bar, and click the left mouse button to pull down the menu.
8. Point to ***R****etrieve* and click the left mouse button. The prompt reads *Document to be retrieved:*.
9. Enter a command as follows:
   - On a hard disk system, type **A:OVERVIEW.WP5** and press Enter↵.
   - On a floppy disk system, type **B:OVERVIEW.WP5** and press Enter↵.

   The drive spins, and the document appears on the screen.

EXPLORING MENUS

10. With the cursor in the upper-left corner of the document, click the right mouse button to display the menu bar.
11. Point to ***L****ayout* and click the left mouse button to pull down the menu.
12. Point to ***L****ine* and click the left mouse button to display the Line Format menu that lists commands you use to format lines of text in a document.
13. Point to *6 - Line* ***S****pacing*, and click the left mouse button. The cursor jumps to the number *1* on the same line as the command.
14. Type **2** and press Enter↵. The cursor returns to the number *0* following the *Selection:* prompt.
15. Click both mouse buttons at the same time to remove the Line Format menu and back up to the Format menu.
16. Click both mouse buttons at the same time to back out of the menus completely, and the document is now double spaced on the screen.

MOVING THE CURSOR

17. Point to a place in the text and click the left mouse button to have the cursor jump to where you pointed. If no text is on the line that you click on, the cursor jumps to the left margin.
18. Point to other places and click the left mouse button.

SELECTING TEXT

19. Point to *U* at the beginning of the first line that reads *USING SOFTWARE.*
20. Hold down the left mouse button.
21. Drag the mouse until the cursor is to the right of the last character on the line and the entire heading is highlighted.
22. Release the left mouse button, and the paragraph remains highlighted. The words *Block on* flash at the lower left of the screen.
23. Press [F8] to underline the highlighted block. Depending on your system, you may or may not see the results on the screen.

SCROLLING THE SCREEN

24. Point to anywhere on the screen,
25. Hold down the right mouse button and drag the mouse downward, trying to move the mouse pointer off the lower edge of the screen. The document scrolls upward.
26. Hold down the right mouse button and drag the mouse upward, trying to move the mouse pointer off the upper edge of the screen. The document scrolls downward.

PRINTING A PAGE

27. Press [Home] twice, and then press [↑] to move the cursor to the top of the document.
28. Click the right mouse button to display the menu bar.
29. Point to ***F**ile* and click the left mouse button to pull down the menu.
30. Point to ***P**rint* and click the left mouse button to display the Print menu.
31. Point to *2 - **P**age* and click the left mouse button to print the page containing the cursor. The heading should be underlined and the document double spaced.

CLEARING THE SCREEN WITHOUT SAVING THE FILE

32. Click the right mouse button to display the menu bar.
33. Point to ***F**ile* and click the left mouse button to pull down the menu.
34. Point to *E**x**it* and click the left mouse button. The prompt reads *Save document? **Y**es (**N**o).*
35. Point to ***N**o* and click the left mouse button. The prompt reads *Exit WP? **N**o (**Y**es).*
36. Point to ***N**o* and click the left mouse button. The Edit screen is now blank.

FINISHING UP

37. You have now completed this tutorial. Either continue with the next activity or exit WordPerfect, turn off the computer, and remove your disk(s).

QUICK REFERENCE

When using a mouse, here are some of the basic commands to remember.

- To cancel a command, click the middle button on a three-button mouse, or hold down either button and click the other on a two-button mouse.
- If you are more than one level down in the menus, clicking both left and right mouse buttons together will back you up through the menus, one level at a time.
- To save time, double-click the left mouse button. This is the same as clicking the left mouse button and pressing Enter←. The first click highlights an item, and the second click selects it. For example, if a prompt like *Document to be saved: FILENAME* is displayed, double clicking on the filename following the prompt with the left mouse button displays the prompt *Replace FILENAME? **No** (**Y**es).*
- Clicking the right mouse button performs one of three procedures:
  - If a pull-down menu is displayed, you exit the menu.
  - If no menu is displayed, it displays the pull-down menu bar. Pressing it again removes the menu bar.
  - Holding down the button and dragging the mouse scrolls the document on the screen.
- Clicking the left mouse button performs several procedures:
  - It moves the cursor to the same position as the mouse pointer.
  - It highlights a menu item pointed to with the mouse pointer.
  - It removes the menu bar and any pulled-down menu if the mouse pointer is not positioned on a menu choice.

You can use a mouse to execute commands listed on the pull-down menus. To do so, you use the commands described in the table "Mouse Commands." For example, to display the menu bar, click the right mouse button, and click it again to remove the menu.

To pull down a menu from the menu bar, point to the menu's name and click the left mouse button. You can also point to any menu name, hold down the left mouse button, and then drag the mouse pointer along the menu bar to pull down other menus.

To select a command from a pulled-down menu (or any other menu), point to the command with the mouse pointer and click the left mouse button. You can also point to any command, hold down the left mouse button, and then drag the mouse pointer to highlight any other command. Once the desired command is highlighted, release the left mouse button.

To exit the menus without making a choice, point anywhere but to a command and click one of the buttons. If you are holding the left mouse button down to drag between choices, release it when not pointing to a command.

MOUSE COMMANDS

To	Do This
Displaying or Removing the Menu Bar	
Display the menu bar	Click right button
Remove the menu bar	Click right button
Pull Down Menu Choices	
Pull down a menu	Point to menu's name and click left button
Make a menu choice	Point to menu choice and click left button
Cancel a command	Hold down left button and click right button
Back up through menus	Click both buttons together
Exit a menu without choosing a command	Point outside of menu and click either button
Commands and Prompts	
Answer save and retrieve prompts	Double click on filename
Answer Yes/No prompts	Click on ***Yes*** or ***No***
Remove help screen	Click right button
Editing and Formatting	
Move the cursor to where the mouse pointer is	Click left button
Scroll the screen	Hold down right button and drag mouse pointer
Block text	Point to first character, hold down left button, and drag

EXERCISE

EXERCISE 1

PRACTICING WITH A MOUSE

Use your mouse to complete the following procedures. (Relax; it may take some practice before you feel comfortable with the mouse.)

1. Display the menu bar and then remove it from the screen.
2. Pull down the File menu and select *List **F**iles*. With the left mouse button, double click on the current directory that appears on the status line to display the List Files screen and menu. Press both buttons to return to the Edit screen.
3. Use the menu bar to display help and then return to the Edit screen.
4. Use the menu bar to exit the program.

TOPIC 3

Saving Documents & Clearing the Screen

After completing this topic, you will be able to:

- Save documents
- Change the default drive or directory
- Specify a path when saving files
- Clear the screen

You should frequently save the file you are working on. If you turn off the computer, experience a power failure, encounter hardware problems, or make a mistake, you may lose files that are in the computer's memory. Your files are not safe from these disasters until you save them onto a disk—a more permanent form of storage. When preparing a document, you should always save it:

- Before experimenting with unfamiliar commands
- Before making major revisions
- Before printing (in case something goes wrong during the process)
- Before exiting the program

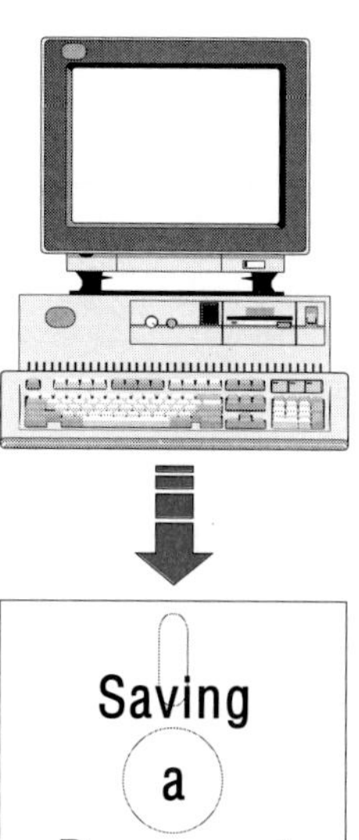

Saving a Document
Saving a document copies it from the computer's memory into a file on the disk.

When you work with application programs like WordPerfect, you save the files that you create onto a disk. On many systems, you save them to a hard disk. On others, especially those you use in school, you save them onto a floppy disk so that you can take your files with you. If you want to save your work onto a floppy disk, you usually insert it into drive A on a hard disk system or into drive B on a floppy disk system. You then use one of WordPerfect's commands to save the file on the screen onto the disk in the drive.

Before you can create a new document with WordPerfect, you must display a blank Edit screen. This happens automatically when you load the program. However, if you are already working on a document and want to create a new one, you first clear the current document from the screen. When you do so, you are given the option of saving or abandoning the document. When you do either, the screen is cleared, and you can then enter a new document. If you want to work on an existing document, you retrieve it onto the screen from the disk on which it is stored in a file.

There are also occasions when you do not want to save the file on the screen. For example, if you make a serious mistake, you may not want to overwrite the file on the disk with the one on the screen. In cases like this, you abandon the file. This removes it from the screen and the computer's memory, and it is lost. If you want to save it without affecting the version already on the disk, you can save it under a new filename.

TUTORIAL

In this tutorial, you explore saving, abandoning, and retrieving files.

GETTING STARTED

1. Load WordPerfect so that the Edit screen is displayed.
2. Insert the disk with your WordPerfect data files on it as follows:
   - On a hard disk system, insert the disk into drive A.
   - On a floppy disk system, insert the disk into drive B.

SAVING A NEW DOCUMENT AND LEAVING IT ON THE SCREEN

3. Type the paragraph of text shown in the figure "The MYFILE Document," then press [Enter←] twice and type your name. Don't worry about making mistakes or typos. You are not concerned at this point with the accuracy or content of the document.

The MYFILE Document
This figure shows the document that you enter to explore saving files in this tutorial.

> I won't be like everyone else. I will save my work frequently so that it won't be lost if the power fails, my computer dies, or I make a mistake. While others are crying about their loss, I'll smile and try not to look too superior.
>
> your name

4. Press [F10], and the prompt reads *Document to be saved:*. (If a screen with the heading *Document Summary* is displayed, press [Enter←] to display the prompt.)
5. Enter a command as follows:
   - On a hard disk system, type **A:MYFILE.WP5** and press [Enter←].
   - On a floppy disk system, type **B:MYFILE.WP5** and press [Enter←].

   The drive spins, and the document is saved onto the disk in the specified drive. The document remains displayed on the screen so that you can continue editing it.

SAVING A DOCUMENT A SECOND TIME

6. Press [F10] to save the document again, and the prompt reads *Document to be saved:* and suggests the name you assigned to the document the last time you saved it.
7. Press [Enter←] to accept the suggested filename, and the prompt reads *Replace x:\MYFILE.WP5?* ***No*** *(**Y**es).*
8. Press [Y], and the drive spins as the document is saved onto the disk.

CHANGING THE DEFAULT DRIVE

9. Press [F5], and the message reads *Dir* followed by the current directory.
10. Press [=] (the equal sign), and the prompt reads *New directory* = followed by the current directory.
11. Enter a command as follows:

- On a hard disk system, type **C:** and press [Enter↵].
- On a floppy disk system, type **A:** and press [Enter↵].

The message reads *Dir* followed by the current directory.

12. Press [F1] to return to the Edit screen, and the default drive is now drive C on a hard disk system or drive A on a floppy disk system.

SAVING A DOCUMENT AND CHANGING ITS NAME

13. Press [F10], and the prompt reads *Document to be saved: x:\MYFILE.WP5.*
14. Press [→] to move the cursor under the period that separates the filename and the extension.
15. Type **2**, and the prompt reads *Document to be saved: x:\MYFILE2.WP5.*
16. Press [Enter↵] to save the file, and you now have two copies of the file on the disk, one under the original name and one under the new name. The file was saved to the original drive even though you changed the default setting because that is the drive it had been retrieved from.

LOOKING AHEAD: DELETING FILES

The error message *Disk Full - Press any Key to Continue* appears when you try to save a file and there is no room for it on the disk. If this happens, either delete some files from the disk and try again, put a new disk into the drive and save the file, or if working from a hard disk, insert a disk into drive A and then save the file on that drive.

SAVING A FILE AND CLEARING THE SCREEN

17. Press [F7], and the prompt reads *Save document?* ***Yes*** *(**N**o).*
18. Press [Y], and the prompt reads *Document to be saved: x:\MYFILE2.WP5.*
19. Press [Enter↵], and the prompt reads *Replace x:\MYFILE2.WP5?* ***No*** *(**Y**es).*
20. Press [Y], and the prompt reads *Exit WP?* ***No*** *(**Y**es).*
21. Press [N], and the Edit screen is now blank.

FINISHING UP

22. You have now completed this tutorial. Either continue with the next activity or exit WordPerfect, turn off the computer, and remove your disk(s).

QUICK REFERENCE

When saving and retrieving files, you have to understand how to specify the drives and directories that you save files to and retrieve them from.

Saving Files and Clearing the Screen

When you save a file the first time, you must assign it a filename that follows DOS conventions. Filenames can have up to eight characters and be followed by an optional period and extension of up to three characters. WordPerfect does not automatically add extensions to files, but you can add your own. If you add the extension .WP5 to your files, you will always be able to identify the program used to create them. The table “Filename Characters” lists the characters that you can use in filenames and extensions.

You use the same command to clear the screen that you use to exit the program; you just respond differently to one of the prompts. When

The file's name can have up to eight characters

 . 

The file's extension must begin with a period and can have up to three characters

Filenames
Files can have a name of up to eight characters and an optional three-character extension separated from the name by a period. Adding the extension .WP5 to your files helps you identify the program that you used to create them.

Character	Example
Letters	A - Z
Letters	a - z
Numbers	0 - 9
Underscore	_
Caret	^
Dollar sign	$
Tilde	~
Exclamation point	!
Number sign	#
Percent sign	%
Ampersand	&
Hyphen	-
Braces	{ }
Parentheses	( )
At sign	@
Grave accent	`
Apostrophe	'

Filename Characters
You can use any of the characters shown here in your file names and extensions.

you press F7 to exit WordPerfect, you have two choices to make when the prompts read *Save document? **Yes** (**N**o)* and *Exit WP? **No** (**Y**es)*.

1. When the prompt reads *Save document? **Yes** (**N**o)*, you normally press Y to save the file. However, if you have already saved it and then made no additional changes, you press N to abandon it. You also press N if you do not want to save the file.
2. When the prompt reads *Exit WP? **No** (**Y**es)*, if you want to work on a new document, press N to clear the screen. If you want to exit the program, press Y to return to the operating system.

→ KEY/Strokes

Saving a File and Leaving It on the Screen

1. Either: Press F10.
   Or: Pull down the File menu and select ***S**ave*.
   The prompt reads *Document to be saved:*. (If a screen with the heading *Document Summary* is displayed, press Enter↵ to display the prompt.)
2. Either: Type a filename and press Enter↵ to save a new file.
   Or: Press Enter↵ if the file's name is displayed following the prompt. The prompt reads *Replace* followed by the path and filename. Press Y to save the file under the current name or press N to edit the filename.

→ KEY/Strokes

Saving a File and Clearing It from the Screen

1. Either: Press F7.
   Or: Pull down the File menu and select *E**x**it*.
   The prompt reads *Save document? **Yes** (**N**o)*.
   - If the document has not been revised since it was last saved, a message on the status line reads *(Text was not modified)*.
   - If a screen with the heading *Document Summary* is displayed, press Enter↵ to display the prompt.
2. Press Y, and the prompt reads *Document to be saved:*.
3. Either: Type a name for the file and press Enter↵ if no name is suggested or you want to save it under a different name.
   Or: Press Enter↵ to save the file under the suggested name if you had saved the file previously, and the prompt reads *Replace FILENAME? **No** (**Y**es)*. Press Y to continue.
   The prompt reads *Exit WP? **No** (**Y**es)*.
4. Press N to stay in the WordPerfect program and clear the screen.

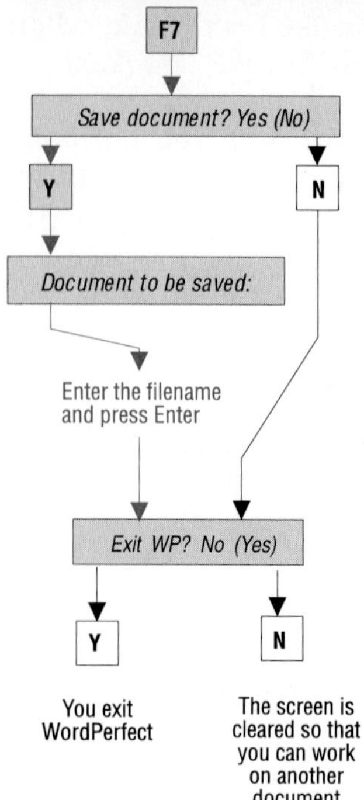

Saving and Clearing Options
When you press F7 to exit WordPerfect, you can save the document on the screen and then either exit the program or clear the screen to work on a new document.

→ KEY/Strokes

Clearing the Screen Without Saving a Document

1. Either: Press F7.
   Or: Pull down the *File* menu and select *Exit.*
   The prompt reads *Save document? **Yes** (**No**).*
   (If the document has not been revised since it was last saved, a message on the status line reads *(Text was not modified)*, so nothing is lost by abandoning it.)
2. Press N, and the prompt reads *Exit WP? **No** (**Yes**).*
3. Press N to clear the document from the screen and remain in the program.

Specifying Drives and Directories

WordPerfect saves files to the default drive and the default directory unless you specify otherwise. You can specify a drive and directory in one of three ways:

- You can specify a path in the Save command. When the prompt asks you to enter a filename, you can specify a drive and directory in front of the filename. For example, to save a file named JOHN.WP5 to a subdirectory named LETTERS on drive C, you would type **C:\LETTERS\JOHN.WP5** and press Enter←.
- You can change the default drive and directory for the session. This is the easiest approach because you need not specify the path when saving files. (To see what the default drive is, you can press F5. The current drive is listed at the left end of the status line. Press F1 to remove the message.)
- You can specify a permanent default drive or directory for all files. After doing so, you can save files to another drive or directory only by changing this setting, overriding this setting with the List Files menu, or by adding a path in front of the filename when saving a file.

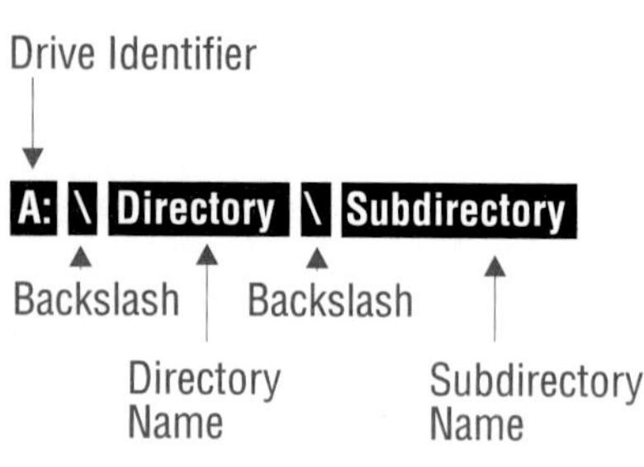

Paths
When you save a file, you can specify a path to save it on a drive or in a directory that is not the current default.

SPECIFYING A NEW PATH OR FILENAME WHEN YOU SAVE A FILE

Whenever you save a file, the prompt reads *Document to be saved:*. The first time you save a file, you type its name and press Enter←. When you save a file again, the program anticipates that you want to save it under the same name on the same drive and directory and displays that suggestion. You can press Enter← to accept the suggestion, or you can redirect the document into a new drive or directory, save it under a new filename, or both. To do so, you specify a new path and filename or edit the one displayed following the prompt.

- To specify a new path and filename, type them in. The first character that you type deletes the entire suggested path and filename.
- To edit the suggested path, press Ins or → to enter edit mode. Then press ← and → to move the cursor through the line of text, inserting or deleting characters.

When you have finished entering or editing the path and filename, press Enter←.

➔ KEY/Strokes

Changing the Default Drive or Directory for a Session

1. Either: Press F5.
   Or: Pull down the ***F****ile* menu and select *List* ***F****iles.*
   The message reads *Dir* followed by the current directory.
2. Press = (the equal sign), and the prompt reads *New directory* = followed by the current directory.
3. Set your drives and directories as follows:
   - On a hard disk system, type the drive and directory (for example, **C:\LETTERS**), or type **A:** to save files to the floppy drive.
   - On a floppy disk system, type **B:** to save files to drive B.
4. Press Enter↵, and the message reads *Dir* followed by the path of the new default drive and directory.
   (If you enter a path that does not exist, a prompt asks if you want to create it. To create a new directory, press Y; to cancel the command, press N.)
5. Either: Press F1 to return to the Edit screen.
   Or: Press Enter↵ to display the List Files screen.

➔ KEY/Strokes

Specifying a Permanent Drive or Directory for Files

1. Press ⇧Shift-F1 to display the Setup menu.
2. Press L (for ***L****ocation of Files*).
3. Press D (for ***D****ocuments*), and the cursor jumps to the directory-listing space on the same line as the command.
4. Type in the drive (and directory) that you want to use for the default and press Enter↵.
5. Press F7 to return to the Edit screen.

The Document Summary Screen

WordPerfect's default settings can be changed so that a document summary form is displayed whenever you save a file or exit the program. The information you enter on the summary sheet can help you locate the document later. When the Document Summary screen is displayed, you press 1 though 7 (or any of the highlighted letters in the command names) to select each entry that you want to make. Enter the information, and press Enter↵. (Press F7 when you have finished entering the abstract.) Press F7 to save your entries and return to the Edit screen.

TOPIC 3

KEY/Strokes

Turning Document Summaries On and Off

1. Press Shift-F1 to display the Setup menu.
2. Press E (for ***E**nvironment*).
3. Press D (for ***D**ocument Management/Summary*).
4. Press C (for ***C**reate Summary on Save/Exit*).
5. Press Y (for ***Y**es*) or N (for ***N**o*).
6. Press F7 to return to the Edit screen.

EXERCISE

EXERCISE 1

SAVING SOME OF YOUR OWN FILES

1. Enter a paragraph or two of your own, perhaps copied from this text.
2. Save the file as ERASE1.WP5.
3. Save the file again as ERASE2.WP5.
4. Clear the screen.

TOPIC 4

Retrieving Documents

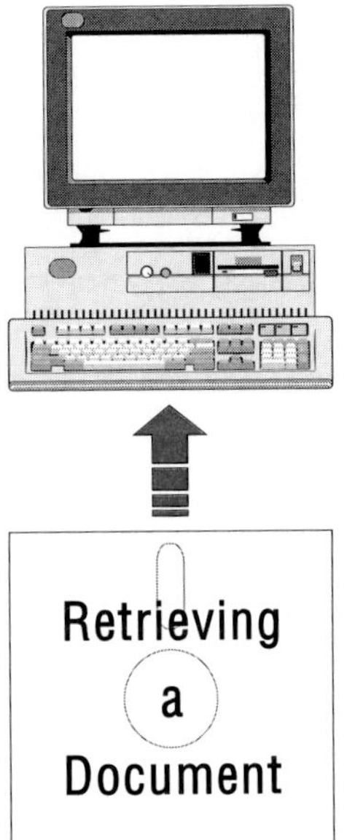

Retrieving Files
When you retrieve a file, it is copied from its file on the disk into the computer's memory and displayed on the screen.

After completing this topic, you will be able to:

- Retrieve files by entering their name
- Retrieve files by selecting their name from the List Files screen and menu

To work on an existing document, you retrieve it onto the screen from the disk on which it is stored. Before retrieving a file:

1. Save any file that is currently displayed on the screen if you want to retrieve it later.
2. Clear the screen so that the file you retrieve is not merged into the one on the screen.
3. If the file was saved onto a floppy disk, insert that disk into one of the computer's disk drives.

When the file is retrieved, the disk drive operates as the computer copies the file from the disk into the computer's memory. The file is then displayed on the screen for you to edit. The copy of the file on the disk remains unchanged until you change the document on the screen and save it back onto the disk.

TUTORIAL

In this tutorial, you explore retrieving files by entering their name or selecting them from a list of files.

GETTING STARTED

1. Load WordPerfect, or clear the screen so that the blank Edit screen is displayed.
2. Insert the disk with your WordPerfect data files on it as follows:
   - On a hard disk system, insert the disk into drive A.
   - On a floppy disk system, insert the disk into drive B.

RETRIEVING A FILE BY ENTERING ITS NAME

3. Press Shift-F10, and the prompt reads *Document to be retrieved:*.
4. Enter a command as follows:
   - On a hard disk system, type **A:MYFILE.WP5** and press Enter.
   - On a floppy disk system, type **B:MYFILE.WP5** and press Enter.

The document appears on the screen just as it was when you saved it.

ABANDONING THE DOCUMENT

5. Press F7, and the prompt reads *Save document?* ***Yes*** *(**N**o)*.
6. Press N, and the prompt reads *Exit WP?* ***No*** *(**Y**es)*.
7. Press N, and the document you were working on is cleared from the screen. However, you remain in the program so that you can enter your own document or retrieve an existing one.

CHANGING THE DEFAULT DRIVE AND DISPLAYING THE LIST FILES SCREEN

8. Press F5, and the message reads *Dir* followed by the current directory.
9. Press = (the equal sign), and the prompt reads *New directory* = followed by the current directory.
10. Enter a command as follows:
    - On a hard disk system, type **A:** and press Enter←.
    - On a floppy disk system, type **B:** and press Enter←.

    The message reads *Dir* followed by the path of the new default drive and directory.
11. Press Enter← again to display a list of the files on the new default drive.

The List Files Screen and Menu
The List Files screen displays the names of the files, their extensions, their size (in bytes), and the date and time they were last saved. Any subdirectory is listed followed by *<Dir>* in the size column. A header indicates the current date and time, the name of the directory, the size of the document currently on the screen, the number of bytes on the disk that are still free and the number already used, and the number of files on the disk or in the directory. The List Files menu at the bottom of the screen lists choices used in file management.

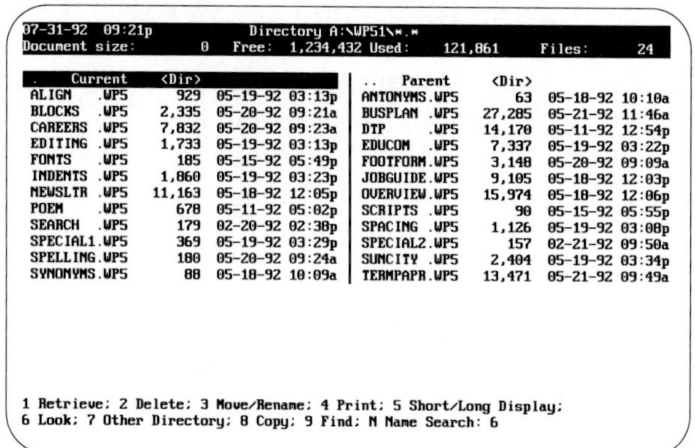

PREVIEWING AND RETRIEVING FILES

12. Press the arrow keys to move the highlight over the file *MYFILE.WP5*.
13. Press L (for ***Look***), and the contents of the file are displayed on the screen so that you can check it (but you cannot edit it).

The Look Command
You can use the Look command on the List Files menu to preview the contents of a file on the disk before you retrieve it.

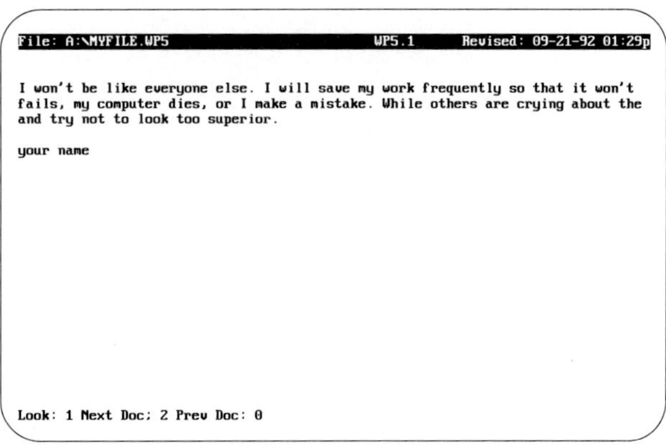
```
File: A:\MYFILE.WP5                    WP5.1      Revised: 09-21-92 01:29p

I won't be like everyone else. I will save my work frequently so that it won't
fails, my computer dies, or I make a mistake. While others are crying about the
and try not to look too superior.

your name

Look: 1 Next Doc; 2 Prev Doc: 0
```

14. Press [F7], and you return to the List Files screen and menu.
15. Press [R] (for ***R****etrieve*), and the file appears on the screen.

FINISHING UP

16. Clear the current document from the screen without saving it, but remain in the program.
17. You have now completed this tutorial. Either continue with the next activity or exit WordPerfect, turn off the computer, and remove your disk(s).

QUICK REFERENCE

When retrieving files, you must understand how to specify the drives and directories that you save files to and retrieve them from.

Retrieving Files

To retrieve a file, press [Shift]-[F10] or pull down the File menu and select ***R****etrieve*, and then enter the name of the file. WordPerfect retrieves files from the default drive and directory unless you specify otherwise. You can specify a drive and directory for retrieving files in the same three ways you use to save files.

- You can change the default drive and directory. This is the easiest approach because you need not specify the path when retrieving files. (To see what the default drive is, you can press [F5]. The current drive is listed at the left end of the status line. Press [F1] to remove the message.)
- You can specify a path in the Retrieve command. When the prompt asks you to enter a filename, you can specify a drive and directory in front of the filename. For example, to retrieve a file named JOHN.WP5 from a subdirectory named LETTERS on drive C, you would type **C:\LETTERS\JOHN.WP5** and press [Enter].
- You can specify a default drive for documents by changing the Location of Files setting on the Setup menu ([Shift]-[F1]).

→ KEY/Strokes

Retrieving a File by Entering Its Name

1. Either: Press Shift-F10.
   Or: Pull down the ***File*** menu and select ***R**etrieve.*
   The prompt reads *Document to be retrieved:*.
2. Type the path if the desired file is not in the current directory, followed by the file's name and extension, and press Enter.
   If you enter a filename that WordPerfect cannot find, the message reads *ERROR: File not found.* If you wait a second, the prompt *Document to be retrieved:* reappears. You can either edit the filename or path or press F1 to cancel the command.

Using List Files to Retrieve Files

WordPerfect's List Files screen and menu simplifies retrieving files and lists many other commands you can use to simplify your work. To display the List Files screen, just press F5 and press Enter or pull down the File menu and select *List **F**iles.*

Moving Around the List Files Screen

When the List Files screen is displayed, an arrow at the top or bottom of the vertical center line indicates that more files are listed in that direction. To see them, press ↑ or ↓, PgUp or PgDn, or the + and - keys on the numeric keypad (with NumLock turned off). To move to the top or bottom of the list, press Home twice, and then press ↑ or ↓.

To move the highlight to a specific file, use the arrow keys or press N (for ***N**ame Search*), and the prompt reads *(Name Search; Enter or arrows to Exit).* Begin typing the file's name. As you type each character, the highlight moves closer to the file. (You can press ←Bksp to delete characters as you type.) When you have typed enough characters to uniquely identify the file, it is highlighted. Press Enter to back up to the menu again.

To see a list of files in a different directory, highlight the directory's name, and press Enter twice. (The directory listed as *Parent <Dir>* is the directory one level up.)

To make the current directory the default directory, highlight *Current <Dir>*, press O (for ***O**ther Directory*), and press Enter twice.

To change the default directory or create a new one, you can also press O (for ***O**ther Directory*), type the new directory (for example, **C:\LETTERS**), and press Enter. If the directory you specify does not exist, the prompt reads *Create:* followed by the name of the directory and the prompt ***N**o (**Y**es).* Press Y to create a new directory.

Retrieving Files

To retrieve a file when the List Files screen is displayed, highlight its name on the list of filenames and press R (for ***R**etrieve*). If a document is already on the screen, the prompt reads *Retrieve into current document? **N**o (**Y**es).* If you press Y, the document on the disk is retrieved into the document on the screen at the cursor's position. At times, you want to do this to assemble a new document from documents already on the disk or to copy text from one document to another.

However, if you press [Y] by mistake, your document on the screen will be expanded by the addition of the document from the disk and you will then have to delete the addition from your file.

If a disk or directory has a lot of files, you can look at just selected ones using wildcards. For example, when you press [F5], the prompt reads *Dir* followed by the current path and then **.**. The **.** is called a filename specification, and it tells WordPerfect to display files with any file name or any extension. To display just selected files, use the question mark or asterisk wildcards.

- The question mark can be used to substitute for any single character.
- The asterisk is more powerful; it represents any character in a given position and all following characters.

For example, if you change the *.* to CHPT?.* all files that begin with CHPT and have one other character are listed when you press [Enter←]. For example, it would list the files CHPT1.DOC, CHPT2.BAK, CHPT3.DOC, and so on.

If you have already displayed the List Files screen, you can change the filename specification by highlighting *Current <Dir>* and pressing [Enter←]. When the message reads *Dir X*.** revise the filename specification. For example, type **B:*.WP5** and press [Enter←] to list all the files on drive B that end with the extension .WP5.

→ KEY/Strokes

Retrieving Files from the List Files Screen and Menu

1. Either: Press [F5] and then press [Enter←].
   Or: Pull down the ***File*** menu and select *List **F**iles.*
2. Highlight the desired file's name.
3. Press [R] (for ***R**etrieve*).

Previewing Files or Directories

To preview the contents of a file that does not contain a document summary, highlight it and then press either [L] (for ***L**ook*) or [Enter←]. (If a document does have a document summary with more than just the name and type, the document summary is displayed instead of the document. To see the document's contents, press [L]—for ***L**ook at text.*) The Look command does not actually load the entire file, so you cannot edit it. It does, however, provide a way for you quickly to scan the contents of several files until you find the one you want. The top of the screen tells you the file's name and size in bytes. If the document is longer than the screen:

- Press [↑] or [↓], or the [+] or [-] key on the numeric keypad with [NumLock] turned off, to scroll through it.
- Press [S] to start and stop continuous scrolling. (You can also press just [S] to stop scrolling.)
- Press [Home] twice, and then press one of the directional arrow keys to move to one of the four edges of the document.
- Press [End] to display the right side of a document that is too wide for the screen.

- Use the Search commands to move the cursor to a specific line in the document.

To view additional documents, you can press PgUp or PgDn or press N (for ***N**ext Doc*) or P (for ***P**rev Doc*) on the Look menu.

You can also highlight a directory (indicated by *<Dir>*) and press Enter← or L (for ***L**ook*). The prompt reads *Dir* followed by the name of the directory. Press Enter← to look at the files in the directory. You can then retrieve a file or press F7 or Spacebar to return to the Edit screen.

Printing a List of Files

When the List Files screen is displayed, you can press ⇧Shift-F7 to print out a list of the files.

EXERCISES

EXERCISE 1

LOADING WORDPERFECT AND RETRIEVING A FILE

When you load WordPerfect, you can automatically retrieve a file by typing the command **WP** *<filename>*. For example, to retrieve a file named EXAMPLE.WP5 from a disk in drive A, type **WP A:EXAMPLE.WP5**. Do this now, and retrieve the document named MYFILE.WP5. Since the file exists, it is retrieved onto the screen after WordPerfect is loaded. When you are finished, press F7 to exit. Then press N twice to clear the screen but remain in the program.

EXERCISE 2

RETRIEVING AND SAVING FILES TO CONVERT AND REFORMAT THEM

There are a number of files on the original *Student Resource Disk* that you should have copied to your own data disk. You use these files in the tutorials, exercises, projects, and applications in this text. Having them on the disk saves you time—you do not have to type them in. To save room on the disk, many of these files have been saved in an ASCII format and must be retrieved and then saved to convert them to WordPerfect format on the disk.

1. Follow the instructions in the KEY/Stroke box "Retrieving Files from the List Files Screen and Menu" to retrieve each of the files listed in the table "Files Supplied on the Student Resource Disk" to be sure they are there and you know how to retrieve them.
2. After looking at each of them, save the files so that they are on the disk in WordPerfect's format (or you cannot print them from the disk later).
3. Check each file's name off in the table after you save it, and then clear the screen before retrieving the next file.

FILES SUPPLIED ON THE STUDENT RESOURCE DISK

Filename	Retrieved
ALIGN.WP5	
ANTONYMS.WP5	
BLOCKS.WP5	
EDITING.WP5	
EDUCOM.WP5	
FONTS.WP5	
FOOTFORM.WP5	
INDENTS.WP5	
JOBGUIDE.WP5	
NEWSLTR.WP5	
POEM.WP5	
SCRIPTS.WP5	
SEARCH.WP5	
SPACING.WP5	
SPECIAL1.WP5	
SPECIAL2.WP5	
SPELLING.WP5	
SUNCITY.WP5	
SYNONYMS.WP5	

CHAPTER 1 REVIEW

- With a program like WordPerfect, you can prepare memos, letters, and reports.
- Programs like WordPerfect are so powerful that you can use them to desktop-publish documents such as catalogs, advertisements, and even books.
- You can load WordPerfect from a floppy or hard disk. To do so, you change to the drive or directory containing the WP.EXE file, type **WP** and press Enter←.
- The Edit screen contains a cursor and a status line. The status line indicates the cursor's position by page and distance from the top and left edges of the paper.
- The *Pos* indicator changes to *POS* when CapsLock is engaged and flashes when NumLock is engaged.
- To exit WordPerfect, press F7 and then answer a series of questions about saving the document on the screen and exiting the program.
- To display help at any point, press F3. To then return to the Edit screen, press Spacebar, Enter←, or 0.
- On floppy disk systems, you will occasionally be prompted to swap disks since the entire program is too large to fit on a single disk.
- You execute most commands by pressing function keys, either alone or in combination with Ctrl, ⇧Shift, and Alt. Many of these commands display menus listing choices that you can make.
- When you use Ctrl, ⇧Shift, or Alt with a function key to enter a command, you hold down Ctrl, ⇧Shift, or Alt while you press the function key. Holding the function key down may cause some commands to repeat.
- To select menu commands, you can press the number (and occasionally, a letter) that precedes the command or the highlighted letter in the command's name.
- To back up through menus, you press 0. To return directly to the Edit screen, you press F7.
- To cancel a command before you complete it, you press F1.
- To answer a prompt, you type a response and press Enter←. If the prompt displays an entry you typed in earlier, you can just press Enter← to accept it.
- To display the pull-down menu bar, you press Alt-= or click the right mouse button.
- To pull down menus from the menu bar, you highlight the menu's name and press Enter← or just press the highlighted letter in the menu's name.
- To select a command with the mouse, you point to it with the mouse pointer and click the left mouse button.
- To save a file, you must assign it a filename with up to eight characters and an optional period and extension with up to three characters.
- You can change a default setting so that a summary sheet is displayed each time you save a new file or exit the program.

- Files are normally saved on the default drive, the one that was the default when you loaded the program. To save files to another drive, you can add a path in front of the filename or specify a default drive or directory for all document files.
- When saving a file, you can leave it on the screen or clear it from the screen.
- To clear the screen, you press F7 and answer No to the prompt that asks if you want to exit WordPerfect.
- You can retrieve a file by pressing Shift-F10 and entering its name or by pressing F5 to display the List Files menu and then selecting it from there.
- When the List Files screen is displayed, you can use the cursor movement keys such as the arrow keys and PgUp and PgDn to display additional files if the screen is full.

CHAPTER 1

QUESTIONS

FILL IN THE BLANK

1. To load WordPerfect, you type ___________ and press Enter.
2. To determine the exact position of the cursor, you look at the ___________ line.
3. When the *Pos* indicator is uppercase (*POS*), it means that ___________ is engaged.
4. When the *Pos* indicator is flashing, it means that ___________ is engaged.
5. To exit WordPerfect, you press ___________.
6. To execute commands, you can press ___________ keys.
7. Before pressing a function key, you can hold down ___________, ___________, or ___________ to execute additional commands.
8. To select a command from a menu, you can press either the ___________ that precedes the choice or the highlighted ___________ in the command.
9. To display the menu bar, you press ___________.
10. To save a file, you press either ___________ or ___________.
11. To retrieve a file, you press either ___________ or ___________.
12. To display the List Files screen, you press ___________.

MATCH THE COLUMNS

1. WP	__ Retrieves a file
2. *Pos* indicator	__ Command that loads the WordPerfect program
3. F7	__ Indicates where the next character that you type will appear
4. F3	__ Saves a file
5. F1	

6. Alt-=
7. F5
8. F10
9. Shift-F10
10. Cursor
11. Status line
12. Mouse pointer

__ Used with a mouse to point to things on the screen
__ Displays the menu bar
__ Indicates the position of the cursor
__ Displays List Files
__ Indicates the status of the NumLock and CapsLock keys
__ Exits menus and the program
__ Displays help screens
__ Cancels commands

WRITE OUT THE ANSWERS

1. What are word processing programs used for?
2. If you are loading WordPerfect from a floppy disk, which disk should you insert first if your program disk is not a system disk? Why?
3. What steps would you follow to load WordPerfect from a floppy disk drive?
4. What steps would you follow to load WordPerfect from a hard disk?
5. What steps do you follow to exit WordPerfect?
6. If you are quitting for the day, what steps should you take?
7. What is the keyboard template? What do the colors indicate?
8. What are help screens? How do you display them?
9. What are function keys? What is their purpose?
10. What are the Ctrl, Alt, and Shift keys used for? How do you use them?
11. What is a pull-down menu? How do you display one?
12. What keys do you press to make menu choices?
13. What key do you press to have the computer accept any menu choices you have made and return directly to the document screen?
14. What key do you press to back up through menus? To cancel a command?
15. What is a prompt? How do you answer prompts?
16. What happens to a file you are working on if you turn off the computer without first saving the file onto a disk?
17. List four stages at which it is prudent to save your files.
18. What two commands can you use to save a file? How do they differ?
19. Which of the following filenames are acceptable to DOS? If not acceptable, why not?

[FILE].DOC	ABC.ABC	A.A	STANFORDS.WP5
1.1	1.1234	LETTER	MEMO.*

20. Assume that you are writing three term papers for each of your classes on a computer. List the filename you would assign to each paper so that you could later identify the course and the papers.
21. Why would you want to abandon a file instead of saving it?

22. You are working on a document named MEMO.DOC and want to save it on a disk or in a directory other than the default. For each of the following, what path and filename would you specify when the prompt reads *Document to be saved:*?

To Save the File on Drive	Directory	I Would Specify This Path
B:	None	________________
A:	None	________________
C:	None	________________
C:	LETTERS	________________
C:	LETTERS\1987	________________

23. What command do you use to retrieve a file from the disk?
24. What command do you use to display the List Files screen and menu?

CHAPTER 1 PROJECTS

PROJECT 1

VIEWING A VIDEO

Many videocassettes about WordPerfect are available. Obtain one of these from your school or public library or from a video rental store and watch it. These videos give you an overview of the procedures offered by the program.

PROJECT 2

PREVIEWING THE PROJECT DOCUMENT FILES

You will use the DTP.WP5 and CAREERS.WP5 files on the *Student Resource Disk* in the end-of-chapter projects in this text. These files should have been copied to your own data disk when you completed Exercise 2 in Topic 1. Retrieve each of these files, and then save them again so that they are converted to the WordPerfect format.

CHAPTER 2

Basic Entering, Editing, & Printing

TOPIC 5

Entering Documents

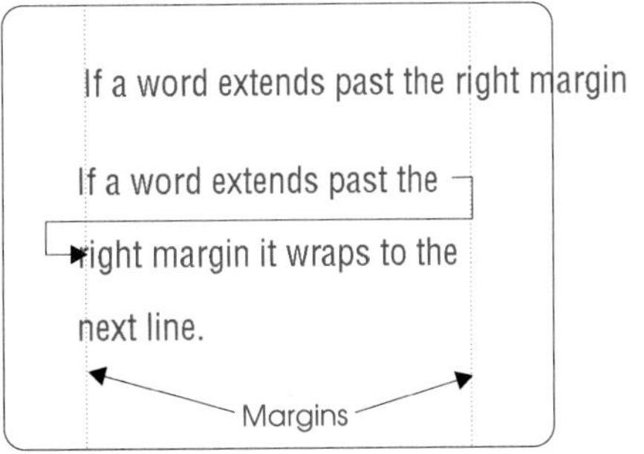

Word Wrap
When you reach the end of a line, the program calculates whether the word you are entering will fit on the line. If it will not fit, the program moves, or wraps, the entire word to the beginning of the next line.

After completing this topic, you will be able to:
- Enter text and correct mistakes
- Explain the difference between hard and soft carriage returns
- Describe how the screen scrolls as you enter text
- Boldface and underline text as you enter it
- Enter special characters

Entering text with WordPerfect is no more difficult than typing it on a typewriter; in many ways, it is easier. With both, you use the keyboard to enter letters, numbers, and symbols. When you open a new document, the cursor rests in the upper-left corner of the screen. As you type a character, the character appears where the cursor is, and the cursor then moves one space to the right.

When you are typing paragraphs, you do not have to press Enter↵ at the end of each line. WordPerfect has a feature, called word wrap, that automatically does this for you. When the end of a line is reached, the word processing program calculates whether the word being entered fits on the line. If it will not fit, the program automatically begins a new line of text by moving the entire word to the next line.

TUTORIAL

NOTE

In this activity, and all later activities, the following things are assumed when you begin:
- The program is loaded and the Edit screen is clear of other documents.
- The data disk on which you save your files is in the default drive.

In this tutorial, you enter text and then save the file. You also underline and boldface some of the text. Relax while you do this tutorial. You can edit the document in later tutorials or even clear the screen and start over.

GETTING STARTED

1. Type in the text for the document shown in the figure "The ENTERING Document—The Body Text." As you enter the document:
   - Notice how the cursor moves as you type. It indicates where the next character you type will appear.

- Do not press Enter↵ at the end of lines. WordPerfect's word-wrap feature automatically does that for you. Press Enter↵ only at the end of the first paragraph to end it. Press Enter↵ one more time to insert a blank line before entering the second paragraph.
- Your lines will probably wrap at places other than the ones shown in the figure; don't worry if they do. Where they wrap depends on your system.
- If you make any typos, press ←Bksp to back up the cursor to erase them, and then enter the correct letter(s).

The ENTERING Document—The Body Text
This figure shows the document that you enter in this tutorial.

> Word processing is probably the most common application of microcomputers. The ease with which you can draft and revise memos, letters, reports, and numerous other documents with a word processing program increases both the speed and the quality of your writing. You can enter, edit, change, reorganize, format, and print text without having to retype all of it each time you make a change. This ease of use encourages you to revise and reorganize your material more frequently so that you can express your ideas more clearly.
>
> There are many word processing programs on the market. They differ from one another in the ease with which you can edit text and in the capacities of the program, especially with respect to formatting documents for printing.

2. Save the document on your data disk under the filename ENTERING.WP5 but leave it on the screen.

ENTERING A HEADING USING BOLDFACING AND UNDERLINING

3. Press Home twice, and then press ↑ to move the cursor to the top of the document.
4. Press Enter↵ to insert a blank line.
5. Press ↑ to move the cursor to the blank line.
6. Press F6 to begin boldfacing, and then press CapsLock to enter all uppercase letters.
7. Type **AN INTRODUCTION TO WORD PROCESSING** and then press F6 to end boldfacing. The words you boldfaced should stand out from the rest of the text. If they do not, adjust your screen's brightness and contrast. If that doesn't make them stand out, your system has not been set up to display boldfaced text.
8. Press Enter↵ to move the cursor down one line.
9. Press F8 to begin underlining.
10. Type your name, and then press F8 to end underlining and CapsLock to stop entering all uppercase letters. The words you underlined should stand out from the rest of the text. If they do not, adjust your screen's brightness and contrast. If that doesn't make them stand out, your system has not been set up to display underlined text.
11. Press Enter↵ to move the cursor down one line.
12. Press F6 to begin boldfacing, and then press F8 to begin underlining.
13. Type today's date (for example, **January 21, 1993**).
14. Press F6 to end boldfacing, and then press F8 to end underlining.

15. Press [Enter ↵], and the words you boldfaced and underlined should stand out from the rest of the text. The document should look like the one in the figure "The ENTERING Document—The Heading."

The ENTERING Document—The Heading
This figure shows the document after you have added a heading.

> **AN INTRODUCTION TO WORD PROCESSING**
> [your name]
> **[today's date]**
>
> Word processing is probably the most common application of microcomputers. The ease with which you can draft and revise memos, letters, reports, and numerous other documents with a word processing program increases both the speed and the quality of your writing. You can enter, edit, change, reorganize, format, and print text without having to retype all of it each time you make a change. This ease of use encourages you to revise and reorganize your material more frequently so that you can express your ideas more clearly.
>
> There are many word processing programs on the market. They differ from one another in the ease with which you can edit text and in the capacities of the program, especially with respect to formatting documents for printing.

ENTERING SPECIAL CHARACTERS

16. Press [Home] twice, and then press [↓] to move the cursor to the end of the document.
17. Position the cursor one character to the right of the last period, press [Spacebar] twice, and type in the sentence shown in the figure "The ENTERING Document—The Special Characters" that begins "For example."

The ENTERING Document—The Special Characters
This figure shows the document after you have added the sentence on special characters and the four examples.

> **AN INTRODUCTION TO WORD PROCESSING**
> [your name]
> **[today's date]**
>
> Word processing is probably the most common application of microcomputers. The ease with which you can draft and revise memos, letters, reports, and numerous other documents with a word processing program increases both the speed and the quality of your writing. You can enter, edit, change, reorganize, format, and print text without having to retype all of it each time you make a change. This ease of use encourages you to revise and reorganize your material more frequently so that you can express your ideas more clearly.
>
> There are many word processing programs on the market. They differ from one another in the ease with which you can edit text and in the capacities of the program, especially with respect to formatting documents for printing. For example, the WordPerfect program makes it easy to enter special characters such as:
>
> The copyright symbol ©
> The registration symbol ®
> A one-half character ½
> A square bullet ■

18. Press Enter twice to insert a blank line.
19. Type **The copyright symbol** and then press Spacebar.
20. Press Ctrl-V, and the prompt reads *Key* =.
21. Type **4,23** and press Enter twice; first to enter the symbol and then to move the cursor down a line. On some systems, the symbol is displayed. If the character cannot be displayed on your screen, you will see a square symbol, but the character may still print correctly.
22. Repeat Steps 19 through 21, but enter the new description for each special character and type the numbers **4,22** (for the registration symbol), **4,17** (for the one-half character), and **4,2** (for the square bullet).

PRINTING A DOCUMENT

23. Save the document again, but leave it on the screen.
24. Press Shift-F7 to display the Print menu.
25. Press F (for ***Full** Document*) to print the document. Notice the following about the printout:
    - The left edge of the printed document starts 1 inch in from the left edge of the paper and 1 inch down from the top edge of the paper.
    - The right margin is justified, that is, evenly aligned.
    - The lines in the heading should be boldfaced, underlined, or boldfaced and underlined.
    - The special characters that you entered should be printed at the bottom of the document.

FINISHING UP

26. You have now completed this tutorial. Either continue with the next activity or quit the program.

QUICK REFERENCE

With WordPerfect, you enter text, including letters, shifted characters, numbers, spaces, and carriage returns. You can also correct mistakes as you go along or boldface and underline text to make it stand out.

Entering Letters, Numbers, and Symbols

You can enter letters, numbers, and shifted characters such as % and &.

To enter uppercase letters, either hold down Shift while typing a letter or press CapsLock to enter all uppercase letters. (The *Pos* indicator on the status line changes to an all-uppercase *POS* when CapsLock is engaged.) Press CapsLock again to return to lowercase. (The *POS* indicator on the status line changes to *Pos* when CapsLock is not engaged.) If you press Shift to enter text when CapsLock is engaged, you enter lowercase letters.

To enter numbers, either use the number keys on the top row of the keyboard or use the numeric keypad. On some computers, the keys on the numeric keypad also move the cursor. When NumLock is engaged, the

Pos indicator flashes, and pressing the keys enters numbers. When NumLock is not engaged, the *Pos* indicator does not flash, and pressing the keys moves the cursor. Some keyboards also have lights that indicate when NumLock is engaged.

If you are an experienced typist and are used to typing a lowercase letter ell (l) for the number one (1), or an uppercase letter oh (O) for zero (0), do not do this on your computer. The computer treats numbers and letters differently, and although you usually won't have problems, you could run into difficulties by disregarding this distinction.

To enter shifted characters like !, @, and # that appear on the top half of some keys, hold down ⇧Shift while you press the key.

Carriage Returns

Carriage returns are codes in the document that indicate where the lines end. When you print the document, these codes tell the printer to move down one line and back to the left margin. WordPerfect has two kinds of carriage returns: soft and hard.

Soft Carriage Returns

WordPerfect automatically enters soft carriage returns at the end of a line as you enter text whenever it reaches the right margin and wraps a word to the next line. Soft carriage returns automatically adjust their position if you revise the text. For example, when you insert or delete text or when you change the margins, existing soft carriage returns are automatically rearranged so that they are always positioned at the end of each line.

Hard Carriage Returns

Unlike soft carriage returns, hard carriage returns remain fixed in place where you enter them by pressing Enter↵. You enter a hard carriage return whenever you want to end a line before you reach the right margin, for example:

- To end a paragraph and start a new one.
- To enter an inside address, a salutation, or a heading.
- To insert a blank line, as you would following an inside address, the date, and the closing of a letter. Each time you press Enter↵, you insert another blank line.

You can enter hard carriage returns as you type a document, or you can enter them into existing text.

- When entering hard carriage returns as you enter text, you press Enter↵ to end a line before it reaches the right margin or to end one paragraph and start a new one. The cursor moves down a line and back to the left margin. If you want a blank line between paragraphs, press Enter↵ again to insert it. Each time you press Enter↵, the cursor moves down another line.
- You enter hard carriage returns in existing text whenever you want to break an existing paragraph or line into two paragraphs or lines. To do so:
  - You move the cursor under the character that you want to be the first character in the new paragraph or line.
  - You then press Enter↵ to insert a hard carriage return. This moves the cursor, the character it was under, and all following

LOOKING AHEAD: REVEALING CODES

When you press Enter←, or when lines wrap automatically, codes are entered into the document. You can see these codes, and many others that are described in Topic 8, by pressing Alt-F3 or F11 to divide the screen in half. The top half shows the document without codes, and the bottom half shows the document with them. To hide the codes, press Alt-F3 or F11 again.

text, down one line and back to the left margin. If you press Enter← a second time, a blank line is inserted above the new paragraph or line.

WordPerfect treats hard carriage returns just like any other character, so you can delete them just like other characters with the ←Bksp or Del key. WordPerfect also has a command (Alt-F3 or F11) that allows you to see where hard returns have been entered so that it is easier to delete them.

Spaces

When entering text, you normally press Spacebar to insert spaces. However, like carriage returns, there are both soft and hard spaces. When you press Spacebar in a document, it enters a soft space. If the word that follows the space will not fit at the end of the line, it wraps to the next line. Certain expressions, though they contain spaces, should not be split to print on different lines, for example:

- A name like Henry VIII or Mrs. Jacqueline Hartwick
- A time like 8 p.m.
- An address like 32 Elm Street
- A formula like 1 + 1 = 2

To keep the two or more parts of the phrase together, press Home and then Spacebar to enter a hard space. This way, if the phrase does not fit on one line, it all wraps to the next line.

Correcting Mistakes

There are several ways to correct mistakes, but when entering text, you usually use the ←Bksp or Del key to do so. If you make any mistakes—and notice them immediately:

- Press ←Bksp to delete characters to the cursor's left; then type the characters correctly.
- You can also use the directional arrow keys (→, ←, ↑, and ↓) to move the cursor through the text and press Del to delete any character the cursor is positioned under.

If you hold these keys down, they delete one character after another until you release them.

Scrolling
As you enter text, the screen gradually fills up. When the last line on the screen is filled, the text begins to scroll, or move, up a line at a time so that the line you are entering is always displayed on the screen. To make room for the new lines, text at the top of the document scrolls off the top of the screen.

Scrolling
When the screen is full, the document scrolls up as you enter new text. The line on which you are entering text always remains displayed on the screen.

Scrolling

As you enter text, the screen gradually fills up. When the last line on the screen is filled, the text begins to scroll, or move, up a line at a time so that the line you are entering is always displayed on the screen. To make room for the new lines, text at the top of the document scrolls off the top of the screen. But it is not gone for good; you can scroll back to it whenever you want using the cursor movement keys and commands. For example, you can press the + and - keys on the numeric keypad (with NumLock off) to scroll up and down through the document a screen at a time. You can press PgUp and PgDn to scroll through it a page at a time.

When you enter enough lines of text so that they will fill a page when you print the document, a dashed line across the screen (——) indicates where the current page will end and a new one will begin. This is called a soft page break. If you insert or delete text above this soft page break, it adjusts its position automatically.

Boldfacing and Underlining

Two frequently used formats, boldfacing and underlining, are assigned to function keys. To boldface text, you press F6; to underline text, you press F8. As you are entering text, you can employ either of two approaches to use these formats:

- Press the function key for the desired format, type the text, and then press the same function key to end the format.
- Press the function key for the desired format, type the text, and then press → to move the cursor to the right of the hidden code that ends the format. (It was inserted automatically when you pressed the function key the first time.)

Any text you enter between the codes that begin and end boldfacing and underlining is formatted as bold or underlined. On some systems, the number following the *Pos* indicator on the status line indicates when the cursor is inside or outside the codes. The way the number is displayed varies. For example, on some systems, the number changes color or intensity; on others, it may be underlined.

Changing the Underline Style

When using underlining, you can choose whether or not spaces and tabs are underlined.

→ KEY/Strokes

Changing the Underline Style

1. Move the cursor to above where you want to change the type of underlining.
2. Either: Press Shift-F8, and then press O (for ***O**ther*).
   Or: Pull down the ***L**ayout* menu and select ***O**ther*.
   The Other Format menu is displayed.
3. Press U (for ***U**nderline*), and the cursor jumps to the line that reads *Spaces **Y**es (**N**o)*.
4. Either: Press Y to underline spaces.
   Or: Press N to not underline spaces.
   The cursor then jumps to the line that reads *Tabs **Y**es (**N**o)*.
5. Either: Press Y to underline tabs.
   Or: Press N to not underline tabs.
6. Press F7 to return to the Edit screen.

Entering Special Characters

WordPerfect has over 1,700 characters that you can print on a graphics-capable printer. These include graphics symbols, Greek letters, foreign currency symbols, and letters with foreign-language accent marks. These are characters that do not appear on your keyboard. If you print a character that is not in one of the fonts available to your printer, WordPerfect prints it as a graphics character. If your printer does not support graphics, you can print only the characters that your printer does support.

Code	Char	Code	Char	Code	Char	Code	Char	Code	Char	Code	Char
001	☺	051	3	101	e	151	ù	201	╔	251	√
002	☻	052	4	102	f	152	¦	202	╩	252	ⁿ
003	♥	053	5	103	g	153	Ö	203	╦	253	²
004	♦	054	6	104	h	154	Ü	204	╠	254	■
005	♣	055	7	105	i	155	¢	205	═		
006	♠	056	8	106	j	156	£	206	╬		
007	•	057	9	107	k	157	¥	207	╧		
008	◘	058	:	108	l	158	₧	208	╨		
009	○	059	;	109	m	159	ƒ	209	╤		
010	◙	060	<	110	n	160	á	210	╥		
011	♂	061	=	111	o	161	í	211	╙		
012	♀	062	>	112	p	162	ó	212	╘		
013	♪	063	?	113	q	163	ú	213	╒		
014	♫	064	@	114	r	164	ñ	214	╓		
015	☼	065	A	115	s	165	Ñ	215	╫		
016	►	066	B	116	t	166	ª	216	╪		
017	◄	067	C	117	u	167	º	217	┘		
018	↕	068	D	118	v	168	¿	218	┌		
019	‼	069	E	119	w	169	⌐	219	█		
020	¶	070	F	120	x	170	¬	220	▄		
021	§	071	G	121	y	171	½	221	▌		
022	▬	072	H	122	z	172	¼	222	▐		
023	↨	073	I	123	{	173	¡	223	▀		
024	↑	074	J	124	|	174	«	224	α		
025	↓	075	K	125	}	175	»	225	ß		
026	→	076	L	126	~	176	░	226	Γ		
027	←	077	M	127	⌂	177	▒	227	π		
028	∟	078	N	128	Ç	178	▓	228	Σ		
029	↔	079	O	129	ü	179	│	229	σ		
030	▲	080	P	130	é	180	┤	230	µ		
031	▼	081	Q	131	â	181	╡	231	τ		
032		082	R	132	ä	182	╢	232	Φ		
033	!	083	S	133	à	183	╖	233	Θ		
034	"	084	T	134	å	184	╕	234	Ω		
035	#	085	U	135	ç	185	╣	235	δ		
036	$	086	V	136	ê	186	║	236	∞		
037	%	087	W	137	ë	187	╗	237	φ		
038	&	088	X	138	è	188	╝	238	ε		
039	'	089	Y	139	ï	189	╜	239	∩		
040	(	090	Z	140	î	190	╛	240	≡		
041	)	091	[	141	ì	191	┐	241	±		
042	*	092	\	142	Ä	192	└	242	≥		
043	+	093	]	143	Å	193	┴	243	≤		
044	,	094	^	144	É	194	┬	244	⌠		
045	-	095	_	145	æ	195	├	245	⌡		
046	.	096	`	146	Æ	196	─	246	÷		
047	/	097	a	147	ô	197	┼	247	≈		
048	0	098	b	148	ö	198	╞	248	°		
049	1	099	c	149	ò	199	╟	249	∙		
050	2	100	d	150	û	200	╚	250	·		

The IBM PC Character Set

This figure illustrates the characters in the IBM extended character set built into the computer's memory. To enter a special character, first locate the character that you want to enter. Then hold down Alt and, using the numeric keypad, type the three-digit number shown in the table. For example, hold down Alt and then type **024** to enter the up arrow, type **013** or **014** to enter the musical notes, or type **171** to enter the ½ character.

You can create special characters in two ways: by typing their decimal code on the numeric keypad or by composing them using WordPerfect's Compose command.

Typing the Decimal Code with WordPerfect

You can hold down the Alt key and type the decimal code for the character on the numeric keypad. (The number keys at the top of the keyboard do not work with this feature.) You can enter any of the characters shown in the figure "The IBM PC Character Set." When you do so, and then release Alt, the character is displayed on the screen. For example, to enter an em dash, hold down Alt, type **196** on the numeric keypad, and then release Alt. (Be sure to check that this character prints on your printer before using it in your documents.)

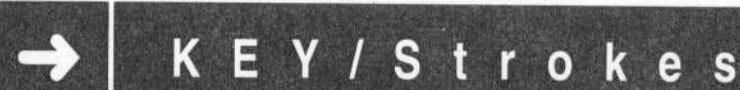

→ KEY/Strokes

Entering Special Characters by Typing Their Decimal Code

1. Position the cursor where you want to create the special character.
2. Hold down Alt.
3. Type the special character's decimal code on the numeric keypad. (See the figure "The IBM PC Character Set.")
4. Release Alt to enter the character.

Composing Characters

You can compose special characters, including digraphs such as Æ and æ, symbols such as an L with a hyphen through it, and diacriticals such as á and ö. To do so, you use the Compose command (Ctrl-V) and then enter the two characters that you want to combine. (You cannot combine uppercase and lowercase letters.) You can also compose characters from any one of 11 predefined character sets. To do so, you use the Compose command and then enter two numbers separated by a comma. The first number identifies the character set; the second, the character within that set. For example, to enter an up arrow symbol, you type **6,23**. The numbers that you enter for some of the most commonly used characters are shown in the figure "Composed Characters" in Exercise 3. For others, refer to the manual that accompanies the WordPerfect program.

→ KEY/Strokes

Composing Special Characters

1. Either: Press Ctrl-V from the Edit screen.
   Or: Pull down the Font menu and select *C**h**aracters*.
   Or: Press Ctrl-2 to begin composing from anywhere in the program. (No prompt is displayed.)
   The prompt *Key* = is displayed unless you pressed Ctrl-2.
2. Either: Type the first and then the second characters.

Or: Type the number of the character set, a comma, and the number of the character, and then press [Enter←].

Only the second character is displayed on the screen; to see both characters, press [Alt]-[F3] or [F11] to reveal codes.

If you enter a character that cannot be displayed on your screen, the character is displayed as a square bullet (■). Characters that cannot be displayed may still print correctly.

EXERCISES

Files Supplied on the Student Resource Disk

Filename	Retrieved
ALIGN.WP5	
ANTONYMS.WP5	
BLOCKS.WP5	
EDITING.WP5	
EDUCOM.WP5	
FONTS.WP5	
FOOTFORM.WP5	
INDENTS.WP5	
JOBGUIDE.WP5	
NEWSLTR.WP5	
POEM.WP5	
SCRIPTS.WP5	
SEARCH.WP5	
SPACING.WP5	
SPECIAL1.WP5	
SPECIAL2.WP5	
SPELLING.WP5	
SUNCITY.WP5	
SYNONYMS.WP5	

EXERCISE 1

ENTERING YOUR NAME IN ALL DOCUMENTS

1. Retrieve from your data disk each of the files listed in the table "Files Supplied on the Student Resource Disk."
2. Enter your name on the last line of the document, with one blank line between it and the line above.
3. Save the document and check the file's name off in the table.

EXERCISE 2

ENTERING SOME DOCUMENTS

1. Enter one or more of the documents shown in the figures "FIRST-01.WP5, FIRST-02.WP5, and FIRST-03.WP5. Don't worry about mistakes; you'll see how to edit your documents in the next topic.
2. Save any document you enter under the same name used as the figure title.
3. Print any document that you entered.

today's date

Mr. Roger McNair
Sales Manager
Penbrook Hotel
Penbrook Plaza East
Long Beach, CA 90801

Dear Roger:

It was a pleasure meeting with you. After our discussion on Monday, I have a clearer picture of your business requirements as well as some exciting ideas on attracting weekend guests to the Penbrook Hotel. Your facilities are impressive indeed.

I have a meeting scheduled with all of CREATIVE DIMENSIONS' department heads tomorrow morning. I know that they will be as eager as I to come up with a great marketing plan for Penbrook. As promised, I will get the advertising and public relations proposal to you as soon as possible.

Sincerely yours,

CREATIVE DIMENSIONS

Sonia Alexander
President

(type your initials)

FIRST-01.WP5
This figure and the next two are reprinted by permission from Patricia A. Custer, *Skill Building Word Processing Exercises*, Prentice-Hall Word and Information Processing on Microcomputers Series, Dennis P. Curtin, series editor (Englewood Cliffs: Prentice, 1992).

CREATIVE DIMENSIONS' BACKGROUND

CREATIVE DIMENSIONS is a full service communications agency with solid experience in all areas of advertising, sales promotion, and public relations. From preplanning investigations to finished production, placement, and follow-up, CREATIVE DIMENSIONS is there constantly to help ensure your success.

At CREATIVE DIMENSIONS we set goals that are both realistic and measurable. We then work until all goals are achieved or surpassed. We are always looking for better ways to enhance the effectiveness of your communications.

There is simply no substitute for hard work and careful planning in today's competitive environment. Our more than 15 years of experience in handling many different types of accounts has taught us this important lesson.

Our executive, account, and creative teams are staffed with only seasoned professionals, so every detail of your business is handled by someone with <u>at least</u> 10 years of advertising or related experience. We believe that there is no part of your business that deserves less.

FIRST-02.WP5

MEMO TO: Word Processing Operators
FROM: your name
DATE: today's date
SUBJECT: Spacing Rules for Punctuation Marks

For your review, below are the standard rules for spacing when keyboarding various marks of punctuation. Please be sure to apply these rules to all documents that you prepare.

Leave two spaces:
after a colon
at the end of every sentence

Leave one space:
after a comma
after a semicolon
after a period following an abbreviation or initial
after a period representing a decimal point
after an exclamation point within a sentence
after a question mark within a sentence

Leave no spaces:
after a period within an abbreviation
before or after a hyphen
before or after a dash (two hyphens)
between any word and the punctuation following it
between parentheses and the enclosed matter
between quotation marks and the enclosed matter

Also, do not separate punctuation from the word it follows, i.e., allowing a dash to begin a new line.

FIRST-03.WP5

TO ENTER	PRESS	EXAMPLE
Open quote	Alt-096	‘
Close quote	Alt-039	’
Em dash	Alt-196	—
Large bullet	Alt-220	■
Small bullet	Alt-254	■
Triangle bullet	Alt-016	➤
Diamond bullet	Alt-004	◆
Pound Sterling	Alt-156	£
Yen symbol	Alt-157	¥
French Franc	Alt-159	ƒ
One-half	Alt-171	½
One-quarter	Alt-172	¼
Division sign	Alt-246	÷
Section symbol	Alt-021	§

Alt-Decimal Number Characters
This figure shows the SPECIAL1.WP5 document that you retrieve to explore entering special characters. To enter a special character shown in the rightmost column, you hold down Alt and then type the three-digit code on the numeric keypad.

COMPOSED CHARACTERS

TYPE	FOR
4,2	■
4,5	¶
4,17	½
4,18	¼
4,22	®
4,23	©
4,28	'
4,29	‘
4,31	”
4,32	“
4,41	™
4,43	☺
5,7	✓
5,14	√
5,23	✓
7,6	Σ

Composed Characters
This figure shows the SPECIAL2.WP5 document that you retrieve to explore entering special characters. To enter a special character shown in the right column, you press Ctrl-V, type the numbers given for that character in the left column, and then press Enter↵.

EXERCISE 3

ENTERING CHARACTERS WITH THE ALT KEY

1. Retrieve the document SPECIAL1.WP5.
2. Enter the special characters described in the first column using the commands shown in the second. To do so:
   - Move the cursor to one of the lines, and press End to move the cursor to the end of the line so it's in the "Example" column.
   - Hold down Alt and type the three-digit code for the character on that line using the numeric keypad.
3. When finished, save the document under its original name and make a printout.

EXERCISE 4

USING THE COMPOSE COMMAND

1. Retrieve the document SPECIAL2.WP5.
2. Enter the special characters described in the first column. To do so:
   - Move the cursor to one of the lines, and press End to move the cursor to the end of the line so it's in the "For" column.
   - Hold down Ctrl and press V to display the prompt *Key* =.
   - Type the first number, the comma, and then the second number shown on that line.
   - Press Enter↵ to enter the character.
3. When finished, save the document under its original name and make a printout.

EXERCISE 5

ENTERING BULLETS IN THE JOBGUIDE DOCUMENT

1. Retrieve the JOBGUIDE.WP5 document.
2. Scroll through the document looking for three sets of lists that currently use asterisks for bullets. Position the cursor under each asterisk, press Del, and then follow the instructions in the KEY/Stroke box “Entering Special Characters by Typing Their Decimal Code” to enter the character **254**.
3. Save the document and print page 1.

EXERCISE 6

ENTERING BULLETS IN THE NEWSLTR DOCUMENT

1. Retrieve the NEWSLTR.WP5 document.
2. Scroll through the document looking for the bulleted list under the heading *Computer Users' Checklist.* Position the cursor under each

asterisk in the list, press Del, and then follow the instructions in the KEY/Stroke box "Composing Special Characters" to enter the special character **4,38**. Square bullets will be displayed on the screen, but other characters will print.

3. Scroll through the document looking for three other sets of lists that currently use asterisks for bullets. Position the cursor under each asterisk, press Del, and then follow the instructions in the KEY/Stroke box "Entering Special Characters by Typing Their Decimal Code" to enter the character **254**.
4. Save the document and print page 2.

EXERCISE 7

ENTERING A COPYRIGHT SYMBOL IN THE EDUCOM DOCUMENT

1. Retrieve the EDUCOM.WP5 document.
2. Press Home twice, and then press ↓ to move the cursor to the end of the document.
3. Position the cursor under the *1* in *1987 EDUCOM and ADAPSO*, and then follow the instructions in the KEY/Stroke box "Composing Special Characters" to enter the special character **4,23**. Press Spacebar to insert a space between the character and the year.
4. Save the document and print the last page.

TOPIC 6

Editing Documents

After completing this topic, you will be able to:

- Move the cursor around a document to edit it
- Explain the differences between inserting and typing over existing text

After you type a document, you proofread and then edit it. To edit a document on the screen, you use the cursor movement keys or commands to move the cursor through the document to delete or insert characters, words, or phrases.

TUTORIAL

In this tutorial, you practice moving the cursor and editing a document to correct mistakes.

GETTING STARTED

1. Retrieve the EDITING.WP5 document.

ENTERING YOUR NAME

2. Position the cursor under the *y* in *your name* on the line between the title and the first paragraph.
3. Press [Ins] so that the status line reads *Typeover*.
4. Type your name. (If it is shorter than the characters already on the line, press [Del] to delete the extra characters.)
5. Press [Ins] again so that the status line no longer reads *Typeover*.

MOVING THE CURSOR

6. Practice moving the cursor through the document with the commands described in the table "Cursor Movement Keys and Commands" in the Quick Reference section. (This is an expanded version of the table in Topic 1's Jump-Start Tutorial.)

   As you move the cursor, notice how it moves through the text. Remember that keys connected with hyphens (for example, [Ctrl]-[←]) are pressed simultaneously, whereas those separated by commas (for example, [Home], [↑]) are pressed one after the other. Hold down some of the keys to see how they repeat until you release them.

Tip

Keys you use to move the cursor and delete text are summarized in the tables in the Quick Reference section. Experiment with these keys as you edit the document.

EDITING THE DOCUMENT

7. Move the cursor through the document to make the corrections shown in the figure "The Unedited EDITING Document." Before doing so, read the suggestions that follow:
   - If you make any serious mistakes, you can clear the screen and retrieve the document again to start over.
   - Use insert mode to enter most of the corrections, but use typeover mode to change the title at the top of the document from lowercase to uppercase. You press [Ins] to toggle between insert and typeover modes. When you are in typeover mode, *Typeover* is displayed on the status line; when you are in insert mode, it isn't. In insert mode, characters move aside to make room for new text that you enter; in typeover mode, they don't.
   - Where it says "See insert #1," insert the following sentence: **WordPerfect's default setting is the insert mode, so if you enter characters into existing text, the text moves over to make room for them.**
   - If you have trouble understanding what changes to make, look at the figure "The Edited EDITING Document" for guidance.

The Unedited EDITING Document

This figure shows the EDITING document as it appears when you retrieve it. Editing changes that were suggested during proofreading are shown in handwriting. These are the corrections that you enter in this tutorial.

Editing Documents with WordPerfect
your name

Wordperfect provides you with seyral ways to move the curser a document. The four arrow keys move the curser one character or line at a time and repeat if you hold it down. On some computers, these directional arrow keys are on the numeric keypad, which is also used to enter all of your numbers. When pressing these keys to move the cursor, be sure the Pos indicator is flashing on the status line at the bottom of the screen. Pressing the arrow keys on the numeric keypad enters numbers. To turn off the flashing Pos indicator at the bottom of the screen., press Num Lock to disengage the key.

To edit your text, you move the cursor through the document and insert characters as needed. To switch back and fourth between insert and typeover mode, press Ins. The message Typeover appears at the left end of the status line when you are in typeover mode. In type over mode, characters you enter type over and replace any existing characters. Pressing Ins toggles between insert and typeover mode.

Deleting text remove it from the screen and the computer's memory. The table "Keys That Delete Text" lists the keys you can delete text with.

As you format a document, you enter codes that control the printer. You will learn about these codes in a later topic, but you may encounter them, even though you don't see them, when you use the Del key to delete text in existing documents. If you use one of these keys to delete a code whose deletion will not have a noticeable effect on the way the document looks on the screen, a prompt may ask you if you want to delete the code. If this prompt appears, press Y to do so or N to leave the code undeleted.

e, o through, directional, o, them, not, If it is, See insert #1, and delete, or Backspace, s

CORRECTING YOUR OWN MISTAKES

8. Now, using what you have learned, correct any additional mistakes. The table "Keys That Delete Text" summarizes the editing commands you have just learned as well as some others. When you have finished, your document should look like the figure "The Edited EDITING Document."

The Edited EDITING Document
When you have finished editing the document, it should look like this.

> EDITING DOCUMENTS WITH WORDPERFECT
> Your Name
> WordPerfect provides you with several ways to move the cursor through a document. The four directional arrow keys move the cursor one character or line at a time and repeat if you hold them down. On some computers, these keys are on the numeric keypad, which is also used to enter numbers. When pressing these keys to move the cursor, be sure the *Pos* indicator is not flashing on the status line. If it is, pressing the arrow keys on the numeric keypad enters numbers. To turn off the flashing *Pos* indicator, press **Num Lock** to disengage the key.
>
> To edit text, you move the cursor through the document and insert and delete characters as needed. WordPerfect's default setting is the insert mode, so if you enter characters into existing text, the text moves over to make room for them. To switch back and forth between insert and typeover mode, press **Ins**. The message *Typeover* appears at the left end of the status line when you are in typeover mode. In typeover mode, characters you enter type over and replace any existing characters. Pressing Ins toggles between insert and typeover mode.
>
> Deleting text removes it from the screen and the computer's memory. The table "Keys That Delete Text" lists the keys you can delete text with.
>
> As you format a document, you enter codes that control the printer. You will learn about these codes in a later topic, but you may encounter them, even though you don't see them, when you use the **Del** or **Backspace** key to delete text in existing documents. If you use one of these keys to delete a code whose deletion will not have a noticeable effect on the way the document looks on the screen, a prompt may ask you if you want to delete the code. If this prompt appears, press **Y** to do so or **N** to leave the code undeleted.

SAVING THE DOCUMENT UNDER A NEW NAME

9. Press [F10], and the prompt reads *Document to be saved: x:\EDITING.WP5* (where *x* stands for your default drive).
10. Press [→] to move the cursor under the period in front of *WP5*.
11. Type **2** to change the filename to *EDITING2.WP5*, and press [Enter ↵] to save the file under the new filename.

FINISHING UP

12. Press [⇧ Shift]-[F7] to display the Print menu.
13. Press [F] (for ***F**ull Document*) to print the entire document.
14. You have now completed this tutorial. Either continue with the next activity or quit the program.

QUICK REFERENCE

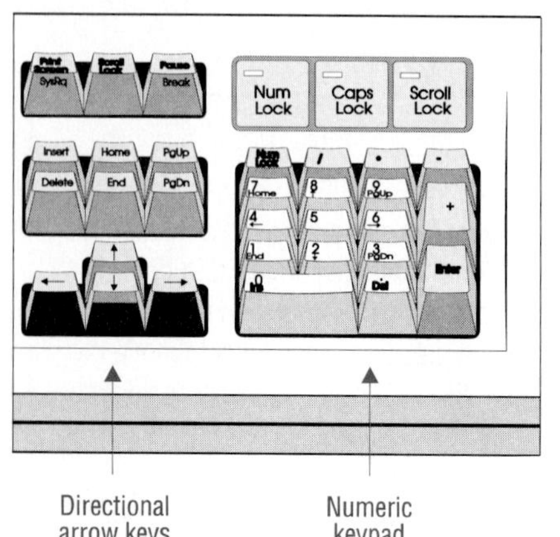

Directional Arrow Keys
The four directional arrow keys (sometimes called cursor movement keys) move the cursor one character or line at a time in the direction of the arrow. All computers have directional arrow keys on the numeric keypad that work only when NumLock is not engaged. Newer computers also have a separate set of directional arrow keys that work at any time.

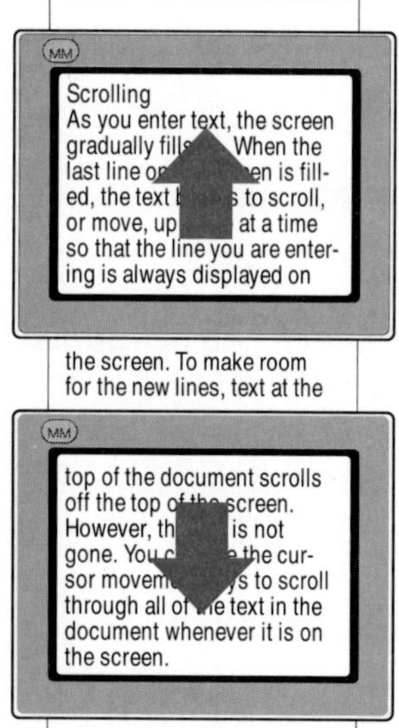

Scrolling the Screen
When the document is longer than the screen, you use cursor movement keys and commands, including ↑ and ↓ or PgUp and PgDn, to scroll the screen up or down to see various parts of the document. You can also scroll horizontally when your document is wider than the screen.

WordPerfect provides you with several ways to move the cursor through a document. The four directional arrow keys move the cursor one character or line at a time and repeat if you hold them down. On some computers, these keys are on the numeric keypad, which is also used to enter numbers. When pressing these keys to move the cursor, be sure the *Pos* indicator is not flashing on the status line. If it is, pressing the arrow keys on the numeric keypad enters numbers. To turn off the flashing *Pos* indicator, press NumLock to disengage the key.

You can also move the cursor in larger jumps with commands; the longer your document, the more important these commands become. The table "Cursor Movement Keys and Commands" describes these cursor movement commands. When moving the cursor with the designated arrow keys, you will notice:

CURSOR MOVEMENT KEYS AND COMMANDS

To Move the Cursor	Press
Horizontally	
One character left or right	← or →
One word left or right	Ctrl-← or Ctrl-→
To left or right edge of text on screen[a]	Home, ← or Home, →
To right edge of document when wider than screen	Home (twice), →
To left edge of document when wider than screen	Home (twice), ←
To beginning of line before all codes	Home (three times), ←
To end of line	End
Vertically	
One line up or down	↑ or ↓
To first line of preceding or following paragraph[b]	Ctrl-↑ or Ctrl-↓
To bottom line and then to next screen[c]	+ or Home, ↓
To top line and then to previous screen[c]	- or Home, ↑
To top line of document	Home (twice), ↑
To top of document before all codes	Home (three times), ↑
To end of document's last line	Home (twice), ↓
To end of document after all codes	Home (three times), ↓
To top of next page[a]	PgDn
To top of previous page[a]	PgUp

[a]You can press Ctrl-Home twice to return to your original position. (See the table "Go To Commands.")
[b]These keys work only on enhanced keyboards.
[c]The + and - keys that scroll the screen are at the far right of the keyboard on the numeric keypad. They work only if NumLock is not engaged.

- When you move the cursor along a line of text, it moves through the text and does not affect it.
- When you move the cursor past the rightmost character on a line, it jumps down to the beginning of the next line.
- When you move the cursor past the leftmost character on a line, it jumps up to the end of the preceding line.
- When you move the cursor up and down through a document, it stays in the same vertical position relative to the edge of the screen unless a line contains less text.

- If the document is longer than the number of lines displayed on the screen, it can be scrolled into view by moving the cursor to the top or bottom of the screen and pressing the up or down arrow keys. Instead of moving off the screen, the cursor stays on the top or bottom row, and the text scrolls into view. You can scroll the screen vertically and horizontally to see the text.
- You cannot move the cursor off the screen, and you cannot move it past the last line of text in the document.
- Pressing the arrow keys moves the cursor one character or line at a time. When you press Home first or hold down Ctrl while pressing the arrow keys, the cursor moves in larger jumps. These keys are like amplifiers. For example, pressing Home once and then pressing an arrow key moves the cursor to the edge of the screen. Pressing Home twice and then pressing an arrow key moves the cursor to the edge of the document even if it is longer or wider than the screen.

Moving Around the Document with a Mouse

You can move the cursor to any point in the document by pointing to it with the mouse pointer and then clicking the left mouse button. If the position you point to contains no text, the cursor jumps to the nearest position that does.

To scroll the document, hold down the right mouse button, and then drag the mouse pointer toward the edge of the screen in the direction you want to scroll. For example, to scroll down through a document, hold down the right mouse button and drag the mouse pointer toward the bottom of the screen. The screen will continue scrolling as long as you hold the button down and position the mouse pointer on the border of the Edit screen.

The Go To Command

WordPerfect's Go To command makes it easy to move the cursor quickly to specific points in a document. To use this command, press Ctrl-Home, or pull down the Search menu and select ***G**oto* to display the prompt *Go to.* Press any of the cursor movement keys or commands described in the table "Go To Commands."

You can also press Ctrl-Home twice to return to where the cursor was originally after using the Go To command, or after pressing Home and any arrow keys, PgUp or PgDn, Search (F2), Replace (Alt-F2), or the + or - keys on the numeric keypad.

GO TO COMMANDS

To Move the Cursor to	Press
Top of current page	Ctrl-Home, ↑
Bottom of current page	Ctrl-Home, ↓
Next occurrence of a specific character	Ctrl-Home, then type character
Next hard carriage return	Ctrl-Home, Enter↵
Next space	Ctrl-Home, Spacebar
Top of specific page	Ctrl-Home, type number of page, Enter↵
Original position after search or move	Ctrl-Home twice

Inserting and Replacing Text

To edit text, you move the cursor through the document and insert and delete characters as needed. WordPerfect's default setting is the insert mode, so if you enter characters into existing text, the text moves over to make room for them. To switch back and forth between insert and typeover mode, press Ins. The message *Typeover* appears at the left end of the status line when you are in typeover mode. In typeover mode, characters you enter type over and replace any existing characters.

← Bksp, Spacebar, and Tab act differently, depending on the mode you are in.

- With insert on, ← Bksp deletes the character to the cursor's left and closes up the space. With typeover on, ← Bksp deletes the character to the cursor's left and inserts a space.
- With insert on, pressing Spacebar inserts a space, and text to the right of the cursor moves over to make room for it. With typeover on, pressing Spacebar deletes the character the cursor is positioned under and moves the cursor one space to the right; text to the right of the cursor does not move over.
- With insert on, Tab pushes text ahead of the cursor to the next tab stop. With typeover on, Tab moves the cursor through the text to the next tab stop without affecting the text.

Deleting Text

Deleting text removes it from the screen and the computer's memory. The table "Keys That Delete Text" lists the keys you can delete text with.

As you format a document, you enter codes that control the printer. You will learn about these codes in a later topic, but you may encounter them, even though you don't see them, when you use the Del or ← Bksp key to delete text in existing documents. If you use one of these keys to delete a code whose deletion will not have a noticeable effect on the way the document looks on the screen, a prompt may ask you if you want to delete the code. If this prompt appears, press Y to do so or N to leave the code undeleted.

KEYS THAT DELETE TEXT

To Delete	Press
The character to the left of the cursor	← Bksp
The character above the cursor	Del
The word containing the cursor or, if the cursor is on a space, the word to the left	Ctrl-← Bksp
From the cursor to the beginning of the word	Home, ← Bksp
From the cursor to the end of the word	Home, Del
From the cursor to the end of the line	Ctrl-End
From the cursor to the end of the page	Ctrl-PgDn

EXERCISES

EXERCISE 1

EDITING THE ENTERING DOCUMENT

1. Retrieve the ENTERING.WP5 document that you created in the previous topic.
2. Edit the document to correct any mistakes you may have made.
3. Save the document under the same name.
4. Print the edited document.

EXERCISE 2

EDITING ON YOUR OWN

1. Retrieve the EDITING.WP5 document from the disk.
2. Without worrying about making mistakes, use the commands described in the table "Keys That Delete Text" to delete every second word in the first paragraph, every second line in the third, and from the beginning of the third paragraph to the end of the document.
3. Print the edited document.
4. Clear the screen without saving your changes.

EXERCISE 3

EDITING YOUR OWN DOCUMENTS

1. Retrieve each of the documents you entered in Exercise 2 in Topic 5 (FIRST-01.WP5, FIRST-02.WP5, or FIRST-03.WP5).
2. Edit each document to correct any mistakes you may have made.
3. Save each document under the same name.
4. Print each edited document.

TOPIC 7

Printing Documents—The Basics

After completing this topic, you will be able to:

- Print documents that are displayed on the screen
- Print documents directly from the disk
- Print documents with the List Files menu
- Preview documents before you print them

To share your documents with others or to make proofreading easier, you make printouts. To begin, you first load the printer with paper, align the paper, and turn the printer on.

TUTORIAL

In this tutorial, you explore printing a document that is displayed on the screen and one that is stored in a file on the disk.

GETTING STARTED

1. Retrieve the OVERVIEW.WP5 document.

PREVIEWING THE DOCUMENT ON THE SCREEN

2. Press Shift-F7 to display the Print menu.
3. Press V (for ***View** Document*), and the document is displayed on the screen just as it will appear when printed. If it does not appear, your system is not equipped to display graphics.

The View Document Command
When you select View Document from the Print menu, the document is displayed on the screen exactly as it will print out. The menu choices at the bottom of the screen allow you to specify the enlargement. Here, a page is shown at 100%.

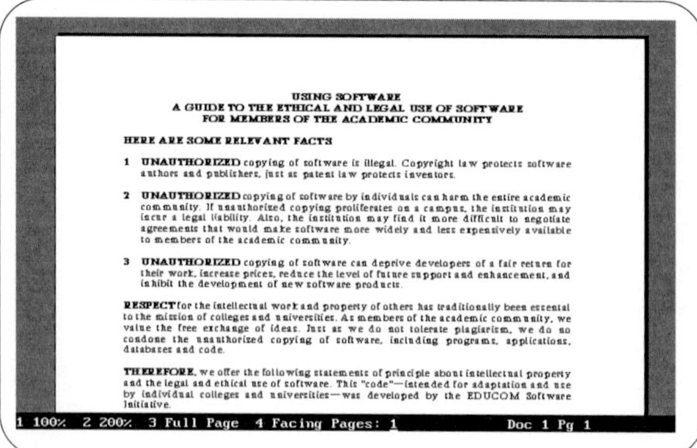

USING SOFTWARE
A GUIDE TO THE ETHICAL AND LEGAL USE OF SOFTWARE
FOR MEMBERS OF THE ACADEMIC COMMUNITY

HERE ARE SOME RELEVANT FACTS

1 **UNAUTHORIZED** copying of software is illegal. Copyright law protects software authors and publishers, just as patent law protects inventors.

2 **UNAUTHORIZED** copying of software by individuals can harm the entire academic community. If unauthorized copying proliferates on a campus, the institution may incur a legal liability. Also, the institution may find it more difficult to negotiate agreements that would make software more widely and less expensively available to members of the academic community.

3 **UNAUTHORIZED** copying of software can deprive developers of a fair return for their work, increase prices, reduce the level of future support and enhancement, and inhibit the development of new software products.

RESPECT for the intellectual work and property of others has traditionally been essential to the mission of colleges and universities. As members of the academic community, we value the free exchange of ideas. Just as we do not tolerate plagiarism, we do no condone the unauthorized copying of software, including programs, applications, databases and code.

THEREFORE, we offer the following statement of principle about intellectual property and the legal and ethical use of software. This "code"—intended for adaptation and use by individual colleges and universities—was developed by the EDUCOM Software Initiative.

1 100% 2 200% 3 Full Page 4 Facing Pages: 1   Doc 1 Pg 1

4. If the status line displays the numbers *1*, *2*, *3*, and *4*, press them in turn to explore the various display options offered on the menu.

5. Press [2] to display the document at 200% enlargement, and then press [+] and [-] on the numeric keypad to scroll within a page.
6. Press [4] to display facing pages, and then press [PgUp] and [PgDn] to scroll between pages.
7. Press [F7] to return to the Edit screen.

PRINTING THE DOCUMENT ON THE SCREEN

8. Press [Home] twice, and then press [↓] to move the cursor to the bottom of the document.
9. Press [⇧Shift]-[F7] to display the Print menu.

The Print Menu
The Print menu lists the commands you use to print documents. The top part of the screen lists the basic commands that allow you to preview documents or print them in full or in part.

```
Print

     1 - Full Document
     2 - Page
     3 - Document on Disk
     4 - Control Printer
     5 - Multiple Pages
     6 - View Document
     7 - Initialize Printer

Options

     S - Select Printer                     HP LaserJet III PostScript
     B - Binding Offset                     0i
     N - Number of Copies                   1
     U - Multiple Copies Generated by       WordPerfect
     G - Graphics Quality                   Medium
     T - Text Quality                       High



Selection: 0
```

10. Press [P] (for ***P**age*) to print just the last page.

PRINTING THE DOCUMENT FROM THE DISK

11. Clear the current document from the screen without saving it, but remain in the program.
12. Press [⇧Shift]-[F7] to display the Print menu.
13. Press [D] (for ***D**ocument on Disk*), and the prompt reads *Document name:*.
14. Type **OVERVIEW.WP5** and press [Enter↵]. The prompt reads *Page(s): (All)*.
15. Type **1** and press [Enter↵] to print just the first page.
16. Press [F7] to return to the Edit screen.

PRINTING A FILE WITH THE LIST FILES MENU

17. Press [F5], and then press [Enter↵] to display the List Files screen and menu.
18. Press the arrow keys to move the highlight over the desired file, in this case, *OVERVIEW.WP5*.
19. Press [P] (for ***P**rint*), and the prompt reads *Page(s): (All)*.
20. Type **2** and press [Enter↵] to print just the second page.
21. Press [F7] to return to the Edit screen.

FINISHING UP

22. You have now completed this tutorial. Either continue with the next activity or quit the program.

QUICK REFERENCE

You can print a file displayed on the screen or any file stored on the disk. When printing a document that is displayed on the screen, you can also preview it before printing. This allows you to save paper because many mistakes will be visible in this preview mode.

Printing Documents from the Print Menu

When you are working on a document, you normally print it using the Print menu. You can press F3 for help on the menu's options. When finished with help, press Spacebar to return to the Print menu.

KEY/Strokes

Printing the Document on the Screen

1. Either: Leave the cursor anywhere in the document if you are printing the entire document.
   Or: Move the cursor to a single page to be printed.
2. Either: Press Shift-F7.
   Or: Pull down the ***File*** menu and select ***Print***.
   The Print menu is displayed.
3. Either: Press F (for ***F****ull Document*) to print the entire document.
   Or: Press P (for ***Page***) to print the page in which the cursor is positioned.
   Or: Press M (for ***M****ultiple Pages*), and the prompt reads *Page(s):*. Type a range of pages (see the box "Specifying Pages to Be Printed") and press Enter.

KEY/Strokes

Printing a Document on the Disk

1. Either: Press Shift-F7.
   Or: Pull down the ***File*** menu and select ***Print***.
   The Print menu is displayed.
2. Press D (for ***D****ocument on Disk*), and the prompt reads *Document name:*.
3. Type the document's name. (If it is not in the default directory, enter a path.)
4. Press Enter, and the prompt reads *Page(s): (All)*.
5. Either: Press Enter to print the entire document.
   Or: Type a range of pages (see the box "Specifying Pages to Be Printed") and press Enter.
6. Press F7 to return to the Edit screen.

SPECIFYING PAGES TO BE PRINTED

When you print a document using the List Files screen and menu or the ***Multiple** Pages* or ***Document** on Disk* command on the Print menu, the prompt reads *Page(s):*. Use the following procedures to print only selected pages when this prompt appears. (Do not enter spaces in the page specifications, for they may create problems.)

- To print from the beginning of the document to a specific page, type a hyphen and then the ending page number. For example, to print from the beginning of the document to page 10, type **-10**.
- To print from a specific page to the end of the document, type the beginning page number followed by a hyphen. For example, to print from page 10 to the end of the document, type **10-**.
- To print a single page, enter the page number. For example, to print page 7, type **7**.
- To print several consecutive pages, enter the starting and ending pages separated by a hyphen. For example, to print pages 2 through 5, type **2-5**.
- To print several nonconsecutive pages, separate them with commas. For example, to print pages 1, 5, and 10, type **1,5,10** and to print page 1 and then pages 6 through 8, type **1,6-8**.

Using List Files to Print

WordPerfect's List Files screen and menu simplifies printing files. To display the List Files screen, press F5 and press Enter↵, or pull down the File menu and select *List **F**iles*. To print out a file on the list, highlight it and press P (for ***P**rint*). When you do so, the prompt reads *Page(s): (All)*. You can either press Enter↵ to print the entire document or specify selected page numbers and press Enter↵ to begin printing. To specify only selected pages, see the box "Specifying Pages to Be Printed."

If you want to print a group of files, you can mark them.

- To mark or unmark individual files, move the highlight over the desired files, and press ⇧Shift-* (or just * on the numeric keypad).
- To mark or unmark all files, press Alt-F5.

When you then press P (for ***P**rint*), a prompt reads *Print marked files? **N**o (**Y**es)*. Press Y to print them or N to cancel the command.

Previewing Documents

The View Document command on the Print menu displays the document on the screen the way it will look when printed so that you can preview it. If you use several formatting commands, you may have a hard time visualizing what the document will look like when it is printed. Many formatting commands do not show their effects on the screen. For example, you do not normally see page numbers, headers, footers, footnotes, top and bottom margins, and font changes on the screen. Though you cannot edit the document when it is displayed with this command, you can see where improvements might be made before you print it out. If you use this command, press + and - on the numeric keypad to scroll within a page. Press PgUp and PgDn to scroll between pages. Press ⇧Shift-F3 to change colors. If your system has a graphics display, you can also use the menu commands to change the size of the page you are viewing or even to view facing pages.

This command first displays the section of the text in which the cursor is positioned. If you want to view a specific page, move the cursor there before executing the View Document command.

EXERCISES

EXERCISE 1

SUMMARIZING YOUR OWN PRINTING PROCEDURES

Depending on the system you are using, your printing procedures may differ from those presented in this text. If that is the case, summarize your printing steps here for future reference.

1. ____________________

2. ____________________

3. ____________________

4. ____________________

5. ____________________

EXERCISE 2

PRINTING MASTER COPIES OF YOUR STUDENT RESOURCE DISK DOCUMENTS

In this exercise, you print out master copies of your documents so that you can use them to compare to later printouts. To conserve paper and time, you may want to print only the first page of each document or divide the list of documents among the class so that each student prints a specific document, which can then be filed along with the others as a class resource.

1. Retrieve from your data disk each of the files listed in the table "Files Supplied on the Student Resource Disk."
2. Follow the instructions in the KEY/Stroke box "Printing the Document on the Screen" to print each document. Check each file's name off in the table as you print it.
3. Save the printouts so that you can compare them to other versions of the same document as you progress through this text.

FILES SUPPLIED ON THE STUDENT RESOURCE DISK

Filename	Printed
ALIGN.WP5	
ANTONYMS.WP5	
BLOCKS.WP5	
EDITING.WP5	
EDUCOM.WP5	
FONTS.WP5	
FOOTFORM.WP5	
INDENTS.WP5	
JOBGUIDE.WP5	
NEWSLTR.WP5	
POEM.WP5	
SCRIPTS.WP5	
SEARCH.WP5	
SPACING.WP5	
SPECIAL1.WP5	
SPECIAL2.WP5	
SPELLING.WP5	
SUNCITY.WP5	
SYNONYMS.WP5	

CHAPTER 2 REVIEW

- When a word will not fit at the end of the line, word wrap moves it to the beginning of the next line.
- You press Enter↵ only at the end of paragraphs or to insert blank lines.
- Soft carriage returns are inserted by the program at the end of lines and are rearranged by the program if line lengths change. Hard carriage returns are entered by pressing Enter↵ and must be deleted to remove them.
- A phrase with words connected by soft spaces will break at a space if it does not fit on a line. A phrase with words connected by hard spaces (**Home**, **Spacebar**) will move to the next line without splitting if it does not fit on the current line.
- Pressing ←Bksp deletes the character to the left of the cursor. Pressing Del deletes the character over the cursor.
- If the document is longer than the screen, the screen scrolls so that you can see the last line as you enter text. You can then press PgUp and PgDn to scroll through the document.
- Pressing F6 turns on boldfacing, and pressing F8 turns on underlining. To turn boldfacing or underlining off, you can press the same key you pressed to turn it on. You can also press → to move the cursor past the hidden code that turns it off.
- You can change the underline styles so that spaces and tabs are underlined or not.
- You can enter special characters by holding down Alt while you type their three-digit number on the numeric keypad. You can also press Ctrl-V and then enter the numbers of a character set and a character separated with a comma.
- When NumLock is engaged, the keys on the numeric keypad enter numbers. When it is not engaged, they move the cursor. When it is engaged, the *Pos* indicator on the status line flashes.
- Pressing Home twice tells the program to move the cursor to the end of the document in the direction of the next arrow key that is pressed.
- To scroll a document with a mouse, you hold down the right mouse button and drag in the direction you want the screen to scroll.
- Pressing Ctrl-Home displays the prompt *Go to*. When you type a page number and then press Enter↵, the cursor moves to the top of that page. When the *Go to* prompt is displayed, you can also press ↑ or ↓ to move to the top or bottom of the current page.
- Pressing Ins toggles the program between insert and typeover modes. In insert mode, any text you type pushes existing text aside. In typeover mode, text types over any existing text in its way. When typeover mode is on, *Typeover* is displayed on the status line.
- To print a document, you press ⇧Shift-F7 to display the Print menu and select one of the choices.
- The View Document command on the Print menu allows you to preview a document before you print it. This saves paper and time because you can see mistakes without making a printout.

- You can use the List Files screen and menu to print files directly from their files on the disk. You can mark a specific file for printing by pressing Shift-* or mark all files by pressing Alt-F5.

CHAPTER 2 QUESTIONS

FILL IN THE BLANK

1. If a word does not fit on the end of a line, ___________ moves it down to the beginning of the next line.
2. To turn boldfacing on and off, you press ___________.
3. To turn underlining on and off, you press ___________.
4. To enter a hard space, you press ___________.
5. To delete the character the cursor is under, you press ___________.
6. To delete the character to the left of the cursor, you press ___________.
7. To enter characters from the IBM PC character set, you hold down ___________ while you type its three-digit code on the ___________.
8. To compose a special character, you press ___________ and then type the character's set and number separated with a ___________.
9. To move the cursor to the end of a document, you press ___________.
10. To move the cursor to the top of the screen and then to the next screen, you press ___________ or ___________ on the ___________.
11. In ___________ mode, text that you enter pushes existing text aside.
12. In ___________ mode, text that you enter is typed over any existing text.
13. To toggle between these two modes, you press ___________.
14. To display the Print menu, you press ___________.
15. To preview what a document will look like when printed, you use the ___________ command.
16. When the prompt reads *Page(s)*, you would type ___________ to print pages 3 through 5 or ___________ to print pages 3, 5, and 8.
17. When the List Files screen is displayed, you can mark individual files for printing by pressing ___________ or mark all of them by pressing ___________.

MATCH THE COLUMNS

1. Enter↵	__ Displays the prompt *Go to*
2. F6	__ Previews a document before printing
3. F8	__ Marks individual files on the List Files screen
4. Home, Spacebar	__ Marks all files on the List Files screen
5. Del	__ Toggles between insert and typeover modes
6. ←Bksp	

7. Ctrl-V	__ New text types over any existing text
8. Alt-**254**	__ Ends a line and moves the cursor down and back to the left margin
9. PgUp and PgDn	__ Turns boldfacing on and off
10. Home, Home, arrow key	__ Turns underlining on and off
11. Ctrl-Home	__ Deletes the character over the cursor
12. Ins	__ Deletes the character to the left of the cursor
13. Typeover mode	__ Scroll through the document on the screen
14. Insert mode	__ Moves cursor to edge of document
15. Shift-F7	__ New text pushes existing text aside
16. View Document command	__ Compose character command
17. *	__ Enters a square bullet
18. Alt-F5	__ Enters a hard space
	__ Displays the Print menu

WRITE OUT THE ANSWERS

1. Describe word wrap. When does it happen?
2. What are carriage returns? What is the difference between a hard and a soft carriage return?
3. How do you break a paragraph into two paragraphs?
4. What is the difference between hard and soft spaces? When would you want to use a hard space?
5. What is the most common way to correct mistakes when entering text?
6. What happens to the document on the screen once the screen is full?
7. What is the cursor used for when editing, and how do you move it?
8. What does scrolling the screen mean? When does it scroll? In which directions can you scroll it?
9. How do you execute the Go To command?
10. What is the basic difference between insert mode and typeover mode?
11. If you press Spacebar to move the cursor, what happens when the program is in insert mode? In typeover mode?
12. Describe three ways of deleting text.
13. If you wanted to print just pages 3 and 4 and 6 through 8, would you print the document from the screen or from a file on the disk? How would you specify pages to be printed?
14. What is the purpose of the View Document command?
15. What command do you use to mark individual files on the List Files screen? All files?

CHAPTER 2 PROJECTS

PROJECT 1

THE DESKTOP PUBLISHING DOCUMENT

1. Retrieve the DTP.WP5 document from your data disk.
2. Enter your name on the second line, and delete the *your name* place holder. Insert a blank line below your name.
3. Save the document and make a printout.

PROJECT 2

THE COMPUTERS AND CAREERS DOCUMENT

1. Retrieve the CAREERS.WP5 document from your data disk.
2. Enter your name on the second line, and insert a blank line below your name.
3. Save the document and make a printout.

CHAPTER 3

Basic Formatting

TOPIC 8

Editing Codes

[BOLD] **Boldfacing** [bold]
[UND] underlining [und]
End of line [SRt]
End of paragraph [HRt]

Codes
Codes that are normally hidden control the format of your document

After completing this topic, you will be able to:

- Describe hidden codes
- Reveal hidden codes and edit them

As you type a document, just the letters and numbers you type are displayed on the Edit screen. However, you often enter invisible codes into the document. Some, like soft carriage returns and soft page breaks, are entered automatically when lines or pages are full. Others, you enter whenever you press Enter↵, Tab⇆, or Spacebar or when you use formatting commands, like those that center, indent, or underline text.

The function of these codes is to override the program's default (built-in) formats and control how your text is printed on a page. When you print out the document, the codes arrive at the printer and give it instructions. For example, a code might tell the printer to move down to the beginning of the next line or to begin boldfacing.

Although these codes are not displayed on the screen, you sometimes sense their presence. When you move the cursor through formatted text, pressing the arrow keys sometimes does not move the cursor. Although the cursor does not appear to be moving on the screen, it is moving through the codes in the document.

TUTORIAL

The paired codes at the beginning and end of this sentence turn boldfacing on and off.
The paired codes at the beginning and end of this sentence turn underlining on and off.

your name

The CODES Document
This figure shows the document that you enter to explore codes in this tutorial.

In this tutorial, you reveal codes when editing a document.

GETTING STARTED

1. Press F6 and then type the first sentence shown in the figure "The CODES Document." After typing the period at the end of the sentence, press F6 again.

2. Press Enter to move the cursor to the next line, press F8, and then type the second sentence shown in the figure "The CODES Document." After typing the period at the end of the sentence, press F8 again.
3. Press Enter twice, and type in your name.
4. Press Home three times, and then press ↑ to move the cursor to the top of the document.
5. Press Shift-F8 to display the Format menu.
6. Press L (for ***L**ine*) to display the Line Format menu.
7. Press M (for ***M**argins*), and the cursor jumps to the number on the line that reads ***M**argins - Left.*
8. Type **2** and press Enter. The cursor moves down to the line that reads *Right.*
9. Type **2** and press Enter. The cursor moves back to the line that reads *Selection: 0.*
10. Press F7 to return to the Edit screen, then press ↓ to reform the document..
11. Save the document using the filename CODES.WP5.
12. Print the document.

REVEALING CODES

13. Press Alt-F3 or F11, and the screen splits horizontally into two parts. The lower half of the screen shows the text with codes. The upper half shows the same text without codes.

Revealing Codes
You can press Alt-F3 or F11 to reveal codes that are normally hidden. The ruler line between the two windows indicates tab stops, indents, and margin settings at the cursor's position.

```
        The paired codes at the beginning and end of this sentence turn
        boldfacing on and off.
        The paired codes at the beginning and end of this sentence turn
        underlining on and off.

        your name




A:\CODES.WP5                                       Doc 1 Pg 1 Ln 1i Pos 2i
[L/R Mar:2i,2i][BOLD:Times Roman Bold 12pt]The paired codes at the beginning and
 end of this sentence turn[SRt]
boldfacing on and off.[bold][HRt]
[UND]The paired codes at the beginning and end of this sentence turn[SRt]
underlining on and off.[und][HRt]
[HRt]
your name[HRt]



Press Reveal Codes to restore screen
```

DELETING CODES

14. Press Home three times, and then press ↑ to move the cursor to the top of the document. If necessary, use the arrow keys to highlight the *[BOLD]* code in the lower part of the screen.
15. Press Del to delete the beginning code, and the second code is automatically deleted. The sentence is no longer boldfaced.
16. Move the cursor to highlight the *[UND]* code at the beginning of the second sentence.
17. Press Del to delete the beginning code in the lower part of the screen, and the second code is automatically deleted. The sentence is no longer underlined.

18. Highlight the code that reads *[L/R Mar:2",2"]* (the 2" may read *2 i* on your system), and press [Del] to delete it.

JOINING PARAGRAPHS

19. Move the cursor to highlight the *[HRt]* code at the end of the first paragraph.
20. Press [Del] to join the two paragraphs.
21. Press [Spacebar] (if necessary) to insert two spaces between the joined sentences.
22. Print the document.

SPLITTING A PARAGRAPH

23. Move the cursor to under the *T* in *The paired codes* at the beginning of the second sentence.
24. Press [Enter←] twice to split the paragraph into two paragraphs and insert a line of space. The first *[HRt]* ends the paragraph, and the second inserts a blank line to separate it from the next paragraph.
25. Press [Alt]-[F3] or [F11] to return to the Edit screen.

FINISHING UP

26. Print the document, and compare it to the first printout you made. The first sentence should no longer be boldfaced, and the margins should be back to 1 inch.
27. Clear the screen without saving your changes.
28. You have now completed this tutorial. Either continue with the next activity or quit the program.

TIPS

- When using typeover mode, you do not type over the codes you entered when formatting text; instead, the codes are automatically pushed to the right to make room for the new text.
- You can adjust the size of the Reveal Codes screen while it is displayed by pressing [Ctrl]-[F3] and then [W] (for ***Window***). Press [↑] or [↓] to change its size; then press [Enter←].
- If you inadvertently delete codes, you can press [F1] to undelete them. However, you cannot see the restored codes unless you reveal codes.
- The position of many open format codes is important. Generally, line format codes should be entered at the beginning of a line, and page format codes at the top of the page.

QUICK REFERENCE

To use WordPerfect successfully, you must understand how to reveal hidden codes so that you can edit them or troubleshoot formatting problems.

Revealing Codes

WordPerfect allows you to reveal the hidden codes in a document. This makes editing much easier. For example, you can see where carriage returns and other formatting codes are located, which makes it simple to delete or change them.

To reveal codes, press [Alt]-[F3] or [F11] or pull down the Edit menu and select ***Reveal Codes***. The lower half of the Reveal Codes screen shows the text with codes, whereas the upper half shows the same text without codes.

The ruler that divides the screen indicates margins with square brackets ([and]) and tabs with ▲ symbols. If the margins and tab stops fall at the same position, braces ({ and }) are displayed instead.

The cursor appears in the top screen as a flashing underscore and in the lower screen as a reverse-video rectangle. The table "WordPerfect Codes" at the end of this topic describes the codes that might be displayed on the Reveal Codes screen. They are usually displayed in a different intensity or color so that they stand out from the rest of the text. With the codes displayed, you can scroll through the document using any of the cursor movement keys and edit as you desire with any of the editing commands. When you have finished, press Alt-F3 or F11 to return to the Edit screen.

→ KEY/Strokes

Revealing Codes

1. Either: Press Alt-F3 or F11.
   Or: Pull down the Edit menu and select ***R**eveal Codes.*
   The Reveal Codes screen is displayed.
2. Edit or revise the document as needed.
3. Either: Press Alt-F3 or F11.
   Or: Pull down the Edit menu and select ***R**eveal Codes.*
   The Edit screen is displayed.

Open Codes
Here an open code has been entered to change the margins after the first paragraph. A second code has then been entered at the end of that paragraph to restore the margins to their original settings. The text above the first code is formatted by the program's default settings. The first code affects all text between it and the second code. The second code affects all text from it to the end of the document.

Paired codes turn a format such as [BOLD] **boldfacing** [bold] on and off.

Paired Codes
Here paired codes have been entered to boldface a word. The first code in the pair turns the format on. The second code in the pair turns the format off.

Types of Codes

You enter two types of codes into a document, called open codes and paired codes. Many of these codes are entered using the Format menu that is displayed when you press ⇧Shift-F8.

Open Codes

Some open codes, like those used to change tab stops or margins, affect all text either from the code to the end of the document or to the next code of the same type. Other open codes, like those that indent text, affect all text until the next hard carriage return.

Paired Codes

Paired codes, like *[BOLD]* and *[bold]*, begin an effect and then end it. For example, when you boldface or underline text, one code is positioned at the beginning of the affected text, and one is at the end. Paired codes often have the same names, but the code that turns the format on is in uppercase, and the code that turns it off is in lowercase.

There are two ways to enter paired codes, depending on whether you are formatting new or existing text.

- To format new text, you enter a beginning code, type text, and then enter an ending code. There is also a shortcut you can use. When you enter a beginning code, the ending code is also automatically entered. After typing the text, you can press → to move the cursor to the right of the ending code so that the rest of the text that you type isn't affected.
- To format existing text, you select a block of existing text (as described in the next topic) and then execute a format command that automatically inserts codes at the beginning and end of the selected block.

If you insert text into a document containing paired codes, the position of the cursor determines the format of the text that you insert.

- If the cursor is between the codes, the text is formatted just like the other text between the code.
- If the cursor is outside the codes, the text is not affected.

On many systems, the number to the right of *Pos* in the status line at the bottom of the screen indicates when the cursor is inside the codes and when it is outside them. The way the number is displayed varies. For example, on some systems, the number changes color or intensity.

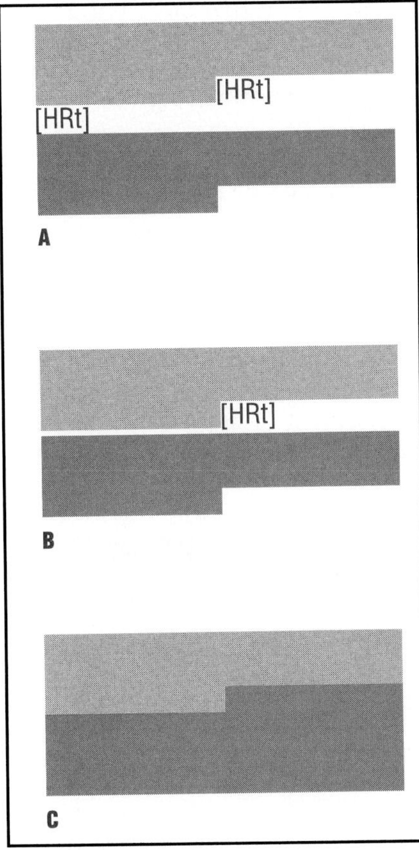

Joining Lines of Text Separated by Hard Carriage Returns
Hard carriage returns are used to separate paragraphs. To separate them with a blank line, you enter two hard carriage returns (A). If you then delete one of these codes (B), the paragraphs close up so that there is no blank space between them. If you delete the second code (C), the two paragraphs join into a single paragraph.

Editing and Deleting Codes

Since codes that you enter into a document affect its format, you can return the affected sections to their default format by deleting the codes that you entered to change the format. For example, if you have indented, boldfaced, superscripted, or centered text, or if you have changed margins, tab stops, or page numbers, you can restore them to their default settings by deleting the appropriate codes. When deleting paired codes, you usually have to delete only one, and the other is deleted automatically. The way you delete codes depends on whether you are in Reveal Codes or not.

When Codes Are Revealed

The easiest way to delete codes is to first reveal them so that you can see them on the screen. When you look at codes in the Reveal Codes screen, some of them can be quite long. However, when you move the cursor through them or delete them, they are like single characters. You only have to press one of the arrow keys twice to move from one side of the code to the other. To delete them, you only have to press ←Bksp or Del once.

When Codes Are Not Revealed

The codes you enter to format text are not normally displayed on the screen. If you try to delete one of these codes with ←Bksp or Del, a prompt may be displayed, for example, *Delete [BOLD]? **No** (**Y**es)*. Press Y if you want to delete the code, or press N if you do not. These prompts appear only when deleting the code will not change the way the document is displayed on the screen. These prompts also do not appear if you select and then delete a block that includes the codes; instead, the codes are deleted along with the selected text.

EXERCISES

EXERCISE 1

EDITING CODES IN THE ENTERING DOCUMENT

1. Retrieve the ENTERING.WP5 document.
2. Reveal codes and practice editing by making each sentence its own paragraph. Then make a printout.
3. Delete the hard carriage return codes to rejoin the sentences into a single paragraph, and make another printout.
4. Delete the codes that you entered to boldface and underline words.

JOINING LINES OF TEXT SEPARATED BY CARRIAGE RETURNS

When editing, you often want to delete blank lines, or join lines and paragraphs that were separated by hard carriage returns. Though not necessarily displayed on the screen, hard carriage returns are much like other characters you enter in a document; therefore, you delete them as you would other characters. To do this accurately, it helps if you can see them. To display hard carriage returns, press Alt-F3 or F11 to display the Reveal Codes screen.

To join two paragraphs, use the arrow keys to position the cursor on or to the right of a hard carriage return code, *[HRt]*. Either press Del to delete the highlighted code or press ←Bksp to delete the code to the left of the cursor so that the line or paragraph below jumps up to join the line above. If necessary, press Spacebar to insert spaces between the last word of the first paragraph and the first word of what was the second paragraph. Press Alt-F3 or F11 to return to the Edit screen.

5. Print the document, and then clear the screen *without* saving your revisions.

EXERCISE 2

IDENTIFYING CODES IN THE OVERVIEW DOCUMENT

1. Retrieve the OVERVIEW.WP5 document.
2. Reveal codes, and then scroll through the document looking for codes.
3. Write down in the table "OVERVIEW Document Codes" some of the codes you find along with a brief description of them drawn from the table "WordPerfect Codes."

OVERVIEW DOCUMENT CODES

Code in Document	Description
______________________	______________________
______________________	______________________
______________________	______________________
______________________	______________________
______________________	______________________
______________________	______________________
______________________	______________________
______________________	______________________
______________________	______________________

WORDPERFECT CODES

Code	Description
[ ]	Hard space
_	Current position of cursor
[-]	Hyphen character
-	Soft hyphen
[/]	Hyphenation canceled
[Adv]	Printer advance
[Bline]	Baseline position
[Block]	Beginning of block
[BlockPro]	Block protection
[Bold]	Bold
[Box Num]	Graphics box caption
[Cell]	Table cell
[Center]	Center
[Center Pg]	Text centered vertically on page
[Cndl EOP]	Conditional end of page
[Cntr Tab]	Centered tab stop
[CNTR TAB]	Hard centered tab
[Col Def]	Column definition
[Col On] [Col Off]	Text columns begin/end
[Color]	Print color
[Comment]	Document comment
[Date]	Date/time function
[Dbl Und]	Double underline
[Dec Tab]	Decimal tab stop
[DEC TAB]	Hard decimal tab stop
[Decml/Algn Char]	Decimal character or thousands separator
[Def Mark:Index]	Index definition
[Def Mark:Listn]	List definition
[Def Mark:ToA]	Table of authorities definition
[Def Mark:ToC]	Table of contents definition
[Dorm HRt]	Dormant hard return
[DSRt]	Deletable soft return
[End Def]	End of index, list, or table of contents
[End Mark]	End of marked text
[End Opt]	Endnote options
[Endnote]	Endnote
[Endnote Placement]	Endnote placement
[Equ Box]	Equation box
[Equ Opt]	Equation box options
[Ext Large]	Extra large print
[Fig Box]	Figure box
[Fig Opt]	Figure box options
[Fine]	Fine print
[Flsh Rgt]	Flush right
[Font]	Base font change
[Footer]	Footer
[Footnote]	Footnote
[Force]	Force odd/even pages
[Ftn Opt]	Footnote/endnote options
[Header]	Header
[Hline]	Horizontal line
[HPg]	Hard page break
[Hrd Row]	Hard row
[HRt]	Hard carriage return
[HRt-SPg]	Hard carriage return and soft page break
[Hyph Off]	Hyphenation ends
[Hyph On]	Hyphenation begins
[HZone]	Change in hyphenation zone
[→Indent]	Indent begins
[→Indent←]	Left/right indent begins
[Index]	Index mark
[Insert Pg Num]	Inserted page number
[ISRt]	Invisible soft return
[Italc]	Italics
[Just]	Right justification
[Just Lim]	Word/letter spacing justification limits
[Kern]	Kern
[L/R Mar]	Left and right margin settings
[Lang]	Language
[Large]	Large print
[Leading Adj]	Leading adjustment
[Link]	Link to spreadsheet file
[Link End]	End of link to spreadsheet
[Ln Height]	Line height
[Ln Num]	Line numbering
[Ln Spacing]	Line spacing
[←Mar Rel]	Left margin release
[Mark:List]	List entry
[Mark:ToC]	Table of contents entry
[Math Def]	Math columns definition
[Math Off]	Math ends
[Math On]	Math begins
[!]	Formula calculation
[t]	Subtotal entry
[+]	Calculate subtotal
[T]	Total entry
[=]	Calculate total
[*]	Calculate grand total
[N]	Negate
[New End Num]	New endnote number
[New Equ Num]	New equation number
[New Fig Num]	New figure number
[New Ftn Num]	New footnote number
[New Tbl Num]	New table number
[New Txt Num]	New text box number
[New Usr Num]	New user box number
[Note Num]	Footnote/endnote reference
[Outline Lvl]	Outline style
[Outline Off]	Outline off
[Outline On]	Outline on
[Outln]	Outline attribute
[Ovrstk]	Overstrike character
[Paper Sz/Typ]	Paper size and type
[Par Num]	Paragraph number
[Par Num Def]	Paragraph numbering definition
[Pg Num]	New page number
[Pg Num Style]	Page number style
[Pg Numbering]	Page numbering
[Ptr Cmnd]	Printer command
[Redln]	Redlining begins/ends
[Ref]	Automatic reference
[Rgt Tab]	Right-aligned tab stop
[RGT TAB]	Hard right-aligned tab stop
[Row]	Table row
[Shadw]	Shadow
[Sm Cap]	Small caps
[Small]	Small print
[SPg]	Soft page break
[SRt]	Soft carriage return
[StkOut]	Strikeout
[Style Off]	Style off
[Style On]	Style on
[Subdoc]	Subdocument
[Subdoc Start]	Subdocument begins
[Subdoc End]	Subdocument ends
[Subscpt]	Subscript
[Suppress]	Page formats suppressed
[Suprscpt]	Superscript
[T/B Mar]	Top and bottom margins
[Tab]	Left-aligned tab
[TAB]	Hard left-aligned tab
[Tab Set]	Tabs reset
[Target]	Automatic reference target
[Tbl Box]	Table box
[Tbl Def]	Table definition
[Tbl Off]	Table ends
[Tbl Opt]	Table box options
[Text Box]	Text box
[ToA]	Table of authorities entry
[Txt Opt]	Text box options
[Und]	Underlining begins/ends
[Undrln]	Underline spaces/tabs
[Usr Box]	User-defined box
[Usr Opt]	User-defined box options
[VLine]	Vertical line
[Vry Large]	Very large print
[W/O Off]	Widow/orphan protection ends
[W/O On]	Widow/orphan protection begins
[Wrd/Ltr Spacing]	Word and letter spacing

TOPIC 9

Selecting Blocks of Text

After completing this topic, you will be able to:

- Select blocks
- Unselect blocks

Many of the commands you use to format, delete, copy, or move text in a document require you to first select the text to be affected. The section of text that you select is called a block and sometimes the process of selecting it is called blocking. After selecting a block, you can use any of the commands that affect blocks of text. For example, you can copy or move it, check its spelling, or save and print it as described in later topics in this text.

TUTORIAL

In this tutorial, you explore selecting blocks of text and then boldfacing and underlining them.

GETTING STARTED

1. Retrieve the EDUCOM.WP5 document.

BOLDFACING PARAGRAPHS

2. Move the cursor to under the *U* in *USING* on the first line.
3. Press Alt-F4 or F12 to turn block on.
4. Press Enter↵ three times to highlight the first three lines of the document.

A Selected Block
When you select a block, it is highlighted in reverse video or in color, as the first three lines in this figure are.

```
USING SOFTWARE
A GUIDE TO THE ETHICAL AND LEGAL USE OF SOFTWARE
FOR MEMBERS OF THE ACADEMIC COMMUNITY

HERE ARE SOME RELEVANT FACTS

1 UNAUTHORIZED copying of software is illegal.  Copyright law protects software
publishers, just as patent law protects inventors.

2 UNAUTHORIZED copying of software by individuals can harm the entire academic
community.  If unauthorized copying proliferates on a campus, the institution ma
liability.  Also, the institution may find it more difficult to negotiate agreem
software more widely and less expensively available to members of the academic c

3 UNAUTHORIZED copying of software can deprive developers of a fair return for t
increase prices, reduce the level of future support and enhancement, and inhibit
of new software products.

RESPECT for the intellectual work and property of others has traditionally been
mission of colleges and universities.  As members of the academic community, we
exchange of ideas.  Just as we do not tolerate plagiarism, we do no condone the
copying of software, including programs, applications, databases and code.

THEREFORE, we offer the following statements of principle about intellectual pro
Block on
                                              Doc 1 Pg 1 Ln 1.58i Pos 1i
```

5. Press [F6] to boldface the heading, and the first three lines may stand out from the rest of the text. If they do not, adjust your screen's brightness and contrast. If that does not work, your system may not be set up to display some types of formatting.
6. Press [Alt]-[F3] or [F11] to reveal codes, and the boldface codes, *[BOLD]* and *[bold]*, can be seen at the beginning and end of the heading.
7. Press [Alt]-[F3] or [F11] to hide codes.

BOLDFACING A LINE

8. Position the cursor at the beginning of the heading that reads *HERE ARE SOME RELEVANT FACTS.*
9. Press [Alt]-[F4] or [F12] to turn block on.
10. Press [End] to highlight the line.
11. Press [F6] to boldface the line.

BOLDFACING WORDS

12. Move the cursor to under the *1* in *1. UNAUTHORIZED.*
13. Press [Alt]-[F4] or [F12] to turn block on.
14. Press [Spacebar] twice to highlight the number *1* and word *UNAUTHORIZED.*
15. Press [F6] to boldface the highlighted number and word.

BOLDFACING OTHER HEADINGS

16. Using [Alt]-[F4] or [F12] and then [Spacebar] or [End], select and boldface each of the following headings (some of which—called run-in headings—are the first word in a paragraph):
    - *2. UNAUTHORIZED*
    - *3. UNAUTHORIZED*
    - *RESPECT*
    - *THEREFORE* (don't include the comma)
    - *SOFTWARE AND INTELLECTUAL RIGHTS*
    - *QUESTIONS YOU MAY HAVE ABOUT USING SOFTWARE*
    - *ALTERNATIVES TO EXPLORE*
    - *Site-Licensed and Bulk-Purchased Software*
    - *Shareware*
    - *Public Domain Software*
    - *A FINAL NOTE*

FINISHING UP

17. Save the document and leave it on the screen.
18. Print the document, and the paragraphs and words you boldfaced should be darker than the rest of the text.
19. You have now completed this tutorial. Either continue with the next activity or quit the program.

> **SELECTING BLOCKS WITH A MOUSE**
>
> If you are using a mouse, you can use it to select a block.
> 1. Point to the beginning or end of the block.
> 2. Press the left button and drag the mouse to highlight the block, and then release the button.
>
> You can manipulate the block or change its size with any of the cursor movement keys or commands. To cancel the selection, click the left button.

QUICK REFERENCE

To work with blocks, you must first select them. After selecting a block of text, you can copy, move, delete, or save it, or append it to the end of another file. When you select a block of text, any codes in the block are also selected. Since you normally do not see these codes, you can encounter problems unless you reveal codes when selecting blocks in heavily formatted documents.

After selecting a block, you can press Alt-F4, F12, or F1 to cancel the selection if you change your mind.

SELECTING BLOCK TIPS

After completing a block procedure, you can select the block again or move the cursor back to the starting point.

- To select the same block again immediately, press Alt-F4 or F12, hold down Ctrl, and then press Home twice.
- To return the cursor to the beginning of a block, hold down Ctrl, and then press Home twice. Use this command after moving a block to return the cursor to the block's original position.

KEY/Strokes

Selecting Blocks

1. Move the cursor to the beginning of the block that you want to select.
2. Press Alt-F4 or F12, and the status line flashes *Block on.*
3. Either: Press any cursor movement keys to highlight the block.

   Or: Type a character to highlight to the next occurrence of that character; for example, type a period to highlight to the end of the sentence.

   Or: Press Spacebar to highlight the word and the trailing space.

   Or: Press Enter← to highlight up to the next hard carriage return.

   Or: Use the Search command (F2) to expand the highlight to the specified string (see Topic 23).

   A selected block appears highlighted so that it stands out from the text you have not selected. It may be in a different color or highlighted in reverse video (dark characters against a bright background).

EXERCISES

EXERCISE 1

EXPLORING SELECTING BLOCKS

1. Retrieve the OVERVIEW.WP5 file.
2. Follow the instructions in the KEY/Stroke box "Selecting Blocks" to practice selecting and unselecting blocks. When the status line reads *Block on*, try pressing the following keys repeatedly. Each should expand the highlight up to the next occurrence of the character (or code) normally entered by the key. Remember that you can press Alt-F4, F12, or F1 to cancel a selection and remove the highlight to start over.

- A lowercase letter such as *e*
- An uppercase letter such as *E*
- A period
- A comma
- Spacebar
- Enter ↵

EXERCISE 2

UNDERLINING HEADINGS IN THE JOBGUIDE DOCUMENT

1. Retrieve the JOBGUIDE.WP5 file.
2. Boldface the title of the paper on the first line.
3. Locate and underline the following headings. (Those marked with an asterisk are the first word in a paragraph.)
   - *Preparing a Cover Letter for a Resume*
   - *Salutation**
   - *Opening**
   - *Body**
   - *Closing**
   - *The Resume*
   - *The Follow-up Letter*
4. Save and then print the document.

EXERCISE 3

BOLDFACING HEADINGS IN THE NEWSLTR DOCUMENT

1. Retrieve the NEWSLTR.WP5 file.
2. Locate and boldface the following headings:
   - *ERGONOMICS AND HEALTH*
   - *Computer Users' Checklist*
   - *SECURITY*
   - *Passwords*
   - *ELECTRONIC SUPERVISION*
   - *END-USER SURVEY REPORT*
3. Save and then print the document.

EXERCISE 4

BOLDFACING AND UNDERLINING HEADINGS IN THE SUNCITY DOCUMENT

1. Retrieve the SUNCITY.WP5 file.
2. Boldface the name and address on the first three lines.
3. Locate and boldface the following headings:
   - *THE TEMPLATE*
   - *CELL INPUT*
   - *CELL OUTPUT*
   - *THE CONSUMER PRICE INDEX*
4. Locate and underline the following headings (so that they are boldfaced and underlined):
   - *THE TEMPLATE*
   - *THE CONSUMER PRICE INDEX*
5. Boldface the *Year*, *Average Consumer*, and *Urban Consumer* column headings for the table of consumer prices.
6. Save and then print the document.

TOPIC 10

Font Appearance & Style

After completing this topic, you will be able to:

- Change the appearance of text in your documents
- Change the size of text

When you want to make characters, words, phrases, or paragraphs stand out, you can change the appearance or size of their type. For example, you can make the type much smaller or much larger. Or you can make it print in italic, boldface, or underlined type. All font appearance and size choices are listed on the Font pull-down menu shown in the figure "Font Appearances and Sizes."

TUTORIAL

Font Appearance

Normal
Bold
Underline
Double underline
Italic
Outline
Shadow
SMALL CAPS

Font Size

Fine
Small
Normal (don't format)
Large
Very large
Extra large

your name

The Formatted and Printed FONTS Document
After formatting the FONTS document, your printout should look similar to this. However, because of variations in fonts, your results will probably vary somewhat.

In this tutorial, you explore changing the appearance and size of text in a document.

GETTING STARTED

1. Retrieve the FONTS.WP5 document.

CHANGING FONT APPEARANCE

2. Move the cursor to under the *B* in *Bold.*
3. Press [Alt]-[F4] or [F12] to turn block on.
4. Press [End] to highlight the line.
5. Press [Ctrl]-[F8] to display the Font menu.
6. Press [A] (for ***A**ppearance*).
7. Press [B] (for ***B**old*), and the word is boldfaced.
8. Repeat Steps 3 through 7 to change the font appearance of the other terms (except Normal) using the appropriate menu command.

CHANGING FONT SIZES

9. Move the cursor to under the *F* in *Fine.*
10. Press [Alt]-[F4] or [F12] to turn block on.
11. Press [End] to highlight the line.
12. Press [Ctrl]-[F8] to display the Font menu.
13. Press [S] (for ***S**ize*).
14. Press [F] (for ***F**ine*), and the word is formatted in a fine font size.

15. Repeat Steps 10 through 14 to change the font size of the other terms (except Normal) using the appropriate menu command.

SAVING AND PRINTING THE DOCUMENT

16. Save the document, but leave it on the screen.
17. Print the document. The results you obtain depend on what fonts are supported by your printer, but they should be similar to the figure "The Formatted and Printed FONTS Document." If your text appears normal, your printer does not support the appearances that you specified. Avoid those formats in later documents when using the same printer.

FINISHING UP

18. You have now completed this tutorial. Either clear the Edit screen and continue with the next activity or quit the program.

QUICK REFERENCE

Font appearance refers to the way the formatted text is printed. The choices range from underlining to boldfacing, and they are listed in the table "Appearance Styles."

Font Appearances and Sizes
You can assign font appearances and sizes by selecting the text and using the choices on the pull-down Font menu.

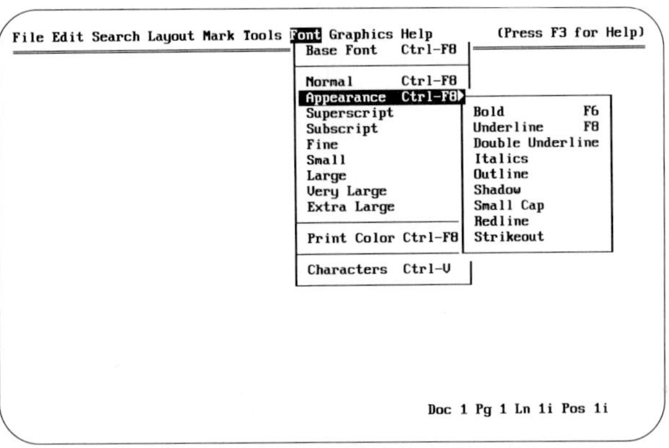

Normal
Bold
Underline
Double underline
Italic
Shadow
SMALL CAPS

Font Appearance
Fonts can be printed in a range of styles, including those shown here.

KEY/Strokes

Changing Font Appearance

1. Move the cursor to where you want the new appearance to begin. (If formatting existing text, select the block.)
2. Either: Press Ctrl-F8, and then press A (for ***A**ppearance*).
   Or: Pull down the Font menu and select ***A**ppearance*.
3. Select any of the styles described in the table "Appearance Styles."
4. If entering new text, type it in, and then use one of the following procedures to turn the format off:
   - Press → to move the cursor to the right of the off code.
   - Press Ctrl-F8, and then press N (for ***N**ormal*).
   - Pull down the Font menu and select ***N**ormal*.

Fine
Small
Normal
Large
Vry large
Ext large

Font Sizes
Font sizes range from fine to extra large.

APPEARANCE STYLES

1 ***Bold*** prints text darker than normal.
2 ***Undln*** prints text underlined.
3 ***Dbl Und*** prints text with a double underline.
4 ***Italc*** prints text in an italic typeface.
5 ***Outln*** prints outline characters.
6 ***Shadw*** prints characters with a shadow effect.
7 ***Sm Cap*** prints all uppercase letters. Characters entered in uppercase print larger than characters entered in lowercase.
8 ***Redln*** highlights text being considered for insertion.
9 ***Stkout*** highlights text being considered for deletion.

Font size refers to how large characters are printed. The choices range from fine to extra large and are listed in the table "Font Sizes." If you specify a size not on your system, WordPerfect will automatically use the closest available size.

KEY/Strokes

Changing Font Sizes

1. Move the cursor to where you want the font size to change. (If formatting existing text, select the block.)
2. Either: Press Ctrl-F8, and then press S (for ***Size***).
   Or: Pull down the Font menu.
3. Select any of the sizes described in the table "Font Sizes."
4. If entering new text, type it in, and then use one of the following procedures to turn the format off:
   - Press → to move the cursor to the right of the off code.
   - Press Ctrl-F8, and then press N (for ***Normal***).
   - Pull down the Font menu and select ***Normal***.

TIPS

- To insert new text at the beginning or the end of formatted text, use the Reveal Codes command to position the cursor. If the new text is to have the same format, position the cursor between the codes. If the new text is to have a different format, position the cursor outside the codes.
- If you select a formatted block of text between codes used to change its size or appearance and then copy or move the block, the copied or moved block will have the same format as the original even if you do not copy the codes.
- You can print the file PRINTER.TST on the *WordPerfect 1* disk to see how your printer prints selected font attributes. Different printers produce different results.

FONT SIZES

1 ***Suprscpt*** prints text in a fine size above the center of the line. You can use this font size to create fractions, formulas, trademark symbols, copyright symbols, registration marks, degrees, and footnote symbols.
2 ***Subscpt*** prints text in a fine size below the center of the line. You can use this font size to create fractions and formulas.
3 ***Fine*** prints text in the smallest font size.
4 ***Small*** prints text in a font size smaller than normal.
5 ***Large*** prints text in a font size larger than normal.
6 ***Vry Large*** prints text in a font size larger than large.
7 ***Ext Large*** prints text in the largest font size.

EXERCISES

1. 1/2

2. Trademarktm

3. RegisteredR

4. 30oF

5. H2O

6. 1 - 3/4 = 1/4

your name

The SCRIPTS Document
You retrieve this document in this exercise.

1. $^{1}/_{2}$

2. Trademark^{tm}

3. Registered^{R}

4. 30°F

5. H_2O

6. 1 - $^{3}/_{4}$ = $^{1}/_{4}$

your name

The Formatted and Printed SCRIPTS Document
When you print your SCRIPTS document, your results should be similar to these.

EXERCISE 1

FORMATTING WITH SUPERSCRIPTS AND SUBSCRIPTS

1. Retrieve the SCRIPTS.WP5 document.
2. Follow the procedures described in the KEY/Stroke box "Changing Font Sizes" to subscript and superscript the appropriate characters. When finished, your document should look like the one shown in the figure "The Formatted and Printed SCRIPTS Document."
3. Save the file under its original name and print the document.

EXERCISE 2

ITALICIZING PARAGRAPHS IN THE EDUCOM DOCUMENT

1. Retrieve the EDUCOM.WP5 document.
2. Follow the procedures described in the KEY/Stroke box "Changing Font Sizes" to change the size of the heading on the first three lines to Extra Large.
3. Follow the procedures described in the KEY/Stroke box "Changing Font Appearance" to italicize the two paragraphs that follow the heading *SOFTWARE AND INTELLECTUAL RIGHTS.*
4. Under the heading *QUESTIONS YOU MAY HAVE ABOUT USING SOFTWARE,* there are a series of letter questions. Each question is followed by a one-paragraph answer. Follow the procedures described in the KEY/Stroke box "Changing Font Appearance" to italicize each of these answer paragraphs.
5. Save and then print the document.

EXERCISE 3

ENLARGING HEADINGS IN THE JOBGUIDE DOCUMENT

1. Retrieve the JOBGUIDE.WP5 document.
2. Follow the procedures described in the KEY/Stroke box "Changing Font Sizes" to make the heading on the first line Large.
3. Save the document and print the first page.

EXERCISE 4

ENLARGING HEADINGS IN THE NEWSLTR DOCUMENT

1. Retrieve the NEWSLTR.WP5 document.
2. Space out the title by entering a space between each pair of letters and two more (for a total of three) between each word.

3. Follow the procedures described in the KEY/Stroke box "Changing Font Sizes" to make the heading on the first line Very Large.
4. Preview the document to check that the title does not wrap to a second line. If it does, change its size to Large. To do so, reveal codes, delete the code for Very Large, and start over.
5. Save the document and print the first page.

EXERCISE 5

ENLARGING HEADINGS IN THE SUNCITY DOCUMENT

1. Retrieve the SUNCITY.WP5 document.
2. Follow the procedures described in the KEY/Stroke box "Changing Font Sizes" to make the heading on the first line Extra Large.
3. Save the document and print the first page.

TOPIC 11

Page Breaks

After completing this topic, you will be able to:

- Explain the difference between hard and soft page breaks
- Control where page breaks fall in your documents

You can control where page breaks fall when you print a document. A page break is the point at which the printer stops printing lines on the current sheet of paper and resumes printing on the next sheet.

Controlling where page breaks occur is important when printing multipage documents because there are certain places where you want to avoid breaks.

- Letters should not end with their closing alone at the top of a page.
- Reports, term papers, and other important documents should often have major sections begin at the top of a new page.
- Tables should be kept together so that they do not break with one part on one page and the rest on the next page.

TUTORIAL

In this tutorial, you explore hard and soft page breaks and protecting blocks and lines of text.

GETTING STARTED

1. Retrieve the EDUCOM.WP5 document.

ENTERING A HARD PAGE BREAK

2. Move the cursor to under the *H* in *HERE ARE SOME RELEVANT FACTS.*
3. Press [Ctrl]-[Enter↵] to enter a hard page break, which is indicated by the double dashed line on the screen. The status line now indicates that the cursor is on *Pg 2.*

PROTECTING A BLOCK OF TEXT FROM A PAGE BREAK

4. Scroll down the document until you find the single dashed line that indicates a soft page break.
5. Move the cursor to the beginning of the first heading paragraph above the line, and press [Alt]-[F4] or [F12] to turn block on.
6. Press [Enter↵] twice to highlight the heading and the following paragraph.

7. Press ⇧Shift-F8, and the prompt reads *Protect block? **No** (**Y**es).*
8. Press Y to protect the block, and since the two paragraphs cannot fit in their entirety onto the page, they both move to the top of the next page.
9. Press Alt-F3 or F11 to reveal codes, and the *[Block Pro:On]* and *[Block Pro:Off]* codes can be seen at the beginning and end of the block.
10. Press Alt-F3 or F11 to hide codes.

TURNING ON WIDOW AND ORPHAN PROTECTION

11. Move the cursor to the top of the document.
12. Press ⇧Shift-F8 to display the Format menu.
13. Press L (for ***L**ine*) to display the Line Format menu.
14. Press W (for ***W**idow/Orphan Protection*).
15. Press Y to turn protection on.
16. Press F7 to return to the Edit screen, and widow and orphan protection is now turned on from the position of the code to the end of the document.

FINISHING UP

17. Save the document.
18. Print the document. The title prints on a page by itself, and the two protected paragraphs both print on a new page.
19. You have now completed this tutorial. Either continue with the next activity or quit the program.

QUICK REFERENCE

To control where page breaks occur, you must understand WordPerfect's three kinds of page breaks: soft, hard, and conditional. You should also understand how to prevent widows and orphans.

Soft Page Breaks

Soft page breaks are automatically entered and adjusted as you enter or delete text. Soft page breaks are indicated on the screen with single dashed lines (-------) and on the Reveal Codes screen with *[SPg]* or *[HRt-SPg]* codes. If you edit the document so that the length of one or more pages changes, the soft page breaks are repositioned automatically. You cannot directly change the position of a soft page break, and you cannot delete it. To move it, you have to change the amount or format of the text above it. For example, if you change top or bottom margins, line height or spacing, or the size of fonts, the soft page breaks will shift.

Hard Page Breaks

You can force a page break to fall at a selected point in a document by entering a hard page break. To do so, you move the cursor to where you want a page to break and press Ctrl-Enter↵. Hard page breaks are indicated on the screen with double dashed lines (=====) and on the

Reveal Codes screen with *[HPg]* codes. To remove or change the position of a hard page break, you must delete the code you entered to create it.

Page Breaks
Soft page breaks are indicated by a single dashed line across the screen, and hard page breaks by a double dashed line.

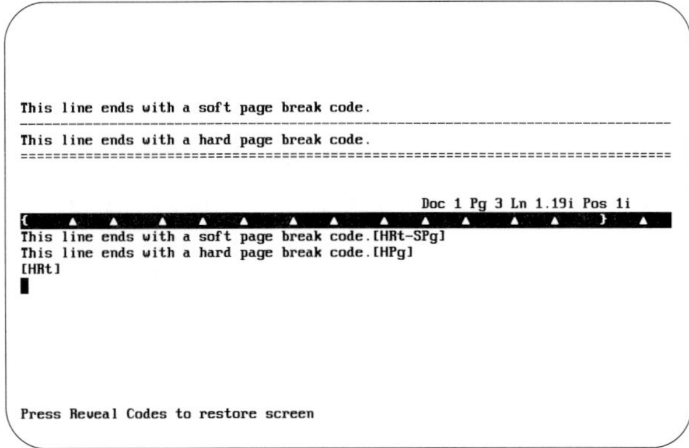

Preventing Page Breaks

You can prevent soft page breaks from occurring in undesirable places by protecting a selected block or a specific number of lines. These commands tell the printer, "If this protected section fits in the remaining space on this page, print it here; otherwise, advance the paper and begin printing it at the top of the next page." This command is extremely useful when you want to:

- Keep the lines of a table on the same page as the table headings
- Keep an illustration on the same page as the text that refers to it
- Keep a heading and at least the first two lines of the following text on the same page

WordPerfect offers two ways to protect sections of your text: You can select the block and then protect it, or you can specify the number of lines to be protected. You usually protect a block when you want to keep it together on the same page if you should add or delete text above it. You specify lines when you want to keep a certain element with another. For example, you can use this command to keep a heading with at least the first two lines of the following paragraph.

Widows and Orphans
A widow is the last line of a paragraph printed by itself at the top of a page. An orphan is the first line of a paragraph that prints by itself at the bottom of a page.

➜ KEY/Strokes

Protecting a Selected Block from a Soft Page Break

1. Move the cursor to under the first character in the block to be protected.
2. Press Alt-F4 or F12 to turn block on.
3. Press the cursor movement keys to highlight the block to be protected.
   - If you protect a block beginning or ending in the middle of a line, the entire line is protected.
   - Do not include the hard carriage return code at the end of the last paragraph.
4. Press ⇧Shift-F8, and the prompt reads *Protect block?* ***No*** *(**Y**es).*
5. Press Y to protect the block.

→ KEY/Strokes

Protecting a Specified Number of Lines from a Soft Page Break

1. Count the number of lines to be protected from a soft page break.
2. Move the cursor to the line above the lines to be protected even if that line has text on it.
3. Either: Press ⇧Shift-F8, and then press O (for ***O**ther*).
   Or: Pull down the Layout menu and select ***O**ther*.
4. Press C (for ***C**onditional End of Page*), and the prompt reads *Number of Lines to Keep Together:*.
5. Type the number of lines to be protected from a page break and press Enter↵.
6. Press F7 to return to the Edit screen.

TIPS

- When a page is filled, WordPerfect automatically inserts a page break. This is shown on the screen as a dashed line (------). If the first line on the new page contains just a *[HRt]* code, that code is automatically converted to a dormant hard return indicated by a *[Dorm Hrt]* code. Lines with this dormant hard return code do not print. This prevents a blank line from being printed at the top of the page. If you edit the document so that the dormant hard return code is no longer the first line on a page, it is automatically converted back into a hard carriage return.
- When you specify lines in the Conditional End of Page command, you must take line spacing into consideration if you have changed it. For example, to protect three lines that have been double-spaced, specify six lines.

Widows and Orphans

When printing documents longer than a single page, you can turn widow and orphan protection on so that at least two lines at the beginning or end of paragraphs are kept together at the bottom and top of each page. This command prevents orphans (the first line of a paragraph printed by itself at the bottom of a page) and widows (the last line of a paragraph printed by itself at the top of the next page).

If WordPerfect calculates that the first or last line of a paragraph is to print at the bottom or top of a page by itself, it moves another line to accompany it. Since single lines are prevented, no three-line paragraphs will be split; the entire paragraph will move to the next page if it will not print on the current page.

→ KEY/Strokes

Turning Widow and Orphan Protection On or Off

1. Move the cursor to where you want to turn widow and orphan protection on or off.
2. Either: Press ⇧Shift-F8, and then press L (for ***L**ine*).
   Or: Pull down the Layout menu and select ***L**ine*.
3. Press W (for ***W**idow/Orphan Protection*).
4. Either: Press Y to turn protection on.
   Or: Press N to turn protection off.
5. Press F7 to return to the Edit screen.

EXERCISE 1

EXPLORING PAGE BREAKS IN THE OVERVIEW DOCUMENT

1. Retrieve the OVERVIEW.WP5 document.
2. Scroll down the document to see if any of the paragraphs are split by a soft page break or a heading is at the bottom of a page by itself. If they are, move the cursor to the line where the paragraph or heading begins, and then add a hard page break. (If the split paragraph is immediately below a heading, insert the page break at the beginning of the heading.)
3. Preview the document with the View Document command, and make a printout.
4. Remove the hard page break codes. Then select the same paragraphs and follow the instructions in the KEY/Strokes box "Protecting a Selected Block from a Soft Page Break" to protect them from soft page breaks.
5. Preview the document on the screen with the View Document command and make a printout.
6. Clear the screen *without* saving the document.

EXERCISE 2

ENTERING A HARD PAGE BREAK IN THE SUNCITY DOCUMENT

1. Retrieve the SUNCITY.WP5 document.
2. Enter a hard page break so that the heading *THE CONSUMER PRICE INDEX* prints at the top of page 2.
3. Save the document.
4. Preview the document on the screen with the View Document command and make a printout of the second page.

TOPIC 12

Page Numbers

After completing this topic, you will be able to:

- Print page numbers in your own documents
- Suppress page numbers on selected pages

WordPerfect prints page numbers only if you tell it to. If you decide to number pages, you can use Arabic (1, 2, 3) or lowercase Roman (i, ii, iii) or uppercase Roman (I, II, III) numbers, and you can suppress them on selected pages—for example, on chapter or part openers.

TUTORIAL

In this tutorial, you add page numbers to a document. When you do so, you use a Roman numeral on the title page. Normally, you do not number such pages, but we do it here only so that you can see how to use Roman numerals.

GETTING STARTED

1. Retrieve the EDUCOM.WP5 document.

TURNING PAGE NUMBERS ON

2. Press Home three times, and then press ↑ to move the cursor to the beginning of the document above all codes.
3. Press ⇧Shift-F8 to display the Format menu.
4. Press P (for ***P**age*) to display the Page Format menu.
5. Press N (for *Page **N**umbering*) to display the Page Numbering menu.
6. Press P (for *Page Number **P**osition*) to display an illustration of page numbering options.

The Page Number Position Menu
The Page Number Position menu illustrates your page number position choices. For example, selecting **1** prints page numbers in the upper-left corner of every page. Selecting **4** prints them in the upper-left corner of even-numbered pages and the upper-right corner of odd-numbered pages.

```
Format: Page Number Position

     Every Page           Alternating Pages
    1   2   3          4                     4

                       Even                Odd

    5   6   7          8                     8

    9 - No Page Numbers



Selection: 0
```

7. Press [6] to enter page numbers at the bottom center of the page, and you return to the Page Numbering Format menu.

SPECIFYING A NEW PAGE NUMBER

8. Press [N] (for ***N**ew Page Number*).
9. Type **i** and press [Enter←].
10. Press [F7] to return to the Edit screen.

SPECIFYING ANOTHER NEW PAGE NUMBER

11. Move the cursor to the beginning of the heading *HERE ARE SOME RELEVANT FACTS* at the top of page 2.
12. Press [⇧Shift]-[F8] to display the Format menu.
13. Press [P] (for ***P**age*) to display the Page Format menu.
14. Press [N] (for *Page **N**umbering*) to display the Page Numbering menu.
15. Press [N] (for ***N**ew Page Number*).
16. Type **2** and press [Enter←].
17. Press [F7] to return to the Edit screen.

FINISHING UP

18. Save and print the document. The first page is numbered at the bottom center with a Roman i, and all subsequent pages are numbered in the same position with Arabic numerals.
19. You have now completed this tutorial. Either continue with the next activity or quit the program.

QUICK REFERENCE

Page Numbers
Page numbers can be printed in Roman or Arabic numerals in a variety of positions on the page.

You can turn page numbering on and then back off anywhere in a document by entering open codes. When you do so, you can also specify where on the page they will print relative to the margins. The figure "The Page Number Position Menu" shows some of the page number positions you can specify. Page numbers are not displayed on the Edit screen but are added as the document is printed. They can be previewed with the View Document command, and their codes can be seen when you reveal codes.

After you turn on page numbering, you can start a new page number sequence anywhere in your document. When you do so, you can specify whether numbers are printed as Arabic numerals (1, 2, 3), lowercase Roman numerals (i, ii, iii), or uppercase Roman numerals (I, II, III).

Page numbers are printed in the text area of the page. The amount of space left available for text is reduced by the line height specified for the page number plus one line.

SPECIFYING PAGES TO BE PRINTED

When you specify the name of the file to be printed and the prompt reads *Page(s):*, you can specify selected pages to be printed and then press Enter↵ to begin printing. When specifying selected pages, use the following procedures if you have changed page numbering within the document. (Do not enter spaces in the page specifications.)

- To print sections where you have specified Roman numbering, enter Roman numerals. For example, to print page 2, type **ii**; to print pages 2 through 5, type **ii-v**; and to print pages 1, 5, and 10, type **i,v,x**.
- If you have specified new page numbers anywhere in the document, those changes divide the document into sections. To print selected pages, follow the preceding rules, but add section numbers followed by a colon. For example, to print pages 2 through 5 in an introduction, and pages 2 through 5 in the second and third sections of the document, type **1:2-5,2:2-5,3:2-5**.

Sections are numbered sequentially beginning at 1 unless you have used both Roman (i, ii, iii or I, II, III) and Arabic (1, 2, 3) numbers in the document. In these cases, each numbering style is numbered separately. For example, to print pages 2 through 5 in an introduction numbered with Roman numerals and pages 2 through 5 in the second and third sections of the document numbered with Arabic numerals, type **1:ii-v,1:2-5,2:2-5**.

KEY/Strokes

Turning Page Numbers On or Off

1. Move the cursor to the beginning of the page (above all other codes) where page numbers are to be turned on or off. (Press Ctrl-Home, and then press ↑ from anywhere on the page.)
2. Either: Press ⇧Shift-F8, and then press P (for ***Page***).
   Or: Pull down the Layout menu and select ***Page***.
3. Press N (for *Page **N**umbering*) to display the Page Numbering menu.
4. Make any of the choices described in the table "Page Numbering Menu Choices."
5. Press F7 to return to the document.

PAGE NUMBERING MENU CHOICES

1 *New Page Number* specifies the page number that is to be printed on the page in which the cursor is positioned and the style it is to be printed in. All subsequent pages are numbered in sequence beginning with the specified number. Type the new page number in the style you want to use, and press Enter↵. For example:
- Type **1**, **2**, or **3** for Arabic.
- Type **i**, **ii**, or **iii** for lowercase Roman.
- Type **I**, **II**, or **III** for uppercase Roman.

2 *Page Number **S**tyle* allows you to combine page numbers with text—for example, *Page 1* or *Page 1 of Chapter 1*. WordPerfect's code for a page number is ^B. (Press Ctrl-B to enter it.) To combine text with the page number in your document, choose this option, and type the text as you want it to appear, using ^B in place of the page number.

3 *Insert Page Number* inserts the page numbering code (*^B*) into the document at the cursor's position, using the format you have specified in *Page Number **S**tyle*. You can also enter ^B directly into a document at any point, including in headers and footers, by pressing Ctrl-B. When the document is printed, the ^B is replaced with the number of the page on which you entered it.

4 *Page Number **P**osition* specifies the position in which page numbers are printed or that there be no page numbering.

Suppressing Page Numbers

If you enter page numbers, you can discontinue them or suppress them on selected pages.

KEY/Strokes

Suppressing Page Numbers

1. Move the cursor to the beginning of the page where page numbers, headers, or footers are to be turned off. (Press Ctrl-Home, and then press ↑ from anywhere on the page.)
2. Either: Press ⇧Shift-F8, and then press P (for ***Page***).
   Or: Pull down the Layout menu and select ***Page***.

3. Press [U] (for ***Suppress** (this page only)*).
4. Select one of the choices listed on the screen. (To select choices 1 and 2, you merely press the number of the option. To select choices 3 through 8, press the number and then [Y] or [N].)
5. Press [F7] to return to the Edit screen.

EXERCISES

EXERCISE 1

ADDING PAGE NUMBERS TO THE EDUCOM DOCUMENT

1. Retrieve the EDUCOM.WP5 document.
2. Follow the instructions in the KEY/Strokes box "Suppressing Page Numbers" to suppress the page number on page 1.
3. Save the document and print the first page.

Page Numbers on Facing Pages
Positioning page numbers at the outside edges of pages that are to be copied or printed back to back makes it easier for the reader to find them.

EXERCISE 2

ADDING MIRRORED PAGE NUMBERS TO THE JOBGUIDE DOCUMENT

1. Retrieve the JOBGUIDE.WP5 document.
2. Move the cursor to the top of the document. Follow the instructions in the KEY/Strokes box "Turning Page Numbers On or Off" to add page numbers so that they print at the outside bottom edges of odd and even pages.
3. Save and then print or preview the document. Hold the printed pages up back to back or display facing pages, and you'll see that the page numbers are positioned at the outside of both pages.

EXERCISE 3

ADDING PAGE NUMBERS TO THE SUNCITY DOCUMENT

1. Retrieve the SUNCITY.WP5 document.
2. Move the cursor to the top of the document, then follow the instructions in the KEY/Strokes box "Turning Page Numbers On and Off" to add page numbers so that they print at the bottom center of each page in uppercase Roman numerals.
3. Follow the instructions in the KEY/Strokes box "Suppressing Page Numbers" to suppress the page number on page 1.
4. Save and then print or preview the document.

TOPIC 13

Paragraph Alignments

After completing this topic, you will be able to:

- Describe the four types of horizontal alignments
- Describe vertical centering
- Align text in various ways in your own documents

One of the key elements of a good design is the alignment of paragraphs. Don't think of paragraphs only as blocks of text. Any line, even if it has only a single character, is a paragraph if it ends with a hard carriage return. This means that text, subheads, footnotes, headers, and almost every other element of a document is considered a paragraph. These paragraphs can be aligned on the type page in one of four ways: justified, flush left, flush right, or centered.

Justified text is evenly aligned with both left and right margins. This alignment is frequently used in books and magazines and gives a very finished appearance to a document. The problem with justified text is that to make the lines equal in length, the spaces between words must vary in width. On short lines, with few words to spread the space among, the spacing between words can be so wide as to make the document look amateurish. To minimize this problem, you can hyphenate the document.

Flush-left text has an even left margin and an uneven (ragged) right margin. It is the alignment you get when you type text on a typewriter. It is a popular alignment for body text because the even spacing between words makes it particularly easy to read.

Flush-right text is the opposite of flush left. Text is evenly aligned with the right margin, and the left margin is ragged. This alignment is used to align page numbers and for special effects, such as aligning dates, addresses, or headings with the right margin so that they stand out.

Centered text is centered horizontally between the left and right margins or vertically between the top and bottom margins. This alignment is most often used for titles, headings, subheadings, illustrations, poems, and dedications.

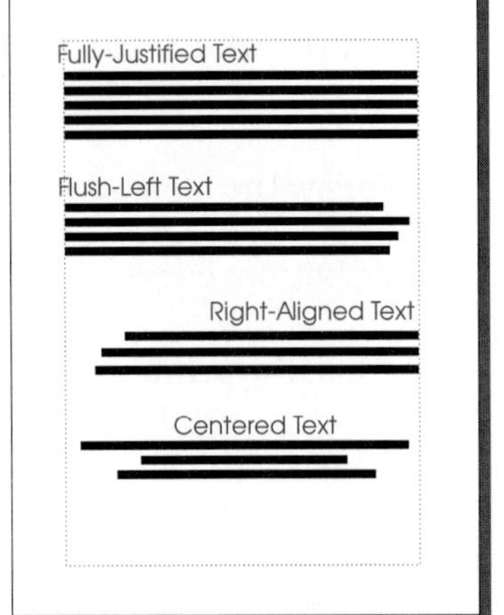

Aligning Text with the Left and Right Margins
You can full-justify text so that both margins are even, align it flush left (with a ragged-right margin), align it flush right (with a ragged-left margin), or center it between the margins.

TUTORIAL

In this tutorial, you explore the different ways of aligning text.

GETTING STARTED

1. Retrieve the ALIGN.WP5 document.

TURNING FULL JUSTIFICATION ON

2. Move the cursor to under the *J* in the heading *Justified Text.*
3. Press [⇧Shift]-[F8] to display the Format menu.
4. Press [L] (for ***Line***) to display the Line Format menu.
5. Press [J] (for ***Justification***) to display the Justification menu.
6. Press [F] (for ***Full***).
7. Press [F7] to return to the Edit screen.

> **WORDPERFECT'S JUSTIFICATION**
>
> WordPerfect has changed the meaning of a standard term in a way that can cause confusion. The term *justified text* universally means text that is aligned flush with both the left and right margins. WordPerfect has used this term to refer to codes that align text in four possible combinations: justified, flush left, flush right, and centered. It then uses the term *full justification* to distinguish true justified text from the other three alignments.

TURNING LEFT JUSTIFICATION ON

8. Move the cursor to under the *U* in the heading *Unjustified Text.*
9. Repeat Steps 3 through 7, but specify ***Left*** instead of ***Full***.
10. Press [F7] to return to the Edit screen.

CENTERING A LINE OF TEXT

11. Move the cursor to under the *C* in the heading *Centered Text.*
12. Press [⇧Shift]-[F6] to center the text. (If necessary, press [↓] to realign the paragraph.)

CENTERING A BLOCK OF TEXT

13. Use [Alt]-[F4] or [F12] to block the entire paragraph under the *Centered Text* heading.
14. Press [⇧Shift]-[F6], and the prompt reads *[Just:Center]? **No** (**Yes**).*
15. Press [Y] to center the paragraph.

RIGHT-ALIGNING A LINE OF TEXT

16. Move the cursor to under the *R* in the heading *Right-Aligned Text.*
17. Press [Alt]-[F6] to right-align the text. (If necessary, press [↓] to align the line with the right margin.)

RIGHT-ALIGNING A BLOCK OF TEXT

18. Use [Alt]-[F4] or [F12] to block the entire paragraph under the *Right-Aligned Text* heading.
19. Press [Alt]-[F6], and the prompt reads *[Just:Right]? **No** (**Yes**).*
20. Press [Y] to right-align the paragraph.

VERTICALLY AND HORIZONTALLY CENTERING TEXT

21. Move the cursor to under the *V* in *Vertically Centered Text* on the second page.
22. Press [⇧Shift]-[F8] to display the Format menu.
23. Press [P] (for ***Page***) to display the Page menu.
24. Press [C] (for ***C**enter Page (top to bottom)*).
25. Press [Y] (for ***Yes***).
26. Press [0] to back up to the Format menu.
27. Press [L] (for ***Line***) to display the Line menu.
28. Press [J] (for ***Justification***) to display the Justification menu.
29. Press [C] (for ***Center***).

30. Press F7 to return to the Edit screen. (If necessary, press ↓ to realign the text.)

FINISHING UP

31. Save and print the document. On the first page, the first paragraph is fully justified, the second has a ragged-right margin, the third is centered, and the fourth is aligned with the right margin. The text on the second page is centered both horizontally and vertically.
32. You have now completed this tutorial. Either continue with the next activity or quit the program.

QUICK REFERENCE

Text in a WordPerfect document is normally justified, but you can change that alignment for large sections, blocks, or specific lines.

Justifying Large Sections of Text

To align large sections of text, you use the Justify command. When you do so without first blocking text, an open code is entered into the document, and all text below the code is formatted with the specified alignment. To end the format, you must enter a different alignment code farther down in the document.

If you first block text and then use one of the Justify commands, a pair of codes is entered. The one at the beginning of the block turns the new alignment on. The code at the end of the block returns the alignment to what it is above the block.

KEY/Strokes

Justifying Text

1. Move the cursor to where you want to change the alignment.
2. Either: Press Shift-F8, and then press L (for ***L**ine*) and **J** (for ***J**ustification*).
   Or: Pull down the Layout menu, select ***L**ine*, and then select ***J**ustification*.
   Or: Pull down the Layout menu and select ***J**ustify*.
3. Select ***L**eft*, ***C**enter*, ***R**ight*, or ***F**ull*.
4. Press F7 to return to the document.

Aligning Text

If you want to center or right-align a single line or a block of text, you use one of the Align commands (Shift-F6 to center it or Alt-F6 to align it flush right).

- If you use one of these commands to align a single line without first blocking it, a code is entered only at the beginning of the line, and the alignment is ended by the hard carriage return code at the end of the line.

- If you block text before using one of these commands, only the block is affected. A code is entered at the beginning of the block to turn the alignment on, and a code is entered at the end of the block to restore the normal alignment that is currently in effect immediately above the newly aligned block.

You can also center text at a specific position. This is useful when preparing tabular material. For example, you can align headings over columns of numbers. You press Tab to move to a tab stop or Spacebar to move to any position on a line. You then press Shift-F6 and enter your text. You can also use Tab or Spacebar to push a line of text until the cursor is in the desired position and press Shift-F6 to center it.

Text Centered at a Specific Position
To center text at a specific position, you move the cursor to that position and press Shift-F6 to begin centering. When you enter a hard carriage return, tab, or indent code at the end of the line, it is centered in the position where the cursor was when you executed the command. Here four lines are centered in two different positions on the page.

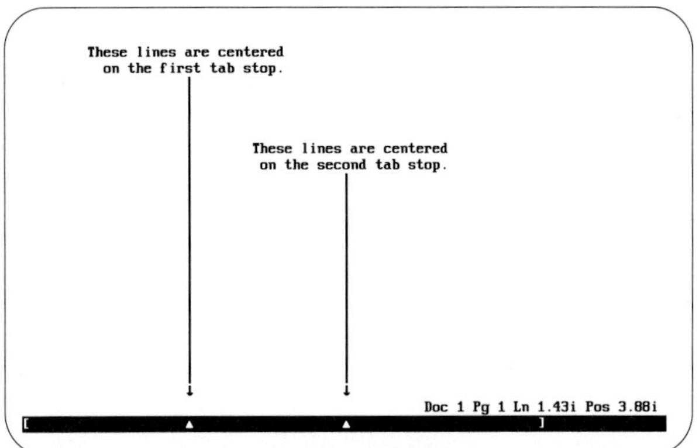

KEY/Strokes

Centering Text or Aligning It with the Right Margin

1. Move the cursor to where you want the alignment to begin:
   - If you are entering new text, move the cursor to a blank line.
   - If you are aligning an existing line, move the cursor under the first character in the line.
   - If you are aligning a block, select the block. (The block can include any part of the first line but must include all the last line.)
   - If you are centering text on a specific column, press Tab or Spacebar to move the cursor to that column.
2. Either: Press Alt-F6 (to right-align) or Shift-F6 (to center).
   Or: Pull down the Layout menu, select ***Align***, and then select ***F****lush Right* or ***C****enter*.
3. This step depends on the selection that you are aligning.
   - If you are entering text, type it in, and press Enter to end the alignment.
   - If you aligned a single line, press ↓ to realign it.
   - If you blocked text, the prompt reads *[Just:Right]?* ***No*** *(**Y**es)* or *[Just:Center]?* ***No*** *(**Y**es)*. Press Y to align the block of text.

WordPerfect 5.1
A Short Course

Final
Manuscript
January 1, 1993

Text Centered Vertically
You can center text vertically on the page. This is useful when you are printing title pages for documents.

Vertically Centering Text

You can center text vertically on the page between the top and bottom margins. This is useful when you are formatting title pages or section openers. The effects of vertical alignment are seen only on printouts or when using the View Document command on the Print menu; the effects are not displayed on the Edit screen. The code for vertical centering must be the first code on the page.

KEY/Strokes

Vertically Centering Text on the Page

1. Move the cursor to the beginning of the page to be centered vertically. (Press Ctrl-Home, and then press ↑ from anywhere on the page.)
2. Either: Press ⇧Shift-F8, and then press P (for ***Page***).
   Or: Pull down the Layout menu and select ***Page***.
3. Press C (for ***Center Page (top to bottom)***).
4. Press Y.
5. Press F7 to return to the Edit screen.

TIPS

- If you type text in front of a *[Just:Center]* or *[Just:Right]* code that you entered to center or align text flush right, the text might not be displayed on the screen (although it will print out). If this happens, press Alt-F3 or F11 to reveal codes and the hidden text.
- When you enter an open code to turn on center or right justification, you cannot use WordPerfect's center, flush-right, or tab-align features. You also cannot hyphenate centered or right-justified text.
- When you are using justified text, hard spaces prevent the program from expanding spaces. To enter a hard space, press Home, and then press Spacebar. This is especially useful when entering formulas.

EXERCISES

EXERCISE 1

CENTERING A TITLE PAGE IN THE EDUCOM DOCUMENT

1. Retrieve the EDUCOM.WP5 document.
2. Follow the instructions in the KEY/Strokes box "Centering Text or Aligning It with the Right Margin" to horizontally center the heading on the first page.
3. Follow the instructions in the KEY/Strokes box "Vertically Centering Text on the Page" to vertically center the heading on the first page.
4. Save the document.
5. Preview the first page of the document and print it out.

EXERCISE 2

CENTERING THE TITLE OF THE JOBGUIDE DOCUMENT

1. Retrieve the JOBGUIDE.WP5 document.
2. Follow the instructions in the KEY/Strokes box "Centering Text or Aligning it with the Right Margin" to horizontally center the title *The Job-Search Kit.*
3. Save the document and print the first page.

EXERCISE 3

CENTERING THE TITLE OF THE NEWSLTR DOCUMENT

1. Retrieve the NEWSLTR.WP5 document.
2. Follow the instructions in the KEY/Strokes box "Centering Text or Aligning it with the Right Margin" to horizontally center the title *THE END USER'S NEWSLETTER.*
3. Save the document and print the first page.

EXERCISE 4

CENTERING THE LETTERHEAD OF THE SUNCITY DOCUMENT

1. Retrieve the SUNCITY.WP5 document.
2. Follow the instructions in the KEY/Strokes box "Centering Text or Aligning It with the Right Margin" to horizontally center the three-line letterhead at the top of the document.
3. Save the document and print the first page.

EXERCISE 5

CENTERING THE POEM DOCUMENT

1. Retrieve the POEM.WP5 document.
2. Follow the instructions in the KEY/Strokes boxes "Centering Text or Aligning It with the Right Margin" and "Vertically Centering Text on the Page" to horizontally and vertically center the poem on the page. You may have to move the cursor down through the text to center it.
3. Save and then print the document.

TOPIC 14

Page Margins

After completing this topic, you will be able to:

- Define the term *text page*, and describe what it contains
- Explain why margin widths are important
- Change margins in your own documents

When a page is printed, the area that is filled with type is called the text page. To establish the text page area, you specify margins. Both their width and proportions have an impact on the visual appeal of a document. The width of the margins determines the amount of white space around the text page. The more white space there is (within reason), the easier and more inviting the material will look.

TUTORIAL

In this tutorial, you explore changing margins.

GETTING STARTED

1. Retrieve the NEWSLTR.WP5 document.

SETTING THE LEFT AND RIGHT MARGINS

2. Press [Home] three times, and then press [↑] to move the cursor to the top of the document before all codes.
3. Press [⇧Shift]-[F8] to display the Format menu.
4. Press [L] (for ***Line***) to display the Line Format menu.
5. Press [M] (for ***Margins***), and the cursor jumps to ***Margins*** *- Left*.
6. Type **.5** and press [Enter↵]. The cursor moves to *Right*.
7. Type **.5** and press [Enter↵]. The cursor moves to *Selection:*.
8. Press [0] to return to the Format menu. (If you return to the Edit screen by mistake, press [⇧Shift]-[F8] again.)

SETTING THE TOP AND BOTTOM MARGINS

9. Press [P] (for ***Page***) to display the Page Format menu.
10. Press [M] (for ***Margins***) and the cursor jumps to ***Margins*** *- Top*.
11. Type **.5** and press [Enter↵]. The cursor moves to *Bottom*.
12. Type **.5** and press [Enter↵]. The cursor moves to *Selection:*.
13. Press [F7] to return to the Edit screen.

FINISHING UP

14. Save and then print the document. Compare the printout to any previous printout to see the effect of changing margins.
15. You have now completed this tutorial. Either continue with the next activity or quit the program if you have finished.

QUICK REFERENCE

The Text Page
The purpose of margins is to frame the text page and set it off.

You change margins for an entire document or for individual paragraphs by entering a margin code. The code is an open code, so it affects all text following it until the end of the document or another margin code occurs. When entering margin settings, you can enter decimals or fractions. For example, to set a margin to 1½ inches, you can type **1.5** or **1 1/2**.

KEY/Strokes

Changing the Left and Right Margins

1. Move the cursor to where the new margins are to begin. (If it is not at the left margin, the program automatically inserts a hard return code, *[HRt]*, in front of the margin code.)
2. Either: Press [Shift]-[F8], and then press [L] (for ***L**ine*).
   Or: Pull down the Layout menu and select ***L**ine*.
3. Press [M] (for ***M**argins*), and the prompt reads ***M**argins - Left*.
4. Enter the left margin setting and press [Enter]. The prompt reads *Right*.
5. Enter the right margin setting and press [Enter].
6. Press [F7] to return to the Edit screen.

KEY/Strokes

Changing the Top and Bottom Margins

1. Move the cursor to the top of the page where the new setting is to begin. (Press [Ctrl]-[Home], and then press [↑] from anywhere on the page.)
2. Either: Press [Shift]-[F8], and then press [P] (for ***P**age*).
   Or: Pull down the Layout menu and select ***P**age*.
3. Press [M] (for ***M**argins*), and the prompt reads ***M**argins - Top*.
4. Enter the top margin setting and press [Enter]. The prompt reads *Bottom*.
5. Enter the bottom margin setting and press [Enter].
6. Press [F7] to return to the Edit screen.

EXERCISES

EXERCISE 1

CHANGING THE EDUCOM DOCUMENT'S MARGINS

1. Retrieve the EDUCOM.WP5 document.
2. Move the cursor to the top of the document. Then follow the instructions in the KEY/Strokes box "Changing the Left and Right Margins" to change the left and right margins to 1½ inches.
3. Follow the instructions in the KEY/Strokes box "Changing the Top and Bottom Margins" to change the top and bottom margins to 1½ inches.
4. Save the document and print the second page. Compare the margins on this printout to those on any previous printout.

EXERCISE 2

CHANGING THE MARGINS FOR A SINGLE PARAGRAPH IN THE EDUCOM DOCUMENT

1. Retrieve the EDUCOM.WP5 document.
2. Move the cursor to the beginning of the paragraph below the heading *SOFTWARE AND INTELLECTUAL RIGHTS*. Then follow the instructions in the KEY/Strokes box "Changing the Left and Right Margins" to change the left and right margins to 2 inches.
3. Move the cursor to the beginning of the heading *QUESTIONS YOU MAY HAVE ABOUT USING SOFTWARE*. Then follow the instructions in the KEY/Strokes box "Changing the Left and Right Margins" to change the left and right margins back to 1½ inches.
4. Save and then print pages 2 and 3 of the document. Compare the margins on this printout to those on the previous printout.

TOPIC 15

Aligning Text with Tab Stops

After completing this topic, you will be able to:

- Display the tab ruler
- Align text with tab stops in your own documents

Using tab stops to align or indent text is critical. If you align or indent text with the Spacebar and print it with proportionally spaced type, your document will print poorly. With proportionally spaced type, the space allocated to a character on the printer depends on its width. However, on the screen, each character takes up the same amount of space. Therefore, columns that align on the screen will not be aligned in a printout. If you use tab stops to align columns, they print correctly.

TUTORIAL

In this tutorial, you align existing text with tab stops.

GETTING STARTED

1. Retrieve the NEWSLTR.WP5 document and notice how the body paragraphs are separated from one another by extra lines. These lines were entered by pressing Enter↵ twice after each paragraph to insert a blank line.

DISPLAYING THE TAB RULER

2. Press Ctrl-F3 to display the Screen menu.
3. Press W (for ***W****indow*), and the prompt reads *Number of lines in this window: 24.*
4. Press ↑ once to display the ruler at the bottom of the screen, and press Enter↵ to return to the document.

The Tab Ruler
You can display the tab ruler so that you know the location of tab stops (▲), left and right margins ([and]), and left or right margins that are in the same position as tab stops ({ and }).

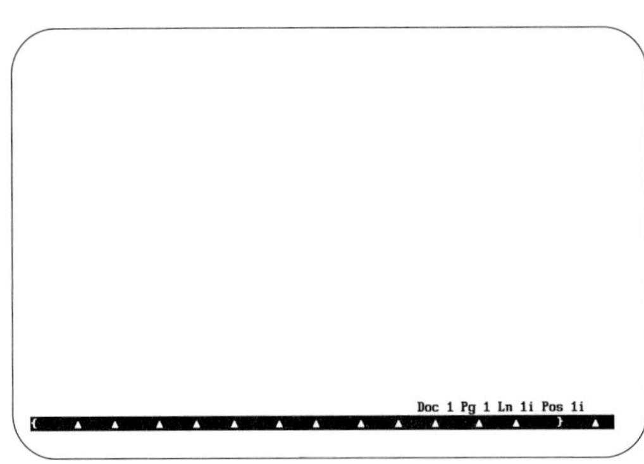

INDENTING THE FIRST LINE OF A PARAGRAPH

5. Move the cursor to the blank line separating the first and second paragraphs under the heading *ERGONOMICS AND HEALTH.*
6. Press Del to delete the hard carriage return code that creates the blank line, and the lower paragraph should move up one line so that no blank line separates it from the paragraph above.
7. Press Tab to indent the first line of the second paragraph to the first tab stop.
8. Move the cursor to each of the blank lines separating paragraphs of body text, and repeat Steps 6 and 7 to indent them. (**Do not** indent the headings, the first paragraph below each heading, or a bulleted list.)

REMOVING THE TAB RULER

9. Press Ctrl-F3 to display the Screen menu.
10. Press W (for ***W****indow*), and the prompt reads *Number of lines in this window: 23.*
11. Press ↓, and then press Enter.

FINISHING UP

12. Save and print the document.
13. You have now completed this tutorial. Either continue with the next activity or quit the program.

QUICK REFERENCE

Aligned with Spaces

Item	Number	Price
Disks	200	5.95
Books	100	3.95
Cables	400	9.95

Aligned with Tabs

Item	Number	Price
Disks	200	5.95
Books	100	3.95
Cables	400	9.95

Tabs
This table shows the difference between printed columns that are aligned with spaces and those aligned with tabs.

Tab stops are initially set every ½ inch, and text tabbed to these tab stops is aligned at the left. You can align text with these tab stops either as you enter it or after you have entered it.

- To align text with a tab stop as you enter the text, press Tab until the cursor is in the desired tab column, and then type the text. If you type enough text to reach past the right margin, the second and subsequent lines wrap back to and align with the left margin, not with the tab stop.
- To align text with a tab stop after you have entered the text, position the cursor under the first character in the text to be aligned. When you then press Tab, the cursor and all text to its right move to the next tab stop. You must be in insert mode to do this. If you are in typeover mode, pressing Tab just moves the cursor through the text.

Although you can set decimal, center, and right-aligned tab stops, you can also align text in a variety of ways using regular left-aligned tab stops.

- To align the decimal points in a column of numbers, press Ctrl-F6 instead of Tab to move the cursor to the desired tab stop. The status line then reads *Align char* = . Type the number—for example, $10.95. Press Tab or Ctrl-F6 to move to the next tab stop, or press Enter to end the line. Repeat the process, and the number you type in the next line will align with the first one on the decimal points.

- To center text on a left-aligned tab stop, press Tab to move the cursor to the tab, press Shift-F6, and then type the text.
- You can right-align text with a left-aligned (or decimal) tab stop. To do so, press Ctrl-F6 to move the cursor to the tab stop, and then type the text without entering an alignment character.

When aligning text with tab stops, you can display a ruler that indicates the positions of margins and tab stops. If you change tab stops (see Topic 16) or margins at any point, the indicators on the ruler change as you move through the document. On the ruler, triangles (▲) indicate tab stops, brackets ([and]) indicate the left and right margins, and braces ({ and }) indicate a left or right margin and tab stop in the same position.

→ KEY/Strokes

Displaying and Removing the Tab Ruler

1. Either: Press Ctrl-F3, and then press W (for ***Window***).
   Or: Pull down the Edit menu and select ***Window***.
   The prompt reads *Number of lines in this window:*. (On most, but not all, systems the prompt will read *Number of lines in this window: 24*.)
2. Either: Press ↑ once to display the ruler at the bottom of the screen. (Pressing it more than once divides the screen into two windows.)
   Or: Press ↓ to remove the ruler.
3. Press Enter to return to the Edit screen.

EXERCISES

EXERCISE 1

EXPLORING SHORTCUTS

1. Follow the procedures in the KEY/Stroke box "Displaying and Removing the Ruler" to display the tab ruler.
2. Enter the heading and the decimal numbers shown in the figure "The SHORTCUT Document." To align the decimal numbers, press Ctrl-F6 four times to move the cursor to the fourth tab stop. The status line then reads *Align char* = . Type the number, and then press Enter to end the line.
3. Enter the heading and the centered text shown in the figure "The SHORTCUT Document." To center text on a left-aligned tab stop, press Tab four times to move the cursor to the fourth tab stop, press Shift-F6, and then type the text.

4. Enter the heading and the right-aligned text shown in the figure "The SHORTCUT Document." To right-align text, press Ctrl-F6 four times to move the cursor to the fourth tab stop, and then type the text without entering an alignment character.
5. Save the document as SHORTCUT.WP5 and make a printout.

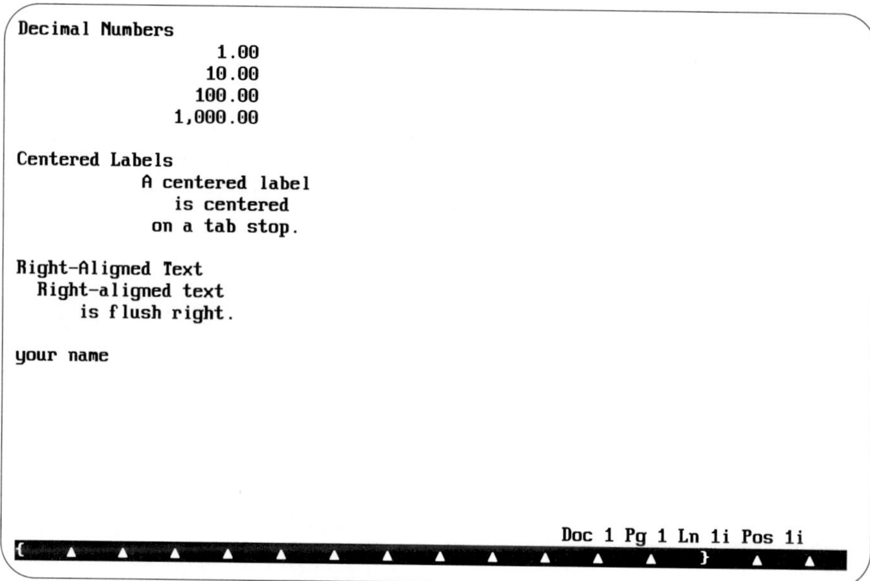

```
Decimal Numbers
                        1.00
                       10.00
                      100.00
                    1,000.00

Centered Labels
              A centered label
                 is centered
               on a tab stop.

Right-Aligned Text
  Right-aligned text
      is flush right.

your name
                                          Doc 1 Pg 1 Ln 1i Pos 1i
```

The SHORTCUT Document
This figure shows the document that you enter to explore shortcuts to aligning text with tab stops in this exercise.

EXERCISE 2

ENTERING THE KEYBOARD TABLE

1. Enter the table shown in the figure "The KEYBOARD Document." As you do so, press Tab on each line between the key and its name.
2. Save the document as KEYBOARD.WP5 and make a printout.

Table of Keyboard Characters
By [your name]

Key	Name
'	apostrophe or foot mark
"	quotation or inch mark
^	circumflex
`	grave
~	tilde
¦	split vertical bar
_	underscore
{}	braces
[]	brackets
()	parentheses
@	at sign
#	pound sign
*	asterisk
\	backslash
/	slash
-	hyphen
=	equal
+	plus
<>	angle brackets
:	colon
;	semicolon

The KEYBOARD Document

EXERCISE 3

ALIGNING HEADINGS IN THE SUNCITY DOCUMENT

1. Retrieve the SUNCITY.WP5 document.
2. There are sections with headings that read *CELL INPUT* and *CELL OUTPUT*. These headings, and the lists that follow them, are separated into two columns with spaces. Delete these spaces, and press Tab once to separate the headings and twice to separate the columns of data below them.
3. Save the document and print the first page. Compare the results to any previous printout. Notice how spaces cause misalignment of the columns and tabs keep them aligned.

TOPIC 16

Setting Tab Stops

After completing this topic, you will be able to:

- Describe the different types of tab stops you can use to align text
- Set tab stops to align your text

You can change the position of tab stops anywhere in a document. When you set tab stops, you have the choice of four possible alignments: left, right, centered, and decimal.

The choice depends on the material you are tabbing. For example, text is usually left aligned in columns, but column headings over numbers may be centered. The numbers below the headings can then be aligned on their decimal points using decimal tab stops. You can also use decimal tab stops to align numbers or letters in enumerated lists. You can change the alignment character from the decimal, the default, to any other character you like. This makes it possible to align commas, pound signs (#), and so on.

You can also specify dot leaders—characters that fill the space between tabbed columns. They make it easier for the eye to move from one column to the next without getting lost.

TUTORIAL

In this tutorial, you change tab stops and then use them to align text and decimals.

GETTING STARTED

1. Retrieve the EDUCOM.WP5 document, and enter your name.

DISPLAYING THE TAB RULER

2. Press Ctrl-F3 to display the Screen menu.
3. Press W (for ***Window***), and the prompt reads *Number of lines in this window: 24.*
4. Press ↑ once to display the ruler at the bottom of the screen, and then press Enter↵ to return to the document.

SETTING TAB STOPS

5. Press Home twice, and then press ↓ to move the cursor to the end of the document.

6. Position the cursor on the blank line above the address that begins *EDUCOM Information.*
7. Press [Shift]-[F8] to display the Format menu.
8. Press [L] (for ***L**ine*) to display the Line Format menu.
9. Press [T] (for ***T**ab Set*) to display the Tab Settings screen.
10. Press [Ctrl]-[End] to delete all existing tab stops.
11. Press [→] to move the cursor to the mark labeled *3"*.
12. Press [L] to enter a left-aligned tab stop.
13. Press [F7] twice to return to the document, and the new tab stop (▲) appears on the ruler at the bottom of the screen.

ENTERING TAB-ALIGNED TEXT

14. The two addresses are separated into columns by spaces. On each line of the addresses delete these spaces, and press [Tab] once so the right address aligns with the new tab you set in Step 11.

REMOVING THE TAB RULER

15. Press [Ctrl]-[F3] to display the Screen menu.
16. Press [W] (for ***W**indow*), and the prompt reads *Number of lines in this window: 23.*
17. Press [↓], and then press [Enter].

FINISHING UP

18. Save the document and print the last page. Compare this page to any other printout. If your printer uses a proportionally spaced type, the earlier spaces did not align the right column, but the new tabs do.
19. You have now completed this tutorial. Either continue with the next activity or quit the program.

QUICK REFERENCE

You can change tab stop settings at any point in a document. The tab stop code is an open code, so it affects all text that follows unless you enter another tab code farther down in the document. If you use decimal tab stops, you can specify the character that is to be aligned at the stop.

Setting Tab Stops

You can set up to 40 tab stops in a document from the left edge of the page to 54½ inches from the left edge. The tab stops you enter remain in effect until the end of the document or until you enter another tab setting code below them.

To change tab stops, you display the Tab Settings screen. With this screen displayed, you have several options.

The Tab Settings Screen
The Tab Settings screen displays the tab stops in effect at the cursor's position. The instructions at the bottom of the screen tell you how to delete and set new tab stops.

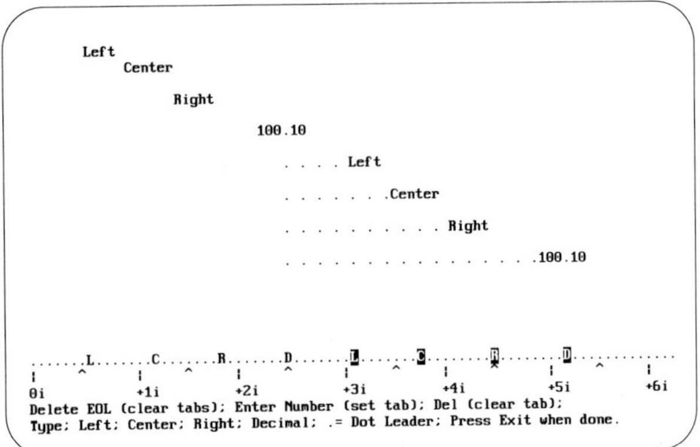

■ You can press [T] and specify if tab stops are relative (the default) or absolute.

- Relative tab stops shift if you change the left margin so that they always stay the same distance from the margin. For example, if you have a relative tab stop ½ inch from the left margin and then increase the left margin by ½ inch, the tab stop shifts to the right ½ inch. When you are setting relative tabs, the *0″* indicator shows where the left margin is positioned. Tabs to the left of the left margin are indicated with negative signs (-1, -2), and those to the right with plus signs (+1, +2).
- Absolute tab stops are set relative to the left edge of the paper you print on so that they do not shift when you change the left margin. When you are setting absolute tabs, the *0″* indicator shows where the left edge of the page is positioned.

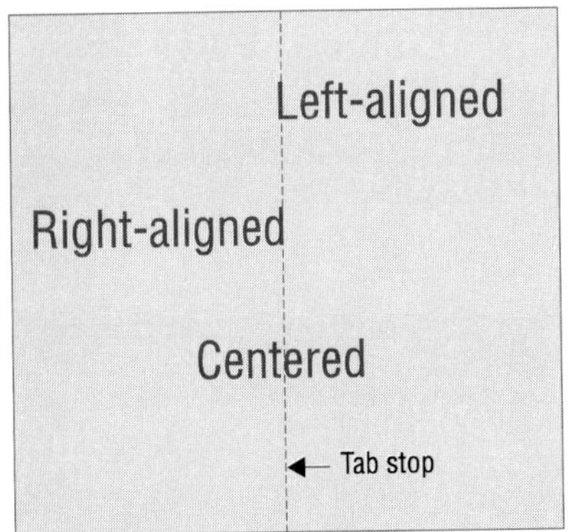

Tab Alignments
You can set tab stops so that text tabbed to them is left-aligned, centered, or right-aligned.

■ You can move the cursor along the ruler line and enter tab stop codes. Enter an **L** for a left-aligned tab, a **C** for a centered tab, an **R** for a right-aligned tab, or a **D** for a decimal tab stop.

■ To delete a specific tab stop, move the cursor under it and press [Del].

■ To specify dot leaders, highlight any tab stop code and press the period. (You can press it again to remove dot leaders.) The tab stop on the Tab Settings screen is displayed in reverse video to indicate that dot leaders have been specified. Dot leaders will then be inserted whenever you press [Tab] to move the cursor to that tab stop in the document.

■ You can move the cursor anywhere on the ruler line and press [Ctrl]-[End] to delete all tab stops to the cursor's right. This is helpful when you want to reset all tabs.

■ To enter a single tab stop, type its position in inches and press [Enter ↵]. If you enter a fractional tab stop position, such as ½, enter it as **0.5** and not **.5** since a leading period indicates a dot leader.

■ To enter tab stops at regular intervals, type the beginning position in inches, a comma, the interval in inches, and then press [Enter ↵]. For example, type **1,1** and press [Enter ↵] to set tab stops every inch beginning at a left margin of 1 inch. The type of tab stop set with this command depends on the type of tab stop set in the beginning position.

- If no tab is set there, this command enters left-aligned tabs (L).
- To set another type, enter that type in the beginning position before using this command. For example, press [D] at 1 inch;

Chapter 1. BASICS 1
Chapter 2. EDITING AND FORMATTING . 10
Chapter 3. MERGE PRINTING 20
Chapter 4. DESKTOP PUBLISHING 30
Chapter 5. SPECIAL FEATURES 40

Dot Leaders
When setting tab stops, if you press the period key after pressing the letter L, R, C, or D, dot leaders are inserted whenever you press [Tab] to move the cursor to that tab stop in the document.

then type **1,1** and press Enter↵ to set decimal tab stops every inch.

- To move a tab code, position the cursor under it, then hold down Ctrl and press → or ←.

→ KEY/Strokes

Setting Tab Stops

1. Move the cursor to where the new tab stops are to take effect.
2. Either: Press ⇧Shift-F8, and then press L (for ***Line***).
   Or: Pull down the Layout menu and select ***Line***.
3. Press T (for ***Tab*** *Set*) to display the Tab Settings screen.
4. Move the cursor to the desired position on the ruler. Then use the tab stop editing commands described in the table "Tab Stop Editing Commands" to enter the tab stop codes described in the table "Tab Stop Codes."
   Press T at any point to display the Tab Type menu, and press A (for ***Absolute***) or R (for ***R****elative to Margin*).
5. Press F7 to return to the Edit screen.

TAB STOP EDITING COMMANDS

To Move the Cursor on the Ruler to	Press
Left edge of screen	Home, ←
Right edge of screen	Home, →
Left or right one tab stop	↓ or ↑
Left edge of ruler line	Home, Home, ←
Right edge of ruler line	End
To Delete Tab Stops	**Press**
At cursor's position	Del
From cursor to end of line	Ctrl-End
All tab stops	Home, Home, ←, Ctrl-End

TIPS

- On enhanced keyboards, you can move the cursor left or right on the ruler by holding down Alt and pressing ← or →. However, do not use the arrow keys on the numeric keypad to do so.
- On enhanced keyboards, you can move a tab stop on the ruler by positioning the cursor over it, holding down Ctrl and pressing ← or →. However, do not use the arrow keys on the numeric keypad to do so.

TAB STOP CODES

Alignment	Code
Text left-aligns	**L**
Text centers on tab stop	**C**
Text right-aligns	**R**
Text aligns with decimal or other specified alignment character	**D**
Text left-aligns (with dot leader)	**L** then . (period)
Text centers on tab stop (with dot leader)	**C** then . (period)
Text right-aligns (with dot leader)	**R** then . (period)
Text aligns with decimal or other specified alignment character (with dot leader)	**D** then . (period)

Numbers	100.00
	50.00
	1.00
List numbers	1.
	10.
	100.
List letters	A.
	B.
	C.

Decimal Tabs
Decimal points can be aligned in columns using decimal tab stops.

Dollar signs	$10
	$100
	$1000
Commas	1,000
	10,000
Pound signs	# 1
	# 10
	# 100
	# 1000

Alignment Character
You can change the alignment character to align characters such as dollar signs, commas, or pound signs instead of decimals.

Decimal Tabs and Alignment Characters

Columns of numbers, including those containing decimal points, can be aligned with decimal tab stops. WordPerfect's default setting is to align decimal points (periods), but you can change the alignment character to any character on the keyboard, including spaces. For example, you can align columns based on commas (,), pound signs (#), dollar signs ($), or a specific letter.

→ KEY/Strokes

Aligning Numbers with Decimal Tab Stops

1. Position decimal tab stops in the desired columns. (See "Setting Tab Stops" in this topic.)
2. Press [Tab] to move the cursor to the decimal tab position, and the status line reads *Align char* = . to indicate that you are in a decimal tab column.
3. Enter the part of the number preceding the decimal point. As you do so, the numbers you enter move to the left while the cursor remains in the decimal tab column.
4. Enter a decimal point using the period key (or any other alignment character that you have specified).
5. Type the numbers that follow the decimal point. As you do so, the decimal remains fixed in place, and all numbers are entered to the right of it.

→ KEY/Strokes

Changing the Alignment Character

1. Move the cursor to where you want the alignment character to change.
2. Either: Press [Shift]-[F8], and then press [O] (for ***O**ther*).
   Or: Pull down the Layout menu and select ***O**ther*.
3. Press [D] (for ***D**ecimal/Align Character*).
4. Enter the new alignment character using any key on the keyboard, including a space (the default is the period), and then press [Enter] twice.
5. Press [F7] to return to the Edit screen.

EXERCISES

EXERCISE 1

SETTING TAB STOPS IN THE JOBGUIDE DOCUMENT

1. Retrieve the JOBGUIDE.WP5 document.

2. Move the cursor to the top of the document.
3. Follow the instructions in the KEY/Stroke box "Setting Tab Stops" to clear all existing tab stops and set a new tab stop at .2".
4. Save the document and print one page. Compare paragraph indents in this printout to ones you made earlier.

EXERCISE 2

SETTING TAB STOPS IN THE NEWSLTR DOCUMENT

1. Retrieve the NEWSLTR.WP5 document.
2. Move the cursor to the beginning of the line that gives the volume and number.
3. Follow the instructions in the KEY/Stroke box "Setting Tab Stops" to clear all tab codes and set a right-align tab at 7.5".
4. Delete the space that separates *Number 1* from *Volume I,* and press Tab to separate the columns. The number should become right-aligned.
5. Position the cursor at the beginning of the line that reads *ERGONOMICS AND HEALTH.*
6. Follow the instructions in the KEY/Stroke box "Setting Tab Stops" to clear all existing tab stops and set a new tab stop at .2".
7. Save the document and print page1. Compare the printout to any that you made earlier.

EXERCISE 3

ALIGNING COLUMNS OF NUMBERS IN THE SUNCITY DOCUMENT

TABLE 1: Consumer Prices (1980-1986)[1]

Year	Average Consumer	Urban Consumer
1980	247.0	246.8
1981	272.3	272.4
1982	288.6	289.1
1983	297.4	298.4
1984	307.6	311.1
1985	318.5	322.2
1986	323.4	328.4

your name

The SUNCITY Table
This figure shows how the table should be aligned in the SUNCITY document.
[1] *Source: U.S. Department of Labor, Bureau of Labor Statistics (BLS)*

1. Retrieve the SUNCITY.WP5 document.
2. Display the tab ruler at the bottom of the screen.
3. Move the cursor to the beginning of the first column under the first *1* in *1980.* Then follow the instructions in the KEY/Stroke box "Setting Tab Stops" to clear all existing tab stops and set new decimal tab stops at 1.5" and 3".
4. Each of the columns is now aligned with spaces. Delete these spaces and press Tab to insert a tab code between each pair of numbers to align them in columns. For example, delete the spaces between *1980* and *247.0,* then put the cursor under the *2* and press Tab. The decimals in each of the numbers will align with the decimal tab stops.
5. Move the cursor to the beginning of the line that begins *TABLE 1.* Then follow the instructions in the KEY/Stroke box "Setting Tab Stops" to clear all existing tab stops and set new centered tab stops at 1.5" and 3".
6. Reveal codes because alignments may temporarily go crazy. Then replace the spaces that align the second and third columns with tab codes. When you have finished, your results should look similar to those shown in the figure "The SUNCITY Table."
7. Save and print the document.

EXERCISE 4

CHANGING THE ALIGNMENT CHARACTER IN THE SUNCITY DOCUMENT

In this exercise, you change the alignment character to colons to correctly align the colons in a memo heading.

1. Retrieve the SUNCITY.WP5 document.
2. Move the cursor to the blank line below the RE: line and follow the instructions in the Key/Strokes box "Setting Tab Stops" to display the Tab Settings Screen. Without changing any tab stops, press F7 to return to the Edit screen. This inserts a tab stop code with the default tab stops.
3. On the blank line below the date, follow the instructions in the KEY/Strokes box "Setting Tab Stops" to clear all existing tab stops, and set a decimal tab stop at .5" and a left-aligned tab stop at .7".
4. Follow the instructions in the KEY/Strokes box "Changing the Alignment Character" to change the alignment character to a colon.
5. Enter tab codes in front of each of the three headings *To:*, *From:*, and *RE:*. Then delete the spaces that follow the colons, and replace them with tabs.
6. Position the cursor on the line below the heading. Then follow the instructions in the KEY/Strokes box "Changing the Alignment Character" to change the alignment character back to a decimal.
7. Save and print the document.

EXERCISE 5

ADDING DOT LEADERS

1. Clear the screen. Then follow the instructions in the KEY/Strokes box "Setting Tab Stops" to clear all existing tab stops and enter a right-aligned tab stop at 6" with dot leaders.
2. Enter the document shown in the figure "The DOTLEAD Document."
3. Save the document as DOTLEAD.WP5 and make a printout.

The DOTLEAD Document
This figure shows the document that you enter to explore dot leaders in this exercise.

your name

Chapter 1. Getting Started 2
Chapter 2. Entering, Editing, & Printing 47
Chapter 3. Basic Formatting 75
Chapter 4. Advanced Editing 137
Chapter 5. Advanced Formatting & Desktop Publishing 168
Chapter 6. Improving Productivity 188
Chapter 7. Real-World Applications 212

TOPIC 17

Paragraph Indenting

After completing this topic, you will be able to:

- Describe the types of indents that you can use in a document
- Describe different ways to visually separate paragraphs
- Indent and space paragraphs in your own document

One way to set off paragraphs in a document is with indents. A regular paragraph indent moves just the first line of the paragraph in from the left margin. But there are three other kinds of paragraph indents you can use: a left indent, a double indent, and a hanging indent.

A left indent moves the whole paragraph in from the left margin. A double indent moves both the left and right sides of the paragraph in by one or more tab stops. Both left and double indents are commonly used to separate quotations, or extracts, from the body of the text so that they stand out.

Hanging indents are the opposite of regular indents. Instead of indenting the first line, they indent every line except the first one from the left margin by one or more tab stops. One of the major applications of hanging indents is for bulleted or numbered lists. The bullets or numbers stand off to the left, and the text following them is indented and aligned.

TUTORIAL

In this tutorial, you indent text. When you are finished, your printout should look similar to the figure "Types of Indents."

GETTING STARTED

1. Retrieve the INDENTS.WP5 document.

INDENTING THE FIRST LINE OF PARAGRAPHS

2. Move the cursor to the blank line between the first and second paragraphs under the heading *I. Indented Paragraphs.*
3. Press Del to delete the *[HRt]* code that separates the paragraphs, and the bottom paragraph moves up so that it and the one above are no longer separated by a blank line.
4. Press Tab to indent the first line of the paragraph to the first tab stop.
5. Move the cursor to the blank line between the second and third paragraphs, and then repeat Steps 3 and 4.

INDENTING A PARAGRAPH FROM THE LEFT MARGIN

6. Move the cursor to the beginning of the first paragraph under the heading *II. Left Indents and Double Indents.*
7. Press [F4], and the cursor and the paragraph move to the first tab stop so that all lines in the paragraph are indented ½ inch from the left margin.

INDENTING A PARAGRAPH FROM BOTH MARGINS

8. Move the cursor to the beginning of the second paragraph, the one that begins *You can also indent ....*
9. Press [⇧Shift]-[F4] twice, and the cursor and the paragraph move to the second tab stop so that both sides of the paragraph are indented 1 inch.

ENTERING HANGING INDENTS

10. Move the cursor to the space following the period in the item numbered 1 under the heading *III. Hanging Indents.*
11. Press [Del] to delete the space, and then press [F4] to indent the paragraph.
12. Move the cursor to the space following the period in the item numbered 2 in the next paragraph, and then repeat Step 11.

FINISHING UP

13. Save and print the document.
14. You have now completed this tutorial. Either continue with the next activity or quit the program.

QUICK REFERENCE

Types of Indents
Indents can take several forms. You can indent the first line of a paragraph. You can indent an entire paragraph from the left margin. You can create double indents to indent a paragraph from both the left and right margins. You can create hanging indents (also called reverse indents or outdents).

You normally indent with either [F4] or [Tab] although you can use the Margin Release command ([⇧Shift]-[Tab]) in special situations. Each time you press these keys, the paragraph is indented one tab stop. To change the distance your text is indented from the margins, change the tab stops.

Indents affect all text up to the next hard return. (You may have to press [↓] to realign the paragraph.) If you indent new text, all text that you enter is affected until you press [Enter]. This automatically ends the indent and returns the cursor to the left margin.

Indenting Text

You can indent the first line of a paragraph ([Tab]), indent the entire paragraph from the left margin ([F4]), or indent the entire paragraph from both margins ([⇧Shift]-[F4]).

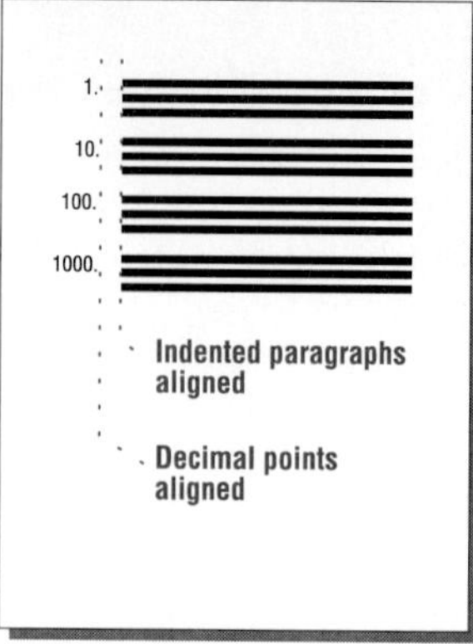

Enumerated Lists
When you use hanging indents to create enumerated lists, the largest number you use determines the amount of the indent that you specify for all entries. Set the tab stop to a position so that there is room for the largest number followed by a period and one or more spaces. You can also set decimal tab stops to align the periods that follow the numbers.

→ KEY/Strokes

Indenting Text

- To indent the first line of a paragraph, move the cursor to the beginning of the first line and press Tab.
- To indent an entire paragraph, move the cursor to the beginning of the paragraph and press F4.
- To double indent a paragraph, move the cursor to the beginning of the paragraph and press Shift-F4.

Hanging Indents

To create a hanging indent in existing text, move the cursor to the place in the first line where you want text to begin indenting, press F4 to insert an indent code, and then press ↓ to reform the rest of the paragraph.

To create a hanging indent as you enter text, type the text to be left hanging—for example, type **1.**—and then press F4 to insert an indent code. Type the rest of the paragraph and press Enter.

You can also enter a hanging indent with the Margin Release command.

 KEY/Strokes

Creating Hanging Indents

- Either: Type the text to be left hanging—for example, type **1**—and press F4 to insert an indent code. Type the rest of the paragraph, and press Enter to return the cursor to the left margin and end indenting.
- Or: Press F4 to move the cursor to the desired tab stop, and press Shift-Tab to move the cursor back one tab stop. Type the text to be left hanging, and press Tab. Type the rest of the paragraph, and press Enter to move the cursor to the left margin and end indenting.

Text — You can align text so that it wraps inside the margins. The left margin is set wider than normal.

Subheads — Subheads can then be entered to the left of the left margin using the Margin Release command. This way, the headings stand out from the text.

Left Margin

Margin Release
The Margin Release command allows you to enter text to the left of the left margin.

The Margin Release Command

You can enter hanging indents with the Margin Release command (Shift-Tab). Every time you press this key combination, the cursor moves left by one tab stop until it reaches the last tab stop.

The Margin Release command acts differently depending on whether you are in insert or typeover mode. With insert on, pressing Shift-Tab inserts a margin release code at the cursor's position. With typeover on, pressing Shift-Tab moves the cursor left one tab stop at a time until it gets to the left margin. Pressing it with the cursor at the left margin inserts a margin release code.

If you use the Margin Release command and then enter new text, the second and subsequent lines of the paragraph you type are aligned with the left margin. Pressing Enter ends the margin release, and the cursor returns to the left margin.

EXERCISES

MARGIN RELEASE AND SUBHEADS

Margin release is a useful procedure when you are working with a page design, like the design of this text, that uses one-third of the page for the headings and two-thirds for the text. You can set the left margin one-third in, and all the body text will then align correctly in the wider column. When you enter a subhead, you then press Shift-Tab to move the cursor to a tab stop set at the left margin of the narrow column. If the subheads are short, they can be set on the same line as the opening line of the paragraph they relate to. If they are longer, they can be set on a line by themselves. If they are on the same line as the first line in the paragraph, set a left tab stop at the left margin setting, and press Tab at the end of the subhead to ensure that the first line of the paragraph remains aligned.

EXERCISE 1

INDENTING NUMBERED AND LETTERED ITEMS IN THE EDUCOM DOCUMENT

1. Retrieve the EDUCOM.WP5 document.
2. Move the cursor to the blank line under the heading *HERE ARE SOME RELEVENT FACTS*. Clear all existing tab stops and set a left-aligned tab stop at .3".
3. Delete spaces and replace them with indent codes following the numbers 1 through 3 under the heading *HERE ARE SOME RELEVANT FACTS*.
4. Delete spaces and replace them with indent codes following the letters (and periods) a through e following the heading *QUESTIONS YOU MAY HAVE ABOUT USING SOFTWARE*.
5. Insert an indent code at the beginning of each answer paragraph following the questions lettered a through e following the heading *QUESTIONS YOU MAY HAVE ABOUT USING SOFTWARE*.
6. Save and print the document.

EXERCISE 2

INDENTING BULLETED LISTS IN THE JOBGUIDE DOCUMENT

1. Retrieve the JOBGUIDE.WP5 document.
2. Delete spaces and replace them with indent codes following all bulleted items.
3. Save and print the document.

EXERCISE 3

INDENTING BULLETED LISTS IN THE NEWSLTR DOCUMENT

1. Retrieve the NEWSLTR.WP5 document.
2. Delete spaces and replace them with indent codes following all bulleted items (but not the list under the heading "Computer User's Checklist").
3. Save and print the document.

TOPIC 18

Line Height & Spacing

After completing this topic, you will be able to:

- Control line spacing
- Control line height

Line height sets the distance from the bottom of one line to the bottom of the next. Line spacing is based on the line height setting. Setting line spacing to 1 sets line spacing to the same distance as the line height setting; setting line spacing to 2 doubles the line height; 3 triples it; and so on.

TUTORIAL

In this tutorial, you change line heights and line spacing.

GETTING STARTED

1. Retrieve the SPACING.WP5 document.

CHANGING LINE HEIGHT

2. Move the cursor to under the *L* in *Line Height Fixed at .3"*.
3. Press [⇧Shift]-[F8] to display the Format menu.
4. Press [L] (for ***L****ine*) to display the Line Format menu.
5. Press [H] (for *Line* ***H****eight*).
6. Press [F] (for ***F****ixed*).
7. Type **.3** and press [Enter↵].
8. Press [F7] to return to the Edit screen.

RESTORING LINE HEIGHT TO AUTO

9. Move the cursor to under the *L* in *Line Height Restored to Auto*.
10. Press [⇧Shift]-[F8] to display the Format menu.
11. Press [L] (for ***L****ine*) to display the Line Format menu.
12. Press [H] (for *Line* ***H****eight*).
13. Press [A] (for ***A****uto*).
14. Press [F7] to return to the Edit screen, and no change is seen on the screen. The results will be seen in your printout if your printer supports this feature.

CHECKING THE RESULTS

15. Print the document, and the spacing between the lines in the first and last paragraphs is what the program thinks appropriate for the size of the type you are using. However, the distance between lines in the middle paragraph is the .3" that you specified (as measured from the bottom of one line to the bottom of the next).

CHANGING LINE SPACING

16. Move the cursor to the top of the document.
17. Press [⇧Shift]-[F8] to display the Format menu.
18. Press [L] (for ***L**ine*) to display the Line Format menu.
19. Press [S] (for *Line **S**pacing*).
20. Type **1.5** and press [Enter↵].
21. Press [F7] to return to the Edit screen.

CHECKING THE RESULTS

22. Print the document, and the spacing between lines in all paragraphs is increased by 50 percent since you changed line spacing from 1 to 1.5.

FINISHING UP

23. Save the document.
24. You have now completed this tutorial. Either continue with the next activity or quit the program.

QUICK REFERENCE

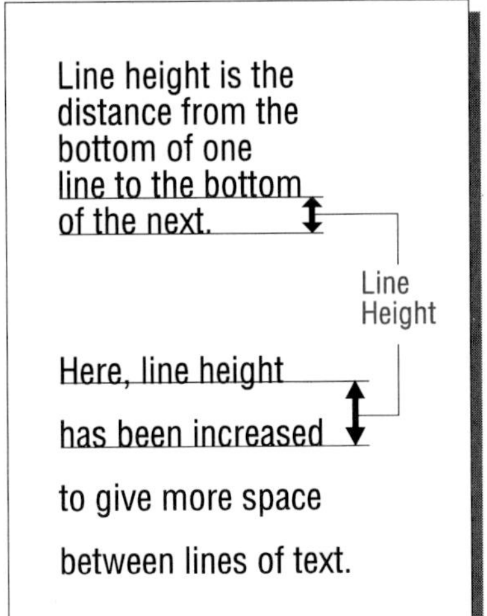

Line Height
Line height is the distance from the bottom of one line to the bottom of the next.

With WordPerfect you can control the space between lines by changing line height or line spacing.

Line Height

You set line height to Auto to have the program adjust line spacing if you change font sizes. You set it to a fixed height if you want all lines to be the same distance from adjacent lines regardless of the type size. However, if you use a fixed line height setting and change font sizes, lines may overlap if the font size is larger than the specified line height.

KEY/Strokes

Changing the Line Height

1. Move the cursor to where you want the line height to change.
2. Either: Press [⇧Shift]-[F8], and then press [L] (for ***L**ine*).
   Or: Pull down the Layout menu and select ***L**ine*.
3. Press [H] (for *Line **H**eight*).
4. Either: Press [A] (for ***A**uto*).
   Or: Press [F] (for ***F**ixed*), type a line height measurement (for example, **.25** for ¼ inch or **.5** for ½ inch between the

bottom of one line and the bottom of the next), and then press [Enter←].

5. Press [F7] to return to the Edit screen.

Line Spacing

To make fine adjustments in line spacing, enter decimals like 1.1 or 1.2. You can change line spacing for an entire document or for individual paragraphs. WordPerfect displays line spacing on the screen to the nearest whole number. For example, 1.5 spacing is displayed as double spacing. When you print the document, the line spacing is whatever you have specified.

Line spacing can be changed throughout a document. Here, one paragraph is single spaced and another is double spaced.

Line spacing can be changed throughout a document. Here, one paragraph is single spaced and another is double spaced.

Line Spacing
Line spacing is a multiple of the line height. If line height is .2", single spacing is .2" and double spacing is .4". If line height is .4", single spacing is .4" and double spacing is .8".

KEY/Strokes

Changing Line Spacing

1. Move the cursor to where you want the line spacing to change.
2. Either: Press [Shift]-[F8], and then press [L] (for ***L**ine*).
   Or: Pull down the Layout menu and select ***L**ine*.
3. Press [S] (for *Line **S**pacing*).
4. Type the desired spacing (for example, type **.5** for half spacing or **2** for double spacing), and then press [Enter←].
5. Press [F7] to return to the Edit screen.

EXERCISES

EXERCISE 1

CHANGING THE EDUCOM DOCUMENT'S LINE SPACING

1. Retrieve the EDUCOM.WP5 document.
2. Follow the procedures in the KEY/Strokes box "Changing Line Spacing" to change the line spacing to 2 for the entire document, including the title page.
3. Print the first and second pages of the document.
4. Clear the screen *without* saving the document.

EXERCISE 2

CHANGING THE JOBGUIDE DOCUMENT'S LINE SPACING

1. Retrieve the JOBGUIDE.WP5 document.
2. Follow the procedures in the KEY/Strokes box "Changing Line Spacing" to change the line spacing to 1.2.
3. Save the document.
4. Print the first page of the document and compare the results to any previous printout.

TOPIC 19

Printing Documents—Advanced Procedures

After completing this topic, you will be able to:

- Select printer options
- Troubleshoot printing problems

Before you can print documents, you must tell your program what printer you are using and what port it is connected to. This is usually done when the program is first installed for use on your system, but you can add printers or change settings at any time. Adding a printer copies the necessary driver from the *Printer* disk to your WordPerfect program disk. This driver lets your program communicate with your printer. For example, if you boldface a word on the screen, the driver translates the command into one the printer understands. You must specify the correct printer driver to get the best results from your printer.

If you add more than one printer to WordPerfect's list of printers and want to change from one to the other to print a document, you must first select the printer so that the correct driver is used. If you do not use the correct driver, you may get strange results when you print a document.

The best way to find out if your printer supports certain features is to make a trial printout using all the program's commands you are interested in. When you print the document, you see how they appear. WordPerfect provides a special PRINTER.TST file for this purpose.

TUTORIAL

In this tutorial, you explore printing a file displayed on the screen and stored on the disk.

GETTING STARTED

1. Retrieve the EDUCOM.WP5 document.

PRINTING THE DOCUMENT

2. Press [Shift]-[F7] to display the Print menu.
3. Press [B] (for ***B**inding Offset*), and the cursor jumps to the 0" on the same line as the command.
4. Type **.5** and press [Enter]. The cursor moves back to the *Selection:* line.
5. Press [F] (for ***F**ull Document*). When the document is printed, hold up pages 1 and 2 and then 3 and 4 back to back as they would appear

if printed on different sides of the same sheet. Notice how the text block has been shifted to increase the margin on the binding side.

FINISHING UP

6. Clear the screen without saving the document.
7. You have now completed this tutorial. Either continue with the next activity or quit the program.

QUICK REFERENCE

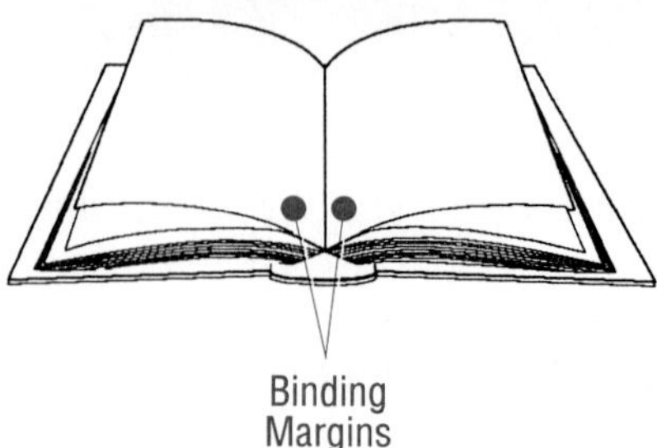

Binding Offset

The Binding Offset command adds to the width of the margin on odd and even pages when you want to bind them back to back. On even-numbered pages, the right margin is increased. On odd-numbered pages, the left margin is increased.

When you press [Shift]-[F7] to display the Print menu, you have a number of options from which you can choose. They are described in the table "Print Menu Options."

PRINT MENU OPTIONS

Print

1 *Full Document* prints the entire document.

2 *Page* prints the page in which the cursor is positioned.

3 *Document on Disk* displays the prompt *Document name:*. Type the name of a document on the disk (you can specify a path in front of the name), and then press [Enter]. This option also allows you to print a document that is formatted for another printer.

4 *Control Printer* displays the Control Printer menu, which is used to manage jobs in the print queue (those documents waiting in line to be printed).

5 *Multiple Pages* specifies which pages of the document on the screen should be printed.

6 *View Document* displays the document on the screen the way it will look when printed so that you can preview it.

7 *Initialize Printer* downloads soft fonts to the printer. You use this command only when you have marked soft fonts with asterisks to indicate that they must be available in the printer when the print job begins.

Options

S *Select Printer* displays a list of printers that have been defined. Highlight the printer you want to use, and then press [S] (for ***Select***). Any document can be printed on any printer. When you select a new printer, WordPerfect reformats the document to match the capabilities of the selected printer as closely as possible.

B *Binding Offset* is used to leave room for a binding when a document is to be reproduced double-sided or printed on a duplex printer and bound. This command shifts the text to the right on odd-numbered right-hand pages and to the left on even-numbered left-hand pages. The net result is to increase the inside margin. The binding offset that you enter is the distance from the edge of the page and is added to the margin settings specified for the document. For example, if the left margin setting is 1" and you set the binding offset to .5", the margin is 1.5" on alternate pages. When you use this command, you can keep margins even on both odd and even pages. To do so, select a binding offset distance and divide it by 2. Enter the result as the binding offset measurement and add the same amount to the desired left and right margin settings. For example, if you want an inside margin of 1½ inches and an outside margin of 1 inch, set the binding offset to .25" and the left and right margins to 1.25". When you print the document, it will be shifted ¼ inch on the page so that the inside (binding) margin is 1½ inches and the outside margin is 1 inch. This command does

> **TIP**
>
> When you specify print options listed on the bottom half of the Print menu, the changes are saved along with the document and remain in effect when you retrieve it again. The only exceptions to this rule are the ***Number of Copies*** and ***Multiple Copies Generated by*** choices. These two choices are automatically restored to their default values when you retrieve a document. All the settings are restored to their default settings when you exit a document.

PRINT MENU OPTIONS (CONTINUED)

not allow you to control the outside margin, however, and works only when you want even margins not counting the binding offset (the distance the block of text is shifted). This is because the binding offset is added to the right margin setting on even pages and the left margin setting on odd pages.

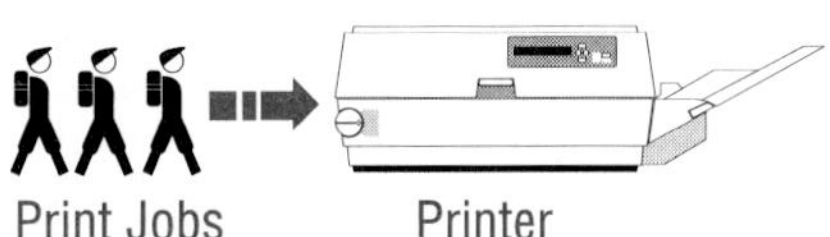

A Print Queue
A print queue is simply a line of jobs waiting to be printed.

N ***N**umber of Copies* specifies the number of copies to be printed.

U ***M**ultiple Copies Generated by* speeds up printing if your laser printer recognizes the command that prints multiple copies.

- If WordPerfect controls multiple copies, they are printed more slowly, especially if they contain graphics or require downloadable fonts. WordPerfect sends the document to the printer all over again for each copy you request. However, copies are collated.
- If the printer controls multiple copies, they are printed faster but are not collated.

G ***G**raphics Quality* controls the resolution used to print graphics. You can choose draft, medium, or high resolution. Higher resolutions take longer to print but give better results. You can also press [N] (for *Do **N**ot Print*) if you want to print just text in the document without the included graphics. You can do this when just editing hardcopy text or when your printer will not print both text and graphics in the same pass.

T ***T**ext Quality* controls the resolution used to print text. The choices and results are similar to those of the ***G**raphics Quality* command.

Troubleshooting Printing Problems

When printing documents, you may occasionally run into problems. If you do, here are some points to consider.

- Before you can print, you must first select a printer.
- If the computer beeps when you try to print a document, press [⇧Shift]-[F7] and then [C] (for ***C**ontrol Printer*) to display a message that tells you how to proceed.

The Control Printer Menu
When you select *Control Printer* from the Print menu, a list of all jobs in the print queue is displayed along with a menu that you can use to manage the jobs. This screen also displays error messages, so if you have problems when printing, you should display it to see whether it identifies the problem. For example, here the message reads *Printer not accepting characters* and suggests *Check cable, make sure printer is turned ON.*

```
Print: Control Printer

Current Job

Job Number: 1                                  Page Number:  1
Status:     End of job                         Current Copy: 1 of 1
Message:    Printer not accepting characters
Paper:      Standard 8.5" x 11"
Location:   Continuous feed
Action:     Check cable, make sure printer is turned ON


Job List

Job  Document          Destination           Print Options
 1   B:\ENTER.WP5      LPT 1
 2   B:\SEARCH.WP5     LPT 1
 3   B:\SPELL.WP5      LPT 1

Additional Jobs Not Shown: 1



1 Cancel Job(s); 2 Rush Job; 3 Display Jobs; 4 Go (start printer); 5 Stop: 0
```

- When you print a document, you may see the message *Disk Full.* The program first prints the document on the screen to a disk file, and this message appears if there is not enough room on the disk for it to do so. If this happens, delete some unneeded files from the disk. You can also use the ***D**ocument on Disk* command to print the file from the disk.
- If your document contains graphics and they do not print completely on a laser printer, you might need to add memory to your printer. A full page of graphics requires at least one megabyte of memory in the printer.

- If you are printing on a network, your document is sent to a print spooler before it is sent to the printer. If it has already been sent to the spooler from your computer, you cannot cancel it. The same is true if you are using a laser printer. If the document has been sent to the printer, you cannot cancel it.
- When you cancel or stop a print job, your printer may continue printing for a while if it has a buffer. To empty the buffer, turn the printer off and then back on again unless you have downloaded fonts or paper is passing through the printer. Once you turn the printer off, all print jobs in the buffer are lost.

EXERCISES

EXERCISE 1

PRINTING THE PRINTER TEST DOCUMENT

WordPerfect supplies a file named PRINTER.TST that you can print to see what features your printer supports. In this exercise, you print this file.

1. Retrieve the PRINTER.TST file onto the screen.
   - On a hard disk system, this file is in the same directory as your WordPerfect program files.
   - On a floppy disk system, it is on the *WordPerfect 1* disk.
2. Enter your name at the bottom of the document.
3. Preview the document using the View Document command on the Print menu. When doing so, select each of the menu choices to see its effect.
4. Make a printout and examine it carefully to see what works and what doesn't. Different printers produce different results.
5. Display the Print menu and note the default settings for ***T**ext Quality* and ***G**raphics Quality*. Change the settings and print the document. Compare the printout to the one you made previously to see any changes. When finished, change the settings back to their original setting.
6. Clear the screen without saving the document.
7. Read one of the printouts you made to see what features are supported by your printer.

EXERCISE 2

EXPLORING PRINTING QUALITY

1. Retrieve any of your documents.
2. Print any page, changing the number of copies and the ***T**ext Quality* setting on the Print menu before you do so. Experiment with the three ***T**ext Quality* settings ***D**raft*, ***M**edium*, and ***H**igh*.
3. Clear the screen *without* saving the document.
4. Compare the printouts to any previous one that you made.

CHAPTER 3

REVIEW

- Pressing Enter←, Spacebar, or Tab⇆ enters hidden codes in a document, as do many of the other commands you use to enter and format text.
- To reveal hidden codes, press Alt-F3 or F11. This splits the screen into two parts, with codes shown in the lower half.
- Open codes, such as those that change margins or tab stops, affect the document all the way to the end or to the next code of the same type.
- Closed codes, such as those used to boldface, come in pairs. One code starts the effect, and another ends it.
- To undo many entering or formatting commands, you just delete the codes that you entered to create them. For example, to join two paragraphs that you separated by pressing Enter←, you delete the *[HRt]* hard carriage return code.
- When you try to delete a code when codes are not revealed, a prompt may ask if you really want to. The prompt appears only when the results of deleting the code would not otherwise be seen on the screen.
- To select a block of text, you position the cursor at the beginning of the block and press Alt-F4 or F12 to turn block on. *Block on* flashes on the status line. You then expand the highlight over the block you want to select.
- When *Block on* is flashing, you can use the arrow keys or press Spacebar, Enter←, or type any character to expand the highlight.
- To select a block with a mouse, you point to the beginning of the block, then hold down the left button and drag the mouse to expand the highlight.
- Once a block is selected, you can format it or copy, move, or delete it.
- Changing font appearance changes the way characters look. For example, you can boldface or italicize them. Changing font sizes changes the size of the characters from fine to extra large.
- To change font appearance or size, you select the text to be formatted and then press Ctrl-F8 or pull down the Font menu.
- A soft page break is inserted by the program when a page is full. It is indicated by a dashed line across the screen. If the text on the page is increased or decreased, the soft page break moves.
- A hard page break doesn't move when text is added or deleted above it. To enter a hard page break, you press Ctrl-Enter←.
- You can protect a block from a soft page break by selecting it and pressing ⇧Shift-F8. You can also press ⇧Shift-F8, select Line, and then turn widow protection on or off.
- Normally, WordPerfect does not print page numbers, but you can turn them on and specify where on the page they will print. You can also specify if they print in Roman or Arabic numbers. Once you have turned them on, you can suppress them on specific pages.
- Normally, text is aligned so that both margins are even. This is called full justification. You can also align it flush with the left or

right margins, leaving the other margin uneven or ragged. A final option is to center text horizontally or vertically on the page.

- You center single lines with [Shift]-[F6] or align them flush right with [Alt]-[F6]. You can also align blocks with these commands if you select them first.
- To align large blocks of text, you enter an open justification code from the Line Format menu. The code affects all text from the code to the end of the document or to the next justification code.
- Margins are usually 1 inch on all four sides of a document but you can change one or more of these margins by entering an open code.
- To align text with tab stops, you normally just press [Tab]. However, you can also press [Ctrl]-[F6] to move the cursor to a tab stop so that decimal points are aligned or press [Shift]-[F6] to center text on a tab stop.
- You can display a tab ruler by pressing [Ctrl]-[F3], selecting ***Window***, and then pressing [↑]. The tab ruler shows tab stops at the cursor's position.
- Tab stops are normally set every ½ inch, but you change them at any point in the document and specify left-aligned, right-aligned, centered, or decimal tab stops.
- When setting tab stops, you can specify if they are relative to the left margin, so that they move when it does, or a fixed distance from the left edge of the page regardless of margin settings.
- You can change the alignment character so that characters other than decimals are aligned at decimal tab stops.
- To indent the first line of a paragraph, position the cursor under the first character and press [Tab].
- To create a hanging indent in an enumerated list, position the cursor after the number or letter and press [F4].
- To indent an entire paragraph, position the cursor under the first character and press [F4].
- To double indent a paragraph, position the cursor under the first character, and press [Shift]-[F4].
- To enter text to the left of the left margin, press [Shift]-[Tab].
- Line height specifies how much space is allocated to a line of type, and it is normally set to Auto so that it changes if type size changes. In special circumstances, however, you can specify a fixed line height so that each line occupies only the specified space.
- Line spacing is based on line height. For example, if you specify a line spacing of 2, the distance between lines will be twice the line height.
- When printing a document, you can specify a binding margin so that text is shifted to the right on odd-numbered pages and to the left on even-numbered pages.
- The Control printer screen lists any problems that may occur during printing and suggests solutions.

CHAPTER 3

QUESTIONS

FILL IN THE BLANK

1. To reveal hidden codes, you press ___________. To then hide them, you press ___________.
2. To join two paragraphs, you delete the ___________ codes that separate them.
3. A code that affects all the document beginning at where you enter it is called a ___________ code.
4. To select a block of text, you move the cursor to the first character in the block and then press ___________ to turn block on.
5. When the status line displays *Block on*, you can press ___________ to expand the highlight to the end of a paragraph or ___________ to expand it to the end of a word.
6. To display the Font menu, you press ___________.
7. If you add or delete text above a ___________ page break, it will move, whereas a ___________ page break will not.
8. To protect a block from a soft page break, you select it and then press ___________.
9. To add page numbers to a document, you press ___________ and then ___________ to display the ___________ menu, which lists the page numbering command.
10. If your document has a three-page introduction with Roman page numbers and the body with Arabic page numbers, you can print page three of the introduction and pages two and three of the body by entering ___________ when the prompt reads *Page(s)*.
11. To center a single line of text, press ___________. To right-align a single line, press ___________.
12. To indent the first line of a paragraph, press ___________.
13. When setting tab stops, you enter ___________ for centered, ___________ for left-aligned, ___________ for right-aligned, and ___________ for decimal.
14. To add dot leaders, you position the cursor over the tab stop on the tab setting screen and press ___________.
15. To align characters other than decimals with decimal tab stops, you change the ___________ character.
16. To indent an entire paragraph from the left margin, press ___________. To indent an entire paragraph from both margins, press ___________.
17. To enter text to the left of the left margin, you press ___________.
18. To change the space between lines of text, you can change either ___________ or ___________.
19. To shift text right on odd pages and left on even pages to leave room for a binding when the pages are to be copied back to back, you use the ___________ command. This command is on the ___________ menu.

MATCH THE COLUMNS

1. Alt-F3
2. *[HRt]*
3. Open code
4. Paired code
5. Alt-F4
6. Ctrl-F8
7. Font appearance
8. Hard page break
9. Ctrl-Enter
10. Shift-F8
11. Widows and orphans
12. Shift-F6
13. Alt-F6
14. Tab
15. Ctrl-F3
16. Alignment character
17. F4
18. Shift-F4
19. Shift-Tab
20. Line height
21. Line spacing
22. Binding offset

__ Protects a selected block from a soft page break
__ Single lines of a paragraph printed by themselves at the top or bottom of a page
__ Centers a line of text
__ Indents the first line of a paragraph
__ Indents the left side of a paragraph
__ Specifies how much space is allocated to a line of text
__ Codes that begin and stop a format
__ Turns block on
__ A hard carriage return code
__ Displays the Font menu
__ Right-aligns a line of text
__ Displays the tab ruler
__ Reveals codes
__ A code that affects text from where it's entered to the end of the document
__ Determines which characters align with decimal tab stops
__ Effects such as bold or italic
__ Doesn't move if text is added or deleted above it
__ Inserts a hard page break
__ Indents both sides of a paragraph
__ Enters text to the left of the left margin
__ Specifies a fraction or multiple of line height to decrease or increase the space between lines of text
__ Command that changes the inside margins on a document that is to be printed and bound like a book

WRITE OUT THE ANSWERS

1. What is the purpose of the codes that you enter in a document?
2. What command do you use to reveal the codes in the document?
3. How do you override default formats in a document? How would you then remove your changes so that the document returns to its original format?
4. What is the difference between an open code and a paired code?
5. When you enter an open code, what part of the document is affected?
6. When you enter a paired code, what part of the document is affected?

7. If two lines or paragraphs were separated by a carriage return, how would you join them?
8. When selecting a block, what keys do you press to turn block on? List and describe three keys (other than the cursor movement keys) that you can press to expand the highlight.
9. List and briefly describe three font appearances you can use.
10. Describe a superscript and a subscript.
11. What is a page break? Why would you want to control page breaks?
12. What is the difference between a soft and a hard page break?
13. What is a conditional page break? Describe the two procedures you can use to enter one.
14. What are the differences between a hard page break and a conditional page break?
15. What are widows and orphans? How can you prevent them from occurring?
16. Does WordPerfect normally print page numbers on each page of a document?
17. List and describe at least two options available for page numbering control.
18. List four ways in which you can align text, and give some examples of when you might want to use the alignments.
19. What does it normally mean to say that text is justified? In what four ways can you "justify" text with WordPerfect?
20. What is a ragged margin?
21. If you want 6-inch lines of text, what should the margin settings be?
22. If you change the top margin so that you print below a letterhead on the first page of a letter, what should you do if the document is more than one page?
23. When would you use text tab stops?
24. In what ways can you align text with a tab stop? Describe two procedures for centering text on tab stops.
25. When would you use decimal tab stops? Describe two procedures for aligning decimal points in numbers with tab stops.
26. List and describe the choices you have when setting tab stops.
27. List and describe three ways to indent text.
28. What is a hanging indent? What is it used for? Describe three ways to create a hanging indent.
29. What command do you use to enter text to the left of the left margin?
30. What does changing the line height do?
31. What does changing the line spacing do?

CHAPTER 3

PROJECTS

PROJECT 1

THE DESKTOP PUBLISHING DOCUMENT

1. Retrieve the DTP.WP5 document from your data disk.
2. Center the heading *Desktop Publishing* and format it as bold and extra large.
3. Center your name on the line below the heading and make it italic.
4. Boldface the following headings:
   - *The Creation Phase*
   - *The Production Phase*
   - *The Manufacturing Phase*
5. Underline the following headings:
   - *Design*
   - *Copyediting*
   - *Typemarking*
   - *Art Preparation*
   - *Typesetting*
   - *Proofreading*
   - *Pasteup*
   - *Printing and Binding*
6. Add pages numbers that print in the bottom center of every page.
7. Change the left margin to 1.5 inches.
8. Set a tab stop at the top of the document at .2" so that the first line of each indented paragraph is indented to this tab stop.
9. Change line spacing for the entire document to 1.2.
10. Save the document and make a printout.

PROJECT 2

THE COMPUTERS AND CAREERS DOCUMENT

1. Retrieve the CAREERS.WP5 document from your data disk.
2. Center the heading *Careers in Information Processing* and format it as extra large.
3. Center your name on the line below the heading and italicize it.
4. Select all uppercase headings and boldface them.
5. Select both subheads under the *TRAINING AND SUPPORT* heading and format them as italic. (If your system does not support italic, use underlining.)
6. Add pages numbers so that they print in the lower-right corner of every page.
7. Change the left and right margins to 1.5 inches.
8. Set a tab stop at the top of the document at .2" so the first line of each paragraph indents to this tab stop.
9. Replace all asterisks with small square bullets (character 4,2).
10. Indent all bulleted items so that the bullet is left hanging.
11. Change line spacing to 1.25.
12. Save the document and make a printout.

CHAPTER 4

Advanced Editing

TOPIC 20

Cutting & Pasting Blocks of Text

After completing this topic, you will be able to:

- Copy, move, and delete blocks
- Append a block to another file
- Undo deletions if you make a mistake

If you are revising typewritten copy, at some point you will likely take a pair of scissors and some glue and reorganize your work by cutting and pasting. With WordPerfect, you do this electronically. Blocks of text are the sections you cut or copy from one place in a document and then paste in at another place.

A block of text can be a character, a word, a phrase, a sentence, a paragraph, a group of paragraphs, or an entire document. However, WordPerfect divides blocks into three basic types: regular blocks, tabular column blocks, and rectangular blocks.

- The regular block option lets you copy, move, delete, or perform any of several other operations on any block of text you specify. The block can begin and end anywhere in the document.

Regular Blocks
Regular blocks can be characters, words, phrases, sentences, or paragraphs. A regular block can begin or end anywhere in the document.

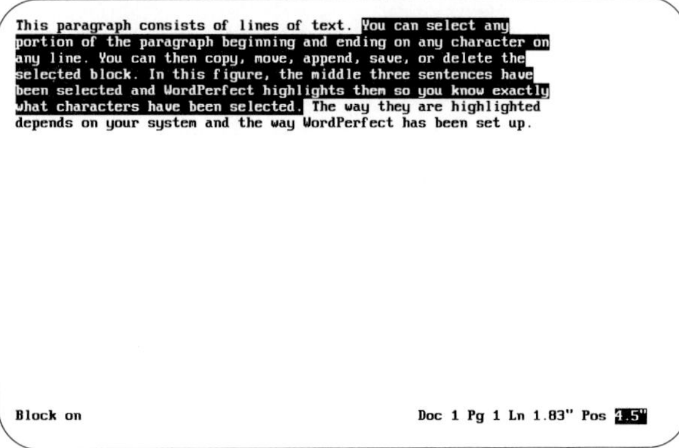

- WordPerfect defines a tabular column block as one or more columns separated from adjoining columns by codes for tabs, tab aligns, indents, or hard carriage returns (but not spaces). With column mode, you can select a column and then copy, move, or delete it in one step.

Tabular Column Blocks
Using column mode, you can copy, move, or delete tabular columns in one step. This figure shows the second column highlighted so that one of these operations can be performed on it.

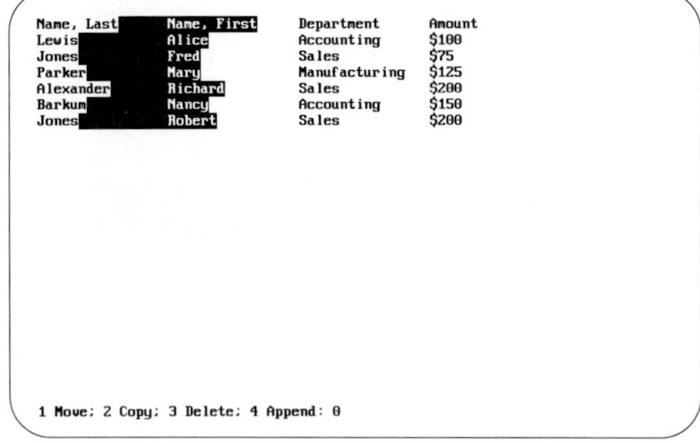

Name, Last	Name, First	Department	Amount
Lewis	Alice	Accounting	$100
Jones	Fred	Sales	$75
Parker	Mary	Manufacturing	$125
Alexander	Richard	Sales	$200
Barkum	Nancy	Accounting	$150
Jones	Robert	Sales	$200

1 Move; 2 Copy; 3 Delete; 4 Append: 0

- Rectangular blocks are like column blocks, but they have no conditions; that is, you specify them by indicating an upper-left corner and a lower-right corner. You select this type of block when you copy or move parts of line drawings or formulas. When you delete or move a rectangular block, the remaining parts of the lines on either side of the rectangle close up individually, as they do with a tabular column block. Thus, deleting or moving a rectangular block from a paragraph of text turns it into nonsense. Each line reads correctly up to where the block was deleted or moved and then continues with the text that was on the same line on the other side of the deleted or moved block. It is much like tearing a lengthwise strip out of the middle of a page and pasting the two remaining halves together.

Rectangular Blocks
A rectangular block is any portion of a document selected by specifying an upper-left corner and a lower-right corner. Here, one part of the organization chart has been selected.

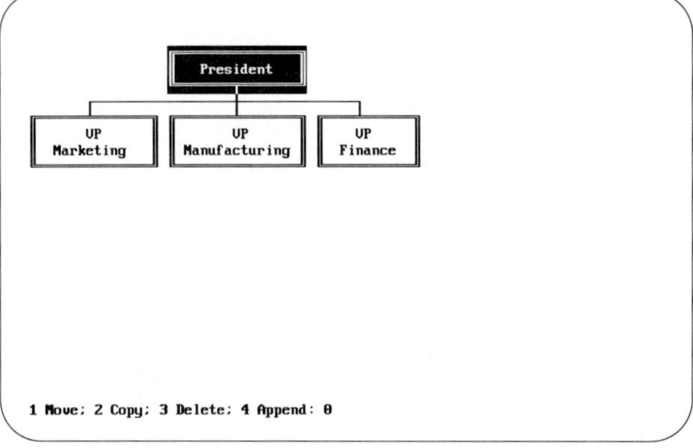

After selecting a block, you can perform a number of functions on it.

- Copying a block leaves it intact and inserts a copy in a new location. When you copy a regular block, the text following it moves over and down to make room for the new copy. When you copy a tabular column block to other columns, the columns to the right move over to make room for it.
- Moving a block deletes it in the original position and then inserts it in the new location. When you move a regular block, it is moved to the new position and deleted from the original position. All text closes up to fill the space the block was moved from. When you move a selected column, the columns originally arranged in one order are arranged in a different order.

- Deleting a block removes it from the screen but not from the computer's memory. When you delete a regular block, all text closes up to fill the space it was deleted from. When you delete a column block, all columns close up to fill the space the column was deleted from. The block is moved into a separate undelete buffer so that you can undo the deletion by pressing F1.
- Appending a block copies it to the end of an already existing file on the disk. When appending a block, you specify the name of the file you want the block appended to. If the filename you enter does not exist, a file by that name is created. The block on the screen is not affected.
- Saving a block copies the selected block to its own file on the disk. You can retrieve the new file and edit it just like any other document file. It can also be retrieved into another position in the document you saved it from or into any other document. Moving blocks to their own files is often used to break large documents into smaller, more manageable files. Working on smaller documents has several advantages:
  - You can get around them more easily.
  - You can save and retrieve them faster.
  - You are less likely to run out of memory.
  - You are less likely to lose your entire document if you make a catastrophic mistake.
- Printing a block sends the selected block to the printer.

TUTORIAL

In this tutorial, you copy, move, and delete blocks of text.

GETTING STARTED

1. Retrieve the BLOCKS.WP5 document.

MOVING A PHRASE

2. Position the cursor under the first *a* in *after selecting a block* in the first line.
3. Press Alt-F4 or F12 to turn block on.
4. Press K to select the text up to the next *k*. This is the entire phrase, not including the period at the end of the sentence.
5. Press Ctrl-F4 to display the Move menu.
6. Press B (for ***B**lock*), and a submenu lists the choices *1 **M**ove; 2 **C**opy; 3 **D**elete; 4 **A**ppend:*.
7. Press M (for ***M**ove*) to move the block into the computer's buffer, and the prompt reads *Move cursor; press Enter to retrieve.*
8. Press Home twice, and then press ← to move the cursor to the beginning of the line.
9. Press Enter↵ to copy the block from the buffer.
10. Edit the sentence so that it reads *After selecting a block, you can perform a number of functions on it.*

MOVING LINES

11. Position the cursor under the first square bullet following paragraph 5.
12. Press Alt-F4 or F12 to turn block on.
13. Press Enter↵ to select the entire line, including the *[HRt]* code.
14. Press Ctrl-F4 to display the Move menu.
15. Press B (for ***Block***), and a submenu lists the choices *1 **M**ove; 2 **C**opy; 3 **D**elete; 4 **A**ppend:.*
16. Press M (for ***Move***) to move the block into the computer's buffer, and the prompt reads *Move cursor; press Enter to retrieve.*
17. Position the cursor on the blank line above the number *6* in the last paragraph and press Enter↵ to copy the block from the buffer and move the line from the beginning of the bulleted list to the end.

COPYING A PARAGRAPH

18. Position the cursor under the *1* in the first numbered paragraph.
19. Press Alt-F4 or F12 to turn block on.
20. Press Enter↵ to highlight the entire paragraph.
21. Press Ctrl-F4 to display the Move menu.
22. Press B (for ***Block***), and a submenu lists the choices *1 **M**ove; 2 **C**opy; 3 **D**elete; 4 **A**ppend:.*
23. Press C (for ***Copy***), and the prompt reads *Move cursor; press Enter to retrieve.*
24. Position the cursor under the *3* in the third numbered paragraph and press Enter↵ to copy the block from the buffer. The list now has two number 1 paragraphs.

DELETING A PARAGRAPH

25. Position the cursor under the *1* in the first numbered paragraph.
26. Press Alt-F4 or F12 to turn block on.
27. Press Enter↵ to highlight the entire paragraph.
28. Press Del, and the prompt reads *Delete Block? **N**o (**Y**es).*
29. Press Y to delete the block.

UNDOING A DELETION

30. Press F1 to display the Undelete menu and the most recent deletion in reverse video.
31. Press R (for ***Restore***), and the deleted block is restored.

MOVING A PREDEFINED BLOCK

32. Position the cursor under the *2* in the second numbered paragraph.
33. Press Ctrl-F4 to display the Move menu.
34. Press P (for ***Paragraph***) to highlight the entire paragraph.
35. Press M (for ***Move***), and the prompt reads *Move cursor; press Enter to retrieve.*
36. Position the cursor under the *3* in the third numbered paragraph and press Enter↵ to copy the block from the buffer. The two number 1 paragraphs are now together.

SAVING A BLOCK

37. Position the cursor under the *1* in the first numbered paragraph.
38. Press [Alt]-[F4] or [F12] to turn block on.
39. Press [Enter←] to select the paragraph.
40. Press [F10], and the prompt reads *Block name:*.
41. Type **MYBLOCK.WP5** and press [Enter←] to copy the block into its own file on the disk.

FINISHING UP

42. Print the document and clear the screen without saving the document.
43. You have now completed this tutorial. Either continue with the next activity or quit the program.

QUICK REFERENCE

When you want to copy, move, or delete a block, you can select any block yourself or use menu commands to select one of WordPerfect's predefined blocks.

Working with Selected Blocks

You can select a block with the cursor movement keys or a mouse and then press [Ctrl]-[F4] to perform a number of functions, including moving, copying, deleting, or appending it. In addition, you can save or print the block.

To save a selected block into its own file on the disk, press [F10], and the prompt reads *Block name:*. Type the name of the new file and press [Enter←].

To print a selected block, press [⇧Shift]-[F7], and the prompt reads *Print block?* ***No*** *(****Yes****)*. Press [Y] to print the block. The block is printed in the same position on the page as if it had been printed with the rest of the text on that page. If you select and print a block at the bottom of the page, it will print at the bottom of the page.

KEY/Strokes

Moving, Copying, Deleting, or Appending a Selected Block

1. Begin by positioning the cursor.
   - If selecting a regular block, move the cursor to the first character to be included in the block.
   - If selecting a tabular column block, move the cursor to under any character in the first line in the desired column.
   - If selecting a rectangular block, move the cursor to the upper-left corner of the block.
2. Press [Alt]-[F4] or [F12] to turn block on.
3. Highlight the block.
   - To highlight a regular block, use the cursor movement keys to highlight the block or use the special commands described

in the KEY/Strokes box "Selecting Blocks" in Topic 9.

- To highlight a tabular column block, position the cursor anywhere on the last line of the desired column.
- To highlight a rectangular block, move the cursor to the lower-right corner of the block.

4. Press Ctrl-F4 to display the Move menu, and then make one of the choices described in the table "The Move Menu for Selected Blocks."
5. Make any of the choices listed in the table "The Move Submenu," and then take the action suggested in that table.

QUICK COPY AND QUICK MOVE ON ENHANCED KEYBOARDS

To copy a block quickly, select it and press Ctrl-Ins. When the prompt reads *Move cursor; press Enter to retrieve*, move the cursor to where you want to insert a copy of the block and press Enter↵.

To move a block quickly, select it and press Ctrl-Del. When the prompt reads *Move cursor; press Enter to retrieve*, move the cursor to where you want to insert the block and press Enter↵.

THE MOVE MENU FOR SELECTED BLOCKS

1 ***B**lock* selects the highlighted block.
2 *Tabular **C**olumn* selects the column positioned between tabs on the selected lines.
3 ***R**ectangle* selects the block indicated by the starting and ending position of the highlight.

THE MOVE SUBMENU

1 ***M**ove* displays the prompt *Move cursor; press Enter to retrieve.* Move the cursor to where you want the block moved and press Enter↵. If you are moving a tabular column block, move the cursor to the first line of the column you want to move the column to, and then press Enter↵.
2 ***C**opy* displays the prompt *Move cursor; press Enter to retrieve.* Move the cursor to where you want the block moved and press Enter↵. If you are copying a tabular column block, move the cursor to the first line of the column you want to copy the column to and press Enter↵.
3 ***D**elete* deletes the block. (You can also delete a block by selecting it and pressing Del.)
4 ***A**ppend* displays the prompt *Append to:* if you have selected a regular block. Type the name of the file you want to append the block to, and press Enter↵.

Working with Predefined Blocks

If you press Ctrl-F4 without first selecting a block of text, a second version of the Move menu is displayed. This menu provides choices that allow you to move, copy, or delete sentences, paragraphs, and pages—the most frequently manipulated blocks. Here is how WordPerfect defines these three blocks:

- A sentence begins with a capital letter and ends with a period (.), question mark (?), or exclamation point (!) followed by up to three spaces.
- A paragraph begins and ends with a hard carriage return code, *[HRt]*.
- A page ends with a hard or soft page break code, *[HPg]* or *[SPg]*. Hard page break codes are moved or copied along with the rest of the page.

TIPS

- When you copy or move text, it is temporarily stored in a buffer until you copy or move another block. To copy the same block that you copied or moved previously, move the cursor to where you want the block inserted, then:
  - Press [Shift]-[F10], and then press [Enter] without specifying a filename.
  - Press [Ctrl]-[F4], and then press [R] (for ***R**etrieve*). Then specify the type of block. Separate buffers are used to store regular blocks, tabular column blocks, and rectangular blocks so that you can retrieve the previous block from each category.
- If you undo a deletion of a tabular column or rectangular block, you cannot insert it back in its original position. To undo a deletion like this, move the cursor to a blank area of the document and undo the deletion. Then move the column or rectangle back to its original position.
- WordPerfect tries to retain formats when you move or delete text and codes.
  - If you select a boldfaced or an underlined block of text between codes used to boldface or underline it and then copy or move the block, the copied or moved block will have the same format as the original.
  - If you block and delete or move one code in a pair, a new code is automatically inserted to retain the original format of the remaining text.

→ KEY/Strokes

Moving, Copying, Deleting, or Appending a Predefined Block

1. Move the cursor to anywhere in the sentence, paragraph, or page.
2. Press [Ctrl]-[F4] to display the Move menu.
3. Make one of the choices described in the table "The Move Menu for Predefined Blocks," and the Move submenu is displayed.
4. Make any of the choices listed in the table "The Move Submenu" and take the action suggested in that table.

THE MOVE MENU FOR PREDEFINED BLOCKS

Choices	Description
1 ***S**entence*	Selects the sentence that contains the cursor up to the next period (.), question mark (?), or exclamation point (!).
2 ***P**aragraph*	Selects the paragraph containing the cursor up to the next hard carriage return.
3 ***P**age*	Selects the page containing the cursor up to the next hard or soft page break.
4 ***R**etrieve*	Retrieves the most recently moved or copied block so that you can insert it into the document one or more times.

Undeleting Text

WordPerfect stores the previous three deletions, including typed-over text, in a buffer—a small portion of the computer's memory allocated to saving material that you delete. It also has an Undelete command ([F1]) that allows you to recover a deletion if you notice the mistake soon enough. Deletions are defined as any sequence of characters that you delete before you move the cursor with one of the cursor movement commands. The buffer stores only the three most recent deletions; thus you must undo mistakes before you make enough additional deletions to move the one out of the buffer that you want to recover.

→ KEY/Strokes

Undeleting Text

1. Move the cursor to where the mistake was originally made. (Text and codes are restored at the cursor's position.)
2. Either: Press [F1].

   Or: Pull down the Edit menu and select ***U**ndelete.*

   The Undelete menu appears along with the most recent deletion in reverse video.
3. Either: Press [R] (for ***R**estore*).

   Or: Press [P] (for ***P**revious Deletion*) repeatedly to cycle through up to three previous deletions (you can also press [↑] or [↓] to display them), and then press [R] (for ***R**estore*) to restore the desired one.

Or: Press [F1] to remove the Undelete menu and return to the Edit screen without restoring a deletion.

EXERCISES

- Use a good grade of letter-sized white bond paper for the final printout.
- Address your letter to a specific person, if possible.
- Be clear, brief, and business-like.
- State exactly the kind of position you are seeking and why you are applying to a particular firm.
- Use care in sentence structure, spelling, and punctuation.
- Enclose a resume.

The JOBGUIDE Document
In this exercise, you reorganize the first bulleted list in the JOBGUIDE document so that it matches the one shown in this figure.

EXERCISE 1

REORGANIZING THE JOBGUIDE DOCUMENT

1. Retrieve the JOBGUIDE.WP5 document.
2. Using the figure "The JOBGUIDE Document" as a guide, follow the instructions in the KEY/Stroke box "Moving, Copying, Deleting, or Appending a Selected Block" to rearrange the items in the first bulleted list.
3. Save the document and make a printout of the first page.

EXERCISE 2

WORKING WITH COLUMN BLOCKS

1. Enter the document shown in the figure "The COLUMN Document." (Press [Tab] once between entries to align them in columns.)
2. Save the document as COLUMN.WP5 and make a printout.
3. Move column B to the right of column C.
4. Copy column D to the right of column E.
5. Delete the first column D.
6. Print the document and clear the screen *without* saving the document.

your name

A	B	C	D	E
1	2	3	4	5
6	7	8	9	10
11	12	13	14	15

The COLUMN Document
This figure shows the document that you enter to explore cutting and pasting column blocks in this exercise.

EXERCISE 3

EXPLORING CUTTING AND PASTING ON YOUR OWN

1. Retrieve the BLOCKS.WP5 document.
2. Follow the instructions in the KEY/Stroke box "Moving, Copying, Deleting, or Appending a Selected Block" to move, copy, and delete words, phrases, sentences, and paragraphs.
3. Follow the instructions in the KEY/Stroke box "Moving, Copying, Deleting, or Appending a Predefined Block" to move, copy, and delete predefined blocks.
4. Print out the document.
5. Clear the screen *without* saving the document.

TOPIC 21

Spell Checking

After completing this topic, you will be able to:

- Explain why spelling checkers cannot be fully trusted
- Spell-check your own documents

WordPerfect includes a spelling checker, an especially valuable aid when you are editing important documents. Spelling checkers are useful, but you cannot rely on them entirely. They check only for spelling, not usage. For example, spelling checkers would find no problems in the sentences *Eye wood like two except you're invitation, butt can not. unfortunately, their are another things i half too due* or *Too bee oar knot two bee.* These sentences, concocted from words that sound like the ones that are intended, will not be flagged by WordPerfect's spelling checker because each word in them is an actual word, correctly spelled, that is in WordPerfect's dictionary. Because of this limitation, you must proofread documents carefully for content and context.

TUTORIAL

Catagory
Trhee
attendence
PREVELENT
definitly
affirmitive

Eye wood like two except you're invitation, butt can not. unfortunately, their are another things i half too due.

your name

The SPELLING Document
This figure shows the document that you retrieve to explore spell checking in this tutorial.

In this tutorial, you use WordPerfect's spelling checker. (If you are working on a floppy disk system, you must have a copy of the WordPerfect *Speller* disk.)

GETTING STARTED

1. Retrieve the SPELLING.WP5 document.
2. If you are working on a floppy disk system, remove your data disk from drive B and insert the *Speller* disk.

SPELL CHECKING A DOCUMENT

3. Press Ctrl-F2 to display the Speller menu.
4. Press D (for ***D**ocument*), and when a word on the screen, like *Catagory*, isn't found in the program's word list, the word is displayed in reverse video, and the Not Found menu and a list of words appear.

The Not Found Screen and Menu
If a word in the document is not found in the dictionary during a spell check, a list of possible replacement words and the Not Found menu are displayed on the bottom half of the screen.

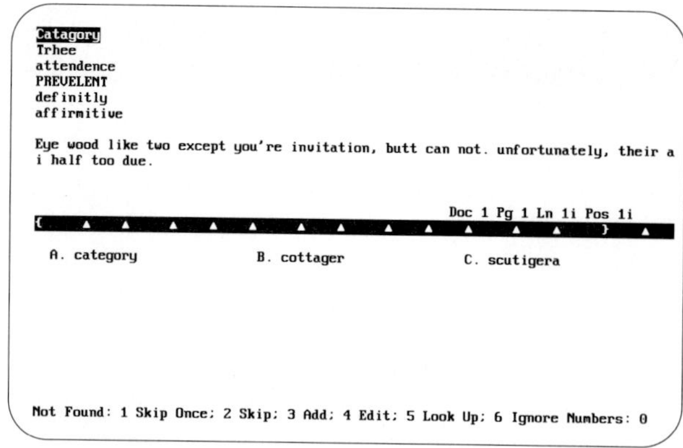

5. To replace the word in the document with one of the words on the displayed list, type the letter that precedes the replacement. When you correct a word, the next misspelled word is displayed. Correct each word until the prompt indicates the number of words in the document and displays the prompt *Press any key to continue*. Press any key to return to editing the document. Notice the following about the spell-checked list:
   - The case of a corrected word remains unchanged. If it began with an uppercase letter, it is replaced with an uppercase letter. If it was all uppercase, it remains all uppercase.
   - The program finds no spelling errors in the sentence because the program checks only your spelling, not your usage or grammar. The words in the sentences are all spelled correctly; they are just used incorrectly.
   - The program probably stopped at your name, not because it isn't spelled correctly but because it isn't in the dictionary. Press 2 (for *Skip*) to skip your name.

COUNTING WORDS

6. Press Ctrl-F2 to display the Speller menu.
7. Press C (for ***C**ount*), and in a moment the status line displays the number of words in the document and the prompt *Press any key to continue*.
8. Press any key to return to the Speller menu.
9. Press F7 to return to the Edit screen.

FINISHING UP

10. If you are using a floppy disk system, remove the *Speller* disk from drive B and insert your data disk.
11. Save the revised document.
12. Print the document.
13. You have now completed this tutorial. Either continue with the next activity or quit the program.

QUICK REFERENCE

The spelling checker compares words in your document to a list of words stored in the dictionary file WP{WP}US.LEX. Words are also checked against a supplemental dictionary, WP{WP}US.SUP, that contains words you add to the dictionary while spell checking documents.

Any words not found in the dictionaries are highlighted, and a list of suggested replacement words is displayed along with the Not Found menu. The spelling checker also looks for words that contain numbers, words that are repeated twice in succession, and words with irregular case, like *HellO* or *washington*. You can select a replacement word from the list, use a menu command to ignore the word, or add the word to your dictionary.

KEY/Strokes

Spell Checking a Document

1. Either: Leave the cursor anywhere in the document to check the entire document.

   Or: Move the cursor to a page if you want to spell-check a specific page.

   Or: Move the cursor to the beginning of a word to be checked.

   Or: Select a block.
2. Either: Press [Ctrl]-[F2] to display the Speller menu.

   Or: Pull down the Tools menu and select *Spell*.
3. Select one or more of the choices described in the table "Speller Menu Choices."

   When you press [W] (for ***W****ord*), [P] (for ***P****age*), or [D] (for ***D****ocument*), the program displays the message **Please wait** and compares the words in the document to the words in its word lists. (You can press [F1] at any point to cancel spell checking.)

   If a word not in the word lists is found, the word is displayed in reverse video, and the Not Found menu and a list of words appear.

   - To replace the word in the document with one of the words on the displayed list, press the letter that precedes the replacement.
   - If a list of suggested replacement words does not appear, or if the list does not contain a choice you like, press [4] (for *Edit*) and type in your corrections. When you have finished, press [F7] to resume spell checking.
   - If the list of words is longer than the screen, press [Enter←] to display more.
   - If you do not want to replace the word with a listed word, you select one of the Not Found menu commands. These commands vary somewhat depending on the situation. The table "Not Found and Double Word Menu Choices" describes choices that might appear and explains what each is used for.

After you spell-check a word, the cursor moves to the next word not found in the dictionaries, and the Not Found menu is displayed again. When spell checking is complete, a message tells you the number of words in the document, and the prompt reads *Press any key to continue*. When you do so:

- If you spell-checked a page or a word, the Edit screen reappears.
- If you spell-checked a page, the cursor moves to the next page, and the Speller menu remains on the screen so that you can check the next page or press F7 to return to the Edit screen.

SPELLER MENU CHOICES

1 ***W**ord* spell-checks the word containing the cursor.
2 ***P**age* spell-checks the page containing the cursor.
3 ***D**ocument* spell-checks the entire document.
4 ***N**ew Sup. Dictionary* specifies a different supplemental dictionary. The prompt reads *Supplemental dictionary name:*. Type a new supplemental dictionary (the default is WP{WP}US.SUP), or press Enter↵ to accept the default and return to the Speller menu.
5 ***L**ook Up* looks up words that sound like the one you enter. (See the description in the table "Not Found and Double Word Menu Choices.")
6 ***C**ount* counts the words in the document. This command is useful for preparing documents with strict length limitations such as school-related projects or articles for magazines and newspapers.

NOT FOUND AND DOUBLE WORD MENU CHOICES

1 *Skip Once* skips the word, and spell checking continues. If the same word is encountered again, it is highlighted.
2 *Skip* skips the word, and spell checking continues. If the same word is encountered again, it is not highlighted.
3 *Add* saves the word in the supplemental dictionary WP{WP}US.SUP.
3 *Delete 2nd* deletes the second word when repeating words are encountered.
4 *Edit* moves the cursor to the word so that you can correct it. (You can also press ← or → to do the same.) When you have finished, press F7. If your correction does not match a word in the dictionary, the word remains highlighted.
5 *Disable Double Word Checking* turns off double word checking so that no further double words are highlighted.
5 *Look Up* displays the prompt *Word* or *word pattern:*. Type the word you want to confirm the spelling of. You can use wildcards to display a list of words that match a specified pattern.
- The question mark (?) substitutes for a single letter.
- The asterisk (*) substitutes for zero or more characters in sequence.

For example, if you want to find how to spell *category*, you can enter *cat** to display all words beginning with those three letters or *cat?gory* if you are unsure of only a single character. If you enter a word without a wildcard, the program displays words that sound like the word you enter. When you have finished looking up words, press F7 to return to the Edit screen.

6 *Ignore Numbers* turns off the spell checking of subsequent words that contain a number, for example, F3 or 3D.

USING THE SPELLING CHECKER ON A FLOPPY DISK SYSTEM

WordPerfect's spelling checker is on a separate disk and is not loaded along with the program. Before executing the Spell command, you should save the file you are working on. If you are working on a floppy disk system, you should also insert the *Speller* disk into drive B. After completing the procedure (and not before), remove the *Speller* disk from drive B, and then reinsert your data disk.

If you execute the Spell command without inserting the *Speller* disk, a message reads *WP{WP}US.LEX not found:*, and a menu offers the following choices: *1 Enter Path; 2 Skip Language; 3 Exit Spell.* If this menu appears, insert the *Speller* disk into drive B and press 1 for *Enter Path.* The prompt reads *Temporary dictionary path:*. Type **B:** and press Enter↵ to display the Speller menu.

EXERCISES

EXERCISE 1

SPELL CHECKING YOUR DOCUMENTS

Some of the documents on the original *Resource Disk* contain misspellings. Retrieve each of the following documents: EDUCOM.WP5, JOBGUIDE.WP5, NEWSLTR.WP5, and SUNCITY.WP5, and follow the instructions in the KEY/Strokes box "Spell Checking a Document" to spell-check them. As you do so:

- If you are working from your own floppy disks and any words are highlighted that you know are spelled correctly, add them to your dictionary. (Do not do this if you are working on the school's hard disk.)
- Save any document in which you correct errors under its original filename.

EXERCISE 2

COUNTING WORDS

1. Retrieve any of the documents that you spell-checked in the previous exercise.
2. Follow the instructions in the KEY/Strokes box "Spell Checking a Document" to count the words in each document without spell checking it.
3. When you have finished, clear the screen without saving the document.

TOPIC 22

Looking Up Synonyms & Antonyms in the Thesaurus

After completing this topic, you will be able to:

- Describe how WordPerfect's thesaurus works
- Use the thesaurus in your own documents

WordPerfect includes a thesaurus for looking up synonyms and antonyms. To use it, you position the cursor anywhere in a word and press Alt-F1 to request the thesaurus to display a list of synonyms and antonyms. For example, when the word *wicked* is highlighted, the thesaurus may display the synonyms *bad, corrupt, evil, sinful, vile, hateful,* and *malevolent* and the antonyms *good, benevolent,* and *mild.* You can select one of the suggested words to replace the word in the document, look up another word, or quit the thesaurus and return to the document.

The Thesaurus Screen

When you press Alt-F1 to invoke the thesaurus, the word you looked up (the headword) is displayed on the screen border. Often, nouns (n), verbs (v), adjectives (a), and antonyms (ant) are listed under separate categories. The words displayed for each form of the headword are called references and are identified by letters. References preceded by dots are also headwords, so you can press the letter in front of them to look up additional words. References with the same connotation are grouped into numbered subgroups.

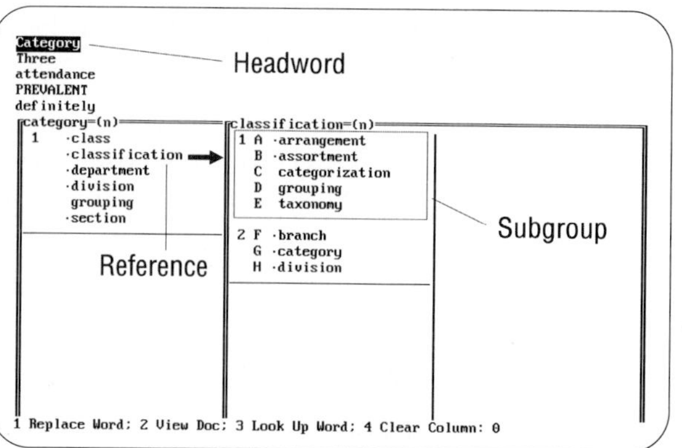

TUTORIAL

In this tutorial, you use WordPerfect's thesaurus. (If you are working on a floppy disk system, you must have a copy of the WordPerfect *Thesaurus* disk.)

GETTING STARTED

1. Retrieve the SPELLING.WP5 document.
2. Before you execute the Thesaurus command on a floppy disk system, insert the *Thesaurus* disk into drive B.

LOOKING UP SYNONYMS

3. Move the cursor to any position in the word *Category*.
4. Press [Alt]-[F1] to display the Thesaurus menu and a list of synonyms for the word *category*.
5. Press [B] (for *classification*) to display additional possibilities branching from the word *classification*.
6. Press [B] again (for *assortment*) to display additional possibilities branching from the word *assortment*.

The Thesaurus Screen and Menu
When you press [Alt]-[F1], a list of words in the thesaurus is displayed along with a menu.

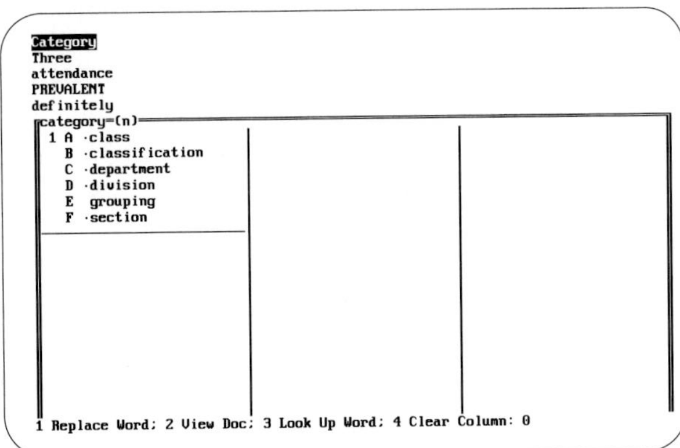

7. Press [4] (for *Clear Column*) to remove the last column.
8. Press [←] to move the selection letters from the second column to the first.
9. Press [1] (for *Replace Word*), and the prompt reads *Press letter for word.*
10. Press [B] (for *classification*), and the word *Category* is replaced with *Classification*. Then the Edit screen reappears.
11. Continue experimenting by moving the cursor to any word and repeating the above steps. Replace each word in the list at the top of the document (except the word *three*) with a synonym or antonym.

FINISHING UP

12. If you are using a floppy disk system, remove the *Thesaurus* disk from drive B and insert your data disk.
13. Save and print the document.
14. You have now completed this tutorial. Either continue with the next activity or quit the program.

QUICK REFERENCE

The thesaurus contains 10,000 headwords (words that can be looked up) and many references, including synonyms and antonyms.

KEY/Strokes

Looking Up Words in the Thesaurus

1. Move the cursor to any position in the word to be looked up.
2. Either: Press Alt-F1.

   Or: Pull down the Tools menu and select *Thesaurus*.

   The Thesaurus menu and list of words appears.

   - If the word you highlight is not in the thesaurus, the prompts read *Word not found* and then *Word:*. Enter a new word and press Enter↵ to continue, or press F7 to return to the document.
   - If the word you highlight is in the thesaurus, the Thesaurus screen and menu are displayed.
3. Use the menu commands described in the table "Thesaurus Menu Choices" and the cursor movement keys described in the table "Thesaurus Screen Cursor Movement Keys" to move the numbers and lists displayed on the Thesaurus screen.
4. Either: Press F7 when you have finished to return to the Edit screen.

   Or: Press Spacebar to return to your document without making changes.

THESAURUS MENU CHOICES

1 *Replace Word* replaces the word in the document with one of the words displayed on the list. Before using it, press → or ← to move the reference menu selection letters (*A*, *B*, *C*, and so on) to the column containing your choice, if necessary. (The table "Thesaurus Screen Cursor Movement Keys" describes other keys you can use to move the cursor through a long list.) Then press 1, and the prompt reads *Press letter for word*. Press the letter preceding the desired replacement, and the Edit screen reappears.

2 *View Doc* returns the cursor to the document so that you can scroll through the document to see the word in context before choosing a replacement. Press F7 to return to the Thesaurus menu.

3 *Look Up Word* displays the prompt *Word:* so that you can enter a word to be looked up.

4 *Clear Column* clears subgroups from the Thesaurus screen. (You can also press ←Bksp or Del to do the same.)

THESAURUS SCREEN CURSOR MOVEMENT KEYS

Code	Press
Move the menu selection letters between columns	← or →
View subgroups too long to fit on the screen	↑ or ↓
Move column up or down	PgUp or PgDn or + or - on the numeric keypad with NumLock off
Move to the first subgroup	Home, Home, ↑
Move to the last subgroup	Home, Home, ↓
Move to a specific subgroup	Ctrl-Home, subgroup number, Enter↵

USING THE THESAURUS ON A FLOPPY DISK SYSTEM

WordPerfect's thesaurus is on a separate disk and is not loaded along with the program. Before executing the Thesaurus command, you should save the file you are working on and replace your data disk in drive B with the *Thesaurus* disk. After completing the procedure (and not before), remove the *Thesaurus* disk from drive B, and then reinsert your data disk.

If you execute the Thesaurus command without inserting the *Thesaurus* disk, a message reads *ERROR: File not found—WP{WP}US.THS*, and the Edit screen reappears. Insert the disk, and then execute the command again.

EXERCISES

Synonyms
Sincerely
Abbreviation
Able
Academic
Accounting
Career
Job
Familiar

your name

The SYNONYMS Document
This figure shows the document that you retrieve to explore looking up synonyms in this exercise.

Antonyms
Happy
Work
Student
Political
Honest
Cheerful

your name

The ANTONYMS Document
This figure shows the document that you retrieve to explore looking up antonyms in this exercise.

EXERCISE 1

FINDING SYNONYMS

1. Retrieve the SYNONYMS.WP5 document.
2. Follow the instructions in the KEY/Strokes box "Looking Up Words in the Thesaurus" to replace each word with a synonym (except the heading, *Synonyms*).
3. Make a printout and clear the screen *without* saving your changes.

EXERCISE 2

FINDING ANTONYMS

1. Retrieve the ANTONYMS.WP5 document.
2. Follow the instructions in the KEY/Strokes box "Looking Up Words in the Thesaurus" to replace each word with an antonym (except the heading, *Antonyms*).
3. Make a printout and clear the screen *without* saving your changes.

TOPIC 23

Searching & Replacing

After completing this topic, you will be able to:

- Search for words or phrases and describe how to replace them
- Use typical search and search and replace options

To have WordPerfect find text within a document, you use the Search command. It provides a quick way to find a section of a long document, for example, or to check whether you used an author's first name or only her initials in an earlier text reference. The Search command can also check words that you frequently misspell in more than one way. For example, using wildcards, you can find all occurrences of the word *similar* even if they have been misspelled *similar, simelar,* and *similer.*

If you want to find text and replace it with new text, you use the Replace command. You can use this command to replace misspelled words with their correct spelling. You can also use it to save typing time. Instead of typing the title of a book over and over again in a long report, for instance, you can type an abbreviation that is unlikely to appear elsewhere in the document. Then you can use the Replace command to replace the abbreviation with the actual title.

TUTORIAL

In this tutorial, you use the Search and Replace commands to find and replace strings.

GETTING STARTED

1. Retrieve the SEARCH.WP5 document.

SEARCHING FOR STRINGS

2. Press [Home] twice, and then press [↑] to move the cursor to the beginning of the document.
3. Press [F2], and the prompt reads -> *Srch:*.
4. Type **THE**.
5. Press [F2] to begin the search, and the cursor moves to the character following the first occurrence of the string *THE*, which is part of the word *THERE.*
6. Press [F2] twice to repeat the command. Continue to do so until no occurrence is found and the message reads * *Not found* *. Notice that the program finds only words that contain uppercase *THE*s.

1. ALL UPPERCASE
THERE
THEIR
THEM
THE
[T] by [A]

2. UPPERCASE AND LOWERCASE
There
Their
Them
The
[T] by [a]

3. ALL LOWERCASE
there
their
them
the
[t] by [a]

your name

The SEARCH Document
This figure shows the document that you retrieve to explore searching and replacing in this tutorial.

7. Repeat Steps 2 through 6, first specifying *The* and then *the* instead of *THE*. When you specify *The*, the program finds words that are all uppercase or that begin with an uppercase letter. When you specify *the*, the program finds words with all combinations of uppercase and lowercase.

SEARCHING IN BOTH DIRECTIONS

8. Press Home twice, and then press ↑ to move the cursor to the beginning of the document.
9. Press F2, and the prompt reads -> *Srch: the.*
10. Type **THEM** and press F2 to search toward the end of the document.
11. Press Home twice, and then press ↓ to move the cursor to the end of the document.
12. Press ⇧Shift-F2, and the prompt reads <- *Srch: THEM.*
13. Press F2 to begin the search toward the top of the document.

REPLACING ALL STRINGS WITHOUT BEING PROMPTED

14. Press Home twice, and then press ↑ to move the cursor to the beginning of the document.
15. Press Alt-F2, and the prompt reads *w/Confirm? **No** (**Yes**).*
16. Press N to replace the string automatically throughout the document, and the prompt reads -> *Srch: THEM.*
17. Type **the** and press F2. The prompt reads *Replace with:.*
18. Type **she** and press F2 to begin the replace operation.
19. Press PgUp to see the document. Since you specified the search string in lowercase and answered No to the prompt *w/Confirm?*, all strings are replaced automatically. Obviously, you can create havoc with this combination of commands.
20. Repeat Steps 14 through 19, but specify *she* as the string to search for and *The* as the string to replace with. This partially restores the file, but the second and third characters in each word in the first section are no longer uppercased.

REPLACING STRINGS ONE AT A TIME

21. Press Home twice, and then press ↑ to move the cursor to the beginning of the document.
22. Press Alt-F2, and the prompt reads *w/Confirm? **No** (**Yes**).*
23. Press Y to confirm each replacement, and the prompt reads -> *Srch: she.*
24. Type **The** and press F2. The prompt reads *Replace with:.*
25. Type **THE** and press F2 to begin the replace operation. Since you answered Yes to the prompt *w/Confirm?*, the command finds the string and pauses. The cursor flashes under the second character, and the prompt reads *Confirm? **No** (**Yes**).* To replace the string, press Y. The cursor then immediately jumps to the next occurrence, and the prompt is displayed again. Replace only the strings in the first section. When all occurrences of the string have been found, the prompt no longer appears.

26. Move the cursor to the line with the heading *ALL LOWERCASE*, and repeat Steps 21 through 25 but replace *The* with *the*. When you have finished, your document should look as it did originally.

REPLACING YOUR OWN ABBREVIATIONS

27. Press Home twice, and then press ↑ to move the cursor to the beginning of the document.
28. Press Alt-F2, and the prompt reads *w/Confirm? **No** (**Yes**).*
29. Press N to replace automatically throughout the document, and the prompt reads *-> Srch: The.*
30. Type **[t]** and press F2. The prompt reads *Replace with:.*
31. Type **Disney Animation: The Illusion of Life** and press F2 to replace all *[T]* and *[t]* codes with the title.
32. Press Home twice, and then press ↑ to move the cursor to the beginning of the document.
33. Press Alt-F2, and the prompt reads *w/Confirm? **No** (**Yes**).*
34. Press N to replace automatically throughout the document, and the prompt reads *-> Srch: [t].*
35. Type **[a]** and press F2. The prompt reads *Replace with:.*
36. Type **Frank Thomas and Ollie Johnston** and press F2 to replace all *[A]* and *[a]* codes with the authors' names.

DELETING STRINGS

37. Press Home twice, and then press ↑ to move the cursor to the beginning of the document.
38. Press Alt-F2, and the prompt reads *w/Confirm? **No** (**Yes**).*
39. Press N to replace the string automatically throughout the document, and the prompt reads *-> Srch: [a].*
40. Type **their** and press F2. The prompt reads *Replace with:.*
41. Press F2 to begin the replace operation without specifying a replacement string. Since you specified the search string in lowercase, did not enter a replacement string, and answered No to the prompt *w/Confirm?* all *their* strings are deleted automatically.

SEARCHING FOR FORMATTING CODES

42. Press Home twice, and then press ↑ to move the cursor to the beginning of the document.
43. Press Alt-F2, and the prompt reads *w/Confirm? **No** (**Yes**).*
44. Press N to make all replacements automatically, and the prompt reads *-> Srch: their.*
45. Press Enter↵, and the prompt reads *-> Srch: [HRt].*
46. Press F2, and the prompt reads *Replace with:.*
47. Type **[CR]** and press F2 to delete all hard carriage return codes and join all lines in the document into a single paragraph. Places where hard carriage return codes were are indicated with the *[CR]* characters.

REPLACING CHARACTERS WITH CODES

48. Press [Home] twice, and then press [↑] to move the cursor to the beginning of the document.
49. Press [Alt]-[F2], and the prompt reads *w/Confirm? **No** (**Y**es).*
50. Press [N] to make all replacements automatically, and the prompt reads *-> Srch: [HRt].*
51. Type **[CR]** and press [F2]. The prompt reads *Replace with:*.
52. Press [Enter←], and then press [F2] to replace all *[CR]* characters with hard carriage returns. This restores the document to its original condition except for the "their"s that you deleted.

FINISHING UP

53. Print the document.
54. Clear the screen without saving the document.
55. You have now completed this tutorial. Either continue with the next activity or quit the program.

QUICK REFERENCE

You can search or replace any string of characters. Strings are simply letters, words, numbers, symbols, sentences, codes, or the like that appear in sequence.

Searching

When you press [F2] or pull down the Search menu and select ***F**orward* or ***B**ackward* to search a document, you are prompted to enter the string you want to find. If the specified string is found, the program moves the cursor to the character or space immediately following it. The search then ends automatically; you then press [F2] twice to continue the search.

The Search Menu
The pull-down Search menu lists all of WordPerfect's Search and Replace commands.

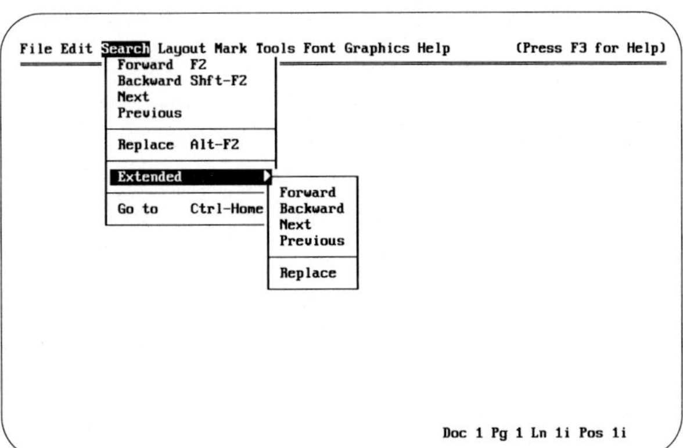

KEY/Strokes

Searching for Strings

1. Move the cursor to where you want to begin the search.
2. Either: Press F2 to search toward the end of the document or press Shift-F2 to search toward the beginning of the document.

   Or: Pull down the Search menu and select ***F**orward* or ***B**ackward*.

   The prompt reads -> *Srch:* or <- *Srch:*.
3. Type the string you want to find.
4. Press F2 (or Esc) to begin the search.

   The cursor moves to the first occurrence of the specified string.
5. Either: Press F2 twice to search toward the end of the document or press Shift-F2 twice to search toward the beginning of the document.

   Or: Pull down the Search menu and select ***N**ext* or ***P**revious*.

   When no occurrence is found, a message reads ** Not found **.

Replacing

You can make dramatic (and sometimes unwanted) changes to a document with the Replace command. When you press Alt-F2 to begin the Replace command, you are prompted *w/Confirm? **N**o (**Y**es)*.

- If you answer Yes to this prompt, each time a string is found a prompt asks if you want to replace it or not.
- If you answer No to this prompt, the command finds all occurrences of a string and automatically replaces them with the new string. You are not prompted to confirm the replacement. Be careful with commands that affect the entire document in this way. You should always save your document first in case something goes wrong. Sometimes the command will not differentiate between whole words or parts of words, for example, *row* and *arrow*. This command also ignores context. For example, if the document contains the sentences *He can read very well* and *She read the book just before class*, and you replace *read* with *write*, the second sentence would end up as *She write the book just before class* and would no longer make sense.

If you replace a string that is in uppercase letters (or in a combination of uppercase and lowercase letters), the replacement reflects this. For example, if you specify that *them* be replaced with *those*, any occurrence of *Them* is converted to *Those* and not *those*.

KEY/Strokes

Replacing Strings

1. Either: Move the cursor to where you want to begin.
   Or: Select a block of text.
2. Either: Press [Alt]-[F2].
   Or: Pull down the Search menu and select ***R**eplace.*
   The prompt reads *w/Confirm? **No** (**Y**es).*
3. Either: Press [Y] to confirm each replacement.
   Or: Press [N] to replace automatically throughout the document.
   The prompt reads *-> Srch:.*
4. Type the string to be replaced.
5. Press [F2], and the prompt reads *Replace with:.*
6. Type the replacement string.
7. Press [F2] to begin the replace operation.
   - If you answered No to the prompt *w/Confirm?* all strings are replaced automatically.
   - If you answered Yes to the prompt *w/Confirm?* the cursor flashes following the string when the first occurrence is found, and the prompt reads *Confirm? **No** (**Y**es).* Press [Y] to replace or press [N] to leave unchanged. The cursor immediately jumps to the next occurrence.

   After all occurrences of the string have been found, the prompt no longer appears.
8. Hold down [Ctrl] and press [Home] twice to return to where you were when you began.

Search and Replace Options

Both search and replace are powerful editing tools. Wildcards and other options make them even more so.

- You can change the direction of search when the prompt reads *Srch:* by pressing [↑] or [↓].
- To find whole words only, for example, *the* but not *there*, enter spaces before and after the word when you enter it. Using this procedure avoids the problem of replacing parts of words when you intended to replace only whole words. For example, searching and replacing *row* with *column* converts *arrow* into *arcolumn* and *rowboat* into *columnboat.* When you specify this option, you should be aware that searching for a singular will not find plurals or possessives; for example, searching for *row* will not find *rows.* You will also not find the string if it ends with a period or other punctuation mark. To do so, you must repeat the procedure, this time specifying *(space)row.*
- To find all occurrences, regardless of case, enter the search string in lowercase letters. This is useful because a word falling at the beginning of a sentence is capitalized, whereas the same word falling elsewhere in a sentence may not be.

- To find strings that match your case, enter the appropriate characters in uppercase when specifying the string to be searched for; for example, *The* finds *The* and *THE* but not *the*, whereas *THE* finds only *THE*.
- To delete strings, enter the string to be deleted when prompted for the string to search for, but leave the replacement string blank. When the replace is completed, all the specified strings are deleted.
- You can use wildcards to substitute for any characters. To enter a wildcard, press Ctrl-V at the appropriate spot in the search string, and the prompt reads *Key* =. Press Ctrl-X, and the *^X* wildcard is displayed on the screen. Do not use this wildcard as the first character or when searching for codes.
- To search for strings in headers, footers, footnotes, endnotes, graphics box captions, and text boxes, you use Extended Search. To use this command, you press Home before executing the Search or Replace command. For example, press Home, F2 (to search forward); Home, Shift-F2 (to search backward); or Home, Alt-F2 (to replace). These Extended Search commands display these entries on the screen if the string being searched for is found in them. If this happens when searching, repeat the Extended Search command to continue, or press F7 to cancel and return to the Edit screen.
- To search for soft and hard carriage returns and page breaks, when the prompt reads *Srch:*, press Ctrl-V to display the prompt *Key* =. Enter one of the codes listed below, and then press F2 to continue.
  - Press Ctrl-M to find a soft carriage return.
  - Press Ctrl-J to find a hard carriage return.
  - Press Ctrl-K to find a soft page break. (This will not find a *[HRt-SPg]* code; to do so, use Ctrl-J instead.)
  - Press Ctrl-L to find a hard page break.
- To find or replace format codes in a document, when the prompt reads *Srch:* or *Replace with:* just press the keys you used originally to enter the code you want to find or replace. (You cannot just type the codes.) For example, press F6 to locate boldface codes, *[BOLD]*. You can also use menus to enter codes following the prompt. For example, to search for margin change codes, press Shift-F8, press L (for ***L**ine*), and then press M (for ***M**argins*).
- When you search for codes and one is found, the cursor stops one space to its right. To delete the code, press ←Bksp. Often, a prompt appears asking if you want to delete the code. To eliminate the prompt when searching for codes, press Alt-F3 or F11 to reveal codes before beginning the search.
- To search or replace format codes that come in pairs, press the format key twice when prompted to enter the string to be searched for or replaced. For example, to replace a boldfaced **the** with an underlined <u>the</u>, when prompted to enter the search string, press F6, type **the**, and then press F6 again. When prompted to enter the replace string, press F8, type **the**, and then press F8 again.
- To search for the second code in a pair, enter both codes following the prompt, and then delete the first one. For example, to find

[bold], press F6 twice to enter *[BOLD][bold]*, and then delete the *[BOLD]* code.

EXERCISES

EXERCISE 1

SEARCHING IN THE JOBGUIDE DOCUMENT

1. Retrieve the JOBGUIDE.WP5 document.
2. Follow the instructions in the KEY/Stroke box "Replacing Strings" to replace each occurrence of the word *resume* with the word *résumé*. When prompted to enter the word to replace with, enter each é by pressing Ctrl-V. Then when the prompt reads *Key* =, type **1,41** and press Enter↵.
3. Save and then print the document.

EXERCISE 2

USING WILDCARDS

1. Retrieve the SEARCH.WP5 document.
2. Explore searching for strings using wildcards. To do so, when the prompt reads -> *Srch:* type any string with one or more wildcards in it. To enter a wildcard, press Ctrl-V, and when the prompt reads *Key* =, press Ctrl-X.
3. Clear the screen *without* saving your changes.

TOPIC 24

Using Windows

After completing this topic, you will be able to:

- Use WordPerfect's two windows to display different documents
- Move or copy text between the windows

WordPerfect has two Edit screens that you use to display different documents so that you can compare, copy, or move text between them. You can switch back and forth between these two screens or display them both on the screen at the same time.

TUTORIAL

In this tutorial, you retrieve a document onto each of WordPerfect's two screens. You then move back and forth between them and copy a block between documents.

GETTING STARTED

1. Retrieve the CODES.WP5 document.

SWITCHING SCREENS

2. Press Shift-F3 to switch to the other screen, and the status line reads *Doc 2.* The screen is blank at the moment.
3. Retrieve the BLOCKS.WP5 document.
4. Practice switching back and forth between the two screens. To do so, press Shift-F3. When you have finished, be sure the status line reads *Doc 2.*

COPYING TEXT BETWEEN WINDOWS

5. Move the cursor under the *1* in the first numbered paragraph.
6. Press Alt-F4 or F12 to turn block on.
7. Press Enter↵ to highlight the entire paragraph.
8. Press Ctrl-F4 to display the Move menu.
9. Press B (for ***B**lock*).
10. Press C (for ***C**opy*), and the prompt reads *Move cursor; press Enter to retrieve.*
11. Press Shift-F3 to display the other screen, and the status line reads *Doc 1.*
12. Press Home twice, and then press ↓ to move the cursor to the end of the document.

13. Press [Enter↵] to copy the block from one document to the other. (If necessary, press [Enter↵] a few times to separate the paragraphs.)

DISPLAYING BOTH SCREENS AT THE SAME TIME

14. Press [Ctrl]-[F3] to display the Screen menu.
15. Press [W] (for ***W****indow*), and the prompt reads *Number of lines in this window: 24*. (On some displays, the number might be different. If yours is, note the number that is listed.)
16. Press [↑] until the prompt reads *Number of lines in this window: 12*, and press [Enter↵] to display the two documents on the same screen.

Windows
You can use WordPerfect's two windows to display different documents. This makes it easy to compare documents or copy and move text from one document to another.

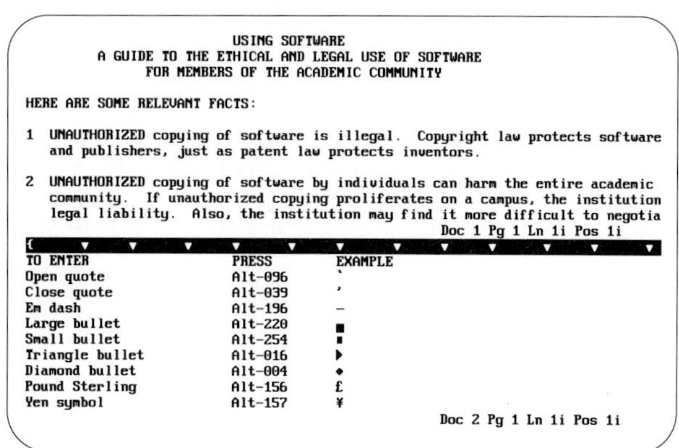

17. Press [⇧Shift]-[F3] to move the cursor between the windows. When you have finished, be sure the cursor is in the top window.
18. Repeat Steps 14 through 16 to return the display to a single screen, but press [↓] until the prompt reads *Number of lines in this window: 24* (or the number of lines listed in Step 15), and then press [Enter↵].

CLEARING BOTH SCREENS WITHOUT SAVING DOCUMENTS

19. Press [F7], and the prompt reads *Save document? **Y**es (**N**o)*.
20. Press [N], and the prompt reads *Exit doc 1? **N**o (**Y**es)*.
21. Press [Y], and the status line reads *Doc 2*.
22. Press [F7], and the prompt reads *Save document? **Y**es (**N**o)*.
23. Press [N], and the prompt reads *Exit WP? **N**o (**Y**es)*.
24. Press [Y] to quit the program, or press [N] to clear the screen and work on your own document.

FINISHING UP

25. You have now completed this tutorial. Either continue with the next activity or quit the program.

QUICK REFERENCE

When the screens are displayed back to back (as they normally are), pressing [⇧Shift]-[F3] switches you back and forth between the two screens. The *Doc* indicator on the status line reads *Doc 1* or *Doc 2* to indicate which of the two documents is currently displayed.

When you split the screen so that both documents can be seen at the same time, the documents are separated from each other with a tab ruler. When the cursor is in the upper window, the triangles indicating tab stop positions point up; when the cursor is in the lower window, the triangles point down. Pressing [Shift]-[F3] moves the cursor back and forth between the two halves of the screen.

TIP

If you have a document open in both windows, you must close each of them before you exit from WordPerfect. When you close the first one, the second one will appear on the screen. If you have two windows open but no document in the second one, the second window is closed automatically when you exit the program from the first window.

KEY/Strokes

Displaying Two Documents on the Screen

1. Either: Press [Ctrl]-[F3], and then press [W] (for ***Window***).
   Or: Pull down the Edit menu and select ***Window***.
   The prompt reads *Number of lines in this window: 24.*
2. Either: Type the number of lines (0 or any number greater than 23 returns you to full-screen display) and press [Enter].
   Or: Press [↑] and [↓] to move the tab ruler to the desired position and press [Enter].
3. Press [Shift]-[F3] to move the cursor between the windows.

EXERCISE

EXERCISE 1

USING BOTH EDIT SCREENS

1. Retrieve a document that you have previously created into each Edit screen.
2. Move blocks from one document to the other and make a printout of the results.
3. Split the screen so that both documents are displayed at the same time.
4. Clear both screens without saving either document.

CHAPTER 4 REVIEW

- WordPerfect has three kinds of blocks that you can copy, move, delete, format, save, print, or append. Regular blocks are those that begin or end anywhere in a document. Tabular column blocks are blocks separated from adjoining columns with tabs. Rectangular blocks are those with specific upper left and lower right corners in the shape of a rectangle.
- To copy, move, delete, or append a selected block, press Ctrl-F4.
- To print a selected block, press ⇧Shift-F7. To save a selected block, press F10.
- Predefined blocks are sentences that end with a punctuation mark, paragraphs that end with a hard carriage return, or pages that end with a soft or hard page break code.
- To undelete a block, move the cursor to where it was deleted from and press F1. You can then restore it or cycle through the previous three deletions and restore any one of them.
- To check the spelling in a document, press Ctrl-F2. You can also use this command to count the words in a document.
- To look up a word in the thesaurus, position the cursor anywhere in the word and press Alt-F1.
- You can search for or replace strings in a document. A string is any sequence of one or more characters, words, phrases, or codes.
- To search for a string in a document, press F2, enter the string, and then press F2 again. To find other occurrences of the same string, press F2 twice. To search toward the top of the document, press ⇧Shift-F2 instead of F2 to begin the process.
- To replace a string in a document, press Alt-F2. Enter the string to be replaced and press F2; then enter the string to replace it with and press F2 again. If you leave the replace string empty, you can delete the string you are searching for.
- Windows allow you to display two different files so that you can compare, copy, or move text. To move the cursor between the windows, you press ⇧Shift-F3. The current document is indicated on the status line as *Doc 1* or *Doc 2*.
- To display two documents on the screen at the same time, press Ctrl-F3, select ***W****indow*, and then press ↑ to scroll the dividing line between the two documents up.

CHAPTER 4 QUESTIONS

FILL IN THE BLANK

1. To copy a selected block of text, press __________.
2. To add a block of text to the end of another document, you __________ it.

3. To print a selected block, you press __________.
4. To save a selected block into its own file, you press __________.
5. To undelete a section of deleted text, press __________.
6. To check the spelling in a document, press __________.
7. To look up a word in the thesaurus, press __________.
8. To search toward the top of the document, press __________. You can also press __________ when the prompt reads *Srch:*.
9. To enter a wildcard in a search string, press __________.
10. To switch between WordPerfect's two Edit screens, press __________.
11. To display two documents on the same screen, press __________.

MATCH THE COLUMNS

1. Three	__ Any sequence of characters
2. F1	__ The number of deleted blocks that WordPerfect stores
3. Ctrl-F4	__ Searches toward the bottom of the document
4. Ctrl-F2	__ Searches toward the top of the document
5. Tabular column block	__ Replace command
6. String	__ Displays the Move menu
7. F2	__ Undeletes text
8. ⇧Shift-F2	__ Enters a wildcard in a search string
9. Alt-F2	__ Switches between windows
10. Ctrl-V then Ctrl-X	__ Spell-checks a document
11. ⇧Shift-F3	__ A column separated from adjoining columns with tab codes

WRITE OUT THE ANSWERS

1. What is a block of text? What kinds of blocks can you work with?
2. What is column mode? When would you use it?
3. What is a rectangular block? When would you select one?
4. What operations can you perform on blocks?
5. What is the difference between moving and copying a block of text?
6. What are the advantages of being able to save a block to a file?
7. What is the purpose of a spelling checker?
8. If the spelling checker stops at a word that is not in its dictionary but that is spelled correctly, what choices do you have?
9. If the spelling checker stops at a word that is spelled incorrectly, but no suggested substitute word is acceptable, what do you do?
10. What is the purpose of a thesaurus?
11. What command do you use to run WordPerfect's thesaurus?
12. When more than one list of synonyms is displayed, what keys can you use to move the menu selection letters between columns?
13. What is a string? Give some examples.

14. What is the Search command, and what is it used for?
15. What is the Replace command, and what is it used for?
16. What is a wildcard used for?
17. List and describe three options when you search or replace.
18. List and describe two advantages of being able to display two documents at the same time.
19. Describe two ways in which two documents can be displayed.
20. What command do you use to move between the two document screens?

CHAPTER 4

PROJECTS

PROJECT 1

THE DESKTOP PUBLISHING DOCUMENT

1. Retrieve the DTP.WP5 document from your data disk.
2. Spell-check the document and correct any mistakes.
3. Count the words in the document.
4. Look up the following words in the thesaurus and substitute a synonym. (Use the Search command to locate them.)
   - *device*
   - *similar*
   - *specialists*
5. Search for the first occurrence of the phrase *desktop publishing* in the text of the file and boldface it.
6. Search for and replace *process* with *sequence*, where the substitute word might be appropriate.
7. Save the document and make a printout.

PROJECT 2

THE COMPUTERS AND CAREERS DOCUMENT

1. Retrieve the CAREERS.WP5 document from your data disk.
2. Move the bulleted paragraph under the *SPECIALIST POSITIONS* heading that begins *Systems analysts ...* above the bulleted paragraph that begins *Programmers ....*
3. Spell-check the document and correct any mistakes.
4. Count the words in the document.
5. Look up the following words in the thesaurus and substitute a synonym. (Use the Search command to locate them.)
   - *executive*
   - *typical*
   - *department*
6. Search for the first occurrence of the words *originators* and *processors* and boldface them.
7. Search for and replace *secretary* with *assistant.*
8. Save the document and make a printout.

CHAPTER 5

Advanced Formatting & Desktop Publishing

TOPIC 25

Changing Typefaces

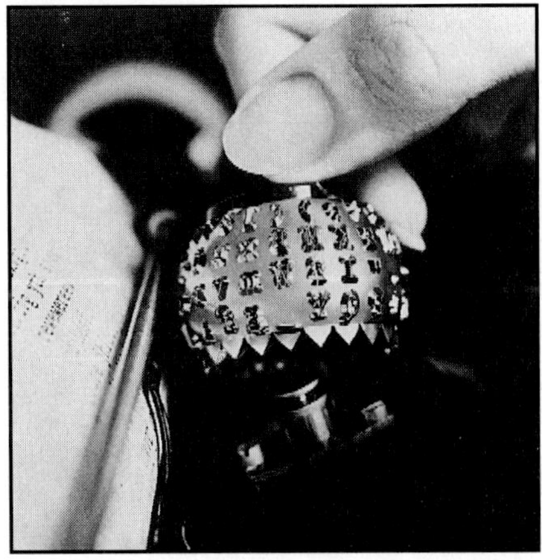

Typeball
A font is much like a typeball because they both contain characters in the same size and style.
Courtesy of International Business Machines Corporation

After completing this topic, you will be able to:
- Explain what a typeface is
- Describe the difference between serif and sans serif typefaces
- Describe situations in which one typeface may be more effective than another
- Change typefaces in your own documents

One of the hallmarks of professionally prepared documents is the tasteful use of different kinds of type. This textbook, for example, uses one type for headings and another for the text itself.

To increase a document's visual impact in this way, you must have a basic understanding of fonts. A font is simply a complete set of the characters that you need to print a document in one typeface, type appearance (which others call *typestyle*), and type size. It includes uppercase (capital) letters, lowercase letters, numbers, punctuation marks, and other special characters. Pick up a typeball from a typewriter, and you are holding a font.

Fonts are available in many designs, called typefaces; each typeface has several type appearances; and each type appearance comes in various sizes. In this topic, we explore the basic design, the typeface. Typical typefaces include Helvetica, Times Roman, Bookman, New Century Schoolbook, and Palatino. The characters in each typeface have distinctive proportions and thicknesses of lines that make them unique. However, typefaces fall into two major categories, serif and sans serif.

- Serif typefaces have smaller lines, called *serifs*, that finish off the main strokes of a letter. The most common serif typeface is Times Roman (called Dutch in some variations).
- Sans serif typefaces do not have the decorative cross marks at the end of main strokes (*sans* is French for *without*). The most common sans serif typeface is Helvetica (called Swiss or Univers in some versions).

Avant Garde Gothic
Bookman
Courier
Helvetica
New Century Schoolbook
Palatino
Times Roman
Zapf Chancery

Typefaces
The term *typeface* refers to the design of a font.

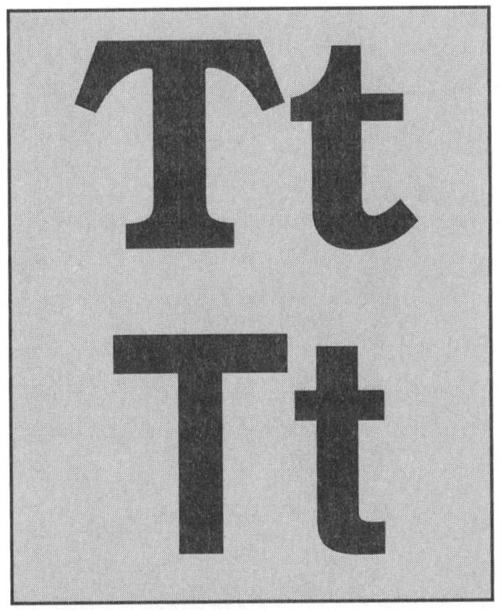

Serif and Sans Serif Type
A serif font (top) is more decorative than a sans serif font (bottom).

In many cases, typeface designs are almost identical, but their names are different. This is because the design itself cannot be protected by copyright, but the name can be. Companies that want to issue a font without permission can do so, as long as they use a different name for their version. This is why some fonts are called Dutch or Swiss when they resemble Times Roman or Helvetica as closely as they possibly can.

When choosing the typefaces to use in a document, there are several things to consider. For example, many people believe that serif typefaces are more readable because the serifs at the bottom of each character guide your eye along the line. However, this is subjective and depends partly on the application, the audience, and other elements of the design. Many publications combine the two types, using a sans serif type for headlines and a serif type for the body of the text.

When choosing typefaces for a document, try to limit your choice to no more than two. Too many typefaces can make a publication look amateurish and cluttered unless handled by someone with a superb sense of design. If you use only two, you can then add impact by changing their sizes and styles (like bold and italic) where needed. The typeface should also be related to the type of document you are creating. Occasionally, one typeface matches up better than others for a specific type of document.

TUTORIAL

In this tutorial, you change the typefaces used to print sections of a document.

GETTING STARTED

1. Retrieve the FONTS.WP5 document.

ENTERING A BASE FONT CODE

2. Move the cursor to the top of the document.
3. Press Ctrl-F8 to display the Font menu.
4. Press F (for *Base **F**ont*) to display a list of the fonts available on your system. The current base font is marked with an asterisk. Scroll through the list, and jot down on the lines below the names of some of the listed fonts. Look in particular for fonts named Helvetica or Swiss (sans serif fonts) and Times Roman, Roman, or Dutch (serif fonts). If the list is longer than the screen, you can use the cursor movement keys to scroll it.

   ____
   ____
   ____
   ____

5. Highlight one of the fonts you wrote down, and press S (for ***S**elect*). On some printers, the prompt reads *Point size:* followed by the current size of the type. If this prompt appears, press Enter↵ to confirm the size.

6. Print the document and compare the results to your previous printout.
7. Reveal codes and delete the base font code.

ENTERING MORE BASE FONT CODES

8. Repeat Steps 3 through 7 to print the document with the other base fonts that you wrote down.

FINISHING UP

9. Clear the screen without saving the document.
10. You have now completed this tutorial. Either continue with the next activity or quit the program.

QUICK REFERENCE

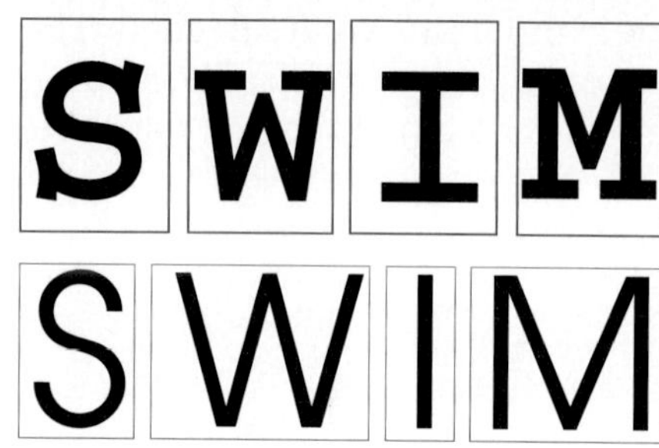

Fixed Pitch and Proportionally Spaced Type
Type can have a fixed pitch or be proportionally spaced. Fixed pitch type (top) assigns the same horizontal space to each character regardless of its width. Proportionally spaced type (bottom) allocates space based on the width of each character.

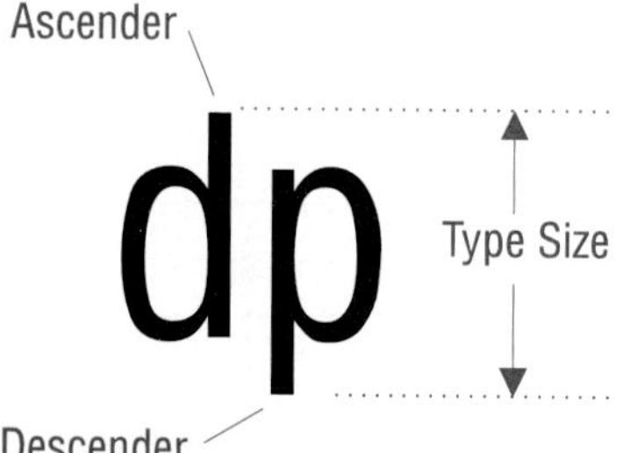

Points
Fonts are measured from the top of ascenders to the bottom of descenders, and the measurement is specified in points—1/72 of an inch.

With WordPerfect, you change typefaces by changing the base font. The initial base font is the default font for your documents. If your documents automatically print in 12-point Times Roman, your base font is 12-point Times Roman. You can specify a new initial base font for all documents or for just the current document.

When specifying base fonts, you have to specify the size of the type you want to use. There are two methods used to measure type: characters per inch and points.

Characters per inch, referred to as CPI, specify type based on the number of characters that print on a 1-inch line. This system of measurement is designed for typefaces in which every character occupies the same amount of space. Ordinary typewriter typefaces are of this sort and are usually designated as pica (which gets 10 characters per inch and is also called 10 pitch) or elite (which gets 12 characters per inch and is also called 12 pitch). Dot-matrix printers, too, may have settings with these names.

Many typefaces are proportionally spaced. That is, the narrower letters such as *i* take up less room than wider letters such as *m*. The CPI system of measurement does not work with proportionally spaced typefaces, and the point system of measurement is used instead. WordPerfect 5.1 measures type in points unless it is set to work like an earlier release of the program.

A point is about 1/72 of an inch, so 72-point type would be 1-inch high, 36-point type would be ½-inch high, and so on. Most documents are printed using 12- or 10-point type, with larger sizes normally reserved for titles and headings. Smaller sizes are typically used for tables, headers and footers, and footnotes.

Keep in mind that changing the size of the base font affects any characters that you have formatted with the Size command on the Font menu. Sizes such as Fine, Small, Large, and Very Large are all relative to the size of the base font. By default, Fine is set to 60% of the base font, Small 80%, Large 120%, Very Large 150%, and Extra Large at 200%. Therefore, a word formatted as Large with a 12-point base font will be smaller than a word formatted the same way with a 14-point base font.

List of Initial Fonts
The Initial Font menu displays a list of all the fonts available for your printer. (The listing on your screen will depend on your printer.)

➔ KEY/Strokes

Specifying the Initial Base Font for All Documents

1. Either: Press [⇧Shift]-[F7] to display the Print menu.
   Or: Pull down the File menu and select ***Print***.
2. Press [S] (for **S***elect Printer*), and the printer that you are currently using is highlighted and marked with an asterisk.
3. Press [E] (for ***E****dit*).
4. Press [F] (for *Initial Base* ***F****ont*) to display a list of the fonts available for your printer.
5. Press the cursor movement keys to highlight the initial base font you want to use. (The current initial base font is marked with an asterisk.)
6. Press [S] (for **S***elect*) to change the initial base font. (If you select a scalable font—one that can be printed in many sizes—the prompt reads *Point size:* followed by the current size. Press [Enter↵], or type a new size and press [Enter↵].)
7. Press [F7] repeatedly to return to the Edit screen.

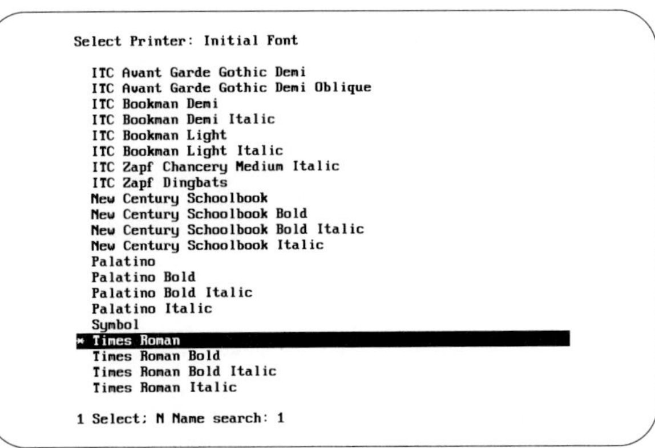

```
Select Printer: Initial Font

  ITC Avant Garde Gothic Demi
  ITC Avant Garde Gothic Demi Oblique
  ITC Bookman Demi
  ITC Bookman Demi Italic
  ITC Bookman Light
  ITC Bookman Light Italic
  ITC Zapf Chancery Medium Italic
  ITC Zapf Dingbats
  New Century Schoolbook
  New Century Schoolbook Bold
  New Century Schoolbook Bold Italic
  New Century Schoolbook Italic
  Palatino
  Palatino Bold
  Palatino Bold Italic
  Palatino Italic
  Symbol
* Times Roman
  Times Roman Bold
  Times Roman Bold Italic
  Times Roman Italic

1 Select; N Name search: 1
```

➔ KEY/Strokes

Specifying the Initial Base Font for the Current Document

1. Either: Press [⇧Shift]-[F8], and then press [D] (for ***D****ocument*).
   Or: Pull down the Layout menu and select ***Document***.
2. Press [F] (for *Initial Base* ***F****ont*) to display a list of the fonts available for your printer.
3. Press the cursor movement keys to highlight the initial base font you want to use. (The current initial base font is marked with an asterisk.)
4. Press [S] (for **S***elect*) to change the initial base font. (If you select a scalable font—one that can be printed in many sizes—the prompt reads *Point size:* followed by the current size. Press [Enter↵], or type a new size and press [Enter↵].)
5. Press [F7] to return to the Edit screen.

TIP

If your system uses downloadable soft fonts, you may have to use WordPerfect's Initialize Printer command on the Print menu (Shift-F7) to download the fonts to the printer. You have to do this only once, at the beginning of a session. The fonts will remain in the printer until you shut it off.

After selecting an initial base font, you can enter a new base font code anywhere in the document to change it. The font specified in the code affects all text from where you insert the code to the next base font code or the end of the document. For example, if you insert a base font code midway down page 1 of your document, the top half of the page is formatted with the initial base font and the lower half with the new base font.

→ KEY/Strokes

Changing the Base Font Within a Document

1. Move the cursor to where you want to change the base font.
2. Either: Press Ctrl-F8, and then press F (for *Base **F**ont*).

   Or: Pull down the Font menu and select *Base **F**ont.*

   A list of fonts available for your printer is displayed.
3. Press the cursor movement keys to highlight the base font you want to use. (The current base font is marked with an asterisk.)
4. Press S (for ***S**elect*) to change the base font, and you return to the Edit screen.

   If you select a scalable font—one that can be printed in many sizes—the prompt reads *Point size:* followed by the current size. Press Enter↵, or type a new size and press Enter↵.

EXERCISES

EXERCISE 1

CHANGING THE BASE FONT FOR ALL DOCUMENTS

Follow the instructions in the KEY/Strokes box "Specifying the Initial Base Font for All Documents" to see which font is the current initial base font for all documents. If you prefer a different font for all documents, select the one that you want to use. If you prefer to leave the setting unchanged, press F7 to return to the Edit screen. If you change the base font, type a sentence and make a printout to compare its typeface to any previous printout.

EXERCISE 2

CHANGING THE BASE FONT FOR A DOCUMENT

Retrieve any of the documents you have been working on, and follow the instructions in the KEY/Strokes box "Specifying the Initial Base Font for the Current Document" to enter a new base font code at the top of the document. Print out one page and compare it to any previous printout. Continue experimenting until you have your documents printing in the typestyles that you prefer.

TOPIC 26

Headers & Footers

Headers and Footers
Headers print in the text area of one or more consecutive pages where the first line of text normally prints. Footers print in the text area of one or more consecutive pages where the last line of text normally prints.

After completing this topic, you will be able to:

- Define the terms *headers, footers, running heads,* and *running feet*
- Enter headers and footers in your own documents

Headers are lines of text printed at the top of the type page, and footers are lines of text printed at the bottom. If they print on more than one page in a sequence, they are called running heads and running feet. Both headers and footers help readers know where they are in the document.

Headers or footers can be aligned with the inside or outside margins or centered between them. However, if the document is to be printed on both sides of the page, the placement of the headers and footers may be affected. To keep them symmetrical (if they are not centered), they may have to alternate from one side to the other on odd-numbered (right-hand) pages and even-numbered (left-hand) pages. When the headers and footers alternate like this, they are said to be mirrored.

TUTORIAL

In this tutorial, you enter headers and footers in a document.

GETTING STARTED

1. Retrieve the EDUCOM.WP5 document.

ENTERING A HEADER

2. Press [Alt]-[F3] or [F11] to reveal codes.
3. Position the cursor to the right of or immediately below the margin code *[L/R Mar:1.5",1.5"]* at the top of the document. Margins for headers and footers are controlled by the open margin code, if any, in effect at the point where they are entered. If you enter a header or footer code above the margin code, the header or footer will align with the default margin settings.
4. Press [⇧Shift]-[F8] to display the Format menu.
5. Press [P] (for ***Page***) to display the Page Format menu.
6. Press [H] (for ***H**eaders*) to display the Header Type menu.
7. Press [A] (for *Header **A***) to display the Header Occurrence menu.
8. Press [P] (for *Every **Page***) to display the Header Entry screen.
9. Press [Alt]-[F6] to right-align the cursor.

10. Type **EDUCOM**.
11. Press F7 to return to the Page Format menu.

ENTERING A FOOTER WITH DATE AND PAGE CODES

12. Press F (for ***F**ooters*) to display the Footer Type menu.
13. Press A (for *Footer **A***) to display the Footer Occurrence menu.
14. Press P (for *Every **P**age*).
15. Type **Date:** and press Spacebar twice.
16. Press Shift-F5 to display the Date menu.
17. Press C (for *Date **C**ode*), and the date taken from the system clock is displayed on the screen. If your system's clock is wrong, the date will be also.
18. Press Alt-F6 to align the cursor with the right margin.
19. Type **Page** and press Spacebar once.
20. Press Ctrl-B to enter a code to number pages.
21. Press F7 twice to save the footer text and return to the Edit screen.

SUPPRESSING HEADERS AND FOOTERS

22. Press Shift-F8 to display the Format menu.
23. Press P (for ***P**age*) to display the Page Format menu.
24. Press U (for ***Su**ppress (this page only)*) to display the Suppress menu.

The Suppress Menu
The Suppress menu lists options for suppressing page numbers, headers, and footers on selected pages.

```
Format: Suppress (this page only)

     1 - Suppress All Page Numbering, Headers and Footers

     2 - Suppress Headers and Footers

     3 - Print Page Number at Bottom Center  No

     4 - Suppress Page Numbering             No

     5 - Suppress Header A                   No

     6 - Suppress Header B                   No

     7 - Suppress Footer A                   No

     8 - Suppress Footer B                   No



Selection: 0
```

25. Press A (for *Suppress **A**ll Page Numbering, Headers and Footers*), and the word *No* following choices 5 through 8 changes to *Yes*.
26. Press F7 to return to the Edit screen.
27. Delete the page numbering codes you entered in a previous topic. These include *{Suppress:PgNum}*, *{PgNumbering:Bottom Center}*, and *{PgNum:i}* at the top of page 1 and *{Pg Num:2}* at the top of page 2.

FINISHING UP

28. Save the document and print the first and second pages. The header and footer are not printed on the first page. On the second page, the header prints at the top of the page aligned with the right margin. The footer prints both the date and page number using the codes you entered.

29. You have now completed this tutorial. Either continue with the next activity or quit the program.

QUICK REFERENCE

You can add two headers and two footers to each page of your document. They are printed where the first or last line of text would normally be printed, with one line inserted to separate them from the text below or above them. Headers or footers are not displayed on the Edit screen, but you can preview them with the View Document command or reveal codes to see their codes. When entering headers or footers, keep the following points in mind:

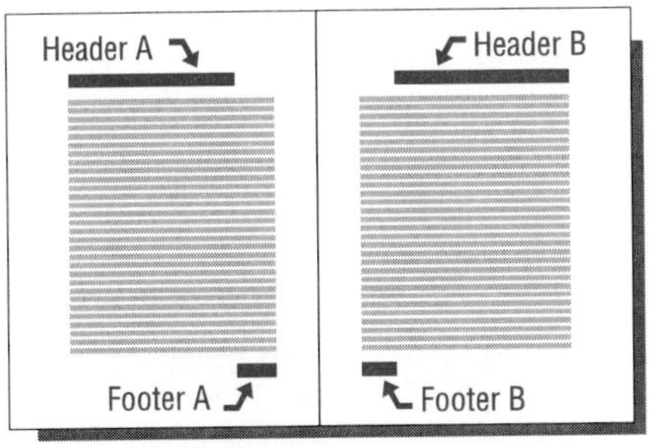

Header A | Header B | Footer A | Footer B

Header and Footer Alignments
When you enter headers or footers, they are automatically aligned with the left margin. However, you can press Shift-F6 to center them or Alt-F6 to align them with the right margin. For example, you can align headers and footers so that they print on the outside or inside edges of pages that are printed or copied back to back.

- Headers or footers print from the place where you enter them to the end of the document or to the next header or footer code that changes or discontinues them.
- The header or footer code must be placed at the top of the page it is to begin on. If the code is not at the top of the page, it will not print until the next page. To be sure the code stays at the top of the page, enter a hard page break immediately before the code if it isn't at the top of the document.
- When entering headers or footers, you can press Enter↵ to insert blank lines above or below the header to add extra space between it and the text. This is useful when you use two headers or footers on the same page and want to keep them on separate lines.
- Your headers or footers can be longer than a single line of text.
- You can enter page numbers in headers or footers by pressing Ctrl-B. This inserts a *^B* code. When you print the document, the page number is printed in the position of the code. If you also turn on page numbers with the Page Format menu, you will have two page numbers printed on each page; to avoid this, turn off normal page numbering.
- You can enter a date or a time in a header or footer using the date and time commands that enter text or codes. To do so, position the cursor in the header or footer, press Shift-F5, and then press T (for *Date **T**ext*) or C (for *Date **C**ode*), or pull down the Tools menu and select *Date **T**ext* or *Date **C**ode*. (To enter a time, you have to use the Date Format command.) The advantage of using codes to enter dates and times is that they change automatically each time the document is retrieved or printed; thus, it is easier to keep track of the various versions of the same document.
- When you enter headers and footers, the program normally aligns them flush left. To change the alignment, use the commands to center them or align them flush right. For example, if you enter two headers or two footers so that they print on the same pages, keep them short, and use the Flush Right command (Alt-F6) to align one of them with the right margin so that they do not overlap on the printout.

To print headers or footers on a document to be printed or copied on both sides of the paper, align them so that they appear on the outside corners. To do so, enter an A header or footer, align it flush left, and specify even pages. Then enter a B header or footer, align it flush right, and specify odd pages.

→ KEY/Strokes

Entering Headers or Footers or Discontinuing Them

1. Move the cursor to the top of the page (above all other codes) where you want the headers or footers to begin. (Press Ctrl-Home, and then press ↑.)
2. Either: Press ⇧Shift-F8, and then press P (for ***Page***).
   Or: Pull down the Layout menu and select ***Page***.
3. Either: Press H (for ***Headers***).
   Or: Press F (for ***Footers***).
4. Select either header or footer type described in the table "Header and Footer Types and Occurrences."
5. Press the number indicating the occurrence of the header or footer (see the table "Header and Footer Types and Occurrences"), and the blank Header/Footer screen appears.
6. Type the header or footer text (you can enter up to one full page of text) and press ⇧Shift-F5 to enter the date or time, or press Ctrl-B to enter a code to number pages.
7. Press F7 twice to save the header or footer text and return to the Edit screen.

→ KEY/Strokes

Editing Headers or Footers

1. Move the cursor to below where the header code is located in the document. (The program searches from the cursor toward the top of the document for the next header or footer code, and that is the header or footer displayed.)
2. Either: Press ⇧Shift-F8, and then press P (for ***Page***).
   Or: Pull down the Layout menu and select ***Page***.
3. Either: Press H (for ***Headers***).
   Or: Press F (for ***Footers***).
4. Select the A or B header or footer and press E (for ***Edit***) to display the next header or footer above the cursor.
5. Edit the header or footer text.
6. Press F7 twice to save the header or footer text and return to the Edit screen.

HEADER AND FOOTER TYPES AND OCCURRENCES

Type

1 *Header* ***A*** or *Footer* ***A*** displays the Occurrence menu so that you can print, edit, or discontinue a header or footer.

2 *Header* ***B*** or *Footer* ***B*** displays the Occurrence menu so that you can print, edit, or discontinue a second header or footer.

Occurrence

1 ***D****iscontinue* discontinues headers or footers for the rest of the document.

2 *Every* ***P****age* prints headers or footers on every page.

3 ***O****dd Pages* prints headers or footers only on odd pages.

4 ***E****ven Pages* prints headers or footers only on even pages.

5 ***E****dit* displays the header or footer for editing.

Suppressing Headers and Footers

If you enter headers or footers, you can suppress them on selected pages.

KEY/Strokes

Suppressing Headers or Footers

1. Move the cursor to the beginning of the page where page numbers, headers, or footers are to be turned off. (Press Ctrl-Home, and then press ↑ from any place on the page.)
2. Either: Press Shift-F8, and then press P (for ***P****age*).

   Or: Pull down the Layout menu and select ***Page***.
3. Press U (for *S****u****ppress (this page only)*).
4. Select one of the choices listed on the screen. (To select choices 1 and 2, you merely press the number of the option. To select choices 3 through 8, press the number, and then press Y or N.)
5. Press F7 once or twice to return to the Edit screen.

EXERCISES

EXERCISE 1

EDITING HEADERS AND FOOTERS IN THE EDUCOM DOCUMENT

1. Retrieve the EDUCOM.WP5 document that you added headers and footers to in the tutorial at the beginning of this topic.
2. Follow the instructions in the KEY/Strokes box "Editing Headers or Footers" to display the Header A text that you entered in the tutorial. Enter a base font code in front of the text for a 10-point typeface.
3. Follow the instructions in the KEY/Strokes box "Editing Headers or Footers" to display the Footer A text that you entered in the tutorial. Enter a base font code in front of the text for a 10-point typeface.

4. Save the document and print just the second page.

EXERCISE 2

ADDING MIRRORED FOOTERS TO THE JOBGUIDE DOCUMENT

In this exercise, you enter mirrored footers that alternate from side to side on odd- and even-numbered pages so that they always print flush with the outside margin.

1. Retrieve the JOBGUIDE.WP5 document.
2. Follow the instructions in the KEY/Strokes box "Entering Headers or Footers or Discontinuing Them" to add a Footer A that prints your last name on odd-numbered pages in all uppercase letters, and align it flush right.
3. Follow the instructions in the KEY/Strokes box "Entering Headers or Footers or Discontinuing Them" to add a Footer B that prints your last name on even-numbered pages in all uppercase letters, and align it flush left.
4. Save and print the document. Your name should be printed on the inside edges of the pages opposite the page numbers printed on the outside edges. You'll see this best by laying pages 2 and 3 side by side as if they were bound together in a book.

TIPS

- If you have specified that page numbers be printed, the headers or footers might print on the same line as the page numbers or even print over them. To avoid this, change the page number position.
- Headers and footers print where the first and last lines of text normally print. To change the line on which they print:
  - Press Enter↵ when the header or footer is displayed on the screen to insert blank lines above or below it.
  - Change the top or bottom margins. For example, you normally have 1-inch top and bottom margins. If you print a header, it prints just below the top margin, and the program adds one line of space below it before the first line of text. If you change the top margin to 3/4 inch, the header prints higher on the page.
- Most format commands work in headers and footers just as they do in normal text. You can boldface or underline text, center or align it with the right margin, and so on.
- To search for or replace text in headers and footers, use the Extended Search (Home, F2) command.
- If headers or footers do not print in a specified font, it is because the new base font code is positioned after the header or footer code. Headers and footers always print in the base font in effect at the place where their code is entered.

TOPIC 27

Footnotes & Endnotes

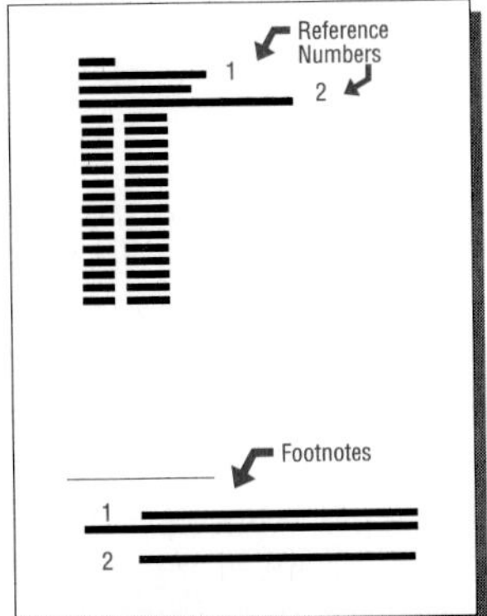

Footnotes
Footnotes print at the bottom of the page on which their reference number appears in the text.

After completing this topic, you will be able to:

- Describe the differences between footnotes and endnotes
- List and describe footnote and endnote options
- Enter footnotes and endnotes in your own documents

Footnotes consist of numbered text printed at the bottom of the page on which a matching reference number appears in the body text. Endnotes are just like footnotes, but instead of printing at the bottom of the page with the matching reference number, they are printed at the end of a section or at the end of the document. When you insert a new footnote or endnote or delete an old one, all footnote or endnote references that follow are automatically renumbered.

TUTORIAL

In this tutorial, you enter footnotes into a document.

GETTING STARTED

1. Retrieve the EDUCOM.WP5 document.

ENTERING A FOOTNOTE

2. Search for the first occurrence of the term *ADAPSO*, and move the cursor under the space to the right of the comma that follows it.
3. Press Ctrl-F7 to display the Footnote menu.
4. Press F (for ***F**ootnote*).
5. Press C (for ***C**reate*), and the screen goes blank except for the number *1*.
6. Type **Now called the Information Technology Association of America.**
7. Press F7 to return to the Edit screen, and the number *1* at the cursor's position is the footnote reference number.
8. Press Alt-F3 or F11 to reveal codes, and notice that the code *[Footnote:1;[Note Num]* also displays the first 30 or so characters in the footnote. It ends with *...]*, indicating that there is more to the footnote that is not displayed.
9. Press Alt-F3 or F11 to hide the codes.

ENTERING A SECOND FOOTNOTE

10. Move the cursor to the end of the paragraph that follows the heading *Shareware.*
11. Repeat Steps 3 through 5 to display the Footnote screen, and type **A good source of this type of software is Public Brand Software, P.O. Box 51315, Indianapolis, IN 46251.**
12. Press F7 to return to the Edit screen, and the new footnote is now numbered *1*. Locate the first footnote number, and you'll see that it's been automatically changed from *1* to *2*.

FINISHING UP

13. Save and print the document, and the footnotes that you entered are printed at the bottom of the page.
14. You have now completed this tutorial. Either continue with the next activity or quit the program.

QUICK REFERENCE

You can enter footnotes and endnotes anywhere in a document by entering codes. You can then specify options to control their numbers and styles.

Footnotes and Endnotes

Footnotes print in the text area of the document, not in the bottom margin. If the footnote is too long to print on a page, ½ inch of it prints on the same page as the reference number, and the rest of the footnote prints on the next page. If there is not enough room to print the first ½ inch of the footnote, both the footnote and the text line that contains the reference number move to the next page.

Endnotes print below the last hard carriage return on the last page of the document. To print endnotes on a separate page, put a hard page break (Ctrl-Enter↵) after the last line of text in the document. To add a heading, type it on the last page, and then press Enter↵ two or three times so that the first endnote prints that number of lines below the heading.

After entering footnotes or endnotes, you can edit them. When you use the command to edit a footnote or an endnote, the program searches for the next note following the cursor and asks if you want to edit that note. You can either press Enter↵ to accept the suggested number or enter a new number and press Enter↵.

KEY/Strokes

Entering or Editing Footnotes or Endnotes or Changing Options

1. Move the cursor to where you want the footnote or endnote reference to appear in the document or above where you want to change the style of all footnotes and endnotes.

2. Either: Press Ctrl-F7, and then press F (for ***Footnote***) or E (for ***Endnote***).

   Or: Pull down the Layout menu and select ***Footnote*** or ***Endnote***.

3. Make one of the selections described in the table "Footnote and Endnote Menu Choices."

FOOTNOTE AND ENDNOTE MENU CHOICES

1	*Create* displays the Footnote or Endnote screen. Type the note and press F7 to return to the Edit screen.
2	*Edit* displays the prompt *Footnote number?* or *Endnote number?* followed by the number of the next note. Press Enter↵ to edit the suggested number (or letter if you have changed the numbering method), or enter the number (or letter) of another note, and then press Enter↵. The note is displayed on the screen. Edit it, and press F7 to return to the Edit screen.
3	*New Number* displays the prompt *Footnote number?* or *Endnote number?* Enter a new number and press Enter↵. This overrides automatic numbering, for example, when different parts of the same document are kept in separate files but you want numbering to be consecutive when you print them out.
4	*Options* displays the Footnote Options or Endnote Options menu. Use any of the choices described in the table "Footnote and Endnote Options." (Only some of the options are offered for endnotes.) When you have finished changing options, press F7 to return to the Edit screen.

Footnote and Endnote Options

You can specify options that include changing the spacing between or within notes, changing starting numbers, or changing the line that separates the notes from the document portion of the page. When you press Ctrl-F7 and select ***Footnote*** or ***Endnote***, you can select Options to display the Options menu. The choices on this menu are described in the table "Footnote and Endnote Options."

The Footnote Options Menu
The Footnote Options menu allows you to specify where and how footnotes are printed.

```
Footnote Options

     1 - Spacing Within Footnotes              1
                 Between Footnotes             0.167i

     2 - Amount of Note to Keep Together       0.5i

     3 - Style for Number in Text              [SUPRSCPT][Note Num][suprscpt]

     4 - Style for Number in Note                   [SUPRSCPT][Note Num][suprscpt

     5 - Footnote Numbering Method             Numbers

     6 - Start Footnote Numbers each Page      No

     7 - Line Separating Text and Footnotes    2-inch Line

     8 - Print Continued Message               No

     9 - Footnotes at Bottom of Page           Yes


Selection: 0
```

T O P I C 27

The Endnote Options Menu
The Endnote Options menu allows you to specify where and how endnotes are printed.

```
Endnote Options

     1 - Spacing Within Endnotes            1
                 Between Endnotes           0.167i

     2 - Amount of Endnote to Keep Together 0.5i

     3 - Style for Numbers in Text          [SUPRSCPT][Note Num][suprscpt]

     4 - Style for Numbers in Note          [Note Num].

     5 - Endnote Numbering Method           Numbers

Selection: 0
```

FOOTNOTE AND ENDNOTE OPTIONS

1 *Spacing Within/Between Footnotes/Endnotes* controls the line spacing within and between the notes. For the spacing within notes, type **1** for single spacing, **1.5** for 1½ spacing, **2** for double spacing, and so on. For the spacing between notes, enter a distance; for example, type **.2** for a spacing of 2/10 inch.

2 *Amount of Note/Endnote to Keep Together* controls the number of lines kept together on the same page when part of the footnote continues onto another page. Enter a measurement; for example, type **1** to keep 1 inch of the note on the page.

3 *Style for Number in **Text*** controls the style of the footnote or endnote reference numbers in the text area of the document. For example, you can change font sizes or appearances.

4 *Style for Number in **Note*** works just like ***3** Style for Number in **Text***, but you can also enter spaces to indent the number from the left margin.

5 *Footnote/Endnote Numbering **Method*** controls the way footnotes are numbered. Press N (for ***N**umbers*), L (for ***L**etters*), or C (for ***C**haracters*) to specify other characters. If you press C, you can specify as many as five characters. (The default is a single asterisk.) If you specify a single character, such as the asterisk, the number of characters indicates the sequence. For example, * indicates the first reference, ** the second, and *** the third. If you specify more than one character, the characters cycle to indicate the sequence.

6 *Start Footnote Numbers each **Page*** specifies whether footnote numbers run consecutively throughout the document or start over on each page of the document.

7 *Line Separating Text and Footnotes* controls whether a line separates footnotes from the last line of the document. Type **N** (for ***N**o line*), **2** (for ***2**-inch line*), or **M** (for ***M**argin to Margin*) to print a line across the entire page.

8 *Print **C**ontinued Message* prints *(Continued...)* on the last line of the first page and *(...Continued)* on the first footnote line of the following page if the footnote continues to the next page.

9 *Footnotes at **B**ottom of Page* specifies where footnotes are to be printed on pages that are not full. You can specify that they be printed at the bottom of the page or just below the last line of text on the page.

TIPS

- When you print selected pages, a single page, or a block, all footnotes for the pages print regardless of how long they are.
- To see an entire footnote, use the View Document command on the Print menu, or print the page on which its reference number

appears. To print all endnotes, print the last page of the document.

- To search and replace in footnotes and endnotes, use the Extended Search command. To do so, press Home, F2 to search or Alt-F2 to replace.
- You can permanently change the footnote and endnote options by changing the Initial Codes setting on the Initial Settings menu of the Setup menu.
- To print endnotes at a place other than the end of the document, press Ctrl-F7 to display the Footnote menu, and then press P (for *Endnote **P**lacement*). The prompt reads *Restart endnote numbering? **Y**es (**N**o)*. Press Y to have endnotes restart numbering below the code, or press N to have endnotes continue in numerical order. This command inserts a comment into the document followed by a hard page break code so that any following text is printed on a separate page. To calculate the space to be occupied by the endnotes, press Alt-F5 to display the Mark Text menu. Press G (for ***G**enerate*), and then press G (for ***G**enerate Tables, Indexes, Automatic References, etc.*). Press Y to generate the space. A new comment is inserted that shows the amount of space occupied by the endnotes.

EXERCISES

EXERCISE 1

EDITING A FOOTNOTE IN THE EDUCOM DOCUMENT

In this exercise, you edit the footnotes that you entered in the tutorial at the beginning of this topic.

1. Retrieve the EDUCOM.WP5 document that you added footnotes to at the beginning of this topic.
2. Follow the instructions in the KEY/Strokes box "Entering or Editing Footnotes or Endnotes or Changing Options" to edit the first footnote. After the ZIP code but before the period, type a comma and a space and then **phone 1-800-426-3475**. When you have finished, press F7 to return to the Edit screen.
3. Save and print the page of the document that contains the first footnote.

EXERCISE 2

ENTERING ENDNOTES IN THE SUNCITY DOCUMENT

1. Retrieve the SUNCITY.WP5 document.
2. Move the cursor to the end of the line on the first page that begins *D12*. Follow the instructions in the KEY/Strokes box "Entering or Editing Footnotes or Endnotes or Changing Options" to enter an

endnote that states **This year must be later than the one you entered into cell D11 but not later than 1986**. Separate it from the number with a space.

3. Move the cursor to the end of the line on the second page that begins *TABLE 1*. Follow the instructions in the KEY/Strokes box "Entering or Editing Footnotes or Endnotes or Changing Options" to enter an endnote that states **Source: U.S. Department of Labor, Bureau of Labor Statistics (BLS)**. Separate it from the number with a space.
4. Save and print the document.

EXERCISE 3

ENTERING FOOTNOTE FORMATS

In this exercise, you enter some standard footnote formats so that you can refer to them should you need to know how to enter footnotes in any of your own documents.

1. Retrieve the FOOTFORM.WP5 document.
2. Follow the instructions in the KEY/Strokes box "Entering or Editing Footnotes or Endnotes or Changing Options" to enter the footnotes shown in the figure "Footnotes to Add to the FOOTFORM Document" at the end of the appropriate line in the document.
3. Save and print the document.

1. Book with one author

2. Book with two or three authors

3. Book with a corporate author

4. Work in several volumes or parts

5. Works in an anthology or a collection

6. Article in a reference work

7. Article from a weekly, biweekly, or monthly magazine or newspaper

8. Article from a daily newspaper

9. Film

10. Interview

The FOOTFORM Document
The FOOTFORM.WP5 document that you retrieve for this exercise looks like this.

[1]First name Last name, Title (City, State: Publisher, copyright date), pages.

[2]First name Last name, First name Last name, and First name Last name, Title (City, State: Publisher, copyright date), pages.

[3]Name of Corporation, Title (City, State: Publisher, copyright date), pages.

[4]First name Last name, Title, Volume or Part (City, State: Publisher, copyright date), pages.

[5]First name Last name, "Title of Article," in Title of Publication, ed. First name Last name (City, State: Publisher, copyright date), pages.

[6]"Title of section," Title of Book, copyright or edition date.

[7]First name Last name, "Title of Article," Name of Periodical, date, section, page.

[8]First name Last name, "Title of Article," Name of Newspaper, date of issue, page.

[9]First name Last name, dir., Film Title, with Major Actor, Studio, date of release.

[10]Personal interview with First name Last name, date.

Footnotes to Add to the FOOTFORM Document
The footnotes shown here are the ones you add to the FOOTFORM.WP5 document.

CHAPTER 5 REVIEW

- Changing the base font (Ctrl-F8, F) changes the overall typestyle for a document. For example, you can print it in Times Roman, Helvetica, or any other typeface your printer supports.
- When you specify a base font, you also specify a type size. The type size of this base font governs how large the type is when formatted with sizes such as Fine or Large on the Font menu.
- You can change the base font in a document by entering a new base font code any place.
- You can specify a base font for all documents using the Edit command on the Print menu.
- You can print two headers or footers at the top and bottom of one or more pages of a document. When you do so, you can press Ctrl-B to have a page number printed or Shift-F5 to enter a date or date code.
- You can enter a footnote or endnote (Ctrl-F7) any place in a document. Footnotes print at the bottom of the page on which the reference number prints. Endnotes print at the end of the document.

CHAPTER 5 QUESTIONS

FILL IN THE BLANK

1. To change the base font, press __________.
2. Fonts that have decorative lines at the end of each stroke are called __________. Those fonts without them are called __________.
3. Font sizes are given in __________ or __________. Of these two methods, the preferred one is to give them in __________.
4. When the space allocated to characters is based on the width of the character, the type is called __________ spaced.
5. When headers print on a series of pages, they are called __________.
6. To enter the date based on the system's clock in a header or footer, press __________.
7. To enter a code where you want page numbers to print in a header or footer, press __________.
8. To enter footnotes or endnotes, press __________.

MATCH THE COLUMNS

1. Ctrl-F8	__	Characters per inch
2. Base font	__	Text printed at the top of the page
3. Serif type	__	Displays the Font menu

4. Sans serif type
5. CPI
6. Point
7. Proportionally spaced
8. Header
9. Footer
10. Shift-F5
11. Ctrl-B

__ Changes the style of type
__ Enters a code in a header or footer so that a page number will be printed
__ 1/72 of an inch
__ Type without serifs
__ Type with lines called serifs at the end of each stroke
__ Text printed at the bottom of the page
__ Displays the date menu
__ Allocating less space to narrow characters and more to wider ones

WRITE OUT THE ANSWERS

1. Describe how changing the base font relates to changing font appearance or size.
2. What are headers and footers? Why are they used?
3. What are headers and footers that appear on more than one page called?
4. List and describe some options you have when printing headers and footers.
5. Assume that your document is to be printed on both sides of the page and then bound. How do you align headers and footers so that they are on the outside edge of each page?
6. What is the difference between a footnote and an endnote?
7. What happens to a footnote reference number if you insert a new reference number above it?
8. List the steps you would follow to edit a footnote.
9. List the steps you would follow to change the spacing between footnotes.

CHAPTER 5 PROJECTS

PROJECT 1

THE DESKTOP PUBLISHING DOCUMENT

1. Retrieve the DTP.WP5 document from your data disk.
2. Change the base font for the entire document to one other than the one you are currently using.
3. Enter a flush-right header on every page with your last name in uppercase letters followed by a code for page numbering.
4. Enter a flush-right footer on every page with a date code (Shift-F5, C).

5. Delete any page number code from the document since page numbers will now be printed in the header.
6. Add the footnote **Sometimes referred to as DTP**. after the phrase *Desktop publishing* in the sentence in the first paragraph that begins *Desktop publishing really began when Apple .....*
7. Save the document, and make a printout.

PROJECT 2

THE COMPUTERS AND CAREERS DOCUMENT

1. Retrieve the CAREERS.WP5 document from your data disk.
2. Change the base font for the entire document to one other than the one you are currently using.
3. Enter a flush-right header on every page with your last name in uppercase letters followed by a code for page numbering.
4. Enter a flush-right footer on every page with a date code (Shift-F5, C).
5. Delete any page number code from the document since page numbers will now be printed in the header.
6. Add the endnote **Federal Express Corporation** immediately after the phrase *One major company* in the first paragraph.
7. Save the document and make a printout. If your heading is misaligned because it is so large, enter a hard carriage return at the end of each line and then center each line.

CHAPTER 6

Improving Productivity

TOPIC 28

Merge Printing

```
To: {FIELD}1~
Department: {FIELD}2~

Your new extension is now {FIELD}3~.
```

Merge Printing
A primary file contains text and merge codes like *{FIELD}1~* that specify where data are to be inserted.

```
John{END FIELD}
Finance{END FIELD}
1003{END FIELD}
{END RECORD}
==========================
Mary{END FIELD}
Production{END FIELD}
1004{END FIELD}
{END RECORD}
==========================
Frank{END FIELD}
Sales{END FIELD}
1005{END FIELD}
{END RECORD}
==========================
```

A secondary file contains the data that are to be inserted into the primary file.

After completing this topic, you will be able to:

- Explain the purpose of merge printing
- Explain the purpose of primary and secondary files and describe how to create them
- Explain the purpose of merge codes
- Enter merge codes in your own documents

Instead of typing a form letter and then editing it over and over again to send to different people, merge printing lets you create one form document that then has personalized data entered into each copy as it is being printed. This procedure can greatly increase your speed in preparing form letters and similar documents that are essentially the same except for minor changes from copy to copy.

The information that personalizes each form letter, such as the name and address, can be entered from the keyboard or kept in a separate file from which it is automatically inserted into the form letter during the merge process. When stored in a separate file, the information can easily be kept up to date and used repeatedly to print letters, envelopes, and mailing labels automatically.

When printing form letters, you begin by creating and coding a primary file. This primary file can contain text, formats, and merge codes. The text and formats appear in each copy that is printed, and the merge codes control the merge-printing process and specify what data are to be inserted where. To merge data automatically, you also create a secondary file that stores the data to be merged in an organized fashion. You edit, save, and retrieve these two types of documents just like any other documents.

The Primary File

The primary file contains the unchanging parts of the document (sometimes called the boilerplate or form letter). It also contains codes, called merge codes, that indicate when data should be inserted from the keyboard or a secondary file during merge printing. The merge codes that refer to a secondary file specify which information from that file is to be inserted into the primary file during merge printing. For example, a merge code might specify that people's names or their addresses be

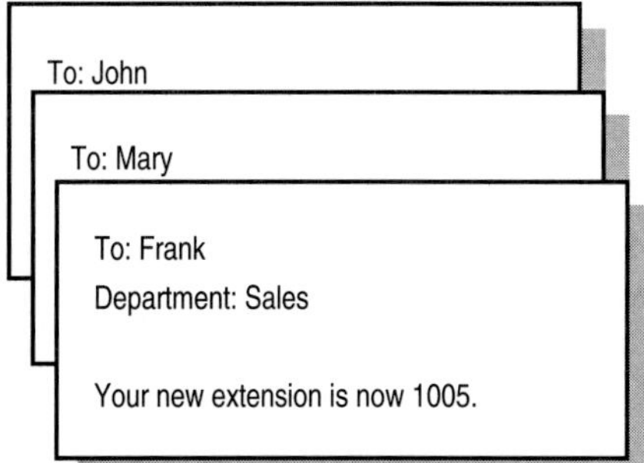

When you merge-print the two files, data from the secondary file are automatically printed in place of the merge codes in the primary file.

inserted. When the document is merge-printed, the codes are replaced with data from the secondary file.

The Secondary File

If you want to insert data into a form letter automatically, you need a secondary file. Secondary files are regular document files that contain information organized into fields and records.

- A field is a specific piece of information, for example, a person's name. Fields can be names (Smith), numbers (100.10), names and numbers (100 Main Street), or formulas (100*3).
- Related fields are stored together as records; for example, one person's name, address, and phone number make up a record.

TUTORIAL

Mr. Robert Smith{END FIELD}
Alf Industries{END FIELD}
Elm Street{END FIELD}
Boston, MA 00120{END FIELD}
Mr. Smith{END FIELD}
{END RECORD}
===========================
Ms. Wendy Lewis{END FIELD}
{END FIELD}
Main Street{END FIELD}
Los Angeles, CA 90020{END FIELD}
Wendy{END FIELD}
{END RECORD}
===========================
Mrs. Mary Lockhart{END FIELD}
Curtis & Mathers{END FIELD}
Oak Road{END FIELD}
Chicago, IL 30010{END FIELD}
Mrs. Lockhart{END FIELD}
{END RECORD}
===========================

The SECOND Document
You enter this document in this tutorial. Data in a secondary file such as this are organized into fields and records.

- A field contains a specific piece of information like a name. To indicate the end of a field, you press [F9] to enter an *{END FIELD}* code.
- A record is a set of related fields that describe an item or a person. To indicate the end of a record, you press [Shift]-[F9] and then [E] (for ***E**nd Record*) to enter an *{END RECORD}* code and a hard page break.

In this tutorial, you merge-print form letters using data stored in a secondary file. You then add merge codes to the document so that you can fill out form letters one after another.

GETTING STARTED

1. Change the default drive to the one that contains the disk that you save your files on. This way you will not have to specify the drive in the following steps.

CREATING A SECONDARY FILE

2. Enter the document shown in the figure "The SECOND Document." As you do so, keep these points in mind:
   - Do not press [Enter←] at the end of each line in an address. Instead, press [F9] to enter the *{END FIELD}* code and move the cursor down one line. Be sure to do this also in the second address on the blank line where a company address would normally go.
   - At the end of each complete address, press [Shift]-[F9] to display the Merge Codes menu, and then press [E] (for ***E**nd Record*) to enter the *{END RECORD}* code and a hard page break.
3. Save the document as SECOND.WP5 so that you can retrieve it later.
4. Compare the document on the screen with the figure "The SECOND Document" to be sure they match. If they do not match exactly, you may have trouble later.

CREATING A PRIMARY FILE

5. Clear the screen.
6. Enter the document shown in the figure "The PRIMARY Document." You enter the *{FIELD}1~* and similar codes by pressing [Shift]-[F9] to display the Merge Codes menu and then pressing [F] (for ***F**ield*). When the prompt reads *Enter Field:* you type the indicated number (note that in the second field you type **2?**) and press [Enter←].

The PRIMARY Document
You enter this document in this tutorial.

{FIELD}1~
{FIELD}2?~
{FIELD}3~
{FIELD}4~
Dear {FIELD}5~:
I am pleased to confirm your appointment at my office.
Sincerely yours,
your name

7. Save the document as PRIMARY.WP5.
8. Compare the document on the screen with the figure "The PRIMARY Document" to be sure they match.

MERGE PRINTING THE PRIMARY AND SECONDARY FILES TO THE SCREEN

9. Clear the screen.
10. Press Ctrl-F9 to display the Merge/Sort menu.
11. Press M (for ***Merge***), and the prompt reads *Primary file:*.
12. Type **PRIMARY.WP5** and press Enter. The prompt reads *Secondary file:*.
13. Type **SECOND.WP5** and press Enter. The message reads ** Merging **, and in a moment, the three personalized letters appear on the screen. Press PgUp and PgDn to scroll through the three letters that you merged. Notice that the fields have been automatically filled from the secondary file. In the one record without a company name, the field has been left blank and the line closed up because you entered a question mark following the field name in the primary file.

USING OPERATOR INPUT

14. Clear the screen without saving the document.
15. Retrieve the PRIMARY.WP5 document.
16. Press Home three times, and then press ↑ to move the cursor to the top of the document.
17. Press Enter twice to insert two blank lines.
18. Move the cursor to the top line.
19. Press Shift-F9 to display the Merge Codes menu.
20. Press M (for ***More***).

Merge Codes More Menu
When you press Shift-F9 to display the Merge Codes menu and then select *More*, a list of additional merge codes is displayed. You can highlight one of them by pressing ↓ or ↑ or by beginning to type its name—without the opening brace ({).

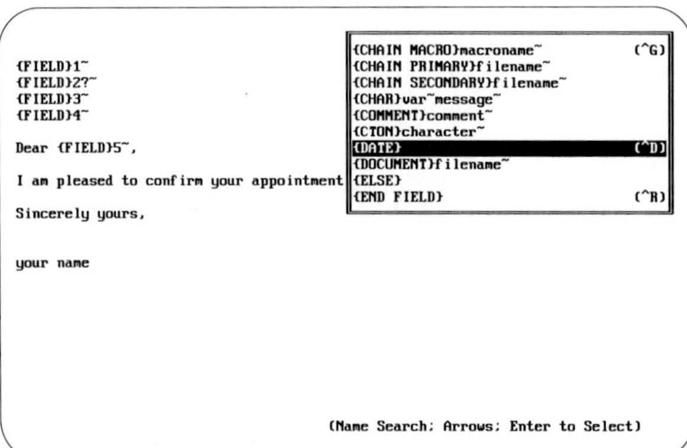

21. Press [D] to move the highlight to *{DATE}*, and press [Enter←] to enter a date code into the document. Your document's first line should now look like the one in the figure "The Primary File Coded for Operator Input."

The Primary File Coded for Operator Input
After you add codes to display prompts for input from the keyboard, your document should look like this.

```
{DATE}
{FIELD}1~
{FIELD}2?~
{FIELD}3~
{FIELD}4~
Dear {FIELD}5~:
I am pleased to confirm your appointment at my office at {INPUT}Enter time: ~ on
{INPUT}Enter date: ~.

Sincerely yours,

your name
```

ADDING OPERATOR INPUT CODES

22. Move the cursor to under the period following *at my office*.
23. Press [Spacebar], type **at** and press [Spacebar] again.
24. Press [⇧Shift]-[F9] to display the Merge Codes menu.
25. Press [I] (for ***I**nput*), and the prompt reads *Enter Message:*.
26. Type **Enter time:** and press [Spacebar].
27. Press [Enter←] to enter the code *{INPUT}Enter time: ~*.
28. Press [Spacebar], type **on** and press [Spacebar] again.
29. Press [⇧Shift]-[F9] to display the Merge Codes menu.
30. Press [I] (for ***I**nput*), and the prompt reads *Enter Message:*.
31. Type **Enter date:** and press [Spacebar].
32. Press [Enter←] to enter the code *{INPUT}Enter date: ~*.

MERGE PRINTING THE FILES

33. Save the revised document.
34. Clear the screen.
35. Press [Ctrl]-[F9] to display the Merge/Sort menu.
36. Press [M] (for ***M**erge*), and the prompt reads *Primary file:*.
37. Type **PRIMARY.WP5** and press [Enter←]. The prompt reads *Secondary file:*.
38. Type **SECOND.WP5** and press [Enter←]. The first letter immediately appears on the screen. Today's date is automatically entered where you placed the *{DATE}* code. The record is for Robert Smith from Alf Industries. The cursor pauses at the first input code (although it isn't displayed on the screen), and the status line displays the prompt *Enter time:* that you entered as a message when entering the code in the primary file.

FILLING OUT THE FIRST LETTER

39. Type **10:00 a.m.** and press F9 to continue. The cursor pauses at the second input code, and the status line reads *Enter date:*.
40. Type **June 10** and press F9 to continue. The second letter appears, and the status line displays the prompt *Enter time:*.

FILLING OUT THE SECOND LETTER

41. Type **11:00 a.m.** and press F9 to continue. The cursor pauses at the second input code, and the status line reads *Enter date:*.
42. Type **June 10** and press F9 to continue. The third letter appears, and the status line displays the prompt *Enter time:*.

FILLING OUT THE THIRD LETTER

43. Type **12:00 noon** and press F9 to continue. The cursor pauses at the second input code, and the status line reads *Enter date:*.
44. Type **June 10** and press F9 to continue. Check your three letters to see if the correct information was entered into each.

FINISHING UP

45. Print the document.
46. Clear the document from the screen without saving it because you can always merge-print it again if you need it.
47. You have now completed this tutorial. Either continue with the next activity or quit the program.

QUICK REFERENCE

Merge printing requires a primary document and an optional secondary document.

The Primary Document

The primary document contains the text that is to appear in every copy and codes that control the printing process.

KEY/Strokes

Inserting Merge Codes into a Primary File

1. Move the cursor to where you want to enter a merge code.
2. Either: Press Shift-F9 to display the Merge Codes menu.
   Or: Pull down the Tools menu and select *Merge Codes*.
3. Enter one of the codes listed on the menu and described in the table "Merge Codes Menu Choices."
4. Repeat Steps 1 through 3 for each merge code in the document.
5. Save the primary file.

MERGE CODES MENU CHOICES

1 ***F**ield* specifies what data are to be inserted from the secondary file. When you select this command, the prompt reads *Enter Field:*. Type the number of the field to be merged at this position from the secondary file, and press [Enter ←] to enter the code *{FIELD}#~* (where # stands for the number of the field that you type). Fields in secondary files end in *{END FIELD}* codes and are numbered from top to bottom. When the cursor is on a field in the secondary file, the number of the field is displayed on the status line.

2 ***E**nd Record* marks the end of a record in a secondary file with an *{END RECORD}* code followed by a hard carriage return.

3 ***I**nput* displays the prompt *Enter Message:*. The message you type is displayed on the screen when the *{INPUT}* code is encountered during the merge process, and the printer pauses and remains stopped until you type information from the keyboard and press [F9] to continue. You can use the message to prompt yourself or another operator for information to enter. For example, the code *{INPUT}Enter time:~* pauses the printer and displays the prompt *Enter time:*. These prompts appear only on the screen; they do not print out.

4 ***P**age Off* turns off hard page breaks after each merge-printed copy so that new records do not begin printing at the top of a new page.

5 ***N**ext Record* directs the merge to the next record. If no such record exists, the merge ends.

6 ***M**ore* displays advanced macro commands that you can use in a merge file.

PLANNING YOUR SECONDARY FILE

When you first create a secondary file, you should plan it carefully so that the data in it are effectively organized.

- If you want to be able to sort a mailing list by ZIP codes, they must be entered into a separate field.
- If you want to use the last name in the salutation, it must be in a separate field. If you have only one field for the entire name, your letter might read "Dear Mr. John Smith" instead of "Dear Mr. Smith."
- The number of lines used in addresses varies. One address might require only three lines, and another might require five. Set up your fields for the greatest number of lines. If a particular address is shorter, you can leave those fields blank.
- If in doubt, break information into smaller fields.

The Secondary File

You enter fields and records on lines from the top of the document to the bottom. Although you do not actually number them, fields are numbered from top to bottom. The first field in each record is field 1, the second field in each record is field 2, and so on. When entering fields and records, keep the following points in mind:

- The status line indicates the number of the field the cursor is in as soon as you press [F9] to indicate the end of the first field.
- Each record must have the same number of fields.
- You can have as many fields in each record as you like and then specify only those you need during a merge. For example, you may want to maintain phone numbers in a name and address file. When printing letters or envelopes, you do not print them.
- Fields can contain any number of lines and both soft and hard carriage returns.
- Each field must contain the same category of information. For example, you cannot have a name in field 1 of the first record and an address in field 1 of the second record.
- The fields in each record are separated from each other with an *{END FIELD}* code that you enter by pressing [F9]. If a field in a record is to be left empty, the *{END FIELD}* code that ends the field must be entered anyway so that the program knows the field is empty.
- Never separate fields or records with an extra hard carriage return or insert spaces between the last word in a field and the *{END FIELD}* code.

■ Records are separated from each other with an *{END RECORD}* code and a hard page break, which you enter by pressing [E] (for ***E**nd Record*) on the Merge Codes menu.

→ KEY/Strokes

Creating a Secondary File

1. Open a new document file.
2. Either: Type the field's contents. (You can press [Enter←] if the data in the field are longer than one line—for example, an inside address—or let word wrap move it to the next line.)

   Or: Leave the field blank.
3. Press [F9] to end the field with an *{END FIELD}* code and move the cursor down to the next line.
4. Repeat Steps 2 and 3 for each field in the record.
5. When the record is complete, press [⇧Shift]-[F9] to display the Merge Codes menu.
6. Press [E] (for ***E**nd Record*) to end the record with an *{END RECORD}* code followed by a hard page break.
7. Repeat Steps 2 through 6 for each record. Be sure to enter each record's information in the same field sequence.
8. When you have finished, save the secondary file.

AVOIDING BLANK LINES

If some of the fields in the secondary file contain no data, you can enter a question mark (?) following the field number to close up the line so that a blank line isn't left when you merge-print the documents.

Merge Printing

After creating the necessary files, you merge-print. Merge printing is the process of printing multiple copies of the primary file. Each copy contains a different set of information inserted in place of merge codes in the primary file. When you merge-print a primary and secondary file, the program goes to the first record in the secondary file, inserts data from the specified fields, and then continues printing. After all the requested fields from the first record have been inserted, the first copy advances from the printer, and the process is repeated for the second copy. But this time the program inserts data from the second record. This continues until all the records in the secondary file have been used.

→ KEY/Strokes

Merge Printing

1. Clear the screen.
2. Either: Press [Ctrl]-[F9], and then press [M] (for ***M**erge*).

   Or: Pull down the Tools menu and select ***M**erge*.

   The prompt reads *Primary file:*.
3. Either: Type the name of the primary file and press [Enter←]. (If necessary, you can enter a path in front of the filename.)

   Or: Press [F5] to display the List Files screen, highlight the file you want to merge-print, and press [R] (for ***R**etrieve*).

The prompt reads *Secondary file:*.

4. Either: Type the name of the secondary file and press [Enter ↵]. (If necessary, you can enter a path in front of the filename.)

   Or: Press [F5] to display the List Files screen, highlight the file you want to merge-print, and press [R] (for ***R**etrieve*).

(To stop a merge in progress, press [⇧ Shift]-[F9].)

More Merge Codes

WordPerfect has 68 merge codes that are very useful. For example, you can enter merge codes that allow you to type text into a document while it is being printed. Moreover, you can specify prompts that appear on the screen when the document is being merge-printed to remind you what information to enter. After you type the data and press [F9] to continue, the program inserts the data you typed into the body of the letter in place of the merge code and continues.

The table "Merge Codes" explains a few of these merge codes. There are three ways to display a menu of these codes so that you can select the one you want:

- Press [⇧ Shift]-[F9] twice.
- Press [⇧ Shift]-[F9], and then press [M] (for ***M**ore*).
- Pull down the Tools menu, select *Mer**g**e Codes*, and then select ***M**ore*.

MERGE CODES

- *{COMMENT}comment~* enters a comment in a primary file that is displayed on the screen when you merge-print the document. You enter the comment in the command where the *comment* is shown.
- *{DATE}* inserts the current date based on the computer's clock.
- *{DOCUMENT}filename~* inserts a file with the specified name into the document when the primary file is merge-printed.
- *{END FIELD}* ends a field in a secondary file.
- *{END RECORD}* ends a record in a secondary file.
- *{FIELD NAMES}name1~nameN~~* assigns names to the fields in a secondary file.
- *{FIELD}field~* specifies the number or name of the field in the secondary file that data are to be inserted from.
- *{INPUT}message~* stops the merge process and displays a message so that you can type in data from the keyboard. After typing data, press [F9] to continue. If you use this code in a file and only want to enter data from the keyboard, merge-print only the primary file. When prompted to enter a secondary file, just press [Enter ↵].
- *{PAGE OFF}* eliminates the hard page break at the end of a document when all fields have been inserted so that the next record does not begin at the top of a new page.
- *{PAGE ON}* inserts a hard page break at the end of a document when all fields have been inserted so that each record prints starting on a new page.
- *{PRINT}* sends text that has already been merged to the printer. You use this when you have too many records to merge-print the files to the screen first.
- *{PROMPT}message~* displays a message on the status line during a merge.
- *{QUIT}* stops a merge when it is encountered in a primary or a secondary file.

MERGE CODES (CONTINUED)

- To merge-print only part of a secondary file, for example, names from *A* through *N*, you can enter a *{QUIT}* code at the point in the secondary file where you want the merge to end.
- When merge printing letters, envelopes, or labels using a secondary file with a lot of records, you may want to enter this code after the first few records and run a test to be sure that your formats and paper alignment are correct. After testing, remove the code and merge-print the entire secondary file.

EXERCISE 1

MERGE PRINTING A FORM LETTER TO COMPUTER COMPANIES

1. Follow the instructions in the KEY/Strokes box "Inserting Merge Codes into a Primary File" to create the primary file shown in the figure "The COMPLTR Document."
   - Enter merge codes so that the *[Company]*, *[Street]*, *[City]*, *[State]*, and *[ZIP]* are entered from the secondary file.
   - Save the file as COMPLTR.WP5 and make a printout as a record.
2. Follow the instructions in the KEY/Strokes box "Creating a Secondary File" to create a secondary document using the data shown in the figure "The COMPLIST Document." Save the file as COMPLIST.WP5 and make a printout as a record.

Your Street
Your City, State ZIP
Today's date

Catalog Department
Field1~
Field2~
Field3~,Field4~ Field5~

Dear Sir or Madam:

Please send me a catalog of your current computer offerings.

Sincerely yours,

Your name

The COMPLTR Document
This figure shows the primary document that you enter to explore merge printing in this exercise.

The COMPLIST Document
This figure shows the secondary document that you enter to explore merge printing in this exercise.

Company	Street	City	State	ZIP
PC Connection	6 Mill Street	Marlow	NH	03456
Northgate Computer Systems	7075 Flying Cloud Drive	Eden Prairie	MN	55344
Dell Computer Corporation	9505 Arboretum Blvd.	Austin	TX	78759
Zeos International, Ltd.	530 5th Avenue N.W.	St. Paul	MN	55112

```
NAME[HRt]
STREET ADDRESS[HRt]
CITY, STATE ZIP{END FIELD}
```

Entering Multiline Fields
You needn't enter only single line fields. For example, in this secondary file, the entire address has been entered as a single field. Each line ends with a hard carriage return, *[HRt]*, except the last, which ends with an *{END FIELD}* code.

3. Follow the instructions in the KEY/Strokes box "Merge Printing" to merge-print the two files to the screen, and make a printout. Don't save the merged copies since you can merge them again should you need them.

EXERCISE 2

MERGE PRINTING A MEMO

1. Enter the memo shown in the figure "The MEMO Document" using the More menu to enter the *{DATE}*, *{INPUT}*, and *{PRINT}* codes.

The MEMO Document
This figure shows the primary document that you enter to explore merge printing in this exercise.

```
{DATE}

To: {INPUT}Type name and press F9~
Fr: {INPUT}Type your name and press F9~
Re: {INPUT}Type subject and press F9~

Please call me as soon as you can regarding {INPUT}Type purpose of memo and
press F9~.
{PRINT}
```

2. Save the memo as MEMO.WP5 and clear the screen.
3. Merge-print the memo (press Enter← when prompted to enter a secondary file name), and enter the names and subjects shown in the figure "Data for the MEMO Document." The document prints one document and then stops.
4. To print one memo after another, enter the merge-code **{NEST PRIMARY}MEMO.WP5~** on the last line after the *{PRINT}* code. This new code will call the primary file up again after the first memo is printed. Save the revised file and merge-print it. Fill out two or more memos. To quit at any point, press ⇧Shift-F9, and then press S (for ***S****top*).

Memo 1
To: John Smith
Fr: (your name)
Re: Meeting
purpose: our plans for Friday's meeting

Memo 2
To: Mary Smith
Fr: (your name)
Re: Inventory
purpose: our current inventory levels

Memo 3
To: Jose Rodriguez
Fr: (your name)
Re: Five-year plan
purpose: your current forecast for sales and profits

Data for the MEMO Document
This figure shows the data that you enter into the MEMO.WP5 document when you merge-print it in this exercise.

TOPIC 29

Automating with Macros

After completing this topic, you will be able to:

- Define macros
- Execute macros
- Edit macros

Since many of the tasks you perform during word processing are repetitive, you often find yourself pressing the same sequence of keys to save, retrieve, or print files; indent paragraphs; boldface or underline words; and so on. Programs such as WordPerfect allow you to create macros that automate these repetitive tasks.

There are two steps to using macros: (1) defining them so they are saved in a file on the disk and (2) executing them. You can define (record) and then automatically execute (play back) any sequence of keystrokes, including text and commands. Defining and executing macros are easy and can save you a lot of time if you use the same series of keystrokes over and over again; for example:

- You can record sections of text and then insert them into documents where needed.
- You can record and then execute a series of commands. If you have to press five or six keys to execute a command, you can store those keystrokes in a macro and execute it by pressing as few as two keys.
- You can enter a pause in a macro when you define it. When you execute the macro, it executes all keystrokes up to the pause and then waits for you to enter text or other keystrokes from the keyboard. When you do so, and then press [Enter ↵], the macro continues. This is useful when all but a few of the keystrokes are the same. For example, you can record all the keystrokes needed to retrieve a file from the disk but enter a pause so that you can type in the desired file's name.

TUTORIAL

In this tutorial, you explore using macros to execute repetitive commands.

GETTING STARTED

1. Press [⇧ Shift]-[F1] to display the Setup menu.
2. Press [L] (for ***Location of Files***).

3. Press [K] (for ***K**eyboard/Macro Files*), and the cursor jumps to the line with that command.
4. Type the letter of the drive in which you place your data disk followed by a colon (for example, type **A:** or **B:**) and press [Enter←].
5. Press [F7] to return to the Edit screen. All macros that you now create will be stored in files on your data disk with the extension .WPM.

ASSIGNING A NAME TO A MACRO FOR BULLETS

6. Press [Ctrl]-[F10] to begin recording, and the prompt reads *Define macro:*.
7. Type **BULLET** and press [Enter←]. The prompt reads *Description:*.
8. Type **Enters a square bullet** and press [Enter←]. The status line flashes *Macro Def* to indicate that keystrokes are now being recorded.
9. Hold down [Alt], type **254** on the numeric keypad, and release [Alt].
10. Press [Ctrl]-[F10] to end recording, and the status line no longer flashes *Macro Def.*

PLAYING BACK THE RECORDED KEYSTROKES

11. Press [Alt]-[F10], and the prompt reads *Macro:*.
12. Type **BULLET** and press [Enter←] to enter a square bullet.

ASSIGNING A KEY TO A MACRO FOR BULLETS

13. Press [Ctrl]-[F10] to begin recording, and the prompt reads *Define macro:*.
14. Press [Alt]-[B], and the prompt reads *Description:*. If a message *ALTB.WPM Already Exists* appears, press [R] (for ***R**eplace*) to overwrite the existing macro unless you have been instructed not to.
15. Type **Enters a square bullet** and press [Enter←]. The status line flashes *Macro Def* to indicate that keystrokes are now being recorded.
16. Hold down [Alt], type **254** on the numeric keypad, and release [Alt].
17. Press [Ctrl]-[F10] to end recording, and the status line no longer flashes *Macro Def.*

PLAYING BACK THE RECORDED KEYSTROKES

18. Press [Alt]-[B] to enter a square bullet.

CHANGING YOUR DEFAULT DRIVE AND DISPLAYING LIST FILES

19. Press [Ctrl]-[F10] to begin recording, and the prompt reads *Define macro:*.
20. Press [Alt]-[D], and the prompt reads *Description:*. (If a message *ALTD.WPM Already Exists* appears, press [R] (for ***R**eplace*) to overwrite the existing macro unless you have been instructed not to.)

21. Type **Changes the default drive** and press [Enter↵]. The status line flashes *Macro Def* to indicate that keystrokes are now being recorded.
22. Press [F5], and then press [=]. The prompt reads *New directory* = followed by the name of the current default directory.
23. Type the path to your data disk, for example, **A:** or **B:**, and press [Enter↵] twice to display the List Files screen.
24. Press [Ctrl]-[F10] to end recording.
25. Press [F7] to return to the Edit screen.

PLAYING BACK THE RECORDED KEYSTROKES

26. Press [Alt]-[D] to change the default drive and display the List Files screen for that drive.
27. Press [F7] to return to the Edit screen.

FINISHING UP

28. You have now completed this tutorial. Either continue with the next activity or quit the program.

QUICK REFERENCE

The first step in using macros is to define them. Once they have been defined, you can execute them.

Defining Macros

When defining macros, you have to assign them a name so that you can play them back. There are three ways to assign names.

- You can enter a name of up to eight characters. If you do so, you have to enter that same name to play the macro back.
- You can assign the macro to an [Alt]-letter key combination so that you can then execute it by holding down [Alt] and pressing the letter you assigned it to.
- You can press [Enter↵] to create a temporary macro that is automatically deleted when you exit WordPerfect.

If you name a macro with a name of an already existing macro, a message informs you that the macro already exists. You can use the displayed menu choices to replace the existing macro, edit it, or view its description.

When the *Macro Def* message is displayed as you define a macro, you can press [Ctrl]-[PgUp] to display the Macro Options menu. (See the table "Macro Options Menu Commands.") You can also use a mouse to execute commands but not to move the cursor.

KEY/Strokes

Defining a Macro

1. Either: Press Ctrl-F10.
   Or: Pull down the Tools menu, select *Macro*, and then *Define*.
   The prompt reads *Define macro:*.
2. Either: Type the name of the macro (up to eight characters) and press Enter↵.
   Or: Hold down Alt and press a letter (A through Z) you want to assign the macro to.
   Or: Press Enter↵ to create a temporary macro that is automatically deleted when you exit WordPerfect. (You cannot edit temporary macros.)
   The prompt reads *Description:*. (If you pressed Enter↵, go on to Step 4.) If a macro by the same name already exists, you are prompted to replace or edit it. Press R (for ***R**eplace*).
3. Type a description of the macro (up to 39 characters) and press Enter↵. The status line flashes *Macro Def.* (When this is flashing, you are recording keystrokes.)
4. Enter the keys to be recorded in the macro. (To enter options at any point, press Ctrl-PgUp. See the table "Macro Options Menu Commands.")
5. Press Ctrl-F10 to end the macro, and the status line no longer flashes *Macro Def.*

MACRO OPTIONS MENU COMMANDS

1	*Pause* pauses the macro during its execution when Ctrl-PgUp is pressed so that you can enter information from the keyboard, for example, to enter a person's name in a salutation or a filename in a file-save or file-retrieve macro. When you then enter text and press Enter↵, the macro resumes.
2	*Display* allows you to see the macro perform or turn off the screen update until the macro is finished.
3	*Assign* assigns values to variables. Refer to the WordPerfect manual's section on advanced macros.
4	*Comment* enters comments into the macro definition to help you understand it later when editing it. Comments that you enter are ignored when the macro is played back.

Executing Macros

When you want to replay the keystrokes that you recorded, you execute the macro. The way you do so depends on how you named it.

- If you assigned it to an Alt-letter key combination, you hold down Alt while pressing the letter key you assigned it to.
- If you assigned it a name, you press Alt-F10, type the name of the macro, and press Enter↵.
- If it is a temporary macro that is automatically deleted when you exit WordPerfect, you press Alt-F10, and then press Enter↵.

KEY/Strokes

Executing a Macro

1. Move the cursor to where you want the macro played back.
2. Either: Press Alt-F10 to display the prompt *Macro:*, type the name of the macro, and press Enter.
   Or: Hold down Alt and press the letter you assigned the keystrokes to.
   Or: Press Alt-F10, and then press Enter to execute a temporary macro created just for the current session.
   Or: Pull down the Tools menu, select ***Ma**cro*, and then ***Ex**ecute*. When the prompt reads *Macro:*, type the name of the macro and press Enter.

Editing Macros

WordPerfect also allows you to edit macros so that you can correct any mistakes you may have made or add procedures without having to redefine the keystrokes. (You cannot edit temporary macros.)

The Macro Edit Screen
The Macro Edit screen displays the macro in a window.

```
Macro: Action

     File            ALTD.WPM

     Description     Changes the default drive

     {List}=A:\{Enter}
     {Enter}

Ctrl-V to Insert next key as command;
Ctrl-PgUp for macro commands:  Press Exit when done
```

KEY/Strokes

Editing a Macro

1. Either: Press Ctrl-F10.
   Or: Pull down the Tools menu, select ***Ma**cro* and then ***D**efine*.
   The prompt reads *Define macro:*.
2. Either: Type the name of the macro you want to edit and press Enter.
   Or: Hold down Alt and press the letter you assigned a macro to.
   Or: Pull down the Tools menu, select ***Ma**cro*, and then ***D**efine*. When the prompt reads *Macro:*, type the name of the macro and press Enter.
   A message tells you the macro has already been defined and displays menu commands to replace or edit it.

TIPS

- You can see the description you entered when defining a macro with the Look command on the List Files menu.
- To stop a macro in progress, press [F1]. (If you press [F1] while defining a macro, it just inserts the cancel code in the macro and does not cancel the macro definition process.)
- When switching between insert and typeover modes in a macro, you can use a command to force the change regardless of what the current mode is. To force typeover mode, press [Home], [Ins]. To force insert mode, press [Home], [Home], [Ins].

3. Press [E] (for ***Edit***) to display the Macro Edit screen and menu. You can edit the macro in this screen just as if it were a document.
   - To insert a keyboard command such as [Enter←], [Tab⇆] or [F4] as a code that will be executed when you run the macro, press [Ctrl]-[V] before pressing it. The result will be displayed as *{Enter}*, *{Tab}* or *{Indent}*.
   - Commands are enclosed in braces, and you can press [Ctrl]-[PgUp] to display a list of additional commands to choose from.
4. Press [F7] to return to the Edit screen.

Saving and Retrieving Macros

When you save a macro, the extension .WPM is automatically assigned to it. You do not have to type this extension when defining or executing a macro, but you will see it in the List Files screen.

Macros are automatically stored in the keyboard/macro directory when they are defined. You specify this directory using the Setup menu's Location of Files command. If you do not specify a directory with this command, macros are saved on the current default directory, which you can change by pressing [F5]. When defining a macro, you can also specify a path in front of the macro name to store the macro in another drive and directory. When you execute the macro, you have to specify the same path and filename when prompted to enter the macro's name. If you have assigned a macro to a letter key and get the message *ERROR: File not found*, change the default directory to the one it is stored in, and try again.

To delete a macro, delete the file with the same name and the extension .WPM. For example, a macro that you assigned to [Alt]-[C] is named ALTC.WPM.

EXERCISES

EXERCISE 1

CREATING MACROS TO ENTER FRACTIONS

1. Change the default drive to the one into which you have inserted your data disk.
2. Follow the instructions in the KEY/Strokes box "Defining a Macro" to create the macros needed to enter the fractions shown in the table "Fractions."
   - When the prompt reads *Define macro:*, enter the name shown in the first column.
   - When prompted for the description, enter the name of the fraction shown in the second column.
   - To enter the fractions when the message *Macro Def* is flashing, press [Ctrl]-[V], and when the prompt reads *Key* =, type the numbers shown in the table.

FRACTIONS

Macro Name	Fraction	Characters
1QUART	One-quarter	4,18
1HALF	One-half	4,17
1THIRD	One-third	4,64
2THIRD	Two-thirds	4,65
1EIGHT	One-eighth	4,66
3EIGHT	Three-eighths	4,67
3QUART	Three-quarter	4,25
5EIGHT	Five-eighths	4,68
7EIGHT	Seven-eighths	4,69

3. Follow the instructions in the KEY/Strokes box "Executing Macros" to enter the fractions.
4. Print the document and clear the screen without saving the document.

EXERCISE 2

USING THE CODES MACRO

WordPerfect comes with a number of useful macros already created for you. One of these is named CODES.WPM. This macro should be located in the same directory as the WordPerfect program files or on one of your floppy disks. This macro goes through a document and recreates it on the other Edit screen with all codes revealed. If you can locate this macro, retrieve the document file CODES.WP5, and execute the CODES macro to reveal its codes. To execute the macro, be sure your printer is on, press Alt-F10, then type **CODES** and press Enter↵. If the CODES.WPM file is not in the current directory, specify a path in front of the macro's name when the prompt reads *Macro:*, For example, if the macro is on drive C in a directory named WP51, type **C:\WP51\CODES** and press Enter↵.

TOPIC 30

File Management

After completing this topic, you will be able to:

- Use commands on the List Files menu to copy, rename, and delete files
- Use commands on the List Files menu to create and remove directories

You can execute several DOS commands from WordPerfect's List Files menu. You can also access DOS without leaving WordPerfect and, when you have finished, return to exactly where you were.

TUTORIAL

In this tutorial, you practice using the List Files screen and menu to manage your files.

GETTING STARTED

1. Change the default drive to the one that contains your data disk.
2. Display the List Files screen and menu.

COPYING FILES

3. Highlight *ENTERING.WP5* on the list of files.
4. Press C (for ***C**opy*), and the prompt reads *Copy this file to:*.
5. Type **ERASE.WP5** and press Enter←. The new ERASE.WP5 file is now listed on the file list.

DELETING FILES

6. Highlight *ERASE.WP5* on the list of files.
7. Press D (for ***D**elete*), and the prompt reads *Delete x:\ERASE.WP5? **N**o (**Y**es)*.
8. Press Y to delete the file.

SEARCHING FOR FILES

9. Press F (for ***F**ind*) to display the Find menu.
10. Press E (for ***E**ntire Doc*), and the prompt reads *Word pattern:*.
11. Type **word processing** and press Enter←. A message indicates that files are being searched for the phrase. When the search is completed, only files that contain the phrase are listed. To see all

the files again, highlight *Current <Dir>* at the top of the list of files on the left side of the screen, and press Enter← twice to update the list.

CREATING DIRECTORIES

12. Press O (for ***O**ther Directory*), and the prompt reads *New directory =* followed by the current directory.
13. Type **MYDIR** and press Enter←. The prompt reads *Create MYDIR? **N**o (**Y**es).*
14. Press Y, and the new directory is added to the list on the screen.

DELETING DIRECTORIES

15. Highlight *MYDIR <Dir>*, and press D (for ***D**elete*). The prompt reads *Delete x:\MYDIR? **N**o (**Y**es).*
16. Press Y, and the new directory is deleted from the list on the screen.

FINISHING UP

17. You have now completed this tutorial. Either continue with the next activity or quit the program.

QUICK REFERENCE

You can execute many DOS commands from the List Files menu (F5, Enter←). These commands are useful when you want to make backup copies of your files or rename or delete them.

Copying Files

You can copy files to other disks or directories or to the same disk or directory if you change its name.

KEY/Strokes

Copying a File

1. Display the directory containing the file to be copied.
2. Use the arrow keys to highlight the name of the file.
3. Press C (for ***C**opy*), and the prompt reads *Copy this file to:*.
4. Type the path of the drive and directory you are copying the file to, and press Enter←.
5. Press F7 to return to the Edit screen.

Moving and Renaming Files

From List Files you can move a file to another disk or directory or rename it and leave it where it is.

➔ KEY/Strokes

Moving or Renaming a File

1. Display the directory containing the file to be moved or renamed.
2. Use the arrow keys to highlight the name of the file.
3. Press [M] (for ***M**ove/Rename*), and the prompt reads *New name:* followed by the name of the file that you highlighted.
4. Either: To rename the file, type the new name and press [Enter←].
   Or: To move the file, type the path you want to move it to, and press [Enter←]. (If you also enter a new filename, it is moved and renamed.)
5. Press [F7] to return to the Edit screen.

Deleting Files and Directories

You can delete files that you no longer need or delete empty directories.

Deleting a File or an Empty Directory

1. Display the directory containing the file or empty directory to be deleted.
2. Use the arrow keys to highlight the name of the file or empty directory.
3. Press [D] (for ***D**elete*), and the prompt reads *Delete* followed by the name of the file to be deleted.
4. Press [Y] to delete.
5. Press [F7] to return to the Edit screen.

Using Directories

To move quickly through directories, highlight the directory (including *Parent <Dir>*, which is the directory one level up), and press [Enter←] twice to display the files it contains. When you locate the directory containing the file you want, highlight the file's name and press [R] (for ***R**etrieve*). You can also press [O] (for ***O**ther Directory*) and press [Enter←] twice to make the highlighted directory the current directory.

To display only selected filenames, highlight *Current <Dir>* and press [Enter←]. The message reads *Dir PATH\ *.**. To display only selected files, use wildcards. For example, type **B:*.WP5** to list all the files on drive B that end with the extension .WP5.

To change the default directory or create a new one, press [O] (for ***O**ther Directory*). Type the new directory (for example, **C:\LETTERS**) and press [Enter←]. If the directory you specify does not exist, the prompt reads *Create:* followed by the name of the directory and the prompt ***N**o (**Y**es)*. Press [Y] to create a new directory.

Accessing DOS

You can access DOS without leaving WordPerfect. When you have finished, you return to exactly where you were.

TIP

To copy or delete a group of files, you can mark them.

- To mark or unmark individual files, move the highlight over the desired files and press [Shift]-[*] (or just press [*] on the numeric keypad).
- To mark or unmark all files, press [Alt]-[F5].

KEY/Strokes

Accessing DOS Without Exiting WordPerfect

1. If using a floppy disk system, insert a disk with the COMMAND.COM file into drive A.
2. Either: Press [Ctrl]-[F1].
   Or: Pull down the File menu and select ***Goto DOS***.
3. Either: Press [G] (for ***Go** to DOS*) to display the command prompt and execute DOS commands. When finished, type **EXIT** and press [Enter].
   Or: Press [C] (for *DOS **Command***), type a command, and press [Enter]. When the command is completed the prompt reads *Press any key to continue*. Do so, and you automatically return to WordPerfect.

EXERCISES

EXERCISE 1

USING LIST FILES TO COPY FILES

If your system has two floppy disk drives, make a backup copy of the disk you saved your files on. Put your original data disk into drive A and a formatted data disk into drive B. Use the List Files screen to display the files on the disk in drive A. Use [Alt]-[F5] to mark them all, and then copy them to drive B.

EXERCISE 2

COPYING FILES INTO A NEW DIRECTORY

1. Using List Files, create a new directory on your data disk named ERASEME.
2. Copy three of your files into the directory.
3. Make the ERASEME directory the current directory.
4. Rename one of the files ICANDOIT.WP5.
5. Press [Shift]-[F7] to make a printout of the files in the current directory.
6. Erase the three files you copied into the directory, including the one you renamed.
7. Delete the directory.

CHAPTER 6 REVIEW

- You can merge-print hundreds or thousands of documents automatically and insert individualized data into each from the keyboard or from a separate file.
- To merge-print, you begin with a primary document that contains codes requesting information from the operator or from a separate file.
- To insert data into a merged document automatically, you store the data in a secondary file. This file is organized into fields and records.
- A field is a single piece of information, such as a name or city. You end a field by pressing F9. A record is a number of fields that define a single entity. For example, a record for you might include your name, your address, and the college that you attend. You end a record by pressing Shift-F9 and E (for ***E**nd Record*).
- WordPerfect has a number of merge-printing codes that perform specific actions such as pausing and displaying a prompt so that you know what to type.
- You can record a series of keystrokes (Ctrl-F10) and then play them back later (Alt-F10). You can assign a name to a macro or attach it to a key so that you can play it back by pressing that key while you hold down Alt.
- You can use commands on the List Files menu to copy, rename, move, and delete files. You can also use the menu to change or create directories.
- You can access DOS without leaving WordPerfect. One command lets you execute a single command and then automatically returns you to WordPerfect. Another leaves you in DOS until you type **EXIT** and press Enter.

CHAPTER 6 QUESTIONS

FILL IN THE BLANK

1. To end a field in a secondary document, press __________.
2. To end a record in a secondary document, press __________ and then __________.
3. To insert a merge code into a primary document, press __________.
4. To merge-print two documents, press __________.
5. You can assign macros names or __________-letter key combinations.
6. Before you can execute a macro, you must first __________ it.
7. To begin recording a macro, press __________.

8. To execute a macro assigned to a key on the keyboard, hold down __________.

9. To execute a macro to which you have assigned a name, press __________.

10. To delete, copy, or move macros, you look for filenames with the extension __________.

11. To return to WordPerfect after accessing the DOS prompt, you type __________.

MATCH THE COLUMNS

1. F9	__	The process of recording a macro
2. Shift-F9, E	__	Closes up a line when a field is empty
3. Field	__	The extension that WordPerfect assigns to macro files
4. Record	__	Ends a field in a secondary file
5. ?	__	Recorded keystrokes that can be played back
6. Define	__	Returns you to WordPerfect after you have accessed DOS from within the program
7. Execute	__	The process of playing back a macro
8. Macro	__	Ends a record in a secondary file
9. .WPM	__	A single piece of data in a secondary file
10. EXIT	__	A set of related fields that defines an item such as a name and address

WRITE OUT THE ANSWERS

1. What are the two files you need for automatic merge printing?
2. Describe a primary file and its function.
3. List and describe two codes that you can enter in a primary file.
4. Describe a secondary file and its function.
5. Describe fields and records.
6. List and briefly describe three merge codes.
7. Describe the purpose of keyboard macros.
8. List the steps you would follow to record a macro.
9. How do you play back a recorded macro?
10. Where are macros stored? How can you specify a different storage area?
11. List and describe three commands on the List Files menu that you can use to manage your files.
12. What command do you use to mark individual files? All files?
13. What command do you use to access DOS without leaving WordPerfect? How do the two versions of this command differ?

PROJECTS

PROJECT 1

MANAGING FILES

1. Erase any back copy files (.BK!) from your data disk.
2. Copy all the files on your data disk to a backup disk and store it in a safe place.

PROJECT 2

USING A MACRO TO ENTER A LETTER CLOSING

Create a macro that will move the cursor to the end of the document, type **Sincerely yours,** move down four lines, and enter your name. Use the macro to enter ten closings, one after the other. Make a printout of the document.

PROJECT 3

USING A MACRO TO ENTER A LETTERHEAD

Create a macro that will enter a centered letterhead that matches the one shown in the figure "A Typical Letterhead." Use the macro to enter ten letterheads, one after the other. Make a printout of the document.

A Typical Letterhead
This figure shows the letterhead that you enter in this exercise.

Curtin & London, Inc.
P.O. Box 363
Marblehead, Massachusetts 01945

CHAPTER 7

Real-World Applications

Now that you have become familiar with WordPerfect, you are ready to put it to work. The applications in this chapter include a job-search kit, a research paper, and a business plan. They test and build on the skills you have developed in the preceding topics.

When completing the applications, keep the following points in mind.

- The applications are based on the procedures already discussed in the text, but they are designed to present new problems for you to solve on your own. Don't be discouraged if they take some thought and effort to work through.
- The Concepts section in each application gives you all the subject-area information you will need to complete the application.
- The Steps section in each application gives you the sequence of steps that you should follow. If you get cannot recall how to perform a procedure, refer to the topic that covers that material.

In the three job-search applications, you prepare a cover letter, a résumé, and a followup letter. The files you use to practice formatting are illustrated and are supplied as unformatted files on the disk. If you think you may need a job-search kit of your own in the future, you are encouraged to use these examples for guidance when you create your own documents.

APPLICATION 1A

The Job-Search Kit—The Cover Letter

When searching for a job, you need a cover letter to accompany a résumé that you mail to prospective employers. In this project, you practice formatting one of the two example cover letters supplied on the *Student Resource Disk*. If you then want to prepare your own cover letter, read the Concepts section and each of the sample cover letters carefully, and highlight ideas you might want to incorporate into your own letter.

Your cover letter should capture the employer's attention, show why you are writing, indicate why your employment will benefit the company, and suggest an interview. The kind of specific information that must be included in a letter means that each must be written individually. Each letter must also be typed perfectly, so word processing helps. Frequently, only the address, first paragraph, and specifics concerning an interview will vary. These items are easily changed on a word processor.

The following guidelines may help you write a cover letter:

- Use care in sentence structure, spelling, and punctuation.
- Use a good grade of letter-sized white bond paper for the final printout.
- Address your letter to a specific person if possible.
- State exactly the kind of position you are seeking and why you are applying to a particular firm.
- Be clear, brief, and businesslike.
- Enclose a résumé.

Letters of application will vary considerably depending on the circumstances in which they are used. Let's go through a typical letter point by point:

Salutation. Each letter should be addressed by name to the person you want to talk with. That person is the one who can hire you. This is almost certainly not someone in the personnel department, and it is probably not the department head either. Most likely it is the person who will actually supervise you once you start work. Call the company to make sure you have the right name. And spell it correctly.

Opening. The opening should appeal to the reader. Cover letters are sales letters. Sales are made after you capture a person's attention. You capture the reader's attention most easily by talking about the company rather than yourself. Mention projects under development, recent awards, or favorable comments recently published about the company. You can find such information in the business press, including the business section of local newspapers and many magazines that are devoted to particular industries. If you are answering an ad, you may mention it. If someone suggested that you write, use his or her name (with permission, of course).

Body. The body of the letter gives a brief description of your qualifications and refers to the résumé, where your sales campaign can continue.

Closing. You cannot have what you do not ask for. At the end of the letter, request an interview. Suggest a time, and state that you will confirm the appointment. Use a standard complimentary close, such as "Sincerely yours," leave three or four lines for your signature, and type your name.

STEPS

1. Retrieve CVRLTR1.WP5 or CVRLTR2.WP5 from your disk.
2. Format the letter so it looks similiar to the one in the illustration.
3. Spell-check the document to find any mistakes you may have missed, and save any changes.
4. Make a printout.

304 Amen Street
San Francisco, California 94102
February 21, 1992

Mr. Wilbert R. Wilson
President, XYZ Company
3893 Factory Boulevard
Cleveland, OH 44114

Dear Mr. Wilson:

Recently I learned through Dr. Robert R. Roberts of Atlantic and Pacific University of the expansion of your company's sales operations and your plans to create a new position of sales director. If this position is open, I would appreciate your considering me.

Starting with over-the-counter sales and order service, I have had progressively more responsible and diverse experience in merchandising products similar to yours. In recent years I have carried out a variety of sales promotion and top management assignments.

For your review, I am enclosing a résumé of my qualifications. I would appreciate a personal interview with you to discuss my application further.

Very truly yours,

John W. Doe

Enclosure

2 Jenevein Avenue
San Bruno, CA 94066
January 1, 1993

Ms. Karen Hernandez
Corporate Development, Inc.
101 4th Street
San Francisco, CA 4107

Dear Ms. Hernandez:

I am responding to your advertisement that appeared in the August 1 issue of the San Jose Mercury News. The possibility of becoming involved in all phases of a computerized learning center is very exciting, and I would welcome the opportunity to discuss it with you in more detail.

I have extensive experience in all phases of Macintosh and IBM PC computer operations. More important, however, I work very well with all kinds of people, and love to convey to them not only knowledge, but a sense of excitement about computers and their applications.

My experience in fund raising is limited to my undergraduate days when I participated in Purdue alumni telethons and fund raising for the Purdue student chapter of a national industrial design association. Although limited in experience, I recognize the importance of this phase of the activity and expect that I would both enjoy it and perform it well, given my ability to convey both enthusiasm and a sense of joining in a shared goal.

I will call you on Monday, August 4, to see if a personal meeting can be arranged at your convenience. I look forward to meeting with you to exchange ideas, to tell you more about myself, and to show you some of the creative computer projects that I have been involved with.

Sincerely yours,

Suzanne Franks

enc. Résumé

Sample Cover Letters
These illustrations show two sample cover letters written to accompany a résumé.

APPLICATION 1B

The Job-Search Kit—The Résumé

When searching for a job, you need a résumé that describes your background. In this application, you practice fomatting one of the two sample résumés supplied on the *Student Resource Disk*. If you then want to prepare your own résumé, read the Concepts section and study the sample résumés, perhaps highlighting or annotating any points you might want to incorporate into your own résumé.

Résumés give the employer written evidence of your qualifications. When creating a résumé, you need two kinds of information: facts about yourself and facts about the job you want. With this information in hand, you can present the facts about yourself in terms of the job you are seeking. A job announcement or advertisement should contain a description of the job's requirements. If the announcement or ad is vague, call the employer to learn what is sought.

Preparing the Résumé

Once you have the information you need, you can prepare a résumé. You may need to prepare more than one master résumé if you are going to look for different kinds of jobs; otherwise, your résumé will not fit the job you seek.

Reverse chronology is the easiest method to use. It is also the least effective because it makes when you did something seem more important than what you did. It is an especially poor format if you have gaps in your work history, if the job you seek is very different from the job you currently hold, or if you are just entering the job market. About the only time you would want to use such a résumé is when you have progressed up a clearly defined career ladder and want to move up a rung.

Résumés that are not chronological may be called functional, analytical, skill oriented, creative, or some other name. The differences among them are less important than their similarity, which is that all stress what you can do. The advantage to a potential employer—and, therefore, to your job campaign—should be obvious. The employer can see immediately how you will fit the job. This format also has advantages for many job hunters because it camouflages gaps in paid employment and avoids giving prominence to irrelevant jobs.

You begin writing a functional résumé by determining the skills the employer is looking for. Again, study the job description for this information. Next, review your experience and education to see when you demonstrated the ability sought. Then prepare the résumé itself, putting first the information that relates most obviously to the job. The result will be a résumé with headings such as "Engineering," "Computer Languages," "Communication Skills," or "Design Experience." These headings will have much more impact than the dates that you would use on a chronological résumé.

The way you arrange your résumé depends on how well your experience seems to prepare you for the position you want. You can either describe your most recent job first and work backward (reverse chronology) or group similar skills together. Whichever format you use, the following advice generally applies:

- Use specifics. A vague description of your duties will make only a vague impression.
- Identify accomplishments. If you headed a project, improved productivity, reduced costs, increased membership, or achieved some other goal, say so.
- Keep the length down to two pages at the most.
- Remember your mother's advice not to say anything if you cannot say something nice. Leave all embarrassing or negative informa-

tion off the résumé, but be ready to deal with it in a positive fashion at the interview.

- Proofread the master copy carefully, and then have someone else do the same.

STEPS

1. Retrieve RESUME1.WP5 or RESUME2.WP5 from the disk.
2. Format the document so it is similar to the one shown in the illustration.
3. Print the document, proofread and edit it, enter the changes into the document, and save it again.
4. Spell-check the document to find any mistakes you may have missed, and save any changes.
5. Make another printout if you made any changes.

Judy L. Antonio
19 Fernwood Drive
Williamsville, New York 14221
(716) 555-1313

EDUCATION	
College	State University College at Buffalo
Degree	Bachelor of Science degree in Education
Certification	Elementary Education
TEACHING EXPERIENCE	
11/87-12/87	Student Teacher Central Elementary School 155 Central Road Williamsville, NY 14221 *Planned and implemented lessons for all subjects in the second and third grades.*
9/87-10/87	Student Teacher Country Parkway Elementary School 35 Hollybrook Drive Williamsville, NY 14221 *Planned and implemented lessons for all subjects in the first grade.*
WORK HISTORY	
3/85-4/87	Teacher Substitute Campus Child Care Center, Inc. SUNYAB Buffalo, NY 14214 *Started as teacher aide and in May, 1985, was promoted to teacher substitute.*
11/84-6/86	Teacher's Assistant Central Day Care Center 15 Jewett Parkway Buffalo, NY 14214 *Before and After School Program: planned and implemented various activities for children, ages 5-7.*
1979-1986	Counselor and Program Staff Cradle Beach Camp (summer resident camp) Old Lake Shore Road Angola, NY 14006 *Responsibilities included: arts and crafts staff, cabin staff, pool staff and cabin counselor with physically handicapped, mentally retarded, and/or deprived boys and girls, ages 9-17. Certified in advanced lifesaving.*
REFERENCES	
	Available upon request from: State University College at Buffalo Grover Cleveland Hall, Room 306 1300 Elmwood Avenue Buffalo, NY 14222

Allison Springs
15 Hilton House
College de l'Art Libre
Smallville, CO 77717
(888) 736-3550

Job sought: Hotel Management Trainee

Skills, education, and experience

Working with people. All the jobs I have had involve working closely with people on many different levels. As vice president of the junior class, I balanced the concerns of different groups in order to reach a common goal. As a claims interviewer with a state public assistance agency, I dealt with people under very trying circumstances. As a research assistant with a law firm, I worked with both lawyers and clerical workers. And as a lifeguard (five summers), I learned how to manage groups. In addition, my work with the state and the law office has made me familiar with organization procedures.

Effective communication. My campaign for class office, committee projects, and fund raising efforts (which netted $15,000 for the junior class project) relied on effective communication in both oral and written presentations.

Organization and management. My participation in student government has developed my organization and management skills. In addition, my work with the state government and a law office has made me familiar with organization procedures.

Chronology

September 1988 to present	Attended College de l'Art Libre in Smallville, Colorado. Will earn a Bachelor of Arts degree in political science. Elected vice president of the junior class, managed successful fund drive, directed Harvest Celebration Committee, served on many other committees, and earned 13 percent of my college expenses
January 1992 to present	Worked as research assistant for the law office of McCall, McCrow, and McCow, 980 Main Street, Westrow, Colorado 77718. Supervisor: Jan Eagelli (666) 654-3211
September 1991 to December 1991	Served as claims interviewer intern for the Department of Public Assistance of the State of Colorado, 226 Park Street, Smallville, Colorado 77717. Supervisor: James Fish (666) 777-7717
1985-1990	Worked as lifeguard during the summer at the Shilo Pool, 46 Waterway, Shilo, Nebraska 77777

Recommendations available upon request

Sample Résumés
These illustrations show two typical résumés: one arranged chronologically and the other functionally.

APPLICATION 1C

The Job-Search Kit—The Followup Letter

After you have had a job interview, you should immediately send a followup letter to the person who interviewed you. In this project, you practice formatting a typical followup letter supplied on the *Student Resource Disk*. If you then want to prepare your own followup letter, read the Concepts section and each of the sample cover letters carefully, and highlight ideas you might want to incorporate into your own letter.

CONCEPTS

The purpose of a followup letter is to remind the person who interviewed you that you are interested in the position you discussed. You might refer to points you made in the interview that you want the interviewer to remember. You are selling yourself in the followup letter just as you did in the cover letter, résumé, and interview. Your advantage in the followup letter is that you have had time to consider how the interview went, so you can address points you forgot to make or would like to reinforce. Keep the letter short, and if possible, itemize key points so that the interviewer can read it quickly and still get the points you are making.

Sample Followup Letter
This illustration shows the text of a sample followup letter that is sent after a job interview.

Dear

Thank you for the interview last (Friday). I am impressed with the quality of your organization and would like to express my continued interest in pursuing the position.

As I mentioned to you, I feel that I could contribute to your company's objectives for a number of reasons.

- I am able to work well with coworkers and am very much a team player.
- My previous experience at (previous job) has given me an understanding of the responsibilities of the position. I hope you will give me the opportunity to share my abilities with your company.

Since the interview, I have given a great deal of thought to our discussion and would like to make the following points:

- While working on the school newspaper, I gained interviewing experience that should make me better at completing the surveys you mentioned would be required as part of the position's responsibilities.
- I have earned over 50 percent of my college expenses and in the process have established a solid employment record over the past four years. I have proved my reliability in this position and hope you will call Mr. Jones at 212-555-1212 to hear his opinions of the contributions that I have made.

Again, thank you for your consideration. If there is any additional information I might be able to supply, please let me know. I am eager to hear from you.

Sincerely yours,

STEPS

1. Retrieve FOLLOWUP.WP5 from the disk.
2. Format the document so it looks similar to the one shown in the illustration.
3. Save your formatted letter and make a printout.
4. Proofread and edit the printout, enter the changes into the document, and save it.
5. Spell-check the document to find any mistakes you may have missed, and save any changes.
6. Make another printout if you made any changes.

APPLICATION 2

The Research Paper—The Body

Many courses in college require the preparation of a research paper. To prepare these papers, you must select a topic, research it, and then prepare a written document. The computer can greatly ease the process of writing, editing, and formatting the paper. You may also find computers in the library that allow you to search for information on specific subjects, easing the research task as well. In this application, you'll be glad to know we have done the research for you. All you have to do is add references, format the document, and proofread the results.

CONCEPTS

Because of the differences among disciplines, different formats are expected in each for presentation of material. These special formats have evolved to communicate a writer's purpose, to emphasize contents by eliminating distracting variations in format, and to make the reader's work easier. Writing in the humanities is less often subject to set formats, although your writing is expected to be well organized, and accepted documentation formats are expected. Writing in the social sciences and natural sciences often calls for using fixed special formats for specific types of writing. For example, if you are writing a case study or a laboratory report, you are expected to use the formats always used for such writings.[1] The paper that follows is based on the style of the Modern Language Association.

[1]Lynn Quitman Troyka, *Simon & Schuster Handbook for Writers* (Englewood Cliffs: Prentice, 1987), pp. 618-19.

STEPS

1. Retrieve the TERMPAPR.WP5 document from your data disk.
2. Enter your name, your instructor's name, the course number, and today's date where indicated.
3. Center the paper title.
4. Fully justify all text that follows and doublespace it.

Key Dates in the History of Microcomputers

Year	**Development**
1972	Intel 8000 series of microprocessors introduced
1974	Microsoft founded by Bill Gates and Paul Allen
1975	MITS Altair on cover of Popular Electronics
1975	Homebrew Computer Club founded
1975	Digital Research founded by Gary Kildall to sell CP/M
1976	Apple I in production
1977	Apple II begins shipments
1977	Radio Shack TRS-80 Model 1 introduced
1977	Commodore PET introduced
1978	VisiCalc prototype shown by Frankston and Bricklin
1980	Apple III introduced
1981	IBM PC announced
1983	Apple Lisa introduced
1983	Lotus 1-2-3 released for sale on IBM PC
1984	Apple Macintosh introduced
1985	Steve Wozniak resigns from Apple
1985	Lotus buys Software Arts, the developers of VisiCalc
1985	VisiCalc production stops
1985	Steve Jobs resigns from Apple

Works Cited

Bashe, Charles J., et al. IBM's Early Computers. Cambridge: MIT P, 1986.

Curtin, Dennis. Microcomputers: Software and Applications. Englewood Cliffs: Prentice, 1986.

Forester, Tom, ed. The Information Technology Revolution. Cambridge: MIT P, 1985.

Gorstine, G.W. 16-Bit Modern Microcomputers: The Intel i8086 Family. Englewood Cliffs: Prentice, 1985.

Hollerbach, Lew. A 60-Minute Guide to Microcomputers. 1st American ed. Englewood Cliffs: Prentice, 1982.

The Research Paper's Table and Works Cited
These illustrations show the formatting of the research paper's table and list of works cited.

NOTES

1 Though the MITS system is no longer manufactured, its method for connecting peripherals and the main computer has become an industry standard. Within three years after it was introduced, Radio Shack, Apple, and Commodore had entered the market.

2 The introduction of VisiCalc is usually credited with making the Apple II the fastest selling computer of its time and with making the microcomputer acceptable in business offices.

5. Use the Search command to locate the headings "Microcomputer Hardware: The Early Years" and "Microcomputer Software: The Early Years" and underline them.
6. Underline the following book and magazine titles. (Use the Search command to locate them.)
   - *IBM's Early Computer*
   - *16-Bit Modern Microcomputers: The Intel i8086 Family*
   - *Popular Electronics*
7. Use the Search command to locate the following strings, and enter the endnotes shown in the box to the left following the period at the end of the sentence:
   - For note 1, search for *companies that supplied its components.*
   - For note 2, search for *VisiCalc did that for them.*
8. The two paragraphs above the heading "Microcomputer Software: The Early Years" are direct quotations. Indent them so that they are 1 inch from the left margin.
9. Enter a hard page break above the table "Key Dates in the History of Microcomputers" at the end of the document. Then format the table as follows:
   - Set a tab stop at 1" to separate the columns.
   - Single space the table, and restore double spacing at the end of it.
   - Boldface the column headings.
10. Enter a right-aligned header so that it prints your last name followed by one space and the page number in the upper-right corner of each page but the first. Have it start page numbering on the second page with the number 2.
11. Format the *Works Cited* page so it is doublespaced and titles are underlined. The second line of each paragraph should be indented ½ inch (use the Margin Release command).
12. Insert a hard page break at the end of the document. Then on the first line of the new page enter the heading **Notes**. Center the heading, and insert two blank lines below it so that the endnotes print starting on the third line.
13. Experiment with base font codes to change the text throughout the document. Use a separate base font for the table and the pages that follow it.

14. Spell-check the document.
15. Print out the document, and proofread it to catch any errors not found by the spell checker.

APPLICATION 3

The Business Plan—The Written Portion

When starting a new business or expanding an existing one, banks and other investors require a business plan. This plan describes in detail what the firm's goals are and how management plans to organize and operate the firm to achieve those goals. A business plan contains two basic parts: a descriptive written section and an analytical financial section. In this application, you deal with the written section of the plan.

CONCEPTS

Business plans are emergent. You start out with a general idea of what you want to accomplish. Next, you develop a set of assumptions that suggest that the plan is feasible. Once this is done, you begin to flesh out the details for each specific area of the operation. As each of these areas is considered and developed, facts may become apparent that will change some of your assumptions in other parts of the plan. This process will continue as you move closer and closer to actually putting the plan into action and even after the venture is launched. There is nothing sacred about the finished document; once made, plans should be reviewed regularly and updated as needed.

The plan consists of two main sections. The first section is the written part of the plan and describes the overall activities of the firm, its position within the marketplace, the important components of the operation, and the purpose of the loan or investment.

The second section contains the financial data and is essentially a quantification of the written portion of the plan. This section can't really be prepared until the written section is essentially finished even though many people do just the reverse—they develop a set of forecasts that seem to make sense and then try to write a plan around the forecasts. However, if the assumptions for the forecasts don't hang together when they are subjected to scrutiny, it's very possible that they won't work once the operation is actually underway.

Finally, documents that support the information presented in either the written or the financial portions of the plan are added as appendices.

The ideas and information that you have collected during the planning process take a specific form when organized into the business plan. This format is designed to lead the reader along a logical path from point to point, answering questions that are likely to arise *before* they are asked, and filling in details of the business project section by section until the story is complete.[2]

[2]William R. Osgood and Dennis P. Curtin, *Preparing Your Business Plan with Lotus 1-2-3* (Englewood Cliffs: Prentice, 1985), pp. 2-3.

STEPS

TABLE 1[a]

Shark System Board Costs[b]					
CPU	Q4 90	Q1 91	Q2 91	Q3 91	Q4 91
486/33 no cache	$550	$500	$475	$450	
486/33 w/cache	$650	$600	$550	$525	
486/50 w/cache	$650	$625	$600	$575	
486/50 w/Intel module support	$600	$550	$525		

Microprocessor Pricing					
CPU	Q4 90	Q1 91	Q2 91	Q3 91	Q4 91
486 20 MHz[c]	$250	$250	$225		
486 25 MHz	$750	$650	$600	$500	$325
486 33 MHz	$950	$850	$700	$500	$400
486 33 w ICEcap	$1,150	$1,050	$900	$700	$600
486 50 MHz	$700	$650	$600		
486 50 module[d]	$1,400	$1,300	$1,200		

[a] Based on Intel estimates 9/90
[b] Includes materials, assembly, testing, and packaging
[c] Intel P23 486/20 no coprocessor
[d] Includes CPU cache controller and 256K cache

The Business Plan's Table
When you have formatted the table in the business plan, it should look similar to this.

Contents

The Business Plan's Table of Contents
Use this illustration as a guide to formatting the headings in the business plan's text.

1. Retrieve the BUSPLAN.WP5 document.
2. Enter your name and today's date in the positions indicated on the first page.
3. Format the company name on the first page as extra large.
4. Enter a hard page break below the date, and center the text on the first page both horizontally and vertically.
5. On the second page, delete hard returns so that the *Contents* heading is on the first line. Boldface and center the heading.
6. Clear all tab stops. Then set a left-aligned tab stop at .5" and a right-aligned tab stop with dot leaders at 6".
7. Delete existing tab codes in front of the contents page numbers, and enter new ones so that the numbers align correctly and the dot leaders are displayed.
8. Enter a hard page break so that the *Summary* heading is on the first line of the third page.
9. Set tab stops on the *Summary* heading line at .3" so that the second and subsequent paragraphs in each section and the two enumerated lists are indented by that amount. Delete the right-aligned tab stop set at 6" and the left-aligned tab stop set at .5".
10. Set right-aligned tab stops to align the columns in Table 1. (Search for *Table 1* to locate the table.) When you have finished, your table should match the table shown in the figure "The Business Plan's Table."
11. Below the table, restore the original tab stops, one left-aligned tab stop at .3".
12. Indent the two numbered lists so that the numbers are left hanging and the other lines are indented to the first tab stop.
13. Enter page numbers so that a Roman numeral ii prints bottom center on the table of contents page and subsequent pages are numbered in the same position beginning with an Arabic number 1.
14. Refer to the figure "The Business Plan's Table of Contents," and notice how the document has two levels of headings. The main headings are called A-heads, and the indented headings below them are called B-heads. Using this figure as a guide, boldface and center A-heads and italicize or underline B-heads in the document. You can use the Search command to quickly locate any heading.
15. Spell-check the document.
16. Save your changes.
17. Print the document. Review the results, and make any changes. If any headings fall at the bottom of the page, enter a hard page break to move them down to the next page where they will accompany the text that immediately follows them.

INDEX

Lotus® 1-2-3®

CHAPTER 1

Getting Started

TOPIC 1

Lotus 1-2-3—An Overview

After completing this topic, you will be able to:

- Describe the terms *spreadsheet*, *worksheet*, *model*, and *template*
- List the steps you follow to create a typical model
- Load Lotus 1-2-3
- Identify and describe the elements of the 1-2-3 worksheet screen display

Spreadsheets are used throughout business to solve and analyze almost any type of problem that involves numbers and calculations. They are used to analyze the performance of products, salespeople, or dealers. They compare costs, prices, and gross margins on individual products in a product line. They also calculate prices, forecast and make budgets for sales, predict expenses and profits, and make cash-flow projections. Their major advantage is that they allow you to explore a number of alternatives quickly and easily.

One of the primary uses of spreadsheets is to build models to analyze financial or other situations and to explore the effects that changes in any assumptions have on the outcome. You use models to simulate real-world situations. Just as a plastic model of an airplane represents, or simulates, a real plane, a spreadsheet model simulates financial or other situations involving numbers. When using a spreadsheet, you should understand four basic terms: *spreadsheet*, *worksheet*, *model*, and *template.*

- A *spreadsheet* is the program that you use on your computer when you want to do financial or numeric analysis.
- A *worksheet* is the arrangement of horizontal rows and vertical columns that appears on the screen. At the intersection of each row and column is a cell into which you enter labels, values, or formulas. These cells are referred to by their coordinates on the worksheet. For example, the cell at the intersection of column B and row 6 is called cell B6.
- A *model* (or file) is the data you enter into the worksheet to solve a problem or perform an analysis. To create a model, you use two basic types of entries: labels and values. *Labels* describe or

CELL ENTRIES

When the cell pointer is positioned in a cell, here are some of the things you can enter:

- *Labels* identify models or individual rows and columns of data.
- *Numbers* can be used in calculations when referred to by formulas.
- *Formulas* can calculate numbers entered into the formula itself or entered into other cells that the formula refers to.
- *Functions* are built-in programs that automatically perform calculations such as mortgage payments, averages, and totals.
- *Formats* control the way numbers are displayed on the screen and the way labels are aligned in their cells.
- *Protection* can prevent data from being entered into the wrong cells.

identify parts of the model. *Values* are the numbers to be analyzed and the formulas and built-in functions that perform the analysis.

- A *template* is a model from which all the numbers have been removed. Since it still retains all the labels, formulas, and functions, you can enter new numbers in the spaces indicated by the labels, and the formulas will calculate an answer. Mastering a spreadsheet and the business principles needed to analyze a problem takes time. In many firms, people who understand the principles behind an application often collaborate with those who understand a spreadsheet to develop templates of great value to others in the firm. These templates are designed to be used again and again by anyone who knows how to move the cell pointer and enter the numbers to be analyzed.

JUMP-START TUTORIAL

In this tutorial, you explore the procedures used to work with spreadsheet models. You complete and then use a model to analyze the purchase of a new automobile. As you work, compare your results to the figure "The Finished Loan Analyzer Model."

The Finished Loan Analyzer Model
When you have finished creating the model in the jump-start tutorial (but before you explore what-ifs), your loan analyzer model will look like the one shown here.

	A	B	C	D	E
1	Your name:	your name			
2	Filename:	OVERVIEW			
3	Date:	today's date			
4	====================	====================	====	====================	====================
5	LOAN ANALYZER		I	Range of	Range of
6	Item	Amount	I	loans	payments
7	------------------------------		I	----------------------	
8	Cost of car	$10,000	I	$6,000	$158.00
9	Down payment	2,000	I	$6,500	$171.17
10	Loan balance	8,000	I	$7,000	$184.34
11	Interest rate	12.0%	I	$7,500	$197.50
12	Term of loan (in months)	48	I	$8,000	$210.67
13		-----------		$8,500	$223.84
14	Monthly payment	$210.67	I	$9,000	$237.00
15	Total payments	$10,112.19	I	$9,500	$250.17
16	Total interest paid	$2,112.19	I	$10,000	$263.34
17	====================	====================	====	====================	====================

GETTING STARTED

1. Load the Lotus 1-2-3 program into your computer's memory.
   - If you load the program from the operating system command prompt (for example, *A:* or *C:*), load the operating system and then refer to the KEY/Strokes box "Loading 1-2-3 from a Floppy Disk" or "Loading 1-2-3 from a Hard Disk" in the Quick Reference section on pages 7 and 8.
   - If you use other procedures to load the program, such as selecting it from a menu, load it and write down the steps that you follow to load the program in Exercise 1 on page 10 so that you have them to refer to later.

THE 1-2-3 SCREEN DISPLAY

The 1-2-3 screen varies slightly from version to version, but all versions look much like this illustration of the Release 2.4 screen. All versions have three basic areas: the control panel, the working area, and the status line. (Only Release 2.4 has icons at the right side of the screen.)

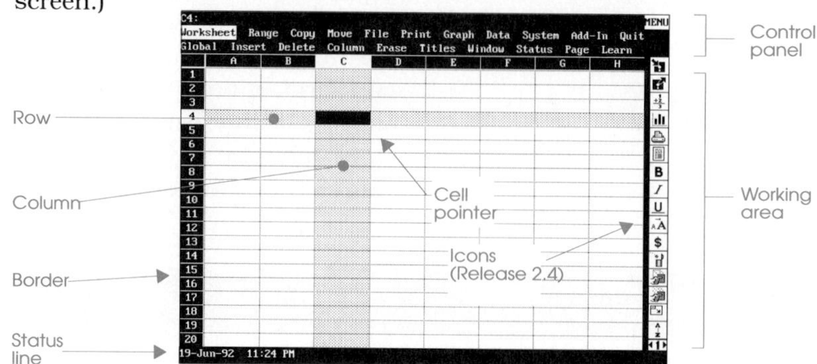

The control panel is located at the top of the screen. Its three lines display the following information:

- The first line provides information about the cell in which the cell pointer is positioned (see the box "The Active Cell"). At the far right end of the line is the mode indicator telling you the current state of the program.
- The second line displays the data you enter or edit in one of the cells. When you press / (the slash key) to begin executing commands, the command menu is displayed on this line. At certain points during command execution, prompts are also displayed on this line.
- The third line displays a brief description of the highlighted menu selection when the menu is displayed. If choosing the highlighted command will display a submenu, the submenu's commands are listed instead of a description.

The working area is where you enter data and create your models. This area contains the following elements:

- A border contains column letters across the top of the worksheet and row numbers down the left side.
  - Columns run vertically down the worksheet and are labeled consecutively across the top border with letters. The first twenty-six columns are labeled A to Z, the next twenty-six are labeled AA to AZ, the next twenty-six are labeled BA to BZ, and so on up to column IV, the 256th column on the full-featured version.
  - Rows run horizontally across the worksheet and are labeled consecutively down the left border with numbers, starting with row 1 at the top of the worksheet and ending at row 8192 on the full-featured version.
- Cells, into which you enter data, fall at the intersection of each column and row (although the dividing lines are displayed only as an option on later releases). Cells are referred to by their coordinates, or address—the column letter followed by the row number. For example, the cell at the intersection of column D and row 8 is cell D8.
- The working area contains a bright highlight, called the *cell pointer*. You move this cell pointer by pressing the pointer movement keys to point to cells when you want to enter, delete, copy, move, or print data. The cell that the cell pointer is positioned in is called the active or current cell.

The status line at the bottom of the screen contains the following information:

- The current date and time (or optionally, the current file's name on Release 2.2 and later versions) are displayed.
- Status indicators are displayed at various points in your procedures.
- Error messages are displayed for some kinds of mistakes.

CHANGING THE DEFAULT DRIVE AND DIRECTORY

2. Insert the *Student Resource Disk* as follows:
   - On a hard disk system, insert the disk into drive A.
   - On a floppy disk system, insert the disk into drive B.
3. Press [/][F][D] (for ***F**ile*, ***D**irectory*), and the prompt reads *Enter current directory:* followed by the name of current default directory.
4. Specify the default directory as follows:
   - On a hard disk system, type **A:\1-2-3** and press [Enter ↵].
   - On a floppy disk system, type **B:\1-2-3** and press [Enter ↵].

RETRIEVING A FILE

5. Press [/][F][R] (for *File, Retrieve*), and the prompt reads *Name of file to retrieve:* followed by a list of files in the current directory.
6. Press [F3] to display a screenful of filenames.
7. Press the arrow keys to highlight *OVERVIEW.WK1* (the extension .WK1 is not displayed on some earlier versions), and press [Enter ↵]. In a moment, the model appears on the screen.

The Loan Analyzer Model on Your Screen
When you retrieve the OVERVIEW model, your screen should look like this.

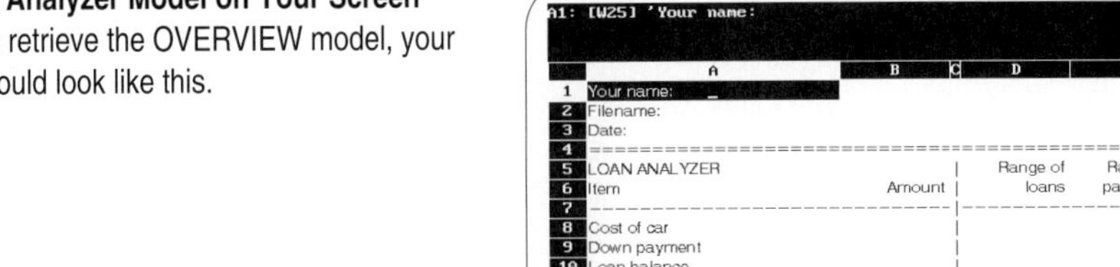

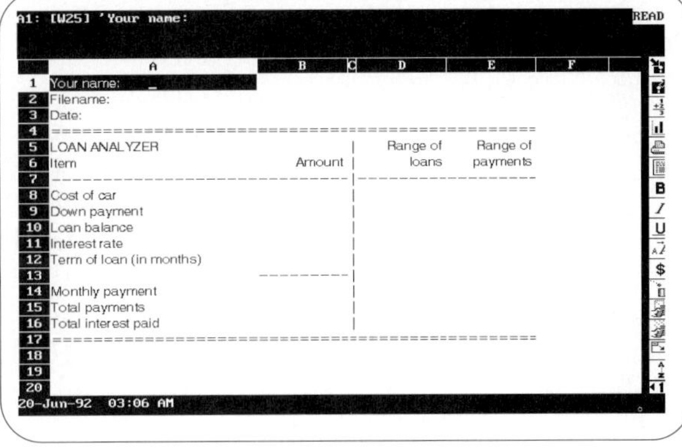

GETTING AROUND THE WORKSHEET

8. Press the arrow keys to move the cell pointer (the bright highlight) around the worksheet. As you do so, notice that the cell address indicator on the first row of the control panel always indicates the cell pointer's position and provides other information about the contents and format of the cell in which it is positioned. For an explanation of some of the things displayed about a cell, see the box "The Active Cell." Notice also that if you try to move the cell pointer to the left of column A or above row 1, the computer beeps.
9. Press [Home] to return the cell pointer to cell A1.

THE ACTIVE CELL

The cell in which the cell pointer is positioned is called the active cell. The first line of the control panel always displays two pieces of information about this cell—its address and its contents. If you have changed any of the settings in the cell, they are indicated between these two basic pieces of information. For example, the line may read *B2: (C0) U [W10] 1000.* Here is what this information means.

B2 The cell address is always listed first.

(C0) The format is listed next if a format has been assigned to the cell with the ***/R**ange* ***F**ormat* command. *C0* is the format for Currency, zero decimal places.

U The protection status is listed next. A *U* means the cell has been unprotected with the ***/** **R**ange* ***U**nprotect* (or ***U**nprot* on some versions) command. A *PR* means the cell is protected and protection has been enabled with the ***/W**orksheet* ***G**lobal* ***P**rotection* ***E**nable* command.

[W10] The column width is listed next if you have changed it from the default width with the ***/W**orksheet* ***C**olumn* ***S**et-Width* command.

1000 The contents of the cell are always listed. If the cell contains a formula, the formula is displayed, not its calculated value.

ENTERING LABELS

10. Use the arrow keys to move the cell pointer to cell B1.
11. Type your name. As you do so, notice that it is displayed on the second line of the control panel at the top of the screen.
12. Press [Enter ←] to enter your name into the cell. It is now displayed on the first line of the control panel.
13. Press [↓] to move the cell pointer to cell B2.
14. Type **OVERVIEW** and press [Enter ←].

ENTERING A FUNCTION

15. Press [↓] to move the cell pointer to cell B3.
16. Type **@NOW** and press [Enter ←] to display the number of days since December 31, 1899 (January 1, 1900, is number 1).
17. Press [/] [R] [F] [D] (for ***R**ange*, ***F**ormat*, ***D**ate*) to display a submenu of date formats.
18. Highlight ***1** (DD-MMM-YY)* and press [Enter ←] twice to format the date.

ENTERING NUMBERS

19. Move the cell pointer to cell B8 (Cost of car), type **10000** and press [Enter ←]. The number is displayed with a dollar sign and a comma because that is the way the cell has been formatted. You'll see how to change cell formats later in this text.
20. Move the cell pointer to cell B9 (Down payment), type **2000** and press [Enter ←]. The number is displayed with a comma.
21. Skip cell B10 and move the cell pointer to cell B11 (Interest rate), type **.12** and press [Enter ←]. The number is displayed as 12.0%.
22. Move the cell pointer to cell B12 (Term of loan), type **48** and press [Enter ←].

ENTERING FORMULAS

23. Move the cell pointer to cell B10, type **+B8-B9** and press [Enter ←]. The formula calculates and displays 8,000 in the cell, and the formula itself is displayed on the first line of the control panel. The formula calculates 8000 by subtracting the contents of cell B9 (2,000) from the contents of cell B8 (10,000).

ENTERING FUNCTIONS

24. Move the cell pointer to cell B14, then type the function **@PMT(B10,B11/12,B12)** and press [Enter ←]. The function calculates and displays the value 211. The function reads in English "Calculate the monthly payment based on the principal in cell B10, the interest rate in cell B11 (divided by 12 to convert it to a monthly interest rate), and the period in cell B12."
25. Press [/] [R] [F] [C] (for ***R**ange*, ***F**ormat*, ***C**urrency*), and the prompt reads *Enter number of decimal places (0..15): 2.*
26. Press [Enter ←] twice to accept the two decimal places, and the cell displays the number $210.67.

ENTERING MORE FORMULAS

27. Move the cell pointer to cell B15, type **+B14*B12** and press [Enter ↵] to calculate total payments.
28. Move the cell pointer to cell B16, type **+B15-B10** and press [Enter ↵] to calculate total interest paid on the loan.

ENTERING AND COPYING FORMULAS

29. Move the cell pointer to cell D8, type **+B10-2000** and press [Enter ↵].
30. Move the cell pointer to cell D9, type **+D8+500** and press [Enter ↵].
31. Press [/][C] (for ***C**opy*), and the prompt asks you what you want to copy or where you want to copy it from and lists the cell you are presently in, D9. The same cell is listed twice because you can copy more than one adjacent cell, called a *range*. The first D9 indicates the beginning of the range to be copied and the second D9 indicates the end.
32. Press [Enter ↵] to accept D9, and the prompt asks where you want to copy it to.
33. Type **D10.D16** and press [Enter ↵]. The formula is copied to cells D10 through D16, and each cell is $500 more than the one immediately above it.
34. Move the cell pointer to cell E8, type **@PMT(D8,B$11/12,B$12)** and press [Enter ↵]. The function calculates the monthly payment of $158.00.
35. Press [/][C] (for ***C**opy*), and the prompt asks you what you want to copy or where you want to copy it from and lists the cell you are presently in, E8.
36. Press [Enter ↵] to accept E8, and the prompt asks where you want to copy it to.
37. Type **E9.E16** and press [Enter ↵]. The function is copied and monthly payments are calculated for each of the loan amounts on the same row in the column to the left.

SAVING THE MODEL

38. Press [/][F][S] (for ***F**ile*, ***S**ave*), and the prompt reads *Enter name of file to save:* followed by the name of the current worksheet. (The filename is preceded by the drive you specified in Step 4.)
39. Press [Enter ↵] to accept the suggested name, and a submenu lists the choices *Cancel* ***R**eplace* (and ***B**ackup* on some later releases).
40. Press [R] (for ***R**eplace*), and the disk drive spins as the model is saved on the disk.

EXPLORING WHAT-IFS

41. To change the term of the loan, move the cell pointer to cell B12, type **60** over the current 48 months, and press [Enter ↵]. The monthly payment in cell B14 falls to $177.96. All of the payments in column E also recalculate to reflect the change in the term of the loan.
42. To change the down payment in cell B9, type **2500** over the current $2,000, and press [Enter ↵]. The loan required in cell B10 falls from $8,000 to $7,500, and the monthly payment falls to $166.83.

43. To change the cost of the car in cell B8, type **9000** over the current $10,000, and press Enter ↵. The loan required in cell B10 falls from $7,500 to $6,500, and the monthly payment falls to $144.59.
44. To lower the interest rate in cell B11, type **.11** over the current 12%, and press Enter ↵. The monthly payment drops to $141.33.

DISPLAYING A GRAPH

45. Press F10 to display a graph of the range of monthly payments. (If the graph isn't displayed on the screen, you do not have a graphics display; press Spacebar to continue.)

    The graph's x-axis (the horizontal axis) plots the range of loans in column D. The bars are the monthly payments in column E. You can locate a bar for any of the calculated loans and read from the top of the bar across to the y-axis to see what the monthly payment would be for that amount.
46. When you have finished looking at the graph, press Spacebar to return to the worksheet.

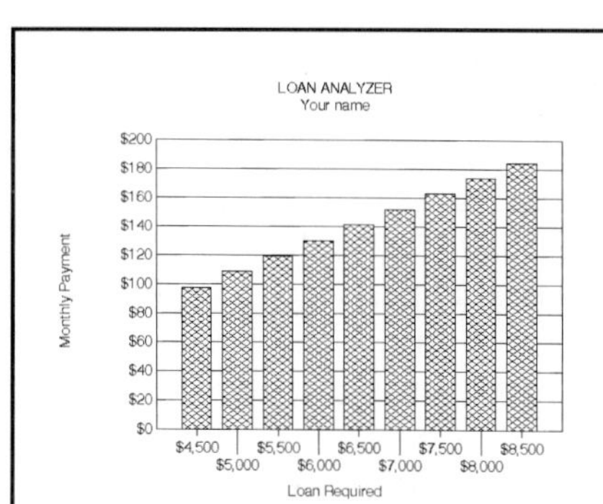

The Loan Analyzer Graph
The graph for the loan analyzer plots loan amounts from column D on the x-axis (the horizontal axis). It then plots monthly payments from column E against the loans. To see how large a monthly payment is, read from the top of its bar across to the y-axis (the vertical axis).

FINISHING UP

47. To erase the model from the screen without saving your most recent changes, press / W E (for ***W**orksheet, **E**rase*), and a submenu lists the choices ***No Yes***.
48. Press Y (for ***Yes***). On later versions of 1-2-3, the computer will beep and display the message *WORKSHEET CHANGES NOT SAVED! Erase worksheet anyway?*. If this prompt appears, press Y to erase the worksheet.
49. To quit 1-2-3, press / Q (for ***Q**uit*), and a submenu lists the choices ***No Yes***.
50. Press Y (for ***Yes***).

QUICK REFERENCE

To use 1-2-3, you must understand the basic procedures that you follow to load and quit the program.

Loading 1-2-3

Before you can load Lotus 1-2-3, you must load the computer's operating system. Once the operating system is loaded, the way you load 1-2-3 depends on the type of computer you are using and the operating system you loaded. If your system is on a network or if you use a menu to load programs, refer to Exercise 1 at the end of this topic.

Loading 1-2-3 from a Floppy Disk

1. On a floppy disk system, insert the 1-2-3 disk labeled *System Disk* into drive A.
2. If the system prompt is not *A>*, type **A:** and press Enter ↵.
3. Type **123** and press Enter ↵ to load the program.

TIP

If you are using Release 2.2 or later versions, you can specify whether the bottom line displays the date and time or the name of the file on the screen. To switch between these two settings, press / W G D O C (for ***W**orksheet*, ***G**lobal*, ***D**efault*, ***O**ther*, ***C**lock*). Press C (for ***C**lock*) to display the date and time, or press F (for ***F**ilename*) to display the filename. Press U (for ***U**pdate*) if you want the change to be there the next time you load the program, and then press Q (for ***Q**uit*) to return to the worksheet.

Loading 1-2-3 from a Hard Disk

1. Change the default drive and directory to the one containing the 123.EXE file. (Some releases name the file 123.COM.)
   - If the system prompt is not *C>* or *C:\>*, type **C:** and press Enter ←.
   - To change the default directory, type **CD** and the name of the directory, and press Enter ←. For example, if the program files are in a directory named 123, type **CD\123** and press Enter ←.
2. Type **123** and press Enter ← to load the program.

THE LOTUS ACCESS SYSTEM

Instead of loading the worksheet directly, you can type **LOTUS** and press Enter ← from the system prompt to load the Lotus Access System. When you do so, a menu is displayed from which you can load either the worksheet or the separate programs that print graphs, convert files, or perform other tasks. To choose one of the commands listed on the menu, press the first letter in its name, or highlight it and press Enter ←. For example, to load the worksheet, press 1 (for ***1**-2-3*), or highlight *1-2-3* and press Enter ←.

On a floppy disk system, you have to swap disks when you execute some of the commands listed on this menu. For example, if you select ***P**rintGraph*, you are prompted to insert the 1-2-3 PrintGraph disk. When one of these prompts appears, remove the current disk from drive A, and then insert the requested disk.

When you quit any of the programs, you automatically return to the Access System menu so that you can load another program. To return to the operating system, you select the ***E**xit* choice listed on the menu.

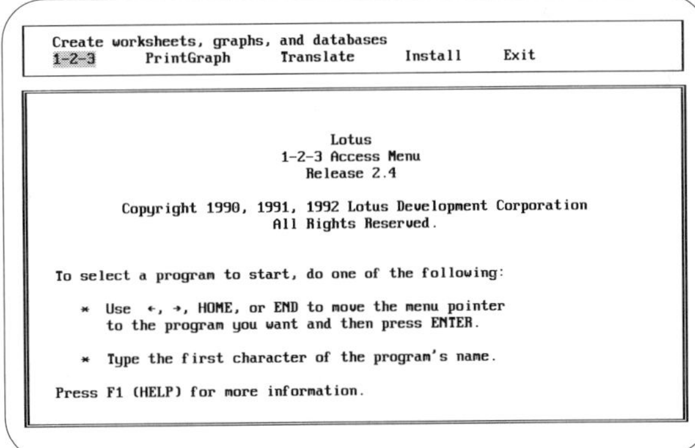

- *1-2-3* displays the worksheet on which you create your models.
- *PrintGraph* displays the Graph menu that you use to print graphs.
- *Translate* converts files between earlier versions of 1-2-3, and other file formats that vary depending on the version you are using.
- *Install* specifies the details of your system.
- *Exit* returns you to the operating system so that you can load another program or quit for the day.

Quitting 1-2-3

At the end of a session, you quit 1-2-3 when you want to load another program or turn the computer off for the day. Release 2.2 and later versions have added a safeguard to ensure that you do not inadvertently lose work when you quit. If you quit the program after making changes to the worksheet that you have not saved, a prompt reads *WORKSHEET CHANGES NOT SAVED! End 1-2-3 anyway?* Press [N] to cancel the Quit command so that you can save the changes, or press [Y] to abandon the changes.

→ KEY/Strokes

Quitting 1-2-3

1. Press [/][Q] (for ***Q**uit*) and a submenu lists the choices ***No Yes***.
2. Press [Y] to quit the program.

EXERCISES

EXERCISE 1

LOADING 1-2-3 ON YOUR SYSTEM

If your 1-2-3 program is on a network, or if your system has been customized, your loading procedures may differ from those discussed in this topic. If they do, list the steps that you follow so that you have them for future reference.

1. ______________________________

   ____
2. ______________________________

   ____
3. ______________________________

   ____
4. ______________________________

   ____
5. ______________________________

   ____

EXERCISE 2

COPYING STUDENT RESOURCE DISK FILES

In this exercise, you copy files from the original *Student Resource Disk* to a formatted data disk. The instructions in this exercise assume that you are working on a system where you can display the DOS command prompt. If you are working on a system connected to a network or with a customized menu, you may have to follow different procedures. If this is the case, ask your instructor for help.

1. Load DOS so that the command prompt is displayed.
2. Insert your disks as follows:
   - On a system with only one floppy disk drive, insert the original *Student Resource Disk* into drive A.
   - On a system with two floppy disk drives, insert the original *Student Resource Disk* into drive A and the disk you want to copy the files to into drive B.
3. Type **A:** and press Enter↵ to make drive A the default drive.
4. Type **CD\1-2-3** and press Enter↵ to make the directory named 1-2-3 the default directory.
5. Type **COPY *.* B:** and press Enter↵. (If you are working on a system with a single floppy disk, ask your instructor if the DOS XCOPY command is available. If it is, type **XCOPY *.* B:** instead of **COPY *.* B** and you won't have to swap disks as often.)
   - On a system with only one floppy disk drive, you will be periodically prompted to swap disks.
   - On a system with two floppy disk drives, the files are listed as they are copied from one drive to the other.
6. When the command prompt reappears, remove the disks and continue with your work.

EXERCISE 3

IDENTIFYING THE ITEMS ON THE SCREEN

1. Load 1-2-3 so that the worksheet is displayed.
2. Turn the printer on.
3. Press / (the slash key) to display the menu.
4. If your instructor approves (check, because this can cause problems on some systems), press ⇧Shift-PrtScr (or just PrtScr on an enhanced keyboard) to make a printout of the screen display.
5. Using the figure "The 1-2-3 Screen Display" as a guide, identify the items on the printout by circling them and writing a brief description of what they indicate. Graphics characters, like those used in borders, may not print or may print as other characters. If this happens, draw them on your printout or ignore them.

TOPIC 2

Moving Around the Worksheet

The Screen Is a Window onto the Worksheet
The display screen is a window onto a large worksheet in the computer's memory.

After completing this topic, you will be able to:

- Move the cell pointer from cell to cell with the arrow keys
- Move the cell pointer in large jumps with [Home], [End], and the GoTo command

The display screen is just a window that allows you to see a small portion of a large worksheet. You can move around this worksheet with the pointer movement keys or with commands that move you more quickly.

TUTORIAL

In this tutorial, you practice moving the cell pointer around the screen.

NOTE ON DISKS

In this, and all computer activities that follow, you use the data disk to which you copied files from the original *Student Resource Disk* in Exercise 2 of Topic 1.

GETTING STARTED

1. Load 1-2-3 so that the worksheet is displayed.
2. Insert the disk with your data files on it as follows:
   - On a hard disk system, insert the disk into drive A.
   - On a floppy disk system, insert the disk into drive B.
3. Press [/][F][D] (for ***F****ile*, ***D****irectory*), and the prompt reads *Enter current directory:* followed by the name of the current default directory.
4. Specify the new default directory as follows:
   - On a hard disk system, type **A:** and press [Enter←].
   - On a floppy disk system, type **B:** and press [Enter←].
5. Press [/][F][R] (for ***F****ile*, ***R****etrieve*), and the prompt reads *Name of file to retrieve:* followed by a list of files in the default directory.
6. Press [F3] to display all of the files, then highlight *OVERVIEW.WK1*, and press [Enter←]. The model appears on the screen. (If the file isn't listed, you probably did not complete Exercise 2 in Topic 1, where you copied files from the master *Student Resource Disk* to your own data disk.)

The OVERVIEW File on the Screen
When you retrieve the OVERVIEW file, it includes all the changes that you entered and saved in the previous topic.

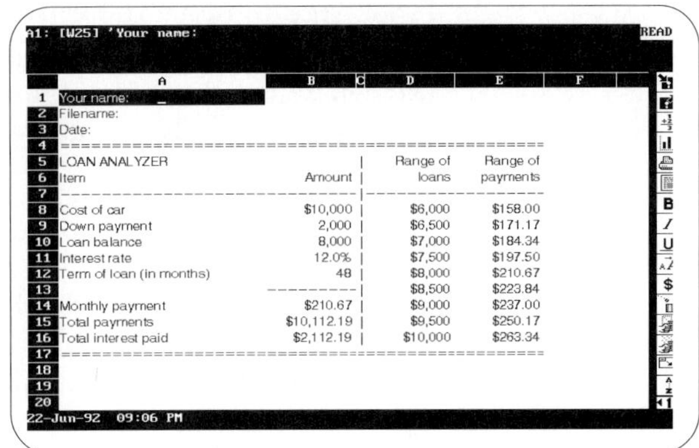

MOVING THE CELL POINTER WITH THE ARROW KEYS

7. Press [Home] to move the cell pointer to cell A1.
8. Hold down [←], and the computer beeps. You cannot move the cell pointer off the worksheet.
9. Hold down [↑], and again the computer beeps.
10. Press [→] once, and the cell pointer moves one cell to the right. The cell address indicator on the first row of the control panel now reads *B1:*, indicating the address of the cell that the cell pointer is positioned in.
11. Press [↓] three times, and the cell pointer moves down one cell at a time until the address indicator reads *B4:*.
12. Hold down [→], and it automatically repeats. When you press [→] with the cell pointer against the right edge of the screen, the screen begins to scroll. The column letters in the border area change when you scroll past the right edge of the screen (although they may not change until you release the key).
13. Hold down [↓] to see what it does.

MOVING THE CELL POINTER WITH THE HOME AND END KEYS

14. Press [Home], and the cell pointer immediately returns to cell A1, the upper-left corner of the worksheet.
15. Press [End], and the *END* indicator is displayed in the lower right-hand corner of the screen.
16. Now press [→], and you jump instantly to the last nonblank cell on the row.
17. Press [End], and the *END* indicator is displayed in the lower right-hand corner of the screen.
18. Now press [→], and you jump instantly to the last column on your worksheet.
19. Now press [End] again, and then press [↓]. The cell pointer moves to the last row in the last column, the lower-right corner of the worksheet. Pressing [End] tells the program to move the cell pointer in the direction of the next key you press until it runs into a boundary. The boundary can be the edge of the worksheet or the boundary between an empty cell and a cell containing data. You will find these key combinations a great help when you navigate large models because they can quickly move you to the end of a row or column of numbers.

20. Press [Home] to move the cell pointer back to cell A1.
21. Press [End], and then press [Home] to move the cell pointer to cell E17, the cell where the last row and column containing data intersect. This command always moves the cell pointer to the lower-right corner of the active area of the worksheet.

MOVING THE CELL POINTER WITH THE PGUP AND PGDN KEYS

22. Press [Home] to return to cell A1.
23. Press [PgDn] a few times to move down a screen at a time.
24. Press [PgUp] a few times to move up a screen at a time.

MOVING THE CELL POINTER WITH THE GOTO COMMAND

25. Press [Home] to return to cell A1.
26. Press [F5] (**GoTo**), and the prompt reads *Enter address to go to:*.
27. Type **B8** and press [Enter←]. The cell pointer immediately jumps to cell B8.

EXPERIMENTING ON YOUR OWN

28. Now experiment with some of the other cell pointer movement keys. (See the tables "Cell Pointer Movement Keys" and "The End Key" in the Quick Reference section.) If you get lost, just press [Home], and the cell pointer will return to cell A1.

FINISHING UP

29. Press [/][W][E] (for ***W****orksheet*, ***E****rase*), and a submenu lists the choices ***N****o* ***Y****es*.
30. Press [Y] (for ***Y****es*) to clear the screen.
31. You have now completed this tutorial. Either continue with the next activity or quit the program. If you quit the program, remove your disks and turn off the computer.

QUICK REFERENCE

When moving the cell pointer around the spreadsheet, you have a number of techniques from which to choose. Your choice should be partly based on how far you have to move. The arrow keys are good for short moves, but the other commands might be better for longer ones.

Moving the Cell Pointer

The four directional arrow keys move the cell pointer a cell at a time and repeat if you hold them down. On some keyboards, these keys are on the numeric keypad, which is also used to enter numbers. When pressing these keys to move the cell pointer, be sure the *NUM* indicator is not displayed on the bottom line of the screen. If it is, pressing the arrow keys on the numeric keypad enters numbers. To turn off the *NUM* indicator, press [NumLock] to disengage the key. (When [NumLock] is engaged, you can move the cell pointer with the arrow keys on the numeric keypad if you hold down [⇧Shift]. [⇧Shift] always reverses the effects of the [NumLock] key as long as you hold [⇧Shift] down.)

As you move the cell pointer down a column or along a row, it eventually runs into one of the boundaries of the screen display. The next time you press the same key, the cell pointer stays against the edge of the screen (it cannot be moved off the screen), but the screen display scrolls to reveal the next row or column of the worksheet. As it does so, the leftmost column or topmost row scrolls off the other side of the screen. You can see this happen if you watch the row and column labels change as you scroll the screen. If the cell pointer runs into one of the boundaries of the worksheet, the computer beeps the next time you press the arrow key that points toward the boundary.

You can move the cell pointer around the worksheet with any of the keys described in the table "Cell Pointer Movement Keys." For example, pressing Home moves the cell pointer to cell A1, the upper-left corner of the worksheet. You can also use the GoTo command to move the cell pointer quickly to a specific cell. Pressing F5 **(GoTo)** displays the prompt *Enter address to go to:*. You then type in the cell address and press Enter↵, and the cell pointer immediately jumps to the specified cell.

CELL POINTER MOVEMENT KEYS

To Move the Cell Pointer	Press
Right or left one column	→ or ←
Up or down one row	↑ or ↓
To cell A1	Home
Right one full screen	Tab⇆ or Ctrl-→
Left one full screen	⇧Shift-Tab⇆ or Ctrl-←
Up or down one full screen	PgUp or PgDn

HOW BIG IS THE 1-2-3 WORKSHEET?

If you have ever used an accountant's ledger pad for financial analysis, you know that even those with only 20 or so columns can be unwieldy. How large would a 1-2-3 worksheet be if it were entirely printed out with each cell 1-inch wide and ¼-inch deep? The size may surprise you. Since 1-2-3 has 256 columns and 8,192 rows for a total of 2,097,152 cells its printout would be 21 feet wide by 171 feet long! Try studying that on the bus to work in the morning.

Scroll Lock

You can engage ScrlLock to keep the cell pointer in the same cell. When you then press the arrow keys, the screen scrolls just as it does when ScrlLock is not engaged, but the cell pointer does not have to be against the edge of the display to make it do so. When the cell pointer reaches the edge of the screen, it stays there, and the worksheet scrolls under it.

The End Key

The **End** key is very useful for moving around the worksheet. Using it in combination with other keys allows you to move the cell pointer to the first or last cell containing data that is preceded or followed by a blank cell. (See the table "The End Key.")

If the worksheet contains data, pressing End and then one of the arrow keys moves the cell pointer to the next data cell in the row or column that is preceded or followed by a blank cell. If the worksheet contains no data in the direction of the arrow key you press, the cell pointer moves to the right boundary of the worksheet.

If the worksheet contains data, press End and then Home to move the cell pointer to the lower-right corner of the working area of the model. If the worksheet contains no data, the cell pointer does not move.

When you press End, the status indicator reads *END* until you press one of the arrow keys or press End again.

THE END KEY

To Move the Cell Pointer to	Press
The lower-right corner of the working area	End, Home
The next data cell on a row preceded or followed by a blank cell or the edge of the worksheet	End and then → or ←
The next data cell in a column preceded or followed by a blank cell or the edge of the worksheet	End and then ↑ or ↓

EXERCISES

EXERCISE 1

IDENTIFYING CELL POINTER MOVEMENT KEYS

Complete the table "Keys That Move the Cell Pointer" by entering the key(s) you would press to move the cell pointer as indicated.

KEYS THAT MOVE THE CELL POINTER

To Move the Cell Pointer	Press
Right one column	______
Left one column	______
Up one row	______
Down one row	______
Right one full screen	______
Left one full screen	______
Up or down one full screen	______
To upper-left corner (cell A1)	______
To lower-right corner of the working area	______
To a specified cell	______

EXERCISE 2

IDENTIFYING END KEY COMBINATIONS

Complete the table "The End Key" by entering the key(s) you would press to move the cell pointer as indicated.

THE END KEY

To Move the Cell Pointer to	Press
The lower-right corner of the working area	End and then ____
The next data cell on a row preceded or followed by a blank cell	End and then ____ or ____
The next data cell in a column preceded or followed by a blank cell	End and then ____ or ____

TOPIC 3

Executing Commands

After completing this topic, you will be able to:

- Execute commands with function keys
- Execute commands with menus
- Explain mode and status indicators

To execute commands, you either make choices from 1-2-3's command menu or press function keys to perform frequently used commands.

TUTORIAL

In this tutorial, you practice executing commands with 1-2-3's command menus and function keys.

GETTING STARTED

1. Load the program so that the worksheet is displayed.

EXPLORING MENUS

2. Press / (the slash key), and the menu appears on the control panel. The mode indicator at the right end of the first line of the control panel reads *MENU.*
3. Press → to move the menu pointer (the highlight) along the list of choices, and watch the descriptions change on the line below.
4. Press Home and End a few times to see how they move the menu pointer to the first and last choices on the menu.
5. Highlight *Worksheet* and press Enter←. A new menu (called a submenu) appears.
6. Press Esc twice to remove the menus from the screen so that the mode indicator reads *READY.*

EXPLORING KEY INDICATORS

7. Press Ins, ScrlLock, CapsLock, and NumLock to see the indicators that are displayed on the bottom line of the screen when these keys are engaged.
8. Press NumLock, ScrlLock, CapsLock, and Ins to turn off the indicators.

	A	B
1	Your name:	
2	Filename:	PROFITS
3	Date:	
4		
5	Sales	1000
6	Costs	600
7	Profit	400

The Profits Model
After completing the model described in this tutorial, your model will look like the one shown here.

COLUMN WIDTHS

The more recent versions of 1-2-3 run in two modes: standard and WYSIWYG (What You See Is What You Get). The number of characters that will fit into a cell vary between these two modes. If any of your labels are not fully displayed, you will see later in this text how to widen the column to fully display them.

CORRECTING MISTAKES

As you enter data, it is displayed on the second line of the control panel along with an edit cursor. If you notice a mistake while entering data, you generally have four choices:

- Press [←Bksp] to delete one or more characters to the left of the edit cursor. The key repeats if you hold it down so that you can delete one character after another.
- Press [Esc] to abandon the entry and start again.
- Press [F2] (**Edit**) to enter edit mode.
- Press [Enter ↵] to complete the entry, and then reenter it correctly.

ENTERING DATA

9. Press [Home] to move the cell pointer to cell A1 so that you can follow the steps below to enter the model shown in the figure "The Profits Model." If you make any typos while entering this model, see the box "Correcting Mistakes."
10. Type **Your name:** and the characters appear on the second line of the control panel and the mode indicator in the upper-right corner reads *LABEL* because you are entering letters.
11. Press [Enter ↵] to enter the characters into the cell, and the first line of the control panel now reads *A1: 'Your name:*. This indicates that the cell pointer is positioned in column A on row 1 and that the cell contains the indicated label. The apostrophe preceding the label is a label alignment character added automatically by the program.
12. Press [→] to move the cell pointer to cell B1, type your last name, and press [Enter ↵].
13. Move the cell pointer to cell A2, type **Filename:** and press [Enter ↵].
14. Press [→] to move the cell pointer to cell B2, type **PROFITS** and press [Enter ↵].
15. Move the cell pointer to cell A3, type **Date:** and press [Enter ↵].
16. Press [→] to move the cell pointer to cell B3.
17. Press ['] to tell 1-2-3 you are entering a label that begins with a number, then type today's date in numbers, using the format month/day/year, and press [Enter ↵].
18. Move the cell pointer to cell A5, type **Sales** and press [Enter ↵].
19. Press [→] to move the cell pointer to cell B5, and type **1000**. The characters appear on the second line of the control panel, and the mode indicator reads *VALUE* because you are entering a number.
20. Press [Enter ↵] to enter the number into the cell, and the first line of the control panel now reads *B5: 1000.*
21. Move the cell pointer to cell A6, type **Costs** and press [→] to move the cell pointer to cell B6.
22. Type **600** and press [Enter ↵].
23. Move the cell pointer to cell A7, type **Profit** and press [→] to move the cell pointer to cell B7.
24. Type **+B5-B6** and press [Enter ↵]. The formula calculates 400 (1000 in cell B5 minus 600 in cell B6). Your screen should now look like the model shown in the figure "The Profits Model."

SAVING THE MODEL

25. Insert your data disk as follows:
    - On a hard disk system, insert it into drive A.
    - On a floppy disk system, insert it into drive B.
26. Press [/][F][D] (for ***F**ile*, ***D**irectory*), and the prompt reads *Enter current directory:* followed by the name of the current default directory.
27. Specify the new default directory as follows:
    - On a hard disk system, type **A:** and press [Enter ↵].
    - On a floppy disk system, type **B:** and press [Enter ↵].
28. Press [/][F][S] (for ***F**ile*, ***S**ave*), and the prompt reads *Enter name of file to save:*.

29. Type **PROFITS** and press [Enter←].

PRINTING THE MODEL

30. Press [/][P][P][R] (for ***P**rint*, ***P**rinter*, ***R**ange*), and the prompt reads *Enter print range:*.
31. Type **A1.B7** and press [Enter←].
32. Press [A][G] (for ***A**lign*, ***G**o*) to print the model.
33. When the Print menu reappears, press [P][Q] (for ***P**age*, ***Q**uit*) to advance the paper out of the printer and leave the Print menu.

USING A MENU COMMAND TO ERASE DATA

34. Press [Home] to move the cell pointer to cell A1.
35. Press [/] to display the command menu.
36. Press [R] (for ***R**ange*) to display a submenu.
37. Press [→] to move the menu pointer over the *Erase* choice, and press [Enter←]. The prompt reads *Enter range to erase: A1..A1*.
38. Press [→] to expand the cell pointer to column B, and the prompt reads *Enter range to erase: A1..B1*.
39. Press [↓] to move the cell pointer to row 3, and the prompt reads *Enter range to erase: A1..B3*.
40. Press [Enter←] to erase the highlighted range.

CLEARING THE SCREEN WITHOUT SAVING THE FILE

41. To erase the model from the screen, press [/][W][E] (for ***W**orksheet*, ***E**rase*), and a submenu lists the choices ***N**o* ***Y**es*.
42. Press [Y] (for ***Y**es*). On newer versions of 1-2-3, the computer will beep and display the message *WORKSHEET CHANGES NOT SAVED! Erase worksheet anyway?*. If this prompt appears, press [Y] to erase the worksheet.

EXPLORING HELP

43. Press [F1] to display the help index. The help screen varies from release to release. Follow the on-screen directions.
44. Press the arrow keys to move the menu pointer (the highlight) around topics in the index.
45. Highlight *About Help* or *About 1-2-3 Help* by pressing the arrow keys, and press [Enter←] to display help on that topic.
46. After reading about 1-2-3's help system, press [F1] or highlight *Help Index* and press [Enter←] to return to the help index.
47. Continue exploring help as follows until you are comfortable with the help system:
    - Press the arrow keys, [Home], or [End] to highlight any keyword, and press [Enter←] to select it.
    - Press [←Bksp] to back up through help screens.
    - Press [F1] or Highlight *Help Index* and press [Enter←] to return to the help index screen.
48. Press [Esc] to return to the worksheet.

EXPLORING HELP ON A COMMAND IN PROGRESS

49. Press [/][F] (for ***File***) to display the File submenu, and the ***R**etrieve* command is highlighted.
50. Press [F1] to display help on the ***R**etrieve* command.
51. Press [Esc] to return to the File menu.
52. Press [Esc] twice more to return to ready mode.
53. Continue experimenting with the Help commands until you feel comfortable using the system.

FINISHING UP

54. You have now completed this tutorial. Either clear the edit screen and continue with the next activity or quit the program.

QUICK REFERENCE

When executing commands, you use function keys or menus, and help is available at all times.

Help Whenever You Need It

1-2-3 contains extensive built-in help facilities that you can display at any time by pressing [F1] (**Help**). The help screens are context sensitive, so the help displayed may be directly related to what you are trying to do at the moment. For example, if you have begun the sequence of commands to save a file and cannot remember how to complete the sequence, pressing [F1] displays help on saving files. Each help screen lists additional help topics. You select a topic by using the arrow keys to move the menu pointer over it and pressing [Enter ↵]. When you have finished with help, press [Esc] to return to where you were in your procedure before you asked for help. If you are using a mouse, releases 2.3 and 2.4 allow you to display help by clicking on a question mark displayed on the screen.

Help
When you press [F1], help is displayed. The help screens vary slightly from release to release. This illustration shows Release 2.4.

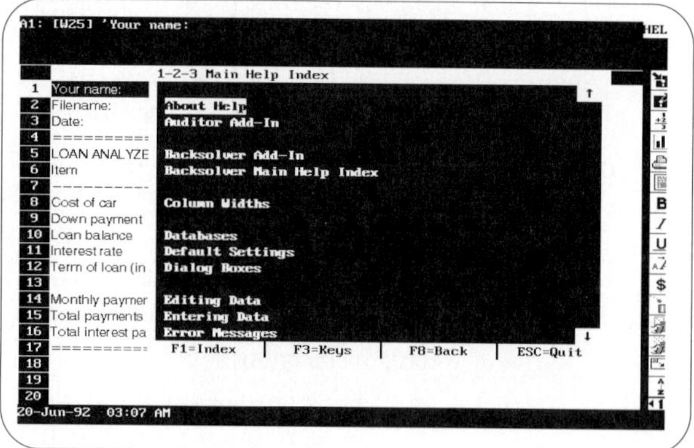

If 1-2-3 encounters any errors, the computer beeps and displays an error message. To find the cause of the error, press [F1] (**Help**). You must then press [Esc] or [Enter ↵] before you can enter any further commands or data.

On a floppy disk system, help is available on all the Lotus 1-2-3 disks. To get help on the appropriate topic, the correct disk must be in drive

A. For example, for help on worksheet commands, the System disk must be in drive A. For help on printing graphs, the PrintGraph disk must be in drive A.

Using 1-2-3's Command Menus

To execute many commands, you use 1-2-3's command menus with the keys described in the table "Keys Used with Menu Commands." To begin, you press [/] (the slash key) to display the menu at the top of the screen. One choice listed on the menu is always highlighted. A brief description of the highlighted choice or the commands on its submenu is displayed on the line below the menu. You can make choices from the menu in one of two ways:

- You can type the first letter in the menu choice's name.
- You can press [→] or [←] to move the highlight, called a *menu pointer*, over your choice, and press [Enter←]. If you position the menu pointer over the first or last choice on the menu and press the arrow key again, the menu pointer wraps around to the other end of the menu. You can quickly move to the first or last menu choice by pressing [Home] or [End].

Most menus have more than one level. Choosing a command listed on a menu may just display another menu on the screen. Getting to the actual command you want to execute occasionally means you must select a series of commands from the displayed submenus.

Menus and Submenus
Multilevel menus frequently display a submenu when you make a menu choice. For example,

A When you press [/], the command menu is displayed in the control panel.
B When you press [F] (for ***F****ile*), the File submenu is displayed.
C When press [S] (for ***S****ave*), a prompt asks you to enter the name of the file.

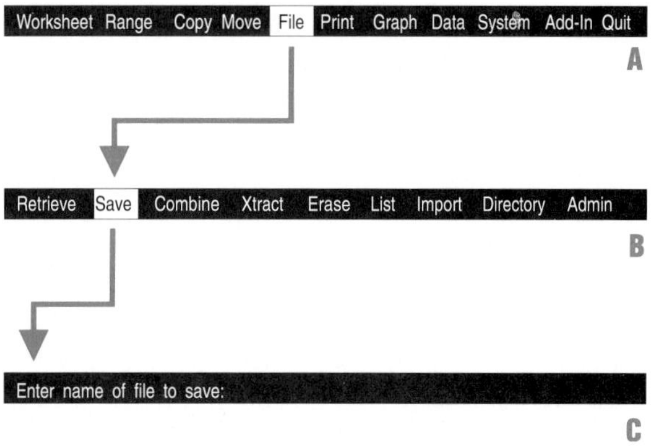

Often, the menu disappears when you complete a command, and you are returned to where you were before you began executing the command. But in some cases, you must select ***Q****uit* from the menu or press [Esc] to remove the menu. These sticky menus stay on the screen, anticipating that you will want to use more than one of the listed choices.

Release 2.2 and later versions have screen displays called *settings sheets* for many commands like those used to print models or create graphs. These settings sheets are simply listings of the current settings that are related to the command in progress. For example, the print settings sheet lists all the settings that affect the way the model will print out. When one of these settings sheets is displayed, you can press [F6] **(Window)** to turn it off. It will remain off until you press [F6] **(Window)** again or return to ready mode and then repeat the command.

Settings Sheets
Release 2.2 and later versions have settings sheets that give you a listing of related commands. For example, when you press / P P (for *Print, Printer*) to print a model, all the current print settings are displayed on the screen. This illustration shows Release 2.4; earlier versions look different.

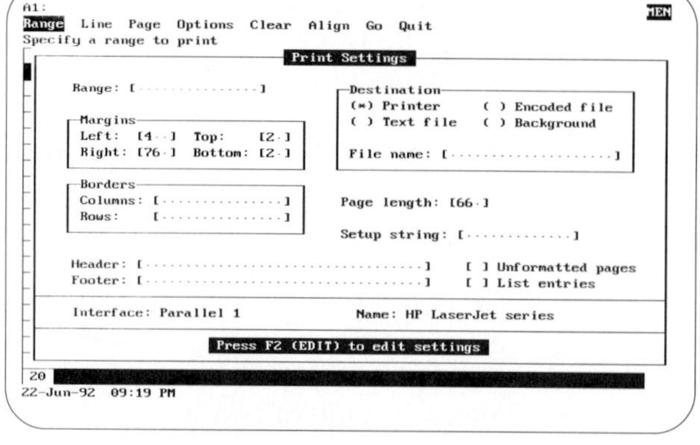

KEYS USED WITH MENU COMMANDS

Key	Function
/	Displays the 1-2-3 command menu
Arrow key	Moves the menu pointer along the menu
Home	Moves the menu pointer to the first selection on the menu
End	Moves the menu pointer to the last selection on the menu
Esc	Backs up though previous menu selections one menu level at a time
Ctrl-Break	Cancels a command in progress and returns the worksheet to ready mode
Enter ↵	Selects the choice highlighted by the menu pointer

Saves a file to the disk

Retrieves a file from the disk

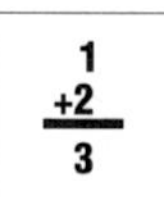
Sums the highlighted range

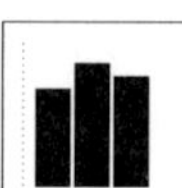
Graphs the highlighted data

Boldfaces the highlighted range

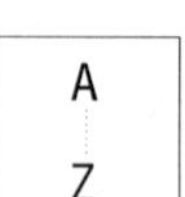
Sorts the highlighted data

Typical SmartIcons
Some of Release 2.4's SmartIcons are shown here along with a brief description of their functions.

Using 1-2-3's SmartIcons

Release 2.4 has icons, called SmartIcons, that provide one-step access to many procedures. An icon is simply a picture, or a graphic representation, of a procedure. For example, after highlighting a range of cells, you can click on the Bold icon, a letter B, to turn boldfacing on or off for the range of cells.

You can pick and choose from any of the 70 SmartIcons included with the program and add them to a palette for easy access. To see a description of any icon, you point to it with a mouse pointer and hold down the right button. To scroll through the available icons, click on the left or right arrow head in the lower right corner or the screen. The number between the arrowheads indicates which set of SmartIcons is currently displayed.

The figure "Typical SmartIcons" illustrates and describes some of the icons included with the program.

Canceling Commands

As you work your way through the menus and submenus, you may find you are on the wrong branch or decide not to continue for some other reason.

- Press Ctrl-Break to return to ready mode.
- Press Esc to retrace your previous choices, a command at a time, to back out of the menu. Sometimes you want to retrace your steps only part way so that you can continue the command down a different branch of the tree.

Answering Prompts

Prompts are questions (displayed on the control panel) that the program wants you to answer. For example, when you press / F S (for

> **1-2-3 RELEASE 2.01 AND 2.2 AND LATER VERSIONS**
>
> Release 2.2 added a number of commands to the menus. To make these new commands fit, some of the names on the old menus were shortened. For example, the *Scientific* format on the Release 2.01 menu was shortened to *Sci* in the Release 2.2. And the *Protect* and *Unprotect* names were shortened to *Prot* and *Unprot*. Some prompts were also revised. For example, when you save a file, the prompt reads *Enter save file name:* on Release 2.01 and *Enter name of file to save:* on Release 2.2 and later versions.
>
> These differences are minor, so you should be able to work with either release without any problems. This text uses the menu names and prompts shown in Releases 2.3 and 2.4.

File, ***Save***) to save a file, the prompt reads *Enter save file name:* (Release 2.01) or *Enter name of file to save:* (Release 2.2 and later versions). Generally, there are three ways to respond to prompts:

- You can type your response. To save a file named BUDGET, you would type **BUDGET**. You can type responses to prompts in any combination of uppercase or lowercase letters. If you make any typos while typing an answer, press [←Bksp] to delete them a character at a time, or press [Esc] to delete the entire response, and then type the answer correctly. When the response is complete and correct, press [Enter↵] to enter it.
- You can make a choice from a menu. For example, when you use the ***/File Retrieve*** command, a list of all the files in the current directory is displayed. You move the menu pointer over the filename you want to retrieve and press [Enter↵].
- You can press [Enter↵] to accept the default response. A default response either is entered by the program's designer or is remembered by the program as your previous response to the same prompt. If the program displays a default response, you can type over it to enter a new response, or you can press [Esc] to clear it and then type your new response.

Critical commands, like those that erase a file you are working on or that save files on top of earlier versions, generally prompt you to confirm them so that you do not inadvertently make a mistake. For example, when you save a file for the second time, 1-2-3 displays a menu that includes commands to ***Cancel*** or ***Replace***. If you select ***Cancel***, you return to where you were before you began the command. If you select ***Replace***, the file is saved, and the previous version is erased.

Mode Indicators

1-2-3 can perform only one task at a time. It can be accepting a new label you are typing, but it cannot also be recalculating, printing, or saving a file. For this reason, the current mode is displayed so that you know what the program is doing or what information it is ready to accept. The mode indicator in the upper-right corner of the screen displays *READY* when you first load the program. In ready mode, the program is in "neutral" awaiting your instructions, and you can move the cell pointer around the worksheet. The mode then changes automatically as you perform various tasks. For instance, when you press [/] to display the menu, the mode indicator reads *MENU*. The table "Mode Indicators" lists many of 1-2-3's mode indicators.

MODE INDICATORS

Indicator	Description
EDIT	Displayed when you press [F2] (**Edit**) to edit the contents of a cell.
ERROR	Displayed when the program detects an error. To obtain help on the cause of the error, press [F1] (**Help**). To remove the indicator and continue, press [Esc] or [Enter↵].
FILES	Displayed whenever a list of files is being displayed.
FIND	Displayed when you use the ***/Data Query Find*** command.
HELP	Displayed when you press [F1] (**Help**).
LABEL	Displayed when entering a label.

MODE INDICATORS (*CONTINUED*)

MENU	Displayed when you press [/] (the slash key) to display the menu.
NAMES	Displayed whenever a list of range names is being displayed.
POINT	Displayed when moving the cell pointer during a command to point to a range and when you press [F5] (**GoTo**).
READY	Displayed when no commands are in progress.
STAT	Displayed when the worksheet's status is being displayed (see **MEM** in the table "Status Indicators").
VALUE	Displayed when entering a number, formula, or function.
WAIT	Displayed when the program is calculating, printing, or otherwise engaged internally. Wait for the *READY* indicator before typing.

Status Indicators

Like mode indicators, status indicators provide information about the program's current status. These indicators are displayed at the bottom of the screen and are described in the table "Status Indicators".

STATUS INDICATORS

Indicator	Description
CALC	Indicates that the worksheet must be recalculated to display the correct result.
CAPS	Displayed when [CapsLock] is engaged.
CIRC	Indicates that the model contains a circular reference.
CMD	Indicates the program is running a macro.
END	Displayed when [End] has been pressed.
LEARN	(Releases 2.2 and later) indicates that learn mode is turned on so that keystrokes are being recorded.
MEM	(Releases 2.2 and later) displayed when fewer than 4,096 bytes of internal memory remain for your model. To see how much memory remains, press [/][W][S] (for ***W**orksheet*, ***S**tatus*), and press any key to return to the worksheet.
NUM	Displayed when [NumLock] is engaged.
OVR	Displayed when [Ins] is engaged to put the program into overtype mode.
RO	(Releases 2.2 and later) displayed when you are using 1-2-3 on a network and do not have a reservation for the file on the screen. The file is read-only, and you cannot save your changes.
SCROLL	Displayed when [ScrlLock] is engaged.
SST	Indicates that a macro is being executed in step mode.
STEP	Indicates that step mode has been turned on.
UNDO	(Releases 2.2 and later) indicates that you can press [Alt]-[F4] (**Undo**) to undo your last procedure.

Undoing Mistakes

Release 2.2 and later versions have an Undo command that allows you to undo changes that you make to a worksheet. When you execute a command, you begin with the program in ready mode. When you complete the command, the program returns to that mode. The Undo command ([Alt]-[F4]) reverses any changes that you made since the program was last in the ready mode. If you change your mind after undoing a change, you can restore the worksheet by pressing Alt-F4 again. Each time you press it, you switch between the two versions of the worksheet: the one before the change and the one after it.

The Undo command works whenever the *UNDO* indicator is displayed on the bottom line of the screen. If this indicator is not displayed, the Undo command will have no effect.

Undo is normally on, but you can turn it off and back on again whenever you want. The undo feature stores a second copy of your worksheet in memory when it is on. To do so, it creates a buffer that saves more than half the computer's available memory for this second copy. This can greatly reduce the amount of memory for the models that you create. For this reason, you may want to turn the undo feature off if you begin to run out of memory.

KEY/Strokes

Turning the Undo Feature On or Off

1. Press /WGDOU (for ***W**orksheet, **G**lobal, **D**efault, **O**ther, **U**ndo*).
2. Either: Press E (for ***E**nable*) to turn undo on.
   Or: Press D (for ***D**isable*) to turn undo off.
3. Press Q (for ***Q**uit*) to return to the worksheet.

EXERCISES

EXERCISE 1

CHECKING A WORKSHEET'S DEFAULT SETTINGS

When working with 1-2-3, there are many settings that you can change to customize the program so that it better meets your needs. When the changes you make affect the entire worksheet, they are called global settings. At any point, you can check these global settings with the ***/W**orksheet **S**tatus* command. (On Release 2.4, you also use the ***/W**orksheet **G**lobal* and ***/W**orksheet **G**lobal **D**efault **S**tatus* commands.) These commands display the current global settings for recalculation, format, label prefix, column width, protection, and so on. Use the ***/W**orksheet **S**tatus* command to see how much memory is available. This is helpful when working on large models.

EXERCISE 2

EXPLORING HELP

Press F1 to display the help menu. Work your way through the index and various screens until you are familiar with the entire help system. As you use the system, read the help keys and other instructions that guide you through the screens.

TOPIC 4

Saving and Retrieving Files & Clearing the Screen

After completing this topic, you will be able to:

- Save and retrieve files
- Clear the screen
- Change the default drive

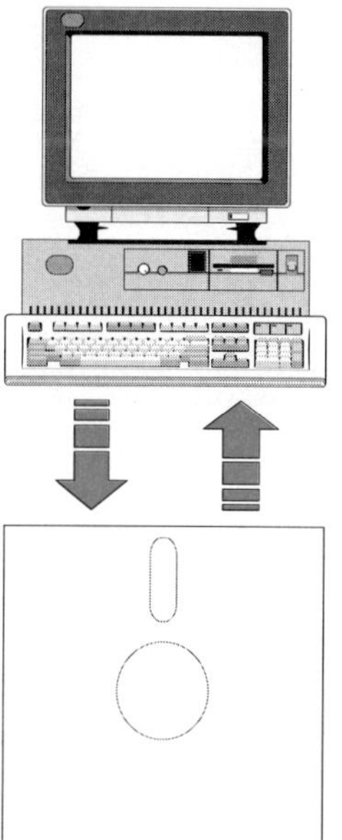

Saving and Retrieving Files
Saving a model copies it from the computer's memory into a file on the disk. Retrieving it copies it from the disk into the computer's memory.

Before you can create a new model, you must display a blank screen. This happens automatically when you load the program. However, if you are already working on a model and want to create a new one, you first clear the current model from the screen. Before doing so, you save the file if you think you may need it again. If you want to work on an existing model, you retrieve it onto the screen from the disk on which it is stored in a file. When saving and retrieving files, you have to understand how to specify the drives and directories that you save files to and retrieve them from.

When creating models, you should save them often, not just when you finish them. If you turn off the computer, experience a power failure, encounter hardware problems, or make a mistake, you may lose files that are in the computer's memory. Your files are not safe from these disasters until you save them onto a disk—a more permanent form of storage. When preparing a model, you should always save your file:

- Before experimenting with unfamiliar commands
- Before making major revisions, like inserting or deleting rows and columns
- Before printing (in case something goes wrong during the process)
- After specifying ranges, changing formats, creating graphs, or changing other settings that are remembered only when the model is saved
- Before quitting the program

TUTORIAL

In this tutorial, you create a small model and then explore 1-2-3's ***/Save*** and ***/Retrieve*** commands and learn how to clear the screen when you want to work on a new model.

GETTING STARTED

1. Load the program so that the worksheet is displayed.

CHANGING THE GLOBAL COLUMN WIDTH

2. Press /WGC (for **W***orksheet*, **G***lobal*, **C***olumn-Width*), and the prompt reads *Enter global column width (1..240): 9.*
3. Type **17** and press Enter ←.

ENTERING A HEADING

4. Press Home to move the cell pointer to cell A1 so that you can begin entering the data shown in the figure "The Heading."
5. Type **Your name:** and press → to move the cell pointer to cell B1.
6. Type your name and press Enter ←.
7. Move the cell pointer to cell A2, type **Filename:** and press → to move the cell pointer to cell B2.
8. Type **AUTOLOAN** and press Enter ←.
9. Move the cell pointer to cell A3, type **Date:** and press → to move the cell pointer to cell B3.
10. Type **@NOW** and press Enter ←.
11. Press /RFD (for **R***ange*, **F***ormat*, **D***ate*) to display a menu of date formats.
12. Press 1 (for ***1*** *(DD-MMM-YY)*), and the prompt reads *Enter range to format: B3..B3.*
13. Press Enter ← to format the suggested range, and your model should look like the one shown in the figure "The Heading."

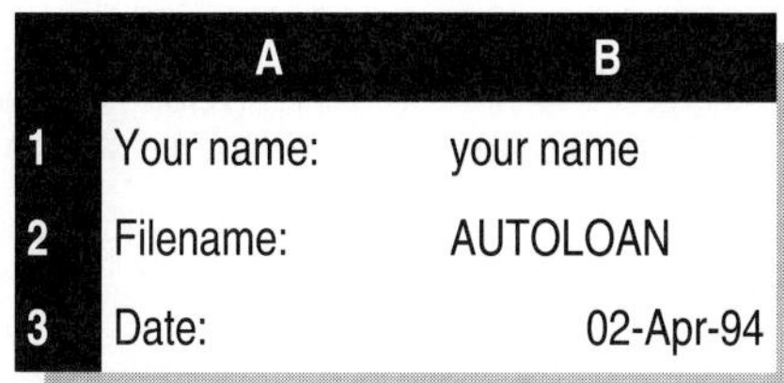

	A	B
1	Your name:	your name
2	Filename:	AUTOLOAN
3	Date:	02-Apr-94

The Heading
After you enter the heading described in this tutorial, it should look like this, although your name and the date will be different.

CREATING A MODEL

14. Enter the labels shown in column A on rows 5 through 8 of the figure "The Auto Loan Model."
15. Enter the numbers shown in column B on rows 5 through 7 of the figure "The Auto Loan Model."
16. With the cell pointer in cell B8 type **@PMT(B5,B6/12,B7)** and press Enter ←. Your model should now look like the one in the figure "The Auto Loan Model."

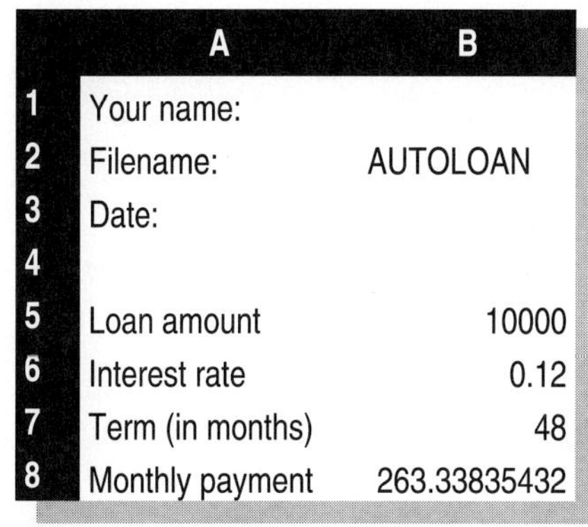

	A	B
1	Your name:	
2	Filename:	AUTOLOAN
3	Date:	
4		
5	Loan amount	10000
6	Interest rate	0.12
7	Term (in months)	48
8	Monthly payment	263.33835432

The Auto Loan Model
After completing the auto loan model described in this tutorial, it should look like this.

SAVING THE FILE

17. Insert your data disk as follows:
    - On a hard disk system, insert the disk into drive A.
    - On a floppy disk system, insert the disk into drive B.
18. Press /FD (for **F***ile*, **D***irectory*), and the prompt reads *Enter current directory:.*
19. Enter the default directory as follows:
    - On a hard disk system, type **A:** and then press Enter ←.
    - On a floppy disk system, type **B:** and then press Enter ←.
20. Press /FS (for **F***ile*, **S***ave*), and the prompt reads *Enter name of file to save:.*
21. Type **AUTOLOAN** and press Enter ← to save the model on the disk.

SAVING THE FILE AGAIN

22. Press /FS (for ***F**ile*, ***S**ave*), and the prompt reads *Enter name of file to save: AUTOLOAN.wk1*. (The filename is preceded by the drive you specified in Step 19.)
23. Press Enter to accept the suggested name, and a submenu lists the choices ***C**ancel* ***R**eplace* (and ***B**ackup* on Releases 2.2 and later).
24. Press R (for ***R**eplace*), and the disk drive spins as the model is saved on the disk again.

CLEARING THE SCREEN

25. Press /WE (for ***W**orksheet*, ***E**rase*), and a submenu lists the choices ***N**o* ***Y**es*.
26. Press Y (for ***Y**es*) to clear the screen.

RETRIEVING THE FILE

27. Press /FR (for ***F**ile*, ***R**etrieve*), and the prompt reads *Name of file to retrieve:*, and a list of files in the current directory is displayed.
28. Press F3 to display a screenful of filenames.
29. Highlight *AUTOLOAN.WK1* and press Enter.

FINISHING UP

30. To clear the screen, press /WE (for ***W**orksheet*, ***E**rase*), and a submenu lists the choices ***N**o* ***Y**es*.
31. Press Y (for ***Y**es*).
32. You have now completed this tutorial. Either continue with the next activity or quit the program.

QUICK REFERENCE

To create and work with spreadsheet files, you need to know how to save and retrieve them as well as clear the screen. You also need to know how to direct the files that you save to the correct drive or directory.

Filenames
Files can have a name of up to eight characters and a three-character extension separated from the name by a period. Lotus 1-2-3 adds the appropriate extension when you save a file.

Saving Files

When you save a file the first time, you must assign it a filename that follows DOS conventions. Filenames can have up to eight characters and are followed by a period and three-character extension automatically assigned by 1-2-3. The figure "Filename Characters" lists the characters that you can use in filenames.

The extension that 1-2-3 adds to your filenames identifies the type of file that it is. The table "1-2-3 Filename Extensions" lists and describes the extensions 1-2-3 uses. You can add your own extension to filenames, but they are not then automatically displayed when you use **/*F**ile* commands.

Releases 2.2 and later have the ability to save backup copies of your models. When you save a file a second or subsequent time, the submenu on Release 2.01 asks if you want to cancel the command or replace the existing file. On Releases 2.2 and later, the submenu also lists the option to back up the file. If you choose this option, the

Character	Example
Letters	A - Z
Letters	a - z
Numbers	0 - 9
Underscore	_
Caret	^
Dollar sign	$
Tilde	~
Exclamation point	!
Number sign	#
Percent sign	%
Ampersand	&
Hyphen	-
Braces	{ }
Parentheses	( )
At sign	@
Grave accent	`
Apostrophe	'

Filename Characters
You can use any of the characters shown here in your file names and extensions.

filename's extension of the current version on the disk is changed to .BAK, and the new version is saved with the same filename and the .WK1 extension.

→ KEY/Strokes

Saving a File

1. Press [/] [F] [S] (for ***F**ile*, ***S**ave*), and the prompt reads *Enter name of file to save:*.
2. Specify the file's name.
   - If no name has been specified for the file, type the name and press [Enter←].
   - If the file was saved previously and you want to use the same name, press [Enter←].
   - To change the file's name, type the new name and press [Enter←]. The first character that you type deletes the previous name.
   - To save the file on another disk or in another directory, press [Esc] one or more times to clear the current path, type a new path and filename, and press [Enter←].
3. If a file by the same name is on the disk:
   - You can select ***C**ancel* or ***R**eplace*.
   - If you are using Release 2.2 or a later version, you can select ***B**ackup*.

1-2-3 FILENAME EXTENSIONS

Extension	Description
.WK1	Worksheets saved using Releases 2.0 and later
.PRN	Print files
.PIC	Graph files
.BAK	Backup copies (Releases 2.2 and later)

Retrieving Files

After you have saved a model into a file on the disk, you can retrieve it with the **/*F**ile **R**etrieve* command. When you do so, the retrieved file erases any file currently on the screen. If you have not saved changes to the worksheet, later releases will display a message that the changes haven't been saved so that you can cancel the command. Releases prior to 2.3 do not have this feature, so be sure to save the file on the screen before retrieving a file from the disk unless you want to lose it. To retrieve a file, it must be on a disk in one of the drives.

- If you are working on a floppy disk system, insert the disk the file was saved on into the disk drive.
- If the file is not stored on the current default drive and directory, specify the drive and directory it is stored in. (See the section "Specifying Drives and Directories" on page 30.)

To retrieve the file, you then execute the **/*F**ile **R**etrieve* command. This displays the prompt *Name of file to retrieve:* and a list of files. (You can press [F3] (**Name**) to display a complete list of the files in the current directory.) The prompt is followed by the path and the filename specification **.wk?*, which displays only those files whose extension begins with the letters WK followed by any third character.

- To change the filename specification, press [Esc] and type in a new specification. For example, to list all files, type ***.***.
- To change the path and filename specification, press [Esc] twice, enter a new path and filename specification, and press [Enter←]. For example, to display all the files on drive A, type **A:*.*** and press [Enter←].

When the file is retrieved, the computer copies the file from the disk into the computer's memory and displays it on the screen. The copy of the file on the disk remains unchanged until you change the file in memory and then save it back onto the disk, at which time it overwrites the old file.

TIP

You can retrieve a file when you load the program. To do so, type **123 -wFILENAME** (where *FILENAME* is the name of the file). Leave no spaces between the w and the filename.

KEY/Strokes

Retrieving a File

1. Press [/] [F] [R] (for ***F****ile*, ***R****etrieve*), and the prompt reads *Name of file to retrieve:*.
2. Press [→] to highlight the name of the file (you can press [F3] (**Name**) to display a screenful of filenames), and press [Enter ↵].

Clearing the Screen

To clear the screen, you use the ***/W****orksheet* ***E****rase* command to erase all data on the worksheet from the screen and the computer's memory. Before using this command, be sure you have saved the file with the ***/ F****ile* ***S****ave* command. If you erase data from the worksheet without first saving it, the data are lost.

KEY/Strokes

Clearing the Screen

1. Press [/] [W] [E] (for ***W****orksheet*, ***E****rase*) to display a submenu.
2. Press [Y] (for ***Y****es*) to clear the screen.

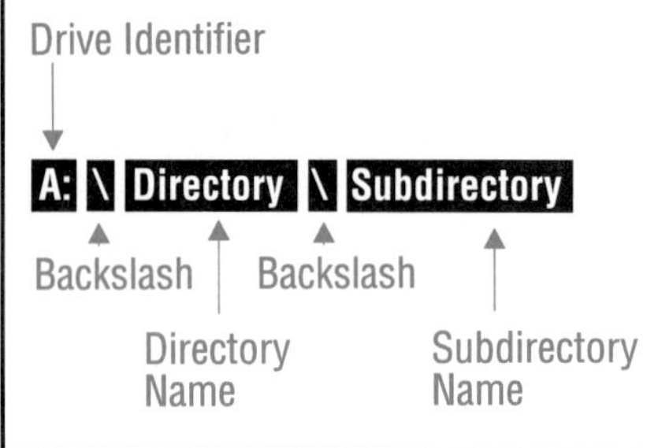

Paths
When you save a file, you can specify a path to save it on a drive or in a directory that is not the current default.

Specifying Drives and Directories

1-2-3 automatically saves files to and retrieves files from the default drive and directory. You can specify another drive and directory in one of two ways:

- You can change the default drive and directory for the current session or for all sessions. This is the easier approach because you then need not specify the path when saving or retrieving files.
- You can specify a path in the ***/S****ave* or ***/R****etrieve* command. When a prompt asks you to enter a filename, you add a drive and directory in front of the filename. For example, to save or retrieve a file named BUDGET to or from a subdirectory named FINANCE on drive C, you type **C:\FINANCE\BUDGET** and press [Enter ↵].

KEY/Strokes

Changing the Default Drive or Directory for a Session

1. Press [/] [F] [D] (for ***F****ile*, ***D****irectory*), and the prompt reads *Enter current directory:*.
2. Type the drive and directory, and press [Enter ↵] to return to the worksheet.

→ KEY/Strokes

Changing the Default Drive or Directory Permanently

1. Press / W G D D (for ***W**orksheet*, ***G**lobal*, ***D**efault*, ***D**irectory*), and the prompt reads *Enter default directory:*.
2. Press Esc to clear the current entry, type the new drive and directory, and press Enter←.
3. Press U (for ***U**pdate*) to save the new setting.
4. Press Q (for ***Q**uit*) to return to the worksheet.

EXERCISES

EXERCISE 1

PRACTICING RETRIEVING FILES

There are a number of files on the original *Student Resource Disk* that you should have copied to your own data disk. You use these files in the tutorials, exercises, and projects in this text. Having them on the disk saves you time—you do not have to type them in.

1. Insert your data disk into one of the drives on your computer.
2. Change the default drive to the drive into which you inserted the disk.
3. Press / F L W (for ***F**ile*, ***L**ist*, ***W**orksheet*) to display a list of files on the disk, and if your instructor approves, press ⇧Shift-PrtScr (or just PrtScr on an enhanced keyboard) to make a printout of the list. If this command causes problems on your system, don't use it.
4. Retrieve three or four of the files listed in the table "Student Resource Disk Files," and check them off as you do so.

STUDENT RESOURCE DISK FILES

Filename	Retrieved
ACCURACY.WK1	
COLUMNS.WK1	
COPYMOVE.WK1	
DOWJONES.WK1	
FORMAT.WK1	
FORMAT2.WK1	
FUNCTION.WK1	
GPA.WK1	
IFFIRE.WK1	
LOGIC1A.WK1	
LOGIC2A.WK1	
LOGIC3.WK1	
MARKET.WK1	
METRIC.WK1	
MYDATES.WK1	
OVERVIEW.WK1	
POWERS.WK1	
PRICING.WK1	
PUBLISH.WK1	
SCHEDULE.WK1	
STAT.WK1	
TEXTBOOK.WK1	
WRONG.WK1	

EXERCISE 2

CHANGING A FILE'S NAME

1. Retrieve the AUTOLOAN file that you saved in the tutorial.
2. Save the file again, but when the prompt reads *Enter name of file to save: AUTOLOAN.WK1*, type **NEWFILE**, and press Enter← to change its name.
3. Retrieve the file using its new name.

TOPIC 5

Printing Models—The Basics

After completing this topic, you will be able to:

- Print part of a model
- Print all of a model

There are times when you need a printed record of a model or want to share your results with others. When it comes time to make a printout, you can print the entire model or only a selected range.

TUTORIAL

In this tutorial, you print first part of and then all of the OVERVIEW model.

GETTING STARTED

1. Retrieve the OVERVIEW model.

PRINTING PART OF THE MODEL

2. Press [/][P][P][R] (for ***P**rint*, ***P**rinter*, ***R**ange*), and the prompt reads *Enter print range:* followed by the address of the cell the cell pointer is in.
3. Move the cell pointer to cell A5.
4. Press the period to anchor the cell pointer, and the prompt reads *Enter print range: A5..A5.*
5. Press [→] to expand the highlight to column B, and the prompt reads *Enter print range: A5..B5.*
6. Press [↓] to expand the highlight to row 16, and the prompt reads *Enter print range: A5..B16.*
7. Press [Enter←] to set the print range and return to the menu.
8. Press [A][G] (for ***A**lign*, ***G**o*) to print the model.
9. When the menu reappears, press [P][Q] (for ***P**age*, ***Q**uit*) to advance the paper out of the printer and leave the Print menu.

PRINTING ALL OF THE MODEL

10. Press [/][P][P][R] (for ***P**rint*, ***P**rinter*, ***R**ange*), and the prompt reads *Enter print range:*, and the previous range you specified is highlighted.
11. Press [Esc] to cancel the previous print range, and the cell pointer moves to cell A5.

12. Press Home to move the cell pointer to cell A1.
13. Press the period to anchor the cell pointer, and the prompt reads *Enter print range: A1..A1.*
14. Press → to expand the highlight to column E, and the prompt reads *Enter print range: A1..E1.*
15. Press ↓ to expand the highlight to row 17, and the prompt reads *Enter print range: A1..E17.*
16. Press Enter ↵ to set the print range and return to the menu.
17. Press A G (for ***A**lign, **G**o*) to print the model.
18. When the menu reappears, press P Q (for ***P**age, **Q**uit*) to advance the paper out of the printer and leave the Print menu.

FINISHING UP

19. Save the model so that you save the print range that you specified.
20. You have now completed this tutorial. Either continue with the next activity or quit the program.

QUICK REFERENCE

To print a model, all you have to specify is the range of cells to be included in the printout.

KEY/Strokes

Printing a File

1. Press / P P (for ***P**rint, **P**rinter*) to display the Print menu. (See the table "Printer Commands.")
2. If you have not specified a range, or if you want to change it, press R (for ***R**ange*), and the prompt reads *Enter print range:*. Specify the range and press Enter ↵.
3. Press A G (for ***A**lign, **G**o*) to begin printing.
4. When the Print menu reappears, press P Q (for ***P**age, **Q**uit*) to advance the paper out of the printer and return to the worksheet.

The Print Settings Sheet
Release 2.2 and later versions have a settings sheet that lists all the current print settings for the current model. (The one shown here is from Release 2.4.) This settings sheet is displayed whenever you press / P P (for *Print, Printer*).

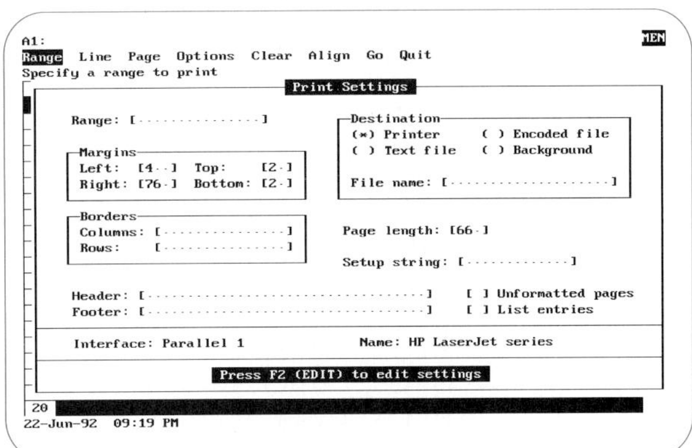

PRINTER COMMANDS

Menu Choice	Description
Range	Specifies the part of the model to be printed.
Line	Advances the paper in the printer one line each time it is selected. If, when selecting this command, the paper reaches the bottom of a page, the paper advances to the top of a new page.
Page	Advances the paper out of the printer and prints a footer at the bottom of the page if you specified one.
Options	Changes the page margins, page length, print font, and several other formats.
Clear	Clears some or all of the print settings previously specified.
Align	Tells the program you have adjusted the paper in the printer, and it is now at the top of the page. When you first load the program, the Align command is executed automatically. If you adjust the paper in the printer after beginning a session, be sure to use the Align command to reset the top of the page.
Go	Starts printing. This command works only if you have specified a range.
Quit	Leaves the Print menu and returns to ready mode.

TIP

If you turn the printer off after pressing Ctrl-Break, the printer's buffer is cleared. After you realign the paper, turn the printer back on, and then use the Align command on the Print menu to tell the program you have reset the top of the page.

Stopping the Printer

To stop the printer while it is printing, hold down Ctrl while you press Break. This stops any further text from being sent to the printer, but the printer may not stop immediately because some printers have buffers that store sections of the text before they are printed. When you press Ctrl-Break, the text stored in the printer's buffer prints, and then the printer stops.

EXERCISE

EXERCISE 1

PRINTING MODELS ON THE STUDENT RESOURCE DISK

In this exercise, you print out master copies of some of your models so that you can use them to compare with later printouts.

1. Using the table "Student Resource Disk Files" in Exercise 1 of Topic 4 as a guide, retrieve one or more of the files and enter your name. Follow the instructions in the KEY/Strokes box "Printing a File" to print each file you retrieve. (Tip: Position the cell pointer in cell A1 when you begin the command. When asked to enter the print range, press the period to anchor the cell pointer, then press End and then Home to highlight the entire model.)
2. After printing each model, save it so that you save the print range that you specified. Also, check the file's name off in the table.
3. Save the printouts so that you can compare them to other versions of the same model as you progress through this text.

CHAPTER 1 REVIEW

- The term *spreadsheet* refers to the program and *worksheet* to the arrangement of rows and columns.
- The term *model* refers to the labels, formulas, and numbers that you enter on the worksheet. The term *template* refers to a model from which numbers have been erased so that you can use it again.
- To load 1-2-3, you type **123** and press Enter←. You can also type **LOTUS** and press Enter← to load the Access System and then select 1-2-3 from the system's menu.
- To quit 1-2-3, you use the ***/Q****uit* command.
- The control panel at the top of the screen displays menus and information about the worksheet.
- The worksheet is divided into rows and columns and is where you enter data into cells.
- Cells are specified by their address—the column and row that intersect to create them. Rows are labeled on the border with numbers and columns are labeled with letters.
- To enter or edit data in the worksheet, you move a bright highlight called the cell pointer from cell to cell.
- To move the cell pointer around the worksheet, you use the arrow keys, PgUp and PgDn, and the **GoTo** (F5) command. To return to cell A1, you press Home.
- The cell in which the cell pointer is positioned is called the active cell. Information about the active cell is always displayed on the first line of the control panel.
- If you press End and then press one of the arrow keys, the cursor moves in the direction of the arrow until it reaches a cell with data next to one without data or the edge of the worksheet.
- Pressing F1 displays context-sensitive help. To return to the worksheet, you press Esc.
- Pressing / displays the command menu. When you make a choice from this menu, submenus are frequently displayed.
- To make a choice from a menu, you can press the first character in the command's name or highlight it with the menu pointer and press Enter←.
- To back up through previous choices you have made while working your way through menus, you press Esc.
- To cancel a command in progress, you press Ctrl-Break.
- Mode indicators in the upper-right corner of the screen, and status indicators on the bottom line, provide you with information about the program's current state.
- To save a file, you use the ***/F****ile* ***S****ave* command.
- To clear the screen so that you can work on a new model, you use the ***/W****orksheet* ***E****rase* command.
- To retrieve a file, you use the ***/F****ile* ***R****etrieve* command. You can then press F3 to display a list of files full screen. When you retrieve a file, any file currently on the screen is removed.

- To change the default drive for a session, you use the ***/File Directory*** command.
- To print a model, you use the ***/Print Printer*** command and then specify a range. You use the ***Align*** command to align the paper in the printer and ***Go*** to begin printing.
- To stop the printer, you press Ctrl-Break.

CHAPTER 1 QUESTIONS

FILL IN THE BLANK

1. To load the 1-2-3 spreadsheet, you type ___________. To load the Access System, you type ___________.
2. When you first load 1-2-3, the program displays a ___________.
3. When you enter labels, formulas, and data into the screen display, you are creating a ___________. If you then delete all of the data and leave only labels and formulas you will have created a ___________.
4. To quit the 1-2-3 program, you type ___________.
5. Cell D12 is at the intersection of row ___________ and column ___________.
6. The bright highlight that you move about the worksheet is called the ___________.
7. The cell in which the bright highlight is positioned is called the ___________ cell. Information about this cell can be found by looking at the ___________.
8. To display help at any point in the program, you press ___________. To then return to the worksheet, you press ___________.
9. To display the command menu, you press ___________.
10. To back up through previously selected menu commands, you press ___________.
11. To cancel a command in progress, you press ___________.
12. To save a file, you press ___________.
13. To change the default drive for a session, you press ___________.
14. To retrieve a file from the disk, you press ___________.
15. To print a file, you press ___________. You must always specify the ___________ to be printed.
16. To stop the printer, you press ___________.
17. To return the cell pointer to cell A1, you press ___________.

MATCH THE COLUMNS

1. Moves the menu pointer to the first selection on the menu.	__ Esc
2. Moves the menu pointer to the last selection on the menu.	__ *WAIT*
	__ *ERROR*

3. Backs up though previous menu selections one menu level at a time.
4. Cancels a command in progress and returns the worksheet to ready mode.
5. Selects the choice highlighted by the menu pointer.
6. Moves the menu pointer along the menu.
7. Displays the 1-2-3 menu.
8. Displays help.
9. Displayed when no commands are in progress.
10. Displayed when you press / (the slash key) to display the Main menu.
11. Displayed when you press **Help** (F1).
12. Displayed when the program detects an error.
13. Displayed when the program is calculating, printing, or otherwise engaged internally.

— /
— Arrow keys
— *READY*
— Ctrl-Break
— Enter ↵
— Home
— End
— *MENU*
— *HELP*
— F1

WRITE OUT THE ANSWERS

1. Describe the difference between a spreadsheet and a model.
2. Describe the difference between a model and a template.
3. What is the purpose of a spreadsheet's functions?
4. How do you change the data in a cell?
5. What is the difference between clearing the screen and quitting the program?
6. 1-2-3 has three lines on the control panel. Briefly describe what each is used for.
7. What is the purpose of the working area?
8. How are cell addresses given? What is the address of a cell in column F and row 30?
9. List three things you can enter into cells, and briefly describe them.
10. List the steps you would follow to load 1-2-3 from a floppy disk drive.
11. List the steps you would follow to load 1-2-3 from a hard disk drive.
12. What happens when you scroll the screen? Can you move the cell pointer off the worksheet? When you scroll the screen, how do you know where you are?
13. What happens when you scroll the screen with ScrlLock engaged?
14. Where does End move the cell pointer on the worksheet when it contains data? When it doesn't contain data?
15. What are modes? Name and briefly describe a few common modes. How do you know what mode the program is in?
16. What key do you press to display help? What does it mean to say help is context sensitive?

17. Do you add an extension to filenames when you save files? Why or why not?
18. When you retrieve a file, what happens to the currently displayed model?
19. What commands do you use to change the default drive and directory for a session? Permanently?
20. When you clear the screen, what happens to the file that is currently displayed?
21. When making a printout, must you print the entire model?
22. How do you stop the printer while it is printing? What is a print buffer?

CHAPTER 1 PROJECTS

PROJECT 1

VIEWING A VIDEO

Many videocassettes about Lotus 1-2-3 are available. Obtain one of these from your school or public library or from a video rental store and watch it. These videos give you an overview of the procedures offered by the program.

PROJECT 2

PREVIEWING AND PRINTING THE PROJECT FILES

There are files on the *Student Resource Disk* that you will use in the end-of-chapter projects in this text. These files should have been copied to your own data disk when you completed Exercise 2 in Topic 1. Retrieve one or more of these files, and make a printout for future reference. Check off their name in the table "Project Files on the Student Resource Disk" as you do so.

PROJECT FILES ON THE STUDENT RESOURCE DISK

Filename	Retrieved
BOXSCORES.WK1	❑
CHARGES.WK1	❑
EXCHANGE.WK1	❑
GRAPHICS.WK1	❑
METRIC.WK1	❑
PUBLISH.WK1	❑

CHAPTER 2

Entering & Editing Data

TOPIC 6

Entering Labels & Numbers

After completing this topic, you will be able to:

- Enter labels and numbers
- Enter repeating labels

You enter data into a worksheet by moving the cell pointer to a cell and typing in the data. Entries are displayed on the second line of the control panel as you type them. You complete the entry by pressing Enter←, which moves the entry from the second line of the control panel to the cell in which the cell pointer is positioned. If the cell already contains an entry, typing a new entry over it and pressing Enter← replaces it.

You can use any of the cell pointer movement keys to complete an entry instead of pressing Enter←. For example, to enter a number into a cell and automatically move down one row, press ↓ instead of Enter← after typing the number. When making several entries along a row or down a column, it is faster to enter data using one of the arrow keys because this enters the data and automatically moves the cell pointer one cell in the direction of the arrow, saving you a keystroke each time.

When you enter data, 1-2-3 distinguishes between labels and values (numbers, formulas, and functions) since it can use values but not labels in most calculations. When you type the first character, the program makes an assumption about which you are entering. For example, 1-2-3 assumes you are entering a value if you type any of the characters listed in the table "Characters That 1-2-3 Assumes Are Values." If you type any other character, the program assumes you are entering a label. You can enter any of the characters listed in the table "Characters That 1-2-3 Assumes Are Values" as a label if you first type a label prefix character such as ', ", or ^. As you will see, label prefixes not only let you enter these characters as labels, they also specify how a label is aligned in a cell.

CHARACTERS THAT 1-2-3 ASSUMES ARE VALUES

Character	Description
0-9	Numbers
+	Positive sign, as in +10+10=20, or cell reference prefix, as in +A1+B2
-	Negation, as in -10+11=1
.	Period used to enter decimals, as in .10
@	Prefix used to enter functions, as in @SUM(A1..A6)
(	Parentheses used to enter formulas, as in (.1*100)+100
$	Currency symbol
#	Pound or number symbol used to enter logical formulas

TUTORIAL

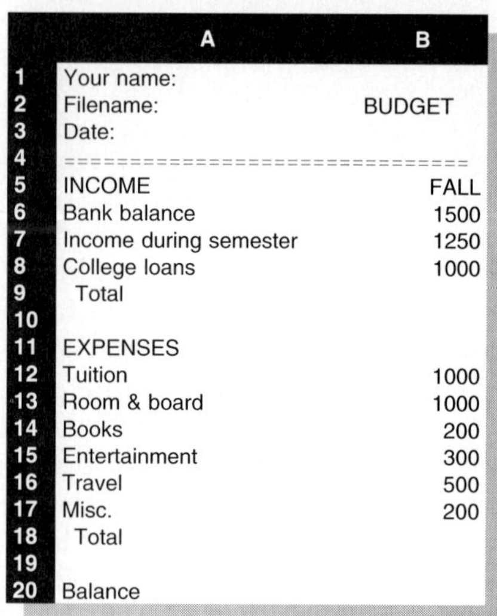

	A	B
1	Your name:	
2	Filename:	BUDGET
3	Date:	
4	================================	
5	INCOME	FALL
6	Bank balance	1500
7	Income during semester	1250
8	College loans	1000
9	Total	
10		
11	EXPENSES	
12	Tuition	1000
13	Room & board	1000
14	Books	200
15	Entertainment	300
16	Travel	500
17	Misc.	200
18	Total	
19		
20	Balance	

The College Budget Model
After you enter the BUDGET model, it should look like this.

In this tutorial, you enter labels and numbers as the first step in preparing a college budget. Your finished model should look like the figure "The College Budget Model." Refer to this figure to check your results as you complete the steps in this tutorial.

GETTING STARTED

1. Load the program or clear the screen.

CHANGING THE WIDTH OF A SINGLE COLUMN

2. Move the cell pointer anywhere in column A.
3. Press [/][W][C][S] (for ***W**orksheet*, ***C**olumn*, ***S**et-Width*), and the prompt reads *Enter column width (1..240): 9.*
4. Type **25** and press [Enter←].

ENTERING A HEADING

5. Enter a heading at the top of your model. To do so, refer to the box "Entering a Heading." Refer to this same box in all subsequent activities where a heading is required.

ENTERING A HEADING

You should enter a heading like the one shown here at the top of all models that you create when completing the activities in this text. To do so, follow these steps whenever you create a new model:

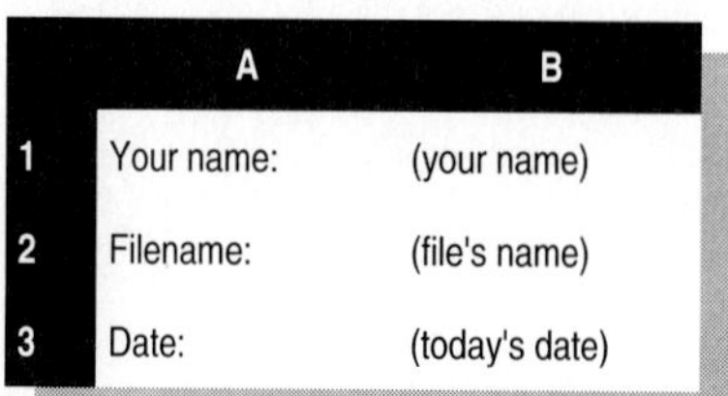

	A	B
1	Your name:	(your name)
2	Filename:	(file's name)
3	Date:	(today's date)

1. Press [Home] to move the cell pointer to cell A1.
2. Type **Your name:** and press [→] to move the cell pointer to cell B1.

3. Type your name and press [Enter←].
4. Move the cell pointer to cell A2, type **Filename:** and press [→] to move the cell pointer to cell B2.
5. Type **BUDGET** (or whatever the name of the current model is) and press [Enter←].
6. Move the cell pointer to cell A3, type **Date:** and press [→] to move the cell pointer to cell B3.
7. Type **@NOW** and press [Enter←].
8. Press [/][R][F][D] (for ***R**ange*, ***F**ormat*, ***D**ate*) to display a menu of date formats.
9. Press [1] (for ***1*** *(DD-MMM-YY)*), and the prompt reads *Enter range to format: B3..B3.*
10. Press [Enter←] to format the suggested range. Asterisks in the cell indicate that the column isn't wide enough to display the formatted date.
11. If necessary, widen columns A and B so that the labels and date are completely displayed. To do so, position the cell pointer in each column, press [/][W][C][S] (for ***W**orksheet*, ***C**olumn*, ***S**et-Width*), and the prompt reads *Enter column width (1..240): 9.* Type the number of characters in your name or **10** (whichever is greater), and press [Enter←].

ENTERING LABELS

6. Enter the labels shown in rows 5 through 20 of column A of the figure "The College Budget Model." To do so, move the cell pointer into the appropriate cell, type the label, and press [Enter←], or even better, press [↓]. Press [Spacebar] twice before entering the Total labels on rows 9 and 18 so that they are indented.

ENTERING REPEATING LABELS

7. With the cell pointer in cell A4, press [\][=], and then press [Enter←].
8. With the cell pointer in cell B4, press [\][=], and then press [Enter←].

ENTERING NUMBERS

9. Enter the label "**FALL** (the " right-aligns the label in the cell) and numbers shown in column B of the figure "The College Budget Model." To do so, move the cell pointer into the appropriate cell, type the label or number, and press [↓] or [Enter←].

PRINTING AND SAVING THE MODEL

10. Save the model as BUDGET.
11. Print the model.
12. Save the model again so that you save the print range that you specified.

FINISHING UP

13. You have now completed this tutorial. Either clear the screen and continue with the next activity or quit the program.

QUICK REFERENCE

LABEL PREFIX CHARACTERS

Character	Effect on Label
'	Left-aligns label in cell (the default)
"	Right-aligns label in cell
^	Centers label in cell

ENTERING LABELS

When entering labels, keep the following points in mind:

- Labels can be as long as 240 characters.
- After typing the first character, the *READY* indicator should change to *LABEL*. If the mode indicator shows *VALUE*, the character you entered is one of those listed in the table "Characters That 1-2-3 Assumes Are Values." If this happens, press Esc to clear the entry, and then reenter it using a label prefix.
- Labels can begin with a number, or any of the characters listed in the table "Characters That 1-2-3 Assumes Are Values," if the first character is a label prefix character.
- Unless you enter a label prefix, the label is aligned with the global setting.
- If a label is longer than its cell is wide, it overflows into the next cell to the right if that cell is empty. If the cell next to it is not empty, only the characters that fit in the cell are displayed. To display the entire label, you can widen the column or erase the contents of the cell to the right.
- If a label flows over into an adjoining column, it won't print completely unless that column is included in the print range.

One of the most basic steps in building models is entering labels and numbers. This is usually a straightforward process, but there are variations and shortcuts that you should be aware of.

Entering Labels

To enter a label, you move the cell pointer to the cell you want to enter it in, type the label, and press Enter↵. This is straightforward with one exception: labels that begin with numbers or certain other characters used in formulas and functions. If the first character you type is one of those shown in the table "Characters That 1-2-3 Assumes Are Values," the program assumes you are entering a value.

To enter a label that begins with a number, for example, 100 Elm Street, you first type a label prefix such as an apostrophe ('). This puts the program into label mode. You then type the label and press Enter↵. Label prefixes do not appear in the cell, but they do appear on the first line of the control panel when the cell pointer is in the cell.

Once a number is entered with a label prefix, it cannot be used in mathematical operations. Be careful when entering text that could also be values. Telephone numbers and ZIP codes, in particular, could cause confusion if entered without a label prefix. For example, if you enter the phone number 555-1212, the last four digits of the number are subtracted from the first thrcc digits, and the result, *-657*, is displayed. No error message results because the program assumes you are entering a formula.

There are three label prefix characters that you can use to enter labels beginning with numbers. You can also use these label prefixes with labels that begin with letters because they also control the alignment of the label in the cell. The table "Label Prefix Characters" describes the three label prefix characters.

→ KEY/Strokes

Entering a Label That Begins with a Value Character

1. Move the cell pointer to where you want to enter a label that begins with a number or one of the characters + - . @ ($ or #.
2. Enter a label prefix character (" to right-align the label, ^ to center the label, or ' to left-align the label).
3. Type the label and press Enter↵.

Entering Numbers

To enter numbers, you move the cell pointer to the desired cell, type the number on either the numeric keypad or the row of number keys, and press Enter↵. When entering numbers, keep the following points in mind:

- When the NumLock key is engaged, you can enter numbers by typing them on the numeric keypad. When NumLock is engaged, the bottom line of the screen displays the *NUM* indicator.

WHAT HAPPENS WHEN YOU PRESS [Enter←]

When you enter data in a cell, the final keystroke is pressing [Enter←] or one of the pointer movement keys. Here is what happens when you press one of these keys:

1. The program checks the entry to see whether it has been typed correctly. If the program finds any errors, the edit cursor moves to where it believes the error is and switches to edit mode. For example, if you type the label **123 Main St.** without a label prefix, and press [Enter←], the computer beeps, and the program changes to edit mode. To enter a label prefix, press [Home], ['], and [Enter←].
2. The program stores the entry into the cell and deletes the previous entry, if any. The entry is no longer displayed on the second line of the control panel but is displayed on the first line when the cell pointer is in the cell.
3. The program recalculates the worksheet to update any formulas so that they display the correct results. Release 2.01 calculates all the cells. Release 2.2 and later versions calculate only those cells that refer directly or indirectly to the changed cells. (This is called minimal recalculation.)
4. The program returns to ready mode.

- To enter numbers with the numeric keypad when [NumLock] is not engaged (*NUM* is not displayed on the screen), hold down [⇧Shift] when you type the numbers.
- After you type the first character, the *READY* indicator should change to *VALUE*. If the mode indicator reads *LABEL*, the character you entered is not one of those listed in the table "Characters That 1-2-3 Assumes Are Values" used to begin a number. If this happens, press [Esc] to clear the entry, and then reenter it correctly.
- Numbers are always right-aligned in their cells.
- You can precede a number with the dollar sign, but it won't be displayed. To display dollar signs, you format the cell with a Currency format.
- Numbers cannot be entered with spaces or commas. For example, enter one thousand dollars as 1000, not 1,000. If you want to format the number, for example, to display dollar signs or commas, use the */**R**ange **F**ormat* and */**W**orksheet **Gl**obal **F**ormat* commands. The format commands can display the number as 1,000, $1,000, or $1,000.00.
- Numbers can have only one decimal.
- To enter a percentage, type the number followed by a percent sign, or type in its decimal equivalent. Either way, you must format the cell as a percentage if you want it displayed with the percent sign. When you enter a percentage as a whole number followed by a percent sign, the program automatically converts it into a decimal by dividing the number by 100. For example, entering a percentage as 10% is the same as entering it as 0.1 or 10/100. If a percentage is less than 50% it may be displayed as 0 if the program is set to a format that rounds numbers off.
- Numbers are always stored in memory with up to 15-digit precision (although only the first 9 digits are displayed on the control panel).

The Label Repeat Command

1-2-3 has a command that lets you repeat a specified character so that it fills the entire width of a cell or row. This command is ideal for entering ruled lines or borders to separate parts of a model. You press [\] (the backslash key) to repeat the next character or characters you type until the cell is full; for example:

- Pressing [\][-] (the hyphen or minus sign) and then pressing [Enter←] fills a cell with a dashed line.
- Pressing [\][=] (the equal sign) and then pressing [Enter←] fills a cell with a double-ruled line.
- Pressing [\][H][-] and then pressing [Enter←] fills a cell with a H-H-H-H-H- border pattern.

You can then copy the ruled line or border to other cells on the row to underline more than one column. The nice thing about repeated labels is that if you change column widths, the labels automatically adjust so that they are always as wide as the columns, no wider or narrower.

KEY/Strokes

Entering a Repeating Label

1. Move the cell pointer to where you want to enter the label.
2. Press [\] (the backslash key).
3. Type one or more characters that you want repeated, and press [Enter←].

EXERCISES

TYPICAL LINE PATTERNS

Ruled Line	Press
————	[\], [-]
========	[\], [=]
H-H-H-H-H	[\], [H], [-]
*************	[\], [*]
....	[\], [.]
________	[\], [_]

EXERCISE 1

ENTERING RULED LINES

1. Clear the screen if it contains any data.
2. Enter the three-line heading. (See the box "Entering a Heading.")
3. Beginning on row 5 in column A, enter samples of the ruled lines shown and described in the table "Typical Line Patterns." Press [Enter←] to enter the ruled line in thc cell after pressing the keys shown in the table.
4. Save the finished model as RULES.
5. Make a printout, and then save the file again so that you save the print settings.

EXERCISE 2

ENTERING LABELS AND NUMBERS IN THE DOW JONES AVERAGES MODEL

The Dow Jones Industrial Average is based on the performance of 30 major industrial stocks. Here you begin expanding a model that helps you understand how this average is calculated and updated.

1. Retrieve the DOWJONES model, and enter your name in cell B1.
2. Enter the labels and numbers of each of the stocks shown on rows 31 through 35 in the figure "The Dow Jones Average Model." Use the label prefix character ^ to center each label in column E.
3. Save the finished model as DOWJONES and make a printout.

The Dow Jones Average Model
After you retrieve the DOWJONES model and enter labels and numbers on rows 31 through 35, your model should look like the one shown here.

	A	B	C	D	E	F	G
31	Union Carbide				UK	28.00	28.00
32	United Technologies				UTX	44.88	44.88
33	USX Corp.				X	32.13	32.13
34	Westinghouse Electric				WX	55.38	55.38
35	Woolworth				Z	54.63	54.63

TOPIC 7

Entering Formulas

After completing this topic, you will be able to:

- Explain what operators are, and describe the order of operations
- Explain the differences between constants and variables
- Enter formulas by typing or pointing

You can enter formulas into worksheet cells that either calculate numbers directly or refer to cells elsewhere on the worksheet into which you enter numbers or other formulas.

TUTORIAL

	A	B
1	Your name:	
2	Filename:	BUDGET
3	Date:	
4	==============================	
5	INCOME	FALL
6	Bank balance	1500
7	Income during semester	1250
8	College loans	1000
9	Total	3750
10		
11	EXPENSES	
12	Tuition	1000
13	Room & board	1000
14	Books	200
15	Entertainment	300
16	Travel	500
17	Misc.	200
18	Total	3200
19		
20	Balance	550

The Revised College Budget Model

After revising the BUDGET model, it should look like this.

In this tutorial, you enter formulas in the BUDGET model. Your finished model should look like the figure "The Revised Budget Model." Refer to this figure to check your results as you complete the steps in this tutorial.

GETTING STARTED

1. Retrieve the BUDGET model that you entered in Topic 6.

ENTERING A FORMULA BY TYPING

2. With the cell pointer in cell B9, type **+B6+B7+B8** and press [Enter ↵] to total the three cells. The formula is displayed on the control panel when the cell pointer is in the cell.

ENTERING A FORMULA BY POINTING

3. With the cell pointer in cell B18, press [+], and the control panel displays [+].
4. Press [↑] six times to move the cell pointer to cell B12, and the control panel displays *+B12.*
5. Press [+], and the cell pointer jumps back to cell B18.
6. Press [↑] five times to move the cell pointer to cell B13, and the control panel displays *+B12+B13.*
7. Press [+], and the cell pointer jumps back to cell B18.
8. Press [↑] four times to move the cell pointer to cell B14, and the control panel displays *+B12+B13+B14.*
9. Press [+], and the cell pointer jumps back to cell B18.
10. Press [↑] three times to move the cell pointer to cell B15, and the control panel displays *+B12+B13+B14+B15.*

11. Press [+], and the cell pointer jumps back to cell B18.
12. Press [↑] twice to move the cell pointer to cell B16, and the control panel displays *+B12+B13+B14+B15+B16*.
13. Press [+], and the cell pointer jumps back to cell B18.
14. Press [↑] once to move the cell pointer to cell B17, and the control panel displays *+B12+B13+B14+B15+B16+B17*.
15. Press [Enter ↵] to enter the formula, and the six cells are totaled. The formula is displayed on the control panel when the cell pointer is in the cell.

ENTERING ANOTHER FORMULA BY POINTING

16. With the cell pointer in cell B20, press [+], and the control panel displays +.
17. Press [↑] to move the cell pointer to cell B9, and the control panel displays *+B9*.
18. Press [-], and the cell pointer jumps back to cell B20.
19. Press [↑] to move the cell pointer to cell B18, and the control panel displays *+B9-B18*.
20. Press [Enter ↵] to enter the formula, and cell B18 is subtracted from cell B9.

EXPLORING WHAT-IFS

21. Save the model under the same name.
22. Change one or more of the numbers, and watch the formulas calculate new results. As you do so, be sure not to type data into cell B9, B18, or B20, or you will overwrite the formulas.

FINISHING UP

23. Print out the model.
24. Clear the screen without saving the model so that your changes are not saved.
25. You have now completed this tutorial. Either continue with the next activity or quit the program.

QUICK REFERENCE

When entering formulas, you must understand a few principles, namely, how operators and the order of operations work and the difference between constants and variables. Once you understand these principles, you can enter formulas by typing them in or by pointing.

Operators—The Basic Building Blocks

When you enter formulas, certain symbols, called *operators*, tell the program what calculations to perform. These operators are used in conjunction with numbers or cell references to create formulas. The table "1-2-3 Operators" lists some of 1-2-3's operators, and the table "Example Formulas with Operators" illustrates how you can use these operators to create formulas.

1-2-3 OPERATORS

Operator	Use
+	Performs addition
-	Performs subtraction
*	Performs multiplication
/	Performs division
^	Raises a number to a specified power

EXAMPLE FORMULAS WITH OPERATORS

Formula	Displayed Result
10+10	20
10*4	40
30-5	25
200/5	40
+A1+A2	The value in cell A1 plus the value in cell A2
+A1*A2	The value in cell A1 multiplied by the value in cell A2
+A1-A2	The value in cell A1 minus the value in cell A2
+A1/A2	The value in cell A1 divided by the value in cell A2
10+A1	10 plus the value entered in cell A1
2*A1	2 multiplied by the value entered in cell A1
4-A1	4 minus the value entered in cell A1
200/A1	200 divided by the value entered in cell A1
2^2	2 raised to the second power

The Order of Operations

When you enter formulas that contain more than one operator, their order of operations becomes important. Each operator is assigned a precedence number that determines the sequence in which it is calculated. The table "Order of Operations" shows these precedence numbers (with Release 2.2, the order of the numbers was reversed).

- Operators with a higher precedence number in Release 2.01 and a lower precedence number in Release 2.2 and later versions are performed first. For example, if you enter the formula 1+1/2, it contains two operators: + (addition) and / (division). Since division has a higher precedence number in Release 2.01 and a lower precedence in Release 2.2 and later versions, it is performed first, so 1/2 = 0.5; then addition is performed, so 1+0.5 = 1.5.
- Operators with the same level of precedence are calculated in the order they appear in the formula from left to right. For example, if you enter the formula 2*3/2, it has two operators: * (multiplication) and / (division), which have the same precedence. Since calculations are performed from left to right, the answer is 3. First multiplication is performed, so 2*3 = 6; then division is performed, so 6/2 = 3.

You can enter formulas so that operations occur in the desired sequence, but it is usually easier to use parentheses to control the order of calculations regardless of the precedence assigned to operators by the program. For example, entering the formula as 1+(1/2) calculates the correct answer since the operations within the parentheses are always performed first. If parentheses are nested—for example, 1+(1/(1/2))—the operations are performed from the innermost parentheses outward; in this formula, the answer would be 3. You can use up to 32 sets of parentheses in any formula.

ORDER OF OPERATIONS

Operator	Description	2.01 (and Earlier) Precedence	2.2 (and Later) Precedence
^	Exponent	7	1
+	Positive value	6	2
-	Negative value	6	2
*	Multiplication	5	3
/	Division	5	3
+	Addition	4	4
-	Subtraction	4	4

Constants and Variables

When you enter formulas, they can contain both constants and variables:

- *Constants* are numbers you do not expect to change. For example, the formula 5*10 contains only numbers; there are no references to other cells. Numbers contained in formulas are called constants because you can change them only with some difficulty, that is, by reentering the formula, for example, by entering it as 6*10.
- *Variables* are numbers you do expect to change to see what effect different numbers have on the outcome of an analysis. For example, the formula 6*A1 contains a constant and a cell reference. The number in the cell that the formula refers to can be easily changed and is thus a variable. You build more powerful models by entering formulas that refer to other cells. This way, you can change the values in the cells that the formula refers to, and it calculates them just as if they were part of the formula.

When creating a model, you first decide what variables you want to explore, and then structure your models accordingly. You should consider almost every number a variable for three reasons:

1. Embedding a number in a formula is making an assumption either that it should not or cannot be changed or that changes in it are unimportant to the outcome of the analysis. When exploring the model, you may find it is very sensitive to changes in that number—a phenomenon you would never discover if the number were embedded in a formula.
2. The next time you use the model, you may forget there is a number embedded in a formula and not take it into consideration.
3. Printouts of models print out only the displayed values, not the formulas behind them. Anyone else trying to follow your analysis might get lost if numbers are embedded in formulas rather than shown on the printout.

TIP

When entering fractions, like ¼, or numbers that contain fractions, like 100¼, you can enter them as decimals. For example, to enter the number 100¼, you enter **100.25**. If you do not know the decimal equivalent, enter the fraction as a formula. For example, to enter the number 100 7/8, enter it as **100+(7/8)**.

Entering Formulas

There are two ways to enter formulas: by typing them in or, if they refer to other cells, by pointing with the cell pointer to the cells they refer to.

Typing Formulas
You can type in a formula that refers to another cell, for example, A1*A2. But this formula begins with a letter, so if you type that letter first, the program assumes you are entering a label. To enter formulas that begin with letters, you first type + (the plus sign) to enter the formula as +A1*A2. You can also begin formulas with any of the value characters listed in the table "Characters That 1-2-3 Assumes Are Values" in Topic 6.

FORMULA RULES

When entering formulas, keep the following points in mind:

- Formulas must begin with a number or one of the value characters + - . # @ (or $. Otherwise, the formula is treated as a label.
- Formulas can be up to 240 characters long.
- Formulas cannot contain spaces.

Pointing to Build Formulas
You can create a formula by using the cell pointer to point to cells referred to in it. Pointing is especially useful when working on larger models where the cells you want to refer to are not displayed on the screen. Experienced users almost always build formulas by pointing because it is faster, more accurate, and easier than typing.

Editing Formulas

If you enter a formula that does not conform to the program's rules, you are automatically placed in edit mode, which you will learn more about in a later topic. For now, should this happen, know that the program moves the cell pointer to where in the line it thinks the error is. For example, if you mean to enter the formula **+A1+A2** but press [Enter←] after typing **+A1+A**, the computer beeps, the edit cursor goes to the second *A*, and you are placed in edit mode. To edit the formula, press [→] to move the cursor to the right of the *A*, type **2** and press [Enter←].

EXERCISES

CALCULATING FORMULAS

Formula	Result
10*.18	________
12*12*12	________
1+(1/2)	________
1+(1/(1/2))	________

EXERCISE 1

USING 1-2-3 AS A CALCULATOR

With the worksheet cleared of data, type each of the formulas listed in the table "Calculating Formulas," but do not press [Enter←]. Instead, press [F9] (**Calc**), and the result of the formula is displayed on the second line of the control panel. You can then press [Esc] to clear it or [Enter←] to enter it into the cell. Enter the result of each calculation into the table. When finished, clear the screen.

EXERCISE 2

EXPLORING THE ORDER OF OPERATIONS

The figure "The Order of Operations Model" shows a simple model that calculates the net price of a product when the list price and discount are known. The formula (100% - discount × list price) requires two operators, subtraction and multiplication. Since these two operators have different orders of precedence, the way the formula is entered in important. Here, the same cell references and operators are used in four combinations, and only two of them calculate the correct result.

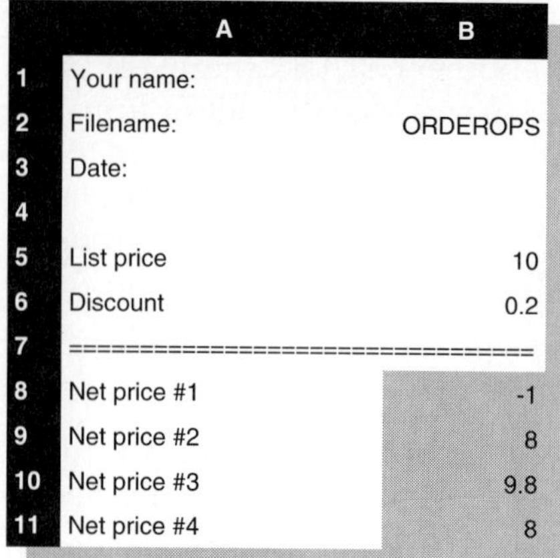

	A	B
1	Your name:	
2	Filename:	ORDEROPS
3	Date:	
4		
5	List price	10
6	Discount	0.2
7	================================	
8	Net price #1	-1
9	Net price #2	8
10	Net price #3	9.8
11	Net price #4	8

The Order of Operations Model
After you enter the order of operations model, your results should look like this.

1. Press /WGC (for ***W**orksheet, **G**lobal, **C**olumn-Width*), type **15** and press Enter↵ to set the global column width to 15 characters. Then, create the model shown in the figure "The Order of Operations Model." The model's formulas are as follows (B5 and B6 are numbers, not formulas):
   - In cell B8, enter **1-B6*B5**
   - In cell B9, enter **(1-B6)*B5**
   - In cell B10, enter **+B5*1-B6**
   - In cell B11, enter **+B5*(1-B6)**

   The formula in cell B9 subtracts the discount in cell B6 (20%) from 1 (100%) and multiplies the result (80%) times the list price ($10.00) in cell B5. The calculated result is correct. The formula in cell B11 is similar, but the two parts are in reverse order.
2. Save the finished model as ORDEROPS.
3. Change the discount to 10% and make a printout.
4. Change the list price to $50.00 and make a printout.
5. Clear the screen without saving the model.

EXERCISE 3

EXPLORING CONSTANTS AND VARIABLES

1. With the cell pointer in column A, press /WCS (for ***W**orksheet, **C**olumn, **S**et-Width*), type **25** and press Enter↵ to set the width of column A to 25 characters. Then create the model shown in the figure "The Constants and Variables Model." As you do so, enter a label prefix character before typing the opening parentheses in the three lettered headings. The model's formulas are as follows:
   (a) All Constants. In cell B6, enter the formula **(1-.2)*10** that contains only constants. Because the numbers are part of the formula, you cannot easily change the discount or price to calculate a new result.
   (b) Part Constants/Part Variables. In cell B11, enter the formula **(1-B10)*B9** that contains both constants and variables. The formula subtracts the value in cell B10 from 1 (100%) and multiplies the result times the price in cell B9. The numbers in cells B9 and B10 are both variables that you can change to explore outcomes.
   (c) All Variables. In cell B16, enter the formula **+B15*B14** with all variables to calculate the discount in dollars. In cell B17, enter the formula **+B14-B16** with all variables to subtract the discount from the list price to calculate the net price.
2. Save the finished model as CONVAR.
3. To change the numbers in the formula with all constants, you have to know how to edit the formula. However, you can easily change them in the other two sections of the model. To see how easy it is to do so:
   - Change the list prices in sections b and c from $10 to $20 and make a printout.
   - Change the discount in sections b and c from .2 (20%) to .3 (30%) and make a printout.

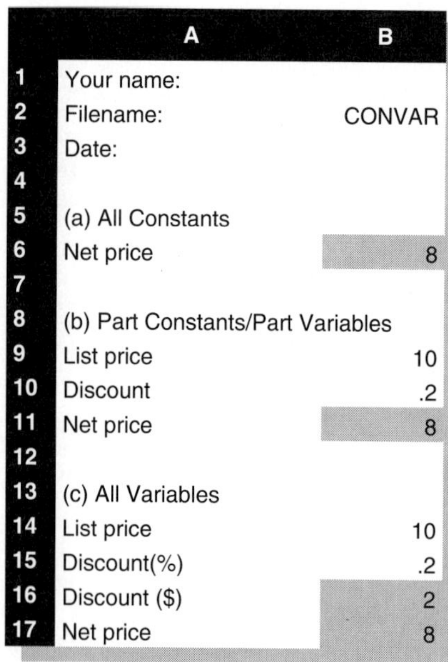

	A	B
1	Your name:	
2	Filename:	CONVAR
3	Date:	
4		
5	(a) All Constants	
6	Net price	8
7		
8	(b) Part Constants/Part Variables	
9	List price	10
10	Discount	.2
11	Net price	8
12		
13	(c) All Variables	
14	List price	10
15	Discount(%)	.2
16	Discount ($)	2
17	Net price	8

The Constants and Variables Model
After you enter the constants and variables model, your results should look like this.

4. Clear the screen without saving the model.

EXERCISE 4

CREATING A PRICING MODEL

Retail businesses purchase their inventory from manufacturers at a discount. They then mark up the goods so that they can sell them at a profit. In this exercise, you create a model that allows you to explore the relationship among prices, discounts, markups, and profits.

1. Retrieve the PRICING model, and enter your name in cell B1.
2. Enter the formulas described in the table "The Pricing Model's Formulas," so your model looks like the figure "The Pricing Model."
3. Save the finished model under its original name.
4. Explore the following what-ifs, and make printouts as you do so:
   - What if the discount is raised to 50%? What happens to the gross profit and gross margin per unit?
   - What if the discount is lowered to 35%? What happens to the gross profit and gross margin per unit?
   - If the discount is 35%, what price do you have to sell it for to obtain a 44% gross margin per unit?

THE PRICING MODEL'S FORMULAS

#	Cell	Formula
1	B12	*The unit cost from manufacturer* is calculated by subtracting the discount from 100% and multiplying the result times the suggested list price.
2	B13	*The total unit cost of goods* is the unit cost from the manufacturer plus the unit cost of freight in.
3	B14	*The gross profit per unit (in dollars)* is your actual selling price minus the total unit cost of goods.
4	B15	*The percentage markup over unit cost of goods* is the gross profit per unit (in dollars) divided by the total unit cost of goods.
5	B16	*The gross margin per unit (%)* is the gross profit per unit (in dollars) divided by your actual selling price.

The Pricing Model
After you retrieve the PRICING model and enter formulas, your model should look like this.

	A	B
11	Part 2. Pricing Analysis	
12	The unit cost from manufacturer	$6.00
13	The total unit cost of goods	$6.20
14	The gross profit per unit (in dollars)	$4.80
15	The percentage markup over unit cost of goods	77%
16	The gross margin per unit (%)	44%

T O P I C 8

Understanding Ranges

After completing this topic, you will be able to:

- Describe what a range is and how you specify ranges
- Explain the difference between global and range commands
- Erase ranges of cells
- Use the */Data Fill* command to enter numbers

When entering data, you usually work with individual cells, but most other commands allow you to work with more than one cell at a time. This greatly speeds up the process of working with models. It is therefore very important that you understand the difference between global and range commands and how you specify ranges.

Global Commands

Global commands affect the entire worksheet. Some of these commands affect the way information is displayed. For example, there are global commands to set the width of columns, align labels, format values, and turn protection on or off.

Normally, you specify a global setting based on what works with most of your data. You then override the global setting with range commands wherever you want data to look different from the global format.

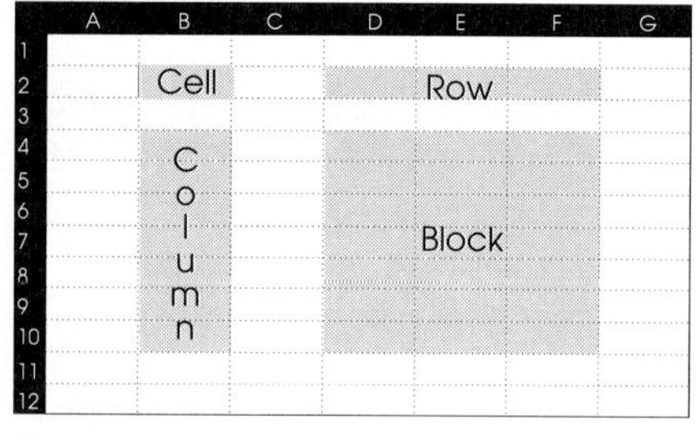

Ranges
A range is a group of adjacent cells arranged in one of four shapes: cells, rows, columns, and blocks.

Range Commands

Range commands affect at least one cell but not necessarily the entire worksheet. You use range commands when changing the width of columns, in functions that make calculations for you, when printing all or part of the worksheet, when erasing groups of cells, when copying or moving data, and when formatting cells.

TUTORIAL

In this tutorial, you practice specifying ranges when using the ***/Data Fill*** and ***/Range Erase*** commands. Your finished model should look like the figure "The Ranges Model" on the next page. Refer to this figure to check your results as you complete the steps in this tutorial.

GETTING STARTED

1. Load the program or clear the screen.
2. Enter the heading on the first three lines. (The filename is NONE because you don't save the file at the end of the tutorial.)

	A	B	C
1	Your name:		
2	Filename:	none	
3	Date:		
4			
5	0	6	12
6	1	7	13
7	2	8	14
8	3	9	15
9	4	10	16
10	5	11	17

The Ranges Model
After you enter the ranges model, it should look like this.

SPECIFYING RANGES BY TYPING THEM

3. Press [/][D][F] (for ***D**ata **F**ill*), and the prompt reads *Enter fill range:*.
4. Type **A5.C10** and press [Enter←]. The prompt reads *Start: 0*.
5. Press [Enter←] three times to accept the suggested numbers, and the range of cells from A5 (the upper-left corner) to C10 (the lower-right corner) is filled with numbers.

ERASING RANGES BY TYPING THEM

6. Press [/][R][E] (for ***R**ange*, ***E**rase*), and the prompt reads *Enter range to erase:*.
7. Type **A5.C10** and press [Enter←] to erase the range.

SPECIFYING RANGES BY POINTING

8. Press [/][D][F] (for ***D**ata **F**ill*), and the prompt reads *Enter fill range:*, and the previous range is highlighted.
9. Press [Esc] to clear the previous range, and the cell pointer returns to cell A5.
10. Press [.] (the period) to anchor the range, and the prompt reads *Enter fill range: A5..A5*.
11. Press [→] to expand the highlight to column C, and the control panel reads *Enter fill range: A5..C5*.
12. Press [↓] to expand the highlight to row 10, and the control panel reads *Enter fill range: A5..C10*.
13. Press [Enter←] to set the fill range, and the prompt reads *Start: 0*.
14. Press [Enter←] three times to accept the suggested numbers, and the range of cells from A5 (the upper-left corner) to C10 (the lower-right corner) is filled with numbers.

PRINTING THE MODEL

15. With the cell pointer in cell A5, press [/][P][P][R] (for ***P**rint*, ***P**rinter*, ***R**ange*), and the prompt reads *Enter print range:*.
16. Press [.] (the period) to anchor the cell pointer, and the control panel reads *Enter print range: A5..A5*.
17. Press [→] to expand the highlight to column C, and the control panel reads *Enter print range: A5..C5*.
18. Press [↓] to expand the highlight to row 10, and the control panel reads *Enter print range: A5..C10*.
19. Press [Enter←] to set the print range and return to the menu.
20. Press [A][G] (for ***A**lign*, ***G**o*) to print the model.
21. When the Print menu reappears, press [P][Q] (for ***P**age*, ***Q**uit*) to advance the paper out of the printer and leave the Print menu.

CHANGING THE ANCHORED CELL

22. Press [/][P][P][R] (for ***P**rint*, ***P**rinter*, ***R**ange*), and the prompt reads *Enter print range:*, and the previous range you specified is highlighted.
23. Press [Esc] to cancel the previous print range, and the cell pointer moves to cell A5.

24. Press [.] (the period) to anchor the cell pointer, and the control panel reads *Enter print range: A5..A5.*
25. Press [→] to expand the highlight to column C, and the control panel reads *Enter print range: A5..C5.*
26. Press [↓] to expand the highlight to row 10, and the control panel reads *Enter print range: A5..C10.*
27. Press [.] (the period) several times. You will see a cursor move from corner to corner around the range when you press the period. (On release 2.3 and later, the highlights on the row and column borders also move along with the cursor.) This cursor indicates the free corner, the one that will move when you press the arrow keys.
28. With the cursor in each corner, press the arrow keys to expand and contract the highlight. Notice how the corner with the cursor moves and the one diagonally across from it is anchored.
29. When you have finished experimenting with the range, set it to C10.A1 (or A1.C10) and press [Enter ←] to set the range.
30. Press [A][G] (for ***A**lign*, ***G**o*) to print the model.
31. When the Print menu reappears, press [P][Q] (for ***P**age*, ***Q**uit*) to advance the paper out of the printer and leave the Print menu.

ERASING RANGES BY POINTING

32. With the cell pointer in cell A5, press [/][R][E] (for ***R**ange*, ***E**rase*), and the prompt reads *Enter range to erase:*.
33. Press [→] to expand the highlight to column C, and the control panel reads *Enter range to erase: A5..C5.*
34. Press [↓] to expand the highlight to row 10, and the control panel reads *Enter range to erase: A5..C10.*
35. Press [Enter ←] to erase the range.

FINISHING UP

36. Clear the screen without saving the model.
37. You have now completed this tutorial. Either continue with the next activity or quit the program.

QUICK REFERENCE

When you use a range command or refer to a range in a function, you specify the range of cells that is to be affected by the command or function. A *range* is a group of adjacent cells and can be as small as a single cell or as large as the entire worksheet. The only rule is that the range must be rectangular. There are essentially four rectangular shapes of ranges: the cell, the row, the column, and the block. These are shown in the figure "Ranges."

Specifying Ranges

When you use range commands, a prompt appears asking you to enter the range. You can specify the range in one of two ways: typing range addresses or pointing to ranges.

Typing Range Addresses
To specify a range by typing, you type two cell addresses that define the range. You can use any combination of cells that are diagonally across from one another, but to be consistent most users always specify the upper-left and lower-right cells in the range. You type two cell addresses separated by a period (called a *delimiter*). For example, when prompted to enter a range, you can type **A1.C3** to indicate the cells falling in the columns between A and C and the rows 1 and 3. When you type one period, two are displayed on the second line of the control panel.

Pointing to Ranges
To specify a range by pointing, you move the cell pointer to one of the corners of the range and press [.] (the period) to anchor that corner of the range. (Some commands, like ***/Range*** *F*ormat or ***/Range Erase***, anchor the range automatically in the cell that the cell pointer is in when you initiate them. When using these commands, you should position the cell pointer in one of the corner cells before you begin typing.)

Once the highlight is anchored, you use the pointer movement keys to highlight the desired range. When you anchor one corner of the range, the corner diagonally across from it becomes the "free corner" of the range. When you press the pointer movement keys, this free corner moves to highlight or unhighlight cells.

The free corner of the highlight is indicated by a small cursor. (On some releases it flashes.) The corner with the cursor is the free corner that moves when you press the cell pointer movement keys. To change the free corner, press [.] (the period) to move this cursor clockwise around the highlight from corner to corner.

Editing Previously Specified Ranges
When using range commands, you can edit the range that is to be affected; for example:

- Range commands remember a range that you previously specified. The second time you use the same command, the previous range is automatically highlighted.
- You may have highlighted the wrong range and want to change it without canceling the command and starting over.

Whenever a range is highlighted, you have the five options listed in the table "Keys Used When Specifying Ranges."

KEYS USED WHEN SPECIFYING RANGES

Key	Effect on Highlighted Range
[Enter ←]	Accepts the highlighted range
[.] (period)	Anchors a range and then moves the anchor cell and the free cell clockwise around the range
[Esc]	Removes the anchor and returns the cell pointer to where the range was anchored
[← Bksp]	Removes the anchor and returns the cell pointer to the cell where it was when the command was begun
[Ctrl]-[Break]	Cancels the command

RANGES IN RELEASE 2.3 AND LATER VERSIONS

In Release 2.3 and later versions, you can select ranges before you execute commands. The advantage to this approach is that the range remains highlighted so that you can use a series of commands, perhaps to format it and then copy it. To select a range in these versions:

1. Move the cell pointer to one of the corners of the range.
2. Press F4 to anchor the range, and the prompt reads *Range:*.
3. Use the cell pointer movement keys to expand the range highlight in any direction.
4. Press Enter← to set the range.
5. Execute any commands on the range.
6. When you have finished, press any cell pointer movement key to remove the range highlight.

Erasing Ranges

To erase the contents of one or more cells, you use the ***/Range Erase*** command. This command erases only the labels, numbers, or formulas, not the formats assigned to the cells.

→ KEY/Strokes

Erasing a Range of Cells

1. Press / R E (for ***R**ange*, ***E**rase*), and the prompt reads *Enter range to erase:*.
2. Specify the range and press Enter←.

The Data Fill Command

The ***/Data Fill*** command enters an equally incremented series of numbers in a row, column, or block of cells. This command is very useful when you want to number the rows of data in a model or when you want to explore a series of numbers, for example, interest rates ranging from 1% to 30%.

When using the ***/Data Fill*** command, you specify the range to be filled and a start, step, and stop value, which can be positive or negative numbers, whole numbers, decimals, formulas, or functions.

- The *start value* is the number the series starts with. The default is 0.
- The *step value* specifies the value each number in the series is to be incremented by. For example, if you start the series at 1 and specify a step value of 2, the series will be 1, 3, 5, 7, and so on. The default is 1.
- The *stop value* is the number the series ends with. Both the fill range and the stop number you enter determine the results. The ***/Data Fill*** command continues to enter numbers until it reaches the end of the range or the stop number, whichever comes first. If you specify a block that includes more than one column, the command fills the first column from the top to bottom of the block and then begins filling adjoining columns. The default is 8191.
- When you use the ***/Data Fill*** command a second time, the program remembers the previous settings, including the range. You can change any of the settings by reentering or editing them or keep them by pressing Enter←.

→ KEY/Strokes

Using the Data Fill Command

1. Move the cell pointer to where you want the numbers to begin.
2. Press / D F (for ***D**ata*, ***F**ill*), and the prompt reads *Enter fill range:*.
3. Specify the range and press Enter←. The prompt reads *Start: 0*.
4. Press Enter← to accept the suggested start value, or type the number that you want the series to start at, and press Enter←. The prompt reads *Step: 1*.

5. Press Enter← to accept the suggested step value, or type the number that you want the series to step by, and press Enter←. The prompt reads *Stop: 8191*.
6. Press Enter← to accept the suggested stop value, or type the number that you want the series to stop at, and press Enter←.

EXERCISES

	A	B	C	D	E	F	G
1	Your name:						
2	Filename:		DATAFILL				
3	Date:						
4	1	191	381	571	761	951	1141
5	11	201	391	581	771	961	1151
19	151	341	531	721	911	1101	1291
20	161	351	541	731	921	1111	
21	171	361	551	741	931	1121	
22	181	371	561	751	941	1131	

The Data Fill Model
The ***/Data Fill*** command can be used to quickly enter an evenly incremented series of numbers into a column, row, or block of cells. Here, numbers step by 10s down the columns in the block.

DATA FILL VARIATIONS

Start	Step	Stop
-100	20	1400
0	.5	30
100	-1	-1
100	45*.25	1000
200	(45/.25)	10000
1	+A5+2	350

EXERCISE 1

EXPLORING DATA FILL

1. Enter the three-line heading at the top of the worksheet.
2. Use the ***/Data Fill*** command to enter the numbers shown in the figure "The Data Fill Model." The numbers start at 1, step by 10, and stop at 1300.
3. Save the document as DATAFILL and make a printout.
4. Without changing the range, use the ***/Data Fill*** command to enter the numbers shown in the table "Data Fill Variations."
5. Clear the screen without saving your changes to the model.

EXERCISE 2

EXPLORING RANGES

1. Enter the three-line heading at the top of the worksheet.
2. Use the ***/Data Fill*** command to fill the range A5.C20 with values that start at 1000, step by -20, and stop at 100.
3. Print out the entire model. It should look like the figure "The Exploring Ranges Model."
4. Use the ***/Range Erase*** command to erase just the range B5.B20.
5. Print out just the range A1.B20.
6. Clear the model from the screen without saving it.

	A	B	C
1	Your name:		
2	Filename:	none	
3	Date:		
4			
5	1000	680	360
6	980	660	340
7	960	640	320
18	740	420	100
19	720	400	
20	700	380	

The Exploring Ranges Model
After you enter the exploring ranges model, it should look like this.

TOPIC 9

Editing Models

After completing this topic, you will be able to:

- Edit the contents of cells
- Insert and delete rows and columns

To improve or expand a model, you can edit the contents of cells and insert or delete rows and columns.

TUTORIAL

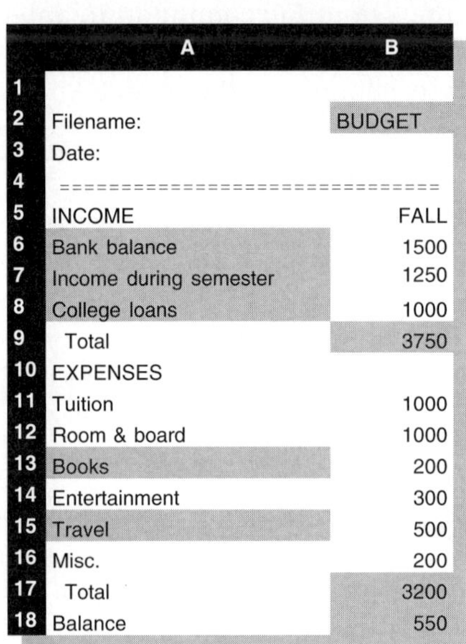

	A	B
1		
2	Filename:	BUDGET
3	Date:	
4	==============================	
5	INCOME	FALL
6	Bank balance	1500
7	Income during semester	1250
8	College loans	1000
9	Total	3750
10	EXPENSES	
11	Tuition	1000
12	Room & board	1000
13	Books	200
14	Entertainment	300
15	Travel	500
16	Misc.	200
17	Total	3200
18	Balance	550

The Corrected WRONG Model
After editing the labels and formulas in the shaded cells, your model should look like this.

In this tutorial, you edit the contents of cells and insert rows and columns into the WRONG model. The shaded cells in the figure "The Corrected WRONG Model" show where corrections should be made and what the final results should look like before you insert new rows.

GETTING STARTED

1. Retrieve the WRONG model and enter your name in cell B1.

CORRECTING A MISTAKE WHILE ENTERING

2. With the cell pointer in cell A1, type **Your naem**.
3. Press [←Bksp] twice so that the line reads *delete Your na.*
4. Type **me:** and press [Enter←] to enter the new revised label.

CORRECTING LABELS AFTER THEY HAVE BEEN ENTERED

5. Correct all the labels on your screen to make them match shaded cells in the figure "The Corrected WRONG Model." To do so:
   - Move the cell pointer to the cell, and press [F2] to enter edit mode.
   - Use the arrow keys to move the edit cursor through the entry on the second line of the control panel, and insert new characters as needed.
   - Press [←Bksp] to delete a character to the edit cursor's left or [Del] to delete the character the edit cursor is under.
   - When finished, press [Enter←] to enter the revised entry into the cell.

CORRECTING NUMBERS AFTER THEY HAVE BEEN ENTERED

6. With the cell pointer in cell B9, press [F2] to enter edit mode. Change the last cell reference in the formula so that it reads *+B6+B7+B8*, and press [Enter←].

7. With the cell pointer in cell B17, press [F2] to enter edit mode. Change the second cell reference in the formula so that it reads *+B11+B12+B13+B14+B15+B16*, and press [Enter←].
8. With the cell pointer in cell B18, press [F2] to enter edit mode. Change the formula so that it reads *+B9-B17*, and press [Enter←].

INSERTING ROWS

9. With the cell pointer anywhere on row 10, press [/][W][I][R] (for ***W**orksheet, **I**nsert, **R**ow*), and the prompt reads *Enter row insert range:*.
10. Press [Enter←] to insert a row above the cell pointer.
11. With the cell pointer anywhere on row 19, press [/][W][I][R] (for ***W**orksheet, **I**nsert, **R**ow*), and the prompt reads *Enter row insert range:*.
12. Press [Enter←] to insert a row above the cell pointer.

FINISHING UP

13. Print the model.
14. Save the model under the same name.
15. You have now completed this tutorial. Either clear the screen and continue with the next activity or quit the program.

QUICK REFERENCE

One of the best features on a spreadsheet is its revisability. You can start with small, simple models, and then add to their power and complexity. To change existing data or formulas in a model, you can edit them or erase them. To expand or condense your model, you can insert or delete rows.

Editing Cell Contents

As you enter labels or values, they are displayed on the second line of the control panel along with an edit cursor. If you notice a mistake while entering data, you can edit the entry. If you notice a mistake after pressing [Enter←], you can return the data to the second line of the control panel for editing. To do this, you move the cell pointer to the cell you want to edit, and press [F2] **(Edit)**. This puts the program into edit mode (the mode indicator reads *EDIT*) and displays the cell's contents on the second line of the control panel along with an edit cursor. In edit mode, you can move the edit cursor freely through the data and insert or delete characters as needed. For example, you can press [Ins] to switch between insert and overtype modes.

- In *insert mode* (the default mode), if you type a character into an existing line of characters, the characters to the right move over to make room for the new character.
- In *overtype mode* (the status indicator reads *OVR*), any character that you type replaces any character the edit cursor is positioned under.

The table "Keys That Move the Edit Cursor and Delete Characters" describes the keys you can use to move the edit cursor and delete characters.

KEYS THAT MOVE THE EDIT CURSOR AND DELETE CHARACTERS

Command	Press
To Move the Edit Cursor	
One character to the left or right	← or →
To the beginning of the line	Home
To the end of the line	End
Five spaces to the right	Tab or Ctrl-→
Five spaces to the left	Shift-Tab or Ctrl-←
To Insert and Delete Characters	
To switch between insert and overtype	Ins
To delete the character to the left of the cursor	← Bksp
To delete the character directly over the cursor	Del
To delete all characters	Esc

Inserting Rows and Columns

Often you may find it necessary to insert rows or columns into the middle of an existing model. You can do this easily, and all formulas automatically adjust so that they continue to refer to the correct cells.

When inserting rows and columns, keep the following points in mind:

- The position of the cell pointer is important.
  - Rows are inserted above the row on which the cell pointer is initially positioned, and the cell pointer then moves to the topmost inserted row.
  - Columns are inserted to the left of the column in which the cell pointer is initially positioned, and the cell pointer then moves to the leftmost inserted column.
  - The cell pointer can be in any cell in the appropriate row or column when you begin the command.
- You can type in a range of rows or columns or point to them when prompted to enter the range to be inserted.
- If rows or columns are inserted within a print range (or a range referred to by a function, as you will see later), the range expands to include the new rows or columns. If rows or columns are inserted on the edge of the range, they are not included.

→ KEY/Strokes

Inserting Rows or Columns

1. Move the cell pointer to the row above which, or the column to the right of which, you want the new rows or columns inserted.
2. Press / W I (for ***W**orksheet, **I**nsert*).
3. Either: Press C (for ***C**olumn*), and the prompt reads *Enter column insert range:*.

   Or: Press R (for ***R**ow*), and the prompt reads *Enter row insert range:*.
4. Point to the range and press Enter.

Deleting Rows and Columns

Deleting rows or columns has almost the same effect as inserting them. The worksheet closes up, and all formulas automatically adjust to refer to the correct cells.

There is one exception to the way formulas automatically adjust. If you delete any cells that remaining formulas refer to, those formulas display error messages. For this reason, it is wise to save a model before making deletions. After making deletions, be sure to check the worksheet to see if any error messages appear in the cells. If you have any doubts, save the model under a new filename so that you do not store it on top of, and erase, the original version. You may also want to convert formulas that refer to parts of the model to be deleted into their currently displayed values before deleting the cells they refer to. (See the TIP in this topic.)

When deleting rows and columns, keep the following points in mind:

- You can type in a range of rows or columns or point to them when prompted to enter the range to be deleted.
- If you do not delete the upper-left or lower-right corner of a range, the range contracts or expands to accommodate the change. If these corners are deleted, the range is erased. If any formulas or functions refer to the range, they display an *ERR* message. If the range is one that you specified in a command like ***/P**rint **P**rinter*, you have to specify the range again the next time you use the command.

KEY/Strokes

Deleting Rows or Columns

1. Move the cell pointer to the topmost or bottommost row, or the leftmost or rightmost column, to be deleted.
2. Press [/] [W] [D] (for ***W**orksheet*, ***D**elete*).
3. Either: Press [C] (for ***C**olumn*), and the prompt reads *Enter range of columns to delete:*.

   Or: Press [R] (for ***R**ow*), and the prompt reads *Enter range of rows to delete:*.
4. Point to the range, and press [Enter←].

EXERCISES

EXERCISE 1

IDENTIFYING EDITING KEYS

Fill out the table "Editing Commands" with the keys that move the edit cursor and that delete characters when editing the contents of a cell.

TIP

You can convert formulas into their calculated values so that they do not change during subsequent recalculations if the cells they refer to are changed or deleted. To do so, move the cell pointer to the cell containing the formula, press F2 (**Edit**) to move the formula to the second line of the control panel, press F9 (**Calc**), and press Enter↵. You can also convert a range of formulas to their calculated values using the ***/Range Value*** command.

EDITING COMMANDS

Action Desired	Press
Move the Edit Cursor	
One character to the right	______
One character to the left	______
To the beginning of the line	______
To the end of the line	______
To Delete	
Character to the left of the cursor	______
Character directly over the cursor	______

EXERCISE 2

EDITING YOUR OTHER MODELS

If you have made any mistakes in your other models, retrieve them now and correct the mistakes. After editing each model, save it, and make a printout.

CHAPTER 2

REVIEW

- To enter data in a worksheet, you position the cell pointer in a cell, type the data, and press Enter← (or any of the cell pointer movement keys).
- The program assumes that you are entering a value if the first character that you type is a number 0 through 9 or one of the characters +, -, ., @, (, $, or #. To begin a label with one of these characters, you must first enter a label prefix character (' ", or ^).
- Label prefix characters can be used to align data in a cell. When entering a label, press ' as the first character to left-align it, " to right-align it, or ^ to center it.
- To enter numbers, type them in without spaces, dollar signs, or commas.
- To enter a repeating label, press \, type the characters that you want repeated, and press Enter←.
- You can type formulas or use the cell pointer to point to the cells you want the formula to refer to.
- Formulas can contain numbers or references to cell addresses. To enter a cell address at the beginning of a formula, enter + first. For example, to enter a formula that adds the numbers in cells A1 and A2, enter the formulas as **+A1+A2**.
- Numbers entered into formulas are called constants, and references in formulas to cells in which numbers are entered are called variables.
- To enter formulas, you use operators; + for addition, - for subtraction, * for multiplication, / for division, and ^ to raise a number to a specified power.
- 1-2-3 assigns priorities to all operators so that formulas are calculated in a predictable sequence. To override this sequence, you enclose parts of a formula in parentheses since calculations within parentheses are always performed first.
- Global commands affect the entire worksheet, whereas range commands affect only specified ranges. When you execute many range commands, you are prompted to enter a range. To do so, you can type in cell addresses that indicate its upper-left and lower-right corners, or you can point to the range with the cell pointer. On Release 2.4, you can also press F4 to anchor a range, then press the cell pointer movement keys to highlight the range.
- To erase a range of cells, you use the ***/Range Erase*** command.
- To fill a range with numbers (formulas or dates), you use the ***/Data Fill*** command. You then specify the number the series is to start with, the number it is to increment by, and the number it is to stop at.
- To edit an entry before you press Enter←, press ←Bksp to delete characters or press F2 to enter edit mode.
- To edit an entry already entered into a cell, press F2. This displays the entry on the control panel, where you can press the arrow keys to move the edit cursor through the entry and type new characters or press Del or ←Bksp to delete existing characters.

- To insert rows or columns, you use the ***/Worksheet Insert*** command. Rows are inserted above and columns are inserted to the left of the cell pointer.
- To delete rows or columns, you use the ***/Worksheet Delete*** command.

CHAPTER 2

QUESTIONS

FILL IN THE BLANK

1. If you enter one of the numbers ___________, or one of the characters ___________, 1-2-3 assumes you are entering a value.
2. To enter a label that begins with a number, you first must type a ___________ character.
3. To align a label in a cell, you first type ___________ to left-align it, ___________ to right-align it, or ___________ to center it.
4. To enter a repeating label that contains just equal signs, you press ___________. To enter the repeating label -X-X-X-X, you press ___________.
5. You can point to cells with the ___________ to enter their cell address into a formula.
6. To enter a formula that subtracts the number in cell B2 from the number in cell B1, you would type ___________.
7. To enter a formula that divides the number in cell B2 by the number in cell B1, you would type ___________.
8. When you enter a number in a formula, it is called a ___________.
9. When you enter a cell address in a formula, it is called a ___________.
10. The operators you use in formulas include ___________ for addition, ___________ for subtraction, ___________ for multiplication, and ___________ for division.
11. The order in which 1-2-3 calculates operators is called the order of ___________. It will calculate multiplication ___________ it calculates subtraction.
12. ___________ commands affect the entire worksheet.
13. ___________ commands affect only the specified cells.
14. To specify a range, you can ___________ or ___________ to the cells with the cell pointer.
15. You press ___________ to anchor a range and ___________ to move the free corner.
16. To erase a range of cells, you press ___________.
17. To enter edit mode, you press ___________.
18. To insert rows, you position the cell pointer on the row ___________ where you want the rows inserted, and press ___________.
19. To insert columns, you position the cell pointer in the column to the ___________ of where you want the columns inserted, and press ___________.

MATCH THE COLUMNS

1. **123**	__ Puts program into edit mode
2. **LOTUS**	__ What you enter in the ***/Data Fill*** command
3. +, -, /, *, and ^	__ Converts a formula to its calculated value
4. ', ", ^	__ A number in a formula
5. [F2]	__ A cell reference in a formula
6. constant	__ Fills the cell with equal signs
7. variable	__ Operators
8. [/][=]	__ Label-prefix characters
9. pointing	__ Affects only specified cells
10. global command	__ One way to enter a formula
11. range command	__ Affects the entire worksheet
12. start, step, and stop values	__ Loads the 1-2-3 program
13. [F2], then [F9]	__ Loads the Lotus Access System

WRITE OUT THE ANSWERS

1. How does a value differ from a label?
2. List three label-prefix characters and describe what they do.
3. Describe how do you enter a label that begins with a number.
4. How would you enter the label 123 Spring Street? The phone number 617-555-1000?
5. What is a repeating label? What can it be used for?
6. List the characters that 1-2-3 assumes are values when they are the first character that you type.
7. How would you enter the number $6,580.00?
8. What happens when you enter a number followed by a percent sign, for example, 20%?
9. What does the ***/Data Fill*** command do? What values must you specify when using it?
10. What are operators? List and describe the functions of four of them.
11. What formula would you enter to multiply the values in cells A1 and C3? To divide A1 by C3? To add them? To subtract A1 from C3?
12. What is the order of operations? If you want to change the order, how can you do so?
13. Describe the difference between a constant and a variable. Why are variables usually preferred?
14. What two ways can you use to enter a formula? Which approach do almost all experienced users prefer? Why?
15. Why do you type a plus sign before entering the first character in a formula, for example, +B2-B3?

16. In what order would the operators in the following formula be calculated: 10+((50/10)*10)-3?
17. When you change a number in a model, what must occur before formulas reflect the change?
18. What is the difference between a global command and a range command?
19. What is a range? Describe some typical shapes of ranges.
20. Describe two ways you specify ranges.
21. Explain the two ways of editing the contents of a cell.
22. What command do you use to delete the contents of a range of cells?
23. How do you insert blank rows into a worksheet model?
24. What happens when you delete cells that remaining formulas refer to?

CHAPTER 2 PROJECTS

PROJECT 1

KEEPING BOX SCORES

We keep beating ourselves, but we're getting better at it.

—Assistant coach Hank Bullough of the Green Bay Packers, quoted in *The Buffalo News*. December 24, 1988, p. B1.

Open the paper any day, turn to the sports section, and you find list after list of sports statistics. One of the first places many persons look is to the box scores, the listings that show the standings in any league or division. As you complete the model described in this project and those in chapters to come, you will create a model that calculates these box scores.

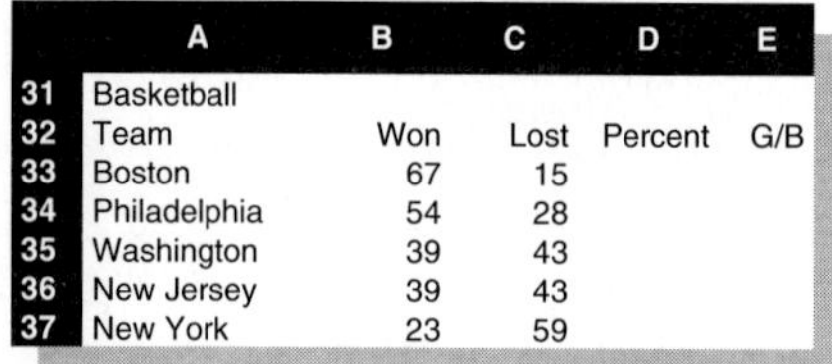

	A	B	C	D	E
31	Basketball				
32	Team	Won	Lost	Percent	G/B
33	Boston	67	15		
34	Philadelphia	54	28		
35	Washington	39	43		
36	New Jersey	39	43		
37	New York	23	59		

The Box Score Model
As you progress though the projects in this text, you will add to, edit, and format the BOXSCORE model, shown here as it will look when you are finished.

1. Retrieve the BOXSCORE model.
2. Enter the labels and numbers shown on rows 31 through 37 in the figure "The Box Score Model." (Note that columns D and E are formulas.)
3. Enter the formulas described in the table "The Box Score Model's Formulas."
4. Save the model under its original name.
5. Edit the model as needed and make a printout.
6. Save the model again.

THE BOX SCORE MODEL'S FORMULAS

#	Cell	Formula
1	E7	Baseball won-lost is calculated by the formula **+B7-C7**.
2	E17	Hockey points are calculated by the formula **(B17*2)+D17**.

	A	B
25	Philippine (Peso)	0.0483
26	Singapore (Dollar)	0.5005
27	United States (Dollar)	1.0000
28	Germany (Mark)	0.5627

The Exchange Rate Model
As you progress though the projects in this text, you will add to, edit, and format the EXCHANGE model, shown here as it will look when you are finished.

PROJECT 2

CALCULATING EXCHANGE RATES

1. Retrieve the EXCHANGE model.
2. Enter the labels and numbers shown on rows 25 through 28 in the figure "The Exchange Rate Model." (Note that columns C and D are formulas which you will enter in the next chapter.)
3. Save the model under its original name.
4. Edit the model as needed and make a printout.
5. Save the model again.

PROJECT 3

CONVERTING BETWEEN ENGLISH AND METRIC UNITS

1. Retrieve the METRIC model.
2. Enter the labels and numbers shown on rows 46 through 50 in the figure "The Metric/English Conversion Model." (Note that column D will be used for formulas.)
3. Enter the formulas described in the table "The Metric/English Conversion Model's Formulas."
4. Save the model under its original name.
5. Edit the model as needed and make a printout.
6. Save the model again.

THE METRIC/ENGLISH CONVERSION MODEL'S FORMULAS

#	Cell	Formula
1	C11	*Multiply by* is calculated by the formula **(D5*(9/5))+32**.
2	D11	*Answer* is calculated by the formula **+C12**.
3	C12	*Multiply by* is calculated by the formula **(D5-32)*(5/9)**.
4	D12	*Answer* is calculated by the formula **+C11**.

	A	B	C
10	Temperature		
11	Fahrenheit	Centigrade	
12	Centigrade	Fahrenheit	
46	Work		
47	Centimeter kilograms	Inch pounds	0.8676
48	Inch pounds	Centimeter kilograms	1.15262
49	Meter kilograms	Foot pounds	7.23301
50	Foot pounds	Meter kilograms	1.3558

The Metric/English Conversion Model
As you progress though the projects in this text, you will add to, edit, and format the METRIC model, shown here as it will look when you are finished.

CHAPTER 3

Revising & Formatting Models

TOPIC 10

Formatting Models

After completing this topic, you will be able to:

- Format text
- Format values

When you want your models, whether on the screen or in printouts, to be attractive and easy to read, you use formats to align labels and format numbers. When you do this, you can use the global or range format commands.

Global Formats

A global format affects all cells on the worksheet. Generally, you select a global format based on the format that will be used most often in a model and then override it in selected cells to display them as desired.

Range Formats

To override the global format in selected cells, you use range formats. Range formats have priority over global formats. For example, if you use a range command to format a group of cells and then change the global format, the format of the cells you formatted with the range command does not change. To make the cells in the range respond again to global commands, you must first reset them to the global format using the Reset command.

When you use range formats, you can see what formats have been assigned to a specific cell by moving the cell pointer to the cell. The formats are displayed on the first line of the control panel. For example, if you have changed a column's width to 11 and its format to currency with two decimal places, the first line of the control panel will read *(C2) [W11]*. If you align a label in a cell, the label prefix is displayed preceding the label.

When you format cells with global commands, the position of the cell pointer is not important. However, when you use range commands, you should try to position the cell pointer in the upper-left corner of the range so that it is easy to expand the highlight over the range. When a prompt asks you to specify the range, you can either type it in or press the cell pointer movement keys to highlight it.

TUTORIAL

In this tutorial, you format cells in the FORMAT model. The figure "Value Formats" shows the model as it will look after you format the cells. Refer to this figure to check your results as you complete the steps in this tutorial.

Value Formats

This figure shows some typical formats and how they are displayed when the number of decimal places is changed. The number 1.5 in cell B5 is the number carried to each of the cells in the model.

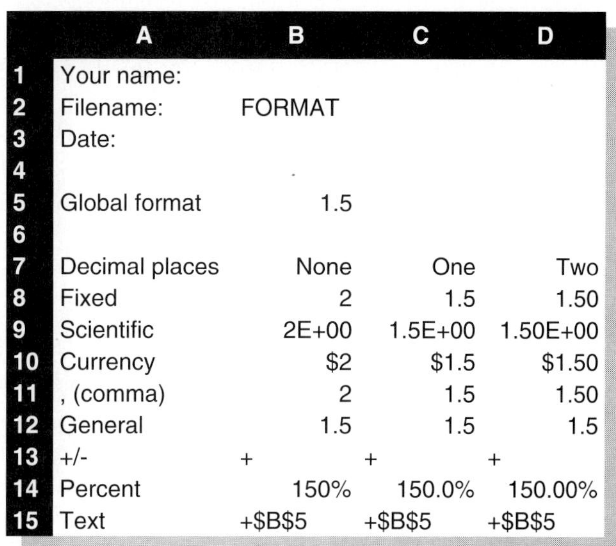

	A	B	C	D
1	Your name:			
2	Filename:	FORMAT		
3	Date:			
4				
5	Global format	1.5		
6				
7	Decimal places	None	One	Two
8	Fixed	2	1.5	1.50
9	Scientific	2E+00	1.5E+00	1.50E+00
10	Currency	$2	$1.5	$1.50
11	, (comma)	2	1.5	1.50
12	General	1.5	1.5	1.5
13	+/-	+	+	+
14	Percent	150%	150.0%	150.00%
15	Text	+$B$5	+$B$5	+$B$5

GETTING STARTED

1. Retrieve the FORMAT model and enter your name.

ALIGNING LABELS

2. With the cell pointer in cell B7, press [/][R][L] (for ***R**ange*, ***L**abel*) to display a submenu.
3. Press [R] (for ***R**ight*), and the prompt reads *Enter range of labels: B7..B7.*
4. Press [→] twice to expand the highlight to cell D7, and press [Enter←] to right-align the labels in their cells.

CHANGING THE GLOBAL FORMAT

5. Press [/][W][G][F][C] (for ***W**orksheet*, ***G**lobal*, ***F**ormat*, ***C**urrency*), and the prompt reads *Enter number of decimal places (0..15): 2.*
6. Press [Enter←] to display all numbers in the model with dollar signs and two decimal places.
7. Press [/][W][G][F][P] (for ***W**orksheet*, ***G**lobal*, ***F**ormat*, ***P**ercent*), and the prompt reads *Enter number of decimal places (0..15): 2.*
8. Type [0] and press [Enter←] to display all numbers in the model with percent signs and no decimal places.

FORMATTING A CELL

9. With the cell pointer in cell B8, press [/][R][F][F] (for ***R**ange*, ***F**ormat*, ***F**ixed*), and the prompt reads *Enter number of decimal places (0..15): 2.*

10. Type **0** and press [Enter←]. The prompt reads *Enter range to format:*.
11. Press [Enter←] to format only the cell containing the cell pointer.
12. With the cell pointer in cell C8, press [/][R][F][F] (for ***R**ange*, ***F**ormat*, ***F**ixed*), and the prompt reads *Enter number of decimal places (0..15): 2*.
13. Type **1** and press [Enter←]. The prompt reads *Enter range to format:*.
14. Press [Enter←] to format only the cell containing the cell pointer.
15. With the cell pointer in cell D8, press [/][R][F][F] (for ***R**ange*, ***F**ormat*, ***F**ixed*), and the prompt reads *Enter number of decimal places (0..15): 2*.
16. Press [Enter←] to accept the suggested number of decimal places, and the prompt reads *Enter range to format:*.
17. Press [Enter←] to format only the cell containing the cell pointer.

FORMATTING OTHER CELLS

18. Move the cell pointer to each of the cells on rows 9 through 15 with a number, and press [/][R][F] (for ***R**ange*, ***F**ormat*). Then:
    - Select the menu choice listed for that cell in column A.
    - If the prompt asks you to enter the number of decimal places (General, +/-, and Text formats don't), type **0**, **1**, or **2** depending on which column you are in.
    - When prompted to enter the range, press [Enter←] to format only the cell containing the cell pointer.
19. Move the cell pointer through the formatted cells, and watch the first line of the control panel. Abbreviations for the formats you entered are given in parentheses.

EXPLORING FORMATS

20. Press [/][W][G][F][C] (for ***W**orksheet*, ***G**lobal*, ***F**ormat*, ***C**urrency*), and the prompt reads *Enter number of decimal places (0..15): 2*.
21. Press [Enter←] to change the global format to dollar signs and two decimal places, but only the number in cell B5 that you did not format with a range format changes.
22. Enter numbers such as 10, 100, 1000, 10000, and 100000 in cell B5 to see the effects the size of the number has on the numbers displayed on the model.
    - When one or more cells displays a row of asterisks, change the global column width by pressing [/][W][G][C] (for ***W**orksheet*, ***G**lobal*, ***C**olumn-Width*). Press the right and left arrow keys to adjust the column widths, and press [Enter←].
    - Do not bother to widen the columns to remove the asterisks from the +/- row since the number of characters is directly related to the number you enter in cell B5. For example, if you enter the number 100, you have to set the column width to 100 to display the results on this row.
23. Repeat Steps 20 and 21 to change the global format a few times. Notice how the cells you formatted with a range format do not respond? Only the number in cell B5, which you did not format with a range format, changes. This is because range formats have precedence over global formats.

FINISHING UP

24. Save the model under the same name.
25. Enter **1.5** into cell B5 and print the model.
26. Save the model again to save the print range.
27. You have now completed this tutorial. Either clear the screen and continue with the next activity or quit the program.

QUICK REFERENCE

Although formatting is not needed to make your models more accurate, it does make them more attractive and more readable. Aligning labels and formatting values is a sign of professionalism.

Formatting Labels

You can align labels with the right or left edge of the cell or center them in the cell. You can also justify long labels so that they are aligned in a specified range of cells.

If you enter a label without a label prefix character, 1-2-3 aligns it based on the global setting (the default setting is left-aligned) and adds the global label prefix character. If you want to change the alignment of labels, you can do so with label prefix characters as you enter them, or you can use the range and global alignment commands after entering them.

LABEL PREFIX MENU CHOICES

To Align All Labels	Choose
With left edge of cells	*Left*
With right edge of cells (with one-space margin)	*Right*
Centered in cells	*Center*

KEY/Strokes

Changing Label Alignments

1. Either: Press / W G L (for ***W**orksheet, **G**lobal, **L**abel-Prefix*) to change the global setting.

   Or: Press / R L (for ***R**ange, **L**abel*) to format a range.
2. Enter one of the choices described in the table "Label Prefix Menu Choices."
3. If aligning a range, specify the range of labels to be aligned, and press Enter↵.

Aligning Labels as You Enter Them

You can change the alignment of all labels to be entered on the worksheet by specifying one of the default alignments described in the table "Label Prefix Menu Choices" with the ***/W**orksheet **G**lobal **L**abel* command. The new alignment affects all labels entered after the global change is made unless a different label prefix is entered with the label or it is realigned with a ***/R**ange **F**ormat* command. Changing the global alignment does not affect labels that have already been entered.

Aligning Previously Entered Labels

You can override the global label alignment in specific cells with the ***/ R**ange **L**abel* command. Blank cells included in the range are not affected by this command. Future labels entered into the range are aligned based on the global prefix. To realign a single label, you can press F2 (**Edit**) to display it on the second line of the control panel and change the label prefix character.

Formatting Values

1-2-3 provides several formats you can use when formatting values in your models. (See the table "Value Formats.") For many of these formats, you can also specify the number of decimal places (up to 15) to be displayed. Formatting numbers does not affect the way they are used in formulas. Numbers are always calculated with accuracy up to 15 decimal places. For example, you can format the number 1000.1425 so that it is displayed as $1,000, $1,000.14, 1000.142, and so on, but it is always calculated by any formulas that refer to it as 1000.1425.

TIPS

- Formats entered with the **/** ***R****ange* ***F****ormat* command are not erased by the **/*R****ange* ***E****rase* command. Any new numbers entered into those cells are displayed in the same format. To erase the format, use the **/*R****ange* ***F****ormat* ***R****eset* command.
- Release 2.2 and later versions allow you to change the display of negative values so that they are displayed with parentheses or negative signs. To use this feature, the numbers must be formatted with the currency or comma format. To choose the type of display, press / W G D O I N (for ***W****orksheet,* ***G****lobal,* ***D****efault,* ***O****ther,* ***I****nternational,* ***N****egative*) to display a submenu of the choices. Select either choice, and press Q (for ***Q****uit*) twice to return to the worksheet.
- You can prevent the display or printing of zeros that you enter or that are calculated by formulas with the **/** ***W****orksheet* ***G****lobal* ***Z****ero* command.
- Release 2.2 and later versions allow you to display a label in all cells that contain a value of zero. To do so, press / W G Z L (for ***W****orksheet,* ***G****lobal,* ***Z****ero,* ***L****abel*), and the prompt reads *Enter label (can include label prefix):*. Type the label and press Enter←.

→ KEY/Strokes

Formatting Values

1. If formatting a range, position the cell pointer in the upper-left cell in the range.
2. Either: Press / W G F (for ***W****orksheet,* ***G****lobal,* ***F****ormat*) to change the global setting.

   Or: Press / R F (for ***R****ange,* ***F****ormat*) to format a range.
3. Enter a choice described in the table "Value Formats." Depending on the format you choose, the prompt may read *Enter number of decimal places (0..15):*. If it does, type the number of decimal places and press Enter←.
4. Specify the range of values to be formatted and press Enter←.

VALUE FORMATS

Format	Description
Fixed	Displays numbers to a specified number of decimal places.
Scientific or *Sci*	Displays numbers as exponential scientific notation, for example, 1E+01.
Currency	Adds a dollar sign ($) before the number, separates thousands with commas, and displays negative numbers in parentheses, for example, ($1,000).
, (comma)	Separates thousands with commas and displays negative numbers in parentheses, for example, (1,000).
General	Displays numbers to the calculated number of decimal places (up to 15) If the column is not wide enough, numbers are displayed in scientific notation or as a row of asterisks.
+/-	Displays positive numbers as a row of +'s and negative numbers as a row of -'s to create simple bar graphs.
Percent	Displays numbers as percentages followed by a percent sign (%) and multiplies the decimal equivalent by 100 to display the number as a whole number. For example, 10% is actually 0.1. When formatted, it is displayed as 10% (0.1*100), but it is still used in formulas as 0.1.
Date	Displays a number in a date format.
Text	Displays formulas as entered instead of as current value. This is helpful when tracing the relationships among cells.
Hidden	Suppresses cell display.
Reset	Resets the range format to the global format.

EXERCISES

	A	B
1	Your name:	
2	Filename:	BUDGET
3	Date:	
4	=================================	
5	INCOME	FALL
6	Bank balance	$1,500
7	Income during semester	1,250
8	College loans	1,000
9	Total	$3,750
10		
11	EXPENSES	
12	Tuition	$1,000
13	Room & board	1,000
14	Books	200
15	Entertainment	300
16	Travel	500
17	Misc.	200
18	Total	$3,200
19		
20	Balance	$550

The Formatted College Budget Model
After you format the BUDGET model, it should look like this.

EXERCISE 1

FORMATTING THE BUDGET MODEL

1. Retrieve the BUDGET model.
2. Format it to match the one shown in the figure "The Formatted College Budget Model."
3. Save the model to save your changes.
4. Print out the formatted model.

EXERCISE 2

EXPLORING FORMATS

1. Retrieve the FORMAT2 model and enter your name in cell B1.
2. Change the global format to currency with two decimal places.
3. Change the global label prefix to centered.
4. Read the labels in column A, and follow the instructions to enter or format data on the same row in column B.
5. Save the finished model under its original name.
6. Make a printout.

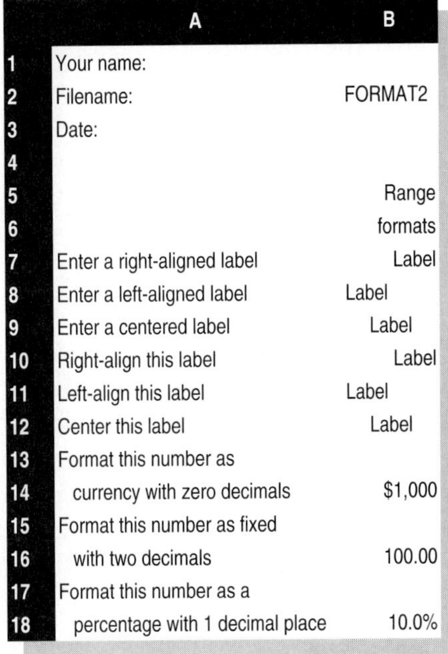

	A	B
1	Your name:	
2	Filename:	FORMAT2
3	Date:	
4		
5		Range
6		formats
7	Enter a right-aligned label	Label
8	Enter a left-aligned label	Label
9	Enter a centered label	Label
10	Right-align this label	Label
11	Left-align this label	Label
12	Center this label	Label
13	Format this number as	
14	currency with zero decimals	$1,000
15	Format this number as fixed	
16	with two decimals	100.00
17	Format this number as a	
18	percentage with 1 decimal place	10.0%

The FORMAT2 Model
After you format the FORMAT2 model, it should look like this.

TOPIC 11

Changing Column Widths

After completing this topic, you will be able to:

- Change column widths
- Reset column widths

When you open a new worksheet, all columns are set to nine characters wide. However, there are a number of situations in which you want to widen or narrow columns.

For example, if you enter a label that is longer than the column is wide, the entire label is displayed only if the adjoining cell is empty. If the adjoining cell contains data, any text that overflows into that column is not displayed. To display the entire label, you can widen the column.

The width of columns also affects whether numbers or values calculated by formulas are displayed correctly. If a number is too large to be displayed in a cell, the program might either:

- Display it in scientific notation, for example, display 100,000 as 1.00E+5.
- Fill the cell with asterisks (******).

To properly display the number, change the column width of the cell or the format of the number. The column width required to correctly display a number depends on:

- The size of the number. Columns must be set at least one character wider than the largest value. If the number is a negative number, there must also be an additional space for the negative sign.
- The format used. Formats that display commas or add dollar or percent signs require additional room for these characters.
- The number of decimal places specified when formatting.

For example, the number 12000 needs a column 6 characters wide. If formatted as currency to two decimal places, $12,000.00, the same number needs 11 characters. If the number might be displayed as a negative value, the column widths should each be one character wider; for example, -12000 requires 7 characters, and ($12,000.00) requires 12 characters.

TUTORIAL

In this tutorial, you change column widths in the COLUMNS model. The figure "The Column Width Model" shows before and after views of the model. Refer to this figure to check your results as you complete the steps in this tutorial.

	A	B
1	Your name:	
2	Filename:	COLUMNS
3	Date:	************************
4		
5	The conten	Contents
6	Number in g	************************
7	Number in c	************************
8	Label that is	Wide label

Before

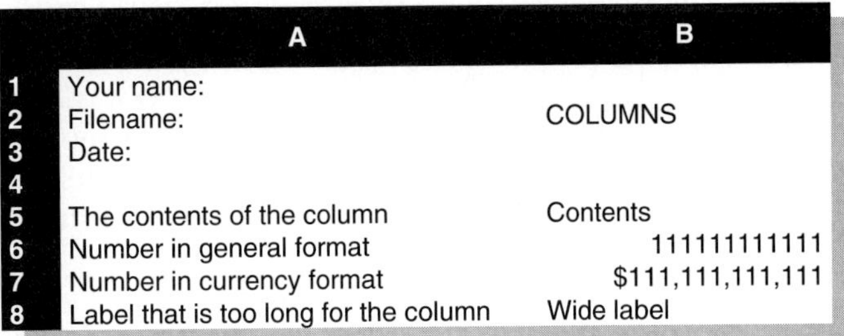

	A	B
1	Your name:	
2	Filename:	COLUMNS
3	Date:	
4		
5	The contents of the column	Contents
6	Number in general format	111111111111
7	Number in currency format	$111,111,111,111
8	Label that is too long for the column	Wide label

After

The Column Width Model

This figure shows the column width model before and after you change column widths.

GETTING STARTED

1. Retrieve the COLUMNS model and enter your name in cell B1.

CHANGING THE WIDTH OF A SINGLE COLUMN

2. Move the cell pointer anywhere in column A.
3. Press [/][W][C][S] (for ***W**orksheet*, ***C**olumn*, ***S**et-Width*), and the prompt reads *Enter column width (1..240): 9.*
4. Type **30** and press [Enter←].

CHANGING THE GLOBAL COLUMN WIDTH

5. Press [/][W][G][C] (for ***W**orksheet*, ***G**lobal*, ***C**olumn-Width*), and the prompt reads *Enter global column width (1..240): 9.*
6. Type **20** and press [Enter←] to change the width of all columns except column A to 20 characters wide.

RESETTING COLUMN WIDTHS

7. With the cell pointer in column A, press [/][W][C][R] (for ***W**orksheet*, ***C**olumn*, ***R**eset-Width*), and the column changes to the global column width of 20 characters wide.

CHANGING THE WIDTH OF A SINGLE COLUMN BY POINTING

8. With the cell pointer in column A, press [/][W][C][S] (for ***W**orksheet*, ***C**olumn*, ***S**et-Width*), and the prompt reads *Enter column width (1..240): 20.*
9. Press [→] to scroll the column wider, and press [←] to scroll the column narrower. As you do so, watch the column width following the prompt change.
10. With the column width set to 40, press [Enter←].

FINISHING UP

11. Print the model.
12. Save the model under the same name.
13. You have now completed this tutorial. Either clear the screen and continue with the next activity or quit the program.

QUICK REFERENCE

The width of a column, as measured in characters, determines how many characters can be displayed in cells falling in the column. When you first load the worksheet, all columns are nine characters wide. You can change the width of any or all columns to between 1 and 240 characters. Narrow columns let you see more on the screen and squeeze more into a printout, so columns should be as narrow as possible. Since column width is always set for an entire column—it cannot be wider or narrower at the top than at the bottom—a column must be set to the width required by the longest entry in the column.

You change the width of individual columns with the ***/W**orksheet* ***C**olumn* commands or the width of all columns with the ***/W**orksheet* ***G**lobal* ***C**olumn-Width* commands.

- You can change column widths before or after you enter data into them. If you use a global command, it changes the width of all columns except those previously changed with a range command. To have those columns respond to a change in the ***/W**orksheet* ***G**lobal* ***C**olumn* command, you must first reset them with the ***/W**orksheet* ***C**olumn* ***R**eset* command. Resetting sets the column to the current global width.
- To see the global column width setting, use the ***/W**orksheet* ***S**tatus* command.
- On Releasc 2.01, you must change the widths of all columns or one column. On Release 2.2 and later versions, you can also change the width of a range of columns.
- When the prompt asks you to enter the column width, you can either type the width (in characters) or press [→] and [←] to scroll the columns wider or narrower. Scrolling is especially useful when making final adjustments to column widths after labels and data have been entered since it lets you see what happens as the width is changed.

KEY/Strokes

Changing Column Widths (All Versions)

1. If changing a single column, position the cell pointer in the column to be changed. If changing column widths globally, the cell pointer can be anywhere.
2. Either: Press [/][W][G][C] (for ***W**orksheet,* ***G**lobal,* ***C**olumn-Width*) to change the global setting, and the prompt reads *Enter global column width (1..240):*.

   Or: Press [/][W][C][S] (for ***W**orksheet,* ***C**olumn,* ***S**et-Width*) to change an individual column, and the prompt reads *Enter column width (1..240):*.
3. Type the column width or press [→] or [←] to scroll it wider or narrower, and press [Enter ↵].

KEY/Strokes

Changing the Widths of a Range of Columns (Release 2.2 and Later Versions)

1. Position the cell pointer in the leftmost column to be changed.
2. Press [/][W][C][C][S] (for ***W**orksheet*, ***C**olumn*, ***C**olumn-Range*, ***S**et-Width*), and the prompt reads *Enter range for column width change:*.
3. Specify the range, and then press [Enter←]. The prompt reads *Select a width for range of columns (1..240):*.
4. Type the column width or press [→] or [←] to scroll the columns, and press [Enter←].

KEY/Strokes

Resetting Column Widths

1. On Release 2.01, position the cell pointer in the column to be reset. On Release 2.2 and later versions, position the cell pointer in the leftmost column to be reset.
2. Either: Press [/][W][C][R] (for ***W**orksheet*, ***C**olumn*, ***R**eset-Width*).
   Or: On Release 2.2 and later versions, press [/][W][C][C][R] (for ***W**orksheet*, ***C**olumn*, ***C**olumn-Range*, ***R**eset-Width*), and the prompt reads *Enter range for column width change:*. Specify the range, and press [Enter←].

EXERCISES

EXERCISE 1

ADJUSTING COLUMN WIDTHS ON OTHER MODELS

Retrieve each of the models you have worked on so far, and adjust column widths so that they are no wider or narrower than necessary. After adjusting each, make a new printout.

EXERCISE 2

REVISING THE DOW JONES AVERAGES MODEL

1. Retrieve the DOWJONES Model.
2. Delete columns B, C, and D.
3. Change the width of column A to 40 characters wide.
4. Reenter your name, the file's name, and the date in the new column B.
5. Save and print the revised model.

TOPIC 12

Copying and Moving Data

After completing this topic, you will be able to:

- Copy data on the worksheet
- Move data on the worksheet

You can copy or move the contents of cells to other locations on the worksheet. These are two of the most powerful spreadsheet features. Copying allows you to save time by entering a formula once and then copying it as needed. For example, you can create a monthly budget by entering the necessary formulas in the first monthly column and then copying them to the other monthly columns. Moving allows you to reorganize models as you create or revise them.

TUTORIAL

In this tutorial, you copy data to and from cells, columns, rows, and blocks. Your finished model should look like the figure "The Copy and Move Model." Refer to this figure to check your results as you complete the steps in this tutorial. Also as you complete the steps in the tutorial, watch the prompts that are displayed on the second line of the control panel. They indicate where you are in the procedure and what cells are involved.

The Copy and Move Model

After you have finished this tutorial, your model will look like this.

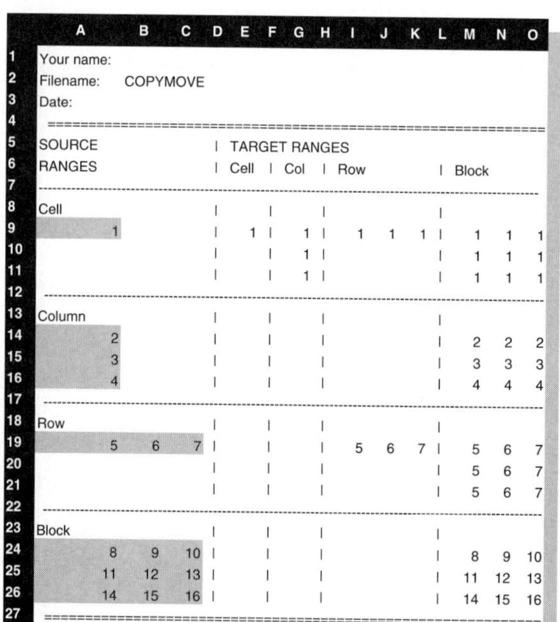

> **PROMPTS**
>
> Through Release 2.2, 1-2-3 displayed the prompts *Enter range to copy FROM:* and *Enter range to copy TO:* when you were prompted to specify the source and target ranges. With Release 2.3, these prompts were changed to *Copy what?* and *Copy where?* and Release 2.4 changed one to *To where?* but all other aspects of the procedure remained unchanged.

GETTING STARTED

1. Retrieve the COPYMOVE model and enter your name in cell B1.

COPYING A CELL TO A CELL

2. With the cell pointer in cell A9, press [/][C] (for ***Copy***), and the prompt displays the source range *A9..A9*.
3. Press [Enter↵] to accept the suggested range, and the prompt displays the target range *A9*.
4. Point to cell E9 and press [Enter↵] to copy the cell to a cell.

COPYING A CELL TO A COLUMN

5. With the cell pointer in cell A9, press [/][C] (for ***Copy***), and the prompt displays the source range *A9..A9*.
6. Press [Enter↵] to accept the suggested range, and the prompt displays the target range *A9*.
7. Point to cell G9 and press [.] (the period) to anchor the range.
8. Press [↓] to expand the highlight to cell G11, and press [Enter↵] to copy the cell to a column.

COPYING A CELL TO A ROW

9. With the cell pointer in cell A9, press [/][C] (for ***Copy***), and the prompt displays the source range *A9..A9*.
10. Press [Enter↵] to accept the suggested range, and the prompt displays the target range *A9*.
11. Point to cell I9 and press [.] (the period) to anchor the range.
12. Press [→] to expand the highlight to cell K9, and press [Enter↵] to copy the cell to a row.

COPYING A CELL TO A BLOCK

13. With the cell pointer in cell A9, press [/][C] (for ***Copy***) and the prompt displays the source range *A9..A9*.
14. Press [Enter↵] to accept the suggested range, and the prompt displays the target range *A9*.
15. Point to cell M9 and press [.] (the period) to anchor the range.
16. Press [→] and [↓] to expand the highlight to cell O11, and press [Enter↵] to copy the cell to a block.

COPYING A COLUMN TO A COLUMN

17. With the cell pointer in cell A14, press [/][C] (for ***Copy***), and the prompt displays the source range *A14..A14*.
18. Press [↓] to expand the highlight to cell A16 and press [Enter↵]. The prompt displays the target range *A14*.
19. Point to cell G14 and press [Enter↵] to copy the column to a column.

COPYING A COLUMN TO A BLOCK

20. With the cell pointer in cell A14, press [/][C] (for ***Copy***), and the prompt displays the source range *A14..A14*.

21. Press [↓] to expand the highlight to cell A16 and press [Enter←]. The prompt displays the target range *A14.*
22. Point to cell M14 and press [.] (the period) to anchor the range.
23. Press [→] to expand the highlight to cell O14, and press [Enter←] to copy the column to a block.

COPYING A ROW TO A ROW

24. With the cell pointer in cell A19, press [/][C] (for ***Copy***), and the prompt displays the source range *A19..A19.*
25. Press [→] to expand the highlight to cell C19 and press [Enter←]. The prompt displays the target range *A19.*
26. Point to cell I19 and press [Enter←] to copy the row to a row.

COPYING A ROW TO A BLOCK

27. With the cell pointer in cell A19, press [/][C] (for ***Copy***), and the prompt displays the source range *A19..A19.*
28. Press [→] to expand the highlight to cell C19 and press [Enter←]. The prompt displays the target range *A19.*
29. Point to cell M19 and press [.] (the period) to anchor the range.
30. Press [↓] to expand the highlight to cell M21, and press [Enter←] to copy the row to a block.

COPYING A BLOCK TO A BLOCK

31. With the cell pointer in cell A24, press [/][C] (for ***Copy***), and the prompt displays the source range *A24..A24.*
32. Press [→] and [↓] to expand the highlight to cell C26 and press [Enter←]. The prompt displays the target range *A24.*
33. Point to cell M24 and press [Enter←] to copy the block to a block.

PRINTING AND SAVING THE MODEL

34. Print out the model.
35. Save the model under the same name.

PRACTICING SOME MORE

36. Hold down [Alt] and press [E] to erase the target ranges in the model. The cells are erased by a macro—keystrokes that have been previously recorded so you can automatically play them back whenever you want.
37. Repeat Steps 2 through 33 to practice copying some more.

FINISHING UP

38. You have now completed this tutorial. Either clear the screen and continue with the next activity or quit the program.

QUICK REFERENCE

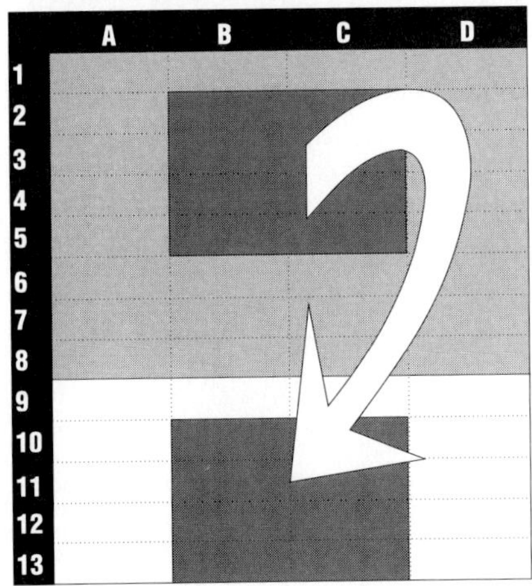

Copying a Range
When you copy a range of cells, a duplicate set of the range's contents and formats is copied from the source range to the target or destination range. Data in the cells in the source range are left unchanged.

One of the primary advantages of working with a spreadsheet is the ability that it gives you to quickly expand or modify your model without having to reenter all the data. The tools you use for this are the ***/Copy*** and ***/Move*** commands.

Copying Data

When you copy a range of cells, a duplicate set of the range's contents and formats is copied from the original cells, called the source range, to a new location, called the target range. The data in the cells in the source range are left unchanged.

- If any cells in the target range contain data, they are overwritten by the copied data.
- When you copy the contents of cells that formulas in other cells refer to, those formulas continue to refer to the original cells, not to the copies.
- When you copy ranges, you must specify cell addresses that define the source and target ranges. The cells you specify to identify the source and target ranges depend on the shape of the range you are copying. Some combinations of source and target ranges are not possible—for example, copying a column to a cell.

KEY/Strokes

Copying Data

1. Press [/][C] (for ***Copy***), and the prompt asks where you want to copy from or what you want to copy and displays the range.
2. Specify the source range and press [Enter↵]. The prompt asks where you want to copy to or where you want to copy and displays the range.
3. Specify the target range and press [Enter↵].

Specifying Ranges When Copying
The cells you specify as the source and target ranges when copying a range are shown tinted. Some combinations of source and target ranges are not possible, for example, copying a column to a cell. These impossible combinations are indicated by Xs. (However, 1-2-3 does have a ***/ Range Transpose*** command that allows you to copy data from columns to rows and vice versa.)

SOURCE RANGE	TARGET RANGE			
Cell	Cell	Column	Row	Block
Column	Cell (X)	Column	Row (X)	Block
Row	Cell (X)	Column (X)	Row	Block
Block	Cell (X)	Column (X)	Row (X)	Block

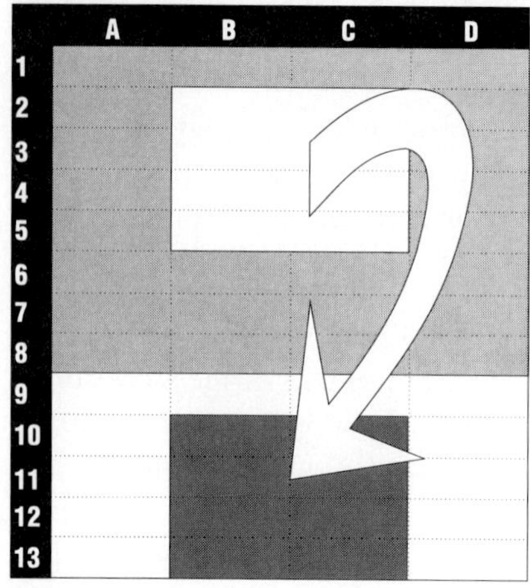

Moving a Range
When you move a range of cells, a duplicate of the cell's contents and formats is moved to the target range, and then the contents of the cells in the source range are automatically deleted. Anything already in the target range is overwritten and lost.

Moving Data

When you move a range of cells, a duplicate of the cells' contents and formats is moved to the target range, and then the contents of the cells in the source range are automatically deleted.

- If the cells in the target range contain any data, they are overwritten, and the old data are lost.
- Any formulas in the source range will continue to refer to the same cells when moved to the target range.
- If any formulas refer to cells in the target range, they display error messages.
- When you move the contents of cells, you must specify cells that define the source and target ranges. The cells you specify vary depending on the shape of the range.

→ KEY/Strokes

Moving Data

1. Press [/][M] (for ***Move***), and the prompt asks where you want to move from or what you want to move and displays the range.
2. Specify the source range and press [Enter←]. The prompt asks where you want to move to or where you want to move and displays the range.
3. Specify the target range and press [Enter←].

Specifying Ranges When Moving
The cells you specify as the source and target ranges when moving a range are shaded. For example, If you are moving a column, you specify the top and bottom cells in the source range and only the top cell in the target range. If you are moving a block, you specify the upper-left and lower-right cells in the source range and only the upper-left cell in the target range.

SOURCE RANGE	TARGET RANGE
Cell	Cell
Column	Column
Row	Row
Block	Block

EXERCISES

EXERCISE 1

EXPANDING THE COLLEGE BUDGET MODEL

In this exercise, you expand the college budget from one semester to four semesters.

1. Retrieve the BUDGET file.
2. Add the new labels on row 5.
3. Copy the ruled line from cell B4 to cells C4 through E4.
4. Copy column B, cells B6 through B20, to columns C through E.
5. In cell C6, enter the formula **+B20**, and copy it to cells D6 through E6. This makes each period's beginning bank balance the same as the previous period's ending balance.
6. Save and print the model. (Be sure to expand the print range to include the new columns.)
7. Change the opening balance in cell B6 to a number that causes the balance in cell E20 to become 0.
8. Make another printout, and clear the screen without saving the model.

The Expanded College Budget Model
After you expand the college budget model to cover four semesters, it should look like this.

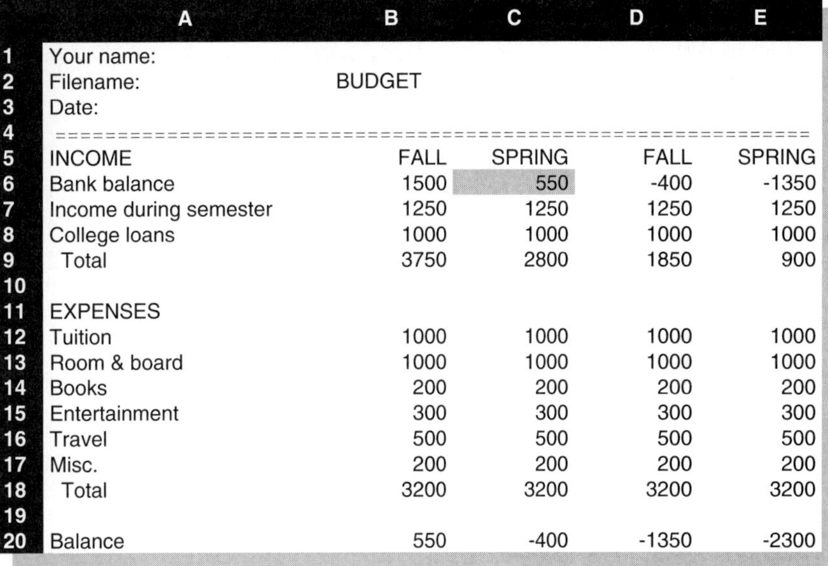

	A	B	C	D	E
1	Your name:				
2	Filename:	BUDGET			
3	Date:				
4	==============================	==========	==========	==========	==========
5	INCOME	FALL	SPRING	FALL	SPRING
6	Bank balance	1500	550	-400	-1350
7	Income during semester	1250	1250	1250	1250
8	College loans	1000	1000	1000	1000
9	Total	3750	2800	1850	900
10					
11	EXPENSES				
12	Tuition	1000	1000	1000	1000
13	Room & board	1000	1000	1000	1000
14	Books	200	200	200	200
15	Entertainment	300	300	300	300
16	Travel	500	500	500	500
17	Misc.	200	200	200	200
18	Total	3200	3200	3200	3200
19					
20	Balance	550	-400	-1350	-2300

EXERCISE 2

CREATING THE GRADE POINT AVERAGES MODEL

In this exercise, you create a model that allows you to calculate your grade point average.

1. Retrieve the GPA model and enter your name in cell B1.

2. In cell E8, enter the formula **+D8*B8**, and copy it to cells E9 through E10.
3. In cell E12, enter the function **@SUM(E7.E11)**, and copy it to B12.
4. In cell B14, enter the formula **+E12/B12**.
5. Save the model under its same name and make a printout.
6. Revise the model so you can use it to record your own grades and calculate your own GPA:
   - Insert 15 rows above the current row 11.
   - Erase all labels and numbers in the range B8.D10.
   - Copy the formula in cell E10 to the range E11.E25
   - Save the file but change its name to GPAMSTR.

The Grade Point Average Model
After you enter the grade point average model, it should look like this.

	A	B	C	D	E
1	Your name:				
2	Filename:	GPA			
3	Date:				
4	====================				
5	Courses taken	Credit	Letter	Grade	Total
6		hours	grades	points	GPs
7	--------------------				
8	Biology	4	A	4.00	16.00
9	English Lit.	3	A	4.00	12.00
10	Intro to Microcomputers	3	A	4.00	12.00
11	--------------------				
12	Totals	10			40.00
13	====================				
14	Grade point average (GPA)	4.00			

EXERCISE 3

DOUBLING A PENNY EVERY DAY

You may remember the childhood puzzle where kids would ask, "What if you put one penny in a bank on the first day and then doubled the amount every day? For example, on day two, you put two pennies in the bank; on day three, you put in four pennies; and so on. How many pennies would you have at the end of the month?" The answer was always surprising. In this exercise, you create a model that answers this question.

1. Enter the model shown in the figure "The Double Penny Model."
2. Use the ***/Data Fill*** command to enter the days.
3. Enter the number **.01** into cell B6.
4. In cell B7, enter a formula that multiplies the amount saved on day 1 (cell B6) times 2. Copy the formula to cells B8 through B36.
5. Format the numbers in column B as currency with two decimal places, and widen the column so that the larger numbers are displayed.
6. Save the finished model as PENNIES.
7. How much would you have at the end of 31 days if you started with $1?

	A	B
1	Your name:	
2	Filename:	PENNIES
3	Date:	
4		
5	Day	Saved
6	1	$0.01
7	2	$0.02
8	3	$0.04
9	4	$0.08
10	5	$0.16
11	6	$0.32
12	7	$0.64
13	8	$1.28
14	9	$2.56
15	10	$5.12
16	11	$10.24
17	12	$20.48
18	13	$40.96
19	14	$81.92
20	15	$163.84
21	16	$327.68
22	17	$655.36
23	18	$1,310.72
24	19	$2,621.44
25	20	$5,242.88
26	21	$10,485.76
27	22	$20,971.52
28	23	$41,943.04
29	24	$83,886.08
30	25	$167,772.16
31	26	$335,544.32
32	27	$671,088.64
33	28	$1,342,177.28
34	29	$2,684,354.56
35	30	$5,368,709.12
36	31	$10,737,418.24

The Doubling Penny Model
After you enter the doubling penny model, it should look like this.

EXERCISE 4

BALANCING A CHECKBOOK

One of the chores that each of us has to perform is balancing our checkbook. If we don't do it, or don't do it correctly, checks begin to bounce. In this exercise, you create a model that makes the checkbook-balancing calculations for you.

1. Enter the model shown in the figure "The Checkbook Model":
   - Set the global format to comma with two decimal places.
   - Use the ' label-prefix when entering check numbers in column A to left-align them in their cells.
   - Enter the number **598.47** into cell F6 and format it as shown.
   - Enter and copy the formulas described in the table "The CHKBOOK Model's Formulas."
   - Align all labels and adjust column widths so your model looks similar to the figure.
2. Save the finished model as CHKBOOK and make a printout.

THE CHKBOOK MODEL'S FORMULAS

#	Cell	Formula	Copy to
1	F8	*Balance* is **+F6+E8-D8.**	
2	F9	*Balance* is **+F8+E9-D9.**	F10.F17

The Checkbook Model
After you enter the checkbook model, it should look like this.

	A	B	C	D	E	F
1	Your name:					
2	Filename:	CHKBOOK				
3	Date:					
4	==					
5						Balance
6	Check #	Date	Check description	Amount	Deposit	$598.47
7	--					
8	1	01/01/199x	Textbook	45.62		552.85
9	2	01/10/199x	Airline ticket	156.50		396.35
10	3	02/12/199x	Dinner	28.70		367.65
11		02/23/199x	Pay check		112.40	480.05
12	4	03/04/199x	Jacket	52.80		427.25
13	5	03/04/199x	Bank charge		-5	422.25
14	6					422.25
15						422.25
16						422.25
17						422.25
18	==					

	A	B	C
1	Your name:		
2	Filename:	SERIES	
3	Date:		
4	=======================================		
5	Arithmetic	Geometric	Exponential
6	---------------------------------------		
7	2	2	2
8	3	4	4
9	4	8	16
10	5	16	256
11	6	32	65,536
12	7	64	4,294,967,296
13	=======================================		

The Number Series Model

After you enter the number series model, it will look like this illustration.

EXERCISE 5

EXPLORING SERIES OF NUMBERS

In math, there are three common types of number series: arithmetic, geometric, and exponential. In this exercise, you enter a model that allows you to see the relationships among these three series.

1. Enter the model shown in the figure "The Number Series Model":
   - Set the global format to comma with zero decimal places.
   - Set the global column width to 15.
   - Align labels to match the figure.
   - Enter the number **2** in cells A7, B7, and C7.
   - Enter and copy the formulas described in the table "The SERIES Model's Formulas."
2. Save the finished model as SERIES and make a printout.

THE SERIES MODEL'S FORMULAS

#	Cell	Formula	Copy to
1	A8	*Arithmetic* is **1+A7.**	A9.A12
2	B8	*Geometric* is **2*B7.**	B9.B12
3	C8	*Exponential* is **+C7^2.**	C9.C12

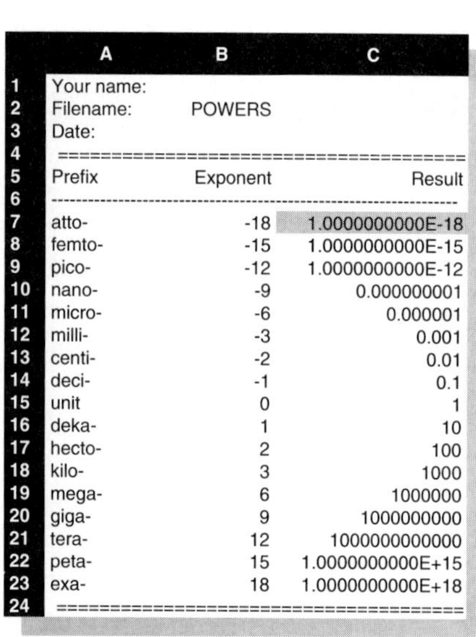

	A	B	C
1	Your name:		
2	Filename:	POWERS	
3	Date:		
4	=======================================		
5	Prefix	Exponent	Result
6	---------------------------------------		
7	atto-	-18	1.0000000000E-18
8	femto-	-15	1.0000000000E-15
9	pico-	-12	1.0000000000E-12
10	nano-	-9	0.000000001
11	micro-	-6	0.000001
12	milli-	-3	0.001
13	centi-	-2	0.01
14	deci-	-1	0.1
15	unit	0	1
16	deka-	1	10
17	hecto-	2	100
18	kilo-	3	1000
19	mega-	6	1000000
20	giga-	9	1000000000
21	tera-	12	1000000000000
22	peta-	15	1.0000000000E+15
23	exa-	18	1.0000000000E+18
24	=======================================		

The Powers of Ten Model

After you complete the powers of ten model, it should look like this.

EXERCISE 6

EXPLORING THE POWERS OF TEN

Many of the numbers used in science and engineering have names you can refer to them by. For example, the kilo in kilobytes stands for 1,000, or 10^3. The mega- in megabytes stands for 1 million, or 10^6. In this exercise, you enter formulas using exponents to create these numbers. Your finished model should look like the figure "The Powers of Ten Model." Refer to this figure to check your results as you complete the steps in this exercise.

1. Retrieve the file POWERS from your data disk.
2. Enter the formula **10^B7** in cell C7 to raise the base 10 to the power listed in column B.
3. Copy the formula to cells C8.C23.
4. Set the width of column C to 30 characters. You results should now match those in the figure. Some of the numbers end in the characters E- followed by two digits. These numbers are too small or too large to be displayed in their cells so they are being displayed in scientific notation.
5. Save the model under the filename POWERS and make a printout.

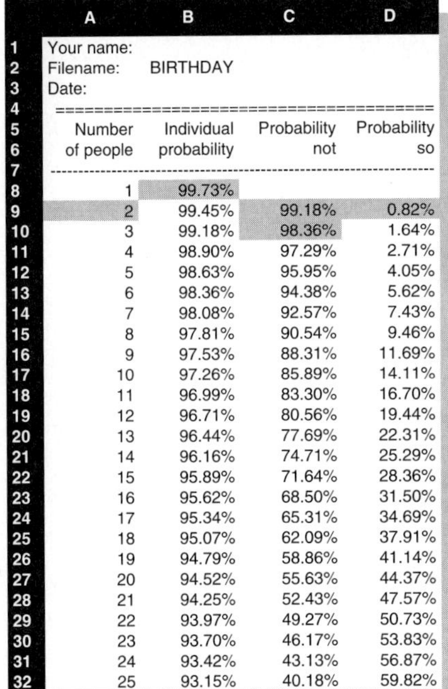

	A	B	C	D
1	Your name:			
2	Filename:	BIRTHDAY		
3	Date:			
4	==========	==========	==========	==========
5	Number	Individual	Probability	Probability
6	of people	probability	not	so
7	----------	----------	----------	----------
8	1	99.73%		
9	2	99.45%	99.18%	0.82%
10	3	99.18%	98.36%	1.64%
11	4	98.90%	97.29%	2.71%
12	5	98.63%	95.95%	4.05%
13	6	98.36%	94.38%	5.62%
14	7	98.08%	92.57%	7.43%
15	8	97.81%	90.54%	9.46%
16	9	97.53%	88.31%	11.69%
17	10	97.26%	85.89%	14.11%
18	11	96.99%	83.30%	16.70%
19	12	96.71%	80.56%	19.44%
20	13	96.44%	77.69%	22.31%
21	14	96.16%	74.71%	25.29%
22	15	95.89%	71.64%	28.36%
23	16	95.62%	68.50%	31.50%
24	17	95.34%	65.31%	34.69%
25	18	95.07%	62.09%	37.91%
26	19	94.79%	58.86%	41.14%
27	20	94.52%	55.63%	44.37%
28	21	94.25%	52.43%	47.57%
29	22	93.97%	49.27%	50.73%
30	23	93.70%	46.17%	53.83%
31	24	93.42%	43.13%	56.87%
32	25	93.15%	40.18%	59.82%

The Birthday Model
After you enter the birthday model, it should look like this.

EXERCISE 7

EXPLORING BIRTHDAY PROBABILITIES

Whenever there is a group of people together, the possibility that any two of them share the same birthday is surprisingly high. For example, if there is one other person in the room, the probability that they do not have the same birthday as you is 364/365, or 99.18%. The probability that the two of you do have the same birthday is therefore 100% – 99.18%, or .82%. If there are two other people in the room, you can calculate the probability that they don't have the same birthday with the formula (364/365)*(363/365). If there were five people, you would use the formula (364/365)*(363/365)*(362/365)*(361/365)*(360/365). If there were 25 people, the formula would be five times as long. Let's see how easy it is to make this calculation by entering and copying a few simple formulas.

1. Clear the screen, and enter the headings and labels shown on rows 1 through 7 of the figure "The Birthday Model."
2. Enter the number **1** in cell A8 and the formula **1+A8** in cell A9. Copy the formula in cell A9 to cells A10 through A32.
3. In cell B8, enter the formula **(365-A8)/365** and copy it to cells B9 through B32.
4. In cell C9, enter the formula **+B9*B8**.
5. In cell C10, enter the formula **+C9*B10** and copy it to cells C11 through C32.
6. In cell D9, enter the formula **1-C9** and copy it to cells D10 through D32.
7. Format the numbers in rows B, C, and D as percentages with two decimal places.
8. Save and print the model. You can see from the table you have created that if 25 people are in the room, the probability that two of them share a birthday is almost 60%.

TOPIC 13

Specifying Relative & Absolute Cell References

After completing this topic, you will be able to:

- Explain the differences among relative, absolute, and mixed cell references
- Specify relative, absolute, and mixed cell references

If you typed in every formula and function that you needed, you would not have to be concerned about relative and absolute cell references. But they become very important when you enter a formula in one cell and then copy it to others to save time.

When you create formulas, they often refer to other cells in the worksheet. The program does not automatically "remember" the actual cell address that the formula refers to; instead, it remembers the position relative to the cell the formula is entered in, for example, one column to the left and two rows up. When you copy the formula to another cell, it refers not to the original cell but to whatever cell is one column to the left and two rows up from the cell you copied it to.

This automatic adjustment occurs because the reference to the cell is a relative reference; that is, the position of the cell referred to is relative to the position of the formula. All formulas you enter have relative references unless you specify otherwise.

You do not always have to keep references to cells relative. You can also make them absolute references so that a formula refers to the same cell wherever it is copied on the worksheet.

You can also use mixed references, which keep the reference to the row or column relative while making the other reference absolute.

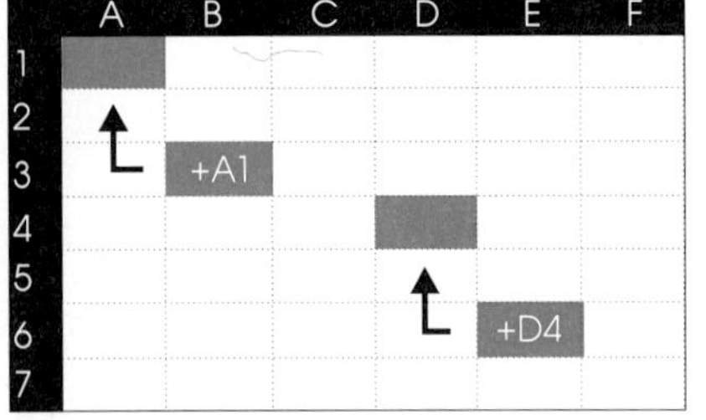

Copying Relative Cell References
When you copy the reference **+A1** from B3to E6 it refers to a cell one column to its left and two rows up.

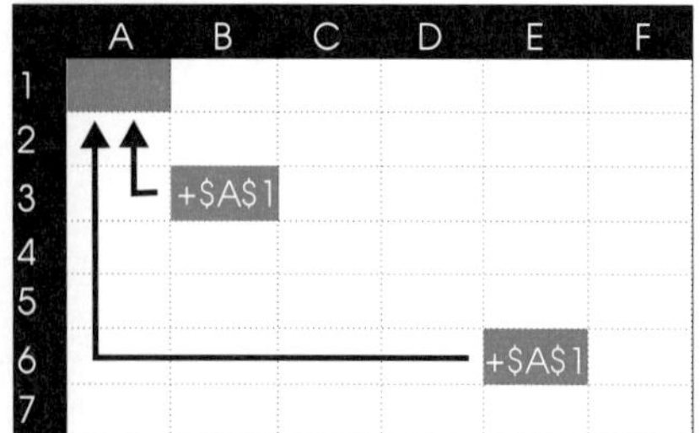

Copying Absolute Cell References
When you copy the reference **+$A$1** from B3 to E6 it continues to refer to cell A1.

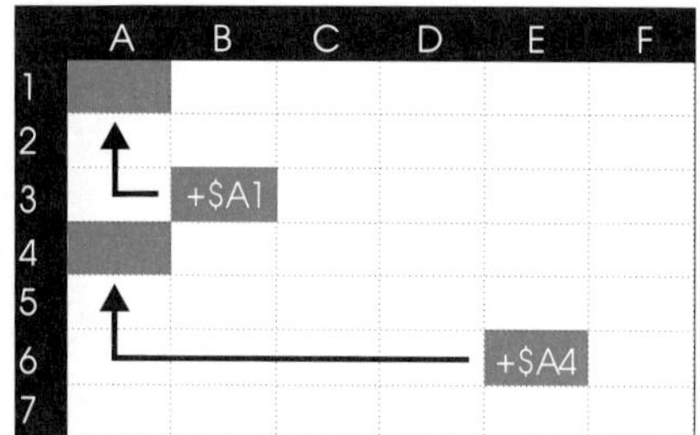

Copying Absolute Column and Relative Row References
When you copy the reference **+$A1** from B3to E6 it continues to refer to column A and whatever row is two up.

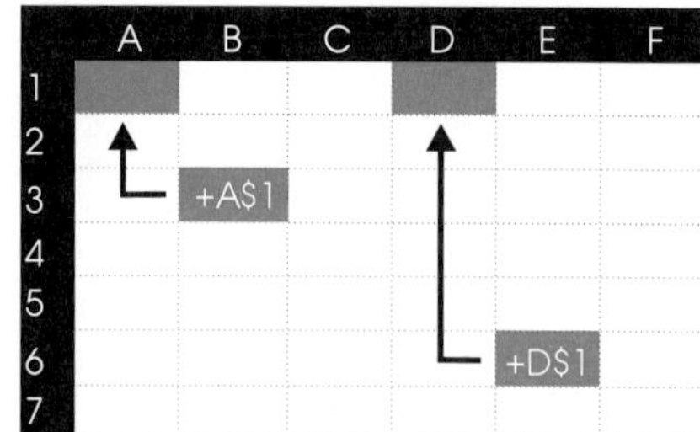

Copying Relative Column and Absolute Row References
When you copy the reference **+A$1** from B3 to E6 it continues to refer to row 1 and whatever column is to its left.

In this tutorial, you use relative and absolute references to create a five-year business plan. Your finished model should look like the figure "The Five-Year Plan Model." Refer to this figure to check your results as you complete the steps in this tutorial.

The Five-Year Plan Model
After you enter the five-year plan model, your results should look like this.

	A	B	C	D	E	F
1	Your name:					
2	Filename:	5YRPLAN				
3	Date:					
4						
5	Part 1. Variables					
6	Initial sales	1,000				
7	Sales growth rate	10%				
8	Cost of goods sold	56%				
9						
10	Part 2. Model					
11	Year	1994	1995	1996	1997	1998
12	Sales	1,000	1,100	1,210	1,331	1,464
13	Cost of goods sold	560	616	678	745	820
14	Gross margin	440	484	532	586	644

GETTING STARTED

1. Load the program or clear the screen.
2. Widen all the columns so that they are 10 characters wide.
3. Since you enter long labels in column A, widen that column so that it is 20 characters wide.
4. Enter the labels shown in column A of the figure "The Five-Year Plan Model." (Remember, you can press ↓ instead of Enter↵ after typing each label.)
5. Enter the variables in cells B6 through B8. Two of the numbers are percentages. To enter them, type **.1** and **.56** and they are displayed as 0 and 1, respectively, because the global format has been set to display all numbers as whole numbers.
6. Set the global format to , (comma) with zero decimal places.
7. Format the numbers in cells B7 and B8 as Percent with zero decimal places.

ENTERING AND CALCULATING DATA FOR 1994

8. In cell B11, enter **1994**.
9. In cell B12, enter the formula **+B6** to carry down opening sales from cell B6 in the variables section.
10. In cell B13, enter the formula **+B8*B12** to calculate cost of goods using the percent figure in the variable section.
11. In cell B14, enter the formula **+B12-B13** to subtract cost of goods from sales.

ENTERING AND CALCULATING DATA FOR 1995

12. In cell C11, enter the formula **+B11+1** to add 1 to the previous year.
13. In cell C12, enter the formula **+B12+($B7*B12)** to calculate sales by adding last year's sales to 10% of last year's sales for a 10% sales

increase. The dollar sign in front of the B7 cell reference will keep the column absolute when the formula is copied.

14. In cell C13, enter the formula **$B8*C12** to calculate cost of goods using the percent figure in the variable section. The dollar sign in front of the B8 cell reference will keep the column absolute when the formula is copied.
15. In cell C14, enter the formula **+C12-C13** to subtract cost of goods from sales.

COPYING THE FORMULAS FOR 1995 TO OTHER YEARS

16. With the cell pointer in cell C11, press [/] [C] (for ***Copy***), and the prompt gives the source range *C11..C11*.
17. Press [↓] to expand the highlight to cell C14 and press [Enter ↵]. The prompt gives the target range *C11*.
18. Press [→] to point to cell D11 and press [.] (the period) to anchor the range.
19. Press [→] twice to expand the highlight to cell F11 and press [Enter ↵] to copy column C to columns D through F.
20. Format the years as Fixed with zero decimal places so that they don't have commas in them.

LOOKING AT THE COPIED FORMULAS

21. Move the cell pointer to various cells in columns C through F to see what happened when formulas with absolute references were copied. All formulas that refer to cells in the variables section continue to refer to the same cells after being copied because they had absolute references to column B. All other references to cells refer to the column to their left because they were relative references.

SAVING AND PRINTING THE MODEL

22. Save the model under the filename 5YRPLAN.
23. Make a printout of the model.

EXPLORING WHAT-IFS

24. Change the sales growth rate in cell B7 from 10 to 15 percent. Sales increase in all but the first year by 15 percent instead of the original 10 percent. Cost of goods also increases but remains a constant 56 percent of sales. Gross margins increase because sales are increasing faster than cost of goods.
25. Change the cost of goods percentage in cell B8 from 56 to 60 percent. Cost of goods increases and gross margins are lower than in the previous what-if. If your goal was to obtain higher gross margins despite increases in cost of goods (perhaps because of increased prices), you have discovered how you can achieve this—increase sales sufficiently to achieve the increase in gross margins despite the increased cost of goods.

FINISHING UP

26. You have now completed this tutorial. Either clear the screen without saving your what-if changes to the model and continue with the next activity or quit the program.

QUICK REFERENCE

You specify absolute references by adding dollar signs ($) in front of the column or row references. You can type them in when you type formulas or use the F4 (**Abs**) key to cycle through the four possible combinations when you are pointing to build a formula. When pointing to a cell in point mode (the mode indicator reads *POINT*), the cell reference you are pointing to is displayed on the second line of the control panel, and its reference changes each time you press F4 (**Abs**). The table "Absolute and Relative Cell References" describes the sequence of choices.

ABSOLUTE AND RELATIVE CELL REFERENCES

Cell Reference	Column	Row
A1	Relative	Relative
$A1	Absolute	Relative
A$1	Relative	Absolute
$A$1	Absolute	Absolute

The F4 (**Abs**) key also works when you press F2 to display a formula for editing. Move the edit cursor to under the cell reference that you want to change, and press F4 (**Abs**) to cycle the cell reference through the four possible combinations.

EXERCISES

	A	B	C
1	Your name:		
2	Filename:	RUNTOTAL	
3	Date:		
4			
5	Month	Sales	Total
6			(to date)
7	Jan	100	100
8	Feb	110	210
9	Mar	120	330
10	Apr	130	460
11	May	140	600
12	Jun	150	750
13	Jul	160	910
14	Aug	170	1080
15	Sep	180	1260
16	Oct	190	1450
17	Nov	200	1650
18	Dec	210	1860

The Running Total Model
After you enter the running total model, your results should look like this.

EXERCISE 1

CALCULATING RUNNING TOTALS

One useful application of absolute and relative references is to anchor one end of a range while letting the other end remain relative. This way, you can enter a function that includes the first number in a range, but when you copy it, additional numbers are included. In this exercise, you use this technique to calculate a running total.

1. Enter the model shown in the figure "The Running Total Model":
   - Use the ***/Data Fill*** command to enter sales starting at 100 and stepping by 10.
   - In cell C7, enter the function **@SUM(B$7..B7)**, and copy it to cells C8 through C18. Notice how column C now calculates a running total on each row. Move the cell pointer down column C, and notice how the formula changed as it was copied.
2. Save the finished model as RUNTOTAL and make a printout.

	A	B	C
1	Your name:		
2	Filename:	RUNAVG	
3	Date:		
4			
5	Month	Sales	Average
6			(to date)
7	Jan	100	100
8	Feb	110	105
9	Mar	120	110
10	Apr	130	115
11	May	140	120
12	Jun	150	125
13	Jul	160	130
14	Aug	170	135
15	Sep	180	140
16	Oct	190	145
17	Nov	200	150
18	Dec	210	155

The Running Average Model
After you enter the running average model, your results should look like this.

EXERCISE 2

CALCULATING RUNNING AVERAGES

You can use the same technique you used in Exercise 1 to calculate a running average.

1. Enter the model shown in the figure "The Running Average Model":
   - Use the ***/Data Fill*** command to enter sales starting at 100 and stepping by 10.
   - In cell C7, enter the function **@AVG(B$7..B7)**, and copy it to cells C8 through C18. Notice how column C now calculates a running average on each row. Move the cell pointer down column C, and notice how the formula changed as it was copied.
2. Save the finished model as RUNAVG and make a printout.

EXERCISE 3

CREATING A MULTIPLICATION TABLE

Every math book you used in grade school probably had a multiplication table in the appendix. In this exercise, you create a multiplication table that allows you to display any range of numbers.

1. Enter the model shown in the figure "The Multiplication Table Model":
   - Set the global column width to 6 and set columns A and B to 10.
   - Enter the formulas described in the table "The MULTTAB Model's Formulas," and copy the formulas to the indicated cells.
2. Save the finished model as MULTTAB.
3. Print the model and save it again to save the print settings.
4. Change the start and increment numbers and watch the table change.

THE MULTTAB MODEL'S FORMULAS

#	Cell	Formula	Copy to
1	A11	Enter the formula **+B5**.	
2	A12	Enter the formula **+A11+B$6** so that the reference to cell B6 has the row reference absolute.	A13.A19
3	B8	Enter the formula **+B5**.	
4	C8	Enter the formula **+B8+$B6** so that the reference to cell B6 has the row reference absolute.	D8.J8
5	B11	Enter the formula **+$A11*B$8** so that the reference to cell A11 has the column absolute and B8 has the row reference absolute.	B11.J19

The Multiplication Table Model
After you enter the multiplication table model, your results should look like this.

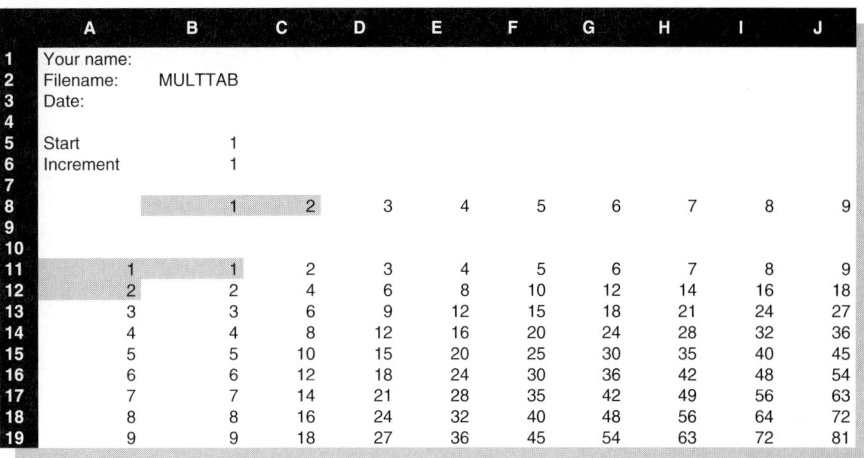

	A	B	C	D	E	F	G	H	I	J
1	Your name:									
2	Filename:	MULTTAB								
3	Date:									
4										
5	Start	1								
6	Increment	1								
7										
8		1	2	3	4	5	6	7	8	9
9										
10										
11	1	1	2	3	4	5	6	7	8	9
12	2	2	4	6	8	10	12	14	16	18
13	3	3	6	9	12	15	18	21	24	27
14	4	4	8	12	16	20	24	28	32	36
15	5	5	10	15	20	25	30	35	40	45
16	6	6	12	18	24	30	36	42	48	54
17	7	7	14	21	28	35	42	49	56	63
18	8	8	16	24	32	40	48	56	64	72
19	9	9	18	27	36	45	54	63	72	81

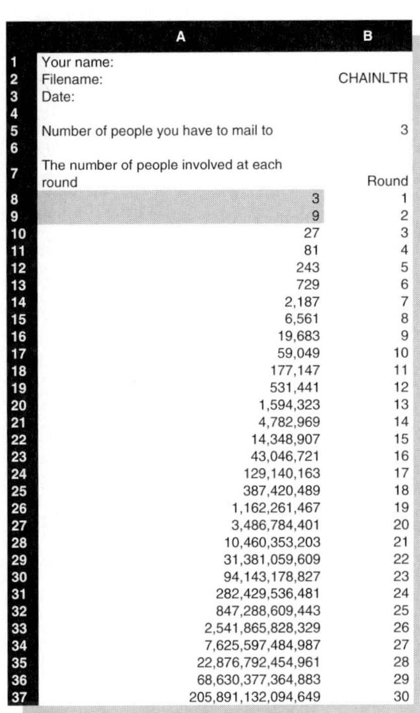

	A	B
1	Your name:	
2	Filename:	CHAINLTR
3	Date:	
4		
5	Number of people you have to mail to	3
6		
7	The number of people involved at each round	Round
8	3	1
9	9	2
10	27	3
11	81	4
12	243	5
13	729	6
14	2,187	7
15	6,561	8
16	19,683	9
17	59,049	10
18	177,147	11
19	531,441	12
20	1,594,323	13
21	4,782,969	14
22	14,348,907	15
23	43,046,721	16
24	129,140,163	17
25	387,420,489	18
26	1,162,261,467	19
27	3,486,784,401	20
28	10,460,353,203	21
29	31,381,059,609	22
30	94,143,178,827	23
31	282,429,536,481	24
32	847,288,609,443	25
33	2,541,865,828,329	26
34	7,625,597,484,987	27
35	22,876,792,454,961	28
36	68,630,377,364,883	29
37	205,891,132,094,649	30

The Chain Letter Model
After you enter the chain letter model, your results should look like this.

EXERCISE 4

EXPLORING CHAIN LETTERS

Have you ever received a chain letter asking you to send money to the sender? These letters always promise great rewards if you do so, and if you send copies of the letter to a number of other people who will then send you money. Because these letters are illegal, they are usually couched in some other terms; for example, you send $5 to the sender to buy mailing labels, which you in turn sell to others. Generally, these chain letters are a great investment—if you are the originator. The problem with them is that the number of people involved grows so fast that before too many mailings, the entire world population has to be involved.

1. Enter the model shown in the figure "The Chain Letter Model":
   - Use the ***/Data Fill*** command to enter the numbers in column B.
   - Set the width of column A to 60.
   - Enter the formulas described in the table "The CHAINLTR Model's Formulas" and copy the formulas to the indicated cells.
2. Save the finished model as CHAINLTR.
3. Print the model and save it again to save the print settings.
4. The variable is the number of people that you have to mail to in cell B3. Change this to 4 and then to 5. How many people are involved on the 10th round? The 30th?

THE CHAINLTR MODEL'S FORMULAS

#	Cell	Formula	Copy to
1	A8	*The number of people you have to mail to* is the number of people you have to mail to carried from cell B5.	
2	A9	*The number of people involved at each round* is the value in cell A8 multiplied by the number of people you have to mail to in cell B5 (an absolute reference).	A10.A37

CHAPTER 3 REVIEW

- Global formats affect the entire worksheet while range formats affect only the specified cells.
- Label formats affect how labels are aligned in their cells.
- Number formats affect how numbers and values calculated by formulas are displayed on the worksheet,
- When you format a range, you override the global format, and changes in the global format will not affect those cells until you reset them.
- If labels are not displayed in their entirety, you can widen the column.
- If asterisks are displayed in a cell, it means that the number is too large to be displayed in the cell in its current format. To display the number, you can change the format or widen the column.
- Copying data duplicates it elsewhere on the worksheet, and the original cells remain unchanged. Moving data duplicates the data elsewhere then deletes the original data.
- When you copy or move data, you specify a source range and a target range. The source range is the location of the current data, and the target range is where you want to move or copy it.
- The source range is always specified using the upper-left and lower-right cell addresses separated by a period. The target range depends on what you are copying or moving and where you are copying or moving it to.
- If you copy or move data into a range that already contains data, you overwrite that old data with the new.
- A relative cell reference refers to a cell or range of cells relative to the position of the reference. For example, it may refer to a cell that is two rows over and three up. Wherever you copy the reference to, it will always refer to a cell that is two rows over and three up from its current position.
- An absolute reference always refers to a specific cell or range of cells. No matter where you copy or move it to, it still refers to the same cell or range.
- You specify absolute references by typing a dollar sign before the column or row reference or by pressing F4 in point or edit mode to cycle through the four combinations.

CHAPTER 3 QUESTIONS

FILL IN THE BLANK

1. To change the format of all cells on the worksheet, you would use a ____________ command.
2. To change the format of selected cells on the worksheet, you would use a ____________ command.
3. To add dollar signs or commas to numbers on the screen, you use a ____________ command.

4. If asterisks are displayed in a cell, it means the number in the cell is ___________.
5. If a label is not entirely displayed in a cell, you should ___________ the column.
6. To copy or move cell contents, you specify both a ___________ and a ___________ range.
7. To specify a source range, you specify the ___________ and ___________ cells in the range.
8. A cell reference that continues to refer to a specific cell even after you have copied it, is called a(n) ___________ reference.
9. A cell reference that refers to a different cell after you copy of move it is called a(n) ___________ reference.
10. The character that you use to indicate that a reference to a column or row is absolute is ___________.
11. The four possible combinations of absolute and relative cells references are ___________, ___________, ___________, and ___________.
12. To cycle through the four possible combinations of absolute and relative cells references, you can press ___________ when the program is in ___________ or ___________ mode.
13. A range of cells that has been formatted with a range format will not respond to changes in a related global format until their format has been ___________.

MATCH THE COLUMNS

1. Global format	__	A cell reference that changes when you move or copy it
2. Range format	__	A cell reference that doesn't change when you move or copy it
3. Reset	__	Both row and column are relative
4. Asterisks	__	Column is relative but row is absolute
5. Source range	__	Affects the format of specific cells
6. Target range	__	Allows a range of formatted cells to respond to changes in global format
7. Relative reference	__	Indicate that a cell is too narrow to display a number
8. Absolute reference	__	Both row and column are absolute
9. F4	__	Column is absolute but row is relative
10. A2	__	Affects the format of all cells on the worksheet
11. $A2	__	The range of cells you copy or move from
12. A$2	__	The range of cells you copy or move to
13. $A$2	__	Cycles through combinations of absolute and relative cell references in point mode

WRITE OUT THE ANSWERS

1. If you format cells with a range command and then change the global format, what happens to the cells formatted with the range command?

2. Why would you want to change the width of a column?
3. What happens if a label is too long to fit into a column?
4. What happens if a value is too long to fit into a column? Describe two ways you can correct the problem.
5. If a cell displays a row of asterisks, what is the cause? How do you correct it?
6. If a cell displays a number in scientific notation, for example, 1.00E+5, what is the cause? How do you correct it?
7. List and briefly describe five formats you can use for values.
8. Describe the difference between copying and moving a range.
9. When copying or moving cells, how do you specify the range to be moved?
10. If you copy or move data into a range that already contains data, what happens to the old data?
11. What is the difference between a relative and an absolute cell reference? What are mixed references?
12. What character is used to specify absolute references? What key do you use to cycle through the four possible combinations of cell references? When can you use this key?
13. If you enter the formula B3 into cell D4 and then copy it to cell G6, what cell will it refer to in its new position?
14. If you enter the formula $B$3 into cell D4 and then copy it to cell G6, what cell will it refer to in its new position?
15. If you enter the formula $B3 into cell D4 and then copy it to cell G6, what cell will it refer to in its new position?

CHAPTER 3 PROJECTS

PROJECT 1

KEEPING BOX SCORES

1. Retrieve the BOXSCORE model.
2. Copy the formula in cell E7 to the range E8.E13.
3. Copy the formula in cell E17 to the range E18.E21.
4. Format the model so labels in columns B through E on row 32 are aligned right.
5. Save the model again.

PROJECT 2

CALCULATING EXCHANGE RATES

1. Retrieve the EXCHANGE model.
2. Enter and copy the formulas described in the table "The Exchange Rate Model's Formulas."

3. Change the global format to comma with 4 decimal places and format the Amount (in $) column as currency with 4 decimal places. (You may have to adjust column widths.)
4. Save the revised model under its original name.
5. Enter a variety of numbers into cell D5 and watch the exchange rates recalculate.
6. Clear the screen without saving your changes in cell D5.

THE EXCHANGE RATE MODEL'S FORMULAS

#	Cell	Formula	Copy to
1	C9	*Amount (in $)* is calculated by the formula **+B9*D$5**	C10.C28
5	D9	*Amount (in local)* is calculated by the formula **+D$5/B9**	D10.D28

PROJECT 3

CONVERTING BETWEEN ENGLISH AND METRIC UNITS

1. Retrieve the METRIC model.
2. Enter the formula **+C15*D$5** into cell D15 and then copy it to the ranges D16.D22, D25.D26, D29.D38, D41.D44, and D47.D50.
3. Quit.

CHAPTER 4 *Displaying Data Graphically*

TOPIC 14 *Creating Graphs—The Basics*

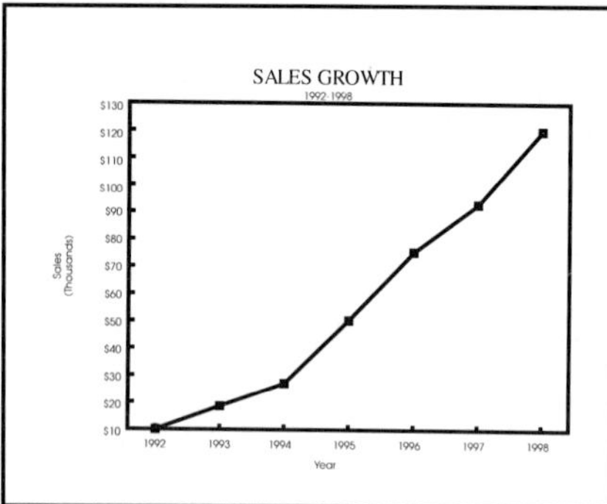

Discrete Data
Discrete data are values representing specific periods of time or other units.

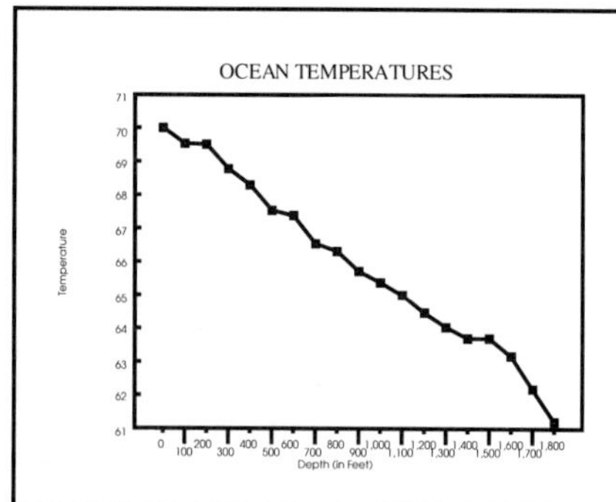

Continuous Data
Continuous data represent an unbroken range of values.

After completing this topic, you will be able to:

- Describe the different types of business graphs and when to use them
- Create and display graphs
- Use graph options to make your graphs more effective

A graphics program is integrated into 1-2-3 so that you can quickly and easily display data on the worksheet as a graph. The power of a 1-2-3 graph is that it graphs the values stored in ranges of cells. This way, when any of the values in those cells are changed, the graph immediately and automatically reflects those changes. This makes graphs powerful analytical tools since you can explore changes in your model graphically instead of trying to interpret columns or rows of numbers.

When creating graphs, one of your most important decisions is choosing the type of graph that best illustrates the data. For example, when creating graphs, you are usually graphing either discrete or continuous data.

Discrete data consist of values measured at a series of selected points. When plotted on a graph, all data between those points are meaningless. Graphs of this kind are frequently called time-series graphs and are used in business to plot sales, profits, inventory, and other important financial values. (For example, the profits from five annual income statements can be plotted to show trends. If you pick a point on the x-axis (the horizontal axis) that falls between periods and read it up to the line connecting data points and then across to the y-axis (the vertical axis), you will not locate the results at that point in time. For example, sales were not necessarily $40,000 midway through 1994. For that reason, a bar graph would be a better choice to illustrate sales.)

Continuous data occur when measurements have been sampled to determine a trend. Although each data point is a discrete value, the points are sampled so that when plotted, values between the measured data points can be estimated from the graph. This estimation of values falling between the points that were actually measured and plotted is called interpolation. When graphing continuous data, a general rule is that the more data points you measure and plot, the more accurate the graph is. (For example, an oceanographer can measure the temperature of the water at various depths in the ocean. If samples are measured at increments of 100 feet from the surface down to 1,800 feet,

VALUES PLOTTED ON XY GRAPH

Cost of Goods Sold	Gross Margin
560	440
616	484
678	532
745	586
820	644

a graph can be plotted using the available data points. When the graph is completed, temperatures can be estimated for any depth by reading up from the x-axis, which shows depth, and across to the y-axis, which shows temperature.)

Line Graphs

A line graph plots a series of values, called the data set (or data range), against the x-axis (the horizontal axis) and can be used to plot both discrete and continuous data.

Bar Graphs

Bar graphs are like a series of snapshots taken at intervals. When the bars on the graph are lined up in some meaningful order, they show relationships, changes, and trends. All bars on a bar graph start at the zero line. Positive values are indicated by bars that extend up from this base line; negative values, by bars that extend down. Bar graphs are particularly appropriate for discrete data—for example, if you want to graph the sales of several divisions within a company or make a comparison of sales by product.

Stacked Bar Graphs

Stacked bar graphs are similar to bar graphs, but instead of the bars being arranged side by side, they are stacked on top of each other. A stacked bar graph can show several sets of data at the same time.

XY Graphs

At first glance, XY graphs can look like line graphs, and under some circumstances, the two are identical. But because XY graphs use values

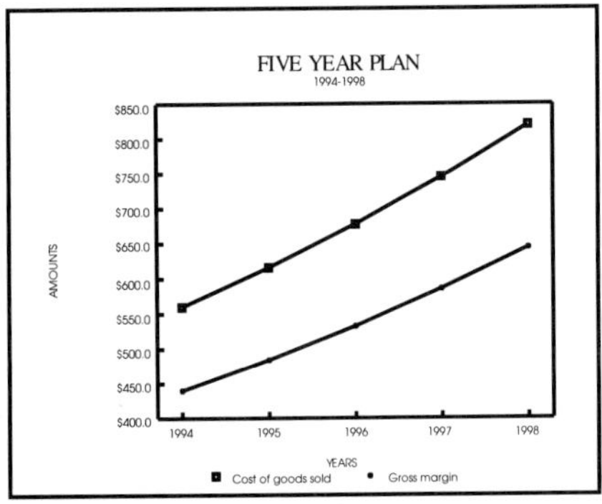

A Line Graph

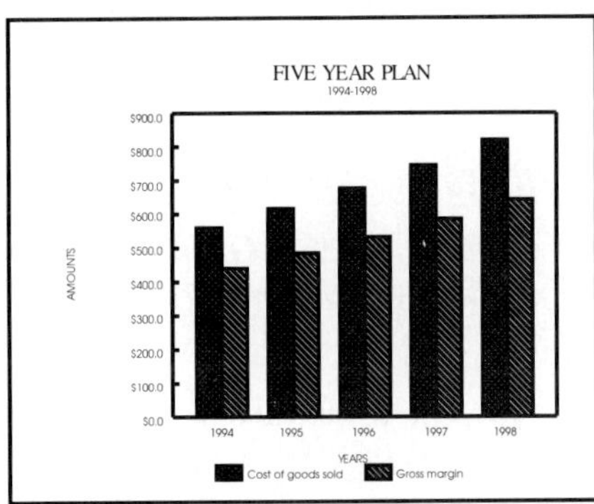

A Bar Graph

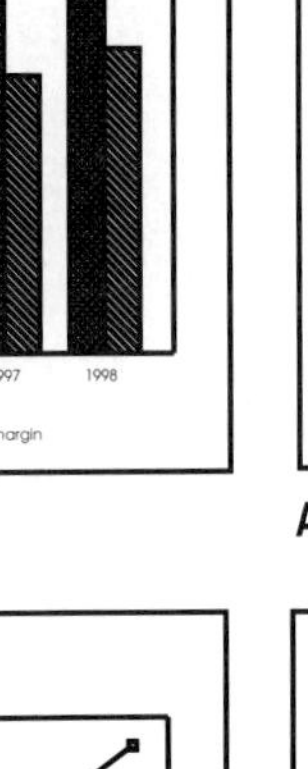

A Stacked Bar Graph

Graph Types

1-2-3 offers the graph types shown here.

An XY Graph

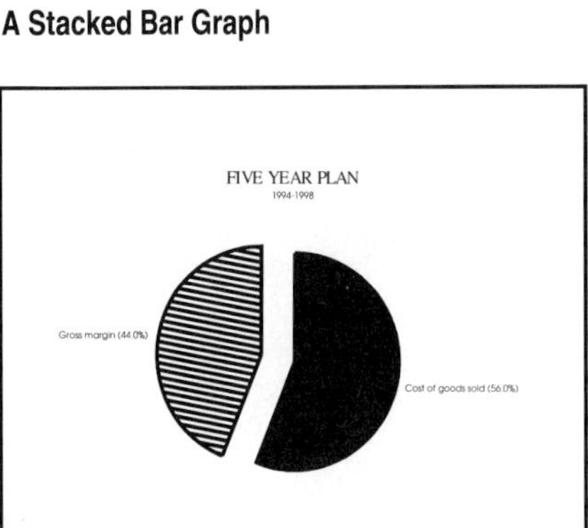

A Pie Chart

instead of labels on the x-axis, they can do much more than line graphs. For example, XY graphs can be used to find correlations between two or more sets of data. Whereas a line graph might show you the increase in a line item over time, an XY graph could show how that increase is related to another line item, such as net sales or profits. The table "Values Plotted on XY Graph" shows the pairs plotted on the graph shown in the figure "An XY Graph." The data points are located above the appropriate values on the scaled x-axis.

Pie Charts

A pie chart is like a single bar on a stacked bar graph; it can show only one set of data at a time. To compare different sets of data (for example, changes between one period and another), you must create and compare more than one pie chart. Pie charts are generally used to illustrate relationships, such as sales of various products in a product line and market shares. The pie represents "the whole" or 100 percent, and the individual slices represent parts of the whole. The relative sizes of the parts are indicated by the sizes of the pie slices.

TUTORIAL

In this tutorial, you explore graphs by creating one for the 5YRPLAN model.

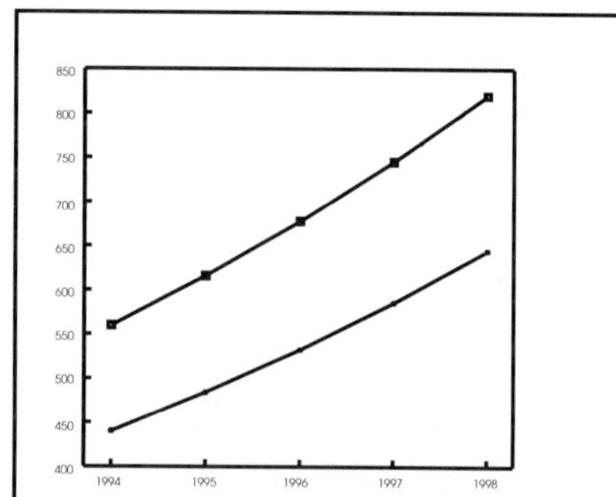

The Five-Year Plan's Line Graph
When you display the graph of the five-year plan, it looks like this.

GETTING STARTED

1. Retrieve the 5YRPLAN model.
2. Change the numbers in the variables section if they are not 1000 as the initial sales (cell B6), 10% as the sales growth rate (cell B7), and 56% as cost of goods sold (cell B8).

CREATING A LINE GRAPH

3. Press [/][G] (for ***G**raph*) to display the Graph menu.
4. Press [X], and the prompt reads *Enter x-axis range:*.
5. Type **B11.F11** and press [Enter ↵].
6. Press [A], and the prompt reads *Enter first data range:*.
7. Type **B13.F13** and press [Enter ↵].
8. Press [B], and the prompt reads *Enter second data range:*.
9. Type **B14.F14** and press [Enter ↵].

DISPLAYING A GRAPH

10. Press [V] (for ***V**iew*) to display the graph that plots cost of goods sold and gross margins over the five-year period of the plan. It should match the one shown in the figure "The Five-Year Plan's Line Graph."
11. Press any key to remove the graph and return to the Graph menu.

CHANGING THE GRAPH TYPE

12. Press [T][S] (for ***T**ype*, ***S**tack-Bar*).

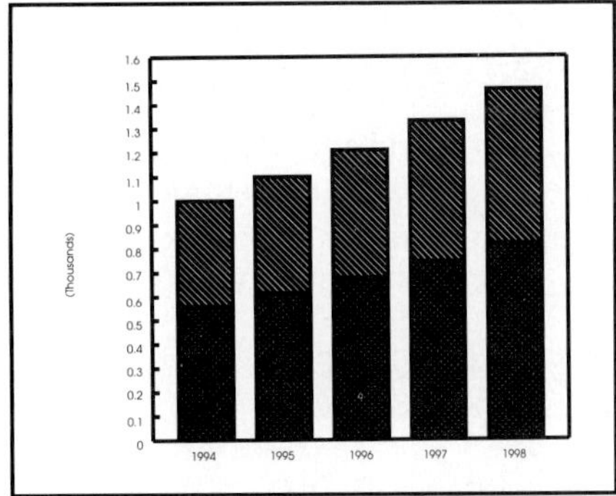

The Five-Year Plan's Stacked Bar Graph
The five-year plan graph looks like this when you display it as a stacked bar graph.

13. Press V (for ***View***) to display the graph as a stacked bar graph that should match the one shown in the figure "The Five-Year Plan's Stacked Bar Graph."
14. Press any key to remove the graph and return to the Graph menu.

ADDING TITLES TO THE GRAPH

15. Press OTF (for ***O**ptions*, ***T**itles*, ***F**irst*), and the prompt asks you to enter the first or top line of the title.
16. Type **FIVE-YEAR PLAN** and press Enter←.
17. Press TS (for ***T**itles*, ***S**econd*), and the prompt asks you to enter the title's second line.
18. Type **1994-1998** and press Enter←.
19. Press TX (for ***T**itles*, ***X**-Axis*), and the prompt reads *Enter x-axis title:*.
20. Type **YEARS** and press Enter←.
21. Press TY (for ***T**itles*, ***Y**-Axis*), and the prompt reads *Enter y-axis title:*.
22. Type **AMOUNTS** and press Enter←.

ADDING LEGENDS

23. Press LA (for ***L**egend*, ***A***), and the prompt asks you to enter the legend for the A or first data range.
24. Type **\A13** and press Enter←.
25. Press LB (for ***L**egend*, ***B***), and the prompt asks you to enter the legend for the B or second data range.
26. Type **\A14** and press Enter←.

FORMATTING THE Y-AXIS VALUES

27. Press SYFC (for ***S**cale*, ***Y**-Scale*, ***F**ormat*, ***C**urrency*), and the prompt reads *Enter number of decimal places (0..15):*.
28. Type **1** and press Enter←.
29. Press Q (for ***Q**uit*) twice to return to the Graph menu.
30. Press V (for ***V**iew*).

    The graph now looks like the one in the figure "The Five-Year Plan's Revised Stacked Bar Graph." (This figure was created on Release 2.2; if you are using Release 2.01 or an earlier version, your graph may look slightly different.)

    - The legends are the labels in cells A13 and A14 carried to the graph by the \A13 and \A14 references you typed when prompted to enter the A and B legends.
    - The y-axis is scaled using the currency format.
31. Press any key to remove the graph and return to the Graph menu.
32. Press Q (for ***Q**uit*) to return to the worksheet.

The Five-Year Plan's Revised Stacked Bar Graph
After you add titles and legends and scale the y-axis, the stacked bar graph looks like this.

FINISHING UP

33. Save the model under the same name so you save all of the graph settings. Be sure to do this; you will use this graph again.
34. You have now completed this tutorial. Either clear the screen and continue with the next activity or quit the program.

QUICK REFERENCE

To create a graph, all you have to do is specify a single data range and an x-axis range that identifies the values being plotted. However, you have the option of adding text and formats to the graph to make it more comprehensible to others.

Specifying Graph Ranges
When you define graph ranges, they must all contain the same number of data points (cells).Here the x-axis has been defined as cells B11 through F11. Two data ranges have been defined on rows 13 and 14, and each contains the same number of data points (cells) as the x-axis.

	A	B	C	D	E	F
1	Your name:					
2	Filename:	5YRPLAN				
3	Date:					
4						
5	Part 1. Variables					
6	Initial sales	1,000				
7	Sales growth rate	10%				
8	Cost of goods sold	56%				
9						
10	Part 2. Model					
11	Year	1994	1995	1996	1997	1998
12	Sales	1,000	1,100	1,210	1,331	1,464
13	Cost of goods sold	560	616	678	745	820
14	Gross margin	440	484	532	586	644

x-axis

Data Ranges

Creating Graphs

There is only one requirement when creating a graph. You must specify a range of cells, called the data range, that is to be graphed. To compare data, you can graph up to six data ranges on the same graph. If you want to label the data points on your graph, you can specify a range of cells on the worksheet as the x-axis range. Any data in the cells in this range are used to label the x-axis of the graph (except an XY graph where they are treated as values).

KEY/Strokes

Creating a Graph

1. Press [/] [G] (for ***Graph***) to display the Graph menu containing the choices described in the table "Graph Menu Commands."
2. Press [X] (for ***X***), and the prompt reads *Enter x-axis range:*.
3. Type in or point to an x-axis range and press [Enter←] to return to the Graph menu.
4. Press [A] (for ***A***), and the prompt reads *Enter first data range:*.
5. Type in or point to a data range and press [Enter←] to return to the Graph menu.
6. Repeat Steps 4 and 5 (but press [B] through [F]) if you want to add additional data ranges.
7. Press [V] (for ***View***) to display the graph.
8. Press any key to clear the graph from the screen and return to the Graph menu.
9. Press [Q] (for ***Quit***) to return to the worksheet.
10. Save the model so that you save the graph settings.

GRAPH MENU COMMANDS

Menu Choice	Description
Type	Selects one of the available graph types: • On Releases 2.2 and earlier, these include ***Line***, ***Bar***, ***XY***, ***Stack-Bar***, and ***Pie***. • Releases 2.3 and 2.4 also include ***Area***, ***HLCO*** (high-low-close), ***Mixed***, and ***Features***. Mixed allows you to combine line and bar graphs. Features displays a submenu that allows you to reverse the x-axis and y-axis positions, stack bars, change the frame around the graph, and add 3D effects.
***X** (range)*	Sets the x-axis range, the range all other ranges are plotted against. When displaying an XY graph, the data in this range are plotted as values. For all other graph types, the data are used to label the x-axis.
A - F	Specifies up to six data ranges plotted against the x-range.
Reset	Cancels all graph settings for the current graph or any of the six ranges. When you reset a graph range, it is no longer displayed on the graph. • ***Graph*** cancels all graph settings. • ***X*** cancels the x-axis range. • ***A*** through ***F*** cancel ranges A through F. • ***Ranges*** (Release 2.2 and later versions only) cancels all ranges. • ***Options*** (Release 2.2 and later versions only) cancels all entries made through the Graph Options menu such as titles and scales. • ***Quit*** returns you to the Graph menu.
View	Displays the current graph. (Press any key to clear the graph.)
Save	Saves the current graph in a .PIC file so that it can be printed from the PrintGraph program.
Options	Specifies various options for enhancing the graph, including legends, formats, titles, and scaling. (See the table "Graph Options Settings.")
Name	Names a graph so that it can be viewed at a later time.
Group	(Release 2.2 and later versions only) allows you to select adjacent rows and columns for graphing rather than specifying each range individually. When you use this command, you are prompted to enter the range. The first row or column in the range is used as the x-axis, and the adjoining rows or columns are the data ranges. After selecting the range, you specify if the range is columnwise or rowwise. • ***Columnwise*** plots the data in each column as a single data range. • ***Rowwise*** plots the data on each row as a single data range.
Quit	Exits from the Graph menu and returns to ready mode.

The Graph Settings Sheet
Release 2.2 and later versions added a settings sheet that lists all the current settings for a graph. This settings sheet is displayed whenever you press / G (for Graph). The settings sheet varies from release to release. This figure shows the Release 2.4 version.

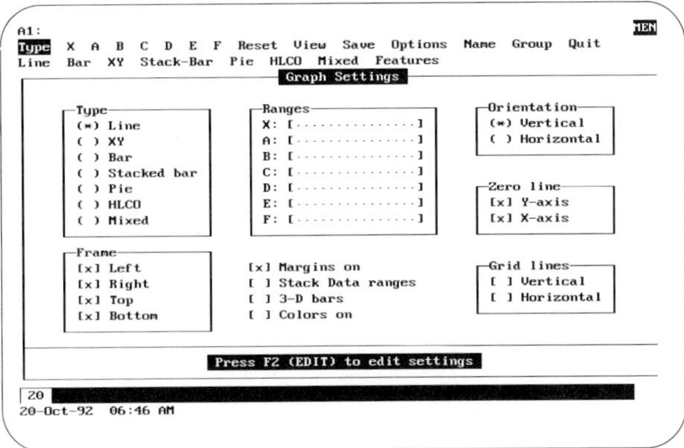

Displaying Graphs

After creating and displaying a graph, you press any key to clear the graph from the screen. Then, pressing F10 (**Graph**) displays the graph again. If your computer does not have the hardware necessary to display graphs on the screen, the computer beeps when you try to view the graph. The only way you can see graphs without replacing or updating the hardware is to save the graphs and then print them out with the PrintGraph program, covered in the next topic.

Options

1-2-3 offers you a lot of control over the way your data are presented on a graph or chart.

→ KEY/Strokes

Changing Graph Options

1. Press / G V (for ***G**raph, **V**iew*) to display the graph, and press any key to return to the Graph menu.
2. Press O (for ***O**ptions*) to display the Graph Options menu.
3. Make any of the choices described in the table "Graph Options Settings."
4. Save the model so that you save the new graph settings.

TIP

You can use the labels that you enter into worksheet cells as titles for your graph or as legends. This makes it easy to revise the graph because changing the labels in the worksheet cells changes the graph automatically. To refer to cells, when prompted to enter a title or legend, enter the backslash followed by the cell's address or its range name (see Topic 19). For example, to refer to a label in cell A1, type **\A1**.

GRAPH OPTIONS SETTINGS

Option	Description
Legend	• Identifies the symbols or patterns used to plot graphs so that data ranges can be distinguished from one another. You can either type in the legend or type a backslash and the cell's address to carry a label from a cell to the graph's legend. • Release 2.2 and later versions have a Range command so that you can enter all the legends in worksheet cells and then specify their range. This adds all legends with a single command.
Format	Formats the entire graph of selected data ranges so that they are displayed with lines, symbols, both, or neither. When data labels are used, the symbols and lines can both be suppressed so that data points are indicated only by the data labels.
Titles	Adds a one- or two-line graph title and x- and y-axis titles. The titles can be up to 39 characters long. The x-axis title describes the range of labels or values against which data are being plotted. The y-axis title describes the data ranges being plotted.
Grid	Grid lines can be displayed vertically, horizontally, or both vertically and horizontally to make data points easier to read across or down to the values on the axes.
Scale	Displays the choices ***Y** Scale*, ***X** Scale*, and ***S**kip*. When you select ***Y** Scale* or ***X** Scale*, your choices are: • ***A**utomatic* scaling is normally the default setting. The y-axis expands to include the largest and smallest data point being plotted. If you generate a series of graphs by changing data in the model, the scale on each may be different.

GRAPH OPTIONS SETTINGS *(CONTINUED)*

- ***Manual*** scaling can be used to override the program's automatic scaling of the y-axis. On XY graphs, the x-axis can also be manually scaled.
- ***Upper*** sets the upper limit of the values to be plotted when using manual scaling.
- ***Lower*** sets the lower limit of the values to be plotted when using manual scaling. If you enter a positive lower limit, it is ignored by bar or stacked bar graphs since they always start at zero.
- ***Format*** controls the way numbers on the axes are displayed.
- ***Indicator*** displays or hides the scale indicator that is displayed when 1-2-3 automatically scales the values on the graph so that they fit better. The scale indicator indicates the order of magnitude that 1-2-3 has chosen and is displayed between the axis title and the axis.
- ***Quit*** returns you to the Graph menu.
- ***Skip*** is used when the x-axis gets crowded with a series of long numbers or dates like January 1994 through December 1998. Sometimes, the labels will even overlap. To prevent this, you can "skip" some labels, for example, so that only every other label is displayed.

Color Displays the graph in colors (if supported by your system).

B&W Displays the graph in monochrome.

Data-Labels

- Data labels are displayed inside the graph area to describe data ranges. To use them, you enter the labels into worksheet cells and specify the range when you are prompted to enter the data label range.
- Release 2.2 and later versions have a ***Group*** command so that you can enter data labels for all ranges with a single command.

Quit Returns you to the Graph menu.

To shade, color, or explode the slices on a pie chart, enter numbers into cells on the worksheet, and specify them as the pie chart's B range. A number between 1 and 7 indicates shading or color, and a 0 or an 8 indicates no shading or color. To explode a slice, add 100 to its corresponding shading number, or just enter the number 100. For example, to explode the first slice, enter 100 in the first cell in the B range. To explode it, and specify its shading or color as 6, enter 106.

EXERCISES

EXERCISE 1

GRAPHING ONE OF YOUR OTHER MODELS

In this exercise, you create a graph for any of the other models that you have entered in previous exercises. To do so, retrieve the model, and then graph the data ranges. When you have finished, save the model so that you save the graph settings. The models to choose from include POWERS, RUNAVG, and RUNTOTAL.

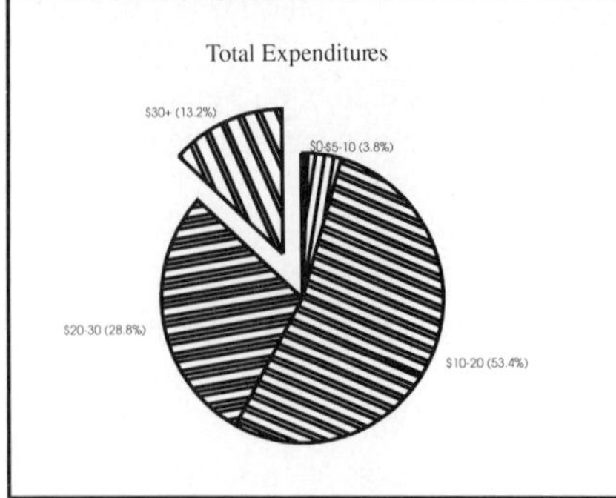

The Market Analysis Model's Graph
After you create the market analysis pie chart, your results should look like this.

THE MARKET MODEL'S GRAPH ELEMENTS

Element	Description
Graph type	Pie
x-axis	B6.F6
First data range	B11.F11
Second data range	B17.F17 (to assign patterns and explode slice)
Graph title	Total Expenditures

THE SERIES MODEL'S GRAPH ELEMENTS

Element	Description
Graph type	Line
X-axis range	A7.A12
First data range	A7.A12
Second data range	B7.B12
Third data range	C7.C12

EXERCISE 2

PERFORMING A MARKET ANALYSIS

In this exercise, you create a model and graph that can be used for market analysis.

1. Retrieve the MARKET model and enter your name.
2. Create the graph shown in the figure "The Market Analysis Model's Graph" using the information supplied in the table "The MARKET Model's Graph Elements."
3. Save the finished model under its original name.
4. To eliminate the overlapping labels, enter 101 into cell B17 and 5 into cell F17. Then view the graph again.
5. Save the revised model.

EXERCISE 3

ADDING OPTIONS TO ANOTHER GRAPH

In this exercise, you add titles and legends to the graph you created in Exercise 1. To do so, retrieve the model and add appropriate titles, legends, grids, and formats. When you have finished, save the model so that you save the graph settings.

EXERCISE 4

GRAPHING THE SERIES MODEL

One thing you should avoid doing is plotting very large and very small data ranges on the same graph. In this exercise, you graph the SERIES model to demonstrate the problems this can cause.

1. Retrieve the SERIES model.
2. Create the graph described in the table "The SERIES Model's Graph Elements." When you view the graph, notice how the small values are not plotted. They are overwhelmed by the larger values. (Programs that offer logarithmic graphs allow you to graph ranges like this on the same graph.)
3. Save the model so that you save the new graph settings.
4. Reset the third data range (C) to remove it from the graph. Then view the graph again. How has the display of the two remaining data ranges changed?

TOPIC 15

Naming & Printing Graphs

After completing this topic, you will be able to:

- Name graphs so that you can save more than one with the worksheet
- Save graphs into files on the disk
- Print graphs

After you have created a graph, you can create additional graphs for the same model and save them to a disk file so that you can print them out with the PrintGraph program. The latest releases of 1-2-3 include WYSIWYG (for "what you see is what you get" and pronounced *wizzy-wig*) features that allow you to display the model just as it will appear when printed. For example, cells that are boldfaced or shaded on printouts will be boldfaced or shaded on the screen. However, these features, called add-ins, change (sometimes dramatically) from release to release. For this reason, this text covers the PrintGraph program that is available on all releases. To learn more about WYSIWYG graphing, refer to your 1-2-3 manual.

TUTORIAL

In this tutorial, you create named graphs for the 5YRPLAN model. You then save graphs and print them.

GETTING STARTED

1. Retrieve the 5YRPLAN model.

NAMING THE GRAPHS

2. Press [/][G][V] (for ***G**raph*, ***V**iew*) to display the graph on the screen. (If it isn't displayed, you did not save the file after adding the graph in Topic 14.)
3. Press any key to clear the graph and return to the Graph menu.
4. Press [N][C] (for ***N**ame*, ***C**reate*), and the prompt reads *Enter graph name:*.
5. Type **BAR** and press [Enter←]. The Graph menu reappears.

CHANGING THE GRAPH TYPE

6. Press [T][L] (for ***T**ype*, ***L**ine*).
7. Press [V] (for ***V**iew*) to display the graph as a line graph.
8. Press any key to remove the graph and return to the Graph menu.

NAMING THE NEW GRAPH

9. Press N C (for ***N**ame*, ***C**reate*), and the prompt reads *Enter graph name:*.
10. Type **LINE** and press Enter←.

DISPLAYING THE TWO NAMED GRAPHS

11. Press N U (for ***N**ame*, ***U**se*), and the prompt reads *Enter name of graph to make current:*.
12. Highlight *LINE* and press Enter←.
13. Press any key to return to the Graph menu.
14. Press N U (for ***N**ame*, ***U**se*), and the prompt reads *Enter name of graph to make current:*.
15. Highlight *BAR* and press Enter←.
16. Press any key to return to the Graph menu.
17. Press Q (for ***Q**uit*) to return to the worksheet.
18. Save the file to save the two named graphs.

SAVING THE GRAPHS TO DISK FILES

19. Use the ***/G**raph **N**ame **U**se* command to display each of the named graphs. After displaying each, press any key to return to the menu and press S (for ***S**ave*). You will be prompted to enter a filename for the graph. Save the line graph as LINE and the stacked bar graph as BAR. (1-2-3 will automatically add the extension .PIC to the files on the disk.) When you have finished, remove the graph menu.

LOADING THE PRINTGRAPH PROGRAM

20. There are two ways to load the PrintGraph program:
    - If you loaded 1-2-3 by typing **LOTUS** to display the Lotus Access System, quit 1-2-3, and then select ***P**rintGraph* from the Access System menu.
    - Load the PrintGraph program directly from the operating system. To begin, quit 1-2-3 and insert the PrintGraph disk into drive A, or change to the 1-2-3 directory on a hard disk. Then type **PGRAPH** and press Enter←.

The PrintGraph Menu
The PrintGraph program contains a menu from which you make choices just as you do from the worksheet's menus. The graphs you select for printing, and the settings you make, are displayed below the menu. There are slight, and insignificant, variations between screens for the various releases. This figure shows the Release 2.4 version.

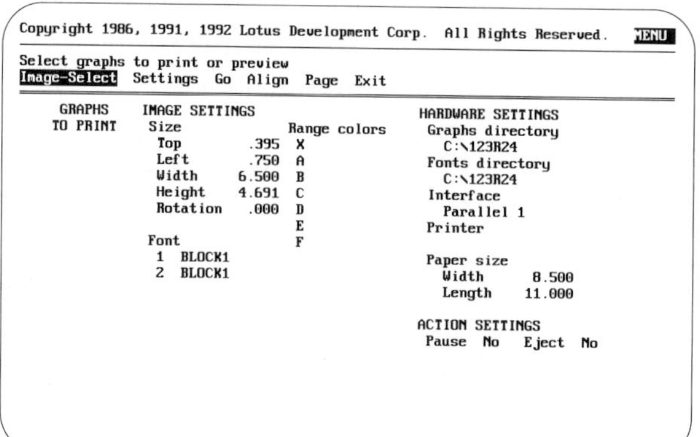

SPECIFYING PRINTGRAPH SETTINGS

21. Press S H G (for ***S**ettings*, ***H**ardware*, ***G**raphs-Directory*).
22. Enter the directory as follows:
    - On a hard disk system, type **A:** and press Enter↵.
    - On a floppy disk system, type **B:** and press Enter↵.
23. Press P (for ***P**rinter*).
24. Highlight the desired printer and press Spacebar to select the printer and place a # symbol in front of it indicating it has been selected.
25. Press Enter↵ to return to the Hardware menu.
26. Press Q (for ***Q**uit*) twice to return to the PrintGraph menu.

SELECTING A GRAPH TO PRINT

27. Press I (for ***I**mage-Select*) to display a list of the graphs on the disk.
28. Highlight *LINE* and press Spacebar to select the graph and place a # symbol in front of it indicating it has been selected.
29. Press F10 to preview the graph (if your computer is equipped to display graphics).
30. Press Spacebar to clear the graph, then press Enter↵ to return to the PrintGraph menu, and the graph that you have selected to print is listed under the heading *GRAPH IMAGES SELECTED* (Release 2.01) or *GRAPHS TO PRINT* (Release 2.2 and later versions).

SPECIFYING HOW THE GRAPH IS TO BE PRINTED

31. Press S I S H (for ***S**ettings*, ***I**mage*, ***S**ize*, ***H**alf*).
32. Press Q (for ***Q**uit*) three times to return to the Graph menu, and the size is indicated under the heading *IMAGE OPTIONS* (Release 2.01) or *IMAGE SETTINGS* (Release 2.2 and later versions).
33. Press S A E Y (for ***S**ettings*, ***A**ction*, ***E**ject*, ***Y**es*).
34. Press Q (for ***Q**uit*) twice to return to the PrintGraph menu, and the current eject setting is indicated under the heading *ACTION OPTIONS* (Release 2.01) or *ACTION SETTINGS* (Release 2.2 and later versions).

PRINTING THE GRAPH

35. Press A G (for ***A**lign*, ***G**o*), and in a few moments, the graph begins printing out.

FINISHING UP

36. When your graph has finished printing, you can print another graph or exit the PrintGraph program. To exit, press E Y (for ***E**xit*, ***Y**es*). This returns you to either the operating system or the Access System depending on how you loaded the program.

QUICK REFERENCE

If you want to have more than one graph for a model, you must name them. To print graphs, you must first save them and then load the separate PrintGraph program.

Naming Graphs

Many times, you want to create more than one graph of the same model. To do so, you create them one at a time and assign each of them a name. You can then refer to their names when you want to display them on the screen. Naming graphs allows you to display a series of graphs from the same model, much like a slide show. That way, you can use graphs to look at more than one aspect of a problem.

KEY/Strokes

Naming Graphs

1. Press [/][G][V] (for ***G**raph*, ***V**iew*) to display the graph that you want to name.
2. Press any key to return to the Graph menu.
3. Press [N] (for ***N**ame*) to display the Graph Name menu.
4. Make any of the choices described in the table "Naming Graphs."

NAMING GRAPHS

Command	Description
Use	Displays the prompt *Enter name of graph to make current:* and a list of previously named graphs. To display one of them, highlight it and press [Enter ←].
Create	Displays the prompt *Enter graph name:*. Do so (up to 14 characters) and press [Enter ←] to name the graph.
Delete	Displays the prompt *Enter name of graph to delete:* and a list of previously named graphs. To delete one of them, highlight it and press [Enter ←].
Reset	Resets all named graphs without any confirmation. If you use this command by mistake, all of your graphs will be lost except the one you displayed most recently. (Press [F10] (**Graph**) to display that one.)
Table	(Release 2.2 and later versions only) prompts for a range. When you point to a cell and press [Enter ←], all named graphs are listed with their name, type, and the first line of the title.

Saving and Printing Graphs

To print a graph with 1-2-3, you first use the Graph menu to display it on the screen and then use the Save command to save it to a disk file. (1-2-3 adds the extension .PIC.) You then load the PrintGraph program. From that program, you can specify which graphs are to be printed, and you can specify a number of options. The PrintGraph program is a separate program. You can load it in one of two ways:

- If you load the Access System, you can quickly switch between the 1-2-3 worksheet and the PrintGraph program. From the Access System, press [1] (for ***1**-2-3*) to display the worksheet, or press [P] (for ***P**rintGraph*) to display the PrintGraph menu. When you quit either program, the Access System menu reappears so that you can move to the other parts of the 1-2-3 program or quit the program.

- You can return to the operating system and run the program named PGRAPH.EXE by typing **PGRAPH** and pressing Enter←. On a floppy disk system, this program is on the PrintGraph disk on earlier releases. On a hard disk system, this program is in the same directory as the 1-2-3 program files.

→ KEY/Strokes

Saving Graphs

1. Press / G V (for ***G**raph, **V**iew*) or / G N U (for ***G**raph, **N**ame, **U**se*) to display the graph on the screen.
2. Press any key to return to the Graph menu.
3. Press S (for ***S**ave*), and the prompt reads *Enter graph file name:*.
4. Type the name you want to save the graph under and press Enter←.

→ KEY/Strokes

Printing Graphs

1. Load the PrintGraph program.
2. Make any changes described in the table "PrintGraph Print Options."
3. Press I (for ***I**mage-Select*) to display a list of graph .PIC files on the disk. Highlight the ones you want to print, and press Spacebar to mark them. (Press Spacebar to unmark files if you change your mind.)
4. Press Enter← to return to the PrintGraph menu.
5. Press S (for ***S**ettings*) if you want to change any of the settings described in the table "The PrintGraph Settings Menu."
6. Press A G (for ***A**lign, **G**o*) to begin printing.

PRINTGRAPH PRINT OPTIONS

Option	Description
***I**mage-Select*	Displays a list of graph .PIC files on the disk. Highlight the ones you want to print, and press Spacebar to mark them. (Press Spacebar to unmark files if you change your mind.) You can also highlight one of the graphs and press F10 (GRAPH) to preview it on the screen. Then press any key to return to the menu. Press Enter← to return to the PrintGraph menu.
***S**ettings*	Displays the menu described in the table "The PrintGraph Settings Menu."
***G**o*	Starts printing the selected graphs.
***A**lign*	Sets the printer so that the current position in relation to the printer's printhead is the top of the page.
***P**age*	Advances the paper in the printer to the top of the next page.
***E**xit*	Returns you to DOS or the Lotus Access System.

TIPS

- When you press F10 (**Graph**), the most recently displayed graph is displayed again.
- If you revise a named graph, be sure to rename it to save the changes.
- Saving a graph saves it only for printing. You cannot recall it for editing. To revise the graph, use the ***/Graph*** commands on the worksheet, and then save it again.

THE PRINTGRAPH SETTINGS MENU

Option	Description
Image	Displays a submenu that allows you to specify the following: ***S**ize* specifies if the graph is to be printed full or half size. You can also manually enter the graph's settings and margins. ***F**ont* specifies the font used for the first line of the title and the font used for the rest of the graph's text. You choose fonts the same way you select graphs for printing. (See the table "PrintGraph Print Options.") ***R**ange-Colors* specifies colors to be used for each range if your printer supports color.
***H**ardware*	Displays a submenu that allows you to specify the following: ***G**raphs-Directory* specifies the directory in which the graph files are stored. ***F**onts-Directory* specifies the directory in which the fonts are stored. ***I**nterface* specifies the port the printer is connected to. ***P**rinter* specifies which printer the graph is to be printed on. ***S**ize-Paper* specifies the length and width of the paper you are printing on.
***A**ction*	***P**ause* pauses the printer after each graph is printed. ***E**ject* ejects paper from the printer after each graph is finished.
***S**ave*	Saves the revised settings in a file named PGRAPH.CNF.
***R**eset*	Cancels any changes you have made and returns to the settings that were last saved in the configuration file.
***Q**uit*	Returns you to the PrintGraph menu.

EXERCISES

EXERCISE 1

PRINTING OTHER GRAPHS

Print any other graphs that you created in previous tutorials and exercises. For example, you created a stacked bar graph and named it BAR for the 5YRPLAN model. You also modified a graph in Exercise 3 of Topic 14. Print one or more of the graphs half size.

EXERCISE 2

GRAPHING TRIGONOMETRY FUNCTIONS

1. Complete the model shown in the figure "The Trigonometry Model" using the formulas described in the table "The TRIG Model's Formulas".
2. Create the two graphs described in the table "The TRIG Model's Graph Elements" and name them COS and SIN.
3. To remove the symbols from the graph, use the command ***/Graph Options, Format, A, Lines***.

	A	B	C
1	Your name:		
2	Filename:	TRIG	
3	Date:		
4			
5	Start	-12.57	
6	Increment	0.16	
7			
8	x	x * COS x	x * SIN x
9	-12.57	-12.57	0.05
10	-12.41	-12.26	-1.93
11	-12.25	-11.64	-3.81
12	-12.09	-10.74	-5.54
13	-11.93	-9.59	-7.09
164	12.23	11.54	-4.04
165	12.39	12.20	-2.17
166	12.55	12.55	-0.21
167	12.71	12.58	1.82
168	12.87	12.28	3.85

The Trigonometry Model
After you enter the trigonometry model, it should look like this.

4. To keep the labels on the x-axis from overlapping, use the command ***/Graph Options, Scale, Skip,*** **10.**
5. Save the model and the graph, and print the graph.

THE TRIG MODEL'S FORMULAS

#	Cell	Formula	Copy to
1	A9	Enter the cell reference **+B5.**	
2	A10	Enter the formula **+A9+B$6.**	A11.A168
3	B9	Enter the formula **+A9*@COS(A9).**	B10.B168
4	C9	Enter the formula **+A9*@SIN(A9).**	C10.C168

THE TRIG MODEL'S GRAPH ELEMENTS

Element	x*COS(x)	x*SIN(x)
Graph type	Line	Line
x-axis	A9.A168	A9.A168
First data range	B9.B168	C9.C168
Name	COS	SIN

The Trigonometry Model's Graph
After graphing the trigonometry model, your graphs of the sine and cosine functions should look like this.

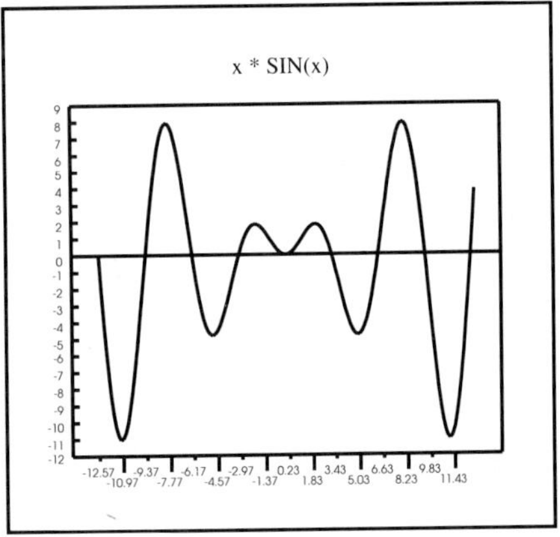

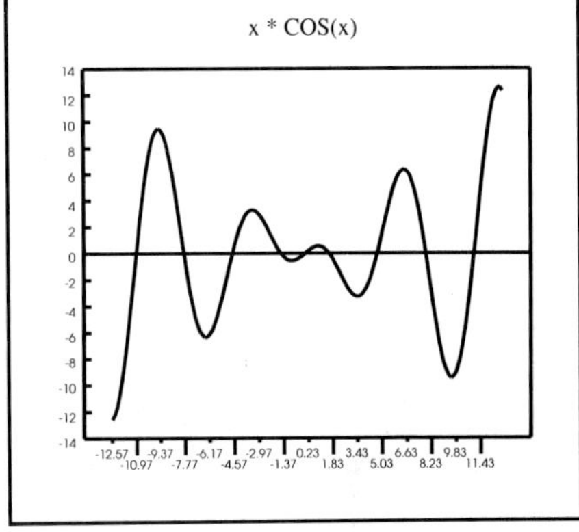

CHAPTER 4

REVIEW

SUMMARY

- When you graph data on the worksheet, the graph automatically changes to reflect any changes you make in the data.
- Discrete data, such as year-end results or sales broken down by territory, are best graphed on bar or stacked-bar graphs.
- Continuous data, such as temperature changes relative to ocean depths, are best graphed as line graphs.
- Pie charts show the breakdown of a whole into its parts. The whole is always 100 percent and the pie slices are subdivisions of that total.
- To create graphs you use the ***/Graph*** command. To add text and formats to the graph, you use the ***/Graph Options*** command.
- You can press F10 to display the most recently displayed graph.
- Labels on the worksheet can be carried to the graph as titles or legends by entering \ followed by the address or name of the cell when prompted to enter the title or legend.
- To have more than one graph of the same model, you must name each graph. You then use the ***/Graph Name Use*** command to choose the graph to be displayed.
- To print a graph, you must first display it and then save it to a file on the disk.
- You print graphs using the separate PrintGraph program. You can load this program from the Lotus Access System or by typing **PGRAPH** and pressing Enter ↵ when you are in the directory on the disk where it is stored.
- When selecting graphs to print, you can highlight a graph's name and press F10 to preview it on the screen.

CHAPTER 4

QUESTIONS

FILL IN THE BLANK

1. To display the graph menu, you press ___________.
2. To add titles to a graph, you select the ___________ command from the Graph menu.
3. To identify the data ranges on a graph, you add ___________.
4. To show how last year's sales were generated by various product lines, you could use a ___________ chart.
5. When changing data on the worksheet, you can press ___________ to display the most recently displayed graph.
6. When a graph is displayed on the screen, you press ___________ to remove it and return to the worksheet.

7. To have more than one graph of the same model, you must ___________ the graphs.
8. When a model has more than one graph, you use the ___________ command to choose which to display.
9. To plot monthly sales and expenses for a 12-month period, a ___________ or ___________ graph would represent the data well.
10. To create a graph, the minimal requirement is to specify a ___________.

MATCH THE COLUMNS

1. ***/Graph***	__ Saves the most recently displayed graph for printing
2. ***/Graph* *Options***	__ Carries a label in cell A1 to a title or legend
3. Data range	__ Displays a list of named graphs
4. x-axis	__ Loads the PrintGraph program from the DOS prompt
5. F10	__ The horizontal axis of a graph
6. \A1	__ Displays the most recently displayed graph
7. **PGRAPH**	__ The extension 1-2-3 adds to graph files
8. y-axis	__ The vertical axis of a graph
9. / G N U	__ Displays the graph menu
10. ***/Graph Save***	__ Displays the Graph Options menu
11. .PIC	__ A range of cells containing the values you want graphed

WRITE OUT THE ANSWERS

1. Describe how discrete data differ from continuous data and list some typical types of graphs or charts you would use for each kind of data.
2. List four basic graph types, and briefly discuss what each type is used for.
3. Under what conditions would an XY graph be more helpful than a line graph?
4. Describe the main advantage of creating graphs with a spreadsheet.
5. Describe the differences between legends and data labels.
6. Describe the difference between manual and automatic scaling.
7. If your graph has labels that overlap on the x-axis, what option would you use to correct the problem?
8. If you want to make printouts of your graphs, what is the first step?
9. What is the name of the program that you use to print graphs? Describe two ways that you can load this program.
10. Once you have loaded the program used to print graphs, what is the first step in printing a graph?

CHAPTER 4 PROJECTS

PROJECT 1

GRAPHING BOX SCORES

1. Retrieve the BOXSCORE model.
2. In column G, add a series of labels that abbreviate the baseball team names as shown on the x-axis of the figure "The Box Score Graph." Put each abbreviation on the same row as the team name in column A.
3. Create a bar graph showing the won-lost (W-L) record of each baseball team. Use the new abbreviated labels as the x-axis for the graph.
4. Add labels and legends so your graph matches the one shown in the figure "The Box Score Graph."
5. Save the model so you save the graph settings.
6. Save your graph as BASEBALL.PIC and make a printout.

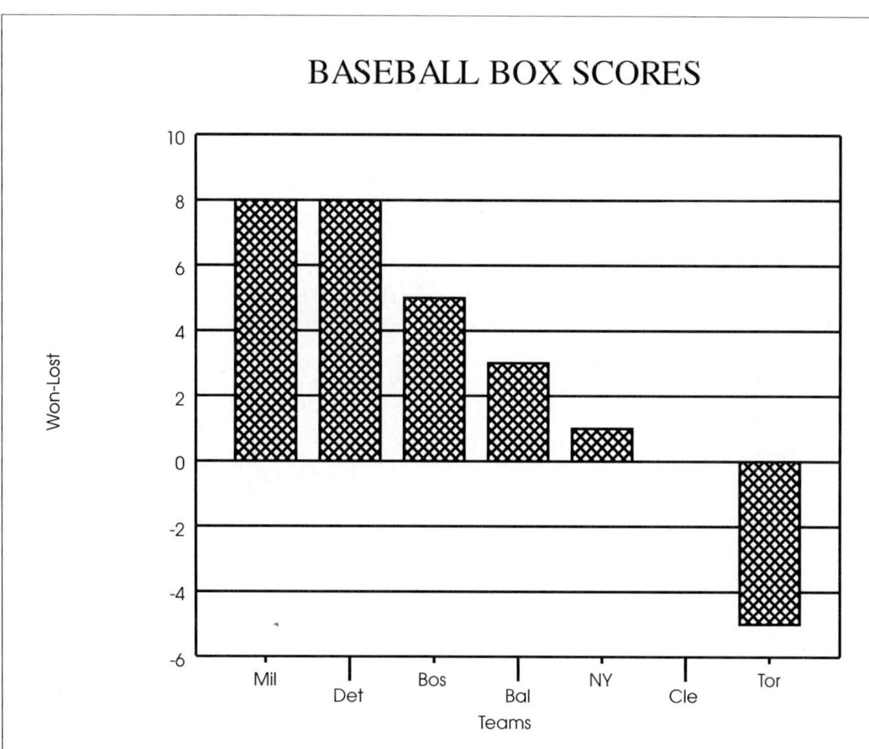

The Box Score Graph
After entering and formatting your graph of the BOXSCORE model, it should look like this.

PROJECT 2

EXPLORING THE POWER OF GRAPHICS

In his book *The Visual Display of Qualitative Information*, Edward Tufte uses an example to show the power of graphs over conventional statistical computations. In this exercise, you complete and then graph a model that demonstrates the point Tufte was making.

1. Retrieve the GRAPHICS model shown in the figure "The Power of Graphics Model," and enter your name in cell B1. The model contains four sets of data. These data are then analyzed with four functions which you'll learn about later: @AVG, @STD, @VAR, and @COUNT. The calculated results for the four sets of data are almost identical.
2. Create and name the four graphs following the instructions provided in the table "The GRAPHICS Model's Graph Elements." When you display the graphs one after another, the differences in the data jump out.
3. Save the finished model as GRAPHICS.

THE GRAPHICS MODEL'S GRAPH ELEMENTS

Element	I	II	III	IV
Graph type	XY	XY	XY	XY
x-axis	B7.B17	D7.D17	F7.F17	H7.H17
First data range	C7.C17	E7.E17	G7.G17	I7.I17
Graph title and name	I	II	III	IV

The Power of Graphics Model
The GRAPHICS model that you retrieve from the disk contains four sets of data that you display as graphs.

	A	B	C	D	E	F	G	H	I
1	Your name:								
2	Filename:	GRAPHICS							
3	Date:								
4									
5	Graph	Graph I		Graph II		Graph III		Graph IV	
6	Ranges	X	Y	X	Y	X	Y	X	Y
7	Values	14	9.96	14	8.1	14	8.84	8	6.58
8		13	7.58	13	8.74	13	12.74	8	5.76
9		12	10.8	12	9.13	12	8.15	8	7.71
10		11	8.33	11	9.26	11	7.81	8	8.84
11		10	8.04	10	9.14	10	7.46	8	8.47
12		9	8.81	9	8.77	9	7.11	8	7.04
13		8	6.95	8	8.14	8	6.77	8	5.25
14		7	4.82	7	7.26	7	6.42	19	12.5
15		6	7.24	6	6.13	6	6.08	8	5.56
16		5	5.68	5	4.74	5	5.73	8	7.91
17		4	4.26	4	3.1	4	5.39	8	6.89
18	Mean	9.0	7.5	9.0	7.5	9.0	7.5	9.0	7.5
19	Std. Dev.	3.2	1.9	3.2	1.9	3.2	1.9	3.2	1.9
20	Variance	10.0	3.8	10.0	3.8	10.0	3.7	10.0	3.7
21	Count	11	11	11	11	11	11	11	11

CHAPTER 5

Advanced Model Building

TOPIC 16

Entering Functions

After completing this topic, you will be able to:

- Explain what built-in functions are
- Use many functions in your own models

	A	B
1	Principal	$10,000
2	Interest	14%
3	Periods	48
4	Payment	$273.26
5		
6	@PMT(B1,B2/12,B3)	

Functions That Refer to Other Cells
The arguments for the @PMT function have been entered into cells B1, B2, and B3. The function then includes references to those cells. The cell references entered in the function in the same order values would be and are separated by commas. The function calculates the same result as if the values had been entered into the function, but now you can easily change any of the three arguments, and it calculates a new result.

	A	B
1	Principal	$10,000
2	Interest	14%
3	Periods	48
4	Payment	$273.26
5	Payment Rounded	$273.00
6		
7	@ROUND(@(B1,B2/12,B3)),0)	

Functions in Combinations
This figure shows the same function entered in the figure "Functions That Refer to Other Cells" nested in another function that rounds the result of the first function's calculation to zero decimal places. The function reads "Round the value of the function @PMT(B1,B2/12,B3) to zero decimal places." The original function calculates the value $273.26, but the new one rounds it to $273.00

1-2-3 contains many built-in functions designed to perform commonly used calculations. Many of the calculations they can perform are quite complicated, so functions simplify the formulas that you have to enter.

Functions have a structure, or syntax, that you must follow. The syntax includes a prefix and arguments.

A prefix must begin every function. The prefix is an at sign (@) followed by the function's name—frequently a contraction of the full name. For example, the prefix for the function that sums the values in a range of cells is @SUM, and the prefix for the function that averages the numbers in a series of cells is @AVG.

Arguments usually must follow the prefix.

- The arguments must be enclosed in parentheses.
- The arguments can be numbers, cell references, ranges, formulas, or other functions.
- If there is more than one argument, they must be separated from each other by commas.
- A few functions, like @PI, @RAND, @FALSE. @TRUE, @ERR, and @NA do not require arguments.

For example, to add the numbers in a range of cells, you would use the function @SUM(A1.A10). The prefix is @SUM, and the argument is the range of cells between A1 and A10. Some functions are slightly more complicated. For example, to calculate monthly payments on a loan, the function syntax is @PMT(Principal, Interest, Period). The prefix is @PMT (for **P**ay**M**en**T**). The arguments are Principal, Interest, and Period and are separated by commas and enclosed in parentheses. You can substitute numbers in the function; for example, the function @PMT(10000,.14,48) calculates and displays monthly payments of $1,402.60.

Instead of entering the values into a function, you can enter them into other cells and then enter references to those cells into the function. The values in these cells are calculated just as if they were a part of the function. Entering the values into their own cells makes them into variables that you can easily change to explore what-ifs. Functions can also be used in combinations.

TUTORIAL

In this tutorial, you enter formulas and functions. Your finished model should look like the figure "The Financial Functions Model." Refer to this figure to check your results as you complete the steps in this tutorial.

The Financial Functions Model
After you enter all functions into the financial functions model, it should look like this.

	A	B	C
1	Your name:		
2	Filename:	FINANCE	
3	Date:		
4			
5	FINANCIAL FUNCTIONS		
6	==========	==========	==========
7	Functions	Arguments	Examples
8	----------	----------	----------
9	@CTERM	Interest rate	10%
10		Future value	$20,000
11		Present value	$5,000
12		Compounding periods	14.55
13			
14	@DDB	Original cost	$10,000
15		Salvage value	$3,000
16		Life (in years)	4
17		Period	1
18		Depreciation	$5,000
19			
20	@FV	Payment	$1,000
21		Rate	10.0%
22		Periods	25
23		Future value	$98,347
24			
25	@IRR	Payments	Guess
26		(1,000)	30.00%
27		500	
28		500	
29		500	IRR
30		500	34.90%
31			
32	@PMT	Principal	$10,000
33		Interest	12.0%
34		Periods	48
35		Payment	$1,205.23
36			
37	@PV	Annual payments	$1,000
38		Rate	8.0%
39		Periods	20
40		Present value	$9,818
41			
42	@RATE	Future value	$20,000
43		Present value	$10,000
44		Term	10
45		Interest rate	7.2%
46			
47	@TERM	Payment	$2,000
48		Interest	12.0%
49		Future value	$10,000
50		Payment periods	4.15
51	==========	==========	==========

GETTING STARTED

1. Retrieve the FUNCTION model and enter your name into cell B1.

ENTERING FUNCTIONS

2. Look carefully at the model and the figure "The Financial Functions Model." Notice how the name of each function is shown in column A of the model. In column B are listed the arguments for each function. Below each set of arguments is the name of the value calculated by the function. For example, the arguments for the @CTERM function are interest rate, future value, and present value. The function then calculates the number of compounding periods needed to turn $5,000 into $20,000 at 10% interest. Enter each of the following functions in the specified cell:
   - In C12, enter **@CTERM(C9,C10,C11)** to calculate how many compounding periods it will take to turn $5,000 into $20,000 at 10% interest.
   - In C18, enter **@DDB(C14,C15,C16,C17)** to calculate depreciation allowance of a $10,000 item being depreciated over 4 years using the double-declining balance method. If you change the value in cell C17 to any year between 1 and 4, you will see the amount that can be depreciated for that year.
   - In C23, enter **@FV(C20,C21,C22)** to calculate the future value of a series of 25 annual $1,000 ordinary annuity payments earning 10% interest.
   - In C30, enter **@IRR(C26,B26.B30)** to calculate the internal rate of return for the stream of cash flows in column B.
   - In C35, enter **@PMT(C32,C33,C34)** to calculate the annual payment on a loan of $10,000 when borrowed for 48 years at 12%.
   - In C40, enter **@PV(C37,C38,C39)** to calculate the present value of an investment on which you have made 20 annual payments of $1,000 at 8%.
   - In C45, enter **@RATE(C42,C43,C44)** to calculate what interest rate is required to turn $10,000 into $20,000 in 10 years.
   - In C50, enter **@TERM(C47,C48,C49)** to calculate how many years it will take an ordinary annuity to turn $2,000 into $10,000 at 12% interest.

SAVING AND PRINTING THE MODEL

3. Save the model under the same name.
4. Print the model.

EXPLORING WHAT-IFS

5. Change any of the arguments for any of the functions and watch the functions calculate new results.

FINISHING UP

6. You have now completed this tutorial. Either clear the screen and continue with the next activity or quit the program.

QUICK REFERENCE

1-2-3 has hundreds of functions, but they can be grouped into categories such as financial, statistical, and mathematical. The following tables describe some of the functions available on 1-2-3.

 KEY/Strokes

Entering a Function

1. Type the function's prefix and the opening parenthesis; for example, if entering the @SUM function, type **@SUM(**.
2. Specify the range to be included in the argument.
3. If there is more than one argument, type, (the comma) and repeat Step 2; otherwise, type **)** (the closing parenthesis) and press Enter←.

FINANCIAL FUNCTIONS

Function	Description
@CTERM(*interest,future value,present value***)**	Calculates the number of compounding periods
@DDB(*original cost,salvage value,life in years,period***)**	Calculates depreciation using the double-declining method
@FV(*regular payment,interest rate,period***)**	Calculates the future value of an annuity
@IRR(*series of cash flows,discount rate***)**	Calculates the internal rate of return of an investment
@NPV(*discount rate,future net cash flows***)**	Calculates the net present value of an investment
@PMT(*principal,interest rate,period***)**	Calculates the payments needed to amortize a loan
@PV(*payments,interest,term***)**	Calculates the present value of a series of equal payments (called an ordinary annuity)
@RATE(*future value,present value,term***)**	Calculates the interest rate needed for present value
@SLN(*original cost,salvage value,life in years***)**	Calculates depreciation using the straight-line method
@SYD(*original cost,salvage value,life in years,period***)**	Calculates depreciation using the sum-of-the-years'-digits method
@TERM(*payment,interest,future value***)**	Calculates the number of payment periods of an investment

TIPS

- Cells containing labels have a numeric value of 0 when referred to in a function's range. For example, if a function reads @SUM(A1.A10) and there is a label in cell A5, it is treated as a zero value.
- The @AVG function treats blank cells and cells containing a zero differently. If you want a cell in the range ignored, leave it blank. If you want it to be treated as a zero value, enter a 0.

STATISTICAL FUNCTIONS

Function	Description
@AVG(*range of values***)**	Calculates the average value
@COUNT(*range of values***)**	Calculates the number of nonblank cells
@MAX(*range of values***)**	Calculates the largest value
@MIN(*range of values***)**	Calculates the smallest value
@STD(*range of values***)**	Calculates the standard deviation
@SUM(*range of values***)**	Calculates the total sum
@VAR(*range of values***)**	Calculates the variance

NUMERIC AND MATHEMATICAL FUNCTIONS

Function	Description
@ABS(*negative number***)**	Calculates the "absolute" value of a number; converts negative numbers to positive numbers
@ACOS(*cosine value***)**	Calculates the radian angle of a cosine value
@ASIN(*sine value***)**	Calculates the angle, in radians, of a sine value
@ATAN(*tangent value***)**	Calculates the radian angle of a tangent value
@ATAN2(*x,y***)**	Calculates the angle, in radians, whose tangent is *y/x*
@COS(*number***)**	Calculates the cosine of a number and displays the result as the angle in radians
@EXP(*number,power***)**	Calculates the base of the natural logarithm (*e*), that is, (2.7182818) to the power of the argument
@INT(*number with at least one decimal place***)**	Calculates the integer part of a number
@LN(*x***)**	Calculates the natural log (base *e*) of *x*
@LOG(*x***)**	Calculates the log (base 10) of *x*
@MOD(*result of a division***)**	Calculates the remainder of any division
@PI	Calculates pi (3.1415926...)
@RAND	Calculates a random number between 0 and 1
@ROUND(*number with at least one decimal place,number of decimal positions to round it to***)**	Rounds a number to a specified number of decimal places
@SIN(*radian angle***)**	Calculates the sine of a radian angle
@SQRT(*number***)**	Calculates the square root of a number
@TAN(*radian angle***)**	Calculates the tangent of a radian angle

EXERCISES

EXERCISE 1

REVISING THE COLLEGE BUDGET MODEL

1. Retrieve the BUDGET model.
2. Replace the formulas in cells B9 and B18 with @SUM functions that sum the cells in the sections immediately above each function.
3. Copy the functions to other columns on the row.
4. Save and print the revised model.

EXERCISE 2

CALCULATING THE DOW JONES AVERAGE

When the Dow Jones Average was first computed, it was based on the prices of 12 stocks. To calculate the average, the prices of the 12 stocks were added, and the total was then divided by 12. However, since stocks split, companies merge, or firms fail, this original approach can no longer be used.

For example, assume two stocks sell at $5 and $10. Their average price is $7.50. If the $10 stock is split two-for-one, each share would be worth $5. Nothing has happened to the value of an investment in these shares, but the average of their prices now is $5.

To keep the average the same, a new divisor is calculated. Using this new divisor, the "average" will remain at $7.50. Here is the formula to calculate a new divisor:

$$\frac{\text{Former divisor}}{\text{Former total value}} = \frac{\text{New divisor}}{\text{New total value}}$$

Since the average was first published, the divisor has been changed frequently and is currently below 0.5. This explains why the Dow Jones Industrial Average can be 3300 when the highest priced stock in the 30-stock group is less than $100. This also explains the wide swings in the average in relation to changes in stock prices. For example, if the divisor was 0.5, an increase of $1 in the price of each of the 30 stocks would result in a 60-point increase in the average. In fact, the use of the term *average* is inaccurate; the Dow Jones Average is actually an index or indicator.

1. Retrieve the DOWJONES model.
2. Enter the labels in cells A36 through A38, and the .7 divisor in cell C37. Then enter the formulas that calculate the average shown in the figure "The Revised Dow Jones Averages Model" using the formulas described in the table "The Dow Jones Average Model's Formulas."
3. Save the model and make a printout.
4. Change the price of Woolworth's stock in column D to $27.32, as it might be if the stock split 2 for 1. What is the new divisor? What is the new average?

The Revised Dow Jones Averages Model
After you enter functions into the Dow Jones Averages model, it should look like this.

	A		B	C	D
31	Union Carbide		UK	28.00	28.00
32	United Technologies		UTX	44.88	44.88
33	USX		X	32.13	32.13
34	Westinghouse Electric		WX	55.38	55.38
35	Woolworth		Z	54.63	54.63
36		Total		1,590.57	1,590.57
37		Divisor		0.70	0.70
38		Average		2,272.24	2,272.24

THE DOW JONES AVERAGE MODEL'S FORMULAS

#	Cell	Formula	Copy to
1	C36	*Total* is the sum of all the stock prices listed on the rows above.	D36
2	D37	The *New divisor* is calculated by multiplying the previous divisor in cell C37 by the new total in cell D36 and dividing the result by the old total in cell C36.	
3	C38	*Average* is the total divided by the divisor in the same column.	D38

EXERCISE 3

ENTERING FUNCTIONS

1. Enter the model shown in the figure "Functions That Refer to Other Cells on page 118."
2. Insert four blank rows at the top of the model and enter the three-line heading using the filename FUNC1.
3. Edit the function to add the @ROUND function so that the function reads *@ROUND(@PMT(B5,B6/12,B7),0)*.
4. Save the model as FUNC1 and make a printout.

EXERCISE 4

CALCULATING LOTTERY PAYMENTS

Almost all state lotteries offer seemingly large prizes, but they spread their payment over a number of years. This stretched-out payment schedule costs the winner a lot of money; in fact, you can say that these lotteries are guilty of false advertising. The tool you use to analyze the true value of payments over time is called present value analysis. This analysis tells you how much a series of payments is worth in today's dollars, after accounting for interest you would have earned had you invested annual payments at a given interest rate. In this exercise, you build a model that allows you to determine how much a lottery prize, or any other payment stretched over a period of years, is worth if you were to receive all of it today.

1. Enter the model shown in the figure "The Lottery Payments Model" using the formulas described in the table "The LOTTERY Model's Formulas." As you can see, $1 million spread in equal payments over 20 years is worth only $490,907 in today's dollars. If you had $490,907 and invested it for 20 years, you would have $1 million.
2. Save the finished model as LOTTERY.
3. Change the size of the prize and see how the present value changes. For example, what is the present value of a $10,000 prize spread over five years?

The Lottery Payments Model
After you enter and format the lottery payments model, it should look like this.

	A	B
1	Your name:	
2	Filename:	LOTTERY
3	Date:	
4		
5	Prize	$1,000,000
6	Payments spread over (in years)	20
7	Annual payments	$50,000
8	Interest rate	8%
9	Present value	$490,907

THE LOTTERY MODEL'S FORMULAS

#	Cell	Formula
1	B7	*Annual payments* are the prize divided by the number of years it is spread over.
2	B9	*Present value* is calculated by the @PV function, whose arguments are annual payments, interest, and the term the payments are spread over.

EXERCISE 5

WORKING WITH STATISTICAL FUNCTIONS

1. Retrieve the STAT model shown in the figure "The Statistical Functions Model" and enter your name into cell B1.
2. Using the labels in Column A on rows 14 through 20 as a guide, enter the specified functions in column B on the same rows. All of the functions use the same range of date, cells B6 through B12. For help, refer to the table "Statistical Functions" in the Quick Reference section.
3. Save the model as STAT and make a printout.
4. Change any of the sales for one or more regions and watch the statistical functions calculate new results.
5. Clear the screen without saving your changes.

	A	B
1	Your name:	
2	Filename:	STAT
3	Date:	
4		
5	Region	Sales
6	Northeast	1515
7	East	1018
8	Southeast	965
9	Central	678
10	Northwest	1956
11	West	1789
12	Southwest	965
13		
14	Average	1269.4285
15	Count	7
16	Max	1956
17	Min	678
18	Standard deviation	447.21323
19	Sum	8886
20	Variance	199999.67

The Statistical Functions Model
After you have entered statistical functions into the STAT model, it will look like this.

TOPIC 17

Date & Time Functions

After completing this topic, you will be able to:
- Describe the purpose of date and time functions
- Use date and time arithmetic in your own models

Dates and times are important elements of many types of analysis. For example, a business's accounts payable and accounts receivables are due on certain dates. The time that a measurement is made in a biology experiment may have an influence on the results. Since dates and times are so important, 1-2-3 provides functions that automatically calculate them for you. You can then format these values to control the way the dates and times are displayed or use them to make calculations.

TUTORIAL

In this tutorial, you use date and time functions. Your finished model should look like the figure "The Time Alive Model" although some numbers will be different because you enter today's date and that date depends on which day you do this tutorial. Refer to this figure to check your results as you complete the steps in this tutorial.

The Time Alive Model
After you enter the time alive model, your results should look like this except that all the dates (other than B6 and C6) and numbers will be different since the @NOW function calculates today's date.

	A	B	C
1	Your name:		
2	Filename:	DATES	
3	Date:		
4			
5		UNFORMATTED	FORMATTED
6	Date of your birth	25,569	01-Jan-70
7	Today's date	33,843	27-Aug-92
8	Number of days alive	8,274	8,274
9	Number of weeks alive	1,182	1,182
10	Number of years alive	23	23

GETTING STARTED

1. Load the program or clear the screen.
2. Change the width of column A to 25 characters and change the global column width to 16 characters.
3. Enter the three-line heading using the filename DATES.
4. Enter the labels shown on rows 5 through 10.

5. Change the global format to , (comma) with zero decimal places.

ENTERING DATES

6. In cell B6, type **@DATE(70,1,1)** and press Enter↵ to display the number of days from December 31, 1899 to January 1, 1970.
7. In cell B7, type **@NOW** and press Enter↵ to calculate the number of days from December 31, 1899 to today.

CALCULATING DATES

8. In cell B8, enter the formula **+B7-B6** to calculate the number of days you have been alive as of today if you were born on January 1, 1970.
9. In cell B9, enter the formula **+B8/7** to calculate the number of weeks you have been alive as of today.
10. In cell B10, enter the formula **+B8/365** to calculate the number of years you have been alive as of today.

FORMATTING THE DATE

11. Copy cells B6 through B10 to the same rows in column C.
12. With the cell pointer in cell C6, press / R F D (for ***R****ange*, ***F****ormat*, ***D****ate*), and a submenu of date formats is displayed.
13. Press 1 (for ***1*** *(DD-MMM-YY)*), and the prompt reads *Enter range to format:*.
14. Expand the highlight to cell C7 and press Enter↵ to format the dates.

FINISHING UP

15. Save the model under the filename DATES.
16. Print the model.
17. Edit the date function in cell C6 so that it is your birth date (or a friend's). Replace the 70 with the year you were born, the first 1 with the month (1-12), and the second 1 with the day of the month (1-31). The numbers in cells C8 through C10 now are accurate for you or your friend.
18. You have now completed this tutorial. Either clear the screen and continue with the next activity or quit the program.

QUICK REFERENCE

To work with dates and times, you first have to generate them as date numbers using one of the functions described in the table "Functions That Calculate Date and Time Numbers." These functions assign a numeric value to days and times.

- The date numbers are the number of days between December 31, 1899 (January 1, 1900 is 1) and December 31, 2099 (36525).
- The time numbers are fractional equivalents of the 24-hour period. Midnight is 0, noon is .5 (½), and just before midnight is .9999. You can enter times as decimals or fractions.

TIPS

- When you use the @NOW function, it updates whenever you recalculate the worksheet. You can use this to display the current time on the screen. To prevent it from updating, type **@NOW** press F9 (**Calc**), and press Enter← to enter the time and date into the cell.
- You can enter a date or time function as the start value in the ***/Data Fill*** command. For example, if you enter the function @NOW as the start value and an increment of 1, the range will fill with the dates starting at today's and stepping by 1 until the stop value or the end of the range is reached. Be sure to specify a very large stop value since date functions generate numbers of 30,000 or more.

After you have generated date or time numbers, you can manipulate them with any of the functions described in the table "Functions That Use Date and Time Numbers."

FUNCTIONS THAT CALCULATE DATE AND TIME NUMBERS

Function	Description
@DATE(*yy,mm,dd***)**	Calculates the date number, the number of days since January 1, 1900
@DATEVALUE(*date string***)**	Calculates the date number of a string like January 1, 1999
@NOW	Calculates the date and time number for the current time if it was entered into the computer system's clock when starting up; no argument is required
@TIME(*hh,mm,ss***)**	Calculates the number of the time
@TIMEVALUE(*time string***)**	Calculates the time number of a time string, like 11:15 a.m.

FUNCTIONS THAT USE DATE AND TIME NUMBERS

Function	Description
@DAY(*date number***)**	Calculates the day number
@HOUR(*time number***)**	Calculates the hour number
@MINUTE(*time number***)**	Calculates the minute number
@MONTH(*date number***)**	Calculates the month number
@SECOND(*time number***)**	Calculates the second number
@YEAR(*date number***)**	Calculates the year number

When you enter a date or time function, the program calculates and displays dates and times as numbers. The number can be formatted so that the date and time are displayed in a variety of other formats. The figure "Date and Time Functions and Formats" shows the results of formatting dates and times calculated with date and time functions, and the table "Date and Time Formats" describes the available formats.

DATE AND TIME FORMATS

Format	Example
Date Formats	
1 (DD-MMM-YY)	11-Jan-92
2 (DD-MMM)	11-Jan
3 (MMM-YY)	Jan-92
4 (Long Intn'l)	01/11/92
5 (Short Intn'l)	01/11
Time Formats	
1 (HH:MM:SS AM/PM)	12:01:45 PM
2 (HH:MM AM/PM)	12:01 PM
3 (Long Intn'l)	12:01:45
4 (Short Intn'l)	12:01

→ KEY/Strokes

Formatting Dates and Times in a Range

1. Move the cell pointer to a cell with a date or time number.
2. Press / R F D (for ***R****ange*, ***F****ormat*, ***D****ate*) to format a range.
3. Press 1 through 5 to format as one of the dates described in the table "Date and Time Formats."

KEY/Strokes

Formatting Dates and Times Globally

1. Press [/][W][G][F] (for ***W**orksheet*, ***G**lobal*, ***F**ormat*) to change the default format.
2. Either: Press [D] (for ***D**ate*), and press [1] through [5] to set the default date format to one of those described in the table "Date and Time Formats."
3. Or: Press [D][T] (for ***D**ate*, ***T**ime*), and press [1] through [4] to set the default time format to one of those described in the table "Date and Time Formats."

Since dates and times are actually numbers, you can add and subtract them, for example, to find the number of days between two dates or the number of hours, minutes, and seconds between two times.

EXERCISE

	A	B
1	Your name:	
2	Filename:	MYDATES
3	Date:	
4		
5	Date Function	@DATE(92,1,11)
6	Serial number	33614
7	DD-MMM-YY	11-Jan-92
8	DD-MMM	11-Jan
9	MMM-YY	Jan-92
10	Long Intn'l	01/11/92
11	Short Intn'l	01/11
12		
13	Time Function	@TIME(12,1,45)
14	Serial number	0.5012152778
15	HH:MM:SS AM/PM	12:01:45 PM
16	HH:MM AM/PM	12:01 PM
17	Long Intn'l	12:01:45
18	Short Intn'l	12:01

Date and Time Functions and Formats
The date and time functions entered into cells B5 and B13 calculate the serial date and time numbers shown in cells B6 and B14. The cells below each serial number show how the available formats affect the number's display.

EXERCISE 1

ENTERING AND FORMATTING DATES AND TIMES

In this exercise, you enter date and time functions and format them using the available formats.

1. Retrieve the MYDATES Model shown in the figure "The Date and Times Functions and Formats."
2. Enter the function **@DATE(92,1,11)** in cell B5 and copy it to cells B6 through B11.
3. Enter the time function **@TIME(12,1,45)** in cell B13 and copy it to cells B14 through B18.
4. Format the cells as follows:
   - Format the functions in cells B5 and B13 as text.
   - Format cell B14 as General.
   - Leave cell B6 unformatted.
   - Format each of the other functions using the formats listed on the same row in column A.
5. Save the finished model under its original name and make a printout.

TOPIC 18

Relational and Logical Operators & Functions

After completing this topic, you will be able to:

- Describe and use relational operators
- Describe and use logical operators
- Use strings in formulas and functions

When entering functions and formulas, some of the most powerful tools that you have are logical and relational operators. These two sets of operators are used to determine the truth or falsity of statements. When used with IF statements, these operators can cause a calculation to branch to two or more possible outcomes. For example, if the statement calculates that a person's sales are above a target figure, his or her commission is increased over what it would be if the sales did not reach the target.

TUTORIAL

In this tutorial, you enter functions that use character strings. Your finished model should look like the figure "The Strings in Functions Model." Refer to this figure to check your results as you complete the steps in this tutorial.

	A	B	C
1	Your name:		
2	Filename:	IFFIRE	
3	Date:		
4			
5	Name	Sales	Action
6	Smith	10,000	PROMOTE
7	Jones	9,000	FIRE
8	Lewis	12,000	PROMOTE
9	Washington	15,000	PROMOTE
10	Lee	23,000	PROMOTE
11	Gonzales	11,000	PROMOTE

The Strings in Functions Model

To include strings in functions, you enclose them in double quotation marks. For example, the IF statement **@IF(B6<10000,"FIRE","PROMOTE")** is entered into cell C6. The function reads "If sales in cell B6 are less than $10,000, then display the string *FIRE;* otherwise, display the string *PROMOTE.*" The function is then copied down the column and indicates who should be fired and who should be promoted.

GETTING STARTED

1. Retrieve the file IFFIRE and enter your name into cell B1.

ENTERING AND COPYING A FUNCTION

2. In cell C6, type **@IF(B6<10000,"FIRE","PROMOTE")** and press Enter↵. The function displays the character string *PROMOTE* because sales in cell B6 are not less than 10000.
3. Copy the function in cell C6 to cells C7 through C11. If sales in a cell in column B are less than 10000, the function in the adjoining cell displays the character string *FIRE.* If any value in a cell in column B is 10000 or more, the function displays *PROMOTE.*
4. Save the model under the filename IFFIRE.
5. Change some of the numbers in column B, and watch the function change the displayed string.

REVISING THE FUNCTION

6. Revise the function in cell C6 so that it reads *@IF(B6=10000,"RETAIN",@IF(B6<10000,"FIRE","PROMOTE")).*

7. Copy the function in cell C6 to cells C7 through C11. The functions now work just as they did before; however, they now display *RETAIN* in any cell where sales are equal to 10000.

FINISHING UP

8. Save the model again under the same name.
9. Print the model.
10. You have now completed this tutorial. Either clear the screen and continue with the next activity or quit the program.

QUICK REFERENCE

You use operators to test the relationship between two items and to specify more than one criterion.

Operator	Meaning
>	greater than
<	less than
=	equal to
<=	less than or equal to
>=	greater than or equal to
<>	not equal to

Relational Operators
The relational operators shown here are used to compare values to determine if they are equal to, greater than, or less than other data.

Operator	Meaning
#AND#	Both conditions must be met
#OR#	either condition must be met
#NOT#	following condition must not be met

Logical Operators
Logical operators are used to connect two or more criteria so both are evaluated by the function or formula.

Relational Operators

You use relational operators to test if a statement is true or false. For example, the relational operator > (greater than) in the formula +A1>1000 calculates TRUE (1-2-3 displays a 1 for TRUE) if the value in cell A1 is larger than 1000 and FALSE (1-2-3 displays a 0 for FALSE) if it is less than or equal to 1000.

Relational operators are used to test two or more numbers to determine their relationship. Using these operators, you can determine if one number is equal to, less than, or greater than another number. Let's say, for example, that you are comparing last year's sales to this year's:

- *Equal to.* If you use a relational operator to determine if last year's sales are equal to this year's, the sales for both years must be the same for the statement to be true. In all other situations, the statement is false. For example, **+A1=1** displays a 1 (true) if the value in cell A1 is equal to 1, and a 0 (false) if it is not.
- *Not equal to.* If you use a relational operator to determine if last year's sales are not equal to this year's, the sales for the two years must be different for the statement to be true. If they are equal, the statement is false. For example, **+A1<>1** displays a 0 (false) if the value in cell A1 is equal to 1, and a 1 (true) if it is not.
- *Greater than.* If you use a relational operator to determine if last year's sales are greater than this year's, the sales for last year must be greater than this year's for the statement to be true. In all other situations, the statement is false. For example, **+A1>1** displays a 1 (true) if the value in cell A1 is greater than 1, and a 0 (false) if it is equal to or less than 1.
- *Less than.* If you use a relational operator to determine if last year's sales were less than this year's, the sales for last year must be less than this year's for the statement to be true. In all other situations, the statement is false. For example, **+A1<1** displays a 1 (true) if the value in cell A1 is less than 1, and a 0 (false) if it is equal to or greater than 1.
- *Greater than or equal to.* If you use a relational operator to determine if last year's sales were greater than or equal to this

year's, the sales for last year must be greater than or equal to this year's for the statement to be true. In all other situations, the statement is false. For example, **+A1>=1** displays a 1 (true) if the value in cell A1 is greater than or equal to 1, and a 0 (false) if it is less than 1.

- *Less than or equal to.* If you use a relational operator to determine if last year's sales were less than or equal to this year's, the sales for last year must be less than or equal to this year's for the statement to be true. In all other situations, the statement is false. For example, **+A1<=1** displays a 1 (true) if the value in cell A1 is less than or equal to 1, and a 0 (false) if it is greater than 1.

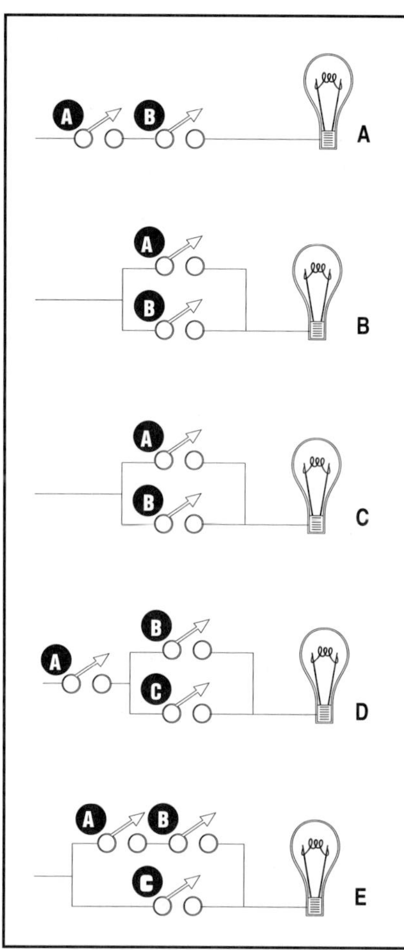

Electrical Circuits and Logical Operators

A AND statements require that all conditions be met. In this example, both switches A and B must be closed for current to flow.

B OR statements require that one condition be met. In this example, either switch can be closed and current will flow.

C NOT statements require that a condition not be met. In this example, switch A OR B must NOT be open for current to flow.

D In compound statements, AND or OR statements can be combined. In this example, switches A AND (B OR C) must be closed for current to flow.

E In this other example of compound statements, switches (A AND B) OR C must be closed for current to flow.

Logical Operators

Logical operators are used to connect one or more statements. For example, the statement +A1>1000#OR#B1>1000 calculates 1 (true) if the value in either cell A1 or B1 is larger than 1000 and 0 (false) if both are less than or equal to 1000.

- AND operators (#AND#) set up tests where two or more conditions must be satisfied before a condition is true. For example, +A1<1#AND#A2>2 displays a 1 (true) only when the value in cell A1 is less than 1 and the value in cell A2 is greater than 2. It displays a 0 (false) for any other combination of values.
- OR operators (#OR#) set up tests where only one of two or more conditions must be satisfied before a calculation is made. For example, +A1=1#OR#A1=2 displays a 1 (true) if the value in cell A1 is equal to 1 or 2. It displays a 0 (false) if the value is anything else.
- NOT operators (#NOT#) set up tests where a calculation is made only when the specified condition is not met. For example, +A1>1#OR##NOT#A1=3 displays a 1 (true) whenever the value in cell A1 is greater than 1 but not 3. It displays a 0 (false) if the value in A1 is less than or equal to 1 or 3.

One way to look at logical operators is the way an engineer would when designing a simple electrical circuit, such as those used in your home to turn lights on and off. For current to flow to the light, the appropriate switches must be closed.

IF Statements

The real power of relational and logical operators is seen when you use them with IF statements. You can use IF statements to "branch" calculations. You do so by establishing a condition that must be met. If the condition is true, one calculation is made. If the condition is false, another calculation is made.

If statements are widely used to prevent *ERR* messages from being displayed in cells. These *ERR* messages are displayed whenever you use the division operator (/) in a formula and the cell containing the denominator is blank. For example, if you enter the formula A1/A2 into cell A3, it displays *ERR* if cell A2 is blank or contains a zero. To prevent error messages, you embed the formula in the IF statement. For example, @IF(A2>0,A1/A2,@NA). This formula now reads, "If the value in cell A2 is greater than 0, then divide the value in cell A1 by the value in cell A2; otherwise, display an NA."

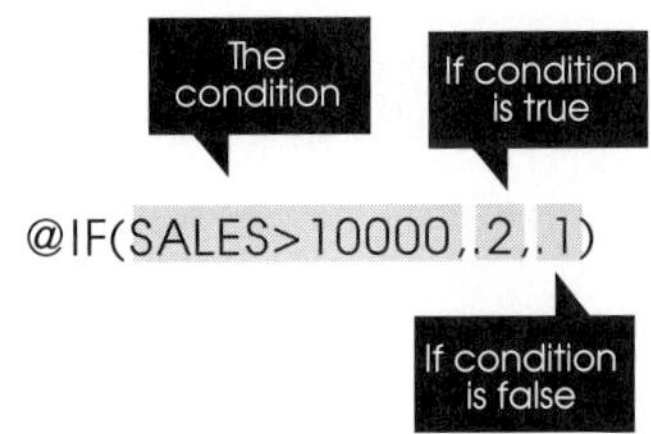

An IF Statement
This IF statement's condition that sales are greater than $10,000 can be true or false. If sales are greater than 10000 THEN the condition is true, and the IF statement branches to .2 (20%), OTHERWISE the condition is false, and the IF statement branches to .1 (10%).

Sometimes, IF statements have to deal with more than two possible outcomes. In these cases, you can nest IF statements within other IF statements. For example, you can specify that if the condition is true, a calculation is made. However, if the condition is false, a second IF statement takes over. If its condition is true, a second calculation is made. If its condition is false, a third calculation is made.

Order of Operations

Relational operators, like arithmetic operators, have orders of precedence. The table "Relational and Logical Operators Order of Operations" lists 1-2-3's orders of precedence. Those with a higher number on Release 2.01 or earlier versions or a lower number on Release 2.2 or later versions are performed first.

RELATIONAL AND LOGICAL OPERATORS ORDER OF OPERATIONS

Operator	Description	2.01 (and Earlier) Precedence	2.2 (and Later) Precedence
=	Equal to	3	5
<>	Not equal to	3	5
<	Less than	3	5
>	Greater than	3	5
<=	Less than or equal to	3	5
>=	Greater than or equal to	3	5
#NOT#	Logical NOT	2	6
#AND#	Logical AND	1	7
#OR#	Logical OR	1	7

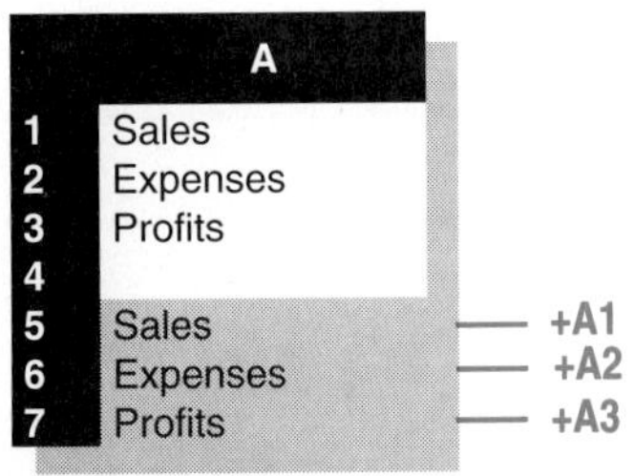

Referring to Strings
Strings are entered into cells A1 through A3. References to those cells are then entered into cells A5 through A7. The references carry the character strings to the cells they are entered into just as they would carry values. If the string is changed, all cells referring to it will automatically change.

Strings

1-2-3 has the ability to handle *strings*, any series of characters used as labels. For example, "100 Elm Street" and "John Lewis" are strings. The ability to manipulate strings has several applications:

- If you use the same labels again and again on a model, you can save time by entering the labels once and then entering references to those cells wherever you want the label to be repeated.
- Strings can be joined into longer strings by *concatenation*. To concatenate strings, the cell references are combined with an ampersand (&).

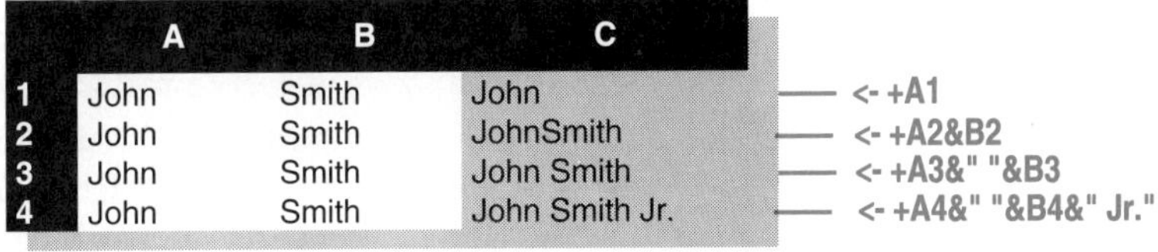

Concatenation
Strings have been entered into columns A and B, and formulas are then entered into column C.

- **+A1** just copies the string in cell A1 to cell C1.
- **+A2&B2** joins two strings in cells A2 and B2.
- You can add a space between the strings by enclosing it in double quotation marks.
- You can add a string to the formula by enclosing it in double quotes.

- Strings can display messages in cells when designated conditions are met.

When entering strings directly into formulas or functions, enclose the strings in double quotation marks, for example, +A1+"string".

EXERCISES

EXERCISE 1

USING STRINGS

1. Enter the labels and cell references shown in the figure "Referring to Strings."
2. Save the model as STRINGS1.
3. Type your name into cell A1 and make a printout. What happens in cell A5?

EXERCISE 2

CONCATENATING STRINGS

1. Create the model shown in the figure "Concatenation." Enter the labels shown in columns A and B, and enter the formulas into column C.
2. Insert four rows at the top of the model and enter a heading using the the filename STRINGS2.
3. Save the model as STRINGS2 and make a printout.

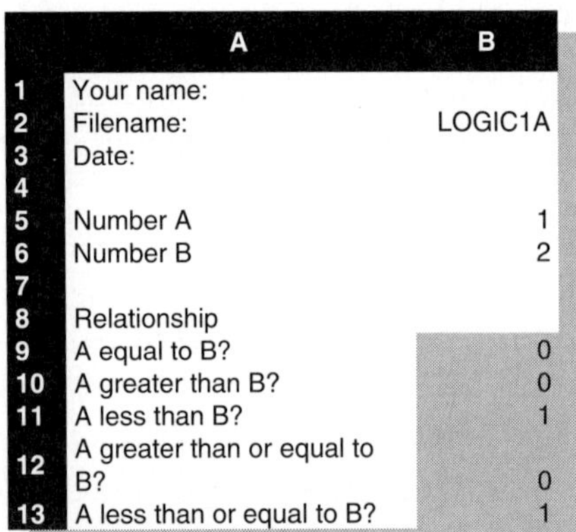

	A	B
1	Your name:	
2	Filename:	LOGIC1A
3	Date:	
4		
5	Number A	1
6	Number B	2
7		
8	Relationship	
9	A equal to B?	0
10	A greater than B?	0
11	A less than B?	1
12	A greater than or equal to B?	0
13	A less than or equal to B?	1

The Relational Operator Model
After you enter the relational operator model, your results should look like this.

EXERCISE 3

EXPLORING RELATIONAL OPERATORS

You can create a truth table for relational operators. By changing the numbers in cells B5 and B6, you can establish if the relationships are true or false.

1. Retrieve the LOGIC1A model shown in the figure "The Relational Operator Model."
2. Enter the formulas described in the table "The LOGIC1A Model's Formulas."

THE LOGIC1A MODEL'S FORMULAS

#	Cell	Formula
1	B9	*A equal to B* is **+B5=B6**.
2	B10	*A greater than B* is **+B5>B6**.
3	B11	*A less than B* is **+B5<B6**.
4	B12	*A greater than or equal to B* is **+B5>=B6**.
5	B13	*A less than or equal to B* is **+B5<=B6**.

3. Save the finished model under its original name and make a printout.

4. Revise the model so that it uses IF statements to display TRUE and FALSE instead of 1 and 0. The formula in cell B9 should be changed to @IF(B5=B6,"TRUE","FALSE"), and the other formulas should be the same except for their conditional statements.
5. Change the filename in the heading to LOGIC1B and save the revised model under that name.

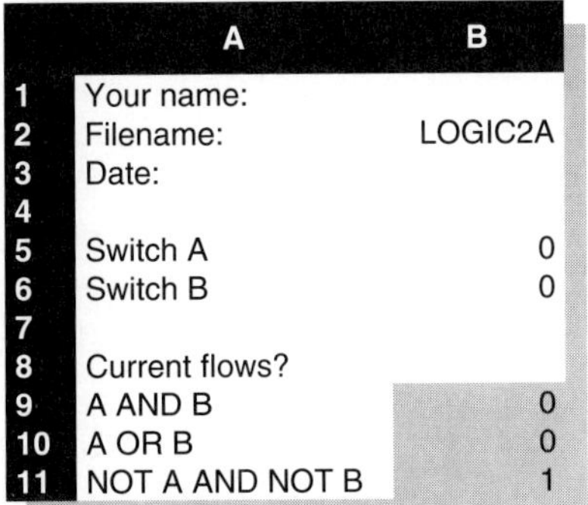

	A	B
1	Your name:	
2	Filename:	LOGIC2A
3	Date:	
4		
5	Switch A	0
6	Switch B	0
7		
8	Current flows?	
9	A AND B	0
10	A OR B	0
11	NOT A AND NOT B	1

The Logical Operator Model
After you enter the logical operator model, your results should look like this.

EXERCISE 4

EXPLORING LOGICAL OPERATORS

You can create a truth table that can be used to analyze the circuits shown in the figure "Electrical Circuits and Logical Operators." The table will show when it is true (1) that current flows and when it is false (0).

1. Retrieve the LOGIC2A model shown in the figure "The Logical Operator Model."
2. Enter the formulas described in the table "The LOGIC2A Model's Formulas."
3. Save the finished model under its original name and make a printout.
4. Enter the label **Closed** into cells B5 and B6.
5. Revise the model so that it uses IF statements to display YES and NO instead of 1 and 0. The formula in cell B9 should be changed to @IF(B5="Closed"#AND#B6="Closed","YES","NO"), and the other formulas should be the same except for their conditional statement.
6. Change the filename in the heading to LOGIC2B and save the revised model under that name.
7. Enter the strings **Open** or **Closed** into cells B5 and B6, and watch the answers to the statement "Current flows?" change.
8. Explore what-ifs by changing the settings for the two switches to various combinations of open and closed.

THE LOGIC2A MODEL'S FORMULAS

#	Cell	Formula
1	B9	*A AND B* is **+B5=1#AND#B6=1**.
2	B10	*A OR B* is **+B5=1#OR#B6=1**.
3	B11	*NOT A AND NOT B* is **#NOT#B5=1#AND##NOT#B6=1**.

	A	B
1	Your name:	
2	Filename:	LOGIC3
3	Date:	
4		
5	Switch A	Closed
6	Switch B	Open
7	Switch C	Closed
8		
9	Current flows?	
10	A AND (B OR C)	YES
11	(A AND B) OR C	YES

The Compound Statement Model
After you enter the compound statement model, your results should look like this.

EXERCISE 5

EXPLORING COMPOUND STATEMENTS

To solve problems like the last two circuits in the figure "Electrical Circuits and Logical Operators," you use more than one logical operator. In this exercise, you enter a model that allows you to explore these more complicated problems.

1. Retrieve the LOGIC3 model shown in the figure "The Compound Statement Model" and enter your name.
2. Enter the formulas described in the table "The LOGIC3 Model's Formulas."
3. Save the finished model under its original name and make a printout.
4. Enter a number of combinations of the two strings **Open** or **Closed** into cells B5, B6, and B7, and watch the answers to the statement "Current flows?" change.

THE LOGIC3 MODEL'S FORMULAS

#	Cell	Formula
1	B10	*A AND (B OR C)* is **@IF(B5="Closed"#AND#(B6="Closed"#OR#B7="Closed"),"YES","NO")**.
2	B11	*(A AND B) OR C* is **@IF((B5="Closed"#AND#B6="Closed")#OR#B7="Closed","YES","NO")**.

TOPIC 19

Ranges—Naming Them

After completing this topic, you will be able to:

- Name ranges
- Refer to named ranges in formulas and commands

You can assign names to ranges of cells. Range names are useful because you can refer to the range name and not have to remember or point to its cell addresses over and over again. Range names are very useful when:

- Entering formulas. For example, the formula +B1-B2 is much harder to enter and understand than an equivalent formula entered as +SALES-EXPENSES. To use words in formulas, you assign a range name to each of the cells that the formula refers to. (Formulas cannot refer to range names that include more than one cell, but functions can).
- Formatting cells. For example, you can specify a currency format for the range of cells named SALES.
- Printing a selected part of the model. For example, you can tell the program to print the range named SUMMARY.
- Copying or moving cells. For example, you can tell the program to copy the range named 1998 to column F.
- Answering the prompt to the GoTo command. To do so, you press F5 **(GoTo)**, type the range's name, and press Enter↵. The cell pointer moves to the upper-left corner of the range.

TUTORIAL

In this tutorial, you practice naming ranges and using commands that refer to range names. You use the COPYMOVE model, which already has a number of named ranges. If you recall, pressing Alt-E erases all the target ranges in this model. This is done with a macro that erases named ranges. A macro is simply a series of keystrokes that has been saved so you can play them back whenever you want to repeat the same keystrokes. The macro you use here was written by the author of this text and saved along with the model on the disk.

GETTING STARTED

1. Retrieve the COPYMOVE model.
2. Press Alt-E to erase all data from the model's target ranges.

LOOKING AT THE MACROS

3. Press [F5] **(GoTo)**, and when the prompt reads *Enter address to go to:*, type **A28** and press [Enter←].

The Erase Macros

The macros in column A erase named ranges. For example, the label */re1A~* in cell A28 is the same as typing **/RE** (for ***R**ange*, ***E**rase*), specifying the range name 1A, and then pressing [Enter←] (the ~ symbol).

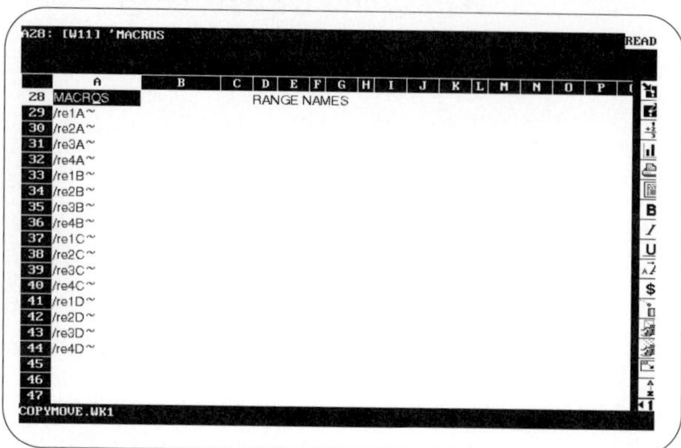

The */re1A~* in cell A29 and similar ones in the cells below are macros. When executed, the slash calls up the command menu; **r** selects ***R**ange*, and **e** selects ***E**rase*. (It is conventional when writing macros to use lowercase letters for keystrokes to distinguish them from cell addresses.) At this point, a prompt asks what range to erase, and 1A is entered since it is the name of the range to be erased. The tilde (~) is the macro command that stands for **Enter**. Let's execute these same macro keystrokes manually to see how they work.

4. Press [F5] **(GoTo)**, and when the prompt reads *Enter address to go to:*, type **1A** and press [Enter←] to move the cell pointer to the first cell in the range named 1A.
5. Type **9** and press [Enter←] to enter some data into the named range.
6. Move the cell pointer to cell B6 so that it isn't in the cell you are about to erase.
7. Press [/][R][E] (for ***R**ange*, ***E**rase*), and the prompt reads *Enter range to erase:*.
8. Type **1A** and press [Enter←] to erase the range that has been named 1A.

LISTING RANGE NAMES

9. Move the cell pointer to cell D29 and press [/][R][N][T] (for ***R**ange*, ***N**ame*, ***T**able*). The prompt reads *Enter range for table:*.
10. Press [Enter←] to list range names and the cells to which they have been applied.
11. Print out the model, expanding the print range to include the table of range names.

NAMING A RANGE

12. With the cell pointer in cell A9, press [/][R][N][C] (for ***R**ange*, ***N**ame*, ***C**reate*), and the prompt reads *Enter name:*.
13. Type **CELL** and press [Enter←]. The prompt reads *Enter range: A9..A9*.
14. Press [Enter←] to name the cell.

COPYING A NAMED RANGE

15. Go to any cell other than A9 so that you can see the effects better.
16. Press [/][C] (for ***C**opy*), and the prompt displays the source range.
17. Type **CELL** and press [Enter←]. The prompt displays the target range.
18. Type **1A** and press [Enter←] to copy the range named CELL to the range named 1A.
19. Repeat Steps 16 through 18, but specify the target range as 1B, then 1C, then finally 1D.

FORMATTING A NAMED RANGE

20. Press [/][R][F][C] (for ***R**ange*, ***F**ormat*, ***C**urrency*).
21. Type **0** and press [Enter←] to format with zero decimal places. The prompt reads *Enter range to format:*.
22. Type **1A** and press [Enter←] to format the range named 1A.
23. Repeat Steps 20 through 22, but specify the range as 1B, then 1C, then finally 1D.

ERASING THE NAMED RANGES

24. Press [/][R][E] (for ***R**ange*, ***E**rase*), and the prompt reads *Enter range to erase:*.
25. Type **1A** and press [Enter←] to erase the range named 1A.
26. Repeat Steps 24 and 25, but specify the range as 1B, then 1C, then finally 1D.

USING THE NAME (F3) KEY

27. Press [/][C] (for ***C**opy*), and the prompt displays the source range.
28. Press [F3] twice to display a list of range names.
29. Highlight *CELL* and press [Enter←]. The prompt displays the target range.
30. Press [F3] to display a list of range names.
31. Highlight *1A* and press [Enter←] to copy the range named CELL to the range named 1A.
32. Repeat Steps 27 through 31, but specify the target range as 1B, then 1C, then finally 1D.

FINISHING UP

33. Print the model.
34. Clear the screen without saving the file.
35. You have now completed this tutorial. Either continue with the next activity or quit the program.

QUICK REFERENCE

When you assign a number of range names to a model, it may become difficult to remember what names have been assigned to which ranges. Two commands help you keep track of the names you have assigned.

- When any prompt asks you to enter a range, you can press F3 (**Name**) to display a list of the range names that you have assigned to the model. If you press it twice, names are displayed full screen—a useful technique if you have assigned a large number of range names. For example, after pressing F5 (**GoTo**), press F3 (**Name**) to display a list of named ranges, or press it twice to display a full-screen listing.

  On Release 2.2 and later versions, you can also list range names when entering formulas. Whenever the mode indicator reads *VALUE*, pressing F3 (**Name**) displays a list of range names assigned to the worksheet.
- You can use the ***/Range Name Table*** command to list on a blank area of the worksheet all range names and the cells they have been assigned to.

The table "Range Name Menu" describes the commands on the Range Name menu. After using these commands, be sure to save the model so that any changes you make are saved.

→ KEY/Strokes

Naming a Range

1. Press / R N C (for ***R**ange*, ***N**ame*, ***C**reate*), and the prompt reads *Enter name:*.
2. Type the name and press Enter↵. The prompt reads *Enter range:*.
3. Specify the range and press Enter↵.

→ KEY/Strokes

Deleting Range Names

1. Press / R N D (for ***R**ange*, ***N**ame*, ***D**elete*), and the prompt reads *Enter name to delete:*. A list of range names is displayed on the line below.
2. Highlight the name of a range to be deleted, or type its name, and press Enter↵.

→ KEY/Strokes

Labeling Cells

1. Enter labels in a row or column next to the row or column that you want to label.
2. Press / R N L (for ***R**ange*, ***N**ame*, ***L**abels*), and the Labels submenu is displayed.
3. Select ***R**ight*, ***D**own*, ***L**eft*, or ***U**p*, and the prompt reads *Enter label range:*.
4. Specify the range that contains the labels you want to assign to the cells and press Enter↵.

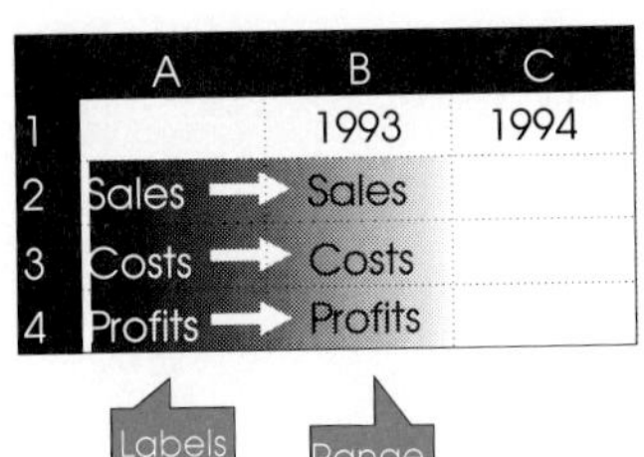

Range Name Labels
The ***/Range Name Label*** command assigns range names to single cells based on the labels in the specified adjoining cells. For example, when you highlight cells A2 through A4, and use the ***/Range Name Label Right*** command, the adjoining cells in column B are assigned the same names as the labels in the cells to their left.

KEY/Strokes

Creating a Table of Range Names

1. Press [/] [R] [N] [T] (for ***Range, Name, Table***), and the prompt reads *Enter range for table:.*
2. Type the address of a cell in the upper-left corner of a blank range, or point to it, and press [Enter ↵]. (The table is two columns wide and overwrites anything in its range, so be careful when indicating the range.)

RANGE NAME MENU

Command	Description
Create	Assigns names to ranges. Names can be up to 14 characters long, in either uppercase or lowercase letters, and can contain spaces.
Delete	Deletes names assigned to ranges.
Labels	Assigns range names to single cells using labels entered into adjacent cells.
Reset	Removes all names assigned to ranges.
Table	Creates a table of range names that gives both the name of the range and the cell address or addresses they have been assigned to. You must specify the cell in the upper-left corner of a range for the table in a blank area of the worksheet since the table will overwrite any cells in the range.

EXERCISE

	A	B
1	Your name:	
2	Filename:	ENGLISH
3	Date:	
4		
5	Sales	1,000
6	Expenses	500
7	Profit	500

The English Language Formula Model
After you enter the English language formula, your results should look like this.

EXERCISE 1

ENTERING AN ENGLISH LANGUAGE FORMULA

In this exercise, you use range names to create a formula.

1. Enter the labels and numbers shown in the figure "The English Language Formula Model."
2. Use the ***/Range Name Labels*** command to assign the names in cells A5 and A6 to the cells to their right.
3. In cell B7, enter the formula **+SALES-EXPENSES**.
4. Save the finished model as ENGLISH, and make a printout.

TOPIC 20

Using Windows & Fixed Titles

After completing this topic, you will be able to:

- Use windows to display different parts of the same model
- Fix titles to keep rows and columns from scrolling off the screen

When a model is too large to be displayed on the screen, you can split the screen into two windows. You can also use fixed titles to view widely separated parts of a model at the same time.

Windows
When the screen is split, you press [F6] (**Window**) to move the cell pointer between the parts.

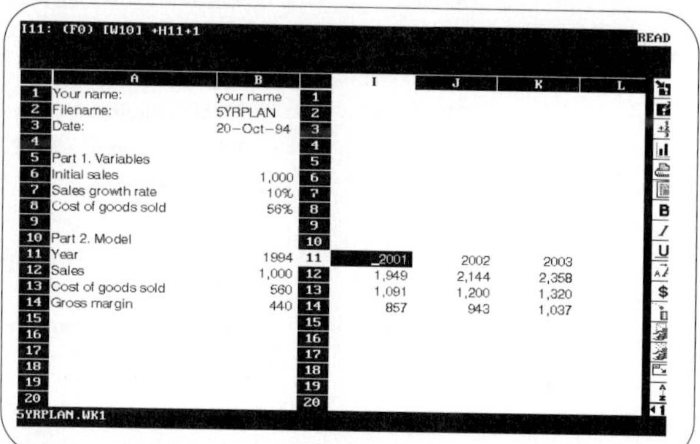

TUTORIAL

In this tutorial, you use windows and fixed titles to display the 5YRPLAN model. Before creating a vertical window, you expand the five-year plan into a ten-year plan. You can return the display to a single window at any time.

GETTING STARTED

1. Retrieve the 5YRPLAN model.

CREATING A HORIZONTAL WINDOW

2. Press [Home] to move the cell pointer to cell A1.
3. Go to A10 and press [/][W][W][H] (for ***W**orksheet*, ***W**indow*, ***H**orizontal*) to split the screen into two windows. The cell pointer is in the top window.
4. Press [F6] (**Window**) repeatedly and watch the cell pointer jump back and forth between the windows.

5. Move the cell pointer to another cell address within one of the windows and press F6 (**Window**) a few more times to see how it always jumps back to the same cell it was in when it last left the window.
6. Move the cell pointer to the lower window and press Home to see the same part of the model in both windows.

CLEARING THE WINDOW

7. Press / W W C (for ***W****orksheet*, ***W****indow*, ***C****lear*).

EXPANDING THE MODEL

8. Press / C (for ***C****opy*), and the prompt displays the source range.
9. Type **F11.F14** and press Enter←. The prompt displays the target range.
10. Type **G11.K11** and press Enter←.

CREATING A VERTICAL WINDOW

11. Go to any cell in column C and press / W W V (for ***W****orksheet*, ***W****indow*, ***V****ertical*) to split the screen vertically.
12. Press F6 (**Window**) to move the cell pointer into the right window. Press → and ← to scroll through the last nine years of the plan to compare them with the first year.
13. To clear the windows, press / W W C (for ***W****orksheet*, ***W****indow*, ***C****lear*).

FIXING COLUMNS AND ROWS

14. Press Home to move the cell pointer to cell A1.
15. Go to C9 and press / W T B (for ***W****orksheet*, ***T****itles*, ***B****oth*).
16. Press → five times, and the columns scroll, but columns A and B remain fixed on the screen.
17. Press PgDn, and the rows scroll, but rows 1 through 8 remain fixed on the screen.
18. Press ↑ until all of Part 2 of the model comes back into view.
19. Continue experimenting with the cell pointer movement keys to see how the fixed titles work.

CLEARING FIXED TITLES

20. Press / W T C (for ***W****orksheet*, ***T****itles*, ***C****lear*), and you can now move freely around the model.

FORMATTING WINDOWS DIFFERENTLY

21. Press Home to move the cell pointer to cell A1.
22. Go to A10 and press / W W H (for ***W****orksheet*, ***W****indow*, ***H****orizontal*) to split the screen into two windows with the cell pointer in the top window.
23. Press F6 (**Window**) to move the cell pointer to the lower window.
24. Press / W G F T (for ***W****orksheet*, ***G****lobal*, ***F****ormat*, ***T****ext*) to display the formulas in the lower window as text.

25. Press [/][W][G][C] (for ***W**orksheet*, ***G**lobal*, ***C**olumn-width*), press [→] to scroll the columns to 15 characters wide so that you can see the complete formulas, and press [Enter←].
26. Press [F6] (**Window**) to move the cell pointer between the windows, and then use the cell pointer movement keys to scroll the windows so that you can compare the formulas in each cell in the lower window with their calculated results in the upper window.
27. When you have finished, press [/][W][W][C] (for ***W**orksheet*, ***W**indow*, ***C**lear*) to return the screen to a single window; the formats in the upper window are the ones that affect the entire worksheet.

FINISHING UP

28. Clear the screen without saving your changes to the model.
29. You have now completed this tutorial. Either continue with the next activity or quit the program.

QUICK REFERENCE

Windows and fixed titles both allow you to bring together distant parts of the same model so that you can compare cells that do not normally appear together on the screen.

Windows

You can divide the screen into two horizontal or vertical windows so that you can display widely separated sections of the worksheet on the screen at the same time. When the screen is divided into two windows, you press [F6] (**Window**) to move the cell pointer between them.

You can divide the screen into horizontal or vertical windows. The **/** ***W**orksheet* ***W**indow* ***H**orizontal* command splits the screen so that the row that the cell pointer is positioned in becomes the topmost row in the lower window. The **/*W***orksheet ***W**indow* ***V**ertical* command splits the screen so that the column that the cell pointer is positioned in becomes the leftmost column in the right window.

The two parts of the worksheet displayed in the windows can be scrolled together (called *synced*) or separately (called *unsynced*) so that you can bring together the sections of the model you want to compare on the screen at the same time. Windows are especially effective in two situations:

- When you want to explore what-if situations. For example, to see the effect of changes in sales and expenses on profits, you create a window that displays the cells you want to monitor and another window that displays the cells you want to change.
- When you want to troubleshoot your model. The same parts of the model can be displayed in both windows, but one can be formatted to display the calculated results of formulas and the other the formulas themselves.

When using windows, keep the following points in mind:

- Entering data in either window affects the underlying worksheet as a whole.

- Titles, column widths, global formats, and label prefixes can be set differently in each window. When the windows are cleared, the format of the upper or left window becomes the format for the entire worksheet.

→ KEY/Strokes

Creating or Removing a Window

1. Move the cell pointer to the row that you want to be the first row in the lower window or the column that you want to be the first column in the right window.
2. Press [/][W][W] (for ***W**orksheet*, ***W**indow*) and select any of the options described in the table "Choices Offered on the Windows Menu."

CHOICES OFFERED ON THE WINDOWS MENU

Menu Choice	Effect
***H**orizontal*	Splits the screen horizontally so that the row containing the cell pointer becomes the topmost row in the lower window; the cell pointer moves to the upper window
***V**ertical*	Splits the screen vertically so that the column containing the cell pointer becomes the leftmost column in the right window; the cell pointer moves to the left window
***S**ync*	Synchronizes scrolling (the default setting) so that the two windows scroll together
***U**nsync*	Unsynchronizes scrolling so that the two windows scroll independently
***C**lear*	Returns to full screen view, and any format changes in the topmost or leftmost window affect the worksheet as a whole

Fixed Titles

Since the topmost rows and leftmost columns are often used for labels identifying the contents of rows and columns, scrolling can make them temporarily disappear from the screen. You can prevent this by fixing, or locking, these titles into position so that the rest of the model scrolls under them. You can fix any rows and columns on the screen, and you are offered four choices:

- Fix rows
- Fix columns
- Fix both rows and columns
- Clear, or unfix, rows and columns

If you are using fixed titles, you can use [F5] **(GoTo)** to move the cell pointer into the titles area. This causes a duplicate of the title rows and columns to appear outside the fixed area.

KEY/Strokes

Fixing or Clearing Titles

1. Move the cell pointer to a cell where you want rows above and/or columns to the left fixed.
2. Press [/][W][T] (for ***W****orksheet*, ***T****itles*) and select any of the options described in the table "Choices Offered on the Titles Menu."

CHOICES OFFERED ON THE TITLES MENU

Menu Choice	Effect
B*oth*	Fixes the columns to the left of, and the rows above, the cell pointer
H*orizontal*	Fixes the rows above the cell pointer
V*ertical*	Fixes the columns to the left of the cell pointer
C*lear*	Unfixes all titles

EXERCISE

EXERCISE 1

WORKING WITH THE DOW JONES AVERAGES MODEL

When models get large, windows can make them much easier to work with. In this exercise, you work with the Dow Jones averages model.

1. Retrieve the DOWJONES model.
2. Create a horizontal window so that rows 1 through 10 are displayed in the top window and rows 33 through 38 are displayed in the bottom window.
3. In column D enter the revised prices shown in the table "DOWJONES What-Ifs," and write down the new divisor. Make the changes one at a time, and do not restore any to their original values so that the changes are cumulative.
4. Clear the screen without saving the changes that you have explored.

DOWJONES WHAT-IFS

Stock	New Price	New Divisor
Alcoa	13.38	________
Allied-Signal	17.32	________
American Express	14.94	________
American T & T	15.75	________
Bethlehem Steel	13.19	________
Boeing	31.63	________
Chevron	24.88	________

TOPIC 21

Using Protection & Security

After completing this topic, you will be able to:

- Protect cells so that you can't erase or overwrite them
- Hide cells and columns so that they cannot be seen by others

1-2-3 provides several options you can use to ensure the integrity and security of your models.

TUTORIAL

In this tutorial, you protect and unprotect cells in your 5YRPLAN model.

GETTING STARTED

1. Retrieve the 5YRPLAN model.

TURNING ON PROTECTION

2. Press [/][W][G][P][E] (for ***W**orksheet*, ***G**lobal*, ***P**rotection*, ***E**nable*) to turn protection on, and all cells on the worksheet are now protected.
3. Try entering data anywhere. The computer beeps when you press [Enter ←] to enter a number into a cell, and it displays the error message *Protected cell*. Press [Esc] to clear the message. The first line of the control panel reads *PR* (for PRotected)

UNPROTECTING A RANGE OF CELLS

4. Press [/][R][U] (for ***R**ange*, ***U**nprot*) and the prompt reads *Enter range to unprotect:*.
5. Type **B6.B8** and press [Enter ←] to unprotect the input cells. (On many systems, unprotected cells are displayed in a different intensity or color).
6. Move the cell pointer around the cells. When it is in an unprotected cell, the first line of the control panel reads *U* (for Unprotected). You can now enter numbers into cells B6, B7, and B8 but nowhere else.

TURNING OFF PROTECTION

7. Press [/][W][G][P][D] (for ***W**orksheet*, ***G**lobal*, ***P**rotection*, ***D**isable*) to turn protection off.

SAVING THE FILE WITH PASSWORD PROTECTION

8. Press [/][F][S] (for ***F****ile*, ***S****ave*), and the prompt reads *Enter name of file to save: 5YRPLAN.*
9. Type **PROTECT** (to change the file's name) and press [Spacebar].
10. Type **P** and press [Enter←]. The prompt reads *Enter password:.*
11. Type **PASSWORD** (it isn't displayed on the screen—dots are), and press [Enter←]. The prompt reads *Verify password:.*
12. Type **PASSWORD** again and press [Enter←] to save the file under the name PROTECT.
13. Now clear the screen and retrieve the PROTECT file. When you do so, the prompt will read *Enter password:.* Type the password and press [Enter←] to retrieve the file. Try retrieving it again, this time entering any other password. (If you enter the password incorrectly, press [Esc] and try again.)

REMOVING PASSWORD PROTECTION

14. Press [/][F][S] (for ***F****ile*, ***S****ave*), and the prompt reads *Enter name of file to save: PROTECT.wk1 [PASSWORD PROTECTED].*
15. Press [←Bksp] once to delete *[PASSWORD PROTECTED]*, and press [Enter←].
16. Press [R] (for ***R****eplace*), and press [Enter←] to save the file on the disk under the name PROTECT but without a password.

FINISHING UP

17. You have now completed this tutorial. Either clear the screen and continue with the next activity or quit the program.

QUICK REFERENCE

You can use cell protection to keep formulas or other important data from being erased or overwritten or to hide cells and columns of data from prying eyes.

Cell Protection

When you first load the worksheet, the cells are unprotected so that you can enter data into them. As you have seen, entering data into a cell deletes any data that was already there. If you enter a number or label into a cell containing a formula, the formula is deleted. This can seriously damage a template.

After you have completed a model, you can protect part or all of it so that you (or another user) cannot inadvertently delete, change, or enter data. You can protect cells so that they cannot be edited, overwritten with new data (by typing, copying, or moving cells into their range), or deleted unless you first remove their protection. If you are planning to use the model as a template, shared by other users, protection is especially important. Others may be less familiar with the model or unfamiliar with the program, thus increasing the likelihood of mistakes.

Protecting cells is like placing a protective shield over the model. 1-2-3 displays unprotected cells in a different intensity or color so that

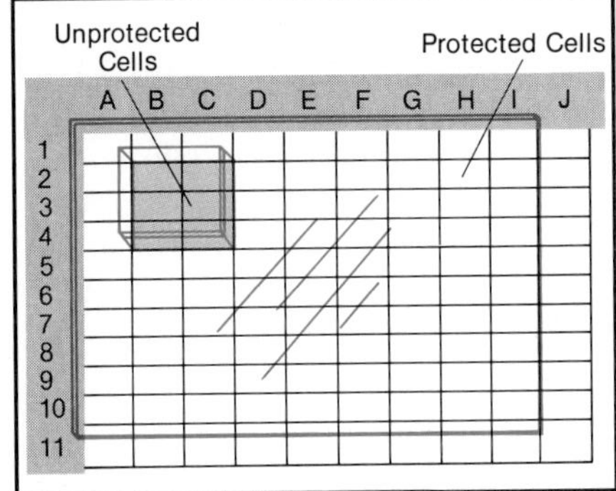

Protection
Enabling protection is like covering the worksheet with a protective shield. You can enter data only in the "holes" in this shield—cells that you have formatted as unprotected.

you can distinguish them from protected cells. It also displays a *U* on the first line of the control panel when the cell pointer is in a cell that is unprotected. (When protection is enabled, a *PR* is displayed on the first line of the control panel when the cell pointer is in a protected cell.)

All cells are protected when you turn protection on. You can also selectively unprotect cells. When protection is off, changes can be made anywhere on the worksheet. When protection is on, changes can be made only in those cells you have specifically designated as unprotected.

→ KEY/Strokes

Turning Protection On and Off

1. Press [/][W][G][P] (for ***W**orksheet, **G**lobal, **P**rotection*).
2. Either: Press [E] (for ***E**nable*) to turn protection on.
   Or: Press [D] (for ***D**isable*) to turn protection off.

→ KEY/Strokes

Protecting or Unprotecting Ranges of Cells

1. Either: Press [/][R][P] (for ***R**ange, **P**rotect* or ***P**rot*) to protect cells, and the prompt reads *Enter range to protect:*.
   Or: Press [/][R][U] (for ***R**ange, **U**nprotect* or ***U**nprot*) to unprotect cells, and the prompt reads *Enter range to unprotect:*.
2. Specify the range and press [Enter ←].

Hiding Cells or Columns

Occasionally, you work at display terminals that people can see as they walk by, or you make printouts that are to be widely circulated, or you share your models with other users. What if sensitive data are on the model, perhaps a list of salaries?

- You can hide cells with the ***/Range Format Hidden*** command so that they cannot be seen or printed unless you first unhide them. To unhide them, you use the ***/Range Format Reset*** command.
- You can hide columns with the ***/Worksheet Column Hide*** command so that the data are not displayed on the screen or in printouts. To unhide them, you use the ***/Worksheet Column Display*** command.

 KEY/Strokes

Hiding or Unhiding a Range of Cells

1. Either: Press [/][R][F][H] (for ***R**ange, **F**ormat, **H**idden*) to hide cells, and the prompt reads *Enter range to format:*.
   Or: Press [/][R][F][R] (for ***R**ange, **F**ormat, **R**eset*) to unhide cells, and the prompt reads *Enter range to format:*.
2. Specify the range and press [Enter ←].

KEY/Strokes

Hiding or Unhiding Columns

1. Either: Press / W C H (for ***W**orksheet*, ***C**olumn*, ***H**ide*) to hide columns, and the prompt reads *Specify column to hide:*.

   Or: Press / W C D (for ***W**orksheet*, ***C**olumn*, ***D**isplay*) to unhide columns, and the prompt reads *Specify hidden columns to redisplay:*.
2. Specify the range (previously hidden columns are indicated by asterisks on the border) and press Enter←┘.

Password Protecting Files

You can assign a password to your files when you save them so that they can be retrieved only by someone who knows the password. If you assign a password and then forget it, you cannot retrieve the file, so be sure to use passwords you will remember.

When you try to retrieve a password-protected file, you are prompted to enter the password. If you cannot, an error message tells you that you have entered an incorrect password. After password protecting a file, you can remove the protection. When you use the ***/File Save*** command, the filename on the control panel is followed with the message *[PASSWORD PROTECTED]*. Press ←Bksp to delete the message, and press Enter←┘.

TIPS

- To check the status of global protection, use the ***/Worksheet Status*** command on releases up through 2.2 and the ***/Worksheet Global*** command on later releases.
- On Release 2.2 and later versions, the contents of hidden cells are not displayed on the control panel when a cell is protected and protection is enabled. On Release 2.01, the contents of hidden cells are displayed.

KEY/Strokes

Protecting a File with a Password

1. Press / F S (for ***F**ile*, ***S**ave*), and the prompt reads *Enter name of file to save:*.
2. Type the filename, press Spacebar, press P, and then press Enter←┘. The prompt reads *Enter password:*.
3. Type a password up to 15 characters long (it isn't displayed on the screen) and press Enter←┘. The prompt reads *Verify password:*.
4. Type the password again and press Enter←┘ to save the file.

EXERCISE

EXERCISE 1

PROTECTING THE PRICING MODE

1. Retrieve the PRICING model.
2. Protect all cells in the worksheet except those in Part 1 where you enter data.
3. Save the model.

TOPIC 22

Printing Models—Advanced Procedures

After completing this topic, you will be able to:

- Use setup strings
- Add headers and footers

When you want to print a model, you can specify headers and footers, change margins, and enter setup strings that change the font used.

TUTORIAL

In this tutorial, you use print options when printing the OVERVIEW model. In one step, you enter a setup string that prints your model in compressed type. Before beginning this tutorial, ask your instructor or lab assistant for the setup string that prints compressed type on the printer you are using. For example, if you are using an Epson printer, the setup string is \015. Write the string for your printer in the space provided here.

Setup string for compressed type:

____

GETTING STARTED

1. Retrieve the OVERVIEW model.

ENTERING A HEADER

2. Press [/][P][P][O][H] (for ***P**rint*, ***P**rinter*, ***O**ptions*, ***H**eader*), and prompt reads *Enter header:*.
3. Type **Date: @ | Your Name | Page #** and press [Enter ←] to return to the Print Options menu.

ENTERING A SETUP STRING

4. Press [S] (for ***S**etup*), and the prompt reads *Enter setup string:*.
5. Type the setup string for compressed type that you wrote in the space above and press [Enter ←] to return to the Print Options menu.
6. Press [Q] (for ***Q**uit*) to return to the Print menu.

PRINTING THE MODEL

7. Press [A][G] (for ***A**lign*, ***G**o*) to print the model.

8. When the printer stops, press [P][Q] (for ***Page***, ***Quit***) to advance the paper out of the printer and leave the Print menu.

FINISHING UP

9. Clear the screen without saving the model.
10. You have now completed this tutorial. Either continue with the next activity or quit the program.

QUICK REFERENCE

DEFAULT PRINTER SETTINGS

Setting	Default
Top margin	Lines 1-2
Header	Line 3
Header margin	Lines 4-5
Lines of text	Lines 6-61
Footer margin	Lines 62-63
Footer	Line 64
Bottom margin	Lines 65-66
Paper length	66 lines
Left margin	Column 4
Right margin	Column 76

When you print a model, 1-2-3 is set up to print it on 8½-by-11-inch continuous form paper using the settings described in the table "Default Printer Settings."

You can, however, change these and other settings since 1-2-3 gives you a great deal of control over the layout of your printouts. But getting a printout just right can require some experimenting. After achieving the results you want, you should save the model because 1-2-3 saves the print settings along with the file. The next time you use the model, you do not have to reenter the print settings.

PRINT OPTIONS

Option	Description
Header	Displays the prompt *Enter header:*. Type a header and press [Enter↵].
Footer	Displays the prompt *Enter footer:*. Type a footer and press [Enter↵].
Margins	Displays a submenu listing ***Left***, ***Right***, ***Top***, and ***Bottom*** (and ***None*** on Release 2.2 and later versions). Select one, and a prompt asks you to enter the margin (in characters). Type in the setting and press [Enter↵]. Selecting *None* on Release 2.2 and later versions sets the top, left, and bottom margins to zero and the right margin to 240.
Borders	Displays a submenu listing ***Columns*** or ***Rows***. Select one, and a prompt asks you to enter the border columns or rows. Specify the range and press [Enter↵].
Setup	Displays the prompt *Enter setup string:*. Type a setup string and press [Enter↵].
Pg-Length	Displays the prompt *Enter lines per page:*. Type in the number of lines per page and press [Enter↵].
Other	Displays the four menu choices described in the table "Other Printing Formats." Make a choice.
Quit	Returns you to the Print menu.

There are two blank lines above a header and two below.

The left and right margins are four spaces wide.

There are two blank lines above a footer and two below.

Page Layout Settings
Page layouts depend somewhat on the printer you are using but generally include the default settings shown here.

Headers and Footers

Headers and footers as long as 240 characters can be added to the model to identify it. As the table "Possible Header and Footer Contents" describes, these may also include page numbers, dates, and times. (A footer is not printed on the last page until you select the Page command from the Print menu.)

On Release 2.2 and later versions, you can enter headers and footers into cells on the worksheet and then refer to those cells when specifying headers and footers. That way, if you change the cell contents, the headers and footers change automatically.

POSSIBLE HEADER AND FOOTER CONTENTS

Entry	Description
Text	Prints as text.
@	Prints current date in the DD-MMM-YY format. Can be combined with text, for example, **Date: @**.
#	Prints a page number. Can be combined with text, for example, **Page #**.
|	Aligns contents within a header or footer. Can be used in combination with text or the date and page number symbols to achieve different effects. For example, **Date:@|text|Page #** left-aligns the date, centers the text, and right-aligns the page number. If used individually in front of an entry, a single | centers the following text, and || right-aligns it.
\cell address	(Releases 2.2 and later) prints the label in the specified cell as a header or footer. For example, to use a label in cell A1 as a header or footer, enter **\A1**.

Margins

You can change left, right, top, and bottom margins. These settings are useful when switching between 8½-by-11-inch and 11-by-14-inch paper. You can tell the program you have changed the paper size or you want to change the layout of a print range by changing the margin settings described in the table "Margin Settings."

Release 2.2 and later versions have a margin command *None* that sets the top, left, and bottom margins to 0 and the right margin to 240 in one step.

MARGIN SETTINGS

Margin	Default Setting	Possible Range
Left	Column 4	0-240
Right	Column 76	0-240
Top	Two lines	0-10
Bottom	Two lines	0-10

Borders

Borders are used when a model is too wide to print on a single sheet of paper. For example, if you use column 1 for labels and print a wide model, column 1 appears only on the first page of the printout. This makes it hard to identify the contents of the rows on the second and subsequent pages. The same is true if you use row 1 for labels and print a long model. The labels appear only at the top of the first page. In either case, if you specify that these columns or rows be treated as borders, they are printed on each page of the printout. When you set borders, be sure that they are not also included in the print range. If they are, duplicate rows and columns will be printed.

Setup

You can send printer setup codes to the printer to change the type size if you are using a dot-matrix printer. Using compressed type allows you to print 132 characters on an 8½-by-11-inch sheet of paper, instead of the normal 85 characters, so that you can squeeze a lot more data onto the sheet of paper. You can specify portrait or landscape orientation if your printer offers a choice.

Unfortunately, different printers use different setup codes. You need to refer to your printer's manual to find the codes used to control printing. You enter setup strings as three-digit numbers preceded by a backslash (\). For example, on an Epson or Epson-compatible printer, the code for compressed print is 015. To use this as a setup string, you would enter \015. If you are entering more than one setup code, enter them one after another. For example, on an Epson printer, the setup string \027\071 turns on double-strike printing. The table "Typical Epson Setup Strings" lists setup strings for Epson printers, and the table "Typical HP LaserJet Setup Strings" lists those for Hewlett-Packard LaserJet printers.

Once a setup string is sent to the printer, the printer remains in that mode. To cancel the setup string, turn the printer off and then back on again.

You can use a pair of split vertical bars (¦¦) to enter setup strings in cells in the worksheet. This allows you to print different sections of the document using different typestyles. For example, on an Epson printer, you can enter ||\015 in a cell to print the first part of a model in compressed type and ||\018 in another cell farther down the worksheet to print the remainder of the model in normal type.

- The ¦ (split vertical bar) is usually on the same key as the \ (backslash). To enter it, hold down Shift. When you enter two split vertical bars, only one is displayed on the screen although both are displayed on the control panel when the cell pointer is positioned in the cell.
- The code must be entered on a row by itself in the leftmost column in the print range. The row on which it is entered does not print out.

TYPICAL EPSON SETUP STRINGS

Print Control	Setup String
Compressed print on	\015
Compressed print off	\018
Boldface	\027\069
Underline	\027\045\049
Double strike on	\027\071
Double strike off	\027\072
Enlarged print	\027\087\049
Print 8 lines per inch	\0270
Print 6 lines per inch	\0272

TYPICAL HP LASERJET SETUP STRINGS

Print Control	Setup String
Portrait mode, normal type	\027E
Portrait mode, compressed type	\027E\027(s16.66H
Landscape mode, normal type	\027E\027&l1O
Landscape mode, compressed type	\027E\027&l1O\027(s16.66H

Page Length

The page length can be set to print between 20 and 100 lines per page. The default length is sixty-six lines on 11-inch paper (six lines per inch). The number of lines from the print range that are actually printed depends on the top and bottom margins you have set and the space reserved for the headers and footers.

To force a page break at any point, use the ***/Worksheet Page*** command to enter a hard page break on any row. The command inserts a new row below the one the cell pointer is on, moves the cell pointer to that row, and enters a page break code (::). When you print the model, the printer will stop printing on the current page when it reaches the code, advance the paper one page, and then resume printing. Nothing on the line with the code is printed. To remove the code, use the ***/Range Erase*** command, or type over it.

TIPS

- You can hide the contents of cells so that they do not appear in the printout.
- If part of long lines print on a second page, you have to reduce your left and right margin settings, print in landscape mode, narrow column widths, use borders, or print in compressed type.
- The split vertical bar is also a label prefix character and can be used to prevent lines from printing. This is useful when you want to enter comments in a model that do not appear in a printout. To use this character to prevent a line from printing, it must be entered in the leftmost column of the range you intend to print. For example, to enter a nonprinting comment on row 1, type **|COMMENT** into cell A1. The split vertical bar will not be displayed on the screen, just the comment.

→ KEY/Strokes

Entering Page Break Code

1. Move the cell pointer to a blank row above the row below which you want to force a page break.
2. Press / W P (for ***Worksheet, Page***) to insert a page break code (::).

Other Printing Formats

Normally when you make a printout, it looks as it does when displayed on the screen. But you can choose any of the printing formats described in the table "Other Printing Formats."

OTHER PRINTING FORMATS

Menu Option	Description
As-Displayed	Prints exactly what is displayed in the print range. This is the default appearance of a printout.
Cell-Formulas	Prints cell entries as a list showing the cell address, the format and protection status, and the cell contents. If cells contain formulas, the formulas are printed instead of the calculated results.
Formatted	Uses all printing specifications selected from the Print menu, including headers, footers, and borders. This is the default printing format.
Unformatted	Suppresses margins, headers, and footers and prints the range in one continuous strip with no page breaks. Use this command to print a text file on the disk that can be read by other programs.

EXERCISES

EXERCISE 1

PRINTING THE COLLEGE BUDGET MODEL

1. Retrieve the BUDGET model.
2. Add a header that prints page numbers and the date, and make a printout.
3. Enter a setup string to print the model in compressed type, and make a printout.
4. Clear the screen without saving the revised model because you do not want to save the new settings.

EXERCISE 2

PRINTING THE AUTO LOAN MODEL

1. Retrieve the AUTOLOAN model.
2. Add a header that prints your name left-aligned and the date right-aligned, and make a printout.
3. Save the model when you are finished so that the new settings are saved.

TOPIC 23

Troubleshooting Models

After completing this topic, you will be able to:

- Display and print out cell formulas
- Print column letters and row numbers on your model's printouts
- Identify circular references
- Describe when recalculation occurs and the order formulas are recalculated in
- Use the @NA function to trace cell references

When entering or testing models, you may occasionally encounter problems or get unexpected results. When this happens, you have to do some troubleshooting. The first step is to identify the problem; then you correct it. Here are some common problems you might encounter.

- The computer beeps when data are entered. This tells you something is wrong. Use the edit commands to correct the entry.
- If you enter a whole number that is too long to be displayed in its cell, it is displayed as a row of asterisks (or in scientific notation if the format is General). To display the entire number, you must widen the column or change the number's format.
- If you enter a decimal number that is too long to be displayed in its cell, it is rounded off.
- An error message is displayed in a cell. This is commonly caused by entering a formula that divides by 0 or by deleting a row or column containing a cell to which a formula refers.
- Recalculation is not performed. If recalculation is set to Manual, you must press F9 (**Calc**) to recalculate the worksheet after making changes so that the changes are reflected in formulas.
- When a formula refers directly to a cell that contains a label, you must treat the label as a string. If you don't, the cell with the formulas will display an *ERR* message or an incorrect result because a label is treated as a number with a zero value. For example, if cell A1 contains a label, the formula 3*A1 calculates zero, 3/A1 displays *ERR*, and 3+A1 displays 3.

TUTORIAL

In this tutorial, you use the @NA (for Not Available) function to trace cell references in the 5YRPLAN model. You then add row and column labels to the model so that you can check which formulas refer to which cells. Your finished model should look like the figure "The Troubleshooting

Model." Refer to this figure to check your results as you complete the steps in this tutorial.

The Troubleshooting Model
After you add the row and column references to the five-year plan model, your results should look like this.

	A	B	C	D	E	F	G	H
1	Your name:						1	I
2	Filename:	5YRPLAN					2	I
3	Date:						3	I
4							4	I
5	Part 1. Variables						5	I
6	Initial sales	1,000					6	I
7	Sales growth rate	10%					7	I
8	Cost of goods sold	56%					8	I
9							9	I
10	Part 2. Model						10	I
11	Year	1994	1995	1996	1997	1998	11	I
12	Sales	1,000	1,100	1,210	1,331	1,464	12	I
13	Cost of goods sold	560	616	678	745	820	13	I
14	Gross margin	440	484	532	586	644	14	I
15								
16	A	B	C	D	E	F		
17	--------------------	--------------------	--------------------	--------------------	--------------------	--------------------		

GETTING STARTED

1. Retrieve the 5YRPLAN model.
2. The three variables in the model are in cells B6, B7, and B8. Type **@NA** into each of these cells, one at a time, and watch what happens to the cells in which formulas refer directly or indirectly to these cells. After entering each @NA, restore the original number before entering it into the next cell.

ENTERING COLUMN LABELS

3. On row 16, enter the column letters **^A** in column A, **^B** in column B, and so on through column F.
4. In cell A17, enter a single ruled line (**\-**), and then copy it to cells B17 through F17.

ENTERING ROW LABELS

5. In cells G1 through G14, use the ***/Data Fill*** command to enter a series of numbers starting at 1 and stepping by 1.
6. In cell H1, type **^ I** and press [Enter ↵].
7. Copy the vertical bar in cell H1 to cells H2 through H14.
8. Change the width of column G to 4 and column H to 3.

PRINTING THE MODEL

9. Press [/][P][P][O][B][C] (for ***P**rint*, ***P**rinter*, ***O**ptions*, ***B**orders*, ***C**olumns*), and the prompt reads *Enter range for border columns:*.
10. Type **G1.H1** and press [Enter ↵].
11. Press [B][R] (for ***B**orders*, ***R**ows*), and the prompt reads *Enter range for border rows:*.
12. Type **A16.A17** and press [Enter ↵].
13. Press [Q] (for ***Q**uit*) to leave the Options menu.
14. Press [R] (for ***R**ange*), and the prompt reads *Enter print range:*.

15. Type **A1.F14** and press [Enter↵].
16. Press [A][G] (for ***A**lign*, ***G**o*) to print the document.
17. When the Print menu reappears, press [P][Q] (for ***P**age*, ***Q**uit*) to advance the paper out of the printer and leave the Print menu. The model is printed with row and column numbers that you can use as a reference when checking cell references. If column F prints on its own page, change the right margin setting to 80 (**/PPOMR**).

The Troubleshooting Model Printout
When you print the five-year plan after adding column letters and row numbers as print borders, your results should look like this.

	A	B	C	D	E	F
1 |	Your name:					
2 |	Filename:	5YRPLAN				
3 |	Date:					
4 |						
5 |	Part 1. Variables					
6 |	Initial sales	1,000				
7 |	Sales growth rate	10%				
8 |	Cost of goods sold	56%				
9 |						
10 |	Part 2. Model					
11 |	Year	1994	1995	1996	1997	1998
12 |	Sales	1,000	1,100	1,210	1,331	1,464
13 |	Cost of goods sold	560	616	678	745	820
14 |	Gross margin	440	484	532	586	644

PRINTING CELL FORMULAS

18. Press [/][P][P][O][O][C] (for ***P**rint*, ***P**rinter*, ***O**ptions*, ***O**ther*, ***C**ell-Formulas*).
19. Press [Q] (for ***Q**uit*) to return to the Print menu.
20. Press [R] (for ***R**ange*), and the prompt reads *Enter print range:*.
21. Type **A10.F14** and press [Enter↵].
22. Press [A][G] (for ***A**lign*, ***G**o*) to print the model.
23. When the Print menu reappears, press [P][Q] (for ***P**age*, ***Q**uit*) to advance the paper out of the printer and leave the Print menu. The contents on the model's formulas have been printed. You can use this printout and the one you made with the column letters and row numbers to check cell references.

FINISHING UP

24. Save the model as TROUBLE.
25. You have now completed this tutorial. Either clear the screen and continue with the next activity or quit the program.

QUICK REFERENCE

When checking models, you can display formulas on the screen or print them out. You can also use the @NA function to check the relationship between cells.

Displaying Formulas on the Screen

You can display all the formulas in a worksheet rather than their calculated results with the ***/Worksheet Global Format Text*** command. If you have changed the formats of any cells containing formulas, you have to reset them to the global format to see the formulas. This is an ideal way to check the relationships among cells. You can also use windows to split the screen and then format one part of the screen to show the formulas and the other part to show the calculated results.

Printing Out Diagnostic Tools

When you make a printout, you can use the ***/Print Options Other Cell-Formulas*** command to make a printout of the contents of each cell. This is a good way to document your models. Further, you can check large models faster and more accurately if you have a printout of the model with row and column labels that match the screen display. To do this, add a column of numbers to the right of and a row of column labels below the model. Print out these labels along with the model.

 KEY/Strokes

Printing Out a Model's Formulas

1. Press [/][P][P] (for ***Print, Printer***) to display the Print menu.
2. If you have not specified a range or if you want to change it, press [R] (for ***Range***), and the prompt reads *Enter print range:*. Type in the coordinates of, or use the cell pointer to point to, the upper-left and lower-right cells in the range and press [Enter ↵]. (If you are printing borders, be sure the print range does not include those rows or columns, or they will be printed twice.)
3. Press [O][O][C] (for ***Options, Other, Cell-Formulas***).
4. Press [Q] (for ***Quit***) to return to the Print menu.
5. Press [A][G] (for ***Align, Go***) to begin printing.
6. Press [P][Q] (for ***Page, Quit***) to advance the paper out of the printer and clear the Print menu.

Using the @NA Function

Relationships can be traced throughout a model by using the @NA function. If you enter the @NA function in any cell containing a value, all formulas referring to that cell, either directly or indirectly, will display *NA* in their cells when the worksheet is recalculated. This is an excellent way to find what formulas are referring to a particular cell, especially before you delete rows and columns.

Circular References

Circular references occur when a formula refers either directly or indirectly to itself. 1-2-3 displays a *CIRC* indicator if the model contains one or more circular references to warn you they exist. If they do exist, you may have to recalculate the worksheet more than once to get the correct result, and even then, a correct result may not be possible. To locate the cell that contains this reference, use the ***/Worksheet Status*** command.

Recalculation

1-2-3 automatically recalculates the formulas in your model every time you enter a new formula or value so that any cells referring to a new or changed value display correct results. Release 2.01 recalculates all the formulas in a model. The larger your model becomes, the longer it takes to recalculate it. Release 2.2 and later versions have a feature called minimal recalculation that speeds up recalculation—only those cells affected by changes are recalculated.

When you first load your worksheet, the default setting controls the type of recalculation used. The default settings are Natural and Automatic. You normally do not need to change these settings, but you can specify when the worksheet recalculates and the number of times it does so. The table "Recalculation Menu Options" describes the choices.

KEY/Strokes

Changing Recalculation

1. Press [/][W][G][R] (for ***W**orksheet, **G**lobal, **R**ecalculation*).
2. Make one of the choices described in the table "Recalculation Menu Options."

RECALCULATION MENU OPTIONS

Menu Choice	Description
***N**atural*	When a formula is recalculated, all other formulas it refers to are recalculated first. (Release 2.2 and later versions' minimal recalculation feature works only when recalculation is set to Natural.)
***C**olumnwise*	Recalculation begins in cell A1, recalculates column A, then goes to cell B1, recalculates column B, and so on.
***R**owwise*	Recalculation begins in cell A1, recalculates row 1, then goes to cell A2, recalculates row 2, and so on.
***A**utomatic*	Recalculates the model every time any data are entered into a cell.
***M**anual*	Recalculation occurs only when you press [F9] (**CALC**). When recalculation is set to Manual and you enter any data, a *CALC* indicator at the bottom of the screen reminds you to press [F9] (**CALC**) for the correct current values in cells containing formulas.
***I**teration*	When a model has circular references or forward references, Iteration determines the number of times the recalculation cycle is repeated. You can set it to any number between 1 (the default) and 50. This setting is ignored if there are no circular references and Natural order is used.

EXERCISES

EXERCISE 1

PRINTING OUT THE FORMULAS IN A MODEL

Retrieve the OVERVIEW model and make a printout of the model's formulas.

EXERCISE 2

EXPLORING CIRCULAR REFERENCES

When you are working with cash flow statements and other financial reports, circular references are sometimes useful. In this exercise, you create a model that shows how a circular reference is used to calculate a loan large enough to cover repayment of both the principal and the interest. Since the interest due is determined by the size of the loan, and the size of the loan required is based partly on the interest due, you have a circular reference.

1. Enter the model shown in the figure "The Circular Reference Model."
   - Change the global format to Currency with zero decimal places.
   - Enter the formulas described in the table "The CIRC Model's Formulas." Notice how the loan is $60,000 (materials plus labor), and interest is $6,000 and the *CIRC* indicator is displayed.
2. Press F9 (CALC) about six times, and watch the loan change as you do so. It finally settles at 6,666.67.
3. Save the finished model as CIRC and make a printout.
4. Change materials and labor to 0, and recalculate the worksheet until the loan and interest both equal zero. Then enter $100,000 for materials and 50,000 for labor. Recalculate the worksheet until you get a final result.

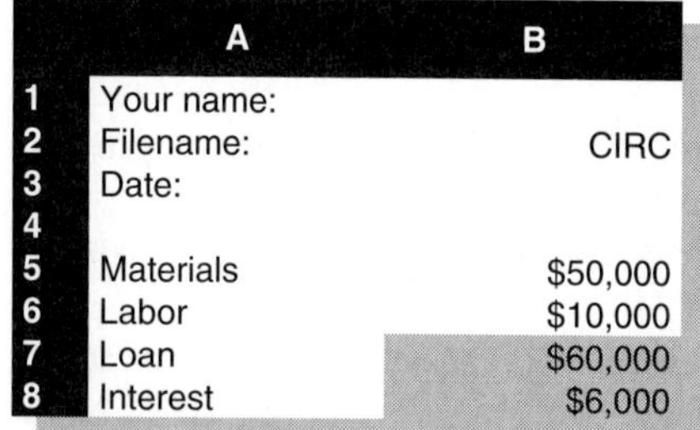

	A	B
1	Your name:	
2	Filename:	CIRC
3	Date:	
4		
5	Materials	$50,000
6	Labor	$10,000
7	Loan	$60,000
8	Interest	$6,000

The Circular Reference Model
After you enter the circular reference model, your results should look like this.

THE CIRC MODEL'S FORMULAS

#	Cell	Formula
1	B7	*Loan* is the sum of the materials, labor, and interest.
2	B8	*Interest* is 10% multiplied times the loan amount.

CHAPTER 5 REVIEW

- Functions are programs built into 1-2-3 that automatically perform calculations for you.
- To enter a function, you type the prefix @, the function's name, and arguments enclosed in parentheses.
- Date and time functions calculate serial numbers that you can format or use in mathematical operations.
- Relational operators such as >, <, or = determine the relationship between numbers or values in cells.
- Logical operators connect two or more statements. For the connected statements to be true, the #AND# operator requires that both connected statements be true; the #OR# operator requires that only one be true; and the #NOT# operator requires that neither be true.
- IF statements can branch calculations so that one operation is performed if the condition is true and another if it is false.
- Strings are one or more text characters or spaces such as you find in labels, names, or street addresses.
- To carry a string from the cell it has been entered into, enter a reference to that cell in the cell you want it carried to.
- To join strings together, you concatenate them with an ampersand. For example, the formula +A1&A2 joins the strings in cells A1 and A2 into a single string.
- You name ranges so you can then refer to them in formulas, functions, and commands by name rather then by cell addresses.
- One big advantage of naming cells is that the names move automatically when you insert or delete rows and columns even though the cell addresses change.
- To assign names to ranges, you use the */**R**ange **N**ame **C**reate* command.
- To divide the screen into two windows, you use the */**W**orksheet **W**indow* command and then select ***H**orizontal* or ***V**ertical.*
- You press F6 to move the cell pointer back and forth between windows.
- To fix rows or columns on the screen so they are not scrolled off, you use the */**W**orksheet **T**itles* command.
- The */**W**orksheet **G**lobal **P**rotection **E**nable* command turns on protection for all cells in the worksheet.
- You can hide columns of data so they do not appear on the screen or on printouts.
- To unprotect selected cells, you use the */**R**ange **U**nprotect* command.
- To protect a file with a password, you enter a space and then the letter P after its name when you save it.
- When printing a model, you can add headers or footers, specify rows or columns that print on every page, and enter a setup string to print it in normal or compressed type. You can also specify the printout's page length and the orientation of the paper in the printer.
- To force a page break, you use the */**W**orksheet **P**age* command.

- When you encounter problems with a model, you can enter the @NA function into a cell and see what other cells display *NA*. Those that do, directly or indirectly, refer to the cell you entered the function into.
- You can display formulas on the screen instead of their calculated results.
- You can print out cell formulas instead of their contents to make a record of a model or to find out how formulas relate to each other.
- When you change a number in a worksheet, formulas display the new results only when the worksheet is recalculated.
- Recalculation controls what cells are recalculated, when they are recalculated, and in what order.
- Release 2.2 and later versions recalculate only those formulas that are affected by a change you make; this is called minimal recalculation.
- Manual recalculation requires you to press a key to recalculate the model. Automatic recalculation recalculates the model each time you enter a number or make a change.
- Iteration controls the number of times a worksheet is recalculated.
- Recalculation is normally set to Natural so that all formulas to which a given formula refers are recalculated first. You can also set recalculation by row or by column in specific circumstances.
- Circular references are cell references in a formula that refer directly or indirectly to the cell it has been entered into.

CHAPTER 5 QUESTIONS

FILL IN THE BLANK

1. To calculate the payments on a loan, you could enter a ___________ to do it automatically.
2. To enter and display today's date or time into the worksheet so it changes when the date or time change you enter a date or time ___________.
3. Date and time functions calculate serial date or time ___________.
4. The serial number for January 1, 1900 is ___________.
5. To determine if the value in cell A1 is greater than the value in cell A2, you could enter the formula ___________ in cell A3. If the value in A1 is greater, the formula will display ___________.
6. To determine if the value in cell A1 is greater than the value in cell A2 and the value in A1 is greater than 100, you could enter the formula ___________ in cell A3.
7. To add cells A1 and A2 if A1 is greater than 100, or display 0 if it isn't, you could enter the IF statement ___________.
8. To carry the label in cell B2 to cell B5, you enter ___________ in cell ___________.

9. To join the label in cell C1 with the label in cell C2 you can enter the formula __________ into any other cell. To add a space between the joined labels, you would enter the formula __________.
10. To assign a name to a range, you use the __________ command.
11. To divide the screen into two windows, you use the __________ command.
12. To move the cell pointer between windows, you press __________.
13. To fix rows or columns on the screen so they don't scroll off, you use the __________ command.
14. To protect all cells on the worksheet, you use the __________ command.
15. To unprotect specific cells, you use the __________ command.
16. If you don't want anyone to see a column of data on your screen or printouts, you can __________ the column with the __________ command.
17. To print a model in compressed type, you have to enter a __________.
18. When recalculation is set to manual, you have to press __________ to recalculate formulas.
19. Circular references mean that a formula is referring directly or indirectly to __________.

MATCH THE COLUMNS

1. @PMT(1000,.3,48)
2. @NOW
3. @DATE(94,1,1)-@NOW
4. +A1<A2
5. +A1=A2#AND#A3<100
6. @IF(A1>0,A1+A2,@NA)
7. +A1&A2
8. +A1&” “&A2
9. / R N C
10. F5, **SALES**, Enter ←
11. / W H
12. / W T B
13. / W G P E
14. / R U
15. F9
16. *CIRC*

__ Concatenates labels in cells A1 and A2
__ Concatenates labels in cells A1 and A2 and adds a space between them
__ Unprotects specific cells
__ Press to recalculate formulas when recalculation is set to manual
__ Displays @NA if A1 is not greater than 0.
__ Creates a range name
__ Creates a horizontal window
__ Fixes rows above and columns to the left of the cell pointer
__ Turns on cell protection
__ Calculates the number of days between today and January 1, 1994.
__ Displays the serial number of today's date
__ Appears when your model contains a circular reference
__ Displays 1 if A1 is less than A2
__ Moves the cell pointer to the upperleft corner of the range named SALES
__ Calculates the payment on a $1,000 loan
__ Displays 1 if A1 is equal to A2 and A3 is less than 100

WRITE OUT THE ANSWERS

1. How would you enter a function to round the value 1.11234? To round the value in cell B4? To round the sum of the values in the range A1..A3?
2. What will the function @SUM(B4..B6) do? What is the term @SUM called? What is the reference B4..B6 called (other than a range)?
3. What is a date function used for? What is date arithmetic?
4. List and describe three date functions and three time functions that generate numbers. List and describe three functions that manipulate date and time numbers.
5. Describe the model you would build to calculate the number of days you have been at college so far.
6. List five relational operators and describe what they are used for.
7. List three logical operators and describe what they are used for.
8. How would the formula @IF(A27>0,A1/A2,0) read if you translated it into normal English?
9. If you want to include a string in a formula or function, what must you do?
10. What are windows? What are they used for?
11. What does the Sync command do? The Unsync command?
12. When you split the screen and then format two windows differently, what happens when you clear the screen? Which window's formatting remains in effect if you had two horizontal windows? If you had two vertical windows?
13. What are fixed titles? What are they used for? List three ways you can fix titles.
14. In what circumstances is cell protection useful? What two steps must you follow to protect a model when you want to enter data in selected cells?
15. What two ways are there to hide the data in cells?
16. What is a password used for? How do you password protect a document? How do you remove password protection?
17. Describe three options that you have when entering headers and footers in a printout of a model.
18. What are borders used for?
19. What is a setup string? Why would you use one?
20. When you change a number in a model, what must occur before formulas reflect the change?
21. What does minimal recalculation mean?
22. What is the difference between Manual and Automatic recalculation?
23. What does Iteration refer to?
24. List and briefly describe three orders that formulas can be recalculated in.
25. What are circular references?
26. Why would you enter the @NA function into a cell?

CHAPTER 5

PROJECTS

PROJECT 1

KEEPING BOX SCORES

1. Retrieve the BOXSCORE model.
2. Enter and copy the functions described in the table "The Box Score Model's Functions."
3. Format all percentage columns as percent with 1 decimal place.
4. Unprotect cell ranges B7.C13, B17.D21, B25.D29, and B33.C37. Enable protection so you can only enter numbers into the unprotected cells.
5. Save the model again.
6. Update one or more of the individual sections with the scores in today's newspaper for the sports that are in season and make a printout.
7. Change the print range to D7.F13 and print out the cell formulas in that range.
8. Clear the screen without saving your changes in the box scores and print range.

THE BOX SCORE MODEL'S FUNCTIONS

#	Cell	Formula	Copy to
1	D7	Baseball *Percent* is calculated by the formula **@ROUND(B7/@SUM(B7.C7),3)**	D8.D13
2	F7	Baseball *Games back* is calculated by the formula **(@MAX(E$7.E$13)-E7)*0.5**	F8.F13
3	E25	Football *Percent* is calculated by the formula **@ROUND((B25+(D25*0.5))/@SUM(B25.D25),3)**	E26.E29
4	D33	Basketball *Percent* is calculated by the formula **@ROUND(B33/@SUM(B33.C33),3)**	D34.D37
5	E33	Basketball *Games back* is calculated by the formula **+C33-@MIN(C$33.C$37)**	E34.E37

PROJECT 2

CALCULATING EXCHANGE RATES

1. Retrieve the EXCHANGE model.
2. Protect all cells except D5 where you enter the number to be converted.
3. Add a footer with the date printed in the center of the page.
4. Print and then save the revised model.

PROJECT 3

CONVERTING BETWEEN ENGLISH AND METRIC UNITS

1. Retrieve the METRIC model.
2. Protect all cells except D5 where you enter the number to be converted.
3. Add a header with the date printed in the upper-right corner of the page.
4. Print and then save the revised model.

CHAPTER 6

Working with Databases

TOPIC 24

Creating and Sorting Databases

After completing this topic, you will be able to:

- Create a database
- Sort a database into ascending or descending order

1-2-3's database capabilities are ideal for organizing and analyzing tables containing sales figures, inventory, mailing or distribution lists, customer accounts, check registers, or any other data that need to be collected, sorted, and analyzed. Databases are created with most of the same commands used to create a model. In fact, a database is just a model organized into fields and records. On a worksheet, records are entered into rows, with one field in each column. There are three key parts in a typical database:

- Field names are placed on the first row and are used to label the columns where data are entered.
- Records are entered on the second and subsequent rows. Records are sets of related data, much like Rolodex[tm] cards that contain a person's name, address, and phone number.
- Fields are the columns of information that make up a record. For example, on a Rolodex[tm] card, the fields might be the person's name, street address, city, state, ZIP code, and phone number.

A Spreadsheet Database
A spreadsheet database is a range of cells containing one or more columns (fields) and at least two rows (records). The first row is always used for field names.

	A	B	C	D	E	F
1	Dept.	Course	Instructor	Day	Time	Bldg.
2	Math	136	Smith	T,T	9:00	Stoner
3	Math	200	Davis	M,W,F	9:00	Widner
4	English	124	Jones	T,T	12:00	Drew
5	Biology	101	Smith	M,W,F	10:00	Hayes

Field name — Record — Field

TUTORIAL

In this tutorial, you explore data management by sorting a database that stores a class schedule. As you follow the tutorial's steps, refer to the figure "The Class Schedule Database Model" that shows the model.

The Class Schedule Database Model
After you enter the class schedule database, your results should look like this.

	A	B	C	D	E	F
1	Your name:					
2	Filename:	SCHEDULE				
3	Date:					
4						
5	DATABASE:					
6	Dept.	Course	Instructor	Day	Time	Bldg.
7	Math	136	Davis	T,T	9:00	Stoner
8	Math	200	Davis	M,W,F	9:00	Widner
9	English	124	Jones	T,T	12:00	Drew
10	Biology	101	Smith	M,W,F	10:00	Hayes
11						

GETTING STARTED

1. Retrieve the SCHEDULE database and enter your name into cell B1.

SORTING THE DATABASE IN ASCENDING ORDER BY COURSE NUMBER

2. Press [/] [D] [S] (for ***D**ata*, ***S**ort*) to display the Sort menu.
3. Press [D] (for ***D**ata-Range*), and the prompt reads *Enter data range:*.
4. Type **A7.F10** and press [Enter←].
5. Press [P] (for ***P**rimary-Key*), and the prompt reads *Primary sort key:*.
6. Point to cell B7 and press [Enter←]. The prompt reads *Sort order (A or D): D.*
7. Press [A] (for ***A**scending*), and then press [Enter←].
8. Press [G] (for ***G**o*) to sort the database by course number in ascending order.

SORTING THE DATABASE IN DESCENDING ORDER BY COURSE NUMBER

9. Press [/] [D] [S] (for ***D**ata*, ***S**ort*) to display the Sort menu.
10. Press [P] (for ***P**rimary-Key*), and the prompt reads *Primary sort key: B7.*
11. Press [Enter←] to accept the key, and the prompt reads *Sort order (A or D): A.*
12. Press [D] (for ***D**escending*), and then press [Enter←].
13. Press [G] (for ***G**o*) to sort the database by course number in descending order.

SORTING THE DATABASE IN ASCENDING ORDER BY BUILDING

14. Press [/] [D] [S] (for ***D**ata*, ***S**ort*) to display the Sort menu.
15. Press [P] (for ***P**rimary-Key*), and the prompt reads *Primary sort key:*.
16. Point to cell F7 and press [Enter←]. The prompt reads *Sort order (A or D): D.*
17. Press [A] (for ***A**scending*), and then press [Enter←].
18. Press [G] (for ***G**o*) to sort the database by building in ascending order.

FINISHING UP

19. Save the model under its original name and make a printout.
20. You have now completed this tutorial. Either clear the screen and continue with the next activity or quit the program.

QUICK REFERENCE

	A	B
1	Last	First
2	Jones	Frank
3	Smith	Ann
4	Jones	Betty
5	Smith	John
6	Jones	Dennis
7	Smith	Liz
8	Jones	Bill
9	Smith	Mike
10	Jones	Lars
11	Smith	Stuart
12	Jones	Hal

	A	B
1	Last	First
2	Jones	Bill
3	Jones	Lars
4	Jones	Betty
5	Jones	Hal
6	Jones	Dennis
7	Jones	Frank
8	Smith	John
9	Smith	Stuart
10	Smith	Liz
11	Smith	Mike
12	Smith	Ann

	A	B
1	Last	First
2	Jones	Betty
3	Jones	Bill
4	Jones	Dennis
5	Jones	Frank
6	Jones	Hal
7	Jones	Lars
8	Smith	Ann
9	Smith	John
10	Smith	Liz
11	Smith	Mike
12	Smith	Stuart

Secondary Key
A secondary key can break ties in a sort. When the file is sorted using just the primary key "Last," first names within the Jones and Smith groupings are not in any specific order. When the "First" field is used as the secondary key, the names are in correct order by both last and first names.

When creating a database, keep the following points in mind:

- Add a row of labels as the first row in the database to name each of the fields. You can name up to 256 fields.
- Do not leave any blank rows in the database. If you do, they will be sorted to the top or bottom of the database.
- Enter either labels or numbers in a field (column), but do not enter both in the same field.

Sorting Databases

Databases can be quickly sorted into ascending or descending order. To do so, you complete four steps:

1. Define the database range. When specifying the range to sort, include only the data records. Do not include field names, or they are sorted along with the data.
2. Specify which columns are to be used as the primary and secondary keys. The primary key specifies the field on which the data range is sorted. The secondary key is specified when there is a possibility of duplicate data in the primary key. For example, if you were sorting a database by name, you would want to use the Lastname field as the primary key and the Firstname field as the secondary key. When the data are sorted, any records with the same last name are subsorted by first name.

   When you use primary and secondary keys, select the keys in descending order of importance. The primary key should be the more important field, and the secondary key should be the less important field.
3. Specify the sort order as ascending or descending. An ascending sort ignores the case of characters and sorts the database in the following sequence:
   - Blank cells
   - Labels beginning with letters in ascending alphabetical sequence
   - Labels beginning with numbers in numeric sequence
   - Labels beginning with any other characters

   A descending sort reverses the order in which these items are sorted.
4. Sort the database.

Sort Order
In an ascending sort (column B), data are arranged in ascending order from the top of the file to the bottom. In a descending sort (column C), data are arranged in descending order from the top to the bottom. Notice how blank cells are sorted to the top in an ascending sort and to the bottom in a descending sort.

	A	B	C
1	Unsorted	Sorted in	Sorted in
2		ascending	descending
3		order	order
4			
5	Smith		4
		Adams	3
6	Jones	Jones	2
7	Adams	Lewis	1
8	Lewis	Melton	Walton
9	Walton	Smith	Smith
10	Melton	Walton	Melton
11	4	1	Lewis
12	2	2	Jones
13	1	3	Adams
14	3	4	

TIPS

- If you want to be able to sort a database back into its original order, you can do so. Before sorting a database, insert a column, and then use the ***/Data Fill*** command to fill it with a sequence of numbers. To sort the database back into its original order at any time, specify the column of numbers as the primary key.
- When you sort a database that contains formulas or to which formulas refer, be sure to follow these rules:
  - Do not refer to cells in other records in the data range.
  - To refer to another cell in the same record, use a relative reference.
  - To refer to cells outside the data range, use an absolute reference.
  - Do not have formulas outside the data range refer to cells within the data range. They will continue to refer to the original cells when the data range is sorted and not to the new position of the data.

→ KEY/Strokes

Sorting a Database

1. Enter data in rows and columns so that the data are organized as a database. (Save the database before sorting so that you have the option of retrieving it in its original form.)
2. Press [/][D][S] (for ***Data, Sort***) to display the Sort menu.
3. Press [D] (for ***D****ata-Range*), and the prompt reads *Enter data range:*.
4. Type in the cell addresses or point to the range (do not include the field names, if any) and press [Enter ↵].
5. Press [P] (for ***P****rimary-Key*), and the prompt reads *Primary sort key:*.
6. Point to any cell in the column you want to use as the primary key and press [Enter ↵]. The prompt reads *Sort order (A or D): D.*
7. Either press [A] (for ***A****scending*) or [D] (for ***D****escending*) and press [Enter ↵].
8. Press [S] (for ***S****econdary-Key*), and the prompt reads *Secondary sort key:*.
9. Point to any cell in the column you want to use as the secondary key and press [Enter ↵]. The prompt reads *Sort order (A or D): D.*
10. Press [A] (for ***A****scending*) or **D** (for ***D****escending*) and press [Enter ↵].
11. Press [G] (for ***G****o*) to sort the database.

The Sort Settings Sheet
Release 2.2 and later versions added a settings sheet that lists all the current settings for a sort. This settings sheet is displayed whenever you press [/] [D] [S] (for ***D**ata*, ***S**ort*). The screens vary slightly from version to version. This illustration shows Release 2.4.

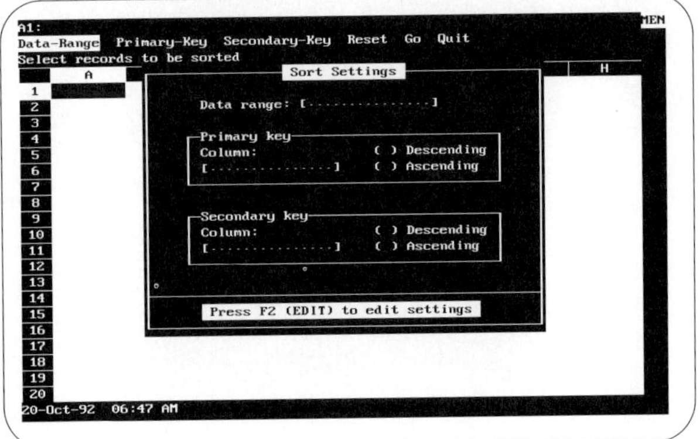

EXERCISES

EXERCISE 1

CALCULATING WHERE YOUR TEXTBOOK DOLLARS GO

In this exercise, you sort a database that shows where your textbook dollars go.

1. Retrieve the TEXTBOOK model shown in the figure "The Textbook Costs Model" and enter your name into cell B1.
2. Save the revised model under its original name.
3. Sort the database into descending order using the $ or % column as the primary key. (They will both give the same sort order.) Make a printout.
4. Sort the database into ascending order using the $ or % column as the primary key. (They will both give the same sort order.) Make a printout.
5. Clear the screen without saving the file.

The Textbook Costs Model
After you enter the textbook costs model, your results should look like this.

	A	B	C	D
1	Your name:			
2	Filename:	TEXTBOOK		
3	Date:			
4				
5	Item	$	%	Order
6	Price	$50.00	100.0%	0
7	Bookstore	$10.50	21.0%	1
8	Paper, printing, & binding	$6.50	13.0%	2
9	Author royalties	$5.75	11.5%	3
10	Preparation costs	$2.50	5.0%	4
11	Editorial costs	$1.75	3.5%	5
12	Production costs	$0.75	1.5%	6
13	Marketing	$5.25	10.5%	7
14	Fulfillment	$2.00	4.0%	8
15	General & administrative	$4.50	9.0%	9
16	Publisher's profit	$10.50	21.0%	10

TOPIC 25

Querying Databases

After completing this topic, you will be able to:

- Query a database to find, extract, and delete information
- Use database statistical functions

You can use a spreadsheet database as a major record-keeping and analysis tool. The */Data Query* commands can be used to:

- Find records meeting specified criteria
- Delete records meeting specified criteria
- Delete duplicate records
- Create a new database containing only selected records or fields

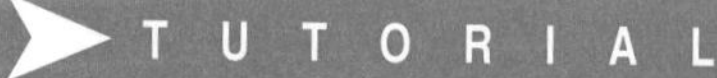

TUTORIAL

In this tutorial, you explore querying the SCHEDULE database. When you have finished, your model should look like the figure "The Revised Course Schedule Database Model."

The Revised Course Schedule Database Model
After you revise the course schedule database model, your results should look like this.

	A	B	C	D	E	F
1	Your name:					
2	Filename:	SCHEDULE				
3	Date:					
4						
5	DATABASE:					
6	Dept.	Course	Instructor	Day	Time	Bldg.
7	Math	136	Davis	T,T	9:00	Stoner
8	Math	200	Davis	M,W,F	9:00	Widner
9	English	124	Jones	T,T	12:00	Drew
10	Biology	101	Smith	M,W,F	10:00	Hayes
11						
12	CRITERIA RANGE:					
13	Dept.	Course	Instructor	Day	Time	Bldg.
14	Biology					
15						
16						
17	OUTPUT RANGE					
18	Dept.	Course	Instructor	Day	Time	Bldg.
19						
20						

GETTING STARTED

1. Retrieve the SCHEDULE model.
2. Enter the label **INPUT RANGE:** in cell A5 that now reads *DATABASE.*

ENTERING A CRITERIA RANGE

3. In cell A12, enter the label **CRITERIA RANGE:**.
4. Copy the field names on row 6 to row 13.

ENTERING AN OUTPUT RANGE

5. In cell A17, enter the label **OUTPUT RANGE:**.
6. Copy the field names on row 6 to row 18.

SPECIFYING THE RANGES

7. Press / D Q I (for ***D**ata, **Q**uery, **I**nput*), and the prompt reads *Enter input range:*.
8. Type **A6.F10** and press Enter←.
9. Press C (for ***C**riteria*), and the prompt reads *Enter criteria range:*.
10. Type **A13.F14** and press Enter←.
11. Press O (for ***O**utput*), and the prompt reads *Enter output range:*.
12. Type **A18.F18** and press Enter←.
13. Press Q (for ***Q**uit*).

EXTRACTING DATA

14. Enter the name **Davis** in cell C14.
15. Press / D Q E (for ***D**ata, **Q**uery, **E**xtract*), and the two records with Davis as the instructor are extracted and listed in the output range on rows 19 and 20.
16. Press Q (for ***Q**uit*).
17. To experiment, erase *Davis* from cell C14 using the **/*R*ange *E*rase** command. Then, enter on row 14 any Dept, Course (these are labels not values), Instructor, Day, Time, or Bldg. that appears in the same column in the input range and press F7 (**Query**). For example, enter **T, T** in cell D14 and press F7 (**Query**) to extract all classes on Tuesday and Thursday. You see that you can extract any records in this way.

EXTRACTING DATA THAT MEET TWO CRITERIA

18. Erase any criteria that you entered on row 14 and enter **Davis** in cell C14 and **Stoner** in cell F14.
19. Press F7 (**Query**), and only one record is extracted because only one record contains both Davis and Stoner in the appropriate columns.
20. Try other combinations on your own. To do so, erase the entries in the criteria range, enter some of your own criteria, and press F7 (**Query**).

EXTRACTING DATA THAT MEET ONE OF TWO CRITERIA

21. Erase any criteria that you entered on row 14, and enter **Biology** in cell A14 and **Jones** in cell C15.
22. Press / D Q C (for ***D**ata*, ***Q**uery*, ***C**riteria*), and the prompt reads *Enter criteria range:*.
23. Press ↓ to expand the highlight to row 15 and press Enter←.
24. Press Q (for ***Q**uit*).
25. Press F7 (**Query**), and two records are extracted. One meets the criterion Jones, and the other meets the criterion Biology.
26. Erase the entries in the criteria range. Then enter some of your own on both rows and press F7 (**Query**).

FINISHING UP

27. Print the model.
28. Save the model under the same name.
29. You have now completed this tutorial. Either clear the screen and continue with the next activity or quit the program.

QUICK REFERENCE

To query a database, you must enter and specify an input range and a criteria range. To extract records from the database, you must also create an output range.

Setting Up a Database to Query

To use the ***/D**ata **Q**uery* commands, you must first specify an input range, a criteria range, and an output range.

The Input Range

The input range is the range of cells the program looks in during a data query. The input range is either the database itself or some portion of it. The range must include the field names on the top row of the database.

The Criteria Range

The criteria range (called the criterion range on Release 2.01 and earlier versions) is the range where the query specifications are listed. The criteria range must be at least two rows. The first row contains copies of some or all of the database's field names (up to 32); the remaining rows are used to enter criteria to be used in the query.

The Output Range

The output range is where data extracted during a query are stored. An output range is necessary only if you are using the Extract or Unique command (see below). The first row of the output range lists the field names from the input range that you want to extract data from (up to 32 fields).

- If you include just the row with the field names in the output range, 1-2-3 will use as many rows below the range as it needs when you execute Query commands. Be sure you have enough blank rows below, or data could be overwritten.

- If you specify more than one row, 1-2-3 restricts its output to just the specified rows. If there are too few rows to hold the data, 1-2-3 displays the error message *Too many records for Output range:*. When you press [Esc] to clear the message, the range is filled with the records that fit.

Querying a Database

Once you have defined the input range, the criteria range, and for some commands, the output range, you can query the database. Pressing [F7] (**Query**) repeats the most recent Query command performed. If you want to find several different groups of data, all you need to do is change the criteria and press [F7] (**Query**).

- The Find command highlights selected records in the input range that meet the requirements specified in the criteria range. If more than one record meets the requirements specified in the criteria range, the first is highlighted.
  - Press [↓] or [↑] to move the cell pointer to other records. If no other records match the criteria, the computer beeps.
  - Press [←] or [→] to move the cell pointer to other fields in the record. (To edit an entry, press [F2] (**Edit**) when the cell pointer is in the field.)
  - Press [Home] to move to the first record or [End] to move to the last record in the database.
  - Press [Enter↵] or [Esc] to end the Find command and return to the Query menu.
- The Extract command copies records from the input range to the output range if they meet the criteria entered into the criteria range. You can use the Extract command to copy selected parts of a database to another range in the worksheet. That range can then be printed or saved as a separate model.
- The Unique command extracts records that meet selected criteria into the output range. If duplicate records exist, only the first one is extracted. You can use the Unique command as a fast way of deleting all duplicate records from a database. Using the Unique command with a blank line in the criteria range copies all records to the output range, but it copies only one copy of those that are duplicated, leaving the other copies behind. You can copy the output range to a new file and use it as the new database.
- The Delete command deletes records from the input range that meet the requirements specified in the criteria range. Delete "closes up" the database, deleting empty rows. Each time you try a delete, you are given the choice of canceling the command or continuing. If you continue, the records are permanently deleted. Before you use the delete option, extract the records you are considering deleting. This gives you the opportunity of checking the records before erasing them. It also gives you a temporary backup copy of the records in the output range. The output range can be copied to another file for later reference, or it can be erased.

→ KEY/Strokes

Querying a Database

1. Enter a database.
2. Copy all the field names, or just those you plan to use, from the database to a blank row where you want to set up criteria and extract ranges.
3. Press [/][D][Q] (for ***D**ata*, ***Q**uery*) to display the Query menu described in the table "Data Query Commands."
4. Press [I] (for ***I**nput*), and the prompt reads *Enter input range:*.
5. Specify the input range and press [Enter ←].
6. Press [C] (for ***C**riteria*), and the prompt reads *Enter criteria range:*.
7. Specify the criteria range and press [Enter ←].
8. If using the Extract, Unique, or Delete command, press [O] (for ***O**utput*), and the prompt reads *Enter output range:*. Specify the output range and press [Enter ←].
9. Use the ***F**ind*, ***E**xtract*, ***U**nique*, or ***D**elete* command described in the table "Data Query Commands."

DATA QUERY COMMANDS

Command	Description
Input	Displays the prompt *Enter input range:*. Do so and press [Enter ←].
Criteria	(***C**riterion* on Release 2.01 and earlier versions) displays the prompt *Enter criteria range:*. Do so and press [Enter ←].
Output	Displays the prompt *Enter output range:*. Do so and press [Enter ←].
Find	Finds records in the input range that match the criteria in the criteria range.
Extract	Extracts records from the input range to the output range that match the criteria in the criteria range.
Unique	Works just like Extract, but it does not extract any duplicate records.
Delete	Deletes records in the input range that match the criteria in the criteria range.
Reset	Resets (cancels) the input, criteria, and output ranges.
Quit	Returns you to the worksheet.

The Data Query Settings Sheet
Release 2.2 and later versions have a settings sheet that lists all the current settings for a query. This settings sheet is displayed whenever you press [/][D][Q] (for ***D**ata*, ***Q**uery*).

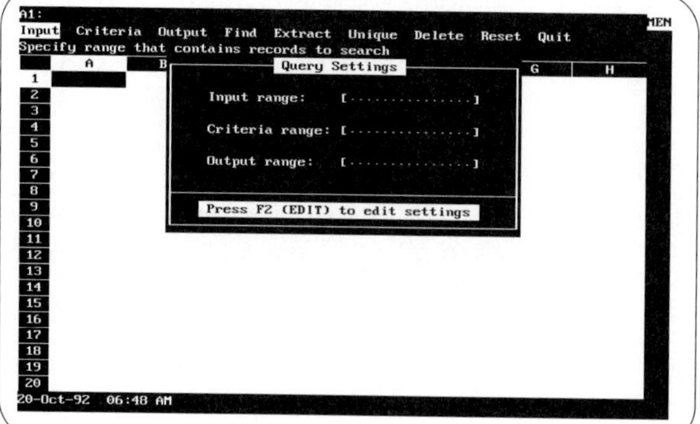

Entering Criteria

When entering criteria in a database, you can search for strings or values and use relational and logical operators to show relationships. Criteria are recalculated once for each record in the database. If the formula evaluates a record as true (not equal to zero), that record is accepted as a match.

When entering criteria, keep in mind that blank rows in the criteria range cause all records to be found.

Searching for Labels

When searching for labels in a database, keep the following points in mind:

- Enter labels exactly as they appear in the input range.
- To find all labels but one, enter ~ (a tilde) before the label. For example, to find all names except Smith, enter ~Smith. To find all names that do not begin with S, enter ~S*.
- You can use the wildcard symbols to find records containing labels.
    - The * (asterisk) substitutes for any characters from the position of the asterisk to the end of the label. For example, the entry John* in the criteria range would find any records that contained John as the first four letters in the appropriate field, including John, Johnny, and John Jacob.
    - The ? (question mark) stands for any single character. For example, h?t would find hut, hat, hot, and hit.

Searching for Values

When searching for values in a database, keep the following points in mind:

- Enter the number you are searching for. The number you enter does not need to have the same format as the ones in the input range.
- When referring to cells in the input range, use relative references.
- When referring to cells outside the input range, use absolute references.

Using Relational Operators

When searching for labels or values, you can use relational and logical operators. For example +A2>1000 finds all records where entries in column A are greater than 1000. +A2<"Jones" finds all records where entries in column A are less than Jones; that is, come before Jones in the alphabet. +B2="Jones" finds all records where entries in column B are equal to Jones.

The cell reference must refer to the cell in the input range that contains the first record for the field being referred to.

Using AND and OR Criteria

You can search for records that meet two or more criteria (an AND criteria) or meet one of two or more criteria.

- If you enter more than one criterion in different fields on the same row, matches occur only if all criteria are met. It is like joining them with logical #AND# operators.

- If you enter criteria in different fields on adjacent rows, records are found if any criterion is met. It is like joining them with logical #OR# operators. When you enter criteria on more than one row, you must expand the criteria range to include them.
- You can also specify AND and OR criteria in the same field using a logical operator. (Do not refer to the row with the field names; refer to the row below it.) For example, +F2="FL"#OR#F2="CA" finds all records where entries in column F are either FL or CA.

Database Statistical Functions

The database statistical functions (see the figure "A Database Statistical Function" and the table "Database Statistical Functions") are similar to the regular statistical functions, except they are designed to be used with a database. Database statistical functions are entered in the form @Function (Input Range, Offset, Criteria Range).

- The input range is the database and must include the field names on the first row and the records on the rows below, just as in a database.
- The offset is the number of the field (column) in the database that contains the specified data. To calculate the offset number, start at the leftmost column in the database and count across, beginning with zero. For example, if your three fields in a database were Name, Price, and Sales, the offset number of the first field (Name) would be 0, the next field (Price) would be 1, and the last field (Sales) would be 2.
- The criteria range is where you enter criteria that specify which records the database statistical functions are to analyze. It must contain one or more field names, with the criteria listed in the cells directly below. (If you leave a cell blank in the criteria range, all records are selected. To prevent this, enter a zero (0) in any empty cell in the criteria range.)

When using database statistical functions, it is easier if you assign names to the input and criteria ranges so that you can refer to them in the functions by name rather than by cell addresses.

	A	B	C
1	Your name:		
2	Filename:	CHARGES	
3	Date:		
4			
5	INPUT RANGE		
6	First Name	Last Name	Amount
7	John	James	$23
8	Bob	James	$23
9	Martha	Smith	$42
10	John	Smith	$35
11	Allen	Smith	$10
12	Avery	James	$12
13	Barbara	Smith	$25
14	Zoro	Smith	$12
15	Zelda	James	$32
16	Yaz	Smith	$75
17	Raymond	Smith	$80
18			
19	CRITERIA RANGE		
20	First Name	Last Name	Amount
21		James	
22			
23	DATABASE STATISTICAL FUNCTIONS		
24	Sum	90	
25	Average	22.5	
26	Count	4	

A Database Statistical Function
A database statistical function has three arguments: the input range, the offset, and the criteria range. For example, the @DSUM function's format is @DSUM(input range,offset,criteria range).

The function in cell B24 of this figure is **@DSUM(TABLE,2,CRITERIA)**.

- The input range includes the range A6.C17 which has been named TABLE.
- The offset is 2, in this case column C.
- The criteria range includes the range A20.C21 which has been named CRITERIA. When a name such as "James" is entered into this range, all records with that name in the specified field are summed. (They are also averaged and counted by the two functions on rows 25 and 26.)

DATABASE STATISTICAL FUNCTIONS

Function	Description
@DAVG(*input,offset,criterion***)**	Averages the values in the offset field that match the specified criteria
@DCOUNT(*input,offset,criterion***)**	Counts all nonblank cells of records in the offset field that match the specified criteria
@DMAX(*input,offset,criterion***)**	Selects the largest value in the offset field that matches the specified criteria
@DMIN(*input,offset,criterion***)**	Selects the smallest value in the offset field that matches the specified criteria
@DSTD(*input,offset,criterion***)**	Finds the standard deviation of the offset field that matches the specified criteria
@DSUM(*input,offset,criterion***)**	Totals the values in the offset field that match the specified criteria
@DVAR(*input,offset,criterion***)**	Finds the variance in the offset field that matches the specified criteria

EXERCISE

EXERCISE 1

QUERYING THE TEXTBOOK COSTS DATABASE

1. Retrieve the TEXTBOOK database.
2. Add the criteria and extract ranges shown in the figure "The Revised Textbook Model."
   - Enter the heading CRITERIA RANGE: into cell A18 and OUTPUT RANGE: into cell A23.
   - Copy the label in cell C5 to cell A19.
   - Copy the labels in the range A5.C5 to cell A24.
   - Specify the input, criteria, and output ranges.
3. Enter the criteria **+C6>.1** into cell A20 and then extract all records where the entry in the % column is greater than 10%.
4. Make a printout of the entire model and then save it.

The Revised Textbook Model
After entering the criteria and output ranges, your model will look like this.

	A	B	C
18	CRITERIA RANGE:		
19	%		
20			
21			
22			
23	OUTPUT RANGE:		
24	Item	$	%

CHAPTER 6 REVIEW

- A 1-2-3 database consists of a row of unique field names followed by one or more rows of data. Each column in the database is a field.
- You can sort a database into an ascending or descending order based on the values in one of the fields. The field you use as the basis of the sort is called the primary key.
- If the field used for the primary key contains identical data in different records (for example, the last name Smith), you can specify another field as the secondary key to break ties.
- You can query a database to find, extract, or delete records.
- To query a database, you must create a criteria range. To extract records, you must also create an output range.
- A criteria range is one or more of the database's field names and one or more of the rows below.
- When you specify one row below the field name(s) in a criteria range, you can specify a single criteria in a field, or enter criteria in more than one field to perform an AND operation.
- When you specify two or more rows below the field name(s) in a criteria range, you can enter criteria in more than one field on different rows to perform an OR operation.
- You can enter relational operators in criteria. For example, +A2>1000 finds all records in column A greater than 1000, and +A2>"Jones" finds all records with names that follow Jones alphabetically.
- You use database statistical functions to calculate values in the database. You enter them in the format @DAVG(*input range,offset,criteria range*). The input range is the database, the offset is the column containing the data (the first column is 0), and the criteria range is the range where you enter the criteria that specify which values are to be included.

CHAPTER 6 QUESTIONS

FILL IN THE BLANK

1. A 1-2-3 database has a row of ___________ followed by rows of ___________.
2. The names used to describe fields in a database must be ___________.
3. When you sort a database in ascending order, the number 1 comes ___________ the number 2.
4. When you sort a database in descending order, the letter A comes ___________ the letter B.
5. To query a database to find records, you need to specify a ___________ range and a ___________ range.

6. To extract records from a database, you must also specify a ___________ range.
7. To extract all records with a value in the SALARY column of less than $10,000, you would enter the criteria ___________. (The field names are on row 1 and the SALARY field is column A.)
8. To extract all records with a value in the SALARY column of more than $10,000, you would enter the criteria ___________. (The field names are on row 1 and the SALARY field is column A.)
9. If you enter criteria into more than one field in the criteria range, you will perform an ___________ operation.
10. If you enter criteria on more than one row in the criteria range, you will perform an ___________ operation.

MATCH THE COLUMNS

1. /DS
2. Primary key
3. Secondary key
4. Descending sort
5. Ascending sort
6. Input range
7. Criteria range
8. Output range
9. Find
10. Extract
11. Unique
12. Delete
13. F7
14. Criteria on same row
15. Criteria on different rows

__ Copies to the output range all records that match the criteria
__ Copies to the output range all records that match the criteria except for duplicate records
__ Repeats the previous query command
__ Performs an AND operation
__ Performs an OR operation
__ Deletes records that match the criteria
__ Arranges all records in the database in ascending order
__ The database
__ Sorts a 1-2-3 database
__ The range into which you enter criteria for a Find, Extract, Delete, or Unique operation
__ The range into which extracted records are copied
__ Displays records one after another that match the criteria
__ The key used as the basis for a sort
__ The key used to break ties in the primary sort
__ Arranges all records in the database in descending order

WRITE OUT THE ANSWERS

1. List some reasons for organizing data in a spreadsheet database.
2. Where are field names entered on a database? Where are records entered?
3. Describe the three key parts of a database.
4. Describe the purpose of the primary and secondary keys.

5. Describe the difference between an ascending and descending sort.
6. What do Query commands allow you to do?
7. Describe the input, criteria, and output range.
8. When must you use an output range?
9. Describe the difference between the Extract and Unique commands.
10. If you wanted to use an OR criterion so that records matched one of the criteria in two or more fields, how would you enter the criterion? How would you do the same with an AND criterion?
11. If you wanted to enter an OR criterion in a single field, how would you do so?
12. What three arguments do you use in a database statistical function?
13. List and briefly describe three database statistical functions.

CHAPTER 6 PROJECTS

PROJECT 1

KEEPING BOX SCORES

1. Update the box scores in each section of the BOXSCORE model by reversing the won and lost numbers for the leader.
2. Sort each section by the category that determines places and make a printout. For example, sort the individual sections as follows:
   - Baseball—sort by Percent
   - Hockey—sort by Points
   - Football—sort by Percent
   - Basketball—sort by Percent
3. Print the model.
4. Clear the screen without saving your changes.

PROJECT 2

USING A DATABASE OF PUBLISHERS

In this project, you sort and query a database containing the names, addresses, and telephone numbers of major college textbook publishers.

1. Retrieve the PUBLISH model and enter your name into cell B1.
2. Sort the database in ascending order by company name and make a printout.
3. Sort the database in ascending order, specifying state as the primary key and company as the secondary key.

4. Add the criteria and extract ranges shown in the figure "The Revised Publishers Model."
5. Extract all records for companies based in NY and make a printout of the entire model.
6. Extract all records for companies based in NY or OH and make a printout.
7. Enter the criteria **Boston** to extract all companies that are based in Boston and make a printout of the model.
8. Enter the criteria **~Boston** to extract all companies that are not based in Boston and make a printout of the model.
9. Enter the criteria **Boston** and **MA** to extract all companies that are based in Boston, MA and make a printout of the model.
10. Enter the criteria **~Boston** and **MA** extract all companies that are based in MA but not in Boston and make a printout of the model.
11. Save the model to save the query ranges.

The Revised Publishers Model
The criteria and output ranges you add to the publishers model, should look like this.

	A	B	C	D	E	F	G
17	Criterion Range						
18	Company	Street	City	State	ZIP	Area	Phone
19							
20							
21							
22	Output Range						
23	Company	Street	City	State	ZIP	Area	Phone
24							

PROJECT 3

USING A DATABASE OF CUSTOMERS AND AMOUNTS DUE

In this project, you sort and query a database of customers and charges they have made.

1. Retrieve the CHARGES model and enter your name into cell B1.
2. Sort the database into ascending order using the Last Name field as the primary sort key and print the sorted database. Notice how records with the same last names are not in alphabetical order by first name. For example, Martha Smith precedes John Smith.
3. Sort the database again using the first name field as a secondary key and make another printout. The database is sorted by last name, with the same last names now sorted by first name. For example, John Smith now precedes Martha Smith.
4. Insert a row above the row of field names and add the label INPUT RANGE.
5. Copy the field names to row 20 and add the label CRITERIA RANGE on the row above.
6. Add the labels shown on rows 23 though 26 in the figure "The Customer Charges Model."
7. Name the input range (A6.C17) INPUT and the criteria range (A20.C21) CRITERIA.

8. Enter the database statistical functions described in the table "The Charges Model's Functions." Instead of cell addresses, the functions refer to the range names.
9. Save the model in case something goes wrong.
10. Enter the last name criteria **James** in the criteria range, and the functions calculate for all Jameses in the database.
11. Replace **James** with **Smith** and the functions recalculate. Make a printout of the model.
12. Enter **Allen** (first name) and **Smith** (last name) in the criteria range, and the functions calculate for anyone by that name.
13. Clear the screen without saving your changes.

THE CHARGES MODEL'S FUNCTIONS

#	Cell	Formula
1	B24	*Sum* is calculated by the formula **@DSUM(INPUT,2,CRITERIA)**
2	B25	*Average* is calculated by the formula **@DAVG(INPUT,2,CRITERIA)**
3	B26	*Count* is calculated by the formula **@DCOUNT(INPUT,2,CRITERIA)**

The Customer Charges Model
After adding the criteria range and database statistical functions to the CHARGES model, your results should look like this.

	A	B	C
19	CRITERIA RANGE		
20	First Name	Last Name	Amount
21		James	
22			
23	DATABASE STATISTICAL FUNCTIONS		
24			
25	Sum	90	
26	Average	22.5	
27	Count	4	

CHAPTER 7

Improving Productivity

TOPIC 26

Recording and Playing Back Macros

After completing this topic, you will be able to:

- Record macros to store keystrokes
- Name macros and play them back

Macros are simply a way to store keystrokes so that they can be played back later. They can save you from having to rekey repetitive data or commands. It is like making a piano into a player piano; the only difference is the computer's keys do not move up and down—it is all done electronically. Macros are created in two ways: by recording them or by typing them in using a macro language. On Release 2.2 and later versions, you can use either method; on Release 2.01, you must type them in.

TUTORIAL

	A	B
16	LEARN RANGE	PRINT
17		/pprMODEL~agpq
18		
19		LINE
20		/gnuLINE~q
21		
22		BAR
23		/gnuBAR~q

The Five-Year Plan with Macros Added
After you record macros in this tutorial, your five-year plan model should look like this.

In this tutorial, you use Release 2.2 and later versions' learn mode to record macros that print the 5YRPLAN model and display the line and bar graphs you created and named in Topics 14 and 15. (If you are using a release prior to 2.2, you can create macros as shown in Topic 27.) Your finished model should look like the one in the figure "The Five-Year Plan with Macros Added." Compare your results with this figure as you complete this tutorial.

GETTING STARTED

1. Retrieve the 5YRPLAN model.

SPECIFYING A LEARN RANGE

2. In cell A16, enter the heading **LEARN RANGE:**.
3. Press [/][W][L][R] (for ***W**orksheet*, ***L**earn*, ***R**ange*), and the prompt reads *Enter learn range:*.
4. Type **A17.A33** and press [Enter←] to store macros that you record in the column immediately below the heading.

NAMING THE PRINT RANGE

5. Press [/][R][N][C] (for ***R**ange*, ***N**ame*, ***C**reate*), and the prompt reads *Enter name:*.
6. Type **MODEL** and press [Enter↵]. The prompt reads *Enter range:*.
7. Type **A1.F14** and press [Enter↵].

RECORDING KEYSTROKES TO PRINT THE MODEL

8. Press [Alt]-[F5], and the *LEARN* indicator is displayed on the bottom line of the screen.
9. Press [/][P][P][R] (for ***P**rint*, ***P**rinter*, ***R**ange*), and the prompt reads *Enter print range:*.
10. Type **MODEL** and press [Enter↵].
11. Press [A][G] (for ***A**lign*, ***G**o*).
12. Press [Q] (for ***Q**uit*).
13. Press [Alt]-[F5], and the *LEARN* indicator is no longer displayed on the bottom line of the screen.
14. Press [↓], and the keystrokes you recorded are displayed in the learn range.

NAMING AND PLAYING BACK THE PRINT MACRO

15. The learn range can store only one macro, so copy the macro in cell A17 to cell B17, and enter the label **PRINT** in cell B16 to identify it.
16. With the cell pointer in cell B17, press [/][R][N][C] (for ***R**ange*, ***N**ame*, ***C**reate*), and the prompt reads *Enter name:*.
17. Type [\][P] and press [Enter↵]. The prompt reads *Enter range:*.
18. Press [Enter↵] to name the cell with the cell pointer.
19. Press [Alt]-[P], and the model prints out on the printer.

RECORDING KEYSTROKES THAT DISPLAY THE LINE GRAPH

20. Press [/][W][L][E] (for ***W**orksheet*, ***L**earn*, ***E**rase*), and you are prompted to confirm.
21. Press [Y] to erase the learn range.
22. Press [Alt]-[F5], and the *LEARN* indicator is displayed on the bottom line of the screen.
23. Press [/][G][N][U] (for ***G**raph*, ***N**ame*, ***U**se*), and the prompt reads *Enter name of graph to make current:*.
24. Type **LINE** and press [Enter↵] to display the line graph.
25. Press [Spacebar] to clear the graph.
26. Press [Q] (for ***Q**uit*).
27. Press [Alt]-[F5], and the *LEARN* indicator is no longer displayed on the bottom line of the screen.
28. Press [↓], and the keystrokes you recorded are displayed in the learn range.

NAMING AND PLAYING BACK THE LINE GRAPH MACRO

29. Copy the macro in cell A17 to cell B20, and enter the label **LINE** in cell B19 to identify it.

30. With the cell pointer in cell B20, press / R N C (for ***R**ange*, ***N**ame*, ***C**reate*) and the prompt reads *Enter name:*.
31. Type **\L** and press Enter←. The prompt reads *Enter range:*.
32. Press Enter← to name the cell with the cell pointer.
33. Press Alt-L to display the line graph.
34. Press any key to return to the worksheet.

RECORDING KEYSTROKES THAT DISPLAY THE BAR GRAPH

35. Press / W L E (for ***W**orksheet*, ***L**earn*, ***E**rase*), and you are prompted to confirm.
36. Press Y to erase the learn range.
37. Press Alt-F5, and the *LEARN* indicator is displayed on the bottom line of the screen.
38. Press / G N U (for ***G**raph*, ***N**ame*, ***U**se*), and the prompt reads *Enter name of graph to make current:*.
39. Type **BAR** and press Enter← to display the graph.
40. Press Spacebar to clear the graph.
41. Press Q (for ***Q**uit*).
42. Press Alt-F5, and the *LEARN* indicator is no longer displayed on the bottom line of the screen.
43. Press ↓, and the keystrokes you recorded are displayed in the learn range.

NAMING AND PLAYING BACK THE BAR GRAPH MACRO

44. Copy the macro in cell A17 to cell B23, and enter the label **BAR** in cell B22 to identify it.
45. With the cell pointer in cell B23, press / R N C (for ***R**ange*, ***N**ame*, ***C**reate*), and the prompt reads *Enter name:*.
46. Type **\B** and press Enter←. The prompt reads *Enter range:*.
47. Press Enter← to name the cell with the cell pointer.
48. Press Alt-B to display the bar graph.
49. Press any key to return to the worksheet.

USING THE GRAPH MACROS

50. Press Alt-L or Alt-B to display the graphs, and then press any key to return to the worksheet.

FINISHING UP

51. Save the model under the same name.
52. You have now completed this tutorial. Either clear the screen and continue with the next activity or quit the program.

QUICK REFERENCE

When you record macros, you follow these steps:

1. Specify the learn range. This is the range of cells that your keystrokes will be recorded in.

2. Turn learn mode on by pressing Alt-F5. The *LEARN* indicator is displayed on the bottom line of the screen.
3. Record keystrokes. You then enter the data or commands you want to use again. The keystrokes are automatically recorded as you run through the sequence of commands or characters you want to record. They are stored in the learn range that you defined.

   You can nest one macro in another by entering its name in braces {}. For example, let's say you have created a macro named PRINT that prints a model. You can then record a macro that saves the file. While doing so, you can have the file print automatically after it is saved by entering {PRINT} in the save macro.
4. Turn learn mode off by pressing Alt-F5. The *LEARN* indicator is no longer displayed on the bottom line of the screen.
5. Name the macro. To name the range, you press / R N C (for ***R****ange*, ***N****ame*, ***C****reate*), and enter a name and specify the range. (You have to name only the first cell in the learn range.) You can assign one of two kinds of names to a macro:
   - To attach the keystrokes to a key, name the macro by pressing \ (the backslash key) and then typing a letter when prompted for the name of the range. You can then execute the macro by holding down Alt while you press the letter you assigned to the macro.
   - To name the range so that you can run it from the menu, type any name up to 15 characters long.
6. Play back the recorded keystrokes.
   - If you attached the macro to a letter key, hold down Alt while you press the letter you assigned the macro to.
   - To run any macro, press Alt-F3 (**Run**) to display a list of named macros, highlight the one you want to run, and press Enter↵.

→ KEY/Strokes

Specifying a Learn Range

1. Press / W L (for ***W****orksheet*, ***L****earn*).
2. Make any of the choices described in the table "Learn Range Menu Commands."

LEARN RANGE MENU COMMANDS

Command	Description
R*ange*	Prompts you to enter the range of cells that your keystrokes will be recorded in. Type the address or point to a column range and press Enter↵.
C*ancel*	Cancels the learn range but leaves any recorded keystrokes on the worksheet.
E*rase*	Erases the learn range but leaves the range defined.

TIP

If you name a macro \0 (the number zero) and the autoexec setting is on, the macro will be automatically executed whenever you retrieve the file. To turn autoexec on or off, press [/][W][G][D][A] (for ***W**orksheet, **G**lobal, **D**efault, **A**utoexec*). Press [Y] (for ***Y**es*) to turn autoexec on, or press [N] (for ***N**o*) to turn it off.

Recording Keystrokes

1. Define a learn range.
2. Press [Alt]-[F5] to turn learn mode on, and the *LEARN* indicator is displayed on the bottom line of the screen.
3. Execute the commands or type the text you want to save.
4. Press [Alt]-[F5] to turn learn mode off.

KEY/Strokes

Playing Back Macros

1. Name the first cell in the learn range.
2. Either: Hold down [Alt] while you press the letter you assigned the macro to.

   Or: Press [Alt]-[F3] (**Run**) to display a list of macros, highlight the one you want to run, and press [Enter↵].

EXERCISE 1

RECORDING MACROS THAT ENTER SETUP STRINGS

In this exercise, record a macro that enters a setup string to print any one of your models in compressed type. Then create one that prints it in normal type. Use both macros to make printouts. Be sure to save the model when you are finished.

EXERCISE 2

RECORDING A MACRO THAT ENTERS THE THREE-LINE HEADING

In this exercise, you record a macro that enters the three-line heading you have been entering at the top of each model that you create. Be sure to save the model when you are finished.

TOPIC 27

Writing and Editing Macros

After completing this topic, you will be able to:

- Write macros
- Test macros in step mode

You can create macros by typing them in, assigning names to them, and then executing them. When entering them like this, you are actually using a macro language. You then enter the keystrokes needed as a label and name the label. The language contains keywords used to indicate keys on the keyboard (see the table "Macro Keywords" in the Quick Reference Section). Until you have all commands memorized, the best way to create a macro is to enter the entire command keystroke by keystroke, noting on a sheet of paper the keys you press.

TUTORIAL

In this tutorial, you create and execute a series of macros. Your finished model should look like the figure "The Macros Model." Refer to this figure to check your results as you complete the steps in this tutorial.

The Macros Model
After you complete the macros model, your results should look similar to this.

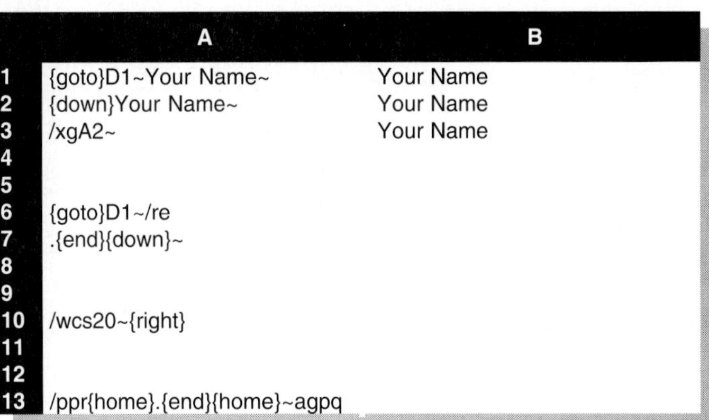

	A	B
1	{goto}D1~Your Name~	Your Name
2	{down}Your Name~	Your Name
3	/xgA2~	Your Name
4		
5		
6	{goto}D1~/re	
7	.{end}{down}~	
8		
9		
10	/wcs20~{right}	
11		
12		
13	/ppr{home}.{end}{home}~agpq	

GETTING STARTED

1. Load the program or clear the screen.
2. Set the global column width to 36.

ENTERING AND EXECUTING A MACRO THAT ENTERS YOUR NAME

3. In cell A1, enter the macro **{goto}D1~Your Name~** and press Enter↵.

NOTE: KEYWORD NAMES

Later releases of 1-2-3 have some macro keystrokes that do not work with earlier versions. Since the old names work with all versions, those are the ones that have been used in this tutorial.

4. With the cell pointer in cell A1, press [/][R][N][C] (for ***R****ange*, ***N****ame*, ***C****reate*), and the prompt reads *Enter name:*.
5. Type [\][N] and press [Enter ←]. The prompt reads *Enter range:*.
6. Press [Enter ←] to name the cell containing the cell pointer.
7. Press [Alt]-[N], and the macro automatically moves to cell D1 and enters your name.

ADDING A LOOP TO THE MACRO

8. In cell A2, enter the macro **{down}Your Name~** and press [Enter ←].
9. In cell A3:
   - If you are using a version later than Release 1A, enter the macro **{BRANCH A2}** and press [Enter ←].
   - If you are using Release 1A, enter the macro **'/xgA2~** and press [Enter ←].
10. Before executing this macro, locate the [Ctrl] and [Break] keys on your keyboard. You must press these keys together to stop the macro.
11. Press [Alt]-[N] to execute the macro.
12. Press [Ctrl]-[Break] to stop the macro, and then press [Esc] to clear the error message.
13. Press [Home] to return to cell A1. The macro automatically moved to cell D1 and entered your name just as it did the last time. The second line of the macro then moved the cell pointer down one cell and entered your name again. The third line told the macro to read the keystrokes in cell A2 again so that it continues to execute the second line, and each time it did, the third line looped it back to the second line and executed those keystrokes again.

ENTERING A MACRO THAT ERASES A RANGE

14. In cell A6, enter the macro **{goto}D1~/re** and press [Enter ←].
15. In cell A7, enter the macro **'.{end}{down}~** and press [Enter ←].
16. With the cell pointer in cell A6, press [/][R][N][C] (for ***R****ange*, ***N****ame*, ***C****reate*), and the prompt reads *Enter name:*.
17. Type **\E** and press [Enter ←]. The prompt reads *Enter range:*.
18. Press [Enter ←] to name the cell containing the cell pointer.
19. Press [Alt]-[E] to erase the range. When you execute the macro, it moves the cell pointer to cell B1 and enters the **/*R****ange* ***E****rase* command. It then presses the period to anchor the range, presses [End] and then [↓] to highlight the range, and presses [Enter ←] to complete the command.

EXECUTING A MACRO IN STEP MODE

20. Press [Alt]-[F2] to display the *STEP* indicator on the bottom row of the screen.
21. Press [Alt]-[N] to execute the name macro.
22. Press [Enter ←] repeatedly to enter the macro a keystroke at a time. Each time you press it, another keystroke or keyword is executed. (On Release 2.2 and later versions, the macro is displayed on the bottom line of the screen, and the highlight indicates which keystroke will be played back the next time you press [Enter ←].)

23. After pressing Enter← enough times to enter your name three or four times, press Ctrl-Break to cancel the macro.
24. Press Alt-E to execute the erase macro, and then press Enter← to execute it a step at a time.
25. After erasing the range, press Alt-F2 to return to ready mode and turn off the step indicator.

CREATING A MACRO THAT CHANGES COLUMN WIDTHS

26. In cell A10, enter the macro **'/wcs20~{right}** and press Enter←.
27. Press / R N C (for ***R**ange*, ***N**ame*, ***C**reate*), and the prompt reads *Enter name:*.
28. Type **\C** and press Enter←. The prompt reads *Enter range:*.
29. Press Enter←.
30. Move the cell pointer to column C and press Alt-C to execute the macro. The column containing the cell pointer is set to 20 characters, and the cell pointer moves one column to the right.
31. Press Alt-C again to set the next column to 20 characters wide.

FINISHING UP

32. Save the model as MACROS and make a printout.
33. You have now completed this tutorial. Either clear the screen and continue with the next activity or quit the program.

QUICK REFERENCE

To write macros, you enter them as labels and then name them.

Creating and Editing Macros

Macros can be used to automate many processes. For example, to print a worksheet, you must press **/**, and then select ***P**rint*, ***P**rinter*, ***A**lign*, ***G**o*, ***P**age*, and ***Q**uit*. But you can create a macro so that this same series of commands is executed when you hold down Alt and press the letter P (or any other key you assign the series of keystrokes to). This macro would be written as **'/ppr{home}.{end}{home}~agpq**.

- The ' enters the / command as a label instead of calling up the menu.
- The / (slash) calls up the Main menu and the letters *ppr* are the same ones you would type to enter the print range from the keyboard.
- The commands *{home}.{end}{home}* highlight the entire model from cell A1 to the lower-right corner of the active area.
- The ~ (tilde) indicates a carriage return (Enter←).
- The *agpq* letters are the commands you would use to align, go, page, and quit the menu.

After entering the macro, you assign it a name; in this example, you name it so that it is executed when you hold down Alt and press P.

When entering macros, keep the following points in mind:

MACRO KEYWORDS

Keys	Keyword
Function Keys	
F2 (Edit)	{edit}
F3 (Name)	{name}
F4 (Abs)	{abs}
F5 (GoTo)	{goto}
F6 (Window)	{window}
F7 (Query)	{query}
F8 (Table)	{table}
F9 (Calc)	{calc}
F10 (Graph)	{graph}
Other Keys	
←	{left}
→	{right}
↑	{up}
↓	{down}
Home	{home}
End	{end}
← Bksp	{bs}
Del	{del}
Esc	{esc}
Enter ↵	~

- You must enter macros as labels. Some keys like the slash key (/) must be preceded by a label prefix character if they are the first character on a line. 1-2-3 ignores the label prefix character when it reads the contents of the cell. If you want a label prefix character to be used at the beginning of a line, you must enter two prefixes; the first converts the second into a label.
- Macros are easier to read and understand if you selectively use uppercase and lowercase letters. For example, put all keystrokes in lowercase letters, and put all range names, cell contents, and cell addresses in uppercase letters. A macro that prints a range named page1 is easier to read when entered as **'/pprPAGE1~agpq** than when entered as **'/PPRPAGE1~AGPQ**.
- Macros usually should not refer to cell addresses because inserting or deleting rows and columns can change those addresses and confuse the macro. Use range names to refer to blocks of cells.
- To end a macro so that you return to ready mode after it has been executed, leave a nonlabel cell at the end (below the last cell containing the macro), or enter a {QUIT} or /XQ command in the last macro cell.
- The first cell in a macro is the only cell that needs to be included in the range name. You can include the rest of the cells, but it is not necessary. 1-2-3 automatically reads each row until it reaches a nonlabel cell or a cell containing the {QUIT} or /XQ command. Macro names consist of \ (the backslash key) followed by a letter of the alphabet or the number zero.
- Macros containing cell pointer movement keywords ({right}, {left}, and so on) may not work the same when ScrlLock is engaged. Always be sure ScrlLock is disengaged before executing a macro containing these commands.
- Always save a file after creating a macro. If a file is not saved after the macro has been created, the macro is not saved.
- Always save a file before executing a new macro. That way if anything changes as a result of the macro (intentionally or not), you have a copy of the original file.
- To stop a macro while it is executing and return to ready mode, press Ctrl-Break. Macros also stop when a {QUIT} or /XQ command or a nonlabel cell is encountered.

Using Operator Input

Macros can be made to pause during execution and accept operator input. For example, you use the {?}~ command to pause the macro for operator input. The macro continues only after you press Enter ↵. The {?} command is followed by ~ (a tilde) since pressing Enter ↵ once completes the entry but does not resume the macro. You can use this pause command with one of the commands described in the table "Macro Commands That Pause for Operator Input."

MACRO COMMANDS THAT PAUSE FOR OPERATOR INPUT

Command	Description
{?}	Causes a pause for operator input when encountered anywhere in a macro. The macro continues only after you press Enter↵. The {?} command is followed by a tilde ({?}~) since pressing Enter↵ once completes the entry but does not resume the macro.
{GETLABEL *prompt,location*}	Displays a prompt on the second line of the control panel and pauses so that you can enter a label. After you press Enter↵, the label you type is entered in the location cell using a left-align prefix character. (On Release 1A, you use the macro command /XL*prompt~location~*.)
{GETNUMBER *prompt,location*}	Displays a prompt on the second line of the control panel and pauses so that you can enter a number, formula, range name, or function. After you press Enter↵, the numeric value of the entry is stored at the location. (On Release 1A, you use the macro command /XN*prompt~location~*.)

Branching Macro Commands

Macros can be made to continue reading macro keystrokes at other locations on a worksheet. This is called branching, and it is useful when using macros to create menus. The table "Branching Macro Commands" describes these branching commands.

BRANCHING MACRO COMMANDS

Command	Description
{*subroutine*}	The macro jumps to the specified location (a range name or cell address) and continues reading keystrokes. If the macro encounters a {RETURN}, /XR, a blank cell, or a numeric cell in the subroutine, control returns to the original macro and the macro continues reading keystrokes on the line below the {*subroutine*} command. (On Release 1A, you use the macro command /XC*location~*.) For example, to have the macro jump to a subroutine named LINE, use the command {LINE} (or /xcLINE~).
{BRANCH *location*}	The macro jumps to the specified location (a range name or cell address) and continues reading keystrokes. (On Release 1A, you use the macro command /XG*location~*.) Unlike the {*subroutine*} command, control does not return to the macro this command was placed in unless you use another {BRANCH *location*} command to refer it back.
{RETURN}	When this command is encountered in a macro that was called as a result of a {*subroutine*} (or /XC) command, control returns to the calling macro. (On Release 1A, you use the macro command /XR.)

BRANCHING MACRO COMMANDS (*CONTINUED*)

{IF *condition*}	If the condition is TRUE (not zero), the macro continues reading keystrokes in the same cell; otherwise, it reads the keystrokes in the cell below. (On Release 1A, you use the macro command /XI*condition.*) For example, the command {IF SALES<10000}{QUIT} (or /XI SALES<10000 / XQ) would end the macro if the number in a cell named SALES were less than 10000. If they were equal to or more than 10000, the macro would continue reading whatever keystrokes it found on the next line.
{MENUBRANCH *location*}	The macro jumps to the cell containing the *location* and displays the menu on the screen. (On Release 1A, you use the macro command /XM*location*~.)
{QUIT}	Ends the macro. (On Release 1A, you use the macro command /XQ.)

Troubleshooting Macros

To work through a macro one step at a time, press Alt-F2 (**Step**). When you are in step mode, the *STEP* indicator is displayed at the bottom of the screen. Then when you invoke a macro, press any key to execute it one keystroke at a time. To leave step mode, press Alt-F2 (**Step**) again. If you press Alt-F2 (**Step**) during the execution of a macro in step mode, pressing any key executes the rest of the macro.

EXERCISE 1

PRINTING THE AUTO LOAN MODEL WITH A MACRO

1. Retrieve the AUTOLOAN model.
2. Enter the macro shown in the figure "The Auto Loan Print Macro."
3. Name the macro so that you can print the model by pressing Alt-P.
4. Make a printout using the macro.

The Auto Loan Print Macro
After you add a print macro to the auto loan model, your results should look like this.

	A	B
1	Your name:	your name
2	Filename:	AUTOLOAN
3	Date:	07-Apr-92
4		
5	Loan amount	10000
6	Interest rate	0.12
7	Term (in months)	48
8	Monthly payment	263.3383543193
9		
10	/ppr{HOME}.{END}{HOME}{UP}~agpq	

CHAPTER 7 REVIEW

- A macro is a series of stored keystrokes that you can replay by entering its name or pressing a key.
- With Release 2.2 and later, you can record macros. On earlier versions, you must type them as labels. To record a macro, you must first use the ***/Worksheet Learn*** command to specify a range of cells where the macro will be stored.
- To execute a macro, you must first name it. To assign it to a key on the keyboard, you name it \\<*key*>, for example, \X. You can then execute the macro by holding down Alt and pressing the key you assigned to the macro.
- To execute a macro that has not been assigned to a key, press Alt-F3, highlight its name, and press Enter.
- With Release 2.2 and later, to begin recording keystrokes, you press Alt-F5, and *LEARN* is displayed on the bottom line of the screen.
- When typing macros, you use a label-prefix character to enter them as labels.
- The ~ (tilde) character is used in a macro to signify Enter.
- Macros are created with keyboard characters such as /, ~, and D1, and keywords. Typical keywords are {left} to move the cursor left, {home} to move it to cell A1, and {graph} to display the most recently displayed graph.
- The {?} macro command pauses the macro until you type data and press Enter.
- The {BRANCH *location*} macro command has the macro continue reading keystrokes at the cell or range name specified as the location.
- The {MENUBRANCH *location*} macro command displays a menu that has been entered with its upper-left corner in the specified location.
- To troubleshoot macros, you press Alt-F2 to turn on step mode and then press any key to execute the macro one keystroke at a time. You then press Alt-F2 again to turn off step mode.

CHAPTER 7 QUESTIONS

FILL IN THE BLANK

1. With Release 2.2 and later, you can ___________ macros. With earlier releases, you must ___________ them in.
2. Before you can execute a macro, you must ___________ it.
3. To assign a macro to a key, you name it with the ___________ character followed by the key you want to use.
4. To execute a macro assigned to the letter P, you would press ___________.

5. To execute a macro named PRINT, you would press __________.
6. The __________ character in a macro tells 1-2-3 to press the [Enter] key.
7. To record macros with learn mode, you must first specify a __________ range with the __________ command.
8. To turn learn mode on and off, you press __________.
9. When writing a macro, the keyword __________ moves the cursor up one cell, __________ moves it to cell A1, and __________ turns on edit mode.
10. When writing a macro, the keyword __________ recalculates the worksheet, __________ moves the cell pointer between windows, and __________ displays the most recently displayed graph.
11. To have a macro in cell A1 continue reading keystrokes in cell G1, you would enter the macro command __________.
12. To display a menu named MYMENU, you would enter the macro command __________.
13. To troubleshoot a macro, you would use __________ mode. To turn this mode on and off, you press __________.

MATCH THE COLUMNS

1. [/][W][L]	__ Pauses a macro until you type data and press [Enter]
2. \P	__ Displays a list of range names so you can select a macro's name to execute it
3. [Alt]-[F3]	__ Turns learn mode on and off
4. [Alt]-[F5]	__ Tells the macro to continue reading keystrokes in the upper-left corner of the range named graphs
5. ~	__ Specifies the learn range for recording macros
6. Label-prefix character	__ [Enter] in a macro
7. {?}	__ Displays the menu entered in the range with its upperleft cell named graph.
8. {BRANCH graphs}	__ Turns step mode on and off
9. {MENUBRANCH graphs}	__ Used to enter macros as text
10. [Alt]-[F2]	__ Macro range name you can execute by pressing [Alt]-[P]

WRITE OUT THE ANSWERS

1. List the steps you follow to record a macro.
2. When you save a macro, you can assign it to a key or give it a name that you can choose from a list. If you assign it to a key, how do you enter its name? If you name it so that it can be selected from a list, how long can its name be?
3. If you assign a macro to a key, how do you play it back? If you assign it a name that you can select from a list, how do you play it back?

4. When using a macro language to write a macro, what are the special terms called that you enter to indicate what keys should be executed?
5. What is the macro command for pressing Enter ↵?
6. What kind of data must macros be entered as?
7. Why should you selectively use uppercase and lowercase letters when entering macros?
8. Should macros often refer to cell addresses? Why or why not?
9. It is important to save a file both after creating a macro and before executing a macro. Why is this?
10. How do you work through a macro a step at a time?
11. Describe the macro command {?}.
12. What are branching macro commands used for? List and describe two of them.

CHAPTER 7

PROJECTS

PROJECT 1

SETUP STRING MACROS

When printing models, you may want to change printer settings back and forth between normal and compressed type. Doing so requires a number of keystrokes to change the setup string and margin settings. Rather than trying to remember the strings and other settings and entering them manually, you can create a menu that changes them automatically.

1. To begin, fill out the "Printer Settings" table for the printer you will be using.

PRINTER SETTINGS

Function	Setup String or Setting
Turn on normal type	________________
Turn on compressed type	________________
Right margin setting for normal type	________________
Right margin setting for compressed type	________________

2. Retrieve one of the models that you have created.
3. In a blank space to the lower-right of the model, enter the macro shown in the figure "The Print Menu Macro:"
   - If you are using Release 1A, replace all occurrences of the command {MENUBRANCH MENU} with the '/xmMENU~ command.
   - Use your own setup string for normal type in place of the 018 shown.
   - Use your own setup string for compressed type in place of the \015 shown.
   - Use your own right margin settings for compressed type in place of the 80 and 132 shown.
   - Name the upper-left cell with the {MENUBRANCH MENU} command \P so you can display the menu by pressing Alt-P.
   - Name the cell with the "Quit Menu" label MENU so the {MENUBRANCH} command reads this cell as the beginning of the menu.
4. When finished, save the model under its original name.
5. Display the menu and select ***C**ompressed*. Then select ***Q**uit Menu* and make a printout of the model.
6. Display the menu and select ***N**ormal*. Then select ***Q**uit Menu* and make a printout of the model.
7. Clear the screen without saving the model

The Print Menu Macro

This macro displays a menu used to change between normal and compressed type. The menu choices are listed on the third row and the descriptions that appear when a choice is highlighted are listed on the row below. The commands on rows that follow contain the commas that enter a new setup string (you should enter your own) and change the right margin setting. The last row redisplays the menu again in case you want to change the setting back.

'{MENUBRANCH MENU}		
Quit Menu	Normal	Compressed
Return to worksheet	Print in normal type	Print in compressed type
	/ppos	/ppos
	X(esc)	X(esc)
	/018~	/015~
	mr80~	mr132~
	qq	qq
	'{MENUBRANCH MENU}	'{MENUBRANCH MENU}

PROJECT 2

DISPLAYING GRAPHS

Retrieve the GRAPHICS model and add a menu that allows you to quit the menu or display the graphs named I, II, III, or IV. When finished, print out the range of cells into which you entered the macro.

CHAPTER 8

Real-World Applications

Now that you have become familiar with Lotus 1-2-3, you are ready to put it to work. The applications in this chapter include a job-search kit, a research paper, and a business plan. They test and build on the skills you have developed in the preceding topics.

When completing the applications, keep the following points in mind:

- The applications are based on the procedures already discussed in the text, but they are designed to present new problems for you to solve on your own. Don't be discouraged if they take some thought and effort to work through.
- The Concepts section in each application gives you all the subject-area information you will need to complete the application.
- The Steps section in each application gives you the sequence of steps that you should follow. If you cannot recall how to perform a procedure, refer to the topic that covers that material.
- The Problems section in some applications is used to explore the finances of the business. The real advantage of using a spreadsheet for the preparation of financial models is the ease with which you can explore alternative outcomes.

APPLICATION 1

The Job-Search Kit—Travel Expenses

When interviewing for many jobs, you have to travel to a regional or home office. When you do so, you are normally reimbursed for your expenses. In this application, you build a model that allows you to keep track of your expenses or make a printout to accompany your followup letter after the interview.

CONCEPTS

The expenses that are reimbursed when interviewing for a position vary from company to company. Normally, they cover only those expenses directly related to the visit. Side trips or entertainment while traveling are not usually covered. Obviously, you do not create a good impression by billing for things that are not covered by the company. Where possible, attach receipts for each item you are billing to support the claim.

STEPS

1. Retrieve the JOBSRCH model shown in the figure "The Job-Search Model."
2. Use date functions to enter the dates on row 6. Enter just one date function into cell B6. Then enter the formula **+B6+1** into cell C6, and copy it to the other columns.
3. Enter the formulas described in the table "The Job-Search Model's Formulas."
4. Format your model to match the figure "The Job-Search Model."
5. When you have finished the model, save it under the same filename and make a printout.
6. Erase all the numbers from the model so that you can use it as a template for your own expenses, and make a printout of the template.

THE JOB SEARCH MODEL'S FORMULAS

#	Cell	Formula	Copy to
1	B16	*Total* is the sum of all numbers entered into column B between rows 8 and 15.	C16.H16
2	I8	*Total* is the sum of all numbers entered on row 8 between columns B and H.	I9.I16

The Job-Search Model
You use this model to calculate your travel expenses when interviewing with a company.

	A	B	C	D	E	F	G	H	I
1	Your name:								
2	Filename:	JOBSRCH							
3	Date:								
4									
5	ITEM	SUN	MON	TUES	WED	THURS	FRI	SAT	TOTAL
6	DATE	05/10/94	05/11	05/12/94	05/13/94	05/14/94	05/15/94	05/16/94	
7	TRAVEL								
8	Air fare	$335.75							$335.75
9	Taxis	26.75	29.00						55.75
10	Parking								0.00
11	Mileage								0.00
12	MEALS								
13	Breakfast	4.95	6.00						10.95
14	Lunch		7.50						7.50
15	Dinner	16.75							16.75
16	TOTAL	$384.20	$42.5	$0.00	$0.00	$0.00	$0.00	$0.00	$426.70

APPLICATION 2

The Research Paper—An Analysis of Computer Costs

Many research papers, especially those in business and science, have statistical tables or analysis sections that can be done with a spreadsheet program. The tables or analysis can then be transferred into the document and formatted or printed on a separate page and inserted manually. In this application, you create a model that is used to calculate the cost of a state-of-the-art computer system that can be used for desktop publishing or other high-end applications.

	A	B
1	Your name:	
2	Filename:	COMPSYS
3	Date:	
4		
5	ELEMENT	PRICE
6	BASIC SYSTEM	$1,500
7	VIDEO DEVICES	
8	Super VGA card	175
9	Display monitor	475
10	MEMORY	
11	STORAGE DEVICES	
12	Floppy disk (5 1/4")	
13	Floppy disk (3 1/2")	
14	Hard disk	450
15	PRINTERS	
16	Laser	1,500
17	Dot-matrix	
18	PostScript cartridge	450
19	PROTECTION DEVICES	
20	Tape backup (60MB)	269
21	Surge protector	25
22	COMMUNICATION DEVICES	
23	Modem (2400 baud)	200
24	Fax card	200
25	MULTIMEDIA DEVICES	
26	Multimedia soundboard	150
27	CD-ROM (with card)	750
28	DESKTOP PUBLISHING DEVICES	
29	Scanner (gray scale)	1,200
30	Mouse	100
31	SOFTWARE	
32	DOS	50
33	MS Windows	75
34	Word processor	250
35	Spreadsheet	250
36	Graphics program	300
37	Database program	300
38	Desktop publishing program	300
39	TOTAL SYSTEM COSTS	8,969
40	Down payment	2,000
41	Loan balance	6,969
42	Interest rate	12.0%
43	Period (in months)	48
44	Monthly payment	$183.52

The Computer System Model
The computer system model allows you to explore the cost of a high-end computer system.

CONCEPTS

Over the past few years, the power of desktop computers has increased dramatically. At the same time, the power required by newer programs such as Microsoft Windows has increased just as dramatically. Many new programs require a great deal of memory and hard disk storage, as well as a fast processor to operate well. In addition, a number of useful peripheral devices, such as scanners and CD-ROM disks, have dropped in price to where they are now affordable for many business and personal applications.

Before you purchase a system, you should carefully analyze your needs over the next five years and buy a system you won't outgrow. Because new programs require more sophisticated systems, older computers can be purchased for less than $1,000. If you don't anticipate needing newer programs, and just want to run character-based programs such as those discussed in this text, one of these systems can be a great buy. However, if you plan on using the latest software, or using your computer for applications such as graphics or desktop publishing, a more powerful and more expensive system may be cheaper in the long run.

STEPS

1. Retrieve the COMPSYS model shown in the figure "The Computer System Model."
2. Enter the formulas described in the table "The Computer System Model's Formulas."
3. Format your model to match the figure "The Computer System Model."
4. When you have finished, save your model under the same filename and make a printout.
5. Using the prices listed in the figure "Typical Computer Prices," experiment with a variety of components to design the system you would like to have.

Typical Computer Prices

A survey of computer catalogs at the time this book was written showed that systems and components were available at the prices shown here. These prices may have changed by the time you complete this application since most prices are falling rapidly.

Basic System		**Memory**	
386SX (16 MHz)	$1,500	2 megabytes	120
386DX (25 MHz)	2,000	4 megabytes	200
486SX (20 MHz)	2,500	**Hard Disks**	
486DX (33 MHz)	3,000	40MB	220
Display Monitors		130MB	450
14" gray scale	200	340MB	1000
14" color	600	**Printers**	
16" or 17" color	1000	Laser printer	1,600
20" color	2000	Dot-matrix printer (24 pin)	300

THE COMPUTER SYSTEM MODEL'S FORMULAS

#	Cell	Formula
1	B39	*Total System Costs* is the sum of all numbers entered into column B.
2	B41	*Loan Balance* is *Total System Costs* minus the down payment.
3	B44	*Monthly payment* is calculated by a function based on the given loan balance, interest rate, and loan period.

APPLICATION 3A

The Business Plan—A Balance Sheet

In this application, you create a balance sheet for a company that compares this year's results with last year's results. After completing this application, you will be able to describe the elements that make up a balance sheet and explain how they relate to one another. You then use this understanding to create a personal balance sheet similar to one you would need to apply for a large loan.

CONCEPTS

The balance sheet is appropriately named, for it must always balance. There are two sections of the balance sheet. The left side shows the firm's assets (what the firm owns), and the right side shows the liabilities (what the firm owes) and the owner equity, which together represent the claims against the assets or how the firm paid for its assets. The balance sheet is a snapshot of a firm's condition at a given point in time, such as the end of the month, quarter, or year. In simple terms, a balance sheet is a record of what the company has done with its income and the money provided by creditors, lenders, and stockholders. Managers and owners use the balance sheet not only for evaluating financial conditions but also for setting management and company goals. The balance sheet is also a window through which others, such as bankers, creditors, and stockholders, can look at a company.

A balance sheet is shown in the figure "The Balance Sheet Model." Instead of being organized into left and right sides, liabilities are entered below assets to simplify its layout on the worksheet. This balance sheet, like most others that you will encounter, contains the following elements:

The Concept of a Balance Sheet
There are two sections of the balance sheet: The left side shows the firm's assets (what the firm owns), and the right side shows the liabilities (what the firm owes) and the owner's equity, which together represent the claims against the assets or how the firm paid for its assets.

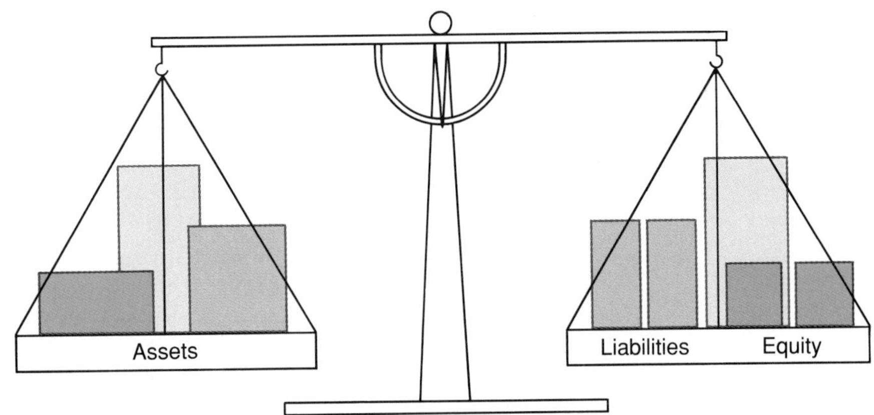

- **Heading for the Statement**. The balance sheet heading should indicate the purpose of the statement, the name of the firm, and the period covered. This statement shows the balance sheet of the firm on the last day of last year and the last day of this year.

- **Current Assets**. The first section of the balance sheet lists the firm's current assets. Current assets are normally expected to flow into cash in the course of the firm's operating year. Typical current assets include cash, marketable securities with maturities of less than a year (such as Treasury bills or money market securities), accounts receivable, notes receivable, inventory, and prepaid expenses such as insurance payments. Total current assets is the sum of the breakdown on the rows above.
- **Fixed Assets**. The next section lists fixed assets. Fixed assets are acquired for the long-term use of the business. These assets are typically not for resale, and they are recorded on the balance sheet at their cost to the business less accumulated depreciation. Fixed assets include land, buildings, leasehold improvements, fixtures, furniture, machinery, tools, and equipment. Total fixed assets are the sum of the itemized items listed on the rows above.
- **Other Assets**. Other assets include anything owned, or to which the firm has legal rights, that is not included in current or fixed assets. Typical other assets include investments in other companies and intangible assets such as goodwill, patents, trademarks, and organizational costs.
- **Total Assets**. Total assets are the sum of total current assets, total fixed assets, and all other assets.
- **Current Liabilities**. Liabilities include claims of creditors against the assets of the business—in other words, debt owed by the business. Current liabilities are short-term obligations due on demand or within a year. Typical current liabilities include accounts payable for merchandise and services, loans payable within the year, taxes, and other accruals. Total current liabilities is the sum of the current liabilities listed on the rows above.
- **Long-Term Debt**. Long-term debt includes debts or loans that are not due for payment within the current year. Typical long-term debt includes bank loans and bonds.
- **Total Liabilities**. Total liabilities are the sums of the itemized long-term debt items entered on the rows above.
- **Owner Equity**. Owner equity is the owners' share of the business and is always equal to the assets of the business minus its liabilities. Owner equity has two parts: the actual investment of the owners in the firm (stock) and retained earnings (any profits left to accumulate in the business). Total owner equity is the sum of the owners' investment and retained earnings entered on the rows above. Total owner equity is also called net worth.
- **Total Equity and Liabilities**. Total equity and liabilities is the sum of all liabilities and owner equity. This sum always equals total assets, and therefore, the balance sheet balances.
- **Current Ratio**. It is hard to tell whether changes in the balance sheet are good or bad unless you compare the relationship between numbers. This comparison is called ratio analysis. One of the key ratios is the current ratio, which measures liquidity (for example, to answer questions like "Can the company pay its bills?"). The current ratio formula divides total current assets by total current liabilities.

	A	B	C
1	Your name:		
2	Filename:	BALANCE	
3	Date:		
4			
5	BALANCE SHEET		
6	PACRIM Enterprises		
7	December 31, 199X		
8		This Year	Last Year
9	CURRENT ASSETS		
10	Cash	$11,200	$6,400
11	Accounts receivable	20,000	20,000
12	Inventory	70,000	70,000
13	Prepaid expense	3,400	3,400
14	Total Current Assets	$104,600	$99,800
15	FIXED ASSETS		
16	Buildings & equipment	$30,000	$30,000
17	Less accumulated depreciation	(10,000)	(5,000)
18	Land	20,000	5,000
19	Total Fixed Assets	$40,000	$30,000
20	OTHER ASSETS		
21	Patents	$10,000	$10,000
22	Total Assets	$154,600	$139,800
23	CURRENT LIABILITIES		
24	Accounts payable	$20,000	$20,000
25	Accrued wages and taxes	10,000	10,000
26	Current portion of long term debt	5,000	5,000
27	Other current liabilities	5,000	5,000
28	Total Current Liabilities	$40,000	$40,000
29	LONG-TERM DEBT		
30	Bank loans	$40,000	$30,000
31	Other	10,000	20,000
32	Total Liabilities	$90,000	$90,000
33	OWNER EQUITY		
34	Common stock	$37,000	$37,000
35	Retained earnings	27,600	12,800
36	Total Owner Equity	$64,600	$49,800
37	Total Equity and Liabilities	$154,600	$139,800
38			
39	Current Ratio	2.62	2.50

The Balance Sheet Model

The balance sheet compares this year's results with last year's results.

STEPS

1. Retrieve the BALANCE model shown in the figure "The Balance Sheet Model."
2. Enter the formulas described in the table "The Balance Sheet Model's Formulas." As you do so, refer to the Concepts section for a description of each of the line items as you enter them.
3. Format your model to match the figure "The Balance Sheet Model."
4. When you have finished with the model, save it under the same filename and make a printout.
5. Create the graph shown in the figure "The Balance Sheet Graph," and add titles and legends to match the illustration. The graph plots total assets, total liabilities, and total owner equity for this year and last year. The x-axis is the range that includes the column headings on row 9. When you are finished, save the graph and make a printout.

THE BALANCE SHEET MODEL'S FORMULAS

#	Cell	Formula	Copy to
1	B14	*Total current assets* is the sum of the *Current assets* broken down on the rows above.	C14
2	B19	*Total fixed assets* is the sum of the *Fixed assets* broken down on the rows above.	C19
3	B22	*Total assets* is *Total current assets* in cell B14 plus *Total fixed assets* in cell B19 plus *Other assets* in cell B21.	C22
4	B28	*Total current liabilities* is the sum of the *Current liabilities* broken down on the rows above.	C28
5	B32	*Total liabilities* is *Total current liabilities* plus the sum of *Long-term debt* in cells B30 and B31.	C32
6	B36	*Total owner equity* is the sum of *Owner Equity* broken down on the rows above.	C36
7	B37	*Total equity and liabilities* is *Total liabilities* in cell B32 plus *Total owner equity* in cell B36.	C37
8	B39	*Current ratio* is *Total current assets* in cell B14 divided by *Total current liabilities* in cell B28.	C39

APPLICATIONS

The Balance Sheet Graph
The graph shows the relationship among assets, liabilities, and equity. If you were to stack the bars for liabilities and equity on top of each other, their height would match the height of the assets bar.

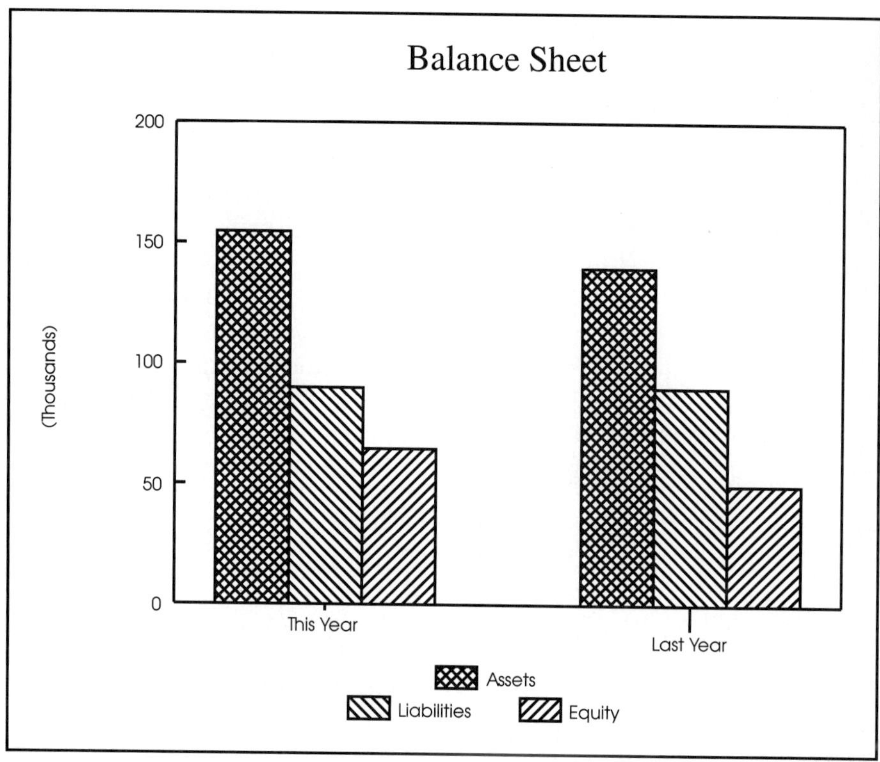

PROBLEMS

1. What if you were making a management decision about how to raise and spend an additional $20,000 so that you improved the company's financial position? Using the balance sheet, explore the following what-ifs, and record the results in the table "Exploring What-Ifs." Compare the results of the changes with the original figures to identify the changes that each what-if caused.
   A. Increase this year's bank loan to $60,000, and put the additional funds into the cash account under current assets.
   B. Reduce cash back to its original $11,200, and use the $20,000 bank loan to pay off accounts payable.
   C. Restore the bank loan to its original $40,000 and accounts payable to $20,000. Reduce inventory by $20,000 to $50,000, and use the proceeds to increase the cash account by $20,000.

EXPLORING WHAT-IFS

What If	Original	A	B	C
Total current assets	______	______	______	______
Total assets	______	______	______	______
Total current liabilities	______	______	______	______
Total liabilities	______	______	______	______
Current ratio	______	______	______	______

2. Using the current ratio as the criterion, which of the alternatives is the best? The worst?

APPLICATION 3B

The Business Plan—An Income Statement

In this application, you create an income statement that shows the sales, expenses, and profits for a three-year period. After completing this application, you will be able to describe the line items that make up an income statement and explain how they are related. You then use this understanding to create a year-end income statement.

CONCEPTS

Business owners and managers must have a way to measure the degree of success or failure of their business or department and to show the net results of subtracting expenses from sales or revenues. The income, or profit-and-loss, statement is the gauge most frequently used to determine profitability. The income statement shows the profit or loss over a period, usually a month, quarter, or year, as shown in the figure "The Income Statement."

The Income Statement
The income statement shows the profitability of the firm over a period of months.

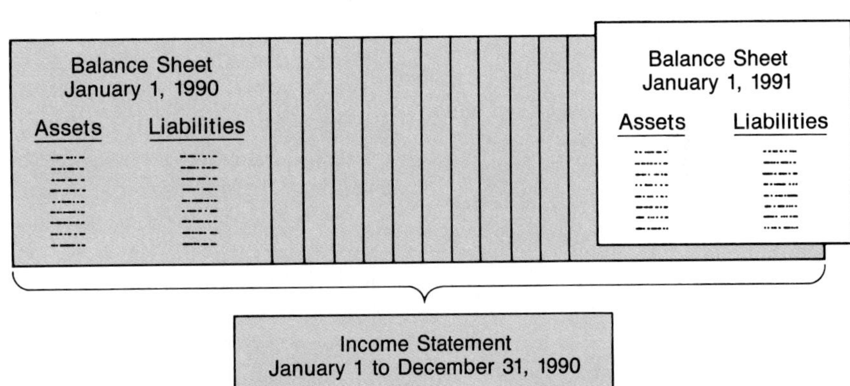

The income statement shown in the figure "The Annual Income Statement Model" has two parts: The first part, variables, is where you enter what-ifs, and the second part is a typical income statement used in business. When you change any numbers in the variables part, the numbers in the income statement part automatically change. The income statement part contains the following line items:

- **Heading for the Statement.** All statements should have headings that identify them. Headings normally include the name of the company and the period covered by the statement.
- **Column Headings.** Typical income statements cover daily, weekly, monthly, quarterly, biannual, or annual periods. You enter each period's figures into a separate column.
- **Sales.** The first section of the income statement records sales activity during the covered period. This section includes:
  - **Gross Sales.** Gross sales are the sales that the firm makes during each period.

- **Discounts, Returns, and Allowances**. Discounts are any price reductions; returns are sales that were made and then returned by customers for refunds or credit; and allowances are credits offered to customers.
- **Net Sales**. Net sales are gross sales minus discounts, returns, and allowances.

- **Cost of Goods Sold**. The next section includes all costs of inventory or raw materials purchased by the firm, including the freight charges of having them delivered. These costs usually vary directly with sales. To make an income statement as accurate as possible, cost of goods sold is generally broken down into individual line items. Total cost of goods sold is the sum of all items listed in the breakdown.
- **Gross Profit**. Gross profit is the money available to the firm after cost of goods sold is deducted from net sales.
- **Operating Expenses**. The next section breaks down the costs, usually fixed or partially fixed and variable, to operate the business. Typical operating expenses include general and administrative costs, selling expenses, interest expenses, and depreciation. Total operating expenses are the sum of all items listed in the operating expense breakdown.
- **Operating Income or Loss**. Operating income or loss is calculated by subtracting total operating expenses from gross profit.
- **Other Income**. Other income is revenue received that is not directly related to the firm's operation.
- **Other Expenses**. Other expenses are costs that are not directly related to the firm's operation.
- **Income Before Taxes**. Income before taxes is calculated by adding other income to net income and loss and then subtracting other expenses.
- **Taxes**. Taxes are the percentage of net income paid to the government.
- **Net Income or Loss**. Net income or loss, frequently referred to as the bottom line, is income before taxes minus taxes.

STEPS

1. Retrieve the INCOME model shown in the figure "The Annual Income Statement Model."
2. Enter the formulas described in the table "The Annual Income Statement Model's Formulas." As you do so, refer to the Concepts section for a description of each of the line items as you enter them.
3. Copy the formula in cell C22 to D22 and the formulas in the range B23.B41 to the same rows in columns C and D.
4. Format your model to match the figure "The Annual Income Statement Model."
5. When you have finished with the model, save it under the same filename and make a printout.
6. Create the graph shown in the figure "The Income Statement Graph," and add titles and legends to match the illustration. The graph plots total cost of goods, total operating expenses, and income

before taxes over the three-year period covered by the statement. The x-axis includes the labels that head the yearly columns. When you are finished, save the graph and make a printout.

The Annual Income Statement Graph

The annual income statement graph shows the annual trend in cost of goods, operating expenses, and profits.

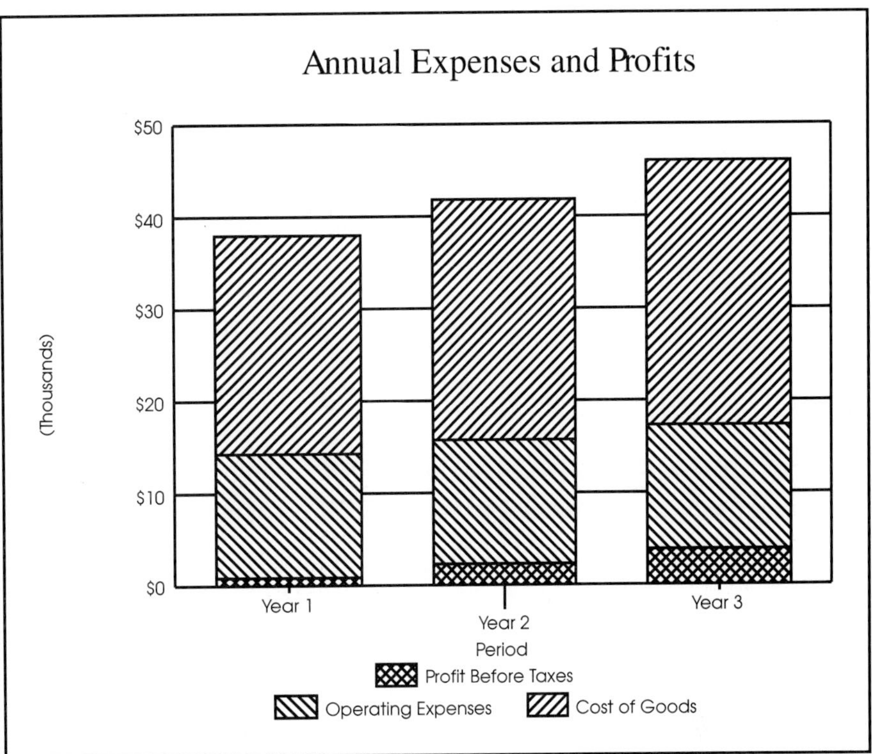

	A	B	C	D	E
1	Your name:				
2	Filename:				
3	Date:	INCOME			
4					
5	VARIABLES:				
6	Starting sales	$40,000			
7	Sales growth rate	5%			
8	Discounts, returns, & allow.	5%			
9	Purchase price	60%			
10	Freight in	4%			
11	General & administrative	$7,500			
12	Selling expense	$3,750			
13	Interest expense	$931			
14	Depreciation	$1,250			
15	Tax rate	25%			
16					
17	PRO FORMA INCOME STATEMENT - FIRST YEAR				
18	PACRIM Enterprises				
19	January 1, 199x -- December 31, 199x				
20			Year 1	Year 2	Year3
21	SALES				
22	Gross sales		$40,000	$42,000	$44,100
23	Discounts, returns, & allow.		2,000	2,100	2,205
24	Net sales		38,000	39,900	41,895
25	COST OF GOODS SOLD				
26	Purchase price		22,800	23,940	25,137
27	Freight in		912	958	1,005
28	Total cost of goods sold		23,712	24,898	26,142
29	Gross profit		14,288	15,002	15,753
30	OPERATING EXPENSES				
31	General & administrative		7,500	7,500	7,500
32	Selling expenses		3,750	3,750	3,750
33	Interest expenses		931	931	931
34	Depreciation		1,250	1,250	1,250
35	Total operating expenses		13,431	13,431	13,431
36	Operating income/loss		857	1,571	2,322
37	Other income				
38	Other expenses				
39	Profit before taxes		857	1,571	2,322
40	Taxes		214	393	580
41	Net income/loss		643	1,179	1,741

The Annual Income Statement Model

The income statement has two parts: variables and the statement itself.

- The variables section is where you enter numbers that automatically generate the numbers on the income statement. Changing these numbers allows you to quickly explore a variety of possible outcomes.
- When you enter numbers into the variables section, the income statement's formulas automatically calculate all the annual numbers (except Other income and Other expenses).

THE ANNUAL INCOME STATEMENT MODEL'S FORMULAS

#	Cell	Formula
1	B22	**Gross sales** for Year 1 are carried down by a reference to *Starting sales* entered into cell B6.
2	C22	**Gross sales** for Year 2 is Year 1 sales in cell B22 (a relative reference) plus the result of multiplying Year 1 sales in cell B22 (a relative reference) by the *Sales growth rate* percentage in cell B7 (an absolute reference).
3	B23	**Discounts, returns, & allow.** are *Gross sales* in cell B22 (a relative reference) times the *Discount, returns, & allow.* percentage in cell B8 (an absolute reference).
4	B24	**Net sales** are *Gross sales* in cell B22 minus *Discounts, returns, & allow.*
5	B26	**Purchase price** is *Net sales* in cell B24 (a relative reference) multiplied by the *Purchase price* percentage in cell B9 (an absolute reference).
6	B27	**Freight in** is the *Purchase price* in cell B26 (a relative reference) multiplied by the *Freight in* percentage in cell B10 (an absolute reference).
7	B28	**Total cost of goods sold** is the sum of the *Cost of goods sold* broken down on the rows above in column B.
8	B29	**Gross profit** is *Net sales* in cell B24 minus *Total cost of goods sold* in cell B28.
9	B31	**General & administrative** is carried down by a cell reference to the *General & administrative* amount in cell B11 (an absolute reference).
10	B32	**Selling expenses** is carried down by a cell reference to the *Selling expenses* amount in cell B12 (an absolute reference).

THE ANNUAL INCOME STATEMENT MODEL'S FORMULAS *(CONT.)*

11	B33	**Interest expenses** is carried down by a cell reference to the *Interest expenses* amount in cell B13 (an absolute reference).
12	B34	**Depreciation** is carried down by a cell reference to the *Depreciation* amount in cell B14 (an absolute reference).
13	B35	**Total operating expenses** is the sum of the *Operating expenses* broken down on the rows above in column B.
14	B36	**Operating income/loss** is *Gross profit* in cell B29 minus *Total operating expenses* in cell B35.
15	B39	**Profit before taxes** is *Operating income* in cell B36 plus *Other income* in cell B37 minus *Other expenses* in cell B38.
16	B40	**Taxes** are *Income before taxes* in cell B39 (a relative reference) multiplied by the *Tax rate* in cell B15 (an absolute reference).
17	B41	**Net income/loss** is *Profit before taxes* in cell B39 minus *Taxes* in cell B40.

PROBLEMS

1. Using the income statement model, explore the following what-ifs, and list the amounts for each item in the table "Exploring Sales What-Ifs." Compare the results of the changes with the original numbers. Which changes are for the better? For the worse?
   A. What if sales are reduced to $37,000?
   B. What if sales are increased to $43,000?
   C. What if sales are $38,000 and the purchase price increases to 65%?

EXPLORING SALES WHAT-IFS

What If	Original	A	B	C
Gross sales	______	______	______	______
Gross profit ($)	______	______	______	______
Gross profit (%)	______	______	______	______
Income before taxes ($)	______	______	______	______
Income before taxes (%)	______	______	______	______

2. Assume that you are the manager of a small store and want to increase your profits. Using the income statement, make the following changes and list the results from the "Year 3" column in the table "Exploring Other What-Ifs." Compare the results of the changes with the original numbers. Which changes are for the better? For the worse?
   A. Assume that with better training, and no additional expenses, your sales help can increase starting sales to $50,000.
   B. Return starting sales to the original $40,000, and then assume that you can strike a better deal with your supplier that will decrease purchase price to 55%.
   C. Return purchase price to the original 60%, and then assume

that by hiring a part-time salesperson sales can be increased. To do so, you must increase general and administrative expenses to $9,000 to increase starting sales to $45,000.

EXPLORING OTHER WHAT-IFS

What If	Original	A	B	C
Gross sales	______	______	______	______
Gross profit ($)	______	______	______	______
Gross profit (%)	______	______	______	______
Income before taxes ($)	______	______	______	______
Income before taxes (%)	______	______	______	______
Net income/loss ($)	______	______	______	______
Net income/loss (%)	______	______	______	______

APPLICATION 3C

The Business Plan—A Bank Loan

In this application, you create a model that calculates the payments due on a loan of any amount, for any period, at any interest rate. The emphasis is on mortgages, but the principles and calculations apply to almost any type of loan. After completing this application, you will be able to describe how interest on a loan is calculated and how it affects the payments due.

CONCEPTS

Shopping for the best mortgage credit available can save you money. Real estate mortgage loans differ in rate of interest, length of repayment period, and size. Some have penalties for prepayment. Because these factors can make a big difference in the ultimate cost of your real estate, it is worthwhile to shop for the type of loan and the terms that best suit your needs.

For each individual, there is a particular set of arrangements for down payment and length of time to repay the loan that will prove best. A desirable contract provides for payments as large as you can afford at the present time, with the right to repay the loan at a faster rate than originally agreed on if you later find that you want to.

The Interest Rate

The interest rate you agree to pay affects the total cost of your loan. Because the amount borrowed is large and repayment extends over many years, a variation of one-half of 1 percent can make a big difference. For example, on a 30-year, $50,000 mortgage, you would pay about $6,960 more in interest on a 12½-percent loan than on a 12-percent loan.

The Term

The length of time you take to repay a loan also has a bearing on the amount of interest you pay. The shorter the time taken to repay the loan, the lower the total cost of interest to you; the longer the time to repay, the higher the total cost. The advantage of spreading payments over a long period is the smaller monthly payment, which may make financing easier for you because it leaves more for current living. The disadvantage is the larger amount paid out in interest for the loan. When the annual rate is 12 percent, the total interest paid on a loan repaid in 20 years is about one-half more than the amount of the original loan, and in 25 years, it will almost double the original loan. If you take as long as 30 years to repay, the amount you pay in interest is almost triple the amount of the original loan.

The Down Payment

Your ability to make a large down payment can save you money on the cost of a mortgage. A large down payment usually has these advantages:

- You may find it easier to obtain a loan.
- You may be able to get a loan at a more reasonable rate of interest.
- Your total interest expense will be lower.
- Your equity in your home will be greater.

On a 25-year, 12-percent loan, every $1,000 of down payment decreases the amount of total interest paid by about $2,160. For example, if you make a down payment of $10,000, the cost of interest over the 25-year period amounts to about $129,580. If you make a down payment of $20,000, the total cost of interest is about $107,990.

STEPS

1. Retrieve the BANKLOAN model shown in the figure "The Bank Loan Model."
2. Enter the formulas described in the table "The Bank Loan Model's Formulas." (You may get a *CIRC* indicator that tells you the model contains a circular reference. This indicator is normal for this model.)
3. Format your model to match the figure "The Bank Loan Model."
4. When you have finished with the model, save it under the same filename and make a printout.
5. Create the graph shown in the figure "The Bank Loan Model's Graph" and add titles and legends to match the illustration. The graph plots the % Interest and % Principal columns. The x-axis is the range of numbers in the Term column. Format them so the labels do not overlap. When you have finished, save the graph and make a printout. What does the graph tell you about the relationship between principal and interest payments over the term of the loan?

The Bank Loan Model
The bank loan model allows you to explore the payments due on loans. You can explore terms by changing the interest rate, principal, and term. You can explore the effect of prepaying a loan by changing the actual payments per period in cell E12. To make this the same as the minimum payment, enter the cell reference **+E11**.

	A	B	C	D	E	F	G
1	Your name:						
2	Filename:						
3	Date:						
4							
5	LOAN AMORTIZATION						
6	Enter annual interest rate				10.00%		
7	Principal ammount				$100,000.00		
8	Indicate term (1=years, 12=months)				1		
9	Enter term (1 to 60)				30		
10							
11	Minimum payments per period				10,607.92		
12	Actual payments per period				10,607.92		
13	Total payments				318,237.74		
14							
15	TERM	BEGINNING	INTEREST	PRINCIPAL	ENDING PRIN.	Graph	Ranges
16		BALANCE	PAID	PAID	BALANCE	%	%
17						Interest	Principal
18	1	100,000.00	10,000.00	607.92	99,392.08	94%	6%
19	2	99,392.08	9,939.21	668.72	98,723.36	94%	6%
20	3	98,723.36	9,872.34	735.59	97,987.77	93%	7%
21	4	97,987.77	9,798.78	809.15	97,178.62	92%	8%
22	5	97,178.62	9,717.86	890.06	96,288.56	92%	8%
23	6	96,288.56	9,628.86	979.07	95,309.49	91%	9%
24	7	95,309.49	9,530.95	1,076.98	94,232.51	90%	10%
74	57	0.00	0.00	0.00	0.00	0%	0%
75	58	0.00	0.00	0.00	0.00	0%	0%
76	59	0.00	0.00	0.00	0.00	0%	0%
77	60	0.00	0.00	0.00	0.00	0%	0%
78	TOT INT. & PRIN.		218,237.74	100,000.00			
79	COMBINED TOTAL		318,237.74				

THE BANK LOAN MODEL'S FORMULAS

#	Cell	Formula	Copy to
1	E11	**Minimum payments per period** are calculated by the function @IF(E8=12,@PMT(E7,E6/12,E9),@PMT(E7,E6,E9)).	
2	E12	**Actual payments per period** are initially set to the minimum payment number by entering a reference to cell E11.	
3	E13	**Total payments** are the *Minimum payments per period* in cell E11 multiplied by the *Term* in cell E9.	
4	A18	**Term** is calculated by the function @IF(E77<0.005,1,A77+1).	
5	A19	**Term** is incremented by the formula 1+A18.	A20.A77
6	B18	**Beginning balance** is carried to this cell by a reference to cell E7.	
7	B19	**Beginning balance** is calculated by the function @IF(E18=B18,0,E18).	B20.B77
8	C18	**Interest paid** is calculated by the function @IF(E$8=12,($E$6/12)*B18,($E$6*B18)).	C19.C77
9	D18	**Principal paid** is calculated by the function @IF(B18>=$E$12,E$12-C18,B18).	D19.D77
10	E18	**Ending principal paid** is the *Beginning balance* in cell B18 minus the *Principal paid* in cell D18.	E19.E77
11	F18	**% Interest** is calculated by the function @IF(C18>0,C18/(C18+D18),0).	F19.F77
12	G18	**% Principal** is calculated by the function @IF(D18>0,D18/(C18+D18),0).	G19.G77
13	C78	**Total interest and principal** is the sum of all *Interest paid* in column C.	D78
14	C79	**Combined total** is *Total interest* in cell +C78 plus *Total principal* in cell D78.	

PROBLEM

1. Using the bank loan model, explore the following what-ifs. Record the results of the what-ifs in the table "Bank Loan What-Ifs." Compare the results of the changes with the original figures to identify the changes that each what-if caused.
   A. Change the term of the loan to 20 years in cell E9.
   B. Change the term of the loan back to 30 years, and increase the actual payments per period in cell E12 to $11,745.96.
   C. Return the payments to $10,607.92 (to do so, enter the cell reference **+E11** into cell E12), and lower the interest rate to 9.5%.

BANK LOAN WHAT-IFS

What If	Original	A	B	C
Total interest paid	_______	_______	_______	_______
Total principal paid	_______	_______	_______	_______
Combined total paid	_______	_______	_______	_______

The Bank Loan Model's Graph

The bank loan model's graph plots principal and interest payments. It shows how interest declines as a percentage of the total payment as time progresses.

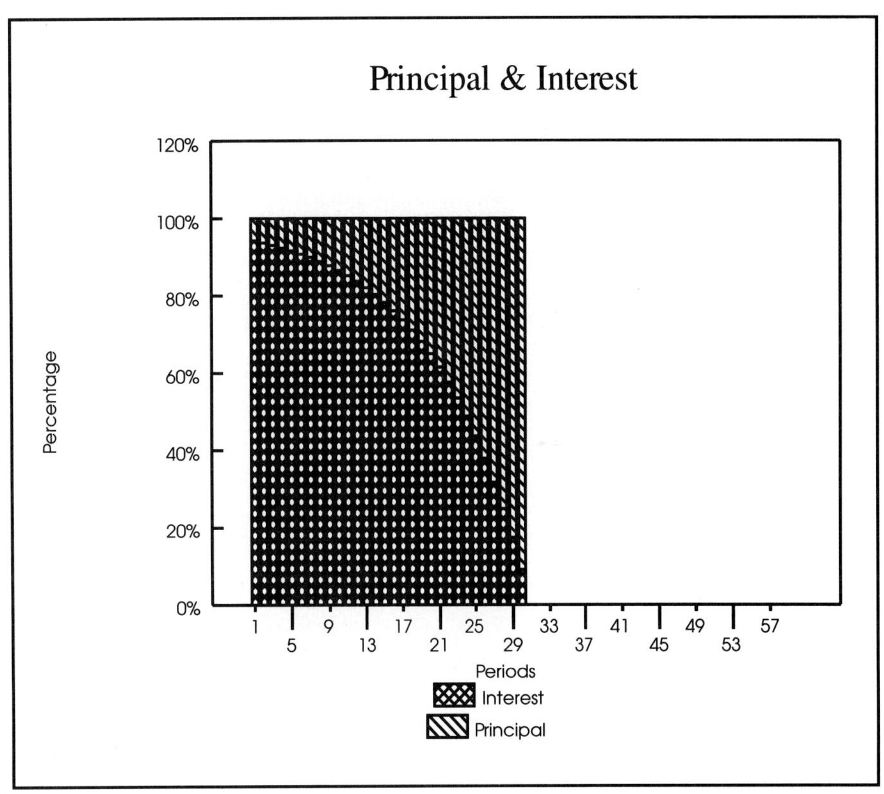

INDEX

INDEX

dBASE III Plus®

CHAPTER 1

Getting Started

TOPIC 1

dBASE III Plus—An Overview

After completing this topic, you will be able to:

- Describe the differences between record management and database management programs
- Explain the concept of a relational database
- Load dBASE III Plus on a floppy or hard disk system
- Open an existing database file with the USE command
- Print data with the SET PRINTER ON and LIST TO PRINT commands
- Clear files from memory with the CLOSE and CLEAR ALL commands
- Quit dBASE III Plus with the QUIT command

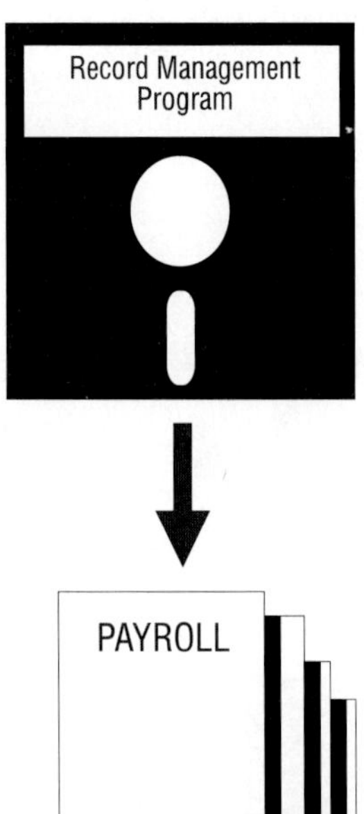

Record Management Programs
Record management programs can work with only one file at a time. To access the data in another file, you must clear the first file from memory and then retrieve the new one.

The management of databases is one of the most important applications of microcomputers. A *database* is simply one or more files that contain an organized body of information. For example, when you make a reservation with an airline, your name and address are entered into its database, and a seat on a specific flight is reserved for you in the same database. Should you call later and give your name, the airline can locate the seat that was assigned by searching the database.

To create, maintain, and use a database, you use a *database management program* such as dBASE III Plus. Such a program allows you to store information, retrieve it when you need it, and update it when necessary. For example, you can:

- Add new information
- Find specific information
- Update information that has changed
- Arrange the information in a specified order
- Delete information that is no longer needed
- Print reports containing all or some of the information
- Create new files that contain information from two other files or part of the information in one file

Because of the power and flexibility of database management programs, the applications are almost endless.

- You can maintain mailing lists for sales and marketing purposes. The data can be used to automatically print letters, envelopes, and mailing labels. You can use the program to get answers to

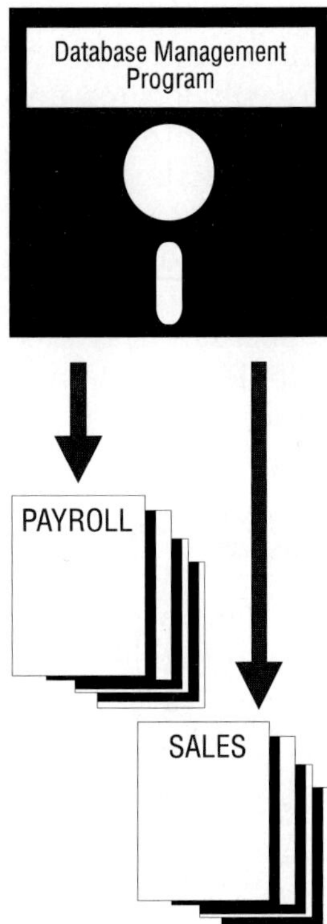

Database Management Programs
Database management programs can manage the data in more than one file. This allows you to relate the data in the two files and reduces the amount of data entry.

questions such as "What phone numbers are listed for SMITH?" or "What phone numbers are listed in area code 617?"

- You can manage inventory by recording products or supplies moving into and out of a business. The program can give you answers to questions such as "How many parts are left in inventory?" or "How many were shipped this month?"
- You can manage assets such as stock portfolios so that you always know what stocks you have and what their value is. You can ask the program questions such as, "How many shares of IBM stock do I own?" "What stocks have increased in value since I bought them?" or "What stocks have I sold this year?"

The expressions *database* and *database management program* are often used very loosely. In fact, two types of programs are used to manage files of highly structured data: record management programs and database management programs. Moreover, strictly speaking, not all highly structured data files are databases.

Record Management Programs

Record management programs (sometimes called *file management* or *flat-file database programs*) are like those integrated into word processing programs such as WordPerfect and spreadsheet programs such as Lotus 1-2-3. These programs store, maintain, and use data in single files. If you use a record management program to store data on various aspects of a business, you must store the data for different applications in separate files—called *record files*. If you need to change an item common to two files, you must change it separately in each of them. Let's say you have one file for names, addresses, and phone numbers and another file for payroll information. If a person's name occurs in both files, it must be separately entered into each file. If the name must be changed or deleted later, it must be separately changed in or deleted from each file.

Database Management Programs

As the amount of data being processed increases, the record management method of using separate files to store information becomes cumbersome because information must be extensively duplicated. An employee's name might appear in several different files—for example, payroll, vacation, and expense accounts. There are disadvantages to this duplication:

- It increases the amount of data entry.
- It increases the risk of errors in the information.
- It requires more storage space.

Using a database management program eliminates these problems. With a database management program, each piece of information can be stored only once because the program can use interrelated data stored in more than one file. Database management programs, therefore, have a major advantage over record management programs since many applications require more than one file. For example, an accounting system requires separate files for the general ledger, accounts receivable, and accounts payable.

DATA VERSUS _DATUM_

The term *data* is one that you frequently encounter when working with databases and other computer programs. It is the plural of *datum*. When you use the term, you should always do so with plural verbs. For example, you would not say, "The data *is* inconclusive." Instead, you would say, "The data *are* inconclusive."

Database Models

When you enter information into a database file, it is organized by the database management program so that it can be easily located and manipulated. The method used by the program to organize data is called the *database model.* Almost all microcomputer database management programs, including dBASE III Plus, use the *relational model.*

A relational database consists of one or more tables, called *relations*. Each table contains rows and columns much like a spreadsheet. Since a database can contain more than one table, the tables can be related to one another. As you will see later, you can manipulate the data in related tables to enter, update, and find information stored in the database.

Relational Database
A relational database file contains columns and rows much like a table. The columns are fields that contain data. The labels at the top of each column are the field names. There are one or more rows of data, and each row is a record.

ID	LASTNAME	FIRST	STREET	CITY	ST	ZIP	AREA	PHONE
122	Kelly	Jim	12 Preston Lane	Orlando	FL	32800	407	555-1011
123	Dougherty	Suzann	10100 Hardy	Los Gatos	CA	95031	415	555-1013
124	Dougherty	Steven	10100 Hardy	Los Gatos	CA	95031	415	555-1013
125	Porsena	Lars	71 North Street	Atlanta	GA	30010	404	555-1014
115	Culman	Tina	100 Elm Street	New Haven	CT	10000	203	555-1001
113	Benjamin	Nancy	25 Oak Street	Cambridge	MA	20000	617	555-1002
116	Kendall	Liz	14 Lark Avenue	Chicago	IL	20000	312	555-1003
120	Hogan	Dennis	40 Main Street	Edgewater	NJ	30000	201	555-1004
119	Morin	Emily	43 Spruce Road	Milpitas	CA	20000	408	555-1005
117	Sobel	Carol	45 Porter Avenue	Fairlawn	NJ	30000	201	555-1006
112	Anthony	William	900 Maple Road	Reading	MA	20000	617	555-1007
118	Morin	Cathy	5 Milk Street	Salem	OR	40000	508	555-1008
114	Morin	Mike	5 Milk Street	Salem	OR	40000	508	555-1009
121	Kendall	Steve	1 Sylvan Avenue	Englewood	NJ	07632	201	555-1010

Field names

Record

Field

JUMP-START TUTORIAL

WHEN THINGS GO WRONG

If you enter a command incorrectly, you may see an error message such as *variable not found* or *unrecognized command verb.* On the second line from the bottom of the screen, a prompt will then read *Do you want some help? (Y/N).* When this message appears, just press N and reenter the command.

In this tutorial, you get a jump start on dBASE by following steps that introduce you to the program using an existing database file. Some of the procedures you will be using may seem confusing at first, but keep in mind that the purpose of this tutorial is to show you the usefulness of the program. You are not expected to retain any of the procedures except those you use to load the program and open your files. All the other procedures will be covered in more depth and at a much slower pace as you proceed through this text. *Relax* and see what dBASE can do for you!

GETTING STARTED

1. Load the dBASE III Plus program into your computer's memory.
   - If you load the program from the operating system command prompt (for example, *A:* or *C:*), load the operating system and then refer to one of the KEY/Strokes boxes "Loading dBASE

from a Floppy Disk" or "Loading dBASE from a Hard Disk" in the Quick Reference section.

- If you use other procedures to load the program, such as selecting it from a menu, load it and then start this tutorial at the section "Opening an Existing Database File." Write down the steps that you follow to load the program in Exercise 1 at the end of this topic so that you have them to refer to later.

THE dBASE OPENING SCREEN

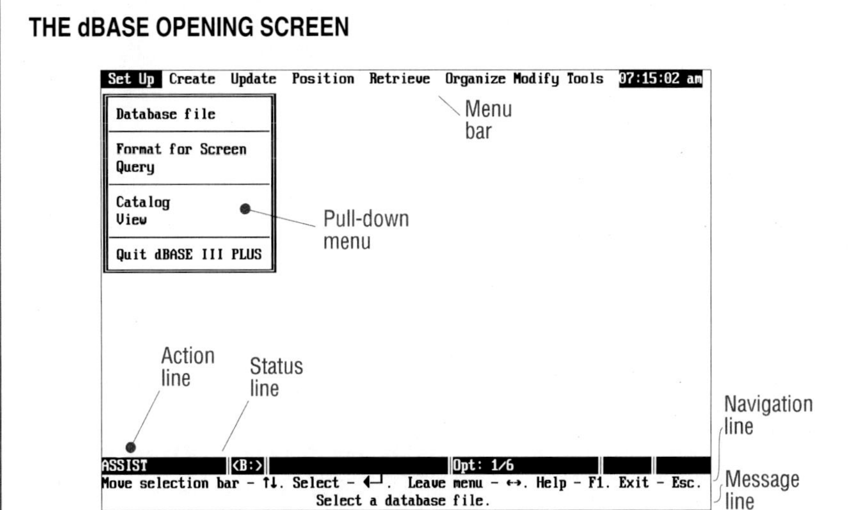

When you load dBASE III Plus, the program's opening screen appears with the Assist menu displayed and the Set Up menu pulled down.

- The Assist menu bar at the top of the screen contains a series of menus, any one of which you can pull down by highlighting its name. This menu bar is optional, and you can execute all dBASE commands without using it.
- The action line lists the commands that you enter as you make selections from the menus. If you do not use the Assist menus, the dot prompt that you use to type in commands is displayed on this same line.
- The status line (displayed in reverse video) displays the command in progress, the current default drive, the name of the current file, and the number of records. It also displays *Ins* (only when the dot prompt is displayed), *Caps*, or *Num* when the Ins, CapsLock, or NumLock key is engaged.
- The navigation line, just below the status line, displays messages listing the keys and commands you can use.
- The message line at the bottom of the screen displays messages when the program wants you to enter information. When the Assist menu is displayed, this line also displays a brief description of the highlighted menu choice.

2. Be sure that your printer is ready since you will be sending data to the printer.

OPENING AN EXISTING DATABASE FILE

3. Press Esc to remove the Assist menu from the top of the screen and display the dot prompt.

4. Insert the original *Student Resource Disk* accompanying this text as follows:
   - On a hard disk system, insert the disk into drive A.
   - On a floppy disk system, insert the disk into drive B.
5. Set the default drive as follows:
   - On a hard disk system, type **SET DEFAULT TO A:** and press Enter←.
   - On a floppy disk system, type **SET DEFAULT TO B:** and press Enter←.

   The status line indicates that the default drive is now *<A:>* or *<B:>*.
6. Set the path as follows:
   - On a hard disk system, type **SET PATH TO A:\DBASE** and press Enter←.
   - On a floppy disk system, type **SET PATH TO B:\DBASE** and press Enter←.

   This PATH command is necessary because the files that you work with are stored on the *Student Resource Disk* in a directory named DBASE (until you copy them to your own disk in Exercise 2 at the end of this topic). The PATH command you entered here tells the dBASE program to look in the DBASE directory when you try to open a database file.
7. Type **USE OVERVIEW** and press Enter← to open the file, and *OVERVIEW* displayed on the status line indicates that the file is now open in the computer's memory.

LISTING AND PRINTING THE FILE'S RECORDS

8. Type **LIST** and press Enter← to list records in the file. The message *EOF/15* on the status line indicates that you are at the end of the file (*EOF* means End of File) and that the file contains 15 records.

Listing the OVERVIEW Database
When you use the LIST command, the database is displayed on the screen in a table format.

```
(DEMO) . LIST
Record#  INVOICE DATE_ORD DATE_OUT PRODUCT      MODEL   PRICE  QTY TESTED
      1  1001    01/03/93 01/04/93 Computer     2006    999.50   2 .T.
      2  1002    01/03/93 01/05/93 Printer       121    100.50   3 .T.
      3  1003    01/03/93 01/03/93 Computer     2006    999.50   1 .T.
      4  1004    01/04/93 01/05/93 Modem        1111    175.00   5 .F.
      5  1005    01/04/93 01/06/93 Monitor       390    500.00   2 .F.
      6  1006    01/05/93 01/05/93 Network card 1258    375.00   5 .F.
      7  1007    01/05/93 01/09/93 Modem        1111    175.00   1 .F.
      8  1008    01/05/93 01/05/93 Tape backup   238    350.00   4 .F.
      9  1009    01/05/93 01/07/93 Keyboard     3456    125.00   4 .F.
     10  1010    01/06/93 01/06/93 Hard disk      35    650.00  10 .F.
     11  1011    01/06/93 01/09/93 CD-ROM        789    500.00   2 .F.
     12  1012    01/06/93 01/07/93 Printer       121    100.50   5 .T.
     13  1013    01/06/93 01/07/93 Monitor       390    500.00   7 .F.
     14  1014    01/07/93 01/07/93 Computer     1010   1250.99  10 .T.
     15  1015    01/07/93 01/10/93 Printer      121     100.50  20 .F.
(DEMO) .
Command Line     |<A:>|OVERVIEW          |Rec: EOF/15       |      |  Caps

                     Enter a dBASE III PLUS command.
```

9. Type **LIST TO PRINT** and press Enter← to print the records in the file. (You may need to type **EJECT** and press Enter← to eject the printed sheet from your printer.)

LISTING AND PRINTING THE FILE'S STRUCTURE

10. Type **LIST STRUCTURE** and press Enter← to display a list of the fields in the database on the screen. This list gives you the name of each field, its type, and width (including decimal places, if any). For example, you can enter 4 digits in the Qty field.

Listing the File's Structure
The LIST STRUCTURE command displays a listing of the fields in the database.

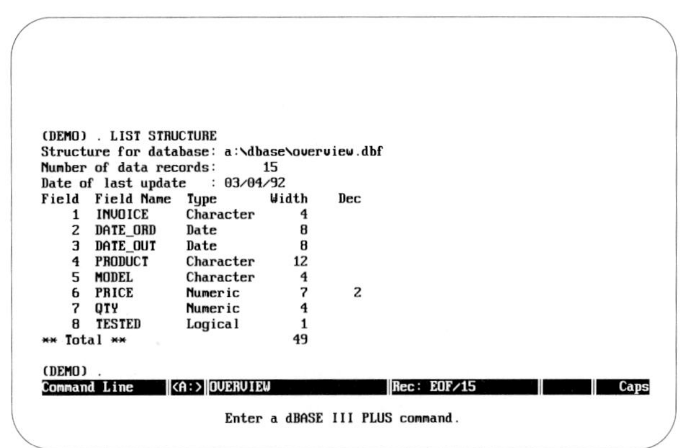

11. Type **LIST STRUCTURE TO PRINT** and press [Enter↵] to print a list of the fields in the database. (Here too, you may need to type **EJECT** and press [Enter↵] to eject the printed page from your printer.)

BROWSING THE FILE'S RECORDS

12. Type **GOTO BOTTOM** and press [Enter↵] to make the last record in the file the current record. The status line now displays *Rec: 15/ 15* to indicate that there are 15 records and the 15th is the current record.
13. Type **GOTO TOP** and press [Enter↵] to make the first record in the file the current record. The status line now displays *Rec: 1/15* to indicate that there are 15 records and the 1st is the current record.
14. Type **BROWSE** and press [Enter↵] to display the database in a tablelike view that you can move the cursor through. Each row on the screen is a record, and each column is a field.
    - A record is the database's description of a person, thing, or activity, for example, all the information on a purchase order.
    - A field is one part of the description stored in the record. Here, for example, the invoice number and the product name are each fields.

Browsing the OVERVIEW Database File
The BROWSE command displays the database in a tablelike format. Each row contains the description of a single record. Each column contains the fields that make up that record.

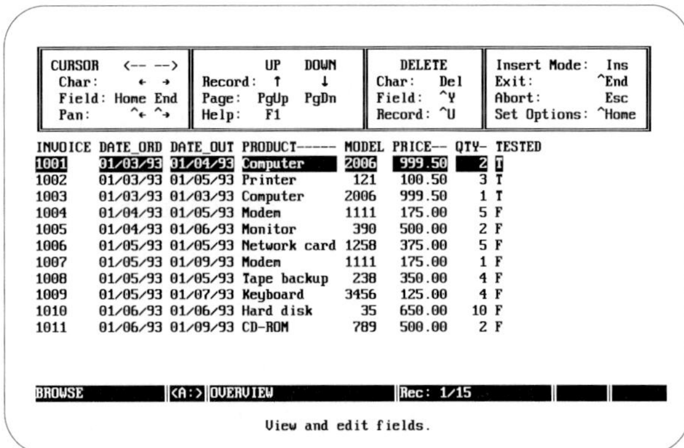

15. Press the arrow keys and [PgDn] and [PgUp] to move around through the records.
16. Press [F1] to remove the help panel from the top of the screen; then press [F1] again to redisplay it.
17. Press [Esc] to leave browse mode and return to the dot prompt.

Fields and Records
A database is always organized into fields and records. Fields contain specific information about a person, item, or other subject. A group of fields makes up a record, a complete description of the person, item, or other subject.

INVOICE	DATE_ORD	DATE_OUT	PRODUCT	MODE	PRICE	QTY	TESTED
1001	01/03/93	01/04/93	Computer	2006	999.50	2	.T.
1002	01/03/93	01/05/93	Printer	121	100.50	3	.T.
1003	01/03/93	01/03/93	Computer	2006	999.50	1	.T.
1004	01/04/93	01/05/93	Modem	1111	175.00	5	.F.
1005	01/04/93	01/06/93	Monitor	390	500.00	2	.F.
1006	01/05/93	01/05/93	Network card	1258	375.00	5	.F.
1007	01/05/93	01/09/93	Modem	1111	175.00	1	.F.
1008	01/05/93	01/05/93	Tape backup	238	350.00	4	.F.
1009	01/05/93	01/07/93	Keyboard	3456	125.00	4	.F.
1010	01/06/93	01/06/93	Hard disk	35	650.00	10	.F.
1011	01/06/93	01/09/93	CD-ROM	789	500.00	2	.F.
1012	01/06/93	01/07/93	Printer	121	100.50	5	.T.
1013	01/06/93	01/07/93	Monitor	390	500.00	7	.F.
1014	01/07/93	01/07/93	Computer	1010	1250.99	10	.T.
1015	01/07/93	01/10/93	Printer	121	100.50	20	.F.

Field names

Record

Field

LISTING SELECTED FIELDS

18. Type **LIST** and press Enter↵ to list all the records.
19. Type **SET FIELDS TO PRODUCT,MODEL,PRICE** and press Enter↵
20. Type **LIST** and press Enter↵ to display only the three fields specified in the SET FIELDS TO command. This limited view is helpful when you want to work with only part of the database.

Listing Selected Fields
When you use the SET FIELDS TO command to specify selected fields, only those fields are shown in subsequent commands.

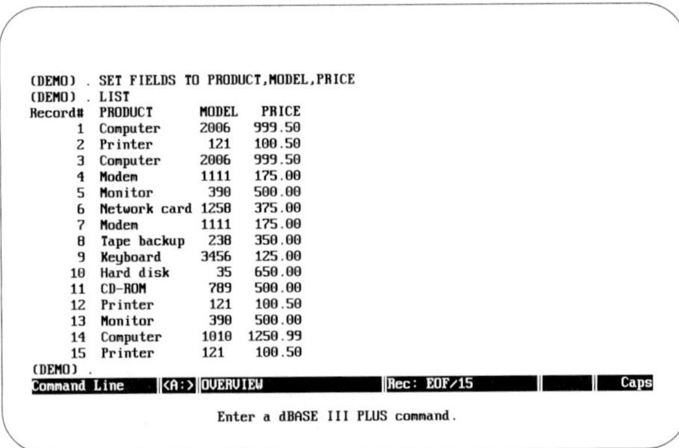

```
(DEMO) . SET FIELDS TO PRODUCT,MODEL,PRICE
(DEMO) . LIST
Record#  PRODUCT      MODEL   PRICE
      1  Computer      2006   999.50
      2  Printer        121   100.50
      3  Computer      2006   999.50
      4  Modem         1111   175.00
      5  Monitor        390   500.00
      6  Network card  1258   375.00
      7  Modem         1111   175.00
      8  Tape backup    238   350.00
      9  Keyboard      3456   125.00
     10  Hard disk       35   650.00
     11  CD-ROM         789   500.00
     12  Printer        121   100.50
     13  Monitor        390   500.00
     14  Computer      1010  1250.99
     15  Printer       121    100.50
(DEMO) .
Command Line  <A:> OVERVIEW   Rec: EOF/15   Caps

Enter a dBASE III PLUS command.
```

21. Type **CLEAR FIELDS** and press Enter↵ so that all fields will be displayed in subsequent commands.
22. Type **LIST** and press Enter↵ to list all the records again.

VIEWING SELECTED RECORDS

23. Type **LIST FOR PRICE>499** and press Enter↵ to display only records with more than 499 in the PRICE field.
24. Type **LIST FOR PRICE<499** and press Enter↵ to display only records with less than 499 in the PRICE field.
25. Type **LIST FOR PRICE=500** and press Enter↵ to display only records with exactly 500 in the PRICE field.

26. Type **LIST FOR PRODUCT="Computer"** and press Enter↵ to display only records with *Computer* in the PRODUCT field. When searching for text as you did here, you enclose it in quotes.
27. Type **LIST FOR DATE_ORD=CTOD("01/05/93")** and press Enter↵ to display only records with dates of 01/05/93 in the DATE_ORD field. The CTOD("01/05/93") part of the command converts the text in the command to dBASE's date format.
28. Type **LIST FOR TESTED** and press Enter↵ to display only records with .T. (for true) in the TESTED field.
29. Type **LIST FOR .NOT.TESTED** and press Enter↵ to display only records with .F. (for false) in the TESTED field.

MAKING CALCULATIONS

30. Type **SUM PRICE** and press Enter↵ to display the total of all numbers in the PRICE field.
31. Type **SUM PRICE*QTY** and press Enter↵ to multiply the contents of the PRICE and QTY fields in each record, and sum the results of those calculations.
32. Type **LIST PRODUCT,PRICE,QTY,PRICE*QTY** and press Enter↵ to display only the PRODUCT, PRICE, and QTY fields for each record along with a calculated field (the rightmost column) where the PRICE and QTY fields in each record are multiplied together.

Calculated Numeric Fields
The command LIST PRODUCT,PRICE,QTY, PRICE*QTY created the new field PRICE*QTY that contains the results of multiplying PRICE times QTY for each record. For example, in the first record, PRICE is 999.50 and QTY is 2, so PRICE*QTY is 1999.00.

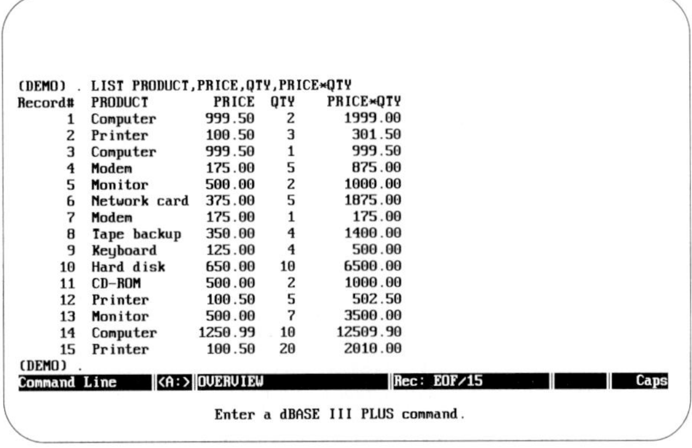

(DEMO) . LIST PRODUCT,PRICE,QTY,PRICE*QTY

Record#	PRODUCT	PRICE	QTY	PRICE*QTY
1	Computer	999.50	2	1999.00
2	Printer	100.50	3	301.50
3	Computer	999.50	1	999.50
4	Modem	175.00	5	875.00
5	Monitor	500.00	2	1000.00
6	Network card	375.00	5	1875.00
7	Modem	175.00	1	175.00
8	Tape backup	350.00	4	1400.00
9	Keyboard	125.00	4	500.00
10	Hard disk	650.00	10	6500.00
11	CD-ROM	500.00	2	1000.00
12	Printer	100.50	5	502.50
13	Monitor	500.00	7	3500.00
14	Computer	1250.99	10	12509.90
15	Printer	100.50	20	2010.00

(DEMO) .
Command Line <A:> OVERVIEW Rec: EOF/15 Caps
Enter a dBASE III PLUS command.

33. Type **LIST PRODUCT,DATE_OUT–DATE_ORD** and press Enter↵ to list each product name along with the number of days between the date it was ordered and the date it was shipped.

Calculated Date Fields
The command LIST PRODUCT,DATE_OUT–DATE_ORD created the new field DATE_OUT–DATE_ORD, in which the date a product is shipped is subtracted from the date it was ordered.

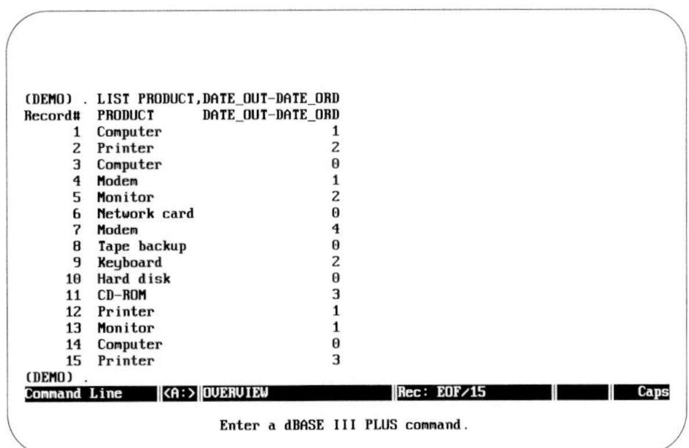

(DEMO) . LIST PRODUCT,DATE_OUT-DATE_ORD

Record#	PRODUCT	DATE_OUT-DATE_ORD
1	Computer	1
2	Printer	2
3	Computer	0
4	Modem	1
5	Monitor	2
6	Network card	0
7	Modem	4
8	Tape backup	0
9	Keyboard	2
10	Hard disk	0
11	CD-ROM	3
12	Printer	1
13	Monitor	1
14	Computer	0
15	Printer	3

(DEMO) .
Command Line <A:> OVERVIEW Rec: EOF/15 Caps
Enter a dBASE III PLUS command.

34. Type **AVERAGE DATE_OUT–DATE_ORD** and press Enter↵ to calculate the average number of days between orders being received and shipped.
35. Type **LIST FOR DATE_OUT–DATE_ORD>2** and press Enter↵ to list records for all products where it took longer than two days to process and ship the order.

ARRANGING THE FILE IN ORDER

36. Type **INDEX ON PRODUCT TO PRODNDX** and press Enter↵. The drives spin and a message then reads *100% indexed.*
37. Type **LIST** and press Enter↵ to see the indexed records listed in alphabetical order by product.
38. Type **INDEX ON PRICE TO PRICENDX** and press Enter↵.
39. Type **LIST** and press Enter↵ to see the indexed records listed in ascending order by price.
40. Type **CLOSE INDEX** and press Enter↵.
41. Type **LIST** and press Enter↵ to see the unindexed records listed in the actual order in which they appear in the database.

PRINTING OUT RECORDS IN THE DATABASE IN ORDER

42. Type **SET INDEX TO PRODNDX** and press Enter↵
43. Type **LIST TO PRINT** and press Enter↵ to print the records in the database in ascending order by product name. (Type **EJECT** and press Enter↵ if you need to.) Compare this printout to the one you made in Step 9.

FINISHING UP

44. Type **CLEAR ALL** and press Enter↵ to remove all files from the computer's memory.
45. You have completed this tutorial. You can continue to the next activity or quit for the day. To quit, type **QUIT** and press Enter↵. Remove your disks and turn off the computer.

QUICK REFERENCE

To use dBASE III Plus, you must first understand the basic procedures for loading the program, opening and closing files, printing data, and quitting the program.

Loading dBASE III Plus

Once the operating system is loaded, the way you load dBASE depends on the type of computer you are using. You have to follow only one of the procedures described below. If your system is on a network or you use a menu to load programs, refer to Exercise 1 at the end of this topic.

KEY/Strokes

Loading dBASE from a Floppy Disk

1. Insert the first dBASE disk (labeled something like *System Disk #1* or *Sampler Disk #1*) into drive A.
2. If the command prompt is not *A>*, type **A:** and press Enter ↵.
3. Type **DBASE** and press Enter ↵ to load the program.

   The copyright screen appears and then a prompt that reads *Press ↵ to assent to the license agreement and begin dBASE III PLUS*. Press Enter ↵ or wait a few moments. Then:

   - If you are using the educational version of dBASE, the prompt reads *Insert Sampler Disk 2 in drive A and a Data Disk in drive B, and press ENTER or press Ctrl-C to abort.*
   - If you are using the full-featured version of dBASE, the prompt reads *Insert System Disk 2 and press ENTER, or press Ctrl-C to abort.*
4. Insert the requested disks and press Enter ↵ to display the dBASE opening screen.

KEY/Strokes

Loading dBASE from a Hard Disk

1. Change the default drive and directory to the one containing the file DBASE.EXE.
   - Change the default drive to the drive containing the dBASE program file DBASE.EXE. For example, if this file is on drive C, type **C:** and press Enter ↵.
   - Change to the directory in which the file DBASE.EXE is stored. It will likely be in a directory named DBASE or, if you are using the educational version, a directory named SAMPLER. To change the directory, use the CD command. For example, to change to the directory named DBASE, type **CD\DBASE** and press Enter ↵. To change to the SAMPLER directory, type **CD\SAMPLER** and press Enter ↵.
2. Type **DBASE** and press Enter ↵ to load the program.

   In a few moments, the copyright screen appears.
3. Press Enter ↵ to continue (or wait for a moment), and the opening screen is displayed.

Changing the Default Drive

When you save or retrieve database files, they are saved to and retrieved from the default drive. You can always tell which drive is currently the default by looking at the status line. It is displayed between angle brackets; for example, *<A:>* means drive A is currently the default drive.

To change the default drive from the dot prompt, use the SET DEFAULT TO <*drive*> command. For example, to change the default drive to drive B, type **SET DEFAULT TO B:** and press Enter ↵.

To specify the default drive from the Assist menu, pull down the Tools menu, highlight *Set drive*, and press Enter↵ to display a list of the system's drives. Highlight the drive that you want to be the default and press Enter↵.

Listing Files on the Disk

To list files on the disk, use the DIR command. For example, to list the database files on the default drive, type **DIR** and press Enter↵. To list the database files on any other drive, follow the command with the drive specifier. For example, type **DIR A:** and press Enter↵ to list the database files on the disk in drive A. This command lists database files (those with the extension .DBF) by default. To list other files, use DOS wildcards or any of the other dBASE filename extensions described in the table "dBASE File Types." For example, to list all the index files on a disk in drive A, type **DIR A:*.NDX** and press Enter↵.

dBASE FILE TYPES

Extension	Description
.CAT	Catalog files that list related files
.DBF	Database files
.DBT	Files that store the contents of memo files
.FMT	Report or screen form files
.FRM	Report format files
.LBL	Label files used to print mailing labels
.MEM	Memory variables files
.NDX	Index files
.QRY	Query files
.SCR	Screen files
.TXT	ASCII text files exported for use by other programs
.VUE	Relationships among files

Setting a Path

If your database files are stored in a subdirectory on a hard disk, you can use the SET PATH TO <*path*> command to have dBASE locate them. For example, if your files are in a directory named DATABASE on drive C, you would type **SET PATH TO C:\DATABASE** and press Enter↵. When entering the path command, separate path names with commas or semicolons and directory names with backslashes. For example, to work with files in a directory named DATABASE on drive A and in the DBASE directory on drive C, type **SET PATH TO A:\DATABASE,C:\DBASE** and press Enter↵.

When you execute a command to open a file, the program first looks to the default drive, and only if it cannot find a file there will it look in the directories specified in the SET PATH TO command. Therefore, if you have two files with the same name, one in the root directory of the default drive and one in a directory listed in the SET PATH TO command, the program opens the one in the root directory of the default drive. SET PATH TO does not affect the DIR command, which lists only files on the default drive.

Opening Database Files

To work with an existing database file, you must first open it with the USE <*filename*> command. For example, to open a file named MEMBERS.DBF, type **USE MEMBERS** and press [Enter←]. (You don't have to specify a filename extension.) This command retrieves the file from the disk into the computer's memory. You can specify a path to the dBASE file or use the command that changes the default drive. If you try to open a file and get the message *File does not exist*, it may be because the file is not on the default drive or you did not specify the correct path.

You can also open files from the Assist menu. To do so, pull down the Set Up menu, highlight *Database File* and press [Enter←]. Highlight the drive that contains the file and press [Enter←] to list database files on the disk. Highlight the name of the file you want to open and press [Enter←]. When the prompt reads *Is the file indexed? [Y/N]*, press [N] for now (you'll learn about indexes later.)

Printing Data

The easiest way to print out the data in a database from the dot prompt is to use the <*command*> TO PRINT command. For example, type **LIST TO PRINT** and press [Enter←] to print out a copy of the data in the open database. (We will see other examples of the LIST command later.)

If you are working on a system that has its own printer, you can also type **SET PRINTER ON** and press [Enter←] or press [Ctrl]-[P]. Both of these commands send everything that appears on the screen to the printer, including the commands that you type. To turn printing off after using one of these commands, you type **SET PRINTER OFF** and press [Enter←] or press [Ctrl]-[P] again. Avoid using either of these commands on shared printers since they tie the printer up, preventing others from making their own printouts.

From the Assist menu, some commands display the prompt *Direct the output to printer? (Y/N)*. When this prompt appears, press [Y] to make a printout.

The EJECT command advances the paper in the printer to the top of the next page. If the paper does not come all the way out of the printer, or if the last line does not print, type **EJECT** from the dot prompt and press [Enter←].

Closing Database Files

Once you open a database file, you must close it before quitting the program or working on another project. If you turn off or reboot the computer without quitting properly, files you have been working on may be damaged and data may be lost. Two commands close files, CLEAR ALL and CLOSE.

The CLEAR Command

The CLEAR ALL command closes all open files and displays the dot prompt so that you can continue working. The dBASE program remains in memory. The CLEAR command used by itself clears the screen and positions the cursor in the lower-left corner.

The CLOSE Command

The CLOSE <*file type*> command is similar to the CLEAR ALL command, but it allows you to close specific types of files. As you will see, you can create index, format, program, and other types of files. To close all these files, including databases, use the CLOSE ALL command, and you achieve the same end as the CLEAR ALL command. To close a specific type of file, you enter the CLOSE command followed by the type of file that you want to close. For example, to close just database files, type **CLOSE DATABASES** and press Enter←. To close INDEX files, type **CLOSE INDEX** and press Enter←. Other files that you can close include ALTERNATE, FORMAT, and PROCEDURE file types.

Quitting dBASE

The QUIT command from the dot prompt removes the dBASE program from memory. To do the same thing from the Assist menu, press S (for ***S**et Up*) to pull down the Set Up menu. Press PgDn to highlight the *Quit dBASE III PLUS* command and press Enter←.

Before quitting, you should use the CLEAR ALL command to be absolutely certain all open database files are closed so that they are not corrupted. Although QUIT is supposed to close the files, sometimes things go wrong and it doesn't. Better to be safe than sorry.

EXERCISES

EXERCISE 1

LOADING dBASE III PLUS ON YOUR SYSTEM

If your dBASE program is on a network or if your system has been customized, your loading procedures may differ from those discussed in this topic. If they do, list the steps that you follow so that you have them for future reference.

1. ____________________
2. ____________________
3. ____________________
4. ____________________
5. ____________________

EXERCISE 2

COPYING STUDENT RESOURCE DISK FILES

In this exercise, you copy files from the original *Student Resource Disk* to your working disk if you have not already done so. The instructions in this exercise assume that you are working on a system where you can display the DOS command prompt. If you are working on a system connected to a network or with a customized menu, you may have to follow different procedures. If this is the case, ask your instructor for help.

1. Load DOS, or quit dBASE, so that the command prompt is displayed.

2. Insert your disks as follows:
   - On a system with only a single floppy disk drive, insert the original *Student Resource Disk* into drive A. (This drive will act as both drive A and B.)
   - On a system with two floppy disk drives, insert the original *Student Resource Disk* into drive A and the disk you want to copy the files to into drive B.
3. Type **A:** and press Enter↵ to make drive A the default drive.
4. Type **CD\DBASE** and press Enter↵ to make the directory named DBASE the default directory.
5. Type **COPY *.* B:** and press Enter↵.
   - On a system with only one floppy disk drive, you will be periodically prompted to swap disks.
   - On a system with two floppy disk drives, the files are listed as they are copied from one drive to the other.
6. When the command prompt reappears, remove the disks.
7. Put the original disk in a safe place, label the new one, and use it to continue with your work.

dBASE III Plus Data Disk
your name
1/01/94
your class

The Disk Label
After copying your dBASE data files to a disk, you should label the new disk so that it doesn't get lost or inadvertently erased.

EXERCISE 3

IDENTIFYING THE ITEMS ON THE SCREEN

1. Load dBASE so that the opening screen is displayed.
2. Turn the printer on.
3. If your instructor approves (this can cause problems on some systems), press ⇧Shift-PrtScr (or just **Print Screen** on an enhanced keyboard) to make a printout of the screen display. Press Esc to display the dot prompt, then type **EJECT** and press Enter↵ to advance the paper out of the printer.
4. Using the figure "The dBASE III Plus Opening Screen" as a guide, identify the items on the printout by circling them and writing a brief description of what they indicate. Graphics characters, like those used in borders, may not print or may print as other characters. If this happens, draw them on your printout or ignore them.

EXERCISE 4

PRACTICING OPENING FILES

In the following topics, it is assumed you know how to load dBASE, change the default drive, and open files. No instructions on these steps are supplied. To be sure you know how to complete these procedures, open the MEMBHOLD, CHARHOLD, EMPLHOLD, and DEPTHOLD files. When each is open, type list and press Enter↵ to display the file's contents. If your instructor approves, type **LIST TO PRINT** and press Enter↵ when one of them is open. (Printing all of them would waste paper.)

TOPIC 2

Executing Commands

After completing this topic, you will be able to:

- Enter commands from the dot prompt
- Use the HISTORY command to repeat commands that you entered previously
- Select commands from the Assist menu that is displayed with the ASSIST command
- Execute commands with function keys
- Display on-line help with the HELP command
- Turn help menus on and off with the SET MENU ON/OFF commands

You can operate dBASE III Plus by typing commands from the dot prompt, by choosing commands from Assist menus, and by pressing function keys. All of dBASE's commands can be typed from the dot prompt, much as you type commands from the DOS command prompt. Many commands can be chosen from the program's pull-down Assist menus. And a few of the most frequently used commands are assigned to function keys so that you can execute them with a single keystroke. On-line help is available whenever the dot prompt or Assist menus are displayed.

DOT-PROMPT TUTORIAL

THE DISK TO USE

Beginning with this tutorial, you use the data disk to which you copied files from the original *Student Resource Disk* in Exercise 2 of Topic 1. If you have not completed that exercise, you must do so before you continue.

In this tutorial, you execute commands by typing them at the dot prompt and by pressing function keys. You also explore dBASE's help system so that you can find help on commands when working on your own.

GETTING STARTED

1. Load dBASE III Plus into the computer's memory.
2. Press Esc to remove the Assist menu and display the dot prompt.

OPENING A FILE

3. Insert the data disk on which you store your database files as follows:
   - On a hard disk system, insert the disk into drive A.
   - On a floppy disk system, insert the disk into drive B.
4. Set the default drive as follows:
   - On a hard disk system, type **SET DEFAULT TO A:** and press

Enter↵ to make drive A the default drive.

- On a floppy disk system, type **SET DEFAULT TO B:** and press Enter↵ to make drive B the default drive.

5. Type **USE OVERVIEW** and press Enter↵ to open the database file.

EXPLORING HELP

6. Type **HELP** and press Enter↵ to display the Help Main menu.

The Help Menu
When you type **HELP** and press Enter↵, the Help Main menu is displayed. For help on a listed topic, press the number that precedes it.

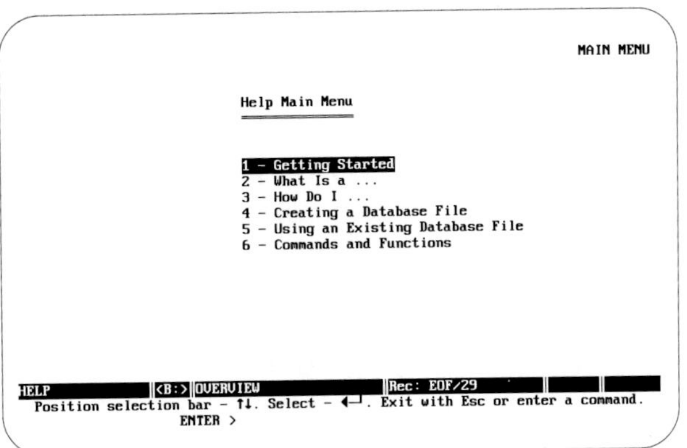

7. Press 1 to select *Getting Started* and execute the command.
8. Press PgDn to scroll through help screens until the computer beeps.
9. Press PgUp the same number of times to scroll back to the Help Main menu.
10. Press ↓ to highlight *3 – How Do I ...* and press Enter↵ to execute the command.
11. Press ↓ to highlight *2 – Turn the Printer On/Off* and press Enter↵.
12. Press F10 twice to back up through previously chosen menus.
13. Continue experimenting on your own until you are comfortable using the help system. Commands that you can use are always listed at the bottom of the screen.
14. When you have finished, press Esc to return to the dot prompt.
15. Type **HELP ASSIST** and press Enter↵ to display help on the Assist menu, and the prompt at the bottom of the screen reads *ENTER* > so that you can get help on other commands.

HELP Commands
When you type **HELP** followed by a command such as **ASSIST**, help on that specific command is displayed. The prompt *ENTER*> at the bottom of the screen lets you type the names of other commands on which you want help.

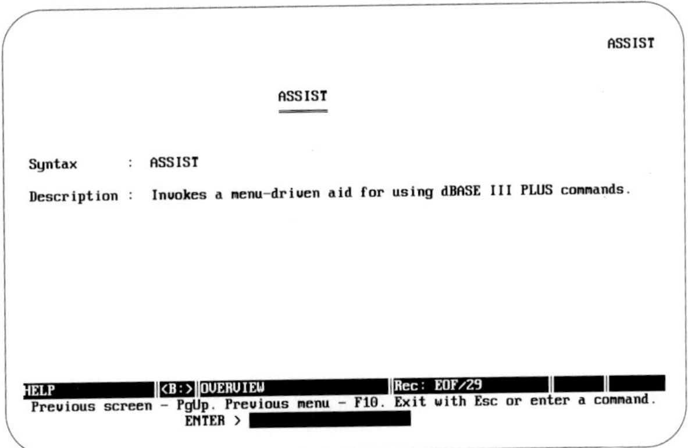

16. Type **QUIT** and press Enter↵ to display help on the QUIT command.

17. Type **CLEAR** and press [Enter←] to display help on the CLEAR command.
18. Type **USE** and press [Enter←] to display help on the USE command.
19. Press [Esc] to return to the dot prompt.
20. Type **HELP LIST** and press [Enter←] for help on the LIST command.
21. Press [Esc] to return to the dot prompt.
22. Type **HELP SET DEFAULT** and press [Enter←] to display help on the command you use to change the default drive.
23. Press [Esc] to return to the dot prompt.

EXPLORING THE HISTORY COMMAND

24. Type **DISPLAY HISTORY** and press [Enter←] to display a list of the commands you have entered previously.

    Depending on how many commands you have typed, the prompt may read *Press any key to continue.* If this prompt is displayed, press any key to display the rest of the commands and return to the dot prompt.
25. Press [↑] to display the last command you entered; then press it a few more times to display other commands one after another.
26. Press [↓] to back up through the commands that you have just scrolled through.
27. Display the command *DISPLAY HISTORY* following the dot prompt.
28. Use the arrow keys and [Del] to revise the command so that it reads *DISP HIST.*
29. Press [Enter←] to execute the revised command.

    The command works just as it did in Step 24 even though it contains only the first four characters from each word. This is true for all dBASE commands. You can abbreviate each word in the command to four or more letters. If the prompt reads *Press any key to continue*, press any key to display the rest of the commands and return to the dot prompt.

EXECUTING COMMANDS WITH FUNCTION KEYS

30. Press [F3] to list the records in the open OVERVIEW database file.
31. Press [F4] to display a list of database files on the default drive.

A List of Database Files
Pressing [F4] displays a list of the database files on the disk in the default drive.

```
(DEMO) . dir
Database Files    # Records    Last Update    Size
BIBLHOLD.DBF              0    10/24/91        354
CHARHOLD.DBF             12    03/04/92        498
COMPHOLD.DBF             30    10/24/91       4584
DEPTHOLD.DBF             20    03/05/92        522
EMPLHOLD.DBF             10    03/06/92       1546
MEMBHOLD.DBF             10    10/16/91       1536
OVERVIEW.DBF             15    03/04/92       1025
SALEHOLD.DBF             18    10/24/91        946
TITLHOLD.DBF              9    10/17/91        852
WRONG.DBF                10    03/05/92       1166

  13029 bytes in     10 files.
1230848 bytes remaining on drive.

(DEMO) .
Command Line    |<A:>|OVERVIEW          |Rec: EOF/15     |     |   Caps

                  Enter a dBASE III PLUS command.
```

32. Press [F5] to display the open database file's structure.

33. Press [F6] to display the current status of the program, and the prompt reads *Press any key to continue.*
34. Press any key to display the status of many commands and function key assignments and return to the dot prompt.
35. Type **GOTO TOP** and press [Enter←].
36. Press [F8] to display the current record, in this case, Record #1.

EXPLORING THE HELP MENU

37. Type **SET MENU ON** and press [Enter←].
38. Type **BROWSE** and press [Enter←] to display a help menu at the top of the screen.
39. Press [Esc] to return to the dot prompt.
40. Type **SET MENU OFF** and press [Enter←].
41. Press [↑] twice to display the BROWSE command following the dot prompt (if you overshoot the command, just press [↓] to return to it) and press [Enter←] to see that the help menu is no longer displayed at the top of the screen.
42. Press [F1] a few times to turn the menu on and off with a function key.
43. Press [Esc] to return to the dot prompt.

FINISHING UP

44. Type **CLEAR ALL** and press [Enter←] to close the open file.
45. You have completed this tutorial. Either continue to the next activity or quit the program. If you quit the program, remove your disks and turn off the computer.

ASSIST-MENU TUTORIAL

In this tutorial, you execute commands using the Assist menus.

GETTING STARTED

1. Load dBASE III Plus into the computer's memory.
2. If the Assist menu is not displayed at the top of the screen, type **ASSIST** and press [Enter←].

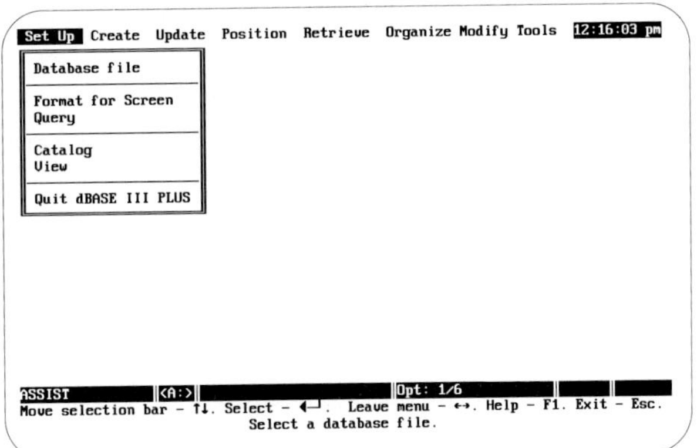

The Assist Menus
Typing **ASSIST** and pressing [Enter←] displays the Assist menus.

3. Insert the data disk on which you store your database files as follows:
   - On a hard disk system, insert the disk into drive A.
   - On a floppy disk system, insert the disk into drive B.

EXPLORING THE ASSIST MENUS

4. Pull down each of the Assist menus, first by pressing the first letter in the menu's name and then by pressing [←] or [→] to move the highlight along the menu bar.
5. Press [T] to pull down the Tools menu.

The Tools Menu
You can pull down any Assist menu by pressing the first letter in its name or by highlighting it and pressing [Enter←┘].

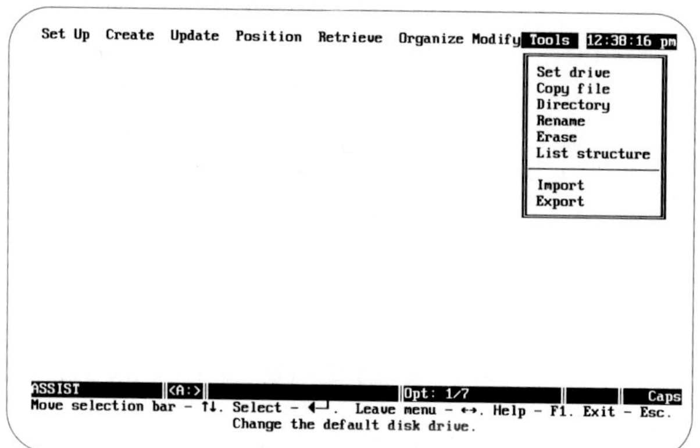

6. Press [↓] and [↑] to move the cursor down and up the list of commands and display a brief description of each on the message line.
7. Press [F1] for help on the currently highlighted command.
8. Press [Esc] to return to the Assist menus.

SETTING THE DEFAULT DRIVE

9. Highlight *Set drive* and press [Enter←┘] to display a list of your system's drives.
10. Highlight *A:* (on a hard disk system) or *B:* (on a floppy disk system) and press [Enter←┘] to change the default drive and return to the Tools menu.
11. Highlight *Directory* and press [Enter←┘] to display a submenu listing your computer's disk drives.
12. Highlight *A:* (on a hard disk system) or *B:* (on a floppy disk system) and press [Enter←┘] to specify the drive you want a directory for and to display a list of filename specifications.
13. Highlight *.* All Files* and press [Enter←┘] to display a list of all files on the default drive and the prompt *Press any key to continue work in ASSIST.*
14. Press any key to return to the Assist menus.

OPENING A FILE

15. Press [S] to pull down the Set Up menu.
16. Highlight *Database file* and press [Enter←┘].
17. Highlight *A:* (on a hard disk system) or *B:* (on a floppy disk system) and press [Enter←┘] to display a list of the files on the disk.

18. Highlight *OVERVIEW.DBF* and press [Enter↵]. The prompt reads *Is the file indexed? [Y/N].*
19. Press [N] and the file's name is displayed on the status line indicating that it is now open.

LISTING RECORDS IN THE FILE

20. Press [R] to pull down the Retrieve menu.
21. Highlight *List* and press [Enter↵].
22. Highlight *Execute the command* and press [Enter↵]. The prompt reads *Direct the output to the printer? [Y/N].*
23. Press [N] to list the records on the screen, and the prompt reads *Press any key to continue work in ASSIST.*

Listing Records in the File
The List command on the Retrieve menu lists all the records in the open database file.

```
Set Up  Create  Update  Position  Retrieve  Organize Modify Tools  10:42:26 am

Record#  INVOICE DATE_ORD DATE_OUT PRODUCT      MODEL  PRICE  QTY TESTED
      1  1001    01/03/93 01/04/93 Computer      2006   999.50   2 .T.
      2  1002    01/03/93 01/05/93 Printer        121   100.50   3 .T.
      3  1003    01/03/93 01/03/93 Computer      2006   999.50   1 .T.
      4  1004    01/04/93 01/05/93 Modem         1111   175.00   5 .F.
      5  1005    01/04/93 01/06/93 Monitor        390   500.00   2 .F.
      6  1006    01/05/93 01/05/93 Network card  1258   375.00   5 .F.
      7  1007    01/05/93 01/09/93 Modem         1111   175.00   1 .F.
      8  1008    01/05/93 01/05/93 Tape backup    238   350.00   4 .F.
      9  1009    01/05/93 01/07/93 Keyboard      3456   125.00   4 .F.
     10  1010    01/06/93 01/06/93 Hard disk       35   650.00  10 .F.
     11  1011    01/06/93 01/09/93 CD-ROM         789   500.00   2 .F.
     12  1012    01/06/93 01/07/93 Printer        121   100.50   5 .T.
     13  1013    01/06/93 01/07/93 Monitor        390   500.00   7 .F.
     14  1014    01/07/93 01/07/93 Computer      1010  1250.99  10 .T.
     15  1015    01/07/93 01/10/93 Printer       121    100.50  20 .F.
ASSIST          <A:> OVERVIEW               Rec: 1/15
                Press any key to continue work in ASSIST.
```

24. Press any key to return to the Assist menus.

DISPLAYING THE FILE'S STRUCTURE

25. Press [T] to pull down the Tools menu.
26. Highlight *List structure* and press [Enter↵]. The prompt reads *Direct the output to the printer? [Y/N].*
27. Press [N] to list the file's structure on the screen, and the prompt reads *Press any key to continue work in ASSIST.*

Listing the File's Structure
The List Structure command on the Tools menu displays a description of the open database file so that you know what fields it contains and what type each of them is.

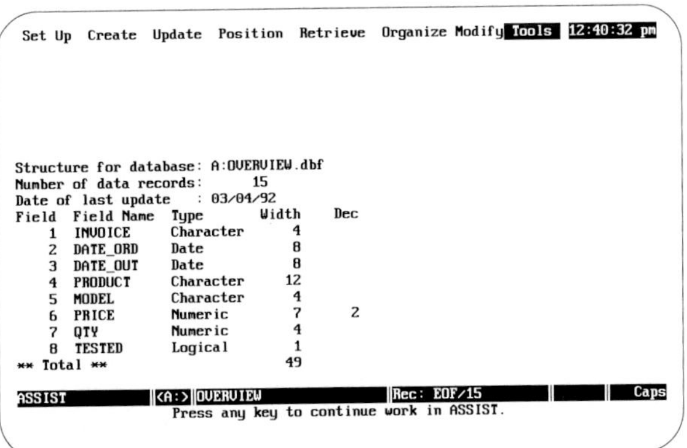

28. Press any key to return to the Assist menus.

FINISHING UP

29. Press [Esc] to display the dot prompt.
30. Type **CLEAR ALL** and press [Enter←] to close the open file.
31. You have completed this tutorial. Either continue to the next activity or quit the program. If you quit the program, remove your disks and turn off the computer.

QUICK REFERENCE

You can execute all commands by typing them from the dot prompt. Many commands can also be executed from the Assist menu, and some can be executed from function keys. At all times, help is available on line should you need it.

Entering Commands from the Dot Prompt

The dot prompt is displayed when the Assist menu isn't. If the menu is displayed, press [Esc] to display the dot prompt. You enter a command at the dot prompt following the rules described here and then press [Enter←] to execute it.

- You can type commands in uppercase letters, lowercase letters, or any combination of the two. For example, to quit the program, you can type **QUIT**, **quit**, or **Quit**.
- Each command must begin with a command verb—for example, DISPLAY, SET, CLEAR, HELP.
- Each command must follow a particular syntax. For example, to display help on the DISPLAY command, you type **HELP DISPLAY** not **HELP ON DISPLAY**.
- Commands can be as long as 254 characters (including spaces).
- Words within a command can be separated by one or more blank spaces.
- When typing longer commands, you need type only the first four characters of each word. For example, typing **DISPLAY STRUCTURE** and **DISP STRU** give the same result.

To edit a command at the dot prompt, use the arrow keys to move the cursor through the characters, press [Ins] to toggle insert mode on and off, or use [Del] and [←Bksp] to delete characters. When you have the command the way you want it, press [Enter←] to execute it.

If you incorrectly enter a command, the program displays an error message and often displays the prompt *Do you want some help? (Y/N).* Press [Y] for help or [N] to return to the dot prompt.

The most frequently used commands are assigned to function keys. The table "dBASE Function Keys" describes these commands.

The HISTORY Command

dBASE keeps your latest 20 commands in memory so that you can repeat them without retyping. To scroll through them from the latest to the earliest, press [↑] when the dot prompt is displayed. Then, to scroll back, press [↓]. When the command you want to repeat is displayed, press [Enter←] to execute it. Remember that you can edit a command on the dot prompt before pressing [Enter←] to execute it.

dBASE FUNCTION KEYS

Key	Command
F1	HELP
F2	ASSIST
F3	LIST
F4	DIR
F5	DISPLAY STRUCTURE
F6	DISPLAY STATUS
F7	DISPLAY MEMORY
F8	DISPLAY
F9	APPEND
F10	EDIT

To change the number of commands the program stores in memory, type **SET HISTORY TO** *<number>* (that is, the number of commands you want stored) and press Enter←.

To display the currently stored commands, type **DISPLAY HISTORY** and press Enter←.

Help
To obtain help when the dot prompt is displayed, use the HELP *<command>* command. For example, for help on the ASSIST command, type **HELP ASSIST** and press Enter←. To look for help on less specific topics, press F1 or type **HELP** without specifying a command and press Enter←. When the Help Main menu is displayed, you can use the commands described in the table "Help Main Menu Commands" to display help on selected topics.

If you enter a command incorrectly, dBASE displays the prompt *Do you want some help? (Y/N)*. If this prompt appears, press Y to display help on the command.

To display or hide help on available keys and commands when performing such operations as browsing records in a file, defining a database, or entering records, press F1 or use the SET MENU ON or SET MENU OFF command.

HELP MAIN MENU COMMANDS

To	Press
Make selection from the Help Main menu	↑ or ↓ to highlight choice, then press Enter← (or the number preceding the desired choice)
Display previous menu (if any)	F10
Display next screen (if any)	PgDn
Display previous screen (if any)	PgUp
Display help on specific command when the prompt reads *ENTER>*	Type the command and press Enter←
Return to dot prompt	Esc

Entering Commands from the Assist Menu
You can execute many but not all commands by making selections from the Assist menu's pull-down menus. To display the Assist menu bar when the dot prompt is displayed, type **ASSIST** and press Enter← or just press F2. One menu is always pulled down.

- To pull down another menu, either press the first letter in its name or press → or ← to highlight it. (Press Home or End to move the cursor to the first or last choice on the menu bar.)
- To make a choice from a pulled-down menu, press ↓ or ↑ to move the highlight between choices. As you do so, the message line displays a brief description of the highlighted choice. You will notice that you cannot highlight choices that are dimmed. These commands are not available from where you are in the program. When you have highlighted the desired choice, press Enter←
- To obtain help, highlight the command on which you want help; then press F1 to display help.

■ To remove the Assist menu from the screen and return to the dot prompt, press [Esc].

The Assist Menus
When the Assist menus are displayed, you can pull down any of the menus and execute a listed command by highlighting it and pressing [Enter ↵].

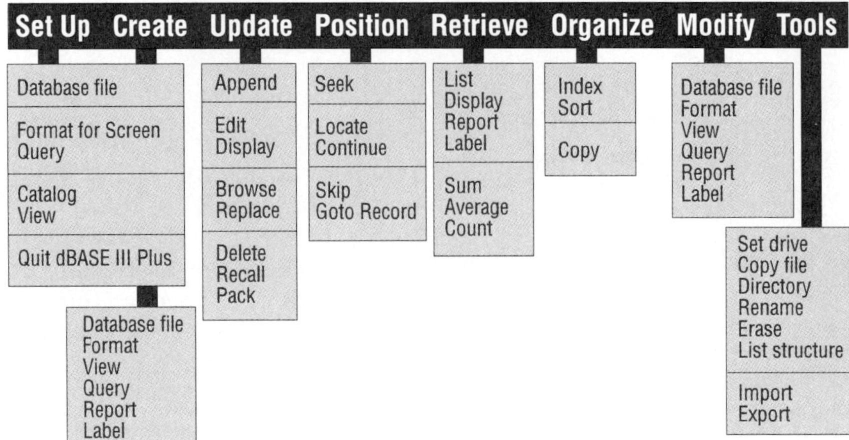

EXERCISES

EXERCISE 1

EXPLORING HELP

Load dBASE III Plus. From the dot prompt, type **HELP HELP** and press [Enter ↵]. When the prompt reads *ENTER* >, press each of the function keys listed in the first column of the table "Help Screens." In the second column, list the title of the help screen that is displayed. When you have finished, exit help and return to the dot prompt.

HELP SCREENS

Key(s)	Description
[F2]	________________
[F3]	________________
[F4]	________________
[F5]	________________
[F6]	________________
[F7]	________________
[F8]	________________
[F9]	________________
[F10]	________________

EXERCISE 2

LOCATING COMMANDS ON PULL-DOWN MENUS

Pull down menus and locate the commands listed in the Command column of the table "Menu Choices." In the Menu column, write down the name of the pull-down menu on which the command is listed. Using help commands, write down a brief description of what each command is used for in the Function column.

MENU CHOICES

Command	Menu	Function
APPEND	________	____________
BROWSE	________	____________
DELETE	________	____________
DIRECTORY	________	____________
DISPLAY	________	____________
EDIT	________	____________
GOTO RECORD	________	____________
INDEX	________	____________
LIST STRUCTURE	________	____________
PACK	________	____________
SET DRIVE	________	____________
SKIP	________	____________
SORT	________	____________

CHAPTER 1 REVIEW

- A database is one or more files that contain an organized body of data.
- To create and use a database, you use a record management program or a database management program. Record management programs can work only with single files. Database management programs can work with one or more files at the same time.
- dBASE is a relational database program, which means that it stores data in tables. These tables can be related to one another so that you can work with more than one at a time.
- Fields are individual pieces of information such as a phone number, a first name, a street address, or a price.
- Records are collections of fields that describe a person, thing, or activity.
- To work with a database file, you must first open the file. This copies the data from the file on the disk into the computer's memory. With dBASE, you open files with the USE <*filename*> command.
- To change the default drive with dBASE, you use the SET DEFAULT TO <*drive*> command.
- To specify that dBASE look for files on a path other than the default, you use the SET PATH TO <*drive:\directory*> command.
- To list database files on the disk, you use the DIR command. To list all files, you use the DIR *.* command.
- To print the records in a file, you can use the LIST TO PRINT command. You can also use the SET PRINT ON command to print most listings that appear on the screen and then use the SET PRINT OFF command when you want printing to cease.
- To remove files from memory, you use the CLEAR ALL or CLOSE <*file type*> command.
- To quit dBASE, you use the QUIT command from the dot prompt or the *Quit dBASE III Plus* command on the Assist menu's File menu.
- You can press [↑] to scroll though the earlier commands. When the one you want is displayed, you can press [Enter←] to execute it again or edit it before you press [Enter←].
- To display the Help Main menu, you type **HELP** from the dot prompt. For help on a specific command, type **HELP** <*command*>. Pressing [F1] also displays help at many points in the program.
- To remove the Assist menu and display the dot prompt, press [Esc].
- To display the Assist menu, type **ASSIST** at the dot prompt and press [Enter←] or simply press [F2].

CHAPTER 1

QUESTIONS

FILL IN THE BLANK

1. The main difference between a database management program and a record management program is that the database management program can work with __________ file.
2. If you use the SET PRINT ON command to begin printing, you then use the __________ command to stop printing.
3. The individual pieces of data that make up a record are called __________.
4. To open a dBASE file named PAYROLL, you would use the command __________.
5. To change the default drive to drive A, you would use the command __________.
6. To list the database files on the disk, you would use the command __________.
7. To close all open files, you could enter the command __________ or the command __________.
8. To quit dBASE, you enter the __________ command.
9. To repeat a command that you entered previously from the dot prompt, you use the __________ command.
10. To scroll through previously entered commands, you press __________.
11. To display the Help Main menu from the dot prompt, type __________ or press __________.
12. To display specific help on the SET command, you would type __________.
13. To display the Assist menu when the dot prompt is displayed, you would type __________ and then press __________.
14. To remove the Assist menu and return to the dot prompt, you would press __________.

MATCH THE COLUMNS

1. Record management program
2. Database management program
3. QUIT command
4. USE command
5. CLEAR ALL command

__ Command to exit the program
__ A database that organizes data into tables
__ A program that can work with multiple files
__ Displays the Help Main menu
__ Opens a database file
__ A description of a person or thing
__ A program that can work only with a single file
__ A single file (as opposed to a database)
__ Changes the default drive

6. Relational database
7. Record file
8. Field
9. Record
10. SET DEFAULT TO
11. LIST TO PRINT
12. ASSIST
13. HELP
14. HELP ASSIST
15. ↑
16. SET MENU ON
17. Database
18. Esc

__ Displays help on the Assist menu
__ Turns on the help menu
__ Displays previous commands from the dot prompt
__ One or more files of related information
__ One part of a record
__ Prints out the records in open file
__ Removes databases from memory
__ Displays the Assist menu
__ Removes the Assist menu and displays the dot prompt

WRITE OUT THE ANSWERS

1. Define the term *database*.
2. Explain the main difference between a record management program and a database management program.
3. What are two or three disadvantages to using a record management program instead of a database management program?
4. What is a database model? Which model is most frequently used for programs that run on microcomputers?
5. What are columns and rows called when discussed in the context of a relational database table?
6. What is a field? A record? Give examples of each.
7. List the steps you would follow to load dBASE from a floppy disk.
8. List the steps you would follow to load dBASE from a hard disk.
9. In what three ways can you execute dBASE commands?
10. What purpose does the Assist menu serve?
11. To display the Help Main menu, what command would you enter?
12. Describe how you display help when you are working from the Assist menu.
13. When you want to quit a dBASE session, what task must you first perform? Why?
14. How do you select a choice from a pull-down menu?

CHAPTER 1

PROJECTS

PROJECT 1

VIEWING A VIDEO

Many videocassettes about dBASE III Plus are available. Obtain one of these from your school or public library or from a video rental store, and watch it. These videos give you an overview of the procedures offered by the program.

PROJECT 2

EXPLORING THE TITLES DATABASE

The *Student Resource Disk* contains a file named TITLHOLD. This file contains a listing of the titles in a book publisher's catalog. The file contains the ISBN (a unique number assigned by the publisher in cooperation with the Library of Congress to each book that is published) along with the book's title, author, edition, version, list price, and the category in which the publisher places it. Open this file and list its records to the printer.

PROJECT 3

EXPLORING THE SALES DATABASE

The *Student Resource Disk* contains a file named SALEHOLD. This file contains the sales in various markets for the titles listed in the TITLHOLD file. Open this file and list its records to the printer.

CHAPTER 2

Creating & Editing Database Files

TOPIC 3

Defining a Database File's Structure

After completing this topic, you will be able to:

- Explain how to plan a database
- Define a database file with the CREATE command
- Describe the different field types available
- Print out a file's structure with the DISPLAY STRUCTURE command

The first step in using a database management program is to plan the file you want to store data in. You then use dBASE's CREATE command to define it. When you define the database, you specify the field names each record is to contain, the maximum width of the data to be entered in each field, and the type of data each field will hold. You can specify fields that store characters, numbers to be calculated, dates, and so on.

As you plan a database, you should make sure you know what types of questions you want to have answered by the data. The number of fields you set up depends on the amount of data you want to store and how you want to manipulate it. For example, if you used only one field for both first and last names and then entered names like John Smith, Betty Lewis, and Roger Wentworth, your file would be limited. You could not sort names based on last names. You might not even be able to find a particular record. To sort persons' names, you set up two fields, one for first names and one for last names. The same principle holds for addresses. For example, if you do not enter ZIP codes in a separate field, you will not be able to sort records by ZIP codes.

Designing a relational database requires very careful planning because it can contain two or more interrelated tables of data. Ideally, each table should have a field that contains information that uniquely identifies each record in the table. If two or more tables have identical fields such as this, they can be used to link the tables for many operations. Fields containing data such as last names will normally not suffice because if the database gets large enough, there will almost certainly be duplication in names. For example, if a field contains two or more Jones, that field can no longer uniquely identify the records. Many kinds of data can uniquely identify records, including:

- Social security numbers
- Part numbers
- Serial numbers
- Vehicle license numbers
- Driver's license numbers
- Bank account numbers
- Dates and times
- Customer account numbers
- Employee serial numbers
- Purchase order numbers
- Telephone numbers
- Credit card numbers
- Policy numbers

Planning a Database
When planning a database, you list the fields you want to include for each record. You then plan the name of each field, its type, and its width. If you want to be able to join the files, one of the fields must be common to both files. For example, in this database for the Ever Hopeful Health Club, we plan to have two files: one to list member names and addresses and another to list charges they make at the club store. The common field, or key attribute, that joins the two files in the database is the ID field.

FIELD	FIELD NAME	TYPE	WIDTH	DEC
Member's ID number	ID	Character	3	-
Member's last name	LASTNAME	Character	15	-
Member's first name	FIRST	Character	15	-
Street address	STREET	Character	17	-
City	CITY	Character	10	-
State	ST	Character	2	-
ZIP code	ZIP	Character	5	-
Area code	AREA	Character	3	-
Phone number	PHONE	Character	8	-
Date enrolled	ENROLLED	Date	8	-
Age	AGE	Numeric	2	0
Any comments	REMARKS	Memo	10	-

A The MEMBERS File

FIELD	FIELD NAME	TYPE	WIDTH	DEC
Member's ID number	ID	Character	3	-
Date a charge is made	DATE	Date	8	-
The amount of the charge	AMOUNT	Numeric	6	2
Has check cleared?	CLEARED	Logical	1	-

B The CHARGES File

DOT-PROMPT TUTORIAL

Two recent college graduates who were interested in physical conditioning together started the Ever Hopeful Health Club. One of their first management steps was to create a database in which they could store their members' names and addresses. Their plan was to use this database to prepare mailings on special events. In this tutorial, you define the MEMBERS database file that stores names, addresses, and phone numbers for members of the Ever Hopeful Health Club.

GETTING OUT OF TROUBLE

Before proceeding, review the following ways for getting out of trouble:

- Press [F1] to display help.
- Press [Esc] to cancel commands and return to the dot prompt.
- Press [←Bksp] to delete characters to the cursor's left if you make a mistake when entering commands or data.

GETTING STARTED

1. Display the dot prompt and set the default drive to the one that contains your data disk.

CREATING A NEW FILE

2. Type **CREATE MEMBERS** and press [Enter←] to display the screen used to define a file.
   - In the upper-right corner, an indicator shows how many bytes of memory are available for your file.
   - Below the line with the bytes-remaining indicator is a help screen that lists the commands you can use when defining the file. You press [F1] to turn this help screen off and on.
   - Across the center of the screen are two sets of four columns used to define fields. The cursor is blinking in the first column with the heading *Field Name*.
   - The status line at the bottom of the screen displays the current command (*CREATE*), the default drive, the name of the file you are creating, and the position of the cursor by field.

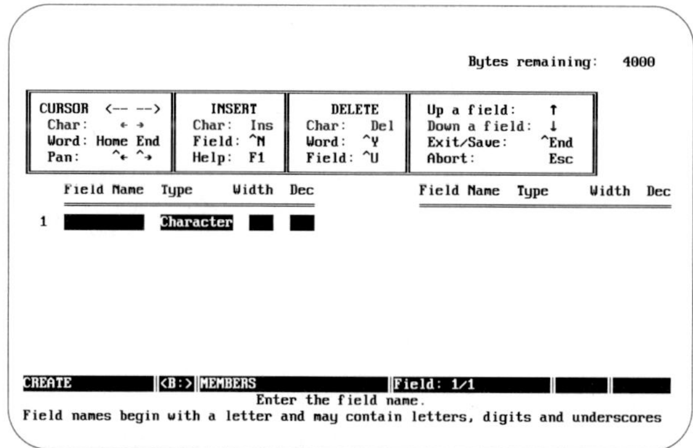

The Database Definition Screen
The CREATE <*filename*> command displays the database definition screen. Each row is used to specify the field's name, type, width, and decimals (if any).

DEFINING THE FILE

3. When you start to define a database file, the cursor should be at the left of the column with the *Field Name* highlighted. The number (*1*) at the far left indicates which field you are defining. To enter field definitions, refer to the table "The MEMBERS File Structure," and follow these procedures:
   - **Field Names**. Type the field's name (all field names are displayed in uppercase characters regardless of the case you use to enter them) and press [Enter←] to move the cursor to the *Type* column.
   - **Field Types**. If you are defining a character field, and the entry reads *Character*, press [Enter←] to leave the type unchanged and move the cursor to the *Width* column. To define a field as other than character, press s to cycle through the available field types. When the field type you want to use is displayed, press [Enter←] to move the cursor to the *Width* column.
   - **Field Widths**. The width depends partly on the field type:
     - When you select *Character*, the cursor moves to the next field so that you can enter the field's width. After entering the

width, press [Enter ↵] to move to the next field.

- When you select *Date* or *Memo*, widths are set automatically, and the cursor moves to the next field.
- When you select *Numeric*, the cursor moves to the next column so that you can enter the field's width. After entering a total width, press [Enter ↵] to move to the next column to enter the portion of the total width that is to be to the right of the decimal point.

THE MEMBERS FILE STRUCTURE

Field	Field Name	Type	Width	Dec
1	ID	Character	3	-
2	LASTNAME	Character	15	-
3	FIRST	Character	15	-
4	STREET	Character	17	-
5	CITY	Character	10	-
6	ST	Character	2	-
7	ZIP	Character	5	-
8	AREA	Character	3	-
9	PHONE	Character	8	-
10	ENROLLED	Date	8	-
11	AGE	Numeric	2	0
12	REMARKS	Memo	10	-

Carefully check your entries against the figure "The Completed MEMBERS File Structure." If you find an error in your definition, move the cursor to the error and correct it.

The Completed MEMBERS File Structure
When you have finished defining the MEMBERS file, your screen should look like this.

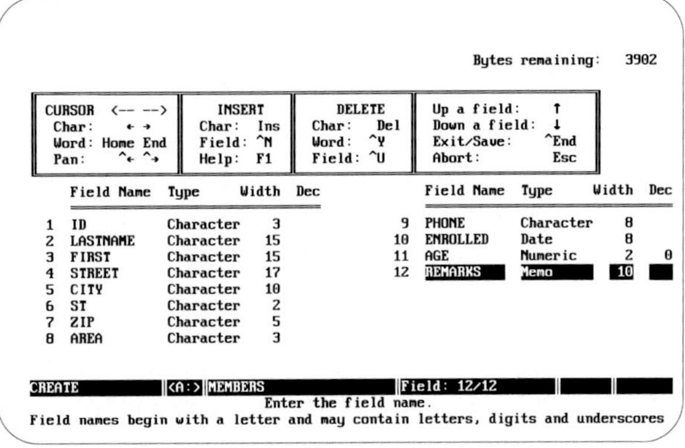

4. Press [Ctrl]-[End] to save the file, and the prompt reads *Press ENTER to confirm. Any other key to resume.*
5. Press [Enter ↵], and in a moment, the prompt reads *Input data records now? (Y/N).*
6. Press [Y] to display a screen into which you enter records. Next to each field name are highlights indicating the field's width. The current field, the one you enter data into when you type, contains the cursor.

The MEMBERS Screen
After defining the MEMBERS file, you can display a blank form to enter a record.

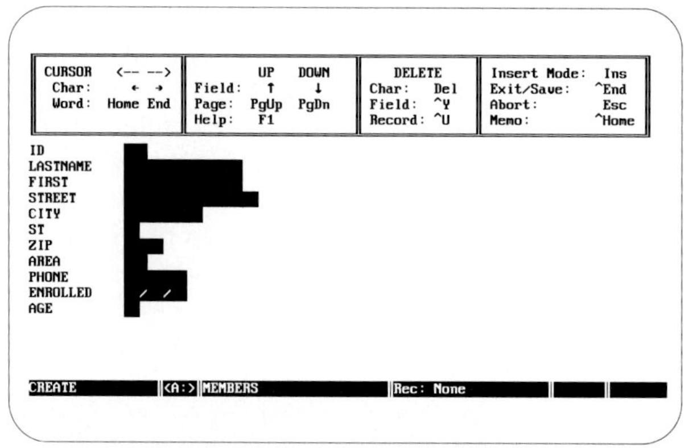

FILE	MEMBERS.DBF
RECORD #	1
ID	122
Last name	Kelly
First name	Jim
Street	12 Preston Beach
City	Orlando
ST	FL
ZIP	32800
Area Code	407
Phone number	555-1011
Date enrolled	01/10/93
Age	26

FILE	MEMBERS.DBF
RECORD #	2
ID	123
Last name	Dougherty
First name	Suzanne
Street	10100 Hardy
City	Los Gatos
ST	CA
ZIP	95031
Area Code	415
Phone number	555-1013
Date enrolled	02/12/93
Age	27

Records to Add to the MEMBERS File
This figure shows the two records that you add to the MEMBERS file.

7. To enter data into the file, refer to the figure "Records to Add to the MEMBERS File" and the following steps.
   - After you complete a field entry, press Enter↵ to move the cursor to the beginning of the next field. If the number of characters you enter equals the field width, the cursor automatically moves to the next field.
   - Type in the data exactly as shown in the two figures. Uppercase and lowercase letters are important because you will look for data, and the program is case sensitive. For example, if you enter *Ca* and later look for *CA*, the program will not find it.
   - If you make a mistake when making an entry, press ←Bksp to delete it, and then correctly reenter it.
   - Enter dates in the format MM/DD/YY. If you enter two digits for each part of the date, you do not have to enter the slashes. If you enter only one digit, you do. For example, you can enter the date January 10, 1993, as **011093** or as **1/10/93**.
   - After entering data into the next to last field (*AGE*), in the first record press PgDn to display a new blank record.

CHECKING AND EDITING YOUR RECORDS

8. After entering both records, press PgUp and PgDn to scroll through them. Don't press PgDn when a blank record form is displayed, or you may be returned to the dot prompt. If this happens, just type **APPEND** and press Enter↵ to display a blank form. Then press PgUp to see the last record in the file in which you entered data. Carefully check your data against the figures for the two records. If you find mistakes in a record, use the arrow keys to move to the mistake, and then edit it with these basic commands:
   - Press Ins to toggle insert mode on and off. When on, *Ins* is displayed on the status line and characters you type push existing characters to the right. When off, characters you type are typed over any existing characters.
   - Press Del to delete the character the cursor is under, or press ←Bksp to delete the character to the left of the cursor.
9. With either record 1 or 2 displayed, press Ctrl-End to save your work and return to the dot prompt. (If a blank record was displayed when you used this command, that blank record would also be saved.)

LISTING AND PRINTING THE FILE'S STRUCTURE AND CONTENTS

10. Type **LIST STRUCTURE** and press [Enter ↵].

The MEMBERS File Structure
The LIST STRUCTURE command displays the structure of the open file.

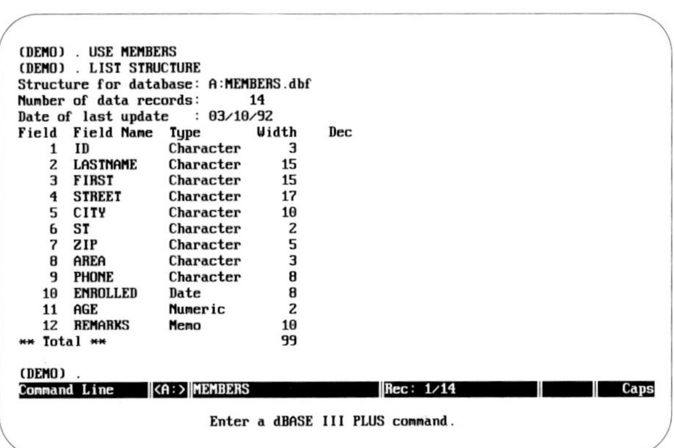

11. Type **LIST STRUCTURE TO PRINT** and press [Enter ↵]. Compare your printout with the figure "The Completed MEMBERS File Structure" to be sure they match. If your database does not match ours, you'll learn how to correct it in the next topic.
12. Type **LIST TO PRINT** and press [Enter ↵]. Compare your printout with the figures in this text for the two records you entered to be sure they match. If your database does not match ours, you'll learn how to correct it in the next topic.

FINISHING UP

13. You have completed this tutorial. Either close all open files and continue to the next activity or quit the program.

ASSIST-MENU TUTORIAL

After creating the MEMBERS file to store member names and addresses, the partners decided that their database could be much more useful. Therefore, they decided to create a file in which to store charges their members made at the club. Since they are using a relational database, they need not enter names and addresses in this new file if it also contains a field that lists members' ID numbers. Since the MEMBERS file also contains the members' ID numbers, charges logged into the new file by ID number can be linked to the member's name and address in the MEMBERS file whenever bills or statement are prepared. In this tutorial, you use the Assist menu to define the CHARGES database file that stores charges made by members of the Ever Hopeful Health Club.

GETTING STARTED

1. Insert your data disk into one of the floppy disk drives.
2. Display the Assist menus and set the default drive to the one into which you inserted your data disk.

CREATING A NEW FILE

3. Press [C] to pull down the Create menu.
4. Highlight *Database file* and press [Enter←] to display a list of the system's drives.
5. Highlight the letter of the drive in which you inserted your data disk and press [Enter←]. The prompt reads *Enter the name of the file:*.
6. Type **CHARGES** and press [Enter←] to display the screen used to define a file.

DEFINING THE FILE

7. When you start to define a database file, the cursor should be at the left of the column with the *Field Name* highlighted. The number (*1*) at the far left indicates which field you are defining. To enter field definitions, refer to the table "The CHARGES File Structure," and follow these procedures:
   - **Field Names**. Type the field's name and press [Enter←] to move the cursor to the *Type* column.
   - **Field Types**. If you are defining a character field, and the entry reads *Character*, press [Enter←] to leave the type unchanged and move the cursor to the *Width* column. To define a field as other than character, press [Spacebar] to cycle through the available field types. When the field type you want to use is displayed, press [Enter←] to move the cursor to the *Width* column.
   - **Field Widths**. The width depends partly on the field type:
     - When you select *Character*, the cursor moves to the next field so that you can enter the field's width. After entering the width, press [Enter←] to move to the next field.
     - When you select *Date* or *Logical*, widths are set automatically, and the cursor moves to the next field.
     - When you select *Numeric*, the cursor moves to the next column so that you can enter the field's width. After entering a total width, press [Enter←] to move to the next column to enter the portion of the total width that is to be to the right of the decimal point.

THE CHARGES FILE STRUCTURE

Field	Field Name	Type	Width	Dec
1	ID	Character	3	-
2	DATE	Date	8	-
3	AMOUNT	Numeric	6	2
4	CLEARED	Logical	1	-

Carefully check your entries against the figure "The Completed CHARGES File Structure." If you find any errors in your definition, move the cursor to the error and correct it.

The Completed CHARGES File Structure
When you have finished defining the CHARGES file, your screen should look like this.

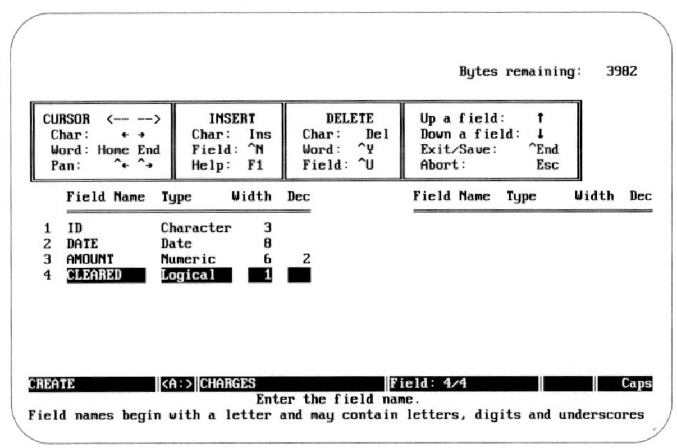

8. With either record 1 or 2 displayed, press Ctrl-End to save the file, and the prompt reads *Press ENTER to confirm. Any other key to resume.*
9. Press Enter↵, and in a moment the prompt reads *Input data records now? (Y/N).*
10. Press Y to display the screen into which you enter data.

The CHARGES Screen
After defining the CHARGES file, you can display a blank form to enter a record.

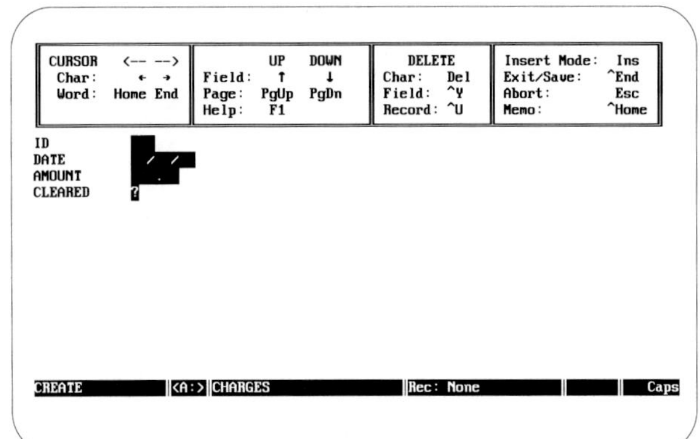

11. To enter data into the file, refer to the figure "Records to Add to the CHARGES File" and the following steps.
    - After you complete a field entry, press Enter↵ to move the cursor to the beginning of the next field. If the number of characters you enter equals the field width, the cursor automatically moves to the next field.
    - Enter dates in the format MM/DD/YY. If you enter two digits for each part of the date, you do not have to enter the slashes. If you enter only one digit, you do. For example, you can enter the date January 10, 1993, as **011093** or as **1/10/93**.
    - When you enter numbers, you can press . (the period key) to automatically move the cursor from the left to the right of the decimal, and type the numbers that follow the decimal.
    - The data you enter in the last field, *CLEARED*, fills the field, so the computer beeps and a new blank record is automatically displayed.
    - When you enter the last field in the second record, a blank record form is displayed (because your last entry fills the field). Press PgUp to see the last record that you entered.

FILE	CHARGES.DBF
RECORD #	1
ID	122
Date	04/10/93
Amount charged	50.00
Cleared	N

FILE	CHARGES.DBF
RECORD #	2
ID	122
Date	04/19/93
Amount charged	75.00
Cleared	N

Records to Add to the CHARGES File
This figure shows the two records that you add to the CHARGES file.

12. After entering both records, press [PgUp] and [PgDn] to scroll through them. Don't press [PgDn] when a blank record is displayed, or you will be returned to the Assist menu. If this happens, just highlight *Append* and press [Enter←] to display the records again. Carefully check your data against the figures for the two records. If you find mistakes in a record, use the arrow keys to move to the mistake, and then edit it with these basic commands:
    - Press [Ins] to toggle insert mode on and off. When on, *Ins* is displayed on the status line, and characters you type push existing characters to the right. When off, characters you type are typed over any existing characters.
    - Press [Del] to delete the character the cursor is under, or press [←Bksp] to delete the character to the left of the cursor.
13. With either record 1 or 2 displayed, press [Ctrl]-[End] to save your work and return to the Assist menus. (If a blank record was displayed when you used this command, that blank record would also be saved.)

LISTING AND PRINTING THE FILE'S STRUCTURE AND CONTENTS

14. Press [T] to pull down the Tools menu.
15. Highlight *List structure* and press [Enter←]. The prompt reads *Direct the output to the printer? [Y/N].*
16. Press [Y] to print the file's structure and when printing is completed, the prompt reads *Press any key to continue work in ASSIST.* (If your page is not ejected from the printer, press [Esc] to return to the dot prompt, then type **EJECT** and press [Enter←]. Type **ASSIST** and press [Enter←] to return to the Assist menus.)

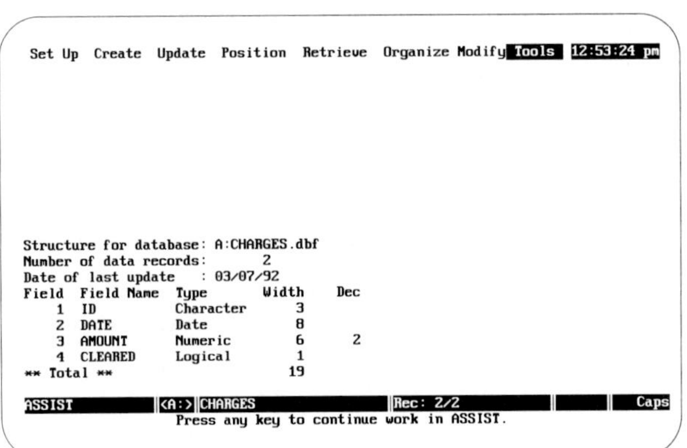

The CHARGES File Structure
The List Structure command on the Tools menu displays the structure of the open file.

17. Press any key to return to the Assist menu. Compare your printout with the figure "The Completed CHARGES File Structure" to be sure it matches. If your file's structure does not match ours, you'll learn how to correct it in the next topic.
18. Press [R] to pull down the Retrieve menu.
19. Highlight *List* and press [Enter←].
20. Highlight *Execute the command* and press [Enter←]. The prompt reads *Direct the output to the printer? [Y/N].*
21. Press [Y] to print the file's records and when printing is completed, the prompt reads *Press any key to continue work in ASSIST.*

22. Press any key to return to the Assist menu. The database has two records. If the last record did not print, press Esc to return to the dot prompt, type **EJECT** and press Enter ←.

    Compare your printout with the figures for the two records to be sure they match. Notice how each N that you entered in the logical fields has been converted to an .F. by the program. If your database does not match ours, you'll learn how to correct it in the next topic.

FINISHING UP

23. You have completed this tutorial. Either continue to the next activity or quit the program. To quit from the Assist menus, press S to pull down the Set Up menu, highlight *Quit dBASE III PLUS*, and press Enter ←.

QUICK REFERENCE

When you define a database, you specify each field's name, type, width, and decimal places, if any.

Defining a Database

To define a database file from the dot prompt, you use the CREATE <*filename*> command. For example, to create a new file named MEMBERS, you type **CREATE MEMBERS** and press Enter ←. To define a database using Assist, pull down the Create menu and select *Database file*. Enter the name of the database and press Enter ←. When the screen used to define a database file appears, use any of the commands described in the table "CREATE Database Commands" to move about the screen and enter or edit descriptions of the fields.

CREATE DATABASE COMMANDS

To	Press
Move the Cursor	
Move cursor to beginning of next column	Enter ← or End
Move cursor to beginning of previous column	Home
Move cursor left or right within a column	← or →
Move cursor up and down through fields	↑ or ↓
Insert and Delete Characters	
Delete character above cursor	Del
Delete character to left of cursor	← Bksp
Delete all characters from cursor to end of word	Ctrl-Y
Insert and Delete Fields	
Insert field above one containing cursor	Ctrl-N
Delete highlighted field	Ctrl-U
Exit a file definition and save definition	Ctrl-End
Exit without saving the file	Esc

Field Names

When naming fields in a database file, observe the following rules:

- The same field name cannot be used twice in the same file.
- Field names must be between one and ten characters long.
- Field names must start with a letter and contain only letters, numbers, and underscores.
- Field names must not have blank spaces. (Underscores are commonly used to separate words in field names, for example, **FIRST_NAME**.)

Field Types

dBASE allows you to store characters, numbers, yes/no responses, dates, times, and comments. Each of these types of data has a specific field type.

- ***Character fields*** store all characters you can enter from the keyboard, including letters, numbers, symbols, and spaces. When numbers such as ZIP codes or phone numbers are entered into a character field, they are treated as text, not values. Numbers entered in character fields cannot be used in calculations but can have leading zeros, such as those used in the ZIP code 01945.
- ***Numeric fields*** store values, including numbers, signs, and decimals. Numbers entered in these fields can be used in calculations. Data in these fields cannot have leading zeros.
- ***Logical fields***, sometimes called *Boolean fields*, store only yes/no or true/false data. You enter true or yes as **T**, **t**, **Y**, or **y** and false or no as **F**, **f**, **N**, or **n**.
- ***Date fields*** store dates, which can then be used in calculations. For example, you can add or subtract dates, or add or subtract numbers to or from them. This allows you to get answers to questions like "What is the average number of days between orders?"
- ***Memo fields*** store general descriptive text. A memo field does not have a fixed width. It expands as you enter up to 5000 characters of data. The data that you enter into a memo field is stored in a separate file with the same name as the database but the extension .DBT. This file is created automatically when you add a memo field to the file's structure. If your database file contains a memo field, you must be sure to copy this accompanying .DBT file whenever you copy the database file. If the program cannot find the memo field file when you try to open a database file with a memo field, you can have problems.

Field Widths

The width of logical, date, and memo fields is set automatically, but you must specify the width of character and numeric fields. The field widths that dBASE III Plus allows are listed in the table "dBASE III Plus Field Widths."

Deciding field widths ought not to be taken lightly. If you make the field too short, you will lose information. For instance, if you allowed only seven characters for the last name, you could enter the name *Smith* but not the name *Hamilton*. But if you make the field too long, you waste storage space in the computer's memory and on the disk and slow down

SMALLEST **LARGEST**

- 9 9 9 9 → 9 9 9 9 9

No decimals places

Two decimal places

Numeric Fields
The width required for a numeric field depends on whether you are planning to enter decimals or minus signs. Here the two fields have the same total width, but one has no decimal places, and the other has two. In the first field, you can enter numbers ranging from -9999 to 99999. In the second field, you can enter numbers ranging from -9.99 to 99.99.

operations. Therefore, you need to balance the amount of information held with the space required to hold that information.

When you specify the width of a numeric field, you must frequently add one character of width for a decimal point or for a leading minus sign. For example, if you specify that a field is five characters wide with two digits to the right of the decimal point, you can enter values from –9.99 to 99.99. You cannot enter numbers lower than –9.99 (for example, –10.00) or higher than 99.99 (for example, 100.00) because each of them would contain six or more characters. When specifying a numeric field, the number you enter in the *Width* column is the total number of characters in the field. If you then enter a number in the *Dec* column, you shift that number of digits to the right of the decimal point.

dBASE III PLUS FIELD WIDTHS

Field Type	Width (in characters)
Character fields	1-254
Numeric fields	1-19 (including 0-15 decimal places)
Logical fields	1 (set automatically)
Date fields	8 (set automatically)
Memo fields	1-5,000 (set automatically)

Displaying a File's Structure

When a database file is in memory, you can use the DISPLAY STRUCTURE command to display its field names, field types, and field widths. To execute this command, you can type **DISPLAY STRUCTURE** and press [Enter←] or just press [F5].

EXERCISES

EXERCISE 1

DEFINING A DATABASE FOR EMPLOYEES

In this exercise, you plan and then define a database that contains information on employees.

1. Work through the Assist menu or from the dot prompt to define a database named EMPLOYEE based on the data provided in the table "The EMPLOYEE File Structure." When you save the definition and are prompted to enter records now, answer no.
2. After creating and saving the structure, make a printout of the database's structure.

THE EMPLOYEE FILE STRUCTURE

Field Name	Description	Type	Width	Dec
EMP_NUM	Unique ID number	C	3	0
LASTNAME	Employee's last name	C	10	0
FIRST	First name	C	10	0
STREET	Street address	C	20	0
CITY	City	C	10	0
STATE	State	C	2	0
ZIP	ZIP code	C	5	0
PAYRATE	Hourly rate of pay	N	5	2

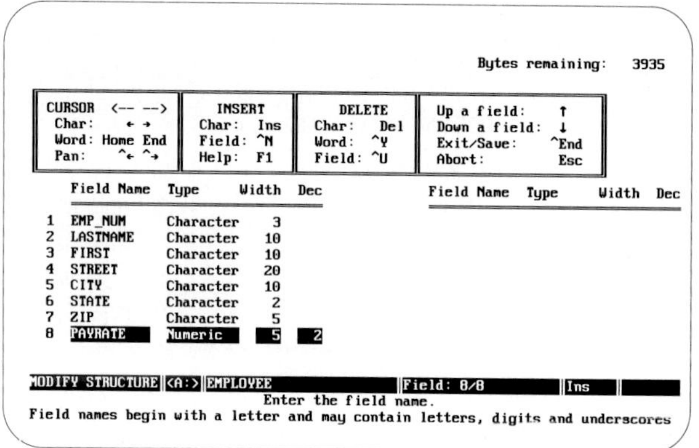

The EMPLOYEE File's Structure
After you define the fields in the EMPLOYEE file, your screen should look like this.

EXERCISE 2

DEFINING A DATABASE FOR DEPARTMENTS

In this exercise, you define a database that contains data on the hours worked by employees.

1. Work through the Assist menu or from the dot prompt to define a database named DEPT based on the data provided in the table "The DEPT File Structure." When you save the definition and are prompted to enter records now, answer no.
2. After creating and saving the structure, make a printout of the database's structure.

THE DEPT FILE STRUCTURE

Field Name	Description	Type	Width	Dec
EMP_NUM	Unique ID number	C	3	0
HOURS	Number of hours worked in previous week	N	5	2
SHIFT	Shift worked: 1, 2, or 3	C	1	0

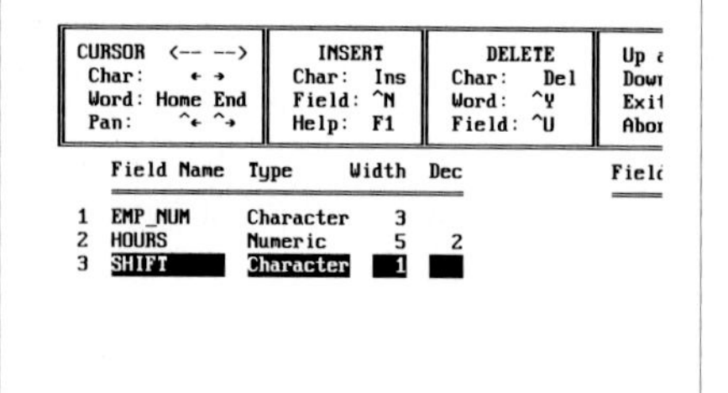

The DEPT File's Structure
After you define the fields in the DEPT file, your screen should look like this.

TOPIC 4

Modifying a Database File's Structure

After completing this topic, you will be able to:

- Modify an existing database with the MODIFY STRUCTURE command
- Redefine existing fields in a database

There are times when a database has to be changed after it has been created. Changes might include adding new fields, deleting existing fields, or modifying the definition of existing ones. For example, a few years ago, many databases had to be restructured when the ZIP code was changed from five to ten characters long. If a change like this is necessary, or if fields must be added or deleted, the file can be restructured.

DOT-PROMPT TUTORIAL

When you defined the MEMBERS database file, you may have made some mistakes. In this tutorial, you retrieve a similar file and correct the file's structure. Using what you have learned, you should then be able to modify your own file so that it is correct.

GETTING STARTED

1. Display the dot prompt and open the WRONG database file.
2. Type **LIST TO PRINT** and press Enter ↵ to print a record of the file's contents.
3. Type **LIST STRUCTURE TO PRINT** and press Enter ↵ to print out a record of the file's structure.

The Original WRONG File Structure
When you print out the file structure for the WRONG.DBF file, it looks like this.

```
(DEMO) . LIST STRUCTURE
Structure for database: A:wrong.dbf
Number of data records:       10
Date of last update   : 03/05/92
Field  Field Name  Type       Width    Dec
    1  ID          Character      3
    2  LSTNAME     Character     10
    3  FIRST       Character     10
    4  STREET      Character     17
    5  CITY        Character     10
    6  ST          Character      2
    7  ZIP         Numeric        5
    8  PHONE       Character      8
    9  ENROLLED    Date           8
   10  AGE         Numeric        2
   11  AGES        Numeric        2
** Total **                      78

(DEMO) .
Command Line  |<A:>|WRONG            |Rec: EOF/10    |    | Caps

              Enter a dBASE III PLUS command.
```

MODIFYING A FILE'S STRUCTURE

4. Type **MODIFY STRUCTURE** and press Enter↵ to display the current definition of each of the fields as shown in the figure "The Original Modify Structure Screen for WRONG."

The Original Modify Structure Screen for WRONG
The MODIFY STRUCTURE command displays a list of the existing fields in the WRONG database so that you can revise or delete existing field definitions or add new ones.

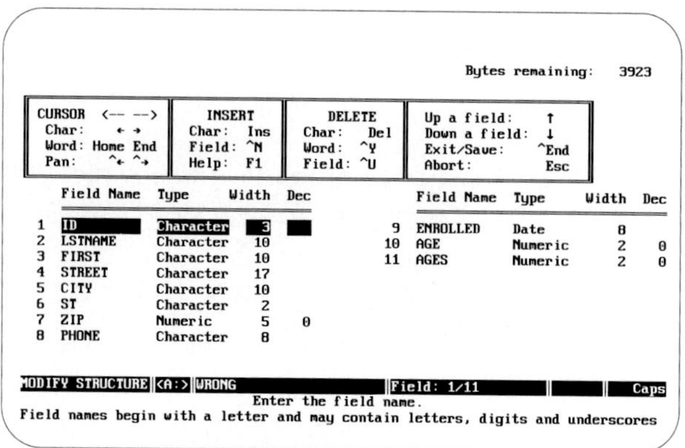

CHANGING A FIELD'S NAME

5. Move the cursor to the second field where LASTNAME is misspelled *LSTNAME.*
6. Move the cursor under the letter *S* and press Ins to turn on insert mode. *Ins* is displayed on the status line.
7. Type **A** and the field's name reads *LASTNAME.*

ADDING A FIELD

8. Move the highlight to field 8, *PHONE.*
9. Press Ctrl-N to insert a blank field above *PHONE.*
10. Enter its name as *AREA*, its type as *Character*, and its width as *3*.

DELETING A FIELD

11. Move the highlight to field 12, *AGES.*
12. Press Ctrl-U to delete the highlighted field.

CHANGING A FIELD'S TYPE

13. Move the highlight to record 7, *ZIP.*
14. Change the type to *Character* and when finished, your screen should look like the one shown in the figure "The Modified WRONG Structure."

The Modified WRONG Structure
After you modify the structure of the WRONG database file, its file structure should look like this.

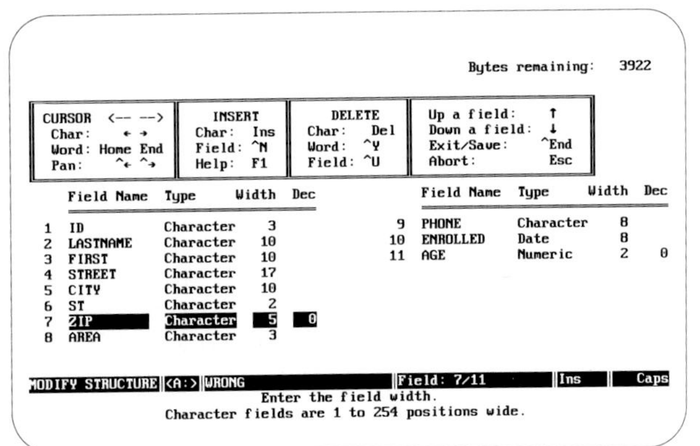

SAVING YOUR CHANGES

15. Press Ctrl-End to save your changes, and the prompt reads *Press ENTER to confirm. Any other key to resume.*
16. Press Enter↵ and in a few moments, the old records are copied from a backup file into the new, restructured database.

PRINTING THE FILE'S CONTENTS AND STRUCTURE

17. Type **LIST TO PRINT** and press Enter↵. Notice how there are no area codes since the new AREA field is empty. Moreover, all last names have been deleted from the field where you changed the field name from LSTNAME to LASTNAME.
18. Type **LIST LASTNAME AREA** and press Enter↵ to see the empty LASTNAME and AREA fields.
19. Type **LIST STRUCTURE TO PRINT** and press Enter↵ to display and print the file's new structure. The ZIP code for the last record has no leading zeros because those are not allowed in numeric fields and that was what this character field originally was before you changed its type.

FINISHING UP

20. You have completed this tutorial. Either close all open files and continue to the next activity or quit the program.

QUICK REFERENCE

To restructure a database, you use the MODIFY STRUCTURE command. This command makes a backup copy of the file and displays a list of the file's fields on the screen so that you can edit them. When you save the revised structure, dBASE copies the records back into the file from the backup file.

When restructuring files, keep the following points in mind:

- If the restructuring adds new fields, those fields are blank.
- When making multiple changes in a field (for example, to change its name and its type), make one change at a time, saving each change and then starting again. Otherwise, the field may be left blank.

- If you change the name of a field, it will be left blank.

To edit an existing field, move the cursor into it, and use any of the editing keys described in the help menu or in the table "MODIFY STRUCTURE Commands."

To add a new field, move the highlight to the last existing field definition and press [↓] to display a new blank field definition.

To insert a new field, position the highlight on the field above where you want to insert it and press [Ctrl]-[N].

To delete an existing field, position the highlight on it and press [Ctrl]-[U].

To save the revised structure, press [Ctrl]-[End], and the prompt reads *Press ENTER to confirm. Any other key to resume.* A message reads *Database records will be APPENDED from backup fields of the same name only!!.*

If you want to abandon any changes and leave the database as it was before you displayed the modify structure screen, press [Esc]. When you do so, the prompt reads *Are you sure you want to abandon operation? {Y/N}.* Press [Y] to abandon your changes.

MODIFY STRUCTURE COMMANDS

To	Press
Move the Cursor	
Move cursor to beginning of next column	[Enter ↵] or [End]
Move cursor to beginning of previous column	[Home]
Move cursor left or right within a column	[←] or [→]
Move cursor up and down through fields	[↑] or [↓]
Insert and Delete Characters	
Delete character above cursor	[Del]
Delete character to left of cursor	[← Bksp]
Delete all characters from cursor to end of word	[Ctrl]-[Y]
Insert and Delete Fields	
Insert field above one containing cursor	[Ctrl]-[N]
Delete highlighted field	[Ctrl]-[U]
Exit a file definition and save definition	[Ctrl]-[End]
Exit without saving the file	[Esc]

EXERCISES

EXERCISE 1

MODIFYING THE MEMBERS AND CHARGES FILE STRUCTURES

If you made any mistakes when defining the MEMBERS and CHARGES database files, use what you have learned in this topic to correct them. After doing so, print out the modified file structure.

EXERCISE 2

MODIFYING THE EMPLOYEE FILE STRUCTURE

1. Open the EMPLOYEE file.
2. Modify the file structure by inserting a field named DEPT (for department) between the existing ZIP and PAYRATE fields. Define the field as a character field with a width of two characters with no decimals.
3. Save the revised structure and then make a printout of it.

The Modified EMPLOYEE File's Structure
After you modify the EMPLOYEE file's structure, your screen should look like this.

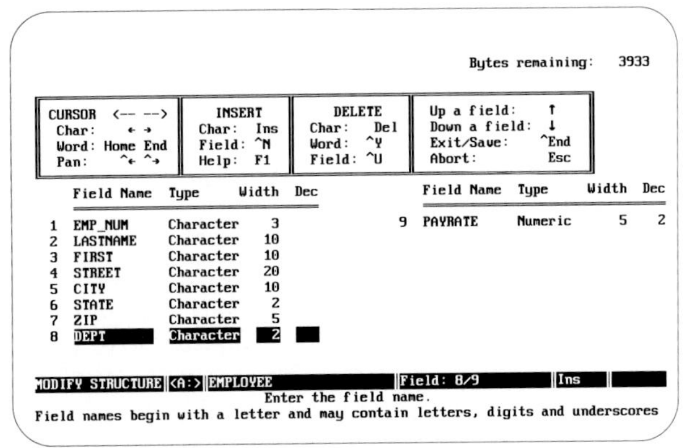

EXERCISE 3

MODIFYING THE DEPT FILE STRUCTURE

1. Open the DEPT file.
2. Modify the file structure by adding a field named WEEKOF above EMP_NUM so that it is the first field in the file. Define the field as a date field.
3. Save the revised structure and then make a printout of it.

The Modified DEPT File's Structure
After you modify the DEPT file's structure, your screen should look like this.

```
Bytes remaining: 3983
CURSOR <-- -->      INSERT       DELETE      Up a field:    ↑
Char:    ← →        Char:  Ins   Char:  Del  Down a field:  ↓
Word: Home End      Field: ^N    Word:  ^Y   Exit/Save:  ^End
Pan:   ^← ^→        Help:  F1    Field: ^U   Abort:       Esc

  Field Name  Type       Width  Dec      Field Name  Type   Width  Dec
1 WEEKOF      Date         8
2 EMP_NUM     Character    3
3 HOURS       Numeric      5     2
4 SHIFT       Character    1

MODIFY STRUCTURE <A:> DEPT            Field: 1/4        Ins
                        Enter the field name.
Field names begin with a letter and may contain letters, digits and underscores
```

TOPIC 5

Entering Data into a Database File

After completing this topic, you will be able to:

- Add records to a database file with the APPEND command
- Append records to a database from another file with the APPEND FROM command
- Save changes to a database with the Ctrl-End command

New records must be added to a database to create it and later to keep the database up to date. If the database file is not already open (when open, its name is displayed on the status line), you use the USE command from the dot prompt or pull down the Set Up menu and use the *Database file* command to open it.

As you enter records, they are automatically saved when you use any of the commands that display another record or a blank data entry form on the screen. You can also copy records from another database with the APPEND FROM <*filename*> command.

Unlike a card index file, where you would want to insert the card in the proper order, the database management program will add it to the end of the file. You can enter new records one after another without worrying about their order. As you will see later, a file can be rearranged in the desired order after you enter the records.

DOT-PROMPT TUTORIAL

In this tutorial, you enter records into the MEMBERS database file using the APPEND command. Then, you copy records into the file from a file on the disk named MEMBHOLD. To do so, you use the APPEND FROM <*filename*> command. The reason you copy the records is to save you typing time. Databases are interesting only when they are too large to take in at a glance. However, why spend lab time typing when dBASE makes it easy to create a large file so easily?

GETTING STARTED

1. Display the dot prompt and open the MEMBERS database file.

ADDING RECORDS

2. Type **APPEND** and press Enter↵.

The screen displays a help menu (which you can turn on or off with [F1]) below which are the fields you enter data into. Next to each field name are highlighted areas that indicate the field's width. The current field, the one you enter data into when you type, contains the cursor.

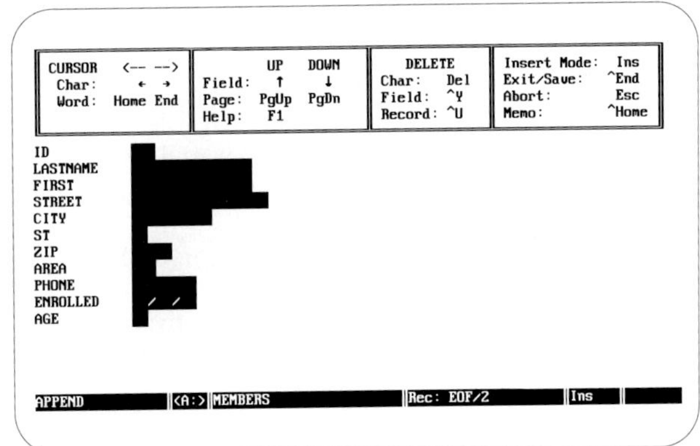

The MEMBERS Append Screen
The APPEND command displays a blank record for the MEMBERS file.

FILE	MEMBERS.DBF
RECORD #	**3**
ID	124
Last name	Dougherty
First name	Steven
Street	10100 Hardy
City	Los Gatos
ST	CA
ZIP	95031
Area Code	415
Phone number	555-1013
Date enrolled	03/01/93
Age	35

FILE	MEMBERS.DBF
RECORD #	**4**
ID	125
Last name	Porsena
First name	Lars
Street	71 North Street
City	Atlanta
ST	GA
ZIP	30010
Area Code	404
Phone number	555-1014
Date enrolled	03/05/93
Age	89

New Records to Append to the MEMBERS File
This figure shows the two records that you add to the MEMBERS file with the APPEND command.

3. To enter data into the file, refer to the figure "New Records to Append to the MEMBERS File" and the following steps.
   - After you complete a field entry, press [Enter←] to move the cursor to the beginning of the next field. If the number of characters you enter equals the field width, the cursor automatically moves to the next field.
   - Type in the data exactly as shown in the two figures. Uppercase and lowercase letters are important because you will look for data, and the program is case sensitive. For example, if you enter *Ca* and later look for *CA*, the program will not find it.
   - If you make a mistake when making an entry, press [←Bksp] to delete it, and then correctly reenter it.
   - Enter dates in the format MM/DD/YY. If you enter two digits for each part of the date, you do not have to enter the slashes. If you enter only one digit, you do. For example, you can enter the date March 1, 1993, as **030193** or as **3/1/93**.
   - After entering data into the next to last field (*AGE*), press [PgDn] to display a new blank record.

CHECKING AND EDITING YOUR RECORDS

4. After entering both records, press [PgUp] and [PgDn] to scroll through them.

   Don't press [PgDn] when a blank record form is displayed, or you may be returned to the dot prompt. If this happens, just type **APPEND** and press [Enter←] to display a blank form. Then press [PgUp] to see the last record in the file in which you entered data.

   Carefully compare the two new records with the figures that you used to enter them. If you find mistakes in a record, use the arrow keys to move to the mistake, and then edit it with these basic commands:
   - Press [Ins] to toggle insert mode on and off. When on, *Ins* is displayed on the status line, and characters you type push

existing characters to the right. When off, characters you type are typed over any existing characters.

- Press [Del] to delete the character the cursor is under, or press [←Bksp] to delete the character to the left of the cursor.

SAVING THE RECORDS

5. Press [Ctrl]-[End] to save your work and return to the dot prompt. When you enter records, they are automatically saved onto the disk when you move to the next record. However, to be sure the last record is saved when you have finished entering data or making corrections, press [Ctrl]-[End].

APPENDING NEW RECORDS FROM ANOTHER FILE

6. Type **APPEND FROM** and press [Enter←]. The prompt reads *Enter file name to append from:*.
7. Type **MEMBHOLD** and press [Enter←]. The message reads *10 records added*, and the dot prompt reappears.

PRINTING THE RECORDS

8. Type **LIST TO PRINT** and press [Enter←] to list the records on the screen and print them out. (Remember to use the EJECT command if necessary to eject your paper from the printer.)

FINISHING UP

9. You have completed this tutorial. Either close all open files and continue to the next activity or quit the program.

ASSIST-MENU TUTORIAL

In this tutorial, you enter records into the CHARGES database file using the Assist menu.

GETTING STARTED

1. Display the Assist menus and open the CHARGES database file.

ADDING RECORDS

2. Press [U] to pull down the Update menu.
3. Highlight *Append* and press [Enter←].
   The screen displays a blank record listing the fields in the file. Next to each field name are highlights indicating the field's width. The current field, the one you enter data into when you type, contains the cursor.

The CHARGES Append Screen
The Append command on the Update menu displays a blank record for the CHARGES file.

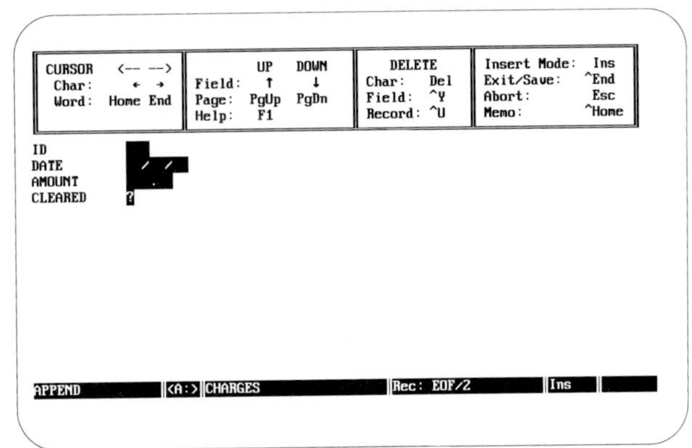

FILE	CHARGES.DBF
RECORD #	3
ID	124
Date	04/19/93
Amount charged	15.00
Cleared	N

FILE	CHARGES.DBF
RECORD #	4
ID	124
Date	04/20/93
Amount charged	13.00
Cleared	N

New Records to Append to the CHARGES File
This figure shows the two records that you add to the CHARGES file with the APPEND command.

4. To enter data into the file, refer to the figure "The Two New Records to Append to the CHARGES File" and the following steps.
   - After you complete a field entry, press Enter↵ to move the cursor to the beginning of the next field. If the number of characters you enter equals the field width, the cursor automatically moves to the next field.
   - Enter dates in the format MM/DD/YY. If you enter two digits for each part of the date, you do not have to enter the slashes. If you enter only one digit, you do. For example, you can enter the date May 19, 1993, as **041993** or as **4/19/93**.
   - When you enter numbers, you can press the period key to automatically move the cursor from the left to the right of the decimal and type the numbers that follow the decimal.
   - When you enter data in the last field, *CLEARED*, it fills the field, so the computer beeps and a new blank record is automatically displayed.
   - When you enter the last field in the second record, a blank form is displayed (because your last entry fills the field). Press PgUp so that the blank record is not saved in the database file.
5. After entering both records, press PgUp and PgDn to scroll through them.

   Don't press PgDn when a blank record is displayed, or you will be returned to the Assist menu. If this happens, just highlight *Append* and press Enter↵ to display the records again.

   Carefully compare the two new records with the figures you used to enter them. If you find mistakes in a record, use the arrow keys to move to the mistake, and then edit it with these basic commands:
   - Press Ins to toggle insert mode on and off. When on, *Ins* is displayed on the status line and characters you type push existing characters to the right. When off, characters you type are typed over any existing characters.
   - Press Del to delete the character the cursor is under, or press ←Bksp to delete the character to the left of the cursor.
6. Press Ctrl-End to save the file and return to the Assist menus.

APPENDING NEW RECORDS FROM ANOTHER FILE

7. Press Esc to return to the dot prompt because the Assist menus do not list a command to append records from another file.

8. Type **APPEND FROM CHARHOLD** and press [Enter ↵]. The message reads *12 records added*, and the dot prompt reappears.

PRINTING THE RECORDS

9. Type **ASSIST** and press [Enter ↵] to display the Assist menus.
10. Press [R] to pull down the Retrieve menu.
11. Highlight *List* and press [Enter ↵] to display a submenu.
12. Highlight *Execute the command* and press [Enter ↵]. The prompt reads *Direct the output to the printer? [Y/N].*
13. Press [Y] to display print out a list of the records. The prompt then reads *Press any key to continue to work in ASSIST.*

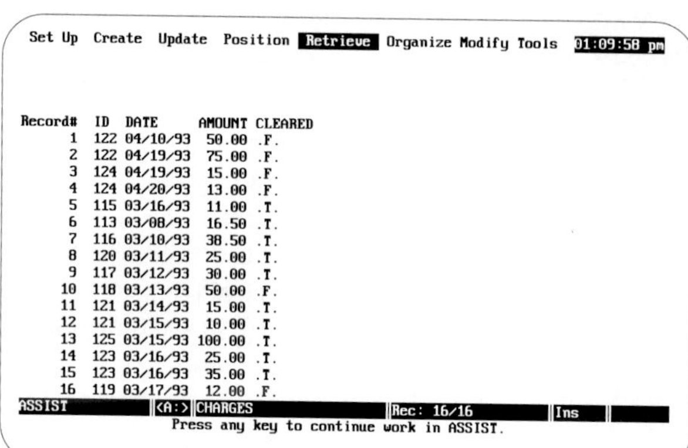

The Added Records
This figure shows all the records you have added to the CHARGES file with the APPEND and APPEND FROM CHARHOLD commands.

14. Press any key to display the Assist menus.

    If your page isn't ejected from the printer, or the last line printed, press [Esc] to return to the dot prompt, type **EJECT** and press [Enter ↵].

FINISHING UP

15. You have completed this tutorial. Either close all open files and continue to the next activity or quit the program.

QUICK REFERENCE

You can use the APPEND command to enter records to the end of the file by typing them in or using the APPEND FROM <filename> to copy them from an existing file.

The APPEND Command

To enter records into a file after it has been defined, the basic command is APPEND [F9], which displays a blank record at the end of the open file. When the field names are displayed, you can use the commands described in the table "APPEND Commands" to enter and edit records.

To save a new record, simply move the cursor to the next record. To be sure all records have been saved, press [Ctrl]-[End] when you want to return to the dot prompt or Assist menu.

APPEND COMMANDS

To	Press
Move the Cursor	
Move cursor left or right one character	← or →
Move cursor up or down one field	↑ or ↓
Display Records	
Display previous record (if any)	PgUp
Display next record (if any)	PgDn
Insert and Delete Characters	**Press**
Toggle between insert and typeover modes	Ins
Delete character	Del
Delete characters from cursor to end of field	Ctrl-Y
Save Records	**Press**
Save records	Ctrl-End

The APPEND FROM Command

The APPEND FROM <*filename*> command adds records to the end of the file that is currently open from any file on the disk that you specify. The only fields that are copied to the open file are those with the same field name and type; moreover:

- If the width of the field is smaller in the file you are appending records to, data is truncated, and numeric data is converted to asterisks.
- Records marked for deletion in the file you are appending from are copied into the new file and are no longer marked for deletion.

EXERCISES

EXERCISE 1

ENTERING RECORDS INTO THE EMPLOYEE FILE

1. Open the EMPLOYEE file.
2. Enter the records shown in the figure "New Records to Append to the EMPLOYEE File."
3. When finished, save the file.
4. Append additional records to the file from EMPLHOLD.DBF. This file is on the original *Student Resource Disk* that came with this text and should have been copied to your data disk earlier.
5. List the records to the printer.

FILE	EMPLOYEE.DBF
RECORD #	1
Employee #	114
Last name	Ames
First name	Roger
Street	400 Hill Avenue
City	Tampa
ST	FL
ZIP	33606
Department	2
Pay rate	7.50

FILE	EMPLOYEE.DBF
RECORD #	2
Employee #	115
Last name	Beecham
First name	Robert
Street	350 Summer Road
City	Tampa
ST	FL
ZIP	33524
Department	1
Pay rate	7.00

New Records to Append to the EMPLOYEE File
This figure shows the two records that you add to the EMPLOYEE file with the APPEND command.

FILE	DEPT.DBF
RECORD #	1
Week of	04/19/94
Employee #	114
Hours	40
Shift	1

FILE	DEPT.DBF
RECORD #	2
Week of	04/19/94
Employee #	115
Hours	40
Shift	1

New Records to Append to the DEPT File
This figure shows the two records that you add to the DEPT file with the APPEND command.

EXERCISE 2

ENTERING RECORDS INTO THE DEPT FILE

1. Open the DEPT file.
2. Enter the records shown in the figure "New Records to Append to the DEPT File."
3. When finished, save the file.
4. Append additional records to the file from DEPTHOLD.DBF. This file is on the original *Student Resource Disk* that came with this text and should have been copied to your data disk earlier.
5. List the records to the printer.

TOPIC 6

Editing & Updating Database Files

After completing this topic, you will be able to:

- Edit fields in edit mode
- Edit memo fields with the **Ctrl-Home** or **Ctrl-PgDn** command
- Describe what a record pointer is and explain how you move it with the GOTO, SKIP, and NEXT commands
- Change data in a specified field with the CHANGE command

It is often necessary to edit or update records in a database file; for example, when employees change addresses, their records must be updated. To do this, you first use the command to find the specific record to be updated and display it on the screen. You then revise the contents of the appropriate fields. Whenever you make changes, they are saved when you move the highlight to another record or press Ctrl-End to return to the dot prompt or Assist menu.

Many of the commands you use to display records move a *record pointer* within the file. This record pointer, which is not displayed, makes the record that it points to the current record. Subsequent commands then start from, or apply to, the current record.

DOT-PROMPT TUTORIAL

In this tutorial, you edit records in the WRONG database file. After correcting this file, you should be able to correct any mistakes you made in your own files.

GETTING STARTED

1. Display the dot prompt and open the WRONG.DBF database file.

MOVING THE RECORD POINTER

2. Type **GO TOP** and press Enter ↵ to move the record pointer to the first record. This is indicated on the status line with the message *Rec: 1/10*. The first number (1) indicates the current record, and the second one (10) indicates the total number of records in the file.
3. Type **GO BOTTOM** and press Enter ↵ to move the record pointer to the last record; *Rec: 10/10*.
4. Type **GO 3** and press Enter ↵ to move the record pointer to the specified record; *Rec: 3/10*.

EDITING RECORDS

5. Type **EDIT 1** and press Enter↵ to display record 1 in edit mode. Compare this record with the figure "The Edited WRONG File." If any fields are highlighted in that figure, correct the same field on the screen so that its contents match the figure's.

   As you move the cursor between fields, it may not move to the leftmost position in the field. In many cases, it helps to press Home or ← to move it there before editing.

ID	LASTNAME	FIRST	STREET	CITY	ST	ZIP	AREA	PHONE	ENROLLED	AGE
115	Culman	Tina	100 Elm Street	New Haven	CT	10000	203	555-1001	01/16/94	33
113	Benjemin	Nancy	25 Oak Street	Cambridge	MA	20000	617	555-1002	01/08/94	26
116	Kendall	Liz	14 Lark Avenue	Chicago	IL	20000	312	555-1003	02/01/94	19
120	Hogan	Dennis	40 Main Street	Edgewater	NJ	30000	201	555-1004	09/06/94	39
119	Morin	Emily	43 Spruce Road	Milpitas	CA	20000	408	555-1005	08/01/94	3
117	Sobel	Carol	45 Porter Avenue	Fairlawn	NJ	30000	201	555-1006	03/06/94	34
112	Anthony	William	900 Maple Road	Reading	MA	20000	617	555-1007	01/07/94	63
118	Morin	Cathy	5 Milk Street	Salem	OR	40000	508	555-1008	06/03/94	22
114	Morin	Mike	5 Milk Street	Salem	OR	40000	508	555-1009	01/10/94	45
121	Dougherty	Steve	1 Sylvan Avenue	Englewood	NJ	07632	415	555-1010	10/15/94	25

The Edited WRONG File
This figure shows the WRONG.DBF file after all corrections have been made. Your file should match this one when you are finished with this tutorial.

6. Press PgDn to display the next record and edit it if necessary.
7. Repeat Step 6 until all records are edited.
8. Press Ctrl-End to save the changes and return to the dot prompt.

EDITING MEMO FIELDS

9. Type **USE MEMBERS** and press Enter↵ to open the MEMBERS file.
10. Type **EDIT 1** and press Enter↵ to display record 1.
11. Press F1 to remove the help menu so that you can see all the fields at the same time.
12. Move the cursor to the *REMARKS* field.
13. Press Ctrl-PgDn to display the memo field.
14. Press F1 to display the help menu again.
15. Type **Special diet**.

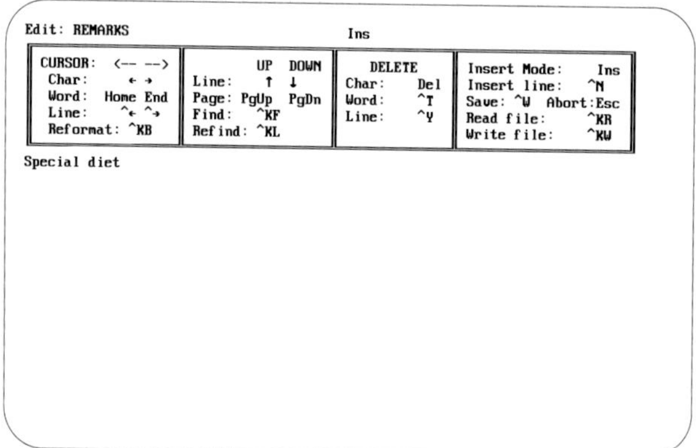

The Memo Field Edit Screen
When you move the cursor into a memo field and press Ctrl-PgDn, the memo field edit screen is displayed.

16. Press Ctrl-End to save the entry and return to the record.
17. List the ID field (List ID) and jot down the record numbers for records with the IDs listed in the table "MEMBERS Memo Field Revisions." For each of those fields, repeat Steps 12 through 16 but enter the data shown in the table. (Press F1 to display the help menu if it isn't displayed.)
18. Press Ctrl-End to save the changes and return to the dot prompt.

MEMBERS MEMO FIELD REVISIONS

ID	Memo Field Entry
119	Gymnastics student
112	Doctor's OK
114	No heart problems

PRINTING THE RECORDS

19. Type **LIST TO PRINT** and press Enter↵ to display and print the revised records. Notice that the contents of the memo fields do not print out.
20. Type **LIST REMARKS** and press Enter↵ to display the contents of all REMARKS fields are displayed, empty or not. Only the record numbers indicate which record the remarks belong to.

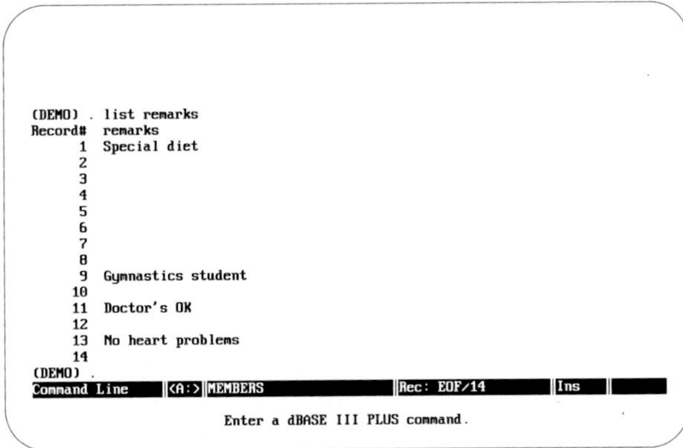

Listed Remarks
The LIST REMARKS command displays the contents of the REMARKS memo field.

21. Type **LIST ID,LASTNAME,REMARKS** and press Enter↵ to list the remarks again, but this time last names indicate who they are for.

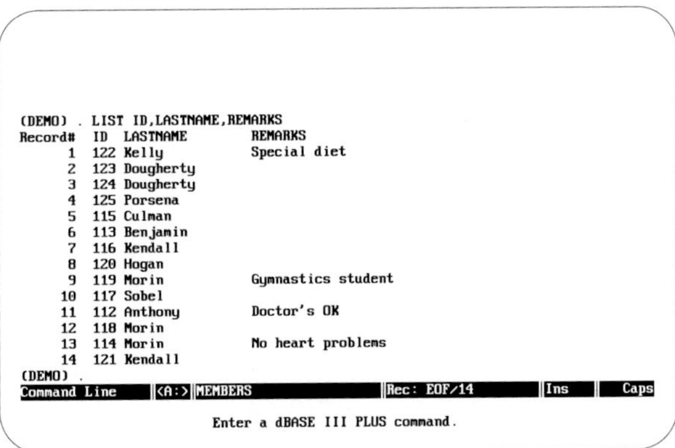

Remarks Listed Along with Other Fields
You can specify other fields in the LIST command so that it's easier to associate remarks with members.

22. Type **LIST ID,LASTNAME,REMARKS TO PRINT** and press Enter↵ to print the last names and remarks.

FINISHING UP

23. You have completed this tutorial. Either close all open files and continue to the next activity or quit the program.

To display records for editing, you use the EDIT command. For example, the command EDIT 1 displays all fields in record 1. You can also move the record pointer to the desired record with the GOTO command and then type **EDIT** and press Enter↵ or just press F10.

Commands That Move the Record Pointer

If you type **GOTO 5** and press Enter↵, the record pointer moves to record 5. If you then type **EDIT** and press Enter↵, record 5 is displayed on the screen. The record marked by the pointer is always listed on the status line as the first digit following *Rec:*. For example, if *Rec: 2/20* is displayed, the record points at record 2, and there are 20 records in the file. Moreover, if you type **?RECNO()** and press Enter↵, the program displays the number of the record that the record pointer points to.

The GOTO Command

When you want to move the record pointer to a specific record, you use the GOTO *<record>* command. You can specify a specific record number or the options TOP or BOTTOM. For example, GOTO 5 displays record number 5, GOTO TOP displays the first record, and GOTO BOTTOM displays the last record when you then use the EDIT command.

The SKIP Command

If you want to jump over records, use the SKIP*<n>* command (where n stands for the number of records to be skipped). For example, if you use the command GOTO TOP and then the command SKIP 5, the record pointer points to record 6. SKIP by itself moves the record pointer to the next record.

Moving the Cursor

When a record is displayed for editing, the commands that you use to move the cursor around the screen are described in the table "Moving the Cursor in Edit Mode."

MOVING THE CURSOR IN EDIT MODE

To move to	Press
Next field	Enter↵
Next field	End
Previous field	Home
Up or down one record	↑ or ↓
Left or right one character	← or →
Next or previous group	PgDn or PgUp

Editing Records

When you are editing records, you can use commands to insert and delete characters and save and abandon your changes. These commands can be displayed by pressing F1 when actually editing, and they are summarized in the table "Editing Commands."

Editing Memo Fields

Memo fields have their own editing commands. To edit a memo field, display the record with the EDIT command. Then move the cursor to the memo field where *memo* is displayed. Press Ctrl-Home or Ctrl-PgDn to display the field in text editing mode. The available editing commands are listed at the top of the screen. If they are not, press F1.

Using the CHANGE Command

The CHANGE command displays specified fields for editing. For example, the command CHANGE ALL FIELD DATE displays all DATE fields one after another so that you can change the dates, and the command CHANGE RECORD 1 FIELD DATE displays the contents of the DATE field for record 1.

EDITING COMMANDS

To	Press
Turn insert mode on or off	Ins
Delete character that cursor is under	Del
Delete character to left of cursor	← Bksp
Delete all characters in field to the right of cursor	Ctrl-Y
Insert new line or field definition	Ctrl-N
Delete word to right of cursor	Ctrl-T
Mark record for deletion	Ctrl-U
Enter a memo field	Ctrl-PgDn or Ctrl-Home
Exit a memo field	Ctrl-PgUp or Ctrl-End
Abort	Esc
Save changes	Ctrl-End

EXERCISES

EXERCISE 1

EDITING THE MEMBERS AND CHARGES FILES

If you made any mistakes when entering the first two records into the MEMBERS and CHARGES database files, use what you have learned in this topic to correct them. After doing so, print out the edited records.

EXERCISE 2

EDITING THE EMPLOYEE AND DEPT FILES

If you made any mistakes when entering the first two records into the EMPLOYEE and DEPT database files, use what you have learned in this topic to correct them. After doing so, print out the edited records.

TOPIC 7

Deleting Records from a Database File

After completing this topic, you will be able to:

- Flag records for deletion with the DELETE and Ctrl-U commands
- Recover flagged records with the RECALL command
- Delete flagged records from a database with the PACK command

As time passes, some of the information in a database becomes out of date. In some cases, this is fixed by editing the data to update them. But when products no longer exist or people are no longer employed, their entire record must be deleted. Deleting records in dBASE is a two-step process. In the first step, you flag records that you want deleted. In the second step, you pack the file to remove the flagged records.

DOT-PROMPT TUTORIAL

In this tutorial, you delete records from the WRONG database file.

Deleting WRONG File Records from the Dot Prompt
In this tutorial, you delete the highlighted records from the WRONG database from the dot prompt.

ID	LASTNAME	FIRST	STREET	CITY	ST	ZIP	AREA	PHONE	ENROLLED	AGE
115	Culman	Tina	100 Elm Street	New Haven	CT	1000	203	555-1001	01/16/94	33
113	Benjemin	Nancy	25 Oak Street	Cambridge	MA	2000	617	555-1002	01/08/94	26
116	Kendall	Liz	14 Lark Avenue	Chicago	IL	2000	312	555-1003	02/01/94	19
120	Hogan	Dennis	40 Main Street	Edgewater	NJ	3000	201	555-1004	09/06/94	39
119	Morin	Emily	43 Spruce Road	Milpitas	CA	2000	408	555-1005	08/01/94	3
117	Sobel	Carol	45 Porter Avenue	Fairlawn	NJ	3000	201	555-1006	03/06/94	34
112	Anthony	William	900 Maple Road	Reading	MA	2000	617	555-1007	01/07/94	63
118	Morin	Cathy	5 Milk Street	Salem	OR	4000	508	555-1008	06/03/94	22
114	Morin	Mike	5 Milk Street	Salem	OR	4000	508	555-1009	01/10/94	45
121	Dougherty	Steve	1 Sylvan Avenue	Englewood	NJ	0763	415	555-1010	10/15/94	25

GETTING STARTED

1. Display the dot prompt and open the WRONG database file.
2. Type **LIST ID TO PRINT** and press Enter↵ to print a record of the records in the database.

FLAGGING RECORDS FOR DELETION

3. Type **DELETE RECORD 2** and press Enter↵. A message reads *1 record deleted*, but the record has not actually been deleted; it has just been flagged for deletion.

4. Type **LIST ID** and press [Enter←] to see that the record numbers and their IDs are listed. Notice how record 2 with ID 113 is marked with an asterisk to indicate that it has been flagged for deletion.
5. Type **EDIT 3** and press [Enter←].
6. Press [Ctrl]-[U] and *Del* is displayed on the status line to indicate the record has been marked for deletion.
7. Press [Ctrl]-[End] to return to the dot prompt.
8. Type **LIST ID** and press [Enter←] to see that records 2 and 3 are flagged.

IGNORING FLAGGED RECORDS

9. Type **SET DELETED ON** and press [Enter←].
10. Type **LIST ID** and press [Enter←] to see that records 2 and 3 are no longer listed. The SET DELETED ON command tells dBASE to ignore flagged records.
11. Type **SET DELETED OFF** and press [Enter←].
12. Type **LIST ID** and press [Enter←] to see that records 2 and 3 are again listed. The SET DELETED OFF command turns off the ON version of the command.

RECALLING RECORDS FLAGGED FOR DELETION

13. Type **RECALL ALL** and press [Enter←]. The message *2 records recalled* indicates the records have been recalled.
14. Type **LIST ID** and press [Enter←] to see that records 2 and 3 are no longer flagged with an asterisk. The RECALL command removed the asterisk.

DELETING RECORDS

15. Type **DELETE RECORD 2** and press [Enter←].
16. Type **DELETE RECORD 3** and press [Enter←].
17. Type **DELE RECO 4** and press [Enter←].
18. Type **DELE RECO 5** and press [Enter←].
19. Type **LIST ID** and press [Enter←] to see that records 2 through 5 are flagged with an asterisk.
20. Type **PACK** and press [Enter←]. The message *6 records copied* indicates the four flagged records have been deleted since originally there were ten records.

FINISHING UP

21. Type **LIST TO PRINT** and press [Enter←] to print out the remaining records.
22. You have completed this tutorial. Either close all open files and continue to the next activity or quit the program.

TOPIC 7

ASSIST-MENU TUTORIAL

Deleting WRONG File Records from the Assist Menus
In this tutorial, you delete the highlighted record from the WRONG database using the Assist menus.

In this tutorial, you use the Assist menu to delete records from the WRONG database file.

ID	LASTNAME	FIRST	STREET	CITY	ST	ZIP	AREA	PHONE	ENROLLED	AGE
115	Culman	Tina	100 Elm Street	New Haven	CT	1000	203	555-1001	01/16/94	33
117	Sobel	Carol	45 Porter Avenue	Fairlawn	NJ	3000	201	555-1006	03/06/94	34
112	Anthony	William	900 Maple Road	Reading	MA	2000	617	555-1007	01/07/94	63
118	Morin	Cathy	5 Milk Street	Salem	OR	4000	508	555-1008	06/03/94	22
114	Morin	Mike	5 Milk Street	Salem	OR	4000	508	555-1009	01/10/94	45
121	Dougherty	Steve	1 Sylvan Avenue	Englewood	NJ	0763	415	555-1010	10/15/94	25

GETTING STARTED

1. Display the Assist menu and open the WRONG database file.

MOVING THE RECORD POINTER TO THE RECORD TO BE DELETED

2. Press P to pull down the Position menu.
3. Highlight *Goto Record* and press Enter←.
4. Highlight *RECORD* and press Enter←. The prompt reads *Enter a numeric value:*.
5. Type **3** and press Enter← to move the record pointer to record 3.

FLAGGING THE CURRENT RECORD FOR DELETION

6. Press U to pull down the Update menu.
7. Highlight *Delete* and press Enter←.
8. Highlight *Execute the command* and press Enter←. The message reads *1 record deleted*, and the prompt reads *Press any key to continue with ASSIST*.
9. Press any key to return to the Assist menus.

DELETING THE FLAGGED RECORD

10. Press U to pull down the Update menu.
11. Highlight *Pack* and press Enter←. The message indicates the number of records copied, and the prompt reads *Press any key to continue work in ASSIST*.
12. Press any key to return to the Assist menus.

LISTING AND PRINTING THE REMAINING RECORDS

13. Press R to pull down the Retrieve menu.
14. Highlight *List* and press Enter←.
15. Highlight *Execute the command* and press Enter←. The prompt reads *Direct the output to the printer? [Y/N]*.
16. Press Y to print the records and the prompt reads *Press any key to continue work in ASSIST*.
17. Press any key to return to the Assist menus. Notice how record 3 with ID 112 has been deleted from the title.

FINISHING UP

18. You have completed this tutorial. Either close all open files and continue to the next activity or quit the program if you have finished.

QUICK REFERENCE

dBASE does not immediately delete records from the disk when you specify that they be deleted. The deleted records are just flagged with an electronic flag. These flagged records can be ignored when other file operations are used, and they can be recovered if needed. They can be permanently removed by a separate operation called packing.

Flagging Records for Deletion
You use the DELETE <*record*> command from the dot prompt to flag a record for deletion. For example, entering DELETE RECORD 5 at the dot prompt flags record 5 for deletion. You can also flag a record for deletion in edit mode (or browse as you will see later) by highlighting it and pressing Ctrl-U.

A record flagged for deletion is indicated with an asterisk next to the record number when you use the LIST or DISPLAY command. It is indicated with the message *Del* on the status line when you use the EDIT (or BROWSE) command and the record is highlighted or displayed full screen.

Ignoring Flagged Records
When records are flagged for deletion but the file has not been packed, you can have commands ignore the flagged records. To do so, use the SET DELETED ON command. To have commands recognize the deleted records, use the SET DELETED OFF command.

Recalling Flagged Records
The RECALL <*record*> command recalls flagged files so that they are not deleted when the file is packed. For example, entering RECALL RECORD 5 at the dot prompt removes the flag from record 5. RECALL ALL unflags all records.

Deleting Flagged Records
The PACK command permanently removes all records flagged for deletion.

The ZAP Command
If you ever want to delete all the records from a database, you use the ZAP command. This command is the same as flagging all records for deletion and then packing the file. If you use the SET SAFETY ON command first, you will be prompted to confirm the procedure when you use this command.

EXERCISES

EXERCISE 1

DELETING RECORDS FROM THE EMPLOYEE FILE

1. Open the EMPLOYEE file.
2. Flag for deletion the record for EMP_NUM 104 (Susan Adams).
3. Pack the database to remove the flagged record.
4. List the remaining records to the printer.

EXERCISE 2

DELETING RECORDS FROM THE DEPT FILE

1. Open the DEPT file.
2. Flag for deletion the records for EMP_NUM 104 (records 3 and 13).
3. Pack the database to remove the flagged record.
4. List the remaining records to the printer.

CHAPTER 2 REVIEW

- Planning a database is important because you want to be able to find data easily.
- To define a database file, you use the CREATE <filename> command.
- When you define a file, you indicate the name of the field, the type of data to be entered, and its width (number of characters).
- Field names must be unique. The same field name cannot be used more than once in a file.
- Fields that contain unique data can be used to link files.
- Field types include character (text), numeric (whose data can be calculated), logical (where you indicate only true and false or yes and no), date, and memo.
- The data entered into memo fields, up to 5,000 characters, are stored in a separate file on the disk that has the same name as the database file but the extension .DBT.
- Field width is important; you don't want to make it so short that you lose information or too long so that you waste memory and disk space.
- To display a file's structure, you can press F5 or enter the DISPLAY STRUCTURE or LIST STRUCTURE command when the file is open.
- If you have an existing database, you can add, delete, or redefine fields with the MODIFY STRUCTURE command.
- To enter records into a database file, you must open the file with the USE <filename> command.
- The APPEND command displays a blank record for the open file so that you can enter a new record at the end of a file.
- Ctrl-End saves the records you have entered into the database.
- You can append records from another file with the APPEND FROM <filename> command.
- One record in an open database file is always marked with the record pointer. The record that it is pointing to is always displayed on the status line following the prompt *Rec:*.
- You can move the record pointer with the GOTO and SKIP commands.
- You can edit records with the EDIT command.
- You can only edit memo fields with the EDIT command. You position the cursor in the memo field and press Ctrl-Home or Ctrl-PgDn to display the memo field's contents.
- The CHANGE command is useful when you only want to change data in a single field.
- You delete records from a database in two steps. You first flag them for deletion and then use the PACK command to remove them.
- If you flag records but don't pack the database, you can have the flagged records ignored by using the SET DELETED ON command.
- To remove the flags from records that have been flagged for deletion, you use the RECALL command.

CHAPTER 2 **QUESTIONS**

FILL IN THE BLANK

1. A ___________ contains unique data like social security numbers.
2. To create a database file named CUST, you would use the command ___________.
3. If you want to calculate numbers, you must store them in a ___________ field.
4. To display the structure of an existing file, you can press ___________ or use the ___________ command.
5. To restructure an open database file, you use the ___________ command.
6. To add new records to the end of an existing database file, you use the ___________ command.
7. Records that you append are added to the ___________ of the file.
8. To add new records from another file named RECADD, you would use the command ___________.
9. One record in a database file is always marked with a ___________.
10. The GOTO and SKIP commands move the ___________.
11. You edit records with the ___________ command.
12. To display the contents of a memo field, you position the cursor in it and then press ___________.
13. To delete records from a database, you must first ___________ them.
14. To remove records that have been flagged, you ___________ the database file with the ___________ command.
15. To remove the flags from records flagged for deletion, you use the ___________ command.
16. To have commands ignore flagged records, you use the ___________ command.

MATCH THE COLUMNS

1. Field with unique data for each record	__ Displays the specified fields for editing
2. CREATE <filename>	__ Adds records to end of file
3. APPEND	__ Lists field definitions in a database file
4. Field width	__ Accept only yes/no or true/false answers
5. LIST STRUCTURE	__ Numbers in these fields can be calculated
6. Logical fields	__ A field that can be used to link files
7. Numeric fields	__ Determines the number of characters that you can enter in a field
	__ Fields with variable widths
	__ Contains dates
	__ Specified only for numeric fields

8. Date fields
9. Memo fields
10. Decimals
11. MODIFY STRUCTURE
12. APPEND FROM
13. GOTO
14. EDIT
15. CHANGE
16. PACK
17. DELETE RECORD <n>
18. SET DELETED ON
19. RECALL

_ Removes flagged records from database
_ The command used to restructure a database
_ Displays all fields for editing
_ Adds records from another file
_ Moves the record pointer
_ Removes delete flags from records
_ Marks a record for deletion
_ Causes flagged records to be ignored
_ Displays the database definition screen

WRITE OUT THE ANSWERS

1. Briefly describe each of the following types of fields:
   a. Character
   b. Numeric
   c. Logical
   d. Date
   e. Memo
2. What widths would you specify for a field into which the largest number you were going to enter was 100.00? 10.00? 1000.00?
3. Why would you not specify the maximum width available for each field so that you do not have to plan field widths so carefully?
4. Why would you not be able to sort names based on last names if you entered both first and last names in one field?
5. Explain what a database structure is and how you make a printout of it.
6. How is a database restructured and why is this done?
7. What happens if you restructure a file and change a field's name?
8. What effect does the record pointer have?
9. When you use the APPEND command, where are records added to the file?
10. In what order do you enter records? Why?
11. Describe the process you follow to delete records from a database.
12. After records are flagged for deletion, describe how you would have them ignored by subsequent commands. Describe how you would then remove the flags.

CHAPTER 2

PROJECTS

PROJECT 1

CREATING THE TITLES DATABASE

1. Create a database file named TITLES.
2. Define the fields using the descriptions in the table "The TITLES Database Fields."

THE TITLES DATABASE FIELDS

Field Name	Description	Type	Width	Dec
ISBN	The book's ISBN	C	13	-
TITLE	The book's title	C	20	-
AUTHOR	The book's author	C	10	-
EDITION	The book's edition	C	1	-
VERSION	Hardcover (H) or paperback (P)	C	1	-
LIST	The list price	N	5	2

3. Print out the file's structure and compare it with the description of the fields in the table.
4. Enter the two records shown in the table "The TITLES Database Records."

THE TITLES DATABASE RECORDS

Field Name	Record 1	Record 2
ISBN	96100	96101
TITLE	American History	Computer Basics
AUTHOR	Smith	Williams
EDITION	1	1
VERSION	P	P
LIST	19.95	24.95

5. Modify the database by adding a new field following the existing LIST field. Name it CATEGORY and define its type as Character and its width as 15.
6. Append records to the file from the TITLHOLD file.
7. Fill in the CATEGORY field for the first two records with **Humanities** (for ISBN 96100) and **Computer Sci** (for ISBN 96101).
8. List the version field and notice how some are uppercase (caps) and some are lowercase. Edit the data in this field so all are uppercase.
9. List all records in the file to the printer.

PROJECT 2

CREATING THE SALES DATABASE

1. Create a database file named SALES.
2. Define the fields using the descriptions in the table "The SALES Database Fields."

THE SALES DATABASE FIELDS

Field Name	Description	Type	Width	Dec
ISBN	The book's ISBN number	C	13	-
TRADE	Sales to the bookstore market	N	7	-
EDUC	Sales to high schools and colleges	N	7	-
MAIL	Sales by direct mail	N	7	-
INTNTL	Sales to the international market	N	7	-

3. Print out the file's structure and compare it with the description of the fields in the table.
4. Enter the two records shown in the table "The SALES Database Records."

THE SALES DATABASE RECORDS

Field Name	Record 1	Record 2
ISBN	96100	96101
TRADE	400	300
EDUC	1200	900
MAIL	200	400
INTNTL	100	75

5. Modify the database by adding a new field between the existing ISBN and TRADE fields. Name it PERIOD and define its type as Character and its width as 6.
6. Append records to the file from the SALEHOLD file.
7. Fill in the PERIOD field for the first two records with **spring** (for ISBN 96100 and 96101).
8. List all records in the file to the printer.

CHAPTER 3

Using the Data in a Database

TOPIC 8

Displaying the Data in a Database

After completing this topic, you will be able to:

- Display records with the LIST, BROWSE, and DISPLAY commands
- Specify the fields to be displayed with the SET FIELDS TO *<field list>* command
- Explain dBASE's syntax for structuring commands

At any point, you can display the data that you have entered into a database with the LIST, DISPLAY and BROWSE commands. The biggest difference between these commands is that you can edit records displayed with the BROWSE command but not with the LIST and DISPLAY commands. These latter two commands are used only to see data in the database.

dBASE COMMAND SYNTAX

For commands to be recognized by dBASE, they must be phrased according to a set of rules. Now that you have some experience with the commands, let's step back for a moment and look at what these rules are.

Commands generally have four parts:

Verb	Scope	Noun	Condition
DISPLAY	ALL	ID,LASTNAME	FOR ID>"101"

Verbs are the commands themselves such as USE, DISPLAY, LIST, APPEND, and SET. A verb must be a part of every command because it specifies the action that is to be performed.

Scope specifies the range of records that will be affected by the command. Scopes include ALL, NEXT n, RECORD n, and REST (where n stands for a record number).

Nouns are optional and almost always refer to a field or another file. For example, in the commands DISPLAY ID and USE MEMBERS, ID is the name of a field, and MEMBERS is the name of a file. (Three exceptions to this are DISPLAY STRUCTURE, DISPLAY STATUS, and the many variations of the SET command.)

Conditions, which are discussed in Chapter 4, set up criteria that filter records so that only those that meet the criteria are affected by the command. Conditions use the phrase FOR, relational operators such as < *and* >, logical operators such as .AND., or a $ sign.

When you display the data in a database file, the command you use displays the data in either form view or table view.

- Form view displays the fields of a single record, and the spaces where you are to enter data are highlighted in reverse video. Form view is what you see when you use the APPEND and EDIT commands. The screen displays a single record and looks like a fill-in form. The advantage of this view is that you can see more fields on the screen. To fill out or edit the form, you move the cursor to the highlighted areas following the field names. The length of the highlight indicates the field width so that you can tell when you are running out of space to enter data.
- Table view displays the fields in many records. Table view is what you see when you use the LIST, DISPLAY and BROWSE commands. If the database is wider or longer than the screen, you can scroll through it both horizontally and vertically. To view, enter, or edit records, you move the cursor through the fields and type data in.

DOT-PROMPT TUTORIAL

In this tutorial, you use the LIST command to explore dBASE syntax and the DISPLAY command to explore the record pointer using the MEMBERS file from the dot prompt. You then experiment with the SET FIELDS TO <*field list*> and BROWSE commands.

GETTING STARTED

1. Display the dot prompt and open the MEMBERS database file.

EXPLORING THE VERB

2. Type **LIST** and press Enter↵ to see how the verb (command) lists all the fields in all the records in the file.

EXPLORING THE SCOPE

3. Type **LIST RECORD 1** and press Enter↵ to see how the scope following the verb specifies which record is displayed.
4. Type **LIST NEXT 5** and press Enter↵ to use another scope to list the next five records, beginning with the one to which the record pointer is pointing.
5. Type **LIST REST** and press Enter↵ to use still another scope to list all remaining records, beginning with the one to which the record pointer is pointing.
6. Type **LIST** and press Enter↵ to list all the records because ALL is the default scope.

EXPLORING THE NOUN

7. Type **LIST LASTNAME,FIRST** and press Enter↵ to see how a noun (LASTNAME,FIRST), specifies which fields are displayed.
8. Type **LIST LASTNAME,FIRST,AREA,PHONE** and press Enter↵ to see how another noun specifies additional fields.

EXPLORING THE CONDITION

9. Type **LIST LASTNAME,FIRST,ST FOR ST="MA"** and press Enter↵ to see how a condition (ST="MA") filters records so that only those that meet the condition are displayed. Only those records with MA in the ST field are displayed.
10. Type **LIST LASTNAME,FIRST,ST FOR ST="CA"** and press Enter↵ to see how a different condition lists different records, in this case those records with CA in the ST field.

USING THE DISPLAY COMMAND TO EXPLORE THE RECORD POINTER

11. Type **DISPLAY RECORD 1** and press Enter↵ to display record 1.
12. Type **2** and press Enter↵ to move the record pointer to record 2. Notice how the status line indicates that the record pointer is on record 2 of 14. Typing just the number of the record moves the record pointer to the record just as a longer command does.
13. Type **DISPLAY** and press Enter↵ to display the second record.
14. Type **SKIP** and press Enter↵ to move the record pointer. A message *Record No. 3* indicates you have skipped to record 3, and the status line indicates the record pointer is on record 3.
15. Type **DISPLAY** and press Enter↵ to display the record.
16. Type **DISPLAY NEXT 3** and press Enter↵ to display three records. The record pointer moves to the last record displayed.
17. Type **GO TOP** and press Enter↵ to move the record pointer to record 1.
18. Press F8 to enter the DISPLAY command.
19. Type **GO BOTTOM** and press Enter↵ to move the record pointer to the end of the file.
20. Press F8 to display the last record.
21. Type **?RECNO()** and press Enter↵ to see the number of the record where the record pointer is positioned.

LISTING ONLY SELECTED FIELDS

22. Type **LIST ID,FIRST,LASTNAME** and press Enter↵ to list the record number, ID, first, and last name of each record. The LIST command must be followed by a list of fields each time you want only selected fields displayed.
23. Type **SET FIELDS TO ID,FIRST,LASTNAME** and press Enter↵ so only the ID, first, and last name fields will be displayed in subsequent commands. It is important to remember that no other fields can be displayed while the SET FIELDS command is on.
24. Type **LIST TO PRINT** and press Enter↵ to display and print the specified fields.

25. Press [F5] to see which fields are listed in a SET FIELDS command. Each field preceded by a > sign has been set. Whenever you want to display fields other than those in the SET FIELDS command, the SET FIELDS command must be turned off.
26. Type **CLEAR FIELDS** and press [Enter←] to reset the program to display all fields.
27. Press [F5] to see that the fields are no longer marked.

USING THE BROWSE COMMAND

28. Type **GO TOP** and press [Enter←] to move the record pointer to the top of the file. The status line displays the number of the record.
29. Type **BROWSE** and press [Enter←] to display a help menu (press [F1] if it isn't) and a list of all the records in the database.

Browsing the MEMBERS File
The BROWSE command displays records in a tablelike view.

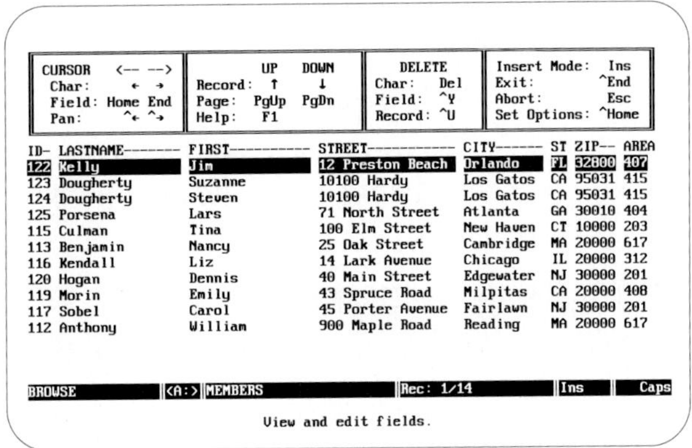

30. Practice moving the cursor and scrolling the screen with the keys listed and described in the table "Moving the Cursor in Browse Mode."

MOVING THE CURSOR IN BROWSE MODE

To move to	Press
Next field	[Enter←] OR [End]
Previous field	[Home]
Up or down one record	[↑] or [↓]
Left or right one character	[←] or [→]
Scroll screen up and down	[PgDn] or [PgUp]
Pan left or right	[Ctrl]-[←] or [Ctrl]-[→]

31. Press [Esc] to return to the dot prompt.
32. Type **SET FIELDS TO ID,FIRST,LASTNAME** and press [Enter←].
33. Type **BROWSE** and press [Enter←] to display only the specified fields.

Setting Fields in the MEMBERS File
The SET FIELDS TO command specifies which fields are displayed when you use the LIST, DISPLAY, or BROWSE command.

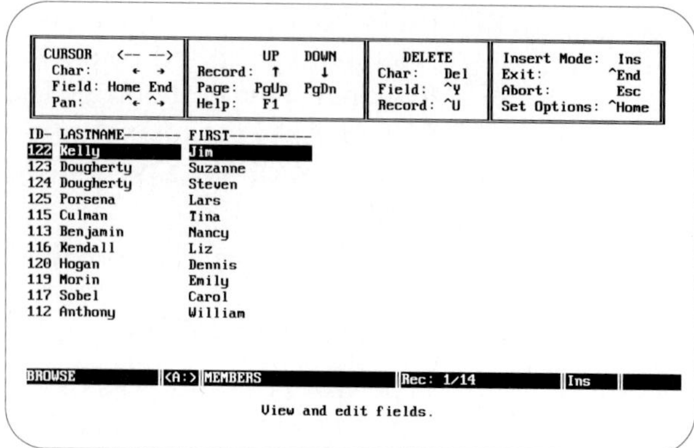

34. Press Esc to return to the dot prompt.
35. Type **CLEAR FIELDS** and press Enter↵ to reset the program to display all fields.

FINISHING UP

36. You have completed this tutorial. Either close all open files and continue to the next activity or quit the program.

ASSIST-MENU TUTORIAL

In this tutorial, you display records in the CHARGES database file with commands from the Assist menu.

GETTING STARTED

1. Display the Assist menu and open the CHARGES database file.

USING THE LIST COMMAND

2. Press R to pull down the Retrieve menu.
3. Highlight *List* and press Enter↵.
4. Highlight *Execute the command* and press Enter↵. The prompt reads *Direct the output to the printer? [Y/N].*
5. Press N to display all the records, and the prompt reads *Press any key to continue to work in ASSIST.*

The LIST Command
The List command on the Retreive menu displays all the records in the database.

```
Set Up  Create  Update  Position  Retrieve  Organize Modify Tools   11:11:05 am

Record#  ID  DATE      AMOUNT CLEARED
      1  122 04/10/93   50.00 .F.
      2  122 04/19/93   75.00 .F.
      3  124 04/19/93   15.00 .F.
      4  124 04/20/93   13.00 .F.
      5  115 03/16/93   11.00 .T.
      6  113 03/08/93   16.50 .T.
      7  116 03/10/93   38.50 .T.
      8  120 03/11/93   25.00 .T.
      9  117 03/12/93   30.00 .T.
     10  118 03/13/93   50.00 .F.
     11  121 03/14/93   15.00 .T.
     12  121 03/15/93   10.00 .T.
     13  125 03/15/93  100.00 .T.
     14  123 03/16/93   25.00 .T.
     15  123 03/16/93   35.00 .T.
     16  119 03/17/93   12.00 .F.
ASSIST          <A:> CHARGES            Rec: 1/16          Ins
              Press any key to continue work in ASSIST.
```

6. Press any key to return to the Assist menus.

USING THE BROWSE COMMAND

7. Press [P] to pull down the Position menu.
8. Highlight *Goto Record* and press [Enter ↵].
9. Highlight *TOP* and press [Enter ↵] to move the record pointer to the top of the file.
10. Press [U] to pull down the Update menu.
11. Highlight *Browse* and press [Enter ↵] to display a list of all records.

Browsing the CHARGES File
The Browse command on the Update menu displays records in a tablelike view.

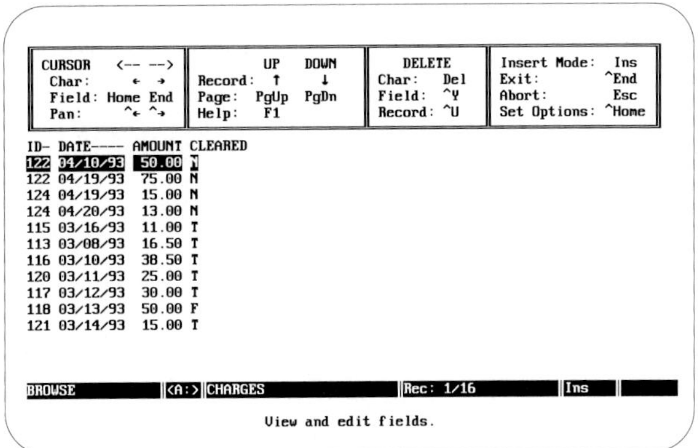

12. Press [Esc] to return to the menu.

DISPLAYING SINGLE RECORDS

13. Press [R] to pull down the Retrieve menu.
14. Highlight *Display* and press [Enter ↵].
15. Highlight *Specify scope* and press [Enter ↵].
16. Highlight *RECORD* and press [Enter ↵]. The prompt reads *Enter a numeric value:*.
17. Type **1** and press [Enter ↵] to move the record pointer to the first record, so it becomes the current record.
18. Highlight *Execute the command* and press [Enter ↵] to display record 1 and the prompt reads *Press any key to continue to work in ASSIST.*
19. Press any key to return to the Assist menus.

DISPLAYING THE NEXT THREE RECORDS

20. Highlight *Display* and press [Enter ↵].
21. Highlight *Specify scope* and press [Enter ↵].
22. Highlight *NEXT* and press [Enter ↵]. The prompt reads *Enter a numeric value:*.
23. Type **3** and press [Enter ↵].
24. Highlight *Execute the command* and press [Enter ↵] to display the current record and the next two. The prompt reads *Press any key to continue to work in ASSIST.*
25. Press any key to return to the Assist menus.

LISTING ONLY SPECIFIED FIELDS

26. Highlight *Display* and press Enter ↵.
27. Highlight *Specify scope* and press Enter ↵.
28. Highlight *ALL* and press Enter ↵.
29. Highlight *Construct a field list* and press Enter ↵ to display a list of the fields in the file.
30. Highlight *DATE* and press Enter ↵.
31. Highlight *AMOUNT* and press Enter ↵.
32. Press → to exit the field menu.
33. Highlight *Execute the command* and press Enter ↵ to display the two specified fields. The prompt reads *Press any key to continue to work in ASSIST.*

Setting Fields in the CHARGES File
The Construct a field list command specifies which fields are displayed when you use the LIST, DISPLAY, or BROWSE command. Here only the DATE and AMOUNT fields are displayed.

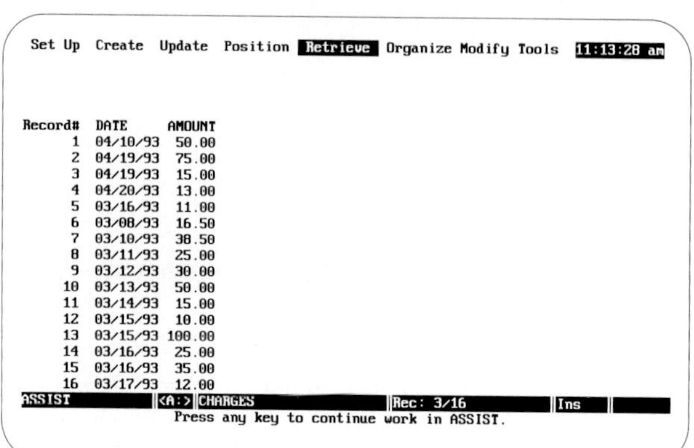

Record#	DATE	AMOUNT
1	04/18/93	50.00
2	04/19/93	75.00
3	04/19/93	15.00
4	04/20/93	13.00
5	03/16/93	11.00
6	03/08/93	16.50
7	03/10/93	38.50
8	03/11/93	25.00
9	03/12/93	30.00
10	03/13/93	50.00
11	03/14/93	15.00
12	03/15/93	10.00
13	03/15/93	100.00
14	03/16/93	25.00
15	03/16/93	35.00
16	03/17/93	12.00

34. Press any key to return to the Assist menus.

FINISHING UP

35. You have completed this tutorial. Either close all open files and continue to the next activity or quit the program.

QUICK REFERENCE

When you want to see the records in a database, but not edit them, you use the DISPLAY or LIST commands. If you follow the command with the TO PRINT option, or use the SET PRINT ON command first, you can also use these commands to print out one or more records in the database. If you want to add or edit records, you use the BROWSE command.

The DISPLAY Command
To display the records in a file, you can use the DISPLAY command with or without the scope ALL, <*n*>, NEXT <*n*>, or REST (where <*n*> stands for any number); for example:

- DISPLAY displays the record with the record pointer.
- DISPLAY ALL (or F8) displays all records in the current database file.

- DISPLAY NEXT 5 displays the next five records beginning with the one to which the record pointer points.
- DISPLAY REST displays all records from the record pointer on.

If there are too many records to be displayed on the screen at one time, the list pauses when the screen is full, and the prompt reads *Press any key to continue*. Press any key to see the next screenful.

The LIST Command

To display the records in a file, you can also use the LIST command. For example, LIST, LIST ALL, or F3 lists all the records in the current database file.

LIST, unlike DISPLAY, does not pause when the screen is full. However, you can press Ctrl-S or the Pause key on enhanced keyboards to stop and restart the scrolling for a large file. You can also restart scrolling by pressing Enter↵ or Spacebar.

The BROWSE Command

The BROWSE command displays as many as 17 records at a time on the screen. When in browse mode, you can press Ctrl-Home to display a menu of GOTO command options. As you move the highlight along the menu bar, a description of each choice is displayed on the bottom line of the screen. These commands are also described in the table "Browse Menu Bar Commands."

When you are in Browse mode, if you move the highlight to the last record and press ↓, the prompt reads *Add new records? (Y/N)*. Press Y and a new, blank record is added which you can then fill in. If the database is large, you can quickly move to the last record with the GOTO BOTTOM command before executing the BROWSE command.

BROWSE MENU BAR COMMANDS

Command	Description
Bottom	Moves the record pointer and highlight to the last record in the data
Top	Moves the record pointer and highlight to the first record in the data base.
Lock	Specifies one or more fields that are to remain displayed on the left side of the screen while you scroll through other fields in the database. Choosing this command displays the prompt *Change number of columns to lock to:*. Type the number you want to lock. (The number refers to the columns displayed on the screen, counting from left to right.) For example, to lock the second and third columns in a database, pan the screen so that these are the leftmost on the screen (column 1 would be off the screen to the left) and then lock 2 columns.
Record No.	Displays the prompt *Enter new record number:*. Type the number of the record that you want to move the record pointer and highlight to and then press Enter↵.
Freeze	Displays the prompt *Enter field name to freeze:*. Type the name of a field, and the highlight will remain in that field as you scroll through records.

Displaying Selected Fields

When you are interested in only the data in specific fields, you can specify which fields are to be displayed by a command. There are two ways to do this: by listing the fields in the command or by using a SET FIELDS TO <*field list*> command so that all subsequent commands are affected.

Specifying Fields in Commands

When you want to list just specific fields, enter a list of the fields following the command. Separate the field names with commas but no spaces. For example, to see just the ID and LASTNAME fields, you would use the following commands:

- BROWSE ID,LASTNAME displays the ID and LASTNAME fields in BROWSE mode.
- LIST ID,LASTNAME lists the ID and LASTNAME fields in all records.
- LIST STREET displays all entries in the field named STREET.
- LIST NEXT 5 STREET displays the contents of the STREET field in the next five records.
- DISPLAY ID,LASTNAME displays the ID and LASTNAME fields in the record marked by the record pointer.
- DISPLAY NEXT 5 STREET displays the contents of the STREET field in the next five records.
- DISPLAY ALL STREET displays all entries in the field named STREET.

Using the SET FIELDS TO Command

To use the same fields in a series of different commands, it is faster to specify them once with the SET FIELDS TO <*field list*> command so that all subsequent commands affect only the specified fields. For example, SET FIELDS TO ID,LASTNAME specifies that when you use the LIST, BROWSE, or DISPLAY command, only the ID and LASTNAME fields are displayed. To see which fields have been set, press F5. The fields marked with greater-than signs (>) are set to be displayed. To list all fields again, use the CLEAR FIELDS command.

EXERCISES

EXERCISE 1

DISPLAYING SELECTED FIELDS IN THE EMPLOYEE FILE

1. Open the EMPLOYEE file.
2. Set fields to EMP_NUM, LASTNAME, FIRST, and PAYRATE.
3. List the records to the printer.
4. Close all files.

The EMPLOYEE File
The EMPLOYEE file contains data such as the names and pay rate shown here. The SET FIELDS TO command is used to display only these fields.

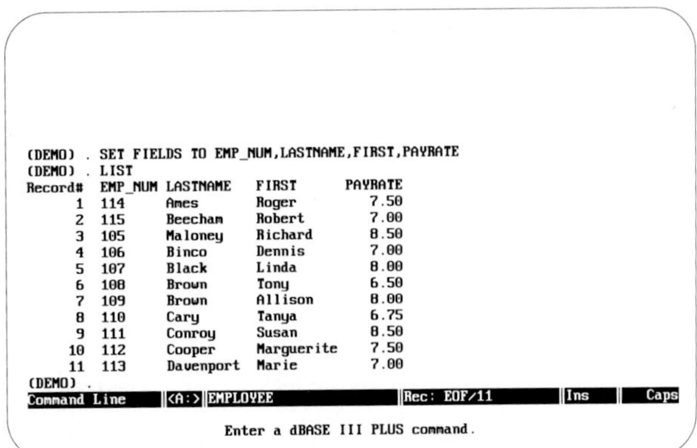

```
(DEMO) . SET FIELDS TO EMP_NUM,LASTNAME,FIRST,PAYRATE
(DEMO) . LIST
Record#  EMP_NUM LASTNAME   FIRST      PAYRATE
      1  114     Ames       Roger         7.50
      2  115     Beecham    Robert        7.00
      3  105     Maloney    Richard       8.50
      4  106     Binco      Dennis        7.00
      5  107     Black      Linda         8.00
      6  108     Brown      Tony          6.50
      7  109     Brown      Allison       8.00
      8  110     Cary       Tanya         6.75
      9  111     Conroy     Susan         8.50
     10  112     Cooper     Marguerite    7.50
     11  113     Davenport  Marie         7.00
(DEMO) .
Command Line   <A:> EMPLOYEE        Rec: EOF/11      Ins    Caps
                 Enter a dBASE III PLUS command.
```

EXERCISE 2

DISPLAYING SELECTED FIELDS IN THE DEPT FILE

1. Open the DEPT file.
2. Set fields to EMP_NUM and HOURS.
3. List the records to the printer.
4. Close all files.

The DEPT File
The DEPT file contains data such as the employee number and hours worked shown here. The SET FIELDS TO command is used to display only these fields.

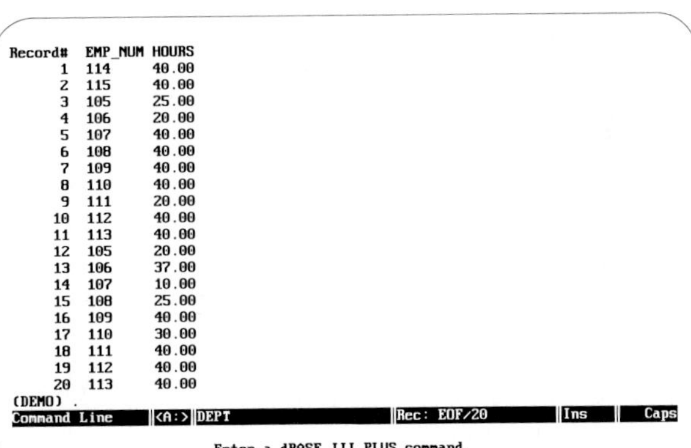

```
Record#  EMP_NUM HOURS
      1  114     40.00
      2  115     40.00
      3  105     25.00
      4  106     20.00
      5  107     40.00
      6  108     40.00
      7  109     40.00
      8  110     40.00
      9  111     20.00
     10  112     40.00
     11  113     40.00
     12  105     20.00
     13  106     37.00
     14  107     10.00
     15  108     25.00
     16  109     40.00
     17  110     30.00
     18  111     40.00
     19  112     40.00
     20  113     40.00
(DEMO) .
Command Line   <A:> DEPT            Rec: EOF/20      Ins    Caps
                 Enter a dBASE III PLUS command.
```

TOPIC 9

Using Relational Operators to Filter Records

After completing this topic, you will be able to:

- Enter relational operators such as greater than (>) and equal to (=) that filter records so that only those records that match the condition are displayed
- Search for character strings by enclosing them in quotation marks
- Search for dates by converting your string to a date with the CTOD (character to date) function
- Specify a filter with the SET FILTER TO command

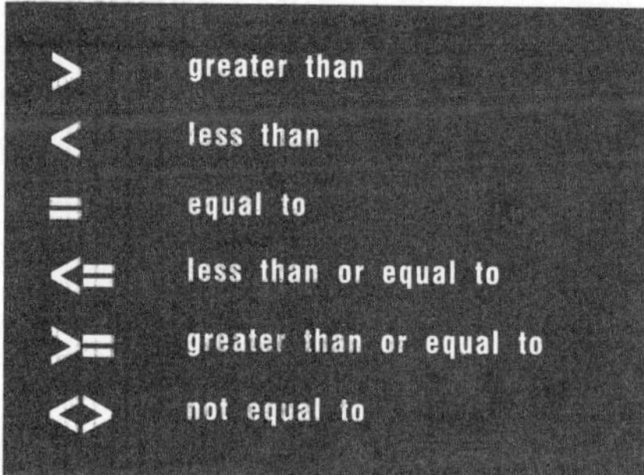

Relational Operators
The relational operators shown here are used to compare data to determine if they are equal to, greater than, or less than other data.

In previous topics, you have used several commands that displayed records so that you could edit or delete them. Those commands were useful in a small database, but when the number of records increases, it becomes harder to find the record you want with the DISPLAY, LIST, and BROWSE command. Database management programs like dBASE III Plus also have commands that let you find one or more records by using relational operators that filter the records that are displayed. Only those records that match the specified criteria are affected by the command.

You use relational operators with commands like DISPLAY to find records. For example, to answer a question such as "What customers have a balance due greater than $25?" you would use the command DISPLAY FOR AMOUNT>25. In this query, the condition FOR AMOUNT>25 has been added as a condition to the command. This command will display only those records of customers whose AMOUNT is greater than $25.

When you use these operators, enclose character strings in quotes. If you do not, you will get an error message *Data type mismatch.* If you see this message, display the file's structure and note down which are numeric fields and which are character fields. Just because there are numbers in a field does not mean it's numeric. For example, ZIP code or department number fields are probably character fields.

Keep in mind that dBASE is case sensitive, so if you refer to the state *MA*, don't enter it as *ma* or *Ma* in your commands.

DOT-PROMPT TUTORIAL

In this tutorial, you use relational operators to filter records in the MEMBERS database file.

GETTING STARTED

1. Display the dot prompt and open the MEMBERS database file.

FILTERING RECORDS WITH RELATIONAL OPERATORS

2. Type **SET FIELDS TO LASTNAME,FIRST,ST,AGE,AREA, ENROLLED** and press [Enter↵].
3. Type **LIST** and press [Enter↵] to display only those fields specified in the SET FIELDS TO command.

The SET FIELDS Command
The SET FIELDS TO command displays only those fields used in this tutorial so that the results of commands are easier to analyze.

```
(DEMO) . USE MEMBERS
(DEMO) . SET FIELDS TO LASTNAME,FIRST,ST,AGE,AREA,ENROLLED
(DEMO) . LIST
Record#  LASTNAME        FIRST           ST AREA ENROLLED AGE
      1  Kelly           Jim             FL 407  01/10/93  26
      2  Dougherty       Suzanne         CA 415  02/12/93  27
      3  Dougherty       Steven          CA 415  03/01/93  35
      4  Porsena         Lars            GA 404  03/05/93  89
      5  Culman          Tina            CT 203  01/16/92  33
      6  Benjamin        Nancy           MA 617  01/08/92  26
      7  Kendall         Liz             IL 312  02/01/92  19
      8  Hogan           Dennis          NJ 201  09/06/92  39
      9  Morin           Emily           CA 408  08/01/92   3
     10  Sobel           Carol           NJ 201  03/06/92  34
     11  Anthony         William         MA 617  01/07/92  63
     12  Morin           Cathy           OR 508  06/03/92  22
     13  Morin           Mike            OR 508  01/10/92  45
     14  Kendall         Steve           NJ 201  10/15/92  25
(DEMO) .
Command Line  |<A:>|MEMBERS          |Rec: EOF/14      |     | Caps

                  Enter a dBASE III PLUS command.
```

4. Type **LIST FOR AGE>50 TO PRINT** and press [Enter↵] to list only records with ages over 50 in the AGE field.
5. Type **LIST FOR ST="MA" TO PRINT** and press [Enter↵] to list only records with MA in the ST field.
6. Type **LIST FOR AREA="201" TO PRINT** and press [Enter↵] to list only records with a 201 area code in the AREA field.
7. Type **LIST FOR ENROLLED>CTOD("12/30/92") TO PRINT** and press [Enter↵] to list only records with dates later than 12/30/92 in the ENROLLED field.
8. Type **CLEAR FIELDS** and press [Enter↵] so all fields will be listed by subsequent commands.

REMEMBER THE HISTORY COMMAND

Many commands in this tutorial are quite long. If you make a mistake and the command does not work, remember that you can press [↑] to return it to the dot command line for editing rather than retype the entire command.

DISPLAYING SELECTED FIELDS IN FILTERED RECORDS

9. Type **LIST LASTNAME FOR ST="MA" TO PRINT** and press [Enter↵] to list only the LASTNAME field for records with MA in the ST field.
10. Type **LIST ID,LASTNAME,FIRST,AREA,PHONE FOR ST="MA" TO PRINT** and press [Enter↵] to list only the specified fields for records with MA in the ST field.

SETTING A FILTER

11. Type **SET FILTER TO AGE>=40** and press [Enter↵] to set a filter so only records with ages of 40 or more will be displayed in subsequent commands.
12. Type **GO TOP** and press [Enter↵] to move the record pointer to the beginning of the database. The status line reads *Rec: 4/14* because the fourth record is the first one in the database that meets the condition specified in the filter.

13. Type **LIST LASTNAME,AGE TO PRINT** and press [Enter←] to list the specified fields in records with ages of 40 or over in the AGE field.
14. Type **BROWSE** and press [Enter←] to display only records with ages of 40 or over in the AGE field.
15. Press [Esc] to return to the dot prompt.
16. Type **SET FILTER TO** and press [Enter←] to remove the filter. (It is turned off when you use the command without specifying a condition.)

CONTINUING ON YOUR OWN

17. The Quick Reference section in this topic describes relational operators. You might want to experiment more with these before proceeding. If you make any mistakes, the program will respond with an error message and may ask if you want help. To try again, press [Esc] to return to the dot prompt.

FINISHING UP

18. You have completed this tutorial. Either close all open files and continue to the next activity or quit the program.

ASSIST-MENU TUTORIAL

In this tutorial, you use relational operators to filter records in the CHARGES database file.

GETTING STARTED

1. Display the Assist menu and open the CHARGES database file.

FILTERING RECORDS

2. Press [R] to pull down the Retrieve menu.
3. Highlight *Display* and press [Enter←].
4. Highlight *Build a search condition* and press [Enter←] to display a list of fields in the database file.
5. Highlight *AMOUNT* and press [Enter←].
6. Highlight = *Equal To* and press [Enter←]. The prompt reads *Enter a numeric value:*.
7. Type **30** and press [Enter←].
8. Highlight *No more conditions* and press [Enter←].
9. Highlight *Execute the command* and press [Enter←] to display the record matching the criterion. The prompt reads *Press any key to continue to work in ASSIST.*
10. Press any key to return to the Assist menus.

DISPLAYING SELECTED FIELDS FROM FILTERED RECORDS

11. Highlight *Display* and press [Enter←].
12. Highlight *Construct a field list* and press [Enter←] to display a list of fields in the database file.

13. Highlight *ID* and press Enter↵.
14. Highlight *AMOUNT* and press Enter↵.
15. Press → to return the highlight to the previous menu.
16. Highlight *Build a search condition* and press Enter↵.
17. Highlight *AMOUNT* and press Enter↵.
18. Highlight >= *Greater Than or Equal To* and press Enter↵. The prompt reads *Enter a numeric value:*.
19. Type **30** and press Enter↵.
20. Highlight *No more conditions* and press Enter↵.
21. Highlight *Execute the command* and press Enter↵ to display the ID and AMOUNT fields for the records that match the criterion of amounts greater than or equal to 30. The prompt reads *Press any key to continue to work in ASSIST.*
22. Press any key to return to the Assist menus.

FINISHING UP

23. You have completed this tutorial. Either close all open files and continue to the next activity or quit the program.

QUICK REFERENCE

The relational operators explained below are used to compare the data in a field to a number, character string, date, or logical statement to determine their relationship. For example, relational operators can determine if one field's value is larger or smaller than another's, has an earlier or later date, or comes before or after it alphabetically. When entering queries containing relational operators, be sure to follow these rules:

- When entering the data to be searched for in character fields, use the same case. For example, when searching for Jones, enter it as Jones, not jones or JONES.
- When searching for text strings, enclose them in matching single or double quotes. For example, to find *Jones*, enter it as "Jones" or 'Jones'. To find the number 101 in a character field, enter it as "101" or '101'. (You can also enclose the string in square brackets [<*string*>].)
- When searching for numbers in numeric fields, no quotes are used.
- When searching for dates in date fields, use the CTOD() (**C**haracter **TO D**ate) function to convert a date entered as characters in your query to a date data type that matches the date in the date field. For example to query a file to find a date equal to January 10, 1993, you would use the command DISPLAY FOR DATE=CTOD("01/10/93").
- If you get the error message *Data type mismatch*, it means you have not used quotes around a string when searching a character field, have used them in a numeric field, or have otherwise entered the wrong data type for the indicated field.

Greater Than

The greater-than operator (>) finds all records greater than the criteria you specify; for example:

- DISPLAY FOR LASTNAME>"Jones" displays all records alphabetically after Jones.
- DISPLAY FOR AMOUNT>10.00 finds all records where the AMOUNT is more than 10.00.
- DISPLAY FOR DATE>CTOD("1/10/93") finds all records where the DATE is later than January 10, 1993.

Less Than

The less-than operator (<) finds all records less than the criteria you specify; for example:

- DISPLAY FOR LASTNAME<"Jones" displays all records alphabetically before Jones.
- DISPLAY FOR AMOUNT<10.00 finds all records where the AMOUNT is less than 10.00.
- DISPLAY FOR DATE<CTOD("1/10/93") finds all records where the DATE is earlier than January 10, 1993.

Equal To

The equal-to operator (=) finds all records exactly equal to the criteria you specify; for example:

- DISPLAY FOR LASTNAME="Jones" finds all records with Jones in the LASTNAME field.
- DISPLAY FOR AMOUNT=10.00 finds all records where the AMOUNT is 10.00.
- DISPLAY FOR DATE=CTOD("1/10/93") finds all records dated January 10, 1993.

Greater Than or Equal To

The greater-than-or-equal-to operator (>=) finds all records greater than or equal to the criteria you specify; for example:

- DISPLAY FOR LASTNAME>="Jones" finds all records with Jones in the LASTNAME field and all entries in that field that follow Jones alphabetically.
- DISPLAY FOR AMOUNT>=10.00 finds all records where the AMOUNT is 10.00 or more.
- DISPLAY FOR DATE>=CTOD("1/10/93") finds all records where the DATE is January 10, 1993, or later.

Less Than or Equal To

The less-than-or-equal-to operator (<=) finds all records less than or equal to the criteria you specify; for example:

- DISPLAY FOR LASTNAME<="Jones" finds all records with Jones in the LASTNAME field and all entries in that field that precede Jones alphabetically.
- DISPLAY FOR AMOUNT<=10.00 finds all records where the AMOUNT is 10.00 or less.
- DISPLAY FOR DATE<=CTOD("1/10/93") finds all records where the DATE is January 10, 1993, or earlier.

Not Equal To

The not-equal-to operator (<>) finds all records not exactly equal to the criteria you specify; for example:

- DISPLAY FOR LASTNAME<>"Jones" displays all records except those with Jones in the LASTNAME field.
- DISPLAY FOR AMOUNT<>10.00 finds all records where the AMOUNT is not 10.00.
- DISPLAY FOR DATE<>CTOD("1/10/93") finds all records not dated January 10, 1993.

The SET FILTER TO command

When you want to use the same filter for a number of commands, you can use the SET FILTER TO <*condition*> command. For example, to display just those records that have over $50 in the AMOUNT field, you use the command SET FILTER TO AMOUNT>50. You turn the filter off by entering the SET FILTER TO command without specifying a criterion.

EXERCISES

EXERCISE 1

FILTERING RECORDS IN THE EMPLOYEE FILE

1. Open the EMPLOYEE file.
2. Set fields to EMP_NUM, DEPT, LASTNAME, FIRST, CITY and PAYRATE.
3. List to the printer only those records that have *1* in the DEPT field.
4. List to the printer only those records that have *Largo* in the CITY field.
5. List to the printer only those records that have less than $7.00 in the PAYRATE field.

EXERCISE 2

FILTERING RECORDS IN THE DEPT FILE

1. Open the DEPT file.
2. List to the printer only those records that have *2* in the SHIFT field.
3. List to the printer only those records that have less than *40* hours in the HOURS field.
4. List to the printer only those records that have employee numbers higher than 110.

TOPIC 10

Using Logical Operators to Filter Records

After completing this topic, you will be able to:

- Enter the logical operators AND and OR to filter records on more than one criterion
- Enter the logical operator NOT to display records that do not meet the specified criteria
- Replace the field contents of selected records with the REPLACE command
- Find records with the LOCATE and CONTINUE commands
- Find records with the $ command

.AND.	both conditions must be met
.OR.	either condition must be met
.NOT.	following condition must not be met

Logical Operators
Logical operators are used to connect two or more criteria so both are evaluated by the command.

You can use the logical operators AND, OR, and NOT to filter records using two or more criteria. You use logical operators along with commands like DISPLAY to find records. For example, to answer the question "What date was a charge made to ID number 101 in the amount of $15?" you would use the query DISPLAY DATE FOR ID="101".AND.AMOUNT=15. In this query, the command specifies that the contents of the date field be displayed for records where both the ID is equal to 101 *AND* the amount is $15. The 101 is enclosed in quotation marks to indicate it is stored in a character field. The logical operator has a period before and after it.

DOT-PROMPT TUTORIAL

In this tutorial, you use logical operators to filter records in the MEMBERS database file. You then apply this procedure to replace data in selected fields and locate records with specific contents.

GETTING STARTED

1. Display the dot prompt and open the MEMBERS database file.
2. Type **SET FIELDS TO ID,LASTNAME,FIRST,ST,ENROLLED,AGE** and press Enter so only the specified fields will be displayed by subsequent commands.

USING THE OR OPERATOR

3. Type **DISPLAY FOR ST="MA".OR.ST="NJ"** and press Enter to display only records with MA or NJ in the ST field.
4. Type **DISPLAY FOR AGE>60.OR.AGE<5** and press Enter to display only records with ages greater than 60 or less than 5.

5. Type **DISPLAY FOR ENROLLED>CTOD("01/05/93").OR.AGE>40** and press Enter↵ to display only records for members enrolled after January 5, 1993, or older than 40.

USING THE AND OPERATOR

6. Type **DISPLAY FOR ST="CA".AND.ID>"120"** and press Enter↵ to display only records with CA in the ST field and IDs higher than 120.
7. Type **DISPLAY FOR ENROLLED>CTOD("01/01/93").AND.AGE>30** and press Enter↵ to display only records for members enrolled after January 1, 1993, and older than 30.

COMPARING RESULTS

8. Type **DISPLAY FOR ST="CA".OR.ID>"120"** and press Enter↵ to display only records that have either the specified state or ID.
9. Type **DISPLAY FOR ST="CA".AND.ID>"120"** and press Enter↵ to display only records that have both the specified state and ID.

Comparing the AND and OR Operators
The command using OR displays those records that have the specified data in either the ST or ID fields. The command using AND displays only those records that meet both criteria.

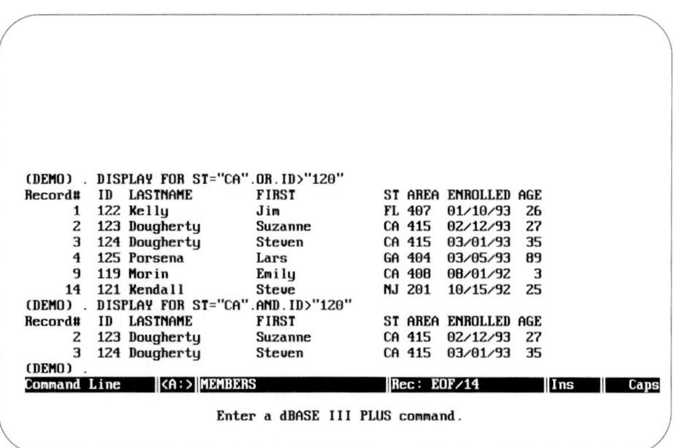

```
(DEMO) . DISPLAY FOR ST="CA".OR.ID>"120"
Record#  ID  LASTNAME        FIRST            ST AREA ENROLLED AGE
      1  122 Kelly           Jim              FL 407  01/10/93  26
      2  123 Dougherty       Suzanne          CA 415  02/12/93  27
      3  124 Dougherty       Steven           CA 415  03/01/93  35
      4  125 Porsena         Lars             GA 404  03/05/93  89
      9  119 Morin           Emily            CA 408  08/01/92   3
     14  121 Kendall         Steve            NJ 201  10/15/92  25
(DEMO) . DISPLAY FOR ST="CA".AND.ID>"120"
Record#  ID  LASTNAME        FIRST            ST AREA ENROLLED AGE
      2  123 Dougherty       Suzanne          CA 415  02/12/93  27
      3  124 Dougherty       Steven           CA 415  03/01/93  35
(DEMO) .
Command Line  <A:> MEMBERS              Rec: EOF/14        Ins    Caps

                    Enter a dBASE III PLUS command.
```

10. Type **DISPLAY FOR ENROLLED>CTOD("01/01/93").OR.AGE>30** and press Enter↵ to display only records that have either the specified date or age.
11. Type **DISPLAY FOR ENROLLED>CTOD("01/01/93").AND.AGE>30** and press Enter↵ to display only records that have both the specified date and age.

More Comparing the AND and OR Operators
The command using OR displays those records that have the specified data in either the ENROLLED or AGE fields. The command using AND displays only those records that meet both criteria.

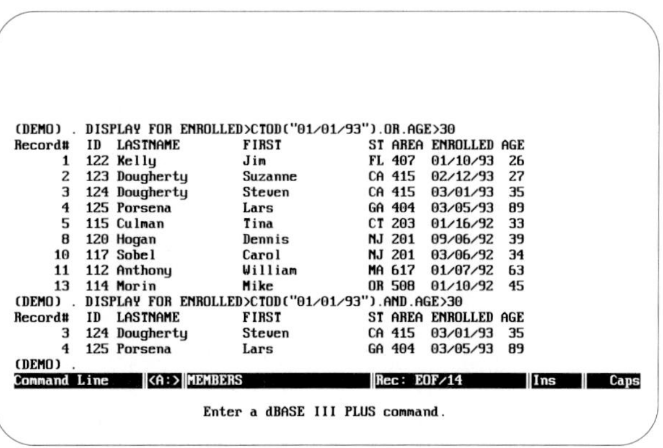

```
(DEMO) . DISPLAY FOR ENROLLED>CTOD("01/01/93").OR.AGE>30
Record#  ID  LASTNAME        FIRST            ST AREA ENROLLED AGE
      1  122 Kelly           Jim              FL 407  01/10/93  26
      2  123 Dougherty       Suzanne          CA 415  02/12/93  27
      3  124 Dougherty       Steven           CA 415  03/01/93  35
      4  125 Porsena         Lars             GA 404  03/05/93  89
      5  115 Culman          Tina             CT 203  01/16/92  33
      8  120 Hogan           Dennis           NJ 201  09/06/92  39
     10  117 Sobel           Carol            NJ 201  03/06/92  34
     11  112 Anthony         William          MA 617  01/07/92  63
     13  114 Morin           Mike             OR 508  01/10/92  45
(DEMO) . DISPLAY FOR ENROLLED>CTOD("01/01/93").AND.AGE>30
Record#  ID  LASTNAME        FIRST            ST AREA ENROLLED AGE
      3  124 Dougherty       Steven           CA 415  03/01/93  35
      4  125 Porsena         Lars             GA 404  03/05/93  89
(DEMO) .
Command Line  <A:> MEMBERS              Rec: EOF/14        Ins    Caps

                    Enter a dBASE III PLUS command.
```

USING THE NOT OPERATOR

12. Type **DISPLAY FOR .NOT.AGE>30** and press Enter← to display only records with ages not greater than 30.
13. Type **DISPLAY FOR .NOT.ST="CA"** and press Enter← to display only records without CA in the ST field.
14. Type **USE CHARGES** and press Enter← to open the CHARGES file.
15. Type **DISPLAY FOR CLEARED** and press Enter← to display only records with .T. in the CLEARED field.
16. Type **DISPLAY FOR .NOT.CLEARED** and press Enter← to display only records with .F. in the CLEARED field.

The NOT Operator
Here the part of the query .NOT.CLEARED told dBASE to display all records that have .F. in the CLEARED field, meaning they have "not cleared."

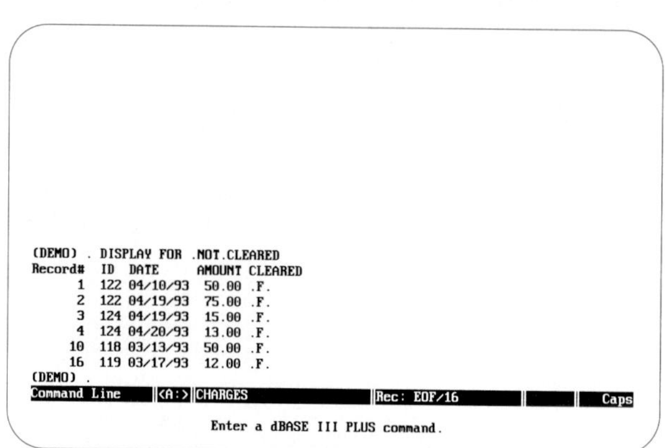

17. Type **DISPLAY FOR AMOUNT>30.AND..NOT.CLEARED** and press Enter← to display only records with AMOUNT larger than 30 and .F. in the CLEARED field.

REPLACING DATA IN SELECTED RECORDS

18. Type **LIST AMOUNT,CLEARED FOR .NOT.CLEARED TO PRINT** and press Enter← to print the contents of the AMOUNT field in records with .F. in the CLEARED field.
19. Type **REPLACE AMOUNT WITH AMOUNT +.50 FOR .NOT.CLEARED** and press Enter←. The message reads *6 records replaced.*
20. Type **LIST AMOUNT,CLEARED FOR .NOT.CLEARED** and press Enter←. Compare the contents of the AMOUNT field with those you printed out. Those records with .F. in the CLEARED field should have been increased by 50 cents.
21. Type **REPLACE AMOUNT WITH AMOUNT -.50 FOR .NOT.CLEARED** and press Enter←. The message reads *6 records replaced.*
22. Type **LIST AMOUNT,CLEARED FOR .NOT.CLEARED** and press Enter←. Again compare the contents of the AMOUNT field with those you printed out. Those records with .F. in the CLEARED field should have been decreased by 50 cents back to their original values.

USING THE LOCATE AND CONTINUE COMMANDS

23. Type **USE MEMBERS** and press **Enter** to open the MEMBERS file.

24. Type **LOCATE FOR ST="CA"** and press [Enter↵]. The message *Record = 2* and *Rec: 2/14* on the status line indicates that record 2 contains CA in the ST field.
25. Type **DISPLAY** and press [Enter↵].
26. Type **CONTINUE** and press [Enter↵] to move the record pointer to record 3 which also contains CA in the ST field.
27. Type **DISPLAY** and press [Enter↵] to display record 3.
28. Type **CONTINUE** and press [Enter↵] to move the record pointer to record 9 which also contains CA in the ST field.
29. Type **DISPLAY** and press [Enter↵] to display the record.
30. Type **CONTINUE** and press [Enter↵]. The message *End of LOCATE scope* indicates that no additional records contain CA in the ST field.

USING THE $ OPERATOR

31. Type **LIST LASTNAME,FIRST,STREET FOR "Hardy" $STREET** and press [Enter↵]. The $ operator tells dBASE to search the STREET field for any entry that contains Hardy.

FINISHING UP

32. You have completed this tutorial. Either close all open files and continue to the next activity or quit the program.

ASSIST-MENU TUTORIAL

In this tutorial, you use logical operators to filter records in the CHARGES database file.

GETTING STARTED

1. Display the Assist menus and open the CHARGES database file.

DISPLAYING RECORDS THAT MATCH MULTIPLE CONDITIONS

2. Press [R] to pull down the Retrieve menu.
3. Highlight *Display* and press [Enter↵].
4. Highlight *Build a search condition* and press [Enter↵] to display a list of the fields in the database file.
5. Highlight *DATE* and press [Enter↵].
6. Highlight > *Greater Than* and press [Enter↵]. The prompt reads *Enter a date value:*.
7. Type **01/01/93**. (Don't enclose the date in quotes when responding to this prompt).
8. Highlight *Combine with .AND.* and press [Enter↵].
9. Highlight *AMOUNT* and press [Enter↵].
10. Highlight > *Greater Than* and press [Enter↵]. The prompt reads *Enter a numeric value:*.
11. Type **20** and press [Enter↵].
12. Highlight *No more conditions* and press [Enter↵].

13. Highlight *Execute the command* and press Enter↵ to display only records with a date later than January 1, 1993, and an amount greater than 20. The prompt reads *Press any key to continue to work in ASSIST.*
14. Press any key to return to the Assist menu.

FINISHING UP

15. You have completed this tutorial. Either close all open files and continue to the next activity or quit the program.

QUICK REFERENCE

Logical operators are used to connect two or more criteria. For example, they can specify that only records meeting two or more criteria are displayed. When you use these operators, remember to enclose character strings in quotes. If you do not, you will get the error message *Data type mismatch.*

AND Operations
When you specify an AND operation, every condition must be met. For example:

DISPLAY FOR AMOUNT=10.00.AND.LASTNAME="Jones"

finds all records where the AMOUNT is 10.00 and the name is Jones. The AND operator is specified as .AND. and is placed between the criteria.

OR Operations
When you specify an OR operation, at least one condition must be met, however, all conditions can also be met. For example:

DISPLAY FOR AMOUNT=10.00.OR.LASTNAME="Jones"

finds all records where the AMOUNT is 10.00 or the name is Jones or where the AMOUNT is 10.00 and the name is Jones. The OR operator is specified as .OR. and is placed between the criteria.

NOT Operations
When you specify a NOT operation, the specified condition must not be met. For example:

DISPLAY FOR AMOUNT=10.00.NOT.LASTNAME="Jones"

finds all records where the AMOUNT is 10.00 and the name is not Jones. The NOT operator is specified as .NOT. and is placed immediately before the criterion that it is to affect.

The REPLACE Command
Updating the contents of fields can be done automatically with the REPLACE command when you want to make the same change to a number of records. For example, if all prices are to increase 5 percent, you needn't edit each record in which a price appears. You can update all the records automatically.

The REPLACE command replaces the current contents of a specified field with new contents. For example, the command REPLACE RECORD

1 AMOUNT WITH 20.00 replaces the existing number in the AMOUNT field in record 1 with 20.00.

You can replace the contents of a field in all records just as easily as you can replace the contents of a field in one record. The command begins with REPLACE ALL and can be executed only from the dot prompt. For example, to increase all numbers in the AMOUNT field by $5.00, you type REPLACE ALL AMOUNT WITH AMOUNT + 5 and press Enter.

In the most common application, you use criteria to filter records so that only specific records are affected. For example, you can type **REPLACE** ALL AMOUNT WITH AMOUNT + 5 FOR AMOUNT >20 to increase all amounts over $20.00 by $5.00. The REPLACE AMOUNT WITH 0 FOR LASTNAME="Smith" command changes amounts to zero only in those fields where the name Smith is in the LASTNAME field.

The LOCATE and CONTINUE Commands

The LOCATE command finds the first record that matches a specified condition, moves the record pointer to that record, and then displays the record's number. The CONTINUE command displays the number of the next record that matches the same condition. For example, the command LOCATE FOR ST="CA" displays the number of the first record that has CA in the ST field. You can then use the DISPLAY or EDIT commands to display the record. To move the record pointer to the next record with CA in the ST field, you use the CONTINUE command.

The $ Operator

When you want to display records based on the partial contents of a field, you can do so using the $ operator. For example, the command LIST FOR "Hardy" $STREET lists only those records where the contents of the STREET field contains the string Hardy in any position.

EXERCISES

EXERCISE 1

FILTERING RECORDS IN THE EMPLOYEE FILE

1. Open the EMPLOYEE file.
2. Set fields to LASTNAME, FIRST, CITY, DEPT, and PAYRATE so that lines do not wrap on the screen.
3. List records to the printer for employees who live in Largo and are assigned to department 1.
4. List records to the printer for employees who live in Largo or are assigned to department 1.
5. List records to the printer for employees who live in Largo and are assigned to department 2.
6. List records to the printer for employees who live in Largo or are assigned to department 2.
7. List records to the printer for employees who live in Tampa and make more than $7.50 per hour.

8. List records to the printer for employees who live in Tampa and make $7.50 per hour.
9. List records to the printer for employees who live in Tampa and make less than $7.50 per hour.
10. List records to the printer for employees who live in Tampa and make $7.50 or more per hour.
11. List records to the printer for employees who do not live in Tampa and make $7.00 or more per hour.
12. List records to the printer for employees who live in Tampa and do not make $7.50 or more per hour.

EXERCISE 2

FILTERING RECORDS IN THE DEPT FILE

1. Open the DEPT file.
2. List records to the printer for employees who worked 40 hours on shift 3.
3. List records to the printer for employees who worked 40 hours or worked on shift 3.
4. List records to the printer for employees who did not work 40 hours.

EXERCISE 3

REPLACING DATA IN THE EMPLOYEE FILE

1. Open the EMPLOYEE file.
2. Increase all numbers in the PAYRATE field by 5 percent (PAYRATE * 1.05) for employees making less than 7.00.
3. List the EMP_NUM, LASTNAME, FIRST, and PAYRATE fields to the printer.

TOPIC 11

Creating & Printing Reports—The Basics

After completing this topic, you will be able to:

- Describe the parts of a typical report
- Create a report with the CREATE REPORT command
- Print a report with the REPORT FORM command
- Modify a report with the MODIFY REPORT command

Most people in a business do not actually use the database itself. Generally, they use reports created from all or part of the information stored in the database. The database might contain information about all aspects of the business. Reports are then designed to organize specific information needed by different people such as the sales manager, the president, or the finance department. Each report provides only the information needed by the person it is printed for. Reports consist of selected fields from selected records.

DOT-PROMPT TUTORIAL

In this tutorial, you create a report for the MEMBERS file that contains only the first name, last name, area code, and phone number fields from all records. You then modify the report to add member enrollment dates.

GETTING STARTED

1. Display the dot prompt and open the MEMBERS file.

CREATING A REPORT

2. Type **CREATE REPORT** and press Enter←. The prompt reads *Enter report file name:*.
3. Type **PHONE** and press Enter← to display the Options menu.

Report Form Screen
When you use the CREATE REPORT command, the report form design screen is displayed with the Options menu pulled down.

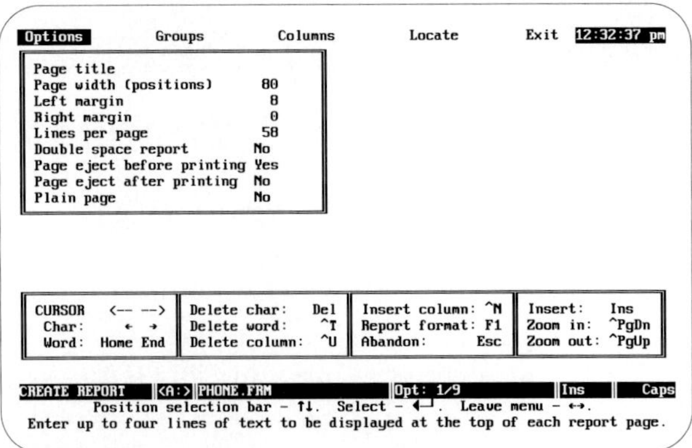

ADDING A HEADING

4. Highlight *Page title* and press [Enter ↵].
5. Type **PHONE NUMBERS** in the page heading area.
6. Press [Ctrl]-[End] to save the title.

DEFINING FOUR COLUMNS

7. Press [C] to pull down the Columns menu.
8. Highlight *Contents* and press [Enter ↵].
9. Press [F10] to display a list of field names.
10. Highlight *FIRST* and press [Enter ↵] twice.
11. Highlight *Heading* and press [Enter ↵].
12. Type **FIRST NAME** and press [Ctrl]-[End].
13. Highlight *Width* and press [Enter ↵].
14. Type **11** and press [Enter ↵].
15. Press [PgDn] to display a new blank form for the next column.
16. Repeat Steps 8 through 15 but select the *LASTNAME* field, enter a heading **LAST NAME** and set the width to **11**.
17. Repeat Steps 8 through 15 but select the *AREA* field, enter a heading **AREA** and set the width to **9**.
18. Repeat Steps 8 through 15 but select the *PHONE* field, enter a heading **PHONE #** and set the width to **9**.

SAVING THE REPORT FORMAT

19. Press [E] to pull down the Exit menu.
20. Highlight *Save* and press [Enter ↵] to save the report form onto the disk as PHONE.FRM, and return to the dot prompt.

DISPLAYING AND PRINTING THE REPORT

21. Type **REPORT FORM PHONE** and press [Enter ↵] to display the report on the screen. All records are listed for just the four fields that you specified. Moreover, the order of the fields is different from the way it appears in the file. First names are now listed before last names.

The PHONE Report
The PHONE report that you create will display the database file on your screen like this.

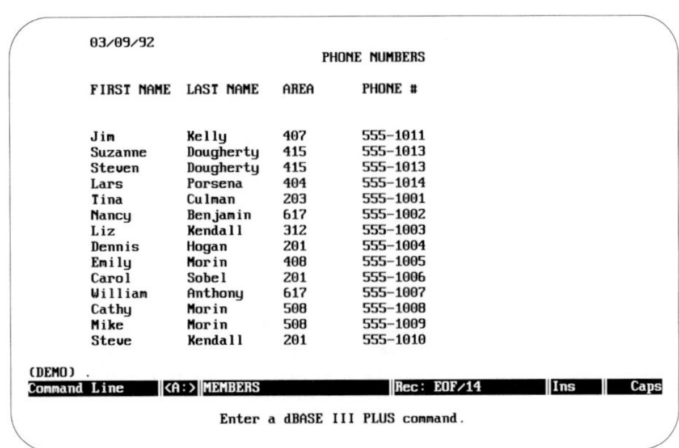

03/09/92

PHONE NUMBERS

FIRST NAME	LAST NAME	AREA	PHONE #
Jim	Kelly	407	555-1011
Suzanne	Dougherty	415	555-1013
Steven	Dougherty	415	555-1013
Lars	Porsena	404	555-1014
Tina	Culman	203	555-1001
Nancy	Benjamin	617	555-1002
Liz	Kendall	312	555-1003
Dennis	Hogan	201	555-1004
Emily	Morin	408	555-1005
Carol	Sobel	201	555-1006
William	Anthony	617	555-1007
Cathy	Morin	508	555-1008
Mike	Morin	508	555-1009
Steve	Kendall	201	555-1010

(DEMO) .
Command Line <A:> MEMBERS Rec: EOF/14 Ins Caps
Enter a dBASE III PLUS command.

22. Type **REPORT FORM PHONE TO PRINT** and press Enter↵ to print a copy of the report.

MODIFYING THE REPORT

23. Type **MODIFY REPORT PHONE** and press Enter↵ to display the Options menu.
24. Press C to pull down the Columns menu.
25. Press PgDn to scroll through the descriptions of the four existing columns and then one more time to display a new blank form for the next column.
26. Highlight *Contents* and press Enter↵.
27. Press F10 to display a list of field names.
28. Highlight *ENROLLED* and press Enter↵ twice.
29. Highlight *Heading* and press Enter↵.
30. Type **ENROLLMENT** and press Enter↵.
31. Type **DATE** and press Ctrl-End.
32. Highlight *Width* and press Enter↵.
33. Type **11** and press Enter↵.
34. Press E to pull down the Exit menu.
35. Highlight *Save* and press Enter↵.

DISPLAYING AND PRINTING THE REPORT

36. Type **REPORT FORM PHONE** and press Enter↵ to display the modified report on the screen.

The Modified PHONE Report
After you modify the report to add the ENROLLED field and the ENROLLMENT DATE heading, your report should look like this.

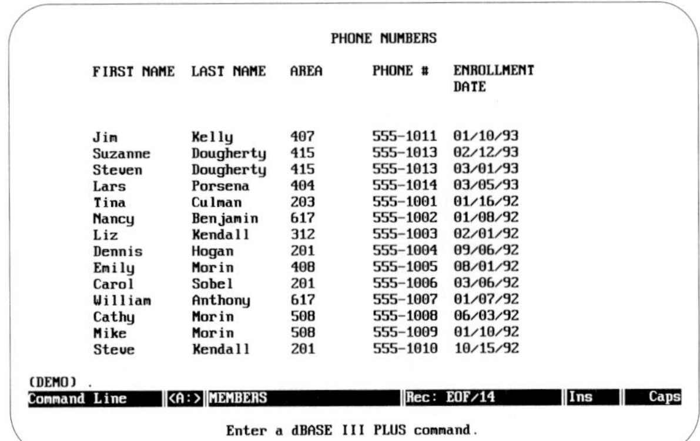

PHONE NUMBERS

FIRST NAME	LAST NAME	AREA	PHONE #	ENROLLMENT DATE
Jim	Kelly	407	555-1011	01/10/93
Suzanne	Dougherty	415	555-1013	02/12/93
Steven	Dougherty	415	555-1013	03/01/93
Lars	Porsena	404	555-1014	03/05/93
Tina	Culman	203	555-1001	01/16/92
Nancy	Benjamin	617	555-1002	01/08/92
Liz	Kendall	312	555-1003	02/01/92
Dennis	Hogan	201	555-1004	09/06/92
Emily	Morin	408	555-1005	08/01/92
Carol	Sobel	201	555-1006	03/06/92
William	Anthony	617	555-1007	01/07/92
Cathy	Morin	508	555-1008	06/03/92
Mike	Morin	508	555-1009	01/10/92
Steve	Kendall	201	555-1010	10/15/92

(DEMO) .
Command Line <A:> MEMBERS Rec: EOF/14 Ins Caps
Enter a dBASE III PLUS command.

37. Type **REPORT FORM PHONE TO PRINT** and press Enter↵ to print a copy of the modified report.

FINISHING UP

38. You have completed this tutorial. Either close all open files and continue to the next activity or quit the program.

QUICK REFERENCE

Since it takes time to format a report, dBASE allows you to save the formats you create so that you can use them again. You assign each format a name, and it is saved on the disk where it can be retrieved the next time you need it.

When preparing a report with dBASE III Plus, you execute the CREATE REPORT <*report filename*> command and then make choices from the menus described in the table "Create Report Menu Commands." If you later want to change the report format, you use the MODIFY REPORT <*report filename*> command. This displays the same menu as the CREATE REPORT command.

CREATE REPORT MENU COMMANDS

Command	Description
Options Menu	
Page title	Displays an input screen where you can enter up to four lines of text that are displayed or printed at the top of each page. Press Enter↵ to start a new line or Ctrl-End to save your entry.
Page width (positions)	Specifies the total number of characters that can be printed on a line.
Left margin	The number of characters left blank for the left margin.
Right margin	The number of characters left blank for the right margin.
Lines per page	The number of lines printed on each page. The default is 58 lines, and the range is from 1 to 500.
Double space report	*Yes* double spaces lines; *No* single spaces them.
Page eject before printing	*Yes* advances the printer to the top of the next page before printing; *No* does not.
Page eject after printing	*Yes* advances the printer to the top of the next page after printing; *No* does not.
Plain page	*No* prints page numbers and the system date on each page; *Yes* does not.
Groups	(Discussed in Topic 18)
Columns	
Contents	Specifies the field to be listed in the column. After selecting, press F10 for a list of fields to choose from.
Heading	Displays an input screen where you can enter up to four lines of text that are displayed or printed at the top of the selected column. Press Enter↵ (or type a semicolon) to start a new line or Ctrl-End to save your entry.

CREATE REPORT MENU COMMANDS (CONTINUED)

Command	Description
Width	The width of the column.
Decimal places	The number of decimal places in the column if it is a numeric field.
Total this column	Specifies if a numeric column is totaled on the report.
Locate	
	Displays a list of fields that have been added to the report. If you highlight one of the fields and press Enter ↵, the Column menu is pulled down, and the definition of the selected field is displayed.
Exit	
Save	Saves your changes and returns you to the dot prompt.
Abandon	Abandons your changes and returns you to the dot prompt.

EXERCISE

THE EMPLOYEE DATABASE REPORT

Field Name	Heading	Width
FIRST	FIRST	10
LASTNAME	LAST NAME	10
STREET	STREET	20
CITY	CITY	10
STATE	ST	2
ZIP	ZIP;CODE	8

EXERCISE 1

CREATING A REPORT FOR THE EMPLOYEE FILE

1. Open the EMPLOYEE file.
2. Create a report named EMPADD using the information provided in the table "The EMPLOYEE Database Report." Give the report the page title "EMPLOYEE REPORT."
3. Double space the report.
4. View the report on the screen and, if necessary, use the MODIFY REPORT EMPADD command to display the menu again so that you can make any necessary corrections.
5. Print the finished report.

The EMPADD Report
The EMPADD report that you create will display the database file on your screen like this.

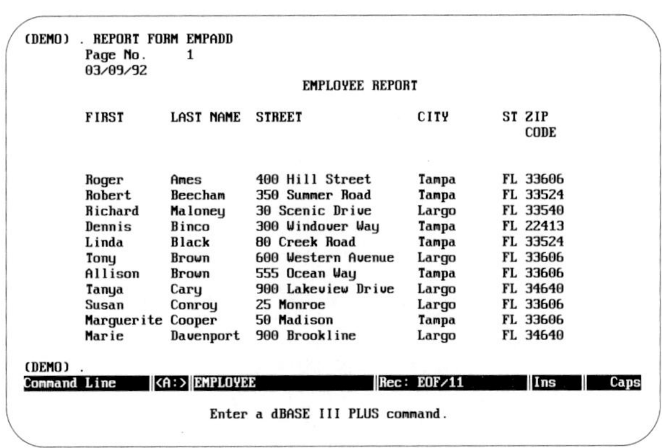

```
(DEMO) . REPORT FORM EMPADD
        Page No.     1
        03/09/92
                               EMPLOYEE REPORT

        FIRST      LAST NAME STREET               CITY       ST ZIP
                                                                CODE


        Roger      Ames      400 Hill Street      Tampa      FL 33606
        Robert     Beecham   350 Summer Road      Tampa      FL 33524
        Richard    Maloney   30 Scenic Drive      Largo      FL 33540
        Dennis     Binco     300 Windover Way     Tampa      FL 22413
        Linda      Black     80 Creek Road        Tampa      FL 33524
        Tony       Brown     600 Western Avenue   Largo      FL 33606
        Allison    Brown     555 Ocean Way        Tampa      FL 33606
        Tanya      Cary      900 Lakeview Drive   Largo      FL 34640
        Susan      Conroy    25 Monroe            Largo      FL 33606
        Marguerite Cooper    50 Madison           Tampa      FL 33606
        Marie      Davenport 900 Brookline        Largo      FL 34640

(DEMO) .
Command Line    <A:> EMPLOYEE          Rec: EOF/11        Ins     Caps

                        Enter a dBASE III PLUS command.
```

TOPIC 12

Making Calculations

After completing this topic, you will be able to:

- Make calculations from the dot prompt with operators such as + and -
- Make calculations with functions such as SUM and AVERAGE
- Use computed criteria to filter records

dBASE has the ability to perform calculations for you. Whenever the dot prompt is displayed, you can add, subtract, multiply, and divide numbers. You can also use three functions that will calculate data stored in fields in database files: SUM, AVERAGE, and COUNT. Finally, you can make calculations using the data stored in two or more fields. For example, you can multiply the contents of the PRICE field times the contents of the QUANTITY field or subtract the date in the DATE_IN field from the date in the DATE_OUT field to calculate how long an item has been in inventory.

DOT-PROMPT TUTORIAL

In this tutorial, you perform a number of calculations using the OVERVIEW database file.

GETTING STARTED

1. Display the dot prompt and open the OVERVIEW database file.

MAKING CALCULATIONS FROM THE DOT PROMPT

2. Type **?100/5** and press Enter← to divide 100 by 5.
3. Type **?100*2** and press Enter← to multiply 100 times 2.
4. Type **?100-33** and press Enter← to subtract 33 from 100.
5. Type **?10^2** and press Enter← to raise 10 to the 2nd power.
6. Type **?SQRT(100)** and press Enter← to calculate the square root of 10.
7. Type **CLEAR** and press Enter← to clear the screen.

USING FUNCTIONS

8. Type **SUM QTY** and press Enter← to total the QTY field of all records.
9. Type **AVERAGE QTY** and press Enter← to average the numbers in the QTY field.
10. Type **COUNT FOR QTY>0** and press Enter← to count the number of records with entries in the QTY field.

11. Type **SUM QTY FOR PRODUCT="Computer"** and press Enter← to total the QTY field only for records with *Computer* in the PRODUCT field.
12. Type **AVERAGE PRICE FOR PRODUCT="Computer"** and press Enter← to average the PRICE field only for records with *Computer* in the PRODUCT field.
13. Type **COUNT FOR PRICE>500** and press Enter← to count the number of records with prices greater than 25.

USING CALCULATED FIELDS

14. Type **SUM PRICE*QTY** and press Enter← to multiply the PRICE and QTY fields in each record and total the results.
15. Type **LIST PRODUCT,PRICE,QTY,PRICE*QTY** and press Enter← to list the PRODUCT, PRICE, and QTY fields for each record along with a calculated field (the rightmost column) where the PRICE and QTY fields in each record are multiplied together.

Calculated Numeric Fields
The command LIST PRODUCT,PRICE,QTY, PRICE*QTY created the new field PRICE*QTY, which contains the results of multiplying PRICE times QTY for each record. For example, in the first record, PRICE is 999.50 and QTY is 2, so PRICE*QTY is 1999.00.

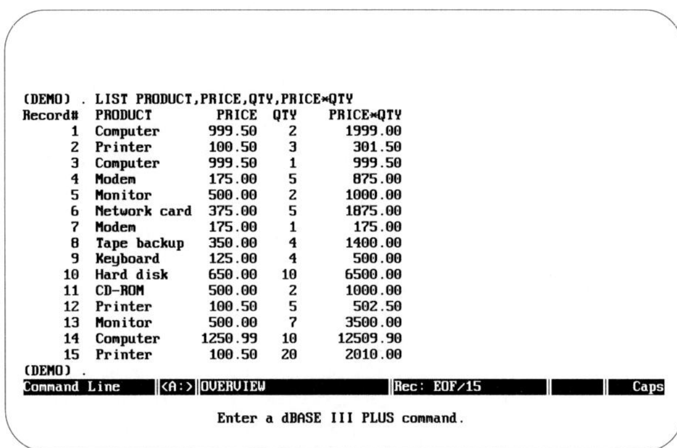

```
(DEMO) . LIST PRODUCT,PRICE,QTY,PRICE*QTY
Record#  PRODUCT        PRICE  QTY   PRICE*QTY
      1  Computer      999.50    2     1999.00
      2  Printer       100.50    3      301.50
      3  Computer      999.50    1      999.50
      4  Modem         175.00    5      875.00
      5  Monitor       500.00    2     1000.00
      6  Network card  375.00    5     1875.00
      7  Modem         175.00    1      175.00
      8  Tape backup   350.00    4     1400.00
      9  Keyboard      125.00    4      500.00
     10  Hard disk     650.00   10     6500.00
     11  CD-ROM        500.00    2     1000.00
     12  Printer       100.50    5      502.50
     13  Monitor       500.00    7     3500.00
     14  Computer     1250.99   10    12509.90
     15  Printer       100.50   20     2010.00
(DEMO) .
Command Line  ||<A:>||OVERVIEW          ||Rec: EOF/15  ||  ||  Caps
                 Enter a dBASE III PLUS command.
```

16. Type **LIST PRODUCT,DATE_OUT–DATE_ORD** and press Enter← to list each product name along with the number of days between the date it was ordered and the date it was shipped.

Calculated Date Fields
The command LIST PRODUCT,DATE_OUT-DATE_ORD created the new field DATE_OUT-DATE_ORD, in which the date a product is shipped is subtracted from the date it was ordered.

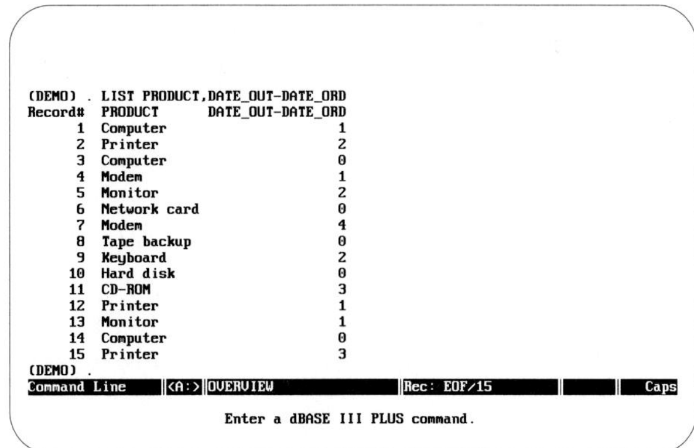

```
(DEMO) . LIST PRODUCT,DATE_OUT-DATE_ORD
Record#  PRODUCT       DATE_OUT-DATE_ORD
      1  Computer                      1
      2  Printer                       2
      3  Computer                      0
      4  Modem                         1
      5  Monitor                       2
      6  Network card                  0
      7  Modem                         4
      8  Tape backup                   0
      9  Keyboard                      2
     10  Hard disk                     0
     11  CD-ROM                        3
     12  Printer                       1
     13  Monitor                       1
     14  Computer                      0
     15  Printer                       3
(DEMO) .
Command Line  ||<A:>||OVERVIEW          ||Rec: EOF/15  ||  ||  Caps
                 Enter a dBASE III PLUS command.
```

17. Type **AVERAGE DATE_OUT–DATE_ORD** and press Enter← to average the number of days between orders being received and shipped.
18. Type **LIST FOR DATE_OUT–DATE_ORD>2** and press Enter← to list all products where it took longer than two days to process and ship the order.

19. Type **LIST FOR PRICE*QTY>2000** and press R to list only those orders that totaled over $2,000.
20. Type **COUNT FOR PRICE*QTY>2000** and press R to count the number of records where inventory value (price times quantity) is over $2,000.

FINISHING UP

21. You have completed this tutorial. Either close all open files and continue to the next activity or quit the program.

QUICK REFERENCE

When the dot prompt is displayed, you can have dBASE make calculations for you. To begin the calculation, enter a question mark and then the formula. You can use any of the following operators in formulas: + (addition), - (subtraction), / (division), * (multiplication), ^ or ** (exponentiation). For example, you can enter ?2+2, ?2-1, ?6/3, ?2*3 or ?2^3. You can also use parentheses to nest parts of a formula. For example, you can enter ?2(3/2). The answers are always displayed on the screen rounded to two decimal places or the number of decimal places you enter in one of the numbers. The program stores numbers with up to 15 decimal places and uses those numbers in calculations.

You can also use the functions described in the table "dBASE Functions" to make calculations. Some function names must be followed by a number in parentheses. For example, you can calculate the square root of the number 10 with the function ?SQRT(10). You can also refer to a field name following the AVERAGE, COUNT, and SUM functions. For example, to total all the numbers in the AMOUNT field, you would use the command SUM AMOUNT. When using functions to calculate fields, the parentheses around the field name are not needed.

dBASE FUNCTIONS

Function	Description
AVERAGE <*field*>	Calculates the average in a specified numeric field
EXP(*n*)	Calculates the value of e^x
SUM <*field*>	Calculates the total of the values in a specified numeric field
COUNT <*field*>	Counts the number of records that meet a specified criterion
LOG(*n*)	Calculates the natural logarithm of a number
ROUND(*n*)	Rounds a number to the specified number of decimal places; for example, ROUND(2.135,2) rounds the number to 2.14
SQRT(*n*)	Calculates the square root of a number

EXERCISES

EXERCISE 1

MAKING CALCULATIONS

Perform the following calculations and write down your results:

1. 2500/2.5
2. 5*3*5
3. 750-123
4. SQRT(15)
5. 123 plus 890
6. (2+3)*6
7. 144/12+6*8
8. 2*4*7-4*3
9. Square root of 400
10. (8-3)*(6*4)
11. (8-3)/(6*4)

EXERCISE 2

MAKING CALCULATIONS IN THE EMPLOYEE FILE

Open the EMPLOYEE file and use functions to make the following calculations:

1. Count the number of records in the file.
2. Average the pay rate for the employees.
3. Count how many employees' pay rate is more than the average pay rate.
4. Count the number of employees whose pay rate is greater than $7.00.

EXERCISE 3

MAKING CALCULATIONS IN THE DEPT FILE

Open the DEPT file and use functions to answer the following queries:

1. How many records are in the file?
2. What is the total number of hours worked by all employees?
3. How many employees worked 40 or more hours in any period?
4. How many employees worked less than 40 hours in any period?
5. What is the average number of hours employees are working per period?
6. How many employees are working more than the average number of hours?

TOPIC 13

Managing Files

After completing this topic, you will be able to:

- Copy entire database files or just selected fields with the COPY TO command
- Copy database file structures with the COPY STRUCTURE TO command
- Copy totaled records to another database with the TOTAL ON command
- Prevent overwriting existing files with the SET SAFETY ON command
- Delete database files with the ERASE command

As the data stored in database files expand, there come times when you need to delete some data that are no longer needed, make backup copies of important files, and even create new databases from those that already exist.

DOT-PROMPT TUTORIAL

In this tutorial, you copy all and parts of the open file to other files on the disk. You then delete those new files from the disk.

GETTING STARTED

1. Display the dot prompt and open the MEMBERS database file.
2. Type **SET SAFETY ON** and press Enter← so you will be prompted if you try to overwrite any existing database files.

COPYING THE OPEN FILE

3. Type **COPY TO NEW1** press Enter←. The message reads *14 Records copied.*
4. Type **USE NEW1** and press Enter←.
5. Type **LIST** and press Enter← to see that the file is the same as the original MEMBERS file.
6. Type **DIR NEW1.*** and press Enter←. The original MEMBERS file has a memo field that stores data in a .DBT file. When you copied MEMBERS to NEW1, dBASE automatically copied and renamed the .DBT file.

COPYING THE FILE'S STRUCTURE

7. Type **USE MEMBERS** and press Enter←.

8. Type **COPY STRUCTURE TO NEW2** and press [Enter ←].
9. Type **USE NEW2** and press [Enter ←] to see that the status line indicates that the file has no records.
10. Type **LIST STRUCTURE TO PRINT** and press [Enter ←] to list and print a copy of file's structure. It is the same as that of MEMBERS but contains no records.
11. Type **LIST** and press [Enter ←] to see that NEW2 contains no data.

COPYING SELECTED FIELDS

12. Type **USE MEMBERS** and press [Enter ←].
13. Type **COPY TO NEW3 FIELDS FIRST,LASTNAME** and press [Enter ←].
14. Type **USE NEW3** and press [Enter ←].
15. Type **LIST TO PRINT** and press [Enter ←]. Only the two fields specified have been copied to the new file and they are arranged in the same order in which they were specified in the COPY command.

COPYING TOTALED RECORDS IN THE CHARGES FILE

16. Type **USE CHARGES** and press [Enter ←].
17. Type **LIST TO PRINT** and press [Enter ←].
18. Type **TOTAL ON ID TO NEW4** and press [Enter ←]. The messages indicate the number of records totaled and the number of new records generated.
19. Type **USE NEW4** and press [Enter ←].
20. Type **LIST TO PRINT** and press [Enter ←]. Compare this with your first printout and note that all records with duplicate ID numbers have been combined so that there is only one record listed for each ID, with the totals from any duplicates added together.

COPYING OTHER FILES

21. Type **COPY FILE PHONE.FRM TO PHONE.HLD** and press [Enter ←] to copy the PHONE report file to a file of the same name but with the extension .HLD.
22. Type **COPY FILE CHARGES.DBF TO CHARGE2.DBF** and press [Enter ←].
23. Type **DIR *.*** and press [Enter ←] to see that the new files PHONE.HLD and CHARGE2.DBF are listed.

PRINTING A DIRECTORY OF THE FILES ON YOUR DISK

24. Ask your instructor if you can route files to your printer with the SET ALTERNATE TO PRN command. If so, continue to the next step. If not, go on to Step 30.
25. Type **SET ALTERNATE TO PRN** and press [Enter ←] to direct a copy of the screen listing to the printer—the alternate device.
26. Type **SET ALTERNATE ON** and press [Enter ←] to turn on the alternate device.
27. Type **DIR *.*** and press [Enter ←]. (Type **EJECT** and press [Enter ←] to eject the paper from the printer.)
28. Type **SET ALTERNATE OFF** and press [Enter ←] to turn printing off.

29. Type **CLOSE ALTERNATE** and press Enter↵ to turn printing off.

DELETING FILES FROM THE DISK

30. Type **ERASE NEW1.DBF** and press Enter↵. The message reads *File has been deleted.*
31. Repeat Step 30 to erase the files NEW2.DBF, NEW3.DBF, NEW4.DBF, PHONE.HLD, and CHARGE2.DBF. Then delete NEW1.DBT.

FINISHING UP

32. You have completed this tutorial. Either close all open files and continue to the next activity or quit the program.

QUICK REFERENCE

Using the following commands, you can copy and delete files as well as create new files from existing ones.

The SAFETY Command
When copying files, the SET SAFETY ON command prompts you if you try to overwrite an existing file on the disk with the same name.

Erasing Files
To delete a file from the disk, you use the ERASE <*filename*> command. You must specify the file's extension in the command. If you delete a database file that contains a memo field, you must delete the memo file separately. This file has the same name as the database file, but its extension is .DBT.

Copying Files
If the file that you want to copy is open, you can use the COPY TO <*filename*> command to copy it to another file on the disk. This command also allows you to copy selected fields or records.

To copy selected fields from the current database, use the command COPY TO <*filename*> FIELDS <*field list*>. For example, to copy the FIRST and LASTNAME fields to a file named TEMP, you would use the command COPY TO TEMP FIELDS FIRST,LASTNAME.

To copy selected records, use the COPY TO <*filename*> FOR <*condition*>. For example, to copy only those records with CA in the ST field to a file named TEMP, you would use the command COPY TO TEMP FOR ST="CA".

To copy any type of DOS file, including those created with dBASE, you use the COPY FILE <*filename*> TO <*filename*> command. Both filenames must include the file extension. If you want to copy to or from a drive that isn't the default, add the drive specifier in front of the filename. For example, to copy a database file named MEMBERS on the default drive to a file named MEMBERS2 on drive B, you would use the command COPY FILE MEMBERS.DBF TO B:MEMBERS2.DBF. If the file contains a memo field, you must also copy the accompanying file of the same name with the extension .DBT. If you do not do so, you will encounter problems when you open the file.

Copying File Structures

If you want to create a new file similar to an existing one, you can copy all or part of the existing file's structure to use in the new file. To do so, you use the COPY STRUCTURE TO <*filename*> command. For example, to copy the entire structure of a file named MEMBERS to a file named MEMBERS2, you would use the command COPY STRUCTURE TO MEMBERS2. To copy just the structure for the LASTNAME and FIRST fields, you would use the command COPY STRUCTURE TO MEMBERS2 FIELDS LASTNAME,FIRST.

Copying Totaled Records

There are times when data in a database become partially duplicated. For example, someone with the ID 101 may make three or more charges, each of which is entered separately. When this happens, you can combine these partially duplicated records into a single record in a new file with the TOTAL ON <*key field*> TO <*filename*> command. For example, TOTAL ON ID TO NEWFILE would add all numeric entries in records with the same ID and save them in a file named NEWFILE. The key field that you specify in the command is not the field being totaled but the field that contains the duplicate entries that you want combined.

The SET ALTERNATE TO Command

You can route data that are displayed on your screen to your printer or to a file on the disk. To do so, you use the SET ALTERNATE TO <*device or filename*> command. You then turn the rerouting on and off with the SET ALTERNATE ON and SET ALTERNATE OFF command. To close the file if you sent data to a disk file, use the CLOSE ALTERNATE command. The data are stored in a file of the name you assigned with the extension .TXT. You can retrieve the file with most word processing programs.

EXERCISES

EXERCISE 1

COPYING THE EMPLOYEE FILE

1. Copy the entire EMPLOYEE file to a file named E1. Open the new file and list its records to the printer.
2. Repeat Step 1 but copy only the fields EMP_NUM, LASTNAME, FIRST, STREET, CITY, STATE, and ZIP to a file named E2.

EXERCISE 2

COPYING THE DEPT FILE

1. Copy the entire DEPT file to a file named D1. Open the new file and list its records to the printer.
2. Repeat Step 1 but copy only the fields EMP_NUM and SHIFT to a file named D2.

CHAPTER 3 REVIEW

- You can display records with the DISPLAY and LIST commands. The DISPLAY ALL command pauses scrolling when the screen is full until you press a key; LIST does not.
- You can specify which fields are to be displayed by entering a list of fields following the LIST or DISPLAY command, separating the fields with commas.
- The SET FIELDS TO command is used to specify which fields are displayed by subsequent commands.
- You can filter records by specifying criteria so that only records that meet the criteria are affected by the command.
- Relational operators such as >, <, =, and <> determine if one item is larger, smaller, equal to, or not equal to another item.
- When specifying the data to be searched for in character fields, you must enclose it in quotes.
- To search for dates in date fields, you must use the CTOD operator to convert the date in your query into a date format.
- The logical operators .AND. and .OR. filter records through two or more criteria.
- The logical operator .NOT. determines if an item matches the criteria.
- You can automatically replace data in a field with the REPLACE command.
- The LOCATE command finds the first record that meets a specified condition. The CONTINUE command finds the next.
- You can use the $ character to do a full field search.
- You can print all or part of the data in a database file by creating reports with the CREATE REPORT <*filename*> command.
- To use an existing report format, you use the REPORT FORM <*report name*> command.
- At the dot prompt, you can enter a question mark followed by a formula to make a calculation.
- You can calculate numbers and fields with functions such as SUM(<*field*> or <*n*>) or LOG(<*n*>).
- You can total records that have identical entries in one field to a new file with the TOTAL ON <*key field*> TO <*filename*> command.
- To delete unneeded files from the disk, you use the ERASE <*filename.ext*> command.
- To copy an open database file, you use the COPY TO <*filename.ext*> command.
- To copy any type of file, you use the COPY FILE <*filename.ext*> TO <*filename.ext*> command.
- To copy the structure of an open database file, you use the COPY STRUCTURE TO <*filename*> command.

CHAPTER 3 QUESTIONS

FILL IN THE BLANK

1. To display records one after another without having the list pause on the screen when it's full, you use the ___________ command.
2. To display records so that the list pauses when the screen is full, you use the ___________ command.
3. To display only the NAME and ADDRESS fields in all subsequent commands, you would use the command ___________.
4. Operators that compare the relative size or order of items are called ___________ operators.
5. The "greater than" operator is specified with the ___________ symbol.
6. Operators that connect criteria so that two or more conditions must be met are called ___________ operators.
7. The operator that you would use to be sure both of two conditions were met would be the ___________ operator.
8. The operator that you would use to be sure either of two conditions was met would be the ___________ operator.
9. To list a record that has CA in the ST field, you could use the command ___________.
10. To find a record that has "Hardy" anywhere in the field, you could use the command ___________.
11. To use the same filter for a number of commands, it would be easier to use the ___________ command.
12. When you refer to data stored in a character field in your queries, you must enclose the data in ___________.
13. When you refer to data stored in a date field in your queries, you must use the ___________ function.
14. To define a new report format, you use the ___________ command.
15. To use an existing report format, you use the ___________ command.
16. To copy an open database file to a file named NEWFILE, you use the command ___________.
17. To copy a file on the disk in drive A named STATE.DBF to a disk in drive B, you type ___________.

MATCH THE COLUMNS

1. DISPLAY ALL	__ Less than
2. LIST	__ Uses a report format
3. SET FIELDS TO	__ Requires that either criterion be met
4. Relational operators	__ Operators used to specify two or more criteria

5. >
6. <
7. <>
8. Logical operators
9. .AND.
10. .OR.
11. .NOT.
12. CTOD
13. SET FILTER TO
14. REPLACE
15. CREATE REPORT
16. REPORT FORM
17. ?
18. SUM
19. AVERAGE
20. ERASE
21. COPY TO
22. TOTAL ON
23. LOCATE
24. CONTINUE
25. $

__ Finds the first record that meets the specified condition
__ Displays all records without pausing
__ Specifies which fields are used in subsequent commands
__ Specifies a filter that remains in effect until removed
__ Not equal to
__ Requires that both criteria be met
__ Operators that compare two items
__ Lists records and pauses when screen is full
__ Greater than
__ Converts characters to dates
__ Combines numeric entries for records with same entry in key field
__ Requires that the criterion not be met
__ Specifies a full-field search
__ Defines a report format
__ Used to enter formulas to be calculated from the dot prompt
__ Totals the numbers in the specified numeric field
__ Deletes files from the disk
__ Finds the next record after using the LOCATE command
__ Copies open file to a new file
__ Averages the numbers in the specified numeric fields
__ Automatically replaces data in a field

WRITE OUT THE ANSWERS

1. Describe three commands you can use to display records and explain how they differ from one another.
2. Describe two ways that you can display selected fields rather than the entire database.
3. Describe what it means to filter records and explain why this is useful.
4. List and describe six relational operators. Give some examples of how they might be used.
5. Briefly describe the logical operators AND and OR. Give some examples of how they might be used.
6. Give the command you would use to display a record with the date 01/01/94 in the DATE field. Describe what each part of the command does.
7. Write out the command that you would use to add 10 percent to all the entries in a numeric field named INTEREST.

8. Briefly describe two ways that you can make calculations at the dot prompt.
9. Describe the steps that you would follow to create and then use a report format.
10. List three commands that you can use to manage your dBASE files and briefly describe what each does.

CHAPTER 3

PROJECTS

PROJECT 1

QUERYING THE TITLES DATABASE

1. Open the TITLES database file and use the SET PRINTER ON or <*command*> TO PRINT commands to print the results of your queries. Using filters and functions, ask the following queries:
   - Which titles have had more than one edition?
   - What is the average list price?
   - How many titles are in the Science category?
   - Which hardcover text(s) have a list price higher than $30?
   - Which paperback text(s) have a list price higher than $30?
   - What is the highest-priced paperback title?
   - What book by Franks is in the Science category?
   - What paperback book is in the third edition?
2. Count the number of titles in the first, second, and third editions.

PROJECT 2

QUERYING THE SALES DATABASE

1. Open the SALES database file and use the SET PRINTER ON or <*command*> TO PRINT commands to print the results of your queries. Using filters and functions, ask the following queries:
   - Which ISBNs had sales in trade of more than 5,000 copies?
   - What is the total trade sale? The average?
   - Which ISBNs had sales of over 3,000 copies in trade and 1,000 copies in education?
   - What were the total spring sales? Fall sales?
   - What was the average spring sale? Fall sale?
2. Use a calculated field to add all sales for each title.

PROJECT 3

PREPARING A REPORT FOR THE TITLES FILE

Prepare a report named TITLEREP for the TITLES database that lists just the ISBN, title, author, edition, version, and price. Use the report format to print out the file.

CHAPTER 4

Sorting & Indexing Databases

TOPIC 14

Sorting Records

After completing this topic, you will be able to:

- Sort databases with the SORT TO command
- Sort files on both primary and secondary keys
- Sort databases in descending order with the /D parameter

Sorting a file rearranges the records into a specified order and saves them to a new file on the disk. To sort a file, you first determine what data are to be arranged in what order. For example, you can sort the file so that the names are arranged alphabetically, or you can sort it so that a given set of numbers is arranged in ascending or descending order. Since these data are stored in fields, you actually specify which field is to be arranged and in what order its data are to be sorted.

When you specify which field is to be used, you are designating it as the key field. You can specify more than one key—one primary key and one or more secondary keys. The primary key is the field that is sorted first. If you are sorting a list of names in the original file, the primary key will sort it so that all the names are in ascending or descending alphabetical order. Ideally, a primary key contains unique information such as a driver's license number, an employee number, or a social security number.

Sometimes a unique field does not exist or serve your purpose. For example, when you sort a file by last names, the file may have more than one person with the same last name. In these cases, a perfect sort is not achieved using just a primary key. A secondary key, like the first name, must be used to break ties.

DOT-PROMPT TUTORIAL

In this tutorial, you sort the MEMBERS database file from the dot prompt.

GETTING STARTED

1. Display the dot prompt and open the MEMBERS database file.

SORTING A FILE IN ASCENDING ORDER

2. Type **LIST FIRST, LASTNAME** and press Enter. Note how the last names are arranged randomly.

The Original File
The last names in the original file are arranged randomly, in the order in which the records were entered.

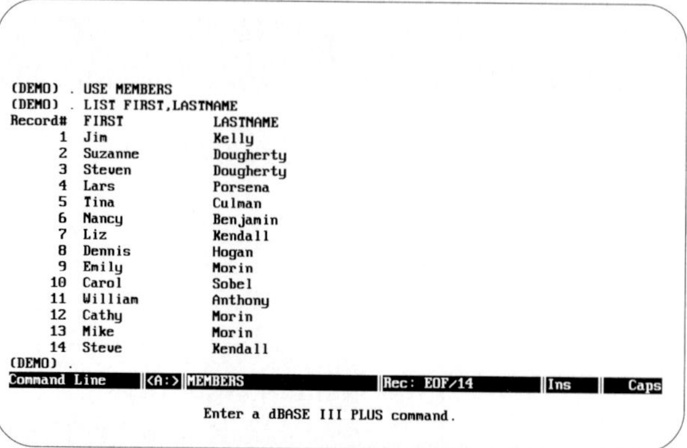

3. Type **SORT ON LASTNAME TO ASCEND1** and press Enter to sort the MEMBERS file to a new file named ASCEND1.
4. Type **USE ASCEND1** and press Enter.
5. Type **LIST FIRST, LASTNAME** and press Enter to see that the new file is arranged alphabetically by last name in ascending order. However, note how some people have the same last names, and the first names of these subgroups are not arranged in alphabetical order.

The File Sorted on LASTNAME
When you sort the file on LASTNAME, it is sorted on the contents of that field to the new file.

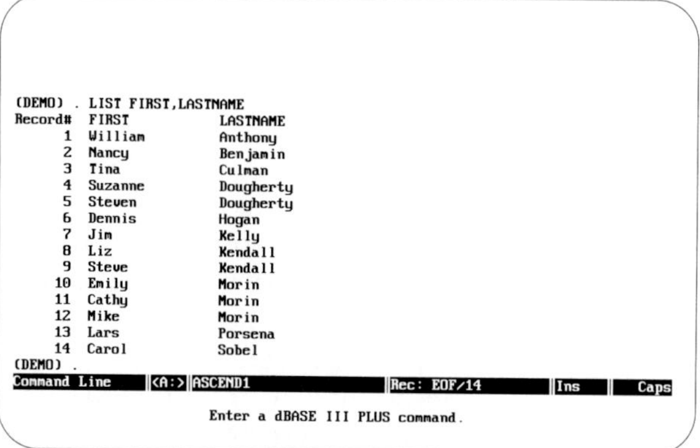

SORTING A FILE USING PRIMARY AND SECONDARY KEYS

6. Type **USE MEMBERS** and press Enter.
7. Type **SORT ON LASTNAME,FIRST TO ASCEND2** and press Enter to sort the MEMBERS file to a new file named ASCEND2.
8. Type **USE ASCEND2** and press Enter.
9. Type **LIST FIRST, LASTNAME** and press Enter to see that all records are still arranged by last name, but now first names within the subgroups with the same last name are also arranged alphabetically.

The File Sorted on LASTNAME and FIRST
When you sort the file on LASTNAME and FIRST, ties within the LASTNAME field are broken and arranged in the order of the contents of the FIRST field.

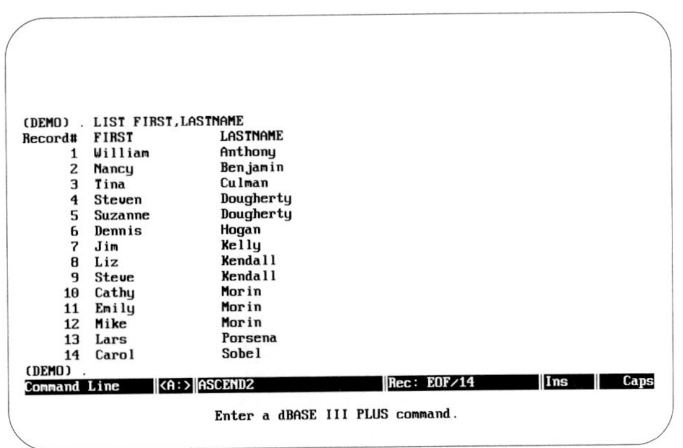

SORTING A FILE IN DESCENDING ORDER

10. Type **USE MEMBERS** and press Enter←.
11. Type **SORT ON LASTNAME/D TO DESCEND1** and press Enter← to sort the MEMBERS file in descending order to a new file named DECEND1.
12. Type **USE DESCEND1** and press Enter←.
13. Type **LIST FIRST, LASTNAME** and press Enter← to see that the file is arranged by last name in descending order.

The File Sorted on LASTNAME in Descending Order
When you sort the file on LASTNAME and add the /D parameter, the file is sorted by last name in descending order.

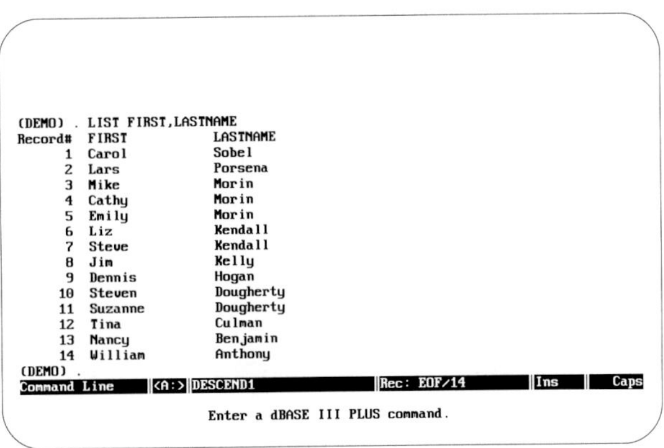

FINISHING UP

14. You have completed this tutorial. Either close all open files and continue to the next activity or quit the program.

QUICK REFERENCE

To sort a file, you use the SORT ON <*field*> TO <*file*> command. The field specified in the command is sorted into order, and all other fields in the records are moved with it. For example, to sort a file on the LASTNAME field to a new file named TEMP, you would use the command SORT ON LASTNAME TO TEMP.

You can sort on both primary and secondary keys. To do so, list the fields on which to sort in descending order of importance, separating the field names from each other with commas. For example, to sort a file on last, first, and middle names, you could use the command SORT ON LAST,FIRST,MIDDLE TO NAMES.

Normally, files are sorted in ascending order. To sort a file in descending order, you use the /D parameter. For example, to sort a file into descending order by LASTNAME, you could use the command SORT ON LASTNAME/D TO NEW.

EXERCISES

EXERCISE 1

SORTING THE EMPLOYEE FILE

1. Open the EMPLOYEE file.
2. Sort the file by LASTNAME to a file named EMPSRT1.
3. Make a printout of the sorted file.
4. Sort the file by both LASTNAME and FIRST to a file named EMPSRT2.
5. Make a printout of the sorted file.

EXERCISE 2

SORTING THE DEPT FILE

1. Open the DEPT file.
2. Sort the file on the EMP_NUM in descending order to a file named DEPTORD.
3. Make a printout of the sorted file.

TOPIC 15

Indexing Records

After completing this topic, you will be able to:

- Explain the advantage of indexing over sorting
- Index files with the INDEX ON command
- Index files on multiple fields

Sorting is not always the best way to arrange a file. It can take a long time to sort a large file, and a file can be sorted in only one order at a time. For example, a name and address file used for mailings might be sorted by last name to produce a reference list. It would then be sorted by ZIP code for printing mailing labels because the post office gives reduced rates for mailings that are presorted by ZIP code. To maintain lists like these in more than one order, you would need separate files, each sorted differently. This can take up a lot of extra room on the disk.

A better way to arrange files is to index them. To index a file, you specify the field you want it indexed by. Ideally, this field contains unique values. Once you specify the field, dBASE creates a shorter companion file for the index with the extension .NDX. The index contains only two things: the record numbers that dBASE assigned when you entered the records and the contents of the indexed field.

An Indexed File
Here a database file has been indexed by LASTNAME. The database file remains in its original order, but the index is arranged alphabetically by last name. When searching for a record such as Culman, dBASE finds the listing in the smaller index file and then uses the record pointer to find the matching record in the database.

Record #	LASTNAME	FIRST	CITY	ST
1	Kelly	Jim	Orlando	FL
2	Dougherty	Suzanne	Los Gatos	CA
3	Dougherty	Steven	Los Gatos	CA
4	Porsena	Lars	Atlanta	GA
5	Culman	Tina	New Haven	CT
6	Benjamin	Nancy	Cambridge	MA
7	Kendall	Liz	Chicago	IL
8	Hogan	Dennis	Edgewater	NJ
9	Morin	Emily	Milpitas	CA
10	Sobel	Carol	Fairlawn	NJ
11	Anthony	William	Reading	MA
12	Morin	Cathy	Salem	OR
13	Morin	Mike	Salem	OR
14	Kendall	Steve	Englewood	NJ

The database file

LASTNAME
Anthony
Benjamin
Culman
Dougherty
Dougherty
Hogan
Kelly
Kendall
Kendall
Morin
Morin
Morin
Porsena
Sobel

The index

When you use an index to find a particular record, you specify the value to be looked for in the indexed field. The program first reads the index file and scans the records there. Since the index is generally much smaller than the database, this can be done quickly. When it finds a record that matches the search criteria you entered, it looks for its record number, or record pointer, and goes directly to where that record is stored on the disk.

Indexes allow you to keep a file in order by several primary keys without having to sort it each time or maintain duplicate .DBF files. For example, the original database file can have two indexes, one arranged by department and another by phone number. You can also index a file on more than one field by joining the field names with plus signs (+) when you create the index. This is similar to sorting a file using a primary and secondary key.

Once you have created an index, dBASE automatically maintains it. If you add, insert, or delete records, or change any data in indexed fields, the index is automatically updated, and the records are moved into the position specified by the index. For example, when you append a record to the end of an indexed file, the new record changes position automatically when you move the cursor to another record. The same thing happens if you revise the field that the file is currently indexed on.

Some commands work only with indexed files. For example, dBASE finds specific records using the SEEK command if a file is indexed. The SEEK command looks in the indexed field for the string you specify in the command. If dBASE finds the string in the index, it moves the record pointer to the matching record in the database. This is fast because the index is already arranged in a specific order so that the command does not have to start at the top of the file and check each entry for a match. It can go directly to the entry you are seeking. The index file is also smaller than the database, so searches within it are faster.

DOT-PROMPT TUTORIAL

In this tutorial, you index the MEMBERS file and explore the SEEK command, which works only with indexed fields.

GETTING STARTED

1. Display the dot prompt and open the MEMBERS database file.
2. Type **SET FIELDS TO LASTNAME,FIRST,CITY,ST** and press R so only the fields that you will be working with are displayed by subsequent commands.

INDEXING A FILE

3. Type **INDEX ON LASTNAME TO LAST** and press R to create an index based on the LASTNAME field. In a moment, the message reads *100% indexed.*
4. Type **LIST** and press R to see that the file is arranged alphabetically by last name in ascending order although the records in the file have not been physically sorted. However, note how some people have the same last names, and the first names of these subgroups are not arranged in alphabetical order.

The File Indexed on Last Name
When you index the file on LASTNAME, the ordered contents of that field are used to arrange the records in the file.

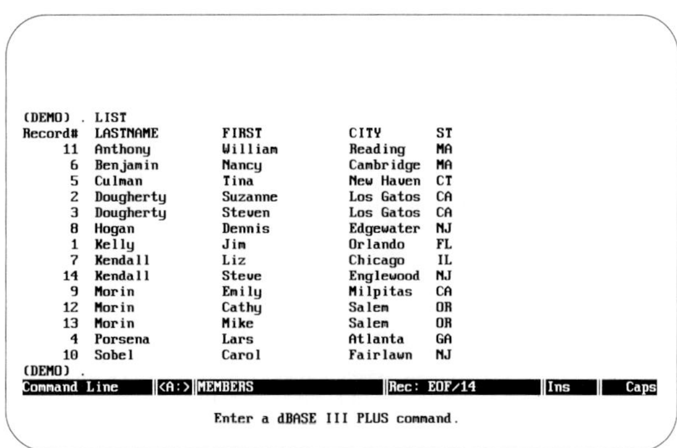

```
(DEMO) . LIST
Record#  LASTNAME         FIRST            CITY         ST
     11  Anthony          William          Reading      MA
      6  Benjamin         Nancy            Cambridge    MA
      5  Culman           Tina             New Haven    CT
      2  Dougherty        Suzanne          Los Gatos    CA
      3  Dougherty        Steven           Los Gatos    CA
      8  Hogan            Dennis           Edgewater    NJ
      1  Kelly            Jim              Orlando      FL
      7  Kendall          Liz              Chicago      IL
     14  Kendall          Steve            Englewood    NJ
      9  Morin            Emily            Milpitas     CA
     12  Morin            Cathy            Salem        OR
     13  Morin            Mike             Salem        OR
      4  Porsena          Lars             Atlanta      GA
     10  Sobel            Carol            Fairlawn     NJ
(DEMO) .
Command Line  |<A:>|MEMBERS          |Rec: EOF/14     |Ins  |Caps
                 Enter a dBASE III PLUS command.
```

5. Type **CLOSE INDEX** and press [Enter←].
6. Type **LIST** and press [Enter←] and the file is listed in its original order.

USING MORE THAN ONE FIELD IN THE INDEX

7. Type **INDEX ON LASTNAME+FIRST TO NAME** and press [Enter←] to create an index based on the LASTNAME and FIRST fields. In a moment, the message reads *100% indexed.*
8. Type **LIST TO PRINT** and press [Enter←] to see that all records are still arranged by last name, but now first names within the subgroups with the same last name are also arranged alphabetically.

The File Indexed on Last Name and First Name
When you index the file on LASTNAME+FIRST, ties within the LASTNAME field are broken and arranged in the order of the contents of the FIRST field.

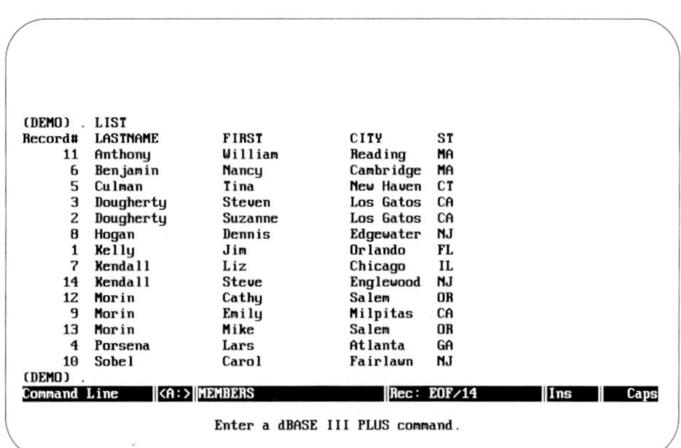

```
(DEMO) . LIST
Record#  LASTNAME         FIRST            CITY         ST
     11  Anthony          William          Reading      MA
      6  Benjamin         Nancy            Cambridge    MA
      5  Culman           Tina             New Haven    CT
      3  Dougherty        Steven           Los Gatos    CA
      2  Dougherty        Suzanne          Los Gatos    CA
      8  Hogan            Dennis           Edgewater    NJ
      1  Kelly            Jim              Orlando      FL
      7  Kendall          Liz              Chicago      IL
     14  Kendall          Steve            Englewood    NJ
     12  Morin            Cathy            Salem        OR
      9  Morin            Emily            Milpitas     CA
     13  Morin            Mike             Salem        OR
      4  Porsena          Lars             Atlanta      GA
     10  Sobel            Carol            Fairlawn     NJ
(DEMO) .
Command Line  |<A:>|MEMBERS          |Rec: EOF/14     |Ins  |Caps
                 Enter a dBASE III PLUS command.
```

INDEXING THE SAME FILE ON ANOTHER FIELD

9. Type **INDEX ON ST TO STATE** and press [Enter←] to create an index based on the ST field. In a moment, the message reads *100% indexed.*
10. Type **LIST** and press [Enter←] to see that the file is now ordered by state.

The File Indexed on State
When the file is indexed on the ST field, it is displayed in ascending order by state.

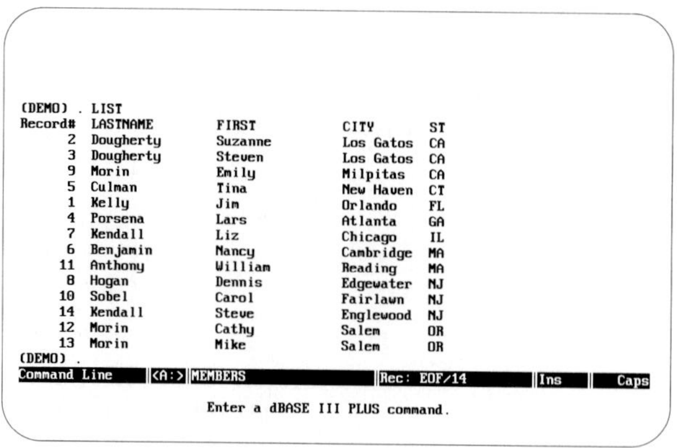

```
(DEMO) . LIST
Record#  LASTNAME       FIRST          CITY         ST
      2  Dougherty      Suzanne        Los Gatos    CA
      3  Dougherty      Steven         Los Gatos    CA
      9  Morin          Emily          Milpitas     CA
      5  Culman         Tina           New Haven    CT
      1  Kelly          Jim            Orlando      FL
      4  Porsena        Lars           Atlanta      GA
      7  Kendall        Liz            Chicago      IL
      6  Benjamin       Nancy          Cambridge    MA
     11  Anthony        William        Reading      MA
      8  Hogan          Dennis         Edgewater    NJ
     10  Sobel          Carol          Fairlawn     NJ
     14  Kendall        Steve          Englewood    NJ
     12  Morin          Cathy          Salem        OR
     13  Morin          Mike           Salem        OR
(DEMO) .
Command Line  <A:> MEMBERS   Rec: EOF/14   Ins   Caps
           Enter a dBASE III PLUS command.
```

SWITCHING AMONG INDEXES

11. Type **SET INDEX TO LAST** and press Enter to make the index based on the LASTNAME field the current index.
12. Type **LIST** and press Enter to see that the file is ordered by last name.
13. Type **SET INDEX TO STATE** and press Enter to change the index.
14. Type **LIST** and press Enter to see that the file is ordered by state.

FINDING OUT WHAT INDEXES ARE OPEN

15. Type **DISPLAY STATUS** and press Enter to display a screen that indicates what files, including indexes, are open. The prompt reads *Press any key to continue.*

The Display Status Screen
The DISPLAY STATUS command shows what indexes are in use.

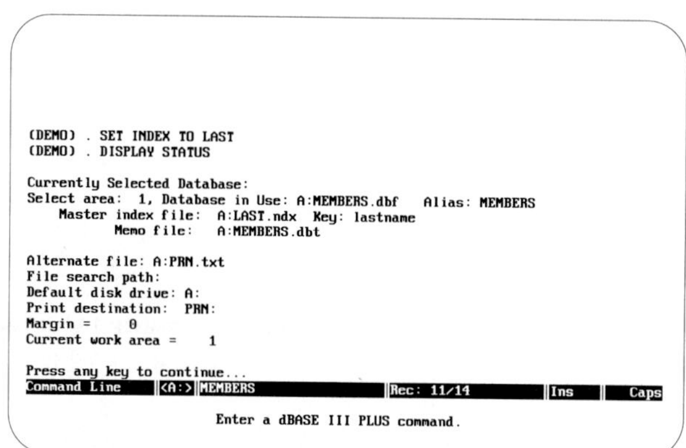

```
(DEMO) . SET INDEX TO LAST
(DEMO) . DISPLAY STATUS

Currently Selected Database:
Select area:  1, Database in Use: A:MEMBERS.dbf    Alias: MEMBERS
    Master index file:  A:LAST.ndx  Key: lastname
           Memo file:   A:MEMBERS.dbt

Alternate file: A:PRN.txt
File search path:
Default disk drive: A:
Print destination:  PRN:
Margin =      0
Current work area =    1

Press any key to continue...
Command Line  <A:> MEMBERS   Rec: 11/14   Ins   Caps
           Enter a dBASE III PLUS command.
```

16. Press any key, and the dot prompt returns.

USING INDEXES TO FIND RECORDS

17. Type **SET INDEX TO LAST** and press Enter.
18. Type **SEEK "Kendall"** and press Enter to locate a record with Kendall in the LASTNAME field—in this case record 7.
19. Type **DISPLAY** and press Enter to display the record.
20. Type **SEEK "Do"** and press Enter to locate a record with Do beginning a word in the LASTNAME field—in this case record 2.
21. Type **DISPLAY** and press Enter to display the record.
22. Type **SEEK "Orlando"** and press Enter to locate a record with Orlando in the CITY field. The program displays the message *No*

find. This is because the program can find only records that have been indexed on the field you want to search. Let's see how this is done.

23. Type **INDEX ON CITY TO CITY** and press Enter← to create a new index based on the CITY field. In a moment, the message reads *100% indexed.*
24. Type **SEEK "Orlando"** and press Enter← to locate a record with Orlando in the CITY field.
25. Type **DISPLAY** and press Enter←. The record appears because you indexed the file on the field being searched and then used that index to locate the record with the SEEK command.

FINISHING UP

26. You have completed this tutorial. Either close all open files and continue to the next activity or quit the program.

QUICK REFERENCE

To index files, you use two basic commands, INDEX ON <*field name(s)*> TO <*index filename*> and SET INDEX TO <*index name*>.

The INDEX ON <*field name(s)*> TO <*index name*> command specifies which field or fields the file is to be indexed by. For example, to index a file on its LASTNAME field to an index named LAST, you would would use the command INDEX ON LASTNAME TO LAST.

You can specify more than one field in the index by connecting the field names with plus signs—for example, INDEX ON LASTNAME+FIRST TO NAME. This is like sorting using a primary and one or more secondary keys. The most important field should always be listed first, and secondary keys should be listed in descending order of their importance for arranging the file.

When you create an index, the file is automatically indexed on it. At other times, you have to specify that it be used with the SET INDEX TO <*index name*> command. For example, to index a file using an existing index named LAST, you could use the command SET INDEX TO LAST. To see which index files are on the disk, use the DIR *.NDX command. To see which indexes are open, use the DISPLAY STATUS command.

You can have more than one index per file. This allows you to maintain the file in different orders at the same time. For example, one index can be by name, another by amount owed, and a third on date of last purchase. If you want to use more than one index at a time, you connect the index names with commas, for example, SET INDEX TO LAST,STATE.

To close open indexes, use the CLOSE INDEX command. This command closes all open indexes in the current work area.

If indexes are not turned on when new records are added to the original file, the REINDEX command can be used to update all the existing index files. After the new records have been appended to the file, turn on all the index files with the SET INDEX TO <*index name(s)*> command. Then, use the REINDEX command. When you do so, a message reads *Rebuilding index* followed by the name of the index file being recreated.

EXERCISES

EXERCISE 1

INDEXING THE EMPLOYEE FILE

1. Open the EMPLOYEE file.
2. Index the file on the DEPT field to an index file named EMPDEPT.
3. List FIRST, LASTNAME, and DEPT to the printer.

EXERCISE 2

INDEXING THE DEPT FILE

1. Open the DEPT file.
2. Index the file on the SHIFT field to an index file named SHIFT.
3. List the indexed file to the printer.
4. Index the file on the EMP_NUM field to an index file named DEPTNUM.
5. List the indexed file to the printer.

CHAPTER 4 REVIEW

- To permanently arrange a file into a new order, you can sort it to a new file with the SORT ON <*filename*> TO <*field*> command. The original file remains unsorted.
- You can sort on more than one field by listing the fields in descending order of importance and separating them with commas.
- The field that you sort on specifies the order of the new file.
- To sort a file into descending order, you use the /D parameter following the name of the field on which the file is being sorted.
- You can index a file so that it appears in a specified order with the INDEX ON <*field name(s)*> to <*index name*> command. Unlike the SORT command, this does not physically resort the file. Instead, it creates a small index file sorted in the specified order that points to records in the database. When an index is turned on, the database appears to be in the order of the index.
- You can create indexes for multiple fields by connecting the field names with plus signs. For example, INDEX ON LAST+FIRST indexes the file by last name and then first name.
- You can open more than one index by separating the index names with commas. For example, the command SET INDEX TO LAST,FIRST opens both indexes at the same time.
- You close indexes with the CLOSE INDEX command.
- If a file is indexed when you add records, they are automatically moved to the position specified by the index's order if the index is open at the time. If the indexes were not open when you added records, you can use the REINDEX command to update the indexes.

CHAPTER 4 QUESTIONS

FILL IN THE BLANK

1. To sort an open file on its ID field to a new file named NEW, you would use the command ___________.
2. To sort the file to a new file named NEW so that it was in descending order, you would use the command ___________.
3. To create an index named IDINDEX based on a field named ID, you would use the command ___________.
4. To create an index named NAME based on the fields named FIRSTNAME and LASTNAME, you would use the command ___________.
5. To open an index named NAME, you would use the command ___________.

6. To open two indexes named ID and NAME, you would use the command __________.

MATCH THE COLUMNS

1. SORT	_	Closes open indexes
2. /D	_	Creates a new file in sorted order
3. INDEX ON	_	Specifies two indexes when opening them
4. SET INDEX TO	_	Opens an existing index
5. CLOSE INDEX	_	Used to sort in descending order
6. LAST+FIRST	_	Specifies two fields when creating an index
7. LAST,FIRST	_	Creates a new index

WRITE OUT THE ANSWERS

1. Describe how you would sort a file in ascending order of LASTNAME to a new file named NEWFILE. Describe how you would do so in descending order.
2. Describe how you would index a file on the NAME field. On both the NAME and CITY fields.
3. What is the difference between sorting and indexing a file? Describe ways in which indexing might be better for you.
4. Describe how you would open two indexes named NAME and ID.

CHAPTER 4

PROJECTS

PROJECT 1

SORTING AND INDEXING THE TITLES DATABASE

1. Open the TITLES database file.
2. Sort the file to a file named CATEGORY based on the CATEGORY field.
3. List the ISBN, AUTHOR, TITLE and fields CATEGORY to the printer.
4. Index the TITLES file on the VERSION field and list the ISBN, AUTHOR, TITLE, and VERSION fields to the printer.

PROJECT 2

SORTING AND INDEXING THE SALES DATABASE

1. Open the SALES database file.
2. Sort the file to a file named ISBN based on the ISBN field.
3. List the ISBN file to the printer.
4. Index the SALES file on the TRADE field and list the indexed file to the printer.

CHAPTER 5

Working with Multiple Database Files

TOPIC 16

Relating Database Files

After completing this topic, you will be able to:

- Specify the relationship between files with the SET RELATION TO command
- Query related files

The big advantage of a database management program is that it allows you to work with more than one file at the same time. To do so, you specify the relationship that you want to establish between the files. The two requirements are that all files have a common field and the file you are relating to must be indexed on that field. To work with more than one file, you must load them all into memory at the same time. To do so, dBASE III Plus allows you to divide the computer's available memory into ten independent work areas. You specify the work areas and make them current with the SELECT command.

Related Database Tables
This database contains two files. One is used to store member names, and the other is used to store their charges. Because the two files share a common ID field, you can relate the two files and then ask queries such as LIST FIRST,LASTNAME,AMOUNT FOR ID=101.

ID	FIRST	LASTNAME
101	Tina	Culman
102	Jacki	Hartwick

ID	AMOUNT
101	10.00
102	20.00

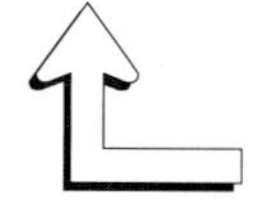

Databases related on their common ID field

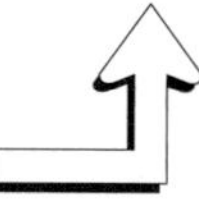

In this tutorial, you establish a relationship between the MEMBERS and CHARGES database files and then query both files at the same time.

GETTING STARTED

1. Load dBASE so that the dot prompt is displayed.

OPENING FILES IN TWO WORK AREAS

2. Type **USE MEMBERS** and press Enter↵.
3. Type **SELECT B** and press Enter↵ to open a second work area.
4. Type **USE CHARGES** and press Enter↵.
5. Type **INDEX ON ID TO CHARGID** and press Enter↵ to index the file on the ID field and name the index CHARGID.

REVIEWING THE STATUS

6. Press F6 to display the program's status. The screen shows that two files are open, one in each work area. It also indicates that the currently selected database file is CHARGES in Select area B.

Displaying the Status
The DISPLAY STATUS command tells you which files are open in which work area and what indexes are being used.

```
(DEMO) . SELECT B
(DEMO) . display status

Select area:  1, Database in Use: A:members.dbf   Alias: MEMBERS
           Memo file:   A:members.dbt
    Related into: CHARGES
    Relation: id

Currently Selected Database:
Select area:  2, Database in Use: A:charges.dbf   Alias: CHARGES
    Master index file:  A:chargeid.ndx  Key: id

File search path:
Default disk drive: A:
Print destination:  PRN:
Margin =     0
Current work area =    2

Press any key to continue...
Command Line    <A:> CHARGES           Rec: EOF/16      Ins      Caps

                    Enter a dBASE III PLUS command.
```

7. Press any key to return to the dot prompt.

RELATING THE FILES

8. Type **SELECT A** and press Enter↵ to return to the first work area. The status line indicates that MEMBERS is the active file.
9. Type **SET RELATION TO ID INTO CHARGES** and press Enter↵. The two databases are now linked to each other on the ID field that both have in common.

QUERYING THE RELATED DATABASES

10. Type **SET FIELDS TO ID,LASTNAME,FIRST,B->AMOUNT,B->CLEARED** and press Enter↵ to specify which fields from the two files are to be displayed. The fields are LASTNAME and FIRST from the MEMBERS file in the current work area (A) and the AMOUNT and CLEARED fields from the CHARGES file that is open in area B.

11. Type **LIST** and press [Enter↵] to list the specified fields from both databases.

Listing Fields from Both Files
After relating the two files, you can list fields from both at the same time.

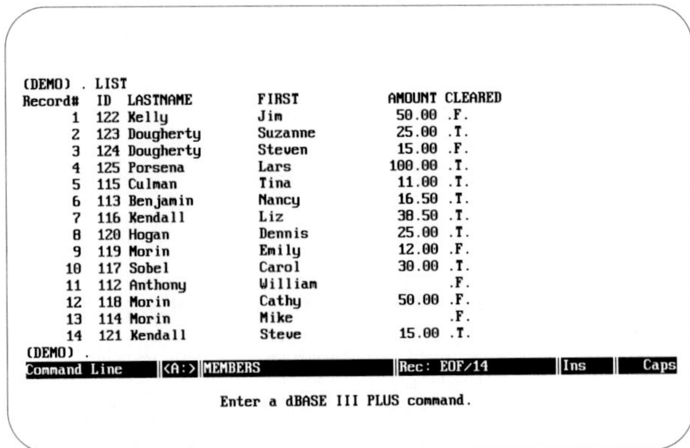

12. Type **LIST TO PRINT** and press [Enter↵].
13. Type **LIST FOR AMOUNT>25.00** and press [Enter↵] to list only those records with amounts greater than 25.00.
14. Type **LIST FOR CLEARED** and press [Enter↵] to list only those files with .T. in the CLEARED field.
15. Type **LIST FOR .NOT.CLEARED** and press [Enter↵] to list only those files with .F. in the CLEARED field are listed. Note that there are no amounts for IDs 112 and 114.

RELATING FILES WITH THE VIEW COMMAND

16. Type **CLOSE ALL** and press [Enter↵] to close all open files.
17. Type **CREATE VIEW MEMBCHRG** and press [Enter↵] to display the create view screen.

The Create View Screen
The CREATE VIEW <*filename*> command displays a screen and menu that you use to relate databases.

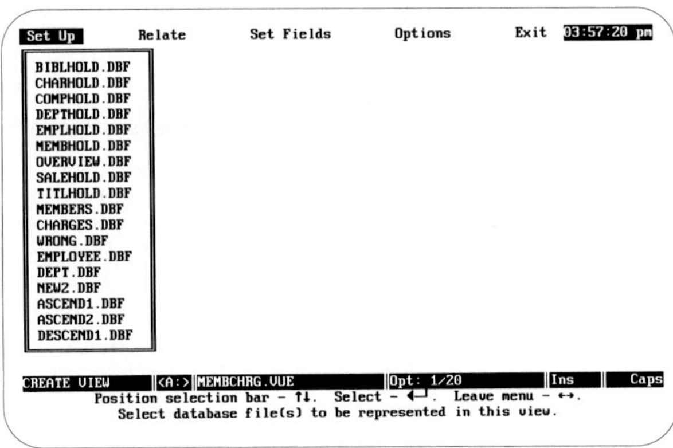

18. Highlight *MEMBERS.DBF* and press [Enter↵] to display a list of its indexes.
19. Press [←] to close the index window and return to the list of files.
20. Highlight *CHARGES.DBF* and press [Enter↵] to display a list of its indexes.
21. Highlight *CHARGID.NDX* and press [Enter↵] to select the index.
22. Press [←] to close the index window and return to the list of files.
23. Press [R] to pull down the Relate menu.

24. Highlight *MEMBERS.DBF* and press [Enter←] to display a window listing the CHARGES.DBF file.
25. Press [Enter←] and then press [F10] to display a list of its fields.
26. Highlight *ID* and press [Enter←] twice.
27. Press [←] to close the window.
28. Press [E] to pull down the Exit menu.
29. Highlight *Save* and press [Enter←] to return to the dot prompt.

USING A VIEW

30. Type **SET VIEW TO MEMBCHRG** and then press [Enter←].
31. Type **SET FIELDS TO LASTNAME,FIRST,B->AMOUNT,B->CLEARED** and press [Enter←] to set fields from both database files. In subsequent commands the only fields listed will be the LASTNAME and FIRST fields from the MEMBERS file in the current work area (A) and the AMOUNT and CLEARED fields from the CHARGES file in area B.
32. Type **LIST** and press [Enter←] to list the specified fields from all records in both databases.

Using a View
After creating a view, you use the command SET VIEW TO <*view name*>, and then you can use the LIST command and other commands to refer to fields from both files at the same time.

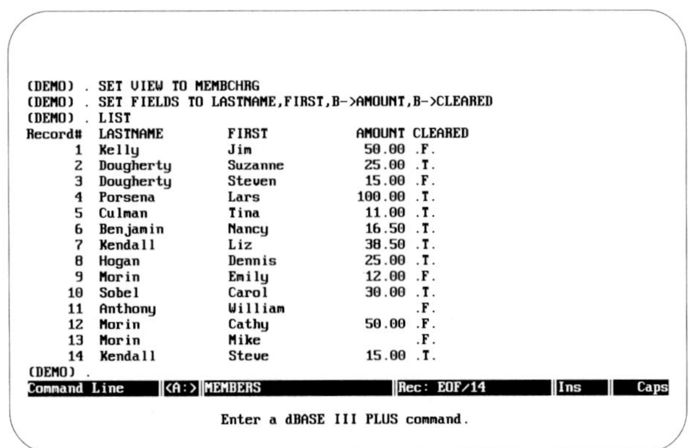

33. Type **LIST TO PRINT** and press [Enter←].

FINISHING UP

34. You have completed this tutorial. Either close all open files and continue to the next activity or quit the program.

QUICK REFERENCE

Two database files can be related if they share a common field. To relate them, you create work areas with the SELECT A, SELECT B, and so on commands. You can also use numbers instead of letters to specify work areas. For example, SELECT 1 and SELECT 2 are the same as SELECT A and SELECT B. You then open the files to be related, each in its own work area. A typical relationship command might be written as shown in the figure "Relating Files—An Example Command."

- SELECT A selects work area A, and USE CHARGES opens the CHARGES file in that work area. (You could also use numbers or

```
SELECT A
USE CHARGES
SELECT B
USE MEMBERS INDEX MEMBID
SELECT A
SET RELATION TO ID INTO MEMBERS
SET FIELDS TO B->LASTNAME,B->FIRST,AMOUNT
```

Relating Files—An Example Command
The command shown here will relate the files named CHARGES and MEMBERS on the ID field which they have in common.

the filename to specify work areas. For example, SELECT 1 is the same command as SELECT A, as is SELECT CHARGES when that is the file open in work area 1.)

- SELECT B selects work area B, and USE MEMBERS INDEX MEMBID opens the MEMBERS file in that work area using the MEMBID index.
- SELECT A returns you to the first work area where CHARGES is the open file.
- SET RELATION TO ID INTO MEMBERS specifies that the CHARGES file in the current work area is to be related to the MEMBERS file based on the common ID field.
- SET FIELDS TO B->LASTNAME,B->FIRST,AMOUNT specifies that you want to work with three fields in the MEMBERS file. The B in the command is known as an alias.

The arrow (a hyphen and a greater-than sign) is an alias symbol and indicates that the field to which it points belongs to the previous file or work area. An alias is assigned to each work area as it is opened. For example, SELECT A or SELECT 1 creates an alias A or 1 for the first work area, SELECT B or SELECT 2 creates an alias B or 2 for the second work area, and so on. You then use the work area's alias to tell the program where to find the fields you want to use. For example, if you are in work area B and want to refer to a field named FIRST in work area A, you would refer to it as A->FIRST. If you were in work area A and wanted to refer to the same field in work area B, you would refer to it as B->FIRST. You do not have to specify the work area if the fields are in the current work area. You can also use the file's name as an alias. In this case, you would enter the same command as the one on the last line of the figure as SET FIELDS TO MEMBERS->LASTNAME,MEMBERS->FIRST,AMOUNT. You can tell which alias is being used for a file with the DISPLAY STATUS command.

EXERCISE

EXERCISE 1

RELATING THE EMPLOYEE AND DEPT FILES

1. Select work area A and open the DEPT file.
2. Select work area B and open the EMPLOYEE file indexed on EMP_NUM.

3. Return to work area A and relate the two files on the EMP_NUM field.
4. Set fields to HOURS and SHIFT in work area A and LASTNAME and FIRST in work area B.
5. List the records to the printer.

The Related DEPT and EMPLOYEE Files
After relating the DEPT and EMPLOYEE files on the EMP_NUM field, you can list fields from both files, as shown here.

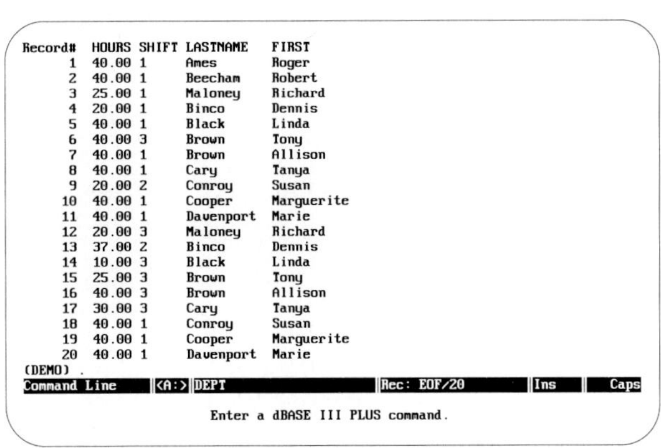

Record#	HOURS	SHIFT	LASTNAME	FIRST
1	40.00	1	Ames	Roger
2	40.00	1	Beecham	Robert
3	25.00	1	Maloney	Richard
4	20.00	1	Binco	Dennis
5	40.00	1	Black	Linda
6	40.00	3	Brown	Tony
7	40.00	1	Brown	Allison
8	40.00	1	Cary	Tanya
9	20.00	2	Conroy	Susan
10	40.00	1	Cooper	Marguerite
11	40.00	1	Davenport	Marie
12	20.00	3	Maloney	Richard
13	37.00	2	Binco	Dennis
14	10.00	3	Black	Linda
15	25.00	3	Brown	Tony
16	40.00	3	Brown	Allison
17	30.00	3	Cary	Tanya
18	40.00	1	Conroy	Susan
19	40.00	1	Cooper	Marguerite
20	40.00	1	Davenport	Marie

(DEMO) .
Command Line <A:> DEPT Rec: EOF/20 Ins Caps
Enter a dBASE III PLUS command.

TOPIC 17

Joining Database Files

After completing this topic, you will be able to:

- Join two database files into a new file with the JOIN command
- Join selected fields from two files into a new file

If you have two files with a common field, you can join them into a new database file. The JOIN command constructs a new file by combining fields from two files provided both have the same value in a specified common field. For example, both your MEMBERS and CHARGES files contain a common ID field that can be used to join them into new files. All records that fail to have the same value in the common field are not included in the new file.

Joined Database Tables
This database contains two files, each of which has an ID field containing unique data. Using that common field, the two files can be joined into a new third file containing some or all the fields from the two files.

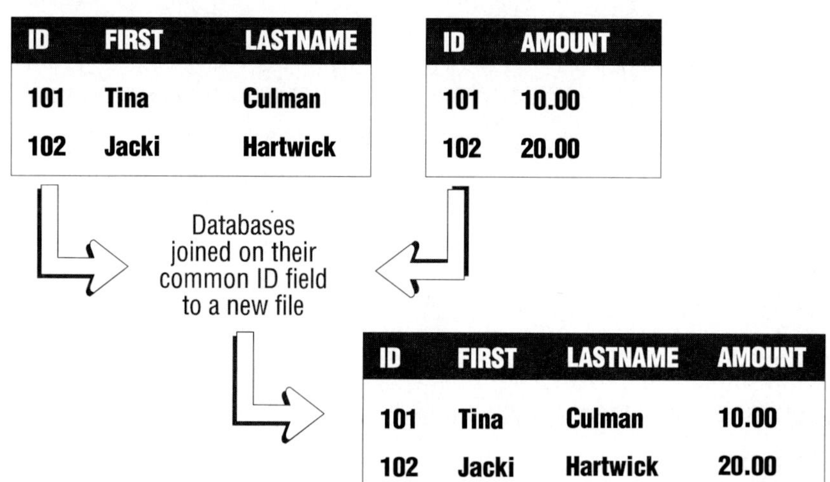

DOT-PROMPT TUTORIAL

In this tutorial, you join the MEMBERS and CHARGES database files to form two new files named NEWFILE1 and NEWFILE2.

GETTING STARTED

1. Load dBASE so that the dot prompt is displayed.

OPENING FILES

2. Type **USE MEMBERS** and press Enter←.
3. Type **SELECT B** and press Enter← to open a second work area.

4. Type **USE CHARGES INDEX CHARGID** and press Enter.

JOINING COMPLETE FILES

5. Type **SELECT A** and press Enter.
6. Type **JOIN WITH B TO NEWFILE1 FOR ID=B->ID** and press Enter. The drive spins, and in a moment, a message indicates the number of records that were joined.
7. Type **USE NEWFILE1** and press Enter to open the new file.
8. Type **DISPLAY STRUCTURE** and press Enter to see that the file's structure now includes the fields from both files.

The NEWFILE1 File's Structure
After joining the MEMBERS and CHARGES files on their common ID field, the new file's structure will look like this.

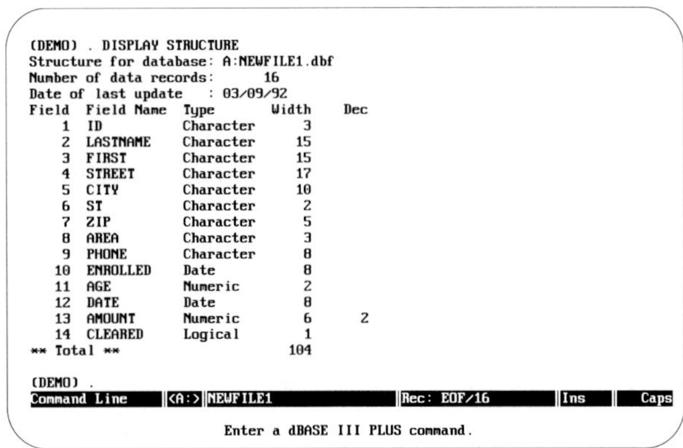

9. Type **SET FIELDS TO ID,FIRST,LASTNAME,AREA,PHONE,AMOUNT** and press Enter.
10. Type **LIST** and press Enter to see that the new file looks just like the original MEMBERS file, but it contains duplicate names and addresses. These duplicates are for those people who had more than one charge in the CHARGES file.

The NEWFILE1 File
All fields from MEMBERS and CHARGES are combined in the new file. The SET FIELDS command is used to display these selected fields.

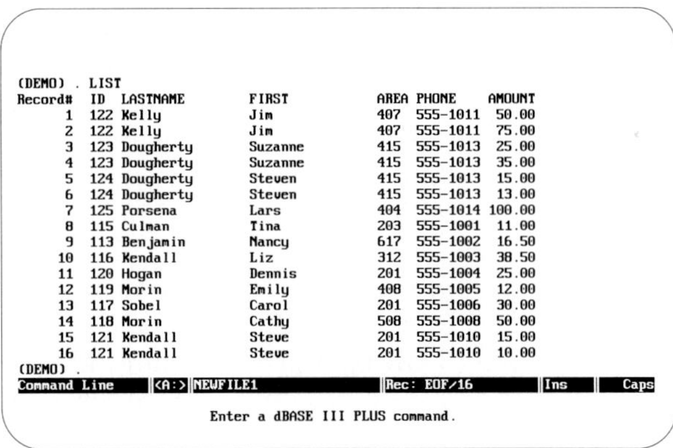

11. Type **LIST TO PRINT** and press Enter.

JOINING SELECTED FIELDS

12. Type **USE MEMBERS** and press Enter to open the file again in work area A.
13. Type **JOIN WITH B TO NEWFILE2 FOR ID=B->ID FIELDS ID,FIRST,LASTNAME,AMOUNT,CLEARED** and press Enter. The

drive spins, and in a moment, a message indicates the number of records that were joined.

14. Type **USE NEWFILE2** and press Enter.
15. Type **LIST** and press Enter to see that the new file contains the specified fields from both files.

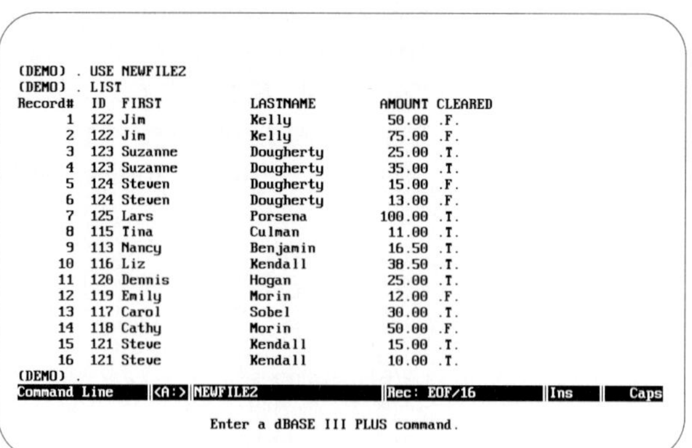

```
(DEMO) . USE NEWFILE2
(DEMO) . LIST
Record#  ID  FIRST            LASTNAME          AMOUNT CLEARED
      1  122 Jim              Kelly              50.00 .F.
      2  122 Jim              Kelly              75.00 .F.
      3  123 Suzanne          Dougherty          25.00 .T.
      4  123 Suzanne          Dougherty          35.00 .T.
      5  124 Steven           Dougherty          15.00 .F.
      6  124 Steven           Dougherty          13.00 .F.
      7  125 Lars             Porsena           100.00 .T.
      8  115 Tina             Culman             11.00 .T.
      9  113 Nancy            Benjamin           16.50 .T.
     10  116 Liz              Kendall            38.50 .T.
     11  120 Dennis           Hogan              25.00 .T.
     12  119 Emily            Morin              12.00 .F.
     13  117 Carol            Sobel              30.00 .T.
     14  118 Cathy            Morin              50.00 .F.
     15  121 Steve            Kendall            15.00 .T.
     16  121 Steve            Kendall            10.00 .T.
(DEMO) .
Command Line  <A:> NEWFILE2          Rec: EOF/16        Ins    Caps

                 Enter a dBASE III PLUS command.
```

The NEWFILE2 File
The specified fields from MEMBERS and CHARGES are combined in the new file.

16. Type **LIST TO PRINT** and press Enter.

FINISHING UP

17. You have completed this tutorial. Either close all open files and continue to the next activity or quit the program.

QUICK REFERENCE

```
SELECT A
USE CHARGES
SELECT B
USE MEMBERS INDEX MEMBID
JOIN WITH CHARGES TO NEWFILE1 FOR ID=A->ID
USE NEWFILE1
LIST
```

Joining Files—An Example Command
The command shown here will join the files named CHARGES and MEMBERS on the ID field which they have in common.

A typical JOIN command might be written as shown in the figure "Joining Files—An Example Command." Here is what each of the commands shown in that figure does.

- SELECT A selects memory area A, and USE CHARGES opens the CHARGES file in that memory area.
- SELECT B selects memory area B, and USE MEMBERS INDEX MEMBID opens the MEMBERS file in that memory area and indexes it on the MEMBID file (the ID field index).
- JOIN WITH CHARGES TO NEWFILE1 FOR ID=A->ID specifies that the MEMBERS file in the current memory area is to be joined with the CHARGES file, and the new file is to be named NEWFILE1. The FOR part of the command specifies that the common field is the ID field. When the JOIN command is executed, a new file is created. The JOIN command automatically deletes duplicate data.
- USE NEWFILE1 opens the new file that was created by joining the MEMBERS and CHARGES files.
- LIST lists the records in the new file.

EXERCISES

EXERCISE 1

JOINING THE EMPLOYEE AND DEPT FILES

1. Open DEPT in work area A.
2. Open EMPLOYEE in work area B and index it on EMP_NUM.
3. From work area A, join the two files on the EMP_NUM field to a new file named EMPDEPT1.
4. Make a printout of the new file's records and its structure.

The EMPDEPT1 File's Structure
After you join all fields from the EMPLOYEE and DEPT files, the new file's structure will look like this.

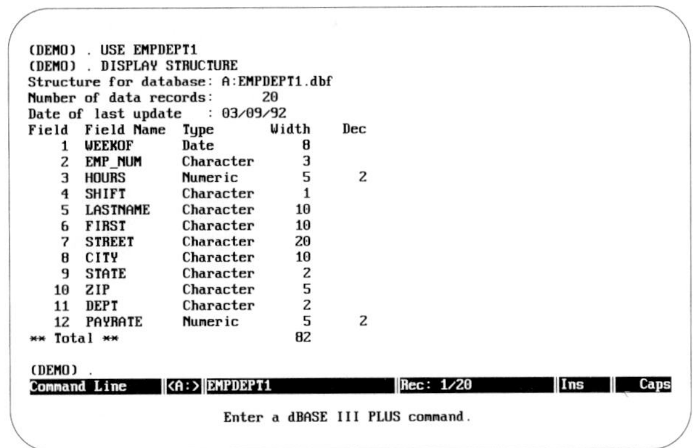

```
(DEMO) . USE EMPDEPT1
(DEMO) . DISPLAY STRUCTURE
Structure for database: A:EMPDEPT1.dbf
Number of data records:      20
Date of last update   : 03/09/92
Field  Field Name  Type       Width    Dec
    1  WEEKOF      Date           8
    2  EMP_NUM     Character      3
    3  HOURS       Numeric        5      2
    4  SHIFT       Character      1
    5  LASTNAME    Character     10
    6  FIRST       Character     10
    7  STREET      Character     20
    8  CITY        Character     10
    9  STATE       Character      2
   10  ZIP         Character      5
   11  DEPT        Character      2
   12  PAYRATE     Numeric        5      2
** Total **                      82

(DEMO) .
Command Line  <A:> EMPDEPT1          Rec: 1/20        Ins   Caps
                  Enter a dBASE III PLUS command.
```

EXERCISE 2

JOINING SELECTED FIELDS FROM THE EMPLOYEE AND DEPT FILES

1. Open DEPT in work area A.
2. Open EMPLOYEE in work area B and index it on EMP_NUM.
3. From work area A, join the two files on the EMP_NUM field to a new file named EMPDEPT2 but include only the EMP_NUM, LASTNAME, FIRST, DEPT, HOURS, and PAYRATE fields in the new file.
4. Make a printout of the new file's records and its structure.

The EMPDEPT2 File's Structure
After you join selected fields from the EMPLOYEE and DEPT files, the new file's structure will look like this.

```
(DEMO) . USE EMPDEPT2
(DEMO) . DISPLAY STRUCTURE
Structure for database: A:EMPDEPT2.dbf
Number of data records:      20
Date of last update   : 03/09/92
Field  Field Name  Type       Width    Dec
    1  EMP_NUM     Character      3
    2  LASTNAME    Character     10
    3  FIRST       Character     10
    4  DEPT        Character      2
    5  HOURS       Numeric        5      2
    6  PAYRATE     Numeric        5      2
** Total **                      36

(DEMO) .
Command Line  <A:> EMPDEPT2          Rec: 1/20        Ins   Caps
                  Enter a dBASE III PLUS command.
```

CHAPTER 5 REVIEW

- You can open more than one file at a time by selecting from up to ten work areas with the SELECT command.
- To work with two or more files, you use the SET RELATION TO <*field name*> INTO <*filename*> command. The file that you are relating into must be indexed on the field you are using to relate the two files.
- To include fields in the noncurrent work area in commands, precede them with the work areas alias. For example, if a field AMOUNT that you want to browse is in work area B and the current work area is A, use the command BROWSE B->AMOUNT.
- To create a new file from two existing files with a common field, use the JOIN command.

CHAPTER 5 QUESTIONS

FILL IN THE BLANK

1. To open work area B, you can use the command ___________ or ___________.
2. When relating two files, the field that must be indexed is the one in the ___________.
3. To relate a file in the current work area to a file named TARGET based on the field named COMMON, you would use the command ___________.
4. To browse fields named FIRST and LAST in the current work area and STREET, CITY, and STATE in work area B, the command would be ___________________________________.
5. To join the file in the current work area with a file named TARGET based on a field named COMMON, the command would be ___________________________________.

MATCH THE COLUMNS

1. SELECT	__ An alias
2. SET RELATION TO	__ Refers to a field in work area B
3. B->AMOUNT	__ Combines two files into one
4. A->AMOUNT	__ Opens work areas
5. JOIN	__ Refers to a field in work area A
6. A or B	__ Specifies a relationship between two files

WRITE OUT THE ANSWERS

1. Describe how you would relate two files and then browse through fields from both at the same time.
2. Describe how you would join two files into one with the JOIN command.
3. Explain what the SELECT command does.

CHAPTER 5

PROJECTS

PROJECT 1

RELATING THE TITLES AND SALES DATABASE FILES

1. Open the TITLES database file in work area A and SALES in work area B. Be sure sales is indexed on the ISBN field.
2. Return to work area A and relate the two files based on the ISBN field.
3. List to the printer only the fields containing data on the title, and sales in trade, educational, mail, and international markets.

PROJECT 2

JOINING THE TITLES AND SALES DATABASE FILES

1. Open the TITLES database file in work area A and SALES in work area B.
2. Join the two files based on the ISBN to a new file called ROYALTY.
3. List the new file to the printer.
4. List to the printer the fields containing data on the ISBN, author, title, period, and sales in the trade, educational, mail, and international markets.

CHAPTER 6

Printing Reports & Designing Custom Input Screens

TOPIC 18

Printing Reports—Advanced Procedures

```
Page No.     1
03/09/92
                         PHONE NUMBERS

FIRST NAME  LAST NAME   AREA      PHONE #   AMOUNTS
                                                DUE

** AREA CODE 201
 Dennis      Hogan       201      555-1004    25.00
 Carol       Sobel       201      555-1006    30.00
 Steve       Kendall     201      555-1010    25.00
** Subtotal **
                                              80.00
** AREA CODE 203
 Tina        Culman      203      555-1001    11.00
** Subtotal **
                                              11.00
** AREA CODE 312
 Liz         Kendall     312      555-1003    38.50
** Subtotal **
                                              38.50
** AREA CODE 404
 Lars        Porsena     404      555-1014   100.00
** Subtotal **
                                             100.00
** AREA CODE 407
 Jim         Kelly       407      555-1011   125.00
** Subtotal **
                                             125.00
** AREA CODE 408
 Emily       Morin       408      555-1005    12.00
** Subtotal **
                                              12.00
** AREA CODE 415
 Suzanne     Dougherty   415      555-1013    60.00
 Steven      Dougherty   415      555-1013    28.00
** Subtotal **
                                              88.00
** AREA CODE 508
 Cathy       Morin       508      555-1008    50.00
** Subtotal **
                                              50.00
** AREA CODE 617
 Nancy       Benjamin    617      555-1002    16.50
** Subtotal **
                                              16.50
*** Total ***
                                             521.00
```

The Indexed and Subtotaled Report
Reports list specified fields and specified records and can be grouped so that subtotals are calculated as they are here for area codes.

After completing this topic, you will be able to:

- Index a report to arrange it into a specific order
- Use conditions to control the records included in a report
- Modify a report with the MODIFY REPORT <*report name*> command
- Group a report on expressions
- Print subtotals and totals

After you have defined a report form, you have much control over how it presents data. You can use indexes and filters to govern the order of the records, specify which fields or records are to be included, and specify if totals and subtotals are to be calculated for numeric fields.

To have subtotals calculated in a report, you specify which field is to be the basis for the subtotal groupings. This field is not the field that contains the numbers to be totaled but any field that contains duplicate data that you want subtotaled. For example, in a report that contains a field named ST (for state) and a field named AMOUNT, the ST field would be specified as the field to group on to generate a report that totaled amounts by state.

DOT-PROMPT TUTORIAL

In this tutorial, you create a report form named AMOUNTS for the NEWFILE1 file you created in Topic 17. As you do so, you explore how to organize the data in reports and create subtotals for fields with identical entries.

GETTING STARTED

1. Display the dot prompt and open the NEWFILE1 file.

CREATING THE REPORT

2. Type **CREATE REPORT AMOUNTS** and press Enter ←.

The Create Report Screen
The CREATE REPORT command displays the screen you use to lay out your reports.

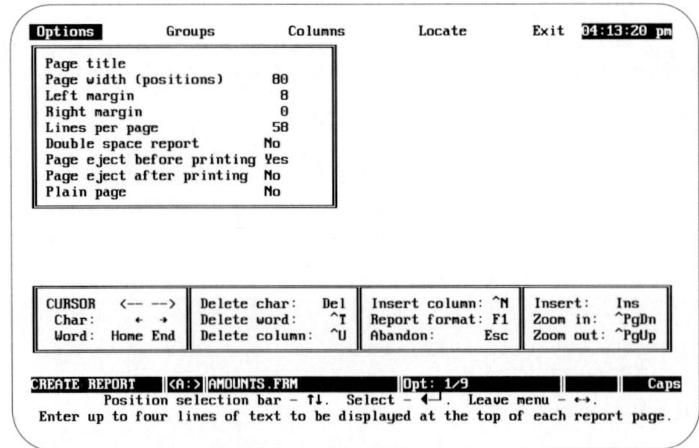

ADDING A HEADING

3. Highlight *Page title* and press Enter←┘.
4. Type **AMOUNTS DUE** in the page heading area.
5. Press Ctrl-End to save the title.

DEFINING FOUR COLUMNS

6. Press C to pull down the Columns menu.
7. Highlight *Contents* and press Enter←┘.
8. Type **FIRST** and press Enter←┘.
9. Highlight *Heading* and press Enter←┘.
10. Type **FIRST;NAME** and press Ctrl-End. The semicolon in the heading causes the second word to print on a second line, as shown in the report format window at the bottom of the screen. We're going to leave the width of this and all following columns at their default settings.
11. Press PgDn to display a new blank form for the next column.
12. Repeat Steps 7 through 11 but type **LASTNAME** for the contents and **LAST;NAME** for the heading.
13. Repeat Steps 7 through 11 but type **AREA** for the contents and **AREA;CODE** for the heading.
14. Repeat Steps 7 through 11 but type **PHONE** for the contents and **PHONE;NUMBER** for the heading.
15. Repeat Steps 7 through 10 but type **AMOUNT** for the contents and **AMOUNTS;DUE** for the heading.
16. Highlight *Total this column* and press Enter←┘ (if necessary) to toggle the answer to *Yes*.

The Column Menu
As you enter definitions for each column in the report, the column headings and widths are displayed in the report format window in the lower part of the screen.

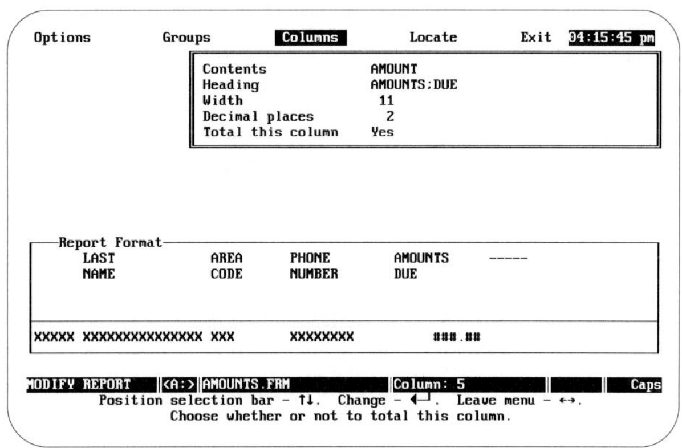

SAVING THE REPORT FORMAT

17. Press [E] to pull down the Exit menu.
18. Highlight *Save* and press [Enter←] to save the report form as AMOUNTS.FRM and return to the dot prompt.

PREVIEWING THE REPORT

19. Type **REPORT FORM AMOUNTS** and press [Enter←] to see the report on the screen with its records in the order that they appear in the file. Notice how there are multiple listings for many people. For example, the last two records are both for Steven Kendall.

The Report Form AMOUNTS with NEWFILE1
The report form AMOUNTS lists NEWFILE1 like this. Notice how there are duplicate names and addresses.

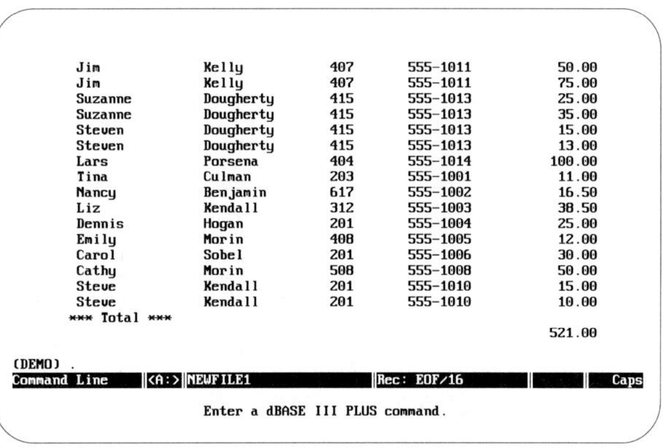

20. Type **TOTAL ON ID TO NEWFILE3** and press [Enter←] to add together all values for the same ID numbers.
21. Type **USE NEWFILE3** and press [Enter←].
22. Type **REPORT FORM AMOUNTS** and press [Enter←] to see that all records with the same ID number have been combined and the values in numeric fields such as AMOUNT are totaled.

The Report Form AMOUNTS with NEWFILE3
The report form AMOUNTS lists NEWFILE3 like this. Notice how all duplicate names have been combined and the numeric values totaled.

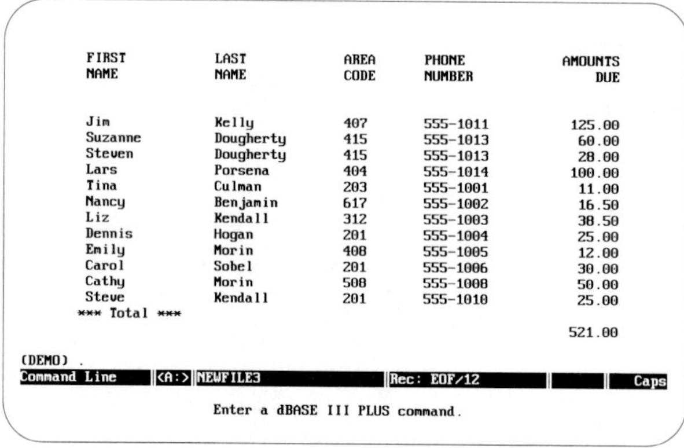

FIRST NAME	LAST NAME	AREA CODE	PHONE NUMBER	AMOUNTS DUE
Jim	Kelly	407	555-1011	125.00
Suzanne	Dougherty	415	555-1013	60.00
Steven	Dougherty	415	555-1013	28.00
Lars	Porsena	404	555-1014	100.00
Tina	Culman	203	555-1001	11.00
Nancy	Benjamin	617	555-1002	16.50
Liz	Kendall	312	555-1003	38.50
Dennis	Hogan	201	555-1004	25.00
Emily	Morin	408	555-1005	12.00
Carol	Sobel	201	555-1006	30.00
Cathy	Morin	508	555-1008	50.00
Steve	Kendall	201	555-1010	25.00
*** Total ***				
				521.00

(DEMO) .
Command Line | <A:> | NEWFILE3 | Rec: EOF/12 | Caps

Enter a dBASE III PLUS command.

ARRANGING THE REPORT IN A DESIRED ORDER

23. Type **INDEX ON AREA TO AREACODE** and press Enter to index the file on area codes.
24. Type **REPORT FORM AMOUNTS** and press Enter to see the report scrolls arranged in order of area codes.

The File Indexed on Area Codes
After you index your database file on the AREA field, the report form lists all records by area code.

FIRST NAME	LAST NAME	AREA CODE	PHONE NUMBER	AMOUNTS DUE
Dennis	Hogan	201	555-1004	25.00
Carol	Sobel	201	555-1006	30.00
Steve	Kendall	201	555-1010	25.00
Tina	Culman	203	555-1001	11.00
Liz	Kendall	312	555-1003	38.50
Lars	Porsena	404	555-1014	100.00
Jim	Kelly	407	555-1011	125.00
Emily	Morin	408	555-1005	12.00
Suzanne	Dougherty	415	555-1013	60.00
Steven	Dougherty	415	555-1013	28.00
Cathy	Morin	508	555-1008	50.00
Nancy	Benjamin	617	555-1002	16.50
*** Total ***				
				521.00

(DEMO) .
Command Line | <A:> | NEWFILE3 | Rec: EOF/12 | Caps

Enter a dBASE III PLUS command.

25. Type **REPORT FORM AMOUNTS TO PRINT** and press Enter to print the report.

SPECIFYING RECORDS

26. Type **REPORT FORM AMOUNTS FOR ST="CA"** and press Enter to see that only those records with CA in the ST field are included in the report.
27. Type **REPORT FORM AMOUNTS FOR AMOUNT>30** and press Enter to see that only those records with amounts greater than 30 are included in the report.

SPECIFYING THE FIELDS TO BE GROUPED ON

28. Type **MODIFY REPORT AMOUNTS** and press Enter.
29. Press G to pull down the Groups menu.
30. Highlight *Group on expression* and press Enter.
31. Press F10 to display a list of field names.
32. Highlight *AREA* and press Enter two times.
33. Highlight *Group heading* and press Enter.
34. Type **AREA CODE:** and press Enter.

The Groups Menu
The Groups menu allows you to specify the field on which records are to be grouped.

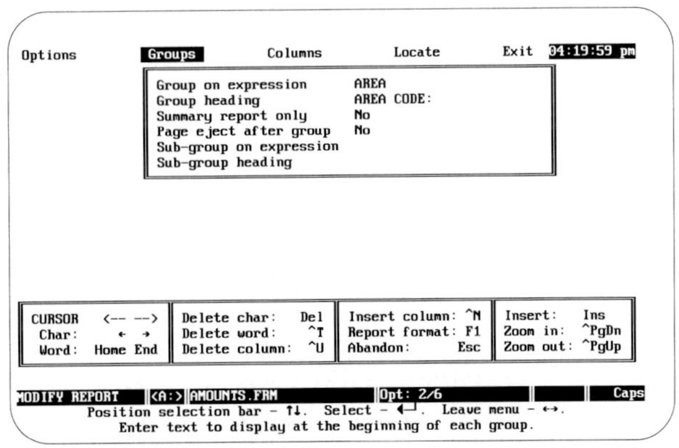

35. Press [E] to pull down the Exit menu.
36. Highlight *Save* and press [Enter ←┘] to save the report form.

DISPLAYING AND PRINTING THE REPORT

37. Type **REPORT FORM AMOUNTS** and press [Enter ←┘] to see that the report is now subtotaled for each area code.

The Modified Report Form AMOUNTS
The modified report form AMOUNTS lists NEWFILE3 like this. Notice how all people in the same area code are grouped together and their amounts subtotaled.

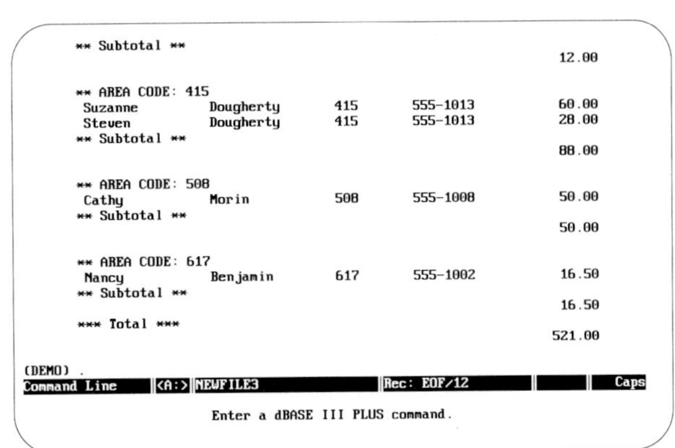

38. Type **REPORT FORM AMOUNTS TO PRINT** and press [Enter ←┘] to print the report.

FINISHING UP

39. You have completed this tutorial. Either close all open files and continue to the next activity or quit the program.

QUICK REFERENCE

Report formats that you create with the CREATE REPORT <*report name*> command can improve on the listings you get with the LIST TO PRINT and similar commands. You can print reports in indexed order, you can total numeric fields, and you can group related records together. Moreover, you can save your report formats so you needn't repeat all of the preparatory steps the next time you need to print a report.

To modify an existing report format, you use the MODIFY REPORT <*report name*> command and then use the same menus and commands you used to create the report.

When you want to organize a report in a specific order, index the field on which you would like it arranged and then display or print the report.

When you create or modify a report format, you can specify if numeric columns are totaled by pulling down the Column menu and displaying the column definition. Set the entry *Total this column* to *Yes*.

When you create or modify a report format, you can specify if related records are grouped by pulling down the Groups menu and specifying which fields are to be used as the basis for groups and subgroups. The choices on the Groups menu are described in the table "Create Report Groups Menu Commands." Choices for the other CREATE REPORT commands are described in the table "Create Report Menu Commands" in Topic 11.

CREATE REPORT GROUPS MENU COMMANDS

Command	Description
Groups	
Group on expression	Specifies the field or expression on which to break for the first level of subtotals.
Group heading	Text that appears at the start of each group.
Summary report only	*Yes* omits detail lines; *No* does not.
Page eject after group	Prints each group on a separate page when set to *Yes*.
Sub-group on expression	Specifies a subgroup under a group. For example, you could group on states and subgroup on cities if those fields were in your database.
Sub-group heading	Text that appears at the start of each subgroup.

EXERCISE

EXERCISE 1

USING THE EMPADD REPORT WITH AN INDEXED FILE

1. Open the EMPLOYEE file.
2. Index the file on the LASTNAME field.
3. Use the EMPADD report form that you created in Topic 11 to display and print the report.

TOPIC 19

Printing Labels

After completing this topic, you will be able to:

- Define, modify, and print labels
- Trim excess spaces from the end of text

Reports are not always in the form of tables. They can also be in the form of printed labels. Think of all the printed labels you encounter from day to day. Letters and packages must be labeled for mailing. Items in a store's inventory are labeled, as are drawers in a filing cabinet and program disks like those you use in this course. If you have to prepare a few labels, any method will suffice, However, if you have to prepare tens, hundreds, or thousands of labels, automation can save an enormous amount of time, especially if the labeling data have already been collected for other purposes or will be used again. One of the major applications of databases is just such automation.

The big advantage of using a database to print labels is the flexibility that it gives you. For example, the post office offers reduced bulk rates to mail that is presorted by ZIP code. Using a database, arranging the labels in order of ZIP codes is fast and easy. Moreover, you need not print all the labels in the database since you can print only those that meet specific criteria.

Many commercially available labels are gummed and mounted on sheets so that they can be run through a printer. By setting up a label file, you can pull names and other information from a database file to fill in these labels.

DOT-PROMPT TUTORIAL

In this tutorial, you create a file that prints mailing labels using names and addresses stored in the MEMBERS database file.

GETTING STARTED

1. Display the dot prompt and open the MEMBERS database file.

CREATING A LABEL DEFINITION

2. Type **CREATE LABEL MAILING** and press Enter ↵ to display the Label menu with the Options menu pulled down.

The Label Menu
The Label menu lists a variety of predefined labels.

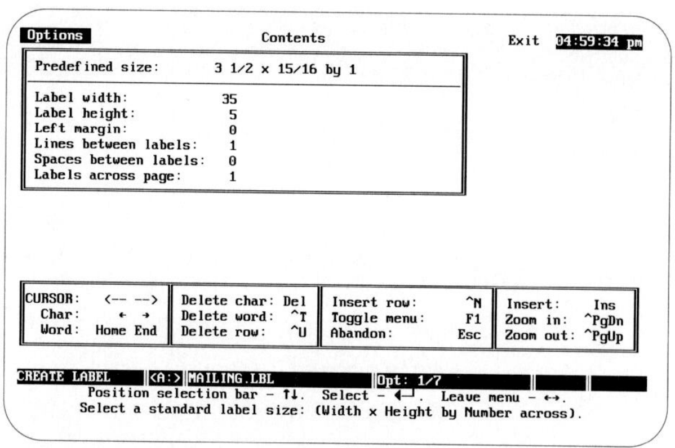

3. Press F1 to turn the cursor-movement key help screen on or off.

SPECIFYING THE LABEL TYPE

4. Highlight *Predefined size:* and press Enter↵ a number of times while watching the text change under the highlight. Each time you press Enter↵, the definition of the label changes in the highlighted field and on the six lines below.
5. Press Enter↵ until the definition reads *3 2/10 x 11/12 by 3 (Cheshire).*

MODIFYING THE LABEL DEFINITION

6. Highlight *Label width* and press Enter↵.
7. Type **25** and press Enter↵. Note that the definition on the top line does not change. It indicates the base label definition that you started with, not the final label design that you end up with after you make changes.

SPECIFYING THE LABEL'S CONTENTS

8. Press C to pull down the Contents menu.
9. Follow the procedures listed here to enter the label definition shown in the figure "The Label's Contents."

The Label's Contents
After you enter the fields that you want printed on the label, your menu should look like this.

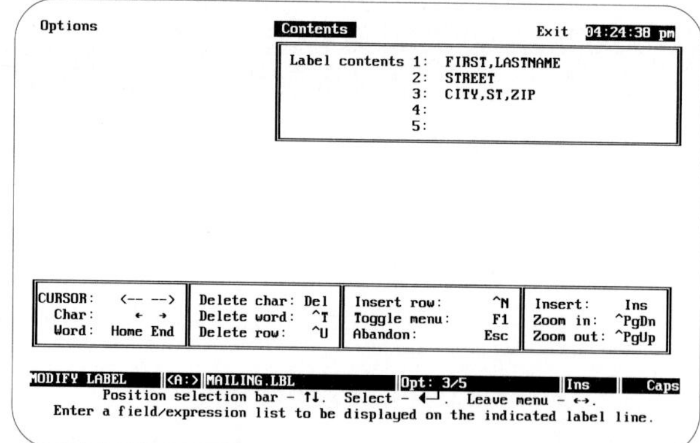

- Use ↓ to move the highlight to the line number that you want to define.
- Press Enter↵ to move the cursor to the space following the number.

- Type in the field names that you want printed on each line. Alternatively, press F10 to display a list of field names in the file, highlight the one you want to use, and press Enter←.
- When you use more than one field name on a line, separate them with commas to insert single spaces between the contents of the fields when they are printed.
- Press Enter← to complete the entry.

SAVING THE LABEL DEFINITION

10. Press E to pull down the Exit menu.
11. Select *Save* to save the definition and return to the dot prompt.

PREVIEWING THE LABELS

12. Type **LABEL FORM MAILING** and press Enter← to preview the labels on the screen. Notice how there are spaces between the city, state, and ZIP code in each label, but there is no comma following the city.

Label Preview
Previewing your labels on the screen makes it easy to find and correct mistakes.

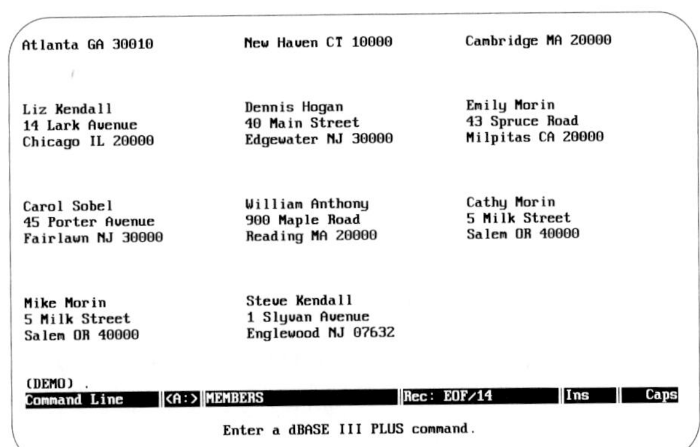

MODIFYING THE CONTENTS

13. Type **MODIFY LABEL MAILING** and press Enter← to display the Label menu with the Options menu pulled down.
14. Press C to pull down the Contents menu.
15. Highlight *3:* and press Enter←.
16. Edit the line so that it reads **TRIM(CITY)+",",ST,ZIP** and press Enter←.

The Revised Label's Contents
After you revise the address line for the city, state, and ZIP code, your screen should look like this.

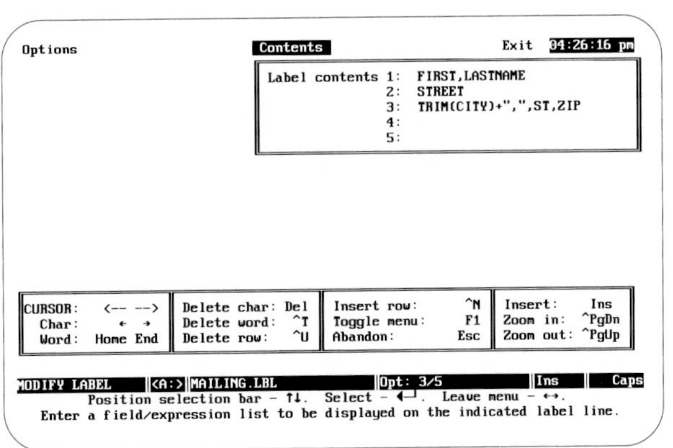

17. Press [E] to pull down the Exit menu.
18. Select *Save* to save the definition and return to the dot prompt.
19. Type **LABEL FORM MAILING** and press [Enter←] to preview the labels on the screen. Now there is a comma between the city and state, followed by a space.

The Revised Labels
Your revised labels should now have commas following the cities.

```
Atlanta, GA 30010          New Haven, CT 10000         Cambridge, MA 20000


Liz Kendall                Dennis Hogan                Emily Morin
14 Lark Avenue             40 Main Street              43 Spruce Road
Chicago, IL 20000          Edgewater, NJ 30000         Milpitas, CA 20000


Carol Sobel                William Anthony             Cathy Morin
45 Porter Avenue           900 Maple Road              5 Milk Street
Fairlawn, NJ 30000         Reading, MA 20000           Salem, OR 40000


Mike Morin                 Steve Kendall
5 Milk Street              1 Sylvan Avenue
Salem, OR 40000            Englewood, NJ 07632

(DEMO) .
Command Line   <A:> MEMBERS            Rec: EOF/14        Ins    Caps
                   Enter a dBASE III PLUS command.
```

PRINTING THE LABELS

20. Type **LABEL FORM MAILING TO PRINT SAMPLE** and press [Enter←] to print one row of labels in graphic form. The prompt then reads *Do you want more samples? (Y/N).*
21. Press [N], and the program prints out a page of labels. (Type **EJECT** and press [Enter←] if your printer does not automatically eject pages.)

PRINTING IN INDEXED ORDER BY ZIP CODE

22. Type **INDEX ON ZIP TO ZIPCODE** and press [Enter←].
23. Type **LABEL FORM MAILING TO PRINT** and press [Enter←] to print the labels in order of their ZIP codes.

PRINTING SELECTED RECORDS

24. Type **LABEL FORM MAILING TO PRINT FOR ST="MA"** and press [Enter←] to print only labels for those people with MA in the ST field are printed.

FINISHING UP

25. You have completed this tutorial. Either close all open files and continue to the next activity or quit the program.

QUICK REFERENCE

To create a new label definition, you use the CREATE LABEL <*filename*> command. To modify an existing input screen, you use the MODIFY LABEL <*filename*> command. Either of these commands displays the Screen menu described in the table "CREATE LABEL and MODIFY LABEL Menu Commands."

CREATE LABEL AND MODIFY LABEL MENU COMMANDS

Command	Description
Options	
Predefined size:	Pressing [Enter←] with the highlight in this field scrolls you through five predefined label definitions. • 3 1/2 x 15/16 by 1 • 3 1/2 x 15/16 by 2 • 3 1/2 x 15/16 by 3 • 4 x 1 7/16 by 1 • 3 2/10 x 11/12 by 3 (Cheshire)
Label width:	Specifies the labels width in characters (1–120). You can type in a number or press [↑] or [↓] to change the value.
Label height:	Specifies the number of lines on the label (1–16).
Left margin:	Specifies the left margin in characters (0–250).
Lines between labels:	Specifies the number of lines between the last line of a label and the first line of the label below (0–16).
Spaces between labels:	Specifies the horizontal space in characters between side-by-side labels (0–120).
Labels across page:	Specifies the number of labels on the page side by side (1–5).
Contents	
1: through <n>	Spaces to enter the field names and other data that are to appear on the label. Use only character fields to fill out labels. To use date fields, convert their contents to characters with the DTOC(field name) function. To convert numeric fields to characters, use the STR(field name) function. The number of lines displayed depends on the number specified in the *Label height:* section of the menu.
Exit	
Save	Saves the current label definition.
Abandon	Abandons the current label definition.

Designing Labels

Labels come in a variety of forms and are generally specified by the size of each label and the number of labels across the page. For example, one common form of label (called a Cheshire label) is 3 $^{2}/_{10}$ inches wide and $^{11}/_{12}$ inch high with three labels across the page. Although predefined labels are listed on the Label menu in inches, you make all modifications such as margin settings and label sizes in characters per inch. To do so, you must understand how labels are laid out on the page. First of all, you determine the size of the type you will use to print the labels. dBASE is designed to work with fixed pitch type such as Courier, where there is a fixed number of characters per inch. For example, 12-point type prints 10 characters per inch, and 10-point type prints 12 characters per inch. If you use a proportionally spaced type, your labels may not print or align correctly. If this happens, print the labels in Courier or a similar fixed pitch font.

Once you know how many characters your printer prints per inch, you can begin laying out a design for labels using a grid with 10 or 12 character spaces per inch. Alternatively, you can measure labels with a ruler and convert to characters per inch. Just multiply the measurement in inches times 10 if you are using 12-point type or times 12 if you are using 10-point type. For example, if you want a left margin of three-quarters of an inch when using 12-point type, multiply .75 times 12 to calculate that the margin is 9 characters wide.

Eliminating Blank Spaces on Printed Labels

Frequently, you specify two or more field names on a line in a label definition. To do so, you concatenate, or join, the fields with the plus symbol—for example, CITY+ST+ZIP. When you do so, the program automatically allocates the same number of characters on the label that are specified as the field's width.

For example, in one database, the fields and their contents may be like those shown in part A of the figure "Label Spacing." When you then use CITY+ST+ZIP to print the labels (B), blank spaces are left if the contents of the FIRST field are shorter than the field's length, and the words run together if the fields are full. To eliminate these two problems, you use the comma or the TRIM command.

When you use more than one field name on a line, you can separate them with commas to indicate that you want one blank space between them. For example, if you specify CITY,ST,ZIP instead of CITY+ST+ZIP (C), you solve the problem of spacing, but you may need a comma separating the city and state. To add one, you use the plus sign followed by a comma in double quotation marks, for example, CITY+",",ST,ZIP (D). The "," part of the command inserts a comma at the end of the defined field width and the comma that follows inserts a space.

When you specify field names in a label definition, the program automatically allocates the same number of characters on the label that are specified as the field's width. Since most fields have data shorter than the allowed field width, spaces are left on the label. To eliminate extra spaces that trail the field's data, you use the TRIM command. For example, if you specify TRIM(CITY)+",",ST,ZIP (C), your label spacing is perfect.

CITY											ST			ZIP					
B	o	s	t	o	n						M	A		0	0	0	0	0	
P	i	t	t	s	b	u	r	g	h		P	A		0	0	0	0	0	
S	a	n		D	i	e	g	o			C	A		0	0	0	0	0	

A The Database's Field's

B	o	s	t	o	n					M	A	0	0	0	0	0
P	i	t	t	s	b	u	r	g	h	P	A	0	0	0	0	0
S	a	n		D	i	e	g	o		C	A	0	0	0	0	0

B Labels printed with CITY+ST+ZIP

B	o	s	t	o	n		M	A		0	0	0	0	0				
P	i	t	t	s	b	u	r	g	h		P	A		0	0	0	0	0
S	a	n		D	i	e	g	o		C	A		0	0	0	0	0	

C Labels printed with CITY,ST,ZIP

B	o	s	t	o	n					,		M	A		0	0	0	0	0
P	i	t	t	s	b	u	r	g	h	,		P	A		0	0	0	0	0
S	a	n		D	i	e	g	o		,		C	A		0	0	0	0	0

D Labels printed with CITY+",",ST,ZIP

B	o	s	t	o	n	,		M	A		0	0	0	0	0				
P	i	t	t	s	b	u	r	g	h	,		P	A		0	0	0	0	0
S	a	n		D	i	e	g	o	,		C	A		0	0	0	0	0	

E Labels printed with TRIM(CITY)+",",ST,ZIP

Label Spacing

dBASE automatically allocates a space for each character in the field's width even when the contents of the field are shorter. However, you can use commas and the TRIM command to correct word spacing problems.

Printing Labels

To print labels, you use the LABEL FORM <*filename*> TO PRINT command. For example, to print labels using a definition saved in the file MAILING, type **LABEL FORM MAILING TO PRINT** and press Enter ←. To print just selected records, use the LABEL FORM <*filename*> TO PRINT FOR <*condition*> version of the command. For example, to print only those records with MA in the ST field, use the LABEL FORM <*filename*> TO PRINT FOR ST="MA" command.

When you work with a large database, the last thing you would want to do is begin printing labels with an untested label definition file. Hundreds or thousands of labels might be printed incorrectly before you noticed the problem or were able to interrupt the program and printer. To preview your results, use the LABEL FORM <*filename*> TO PRINT SAMPLE command. This prints a single page of labels and shows how fields are laid out using Xs for characters, 9s for numbers in numeric and date fields, Ls in logical fields, and MEMOs in memo fields.

EXERCISES

EXERCISE 1

MODIFYING THE MAILING LABEL DEFINITION

Open the MEMBERS database file and modify the MAILING label definition by using the Contents menu to change the third line as follows:

a. CITY+ST+ZIP
b. CITY+",",ST,ZIP
c. TRIM(CITY)+",",ST,ZIP

After making each change, print the labels and write down on the page the entry in line 3 that was used to print them. When finished with all three versions, compare them carefully and indicate the differences among them.

EXERCISE 2

PRINTING LABELS FROM THE EMPLOYEE DATABASE FILE

Open the EMPLOYEE database file and define 2-across mailing labels (3 1/2 x 15/16 by 2), each of which looks like the following:

ROGER AMES
400 HILL DRIVE
TAMPA, FL 33606

Name the form EMPLABL and use it to print the records in the EMPLOYEE file.

TOPIC 20

Creating Customized Input Screens

After completing this topic, you will be able to:

- Create customized input screens
- Protect data from being changed
- Restrict the type of data that can be entered

The commands such as APPEND and EDIT that you have used to enter or edit data in a database use the file's field names to label the fields. At times you may want to add other information to the input screen—for example, prompts that explain what should be entered. To do this, you design your own customized input screens. When doing so, you can enter text that describes fields, allow data in fields to be seen but not changed, specify the type of data that can be entered, or even omit fields from the screen so that the user does not know they exist. Once the input screen is defined, you can call it up whenever you use the APPEND, CHANGE, EDIT, or INSERT command.

DOT-PROMPT TUTORIAL

In this tutorial, you design an input screen for the MEMBERS database. When finished with the screen, you can use it to view, enter, and edit records in the database. The figure "The Customized Input Screen at Work" shows how the screen will look when you use it at the end of the tutorial.

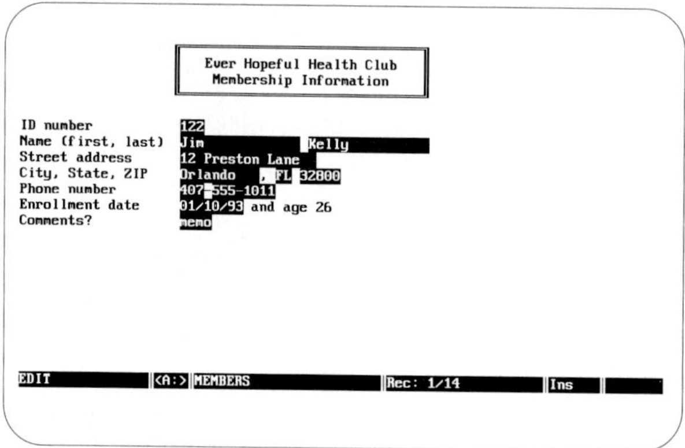

The Customized Input Screen at Work
In this tutorial, you create a customized input screen that simplifies entering data into the database. After you have designed the form, it will look like this when you use it in conjunction with the EDIT or APPEND command.

GETTING STARTED

1. Display the dot prompt and open the MEMBERS database file.

CREATING A SCREEN DEFINITION

2. Type **CREATE SCREEN MEMBERS** and press [Enter←] to display the Screen menu with the Set Up menu pulled down.

The Screen Menu
When you display the Screen menu, the Set Up menu is pulled down.

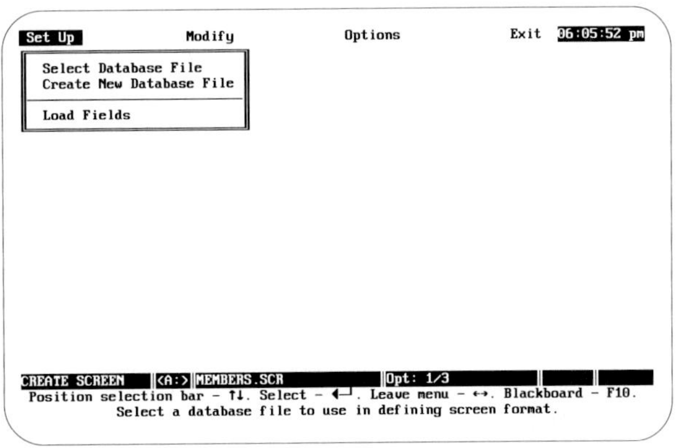

LABEL POSITIONS FOR MEMBERS.SCR

Row	Col	Label
2	23	Ever Hopeful Health Club
3	24	Membership Information
6	0	ID number
7	0	Name (first, last)
8	0	Street address
9	0	City, State, ZIP
10	0	Phone number
11	0	Enrollment date
11	29	and age
12	0	Comments?

ENTERING LABELS

3. Press [F10] to remove the menu and display a screen called the blackboard.
4. Press the arrow keys to move the cursor to the row and column indicated for each label in the table "Label Positions for MEMBERS.SCR" and type in the indicated label. The position of the cursor on the blackboard is always indicated on the right side of the status line.

The Blackboard
After you enter your labels on the blackboard, your screen should look like this.

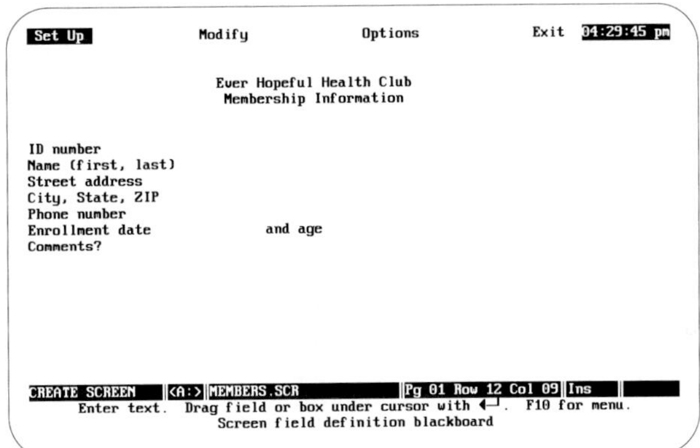

ENTERING FIELDS

5. Move the cursor to row 6, column 20.
6. Press [F10] to display the menu.
7. Press [S] to pull down the Set Up menu.
8. Highlight *Load Fields* and press [Enter←] to display a list of the fields in the MEMBERS database.
9. Highlight *ID* and press [Enter←] to select it.
10. Press [F10] to return to the blackboard. The name of the field and the field itself are now on the blackboard. The field is in reverse video with three *X*s in it to indicate its length and type. (*X* indicates a character field.) To move the highlighted field to where we want it, you will delete the field name and spaces to drag it into position.

The ID Field
When you enter the ID field onto the blackboard, both the field name and the field itself are entered.

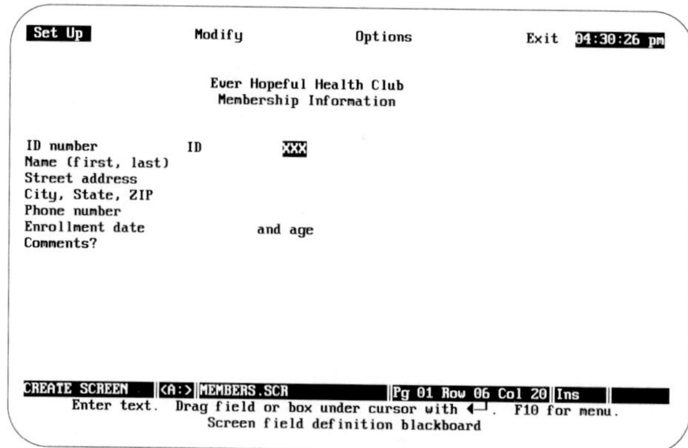

FIELD POSITIONS FOR MEMBERS.SCR

Field	Row	Col
FIRST	7	20
LASTNAME	7	36
STREET	8	20
CITY	9	20
ST	9	32
ZIP	9	35
AREA	10	20
PHONE	10	24
ENROLLED	11	20
REMARKS	12	20

11. Press [Del] to delete the label and the spaces in front of the field's highlight until the cursor is under the first *X*. (If you delete one or more *X*s by mistake, press [Ins] to reenter them.)
12. Repeat Steps 6 through 11 to enter each of the remaining fields listed in the table "Field Positions for MEMBERS.SCR." This table lists the row and column in which the cursor should be positioned when you begin Step 6. (If you add a field to the blackboard by mistake, position the cursor in the highlighted area and press [Ctrl]-[U], then press [N] when the prompt asks if you want to also delete it from the database.)
13. Notice how entering the ENROLLED field overwrote the text *and age* that you entered. Move the cursor to row 11, column 29 and type **and age** again.
14. Copy the AGE field in with the cursor in row 11, column 37.
15. With insert turned off, type in a comma between the CITY and ST fields and a hyphen between the AREA and PHONE fields.

Final Screen Layout
After you enter labels and fields, your blackboard should look like this.

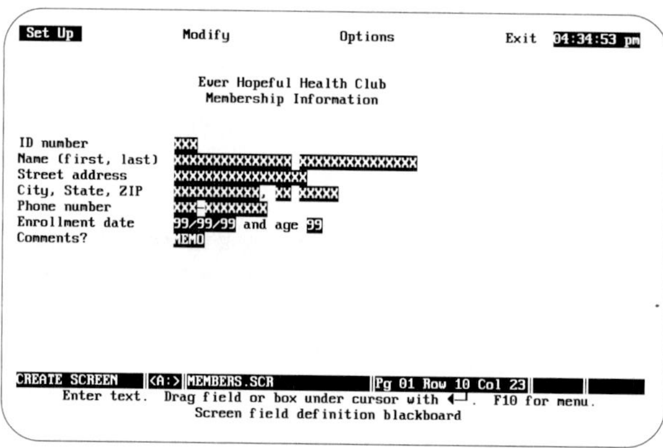

DRAWING BOXES

16. Press [F10] to display the menu.
17. Press [O] to pull down the Options menu.
18. Highlight *Double bar* and press [Enter ↵]. The prompt reads *Position cursor to box corner with ↑↓←→. Complete with ↵. Exit with Esc.*
19. Move the cursor to row 01, column 19 and press [Enter ↵] to specify the box's upper-left corner. The prompt reads *Position cursor to other corner with ↑↓←→. Complete with ↵. Exit with Esc.*

20. Move the cursor to row 04, column 51 and press [Enter←] to specify the box's lower-right corner.
21. Move the cursor anywhere in the double line that forms the right side of the box.
22. Press [Enter←] to turn on drag mode.
23. Press [←] once to change the box's width slightly, and press [Enter←].

Adding a Box
After you enter a box around the heading, your blackboard should look like this.

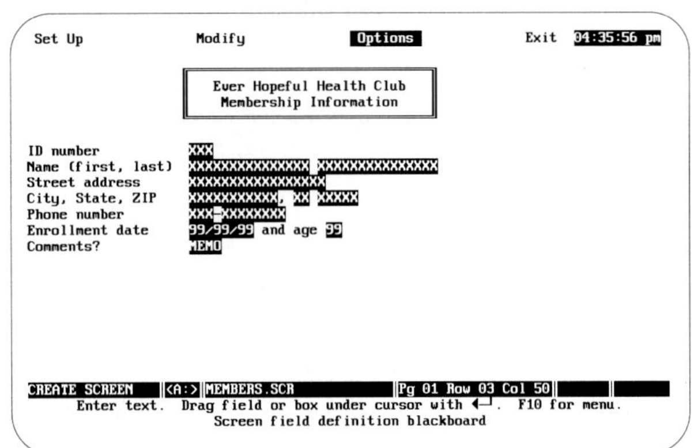

PREVENTING DATA FROM BEING ENTERED INTO SELECTED FIELDS

24. Move the cursor into the reverse video area following the text *and age.*
25. Press [F10] to display the menu, and the Modify menu is pulled down.
26. Highlight *Action:* and press [Enter←] to change the entry from *Edit/GET* to *Display/SAY.*
27. Press [F10] to return to the blackboard and the AGE field is no longer displayed in reverse video. This indicates that data can no longer be entered or altered in the field.

SPECIFYING THE TYPE OF DATA THAT CAN BE ENTERED

28. Move the cursor into the reverse video area following the *ID number* label.
29. Press [F10] to display the menu, and the Modify menu is pulled down.
30. Highlight *Picture Template:* and press [Enter←] to display a list of options and the prompt *Picture value.*
31. Type **999** and press [Enter←] to allow only digits to be entered into the field.
32. Press [F10] to return to the blackboard, and the Xs in the field are replaced by 9s.

Specifying Data Types
After you convert the AGE field to Display/Say and create a picture template for the ID field, your screen should look like this.

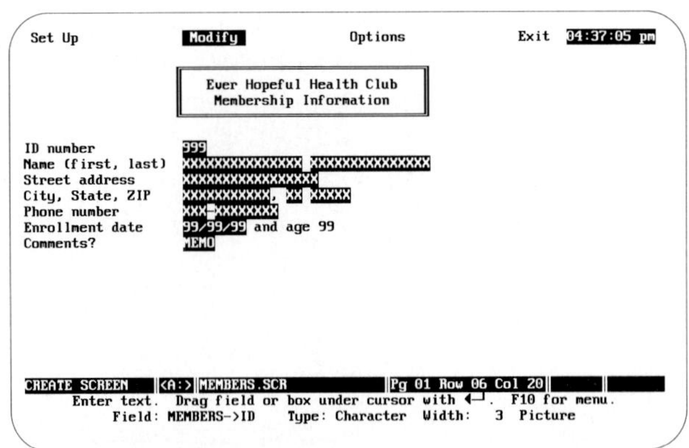

SPECIFYING THE FORMAT OF DATA THAT CAN BE ENTERED

33. Move the cursor into the reverse video area following the hyphen in the *Phone number* field.
34. Press F10 to display the menu, and the Modify menu is pulled down.
35. Highlight *Picture Template:* and press Enter←┘ to display a list of options and the prompt *Picture value.*
36. Type **999-9999** and press Enter←┘ to allow only a hyphen in the fourth position and numbers in the others.
37. Press F10 to return to the blackboard, and the Xs change to 9s with a hyphen in the fourth position.

SAVING A COPY OF THE SCREEN DISPLAY

38. Press F10 to display the menu.
39. Press O to pull down the Options menu.
40. Highlight *Generate text file image* and press Enter←┘.

    Nothing appears to happen, but the screen and its specifications will be saved in an ASCII text file when you exit.

SAVING AND PRINTING THE SCREEN

41. Press E to pull down the Exit menu.
42. Highlight *Save* and press Enter←┘ to save the screen definition and return to the dot prompt.
43. Type **TYPE MEMBERS.SCR TO PRINT** and press Enter←┘ to print out the screen that you generated in Step 40.

USING THE INPUT SCREEN

44. Type **CLOSE ALL** and press Enter←┘.
45. Type **USE MEMBERS** and press Enter←┘.
46. Type **GO TOP** and press Enter←┘.
47. Type **EDIT** and press Enter←┘ and you see the Edit screen as it normally appears. This layout is supplied automatically.
48. Press Esc to return to the dot prompt.
49. Type **SET FORMAT TO MEMBERS** and press Enter←┘.
50. Type **EDIT** and press Enter←┘ to display the database using the customized input screen that you just created.

51. Press [Enter ↵] to move the cursor between fields and [PgUp] and [PgDn] to move between records. Display the record for ID 115 (Tina Culman) and try the following:
    - Change the street address from 100 Elm Street to 200 Elm Street.
    - Note that the data in the AGE field are not displayed in reverse video and you cannot move the cursor to that field.
    - Notice that you cannot enter letters into the ID field.
    - Notice that you cannot enter a phone number without a hyphen in the fourth character position. (After typing three digits, the hyphen is automatically inserted.)

FINISHING UP

52. Press [Esc] to display the dot prompt.
53. Type **CLOSE FORMAT** and press [Enter ↵] to close the format file.
54. You have completed this tutorial. Either close all open files and continue to the next activity or quit the program.

QUICK REFERENCE

To create a new input screen, you use the CREATE SCREEN <*filename*> command. To modify an existing input screen, you use the MODIFY SCREEN <*filename*> command. Either of these commands displays the Screen menu described in the table "CREATE SCREEN and MODIFY SCREEN Menu Commands." In addition to the Screen menu, you work with the blackboard, the area on which you lay out the input screen. You toggle between the menu and the blackboard by pressing [F10].

Entering and Aligning Text

Press [Ins] to toggle insert mode on or off. In insert mode, press [Spacebar] to insert spaces that push text and fields to the right. Press [Del] or [← Bksp] to delete spaces so that text and fields move to the left.

Moving Fields

To move a field, position the cursor in the reverse video (or color) highlight that indicates the field's length and press [Enter ↵] to turn on drag mode. At this point, the prompt reads *Move field with ↑↓←→. Complete with ↵. Exit drag with Esc.* Move the cursor to where you want the first character of the field to be and press [Enter ↵] a second time to move the field.

Inserting and Deleting Lines

To insert lines on the blackboard, move the cursor to a line above where you want to insert a line and press [Ctrl]-[N]. To delete a line, position the cursor on the line to be deleted and press [Ctrl]-[Y]. When you delete a line, the line below moves up to take its place.

CREATE SCREEN AND MODIFY SCREEN MENU COMMANDS

Commands	Description
Set Up	
Select Database File	Highlight this choice and press Enter↵ to display a list of available databases from which to choose.
Create New Database File	Highlight this choice and press Enter↵ to display the prompt *Enter name for new Database file:*.
Load Fields	This command loads the database's fields onto the blackboard. The field names are in uppercase letters, and the fields are in reverse video with an X in each character position.
Modify	
Screen Field Definition	Specifies characteristics of the field. (The cursor must be in a field for these commands to be activated.) • *Action*: can be toggled between Edit/GET and Display/SAY by pressing Enter↵. In Edit/GET mode, you can enter and change data in the field. In Display/SAY mode, you cannot. • *Source*: indicates the name of the database file(s) the screen is being used with. • *Content:*, *Type:*, *Width:*, and *Decimal:*, indicate details about the field that you are modifying.
Picture Functions:	Specifies the type of data that you can enter into a field or the way that data are displayed. The choices you are offered depend on the action you have specified. For details, see the dBASE III Plus Manual or a more advanced textbook.
Picture Template:	Specifies the format in which data can be entered into a field or the way that data are displayed. For details, see the dBASE III Plus Manual or a more advanced textbook.
Range:	Specifies the maximum and minimum values that can be entered into fields.
Options	
Generate text file image	Saves a "picture" of the current blackboard in an ASCII text file so that you can retrieve it from DOS or into a word processing program. The printout also lists specifications describing the screen format.
Draw a window or line	After highlighting a single- or double-ruled line or box and pressing Enter↵, move the cursor to where you want a line or box to begin and press Enter↵. Move the cursor to where you want the line or box to end, and press Enter↵ again.
Exit	
Save	Saves the input screen into a file with the extension .SCR.
Abandon	Abandons any changes made to the input screen.

Deleting Fields

When creating custom input screens, you can edit them as you go along. For example, to delete characters in a label, press Del or ←Bksp.

To delete a reverse video field, position the cursor in the field, press Ctrl-U, and the prompt reads *Do you wish to also delete field from database? [Y/N]*. Press N to delete the field just from the customized input screen or press Y to delete it from both the customized input screen and from the database.

Drawing Boxes

After selecting a single- or double-ruled line from the Options menu, move the cursor to where you want the upper-left corner of the box to be and press Enter↵. Move the cursor to where you want the lower-right corner of the box to be and press Enter↵ again. As you move the cursor about the screen, its position is always listed on the status line by page, row, and column. You can use this position indicator as a guide when you draw boxes.

When drawing boxes around text, it's usually easier to enter text first and then draw boxes. If you add text after a box is drawn, you can change the size of the box by moving the cursor onto the line you want to move and pressing Enter↵ to enter drag mode. Use the arrow keys to change the size of the box and press Enter↵ again.

Using a Screen Form

Once you have designed and saved a screen definition, you use the SET FORMAT TO <*filename*> command. When you then use the APPEND, EDIT, CHANGE, or INSERT command, the screen form appears instead of the original default form. To turn off the screen form, use the CLOSE FORMAT command.

EXERCISES

LABEL POSITIONS FOR EMPLOYEE.SCR

Row	Col	Label
1	29	Employee records
4	0	Employee ID number
6	0	Name (first, last)
8	0	Street
10	0	City, State, ZIP
12	0	Department
14	0	Pay rate

EXERCISE 1

CREATING AN INPUT SCREEN FOR THE EMPLOYEE FILE

Open the EMPLOYEE database file and define an input screen named EMPLOYEE to match the one shown in the figure "The EMPLOYEE Customized Input Screen" and described in the tables "Label Positions for EMPLOYEE.SCR" and "Field Positions for EMPLOYEE.SCR." When finished, generate a text file image and make a printout.

FIELD POSITIONS FOR EMPLOYEE.SCR

Field Name	Row	Col
EMP_NUM	4	19
FIRST	6	19
LASTNAME	6	30
STREET	8	19
CITY	10	19
STATE	10	31
ZIP	10	34
DEPT	12	19
PAYRATE	14	19

TOPIC 20

The EMPLOYEE Customized Input Screen
After you lay out the input screen for the EMPLOYEE database file, your blackboard should look like this.

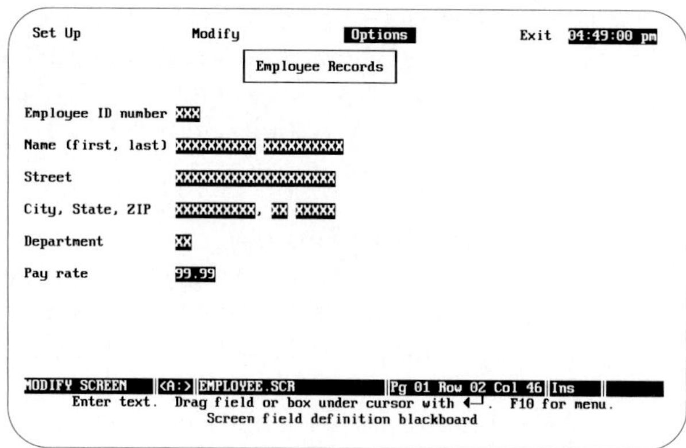

LABEL POSITIONS FOR DEPT.SCR

Row	Col	Label
1	32	Department records
4	0	Employee number
6	0	Week starting
8	0	Shift worked
10	0	Number of hours

EXERCISE 2

CREATING AN INPUT SCREEN FOR THE DEPT FILE

Open the DEPT database file and define an input screen named DEPT to match the one shown in the figure "The DEPT Customized Input Screen" and described in the tables "Label Positions for DEPT.SCR" and "Field Positions for DEPT.SCR." When finished, generate a text file image and make a printout.

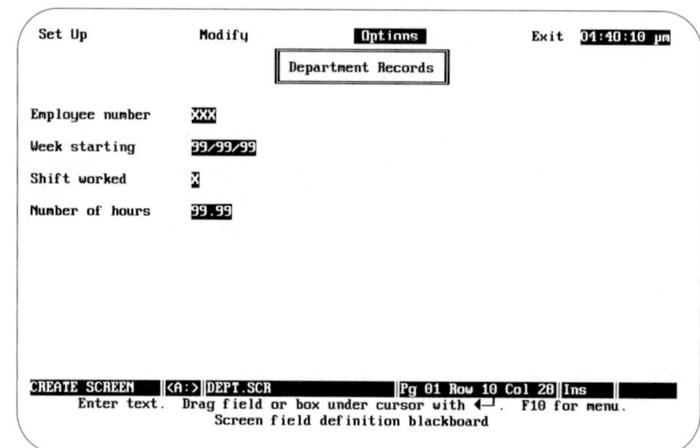

The DEPT Customized Input Screen
After you lay out the input screen for the DEPT database file, your blackboard should look like this.

FIELD POSITIONS FOR DEPT.SCR

Field Name	Row	Col
EMP_NUM	4	20
WEEKOF	6	20
SHIFT	8	20
HOURS	10	20

CHAPTER 6 REVIEW

- You can index a database to control the way the records appear in reports.
- You can modify report formats with the MODIFY REPORT <*report name*> command.
- You can group records in a report so that records with common entries in the same field are grouped together.
- You can have dBASE total and subtotal numeric fields in a report.
- You can define a report for mailing labels with the CREATE LABEL <*filename*> command.
- The TRIM command can be used to delete blank spaces from the end of a field's data.
- To print labels, you use the LABEL FORM <*filename*> TO PRINT command.

CHAPTER 6 QUESTIONS

FILL IN THE BLANK

1. To change the order in which records appear in a report, you use an ____________.
2. To control the records that are included in a report, you can use ____________.
3. To modify a report format named MAIL, you would use the command ____________.
4. To create a format for mailing labels, you use the ____________ command.
5. To remove trailing blanks from data, you use the ____________ command.
6. To print mailing labels using an existing form, you use the ____________ command.

MATCH THE COLUMNS

1. MODIFY REPORT <*filename*>	__ Removes blank spaces from the end of data
2. Group on expression	__ Creates and revises formats for mailing labels
3. MODIFY LABEL <*filename*>	__ Revises a report format
	__ Gathers together records with similar entries in a field
	__ Prints mailing labels

4. LABEL FORM <*filename*> TO PRINT
5. TRIM

WRITE OUT THE ANSWERS

1. What command do you use to rearrange information in a report after you have created its format?
2. Describe how you would generate subtotals and totals for contributions in a report where:
   - A field named MEMBER indicated whether people were members or not.
   - A field named AMOUNT listed their contributions.

CHAPTER 6

PROJECT

PROJECT 1

PREPARING A REPORT FOR THE ROYALTY DATABASE FILE

Prepare a report format for the ROYALTY file that lists ISBN, author, title, edition, and version. Group the report on author names, then index the file on author names and use the report to print the file.

CHAPTER 7

Programming with dBASE

TOPIC 21

Creating Command Files—The Basics

After completing this topic, you will be able to:

- Create and modify command files
- Execute and print command files

When you first begin using dBASE, you enter commands one at a time. However, once you are familiar with the dBASE program, you will find that it allows you to improve your productivity by saving frequently used commands in command files also called programs. This not only saves you time the next time you use the commands, it also makes dBASE easier to operate for people with little or no experience. All they have to know is how to execute the command files that you have created and saved. These command files can range from very simple ones that open files to complex ones that display menus from which you make choices to work with your applications.

DOT-PROMPT TUTORIAL

In this tutorial, you create and execute a series of command files that illustrate the basic procedures you use to create, print, and execute dBASE's command files. As you create and execute these files, you'll see how many repetitive tasks can be automated so that you can execute them with a single command. The command files you will create include the following:

- The BEGIN command file introduces you to the edit screen and editing commands.
- The STARTUP command file sets the default drive, opens the MEMBERS file, and then executes the BROWSE command.
- The SCREEN command file sets the screen form to SCREEN.SCR and then displays the MEMBERS file in edit mode.
- The INDEXING command file opens the MEMBERS file; sets the index to LASTNAME; and sets the fields to FIRST, LASTNAME, AREA, and PHONE. It then displays the database in browse mode.
- The LINKING command file opens the MEMBERS and CHARGES files, relates them based on the ID numbers, and then displays selected fields from each file.

- The QUERY command file is a modification of the LINKING file where a filter is added so that only those records from the state of MA are displayed.

After completing these command files, you should have a basic understanding of dBASE command files. When entering the command files, keep the following points in mind:

- To save time, commands are not explained each time they are used, but the commands that are introduced in this topic are described in the Quick Reference section that follows.
- When the edit screen is displayed, you can press F1 to turn the help menu on and off. This menu lists the commands you use to edit and save the command file. The commands listed on the menu are also described in the table "Edit Screen Commands" in the Quick Reference section that follows.
- The lines in each command file that begin with an asterisk are comment lines that are not executed when the command files are run. They are used to document the command files, but they are not necessary to successfully execute the programs. Read these lines carefully because they describe what each part of the command file is doing.
- If you encounter any problems while executing your programs, refer to "Troubleshooting Command Files" in the Quick Reference section that follows.
- If your printer does not automatically eject pages, type **EJECT** and press Enter↵ to eject the page before making another printout.

THE BEGIN COMMAND FILE

```
* BEGIN.PRG by [enter your name here]
* Prepared on [enter today's date here]
* Clear the screen
CLEAR
* Display a prompt
@ 1,0 SAY "Hello, my name is [your name ]."
* Pause the program until a key is pressed
WAIT
* Display another prompt
@ 3,0 SAY "The WAIT command worked!"
```

The BEGIN Command File
This figure shows the BEGIN command file that you enter in this tutorial. (Don't enter the line numbers in your program; they are there only to help you keep track of the program and troubleshoot it.)

1. Type **MODIFY COMMAND BEGIN** and press Enter↵ to display the edit screen.
2. Enter the command file shown in the figure "The BEGIN Command File." Be sure to enter the quotation marks around the text on the two lines that begin with the @ character. All editing commands are described in the table "Edit Screen Commands" in the Quick Reference section.
3. Press Ctrl-W to save the command file.
4. Type **TYPE BEGIN.PRG TO PRINT** and press Enter↵ to print out the command file. Compare the printout with the figure "The BEGIN Command File." If there are any differences, repeat Steps 1 through 3 to edit and save the corrected file.
5. Type **DO BEGIN** and press Enter↵ to run the command file. The text you enclosed in quotes in the line beginning *@ 1,0 SAY* appears on the screen. The *Press any key to continue....* prompt is automatically displayed by the WAIT command, which also pauses the command file.
6. Press any key to continue and the line of text specified in the second SAY command is displayed on the screen.

THE STARTUP COMMAND FILE

7. Type **MODIFY COMMAND STARTUP** and press Enter↵ to display the edit screen.

```
1. * STARTUP.PRG by [enter your name here]
2. * Prepared on [enter today's date here]
3. * Set default drive
4. SET DEFAULT TO B:
5. * Open database file
6. USE MEMBERS
7. * Browse the database file
8. BROWSE
9. CLOSE ALL
```

The STARTUP Command File
This figure shows the STARTUP command file that you enter in this tutorial. On line 5, change the drive you want to use as the default if it isn't drive B. (Remember not to enter the line numbers.)

8. Enter the command file shown in the figure "The STARTUP Command File." (Be sure to change the default drive in the SET DEFAULT command if you are not using drive B.)
9. Press [Ctrl]-[W] to save the command file.
10. Type **TYPE STARTUP.PRG TO PRINT** and press [Enter←] to print out the command file. Compare the printout with the figure "The STARTUP Command File." If there are any differences, repeat Steps 7 through 9 to edit and save the corrected file.
11. Type **DO STARTUP** and press [Enter←] to run the command file so it displays the MEMBERS file in browse mode.
12. Press [Esc] to return to the dot prompt and use the CLOSE ALL command to close all database files.

THE SCREEN COMMAND FILE

13. Type **MODIFY COMMAND SCREEN** and press [Enter←] to display the edit screen.
14. Enter the command file shown in the figure "The SCREEN Command File." (Be sure to change the default drive in the SET DEFAULT command if you are not using drive B.)
15. Press [Ctrl]-[W] to save the command file.
16. Type **TYPE SCREEN.PRG TO PRINT** and press [Enter←] to print out the command file. Compare the printout with the figure "The SCREEN Command File." If there are any differences, repeat Steps 13 through 15 to edit and save the corrected file.
17. Type **DO SCREEN** and press [Enter←] to run the command file so it displays the MEMBERS file in edit mode using the customized input screen named MEMBERS.
18. Press [Esc] to return to the dot prompt and use the CLOSE ALL command to close all database files.

```
1. * SCREEN.PRG by [enter your name here]
2. * Prepared on [enter today's date here]
3. * Set default drive
4. SET DEFAULT TO B:
5. * Open the MEMBERS file
6. USE MEMBERS
7. * Set the screen form
8. SET FORM TO MEMBERS
9. * Display the file in Edit mode
10. EDIT
```

The SCREEN Command File
This figure shows the SCREEN command file that you enter in this tutorial. On line 4, change the drive you want to use as the default if it isn't drive B. (Remember not to enter the line numbers.)

THE INDEXING COMMAND FILE

19. Type **MODIFY COMMAND INDEXING** and press [Enter←] to display the edit screen.
20. Enter the command file shown in the figure "The INDEXING Command File." (Be sure to change the default drive in the SET DEFAULT command if you are not using drive B.)

```
1. * INDEXING.PRG by [enter your name here]
2. * Prepared on [enter today's date here]
3. * Set default drive and open a database
4. SET DEFAULT TO B:
5. USE MEMBERS
6. * Specify an index
7. SET INDEX TO LAST
8. * Specify the fields to be displayed
9. SET FIELDS TO LASTNAME,FIRST,AREA,PHONE
10. * Browse the database
11. BROWSE
```

The INDEXING Command File
This figure shows the INDEXING command file that you enter in this tutorial. On line 4, change the drive you want to use as the default if it isn't drive B. (Remember not to enter the line numbers.)

21. Press Ctrl-W to save the command file.
22. Type **TYPE INDEXING.PRG TO PRINT** and press Enter ↵ to print out the command file. Compare the printout with the figure "The INDEXING Command File." If there are any differences, repeat Steps 20 and 21 to edit and save the corrected file.
23. Type **DO INDEXING** and press Enter ↵ to run the command file. The specified fields in the MEMBERS file are displayed in browse mode, and the file is arranged alphabetically by last name.[1]
24. Press Esc to return to the dot prompt and use the CLEAR ALL and CLOSE ALL commands to close all open files.

THE LINKING COMMAND FILE

25. Open the MEMBERS file, type **INDEX ON ID TO MEMBERS** and press Enter ↵.
26. Open the CHARGES file, type **INDEX ON ID TO CHARGES** and press Enter ↵.
27. Type **MODIFY COMMAND LINKING** and press Enter ↵ to display the edit screen.
28. Enter the command file shown in the figure "The LINKING Command File." (Be sure to change the default drive in the SET DEFAULT command if you are not using drive B.)

The LINKING Command File
This figure shows the LINKING command file that you enter in this tutorial. On line 7, change the drive you want to use as the default if it isn't drive B. (Remember not to enter the line numbers.)

```
1.  * LINKING.PRG by [enter your name here]
2.  * Prepared on [enter today's date here]
3.  * Clear memory
4.  CLOSE ALL
5.  CLEAR ALL
6.  * Set default drive
7.  SET DEFAULT TO B:
8.  * Open memory area A and indexed MEMBERS file
9.  SELECT A
10. USE MEMBERS INDEX MEMBERS
11. * Open memory area B and indexed CHARGES file
12. SELECT B
13. USE CHARGES INDEX CHARGES
14. * Return to memory area A
15. SELECT A
16. * Set the relation between the two files
17. SET RELATION TO ID INTO CHARGES
18. * Specify the fields from each file to be listed
19. LIST OFF LASTNAME,FIRST,B->AMOUNT,B->CLEARED
```

29. Press Ctrl-W to save the command file.
30. Type **TYPE LINKING.PRG TO PRINT** and press Enter ↵ to print out the command file. Compare the printout with the figure "The LINKING Command File." If there are any differences, repeat Steps 27 through 29 to edit and save the corrected file.
31. Type **DO LINKING** and press Enter ↵ to run the command file. The two database files are joined, and two fields from each database are displayed on the screen.
32. Use the CLEAR ALL and CLOSE ALL commands to close all open files.

THE QUERY COMMAND FILE

33. Type **MODIFY COMMAND LINKING** and press Enter↵ to display the edit screen.
34. Press Ctrl-KW to copy the file and the prompt at the top of the screen reads *Enter file name:*.
35. Type **QUERY.PRG** and press Enter↵ to copy the file into a file on the disk named QUERY.PRG.
36. Press Esc to return to the dot prompt.
37. Type **MODIFY COMMAND QUERY** and press Enter↵ to display the new file on the edit screen.
38. Change the first line so the program name is QUERY.PRG and then edit the last two lines of the program so that they match those shown in the figure "The QUERY Command File."

The QUERY Command File
This figure shows the QUERY command file that you enter in this tutorial. On line 7, change the drive you want to use as the default if it isn't drive B. (Remember not to enter the line numbers.)

```
 1. * QUERY.PRG by [enter your name here]
 2. * Prepared on [enter today's date here]
 3. * Clear memory
 4. CLOSE ALL
 5. CLEAR ALL
 6. * Set default drive
 7. SET DEFAULT TO B:
 8. * Open memory area A and indexed MEMBERS file
 9. SELECT A
10. USE MEMBERS INDEX MEMBERS
11. * Open memory area B and indexed CHARGES file
12. SELECT B
13. USE CHARGES INDEX CHARGES
14. * Return to memory area A
15. SELECT A
16. * Set the relation between the two files
17. SET RELATION TO ID INTO CHARGES
18. * List names of people who have not paid
19. LIST OFF LASTNAME,FIRST,B->AMOUNT,B->CLEARED FOR .NOT.B->CLEARED
```

39. Press Ctrl-W to save the command file.
40. Type **TYPE QUERY.PRG TO PRINT** and press Enter↵ to print out the command file. Compare the last two lines with the figure "The QUERY Command File." If there are any differences, repeat Steps 37 through 39 to edit and save the corrected file.
41. Type **DO QUERY** and press Enter↵ to run the command file; only records with .F. in the CLEARED field are displayed on the screen.
42. Use the CLEAR ALL and CLOSE ALL commands to close all open files.

FINISHING UP

43. You have completed this tutorial. Either continue to the next activity or quit the program.

To write or edit a command file, you use the MODIFY COMMAND <*filename*> command, which puts dBASE into edit mode. This mode is much like a word processing program. You can type and edit commands and then save them into their own file on the disk. For example, to write or edit a command file named MENU, you would use the command MODIFY COMMAND MENU. If you are writing the command file, the text edit screen appears blank. If the file already exists and is on the default drive, it is displayed on the screen. You do not have to specify an extension for the command file's name because dBASE automatically adds the extension .PRG to all command files.

Help When Editing

When the edit screen is displayed, you can press F1 to turn the help menu on and off. When on, the character ^ stands for the Ctrl key. For example, the command ^← means that you should hold down the Ctrl key while you press the left arrow key. The commands listed on this menu are described in the table "Edit Screen Commands."

Displaying and Printing Command Files

You display the commands stored in a command file with the TYPE <*filename*> command. When using the TYPE command, you must specify the file's extension. For example, to display the contents of a command file named MENU, you type **TYPE MENU.PRG** and press Enter↵ to display the command file on the screen. To print the file, just add the command TO PRINT to the program's name. For example, to print the file named MENU, type **TYPE MENU.PRG TO PRINT** and press Enter↵.

Executing Command Files

After writing or editing a command file, you execute it with the DO <*filename*> command. For example, to execute a command file named MENU, you type **DO MENU** and press Enter↵. The commands stored in the command file are then automatically executed.

Understanding the Commands Used in the Programs in This Topic

Here are brief descriptions of each of the commands introduced in the programs in this topic.

- *@ row n, col n SAY* displays on the screen in the specified position the text that follows. The text to be displayed must be enclosed in double quotation marks. For example, the command @ 1,0 SAY "Hello" displays the word *Hello* on the screen beginning in row 1 and column 0. Rows are counted from top to bottom beginning with row 0. Columns are counted from left to right beginning with column 1.
- *CLEAR* clears all data from the screen and returns the cursor to the upper-left corner.
- *WAIT* pauses the program and displays the prompt *Press any key to continue*. When you press any key, the command file continues to the next step.Edit Screen Commands

EDIT SCREEN COMMANDS

To	Press
Cursor Movement Commands	
Move cursor one character left or right	← or →
Move cursor to beginning or end of word	Home or End
Move cursor to beginning or end of line	Ctrl-← or Ctrl-→
Move cursor up or down one line	↑ or ↓
Realign lines of text with margins after making inserts	Ctrl-K B
Page up or down	PgUp or PgDn
Find string	Ctrl-K F
Repeat previous Find command	Ctrl-K L
Editing Commands	
Delete character	Del or ←Bksp
Delete word containing cursor	Ctrl-T
Delete line containing cursor	Ctrl-Y
Turn insert mode on and off	Ins
Insert line	Ctrl-N
Save and Retrieve Commands	
Save file	Ctrl-W
Abandon file without saving changes	Esc
Copy a file on disk into file on screen at cursor's position	Ctrl-K R
Copy file on screen into a file on disk	Ctrl-K W

Troubleshooting Command Files

To troubleshoot a command file, you can use the SET STEP ON command. When you then use the DO <*filename*> command to execute the command file, a prompt at the bottom of the screen reads *Press SPACE to step, S to suspend, or Esc to cancel.* Each time you then press Spacebar, another line of the command file (another step) is executed. If you press S to suspend the program, *Suspend* is displayed on the status line. To continue, type **RESUME** and press Enter←. To quit, type **CANCEL** and press Enter←.

When finished, use the SET STEP OFF command to turn step mode off so that you can run command files without pressing Spacebar.

When dBASE encounters a problem with your program during execution, it displays an error message and places a question mark above the command that caused the problem to indicate that the problem occurred above that point in the program. Typical situations where this happens include the following:

- *Syntax error* indicates that some part of your command is not written correctly or a word in a command is not spelled correctly. For example, if you enter SET INDX TO ZIPCODE instead of SET INDEX TO ZIPCODE, you will see this message. Check through the program carefully looking for misspellings or other errors.
- *Variable not found* indicates that a field of data or a memory variable asked for in the command does not match the fields in the active database file or any established memory variables. For example, if you enter LIST LAST,FIRSTNAME instead of LIST

LASTNAME,FIRST, you will see this message. Check the command carefully to ensure that the variables are correct and correctly spelled for the active database file and any memory variables.

- *File already open* means you have left a program using Suspend or Ignore without closing all files. To correct this problem, just type **CANCEL** and press Enter←.

EXERCISES

EXERCISE 1

CREATING AN EMPLOYEE COMMAND FILE

Write a command file that opens the EMPLOYEE database file; sets fields to FIRST, LASTNAME, and PAYRATE; and then displays the file in browse mode. Print out a copy of the program.

EXERCISE 2

CREATING A DEPT COMMAND FILE

Write a command file that opens the DEPT database file; sets fields to EMP-NUM and HOURS; and then display the file in browse mode. Print out a copy of the program.

TOPIC 22

Creating Command Files—Advanced Procedures

After completing this topic, you will be able to:

- Use DO WHILE statements to create loops in your command files
- Use IF statements to branch programs based on conditions
- Use TEXT commands to create menus
- Use CASE commands to branch programs based on user selections

Command files can do more than just store commands to be executed. They can also contain decision points that take specific actions based on operator input or on the outcome of prior actions by the program. For example, a command file can repeat a process over and over until it is finished (called a loop) or run one set of commands if the condition is true and another set if the condition is false (called a branch). These capabilities make the program extremely flexible. A knowledgeable user can program it to perform almost any task.

DOT-PROMPT TUTORIAL

In this tutorial, you create and execute a series of programs that illustrate many features of dBASE's command files.

- The LOOPING command file displays a series of numbers on the screen. The purpose of this command file is to introduce you to the DO WHILE command and memory variables.
- The CHARGEN command file displays the 254 characters in the IBM PC's character set. This command file is an application of the principles you first explored in LOOPING.
- The PRINTER command file allows you to set some printers to compressed or normal type. The numbers 15 and 18 in the SAY CHAR(15) and SAY CHAR(18) commands are the setup codes that turn on compressed or normal type on an Epson or an IBM ProPrinter dot matrix printer. They may not work with your printer but your instructor may be able to suggest alternative codes for you to use.
- MENU displays a menu on the screen so that you can make choices to add records or browse through the records in the MEMBERS and CHARGES database files.

After completing these command files, you should have a basic understanding of dBASE command files. When entering the command files, keep the following points in mind:

- To save time in these tutorials, commands are not explained each time they are used, but the commands introduced in this topic are described in the Quick Reference section that follows.
- You will notice that some lines are indented. (To indent a line, press Tab or the left or right arrow keys.) The indents are not necessary, but they help you identify where decisions are being made by the command file.

THE LOOPING COMMAND FILE

1. Type **MODIFY COMMAND LOOPING** and press Enter to display the edit screen.
2. Enter the command file shown in the figure "The LOOPING Command File."

The LOOPING Command File
This figure shows the LOOPING command file that you enter in this tutorial.

```
* LOOPING.PRG by [enter your name here]
* Prepared on [enter today's date here]
* Clear the screen
CLEAR
* Prevent dBASE messages from being displayed
SET TALK OFF
* Enter the value 0 in the memory variable area named COUNTER
COUNTER = 0
* Specify the value that number in the counter must be less
* than or equal to for the command file to continue operating
DO WHILE COUNTER <= 100
* Display the current number in the counter on the screen
* (one question mark lists numbers vertically; two question
* marks list them across the screen and then down).
?? COUNTER
* Increment the number in the counter by 1
COUNTER = COUNTER + 1
* End the DO WHILE when specified number in the counter
* is exceeded.
ENDDO
* Display a closing message on the screen
? "I've counted as high as you asked."
```

3. Press Ctrl-W to save the command file.
4. Type **TYPE LOOPING.PRG TO PRINT** and press Enter to print out the command file. Compare the printout with the figure "The LOOPING Command File." If there are any differences, repeat Steps 1 through 3 to edit and save the corrected file.
5. Type **DO LOOPING** and press Enter to run the command file and list the numbers 1 through 100 on the screen. The message then reads *I've counted as high as you asked.*

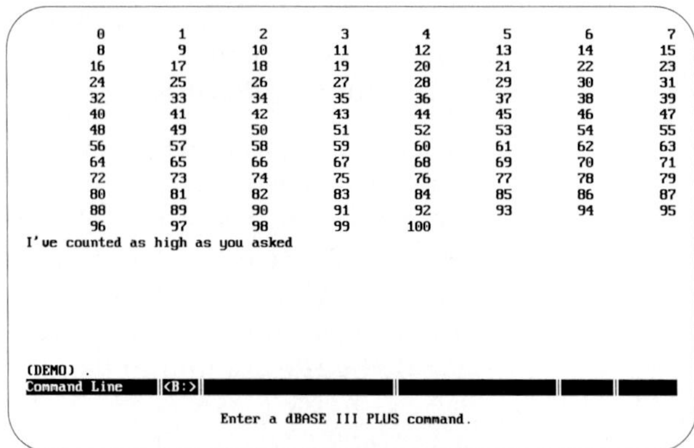

The LOOPING Program
When you execute the LOOPING program, your screen should look like this.

6. Repeat Step 1, change the number in the line *DO WHILE COUNTER <= 100* to 200 and press Ctrl-W to save the change.
7. Type **DO LOOPING** and press Enter↵ to run the command file. The command file now lists the numbers 1 through 200 on the screen and then displays the message *I've counted as high as you asked.*

THE CHARGEN COMMAND FILE

8. Type **MODIFY COMMAND CHARGEN** and press Enter↵ to display the edit screen.
9. Enter the command file shown in the figure "The CHARGEN Command File."

The CHARGEN Command File
This figure shows the CHARGEN command file that you enter in this tutorial.

```
* CHARGEN.PRG by [enter your name here]
* Prepared on [enter today's date here]
* Set up the system
SET TALK OFF
CLEAR
* Open memory variables and store values in them
ROW = 1
COUNTER = 0
* Set up a loop for 256 characters
DO WHILE COUNTER < 256
COL = 0
* Set up a loop for individual rows
DO WHILE COL <=72 .AND. COUNTER < 256
    @ ROW,COL SAY STR(COUNTER,3)+" "+CHR(COUNTER)
    COL = COL + 6
    COUNTER = COUNTER + 1
ENDDO
ROW = ROW + 1
ENDDO
```

10. Press Ctrl-W to save the command file.
11. Type **TYPE CHARGEN.PRG TO PRINT** and press Enter↵ to print out the command file. Compare the printout with the figure "The CHARGEN Command File." If there are any differences, repeat Steps 8 through 10 to edit and save the corrected file.
12. Type **DO CHARGEN** and press Enter↵ to run the command file and display a table of the 254 characters in the IBM PC character set.

The CHARGEN Program
When you execute the CHARGEN program, your screen should display the 254 characters in the IBM PC character set.

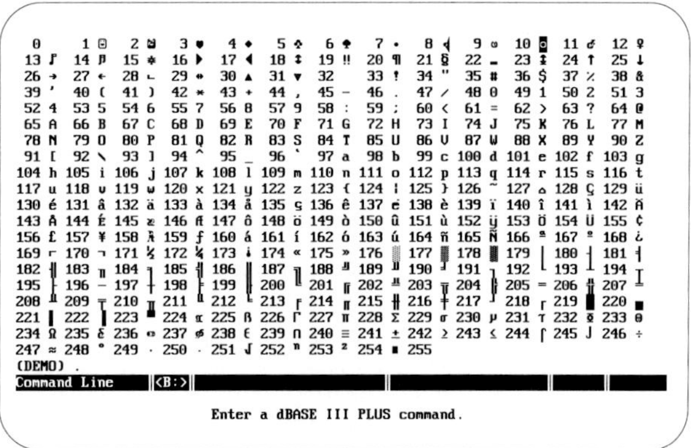

THE PRINTER COMMAND FILE

13. Type **MODIFY COMMAND PRINTER** and press Enter↵ to display the edit screen.
14. Enter the command file shown in the figure "The PRINTER Command File."

The PRINTER Command File
This figure shows the PRINTER command file that you enter in this tutorial.

```
* PRINTER.PRG by [enter your name here]
* Prepared on [enter today's date here]
* Set up the system
SET TALK OFF
SET PRINT OFF
CLEAR
* Display a prompt and store answer in a memory variable
ACCEPT "Print in compressed type? (Y/N) " TO YesNo
* If answer is yes send CHAR(15) for compressed type
IF UPPER(YesNo) = "Y"
SET DEVICE TO PRINT
@PROW(),PCOL() SAY CHR(15)
SET DEVICE TO SCREEN
* If answer is no send CHAR(18) for normal type
ELSE
SET DEVICE TO PRINT
@PROW(),PCOL() SAY CHR(18)
SET DEVICE TO SCREEN
* End the IF statement
ENDIF
* Restore system
SET TALK ON
```

15. Press Ctrl-W to save the command file.
16. Type **TYPE PRINTER.PRG TO PRINT** and press Enter↵ to print out the command file. Compare the printout with the figure "The PRINTER Command File." If there are any differences, repeat Steps 13 through 15 to edit and save the corrected file.
17. Type **DO PRINTER** and press Enter↵ to run the command file and the prompt reads *Print in compressed type? (Y/N).*
18. Press Y and then press Enter↵ to return to the dot prompt.
19. Type **USE MEMBERS** and press Enter↵.
20. Type **LIST TO PRINT** and press Enter↵ to print the file in compressed type.

THE MENU COMMAND FILE

21. Type **MODIFY COMMAND MENU** and press [Enter ↵] to display the edit screen.
22. Enter the command file shown in the figure "The MENU Command File."
    - To align the menu on lines 13 through 27, press [Tab] four times and then enter the text. To enter the ruled lines in the menu, use the equal sign (=) key.
    - Enter single spaces between characters and three spaces between words in the menu's title on line 14. Press [Spacebar] or [Del] in insert mode to center the title horizontally in the space between the ruled line.
    - The 16 spaces that follow the opening quotation mark in the line *INPUT "   Enter choice, press Enter: " TO MChoice* on line 32are used to align the prompt under the menu.
    - Enter quotation marks around the text ********* TRY AGAIN ******** on line 56.
23. Press [Ctrl]-[W] to save the command file.
24. Type **TYPE MENU.PRG TO PRINT** and press [Enter ↵] to print out the command file. Compare the printout with the figure "The MENU Command File." If there are any differences, repeat Steps 21 through 23 to edit and save the corrected file.
25. Type **DO MENU** and press [Enter ↵] to run the command file and display the menu. A flashing cursor is displayed on the line that reads *Enter choice, press Enter:*.

```
1.  * MENU.PRG prepared by [enter your name here]
2.  * Prepared on [enter today's date here]
3.  * Set up the system
4.  CLOSE ALL
5.  SET TALK OFF
6.  SET STATUS OFF
7.  SET BELL OFF
8.  * Set up a loop
9.  DO WHILE .T.
10. * Display menu choices and get user input
11. CLEAR
12. TEXT
13.         ==================================
14.             M A I N   M E N U
15.         ==================================
16.
17.         1. Append Names to Members File
18.
19.         2. Browse Records in Members File
20.
21.         3. Add Credits to Charges File
22.
23.         4. Browse Records in Charges File
24.
25.         5. Exit and Return to Dot Prompt
26.
27.         ==================================
28. ENDTEXT
29. * Set the MChoice memory variable to zero
30. STORE 0 TO MChoice
31. * Display prompt store response in MChoice memory variable
32. INPUT "                Enter choice, press Enter: " TO MChoice
33. * Execute the selection stored in MChoice
34. DO CASE
35.      CASE MChoice = 1
36.           USE MEMBERS
37.           APPEND
38.      CASE MChoice = 2
39.           USE MEMBERS
40.           BROWSE
41.      CASE MChoice = 3
42.           USE CHARGES
43.           APPEND
44.      CASE MChoice = 4
45.           USE CHARGES
46.           BROWSE
47.      CASE MChoice = 5
48.           CLOSE ALL
49.           CLEAR
50.           SET TALK ON
51.           SET STATUS ON
52.           CANCEL
53.      OTHERWISE
54.           CLEAR
55.           @ 12,16 SAY "You Must Enter 1 through 5!"
56.           @ 14,16 SAY "****** Try Again *********"
57. * Move cursor to bottom line of the screen
58.           @ 24, 16 SAY ""
59. * Pause screen until a key is pressed
60.           WAIT
61.      ENDCASE
62. ENDDO
```

The MENU Command File
This figure shows the MENU command file that you enter in this tutorial.

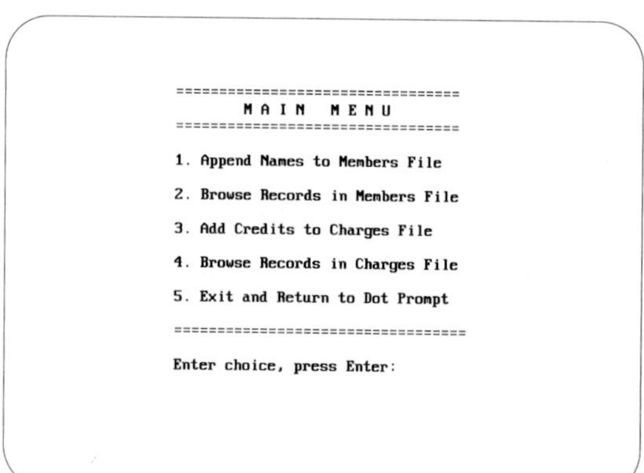

The MENU Program
When you execute the MENU program, the menu is displayed on the screen.

26. Press [1] and the press [Enter ↵] to display a new, blank record for the MEMBERS file.
27. Press [Esc] to cancel the command and return to the menu.
28. Continue making choices and press [Esc] to return to the menu.
29. Try entering any number other than 1 through 5 and watch what happens.
30. When finished, press [5] (for *Exit*) to return to the dot prompt.

FINISHING UP

31. You have completed this tutorial. Either close all open files and continue to the next activity or quit the program.

To write powerful programs, you need to understand the concepts behind memory variables and DO WHILE, IF, and CASE commands.

Memory Variables

Memory variables are parts of the computer's memory that are named during the execution of a command file. Data can then be stored in these areas and retrieved from them. There are two ways to store data in a memory variable: STORE <*expression*> TO <*memory variable*> and <*memory variable*>=<*expression*>. For example, the command STORE 1 TO COUNTER stores the number 1 in a memory variable named COUNTER. The expression COUNTER=1 does the same thing. To see the contents of memory variables, press F7 from the dot prompt or type a question mark followed by the name of the memory variable. For example, to see the contents of the memory variable COUNTER, type **? COUNTER** and press Enter ↵.

DO WHILE Commands

There are situations in which you want a command repeated over and over again until a specified condition is met. It's like telling someone to "empty all those boxes and put their contents on the shelves until there are no more boxes to empty." In dBASE, you structure this kind of command as follows:

```
DO WHILE <condition>
<commands>
ENDDO
```

dBASE tests to see if the condition is true, and then executes the commands that follow. When it reaches ENDDO, it jumps back up to the DO WHILE line and checks whether the condition is still true. If it is, the program executes the commands again. It continues looping like this until it finds that the condition no longer evaluates as true and then jumps to the command that follows the ENDDO statement.

In the LOOPING command file, the program creates a memory variable named COUNTER and stores the number 1 in it. The DO WHILE statement then checks the number to see if it is less than or equal to 100. If it is, the program displays the number (?? COUNTER) and then adds 1 to the number in the counter. The program then loops back to the DO WHILE line and reads the counter again. (This time it is 2.) If it is still less than or equal to 100, the commands are repeated one more time. Eventually, the counter reaches 101, and at that point, the condition is false, so the program jumps to whatever command follows the ENDDO line.

```
COUNTER = 0
DO WHILE COUNTER <= 100
?? COUNTER
COUNTER = COUNTER + 1
ENDDO
```

IF Commands

There are situations in which you want a program to branch in one of two directions based on the truth or falsity of a condition you set up for it to evaluate. In these situations, you can use an IF statement. Such a statement basically says, "If this condition is met, then do one thing; if it is not met, do another." It's as if a rich uncle were to say to you, "If you get an A in this course, I'll buy you a convertible; if you don't, you agree to stay in your room all next semester and study day and night." In dBASE, this kind of statement is structured as:

IF you get an A in this course
I'll buy you a convertible
ELSE
You'll stay in your room and study all semester
ENDIF

Or, in more schematic form:

IF <*condition*>
<commands>
ELSE
<*commands*>
ENDIF

In the PRINTER.PRG, the user's input from the ACCEPT statement is stored in a character memory variable and then evaluated by the IF statement. If the uppercase equivalent of the response is a Y, then CHR(15) is sent to the printer. (UPPER is a dBASE function that changes the characters in the parentheses following it from lowercase to uppercase.) If the response isn't Y, then CHR(18) is sent.

```
ACCEPT "Print in compressed type? (Y/N) " TO YesNo
IF UPPER(YesNo) = "Y"
SET DEVICE TO PRINT
@PROW(),PCOL() SAY CHR(15)
SET DEVICE TO SCREEN
ELSE
SET DEVICE TO PRINT
@PROW(),PCOL() SAY CHR(18)
SET DEVICE TO SCREEN
ENDIF
```

The ELSE part of the IF statement is optional in some situations. If you eliminate it and the condition in the IF statement evaluates to false, the program jumps to the first command that follows the ENDIF statement.

CASE Commands

CASE statements are similar to IF statements but are easier to use when there may be a number of possible responses to a command. In their simplest form, they can be set up to do the same thing the IF statement does; for example:

DO CASE
CASE <*condition*>
        <*commands*>
OTHERWISE
        <*commands*>
ENDCASE

In this example, if CASE evaluates to true, the commands that follow it are executed. If it evaluates to false, the commands under the OTHERWISE statement are executed.

Usually, the command is set up more like the one in the MENU command file. There, five possible correct choices can be made, numbered 1 through 5. Each of them is listed as a CASE and separate commands are executed depending on which is chosen. If any input other than a correct one is made, the commands under the OTHERWISE portion of the file are executed.

Understanding the Commands Used in the Programs in This Topic

Here are brief descriptions of each of the commands introduced in the programs in this topic.

- ? and ?? display or print an expression list. A single question mark displays or prints each item on a separate line; double question marks display or print them on the same line until the line is full.
- ACCEPT displays a prompt on the screen and then stores your response in a character memory variable. The prompt following the ACCEPT command must be enclosed in single or double quotes or in square brackets ([]). For example, the command ACCEPT "Answer Y for yes or N for no" TO ANS displays the prompt *Answer Y for yes or N for no.* When you then press Y or N, it stores the letter in the character memory variable ANS.
- INPUT is like ACCEPT but is used when you want to store numeric data.
- CHR() sends the ASCII code for a keyboard or other character to the printer. This command can be used in many cases to control the printer's operation. For example, sending the command CHR(15) to an Epson dot-matrix printer sets it to compressed type. Sending the command CHR(18) resets it to normal type.
- CLEAR clears the screen before the menu is displayed.
- TEXT and ENDTEXT specify the beginning and end of a text block that will be displayed on the screen when that part of the command file is executed.
- DO CASE and ENDCASE indicate the beginning and end of a decision area. Between these two lines is listed a series of options from which the user can choose. If the OTHERWISE command is used and a user makes any input other than one specified in one of the CASE commands, the commands that follow the OTHERWISE option are executed.
- DO WHILE and ENDDO indicate the beginning and end of a loop. The commands between these two statements will be executed as long as the specified condition is met.
- GET displays a memory variable or field name with the READ statement and allows you to put a value into a field. For example, the command GET MChoice gets data from the memory variable MChoice.
- IF, ELSE, and ENDIF indicate a decision area. If the condition specified following the IF statement is true, the commands immediately below it are executed. If the condition is false, the commands that follow the ELSE statement are executed. If there is no ELSE statement and the condition following the IF statement is false, then the commands that follow the ENDIF command are executed.

- PCOL() and PROW() are the column and row position of the printer's printhead.
- SET BELL OFF/ON specifies if the computer beeps or not when you enter a menu choice.
- SET DEVICE TO SCREEN/PRINT specifies if the @ ... SAY commands that follow are sent to the screen or printer.
- SET STATUS OFF/ON turns the status line at the bottom of the screen off or back on during full-screen operations.
- SET TALK OFF/ON specifies if information such as record numbers, memory variables, or command results are displayed on the screen or not when commands are executed. The command can be used to suppress unnecessary information from being displayed.
- STORE stores data in a memory variable. For example, STORE 0 TO MCOUNT stores the number zero in the memory variable MCOUNT.

EXERCISE

EXERCISE 1

CREATING A MENU PROGRAM FOR THE EMPLOYEE AND DEPT FILES

Write a command file that presents a menu with choices to add records or edit records in the EMPLOYEE and DEPT files. The command file should also include a choice to exit and return to the dot prompt. Pattern your command file after the MENU.PRG shown in the figure "The MENU.PRG Command File." When finished, make a printout of your command file.

CHAPTER 7 REVIEW

- You create and edit programs with the MODIFY COMMAND <*filename*> command.
- When the edit screen is displayed, you can press F1 to turn the help menu on and off.
- After entering or editing a program, press Ctrl-End to save it and return to the dot prompt.
- To add comment lines, begin them with an asterisk. These lines are ignored when the program is run but can be used to document the program.
- You execute programs with the DO <*filename*> command.
- To execute a command file a line at a time, use the SET STEP ON command before executing it. Then press Spacebar to execute the next line of the program.
- You display programs with the TYPE <*filename*> command, and the TYPE <*filename*> TO PRINT command makes a printout of the program.
- DO WHILE commands are used to repeat all or part of a program until a specified condition is met.
- IF commands branch programs based on the evaluation of a criteria. If the criteria is true, the program does one thing. If it is false, the program does another.
- DO CASE commands are used to provide a list of possible choices and branch the program depending on which is selected.
- TEXT and END TEXT statements identify the beginning and end of text blocks that are to be displayed on the screen.

CHAPTER 7 QUESTIONS

FILL IN THE BLANK

1. To create or edit a command file named PROGRAM, you would type ___________.
2. To execute a command file named PROGRAM, you would type ___________.
3. To display the contents of a command file named PROGRAM, you would type ___________.
4. To print the contents of a command file named PROGRAM, you would type ___________.
5. To troubleshoot a command file during its execution, you would first use the ___________ command.
6. To have a series of commands repeat until a specified condition was met, you would use a ___________ command.

7. To display a block of text on the screen, you would mark its beginning with __________ and its end with __________.
8. To have a program branch based on the evaluation of a criteria, you would use an __________ statement.
9. To list a number of menu choices and have the program branch based on which choice is made, you could use a __________ statement.

MATCH THE COLUMNS

1. MODIFY COMMAND <*filename*>	__ Executes a command file
2. DO <*filename*>	__ Branches the program based on the evaluation of some criteria
3. TYPE <*filename*>	__ Saves a command file
4. Ctrl-W	__ Displays a command file
5. SET STEP ON	__ Creates or edits a command file
6. DO WHILE	__ Executes a command file one line at a time
7. IF statements	__ Repeats a command or series of commands until a specified condition is met
8. DO CASE	__ Begins a block of text that is to appear on screen
9. TEXT	__ Useful when entering lists of commands from which to choose

WRITE OUT THE ANSWERS

1. What command do you execute to write or edit a command file?
2. What command do you execute to display the contents of a command file?
3. What command do you use to execute a command file?
4. What is a memory variable?

CHAPTER 8 Real-World Applications

Now that you have become familiar with dBASE III Plus, you are ready to put it to work. The applications in this chapter include a job-search kit, a research paper, and a business plan. They test and build on the skills you have developed in the preceding topics.

When completing the applications, keep the following points in mind.

- The applications are based on the procedures already discussed in the text, but they are designed to present new problems for you to solve on your own. Don't be discouraged if they take some thought and effort to work through.
- The Concepts section in each application gives you all the subject-area information you will need to complete the application.
- The Steps section in each application gives you the sequence of steps that you should follow. If you get cannot recall how to perform a procedure, refer to the topic that covers that material.

APPLICATION 1 The Job-Search Kit—Company Contacts

To find a job in today's employment market, you must be organized and relentless in pursuit of possible employers. One key to success is accurate record keeping and followup. You will help your chances if you follow up an interview with a well-written letter emphasizing your strong points. In this application, you create a database file that can organize your search, making followup easier and more effective.

CONCEPTS

When looking for employment, you need to tip the balance in your favor at every opportunity. To begin, research the companies you want to contact. You need to know something about who they are and what they do so you can write an effective cover letter and target your résumé. Most importantly, try to contact a specific individual by name. Addressing a letter to a company or to a personnel department is an immediate sign that you haven't done your research. Since most published corporate listing are out of date, call the company and ask to whom you should address your application. For example, if you are applying for a sales position, call the sales department and ask the person who answers the phone for the name, title, and address of the person who makes the hiring decisions. You can then address your letter to that person by name, and follow up with a phone call to make sure the letter arrived. Be sure you get the correct spelling of the name, and the correct address, and save that information in your database file for future reference and followup.

STEPS

1. Review the records illustrated in the figure "The JOBSRCH Records" and use them to plan a database with the fields listed in the table "The JOBSRCH Database." Indicate each field's name, its type, and its length.

THE JOBSRCH DATABASE

Description	Field's Name	Type	Width
Company name	________	___	___
Company street	________	___	___
Company city	________	___	___
Company state	________	___	___
Company ZIP code	________	___	___
Contact's salutation (Mr., Mrs., or Ms.)	________	___	___
Contact's first name	________	___	___
Contact's last name	________	___	___
Date of first interview	________	___	___
Date of second interview	________	___	___
Date of third interview	________	___	___
Job offered (Y or N)	________	___	___
Starting salary offered	________	___	___
Comments	________	___	___

2. Create a database file named JOBSRCH and define its fields using the plan you have created in Step 1.
3. List the file's structure to the printer.
4. Enter the records into the database file shown in the figure "The JOBSRCH Records".
5. Append additional records to the database from the file JOBSHOLD.DBF that came on the *Student Resource Disk.*
6. List the file's records to the printer. Proofread the printout and then edit records as necessary so that your database contains the exact data shown in Step 4.
7. List to the printer just those records where a job was offered.
8. Calculate the average salary offered. Calculate it only for those records where it was greater than zero.

JOBSRCH Records
After defining the JOBSRCH database file, you enter these records into it.

	Company 1	Company 2	Company 3
Firm	Marble Harbor Press	ComputerPlace	The Driftwood
Street	100 Atlantic Avenue	16010 Adams Street	4 Front Street
City	Marblehead	Fresno	Boca Raton
State	MA	CA	FL
ZIP code	01945	93710	33433
Salutation	Mr.	Ms.	Mr.
First name	William	Matilda	Richard
Last name	Kinsman	Smith	Ashley
Resume sent	1/6/94	1/6/94	1/6/94
Interview 1	3/10/94	3/15/94	5/11/94
Interview 2	4/20/94		5/13/94
Interview 3			5/18/94
Offer?	Yes	No	Yes
Salary	$19,000		$20,000
Comments	I like the office environment		I'll take it!

9. List to the printer just the contact's name and address for those records where a job was offered.
10. Prepare mailing labels that print out just the names of the people you interviewed with (using their salutations) and the name and address of their firm. Printout the labels.
11. Index the file on the ZIP code and print the labels again.
12. Copy the file's structure to a file named MYJOBS so you can use it in your own job search.

APPLICATION 2

The Research Paper—Works Cited

Many types of documents, including research papers, require a bibliography or list of works cited that gives publication details of the documents you used as sources. Traditionally, you would enter each publication on an index card and then manually arrange the cards in the proper order. Using a database to maintain a list of publications allows you to easily update your references and arrange them in order by indexing or sorting. In this application you create a database file to maintain a list of sources for a research paper.

CONCEPTS

The term *documentation style* refers to the various systems for providing information about the sources you have used in a research paper. Documentation styles vary among the disciplines. Some styles use footnotes or endnotes; other put reference information in parentheses within the text. Styles also differ in requirements for the complete list of sources at the end of a paper.

Before you start consulting sources, know what documentation style you will be using in your paper. If your assignment does not specify a documentation style, ask your instructor which to use. Be aware of what information the style calls for about each source. Then as you take notes on each source, keep a record of that information so you can document your sources correctly and fully.

The **Modern Language Association (MLA)** has developed the documentation styles used in most of the humanities. Before 1984, "MLA style" called for footnotes or endnotes, and the list of sources was named Bibliography. Current MLA style, introduced in 1984, calls for parenthetical references instead of footnotes or endnotes. It also changed the name of the list of sources used to Works Cited. The list includes only the sources from which you use paraphrases or summaries or quotations. It does not include sources you consulted but did not actually refer to in the paper. This list follows any endnotes and begins on a new page, numbered sequentially with the rest of the paper. Entries are alphabetized according to the author's last name. Each entry starts at the left margin, and the second and subsequent lines indent five spaces (½-inch). Double spacing is used within and between entries.

The **American Psychological Association (APA)** has developed another documentation style commonly used for research papers, especially in the social sciences. Like MLA style, APA style uses parenthetical references and a list of sources. The sources used in this application are shown in MLA style.*

*This Concepts section is drawn from Lynn Quitman Troyka, *Simon & Schuster Handbook for Writers*, 2nd ed. (Englewood Cliffs: Prentice, 1990) 611, 666. The first two paragraphs are direct quotations.

STEPS

Curtin, Dennis. Microcomputers: Software and Applications. Englewood Cliffs: Prentice, 1989.
Burks, Alice R., and Arthur W. Burks. The First Electronic Computer: The Atanasoff Story. Ann Arbor: U of Michigan P, 1988.
Hollerbach, Lew. A 60-minute Guide to Microcomputers. 1st American ed. Englewood Cliffs: Prentice, 1982.
Forester, Tom, ed. The Information Technology Revolution. Cambridge: MIT P, 1985.
Dubbey, John Michael. The Mathematical Work of Charles Babbage. Cambridge UP, 1978.
Bashe, Charles J., et al. IBM's Early Computers. Cambridge: MIT P, 1986.
Gorstine, G.W. 16 Bit Modern Microcomputers: The Intel I8086 Family. Englewood Cliffs: Prentice, 1985.

The TERMPAPR Records

1. Review the sources shown in the figure "The TERMPAPR Records" and use them to plan a database with the fields listed in the table "The TERMPAPR Database." Indicate the field's name, its type, and its length.

THE TERMPAPR DATABASE

Description	Field's Name	Type	Width
Author's name	________	___	___
Title of book	________	___	___
City in which book was published	________	___	___
Name of the publisher	________	___	___
Copyright date	________	___	___

2. Create a database file named TERMPAPR and define its fields using the plan you have created in Step 1.
3. List the file's structure to the printer.
4. Enter the records into the database file shown in the figure "The TERMPAPR Records."
5. List the file's records to the printer. Proofread the printout and then edit records as necessary so that your database contains the exact data shown in Step 4.

6. List to the printer all books published in Englewood Cliffs. List to the printer all books published in Cambridge.
7. Prepare a report format named TERMPAPR that prints out just the author and title of each work Use the report format to print the contents of the file.
8. Index the file on the author's last name and then use the report format to print the file again.
9. Copy the file's structure to a file named MYPAPER so you can use it for your own term papers and other library research.

APPLICATION 3

The Business Plan—Inventory Records

When you start or manage a small business, inventory can be one of the largest costs you will encounter. To control inventory, you need to develop a system that tells you what is on hand and on order. In this application, you create a simple database to keep track of inventory on order.

CONCEPTS

The purpose of controlling inventory is to provide maximum service to your customers at the lowest cost to your business. Your aim should be to achieve a rapid turnover of your inventory. The less money and space you tie up in raw materials, work in process, and finished goods inventories, the better. In other words, the faster you get back your investment, the faster you can reinvest your capital for other business purposes.

A glimpse at some industry statistics should clarify this point. The average firm has 15 to 25% of its capital invested in inventory. Additionally, the costs involved in carrying an inventory can be as high as 35% of the average inventory value, although the average annual cost in most industries is somewhat over 20% of the inventory value.

The benefits of a reduced inventory are clear. A manufacturer who carries a $300,000 inventory is likely to pay In excess of $60,000 a year in carrying costs. Reducing inventory not only frees some of the capital previously Invested in inventory, but the carrying costs will also drop proportionately. A good rule of thumb for inventory control is to carry only that amount of inventory necessary to provide good service to customers and to supply the production schedule so interruptions are prevented.

STEPS

1. Review the records shown in Step 4 and use them to plan a database with the fields listed in the table "The INVENTRY Database." Indicate the field's name, its type, and its length.

THE INVENTRY DATABASE

Description	Field Name	Type	Width
Part's stock number	________	____	____
Part's name	________	____	____
Part's description	________	____	____
Part's cost	________	____	____
Order date	________	____	____
Instock date	________	____	____
Quantity in order	________	____	____
Quantity received	________	____	____
Unit cost	________	____	____

2. Create a database file named INVENTRY and define its fields using the plan you have created in Step 1.
3. List the file's structure to the printer.
4. Enter the records into the database file shown in the figure "The Inventry Records."

The INVENTRY Records
After defining the INVENTRY database file, you enter these records into it.

	Part 1	Part 2	Part 3
Manufacturer	IBM	Compaq	HP
Description	Hard disk drive	Tower computer	ScanJet
Stock number	10010	MD50	L300
Unit cost	325	1250	1200
Order date	9/10/94	9/11/94	9/11/94
Instock date	9/20/94	9/25/94	9/20/94
Qty. ordered	75	5	10
Qty. received	73	5	10
Selling price	650	2500	1800

5. Append additional records to the database from the file INVHOLD.DBF that came on the *Student Resource Disk.*
6. List the file's records to the printer. Proofread the printout and then edit records as necessary so that your database contains the exact data shown in Step 4.
7. List to the printer any record where the quantity received is less than the quantity ordered.
8. List to the printer and records where the number of days between ordering and receiving is greater than 7 days.
9. Calculate the total inventory cost for each item by multiplying the quantity received times the unit cost. List the results to the printer.
10. Calculate the average time between ordering and receiving inventory.
11. Prepare a report format named INVENTRY that prints out only the stock number, the unit cost, the quantity received, and the selling price.
12. Index the file on the selling price and then use the report format to print the file again.

APPENDIX

Installing the Educational Version of dBASE III Plus

If you are using the educational (also called the sampler) version of dBASE III Plus, you need to install it for use on your system if this hasn't already been done. To install the program, just follow the steps in this brief tutorial. If you are using the full-featured version, or if the educational version has already been installed on your hard disk drive, you should skip this tutorial.

WARNING TO INSTRUCTORS

Do not install the educational or sampler version onto a hard disk system without first understanding what it does (use the TYPE command to look at the INSTALL.BAT file). The install program renames your existing CONFIG.SYS file CONFIGS.OLD. It then copies its own CONFIG.SYS file to your disk. This new CONFIG.SYS file contains only the statements FILES = 20 and BUFFERS = 15. On most systems, you can recover your old CONFIG.SYS file by deleting CONFIG.SYS and then renaming the CONFIGS.OLD file CONFIG.SYS. However, if your system already has a CONFIGS.OLD file when you run install, your original CONFIG.SYS file is dumped, and you cannot recover it. Many programs that add lines to your CONFIG.SYS file when you install them, rename the original version. For this reason, if you have a lot of programs on your system, you may have a CONFIGS.OLD file.

To be safe, create a directory on the hard disk and copy the dBASE files into it with the COPY *.* command. Then create your own CONFIG.DB file. The one that comes with the program is as follows:

```
STATUS = ON
COMMAND = ASSIST
DEFAULT = A
```

You can use these lines as is or customize them for your system, for example to change the default drive from A to B.

GETTING STARTED

1. Load the operating system so the command prompt is displayed.
2. Insert the dBASE III Plus disk labeled *SYSTEM DISK #1* into drive A.
3. Type **A:** and press Enter↵ to make drive A the default drive.

INSTALLING THE PROGRAM

4. Type **INSTALL** and press Enter↵ to display the Memory and Drive Selection menu. The prompt reads *Type the letter corresponding to your computer's configuration:*.

5. Press one of the letters [A] through [D] that best describes your system.
   - On a floppy disk system, the prompt reads: *put Sampler disk 1 in drive A, and your Dos Disk in drive B (Remember to remove any write protect tabs from disk) Press any key to continue. . .* Insert the disks as instructed and press the designated key to continue. The drives spin, and in a moment, the command prompt reappears and the prompt reads: *Now reboot your computer with your Dos disk in drive A (CONTROL - ALT - DEL). Then place Sampler disk 1 in drive A and type DBASE.*
   - On a hard disk system, the files are copied from the disk in drive A to a directory named SAMPLER on the disk in drive C. When the files are copied, the prompt reads: *Place Sampler disk 2 in drive A Press any key to continue.* Remove the *SYSTEM DISK #1* from drive A, insert the disk labeled *SYSTEM DISK #2* and press any key. The files from that disk are copied to drive C. When the files are copied, the prompt reads: *Reboot your computer (CONTROL - ALT - DEL) and type CD \SAMPLER, then type DBASE.* When all the files have been copied, the command prompt reappears.

FINISHING UP

6. You have completed the installation of the program.
   - To quit, remove your disks and turn off the computer.
   - To continue, you must first reboot the computer so that the program reads the configuration file created when you installed the program. (On a floppy disk system, begin by inserting the DOS disk into drive A.) On an IBM PC or compatible computer, press [Ctrl]-[Alt]-[Del] or turn off the computer and then turn it back on. Once the system is rebooted, loading instructions can be found in Topic 1.

INDEX

INDEX

Exchanging Files Among Programs

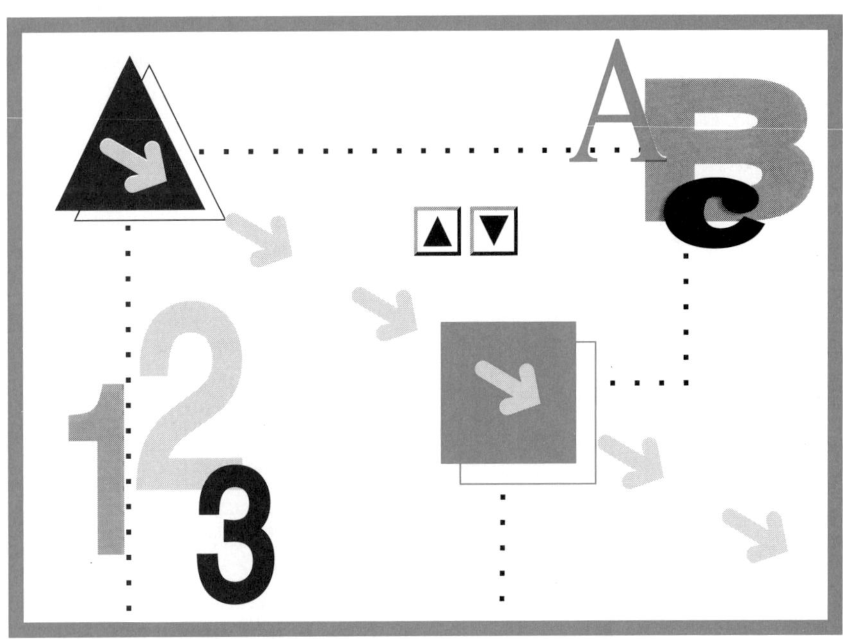

Exchanging Files Among Programs

TOPIC 1 Transferring Files to and from WordPerfect

After completing this topic, you should be able to:

- Import a spreadsheet file into a WordPerfect document
- Link a spreadsheet file with a WordPerfect document
- Import ASCII text files, including dBASE files, into WordPerfect
- Export WordPerfect files as ASCII text files

Whenever you create a file with a program such as WordPerfect, 1-2-3, or dBASE, it contains codes that are specific to the program you are using. For example, when you underline or boldface words, insert tab stops, or add headers and footers, you are entering codes into the file. There is no established industrywide standard for what codes should be used, so each software publisher makes up its own. The result is that files created on one program cannot be directly read by another. To transfer such files to another program you must either save them in a format that can be read by another program or convert them to the other format using a file conversion program.

The most reliable, but least sophisticated, way to transfer a file between two programs is to convert it to what is known as an ASCII text file. A file in this format follows a standard convention and can be read by most other programs. The problem with ASCII text files is that they contain no formatting codes, so all of your formatting is lost in the transfer. Also, soft carriage returns are converted to hard carriage returns, and tabs are replaced with spaces. When you retrieve the file into another program, you have to reformat it, removing the hard returns and reconverting the spaces to tab stops.

A more sophisticated way to move data between programs is to convert one file format into another. With file conversion, the codes entered with one program are converted into those used by another. This allows many formats to be retained.

Many of the newest programs contain filters for converting other programs' files. You just use a command to retrieve the file and it is automatically converted. by filters that are attached to the main program. For example, if a WordPerfect document contains a table, you can use 1-2-3 to perform the calculations, then *import* the 1-2-3 file into your document or *link* the 1-2-3 file to it.

The difference between importing and linking is the flexibility that linking gives you. For example:

- When you import a file, it is copied from the spreadsheet file into the document, and no permanent connection is established.
- When you link the spreadsheet file to your document, you can automatically update the data in your document if the data in the spreadsheet file change.

WordPerfect, like many other programs, also supports 1-2-3's graphics file format so you can retrieve a graph directly into a document. You can also save WordPerfect files as ASCII text files so that they can be imported into any program that reads ASCII files.

When you transfer data from WordPerfect to a spreadsheet or database program, you have to add commas to indicate the division of the data into columns or fields. These commas are called delimiters. For example, if you transfer a line that reads FIRST,LAST,MIDDLE to a spreadsheet, each of the three words is placed in a separate column. If you transfer the same line to a database, each word is placed in a separate field. In some situations you also have to add quotes around labels so programs can distinguish labels from numbers.

TUTORIAL

In this tutorial, you import 1-2-3 and dBASE files into a WordPerfect document. After importing files, you then export parts of the WordPerfect document so they can be retrieved by 1-2-3 and dBASE III Plus. All but one of the files that you import in this tutorial have been provided in the EXCHANGE directory on the original *Student Resource Disk*. The only file not in this directory is the LINE.PIC graphics file that you saved in the topic on saving and printing graphics. Before proceeding, be sure the files in the EXCHANGE directory and the LINE.PIC file are copied to your data disk. If you need to quit before finishing the tutorial, finish the section on which you are working, save the document, and resume at the next section later.

GETTING STARTED

1. Load WordPerfect and set the default drive to the one in which you inserted your data disk.
2. Retrieve the EXCHANGE.WP5 document.

The EXCHANGE.WP5 File
When you retrieve the EXCHANGE.WP5 file it will look like this on your screen.

```
Name:
Date:
Filename: EXCHANGE.WP5

Linking a 1-2-3 Spreadsheet File
In this section, you link the Lotus 1-2-3 file named PANDL.WK1 to this document.

Importing a 1-2-3 Spreadsheet File
In this section, you import the 1-2-3  file named SALES.WK1.

Importing a 1-2-3 Print File
In this section, you import a 1-2-3 file named EXPENSES.PRN that was printed to
1-2-3.

Importing a dBASE File Saved in ASCII Text Format
In this section, you import a dBASE file that was saved by that program in the A
format.

Importing a 1-2-3 Graph
In this section you place a 1-2-3 graph of the five-year plan model named LINE.P
created in a previous tutorial.

Exporting a Nondelimited File
In this section, you export the PANDL.WK1 file as an ASCII text file named PANDL
                                                  Doc 1 Pg 1 Ln 1i Pos 1i
```

LINKING A 1-2-3 SPREADSHEET FILE

3. Move the cursor to the blank line following the section "Linking a 1-2-3 Spreadsheet File."
4. Press Ctrl-F5 to display the Text In/Out menu.
5. Press S (for ***S**preadsheet*).
6. Press C (for ***C**reate Link*).
7. Press F (for ***F**ilename*), and the prompt reads *Enter filename:*.
8. Press F5 and then Enter↵ to display a list of files on the default drive/directory.
9. Highlight *PANDL.WK1* and press R (for ***R**etrieve*). The Create Link menu reappears and the file's name is listed.

The Create Link Menu
When you link with the PANDL file its name is listed on the Create Link screen.

```
Spreadsheet: Create Link

     1 - Filename                A:\PANDL.WK1

     2 - Range                   <Spreadsheet>        A1..E5

     3 - Type                    Table

     4 - Perform Link

Selection: 0
```

10. Press P (for ***P**erform Link*), and a message reads ** Importing Spreadsheet **. In a moment the Edit screen reappears with the spreadsheet file in a table preceded and followed by comments. These tables are beyond the scope of this text, so refer to the WordPerfect manual if you want to know more about them.

The Linked PANDL File
When you link the PANDL file to the document, it appears as a table preceded and followed by comments.

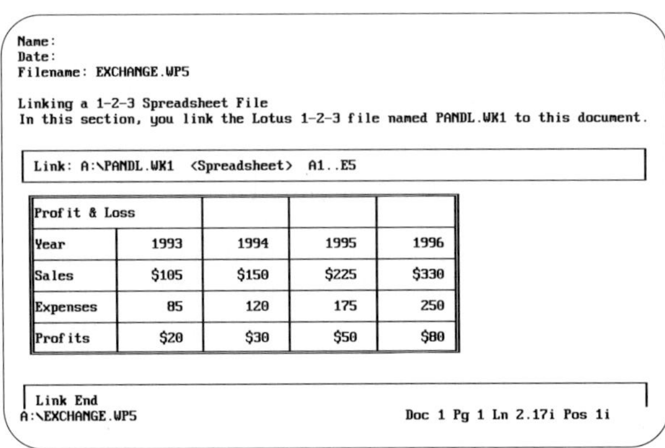

Name:
Date:
Filename: EXCHANGE.WP5

Linking a 1-2-3 Spreadsheet File
In this section, you link the Lotus 1-2-3 file named PANDL.WK1 to this document.

Link: A:\PANDL.WK1 <Spreadsheet> A1..E5

Profit & Loss				
Year	1993	1994	1995	1996
Sales	$105	$150	$225	$330
Expenses	85	120	175	250
Profits	$20	$30	$50	$80

Link End
A:\EXCHANGE.WP5 Doc 1 Pg 1 Ln 2.17i Pos 1i

IMPORTING A 1-2-3 SPREADSHEET FILE

11. Move the cursor to the blank line following the section "Importing a 1-2-3 Spreadsheet File."
12. Press Ctrl-F5 to display the Text In/Out menu.
13. Press S (for ***S**preadsheet*).
14. Press I (for ***I**mport*).
15. Press F (for ***F**ilename*), and the prompt reads *Enter filename:* followed by the name of the file you just linked.

16. Press F5 and then Enter← to display a list of files on the default drive/directory.
17. Highlight *SALES.WK1* and press R (for ***R**etrieve*). The Create Link menu reappears and the file's name is listed.
18. Press P (for ***P**erform Import*), and a message reads ** Importing Spreadsheet **. In a moment the Edit screen reappears with the spreadsheet file in a table.

IMPORTING A 1-2-3 PRINT FILE

19. Move the cursor to the blank line following the section "Importing a 1-2-3 Print File."
20. Press Ctrl-F5 to display the Text In/Out menu.
21. Press T (for *DOS **T**ext*).
22. Press R (for ***R**etrieve (CR/LF to [HRt]*), and the prompt reads *Document to be Retrieved:*.
23. Type **EXPENSES.PRN** and press Enter← to retrieve the model into the document.

The Imported EXPENSES.PRN File
When you import the EXPENSES.PRN file, it appears on the screen with columns aligned.

```
Importing a 1-2-3 Print File
In this section, you import a 1-2-3 file named EXPENSES.PRN that was printed to
1-2-3.
    Expense Forecast
    Year              1993      1994      1995      1996
    G&A                $35       $60      $100      $150
    Marketing           35        50        65        90
    Debt service        10        10        10        10
    Total              $80      $120      $175      $250

Importing a dBASE File Saved in ASCII Text Format
In this section, you import a dBASE file that was saved by that program in the A
format.

Importing a 1-2-3 Graph
In this section you place a 1-2-3 graph of the five-year plan model named LINE.P
created in a previous tutorial.

--------------------------------------------------------------------------------
Exporting a Nondelimited File
In this section, you export the PANDL.WK1 file as an ASCII text file named PANDL

Profit & Loss
                                                  Doc 1 Pg 1 Ln 8.21i Pos 1i
```

IMPORTING A DBASE FILE SAVED IN ASCII TEXT FORMAT

24. Move the cursor to the blank line following the section "Importing a dBASE File Saved in ASCII Text Format."
25. Press Ctrl-F5 to display the Text In/Out menu.
26. Press T (for *DOS **T**ext*).
27. Press R (for ***R**etrieve (CR/LF to [HRt]*), and the prompt reads *Document to be Retrieved:*.
28. Type **MEMBHOLD.TXT** and press Enter← to retrieve the model into the document. The fields in the file are delimited (serarated) with one or more commas. To convert the imported file to tabular columns, you need to replace these commas with other codes.
29. Search and replace three commas (,,,) with a tab character ([Tab]).
30. Search and replace two commas (,,) with a hard carriage return ([HRt]).
31. Search and replace all single commas (,) with nothing to remove them.
32. Delete all columns to the right of the phone number to narrow the table.
33. Set tab stops to align the columns.

RETRIEVING A 1-2-3 GRAPH

34. Move the cursor to the blank line following the section "Importing a 1-2-3 Graph."
35. Press Alt-F9 to display the Graphics menu.
36. Press F (for ***F**igure*).
37. Press C (for ***C**reate*) to display the Graphics Definition screen and menu.
38. Press F (for ***F**ilename*), and the prompt reads *Enter filename:*.
39. Press F5, and press Enter↵ to display a list of the files on your disk.
40. Highlight *LINE.PIC* and press R (for ***R**etrieve*).

The Figure Definition Menu
When you select the graphic file to be included, the Figure Definition menu is displayed. The commands on this menu specify the size and position of the graphic.

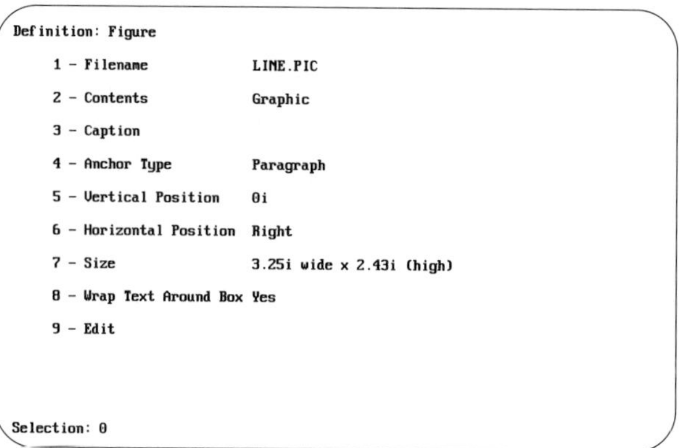

41. Press H (for ***H**orizontal Position*).
42. Press C (for ***C**enter*).
43. Press F7 to return to the Edit screen. The figure number and the top of the figure box are displayed on the screen.
44. Move the cursor under the first character in the heading "Exporting a nondelimited file" and press Enter↵ to move the heading (and the text that follows) below the bottom of the box.
45. Use the Print menu's View Document command to preview your results.
46. Press F7 to return to the Edit screen.

CREATING A NONDELIMITED ASCII FILE

47. Block the table below the heading "Exporting a Nondelimited File" including the tab setting code in front of the table's title.
48. Press Ctrl-F4 to display the Move menu.
49. Press B (for ***B**lock*).
50. Press C (for ***C**opy*) and the prompt reads *Move cusor; press enter to retrieve.*
51. Press ⇧Shift-F3 to display the Doc 2 screen and then press Enter↵ to copy the table to the screen by itself.
52. Press Ctrl-F5 to display the Text In/Out menu.
53. Press T (for *DOS **T**ext*) to display a submenu.
54. Press S (for ***S**ave*), and the prompt reads *Document to be saved (DOS text):*.
55. Type **PANDL.TXT** and press Enter↵ to save the files in ASCII text format under the name PANDL.TXT.

56. Clear the Doc 2 screen and press Shift-F3 to return to the Doc 1 screen and the EXCHANGE.WP5 document.

CREATING A DELIMITED ASCII FILE TO IMPORT INTO 1-2-3

```
"Sales Forecast"
"Year","1993","1994","1995","1996"
"Hardware",50,50,50,50
"Software",50,50,75,100
"Services",5,50,100,180
"Total",105,150,225,330
```

The 1-2-3 Delimited ASCII Text File
After you add quotes and commas to the file, it should look like this.

57. Copy the table below the heading "Exporting a Delimited File" to the Doc 2 screen as you did with the other table in Steps 47 through 51.
58. Follow the instructions below to add delimiters that tell 1-2-3 which characters are text and which are numbers. When you have finished, your document should look like the one in the figure "The 1-2-3 Delimited ASCII Text File."
    - Enclose all text strings that you want to import in quotes (""). In this file, the text strings are in the first column and the years 1993, 1994, 1995, and 1996 on the second row.
    - Delete the dollar signs ($) from all numbers.
    - Replace all tabs with commas.
59. Press Ctrl-F5 to display the Text In/Out menu.
60. Press T (for *DOS **T**ext*) to display a submenu.
61. Press S (for ***S**ave*), and the prompt reads *Document to be Saved:*.
62. Type **SALES1.TXT** and press Enter to save the document in ASCII format.

CREATING A DELIMITED ASCII FILE TO IMPORT INTO DBASE

```
Hardware,50,50,50,50
Software,50,50,75,100
Services,5,50,100,180
```

The dBASE Delimited ASCII Text File
After you delete rows and dollar signs and add commas to the file, it should look like this.

63. Clear the Doc 2 screen and then press Shift-F3 to return to the Doc 1 screen and the EXCHANGE.WP5 document.
64. Copy the table below the heading "Exporting a Delimited File" to the Doc 2 screen as you did with the other tables.
65. Revise the document as follows (when you have finished, your document should look like the one in the figure "The dBASE Delimited ASCII Text File"):
    - Delete the first and second rows, those with the title of the table and the dates.
    - Delete the dollar signs in front of numbers.
    - Delete the last row that contains totals.
    - Replace all tabs with commas so dBASE knows where fields end.
66. Press Ctrl-F5 to display the Text In/Out menu.
67. Press T (for *DOS **T**ext*) to display a submenu.
68. Press S (for ***S**ave*), and the prompt reads *Document to be Saved:*.
69. Type **SALES2.TXT** and press Enter to save the document in ASCII format.
70. Clear the Doc 2 screen and then press Shift-F3 to return to the Doc 1 screen and the EXCHANGE.WP5 document.

FINISHING UP

71. Save and print the document. Note that the comments above and below the first two tables do not print. If the columns in the third table are not aligned, it is because your printer is using a proportional font. Reveal codes and you will find that the columns

are aligned with spaces, not with tab codes. To align these columns you can specify a base font of Courier or replace all spaces between the columns with tab codes and then set tab stops to align the columns correctly.

72. You have now completed this tutorial. Either continue with the next activity or quit the program.

QUICK REFERENCE

When you want to transfer files to and from WordPerfect, the procedure you use depends on the type of file you want to use or create. If you are importing data from a spreadsheet model you can import it or link it to the document. If you are transferring data to spreadsheets or other programs, you save it as an ASCII text file.

Importing or Linking with a Spreadsheet File

WordPerfect allows you to import a spreadsheet file or link it to your document file. When you import a spreadsheet file, column widths are based on the base font at the cursor's position. If tables are too wide, delete the file, insert a base font code for a smaller font, and then import the spreadsheet again.

 KEY/Strokes

Importing or Linking with a Spreadsheet File

1. Either: Press Ctrl-F5 and press S (for ***S**preadsheet*).
   Or: Pull down the File menu, select *Text **I**n*, and then select ***S**preadsheet*.
2. Make one of the menu choices described in the table "Spreadsheet Menu Options."

SPREADSHEET MENU OPTIONS

1 ***I**mport* imports the data in the specified file but does not establish a permanent link.
- **1** ***F**ilename* is the name of the file to be imported (you can press F5 to display the List Files screen to locate it, and press R (for ***R**etrieve*).
- **2** ***R**ange* is the name of the range or the cell address of the upper-left and lower-right corner cells, separated by a colon or one or two periods. If you do not specify a range, the entire file is imported.
- **3** ***T**ype* specifies if the file is to be imported as a table or as text.
- **4** ***P**erform Import* imports the specified file.

2 ***C**reate Link* establishes a permanent link with a spreadsheet file.
- **1** ***F**ilename* is the same as on the Import menu.
- **2** ***R**ange* is the same as on the Import menu.
- **3** ***T**ype* is the same as on the Import menu.
- **4** ***P**erform Link* enters codes into your document that refer to the linked file.

3 ***E**dit Link* displays a menu with the same choices as ***2 C**reate Link*.

4 ***L**ink Options* specifies options that define your link.
- **1** *Update on **R**etrieve* automatically updates your document whenever you retrieve it.
- **2** ***S**how Link Codes* displays or hides the link codes in your document.

- **3** *Update All Links* updates all tables in your document to reflect any changes in the files to which they are linked.

Saving and Retrieving ASCII Text Files

WordPerfect has several menu commands that save or retrieve ASCII text files. There is also a command to save the document on the screen in a generic word processing format or so that it can be retrieved by earlier versions of WordPerfect.

→ KEY/Strokes

Saving and Retrieving ASCII Text Files

1. Press Ctrl-F5 to display the Text In/Out menu.
2. Select any of the menu options described in the table "Document Conversion, Summary, and Comments Menu Choices," and the prompt reads *Document to be saved:* or *Document to be retrieved:*.
3. Type the name of the document, and then press Enter←. (Or press Enter← to accept the suggested name, if any.)

DOCUMENT CONVERSION, SUMMARY, AND COMMENTS MENU CHOICES

1 *DOS **T**ext* saves and retrieves ASCII text files and displays a menu with the following choices:
  - *1 **S**ave* deletes many WordPerfect formatting codes. Indents, tabs, centering, and margins are converted to spaces. If you want to preserve formats such as columns, centered text, footnotes and endnotes, and headers and footers, see "Printing to Disk" in the WordPerfect manual accompanying the program.
  - *2 **R**etrieve (CR/LF to [HRt])* converts all soft and hard carriage returns to hard carriage returns.
  - *3 R**e**trieve (CR/LF to [SRt] in HZone)* converts all carriage returns that fall in the hyphenation zone to soft carriage returns. All carriage returns that occur in pairs, as they do between paragraphs, are converted to hard carriage returns.

2 ***P**assword* adds, changes, or removes a password from a document.

3 *Save **A**s* saves files in a generic file format that can be read by other word processing programs
  - *Generic* removes all codes specific to WordPerfect, but the following formats are replaced: Codes for centering, indenting, flush right, and soft carriage returns are replaced with spaces, and hard carriage returns are replaced by soft carriage returns and line feeds. Tab codes are retained. Footnotes and endnotes are deleted.
  - ***W**ordPerfect 5.0* removes all codes specific to version 5.1 so that the file can be retrieved with version 5.0.
  - *Word**P**erfect 4.2* removes all codes specific to version 5.1 so that the file can be retrieved with version 4.2.

4 ***C**omment* creates or edits document comments.

5 ***S**preadsheet* imports or links spreadsheet models and documents.

EXERCISE 1

IMPORTING AND LINKING SPREADSHEET FILES

1. Open a new document.
2. Link one of the spreadsheet models on your disk to the document.
3. Import another copy of the same model
4. Save the document as LINKTEST.WP5.
5. Quit WordPerfect and load 1-2-3.
6. Load the model that you linked to the document.
7. Change one or more numbers in the model and then save it again.
8. Quit 1-2-3 and load WordPerfect.
9. Retrieve the LINKTEST.WP5 document.
10. Press Ctrl-F5 then S (for ***S**preadsheet*) and L (for ***L**ink Options*). Press U (for ***U**pdate All Links*) and notice how the linked table in the document is updated to reflect the changes you made to the 1-2-3 file. The copy that you imported remains unchanged.

TOPIC 2

Transferring Files to and from 1-2-3

After completing this topic, you should be able to:

- Import delimited text files
- Import and parse nondelimited text files
- Save files as ASCII (.PRN) text files

There are two ways you can transfer files created on other programs to 1-2-3. You can import them as ASCII text files, or you can convert them if they were created on a program that 1-2-3 supports, like dBASE. If you import a nondelimited ASCII text file, you use a procedure called parsing, to break long lines up into individual cells.

To transfer data from 1-2-3 to another program, you print the file to the disk. These 1-2-3 print files are ASCII files with a slight difference. All format codes are first interpreted before they are removed from the file. A print file is created just like a printout on the printer but the output is sent to a file on a disk instead of to the printer. Formats like headers, footers, page numbers, and top and bottom margins that would appear on a printout also appear in the print file on the disk.

TUTORIAL

In this tutorial, you import nondelimited and delimited ASCII text files. You then save a file as an ASCII text file by printing it to a disk file and convert a dBASE file for use with 1-2-3 and vice versa. The ASCII files you use are the ones you copied onto your data disk in topic1. The dBASE file that you convert is MEMBHOLD.DBF. This file was supplied on the *Student Resource Disk* and used in the dBASE section of this text. If it isn't on the data disk you are currently using, copy it and its accompanying MEMBHOLD.DBT file there from the dBASE directory of the *Student Resource Disk* or another of your data disks.

GETTING STARTED

1. Load 1-2-3, preferably by way of the Lotus Access System, and set the default drive to the drive into which you inserted your data disk.

IMPORTING THE SALES.TXT DELIMITED FILE

2. Go to cell A1 and press / F I N (for ***F**ile*, ***I**mport*, ***N**umbers*). The prompt reads *Enter name of file to import.*
3. Type **SALES1.TXT** and press Enter ↵. The file appears on the screen just as if it had been created by 1-2-3.

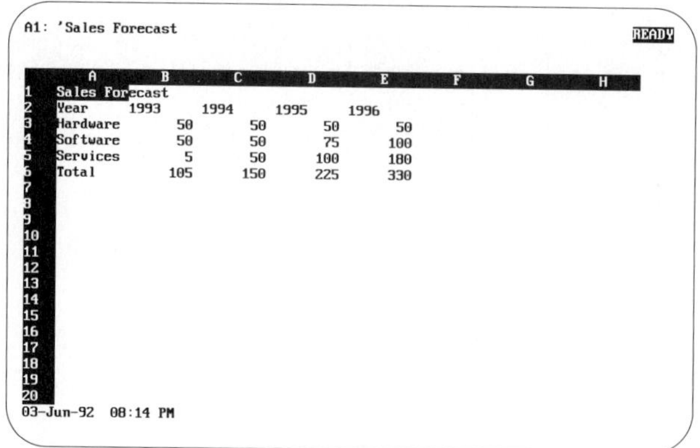

4. Format the numbers on rows 3 and 6 as currency with no decimal places and right-align the dates on row 2.
5. Save the file as **SALES1**, make a printout, and then clear the screen.

IMPORTING THE PANDL.TXT NONDELIMITED FILE

6. Go to cell A1 and press [/] [F] [I] [T] (for ***F**ile*, ***I**mport*, ***T**ext*). The prompt reads *Enter name of file to import:*.
7. Type **PANDL.TXT** and press [Enter ←]. The file is imported with each line entered as a label in column A. To see this, move the cell pointer up and down the cells in column A. As you do so, you see the entire label displayed on the first line of the control panel. If you then move the cell pointer to columns B through H, you will see that they contain no data.

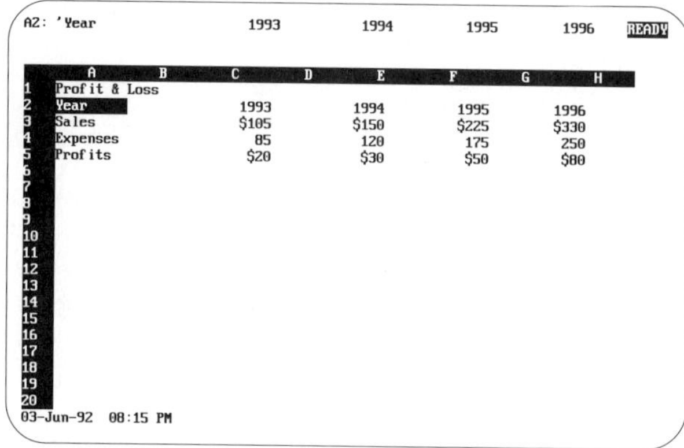

PARSING THE LABELS

8. Go to cell A2 and press [/] [D] [P] (for ***D**ata*, ***P**arse*).
9. Press [F] [C] (for ***F**ormat-Line*, ***C**reate*) to display a format line above the labels (Release 2.01) or a settings sheet (Releases 2.2 and later).
10. Press [Q] (for ***Q**uit*) to remove the menu. Look carefully at the format line. The *L>>>>>>>* code indicates that when you parse the file, the entries in the first column will be treated as labels. The *V>>>>>>>* codes indicate that when you parse the file, the entries in the next four columns will be treated as values.

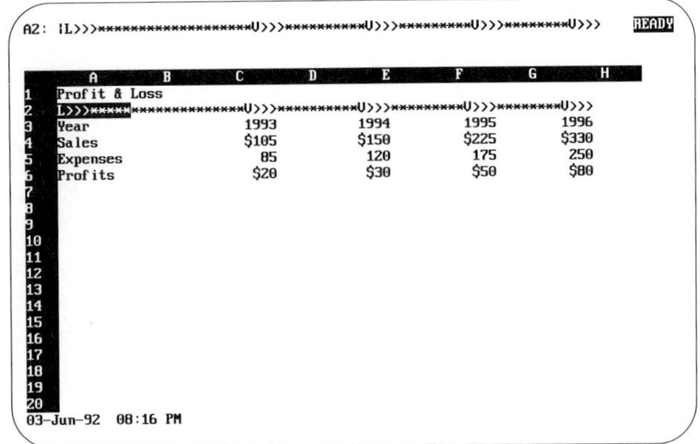

11. With the cell pointer in A2, press [/][D][P] (for ***D**ata*, ***P**arse*).
12. Press [I] (for ***I**nput-Column*), and the prompt reads *Enter column of labels to parse:*.
13. Type **A2.A6** and press [Enter←].
14. Press [O] (for ***O**utput-Range*), and the prompt reads *Enter output range:*.
15. Type **A8** and press [Enter←].
16. Press [G] (for ***G**o*) to parse the labels. Move the cell pointer to each cell in the output range on rows 8 through 11 and you will see that the entries are no longer long labels extending from column A as they are in the input range.

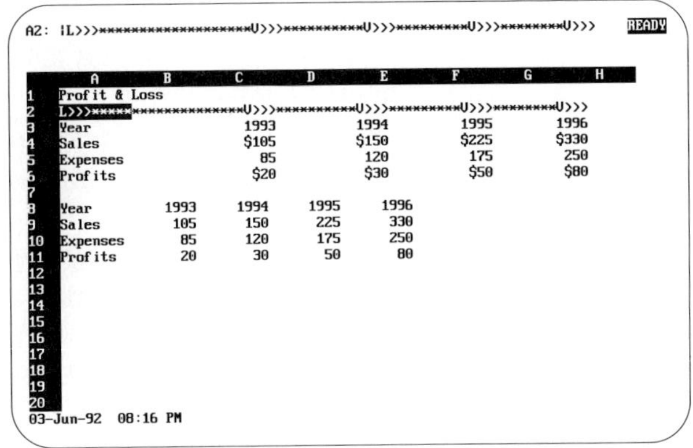

17. Delete rows 2 through 7.
18. Make a printout
19. Save the file as PANDL2.

PRINTING TO A PRINT FILE

20. Press [/][P][F] (for ***P**rint*, ***F**ile*), and the prompt reads *Enter print file name:*.
21. Type **PANDL** and press [Enter←] to display the Print menu.
22. Press [O][O][U][Q] (for ***O**ptions*, ***O**ther*, ***U**nformatted*, ***Q**uit*).
23. Press [R] (for ***R**ange*), and the prompt reads *Enter print range:*.
24. Type **A1.E5** and press [Enter←].
25. Press [A][G][Q] (for ***A**lign*, ***G**o*, ***Q**uit*) to print the file to the disk with the extension .PRN that 1-2-3 automatically adds.

TRANSLATING A DBASE FILE FOR USE WITH 1-2-3

26. Quit 1-2-3 and load the Lotus Access System, if you are not already in it.
27. Press T (for ***T**ranslate*) from the Access System menu, and the prompt reads *What do you want to translate FROM?* and a list of programs is displayed. (On a floppy disk system, the prompt reads *Insert Utility disk into your diskette drive. Press [RETURN] to continue or [ESCAPE] to quit.* Insert the Utility disk into drive A, and press Enter to display the Translate Utility menu.)

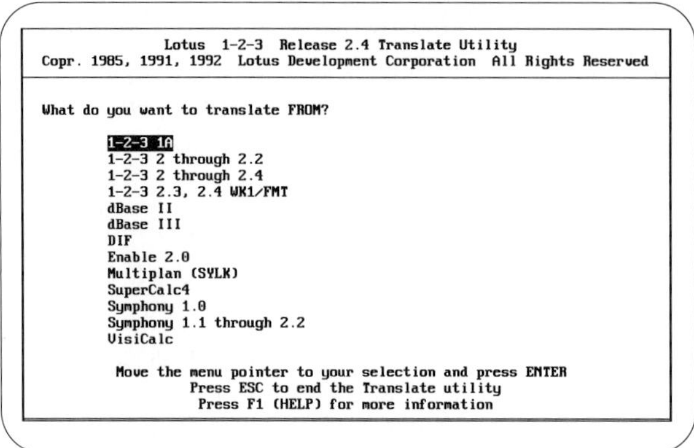

28. Highlight *dBASE III* and press Enter. The prompt reads *What do you want to translate TO?* and a list of programs is displayed.
29. Highlight the release of 1-2-3 you are using and press Enter. A screen of descriptive text is displayed, and the prompt reads *Press [ESCAPE] to continue.*
30. Press Esc to clear the text and display a path to the source file.
31. Press Esc to delete the current path until the prompt reads *Source file:* without a filename. (You may have to press it more than once).
32. Type **B:** (on a floppy disk system) or **A:** (on a hard disk system) and press Enter to display a list of files with the .DBF extension on the disk in the specified drive.
33. Highlight *MEMBHOLD.DBF* and press Enter to list that file as the *Destination* or *Target* file.
34. Press Enter to confirm your choices, and the prompt reads *Proceed with translation.*
35. Press Y, and the message reads *Translation in progress...please wait.* In a moment the message reads *Translation Successful.*
36. Press Esc twice, and the prompt reads *Do you want to leave Translate?.*
37. Press N, and the prompt reads *What do you want to translate FROM?.*

TRANSLATING A 1-2-3 FILE FOR USE WITH DBASE

38. Highlight the release of 1-2-3 you are using and press Enter. The prompt reads *What do you want to translate TO?.*
39. Highlight *dBase III* and press Enter. A screen of text is displayed, and the prompt reads *Press [ESCAPE] to continue.*
40. Press Esc twice to clear the text and display a path to the source file.

41. Press [Esc] to delete the current path and the prompt reads *Source file:* without a filename.
42. Type **B:** (on a floppy disk system) or **A:** (on a hard disk system) and press [Enter←] to display a list of files with the .WK1 extension on the disk in the specified drive.
43. Highlight *STAFF.WK1* and press [Enter←] to list that file as the *Destination* or *Target* file.
44. Press [Enter←] to accept the path and filename, and the prompt reads *Worksheet Range.*
45. Press [W] (for ***W**orksheet*), and the prompt reads *Proceed with translation.*
46. Press [Y], and the message reads *Translation in progress...please wait.* In a moment the message reads *Translation Successful.*
47. Press [Esc] twice, and the prompt reads *Do you want to leave Translate?.*
48. Press [Y] to return to the Access System menu.

RETRIEVING THE TRANSLATED FILE

49. Load the 1-2-3 worksheet and retrieve the MEMBHOLD.WK1 file that you translated.
50. Set columns widths correctly and then make a printout.
52. Save the file so the new column widths and print range are saved.

FINISHING UP

52. You have now completed this tutorial. Either continue with the next activity or quit the program.

QUICK REFERENCE

You can import either delimited or nondelimited ASCII text files. If you import nondelimted files, you have to parse them to break the long lines of data up into individual cells. You can also use 1-2-3's Translate program to convert files to and from other formats supported by the program.

Importing Files

You use 1-2-3's ***/F**ile **I**mport* command to import any files that have been saved as ASCII text files. When using this command, you must understand the difference between a delimited and a nondelimited text file.

- Delimited text files contain characters like commas, called delimiters, that separate data. The delimiters specify where the data should be broken up into columns. To import a delimited text file, you use the ***/F**ile **I**mport **N**umbers* command, which imports numbers and any labels enclosed in quotes (""). (Do not use the ***/F**ile **I**mport **T**ext* command to import this type of file.) To import a delimited text file correctly, follow these rules:
  - Labels must be enclosed in quotation marks ("").

- Labels and numbers must be separated by commas, spaces, colons, or semicolons.
- Numbers must not contain commas because they can be mistaken for delimiters.

■ A nondelimited text file does not separate data with delimiters. To import this type of file, you use the ***/File Import Numbers*** command to import numbers and labels enclosed in quotes. To import a nondelimited text file correctly, follow these rules:

- Labels must be enclosed in quotation marks ("").
- Each line must end with a hard carriage return and a line feed.
- No line may exceed 240 characters.

If you do not want to enclose labels in quotes, you can use the ***/File Import Text*** command to import the file. This command enters each line of text into a single cell as a long label. Although the data on the screen may appear to be broken up into cells, they aren't. If you position the cell pointer in one of the cells in the first column, you will see the entire line displayed on the control panel. To break up a label—for example, to use numbers it contains in calculations—you must use the ***/Data Parse*** command.

→ KEY/Strokes

Importing a File

1. Move the cursor to the upper-left cell in the range you want to import the data into.
2. Press / F I (for ***File, Import***) to display a submenu.
3. Specify ***Text*** or ***Numbers*** (see the table "File Import Menu Options"), and the prompt reads *Enter name of file to import:*
4. Highlight the name of the file and press Enter↵.

FILE IMPORT MENU OPTIONS

Option	Description
Text	• When used with a nondelimited text file, each line is imported as a long label. • Do not use with delimited files.
***N**umbers*	Imports numbers and labels that have been enclosed in quotes.

Parsing Files

When you use the ***/File Import Text*** command to import data as long labels, you can break them up into individual cells with the ***/Data Parse*** command. To use the ***/Data Parse*** command, you must specify the format line, the input column, and the output range.

The Format Line

When you use the ***/Data Parse*** command, you select ***Create*** from the menu to create a format line. When you do so, 1-2-3 analyzes the line the cursor is positioned on and determines where labels, values, dates, and times are located. It then places a format line above the row to indicate where it thinks data below the line should be divided into cells. The individual sections into which a line is parsed are called data blocks. The type of data into which the blocks are broken is called the block type. There are four block types: value, label, date, and time.

When parsing data, keep the following points about the format line in mind:

- The format line is a label with a split vertical bar as the label prefix. The characters on the line can be any of those described in the table "Format Line Symbols."
- The format line is based on 1-2-3's analysis of the first label in the data. It shows 1-2-3's best guess as to how the data should be parsed.
- Spaces in the label indicate to 1-2-3 where it should begin a new data block. Therefore the label 100 Elm Street would be divided into three data blocks. The label 123-Elm-Street would be treated as one label block.
- The total number of > and * characters specifying a data block on the format line must be at least equal to the longest entry in that data block on the rows below or data may be lost when you parse.

FORMAT LINE SYMBOLS

Symbol	Description
Data Types	
L	The first character of a label block, for example, L>>>>.
V	The first character in a value block, for example, V>>>>.
D	The first character in a date block, for example, D>>>>>>>>.
T	The first character in a time block, for example, T>>>>.
Data Includes	
>	Characters in a data block. When you use the menu command to enter a format line, the number of these characters assigned to each data block is determined by the number of characters in the data blocks on the first row of data.
*	Blank spaces that can become part of a data block if that block requires extra characters. For example, if the first row contains the name IOWA and you enter a format line, it might be L>>>. However, the next entry might be New Hampshire. To insure that a sufficient number of characters is allocated for the widest entry in the column, you reserve spaces with this character. For example, to print both IOWA and New Hampshire in the same column, the format line might read L>>>>>>>>>>>> or L>>>*********.
Data Deletes	
S	Specifies that the data block immediately below is to be skipped when the data are parsed. For example, to skip a five-character block, the format line would contain S>>>>.

Although 1-2-3 guesses about the layout of the format line, it is usually quite accurate. However, in some situations you may find it necessary to edit the line.

- If any data block on the format line is not wide enough to contain the data on rows below the first.
- If 1-2-3 assigned the wrong data type to any data block. For example, if your dates are entered as 1/1/99, 1-2-3 will interpret them as dates and you may want to keep them as labels. To do so, you change the first letter in the data block on the format line from D to L to keep them as labels.
- If any block containing a space was divided into two data blocks but you want it to be treated as one.

If you find that you have to edit the format line, there are two methods you can use:

- The ***/Data Parse Format-Line Edit*** command moves the cursor to the format line and changes the mode to overstrike so any character that you type replaces the character that you type it over. Also, you can press ↓, ↑, PgDn, and PgUp to scroll the labels to be parsed while the format line remains fixed on the screen. This allows you to compare the data to be parsed with the format line. You can also press Esc to erase the format line (press it repeatedly until the line appears again in its original form).
- Moving the cell pointer to the cell containing the format line, and pressing F2 (**Edit**) displays the format line on the control panel just like any other label. Just move the cursor through the label and insert and delete characters as needed. When finished, press Enter↵.

Sometimes, editing the line is not enough. There may be so much variety in the data to be parsed that one format line cannot define it all. In these cases you can enter more than one format line. This is usually necessary when data in labels below the first contain data blocks that do not match the data type specified for the first label or when different labels have different data block lengths that can't be accommodated on the same format line.

The Input Column

The input column specifies the single column range that contains the labels to be parsed. The format line must be the first cell in the range. If there is more than one format line, the others should also be included. Blank rows in the input column are ignored.

The Output Range

If you specify one cell as the output range, 1-2-3 uses that cell as the upper-left corner of the range and uses as many rows and columns for the data as it needs. If you specify an output range that overlaps the input column, data in the input column will be overwritten. This saves memory, but be sure you save the file before doing so deliberately in case something goes wrong.

KEY/Strokes

Using the Data Parse Command

1. Import an ASCII text file with the ***/File Import Text*** command.
2. Move the cell pointer to the cell that contains the first label in the column to be parsed.
3. Press [/] [D] [P] (for ***Data, Parse***) to display the Data Parse menu described in the table "Data Parse Menu Commands."
4. Press [F] [C] (for ***Format-Line, Create***) to automatically insert a format line.
5. Press [F] [E] (for ***Format-Line, Edit***) to edit the line or scroll the data to compare it with the format line. When finished, press [Enter←] to return to the menu.
6. Press [I] (for ***Input-Column***), and the prompt reads *Enter column of labels to parse:*
7. Specify the range of cells in the column that contains the labels to be parsed. Be sure to include the format line and all cells with labels.
8. Press [O] (for ***Output-Range***), and the prompt reads *Enter output range:*.
9. Specify the upper-left corner of the output range and press [Enter←].
10. Press [G] (for ***Go***) to parse the labels.

DATA PARSE MENU COMMANDS

Command	Description
Format-Line	Creates or edits the line that specifies how data blocks are to be broken up and what their data types are to be.
Input-Column	Specifies the cells in the column that contain the labels to be parsed. The input column must contain the format line.
Output-Range	Specifies the range the labels will be parsed to.
Reset	Resets the input and output ranges.
Go	Parses the labels.
Quit	Returns you to *READY* mode.

Translating Files

To translate files to or from other programs, you can use the Translate program. You can load this program in one of two ways:

- If you load the Lotus Access System, you can quickly switch between the 1-2-3 worksheet and the Translate program. From the Access System, press [1] (for *1-2-3*) to display the worksheet, or press [T] (for ***Translate***) to display Translate. When you quit either program, the Access System menu reappears so that you can move to the other parts of the 1-2-3 program or quit 1-2-3.
- You can return to the operating system and run the program named TRANS.COM.

- On a floppy disk system, insert the Translate disk into drive A. Type **A:** and press [Enter↵] to change the default drive to drive A. Type **TRANS** and press [Enter↵] to load the program.
- On a hard disk system, change to the directory that holds the 1-2-3 program files. For example, if the files are in a directory named 123, type **CD\123** and press [Enter↵] to change the directory. Then type **TRANS** and press [Enter↵] to load the program.

When you translate files, you convert a source file created on a source product to a target file for use on a target product. For example, if you have used dBASE to create a database that you now want to use with 1-2-3, the original dBASE file is a source file and dBASE is the source product. The new 1-2-3 file is the target file and 1-2-3 is the target product. Source files that can be converted vary from release to release but generally include programs such as dBASE and other versions of 1-2-3. Source files must have the extension .WK1. If they do not, rename them before attempting to translate them.

To convert a 1-2-3 worksheet to a dBASE format, you must first specify the input range in the worksheet with the ***/DQI*** (for ***D****ata*, ***Q****uery*, ***I****nput*) command.

→ KEY/Strokes

Translating Files

1. Display the Lotus Access System.
2. Press [T] (for ***T****ranslate*), and the prompt reads *What do you want to translate FROM?*.
3. Highlight the source program that created the file you want to translate and press [Enter↵] (the prompt reads *What do you want to translate TO?*).
4. Highlight the target program that you want to use the file with and press [Enter↵].
5. Follow the instructions that are displayed on the screen.

Saving Files as ASCII Text Files

To save a file in the ASCII text file format, you use 1-2-3's ***/P****rint* ***F****ile* command. This command prints only the calculated values, not the formulas and functions. Since formulas are not printed, the print file cannot be used as a working file. When printing to a disk file, you must specify a name for the file; 1-2-3 automatically adds the extension .PRN to the file to distinguish it from the original file.

Before printing to the disk, you might consider changing the following options.

- To prevent headers, footers, and page breaks in the file, use the ***/P****rint* ***F****ile* ***O****ptions* ***O****ther* ***U****nformatted* command.
- To prevent distracting line breaks, set the left margin to 0 and the right margin to 65. This should give you a line length of 65 characters, or 6½-inches. When you retrieve the file with a word processing program, you can then set the left and right margins to 1" and the model will print correctly on an 8½-inch-wide page.

- To keep the text from printing off the right edge of the page, set the right margin to less than 80 characters.

When printing to a text file, you can print several different ranges in the same model by specifying a new range after each Go command. The ranges are printed to the same text file, one after the other. You can continue adding ranges to the text file until you press the Print menu's Quit command. Once you quit the print session, the text file is closed. (Setup strings are ignored when you print to a file.)

When you print to a file on the disk, you can then use the DOS TYPE command to display the file on the screen and the DOS PRINT command to print it. For example,

- If the file is named BUDGET.PRN (1-2-3 automatically adds the .PRN extension) and is on drive A, type **TYPE A:BUDGET.PRN** and press [Enter←]. Sometimes, long files scroll by too fast to read. You can pause the screen while it is scrolling by pressing [Ctrl]-[S], or if your computer has such a key, [Pause]. To resume scrolling, press any key.
- If the same file is on drive B and the DOS disk is in drive A (PRINT is an external command), type **A:PRINT B:BUDGET.PRN** and press [Enter←]. When you use the PRINT command the first time in a session, a prompt asks you for the name of the print device and suggests LPT1 (the normal printer port). If your printer is attached to that port, you just press [Enter←] to print the file. If your printer is attached to a different port, for example, LPT2, COM1, or COM2, you type the name of the port and press [Enter←]. You are asked for the port only when you first use the command.

→ KEY/Strokes

Printing to a Disk File

1. Be sure there is a disk in the drive you are printing to.
2. Press [/][P][F] (for ***P**rint*, ***F**ile*), and the prompt asks you to enter the name of the file that you are printing to.
3. Type the name of the file and press [Enter←] to return to the Print menu.
4. If you have not specified a range or if you want to change it, press [R] (for ***R**ange*), and the prompt reads *Enter print range:*. Specify the range and press [Enter←]. (If you are printing borders, be sure the print range does not include those rows or columns, or they will be printed twice.)
5. If you want to specify or change print options, do so now.
6. Press [A][G] (for ***A**lign*, ***G**o*) to begin printing. (Printing will not actually begin until after Step 7.)
7. Specify another print range if you want to print it on the same page.
8. Press [P][Q] (for ***P**age*, ***Q**uit*) to close the file and return to the worksheet.

KEY/Strokes

Translating Files

1. Display the Lotus Access System.
2. Press [T] (for ***T****ranslate*), and the prompt reads *What do you want to translate FROM?*.
3. Highlight the program that created the file you want to translate and press [Enter←] (the prompt reads *What do you want to translate TO?*).
4. Highlight the program that you want to use the file with and press [Enter←].
5. Follow the instructions that are displayed on the screen.

EXERCISE

EXERCISE 1

EXPERIMENT WITH THE PRINT FILE COMMAND

1. Retrieve any of the 1-2-3 models on your data disk.
2. Print the file to a disk file.
3. Quit 1-2-3 and load WordPerfect.
4. Retrieve the print file and format it.
5. Save the new document as PRTFILE.WP5 and make a printout.

TOPIC 3

Transferring Files to and from dBASE III Plus

After completing this topic, you should be able to:

- Retrieve files translated by Lotus 1-2-3
- Retrieve delimited ASCII text files
- Save dBASE files as ASCII text files

dBASE accepts delimited ASCII text files and files converted by other programs such as 1-2-3. To use the data in a delimited text file, you must first create the database and then append the data to it. Files converted by programs such as 1-2-3 can be used directly, just as if they had been originally created in dBASE.

TUTORIAL

In this tutorial, you open the 1-2-3 file that you converted to a dBASE file with the Lotus Translate program. You then define a new file into which you will append the data in the delimited ASCII text file that you created with WordPerfect. Finally, you will save a dBASE file as an ASCII text file so it can be imported into WordPerfect or 1-2-3. The dBASE file that you convert is MEMBHOLD.DBF, which you created in the dBASE section of this text. This file, and its accompanying MEMBHOLD.DBT file, must both be on the data disk that you are currently using. If they are not, copy them from the disk they are on or use that disk for the appropriate section of the tutorial.

GETTING READY

1. Load dBASE so the dot prompt is displayed and set the default drive to the one into which you inserted your data disk.

USING A FILE TRANSLATED BY 1-2-3

2. Type **USE STAFF** and press Enter↵ to open the file that you translated from the Lotus Access System menu.
3. Type **BROWSE** to display the contents of the file.

The STAFF File
When you retrieve the STAFF file that you converted with the 1-2-3 Translate program, it looks like this in BROWSE mode.

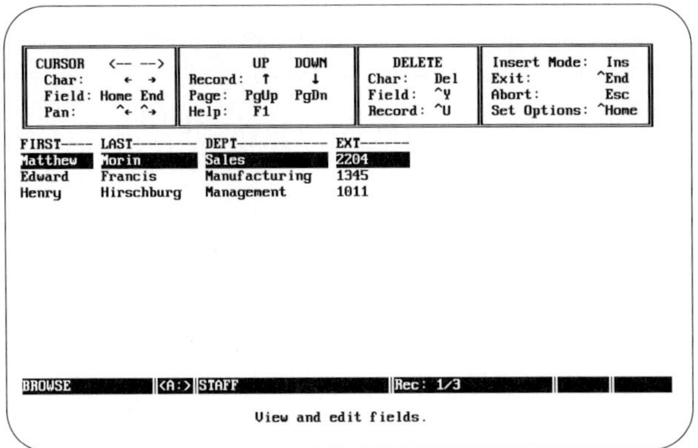

4. Press [Esc] to return to the dot prompt.

DEFINING A NEW FILE FOR IMPORTED DELIMITED ASCII TEXT

5. Type **CREATE SALES2** and press [Enter←┘] to display the file definition screen. Define the database file described in the table "The SALES2 Database Fields."

THE SALES2 DATABASE FIELDS

FIELD	FIELD NAME	TYPE	WIDTH	DEC
1	PRODUCT	Character	10	-
2	FIRST	Numeric	5	0
3	SECOND	Numeric	5	0
4	THIRD	Numeric	5	0
5	FOURTH	Numeric	5	0

Carefully check your entries against the figure "The Completed SALES2 Definition." If you find an error in your definition, move the cursor to the error and correct it.

The Completed SALES2 Definition
After you have defined the SALES2 database file, your definition should match the one shown here.

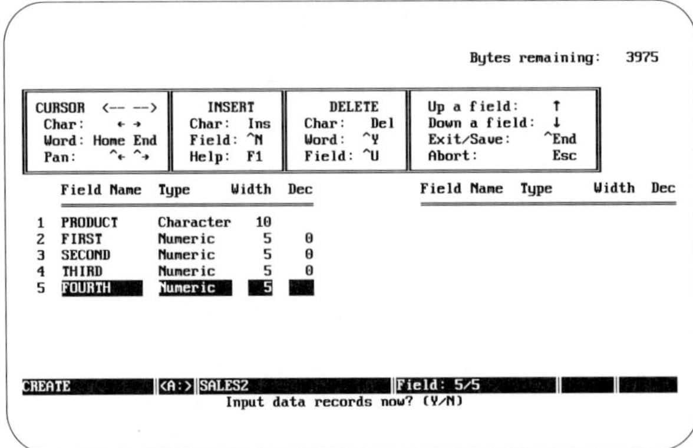

6. Press [Ctrl]-[End] to save the file, and the prompt reads *Press ENTER to confirm. Any other key to resume.*
7. Press [Enter←┘] to save the file definition on the disk, and in a moment the prompt reads *Input data records now? (Y/N).*
8. Press [N] to return to the dot prompt.

APPENDING RECORDS FROM THE SALES2.TXT FILE

9. Type **APPEND FROM SALES2.TXT DELIMITED WITH ,** (be sure to include the comma in the command) and press Enter←. In a moment the message reads *3 Records Added*, and the dot prompt reappears.
10. Type **GOTO TOP** and press Enter←.
11. Type **BROWSE** and press Enter← to display the records in the file.

The SALES2 Database File
After you append records to the SALES2 database file and display it in browse mode, it should look like the one shown here.

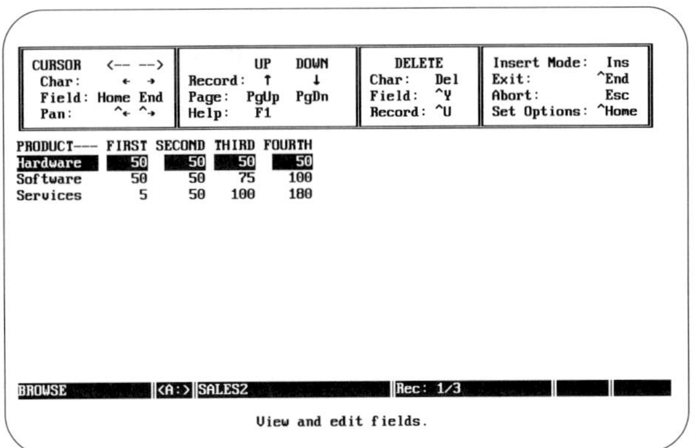

12. Press Esc to return to the dot prompt.

SAVING AN ASCII TEXT FILE

13. Open the **MEMBHOLD.DBF** file.
14. Type **COPY TO MEMBERS1.TXT DELIMITED WITH ,** and press Enter←. (Be sure to include the comma in the command.) In a moment the prompt indicates the number of records that were copied.
15. Type **COPY TO MEMBERS2.TXT FIELDS FIRST,LASTNAME, STREET,CITY,ST,ZIP DELIMITED WITH ,** and press Enter←.

FINISHING UP

16. You have now completed this tutorial. Either continue with the next activity or quit the program.

QUICK REFERENCE

The most common way to import data into dBASE from other programs is using ASCII text files. When you create a delimited ASCII text file with a program such as WordPerfect, you do not enter field names in the file. To import such a file into dBASE you then need an existing file with the same number of fields and they must be in the same order as the delimited file you are importing. Also, if you are importing numeric data, you can define the field for it as either character or numeric depending on how you want it stored in dBASE.

To import data, you use the command APPEND FROM <*ASCII text filename*> DELIMITED WITH <*delimiter*>. For example, if you have a database file open and want to append comma-delimited data to it from a file named PAYROLL.TXT, you would use the command APPEND FROM PAYROLL.TXT DELIMITED WITH , to import it . If the data were delimited with quotation marks, you would use the command APPEND FROM PAYROLL.TXT DELIMITED WITH ".

To export data for use in other programs, you use dBASE to create delimited files for you. To begin, you must know what delimiters are used by the program that you are transferring the data to. You can then specify that delimiter in the command COPY TO <*filename*> DELIMITED WITH <*delimiter*>. For example, with a database file open, you could use the command COPY TO NEWFILE DELIMITED WITH , to generate a comma-delimited file. If you do not specify a delimiter, the command creates a file with quotes around data in character fields (none are used around numeric data), and separates fields with commas.

EXERCISES

EXERCISE 1

RETRIEVING CONVERTED FILES

Load WordPerfect and retrieve the two files you saved as ASCII text files in this topic, MEMBERS1.TXT and MEMBERS2.TXT. Print both of them out.

EXERCISE 2

EXPLORING DELIMITERS

1. Open the SALES2 database file and copy it with the **COPY TO SALES3.TXT DELIMITED WITH ,** command.
2. Copy the SALES2 file again with the command **COPY TO SALES4.TXT DELIMITED** command.
3. Retrieve the two files SALES3.TXT and SALES4.TXT with WordPerfect and make printouts of each. What are the differences between the two files?

REVIEW

- You can transfer information between programs by saving it in a form the other program can understand or by converting it to the other program's format.
- The most common format for files that are to be exchanged is the ASCII text file format. This format contains no formatting codes; each line ends with a hard carriage return; and any tabs in a document are converted to spaces.
- Newer programs allow you to import data from other programs directly, using built-in filters.
- Delimited text files contain characters such as commas that indicate where data should be broken up into columns.
- A nondelimited text file does not separate data with delimiters.
- WordPerfect can read 1-2-3 files directly, without conversion. You can either import them into a document or link them to it. A document with a linked file can be updated if you change the data in the 1-2-3 file.
- For a delimited text file to be imported into 1-2-3 correctly, labels must be enclosed in quotation marks, and labels and numbers must be separated by commas, spaces, colons, or semicolons. You then use the ***/File Import Numbers*** command to import the file.
- To import a nondelimited text file into 1-2-3, each line must end with a hard carriage return and a line feed, and no line may exceed 240 characters. You then use the ***/File Import Text*** command to import the file. Finally, you use the ***/Data Parse*** command to break long labels up into individual cells.
- Files created on some programs, like dBASE, can be translated for use with 1-2-3. To translate a file, you use the Translate program on the Access System menu. You can also use the Translate program to convert 1-2-3 files for use on other programs.
- 1-2-3 can save ASCII text files using the ***/Print File*** command. This command prints only the calculated values, not the formulas and functions. 1-2-3 adds the extension .PRN to a file printed to the disk to distinguish it from the original file.
- To transfer a delimited ASCII text file into dBASE, you must first define the database. You then use the APPEND FROM <*filename*> DELIMITED WITH <*delimeter*> command to append the records to the file.
- To transfer a dBASE file to another program, you use the command COPY TO <*filename*> DELIMITED WITH <*delimeter*>.

QUESTIONS

FILL IN THE BLANK

1. You can use a ___________ to convert the codes of one program to the codes used by another.
2. A delimited text file can use ___________ to indicate where data are to be broken into columns or fields.
3. An ___________ file is a file format that is frequently used to transfer data between programs.
4. If you ___________ a 1-2-3 file to a WordPerfect document, you can update it later if you change data in the 1-2-3 file.
5. To import a delimited ASCII text file into 1-2-3 it should have ___________ to indicate where data are to be broken into columns or fields and ___________ around labels.
6. The save a file in ASCII format with WordPerfect, you begin by pressing ___________.
7. When you import a ___________ text file into 1-2-3, all rows are entered into column A as labels. To break these long labels in column A up into cells, you ___________ the data.
8. To save a 1-2-3 file as an ASCII text file you must ___________ it to a file on the disk.
9. To save a dBASE file as an ASCII text file, you use the command ___________.

MATCH THE COLUMNS

1. File conversion program	__ Converts one program's codes into another's
2. ASCII text file	__ A standard file format that can be read by most programs
3. Delimited	__ A file with commas added to separate fields
4. Nondelimited	__ A file without commas added to separate fields
5. Imported 1-2-3 file	__ A file in WordPerfect that can't be automatically updated
6. Linked 1-2-3 file	__ A file in WordPerfect that can be automatically updated because a permanent link has been established
7. Parsing	__ Breaking up long lines into individual cells
8. COPY TO	__ The dBASE command that creates an ASCII text file

WRITE OUT THE ANSWERS

1. What is the difference between a delimited and a nondelimited text file?
2. What command do you use to import a delimited text file into 1-2-3? into dBASE III Plus?
3. What command do you use to import a nondelimited text file into 1-2-3?
4. If you import a file into 1-2-3 as text, what command must you use to break up the labels into cells?
5. Why might you want to print your 1-2-3 model to a file on the disk?
6. What 1-2-3 command do you use to print a file to the disk?
7. If you wanted to transfer one of your 1-2-3 files to dBASE, what procedure would you use?
8. If you want to add an ASCII text file to dBASE III Plus, should the file be delimited? How do you then add it to the dBASE file?
9. How do you save a dBASE III Plus file as an ASCII text file?

DOS

Warm-boot the system	Ctrl-Alt-Del
Display version number	VER
Change the prompt	PROMPT PG
Cancel a command	Ctrl-Break
Display help (DOS 5)	HELP <command>
Load DOSKEY (DOS 5)	DOSKEY
Format a data disk	FORMAT <drive>
List all files	DIR <drive>*.*
Copy all files	COPY *.* <drive>

Recall one character from the previous command	Recall the previous command up to the specified character	Recall all of the previous command	Clear the previous command up to the specified character	Replace the previous command with the current command	Insert ^Z end-of-file code (same as Ctrl-Z)

WordPerfect® 5.1

Hold down: Ctrl Alt Shift None when you press function key

Change the default drive	F5, =, <drive>, Enter
Display/remove help	F3/Spacebar
Exit WordPerfect	F7
Display menu bar	Alt-=
Save a file	F10
Retrieve a file	Shift-F10
Print a file	Shift-F7
Reveal/hide codes	Alt-F3 or F11
Turn block on/off	Alt-F4 or F12

	F1	F2	F3	F4	F5	F6	F7	F8	F9	F10	F11	F12
Ctrl	Shell	Spell	Screen	Move	Text In/Out	Tab Align	Footnote	Font	Merge/Sort	Macro Def.		
Shift	Setup	< Search	Switch	>Indent<	Date/Outline	Center	Print	Format	Merge Codes	Retrieve		
Alt	Thesaurus	Replace	Reveal Codes	Block	Mark Text	Flush Right	Columns/Tables	Style	Graphics	Macro		
None	Cancel	Search >	Help	>Indent	List Files	Bold	Exit	Underline	End Field	Save	Reveal Codes	Block

Lotus® 1-2-3®

Hold down: Alt when you press key (Release 2.01 and later only)

Display command menu	/
Display help	F1
Change default drive/directory	/FD
Cancel a command	Ctrl-Break
Save a file	/FS
Retrieve a file	/FR
Goto	F5
Edit cell contents	F2
Format range of values	/RF

	F1	F2	F3	F4	F5	F6	F7	F8	F9	F10
Alt	Compose	Step	Run	Undo	Learn		App1	App2	App3	App4
	Help	Edit	Name	ABS	GoTo	Window	Query	Table	Calc	Graph

dBASE III Plus®

Change the default drive	SET DEFAULT TO <drive>
Load a file	USE <filename>
Browse a file	BROWSE
Move record pointer	GOTO <TOP>, <BOTTOM>, or <#>
Display help	HELP <command>
Display Assist menus	ASSIST
Print records	LIST TO PRINT
Edit record	EDIT <number>
List all records	LIST ALL

F1	F2	F3	F4	F5	F6	F7	F8	F9	F10
Help	Display Assist Menu	List Records	Directory of Files	Display Structure	Display Status	Display Memory	Display Current Record	Append	Edit Current Record

DOS

Recall one character from the previous command

Recall all of the previous command

Replace the previous command with the current command

Recall previous command up to specified character

Clear the previous command up to the specified character

Insert ^Z end-of-file code (same as Ctrl-Z)

Warm-boot the system	Ctrl-Alt-Del
Display version number	VER
Change the prompt	PROMPT PG
Cancel a command	Ctrl-Break
Display help (DOS 5)	HELP <command>
Load DOSKEY (DOS 5)	DOSKEY

WordPerfect® 5.1

Shell
Setup
Thesaurus
Cancel

Screen
Switch
Reveal Codes
Help

Text In/Out
Date/Outline
Mark Text
List Files

Footnote
Print
Columns/Tables
Exit

Merge/Sort
Merge Codes
Graphics
End Field

<
Re
Sea

Mo
>Ind
Blo
>Inde

Tab Alig
Center
Flsh Rgt
Bold

Font
Format
Style
Underline

Macro Def.
Retrieve
Macro
Save

Hold down:
Ctrl Alt
Shift None
when you press key

Change the default drive	F5
Display/remove help	F3/Spacebar
Display menu bar	Alt-=
Save a file	F10
Retrieve a file	Shift-F10
Exit WordPerfect	F7

Lotus® 1-2-3®

Compose
Help

Run
Name

Learn
GoTo

App1
Query

App3
Calc

Step
Edit

Undo
ABS

Window

App2
Table

App4
Graph

Hold down Alt when you press key

Display command menu	/
Display help	F1
Change default drive/directory	/FD
Cancel command	Ctrl-Break
Save a file	/FS
Retrieve a file	/FR

dBASE III Plus®

Help

List Records

Display Structure

Display Memory

Append

Display Assist Menu

Directory of Files

Display Status

Display Current Record

Edit Current Record

Change the default drive	SET DEFAULT TO <drive letter>:
Load a file	USE <filename>
Browse a file	BROWSE
Move record pointer	GOTO <TOP>, <BOTTOM>, <#>
Display help	HELP <command>
Display Assist menus	ASSIST

Checking Disks

Indicate status of memory and disk space	CHKDSK
Look for noncontiguous blocks	CHKDSK *.*
Fix lost clusters	CHKDSK /F

Displaying and Printing ASCII Text Files

Display ASCII text file	TYPE <*filename*>
Pause a file display	TYPE <*filename*> |MORE
Print an ASCII text file	PRINT <*filename*>
Print screen display from enhanced keyboard	**PrintScreen**
Print screen display from standard keyboard	Shift-PrtScr
Print all text as it appears on the screen	Ctrl-PrtScr
Turn off printing all text as it appears on the screen	Ctrl-PrtScr
Pause scrolling screen display	Ctrl-S or Pause

Creating and Using Batch Files

Create a batch file	COPY CON <*filename.bat*>
End a batch file	Ctrl-Z or F6
Display contents of a batch file	TYPE <*filename.bat*>
Edit a batch file (DOS 5 only)	EDIT <*filename.bat*>

Using the Shell (DOS 4 and 5 only)

Display the Shell	DOSSHELL
Activate the menu bar	F10 or Alt
Exit menus without making choice	Esc
Display help	F1
Move between areas of the Shell	Tab
Select files	Shift-F8 then Spacebar
Exit the DOS Shell	F3

DOS Pocket Guide

Basic Commands

Display the version of DOS in memory	VER
Display system date	DATE
Display system time	TIME
Change the prompt to display directories	PROMPT PG
Reboot the system	Ctrl-Alt-Del
Cancel a command in progress	Ctrl-Break
Display help index (DOS 5 only)	HELP
Display help on specific command (DOS 5 only)	HELP <*command*>
Load DOSKEY (DOS 5 only)	DOSKEY
Display all commands saved by DOSKEY	DOSKEY /HISTORY
Display last command saved by DOSKEY	↑

Changing the Default Drive

Make drive A the default drive	A:
Make drive B the default drive	B:
Make drive C the default drive	C:

Formatting Data Disks

Format a data disk	FORMAT <*drive:*>
Format a data disk w/volume name	FORMAT <*drive:*>/V
Load the MIRROR program (DOS 5 only)	MIRROR <*drive:*>
Unformat a disk (DOS 5 only)	UNFORMAT <*drive:*>
Label a formatted disk	LABEL <*drive:*>
Display volume label	VOL <*drive:*>

Formatting System Disks

Format disk as a system disk	FORMAT <*drive:*>/S
Format a system disk with a volume name	FORMAT <*drive:*>/S/V

Hand pointing right	Ctrl-V 5,21
Hand pointing left	Ctrl-V 5,22
Em dash	Ctrl-V 4,34

Aligning Text

Set tabs	Shift-F8, L, T
Display tab ruler	Ctrl-F3, W, ↑
Indent text	F4
Double indent text	Shift-F4
Use margin release	Shift-Tab
Center line	Shift-F6
Right-align a line	Alt-F6
Align paragraphs with left and right margins	Shift-F8, L, J
Align decimal point with left-aligned tab stops	Ctrl-F6
Center text on left-aligned tab stops	Shift-F6
Right-align text on left-aligned tab stops	Ctrl-F6

Merge-Printing

Insert merge codes into document	Shift-F9, F
End a field in secondary file	F9
End a record in secondary file	Shift-F9, E
Merge-print documents	Ctrl-F9, M

Using Macros

Define a macro	Ctrl-F10
Execute a macro	Alt-F10
Edit a macro	Ctrl-F10 <*macro name*>

WordPerfect Pocket Guide

Getting Started

Load WordPerfect from a floppy disk	WP Enter
Load WordPerfect from a hard disk	CD\\<*directory*> Enter WP Enter
Change the default drive	F5, = <*drive:*>, Enter
Display help	F3
Return to edit screen from help	Enter or Spacebar
Cancel a command	F1
Exit WordPerfect	F7

Displaying and Using Menus

Display the menu bar	Alt-=
Pull down a highlighted menu	↓
Exit menus without making a choice	F1 or Esc

Saving Files and Clearing the Screen

Save the file on the screen	F10
Save the file on the screen as you exit	F7, Y, Y
Clear the screen and save the file	F7, Y, N
Clear the screen without saving the file	F7, N, N
Save files to exchange with other programs	Ctrl-F5

Retrieving Files

Retrieve a file by name	Shift-F10
Display List Files screen	F5, Enter, Enter
Print a list of the files displayed in List Files	Shift-F7

Moving the Cursor

Move between pages	PgUp and PgDn

Listing Files

List all files	DIR <drive:>
List all files in a directory	DIR <drive:\directory>
List files in five columns	DIR <drive:>/w
List files so screen pauses when full	DIR <drive:>/P
List files with specified filename	DIR <drive:> <filename>.*
List files with specified extension	DIR <drive:> *.<ext>
Wildcard that stands for a single character	?
Wildcard that stands for all characters to end of name or extension	*
Print directory listing	DIR *.* >PRN
Store directory listing in a disk file	DIR ><drive:/filename>
Pause a directory listing	DIR |MORE

Sorting Directories (second set of commands for DOS 5 only)

Sort directory by filename	DIR | SORT or DIR /ON
Sort directory by extension	DIR | SORT /+10 or DIR /OE
Sort directory by file size	DIR | SORT /+14 or DIR /OS
Sort directory by date	DIR | SORT /+24 or DIR /OD

Copying Files

Copy individual file from drive A to B	COPY A:<filename> B:
Copy all files from drive A to B	COPY A:*.* B
Copy all files from drive B to A	COPY B:*.* A

Duplicating Disks

Duplicate a disk in drive A to a disk in drive B	DISKCOPY A: B:

Comparing Disks

Compare a disk in drive A with a disk in drive B	DISKCOMP A: B:

Renaming Files

Rename a file	RENAME <old name> <new name>

Deleting Files

Delete file from disk	DEL <filename> or ERASE <filename>
Delete all files with the specified extension	ERASE *.<ext>
Delete all files with the specified filename	ERASE <filename>.*
Delete all files	ERASE *.*
Undelete files (DOS 5 only)	UNDELETE <filename>
List deleted files (DOS 5 only)	UNDELETE <drive:> /LIST
Mirror deleted files (DOS 5 only)	MIRROR/T<drive:>

Making Directories

Create new directory below current directory	MD <directory name>
Specify a path	<drive:>\<directory>\<subdirectory>

Removing Directories

Remove directory from current directory	RD <directory name>

Changing Directories

Change the default directory	CD <directory name>
Return to the root directory	CD\
Move up one directory level	CD ..
Display the default directory on another drive	CD <drive:>

Listing Directories

List directories	DIR *.
List directories	TREE <drive:>
List directories and files	TREE <drive:>/F

Move a screen at a time	+ or - on numeric keypad
Move to any edge of document	Home, Home, arrow key

Editing Text

Toggle between insert and typeover	Ins
Reveal/hide codes	Alt-F3 or F11
Delete single characters	Del or ←Bksp
Delete word	Ctrl-←Bksp
Delete from cursor to end of line	Ctrl-End
Delete from cursor to the end of page	Ctrl-PgDn
Enter date or time code	⇧Shift-F5

Working with Blocks

Turn block on/off	Alt-F4 or F12
Display Move menu	Ctrl-F4
Copy last block moved or copied	⇧Shift-F10, Enter↵
Protect block from soft page break	⇧Shift-F8

Using Editing Tools

Search forward for a string	F2
Search backward for a string	⇧Shift-F2
Search for next occurrence of same string	F2, F2
Replace a string	Alt-F2
Spell-check a document	Ctrl-F2
Use thesaurus	Alt-F1

Using Windows

Switch between windows	⇧Shift-F3
Display both windows at the same time	Ctrl-F3, ↑

Printing Documents

Preview document on the screen	⇧Shift-F7, V
Display Print menu	⇧Shift-F7
Display List Files menu	F5
Display Control Printer menu	⇧Shift-F7, C

Page Layout

Enter a hard page break	Ctrl-Enter↵
Enter page numbers	⇧Shift-F8, P, N
Enter headers	⇧Shift-F8, P, H
Enter footers	⇧Shift-F8, P, F
Change top/bottom margins	⇧Shift-F8, P, M
Change left/right margins	⇧Shift-F8, L, M
Center page top to bottom	⇧Shift-F8, P, C
Change justification	⇧Shift-F8, L, J
Change line height	⇧Shift-F8, L, H
Change line spacing	⇧Shift-F8, L, S
Enter footnotes	Ctrl-F7, F
Enter endnotes	Ctrl-F7, E
Suppress headers/footers/page numbers	⇧Shift-F8, P, U

Changing Fonts

Boldface selected text	F6
Underline selected text	F8
Change font sizes	Ctrl-F8, S
Change font appearance	Ctrl-F8, A
Change the base font	Ctrl-F8, F

Composing Special Characters

Trademark symbol	Ctrl-V 4,41
Registration symbol	Ctrl-V 4,22
Round bullet	Ctrl-V 4,0
Square bullet	Ctrl-V 4,2
Checkmark	Ctrl-V 5,23
Copyright symbol	Ctrl-V 4,23

Using Numeric and Mathematical Functions

Absolute value of a number	**@ABS(***negative number***)**
Integer part of a number	**@INT(***number***)**
Natural log (base *e*) of *x*	**@LN(***x***)**
Log (base 10) of *x*	**@LOG(***x***)**
Pi (3.1415926..)	**@PI**
Round a number	**@ROUND(***number,number of places***)**
Square root of a number	**@SQRT(***number***)**

Calculating Date and Time Numbers

Number of days since Jan 1, 1900	**@DATE(***yy,mm,dd***)**
Date number of a text string	**@DATEVALUE(***date string***)**
Current date and time of system's clock	**@NOW**
Time number	**@TIME(***hh,mm,ss***)**
Time number of a text string	**@TIMEVALUE(***time string***)**

Using Date and Time Numbers

Calculate the day number	**@DAY(***date number***)**
Calculate the month number	**@MONTH(***month number***)**
Calculate the year number	**@YEAR(***year number***)**

Using Relational and Logical Operators

Greater than operator	>
Less than operator	<
Equal to operator	=
Less than or equal to operator	<=
Greater than or equal to operator	>=
Not equal to operator	<>
AND operator	#AND#
OR operator	#OR#
NOT operator	#NOT#

Lotus 1-2-3 Pocket Guide

Getting Started

Load the program	123
Load the Access System	LOTUS
Display help	F1
Display the command menu	/
Cancel command in progress	Ctrl-Break
Back up through menus	Esc
Quit the program	/Q
Check the worksheet's status	/WS
Erase the worksheet	/WE

Saving and Retrieving Files

Change the default drive/directory for the session	/FD
Change the default drive/directory permanently	/WGDD
Save a file	/FS
Retrieve a file	/FR

Moving the Cell Pointer

Move the cell pointer to cell A1	Home
Move cell pointer to lower right corner of the active area	End, Home
Move to a specific cell	F5
Move right one screen	Ctrl-→
Move left one screen	Ctrl-←
Move down one screen	PgDn
Move up one screen	PgUp

Entering and Editing Cell Contents

Display cell's contents on the edit line	F2
Enter label that begins with a number	"

Print labels	LABEL FORM <*filename*> TO PRINT

Creating and Using Customized Screens

Create a screen definition	CREATE SCREEN <*filename*>
Print a screen definition	TYPE <*filename*> TO PRINT
Use a screen definition	SET FORMAT TO <*filename*>
Close a screen display	CLOSE FORMAT

Calculating Fields

Average a field	AVERAGE <*field name*>
Total a field	SUM <*field name*>
Count a field	COUNT <*field name*>
List calculated fields	LIST FOR <*field*><*+, -, /, or **><*field*>

Creating New Files from Old Files

Copy a file	COPY TO <*filename*>
Copy a file's structure	COPY STRUCTURE TO <*filename*>
Copy specific fields	COPY TO <*filename*> FIELDS <*field list*>
Copy specific records	COPY TO <*filename*> FOR <*filter*>

Relating and Joining Files

Select memory areas	SELECT <*area A or 1, B or 2 and so on*>
Set relation	SET RELATION TO <*field*> INTO <*filename*>
Create a view	CREATE VIEW <*filename*>
Use a view	SET VIEW TO <*filename*>
Join with file in area B	JOIN WITH B TO <*filename*> FOR <*field*>=B-><*field*>

Creating and Using Command Files

Create a command file	MODIFY COMMAND <*filename*>
Print a command file	TYPE <*filename*> TO PRINT
Execute a command file	DO <*filename*>

dBASE III Plus Pocket Guide

Getting Started

Load the program	DBASE
Quit the program	QUIT
Change the default drive	SET DEFAULT TO <*drive:*>
Specify a directory	SET PATH TO <*path*>
Turn menus on/off	SET MENU ON/OFF
Display directory of .DBF files	F4 or DIR

Displaying Menus and Help

Display the Assist menus	F2 or ASSIST
Display the dot prompt	Esc
Display help menu	F1 or HELP
Display help on a specific command	HELP <*command*>
List previous commands	DISPLAY HISTORY

Creating, Modifying, and Saving Files

Create a file	CREATE <*filename*>
Open an existing file	USE <*filename*>
Close open files	CLEAR ALL
Modify a file's structure	MODIFY STRUCTURE
Display a file's structure	F5 or LIST STRUCTURE
Print a file's structure	LIST STRUCTURE TO PRINT
Save changes	Ctrl-End

Adding Records

Add records	F9 or APPEND
Insert a record	INSERT
Add records from another file	APPEND FROM <*filename*>

Align label left	'
Align label right	"
Align label in center of cell	^
Erase cells	/RE
Enter repeating label	\<*character to be repeated*>
Fill a range with values	/DF
Cycle through absolute/relative combinations in POINT mode	F4
Name a range	/RN
Create windows	/WW
Move between windows	F6
Fix or clear titles	/WT

Protecting Data

Protect ranges of cells	/RP
Unprotect ranges of cells	/RU
Enable cell protection	/WGPE
Disable cell protection	/WGPD

Formatting Cells

Format values; in ranges	/RF
Format values; globally	/WGF
Change column widths; globally	/WGC
Change column width; single column	/WCS
Change column widths; in ranges	/WCCS
Reset column width to global setting	/WCR
Align labels; in ranges	/RL
Align labels; globally	/WGL

Reorganizing Data on the Worksheet

Copy a range	/C
Move data	/M
Insert columns	/WIC
Insert rows	/WIR
Delete columns	/WDC
Delete rows	/WDR

Printing Models

Print the model	/PP
Print to a file	/PF

Creating and Displaying Graphs

Display the graph menu	/G
Display most recently displayed graph	F10

Using Macros

Turn on step mode	Alt-F2
Display list of macros	Alt-F3

Using Financial Functions

Number of compounding periods	**@CTERM(***int,fut val.,present val.***)**
Future value of an annuity	**@FV(***regular payment,interest rate,term***)**
Internal rate of return	**@IRR(***guess,range of cash flows***)**
Net present value	**@NPV(***interest rate,range***)**
Payment to amortize a loan	**@PMT(***principal,interest rate,term***)**
Present value of an ordinary annuity	**@PV(***payments,interest,term***)**
Interest rate for present value	**@RATE(***future val.,present val.,term***)**
Number of payment periods	**@TERM(***payment,interest,future value***)**

Using Statistical Functions

Sum of values	**@SUM(***range of values***)**
Average value	**@AVG(***range of values***)**
Number of nonblank cells	**@COUNT(***range of values***)**
Largest value	**@MAX(***range of values***)**
Smallest value	**@MIN(***range of values***)**
Standard deviation	**@STD(***range of values***)**
Variance	**@VAR(***range of values***)**

Printing Records

List records to the printer	LIST TO PRINT
Turn the printer on or off	SET PRINT ON/OFF
Eject pages from the printer	EJECT

Editing Records

Edit records	F10 or EDIT
Replace data	REPLACE ALL <*field*> WITH <*replacement*>
Zoom into a memo field	Ctrl-Home or Ctrl-PgDn
Edit specific fields	CHANGE ALL FIELD <*field list*>

Deleting Records

Flag a record for deletion	DELETE RECORD <#>
Flag a record for deletion in browse mode	Ctrl-U
Remove flags	RECALL <*record # or ALL*>
Have dBASE ignore flagged records	SET DELETED ON
Pack the database to remove flagged records	PACK
Delete all records	ZAP

Moving the Record Pointer from the Dot Prompt

Move to the first record	GOTO TOP
Move to the last record	GOTO BOTTOM
Move to any record	GOTO <#>

Displaying Records

List all records	F3, LIST, or DISPLAY ALL
List a specific record	LIST RECORD <#>
List records in table view	BROWSE
Leave browse mode	Esc
Display selected fields	SET FIELDS TO <*field list*>
Clear set fields	CLEAR FIELDS
Display contents of memo fields	LIST <*field name*>

Using Logical and Relational Operators

Specify logical operators in a command	LIST FOR <*filter*>
Set a filter	SET FILTER TO <*filter*>
Remove a filter	SET FILTER TO
Locate a record	LOCATE FOR <*filter*>
Greater than operator	>
Less than operator	<
Equal to operator	=
Less than or equal to operator	<=
Greater than or equal to operator	>=
Not equal to operator	<>
AND operator	.AND.
OR operator	.OR.
NOT operator	.NOT.

Arranging Records

Sort records	SORT ON <*field*> TO <*filename*>
Sort on two fields	SORT ON <*field1*>,<*field2*> TO <*filename*>
Sort in descending order	SORT ON <*field*>/D TO <*filename*>
Index records	INDEX ON <*field*> TO <*index name*>
Index on two fields	INDEX ON <*field1*>+<*field2*> TO <*index name*>
Specify an existing index	SET INDEX TO <*index name*>
Close an index	CLOSE INDEX

Creating and Using Reports

Create a report format	CREATE REPORT <*report name*>
Modify a report	MODIFY REPORT <*filename*>
Use a report format	REPORT FORM <*report name*>
Print a report	REPORT FORM <*report name*> TO PRINT
Create a label definition	CREATE LABEL <*filename*>
Use a label definition	LABEL FORM <*filename*>
Modify a label definition	MODIFY LABEL <*filename*>